ZELMA R. LONG

AMERICAN WINE

Village Spirits

AMERICAN WINE

A COMPREHENSIVE GUIDE

By Anthony Dias Blue

Best wishes

*Carol Wilson
5/28/86
To future
dine
trips!
cw*

Anthony D. Blue

Disney World 1986

DOUBLEDAY & COMPANY, INC.
Garden City, New York
1985

Library of Congress Cataloging in Publication Data

Blue, Anthony Dias
    American wine.

    1. Wine and wine making—United States. I. Title.
TP557.D5C 1985   641.2'22'0973   84-28631
ISBN 0-385-19191-X

First Edition

In loving memory of Sidney Daniel Blue
and Stephen Abraham Koshland,
who taught me about taste.

Contents

Acknowledgments

A book of this magnitude and complexity could not have been written without the dedication and hard work of many people. The key participants in this enormous project were Nancy Lynn Gray, William B. Smith, and Pamela Mosher. As my chief researcher, Nancy accumulated thousands of facts and figures and made sense out of them. She pursued reluctant vintners, tracked down elusive wines, and discovered obscure wineries. And Bill, our resident computer expert, made this impossible project possible. He taught us how DBASE II and DBASE III could coordinate all these bits of information and form them into a coherent whole. Then he created the program that made this mountain of raw data come out looking like a book. Editor Pamela Mosher worked tirelessly on the manuscript, supervised the design, and worked closely with Bill, the typographer, and publisher to bring the book to print. I also thank my wonderful fact-checking staff: Robin Richardson, Lisa King, Mark Lupher, and Jonna Carl.

Special thanks go to my good friend Hank Rubin, who carefully coordinated the weekly tastings and analyzed the results. Thanks also to my fellow tasters, whose input was of considerable help: Richard Carey, Scott Clemens, Arthur Damond, Jim Gordon, Mike Higgins, Richard Paul Hinkle, Professor Joseph Koppel, Jim Laube, Nancy Peach, Norman Roby, Stu Smith, Harvey Steiman, and Jean Wolfe Walzer.

Thanks to my editors, Fran McCullough and James Raimes, and my agent, Don Cutler. Their unflagging belief in this book pulled me through some of the darkest hours.

Thanks again to Pamela Mosher, who shepherded the book at the end and got it out on time. Thanks go to my regular editors, whose patience and understanding allowed me to complete this project: Marilou Vaughan, Bill Garry, Barbara Varnum, and Laurie Buckle at *Bon Appétit*, Marvin Shanken and Harvey Steiman at *The Wine Spectator*, Lou Schwartz and Stu Troup at *Newsday*, Paul Jeffers at WCBS, Kit Snedaker at the *Los Angeles Herald Examiner*, and Stuart Dodds and Stan Arnold at Chronicle Features. And there are a few more people and institutions that for one reason or another deserve my thanks: Robert Lawrence Balzer, Steve Birnbaum, Stan Bromley, Jack Daniels, Frank and Ron George, Jerry Goldstein, Eric Hansen, Mike Klauber, Bob Mondavi, Ed Schwartz, Philip Seldon, Stephen Spector, André Tchelistcheff, Rich Thomas, Jim Wallace, Win Wilson, Steve Winston, the Alameda County Fair, the California Wine Festival at Monterey, the California Wine Experience, the Central Coast Wine Judging, the Napa Symposium, the Santa Cruz Wine Judging, and the Sonoma County Harvest Fair.

Finally, thanks go to my wife, Kathy, and my children, Caitlin, Toby, Jessica, and Amanda, for putting up with more than two years of book mania.

Introduction

Wine is very special.

It is one of the most delicious potables known to man, but also one of the most complex and variable. There are enormous differences between the many wine grape varieties, each of which responds to varying environmental factors, such as soil, weather, and viticultural techniques. Each individual wine ends up as subtly unique as a snowflake or a human fingerprint. That's why there is such a thing as a book like this about wine and not one about catsup or peanut butter.

Wine writers have differing responses to their subject. Some are products of the time when wine was sipped only in baronial dining rooms, while the peasantry made do with ale. These elitist wine experts like to talk about the 1929 Mouton-Rothschild, but they would never condescend to mention the very accessible charms of a three-dollar white table wine. For them the enjoyment of wine is very much like an exclusive men's club. They perpetuate a mystique that they hope will serve as a barrier against the onslaught of the barbarians. Their greatest dread is that wine will be accepted as a normal part of everyday life, thus causing their feeling of superiority to evaporate.

Some other wine writers take their subject and themselves so seriously that you'd think they were talking about brain surgery or microelectronics. People whose job it is to tell other people what to do, what to buy, or what to think tend to develop an exaggerated opinion of their own importance. In the wine business, as in other areas, it is essential to remember that the really important people are the ones who make the product, not the ones who write about it.

I am a loudmouth who tends to be quite opinionated. My judgments about wines are based on knowledge, long experience, a prodigious memory, and a fairly good palate, but they should be taken with a grain of salt. Any assessment of wine, even by so-called experts, should be read with a skeptical eye. Criticism is never more than the opinion of one person—a person who may have different experiences, different sensory memories, and different tastes than you.

Therefore, please think of this book as a guide, not as the final word. Aside from the idiosyncrasies of personal taste, wine criticism may be less than exact because its subject is always changing. Unlike a movie, book, or play, wine is constantly evolving; it is always a work in progress, and wine writing is just a signpost along the way. In this guide, I have tried to unearth discoveries in every price range; I also haven't hesitated to point out wines that I think should be avoided. But don't take me *too* seriously. Don't run out and buy a case of a wine I recommend highly without buying one bottle first. If you don't taste for yourself, you may find your cellar filled with expensive disappointments.

I don't, however, want to minimize the usefulness of this volume (I'd be doing myself a disservice if I did). I love wine and I want to share my enthusiasm with you, in the hope that those of you who are not yet convinced will find my ardor contagious. I approached every wine mentioned on these pages with a sense of anticipation and excitement. If my words can stimulate just a little of that feeling in you, I will have succeeded.

Wine is not crucial—entire lives can be lived without it. But this magical liquid can add so much pleasure, so much enrichment. I would like to provide the key to those experiences for you.

American Wines: Ready to Take on the World

On December 5, 1933, America emerged from the thirteen-year nightmare of Prohibition. But despite this historic reversal of national policy, the American wine industry did not spring into action immediately. This was quite understandable, since there was no wine industry to speak of—the "noble experiment" had all but wiped it out.

The story had been quite different before 1920. California wines had been growing in volume and quality since the late 1800s. New techniques, new varieties, and a heightened sophistication were leading American wines to a surprising level of acceptance. Some California bottlings were reaching Europe and actually winning medals at important competitions. But the Volstead Act put an end to this encouraging growth and practically finished off the American wine industry. A few producers were able to hold out by producing "sacramental" or cooking wine, but essentially American wine ceased to exist.

When Prohibition was over, the wine business got off to a poor start as producers rushed badly made wines to market in December 1933. Bottles exploded because of unfinished fermentation, and wines tasted of mold, vinegar, and other more exotic spoilages; most wines coming from abroad were not much better. Consumers turned to gin and beer, and the American wine industry settled down to making dessert wines—port, sherry, muscatel, and other sweet wines fortified with brandy.

For twenty-five years very few people knew a serious American wine industry existed. But during that time great wines were being made—not many, but enough to indicate the enormous potential of our vineyards. At the Inglenook winery in the Napa Valley, fine Cabernet Sauvignons were produced throughout the 1940s and 1950s. Across the highway at Beaulieu Vineyard, under the guidance of Russian-born and French-trained André Tchelistcheff, great Cabernets and Pinot Noirs were commonplace. Many of the Inglenook and Beaulieu wines of this period are still very much alive and quite delicious; they have become much sought after and highly valued at wine auctions both here and in Europe.

Nevertheless, it took a dramatic event, a family feud, to get the American wine boom going. In 1966 Robert Mondavi, co-owner of the Charles Krug Winery, left the winery because of a dispute with his brother Peter. Robert, whose energy and determination are legendary, immediately built his own winery, the first major new winery in California since Prohibition.

Mondavi's confidence in the future of the American wine industry was infectious. Others took the cue, and wineries began springing up from Ukiah to Santa Cruz. Soon afterward premium vineyards were planted in Monterey, Paso Robles, and the Santa Ynez Valley. In 1960 the Napa Valley had hit a low of twenty-five wineries, only twelve of which sold wine outside the county; by 1975 it had forty-five active wineries (today the count is well over one hundred). The boom was on in earnest.

In the East, wineries began to appear around New York's Finger Lakes, on the banks of Lake Erie, and in Maryland, Virginia, and Ohio. Home winemakers in Oregon and Washington began converting their garages to commercial wineries.

But despite the talk and the brave new world attitude of these pioneer vintners, no one believed for a minute that their wines could be compared to the great bottlings of Europe, particularly France. After all, the French had been making great wines for hundreds of years; the upstart American wine industry only really got started at the end of 1933.

After 1955 things began moving, slowly at first. Then between 1965 and 1975 great strides were made. The world-famous viticulture and enology department at the University of California at Davis began turning out talented winemakers and growers, tyros who had been thoroughly educated in how to avoid making the mistakes of the past. American wines were cleaner, more complex, and better made than they had ever been before.

In addition, discoveries were being made regularly in the winery laboratories. In Modesto the Gallo labs were finding out new things every day; so was Mondavi in Napa. Meanwhile, Dr. Konstantin Frank and Charles Fournier were making great advances in the use of vinifera grapes in the cooler northeastern climate, and vineyards of new French-American hybrid grapes were appearing all over the country.

Stephen Spurrier, a young English wine merchant in Paris, thought California wines were good, but just how good he wasn't sure. In May 1976 he decided to put them to the test. He assembled four of California's best Chardonnays and four of the best Cabernet Sauvignons. He then assembled four of France's best white Burgundies, wines that are also made from the noble Chardonnay grape, and four Grand Cru Classe red Bordeaux wines (including such notables as Château Mouton-Rothschild), also made from the elegant Cabernet Sauvignon grape. Mr. Spurrier brought together nine of the greatest wine palates in Paris, including top restaurateurs, wine stewards, wine journalists, château owners, and Pierre Brejoux, Inspector General of the Institut National des Appellations d'Origine, France's top wine judge. He masked the bottles so nobody knew which wines were from France and which were from California.

Those in attendance did know that they were tasting California wines as well as French wines, and as the tasting progressed their comments about the wines they identified as being from the United States became more and more cutting and patronizing. Imagine their surprise and chagrin when the wines were finally unmasked, and they saw that the wines they had guessed to be French were in fact mostly American, and the wines they had denigrated turned out to be mostly French. The tasters were mortified, and wine history was made.

Before the unmasking, the French wine experts had been asked to rank the wines. When these rankings were tabulated, the upstart wines from California won the day decisively. Judged best were wines from two small and relatively new Napa Valley wineries. The Chardonnay category was led by the 1973 vintage made by Château Montelena, a winery in Calistoga whose first releases had been from the 1972 vintage. The winning Cabernet Sauvignon was the 1973 vintage from Stag's Leap Wine Cellars, also the winery's second release of this variety.

These resounding victories sent shock waves throughout the wine world. The news was carried by all the major television networks in the United States and featured in such national publications as *Time* magazine. The perception of California's wines was changed overnight and forever. Americans could now shed their feelings of enological inferiority and be confident that the best domestic wines were at least the equal of Europe's best.

The immediate result of this breakthrough was that American wine snobs, people who stocked their cellars with only fine French and German wines, began to think of America's products as more than just impertinent domestic plonk. Many of them actually tried California wine for the first time and came away believers. American wines became chic. Wine lovers who used to compare notes about the latest Bordeaux vintage now searched the marketplace for the latest releases of the newest and most obscure California "boutique" wineries—small wineries specializing in a few premium wines.

But Europeans, especially the French, were still unimpressed. So in 1980 food and wine jounalists Henri Gault and Christian Millau held a big international tasting of wines from France, Australia, Germany, Italy, Switzerland, Greece, and the United States. Among the tasters were important wine professionals from all over the world, a majority of whom were French.

Once again American wines fared remarkably well. Among whites, for example, Chardonnays by Trefethen, Freemark Abbey, and Robert Mondavi finished in the first six. The 1976 Trefethen Chardonnay, which finished first, outdistanced among others the much more expensive 1976 and 1978 Puligny-Montrachet Premier Crus shipped by the well-respected Burgundy house of Joseph Drouhin.

International recognition has not been limited to California wines. Such Oregon and Washington wineries as the Eyrie Vineyards, Tualatin Vineyards, and Château Ste. Michelle have won many competitions and, more importantly, the respect of influential European palates.

Price has become something of a stumbling block along the road to worldwide acceptance of California wines. The recent strength of the dollar in comparison to European currencies, plus the substantial subsidies that foreign governments pay to support wine exports, seem to give French and Italian wines a definite price advantage in the marketplace. But a careful comparison of wines in the same price range shows that the plucky Americans are able to hold their own.

This was borne out in the results of a 1981 London tasting of twenty similarly priced French and American Cabernet Sauvignons, in which the first five places went to California wines. They were, in order of finish: 1977 Trefethen, 1977 Joseph Phelps, 1976 Freemark Abbey, 1977 Robert Mondavi, and 1977 Iron Horse.

But it is not just the small premium producers who are showing well in comparison to the fine wines of Europe. Almadén's very good Monterey Cabernet Sauvignons have done quite well in such comparative tastings. (I have actually seen Almadén's wines on supermarket shelves in France.) Gallo's fine Cabernet has also scored very well in competitions in England and elsewhere.

Recently a group of French people came to visit the California wine country. I was one of their hosts and was put in charge of selecting the wines for their visit, which was to include a large tasting. The varieties that these people, who were mostly restaurateurs and wine professionals, knew best were Chardonnay, Sauvignon Blanc, Pinot Noir, and Cabernet Sauvignon. They tasted California versions of these and were so enthusiastic about most of them that they took many bottles back to France.

The point of all this is that American wines are no longer taking a back seat to any other wines. Great wines are made in France, Germany, and Italy, but great wines are also being made in California, New York, and Virginia—wines that are certainly in the same league as the greatest Europe has to offer. And in fine homes and restaurants here and abroad, American wines have taken their place at the best tables. Not only are the wines of America acceptable in polite company, they are actually sought after, which is quite an accomplishment for an industry that is just a bit more than 50 years old.

What is Wine?

No one knows when the first wine was made; its origins are lost in the mists of prehistory. We do know that wine played an important part in most ancient civilizations. The temperate zones where people first came together in rudimentary political units were also the areas where grapevines happened to originate.

I can just imagine that momentous event, the making of the first wine. Like many great discoveries, it was, I'm sure, an accident. Someone came across grapevines laden with ripe fruit. Overjoyed by his (or her) great fortune, he quickly picked the grapes, piled them into some rough container or sack, and triumphantly carried them home.

Upon arriving at the family cave or hut, he noticed that the weight of the fruit was causing the bunches at the bottom of the pile to exude a delicious, sweet juice. Growing more excited, he crushed the rest of the grapes with a rock, his hands, or maybe his feet. Filling a number of open-topped containers with this sweet juice, our first enologist figured he had enough for his family to drink for many days.

His prehistoric abode, not exactly a model of hygiene, was loaded with all sorts of microbiological specimens. Among these was a colony of wild yeast spores that, freely floating through the air, came upon the open containers of grape juice.

The rest, as they say, is history. The yeast began devouring the sugar in the grape juice, turning it into alcohol. Imagine the surprise of our ancient friend when he returned to his grape juice and found that it had changed. Not only was it less sweet than it had been before, but it had a new, more interesting taste and a bite that hadn't been there before. Imagine his delight when he discovered how good the grape juice made him feel.

I'm sure that he and his family then partook greedily of this strangely appealing drink, perhaps to excess. The next morning our hero awoke to find that he had not only invented wine but had the first hangover.

Wine is still made by that simple, basic process. Grape juice combines with yeast, which converts its sugar to alcohol. The only difference today is that we have learned to control the process and to protect the final product so it doesn't have to be consumed immediately. But if we drink too much we still get a hangover.

In the fall of 1981 my son, Toby, and I made our own Chardonnay, with the help of Beringer Vineyards. We went through all the steps taken by a full-sized commercial winery; we just made a very small amount.

We began at 7:15 A.M. on a mid-September morning. The sun was just peeking through the fog as it rose over the Napa Mountains. Most picking is done in these morning hours so the fruit can be delivered to the winery when it is still cool. The temperature at which grapes ferment is very important—the cooler the juice is to begin with the slower and more gentle the process.

First, with the use of a refractometer, we tested the sugar level of the grapes. The juice of a ripe grape should be between 21 percent and 24 percent sugar, which allows the fermentation to convert the sugar to a desirable alcohol level. Generally the conversion rate is about 55 percent, which means that 22 percent sugar will result in a dry wine containing about 12 percent alcohol. (Sometimes, without warning or explanation, the conversion rate jumps to 60 or 65 percent, and winemakers find themselves with a wine much higher in alcohol than expected.)

Wielding hook-bladed knives, we had picked fourteen lug-boxes of grapes by 10 A.M. We loaded our haul, about one third of a ton, into a truck. By the time the last heavy box was hoisted in, we were tired, blistered, and in awe of the efficient professional pickers we had seen speeding through a nearby block of Sauvignon Blanc.

We trucked the grapes back to the Beringer winery in St. Helena, a few miles from the vineyard, and unloaded them at the stemmer-crusher, a machine that removes the grapes from their stems and breaks their skins. We used a small machine that was identical to the big stainless steel stemmer-crusher the winery uses for large loads of fruit.

For an hour or so we fed our grapes into the machine (with the big stemmer-crusher the process is much faster). The stems were collected in a basket, and the crushed grapes and free-run juice were collected in a vat.

The grape skins, pulp, and juice were then held in contact with each other for ten hours. During this time the skins impart varietal character and complexity to the juice.

This is one of the many decisions the winemaker makes during the winemaking process: How much skin contact should the wine have? For some simple white varieties, such as Chenin Blanc or Riesling, the period is usually very short.

Another choice, especially when making Chardonnay, is whether to ferment the wine in oak barrels or in stainless steel vats. Both ways are common; it depends on what style of wine the winemaker wants to make. Barrel fermentation gives the wine an earthy, rich, oaky flavor. Stainless steel fermentation generally results in a crisper, lighter wine. Some winemakers compromise by starting the fermentation in stainless and then transferring the still-fermenting juice to oak. Another method is to combine separate lots of barrel-fermented and stainless-steel-fermented wines in the same blend. We chose to barrel ferment our Chardonnay.

The next step was putting our grapes and juice into a press. The oldest style of press, called a basket press, consists of upright wooden slats that are filled with the grapes and then pressed with the use of a ratchet and rod that squeezes down, compressing the grapes into a dense cake. The pressed juice flows out the bottom, through a funnel, and into a French oak barrel. Most wineries have abandoned this rudimentary type of device in favor of big electric presses that use centrifugal force or gentle pressure to extract the juice.

The next decision is what kind of yeast to use. There are hundreds of different strains of yeast to choose from, and each imparts a particular character to the finished wine. Different yeasts are used for different varieties. Almost all modern wineries "innoculate" their wines with yeast rather than depend on wild yeasts, which allows the vintner greater control over the winemaking process.

We used a French Champagne yeast, a type used by many American wineries in the making of Chardonnay. We mixed the dry, powdered yeast with a small amount of the grape juice to "proof" it, very much as in bread making. The yeast shows that it is active and alive by bubbling and foaming as it feeds on the sugar in the fresh grape juice.

We poured the bubbling liquid into the oak barrel, and the fermentation process began in earnest. We inserted a glass fermentation valve in the bung hole of the barrel to allow the carbon dioxide that is produced in the chemical reaction to escape. (In the Champagne-making process the carbon dioxide is trapped within the bottle, creating those delightful bubbles.)

In the cool winery, it takes several days for all of the sugar to be converted and the wine to become dry. When making Johannisberg Riesling, Gewürztraminer, Muscat, or Chenin Blanc, the stainless steel fermenting vat is usually equipped with a refrigeration jacket that can quickly cool its contents. This is how winemakers who want to leave a bit of residual sugar in their wines can stop the fermentation process when the desired sugar level is reached. At this point the new wine is "racked"—pumped out of the tank—and filtered so all the yeast is removed and further fermentation is impossible.

When fermentation of our Chardonnay was completed, we racked the new wine to separate it from the spent yeast and other solids that had dropped to the bottom of the barrel. We returned the wine to a clean barrel, where it aged undisturbed for several months. Once again there are decisions to be made by the winemaker: How long should the wine remain in oak? How new should the oak be? What kind of oak should it be? Each decision will have a profound effect on the flavor of the finished product.

Our Chardonnay turned out quite well. In fact, it won a bronze medal at the 1983 California State Fair amateur winemaking competition. Next time I'll pick my grapes when they are a little less ripe and take the wine out of the oak a bit sooner, but this is how most winemakers learn, by experience.

The following year Toby, then twelve years old, and I tried our now-seasoned hands at making red wine. We helped John Buehler of Buehler Vineyards in Napa to make his 1982 Cabernet Sauvignon. The differences between making red and white are fairly simple.

Red wines are allowed much longer skin contact so the wine will extract the full measure of color, tannin, and other character complexities from the skin. The grapes are crushed perhaps a bit more forcefully than when making whites, and they are eventually fermented with the skins still in contact with the juice. After fermentation the grape skins and pulp fall to the bottom of the fermenter and the clear wine is drawn off. Reds, except Beaujolais-style wines, are almost always aged in oak barrels. They can spend a year or two in barrels followed by a year or two in bottles before being released. Because of their greater complexity and their harsh tannins when young, reds require considerably more age before they are drinkable.

There are three ways to make sparkling wines: the original Champagne method, the transfer method, and the Charmat or bulk process. In the *méthode champenoise* a still wine is made and bottled. To this young wine is added some sugar and yeast. Then the bottle is capped, and a secondary fermentation takes place in the bottle. The carbon dioxide bubbles, trapped in the bottle, go into solution and appear only when the wine is finally opened and consumed.

The most complicated part of the Champagne method is removing the residue of spent yeast after the secondary fermentation is completed. This is accomplished by gradually tilting the bottle, over a period of several days or weeks, until the sediment is resting next to the cork. (This procedure is called *remuage*.) The neck of the bottle is then quickly frozen, the ice plug containing the yeast is removed, and the bottle is recorked. This process is called *degorgement*. American wines made in this painstaking way are usually labeled: "Naturally fermented in *this* bottle."

In the transfer method, the wines are cooled after the secondary fermentation and emptied from the bottle into a tank. Kept under pressure, the wine is filtered and returned to clean bottles. These wines are labeled: "Naturally fermented in *the* bottle."

In the bulk process, the secondary fermentation takes place in large vats, and the wine is then bottled under pressure.

Blanc de Noir wines are new, very popular wines that represent a creative solution by American vintners for disposing of a surplus of red grapes in the midst of a white wine boom. They are white wines made from red grapes. The grapes are gently crushed and the juice is quickly removed from contact with the grape skins, which hold the pigment that tints the wine red. Sometimes these wines look like white wines, but most of the time a little color slips in, giving them a slightly pink cast.

Even at their ruddiest, Blanc de Noir wines are lighter in color than rosé wines. The classic method for making rosé calls for the wine to ferment for a day or so in contact with the skins. Once the optimum amount of color has been absorbed, the wine is drawn off, completing its fermentation away from the skins. Some cheap rosés are actually made by combining red and white wines.

There are other methods and an infinite number of variations and nuances that winemakers learn during four years at U.C. Davis or at Fresno State University. But although we've come a long way towards perfecting techniques of winemaking, most of what has been discovered in the past few thousand years has just been fine-tuning. Our prehistoric friend might be befuddled by all the shiny stainless steel, pumps, centrifuges, and bottling lines in the modern winery, but the basic process is still the same one he discovered on that great day when he took his first sip of that strangely appealing transformed grape juice.

How to Use This Book

I want this book to help you get as much enjoyment from American wines as possible, and therefore I have tried to provide accurate statistical and historical profiles of each functioning winery in the country, along with tasting notes on thousands of currently available wines.

Buying American wine can be a hit-or-miss affair. All a buyer learns from most labels is the grape variety, the winery name, the year, the appellation, and the price. For most European wines this information might be enough, but it doesn't do the job for American wines. The American wine industry is young and still quite volatile; a great Chardonnay from a particular winery one year doesn't guarantee an equally delicious effort the next year. With established French or Italian wines the differences between bottlings from different years are mainly attributable to variations of weather. But in the United States, even if the climate remains the same over the different years, the winery may have changed winemakers, purchased its grapes from a different source, or just made its wine in a different style. In every case the wine will taste different.

Consequently, I want this book to take the unpleasant surprises out of your wine buying. Over the past year or two I have tasted and rated more than 5,000 wines. Although I was unable—as much as I may have wished otherwise—to taste absolutely everything on the market, I would guess that the wines rated in this book represent more than 90 percent of the American wines you are likely to encounter at your local wine shop.

I tasted the vast majority of wines "blind"—with the label hidden—and I tasted most of them more than once. Twice every week I meet with a small group of wine professionals to taste between thirty and fifty wines. These intensive exercises, carried out under the aegis of *Bon Appétit* magazine and *The Wine Spectator*, allow me to keep up with the continuous flow of new releases.

In addition, I have judged a host of comprehensive wine events in California and elsewhere. I also attend many industry wine tastings, and I constantly sample wines at home, where my wife is not at all delighted with the half-empty wine bottles that are always cluttering up the kitchen.

So I've tasted many wines—what qualifies me to judge them? I can tell you that I have an excellent, well-trained palate, and I can spot volatile acidity or mercaptans at fifty paces. But that's not enough. I am also extremely consistent. When I hold a wine up to a standard set of criteria, I come away with a judgment that complements all the judgments that have gone before. I have tested myself frequently by tasting the same wine at several different times and comparing the notes recorded at each tasting, and there is almost never a serious disparity in my ratings.

The tasting notes set this book apart from the other American wine books that have come before it. They represent my personal opinions, but they are thorough, informed, carefully achieved, and consistent. So if you agree with me on one or two wines, you will probably agree with me on most of them.

Every professional taster agrees that there are certain characteristics that make some wines unacceptable. Oxidation (spoilage due to excessive exposure to oxygen), volatile acidity (sour, vinegary acid), and dirtiness or bacterial spoilage (the result of sloppy winemaking) are some of the most noticeable problems. Luckily not many wines are so blatantly flawed, so most wines are not so clearly classifiable.

Too many people who taste wine will break a wine down into its various components—clarity, aroma, balance, mouth feel, sweetness, varietal character, finish, aging potential—but will neglect to form an impression of the wine as a whole. Many winemakers and enology professors will criticize a wine that has a minor flaw, despite the fact that it may be delicious and quite enjoyable to drink.

For me, the bottom line in wine judging is, "Does it taste good?" I like to think that I have a consumer's palate; I steer clear of technical terminology and pretentious pronouncements. In my tasting notes I haven't tried to reach dizzying literary heights. In fact, you'll find the notes fairly repetitive, because I use the same words to describe the same characteristics. Here are some of the most frequently used descriptives:

Clean: This is one of the most important characteristics of good wine. Modern technology has made it possible to avoid the dirt and spoilage that used to plague the winemaking process. Well-made wines should always be clean.

Crisp: This refers to fresh, fruity acidity which is a highly desirable quality, especially for white wines.

Fruity: The taste of fresh fruit (especially grapes). This is characteristic of well-made young wines.

Oxidized: A spoilage condition caused by excessive exposure to air. Oxidation causes a wine to lose its fruitiness and freshness.

Structured: A very important element of any wine, especially reds. A good Cabernet Sauvignon, for example, should have a firm backbone of acidity, upon which all of its other characteristics hang. This backbone gives the wine structure and indicates that it will age well. Without structure a wine is flabby, shapeless, lacking in promise, and ultimately flawed.

Tannic: Characteristic of young red wines, tannin manifests itself as an astringent, puckery feeling in the mouth. Eventually—in the ideal scenario—the tannin softens and allows the fruit and varietal character of the wine to show through.

Vegetal: Smelling and/or tasting of vegetables. This could manifest itself in a number of ways, all of them unattractive. Some of the more common vegetable likenesses that crop up are bell peppers, asparagus, and broccoli.

Vinous: A heavy, sometimes oily quality that tastes more of leaves and stems than fruit.

Varietal Character: The particular flavor of the grape variety used in making the wine. Definitely a desirable characteristic.

Volatile Acidity: A vinegary taste brought about by the presence of acetic acid and ethyl acetate. Acceptable in small amounts but very undesirable in large quantities.

The rest of my descriptive terms should be easily understandable, but a few technical terms need defining. They are:

Botrytis: Short for *botrytis cenera*, the Latin name for a mold that attacks grapes on the vine and dehydrates them, thereby intensifying their sugar content. Wines made from these grapes are sweet and rich. In the United States such wines are usually designated as "late harvest."

Carbonic Maceration: The technique used most frequently in France's Beaujolais district, in which whole uncrushed clusters of grapes are put into the fermenting tank. The resulting wine is fruity and ready to drink when quite young.

Solera: A stack of barrels that is used in making sherry. The young wine is placed in the top barrels, which are exposed to the heat of the sun, thus giving the wine its nutty flavor. As the wines age, they are transferred to lower barrels in the solera until they reach the bottom level, from which they are bottled.

I must confess some preferences and prejudices. Everyone can look back at magical moments—crucial events that changed the direction of their lives. I like to think about the summer of 1952, when at age eleven I was dragged kicking and screaming to France. My parents wanted me to get some culture; all I wanted to do was play baseball with my friends at home.

One of our stops was Beaune because my father was particularly fond of the wines of the Burgundy region. I remember one morning in particular: We drove to Pommard, where we visited the cellar of a small producer. The place was dark and rank. The farmer— a fellow with wide suspenders and a two-day growth of beard—offered me a taste of wine in a chipped and dirty glass. Before my parents could object I put the glass to my lips and drank.

Then came the thunderclap, the drum roll. This glorious wine from the 1949 vintage jolted me like nothing I had experienced before. In an instant I was transformed from a reluctant traveler into a wine lover. I'll never forget that velvety, rich, explosive flavor; it has stood as a model for all the other wine experiences of my life.

Aside from its dramatic aspects, this event made me a lover of Pinot Noir and an appreciator of French wines. Even today, thirty-three years later, I am a great fancier of Pinot Noir, and I also tend to like wines that are French in style—which means I generally prefer wines with good, firm acidity.

I am very sensitive to the vegetative qualities that show up in many American Cabernet Sauvignons and Merlots. I like my wines on the young side—one to three years old for whites, two to five years old for reds—and I appreciate the judicious use of oak barrels in the making of wine.

In my comments about some Cabernets and a few other wines I have tried to project when the better ones will reach their optimum drinkability. When I say "drink 1988" I don't mean 1988 is the only year in which the wine should be consumed. If a good wine reaches its maturity in 1988 it should stay at that level for at least three or four years, maybe more. If, like me, you prefer wine on the youthful side, you should probably shave a year or two off the ready date; if you like them well aged, hold them for a year or two after the date given.

I have tried to identify each wine as fully as possible. In most cases you will find the year, the variety, the vineyard, the appellation, the price, and any special designations, such as "Reserve" or "Late Harvest," that are recorded on the label. These distinctions are important, because many wineries produce a number of wines of the same variety in the same year. When you want to pair a wine up with a rating in the book, be sure to pay attention to all of these. Also, you will see that throughout the book I've located the wineries by state with the exception of those in California. In California, where the total acreage devoted to wine grapes equals more than that of all the other states combined, viticulture is so pervasive and the various grape-growing regions—from Mendocino to San Diego—so distinct that I decided it would be more useful and informative to locate its wineries by county.

Price is the most inexact of the book's elements. I have tried to list the suggested retail price, which is usually the price charged in the winery tasting room. But in the highly competitive wine market, very few retail establishments actually take the full markup, which means you are likely to find many of the wines at prices 10 to 25 percent below those listed in the book. If you live in or near a large metropolitan area, you are more likely to be able to buy wines at discounted prices. If you are unfortunate enough to live in a state where wine sales are still controlled by the state, the prices may very well be higher.

For older wines I have tried to list the current retail price if the wines are still available. Wines that have virtually vanished from the marketplace are listed—for those who may have some of them in their cellars—but without prices.

In this book I have used six different ratings: ☆☆☆☆, ☆☆☆, ☆☆, ☆, no stars, and ○. Let me explain each of these:

☆☆☆☆   This is the top rating, given to only a very few "outstanding" or "extraordinary" wines. Some of these show great aging potential, but most of them are wines that will provide you with a superb, world-class drinking experience right now. For those who are familiar with the twenty-point rating system, these four-star wines would correspond to those rated eighteen points or better. (Of 5,884 wines rated, 126 were awarded ☆☆☆☆. This represents 2.1 percent of all wines rated.)

☆☆☆   These are wines I have rated "excellent," among the very best wines in the marketplace. These are wines for special occasions, wines for cellaring. Most three-star wines finished close to the top in their tastings. Three stars corresponds to sixteen or seventeen points on the twenty-point scale. (1,517 wines were awarded ☆☆☆. This represents 25.8 percent of all wines rated.)

☆☆   These are wines that I have judged to be "very good." Two-star wines are appealing, everyday wines with no pronounced faults. These are luncheon wines, pizza wines, picnic wines, casual wines that are quite pleasant without demanding a great deal of attention. Two stars corresponds to fifteen points on the twenty-point scale. (2,000 wines were awarded ☆☆, which represents 33.9 percent of all wines rated.)

☆   These are wines that I have rated "good." One-star wines are drinkable but lack depth, charm, style, or a combination of these traits. These wines are not repugnant, but they offer little more than liquid refreshment. One star corresponds to fourteen points on the twenty-point scale. (1,192 wines were awarded ☆. This represents 20.3 percent of all wines rated.)

No Stars   These are wines that I have rated "fair," marginal wines that suffer from one, two, or a combination of flaws. These wines should be avoided if possible. No stars corresponds to thirteen points on the twenty-point scale. (787 wines were awarded no stars, which represents 13.4 percent of all wines rated.)

○   These are wines that I have judged to be "poor," seriously flawed wines that should be avoided at all costs. They have characteristics that render them undrinkable. This rating corresponds to less than thirteen points on the twenty-point scale. (262 wines were rated ○, representing 4.5 percent of all wines rated.)

In addition to these ratings I have occasionally designated a wine as a "good value." Good-value wines are the entries in red. There are no set rules for these wines except that they impressed me as being good or very good wines that were definitely underpriced. For this reason a good-value Chenin Blanc might have to be less than $4 while a good-value Chardonnay could easily cost $7.

Many wines are released without a vintage date. These non-vintage wines are denoted by the letters "NV."

As I worked on this book and got to know the people who make up our domestic wine industry, I was struck by the differences between American winemakers and those I have encountered in Europe. Unlike the vintners of France and Italy, who come out of an agricultural tradition that goes back hundreds of years and many generations, most American winemakers are new to wine and have made a conscious, deliberate choice of winemaking as a career. For many, being in the wine business is the fulfillment of a lifelong dream. American vintners are a dedicated band of individualists who are in the business by choice. They do what they do because they love it, not because they have to or because they think they are going to get rich. (One of the favorite quips among winemakers in California is, "Do you know how to make a small fortune in the wine business? Start with a big fortune.")

I have been very impressed by the generally high quality of the wines that are being produced in the United States. Fine wines are being made in California, New York, Oregon, and Washington—that we know. But they are also beginning to appear with regularity from such places as Maryland, Virginia, Ohio, New Jersey, Idaho, and Texas.

Although there are a substantial number of "fair" and "poor" ratings in the book, there are also a remarkable number of "very good" and "excellent" wines. I have subjected all these wines to tough, uncompromising scrutiny; there has been no room for chauvinism. In fact, many of the tastings at which these judgments were made were not limited to American wines. Foreign wines were judged along with the products of domestic wineries.

American wines easily hold their own when judged against wines from abroad. And even with the dollar high and European currencies in the doldrums, the best American wines still represent a good value by comparison. Among inexpensive wines there is no contest—American jug wines offer considerably more consistency and depth than the ordinary plonk that is exported to the United States from abroad.

The American wine industry has arrived. It offers endless variety as well as excellent quality. I hope this book helps maximize your enjoyment of the many enological delights that await you.

The Wineries and the Wines

Acacia Winery
NAPA COUNTY

2750 Las Amigas Road, Napa, California 94558 (707-226-9991). FOUNDED: 1979. ACREAGE: 42 acres. PRODUCTION: 22,000 cases. DISTRIBUTION: Nationwide. OWNERS: Partnership. Michael Richmond, Jerry Goldstein, and Larry Brooks. WINEMAKER: Larry Brooks. Tours by appointment.

Gravel-voiced Los Angeles attorney Jerry Goldstein and soft-spoken Texan Mike Richmond are an unlikely duo, but their winery has been a raging success from the beginning. Together with winemaker Larry Brooks, a former Toyota salesman, they specialize in vineyard-designated Chardonnays and Pinot Noirs. Most of their grapes come from the cool Carneros region in southern Napa County near where their modern and functional winery gazes out over San Pablo Bay. Acacia has been such a hit that Jerry and Mike are starting a new winery with ex-Robert Keenan winemaker Joe Cafaro that will specialize in Cabernet and Sauvignon Blanc.

WHITE

☆☆☆ 1979 CHARDONNAY ($14.00) Winery Lake, Napa Valley-Carneros. *Ripe, rich, fruity and intense.*

☆☆☆ 1980 CHARDONNAY ($12.50) Napa Valley. *Rich and complex. Coarser than the other Acacia '80s.*

☆☆☆☆ 1980 CHARDONNAY ($14.00) Napa Valley-Carneros. *Buttery, toasty, elegant, complex; a masterpiece.*

☆☆☆ 1980 CHARDONNAY ($17.50) Winery Lake, Napa Valley-Carneros. *Rich and complex, full-bodied, oaky and big.*

☆☆☆☆ 1981 CHARDONNAY ($12.50) Napa Valley. *Lovely, crisp, clean, varietal and oaky. Very stylish.*

☆☆☆ 1981 CHARDONNAY ($14.00) Napa Valley-Carneros. *Clean, well made, nice but not brilliant.*

☆☆☆ 1981 CHARDONNAY ($17.50) Winery Lake, Napa Valley-Carneros. *Smooth, fruity, clean, complex. Drink now or hold until 1988.*

☆☆☆ 1982 CHARDONNAY ($12.50) Napa Valley. *Crisp, clean, lovely fruit, good balance.*

☆☆ 1982 CHARDONNAY ($14.00) Napa Valley. *Rich, vinous, dense, lacking in the middle; disappointing.*

☆☆☆ 1982 CHARDONNAY ($16.00) Marina, Napa Valley-Carneros. *Vinous, good oak, rich and clean.*

☆☆☆ 1982 CHARDONNAY ($17.50) Winery Lake, Napa Valley-Carneros. *Lovely, rich oak; great varietal character and ripe fruit.*

☆☆ 1983 CHARDONNAY ($10.00) Napa Valley. *Heavy, rich, intense, varietal, balanced.*

☆☆☆ 1983 CHARDONNAY ($12.50) Napa Valley. *Fatter than the others. Ripe, oaky, very nice.*

☆☆☆ 1983 CHARDONNAY ($14.00) Napa Valley-Carneros. *Oaky, fruity, charming.*

☆☆☆ 1983 CHARDONNAY ($15.00) Marina, Napa Valley-Carneros. *Crisp, balanced, slightly vinous, lovely.*

☆☆☆ 1983 CHARDONNAY ($17.50) Winery Lake, Napa Valley-Carneros. *Oaky, rich, firm fruit, deep. Drink 1986.*

☆☆☆ 1984 CHARDONNAY ($15.00) Marina, Napa Valley-Carneros. *Lovely fruit, clean flavors, good balance.*

☆ 1982 CAVISTE JOHANNISBERG RIESLING ($4.00) Napa Valley-Carneros. *Dry, bitter, not much varietal character or charm.*

☆☆ 1983 CAVISTE JOHANNISBERG RIESLING ($4.00) Napa Valley. *Better—fresh, clean, varietal, some softness and charm.*

RED

☆☆☆ 1979 PINOT NOIR ($15.00) Iund, Napa Valley-Carneros. *Cherry, spice and snappy fruit. Drink now.*

☆☆☆ 1979 PINOT NOIR ($15.00) Lee, Napa Valley-Carneros. *Fruity and crisp. A little less stuffing than the other two.*

☆☆☆ 1979 PINOT NOIR ($15.00) St. Clair, Napa Valley-Carneros. *Balanced, clean and fruity. Good varietal character.*

☆☆☆ 1980 PINOT NOIR ($15.00) Iund, Napa Valley-Carneros. *Earthy and firmly structured.*

☆☆ 1980 PINOT NOIR ($15.00) Lee, Napa Valley-Carneros. *Dense, rich and fruity but essentially clumsy.*

☆☆☆☆ 1980 PINOT NOIR ($15.00) Madonna, Napa Valley-Carneros. *Earthy, lush, deep with a hint of cherries. Stunning.*

☆☆☆☆ 1980 PINOT NOIR ($15.00) St. Clair, Napa Valley-Carneros. *Snappy and crisp, graceful, balanced, superb.*

☆☆☆ 1981 PINOT NOIR ($15.00) Iund, Napa Valley-Carneros. *Toasty and fruity but with a touch of tar.*

☆☆☆ 1981 PINOT NOIR ($15.00) Lee, Napa Valley-Carneros. *Perhaps the best Acacia of 1981. Soft, lush and lovely.*

☆☆☆ 1981 PINOT NOIR ($15.00) Madonna, Napa Valley-Carneros.

☆☆ 1981 PINOT NOIR ($15.00) St. Clair, Napa Valley-Carneros.

☆☆ 1981 PINOT NOIR ($15.00) Winery Lake, Napa Valley-Carneros. *Meaty and well structured. Long aging potential.*

☆☆ 1982 PINOT NOIR ($15.00) Iund, Napa Valley-Carneros. *Peppery, vegetal, lean and crisp. Drink 1986.*

☆☆☆ 1982 PINOT NOIR ($15.00) Lee, Napa Valley-Carneros. *Rich, hard, lovely structure. Drink 1986 and beyond.*

☆☆☆ 1982 PINOT NOIR ($15.00) Madonna, Napa Valley-Carneros. *Toasty nose, rich berries, earth and some hardness. Drink 1986.*

☆☆☆☆ 1982 PINOT NOIR ($15.00) St. Clair, Napa Valley-Carneros. *Cherry-berry flavors, lush, full, fat, balanced. Drink now.*

☆☆☆☆ 1982 PINOT NOIR ($15.00) Winery Lake, Napa Valley-Carneros. *Deep, brooding, complex, incredible. Drink now.*

☆☆☆ 1983 PINOT NOIR ($15.00) Iund, Napa Valley-Carneros. *Peppery, nice, lush, soft intense richness. Drink 1986.*

☆☆☆ 1983 PINOT NOIR ($15.00) Lee, Napa Valley-Carneros. *A bit softer than the '82; lovely. Drink 1986.*

☆☆☆☆ 1983 PINOT NOIR ($15.00) Madonna, Napa Valley-Carneros. *Dark, rich, lush and superb. Drink 1987.*

☆☆☆☆ 1983 PINOT NOIR ($15.00) St. Clair, Napa Valley-Carneros. *Rich, fat, with berries and depth of fruit. Drink 1986.*

☆☆☆ 1983 PINOT NOIR ($15.00) Winery Lake, Napa Valley-Carneros. *Lush, fruity and remarkably complex. Drink 1987.*

Adams County Winery
PENNSYLVANIA

Peach Tree Road, R.D. 1, Orrtanna, Pennsylvania 17353 (717-334-4631). FOUNDED: 1975. ACREAGE: 10 acres. PRODUCTION: 1,250 cases. DISTRIBUTION: At winery. OWNERS: Ron and Ruth Cooper. WINEMAKER: Ron Cooper. Tours and tasting Thursday–Monday 12:30 P.M.– 6 P.M.

Ron and Ruth Cooper came over from England and settled down on a fruit farm near Gettysburg. "We decided on this area because of the peaches; grapes seem to grow very well in areas that grow peaches," says Ruth. Ron had been making wine since he was a child. His work as a fiber optics engineer did not prevent his wanting to start a serious wine operation of his own. The peach trees were replaced with vinifera and, eventually, French-American hybrids. A 110-year-old barn became the winery.

Adelaida Cellars
SAN LUIS OBISPO COUNTY

Adelaida Star Route, Paso Robles, California 93446 (805-239-0190). FOUNDED: 1983. ACREAGE: None. PRODUCTION: 5,000 cases. DISTRIBUTION: California. OWNERS: John and Andrée Munch. WINEMAKER: John Munch. No tours or tasting.

Originally, Adelaida Cellars was meant to be a company name for John Munch's first priority, "Tonio Conti" champagne. John had been making this champagne since 1982 at Estrella River Winery for a group of Swiss investors—all wine devotees with money to burn. "Adelaida Cellars was a pre-marketing plan," says John. "It was a tool to help introduce Tonio Conti champagne into the market once it became available. But somehow the wines took off on their own, and now Adelaida is totally independent." John Munch, who has a master's degree in Anglo-Saxon poetry and a supplementary career restoring Victorian houses, never intended to become a winemaker until he started investigating the wine business for his friends in Geneva.

WHITE

☆☆ 1982 CHARDONNAY ($7.75) Paso Robles. *Clean, rich, good fruit and oak. A nice first effort.*

SPARKLING

☆☆☆ 1982 TONIO CONTI BLANC DE BLANCS ($17.00) Paso Robles. *Clean, fresh, balanced, very attractive.*

RED

☆☆ 1981 CABERNET SAUVIGNON ($7.25) Paso Robles. *Herbal, clean, rich, nicely made, short on middle palate.*

꙳

Adelsheim Vineyard
OREGON

Route 1, Box 129D, Newberg, Oregon 97132 (503-538-3652). FOUNDED: 1972. ACREAGE: 18 acres. PRODUCTION: 8,000 cases. DISTRIBUTION: Major U.S. markets. OWNERS: David and Virginia Adelsheim. WINEMAKER: David Adelsheim. Tours and tasting by appointment. Invitational tasting events.

In the hills overlooking the Willamette Valley, Dave and Ginny Adelsheim have built their home and their winery. Dave is a former banker and craftsman, and Ginny is a talented potter and sculptor. The Adelsheims eschew spraying and cover their vineyard with nets instead—an effective yet expensive and time-consuming practice. Dave served an apprenticeship at the Eyrie Vineyards under David Lett and was a prime mover in getting Oregon to enact the toughest labeling laws in the nation. Although much of the Adelsheim production comes from estate-grown grapes, some are purchased from growers in Oregon and Washington.

WHITE

☆☆ 1981 CHARDONNAY ($11.00) Yamhill, Oregon. *Rich, deep, good oak, slightly dried out fruit.*

☆☆ 1982 CHARDONNAY ($11.00) Yamhill, Oregon. *Attractive fruit and rich flavors balanced by crisp acidity.*

☆☆ 1982 SEMILLON ($7.50) Sagemoor Farms, Washington. *Fruity, dense, clean.*

☆☆ 1982 WHITE RIESLING ($6.95) Yamhill, Oregon. *Crisp, clean, decent varietal character.*

RED

☆ 1981 MERLOT ($9.00) Sagemoor Farms, Washington. *Vegetal and simple.*

☆☆☆ 1981 MERLOT ($12.00) Limited Bottling, Sagemoor Farms, Washington. *Tart, fruity, clean and lovely.*

☆☆☆ 1982 MERLOT ($9.00) 90% Washington, 10% Oregon, 5% Cabernet. *Rich, spicy, clean and well built.*

☆☆☆ 1981 PINOT NOIR ($10.00) Yamhill, Oregon. *Thin but balanced and elegant.*

Adler Fels Winery
SONOMA COUNTY

5325 Corrick Lane, Santa Rosa, California 95405 (707-539-3123). FOUNDED: 1980. ACREAGE: None. PRODUCTION: 6,000 cases. DISTRIBUTION: Major U.S. markets. OWNERS: David Coleman, Ayn Ryan, and Lila Buford. WINEMAKERS: Pat Heck and David Coleman. Tours and tasting by appointment.

Graphic designer Dave Coleman and his wife, Ayn Ryan, didn't seem to take their winery seriously at first but all that has changed. Ms. Ryan's mother, Lila Burford, a partner in the winery, is a Merzoian (see Château St. Jean). The renovated barn-winery sits on a perch overlooking the Valley of the Moon at a spot known locally as "Eagle Rock," which translates into German as *Adler Fels*. Mr. Coleman designed the label, which has run into some consumer resistance because of its resemblance to the eagle symbol of the Third Reich.

WHITE

O   1981 CHARDONNAY ($9.00) Hiatt, Mendocino.

☆☆ 1981 CHARDONNAY ($12.00) St. Francis, Sonoma.

☆☆ 1982 CHARDONNAY ($8.00) Barra, Mendocino. *Lush, rich, oaky, attractive.*

☆☆ 1983 CHARDONNAY ($10.50) Nelson, Sonoma Valley. *Decent, varietal, oaky.*

☆☆ 1982 FUME BLANC ($8.25) Salzgeber-Chan, Sonoma.

☆☆☆ 1983 FUME BLANC ($8.50) Salzgeber-Chan, Sonoma.

☆☆ 1981 JOHANNISBERG RIESLING ($6.50) Bacigalupi, Sonoma. *Lush, fat, good fruit.*

SPARKLING

1981 MELANGE A DEUX ($15.00) Sonoma. *50% Johannisberg Riesling, 50% Gewürztraminer.*

RED

☆☆ 1976 CABERNET SAUVIGNON ($12.00) Napa Valley. *Made by Heitz. Raisiny, rich and complex.*

1980 CABERNET SAUVIGNON ($10.00) Napa Valley. *Veggie, muddy, some decent fruit.*

☆   1982 CABERNET SAUVIGNON ($10.00) Napa Valley. *3% Merlot. Weedy, dense, balanced.*

AEOLUS *see* San Pasqual Vineyards

Ahern Winery
LOS ANGELES COUNTY

818 Arroyo Avenue, San Fernando, California 91340 (818-365-3106). FOUNDED: 1978. ACREAGE: None. PRODUCTION: 7,000 cases. DISTRIBUTION: Nationwide. OWNERS: Jim and Joyce Ahern. WINEMAKER: Jim Ahern. Tours and tasting by appointment.

Jim and Joyce Ahern run the second-largest winery in Los Angeles. Jim started as a home winemaker in 1971 and still is an active instructor for hobbyists. Their charmless but efficient warehouse-winery produces mainly barrel-fermented Chardonnay (mostly bought from the Edna and Santa Maria valleys).

WHITE

☆☆☆ 1981 CHARDONNAY ($11.00) MacGregor, San Luis Obispo.

☆ 1982 CHARDONNAY ($10.00) Edna Valley. *A trifle weedy but pleasant.*

☆ 1982 CHARDONNAY ($12.00) MacGregor, San Luis Obispo. *Snappy, crisp and smooth but with some strong vegetal notes.*

☆☆☆ 1982 CHARDONNAY ($12.00) Paragon, San Luis Obispo. *Rich, full and oaky. Good lemony fruit.*

☆☆☆ 1981 WHITE RIESLING ($6.00).

RED

☆☆ 1980 ZINFANDEL ($7.50) Amador.

ᘏ᙭

Ahlgren Vineyard
SANTA CRUZ COUNTY

20320 Highway 9, Boulder Creek, California 95006 (408-338-6071). FOUNDED: 1976. ACREAGE: 2 acres. PRODUCTION: 1,400 cases. DISTRIBUTION: California, New York, Rhode Island, Boston, and New Jersey. OWNERS: Dexter and Valerie Ahlgren. WINEMAKERS: Dexter and Valerie Ahlgren; Dennelle Ahlgren Borelli, assistant winemaker. Tours and tasting by appointment.

Dexter Ahlgren is a consulting civil engineer and his wife, Valerie, was an English teacher until she decided to devote full time to their winery, one of the smallest in California. Located at their mountainside country home, the winery uses antique basket presses and small wooden fermenters with open tops. A new winery and (slightly) expanded production are planned but the "handmade" style of the wine won't change.

WHITE

1980 CHARDONNAY ($12.50) Ventana, Monterey. *Vinous, overdone, weedy.*

☆☆ 1981 CHARDONNAY ($12.00) Ventana, Monterey. *Big and oaky. A fine example of "California-style."*

☆ 1982 CHARDONNAY ($13.00) Ventana, Monterey. *Earthy, rich, fat and hot with a touch of volatile acidity.*

☆☆ 1981 SEMILLON ($8.50) Ruby Hill, Livermore Valley.

1982 SEMILLON ($8.50) Santa Cruz Mountains. *Tanky, harsh, very unattractive.*

1982 SEMILLON ($8.50) Alma, Santa Cruz Mountains. *Ripe, overdone, not clean.*

RED

☆☆ 1977 CABERNET SAUVIGNON ($7.50) Bates Ranch, Santa Cruz Mountains. *Deep, rich, raisiny, fat. Drink 1986.*

☆☆☆ 1978 CABERNET SAUVIGNON ($12.00) Napa Valley.

☆☆ 1979 CABERNET SAUVIGNON ($10.00) 79% Tepusquet, 17% Petite Sirah, 4% Merlot. Ventana, Central Coast. *Inky and intense, rich, fruity and harsh but very good.*

☆ 1980 CABERNET SAUVIGNON ($10.50) Rutherford-Napa Valley. *Intense, dark, tannic, chocolatey, a monster.*

☆☆ 1980 CABERNET SAUVIGNON ($10.50) Bates Ranch, Santa Cruz Mountains. *Herbs and berries. Rich, dense, tannic. Drink 1986.*

☆☆ 1981 CABERNET SAUVIGNON ($10.00) Cristina, Napa Valley. *Herbal, balanced, clean, lovely structure. Drink now.*

☆ 1979 ZINFANDEL ($9.00) Livermore Valley.

☆ 1980 ZINFANDEL ($7.50) California. *Intense, berried, overdone, too concentrated.*

☆ 1981 ZINFANDEL ($6.75) Livermore Valley. *Hard, lacking freshness.*

ᘏ᙭

Alamara Vineyards
MISSISSIPPI

Frost Bridge Road, Mathersville, Mississippi 39360 (601-687-5548). FOUNDED: 1979. ACREAGE: 40 acres. PRODUCTION: 10,000 cases. DISTRIBUTION: Mississippi, Louisiana, and Florida. OWNERS: Margaret and Alex P. Mathers. WINEMAKER: Alex P. Mathers. Tours and tasting Monday through Saturday 9 A.M.–5 P.M.

After working twelve years as chief chemist for the Bureau of Alcohol, Tobacco and Firearms, Alex Mathers started planning for retirement. Although he worked in Washington, D.C., Alex moved to a 140-acre farm in Mississippi, where he planted a small vineyard. When he retired in 1974, he built the winery and began doing research on which grapevine types could withstand Mississippi's climate. "The weather in Mississippi is just fine for growing grapes," says Alex, "but the heat, humidity, and moisture are just as excellent for promoting mold and disease." Before expanding either his vineyards or his winery, Alex is awaiting further research on disease resistance and vine yields.

WHITE

NV   SCUPPERNONG ($2.50) Chablis, Mississippi.
NV   SCUPPERNONG ($2.50) Chablis-Pale Dry, Mississippi.
NV   SCUPPERNONG ($2.50) Sauterne, Mississippi. *Sweet.*

ROSE

O   NV   PINK MUSCADINE ($2.50) Mississippi.

Alaqua Vineyards Winery
FLORIDA

Route 1, Box 97-C4, Freeport, Florida 32439 (904-835-2644). FOUNDED: 1981. ACREAGE: 9 acres. PRODUCTION: 2,700 cases. DISTRIBUTION: Florida. OWNERS: Foster and Rebecca Burgess. WINEMAKER: Foster Burgess. Tours and tasting Wednesday–Saturday 10 A.M.–5 P.M., Sunday 1 P.M.–5 P.M.

Physicist Foster Burgess was annoyed when he couldn't find a single bottle of Florida wine on the wine list of a local restaurant. To rectify this situation, Foster started an experimental vineyard in 1977 and drew up plans for a Tudor-style winery. Foster buys locally grown grapes to supplement his own production. He specializes in three varieties: Carlos, Noble, and Muscadine—the only native Florida grape produced commercially in the state.

Alderbrook Winery
SONOMA COUNTY

2306 Magnolia Drive, Healdsburg, California 95448 (707-433-9154). FOUNDED: 1982. ACREAGE: 55 acres. PRODUCTION: 10,000 cases. DISTRIBUTION: California. OWNERS: Partnership. John Grace, Philip Staley, and Mark Rafanelli. WINEMAKER: Philip Staley. Tours and tasting by appointment.

John Grace left the restaurant business to look for a job in the wine industry. At just about the same time, his high school buddy Mark Rafanelli was ripping prune trees off his recently purchased Healdsburg property. Mark, son of Americo Rafanelli, owner-winemaker of A. Rafanelli Winery (see), recruited another friend, Phil Staley, a dentist who frequently moonlighted as a winemaker. Together, the three partners have planted the property with grapevines and turned the old prune barn into a winery.

WHITE

☆☆ 1982 CHARDONNAY ($8.25) Sonoma. *Clean, vinous, lovely with a charming oak sweetness.*

☆☆☆ 1983 CHARDONNAY ($8.75) Sonoma. *Crisp, clean, balanced, complex, lovely.*

☆☆ 1982 SAUVIGNON BLANC ($7.00) Sonoma.

☆☆ 1983 SAUVIGNON BLANC ($7.50) Sonoma. *Tart, snappy, clean, fresh.*

☆☆☆ 1983 SEMILLON ($6.00) Sonoma. *Oaky, crisp, snappy, clean and balanced; lovely.*

る

Alexander Valley Vineyards
SONOMA COUNTY

8644 Highway 128, Healdsburg, California 95448 (707-433-7209). FOUNDED: 1975. ACREAGE: 240 acres. PRODUCTION: 18,000 cases. DISTRIBUTION: Major market states. OWNER: Hank W. Wetzel, managing general partner; Katie Wetzel Murphy, marketing director. WINEMAKER: Hank W. Wetzel. Tasting daily 10 A.M.–5 P.M. Tours by appointment.

Aerospace executive Harry Wetzel bought the Cyrus Alexander homestead in 1963 and developed it into one of California's most beautiful vineyard sites. All the grapes are home grown and the wines are made by Harry's son Hank; his daughter Katie Murphy works in marketing. One of the established wineries of the area, Alexander Valley Vineyards has built a solid reputation for consistent quality.

WHITE

☆☆☆ 1975 CHARDONNAY Alexander Valley.

☆☆ 1979 CHARDONNAY ($8.25) Estate, Alexander Valley. *Buttery, rich, vinous, attractive.*

☆ 1980 CHARDONNAY ($10.25) Estate, Alexander Valley.

☆ 1981 CHARDONNAY ($10.00) Estate, Alexander Valley. *Crisp and full but with a troublesome touch of oxidation.*

☆☆☆ 1982 CHARDONNAY ($10.00) Estate, Alexander Valley. *Rich, crisp, clean and lovely.*

☆☆☆ 1983 CHARDONNAY ($10.00) Estate, Alexander Valley. *Lush, rich yet more elegant than the '82.*

☆☆☆ 1982 CHENIN BLANC DRY ($6.00) Estate, Alexander Valley. *Crisp, fresh and dry with lots of appeal.*

☆☆☆ 1983 CHENIN BLANC ($6.00) Estate, Alexander Valley. *Fresh, clean, fruity, soft and round.*

☆☆ 1982 GEWURZTRAMINER ($6.25) Estate, Alexander Valley. *1.2% residual sugar. Fresh, richly varietal, pleasant.*

☆☆☆ 1983 GEWURZTRAMINER ($6.50) Estate, Alexander Valley. *1.5% residual sugar. Tart, crisp, clean, lively, varietal.*

☆ 1981 JOHANNISBERG RIESLING ($6.25) Estate, Alexander Valley. *Pleasant but a bit flabby.*

☆☆ 1984 JOHANNISBERG RIESLING ($6.00) Estate, Alexander Valley. *Floral, spicy, clean, good acidity.*

RED

☆☆ 1975 CABERNET SAUVIGNON Alexander Valley.

☆☆☆ 1978 CABERNET SAUVIGNON ($6.50) Estate, Alexander Valley. *This wine has matured beautifully. Rich, balanced, elegant.*

☆☆ 1979 CABERNET SAUVIGNON ($7.00) Estate, Alexander Valley. *Balanced, attractive, well made.*

☆☆ 1980 CABERNET SAUVIGNON ($9.00) Estate, Alexander Valley. *Rich, intense, clean and raisiny.*

☆☆☆ 1981 CABERNET SAUVIGNON ($9.00) Estate, Alexander Valley. *Rich, intense, balanced. Drink 1986 and beyond.*
 ☆☆ 1982 CABERNET SAUVIGNON ($10.00) Estate, Alexander Valley. *Lush, clean, rich, good finish. Drink 1988 and beyond.*
 ☆☆ 1982 CABERNET SAUVIGNON ($10.00) Estate, Alexander Valley. *Herbal, clean, lush, should mature quickly. Drink 1986.*
 ☆☆ 1980 PINOT NOIR ($6.00) Estate, Alexander Valley.
 ☆☆ 1981 PINOT NOIR ($6.00) Estate, Alexander Valley. *Rich and attractive; simple with a touch of weediness.*
 ☆☆ 1982 PINOT NOIR ($6.50) Estate, Alexander Valley. *Rich, snappy, very pleasant.*
  ☆ NV SIN ZIN ($6.00) Alexander Valley. *Fat, berried, overdone.*

Allegro Vineyards
PENNSYLVANIA

R.D. 2, Box 64 Sechrist Road, Brogue, Pennsylvania 17309 (717-927-9148). FOUNDED: 1980. ACREAGE: 15 acres. PRODUCTION: 2,000 cases. DISTRIBUTION: Pennsylvania, Washington D.C., and Maryland. OWNERS: John H. and Timothy Crouch. WINEMAKERS: John H. and Timothy Crouch. Tours and tasting Wednesday–Friday 2 P.M.–7 P.M., weekends 12–5 P.M.

Backyard grape growers, amateur winemakers, John and Timothy Crouch invested in what they thought was a pretty good deal. They purchased a rundown vineyard at bare land prices. "It probably took as much if not more work to bring the old vines back into production than it would have if we had started from scratch," says John. Tim, his brother, works as a project manager for an electrical contractor while John runs the winery and vineyards. "Tim makes the money and I spend it," says John, laughing. The brothers make only estate-grown wines, both vinifera and French-American hybrids. The stark, utilitarian, garage-style winery has a lovely tasting room paneled in white cedar, an outside terrace, and a picnic area.

Almadén Vineyards
SANTA CLARA COUNTY

1530 Blossom Hill Road, San Jose, California 95118 (408-269-1312). FOUNDED: 1852. ACREAGE: 5,630 acres. PRODUCTION: 10 million cases. DISTRIBUTION: Nationwide and foreign. OWNER: National Distillers and Chemical Corp. Ron Siletto, vice president and general manager. WINEMAKER: Klaus Mathes, vice president. OTHER LABELS: Charles Lefranc, Caves Laurent Perrier, Le Domaine. Tours daily 9 A.M.–3 P.M. Tasting at Almadén's Don Pacheco Tasting Room, 8090 Pacheco Pass Highway, Hollister, California. April–October: 10 A.M.–6 P.M., November–March: 10 A.M.–5 P.M.

"California's oldest producing winery" was founded in 1852 by Charles Lefranc, Paul Masson's father-in-law, and built into a behemoth in post-Prohibition days by San Francisco financier Louis Benoist. Since 1967 the parent company has been giant National Distillers. Almadén has ridden to fame and fortune on "Chablis" (2,800,000 cases produced last year) and sparkling wines. San Jose's urban sprawl is crawling right in the back door of the historic old winery, and snazzy new facilities have been built near the 4,000-plus acres in San Benito County (to the south) and in Monterey County (farther south). Almadén is now in third place in total volume of production. It trails Gallo and aggressive Seagram's, which markets the Taylor California Cellars and Paul Masson brands. Nevertheless, Almadén still retains a good reputation with consumers which winemaster Klaus Mathes is trying hard to perpetuate. The Charles Lefranc line is Almadén's semi-successful attempt to compete in the premium market.

WHITE

☆ NV GOLDEN CHABLIS ($2.85) California. *Soft, round, off-dry; tastes mostly of Thompson Seedless.*

NV MONTEREY CHABLIS ($2.88) Monterey.

☆☆ NV MOUNTAIN RHINE ($2.88) California. *Sweet, lush, fresh and appealing.*

☆ NV MOUNTAIN WHITE CHABLIS ($2.88) California. *Fruity, off-dry, dull but decent.*

O NV MOUNTAIN WHITE SAUTERNE ($2.88) California. *Oxidized and dull.*

☆ 1982 CHARLES LEFRANC MAISON BLANC ($3.13) San Benito. *Decent, clean, lacking character.*

☆☆ 1983 CHARLES LEFRANC MAISON BLANC ($3.40) San Benito. *85% Pinot Blanc. Decent, soft, round, clean.*

☆☆ 1979 CHARLES LEFRANC CHARDONNAY ($8.45) San Benito. *Clean but vinous and heavy.*

☆ 1981 CHARDONNAY ($6.50) San Benito. *Clean and balanced.*

1981 CHARLES LEFRANC CHARDONNAY ($8.80) San Benito. *Tanky nose, decent but tarnished.*

1981 CAVES LAURENT PERRIER CHARDONNAY ($12.00) California.

1982 CHARDONNAY ($5.75) San Benito. *Flat and lacking varietal character.*

1982 CAVES LAURENT PERRIER CHARDONNAY ($12.50) California. *Perfumy, strange, unappealing.*

☆ 1983 CHARDONNAY ($5.50) San Benito. *Dull, lacking varietal character.*

1983 CHARLES LEFRANC CHARDONNAY ($8.80) San Benito. *Dull, lacking fruit.*

NV CHENIN BLANC ($3.50) California.

☆ 1982 CHENIN BLANC ($3.75) California. *Sweet, vegetal, quite decent.*

☆☆ 1982 FUME BLANC ($6.50) Monterey.

☆☆ 1983 CHARLES LEFRANC FUME BLANC ($8.25) California. *Lush, varietal, delicious.*

☆ 1979 CHARLES LEFRANC GEWURZTRAMINER ($7.00) Late Harvest, Paicines, San Benito. *6.6% residual sugar. Melony, soft and a little dull.*

☆☆☆ 1982 GEWURZTRAMINER ($5.85) San Benito. *Round, full, clean, fresh, off-dry, delightful.*

☆☆☆ 1976 CHARLES LEFRANC JOHANNISBERG RIESLING ($10.00) Special Harvest, San Benito. *7% residual sugar. Dark, rich, honied, botrytised, lovely.*

1977 CHARLES LEFRANC JOHANNISBERG RIESLING ($8.50) Late Harvest, San Benito. *5.6% residual sugar. Minty and somewhat dull fruit.*

1979 CHARLES LEFRANC JOHANNISBERG RIESLING ($12.00) Select Late Harvest, Paicines, San Benito. *375ml. Oxidized, no fruit.*

☆☆ 1981 JOHANNISBERG RIESLING ($5.35) San Benito.

☆☆ NV RIESLING ($3.75) California. *1.5% residual sugar. Sweet, spicy, clean.*

☆ 1980 SAUVIGNON BLANC ($5.25) Monterey.

☆ 1982 SAUVIGNON BLANC ($4.50) Monterey. *Soft, sweet and grassy.*

☆ 1982 CHARLES LEFRANC SAUVIGNON BLANC ($9.75) Late Harvest, Monterey. *11.3% residual sugar. Lush, thick, grassy, vegetal.*

☆☆ 1982 CHATEAU LEFRANC SAUVIGNON BLANC ($9.75) Monterey. *11.5% residual sugar. Herbal and rich, clean, smooth.*

SPARKLING

O NV PINK CHAMPAGNE ($2.50) California. *Very sweet and syrupy.*

NV LE DOMAINE ($4.48) California. *Sweet and oily.*

☆ 1976 GRAND CUVEE, NATURE ($8.90) California. *Heavy. Made from Chardonnay grapes.*

O 1977 EYE OF THE PARTRIDGE ($8.00) California. *Sweet and syrupy.*

1979 EXTRA DRY CHAMPAGNE ($7.20) California.

1979 EYE OF THE PARTRIDGE ($8.90) California. *Dull, heavy.*
☆ 1981 BRUT ($7.20) California. *Transfer.*
1981 EYE OF THE PARTRIDGE ($8.90) California. *Dull, decent fruit, better than the '79.*

BLANC DE NOIR

☆☆ 1984 CHARLES LEFRANC WHITE ZINFANDEL ($4.50) California. *Sweet, varietal, charming, clean, very pleasant.*

RED

☆ NV MOUNTAIN RED BURGUNDY ($2.87) California.
NV MOUNTAIN RED CHIANTI ($2.87) California.
☆☆ NV MONTEREY BURGUNDY ($3.52) Monterey. *A consistent winner among red jug wines. Fruity and fresh.*
☆ 1981 CHARLES LEFRANC MAISON ROUGE ($3.25) San Benito. *Mostly Pinot Noir.*
☆ 1983 CHARLES LEFRANC MAISON ROUGE ($3.00) San Benito. *Crisp, clean, snappy, a bit thin.*
1975 CHARLES LEFRANC CABERNET SAUVIGNON ($7.00) Monterey. *Sweet, dull.*
☆ 1977 CHARLES LEFRANC CABERNET SAUVIGNON Monterey. *Nice but this one has seen better days.*
☆☆ 1977 CABERNET SAUVIGNON ($4.50) Monterey. *Soft and elegant, earthy and very good.*
☆☆ 1978 CABERNET SAUVIGNON ($4.50) Monterey. *Clean, balanced, varietal, herbal, lovely.*
☆☆ 1979 CABERNET SAUVIGNON ($5.00) Monterey. *Slightly vegetal, thick, rich, lacks grace.*
☆☆ 1979 CHARLES LEFRANC CABERNET SAUVIGNON ($8.45) Monterey. *Herbal, ripe, rich, well made. Drink 1986.*
☆☆☆ 1980 CABERNET SAUVIGNON ($5.50) Monterey. *Ripe, soft and beautifully structured.*
1980 CHARLES LEFRANC CABERNET PFEFFER ($7.65) Cienaga Valley. *Dull, odd, not very Cabernet-like.*
☆☆☆ 1981 CABERNET SAUVIGNON ($4.00) Monterey. *Clean, fruity, varietal, charming. Drink now or hold.*
☆☆☆ 1981 CHARLES LEFRANC CABERNET SAUVIGNON ($8.50) Monterey. *Rich, lush, fat, complex, delightful. Drink 1986.*
☆ 1977 PINOT NOIR ($5.00) San Benito.
☆ 1978 PINOT NOIR ($4.75) San Benito. *Decent but with stemmy, celery flavors.*
1979 PINOT NOIR ($5.00) San Benito. *Oily, herbal, low acidity.*
☆ 1982 PINOT NOIR ($5.85) San Benito. *Green, hard, decent but not likable. Maybe time will smooth it.*
1978 ZINFANDEL ($2.85) Monterey.
1978 CHARLES LEFRANC ZINFANDEL ($6.00) Royale, San Benito. *Muddy and flabby.*
☆☆ 1979 ZINFANDEL ($3.75) 34% Monterey, 64% San Benito. *Clean and well made.*
☆☆☆ 1980 CHARLES LEFRANC ROYALE ZINFANDEL ($7.50) San Benito. *3.2% residual sugar. Crisp, fruity, balanced, very good.*

Alpine Vineyards
OREGON

Green Peak Road, Alpine, Oregon 97456 (503-424-5857). FOUNDED: 1980. ACREAGE: 20 acres.
PRODUCTION: 3,000 cases. DISTRIBUTION: California, Hawaii, Oregon, and Washington.
OWNERS: Dan and Christine Jepsen. WINEMAKER: Dan Jepsen. Tours and tasting June 15–

September 15: 12–5 P.M. weekends. September 16–June 14: 12–5 P.M. Sunday only. Weekday tours by appointment only.

Dan Jepsen is a doctor in Eugene and his wife, Christine, is a nurse. Their remote mid-Willamette Valley 60-acre ranch and small winery-home is the fulfillment of a dream that began with Dan's study of chemistry and that was fully formed by his travels in Europe. He came back determined to make first-rate Burgundian-style Pinot Noir.

WHITE

☆   1981 BLANC DE BLANCS ($6.00) Estate, Oregon.
☆☆   1980 CHARDONNAY ($8.50) Estate, Oregon.
☆☆☆ 1981 WHITE RIESLING ($7.00) Estate, Oregon.
☆☆☆ 1982 WHITE RIESLING ($7.50) Estate, Willamette Valley, Oregon. *Melony nose, fresh and fruity.*

RED

☆☆☆ 1982 PINOT NOIR ($9.00) Estate, Willamette Valley, Oregon. *Lovely, elegant, light, balanced.*

Alta Vineyard Cellar
NAPA COUNTY

1311 Schramsberg Road, Calistoga, California 94515 (707-942-6708). FOUNDED: 1878. ACREAGE: 10 acres. PRODUCTION: 2,000 cases. DISTRIBUTION: California and other states. OWNERS: Benjamin and Rose Falk. WINEMAKER: Jon P. Axhelm. Tours by appointment.

Benjamin and Rose Falk have become Napa Valley fixtures since they moved to California and revived this old property in 1970. Back in 1880 Alta was visited by Robert Louis Stevenson during his honeymoon, as reported in his *Silverado Squatters.* There have been financial setbacks, but Alta continues to produce small quantities of Chardonnay.

WHITE

1980 CHARDONNAY ($13.50) Napa. *Dull and lifeless.*
☆☆   1981 CHARDONNAY ($14.50) Estate, Napa Valley. *Crisp and richly varietal. Very classy.*

Amador City Winery
AMADOR COUNTY

Highway 49 and O'Neill Alley, Amador City, California 95601 (209-267-5320). FOUNDED: 1967. ACREAGE: None. PRODUCTION: 8,000 cases. DISTRIBUTION: California. OWNERS: Harry and Leslie Ahrendt. WINEMAKER: Harry Ahrendt. Tasting daily 10 A.M.–6 P.M.

This winery was started by Lee Merrill in 1967. Harry Ahrendt, a printer who joined Lee in 1970, assumed management of the winery after Lee died in 1978. Harry and his wife, Leslie, are making generic wines such as "Sauternes" and Chablis as well as a spiced wine that is served hot. Harry still has his printing press, but he only uses it for winery materials such as labels and brochures.

BLANC DE NOIR

☆☆☆ 1982 WHITE ZINFANDEL ($5.00) Amador. *Fresh, clean, snappy, delicious.*

Amador Foothill Winery
AMADOR COUNTY

12500 Steiner Road, Plymouth, California 95669 (209-245-6307). FOUNDED: 1980. ACREAGE: 10 acres. PRODUCTION: 7,500 cases. DISTRIBUTION: Alaska, California, Colorado, Nevada, New York, Texas, and Washington D.C. OWNER: Ben Zeitman. WINEMAKER: Ben Zeitman. Tours and tasting weekends and holidays 12–5 P.M. or by appointment.

Ben Zeitman, a former NASA research chemist, is a Zinfandel activist; he is extremely vocal in his championing of this most American variety. His winery is very energy efficient and includes a rock bed cooling system which uses no mechanical refrigeration. In 1983 the winery's own vineyard was harvested for the first time. Sauvignon Blanc, Cabernet Sauvignon, and Semillon were picked in 1984. Production is projected to reach 10,000 cases.

WHITE

☆☆ 1983 AMADOR FUME BLANC ($7.50) Amador. *Snappy, clean, lovely roundness and richness. Bottle variation.*

BLANC DE NOIR

☆☆☆ 1984 WHITE ZINFANDEL ($5.25) Amador. *Lovely, fruity, delicious.*

RED

☆☆ 1980 ZINFANDEL ($6.00) Amador.
☆☆☆ 1980 ZINFANDEL ($8.00) Eschen Vineyard, Fiddletown, Amador. *Super fruit and varietal character. Good aging potential.*
☆ 1981 ZINFANDEL ($6.00) Amador. *Raisiny, tannic, intense.*

Amador Winery
AMADOR COUNTY

Highway 49 and O'Neill Alley, Box 65, Amador City, California 95601 (209-267-5320). FOUNDED: 1967. ACREAGE: None. PRODUCTION: 6,000 cases. DISTRIBUTION: At winery. OWNERS: Harry L. and Leslie Ahrendt. WINEMAKER: Harry L. Ahrendt. No tours. Tasting daily 10 A.M.– 6 P.M.

The American wine industry is full of individualists and Harry Ahrendt is certainly one of them. He started by printing labels for the hobbyist owner-winemaker Lee Merrill who built the winery—one of the oldest in Amador. Lee taught Harry about winemaking and then "messed up and died" as Harry puts it. Harry now runs the show with his wife. For the most part, the winery makes only generic wines, some of which have rather fanciful names.

Amity Vineyards
OREGON

Route 1, Box 348B, Amity, Oregon 97101 (503-835-2362). FOUNDED: 1976. ACREAGE: 15 acres. PRODUCTION: 8,000 cases. DISTRIBUTION: Major U.S. markets. OWNERS: Myron Redford, Ione Redford, and Janis Checchia. WINEMAKER: Myron Redford. OTHER LABEL: Redford Cellars. Self-guided tours and tasting at the winery. Group tours by appointment. Tasting room at Amity Oregon Wine Tasting Room, Highway 18, Bellevue. Call for information.

Myron Redford is one Oregon's most vocal spokesmen. He is convinced that the best American Pinot Noirs will come, eventually, from his state. A former researcher at the University of Washington, Myron is a thoughtful and analytical winemaker. His brother Stephen produces a small amount of Merlot and Cabernet under the Redford Cellars label.

WHITE

NV SOLSTICE BLANC ($4.75) Washington-Oregon. *Varnishy, dull.*

☆ 1982 SOLSTICE BLANC ($5.00) 58% Oregon, 42% Washington. *Six-variety blend. Dry, somewhat heavy and dull.*

☆ 1983 SOLSTICE BLANC ($5.00) 83% Washington, 17% Oregon. *Clean, herbal, decent.*

☆☆ 1980 CHARDONNAY ($10.00) Oregon.

O 1981 CHARDONNAY ($10.00) Oregon. *Oxidized, unattractive.*

O 1982 CHARDONNAY ($10.00) Oregon. *Oxidized, dirty.*

☆ 1983 GEWURZTRAMINER ($7.00) Oregon. *0.06% residual sugar. Dry, bitter, well made but not likable.*

☆☆ 1982 WHITE RIESLING ($7.00) Dry White Riesling, Amity, Red Hills, Feltz and three others, Oregon.

☆☆ 1983 WHITE RIESLING ($7.00) Dry White Riesling, Oregon. *Very spritzy, clean, dry, pleasant.*

RED

☆☆ 1980 REDFORD CABERNET-MERLOT ($8.00) Washington. *44% Merlot. Dense, soft, some weediness but nice.*

☆ 1980 REDFORD CELLARS CABERNET SAUVIGNON ($5.00) Oregon-Washington. *54% Cabernet, 46% Merlot. Varietal with some weediness.*

☆☆ 1978 PINOT NOIR ($8.00) Oregon. *Burgundian and elegant.*

☆☆ 1978 PINOT NOIR ($20.00) 76% Windhill Pinot, 24% Amity Gamay, Oregon.

☆☆☆ 1978 PINOT NOIR ($20.00) Winemaker's Reserve, 76% Windhill, 24% Estate Gamay, Oregon. *Rich, earthy and complex with very Burgundian finesse.*

☆☆ 1979 PINOT NOIR ($9.00) 50% Washington, 50% Oregon. *50% carbonic maceration. Pale, underripe and shallow.*

☆☆ 1980 PINOT NOIR ($8.00) Oregon. *Lush fruit in nose but somewhat slim on the palate.*

☆☆ 1980 PINOT NOIR ($15.00) Winemaker's Reserve, Oregon. *Rich, stemmy, earthy and complex.*

☆ 1981 PINOT NOIR ($7.00) Four vineyards, Oregon. *Thin, dull.*

☆ 1982 PINOT NOIR ($7.00) Four vineyards, Oregon. *Pale, dull, lacking varietal character.*

಼

Anderson Valley Vineyards
NEW MEXICO

1500 Montano Road Northwest, Albuquerque, New Mexico 87107 (505-344-7266). FOUNDED: 1984. ACREAGE: 18 acres. PRODUCTION: 5,000 cases. DISTRIBUTION: New Mexico. OWNER: Patty Anderson. Chris Anderson, winery manager. WINEMAKER: Chris Anderson. Tours and tasting May–December: Tuesday–Saturday 12–5 P.M. or by appointment.

Maxie Anderson was a famous balloonist, the first to fly a balloon across the Atlantic. When he wasn't breaking ballooning records, he was working as a chief executive for Rancher's Exploration, a silver mining firm in New Mexico. A great connoisseur of wine with a deep interest in winemaking and viticulture, Maxie started planting grapes in 1976 in hopes of eventually starting a small winery with his wife, Patty, and their son Chris. But in 1983, Maxie was killed in a ballooning accident during the World Cup Race in Germany. "It was about that same time that the vineyards were really coming into production," says Chris, "so we decided to go ahead with Dad's plans for the winery." Chris is an electrical engineer, but he is managing the winery with the help of a consultant.

S. Anderson Vineyard
NAPA COUNTY

1473 Yountville Crossroad, Napa, California 94558 (707-944-8642). FOUNDED: 1979. ACREAGE: 49 acres. PRODUCTION: 3,500 cases. DISTRIBUTION: Major U.S. markets. OWNERS: Stanley B. and Carol G. Anderson. WINEMAKER: Stanley B. Anderson. Tours available on weekends by appointment. No tasting. Retail sales by appointment.

Stanley Anderson is a dentist from Pasadena who has been growing high-quality Chardonnay grapes in Yountville for a number of years. When he decided to make his own wine he sent his wife, Carol, to take a few courses at U.C. Davis. The Anderson's new winery will allow production to expand to 10,000 cases (3,000 Chardonnay and 7,000 sparkling). To accommodate this expansion, the Andersons recently dug storage caves deep into the hillside behind the winery.

WHITE

☆☆ 1980 CHARDONNAY ($12.50) Estate, Napa Valley. *Oily, heavy, rich and oaky with good acidity.*
☆☆☆ 1981 CHARDONNAY ($12.50) Estate, Napa Valley. *Fresh and beautifully balanced.*
☆☆☆ 1982 CHARDONNAY ($12.50) Napa Valley. *Fresh, crisp, fruity with nice oak and balance.*

SPARKLING

☆☆☆ 1980 BLANC DE NOIRS ($15.50) Estate, Napa Valley. *Fresh, clean and attractive.*
☆☆☆ 1982 CUVEE DE LA CAVE ($14.00) Napa Valley. *Yeasty, fresh, lush, lovely.*

Anderson Wine Cellars
TULARE COUNTY

20147 Avenue 306, Exeter, California 93221 (209-592-4682). FOUNDED: 1980. ACREAGE: 20 acres. PRODUCTION: 1,800 cases. DISTRIBUTION: California. OWNERS: Cathy and Don Anderson. WINEMAKER: Don Anderson. Tours and tasting by appointment only.

A dentist in Newport Beach and a grapegrower-winemaker in the Central Valley, Don Anderson travels back and forth, running both businesses. When Don and his family first moved to Exeter, they grew mostly table grapes. As the demand for wine grapes grew, they planted more. Then in 1980, the Andersons discovered that wine grapes become even more profitable if they are made into wine. They built a 4,000-square-foot building, and Dr. Don started a small commercial winery.

ANDRE *see* E. & J. Gallo Winery

Antuzzi's Winery
NEW JERSEY

Bridgeboro-Moorestown Road, Delran, New Jersey 08075 (609-764-1075). FOUNDED: 1974. ACREAGE: 3 acres. PRODUCTION: 10,000 cases. DISTRIBUTION: New Jersey. OWNER: Matthew J. Antuzzi. WINEMAKER: Matthew J. Antuzzi. Tours and tasting Monday–Wednesday 10 A.M.–6 P.M., Thursday–Saturday 10 A.M.–8 P.M., Sunday 12–5 P.M.

While working as an industrial chemical salesman, Matthew Antuzzi was on the road a good deal. He was tiring of this peripatetic life when he inherited his grandfather's old winemaking equipment. He started making wine at home, then he got serious. He found himself traveling to California just to attend enology classes at U.C. Davis and to visit a few wineries. The traveling finally stopped when he purchased land and planted his first vines. Mathew's winery specializes in meeting the tastes of local wine enthusiasts and 95 percent of his wine is sold at the winery.

Arbor Crest
WASHINGTON

4506 East Buckeye, Spokane, Washington 99207 (509-484-WINE). FOUNDED: 1982. ACREAGE: 120 acres. PRODUCTION: 25,000 cases. DISTRIBUTION: Nationwide. OWNERS: David and Harold Mielke. WINEMAKERS: Scott Harris and Bruce McCarthy. Tours and tasting daily 12–5:30 P.M.

Longtime fruit growers, David and Harold Mielke instinctively knew that their 100-acre farm had the potential to grow fine wine grapes. Harry, a research hematologist, decided to plant an experimental vineyard of vinifera and French-American hybrids in their cherry orchard. Once the vineyards began to show promise, the brothers went to a bankruptcy sale and bought the equipment of the defunct Veedercrest Winery in Emeryville, California. The Mielkes trucked their purchases to Spokane, set up shop in a cherry processing shed, and hired winemaker Scott Harris, a U.C. Davis enology graduate, formerly with Davis Bynum Winery.

WHITE

☆☆☆ 1982 CHARDONNAY ($10.00) Sagemoor, Washington. *Crisp, clean, balanced, citric; a delightful wine.*

☆☆ 1982 GEWURZTRAMINER ($6.43) Late Harvest, Washington. *5.1% residual sugar. Soft, lush, clean and fruity.*

☆ 1982 JOHANNISBERG RIESLING ($6.25) Dionysus, Washington.

☆☆ 1982 JOHANNISBERG RIESLING ($15.00) Selected Late Harvest, Stewart's Sunnyside, Washington. *375ml. 8.6% residual sugar. Soft, fruity, clean, nice.*

☆☆ 1983 SAUVIGNON BLANC ($9.50) Cameo Reserve, Washington. *Crisp, fruity, pleasant but with some strange flavors.*

RED

☆☆ 1982 MERLOT ($7.50) Bacchus, Washington. *18% Cabernet Sauvignon. Rich, woody, clean and complex.*

Arbor Knoll Winery
TULARE COUNTY

P.O. Box 495, Springville, California 93265 (209-539-2492). FOUNDED: 1982. ACREAGE: 4 acres. PRODUCTION: 450 cases. DISTRIBUTION: California. OWNER: Glenn Wallace. WINEMAKER: Glenn Wallace. Tours and tasting by appointment.

Glenn Wallace, a financial consultant, wanted to get out of the Los Angeles fast lane, so he bought some property, planted a vineyard, and built a winery. Glenn only makes one wine from a grape variety he had bred just for himself, called "Glennel." It is a cross between Semillon and Folle Blanche, and Glen has the exclusive rights to it.

Argonaut Winery
AMADOR COUNTY

13675 Mt. Echo Drive, Ione, California 95640 (209-274-4106). FOUNDED: 1976. ACREAGE: 2 acres. PRODUCTION: 2,000 cases. DISTRIBUTION: California. OWNERS: Partnership. Jim Payne, Harly Harty, Bill Bilbo, and Paul Loyd. WINEMAKER: Steven Burrall. Tours by appointment.

This "weekend winery" is a business-hobby of four active partners, three of whom are engineers during the week. Although Zinfandel has been the predominant variety since the first crush in 1976, the winery also owns a small Barbera vineyard and made some Sauvignon Blanc for the first time in 1983. There are no plans at present to expand.

RED

☆☆   1980 BARBERA ($6.00) Amador.
☆☆   1980 ZINFANDEL ($3.00) Calaveras.
☆☆   1980 ZINFANDEL ($5.00) Amador.

ARROYO SONOMA *see* California Wine Company

Arterberry Limited
OREGON

905 East 10th Avenue, McMinnville, Oregon 97128 (503-472-1587). FOUNDED: 1979. ACREAGE: None. PRODUCTION: 5,000 cases. DISTRIBUTION: Oregon and Washington. OWNER: Margaret Arterberry, president; Fred Arterberry, Jr., vice president. WINEMAKER: Fred Arterberry, Jr. OTHER LABELS: Red Hills Vineyard, Arterberry Cider. Tours and tasting. Call for information.

The Arterberry Winery started when truck manufacturing executive Fred Arterberry, Sr., was looking for a tax shelter. Since his son Fred Jr. had been making wine for other wineries, a winery business seemed a logical solution. They leased a stark, utilitarian building, and Fred started making low-alcohol cider and méthode champenoise sparkling wine from Pinot Noir and Chardonnay. Three years later, in 1982, he began making still wines. The winery doesn't own any of its own vineyards; Fred Jr. buys almost all his grapes from his father-in-law.

Artisan Wines
NAPA COUNTY

6666 Redwood Road, Napa, California 94558 (707-252-6666). FOUNDED: 1984. ACREAGE: None. PRODUCTION: 10,000 cases. DISTRIBUTION: California and Hawaii; Japan. OWNERS: Jeffrey Caldewey and Michael Fallow. WINEMAKER: Michael Fallow. OTHER LABELS: Michael's, Ultravino, Cru Artisan. No tours or tasting.

If ever there was a winery tailored to the young and upwardly mobile, this is it. Michael Fallow, winemaking consultant at William Hill Winery, and Jeffrey Caldewey, celebrated designer, have combined stylish graphics, an up-scale attitude, and a three-tier wine production. They are marketing three different labels, each with its own extravagant label design, each reflecting "an aura of sophistication and status." The "Michael's" label is on wines produced and bottled by the winery, the "Ultravino" wines are purchased and blended "for the modern palate," and the "Cru Artisan" is imported wine selected by Master of Wine, Kenneth Christie. Referring to their wines as "neo-classical creations," Caldewey and Fallow are trying to produce "a product with a discernible attitude—one that makes a statement about ourselves and those who drink our wines."

WHITE

☆☆☆   1982 MICHAEL'S CHARDONNAY ($15.00) Napa Valley. *Barrel fermented. Rich, clean, very nice.*

☆☆   1983 ULTRAVINO CHARDONNAY ($8.00) Napa Valley. *Clean, fresh, attractive.*

RED

☆☆☆   1982 MICHAEL'S CABERNET SAUVIGNON ($12.00) Napa Valley. *Herbal, earthy, Bordeaux-like, smooth, elegant. Drink 1988.*

❧

ASSOCIATED VINTNERS (AV) *see* Columbia Winery

Au Bon Climat
SANTA BARBARA COUNTY

2800 San Marcos, Box 113, Los Olivos, California 93441 (805-344-3035). FOUNDED: 1982. ACREAGE: None. PRODUCTION: 3,500 cases. DISTRIBUTION: Nationwide. OWNERS: Adam Tolmach and Jim Clendenen. WINEMAKERS: Adam Tolmach and Jim Clendenen. Tours by appointment.

Jim Clendenen and Adam Tolmach became good friends while working together at Zaca Mesa winery. Adam had a degree in enology and Jim had a background in winemaking from his travels to France and Australia. Since the two winemakers shared many of the same winemaking goals and Burgundian ideas, they decided to start their own winery. They approached several grape growers and winery owners in hopes of leasing land and facilities. In 1982 they rented an abandoned winery on 350 acres of vineyard. "We have the pick of all three hundred and fifty acres," says Jim. The two winemakers claim to be combining the best of California's winemaking technology with unadulterated Burgundian methods to make their Pinot Noir and Chardonnay.

WHITE

☆☆   1982 CHARDONNAY ($10.00) Santa Barbara. *Toasty, buttery, nice.*

☆☆☆   1983 CHARDONNAY ($10.00) Santa Barbara. *Crisp, tight, Burgundian, elegant, slightly vinous; superb.*

☆☆☆   1983 CHARDONNAY ($10.00) Los Alamos, Santa Barbara. *Toasty, oaky, ripe fruit, complex.*

☆☆☆☆   1983 CHARDONNAY ($20.00) Babcock, Santa Barbara. *Soft, rich, balanced, complex, remarkable.*

RED

1984 NOUVEAU ROUGE ($5.00) Santa Barbara. *Made from Pinot Noir. Major volatile acidity problem.*

☆☆   1982 PINOT NOIR ($12.00) Santa Barbara. *Rich, Burgundian, some vegetal overtones, quite good.*

❧

Austin Cellars
SANTA BARBARA COUNTY

1516 Copenhagen, Solvang, California 93463 (805-688-9665). FOUNDED: 1981. ACREAGE: None. PRODUCTION: 12,000 cases. DISTRIBUTION: East and West Coast states. OWNERS: Partnership. Tony Austin, general manager. WINEMAKER: Tony Austin. Tours by appointment.

Tony Austin was the winemaker at Firestone Vineyards for seven years before he quit for "artistic reasons." He started his own winery in 1981 to "explore the quality of the fruit in this area," says Tony. A speedy talker and a very opinionated winemaker, Tony explains the advantages of being a vineyardless winery. "With 8,000 acres of grapes to chose from as a buyer, I don't care to grow my own grapes. With this selection, it is so much better to buy. If contracted grapes are not up to standard, the contract can be canceled within twenty-four hours of picking." Tony started the winery on his own and made wine in rented facilities, but fifteen partners were soon found to help with the acquisition of a 100-acre site for a new winery building.

WHITE

☆☆☆ 1982 GEWURZTRAMINER ($8.00) Bien Nacido, Santa Barbara. *Spicy, delicate, off-dry, delicious.*

☆☆☆ 1982 JOHANNISBERG RIESLING ($6.90) Bien Nacido, Santa Barbara. *Lovely varietal character.*

☆ 1981 SAUVIGNON BLANC ($8.50) Sierre Madre, Santa Barbara. *Controversial. Assertively grassy.*

☆☆☆ 1981 SAUVIGNON BLANC ($8.50) Botrytis, Sierra Madre, Santa Barbara. *13.2% residual sugar. Grassy and lovely. Sauternes-like.*

RED

☆☆ 1981 PINOT NOIR ($10.00) Santa Barbara.

☆☆ 1981 PINOT NOIR ($18.00) Sierra Madre, Santa Barbara. *Lush, fat, clean.*

☆☆☆ 1982 PINOT NOIR ($10.00) Bien Nacido, Santa Barbara. *Ripe, clean, smooth, powerful, deep, lovely.*

☆☆☆ 1982 PINOT NOIR ($12.00) Sierra Madre, Santa Barbara. *Rich, complex, superb, a classic. Drink now.*

Babcock Vineyards
SANTA BARBARA COUNTY

5175 Highway 246, Lompoc, California 93436 (805-736-1455). FOUNDED: 1983. ACREAGE: 40 acres. DISTRIBUTION: California. OWNERS: Walter and Mona Babcock. WINEMAKER: John Kerr. Tours and tasting by appointment.

The Babcocks sold their Seal Beach restaurant, Walt's Wharf, and bought an insignificant piece of property in Lompoc. "We didn't buy the property to plant grapes," says Mona Babcock, "but the soil was so terrible, grapes were the only thing that would grow." Besides grapes, the Babcocks also grow and sell apples, "and soon we'll have flower fields," says Mona. The Babcocks had become very interested in wine while putting together the wine list for their restaurant, so when their grapes became very popular among local wineries, such as J. Carey Cellars and Au Bon Climat, they decided to make their own wine. Bryan Babcock, their son, helped out for the first two years while he was finishing his master's degree in enology. Besides managing the vineyard and winery and selling apples, Walter Babcock works three days a week as a dentist.

William Baccala Winery
MENDOCINO COUNTY

10400 South Highway 101, Ukiah, California 95482 (707-468-8936). FOUNDED: 1981. ACREAGE: 111 acres. PRODUCTION: 15,000 cases. DISTRIBUTION: Major market states. OWNER: William P. Baccala. WINEMAKER: Miles Karakasevic. OTHER LABELS: Villa Baccala, Fawn's Glen. Tours by appointment. Tasting and sales daily 10 A.M.–5 P.M

William Baccala, an insurance man of many interests, bought a rolling hillside ranch in Men-docino County. There were a few vines, a few sheep, and a two-story 100-year-old house on the property. While his vines were maturing, Bill had his wine made elsewhere. Located right off the highway, the ranch house became the tasting room, a deli, and a formal dining room for special parties. The winery and brandy distillery were built right next to the house. While the first wines were released under two different labels, Villa Baccala and Fawn's Glen, they are currently all under one Estate Label: William Baccala.

WHITE

☆ 1981 VILLA BACCALA CHARDONNAY ($5.50) Mendocino. *Minty, fruity and quite strange.*

☆☆ 1982 FAWN'S GLEN CHARDONNAY ($5.00) Mendocino. *Fresh and appealing but a bit thin and watery.*

☆☆☆☆ 1983 CHARDONNAY ($11.00) Mendocino. *Crisp fruit, fragrant oak, elegance, finesse. It's got it all.*

Bacchanal Vineyards
VIRGINIA

Route 2, Box 806, Afton, Virginia 22920 (804-272-6937). FOUNDED: 1984. ACREAGE: 6 acres. PRODUCTION: 2,500 cases. DISTRIBUTION: Virginia. OWNERS: David and Betty Medford. WINEMAKER: David Medford. Tours not yet available.

David and Betty Medford purchased property on Afton Mountain several years ago. They wanted to grow grapes and eventually start a winery as a retirement project. Since David works in pharmaceuticals in Richmond, two hours away from the vineyard site, the Medfords have been caring for the vineyards on weekends, recruiting the help of their friends and their youngest son at harvest time. In 1984 the Medfords constructed a contemporary-style winery built of native, natural materials complete with an outdoor tasting patio.

BACIGALUPI *see* Belvedere Wine Company

Stephen Bahn Winery
PENNSYLVANIA

R.D. 1, Box 758, Brogue, Pennsylvania 17309 (717-927-9051). FOUNDED: 1981. ACREAGE: 6 acres. PRODUCTION: 1,050 cases. DISTRIBUTION: At winery and wine shop. OWNERS: Stephen H. and Anne Bahn. WINEMAKER: Stephen H. Bahn. Tours and tasting Saturday 12–5 P.M., Sunday 1 P.M.–6 P.M. Wine shop Wednesday–Saturday 12–5 P.M.

After drifting through his first years at Pennsylvania State University, wine lover Stephen Bahn went to California to study viticulture and enology at Fresno State University. Stephen returned to Pennsylvania with a degree, purchased land, and planted vinifera vines. He lives above the winery with his wife, Ann, and their three children. Steven still works full time with an industrial equipment supply business.

Alexis Bailly Vineyard
MINNESOTA

18200 Kirby Avenue, Hastings, Minnesota 55033 (612-437-1413). FOUNDED: 1976. ACREAGE: 12 acres. PRODUCTION: 3,000 cases. DISTRIBUTION: Minnesota. OWNER: Bailly family.

WINEMAKER: Nan Bailly. Tours by appointment. Tasting June–October: Friday–Sunday 12–5 P.M.

David Bailly, a Minneapolis lawyer, started his gentleman's farm by planting French-American hybrids in 1973. A serious wine buff, David became a grapegrower with the encouragement of vigneron friends from France. He learned how to protect his vines during the hard winters, and by 1977 his first grapes were harvested. While a two-story log-building winery was under construction, David's daughter Nan went to France to learn winemaking. While Nan has concentrated on red hybrid varieties, she has also started experimenting with vinifera grapes.

RED

☆☆   1979 LEON MILLOT ($8.00) Minnesota. *Earthy, rich, balanced, rather attractive.*

Bainbridge Island Winery
WASHINGTON

682 State Highway 305 Northeast, Bainbridge Island, Washington 98110 (206-842-9463). FOUNDED: 1982. ACREAGE: 2 acres. PRODUCTION: 1,700 cases. DISTRIBUTION: At winery. OWNERS: JoAnn and Gerard Bentryn. WINEMAKER: Gerard Bentryn. Tours and tasting Wednesday–Sunday 12–5 P.M.

A geographer and climatologist, Gerard Bentryn searched the United States for an area with a climate similar to Germany's finest grape growing regions. Gerard and his wife, JoAnn, had come to the United States from Germany when he was studying for his master's degree. During his studies he became convinced that the Puget Sound area was the climatic Rheingau of the United States. While working for the National Park Service, Gerard began planting his Bainbridge Island vineyards (most of the acreage devoted to the Muller-Thurgau variety). He then built "the prettiest little winery in the state of Washington," according to JoAnn. Just a ferry ride away from Seattle, the winery is a quaint turn-of-the-century farm building with a flower garden, small pond, windmill, and Victorian-style tasting room–wine museum, filled with antique glasses, bottles, and other wine artifacts.

WHITE

1982 CHARDONNAY ($6.00) Late Harvest, Washington. *375ml. Grapey, sweet, awkward.*

Baldinelli Vineyards
AMADOR COUNTY

Route 2, Box 7A, Shenandoah Road, Plymouth, California 95669 (209-245-3398). FOUNDED: 1979. ACREAGE: 60 acres. PRODUCTION: 12,000 cases. DISTRIBUTION: 30 states. OWNERS: Ed Baldinelli and John Miller. WINEMAKER: Ed Baldinelli. Tours and tasting weekends 11 A.M.– 4 P.M.

"I retired from a five-day-a-week job to a seven-day-a-week job," says Ed Baldinelli of his transition from Kaiser engineer to winery owner. He and his partner John Miller, who used to be with the Amador County Department of Agriculture, have been growing and selling grapes since 1972. In 1979 they began to produce their own wines.

WHITE

☆ 1982 SAUVIGNON BLANC ($6.25) Shenandoah Valley, Amador. *Varietal, but the flavors are a bit muffled.*

BLANC DE NOIR

1982 WHITE ZINFANDEL ($5.00) Estate, Shenandoah Valley. *Stinky, odd flavors, O.K. fruit but quite strange.*
○ 1983 WHITE ZINFANDEL ($5.45) Shenandoah Valley. *Awful.*

RED

☆☆ 1980 RED TABLE WINE ($3.80) Estate, Shenandoah Valley. *100% Zinfandel. Nice, clean, softly fruity.*
☆☆☆ 1979 CABERNET SAUVIGNON ($7.00) Estate, Amador. *Soft, clean, intense, spicy.*
☆☆ 1980 CABERNET SAUVIGNON ($7.70) Estate, Amador. *Dense, concentrated, violets in the nose. Drink 1987.*
☆☆ 1981 CABERNET SAUVIGNON ($7.50) Shenandoah Valley, California. *Intense, concentrated, fruity. Drink 1987 and beyond.*
1979 ZINFANDEL ($6.60) Estate, Shenandoah Valley, Amador.
☆☆☆ 1980 ZINFANDEL ($6.00) Lot 1, Shenandoah Valley, Amador. *Crisp, fruity, delightfully elegant.*

Baldwin Vineyards
NEW YORK

Hardenburgh Road, Road 2, Box 36, Pine Bush, New York 12566 (914-744-2226). FOUNDED: 1982. ACREAGE: 11 acres. PRODUCTION: 1,250 cases. DISTRIBUTION: New York. OWNERS: Jack and Patricia Baldwin. WINEMAKERS: Jack and Patricia Baldwin. Tours and tasting Tuesday–Sunday 12–7 P.M.

Real wine aficionados, Jack and Pat Baldwin started a gourmet dinner and wine tasting group. These bacchanalian get-togethers were fun, but they weren't enough for the Baldwins. They began running one of the most active Les Amis du Vin chapters in New Jersey. Discovering that they could in fact work well together, they decided to take their wine neurosis one step further. Moving to New York, they bought a 200-year-old house on the banks of the Shawangunk River and converted the surrounding out-buildings into a winery. Jack is a full-time marketing executive for a pharmaceutical company; Patricia and her daughter Wendy do the winemaking.

Ballard Canyon Winery
SANTA BARBARA COUNTY

1825 Ballard Canyon Road, Solvang, California 93463 (805-688-7585). FOUNDED: 1974. ACREAGE: 50 acres. PRODUCTION: 10,000 cases. DISTRIBUTION: California, Hawaii, Alaska, Washington, and New Jersey. OWNERS: Gene and Rosalie Hallock. WINEMAKER: Fred Holloway. Tours and tasting daily 11 A.M.–4 P.M. Groups by appointment.

Gene Hallock was a Santa Barbara dentist before he developed an interest in viticulture in 1974. He started making his own wine in 1978 because he was dissatisfied with the prices he was getting for grapes from the wineries he supplied. Ballard Canyon's goal is to emphasize fruitiness in its wine, which is easy to do since the region's coolness tends to produce fruity, high-acid grapes.

WHITE

1981 CHARDONNAY ($12.00) Estate, Santa Barbara. *Crisp, vinous, smooth but with a distracting touch of sweetness.*

☆ 1982 CHARDONNAY ($8.95) Tepusquet, Santa Barbara. *Earthy, herbaceous, lacking charm or varietal character.*

☆☆ 1982 CHARDONNAY ($13.00) Santa Barbara.

☆☆ 1982 FUME BLANC ($8.50) Santa Barbara. *Good fruit and varietal character. Sugar is a bit odd.*

☆☆ 1983 FUME BLANC ($7.95) Santa Barbara. *Fresh, grassy, some sweetness, good.*

☆☆☆ 1981 JOHANNISBERG RIESLING ($6.25) Santa Ynez Valley. *2.35% residual sugar. Crisp, sweet and very clean.*

☆☆☆ 1981 JOHANNISBERG RIESLING ($8.25) Reserve, Santa Ynez Valley. *3.9% residual sugar. Rich, fruity, clean and complex.*

☆☆ 1982 JOHANNISBERG RIESLING ($7.00) Santa Ynez Valley. *2.5% residual sugar. Slightly syrupy, fresh but a bit odd.*

☆☆☆ 1982 JOHANNISBERG RIESLING ($8.75) Reserve, Santa Ynez Valley. *3.9% residual sugar, 20% botrytis. Fresh, clean and crisp.*

☆☆ 1983 JOHANNISBERG RIESLING ($7.50) Estate, Santa Ynez Valley. *2.4% residual sugar. Spritzy, clean, fragrant, very nice.*

☆☆ 1983 JOHANNISBERG RIESLING ($9.00) Reserve, Santa Ynez Valley. *4% residual sugar. Thick, sweet, simple, clean and fruity.*

☆☆☆ 1984 JOHANNISBERG RIESLING ($7.50) Estate, Santa Barbara. *2.3% residual sugar. Varietal, delicate, fruity, superb.*

☆☆ 1983 MUSCAT ($8.00) Santa Barbara. *3.2% residual sugar. Fresh, varietal, pleasant.*

BLANC DE NOIR

☆☆ 1982 CABERNET SAUVIGNON ($6.00) Rosalie Blushing Brunch, Estate, Santa Ynez Valley. *3.6% residual sugar. Fresh and varietal.*

☆☆ 1983 CABERNET SAUVIGNON BLANC ($5.75) Estate, Santa Ynez Valley. *1.4% residual sugar. Snappy, fruity, varietal, clean.*

☆☆ 1984 CABERNET SAUVIGNON BLANC ($5.75) Santa Barbara. *1.3% residual sugar.*

RED

O 1980 CABERNET SAUVIGNON ($9.00) Estate, Santa Ynez Valley. *Intensely vegetal, berried, overripe, short finish.*

☆ 1981 CABERNET SAUVIGNON ($9.00) Estate, Santa Ynez Valley. *Vegetal and muddy, some decent fruit.*

O 1980 ZINFANDEL ($8.00) Estate, Santa Barbara. *Weedy.*

BALLATORE *see* E. & J. Gallo Winery

Balverne Winery & Vineyards
SONOMA COUNTY

10810 Hillview Road, Windsor, California 95492 (707-433-6913). FOUNDED: 1979. ACREAGE: 753 acres. PRODUCTION: 25,000 cases. DISTRIBUTION: California, Oregon, Washington, Massachusetts, and Eastern states. OWNER: Corporation. B. J. Bird, president and general manager. WINEMAKER: Michael Duffy. Tours by appointment only.

The owners of Balverne Vineyards have divided their large vineyard holding into seven different parcels, each designated with its own romantic name. The entire 710-acre parcel, once part of the Rancho Sotoyome land grant, climbs through the rolling terrain of the Chalk Hill area in Sonoma County. With 250 acres of vineyard, the partners at Balverne are more comfortable being characterized as winegrowers than winemakers. They want each of their wines to be the best in its category and they believe that top quality viticulture is the key.

WHITE

☆☆ 1983 HEALDSBURGER ($6.00) Sonoma. *41% Riesling, 34% Scheurebe, 25% Gewürz-traminer. Fresh, fruity.*

☆☆ 1980 CHARDONNAY ($17.00) Deerhill, Sonoma. *Lemony, angular, a bit short on varietal character.*

☆☆☆ 1981 CHARDONNAY ($13.00) Deerfield, Sonoma. *Rich, complex, earthy, very attractive.*

☆☆☆ 1982 CHARDONNAY ($12.00) Deerfield, Sonoma. *Clean, austere, good structure, varietal, very good.*

☆☆ 1982 GEWURZTRAMINER ($8.00) Dry, Pepperwood Estate, Sonoma.

☆☆ 1981 SAUVIGNON BLANC ($10.00) Stonecrest, Sonoma. *12% Semillon.*

1982 SAUVIGNON BLANC ($8.50) Sonoma. *12% Semillon.*

☆☆ 1982 SAUVIGNON BLANC ($10.00) Stonecrest Estate, Sonoma.

RED

☆☆☆ 1980 CABERNET SAUVIGNON ($25.00) Sonoma.

☆ 1980 ZINFANDEL ($10.00) Estate, Sonoma. *Decent but muddy and a bit vegetal.*

BANDIERA *see* California Wine Company

Banholzer Winecellars
INDIANA

5627 East 1000 North, Hesston, Indiana 46340 (219-778-2448). FOUNDED: 1971. ACREAGE: 72 acres. PRODUCTION: 10,000 cases. DISTRIBUTION: At winery. OWNERS: Carl and Janet Banholzer. Carl Banholzer, general manager. WINEMAKER: Carl Banholzer. Tours and tasting Friday–Sunday 11 A.M.–5 P.M. Gift shop.

The product of a long line of German winemakers, Carl Banholzer established some of the very first plantings of vinifera in the Midwest when he and Leonard Olsen established their Tabor Hill Vineyards in Michigan in 1965. Carl started this family winery and vineyards in 1971 on what used to be a dairy farm. He produced vinifera and French-American hybrid wines, plus an Indian champagne that received wide acclaim. Things were looking extremely positive until the devastating sub-zero winters of 1977, 1978, and 1979. By the end of this period the winery was in serious financial trouble. It was rescued, however, by a group of investors who brought in additional capital, saved the damaged vineyards, bottled the wines already in tanks, and implemented a program of winery expansion.

Barboursville Vineyards
VIRGINIA

Route 777, Box 136, Barboursville, Virginia 22923 (703-832-3824). FOUNDED: 1976. ACREAGE: 45 acres. PRODUCTION: 7,000 cases. DISTRIBUTION: Virginia and other eastern states. OWNER:

Zonin S.P.A. Adriano Rossi, general manager. WINEMAKER: Adriano Rossi. Tours and tasting Saturday 10 A.M.–5 P.M. Appointments appreciated.

On the Barboursville Plantation, in the shadow of the historic brick ruins of the late governor James Barbour's mansion, the Zonin family, owners of a large and very successful winery in Veneto, Italy, planted vinifera vineyards. The U.S. Department of Agriculture and the Virginia Polytechnic University had warned them against vinifera planting; apparently all attempts since Prohibition had failed miserably. They advised the region was unfit for any grape vine except Concord. But the Zonins weren't deterred. Starting their own nursery in 1978, they cultivated vinifera for themselves and for other growers. They battled cold winters, spring frosts, black rot, and Japanese beetles, and made Barboursville Vineyards the first in Virginia to grow vinifera of commercial quality. They inspired others, and the modern Virginia wine industry was born.

WHITE

☆   1982 CHARDONNAY ($7.00) Virginia.
☆   1983 GEWURZTRAMINER ($6.00) Medium Dry, Virginia. *Lush, heavy, lacking fruit acidity, varietal.*
☆☆ 1983 RIESLING ($6.00) Virginia. *Dry, crisp, good balance, lacking freshness.*

RED

☆   1980 CABERNET SAUVIGNON ($6.50) Virginia. *15% Merlot. Soft, herbal and elegant. Simple but clean.*
    1982 MERLOT ($7.00) Virginia. *Spicy, leathery, some dirty flavors.*

Bardenheier's Wine Cellar
MISSOURI

1019 Skinker Parkway, St. Louis, Missouri 63112 (314-862-1400). FOUNDED: 1873. ACREAGE: 65 acres. PRODUCTION: 400,000 cases. DISTRIBUTION: 12 states. OWNER: Futura Coatings Company. Rodney D. Jarbo, president; E. Dean Jarbo, chairman. WINEMAKER: Edward Lemay. Tours and tasting daily 9 A.M.–4:30 P.M.

After Prohibition, Joseph Bardenheier reopened his father's winery. The operation grew steadily over the years and had to move to larger quarters several times. In 1955 the winery was finally settled in an abandoned public garage. Joseph died in 1962, but his sons continued operating the winery. Recently, the winery was sold to Futura Coatings, a company whose business includes relining wine tanks. Futura brought in new equipment and expertise while continuing to expand production. John Bardenheier and his son John Jr. have stayed with the winery as consultant and operations manager, respectively.

Bargetto Winery
SANTA CRUZ COUNTY

3535 North Main Street, Soquel, California 95073 (408-475-2258). FOUNDED: 1933. ACREAGE: None. PRODUCTION: 40,000 cases. DISTRIBUTION: California, Colorado, Ohio, Nevada, Texas, and Wisconsin. OWNER: Bargetto family. Beverly Bargetto, president; Martin Bargetto, general manager. WINEMAKER: John Bargetto. Tours weekdays 11 A.M. and 2 P.M. Tasting room open daily 10 A.M.–5:30 P.M.

The largest winery in Santa Cruz County, Bargetto has a long-standing reputation for making excellent fruit and berry wines. Since third-generation Bargettos became involved in the winery operation, emphasis has been on grape wines. All the fruit is purchased, and most of the grapes come from the Tepusquet Vineyard in Santa Maria as well as other locations in Napa, Santa Barbara, and San Luis Obispo counties.

WHITE

☆☆ 1981 CHARDONNAY ($9.50) Tepusquet, Santa Barbara. *Vinous, big, nice fruit. Some bottles show off flavors.*

☆ 1982 CHARDONNAY ($9.50) Tepusquet, Santa Barbara. *Decent but essentially dull.*

1982 CHENIN BLANC ($5.50) Tepusquet, Santa Barbara. *1.77% residual sugar. Vegetal, odd, but with lovely fruit acid.*

☆ 1983 CHENIN BLANC ($5.50) Tepusquet, Santa Maria Valley. *Decent acidity, some strange flavors.*

☆☆ 1982 GEWURZTRAMINER ($6.25) Dry, Tepusquet, Santa Barbara. *Fragrant, clean and attractive.*

☆☆ 1981 JOHANNISBERG RIESLING ($6.00) Santa Barbara. *2.24% residual sugar.*

☆ 1982 JOHANNISBERG RIESLING ($6.00) 50th Anniversary, Santa Barbara. *Grassy but attractive.*

☆ 1982 JOHANNISBERG RIESLING ($9.00) Late Harvest, Santa Barbara. *A bit musty but pleasant enough.*

☆ 1983 JOHANNISBERG RIESLING ($6.00) Tepusquet, Santa Maria Valley. *Crisp, clean, dense.*

SPARKLING

☆☆☆ 1981 BLANC DE NOIR ($12.50) Monterey. *Lovely, lush, balanced, 1% dosage. Méthode champenoise.*

BLANC DE NOIR

☆☆ 1983 WHITE ZINFANDEL ($5.00) Central Coast. *Fresh, clean, appealing.*

☆☆☆ 1984 WHITE ZINFANDEL ($5.75) California. *1.5% residual sugar. Crisp, fresh, assertive, charming.*

RED

☆ NV BURGUNDY ($3.00) California. *Weedy but lush and attractive.*

☆ 1978 CABERNET SAUVIGNON ($7.00) Soma, Santa Clara.

☆☆☆ 1981 CABERNET SAUVIGNON ($12.00) Dedication, St. Regis, Sonoma. *Clean and delicious with good fruit and acid. Drink now.*

☆☆ 1981 ZINFANDEL ($7.00) Napa Valley. *Berried, fruity, clean, nice.*

The Barry Wine Company
NEW YORK

7107 Vineyard Road, Conesus, New York 14435 (716-346-2321). FOUNDED: 1937. ACREAGE: 30 acres. PRODUCTION: 50,000 cases. DISTRIBUTION: Eastern states. OWNER: Eagle Crest Vineyards, Inc. Austen Wood, president. Tours and tasting June–October 12–5 P.M.

Almost a century old, this stone winery with its vaulted cellars was built by Bishop McQuaid to make sacramental wines. Situated on a western slope facing Hemlock Lake, surrounded by hemlock trees, the winery and vineyards were bought in the 1960s by the Cribari family of California (see Guild Wineries), who continued to make sacramental wines a large part of their total production. In 1982 the fourth generation Cribari cousins, Ted and Albert, sold the winery to Eagle Crest Vineyards. The Cribaris continue to manage operations.

Barrywine Plantations Winery
MARYLAND

13601 Glisans Mill Road, Mount Airy, Maryland 21771 (301-662-8687). FOUNDED: 1976. ACREAGE: 40 acres. PRODUCTION: 3,000 cases. DISTRIBUTION: Maryland. OWNERS: John and Lucille Allen. WINEMAKERS: John and Anthony Allen. Tours and tasting daily 10 A.M.–6 P.M. Seasonal concerts—Strawberry Wine Festival in June; Wine Harvest Festival in October.

"The first mistake was buying the farm, the second mistake was planting grapes, and the third mistake was accepting my father-in-law's gift of all his old winemaking equipment," explains John (Jack) Allen. "These mistakes just kept multiplying until we got ourselves to where we are now." John started as a quiet, hobby winemaker until the hobby outgrew itself. His family transformed the old dairy farm and its complex puzzle of buildings into a winery-visitor center. The cattle sheds are used for tasting and sales, and the winery is on the second floor of the old barn.

Batavia Wine Cellars
NEW YORK

School Street and Hewitt Place, Batavia, New York 14020 (716-344-1111). FOUNDED: 1940. ACREAGE: None. PRODUCTION: 625,000 cases. DISTRIBUTION: Eastern states. OWNER: Cannon Bagel Company. WINEMAKER: Ned Cooper. No tours or tasting.

During World War II it became impossible for importer Harry Robinson to bring in French Champagne. Shipments had been cut off and Harry was out of a job. That's when he and his friend Albert Cooper started making their own sparkling wine in the heart of New York City. After a series of moves, they settled the winery in a building previously used for manufacturing tractors. Now, following in their fathers' footsteps, Harry's son Leon and Albert's son Ned make other wines, though sparkling wines are still a specialty. Ned was the one to actually start making the wine for the sparkling cuvées. In Harry and Albert's day, all the still wines were purchased. Now the winery makes 100 percent of the wines they sell. "And we make it all: sherries, ports, even retsina," says Ned. "Just ask for it and we make it."

Bay Cellars
ALAMEDA COUNTY

1401 Stanford Avenue, Emeryville, California 94608 (415-526-0469). FOUNDED: 1982. ACREAGE: None. PRODUCTION: 1,250 cases. DISTRIBUTION: Local. OWNER: Richard L. Rotblatt. WINEMAKER: Richard L. Rotblatt; John Reynold, enologist; Mike McKinney, cellarmaster. Tours by appointment.

Richard Rotblatt and good friend Mike McKinney have always been serious about winemaking. From the start in 1970, when they made wine at home, there was little doubt that eventually they would make great Pinot Noir and Chardonnay. In 1982 Richard, a full-time engineer, opened the winery on Stanford Avenue in Berkeley. "Originally, I had wanted to keep the winery in the basement of my home, but the neighbors had visions of huge trucks hauling enormous loads of grapes into their neighborhood," says Richard. Now the winery is sharing the old Veedercrest Winery in nearby Emeryville with Rosenblum Cellars and St. George Spirits.

WHITE

☆☆☆   1982 CHARDONNAY ($12.00) Tepusquet, Santa Maria. *Rich, vinous, clean, good fruit, lovely.*

RED

☆☆   1982 CLARION ($10.50) Napa Valley. *66% Merlot, 24% Cabernet, 10% Cabernet Franc. Oaky, rich. Drink 1986.*
☆☆☆   1982 PINOT NOIR ($13.50) Buena Vista, Carneros District. *Fruity, rich, varietal, clean and very lovely. Drink now.*

Beaulieu Vineyard
NAPA COUNTY

1960 St. Helena Highway, Rutherford, California 94573 (707-963-1451). FOUNDED: 1900. ACREAGE: 1,500 acres. PRODUCTION: 400,000 cases. DISTRIBUTION: Nationwide. OWNER: Hueblein, Inc. Legh F. Knowles, chairman; Thomas Selfridge, president. Tours and tasting daily 10 A.M.–3:15 P.M.

Founded by Frenchman Georges de Latour, Beaulieu Vineyard—BV—has been a leading winery for 85 years. In 1938 de Latour hired a young Russian enologist named André Tchelistcheff, whose old world experience and enormous natural talent revolutionized the American wine industry. Tchelistcheff identified Cabernet Sauvignon as the variety with the most potential for the central Napa Valley, and he proceeded to make a series of dazzling, world-class Cabernets. In the 1940s, 1950s and 1960s, BV was the standard by which all other wines were judged. Later Tchelistcheff decided that the cool Carneros region in the southern part of Napa would be ideal for growing Pinot Noir. In 1962 de Latour's daughter, Helene de Pins, installed ex-Glenn Miller trumpet player Legh Knowles as national sales manager of the winery and then, in 1969, she sold BV to Heublein which, in turn, was gobbled up by R. J. Reynolds in 1982. Despite this new ownership, the winery has attempted to maintain its previous standard of excellence while expanding its line.

WHITE

☆☆☆ 1982 CHABLIS ($5.25) Estate, Napa Valley. *Charming blend of seven varieties. Crisp, dry and attractive.*

☆☆ 1983 HOCK ($7.00) Napa Valley. *1.5 liter. 100% Johannisberg Riesling. Fresh, fruity, clean.*

☆☆ 1980 CHARDONNAY ($9.00) Beaufort, Napa Valley. *Clean and attractive. Good acidity.*

☆ 1981 CHARDONNAY ($14.00) Los Carneros Region, Napa Valley. *Open, fruity, simple, decent.*

☆ 1982 CHARDONNAY ($11.00) Beaufort, Napa Valley. *Clean, crisp, decent, short and simple.*

☆☆☆ 1982 CHARDONNAY ($14.00) Los Carneros Region, Napa Valley. *Lovely, sweet oak, rich flavors, intense, balanced—superb.*

☆☆☆ 1982 JOHANNISBERG RIESLING ($7.50) Beauclair, Estate, Napa Valley. *Snappy, clean, varietal.*

☆☆☆ 1982 MELON ($8.50) Estate, Napa Valley. *Crisp, fruity and very appealing. Great with seafood.*

☆☆ 1981 SAUVIGNON BLANC ($8.75) Napa Valley.

☆☆☆ 1983 SAUVIGNON BLANC ($8.00) Estate, Napa Valley. *Fresh, round, crisp fruit. Lovely oak finish.*

SPARKLING

☆ 1979 BRUT ($13.25) Napa Valley.

☆ 1980 BRUT ($14.00) Napa Valley. *Dull.*

ROSE

☆☆ 1983 BEAUROSE ($5.00) Estate, Napa Valley. *67% Cabernet, 23% Gamay, 8% Pinot Noir. Snappy, clean, dry.*

RED

☆☆☆ 1968 BURGUNDY Napa Valley. *Velvety, clean and lovely.*

☆☆☆ 1958 CABERNET SAUVIGNON Private Reserve, Estate, Napa Valley. *Surprisingly rich, fruity and fresh. Many years to go.*

☆☆☆☆ 1966 CABERNET SAUVIGNON Private Reserve, Estate, Napa Valley. *Deep, complex and still youthful. Elegant.*

☆☆ 1968 CABERNET SAUVIGNON Private Reserve, Estate, Napa Valley.

☆☆☆☆ 1970 CABERNET SAUVIGNON Private Reserve, Estate, Napa Valley. *Remarkable finesse and depth. Elegant, rich and holding well.*

☆☆☆ 1973 CABERNET SAUVIGNON Private Reserve, Estate, Napa Valley. *Delicate but lovely, supple and ready to drink now.*

☆☆☆ 1974 CABERNET SAUVIGNON Private Reserve, Estate, Napa Valley. *Spicy, rich, deep and nicely structured. Drink near term.*

☆ 1975 CABERNET SAUVIGNON ($15.00) Private Reserve, Estate, Napa Valley. *Somewhat dull and lacking depth. Decent but disappointing.*

☆☆☆ 1976 CABERNET SAUVIGNON ($18.00) Private Reserve, Estate, Napa Valley. *Elegant, clean and firmly structured. Should improve.*

☆☆ 1977 CABERNET SAUVIGNON ($18.00) Private Reserve, Estate, Napa Valley. *Earthy, complex, but lacking style. Will last a long time.*

☆☆☆ 1978 CABERNET SAUVIGNON ($18.00) Private Reserve, Estate, Napa Valley. *Minty, oaky, ripe, very classy. Drink 1987 and beyond.*

1979 CABERNET SAUVIGNON ($7.00) Beau Tour, Napa Valley. *Vegetal, stemmy, decent.*

☆ 1979 CABERNET SAUVIGNON ($8.00) Rutherford, Napa Valley.

☆☆ 1979 CABERNET SAUVIGNON ($20.00) Private Reserve, Estate, Napa Valley. *Big, fruity, complex, balanced but a bit clumsy. Drink 1986.*

☆ 1980 CABERNET SAUVIGNON ($8.00) Beau Tour, Napa Valley. *Simple, pleasant, drinkable; a little too vegetal.*

☆☆ 1980 CABERNET SAUVIGNON ($9.00) Rutherford, Estate, Napa Valley. *Coffee nose, herbal flavors, simple and clean. Drink now.*

☆ 1981 CABERNET SAUVIGNON ($7.25) Beau Tour, Estate, Napa Valley. *Decent but lacking finesse and middle range. Drink now.*

☆☆ 1981 CABERNET SAUVIGNON ($8.00) Rutherford, Napa Valley. *Charming, round, oaky, varietal. Drink now.*

☆ 1982 CABERNET SAUVIGNON ($6.00) Beau Tour, Napa Valley. *Decent, earthy.*

1982 CABERNET SAUVIGNON ($10.00) Claret, Napa Valley. *1.5 liter. Weedy, rough and unattractive.*

☆☆☆ 1976 PINOT NOIR ($8.00) Los Carneros Region-Napa Valley. *Elegant and rich with hints of cherry and violet.*

☆☆ 1977 PINOT NOIR Los Carneros, Napa Valley. *Tannic and richly varietal.*

☆ 1978 PINOT NOIR ($6.50) Beaumont, Estate, Napa Valley.

1979 PINOT NOIR ($9.00) Los Carneros, Napa Valley. *Stemmy, raisiny. This one has not aged gracefully.*

☆ 1980 PINOT NOIR ($9.00) Los Carneros. *Clean, balanced, decent.*

Beau Val Wines
AMADOR COUNTY

Star Route #2, Box 8D, 10671 Valley Drive, Plymouth, California 95669 (209-245-3281). FOUNDED: 1979. ACREAGE: 7.5 acres. PRODUCTION: 1,000 cases. DISTRIBUTION: California. OWNERS: Robert and Nan Francis, and Vernon and Jean Gilman. WINEMAKER: Vernon Gilman. Tours and tasting by appointment.

Vernon and Jen Gilman, a home winemaking team turned professional, specialize in Zinfandel. They aim for a lower alcohol wine that is ready to drink early. The winery occupies their basement and garage.

RED

☆☆ 1979 ZINFANDEL ($7.50) Special Selection, Amador.
☆☆ 1980 ZINFANDEL ($5.75) Amador.

BEL ARBRES *see* Fetzer Vineyards

BELL CANYON CELLARS *see* Burgess Cellars

Bella Napoli Winery
SAN JOAQUIN COUNTY

21128 South Austin Road, Manteca, California 95336 (209-599-3885). FOUNDED: 1934. ACREAGE: 60 acres. PRODUCTION: 5,000 cases. DISTRIBUTION: At winery. OWNER: Lucas G. Hat. WINEMAKER: Lucas G. Hat. No tours or tasting. Retail sales available.
     This Central Valley winery is virtually a one-man operation. Lucas Hat, son of founder Tony Hat, produces four-liter jug wines under four labels. These include one of the few "Sauternes" still made in California. The wines are sold locally in stores and restaurants.

Belle Creek Ranch
BUTTE COUNTY

576 Belle Creek Lane, Paradise, California 95964 (916-877-4124). FOUNDED: 1983. ACREAGE: None. PRODUCTION: 800 cases. DISTRIBUTION: California. OWNER: J. P. Bowman WINE-MAKER: J. P. Bowman. Tours by appointment.
     J. P. Bowman has discovered the advantages of using wine in raising cows. "It's important for those cows to stay real calm and happy if they are going to become prime beef," says J. P., "so I've been putting some of my wine on their corn. They love it, and they're some of the calmest cows you ever did see." When he is not making wine in his basement or fattening up his cows, J. P. works in construction, "but I want to retire from construction soon," says a tired J. P. His wife works as a schoolteacher.

Bellerose Vineyard
SONOMA COUNTY

435 West Dry Creek Road, Healdsburg, California 95448 (707-433-1637). FOUNDED: 1979. ACREAGE: 52 acres. PRODUCTION: 5,000 cases. DISTRIBUTION: Major market states. OWN-ERS: Charles and Nancy Richard. WINEMAKER: Charles Richard; Lloyd Chan, consulting enologist. Tours by appointment. No tasting. Retail sales available by appointment.
     Charles Richard speaks softly about his decision to become part of Sonoma County's wine renaissance. Born into the hotel and restaurant trade in Pennsylvania, Charles wanted to be a classical musician before he became intrigued with the idea of making great wine. He purchased an old winery site with existing Cabernet Sauvignon and Merlot vines on a slope of the Dry Creek Valley and, after extensive clearing and renovating, started planting three other red Bordeaux varieties. His goal is to emulate, not copy, the style of Bordeaux by blending Cabernet Sauvignon, Merlot, Cabernet Franc, Malbec, and Petite Verdot.

RED

☆☆   1979 CABERNET SAUVIGNON ($8.00) Sonoma.
☆☆☆   1980 CABERNET SAUVIGNON ($12.00) Cuvée Bellerose, Sonoma. *70% Cabernet, 18%
       Merlot, 10% Cabernet Franc, 2% Malbec. Classic.*

ح&

Belli and Sauret Vineyards
SAN LUIS OBISPO COUNTY

4360 Estrella Route, Paso Robles, California 93451 (805-467-3885). FOUNDED: 1982. ACREAGE:
93 acres. PRODUCTION: 5,000 cases. DISTRIBUTION: Nationwide. OWNERS: Richard Sauret
and Remo Belli. WINEMAKER: Various winemakers. Tasting by appointment.

Richard Sauret has been growing almonds in the Paso Robles area since 1955 and grapes since
1970. In 1979 Remo Belli of Remo Incorporated, an important manufacturer of drumheads located
in North Hollywood, purchased a ranch from Richard and later became his partner in another
property. In 1982 the two growers decided to start their own wine label which would utilize only
their own grapes. Their wines are made at HMR Vineyards.

WHITE

☆   1983 CHARDONNAY ($7.00) Paso Robles.
☆☆   1983 SAUVIGNON BLANC ($6.25) Paso Robles. *Crisp, varietal, grassy, clean.*

RED

☆☆☆   1982 ZINFANDEL ($6.75) Paso Robles. *Lush, rich, fruity, clean and delicious.*

ح&

Belvedere Wine Company
SONOMA COUNTY

4035 Westside Road, Healdsburg, California 95448 (707-433-8236). FOUNDED: 1979. ACREAGE:
2.5 acres. PRODUCTION: 35,000 cases. DISTRIBUTION: Major market states. OWNERS: Peter
S. Friedman and William R. Hambrecht. WINEMAKER: Donald Frazer; James Wolner, production
manager. OTHER LABELS: Bacigalupi, York Creek, Robert Young, Wine Discovery, Winery Lake.
No tours or tasting.

Gregarious Pete Friedman, a former executive at Sonoma Vineyards, has entered into agree-
ments with some of Napa and Sonoma's most prestigious vineyards (Bacigalupi and Robert Young
in Sonoma, Winery Lake and York Creek in Napa) and has had great success in releasing wines
under their names. He also markets a line of low-priced varietals. Pete's partner in this venture is
investment banker Bill Hambrecht, who also owns a piece of Chalone Vineyard.

WHITE

☆☆   1980 BACIGALUPI CHARDONNAY ($15.00) Estate, Sonoma. *Crisp, clean and varietal.*
      1981 BACIGALUPI CHARDONNAY ($13.50) Sonoma. *Sour, unpleasant.*
☆   1982 WINE DISCOVERY CHARDONNAY ($4.00) Santa Barbara. *Sappy, big, earthy,
       rich, decent.*
☆   1982 WINE DISCOVERY CHARDONNAY ($4.75) Santa Maria. *Clean, hard and vinous.*
☆   1982 WINE DISCOVERY CHARDONNAY ($4.75) Monterey. *Earthy, clean, decent fruit.*
☆☆   1982 WINERY LAKE CHARDONNAY ($12.00) Estate, Los Carneros. *Big, vinous, a bit
       overripe, lovely fruit and oak.*
☆   1983 CHARDONNAY ($4.75) Discovery Series, Central Coast. *Clean, varietal, decent.*

☆☆☆ 1983 BACIGALUPI CHARDONNAY ($12.00) Sonoma. *Crisp, complex, elegant, richly fruity, superb.*

☆☆☆ 1983 WINERY LAKE CHARDONNAY ($12.00) Napa Valley. *Clean, balanced, rich, fruity, classic.*

☆ 1982 WINE DISCOVERY GEWURZTRAMINER ($4.75) Winery Lake, Napa Valley. *Full, lush, overripe, lacking fruitiness.*

☆☆☆ 1984 WINERY LAKE GEWURZTRAMINER ($6.50) Napa Valley. *Lush, clean, varietal, very attractive.*

BLANC DE NOIR

☆ 1984 WINE DISCOVERY WHITE ZINFANDEL ($3.00) California. *Decent, fresh, clean, simple, off-dry.*

RED

O NV WINE DISCOVERY CABERNET SAUVIGNON ($3.00) Monterey. *Jalapeño peppers.*

O 1980 WINE DISCOVERY CABERNET SAUVIGNON ($3.00) Napa Valley. *Stinky, unpleasant.*

1980 WINE DISCOVERY CABERNET SAUVIGNON ($3.90) Sonoma. 7% Merlot. *Dull, decent but lacking depth or charm.*

☆☆☆☆ 1980 ROBERT YOUNG CABERNET SAUVIGNON ($12.00) Sonoma. *Elegant, rich, superb. Will age well.*

☆ 1981 WINE DISCOVERY CABERNET SAUVIGNON ($3.75) Napa Valley. *Vegetal but decent.*

☆☆ 1982 CABERNET SAUVIGNON ($4.00) Discovery Series, Lake. *Herbal, lush, clean, simple but attractive.*

☆☆☆ 1982 ROBERT YOUNG CABERNET SAUVIGNON ($10.00) Alexander Valley. *Very crisp, clean, lovely. Drink 1988.*

☆☆☆ 1982 YORK CREEK CABERNET SAUVIGNON ($12.00) Napa Valley. *Tart, well-built, hard, intense. Drink 1988.*

☆☆☆ 1982 ROBERT YOUNG MERLOT ($10.00) Alexander Valley. *Soft, herbal, super rich, lovely. Drink 1986.*

☆☆☆ 1979 BACIGALUPI PINOT NOIR ($15.00) Sonoma. *Spicy and tannic. Good aging potential.*

☆☆☆ 1981 BACIGALUPI PINOT NOIR ($11.00) Sonoma. *Rich, deep, clean, fruity, varietal, lovely.*

☆☆☆☆ 1981 WINERY LAKE PINOT NOIR ($12.00) Estate, Los Carneros. *Rich, varietal, fruity with sweet oak; very Burgundian.*

☆☆☆ 1982 BACIGALUPI PINOT NOIR ($12.00) Sonoma. *Rich, deep, soft, fruity, complex, varietal, and lovely.*

☆☆ 1982 WINERY LAKE PINOT NOIR ($12.00) Napa Valley. *Light, crisp, clean, varietal, charming but a bit underripe.*

ぞ**

Benmarl Wine Company
NEW YORK

Highland Avenue, Marlboro, New York 12542 (914-236-7271). FOUNDED: 1971. ACREAGE: 75 acres. PRODUCTION: 10,000 cases. DISTRIBUTION: New York, New Jersey and by mailing list. OWNER: Benmarl Wine Company. Mark and Dene Miller, managers. WINEMAKER: Mark Miller. Tours by appointment.

Mark Miller, a former illustrator and recent author, loves to experiment. He planted vines on his estate in 1957 in an effort to discover the ultimate grape varieties for the Hudson River Valley region. He added a winery in 1969 and dreamed up an unusual marketing concept called the *Société des Vignerons*, or "vine owners club." Each member buys a pair of Benmarl grapevines or, rather, sponsors the vines' production by paying a membership fee. In return, the "Vignerons" are treated to a wine tasting in the spring, where they can each select one case of wine produced by the society-funded vineyards.

WHITE

1981 MARLBORO VILLAGE WHITE ($5.00) Hudson River Region. *Dry, odd mustiness, weak fruit.*

☆ 1981 SEYVAL BLANC ($7.00) Hampton Estate, Hudson River Region. *Soft, barrel fermented.*

RED

☆☆ 1981 MARLBORO VILLAGE RED ($9.00) Hudson River Region. *Baco Noir, Chelois, Marechal Foch, and Chancellor.*

☆☆ 1979 BACO NOIR ($12.00) Estate, Hudson River Region, New York. *Earthy, rich, fruity, clean, rather pleasant.*

Beringer Vineyards
NAPA COUNTY

2000 Main Street, St. Helena, California 94574 (707-963-7115). FOUNDED: 1876. ACREAGE: 2,200 acres. PRODUCTION: 500,000 cases. DISTRIBUTION: Nationwide and some foreign countries. OWNER: Corporation. Michael Moone, president. WINEMAKER: Ed Sbragia. OTHER LABEL: Los Hermanos. Tours and tasting daily 10 A.M.–4 P.M. Gift shop.

The oldest continuously operating winery in the Napa Valley, and one of the Napa Valley's leading tourist attractions, Beringer has been miraculously converted from a lackluster producer of undistinguished wines to one of America's best and most prestigious wineries. This was the result of intelligent management by New Yorker Dick Maher, who has since moved back East to head up Seagram's big wine operation; splendid winemaking by veteran Myron Nightingale and Ed Sbragia; and considerable capital investment by parent company Nestlé. This state-of-the-art winery, built across the street from the gingerbread Victorian "Rhine House," turns out premium quality Beringer wines and jug wines sold under the Los Hermanos label.

WHITE

☆ NV LOS HERMANOS CHABLIS ($2.50) California. *Clean, crisp, decent.*

☆ 1982 CHABLIS ($4.50) North Coast. *Decent flavors, a bit watery.*

☆☆☆ 1979 CHARDONNAY ($11.00) Gamble Ranch, Napa Valley. *Big, vinous, buttery, clean and nicely balanced. Drink now.*

☆☆ 1979 CHARDONNAY ($12.50) Private Reserve, Napa Valley. *Rich, full-bodied and fruity. Drink now.*

☆☆ 1980 CHARDONNAY ($8.50) Estate, Napa Valley. *Vinous, ripe and nice.*

☆☆☆ 1980 CHARDONNAY ($11.50) Gamble Ranch, Napa Valley. *Toasty oak (barrel fermentation), good fruit and depth.*

☆☆☆ 1980 CHARDONNAY ($13.50) Private Reserve, Estate, Napa Valley. *Toasty, heavy with intense fruit and varietal character.*

☆☆ 1981 CHARDONNAY ($9.75) Estate, Napa Valley. *Hard and clean with good fruit and acid. Should age well.*

☆☆ 1981 CHARDONNAY ($12.50) Gamble Ranch, Napa Valley. *Toasty barrel fermentation flavor, good fruit and acid.*

☆☆☆ 1981 CHARDONNAY ($13.00) Private Reserve, Napa Valley. *Rich, oaky and aristocratic in style.*

☆☆ 1982 CHARDONNAY ($9.75) Beringer Estates, Napa Valley. *Fresh, clean, attractive. Nicely balanced, short on depth.*

☆☆☆ 1982 CHARDONNAY ($9.75) Estate, Napa Valley. *Vinous, rich and clean; well made.*

☆☆ 1982 CHARDONNAY ($15.00) Private Reserve, Napa Valley. *Big, rich, deep, fruity.*

☆☆ 1983 CHARDONNAY ($9.50) Napa Valley. *Clean, fresh, attractive.*

☆☆☆ 1983 CHARDONNAY ($12.00) Gamble Ranch, Napa Valley. *Barrel fermented. Toasty, lush, big, yet balanced.*

☆☆ 1983 CHENIN BLANC ($4.75) Napa Valley. *Round, lush, attractive.*

☆☆ 1982 FRENCH COLOMBARD ($5.50) Dry, Napa Valley. *Crisp, clean, simple and appealing.*

☆☆ 1981 FUME BLANC ($7.25) Knights Valley Estate, Sonoma.

☆☆ 1981 FUME BLANC ($8.00) Napa Valley. *Crisp and soft.*

☆☆ 1982 FUME BLANC ($7.50) Napa Valley. *Clean and pleasant.*

☆☆ 1982 FUME BLANC ($7.80) Sonoma. *Grassy, intense, lovely fruit and acid. Sancerre style.*

☆☆ 1983 FUME BLANC ($6.25) Napa Valley. *Pleasant, some grassiness, clean, attractive.*

☆☆☆ 1983 FUME BLANC ($7.50) Sonoma. *Snappy, good varietal character, rounded, lovely.*

☆☆☆ 1983 FUME BLANC ($12.00) Reserve, Sonoma. *Lovely, rich, oaky, loaded with tangy fruit. Stunning.*

☆☆ 1982 JOHANNISBERG RIESLING ($7.25) Estate, Napa Valley. *Delicate, clean and snappy.*

☆☆☆ 1982 JOHANNISBERG RIESLING ($15.00) Botrytised, Napa Valley. *375ml. 20.3% residual sugar. Lush, smooth, lovely.*

☆☆☆ 1982 JOHANNISBERG RIESLING ($15.00) Special Select Late Harvest, Napa Valley. *375ml. 20.3% residual sugar. Lush, rich, clean, superb.*

☆☆ 1980 SEMILLON ($30.00) Nightingale, Napa Valley. *15.7% residual sugar. Induced botrytis, nicely made, interesting.*

BLANC DE NOIR

☆☆ 1984 LOS HERMANOS WHITE CABERNET ($2.00) California. *Herbal, clean, attractive.*

☆ 1984 LOS HERMANOS WHITE ZINFANDEL ($2.00) California. *Fresh, simple, decent.*

☆☆ 1984 WHITE ZINFANDEL ($6.00) Napa Valley.

RED

☆☆ NV LOS HERMANOS CABERNET SAUVIGNON ($2.00) California. *Crisp, snappy, clean, very attractive.*

☆☆☆ 1973 CABERNET SAUVIGNON Centennial Cask Selection, Estate, Napa Valley. *Deep, rich, full, aging gracefully.*

☆☆☆ 1977 CABERNET SAUVIGNON ($18.00) Private Reserve, Lemmon Ranch, Napa Valley. *Complex, velvety, fruity, superb. Will improve for years.*

☆☆☆☆ 1978 CABERNET SAUVIGNON ($22.00) Private Reserve, Lemmon Ranch, Napa Valley. *Depth, richness and fruit. A classic. Will improve for years.*

☆☆ 1979 CABERNET SAUVIGNON ($8.00) Knight's Valley, Sonoma. *Elegant, clean, but a little simple. Lovely velvety texture.*

☆☆☆ 1979 CABERNET SAUVIGNON ($9.00) State Lane, Napa Valley. *Their best '79 Cabernet—rich, unctuous, complex and lovely.*

☆☆ 1980 CABERNET SAUVIGNON ($8.00) Knight's Valley, Sonoma. *Berried, sweet fruit, clean and attractive. Drink now.*

☆☆☆ 1980 CABERNET SAUVIGNON ($15.00) State Lane, Napa Valley. *Rich, complex, clean, a real beaut'. Drink 1986 and beyond.*

☆☆☆☆ 1980 CABERNET SAUVIGNON ($20.00) Private Reserve, Lemmon-Chabot, Napa Valley. *Rich, structured, deep, complex, stunning. Drink 1986.*

☆☆ 1981 CABERNET SAUVIGNON ($7.00) Napa Valley. *Fruity, clean, oaky, appealing. Drink now.*

☆☆ 1981 CABERNET SAUVIGNON ($10.00) Knight's Valley, Sonoma. *Clean, varietal, attractive. Drink now.*

☆☆☆ 1981 CABERNET SAUVIGNON ($15.00) Private Reserve, State Lane, Lemmon-Chabot, Napa Valley. *Soft, rich, clean, mellow. Drink 1986.*
☆☆☆☆ 1981 CABERNET SAUVIGNON ($25.00) Lemmon-Chabot, Napa Valley. *Powerful, rich, clean, lovely, fruity, complex. Drink 1988.*
☆ 1977 PETITE SIRAH ($6.50) Estate, Napa Valley. *Off nose, good fruit, lacking depth.*
☆☆ 1978 PETITE SIRAH ($6.50) Napa Valley. *Sweet oak, rich fruit, intense.*
1978 PINOT NOIR ($6.00) Napa Valley. *Oily, odd, unattractive.*
☆ 1979 PINOT NOIR ($5.80) Sonoma. *Light, clean, decent.*
☆ 1980 PINOT NOIR ($10.00) Small Lot, Knights Valley Estate, Sonoma.

FORTIFIED

☆☆ 1979 PORT ($6.00) Napa Valley. *Made from Cabernet grapes. Rich and clean with good depth.*
☆☆ CABERNET SAUVIGNON PORT ($6.00) Estate, Napa Valley. *Vanillin, lush, fat, sweet, clean.*

Berkeley Wine Cellars
ALAMEDA COUNTY

907 University Avenue, Berkeley, California 94710 (415-549-1266). FOUNDED: 1970. ACREAGE: None. PRODUCTION: 4,000 cases. OWNER: Peter Brehm. WINEMAKER: Frank Churchill, cellarmaster. No tours or tasting. Beer and winemaking supplies for sale.

Wine and the People, a home winemaking and beer-making supply store, had business relationships with some of the finest vineyards in California before they became famous. Owner Peter Brehm, a man with an uncanny instinct for vineyard selection, would sell the grapes or juice from these vineyards to his winemaking customers, but he would often save some of the finest lots for himself. In 1970 Peter contracted with Winery Lake Vineyard in Napa, long before René de Rosa's vineyard became famous. It was the Pinot Noirs Peter made from this vineyard that encouraged him to start a winery in the back of his store. Pinot Noir was Peter's love, but the winery also became known for its Zinfandels and heavier red wines. In 1984 Berkeley Wine Cellars ceased making wine.

RED

☆☆ 1980 PINOT NOIR ($12.00) Winery Lake, Carneros, Napa Valley. *Snappy and fresh-faced. Good aging potential.*
☆☆☆ 1977 ZINFANDEL Kelley Creek, Dry Creek Region, Sonoma.
☆☆ 1978 ZINFANDEL Kelley Creek, Dry Creek Valley, Sonoma.
☆☆☆ 1979 ZINFANDEL ($7.25) Kelley Creek, Dry Creek Region, Sonoma. *Soft, fruity, charming.*
☆ 1981 ZINFANDEL ($6.00) Kelley Creek, Sonoma. *Berried, clean, a bit overripe, raisiny.*

Bernardo Winery
SAN DIEGO COUNTY

13330 Paseo Del Verano Norte, San Diego, California 92128 (619-487-1866). FOUNDED: 1889. ACREAGE: 75 acres. PRODUCTION: 3,500 cases. DISTRIBUTION: At winery. OWNER: Ross Rizzo, president. WINEMAKER: Ross Rizzo. Tours and tasting daily 9 A.M.–5 P.M. Gift shop open Wednesday–Sunday 11 A.M.–5 P.M.

This small Southern California operation sells most of its wine through its own food market and gift shop, where tourists can also buy a bottle of Bernardo olive oil. Ross Rizzo, whose father ran the winery before him, uses mainly redwood tanks and grows, among others, Tokay, Carigane, and Mission grapes.

Bias Vineyards & Winery
MISSOURI

Route 1, Box 93, Berger, Missouri 63014 (314-834-5475). FOUNDED: 1980. ACREAGE: 7 acres. PRODUCTION: 1,200 cases. DISTRIBUTION: Missouri. OWNERS: Jim and Norma Bias. WINE-MAKER: Jim Bias. Tours and tasting daily 12–6 P.M.

Weary of city life, Jim Bias, an airline pilot, bought a farm and moved to the country with his wife Norma. There happened to be a vineyard on the property they acquired, so the couple began to sell grapes to nearby wineries. Even then, they had no idea that their country retreat would become a real commercial winery. It didn't take too long, however, before they were filling a new building with stainless steel tanks and presiding over their first crush.

The Biltmore Estate Company
NORTH CAROLINA

One Biltmore Plaza, Asheville, North Carolina 28803 (704-274-1776). FOUNDED: 1978. ACREAGE: 125 acres. PRODUCTION: 35,000 cases. DISTRIBUTION: At Biltmore Estate only. OWNER: Cecil family. William Cecil, Jr., general manager. WINEMAKER: Philippe Jourdain. Tours daily 10 A.M.–6 P.M.

William Cecil, Jr., felt a few vines and a winery might increase the number of visits by tourists to the historic Biltmore House and Gardens. In his capacity as estate manager, William had twelve acres of experimental vineyards planted. Satisfied with the small batches of wine made from those vines, he installed a winery in the downstairs building of the estate greenhouse. Then, as his confidence grew in the enological potential there, he converted the dairy barn into a new, larger, rustic-style winery.

Bjelland Vineyards
OREGON

Bjelland Vineyards Lane, Roseburg, Oregon 97470 (503-679-6950). FOUNDED: 1969. ACREAGE: 22 acres. PRODUCTION: 12,000 cases. DISTRIBUTION: Oregon. OWNERS: Paul and Mary Bjelland. WINEMAKERS: Paul and Mary Bjelland. Tours and tasting daily 11 A.M.–5 P.M. Picnic facilities.

Paul Bjelland moved to the Umpqua Valley to escape urban life. In 1968 he started one of Oregon's earliest vinifera wineries and founded the Oregon Winegrowers Association. His farm produces other crops and is home for livestock as well. Mary Bjelland, his wife, makes quite creditable fruit and berry wines.

Blackwood Canyon Vintners
WASHINGTON

Route 2, Box 2169-H, Sunset Road, Benton City, Washington 99230 (509-588-6249). FOUNDED: 1982. ACREAGE: 30 acres. PRODUCTION: 5,000 cases. DISTRIBUTION: Major market states.

OWNER: M. Taylor Moore. WINEMAKER: M. Taylor Moore. Tours and tasting weekends 10 A.M.–6 P.M. Weekdays by appointment.

After earning a degree in fermentation science at U.C. Davis, Mike Moore worked in several California wineries. Then friends from Oregon introduced him to the world of northwestern wines, and he began thinking about starting his own winery. He moved to Washington, "because I was excited about the wines, the grapes, and the potential of the area," says Mike. He managed vineyards and did consulting while he was "searching every part of the state," studying climates and soils. He decided on the Red Mountain area for his winery site and with the help of his parents and uncle built a beautiful "old Dutch barn" winery with diagonal cedar siding.

Blanc Vineyards
MENDOCINO COUNTY

10200 West Road, Redwood Valley, California 95470 (707-485-7352). FOUNDED: 1983. ACREAGE: 140 acres. PRODUCTION: 1,500 cases. DISTRIBUTION: California and Utah. OWNERS: Partnership. Robert and Marlys Blanc, managers. WINEMAKER: Christy Scollin. Tours and tasting by appointment.

While living in Orange County and working for the Getty Mining Company, Robert and Marlys Blanc bought a 100-acre parcel in the Redwood Valley containing 40 acres of vines. They later added 100 additional acres and hired grape grower Bill Pauli to help their son Jeff manage the vineyards. Meanwhile, daughter Christy was working as a chemist and becoming very interested in winemaking. In 1982 came the inevitable—with Christy as winemaker, the first Blanc vintage was custom-crushed at Fetzer Vineyards. Now the winery is located in a renovated dairy barn on the property.

WHITE

☆   1983 SAUVIGNON BLANC ($7.95) Mendocino.

Blenheim Vineyards
VIRGINIA

Highway 727, Route 6, Charlottesville, Virginia 22901 (804-295-7666). FOUNDED: 1979. ACREAGE: 10.5 acres. PRODUCTION: 600 cases. DISTRIBUTION: Virginia. OWNER: John J. Marquis, Jr. WINEMAKER: John J. Marquis, Jr. Tours by appointment.

John Marquis got his degree in business administration, yet he wanted to become a farmer. As soon as he graduated, John and his father, John Marquis, Sr., moved from Ohio to Virginia "to get out of the cold," says John. They bought a cattle ranch that had once been part of a larger estate established in 1745. In 1979 John planted vinifera grapes there; four years later he started making wine in the old smokehouse on the farm.

Blue Ridge Winery
PENNSYLVANIA

1101 Pine Road, Carlisle, Pennsylvania 17013 (717-486-5030). FOUNDED: 1982. ACREAGE: 7 acres. PRODUCTION: 2,000 cases. DISTRIBUTION: At winery. OWNER: Peter Capozzi. WINEMAKER: Peter Capozzi. Tours and tasting Wednesday–Sunday 12–6 P.M., or by appointment.

When Peter Capozzi saw that great big 185-year-old barn, he knew exactly what he wanted to do. He had been making wine all his life; his father and grandfather had taught him how. Peter, who runs a heating and plumbing business, bought the barn, converted it into a winery, leased vineyards, and began making dry red and rosé table wines.

Boeger Winery
EL DORADO COUNTY

1709 Carson Road, Placerville, California 95667 (916-622-8094). FOUNDED: 1973. ACREAGE: 35 acres. PRODUCTION: 10,000 cases. DISTRIBUTION: Major U.S. markets. OWNERS: Greg and Susan Boeger, and George and Lillian Babbin. WINEMAKER: Greg Boeger. Tours and tasting Wednesday–Sunday 10 A.M.–5 P.M.

Greg Boeger, a member of the Nichelini family of Napa, grew up in the wine business. He got a master's degree at U.C. Davis and then went off on his own, establishing one of the first "new generation" wineries in the Sierra Foothills. The property had been a pear ranch and, before that, a vineyard and winery in the 1860s. The vines are planted at a 2,300- to 3,000-foot elevation where cool Sierra breezes contribute to the harvest of white varieties that are not generally successful in nearby Amador County.

WHITE

☆☆ 1983 SIERRA BLANC ($4.50) El Dorado. *1% residual sugar. Fruity, soft and quite lovely.*
☆ 1981 CHARDONNAY ($9.00) El Dorado. *Nice but oafish.*
☆☆☆ 1982 CHARDONNAY ($9.00) El Dorado. *Nice, fruity, clean, rich, long finish, very good.*
☆☆☆ 1983 CHENIN BLANC ($5.50) El Dorado. *1% residual sugar. Charming, fruity, crisp.*
☆☆☆☆ 1982 SAUVIGNON BLANC ($6.00) 10th Anniversary, El Dorado. *Fruity, clean and de-licious—atypical but superb.*
☆☆☆ 1983 SAUVIGNON BLANC ($7.50) El Dorado. *Almost as good as the 1982—round, fresh, balanced, superb.*
☆ 1984 SAUVIGNON BLANC ($7.50) El Dorado. *0.7% residual sugar. 16% Semillon. Fruity fresh, charmingly varietal, clear, but too sweet.*

BLANC DE NOIR

☆ 1982 WHITE ZINFANDEL ($4.50) El Dorado. *1.5% residual sugar. Sweet, dense, heavy.*
☆☆ 1983 WHITE ZINFANDEL ($5.00) El Dorado. *Crisp, snappy, food wine with a nice rounding of sugar (1.4%).*
☆☆ 1984 WHITE ZINFANDEL ($5.00) El Dorado. *1.8% residual sugar. Decent, fruity, a bit heavy.*

RED

☆☆ 1981 HANGTOWN RED ($3.95) California. *Lush, fat and intense. A very appealing glass of wine.*
☆ 1982 HANGTOWN RED ($4.00) California. *Raisiny, spicy, rich, decent.*
☆ 1979 CABERNET SAUVIGNON ($8.00) Estate, El Dorado.
☆☆ 1980 CABERNET SAUVIGNON ($8.50) El Dorado. *Good fruit and earth, clean and fat, simple. Drink now.*
☆☆ 1980 MERLOT ($8.50) 10th Anniversary, Estate, El Dorado. *Soft and delicate, balanced.*
☆☆ 1981 MERLOT ($9.50) Estate, El Dorado. *Soft and appealing with a nice lushness.*
☆☆ 1982 MERLOT ($10.00) Estate, El Dorado. *Fruity clean, attractive.*
☆ 1979 ZINFANDEL ($5.25) El Dorado. *Dull, lacking depth.*
☆☆ 1980 ZINFANDEL ($5.50) El Dorado.

☆☆   1981 ZINFANDEL ($6.00) El Dorado. *Leathery, soft textured, clear, decent.*
  ☆   1981 ZINFANDEL ($6.00) El Dorado. *Soft, clean and decent.*

Bogle Vineyards
YOLO COUNTY

Route 1, Box 276, Clarksburg, California 95612 (916-744-1139). FOUNDED: 1979. ACREAGE: 300 acres. PRODUCTION: 8,000 cases. DISTRIBUTION: Nationwide. OWNER: Warren V. Bogle, president; Frances C. Bogle, vice president; Chris C. Bogle, secretary. WINEMAKER: Mark Shannon. Tours and tasting by appointment.

Warren and Frances Bogle have grown grapes on Merritt Island in the Sacramento River Delta region since the late 1960s. They were so impressed with the high quality of their fruit that they built a small winery in the mid-1970s. In addition to their large vineyard, the Bogles also have seven-hundred acres of other crops. Grapes are machine harvested, field-crushed, and fermented very cold and long.

WHITE

  ☆   1982 CHENIN BLANC ($3.75) Clarksburg. *Slightly sweet and a bit weedy.*
☆☆☆☆   1982 CHENIN BLANC ($5.00) Dry, Clarksburg. *Crisp and delicious with subtle oak and bright fruitiness.*
 ☆☆☆   1983 CHENIN BLANC ($4.50) Clarksburg. *1.4% residual sugar. Crisp and fruity.*

BLANC DE NOIR

  ☆   1982 SARAH'S BLUSH ($3.50) Clarksburg. *Made from Petite Sirah. Tart and fruity. 1.4% residual sugar.*

RED

  NV   VIN ROUGE ($3.75) Clarksburg. *Petite Sirah. Weedy and lacking acidity.*

Jean-Claude Boisset
NAPA COUNTY

8440 St. Helena Highway, Rutherford, California 94573 (415-957-9716). FOUNDED: 1980. ACREAGE: 46 acres. PRODUCTION: 10,000 cases. DISTRIBUTION: Major U.S. markets. OWNER: Jean-Claude Boisset. WINEMAKER: Bob Levy. No tours or tasting. All sales through Lion Imports.

This well-located Rutherford vineyard is owned by Frenchman Jean-Claude Boisset, a shipper of Burgundy wines. The first few vintages of Cabernet Sauvignon (and a little Chardonnay) were crushed and vinified at Conn Creek Winery. More recent wines were made at Rombauer Vineyards.

WHITE

 ☆☆   1983 CHARDONNAY ($9.00) Napa Valley. *Austere, good fruit, balanced.*
 ☆☆☆   1983 SAUVIGNON BLANC ($7.50) Napa Valley. *Tangy fruit, clean, fresh, charming.*

RED

 ☆☆   1979 CABERNET SAUVIGNON ($10.00) Estate, Napa Valley. *Lush, deep, clean and complex. Drink 1986.*
 ☆☆   1981 CABERNET SAUVIGNON ($9.00) Estate, Napa Valley. *Lush, earthy, nicely structured. Drink 1986.*

Bonny Doon Vineyard
SANTA CRUZ COUNTY

10 Pine Flat Road, Santa Cruz, California 95060 (408-425-3625). FOUNDED: 1981. ACREAGE: 20 acres. PRODUCTION: 4,500 cases. DISTRIBUTION: California, Illinois, Massachusetts, and New York. OWNER: Alan Grahm. WINEMAKER: Randall Grahm. Tasting May–October: Tuesday–Sunday 12–6 P.M., November-April: weekends 12–6 P.M.

After traveling in Europe, Randall Grahm worked in a retail wine store in Los Angeles where he got hooked on old Burgundies. He proceeded to get his enology degree at U.C. Davis, after which he "became a complete 'Burgund-o-phile'. I wanted to make The Great American Pinot Noir," says Randall. He tried to learn all he could by talking to other growers and winemakers in California and France, then he bought Bonny Doon and went to great lengths to ensure a most Burgundian atmosphere for his new vines. He hauled in limestone, ten tons per acre, and used Burgundian vine spacings. Randall has had to buy outside fruit that doesn't measure up to his stringent standards while waiting for his own vines to produce. And his wines were made at other wineries until he converted an old barn into a winery in 1983.

WHITE

☆☆☆ 1983 VIN DE PAILLE ($12.00) Central Coast. *375ml. 12.5% residual sugar. Muscat, rich, grapey.*

☆☆☆ 1983 CHARDONNAY ($12.00) La Reina, Monterey. *Rich, complex, deep, attractive.*

BLANC DE NOIR

☆ NV PINOT NOIR ($6.50) Vin Gris, Cuvée 823, Sonoma. *20% Chardonnay, 80% Pinot Noir. Crisp, complex, dry.*

RED

☆☆ 1982 VIN ROUGE ($6.00) California. *Peppery, rich, interesting. Read the label notes.*

☆☆ 1982 CLARET ($9.00) Mendocino. *Vegetal but nicely made, clean and complex. Drink now.*

☆☆☆ 1983 CLARET ($9.00) Central Coast. *75% Cabernet, 25% Merlot. Rich, clean, lush.*

☆☆ 1981 PINOT NOIR ($9.00) Arrendell, Sonoma. *Earthy and balanced, soft fruit, a bit underripe.*

☆☆☆ 1983 PINOT NOIR ($18.00) Bethel Heights, Willamette Valley, Oregon. *Rich fruit, elegant, clean, charming.*

☆☆☆ 1983 SYRAH ($10.50) Central Coast. *Crisp, complex, graceful, very Rhone-like.*

BOONE'S FARM *see* E. & J. Gallo Winery

Boordy Vineyards
MARYLAND

12820 Long Green Pike, Hydes, Maryland 21082 (301-592-5015). FOUNDED: 1945. ACREAGE: 32 acres. PRODUCTION: 6,000 cases. DISTRIBUTION: Maryland, Washington D.C., Virginia, and Georgia. OWNER: Deford family. Robert Deford III, president; Robert Deford, Jr., vice president. WINEMAKER: Robert Deford III; Benjamin Allen, cellarmaster. Tours and tasting Tuesday–Saturday 10 A.M.–5 P.M., Sunday 1 P.M.–4 P.M. Large groups by appointment.

Philip M. Wagner, one of America's great winemaking pioneers, was the man who brought French-American hybrid grape varieties to the eastern United States and Canada. Prior to the cultivation of these hybrids, eastern wineries were making wines from native Labrusca grapes which, to Wagner's taste, made unappealing wines. Constantly experimenting with new vineyards, Wagner needed a place for all the juice, so he built this small stucco winery. The Deford family, long time grape growers who had sold grapes to Wagner, were immediately interested when they learned the winery was for sale. Robert Deford III bought the winery with his family and in 1980 moved the winery to rural northeastern Baltimore County. There he modernized the equipment and reintroduced varietal wines.

WHITE

☆   1982 SEYVAL BLANC ($4.50) Maryland.
☆   1983 VIDAL BLANC ($5.00) Maryland. *Sweet, snappy.*

BLANC DE NOIR

☆   NV PINOT NOIR ($5.00) Vin Gris, Maryland. *Fresh, clean.*

Borra's Cellar
SAN JOAQUIN COUNTY

1301 East Armstrong Road, Lodi, California 95240 (209-368-5082). FOUNDED: 1975. ACREAGE: 30 acres. PRODUCTION: 1,500 cases. DISTRIBUTION: Northern California. OWNERS: Steven J. and Beverly V. Borra. WINEMAKER: Steven J. Borra. Tastings weekends 10 A.M.–4 P.M.

Steve Borra retired in 1983 from his job at the telephone company to devote full time to his small winery. The vineyards were planted by Steve's grandfather and they are now mainly Zinfandel and Barbera. Traditional winemaking practices are used: natural yeast fermentation, redwood fermenters, and long oak aging.

BLANC DE NOIR

☆   1984 BARBERA BLANC ($4.95) Lodi. *Some sulfur in nose, decent, fruity, a bit dull.*

RED

☆   NV BARBERA ($4.95) Trois Cuvées, Lodi. *Snappy, decent, clean.*
☆☆   1978 BARBERA ($5.00) Estate, California.
☆   1978 CARIGNANE ($5.00) Estate, California.

Boskydel Vineyard
MICHIGAN

Route 1, Box 522, Lake Leelanau, Michigan 49653 (616-256-7272). FOUNDED: 1976. ACREAGE: 25 acres. PRODUCTION: 2,000 cases. DISTRIBUTION: Michigan. OWNER: Bernard C. Rink. WINEMAKER: Bernard C. Rink. Tours and tasting daily 1 P.M.–6 P.M.

Living on a southwest slope overlooking Lake Leelanau, the Rink family began experimenting with thirty-five different grape varieties in 1964. By 1971, Bernard Rink had selected six French-American hybrids that he felt could withstand the harsh Michigan winters. Bernard's interest in wine began at home where, during Prohibition, his father converted grapes grown from near Lake Erie into a little illicit wine. The barrels were kept hidden in the kitchen. Now, as Dean of Library Services at Northwestern Michigan College, Bernard sees his winemaking adventure as a means of teaching his five sons a sense of responsibility and the principles of hard, honest work.

WHITE

☆ 1981 RAVAT VIGNOLES Leelanau Peninsula, Michigan. *Lacking fruit, grassy, dry.*
☆☆ 1982 SEYVAL BLANC Leelanau Peninsula, Michigan. *Off-dry.*

ROSE

○ 1981 DECHAUNAC Leelanau Peninsula, Michigan.

The Brander Vineyard
SANTA BARBARA COUNTY

P.O. Box 92, Los Olivos, California 93441 (805-688-2455). FOUNDED: 1979. ACREAGE: 40 acres. PRODUCTION: 6,000 cases. DISTRIBUTION: California and major market states. OWNER: C. Frederic Brander. WINEMAKER: C. Frederic Brander. OTHER LABEL: St. Carl. Tours by appointment.

Fred Brander's vision is to create a Bordeaux-style estate in the Santa Ynez Valley. From his Latour-like label to his carefully constructed Cabernet—under the St. Carl label (with Merlot and Cabernet Franc)—and his Sauvignon Blanc (with Semillon), he has succeeded. Fred, a youthful and pensive U.C. Davis graduate, is a perfectionist and it shows. He is also a partner at Santa Ynez Valley Winery.

WHITE

☆☆☆ 1980 SAUVIGNON BLANC ($7.00) Santa Ynez Valley. *35% Semillon. Toasty, rich, earthy.*
☆☆☆ 1981 SAUVIGNON BLANC ($7.50) Estate, Santa Barbara. *Crisp, lean and varietal.*
☆☆ 1982 SAUVIGNON BLANC ($8.00) Santa Ynez Valley. *Crisp, clean, toasty and tannic.*
☆☆☆ 1983 SAUVIGNON BLANC ($8.25) Santa Ynez Valley. *18% Semillon. Crisp, clean, subdued varietal character.*

BLANC DE NOIR

☆☆ 1983 ST. CARL CABERNET BLANC ($4.75) Santa Ynez Valley. *0.7% residual sugar. Herbal, crisp, attractive, clean.*
☆☆ 1983 ST. CARL CABERNET FRANC BLANC ($5.75) Santa Ynez Valley. *0.6% residual sugar. Fresh, crisp and snappy; well balanced.*
☆☆☆ 1983 ST. CARL MERLOT BLANC ($4.75) Santa Ynez Valley. *1.4% residual sugar and good crisp acid give this one snap.*

Brandywine Vineyards
PENNSYLVANIA

Box A, Kemblesville, Pennsylvania 19347 (215-255-4171). FOUNDED: 1982. ACREAGE: 15 acres. PRODUCTION: 4,100 cases. DISTRIBUTION: Pennsylvania, Delaware, and Maryland. OWNER: Corporation. Tom McKeon and Bill Wingate. WINEMAKER: Tom McKeon. Tours and tasting Monday–Saturday 11 A.M.–6 P.M., Sunday 12–5 P.M.

Tom McKeon, a research chemist who likes wine, reached what some would call a mid-life crisis. He needed to break away and explore a new lifestyle, so he searched for a vineyard and potential winery, plus some creative financing. He found a piece of bare land owned by one of his winery partners, Bill Wingate, and built the winery first before starting to plant vineyards. Tom is currently buying grapes until his own vineyard starts producing.

Braren Pauli Winery
MENDOCINO COUNTY

12507 Hawn Creek Road, Potter Valley, California 95469 (707-778-0721). FOUNDED: 1979. ACREAGE: 100 acres. PRODUCTION: 4,000 cases. DISTRIBUTION: California. OWNERS: Larry Braren and Bill Pauli. WINEMAKER: Larry Braren. Tours by appointment. Additional tasting and business offices at 1611 Spring Hill Road, Petaluma.

When Bill Pauli purchased a renowned block of Zinfandel vineyard, he and his partner Larry Braren knew that their next step would be to make wine. An established grape grower in Mendocino's Potter Valley, Bill first met Larry while managing a vineyard in which Larry had an interest. The partners built a winery in a barn on Bill's property.

WHITE

☆☆ 1981 CHARDONNAY ($9.37) Potter Valley, Mendocino. *Lovely, rich bouquet; simple, lemony with attractive flavors.*

☆ 1982 CHARDONNAY ($7.00) Mendocino.

☆ 1983 SAUVIGNON BLANC ($3.25) Potter Valley, Mendocino. *Oaky and lacking fruit; decent.*

BLANC DE NOIR

☆☆ 1984 WHITE ZINFANDEL ($4.50) Mendocino. *1.3% residual sugar. Snappy, earthy, attractive.*

RED

☆☆ 1980 ZINFANDEL ($8.50) Redwood Valley, Mendocino. *Big, fat, lush, intense, old style.*

Breitenbach Wine Cellars
OHIO

Rural Route 1, Dover, Ohio 44622 (216-343-3603). FOUNDED: 1980. ACREAGE: None. PRODUCTION: 4,000 cases. DISTRIBUTION: At winery. OWNER: Cynthia Bixler. WINEMAKER: Dalton Bixler. No tours. Tasting daily 11 A.M.–6 P.M.

After running an alarm business and working in land sales, Dalton Bixler wanted to sink his teeth into something he and his wife, Cynthia, could manage together. They built a simple two-story structure on a large piece of property within this small German-American community. The winery, downstairs, is beneath a folksy country market that sells trinkets and local foods plus Breitenbach fruit wines and grape wines.

Brenner Cellars
SONOMA COUNTY

P.O. Box 7018, Cotati, California 94928 (707-792-0258). FOUNDED: 1980. ACREAGE: None. PRODUCTION: 3,000 cases. DISTRIBUTION: California and major market states. OWNER: Allan Brenner. WINEMAKER: Allan Brenner, cellarmaster. No tours or tasting.

Allan Brenner, an enterprising young winelover, decided one day to create his own label to blend and bottle his own wines. He usually releases one wine per year, a wine that he either buys or has made for him. Occasionally he even involves himself in the winemaking procedure. His first wine was a Zinfandel purchased from Lytton Springs Winery in Sonoma County. Subsequent wines have been various varieties made at different wineries. To be closer to his wine sources, Allan moved from Los Angeles to Sonoma County in 1984.

RED

☆☆ 1981 CABERNET SAUVIGNON ($8.50) San Luis Obispo. *Varietal, fruity, charming.*
     Drink now.
☆ 1979 ZINFANDEL ($7.50) Sonoma. *Decent, simple, clean and bland.*

Leslie J. Bretz
OHIO

P.O. Box 17, Middle Bass, Ohio 43446 (419-285-2323). FOUNDED: 1935. ACREAGE: 15 acres. PRODUCTION: 6,200 cases. DISTRIBUTION: Ohio and at winery. OWNER: Walter C. Bretz. WINEMAKER: Walter C. Bretz. Tours in summer only: Monday–Saturday 1 P.M.–5 P.M.

The old cellar of this winery dates back to 1867 when Walter Bretz's great grandfather established the family winery, and some of the vines on the surrounding property are more than 50 years old. Recently, a three-story concrete winery was built on the remains of the original arched cellar. Like his father before him, Walter was born and raised on this property and seemed to have always been destined to grow grapes and make wine. He makes six wines, the same type and style every year. Three are semi-sweet; three are dry.

Bridgehampton Winery
NEW YORK

P.O. Box 979, Bridgehampton, New York 11932 (516-537-3155). FOUNDED: 1982. ACREAGE: 26 acres. PRODUCTION: 1,500 cases. DISTRIBUTION: New York. OWNER: Lyle Greenfield. WINEMAKER: Richard Harbich. Tours weekends 12–6 P.M. Tasting daily 11 A.M.–5 P.M.

When New York advertising man Lyle Greenfield wanted to get away from the pressures of the city, he would escape to his summer home on Long Island. Through the years, he watched the potato fields around him being replaced by vineyards. He also heard reports that Long Island had potential as a vinifera producing area. Lyle purchased a 70-acre parcel in Bridgehampton and began planting vinifera in 1979. The brand new winery, of potato-barn-style, has a sleek A-line roof that sits just above the ground; the entire first floor is buried in the earth. The first wines, a Chardonnay and a Riesling, were made at the Hermann J. Wiemer Winery before Cornell graduate Richard Harbich became Bridgehampton's winemaker.

WHITE

☆ 1982 CHARDONNAY ($12.00) Long Island. *Clean and fruity.*
☆☆ 1982 JOHANNISBERG RIESLING ($12.00) Long Island. *Dry, crisp and varietal with*
      lovely fruit.

Brimstone Hill Vineyards
NEW YORK

Road 2, Box 142, Pine Bush, New York 12566 (914-744-2231). FOUNDED: 1979. ACREAGE: 5 acres. PRODUCTION: 625 cases. DISTRIBUTION: Local. OWNERS: Richard and Valerie

Eldridge. WINEMAKER: Richard Eldridge. Tours and tasting summer: Monday–Friday 10 A.M.–5 P.M., Sunday 12–5 P.M; winter by appointment.

Valerie Eldridge comes from a prominent French winemaking family. Her husband Richard, a college professor, was so impressed by her family's wines that in 1969 he bought some land in the foothills of the Shawangunk Mountains on the west bank of the Hudson River and planted vineyards. He sold grapes to other winemakers while experimenting with small lots of his own. Since he had planted some twenty different and fairly unusual varieties, his grapes were very much in demand. But now that Richard has finally started his own winery, and has planned to double his current production, he keeps his entire vineyard production for himself.

&

Bristle Ridge Vineyards
MISSOURI

P.O. Box 95, Nob Noster, Missouri 65336 (816-229-0961). FOUNDED: 1979. ACREAGE: 5 acres. PRODUCTION: 2,100 cases. DISTRIBUTION: Missouri. OWNER: Edward Smith. WINE-MAKER: Edward Smith. Tours and tasting Saturday 10 A.M.–6 P.M., Sunday 12–6 P.M.

The result of a hobby gone wild, Bristle Ridge Vineyards was started by Edward Smith after he left his job as service manager for a printing equipment company. He and his wife looked for several years before they found a three-story concrete block building with surrounding land that could easily be planted in vines. Happy in his new agrarian lifestyle, Edward pays the bills by free-lancing in the printing industry.

&

JFJ Bronco Winery
STANISLAUS COUNTY

6342 Bystrum Road, Ceres, California 95307 (209-538-3131). FOUNDED: 1973. ACREAGE: None. PRODUCTION: 1,500,000 cases. DISTRIBUTION: Nationwide. OWNERS: John, Fred and Joseph Franzia, management. WINEMAKER: John Franzia. OTHER LABEL: CC Vineyard Brand. No tours or tasting.

When John, Fred, and Joe Franzia sold their winery to Coca-Cola of New York in 1973, they started a wholesale wine distributorship in Southern California. The following year Bronco built its Ceres facility and, several years later, built another winery at Fresno after Bronco and the Getty Oil Company entered into a lease agreement for Getty's grapes. Bronco is ranked fourth among wineries in total storage capacity. Fred Franzia, spokesman, president, and grape contractor for Bronco, is proud to admit that Gallo is his model. "We're trying to be No. 1," he says.

&

Bronte Champagne & Wine Company
MICHIGAN

930 West Eight Mile Road, Detroit, Michigan 48220 (616-621-3419). FOUNDED: 1932. ACREAGE: None. PRODUCTION: 62,500 cases. DISTRIBUTION: Midwestern states. OWNER: Robert E. Wozniak. WINEMAKER: Angelo Spinazze. Tours and tasting daily 10 A.M.–5 P.M.

The Bronte Winery, oldest in the state, has a long, colorful history. Founded by a dentist, Dr. Wozniak, the winery started in the old Columbia brewery; then it moved to a vineyard site where the Keeler Bonnybrook Harness Races had been run. Ironically, this same site was later used as the meeting place for the Women's Christian Temperance Union of Keeler. One of the most interesting local historical attractions today is winemaker Angelo Spinazze, first hired by Dr. Wozniak in 1937. Under his direction, the winery planted the first commercial French-American hybrid grapes in Michigan. The winery also claims that in 1946 it was the first in Michigan to make "Champagne." Later, it added the dubious distinction of being the first to make Cold Duck. Angelo and Dr. Wozniak's son Robert run the winery.

ટે

Brookside Vineyard Company
SAN BERNARDINO COUNTY

2801 East Guasti Road, Guasti, California 91743 (714-983-2787). FOUNDED: 1832. ACREAGE: 500 acres. PRODUCTION: 300,000 cases. DISTRIBUTION: Nationwide. OWNER: Corporation. Norman Scheidt, president. WINEMAKER: Primo Scorsatto. OTHER LABELS: E. Vache, Guasti. Tours weekends 10 A.M.–6 P.M. Gift shop and picnic facilities.

This large operation used to function more as a chain of tasting rooms than as a winery. In 1982, however, a group of San Francisco private investors bought Brookside from Beatrice Foods. Since then all but six of the tasting rooms have been closed—those remaining open are mainly in Southern California. Ninety-five percent of the winery's production comes from its own vineyards. Brookside produces an enormous line of products under several labels.

ટે

Brotherhood Winery
NEW YORK

35 North Street, Washingtonville, New York 10992 (914-496-3661). FOUNDED: 1839. ACREAGE: None. PRODUCTION: 100,000 cases. DISTRIBUTION: Eastern states. OWNER: Mrs. E. D. Farrell, president. WINEMAKERS: Steve Price and Mark Diagle. Tours and tasting weekends 11 A.M.–4 P.M. except February and November. Weekday hours vary according to season.

The Brotherhood Winery survived Prohibition by making sacramental wine. It is the oldest continuously operated winery in the United States. The popular tours of the large, ancient underground aging cellars and 150-year-old handmade oak casks attract so many visitors every day (who also purchase most of the wine made at the winery) that the winery had to pull out the vineyards to put in a parking lot. All this began with a Frenchman, Jean Jaques, who in 1810 preferred selling his wine for sacramental purposes. Later the winery was sold to a Mr. Emerson, a customer of the winery who also purchased wine made by a Hudson Valley religious community called the Brotherhood. Mr. Emerson changed the winery's name to Brotherhood Winery. Today Mrs. Eloise Farrell and her daughter Anne maintain the historic and somewhat mystical atmosphere of the winery for visitors, while equipping it with all the latest enological equipment.

WHITE

☆ 1982 CHARDONNAY ($10.00) New York State.

FORTIFIED

☆ CREAM SHERRY ($3.85) New York State. *Sweet, nutty, some nice acidity.*
☆☆ RUBY PORT ($3.85) New York State. *Deep, spicy, rich, good acidity.*

☆   CELEBRATION PORT ($5.95) New York State. *Tawny color, rich, deep, sweet,
        18% alcohol, short.*
☆☆   FINO SHERRY ($7.00) New York State. *Dry, nutty, crisp and fruity. Solera of white
        hybrids.*

FLAVORED

☆   HOLIDAY ($3.75) New York State. *Spicy, cinnamon-flavored white wine.*
☆☆   MAY WINE ($3.75) New York State. *Sweet, charming rosé, flavored with woodruff
        and strawberry.*

乡

David Bruce Winery
SANTA CRUZ COUNTY

21439 Bear Creek Road, Los Gatos, California 95031 (408-354-4214). FOUNDED: 1964.
ACREAGE: 25 acres. PRODUCTION: 20,000 cases. DISTRIBUTION: Major market states.
OWNER: Corporation. David Bruce, chairman; Dennis Marion, president. WINEMAKER: Keith
Hohlfeldt. Tours and tasting on Saturdays 11 A.M.–5 P.M. or by appointment.

David Bruce is a retired San Jose dermatologist whose mountaintop "hobby" winery has become
one of the biggest in Santa Cruz County. In the beginning, Bruce, a disciple of eccentric winemaker
Martin Ray, was known for outlandish, high-extract wines. Lately he has trimmed his product line
and hired Keith Hohlfeldt, former winemaker at Sunrise Winery. The winery has since become
more establishment than maverick.

WHITE

O   NV OLD DOG WHITE ($3.95) California. *Dull, no fruit, watery.*
      1979 CHARDONNAY ($6.50) Lot 2, San Luis Obispo. *Lifeless and watery.*
O   1981 CHARDONNAY ($12.00) Wasson, Sonoma.
☆☆   1981 CHARDONNAY ($12.50) California, 72% Santa Barbara, 28% Chamisal, Edna
          Valley. *Simple, clean and crisp.*
☆☆☆   1981 CHARDONNAY ($18.00) Estate, Santa Cruz Mountains. *Toasty and rich but with
          good, firm acidity. Will age well.*
      1982 CHARDONNAY ($10.00) California. *Flabby and dull.*
O   1982 CHARDONNAY ($18.00) Estate, Santa Cruz Mountains. *Odd, unattractive.*
☆   1983 CHARDONNAY ($10.00) California. *Vinous, rich, unbalanced, clumsy.*
      1980 SAUVIGNON BLANC ($8.00) Santa Barbara.

RED

      NV OLD DOG RED ($3.95) California.
☆   1979 CABERNET SAUVIGNON ($9.00) California.
☆   1980 CABERNET SAUVIGNON ($12.50) Vintner's Selection, Santa Clara. *Weedy, some
          volatile acidity.*
☆☆☆   1981 CABERNET SAUVIGNON California. *Rich, berried, tannic, dense, good. Drink
          1988 and beyond.*
☆☆☆   1982 CABERNET SAUVIGNON ($12.50) Vintners Select, California. *Lush, structured,
          classic. Drink 1986.*
☆   1975 PINOT NOIR Santa Cruz. *For lovers of old wines. Chocolatey, raisiny, smooth,
          ripe.*
☆   1978 PINOT NOIR ($12.00) Estate, Santa Cruz. *Chocolate and walnuts. Decent but past
          its prime.*
☆   1979 PINOT NOIR ($12.00) Estate, Santa Cruz Mountains. *Spicy, with some veggie
          characteristics. Decent balance, smooth.*

☆☆☆ 1980 PINOT NOIR ($15.00) Estate, Santa Cruz. *High alcohol, cherry flavors; complex and delicious.*

☆☆☆ 1981 PINOT NOIR ($12.50) Estate, Santa Cruz Mountains. *Earthy, rich and loaded with lovely cherry flavors. Drink 1986.*

☆☆☆ 1982 PINOT NOIR ($12.50) Estate, Santa Cruz Mountains. *Crisp, soft, lovely fruit and varietal character. Drink 1986.*

☆☆☆ 1983 PINOT NOIR ($12.50) Estate, Santa Cruz Mountains. *Tangy, rich, varietal, attractive. Drink 1987.*

☆☆ 1979 ZINFANDEL ($8.50) Santa Clara.

☆ 1980 ZINFANDEL ($6.50) Amador.

☆ 1981 ZINFANDEL ($5.50) Mendocino. *Rich, buttery oak, some odd flavors, decent.*

Brundage Cellars
IDAHO

311 Lake Street, McCall, Idaho 83638 (208-634-7665). FOUNDED: 1981. ACREAGE: None. PRODUCTION: 400 cases. DISTRIBUTION: Idaho. OWNER: Corporation. Bill Crowley, president. WINEMAKER: Rick Fereday. No tours or tasting.

This winery may be named after Brundage Mountain, but the wine is made in the basement of Rick and Bob's Hardware Store. Rick, Bob, and Bill, a financial consultant, had been making wine as a hobby at Bill's house. The more equipment they bought and the more wine they made, the more serious they became about starting a real winery. Forming a corporation with Bill as president, the boys moved their equipment to the store. According to Bob, the scene on the wine label is the view of Big Payette Lake seen from the back of the hardware store.

Brushcreek Vineyards
OHIO

12351 Newkirk Lane, Rural Route 4, Peebles, Ohio 45660 (513-588-2618). FOUNDED: 1977. ACREAGE: 3.5 acres. PRODUCTION: 1,250 cases. DISTRIBUTION: Local. OWNERS: Ralph and Laura Wise. WINEMAKER: Ralph Wise. Tours and tasting Monday–Saturday 11 A.M.–8 P.M.

Ralph Wise, with full support from his wife and five children, decided to make his winemaking hobby a family affair. He began by converting a large structure built from huge logs (some of which are two feet wide and sixty feet long) into a winery. Despite the demands of his job as a quality control engineer, Ralph keeps a close eye on the winemaking process, but he relies heavily on the rest of the family for the day-to-day work. Presently all grapes are purchased, but Ralph figures that some day one of the kids may want to be a vineyard manager.

Buccia Vineyard
OHIO

518 Gore Road, Conneaut, Ohio 44030 (216-593-5976). FOUNDED: 1978. ACREAGE: 4 acres. PRODUCTION: 700 cases. DISTRIBUTION: At winery and local outlets. OWNER: Fred Bucci, manager; Joanna Bucci. WINEMAKERS: Fred and Joanna Bucci. Tours April–December: weekdays 2 P.M.–7 P.M., Saturday 2 P.M.–9 P.M. Tasting year-round: Monday–Saturday 2 P.M.–7 P.M. Closed Sundays.

Five years of working with American Telephone and Telegraph in Cleveland was enough for Fred Bucci. He took off for the country, preferring the life of grapes and wine. This was no snap decision, but an idea that sprung from the Italian winemaking tradition inherited by Fred from his grandfather, Pasquale Bucci. While continuing to work as a tax appraiser, Fred planted vineyards in 1975 and opened the winery in his basement in 1978. He adheres to an old world winemaking style, relying more on manpower than fancy equipment. The newest addition to the winery is the tasting room next to the Bucci home.

Buckingham Valley Vineyards
PENNSYLVANIA

Box 371, Route 413, Buckingham, Pennsylvania 18912 (215-794-7188). FOUNDED: 1966. ACREAGE: 16 acres. PRODUCTION: 8,000 cases. DISTRIBUTION: At winery. OWNERS: Gerald C. and Kathleen Forest. WINEMAKER: Gerald Forest. Tours and tasting Tuesday–Friday 12–6 P.M., Saturday 10 A.M.–6 P.M., Sunday 12–4 P.M. January–February: weekends only.

It was the farmer's way of life, "the good life," that drew Jerry and Kathleen Forest to Buckingham to grow grapes. Jerry is a self-taught winemaker who worked as advertising director for a newspaper chain while the newly established vineyards and colonial-style house and winery were completed. The winery is connected to the house and has been expanded gradually by Jerry and his two sons. Kathleen puts most of her energy into the vineyards, though her sons are beginning to help out there as well.

WHITE

☆   1983 VIDAL BLANC ($4.00) Pennsylvania. *Decent, clean.*

Bucks Country Vineyards
PENNSYLVANIA

Route 202, R.D. 3, Box 167, New Hope, Pennsylvania 18938 (215-794-7449). FOUNDED: 1973. ACREAGE: 1 acre. PRODUCTION: 40,000 cases. DISTRIBUTION: At tasting locations. OWNER: Corporation. Arthur Gerold, president; Peter Gerold, general manager. WINEMAKERS: David Thiebeau and Steve Shepard. Tasting at several locations. Call for information.

Once the owner of Brooks–Van Horn Costumes, one of the largest theatrical costumers in New York, Arthur Gerold created a farm-winery in a bigger-than-life theatrical style. He established the main winery on a William Penn land grant, then proceeded to build three branches in different areas of the state. These funky, country-barn-style stores sell Bucks Country wines, homemade breads, and cheeses made by the "Pennsylvania Cheesemaker." More diversion for the tourists include gift shops full of glassware, china, and gourmet items. At the winery location there is a museum featuring the history of wine and Champagne making, and a collection of glasses from the Metropolitan Museum of Art in New York. Dramatic flare is supplied by an exhibition of theatrical costumes made by Brooks–Van Horn and once worn by famous stage and movie stars.

Buehler Vineyards
NAPA COUNTY

820 Greenfield Road, St. Helena, California 94574 (707-963-2155). FOUNDED: 1978. ACREAGE: 61 acres. PRODUCTION: 10,000 cases. DISTRIBUTION: California and some other states. OWNER:

John P. Buehler, Sr.; John P. Buehler, Jr., general manager. WINEMAKER: Heidi Peterson. No tours or tasting. Visits by appointment.

John Buehler, Sr., is a former Bechtel executive who bought this beautiful 75-acre hilltop estate on the eastern side of the Napa Valley as a retirement home. After growing grapes and selling them to others, his son John Jr., who also lives on the property, decided to build a small winery. Although grapes are still sold to others, winery production has steadily increased and is projected to reach 15,000 cases. John Jr. and his wife, Lisa, have built a striking château-style home on the property. Winemaker Heidi Peterson is the daughter of Taylor California Cellars' Dick Peterson.

WHITE

☆☆ 1981 PINOT BLANC ($9.00) Estate, Napa Valley.
☆☆ 1982 PINOT BLANC ($8.00) Estate, Napa Valley. *Soft, rich, balanced, a lovely wine.*
☆☆☆ 1983 PINOT BLANC ($8.00) Estate, Napa Valley. *Lovely fruit, clean, rich, delightful.*

BLANC DE NOIR

☆☆☆ 1983 WHITE ZINFANDEL ($5.50) Estate, Napa Valley. *1.5% residual sugar. Pretty, charming, crisp, fresh, lovely.*
☆☆ 1984 WHITE ZINFANDEL ($5.50) Estate, Napa Valley. *Crisp, clean and fruity. Delicious.*

RED

☆☆☆ 1978 CABERNET SAUVIGNON ($9.00) Estate, Napa Valley. *Soft and lush with some sugar and good varietal character.*
☆☆ 1980 CABERNET SAUVIGNON ($12.00) Estate, Napa Valley.
☆☆ 1981 CABERNET SAUVIGNON ($12.00) Estate, Napa Valley. *Intense, tight and tannic. Drink 1986.*
☆☆☆ 1982 CABERNET SAUVIGNON ($10.00) Estate, Napa Valley. *Lush, rich, dense, good structure (I'm prejudiced). Drink 1988.*
☆☆☆ 1979 ZINFANDEL ($7.00) Estate, Napa Valley.
☆☆☆ 1980 ZINFANDEL ($8.00) Estate, Napa Valley. *Lush, velvety and rich.*
☆☆ 1981 ZINFANDEL ($7.00) Napa Valley. *Soft, lush and big. Needs a year or two of age.*
☆☆ 1982 ZINFANDEL ($6.00) Estate, Napa Valley. *Crisp, clean, tart and attractive.*
☆☆☆ 1982 ZINFANDEL ($7.00) Napa Valley. *Lush, smooth, lovely fruit, rich, balanced.*

Buena Vista Winery
SONOMA COUNTY

27000 Ramal Road, P.O. Box 182, Sonoma, California 95476 (707-938-8504). FOUNDED: 1857. ACREAGE: 1,700 acres. PRODUCTION: 100,000 cases. DISTRIBUTION: Nationwide. OWNER: A. Racke of West Germany. Marcus Moller-Racke, president. WINEMAKER: Jill Davis. Self-guided tours and tasting daily 10 A.M.–5 P.M. at the Old Winery (Haraszthy Cellars) 1 mile east of Sonoma. Picnic area, gift shop, art gallery. Special events, theater and art exhibits held throughout the year. Mozart concerts in August.

Agoston Haraszthy built the original Buena Vista in 1857, making it California's oldest premium winery. The property was revived in the 1940s by newspaperman Frank Bartholomew who sold out to Southern California's Young's Markets in the early 1970s. The new owners planted a big new vineyard in the cool Carneros region and built a new, ultramodern winery. Another 1,000 acres in the Carneros region were purchased in 1984, making Buena Vista the largest vineyard estate in that region. In 1979 the West German wine and spirits firm A. Racke acquired Buena Vista. The new vineyards and new owners, whose style is definitely "hands on," have certainly made this winery one of the most important and most successful in Sonoma County.

WHITE

☆☆ 1981 CHABLIS ($4.00) North Coast. *Crisp, tart, some nice vinous character.*

☆☆ 1982 SPICELING ($5.50) Sonoma Valley. *1.25% residual sugar. 60% Gewürztraminer, 40% Johannisberg Riesling. Snappy.*

☆☆☆ 1983 SPICELING ($5.00) Estate, Sonoma Valley. *55% Gewürztraminer, 45% Riesling. 0.85% residual sugar. Fresh, crisp, fruity.*

☆☆ 1979 CHARDONNAY ($18.00) Heritage, Sonoma. *Intense, rich, unctuous, beginning to show its age.*

☆☆ 1980 CHARDONNAY ($9.00) Sonoma Valley. *At best floral and clean; can develop an oily heaviness.*

☆☆☆ 1980 CHARDONNAY ($15.00) Special Selection, Sonoma Valley. *Rich, buttery, lovely oak and varietal flavors.*

☆☆ 1981 CHARDONNAY ($9.00) Sonoma Valley.

☆☆ 1981 CHARDONNAY ($15.00) Special Selection, Estate, Sonoma Valley. *Earthy, fruity and varietal.*

☆☆ 1982 CHARDONNAY ($9.00) Sonoma Valley. *Crisp, clean, simple, attractive.*

☆☆ 1983 CHARDONNAY ($9.00) Sonoma Valley-Carneros. *Clean, crisp, dense, not much depth.*

☆☆ 1982 FUME BLANC ($7.50) Sonoma.

1980 GREEN HUNGARIAN ($5.50) Napa Valley. *0.93% residual sugar. Vinous, unattractive.*

1980 JOHANNISBERG RIESLING ($7.50) Sonoma. *Vinous, heavy.*

☆ 1981 JOHANNISBERG RIESLING ($6.50) Sonoma Valley, Carneros. *Crisp and fruity with some finesse.*

☆☆☆ 1981 JOHANNISBERG RIESLING ($8.90) Special Selection, Sonoma Valley, Carneros. *3.5% residual sugar. Dull nose but ripe apple fruit flavors.*

☆☆ 1981 JOHANNISBERG RIESLING ($18.00) Late Harvest, Carneros-Sonoma Valley. *10% residual sugar.*

1980 SAUVIGNON BLANC ($7.50) Vineyard Selection, Sonoma-Cutrer, Sonoma. *Overwhelmingly vegetal.*

BLANC DE NOIR

☆☆ 1983 BLANC DE PINOT NOIR ($4.65) Estate, Sonoma Valley-Carneros. *1.6% residual sugar.*

☆☆☆ 1984 BLANC DE PINOT NOIR ($5.50) Sonoma Valley-Carneros. *1.74% residual sugar. Crisp, fresh, varietal, tart, charming.*

ROSE

☆ 1983 PINOT NOIR ROSE ($5.00) Sonoma Valley-Carneros. *0.77% residual sugar.*

RED

☆☆ 1979 BURGUNDY ($4.00) Sonoma Valley. *Some stems, definite Pinot Noir character. Very nice.*

☆☆☆ 1983 PINOT JOLIE ($5.00) Sonoma Valley. *2% residual sugar. Pinot Noir. Snappy, fresh and delicious.*

☆☆☆ 1984 PINOT JOLIE ($5.50) Sonoma Valley. *1.9% residual sugar. Pinot Noir. Snappy, fresh, fruity, delicious.*

☆☆ 1968 CABERNET SAUVIGNON Cask 102, Sonoma. *Big, full, still attractive and with a number of years to go.*

☆☆ 1977 CABERNET SAUVIGNON Cask 34, Sonoma Valley. *Elegant, clean and nicely balanced.*

☆☆☆ 1978 CABERNET SAUVIGNON ($18.00) Special Selection, Estate, Sonoma Valley. *Rich and ripe, great depth and structure, herbal and deep.*

☆☆☆ 1979 CABERNET SAUVIGNON ($18.00) Special Selection, Estate, Sonoma Valley. *Rich, complex, supple, forward. Will improve for years.*

☆☆ 1980 CABERNET SAUVIGNON ($9.00) Sonoma. *Soft, well-structured, nice herbal notes. Drink now.*

☆☆☆ 1980 CABERNET SAUVIGNON ($18.00) Special Selection, Estate, Sonoma Valley. *Lush and berried, rich, complex. Needs time.*

☆☆☆ 1981 CABERNET SAUVIGNON ($9.00) Sonoma Valley-Carneros. *Grapey, rich, clean flavors. Drink now or hold two years.*

☆☆☆ 1981 CABERNET SAUVIGNON ($11.00) Sonoma-Carneros. *Silky, lush, concentrated, attractive. Drink 1986.*

☆☆☆☆ 1981 CABERNET SAUVIGNON ($18.00) Special Selection, Estate, Sonoma Valley-Carneros. *Crisp, fresh, clean, lovely, complex, balanced. Drink 1987.*

☆☆☆ 1982 CABERNET SAUVIGNON ($11.00) Napa Valley-Carneros. *Soft, bright, fruity, clean, lovely. Drink now.*

☆ 1980 GAMAY BEAUJOLAIS ($6.00) Late Harvest, Sonoma Valley, Carneros. *Interesting but not wholly successful.*

☆☆ 1983 GAMAY BEAUJOLAIS ($5.50) Sonoma Valley. *Snappy, fruity, clean with some nice depth.*

☆☆ 1976 PINOT NOIR ($8.25) Sonoma Valley. *Lush, soft and attractive. Relatively simple.*

☆ 1979 PINOT NOIR ($7.50) Sonoma Valley. *Raisiny, dull, lacking varietal character.*

☆ 1980 PINOT NOIR ($7.00) Sonoma Valley. *Fruity with some green flavors. Vinous, lacking depth.*

☆☆☆ 1981 PINOT NOIR ($12.00) Special Selection, Sonoma Valley. *Rich, clean, soft yet beautifully structured.*

☆☆ 1982 PINOT NOIR ($12.00) Estate, Carneros, Sonoma.

☆☆ 1981 ZINFANDEL ($6.00) Sonoma. *Crisp, fresh, spicy, charming.*

☆☆☆ 1981 ZINFANDEL ($12.00) Special Selection, Sonoma Valley. *Spicy, crisp, clean and very elegant.*

☆ 1982 ZINFANDEL ($6.00) Sonoma County-Carneros. *Varietal, a bit heavy on the sulfur.*

☆ 1982 ZINFANDEL ($6.00) Sonoma. *Vegetal, smokey, decent.*

☆☆☆ 1982 ZINFANDEL ($10.00) Vineyard Selection, Barricia, Sonoma Valley. *Crisp, fruity, clean, delightful. The way Zinfandel should be made.*

Buffalo Valley Winery
PENNSYLVANIA

Buffalo Road, R.D. 2, Lewisburg, Pennsylvania 17837 (717-524-4850). FOUNDED: 1979. ACREAGE: None. PRODUCTION: 3,000 cases. DISTRIBUTION: Local. OWNERS: Charles Pursel and Thomas Amabile; Jerry Evitts, general manager. WINEMAKER: Thomas Amabile. Tours and tasting Wednesday–Thursday 1 P.M.–5 P.M., Friday 1 P.M.–6 P.M., Saturday 10 A.M.–6 P.M., Sunday 12–5 P.M

Charles Pursel had acquired several different land parcels as a result of his construction business. One of these lots contained a building that had once been a teen center, and before that, a chicken coop. He and his winemaking friend Tom Amabile decided that—utilizing Charles's construction skills and connections—the now-vacant building could be transformed into a winery. Limited to approximately two acres of plantable land, the partners buy grapes and juice from Pennsylvania producers. Tom works as the winemaker while holding down a full-time job in New Jersey.

Bully Hill Vineyards
NEW YORK

Greyton Taylor Memorial Drive, Hammondsport, New York 14840 (607-868-3610). FOUNDED: 1960. ACREAGE: 125 acres. PRODUCTION: 50,000 cases. DISTRIBUTION: 21 states. OWNER:

Walter S. Taylor. WINEMAKER: Greg Learned. Tours and tasting. Retail sales. Call for information. Wine Museum of Greyton H. Taylor.

The man without a name, Walter S. Taylor has stretched his misfortune to its promotional limits. He did overreact just a bit when the Taylor Wine Company, founded by Walter's grandfather, fired him in 1970 from the board of directors and then took him to court in 1977 to prevent him from using his own name—"Taylor"—on the wines he was making at Bully Hill vineyards. Walter sees himself as a noble knight on a crusade against the evil power of the New York State wine industry and the U.S. Federal Court System. An artist, author and poet, Walter has created brochures, labels, and drawings to tell his "nameless man" story. Bully Hill produces wines made from French-American hybrid grapes.

Burgess Cellars
NAPA COUNTY

1108 Deer Park Road, P.O. Box 282, St. Helena, California 94574 (707-963-4766). FOUNDED: 1972. ACREAGE: 72 acres. PRODUCTION: 30,000 cases. DISTRIBUTION: Nationwide. OWNERS: Tom and Linda Burgess. WINEMAKER: Bill Sorenson. OTHER LABEL: Bell Canyon Cellars. Tours by appointment only. Retail sales daily 10 A.M.–4 P.M.

In the early 1970s, Tom Burgess, a burly former corporate pilot, bought this old vineyard site in the hills east of Napa. The winery, since modernized, was the original location for the now-defunct Souverain Cellars of Rutherford. In addition to vineyards located at the winery, a relatively new vineyard in Yountville is now producing estate-grown fruit. Burgess is one of the Napa Valley's older boutique wineries.

WHITE

☆☆ 1979 CHARDONNAY ($12.00) Napa Valley. *Lush, deep, still attractive.*

☆ 1980 CHARDONNAY ($12.75) Napa Valley. *Varietal, clean but coarse, lacking finesse.*

☆☆☆ 1981 CHARDONNAY ($12.75) Napa Valley. *Fresh, elegant, complex and beautifully balanced.*

☆☆ 1982 BELL CANYON CELLARS CHARDONNAY ($6.75) Sonoma. *Crisp, fruity, grassy, Sauvignon Blanc style.*

☆☆☆ 1982 CHARDONNAY ($11.75) Vintage Reserve, Napa Valley. *Crisp, lean, balanced, nicely structured. Very good.*

☆☆☆ 1983 CHARDONNAY ($12.00) Vintage Reserve, Napa Valley. *Fresh, fruity, clean, balanced, showing lovely finesse.*

☆ 1981 CHENIN BLANC ($7.50) Dry, Napa Valley. *Some fruit, some wood but essentially dull.*

BLANC DE NOIR

☆ 1984 BELL CANYON CELLARS WHITE ZINFANDEL ($4.95) Napa Valley. *Dull, soft, lacking fruit.*

RED

☆☆☆☆ 1978 CABERNET SAUVIGNON ($16.00) Vintage Selection, Napa Valley. *Classy, deep, lovely oak and fruit. Drink 1987.*

☆☆ 1979 CABERNET SAUVIGNON ($9.50) Napa Valley.

☆☆☆ 1979 CABERNET SAUVIGNON ($16.95) Vintage Selection, Napa Valley. *Superb, rich, deep, tremendous aging potential. Drink 1986.*

☆☆ 1980 CABERNET SAUVIGNON ($10.50) Napa Valley.

☆☆☆ 1980 CABERNET SAUVIGNON ($15.95) Vintage Selection, Napa Valley. *Lean, super crisp, complex and elegant. Drink 1986 and later.*

☆☆ 1981 CABERNET SAUVIGNON ($15.95) Selection, Napa Valley. *Intense, concentrated, rich but austere and hard-edged. Drink 1989.*

☆☆ 1976 PINOT NOIR ($8.00) Winery Lake, Napa Valley. *Classy and well made but not Burgundian.*

☆☆ 1979 PINOT NOIR ($9.00) Napa Valley. *Simple, clean and attractive.*

☆☆ 1980 PINOT NOIR ($6.00) Napa Valley. *Crisp, toasty, clean.*

☆☆☆ 1977 ZINFANDEL ($6.75) Napa Valley. *Rich and berried, balanced and clean. Ready to drink.*

☆☆ 1978 ZINFANDEL ($7.00) Napa Valley. *Clean, lush, lovely fruit. Drink now.*

☆☆ 1980 ZINFANDEL ($7.00) Napa Valley. *Spicy, brambly, intense.*

☆☆ 1981 ZINFANDEL ($5.95) Napa Valley. *Varietal, clean, intense but nicely balanced.*

☆☆☆ 1982 ZINFANDEL ($6.50) Napa Valley. *Rich, dark, concentrated with lovely berry fruit. Drink 1986.*

BUZZARD LAGOON *see* Cook-Ellis Winery

Davis Bynum Winery
SONOMA COUNTY

8075 Westside Road, Healdsburg, California 95448 (707-433-5852). FOUNDED: 1965. ACREAGE: None. PRODUCTION: 25,000 cases. DISTRIBUTION: Nationwide. OWNER: Corporation. Dave Bynum, general manager. WINEMAKER: Gary Farrell. OTHER LABELS: River Bend, Barefoot Bynum. Tours by appointment. Tasting and sales daily 10 A.M.–5 P.M.

A quiet, grandfatherly fellow, Davis Bynum started his winery in Albany (next to Berkeley and across the bay from San Francisco) in 1965. Encouraged by a grape grower friend, Davis moved his winery in 1973 to its present location in Sonoma County. The dimly lit, cramped building holds several small, dark rooms separated by thick concrete walls. Inside, the rebuilt equipment and older barrels and puncheons provide a pre-Prohibition winery atmosphere. The winery gets most of its grapes from vineyards owned by Bynum shareholders in Sonoma County.

WHITE

☆☆☆ 1982 BELLEFLEUR ($4.00) Sonoma. *Made from French Colombard. Crisp and fruity, clean and dry.*

☆☆ 1981 CHARDONNAY ($10.00) Sonoma.

☆☆☆ 1981 CHARDONNAY ($10.00) Allen-Hafner Reserve, Allen, Alexander Valley. *Beautifully balanced, clean and fresh.*

1981 CHARDONNAY ($10.00) Reserve, 17% Alexander Valley, 83% Russian River. *Short on varietal character and charm.*

☆☆ 1982 CHARDONNAY ($10.00) Reserve, Sonoma. *Crisp, clean, fresh, attractive.*

☆☆☆ 1983 CHARDONNAY ($12.50) Allen-Hafner Reserve, Sonoma. *Clean, rich yet delicate, great balance.*

☆ 1981 FUME BLANC ($9.00) Rochioli-Harrison, Sonoma.

☆☆☆ 1982 FUME BLANC ($8.00) Rochioli-Harrison Reserve, Sonoma. *Rich, round and fully fruited.*

☆ 1983 FUME BLANC ($7.50) Westside Road, Sonoma.

☆☆   1983 FUME BLANC ($8.00) Rochioli-Harrison, Reserve, Sonoma. *Grassy, rich, deep.*
☆☆   1982 GEWURZTRAMINER ($5.00) Sonoma. *Rich, clean, varietal.*
☆   1983 GEWURZTRAMINER ($5.50) Westside Road, Sonoma. *1% residual sugar. Lush, overripe, full, lacking acidity.*

BLANC DE NOIR

☆☆☆ 1983 WHITE ZINFANDEL ($4.50) Sonoma. *Crisp, fruity, clean and delicious.*

ROSE

1983 ZINFANDEL ROSE ($3.50) Sonoma. *Dull, skunky.*

RED

☆☆   1979 CABERNET SAUVIGNON ($8.00) Sonoma.
☆☆   1980 CABERNET SAUVIGNON ($8.00) Sonoma. *Intense and overripe, but clean and balanced. Drink now.*
☆☆   1981 CABERNET SAUVIGNON ($9.00) Sonoma. *15% Merlot. Crisp, clean, quite nice. Drink 1986.*
☆   1980 MERLOT ($10.00) Jack Long, Dry Creek Valley, Sonoma. *Marred by dirty flavors and aromas.*
     1980 MERLOT ($12.00) Reserve Bottling, 93% Jasper Long, Sonoma. *Earthy, weedy, not pleasant.*
☆   1975 PINOT NOIR Unfiltered, Rochioli, Sonoma. *Fragrant but lacking depth.*
     1976 PINOT NOIR Rochioli-Allen, Sonoma.
☆   1978 PINOT NOIR Late Bottling, Rochioli-Allen, Sonoma. *Earthy, tart, fruity; O.K.*
☆☆   1980 PINOT NOIR ($8.00) Russian River Valley, Sonoma. *Earthy and intense.*
☆☆   1980 PINOT NOIR ($10.50) Reserve, Sonoma. *Big, lush, a bit stemmy, aging potential.*
☆☆☆ 1982 PINOT NOIR ($10.00) Westside Road, Russian River Valley. *Fresh, clean, rich flavors, lovely textures. Stunning.*
☆☆☆ 1982 PINOT NOIR ($10.00) Westside Road, Sonoma. *Rich, deep, varietal, well made.*

Byrd Vineyards
MARYLAND

Church Hill Road, Myersville, Maryland 21773 (301-293-1110). FOUNDED: 1976. ACREAGE: 30 acres. PRODUCTION: 5,000 cases. DISTRIBUTION: Maryland and Washington D.C. OWNERS: Brett and Sharon Byrd. WINEMAKER: Curt Sherrer. Tours and tasting weekends. Call for information. Closed January. Annual Wine Harvest festival first weekend in October.

Brett Byrd's property was destined for a housing development, a patchwork of split lots and jigsaw homes. But after the Byrds finished their own house, they looked out the front door, across 40 acres of lush landscape, and knew they just couldn't bring themselves to cover that land with buildings. "The property was too small for cows or corn so we decided to plant grapes," says Brett. Then, after an inspirational visit to California's Stony Hill Vineyard, the Byrds became determined to make world-class wines in Maryland. They feel they are well on the way.

WHITE

☆☆   1983 CHARDONNAY ($7.50) Estate, Catoctin, Maryland. *Toasty, rich, balanced.*
☆☆☆ 1983 SAUVIGNON BLANC ($8.00) Maryland. *Fresh, varietal, charming.*

RED

☆   1982 CATOCTIN ($10.00) Estate, Maryland. *Thin, snappy, decent, clean.*
☆☆☆ 1980 CABERNET SAUVIGNON ($12.00) Maryland. *Violets, fruit, oak—all nicely balanced. Superb.*

Cache Cellars
SOLANO COUNTY

Route 2, Box 2780, Davis, California 95616 (916-756-6068). FOUNDED: 1978. ACREAGE: None. PRODUCTION: 4,500 cases. DISTRIBUTION: California, Hawaii, Nevada, and Texas. OWNERS: Charles and Elizabeth Lowe. WINEMAKER: Charles Lowe. Tours by appointment.

After attending U.C. Davis, Charles Lowe bought an old dairy building right in Davis. An Air Force pilot from Alabama, Lowe still flies as a part-time profession, but his wine business is becoming more and more involving. Grapes are purchased from some of the best vineyards in the state, and the winemaking style—while using very modern equipment—is quite traditional.

WHITE

☆☆☆ 1981 CHARDONNAY ($11.00) Ventana, Monterey. *Soft, mellow; good, controlled oakiness. Elegant.*

☆☆ 1982 CHARDONNAY ($11.00) La Reina, Monterey. *Crisp, complex, fruity; not as rounded as the '81.*

☆☆☆ 1983 CHARDONNAY ($11.00) La Reina, Monterey. *Great fruit and nice oak plus good finesse.*

☆☆ 1981 SAUVIGNON BLANC ($7.50) Rancho Tierra Rejada, San Luis Obispo. *Grassy, floral, angular with a touch of bitterness.*

☆☆ 1982 SAUVIGNON BLANC ($7.50) Rancho Tierra Rejada, San Luis Obispo. *Unusual but attractive. Toasty, intense, not varietal.*

RED

☆☆☆ 1983 CABERNET SAUVIGNON Napa Valley. *Supple, complex, herbs and cherries.*

☆☆ 1979 PINOT NOIR ($7.50) Sonoma. *Pleasant, clean, fruity, nice oak, some tannic hardness.*

☆☆ 1982 PINOT NOIR ($7.50) Vinco, Monterey. *Clean, earthy, light, pleasant.*

☆ 1980 ZINFANDEL ($6.00) Baldinelli, Amador. *Spicy, good balance, lacking charm.*

☆☆☆ 1981 ZINFANDEL ($6.50) Baldinelli, Amador. *Intense but beautifully balanced. Good acid and fresh fruit.*

Cadenasso Winery
SOLANO COUNTY

1955 West Texas Street, P.O. Box 22, Fairfield, California 94553 (707-425-5845). FOUNDED: 1906. ACREAGE: 200 acres. PRODUCTION: 42,000 cases. DISTRIBUTION: Northern California. OWNERS: Frank and Joan Cadenasso. WINEMAKER: Frank Cadenasso. Tasting daily 8 A.M.–5:30 P.M.

Giovanni Cadenasso arrived from Italy with eight dollars in his pocket and not a word of English in his vocabulary. Within a week he was in business. His son Frank, who now runs the business, is cutting down on the varieties produced: "A winemaker with too many wines is like a doctor with too many patients—he can't take good enough care of all of them." Most of the wines are sold to other wineries.

Cagnasso Winery
NEW YORK

Route 9 W, Marlboro, New York 12542 (914-236-4630). FOUNDED: 1977. ACREAGE: 10 acres. PRODUCTION: 2,500 cases. DISTRIBUTION: At winery. OWNERS: Joseph Cagnasso and June

Ramey. WINEMAKER: Joseph Cagnasso. Tours by appointment only. Tasting weekdays April–December: 12–4:30 P.M.; weekends 10 A.M.–4:30 P.M.

A graduate of the Alba School in Italy, Joseph Cagnasso has made wine professionally both in Europe and in the United States. After making champagne for E. & J. Gallo in California, he and his wife, June, moved to New York in 1972, where he worked for Brotherhood Winery. When the Farm Winery Act was passed, Joseph immediately quit his job and began planting vines on his own property. His barn became the tasting room and a metal winery building was constructed nearby. Dissatisfied with the way vinifera vines adapt to New York's climate, Joseph has since pulled them out and substituted French-American hybrid varieties.

Cain Cellars
NAPA COUNTY

3800 Langtry Road, St. Helena, California 94574 (707-963-1616). FOUNDED: 1981. ACREAGE: 70 acres. PRODUCTION: 10,000 cases. DISTRIBUTION: Nationwide. OWNERS: Jerry and Joyce Cain. WINEMAKER: Lester Hardy. Tours by appointment. No sales or tasting.

When he saw the McCormick Ranch in Napa, Jerry Cain began thinking. After living in affluent Palm Springs for a while, Jerry and his wife were eager for an alternative lifestyle. The McCormick Ranch presented the perfect opportunity to break away. A careful planner, Jerry researched the economics of becoming a Napa Valley vintner. "My wife is always accusing me of 'long-range-itis'," says Jerry. Although they started small, the winery and vineyards are gradually expanding toward a 30,000 case production.

WHITE

☆☆☆   1981 CHARDONNAY ($9.00) Napa Valley.

       1983 CHARDONNAY ($10.00) Napa Valley. *Toasty and rich, but marred by spoilage.*

☆☆   1981 SAUVIGNON BLANC ($10.00) Napa Valley.

☆☆☆   1982 SAUVIGNON BLANC ($7.50) Napa Valley. *Angular, fruity and clean.*

       1983 SAUVIGNON BLANC ($7.50) Napa Valley. *Odd nose, weedy, strange.*

RED

☆☆☆   1982 MERLOT ($11.00) Napa Valley. *Fruity, crisp, lovely structure. Drink 1988.*

Cakebread Cellars
NAPA COUNTY

8300 St. Helena Highway, Rutherford, California 94573 (707-963-5221). FOUNDED: 1973. ACREAGE: 35 acres. PRODUCTION: 34,000 cases. DISTRIBUTION: Major market states and some foreign countries. OWNERS: Jack and Dolores Cakebread. WINEMAKER: Bruce Cakebread. Tours by appointment.

Jack Cakebread is a commercial photographer and had a successful auto repair business in Oakland when he and his wife, Dolores, bought their property in the Napa Valley in 1973. They built a handsome, modern winery and sent their son Bruce to U.C. Davis to learn about winemaking. He seems to have learned his lessons well; Cakebread has become a respected Napa boutique winery. Some grapes are purchased and others are home grown.

WHITE

☆   1980 CHARDONNAY ($12.50) Napa Valley. *Very vinous and coarse.*

☆☆   1981 CHARDONNAY ($13.75) Napa Valley. *Crisp, steely, but lacking great depth; clean.*

☆☆☆ 1982 CHARDONNAY ($13.75) Napa Valley. *Fresh, clean, some oak complexity. Best Cakebread Chardonnay yet.*

☆☆ 1983 CHARDONNAY ($13.50) Napa Valley. *Clean, pleasant but not as good as the '82.*

☆☆ 1981 SAUVIGNON BLANC ($9.50) Napa Valley.

1982 SAUVIGNON BLANC ($9.50) Special Decade Bottling, Napa Valley. *Earthy, weedy, not well balanced.*

☆☆☆ 1983 SAUVIGNON BLANC ($9.50) Napa Valley. *Varietal, clean, balanced, fruity and lovely.*

RED

☆☆ 1978 CABERNET SAUVIGNON ($12.00) Jt-L1, Napa Valley. *Minty, woody, fat, chewy. Drink now.*

☆☆☆ 1979 CABERNET SAUVIGNON ($14.00) Napa Valley. *Herbal, ripe, forward, oaky, should age well.*

☆☆☆ 1980 CABERNET SAUVIGNON ($14.00) Rutherford Reserve, Napa Valley. *Big but nicely balanced. Lovely oak. Drink 1987 and beyond.*

☆ 1980 CABERNET SAUVIGNON ($16.00) Napa Valley. *Herbal, tight, not much.*

☆☆ 1981 CABERNET SAUVIGNON ($10.50) Napa Valley. *Smokey, deep fruit. Drink 1986.*

☆☆ 1979 ZINFANDEL ($10.00) Beatty Ranch, Howell Mountain, Napa Valley.

☆☆ 1980 ZINFANDEL ($10.75) Beatty Ranch, Howell Mountain, Napa Valley. *Brambly, big and fruity.*

☆☆☆ 1981 ZINFANDEL ($10.75) Napa Valley. *Clean, fresh, balanced, crisp. Cakebread's best and last Zinfandel.*

Calafia Cellars
NAPA COUNTY

629 Fulton Lane, St. Helena, California 94574 (707-963-0114). FOUNDED: 1979. ACREAGE: 2 acres. PRODUCTION: 2,500 cases. DISTRIBUTION: Major market states. OWNER: E. M. Johnson family. Randle Johnson, general manager. WINEMAKER: Randle Johnson. Tours by appointment.

Randle Johnson is the winemaker for Vintage Vineyards in Napa, and Calafia Cellars is his own label. Calafia was a legendary Amazon queen who—as the tale goes—lived on the West Indian island Matinino, where her great wealth was guarded by griffins. The legend was popularized in a sixteenth-century Spanish novel which was familiar to Spanish explorers, including Cortez. When Cortez first saw Baja he thought it was an island and named it "Calafia's Land" or *California*. Calafia Cellars' grapes are purchased mostly from Napa's Mount Veeder district.

WHITE

1982 SAUVIGNON BLANC ($8.00) Napa Valley. *Weedy, sulfurous and unattractive.*

☆☆☆ 1983 SAUVIGNON BLANC ($7.50) Honig, Napa Valley. *Oaky, rich, clean, charming.*

RED

☆ 1979 CABERNET SAUVIGNON ($11.50) Sonoma Valley. *Some off odors, but good firm fruit.*

1980 CABERNET SAUVIGNON ($12.00) Glen Ellen, Sonoma Valley. *Tanky.*

☆☆☆ 1981 CABERNET SAUVIGNON ($11.00) Kitty Hawk, Napa Valley. *Fruity, crisp, lean and attractive. Drink now.*

☆☆ 1979 MERLOT ($10.00) Napa Valley. *Fruity, rich with good, long finish.*

☆☆ 1981 MERLOT ($13.50) Pickle Canyon, Napa Valley. *Rich, velvety, lush and lovely.*

☆☆☆ 1982 MERLOT ($12.00) Pickle Canyon, Napa Valley. *Lovely fruit, rich, clean, nicely structured. Drink 1986.*

☆☆☆ 1980 ZINFANDEL ($7.50) Pickle Canyon, Napa Valley. *Lush fruit and rich flavors.*

Calera Wine Company
SAN BENITO COUNTY

11300 Cienega Road, Hollister, California 95023 (408-637-9170). FOUNDED: 1975. ACREAGE: 24 acres. PRODUCTION: 10,000 cases. DISTRIBUTION: Major market states. OWNER: Josh Jensen, president; Jeanne Jensen. WINEMAKER: Steve Doerner. Tours by appointment Saturdays at 11 A.M. No tasting.

   Josh Jensen, who looks more like a professional athlete than a vintner, spent two years in Burgundy trying to discover the secret of the great Pinot Noirs of that region. He decided that limestone in the soil was crucial and returned to his native California to find an ideal location for a vineyard. Finally, in the mountains of San Benito County, he found his limestone and built Calera (Spanish for "lime kiln") there. Jensen makes small quantities of Pinot Noir from his three tiny vineyards, and Zinfandel, Pinot Noir, and Chardonnay from purchased grapes.

WHITE

☆☆   1982 CHARDONNAY ($9.75) Santa Barbara. *Toasty, rich, eclectic.*
☆☆   1983 CHARDONNAY ($10.75) Santa Barbara. *Fat, heavy, decent, but with some off flavors.*

RED

O   NV   ROUGE DE ROUGES ($4.00) California. *Weird.*
☆☆☆   1978 PINOT NOIR ($9.00) Jensen, California. *Only 744 375ml bottles made. Fragrant, berried, silky, mellow.*
☆☆   1978 PINOT NOIR ($9.00) Reed, California. *Only 600 375ml bottles made. Silky, smooth, deep.*
☆☆☆   1978 PINOT NOIR ($9.00) Selleck, California. *Only 432 375ml bottles made. Violet, earthy, silky, supple.*
☆☆   1979 PINOT NOIR ($18.00) Jensen, California. *Somewhat thin and stemmy, but complex and interesting.*
☆☆☆   1979 PINOT NOIR ($18.00) Reed, California. *Earthy, rich, fruity, very complex and balanced. Will age.*
☆☆☆   1979 PINOT NOIR ($18.00) Selleck, California. *Firm, rich, varietal, some stems, very complex. Will age.*
     1980 PINOT NOIR ($10.00) Santa Barbara. *Stemmy, weedy, crude.*
☆   1980 PINOT NOIR ($18.00) Jensen, California. *Stemmy, green, clean but harsh.*
☆   1981 PINOT NOIR ($9.00) Santa Barbara.
☆☆☆   1981 PINOT NOIR ($18.00) Jensen, California. *Deep, tannic, leathery, chalky. Should age well for twenty years.*
☆☆   1981 PINOT NOIR ($18.00) Selleck, California. *Green and hard, clean, fresh and spicy. Drink 1988.*
☆☆☆   1982 PINOT NOIR ($23.00) Jensen, California. *Rich, stemmy, angular, intense. Drink 1987.*
☆☆☆   1982 PINOT NOIR ($23.00) Reed, California. *Herbal, rich, with deep lovely varietal flavors. Drink 1987.*
☆☆☆   1983 PINOT NOIR ($23.00) Jensen, California. *Edgy, crisp, beautifully structured, varietal. Drink 1988.*
☆☆☆   1983 PINOT NOIR ($23.00) Selleck, California. *Fresh, lush, beautifully structured. Drink 1988.*
☆☆   1979 ZINFANDEL ($7.50) Cienega District. *Big, dark, berried.*
☆☆   1979 ZINFANDEL ($8.50) Reserve, Cienega District. *Big, overdone, ripe and intense.*
☆   1980 ZINFANDEL ($6.00) Doe Mill.
☆☆   1980 ZINFANDEL ($7.00) Reserve, Doe Mill. *Big, dark and rich. Lacking finesse.*
☆☆   1981 ZINFANDEL ($7.00) Templeton. *Jammy and clean.*
☆☆   1981 ZINFANDEL ($8.50) Reserve, Cienega Valley. *Round, crisp, full and fresh.*

California Cellar Masters
SAN JOAQUIN COUNTY

212 West Pine Street, P.O. Box 1300, Lodi, California 95240 (209-368-6681). FOUNDED: 1860. ACREAGE: None. PRODUCTION: 10,000 cases. DISTRIBUTION: At tasting rooms. OWNER: Corporation. Marlow E. Start, president. WINEMAKER: Wine is made elsewhere, blended at the winery. OTHER LABELS: Coloma Cellars, Gold Mine Winery, Mother Lode. Tasting daily 10 A.M.–5 P.M. at several locations. Call for information.

While this operation is essentially a blending and bottling plant for bulk wines purchased in almost every California county, the Coloma Cellars label has a fascinating history. Established in 1860 during the Gold Rush days by Martin Allhoff, an unsuccessful gold miner, the winery was quite successful. Allhoff ran afoul of the law and, rather than go to prison, committed suicide. The winery operates a number of sales and tasting rooms.

California Cooler
SAN JOAQUIN COUNTY

2601 Teepee Drive, Stockton, California 95205 (209-466-7000). FOUNDED: 1981. ACREAGE: None. PRODUCTION: 7 million cases. DISTRIBUTION: Nationwide. OWNER: Brown-Forman Corporation. WINEMAKERS: Stuart Bewley and Michael Crete. No tours or tasting.

Stuart Bewley and Michael Crete had been making their special concoction of white wine and slightly carbonated fruit juice (with fruit particles) at home for years before they decided to see if it might be marketable. They put their original version—a citrus blend—in beer bottles, marketed it through a beer distributor, and sat back to watch the sales soar. Their success prompted them to introduce an orange version of the beverage in 1984, which also became very popular. The coolers have been so popular, in fact, that last year Stuart and Michael sold their business to the Brown-Forman Corporation for over $100 million.

FLAVORED

☆☆ CALIFORNIA COOLER–CITRUS ($.75) California. *12 oz. 6% alcohol. Fresh fruity flavors, with some interesting almond/spice nuances. Tangy and well balanced.*

☆☆ CALIFORNIA COOLER–ORANGE ($.75) California. *12 oz. 6% alcohol. Fresh orange flavors; crisp, clean and attractive.*

California Growers Winery
TULARE COUNTY

38558 Road 128, Cutler, California 93615 (209-528-3033). FOUNDED: 1936. ACREAGE: None. PRODUCTION: 300,000 cases. DISTRIBUTION: Selected U.S. markets. OWNER: Corporation. Bruno Bisceglia, president. WINEMAKER: Charles Asher. OTHER LABELS: Growers, Le Blanc, Bounty, Jean Escalle. No tours or tasting.

The winery began as a cooperative, owned by local growers. At first, most of the production was sweet dessert wines. In 1970 a large corporation bought the winery from the growers. While still producing wine in bulk, the transition has slowly been made from dessert wines to table wines. Volume has tripled, and equipment and cooperage have been modernized.

California Wine Company
SONOMA COUNTY

155 Cherry Creek Road, Cloverdale, California 95425 (707-894-4295). FOUNDED: 1937. ACREAGE: 375 acres. PRODUCTION: 65,000 cases. DISTRIBUTION: Major market states. OWNER: Corporation. John B. Merritt, general manager. WINEMAKER: John B. Merritt. OTHER LABELS: Arroyo Sonoma, Potter Valley, Bandiera, Sage Creek, John B. Merritt. Tours by appointment. Tasting daily 10 A.M.–5 P.M.

California Wine Company operates out of what was the Bandiera family winery in Sonoma and produces lower priced, Fetzer-style wines under the Bandiera name. John B. Merritt, formerly of Gundlach-Bundschu, is the winemaker, and the line bearing his name is a bit more expensive and receives more care and aging. Sage Creek wines are made only from the company's Napa Valley vineyards. Two other labels, Arroyo Sonoma and Potter Valley, were made for Schenley Distilleries and have been dropped.

WHITE

☆ 1983 BANDIERA WILDFLOWER ($4.00) California. *Mostly Chenin Blanc. Grassy, intense, O.K. fruit, a bit heavy.*

☆ 1981 JOHN B. MERRITT CHARDONNAY ($7.25) Sonoma.

☆ 1981 SAGE CREEK CHARDONNAY ($8.75) Napa Valley.

1982 BANDIERA CHARDONNAY ($4.00) Mendocino. *Clean but not at all varietal; strange.*

☆ 1982 SAGE CREEK CHARDONNAY ($10.75) Napa Valley. *Crisp but somewhat atypical; strange.*

1983 ARROYO SONOMA WINERY CHARDONNAY ($6.00) California. *Thin, unpleasant.*

1983 BANDIERA CHENIN BLANC ($4.50) Napa Valley. *Heavy, bitter.*

☆ 1982 BANDIERA JOHANNISBERG RIESLING ($4.95) Mendocino. *1.1% residual sugar.*

1982 JOHN B. MERRITT JOHANNISBERG RIESLING ($6.00) Mendocino. *1.1% residual sugar.*

☆☆☆ 1982 JOHN B. MERRITT JOHANNISBERG RIESLING ($15.00) Potter Valley, Mendocino. *12.58% residual sugar. Fresh, balanced, botrytized, lovely.*

☆ 1981 SAGE CREEK SAUVIGNON BLANC ($5.25) Napa Valley.

☆☆ 1982 BANDIERA SAUVIGNON BLANC ($4.50) Mendocino. *Great varietal grassiness, rich, delightful.*

☆ 1982 BANDIERA SAUVIGNON BLANC ($5.00) Mendocino.

BLANC DE NOIR

☆☆ 1983 BANDIERA WHITE ZINFANDEL ($4.50) North Coast. *2.45% residual sugar. Fruity, clean, pleasant.*

☆☆☆ 1984 BANDIERA WHITE ZINFANDEL ($4.25) Sonoma. *2.85% residual sugar. Snappy, fruity, delicious, great color.*

ROSE

☆ 1983 BANDIERA ROSE OF ZINFANDEL ($3.75) Napa Valley. *2.4% residual sugar. Fresh, clean, decent.*

RED

☆☆ NV BANDIERA DRY RED ($3.73) North Coast. *Soft, clean and decent.*

☆☆☆ 1978 ARROYO SONOMA SPECIAL RESERVE CABERNET SAUVIGNON ($12.00) Sonoma. *Lush, sweet oak, balanced with firm fruit. Drink now.*

☆ 1980 BANDIERA CABERNET SAUVIGNON ($4.50) Sonoma. *Decent, simple, clean, a bit low in fruit.*

☆ 1981 BANDIERA CABERNET SAUVIGNON ($7.25) North Coast. *Simple, dull, vegetal.*
☆☆☆ 1981 JOHN B. MERRITT CABERNET SAUVIGNON ($8.00) Sonoma. *A lovely wine—crisp, varietal, delightful. Drink now.*
☆ 1981 SAGE CREEK CABERNET SAUVIGNON ($10.00) Napa Valley. *Muddy, earthy, dull.*
☆ 1981 SAGE CREEK CABERNET SAUVIGNON ($10.75) Napa Valley. *Intense, overripe, chocolatey.*
☆☆ 1980 JOHN B. MERRITT PINOT NOIR ($6.50) Carneros, Sonoma. *Soft, good varietal character.*
☆☆☆ 1980 BANDIERA ZINFANDEL ($4.25) North Coast. *Varietal, clean and crisp.*
1981 BANDIERA ZINFANDEL ($4.00) Napa County. *Thin, lacking fruit.*

CALISTOGA VINEYARDS *see* Cuvaison Vineyard

Callaway Vineyards and Winery
RIVERSIDE COUNTY

32720 Rancho California Road, Temecula, California 92390 (714-676-4001). FOUNDED: 1974. ACREAGE: 340 acres. PRODUCTION: 144,000 cases. DISTRIBUTION: Major market states. OWNER: Hiram Walker and Sons, Inc. Ely R. Callaway, chairman; Terrance Clancy, president. WINEMAKER: Dwayne Helmuth. Tours and tasting daily 10 A.M.–4 P.M.

Ely Callaway, former president of Burlington Industries and a non-winedrinker, decided to prove that premium varietal wines could be made from grapes grown in Temecula, north of San Diego. Callaway's marketing wizardry has not only kept his winery afloat but it made the place a big enough success to attract the attention of the Hiram Walker company, which came in and bought the whole thing in 1982. Callaway stayed on, weaving his own special brand of hype, as did winemaker Steve O'Donnell who, until his death in 1983, made the best of a difficult climatological situation. Since 1983 the winery has made only white wines.

WHITE

☆☆ 1984 VIN BLANC ($4.75) California. *Clean, fresh, with some Riesling qualities; attractive.*
☆☆ 1981 CHARDONNAY ($8.50) Estate, Temecula. *Heavy and vinous, but quite clean and well made.*
☆☆☆ 1982 CHARDONNAY ($8.50) Temecula. *No oak used. Clean, lemony and uncomplicated; delightful.*
☆☆ 1983 CHARDONNAY ($8.75) Temecula. *Oaky, rich, balanced.*
O 1982 CHENIN BLANC ($6.45) Temecula.
☆ 1983 CHENIN BLANC ($6.00) Dry, Temecula. *Vinous, grapey, grassy. 0.85% residual sugar. Heavy.*
1984 CHENIN BLANC ($5.00) Temecula. *0.8% residual sugar. Vinous, unpleasant.*
1981 FUME BLANC ($7.25) Temecula. *Green, unattractive.*
☆☆ 1982 FUME BLANC, VERY DRY ($7.00) Temecula.
☆ 1983 FUME BLANC ($7.25) Temecula. *Clean, earthy, some sweetness, odd.*
☆ 1983 SAUVIGNON BLANC ($7.25) Temecula. *0.8% residual sugar. Sweet, fat, unusual.*
☆☆ 1981 WHITE RIESLING ($6.25) Temecula. *0.7% residual sugar.*
☆☆☆ 1983 WHITE RIESLING ($5.25) Temecula. *Fragrant, clean, fresh, snappy.*
☆☆☆ 1984 WHITE RIESLING ($5.50) Temecula. *1.4% residual sugar. Rich, varietal, fresh, appealing.*

RED

O NV RONDEUR ($6.00) Temecula. *Made from Zinfandel grapes.*
☆☆ 1979 CABERNET SAUVIGNON ($8.50) Estate, Temecula.

☆   1980 CABERNET SAUVIGNON ($7.00) Temecula. *Weedy and dense, lush and decent.*
    1980 PETITE SIRAH ($8.50) Estate, Temecula. *Muddy and dull.*

Calvaresi Winery
PENNSYLVANIA

832 Thorn Street, Reading, Pennsylvania 19601 (215-373-7821). FOUNDED: 1981. ACREAGE:
None. PRODUCTION: 1,500 cases. DISTRIBUTION: At winery. OWNER: Thomas Calvaresi.
WINEMAKER: Thomas Calvaresi. Tours and tasting evenings by appointment. Monday–Friday
7 P.M.–9 P.M., Saturday–Sunday 1 P.M.–5 P.M.

Every night Tom Calvaresi would come home from his job as an auto parts salesman and
disappear into the cellar, his winemaking workshop. Ever since learning the art from his grandfather,
Tom had been making wine at home. Eventually he decided to "go through all the rigamarole" to
get his winery bonded. Now producing about ten different varieties, the winery has expanded a
little each year, but it is still reached by walking down the Calvaresi cellar stairs.

Camas Winery
IDAHO

521 Moore, Moscow, Idaho 83843 (208-882-0214). FOUNDED: 1983. ACREAGE: None. PRO-
DUCTION: 1,000 cases. DISTRIBUTION: Idaho, Washington. OWNERS: Stewart and Susan Scott.
WINEMAKER: Stewart Scott. Tours by appointment. No tasting.

When the Scotts decided to move to Idaho, they had dreams of growing grapes and making
wine. After serving an apprenticeship with Thomas Kruse at his winery in Gilroy, California,
Stewart—a third generation San Franciscan—had considered starting a winery there. But with two
small children, he needed to live where he could support his growing family and start a winery as
well. Stewart works for the Federal government in the U.S. District Court in Idaho. Before starting
the winery, he tried planting a few grapes and quickly learned that it was winemaking, not grape
growing, that interested him. Cautiously—keeping his overhead down, purchasing very little new
equipment—Stewart started his winery in the basement, the garage, and the backyard of his house.
The plan is to keep things small until he gets a feel for the market. So far, the winery has been self-
supporting.

Cambiaso Vineyards
SONOMA COUNTY

1141 Grant Avenue, P.O. Box 548, Healdsburg, California 95448 (707-433-5508). FOUNDED:
1934. ACREAGE: 52 acres. PRODUCTION: 75,000 cases. DISTRIBUTION: 10 major market
states and England. OWNER: Four Seas Investment Corporation. Somchi Likitprakong, general
manager. WINEMAKER: Robert Fredson. Tours daily 10 A.M.–4 P.M. by appointment. No tasting.

This is one of Sonoma's Italian family wineries, founded right after the end of Prohibition. A
few years ago, the property was sold to Four Seas Investment Corporation. The president of Four
Seas is a wealthy wine buff from Thailand, Supasit Mahaguna, who has built a brand new winery,
keeping the old one as a tourist attraction. He hired General Manager Somchi Likitprakong, who
doesn't drink wine since he is allergic to alcohol. Wines are generally low-priced premium varietals.

WHITE

O   1981 CHARDONNAY ($6.50) Sonoma. *Horrible.*
☆☆   1982 CHARDONNAY ($6.50) Sonoma. *Simple, clean, fruity, fresh.*

☆☆☆ 1983 CHENIN BLANC ($4.00) Clarksburg. *Fresh, tangy, clean, delightful.*
1981 FUME BLANC ($6.55) Chalk Hill, Sonoma.

ROSE

○ NV VIN ROSE ($2.50) California. *1.2% residual sugar.*

RED

☆☆ 1981 CABERNET SAUVIGNON ($4.75) Dry Creek Valley. *Decent, clean, simple, lacking character.*
1979 PETITE SIRAH ($4.00) Clarksburg. *Vinous, vegetal, heavy.*
☆☆ 1981 ZINFANDEL ($5.00) Chalk Hill, Sonoma. *Fruity, clean, simple.*

Canandaigua Wine Company
NEW YORK

116 Buffalo Street, Canandaigua, New York 14424 (716-394-3630). FOUNDED: 1945. ACREAGE: None. PRODUCTION: 6 million cases. DISTRIBUTION: Nationwide. OWNER: Corporation. Marvin Sands, president; Bertram Silk, vice president winery operations. WINEMAKER: Greg Failing. OTHER LABELS: Many different labels. No Tours. Tasting in summer daily 12–6 P.M. Four additional premises: Bisceglia Brothers Wine, Richard's Wine Cellars, Tenner Brothers, and Batavia Wine Company.

Representing over six dozen different labels, with five different bonded premises, the Canandaigua Wine Company works like a huge winemaking machine, churning out all kinds, shapes, and sizes. One of their brands, Virginia Dare, is America's oldest wine brand, dating back to 1835. Their best-seller, Wild Irish Rose, a fortified, 20-percent alcohol dessert wine, has made this winery of humble beginnings into the fifth-largest producing winery in the United States. With money to spend, the winery began buying up struggling smaller wineries, acquiring new brands and new winery locations. Marvin Sands, founder and president, sees himself as a man who not only knows how to make wine but knows how to build an incredibly successful wine business.

SPARKLING

NV J. ROGET EXTRA DRY ($4.00) American Champagne. *Sweet and caramel flavored. Charmat bulk process.*
☆ NV J. ROGET SPUMANTE ($4.00) American. *Muscat-like and sweet. Bulk process.*

FORTIFIED

RICHARD'S WILD IRISH ROSE ($3.00) American. *18% Alcohol. Syrupy sweet like liquid grape jelly.*

FLAVORED

☆ SUN COUNTRY COOLER—CITRUS ($.75) American. *12 oz. 6% alcohol. Lemony, simple, dull.*
☆☆ SUN COUNTRY COOLER—ORANGE ($.75) American. *12 oz. 6% alcohol. Fresh orange flavors; lovely, with clean fruit and a crisp finish.*
☆☆ SUN COUNTRY COOLER—TROPICAL FRUIT ($.75) American. *12 oz. 6% alcohol. Crisp, clean, tangy, with interesting flavors.*

Caparone Winery
SAN LUIS OBISPO COUNTY

Route 1, Box 176 G, San Marcos Road, Paso Robles, California 93446 (805-467-3827). FOUNDED: 1980. ACREAGE: 8 acres. PRODUCTION: 3,000 cases. DISTRIBUTION: California and major market states. OWNERS: Dave and Mary Caparone. WINEMAKER: Dave Caparone. Tours daily 11 A.M.–5 P.M.

The proprietor of this small Central Coast winery, Dave Caparone, is fascinated by Italian red wine varieties. He is experimenting with Nebbiolo and Brunello (Sangiovese Grosso) and hopes to be America's first successful producer of wines made from these noble grapes. The one-man winery is very simple, and the only cellar treatment the wines receive is racking. The fruit (now mostly Merlot, Pinot Noir, and Cabernet) is picked very ripe and fermented at high temperatures.

RED

☆   1979 CABERNET SAUVIGNON ($9.50) Tepusquet, Santa Maria Valley.

○   1980 CABERNET SAUVIGNON ($10.00) Lot 1, Tepusquet, Santa Maria Valley. *Extremely vegetal, unattractive.*

    1980 CABERNET SAUVIGNON ($10.00) Lot 2, Tepusquet, Santa Maria Valley. *Crisp, some volatile acidity, somewhat vegetal.*

    1981 CABERNET SAUVIGNON ($8.50) Tepusquet, Santa Maria Valley. *Big, lush and weedy.*

    1981 MERLOT ($12.00) Tepusquet, Santa Maria Valley. *Weedy, tannic, bitter.*

☆☆ 1982 MERLOT ($8.50) Santa Maria. *Earthy, rich, dark, deep, lush, intense. Drink 1986.*

Carano Cellars
SONOMA COUNTY

1499 Moody Lane, Geyserville, California 95441 (707-857-3533). FOUNDED: 1982. ACREAGE: 300 acres. PRODUCTION: 3,000 cases. DISTRIBUTION: California and Nevada. OWNERS: Don and Ronda Carano; Steven Spangler, manager. No tours or tasting.

Don Carano, an attorney and hotel owner, bought vineyards in the Alexander Valley in 1979. Each year he bought more and more acreage while entertaining the idea of eventually starting a winery. In 1982 he took the initial step of bonding a small wine cellar for aging his wines. Crushing and processing took place at a nearby winery. In 1983 Don purchased 60 acres in the north end of Dry Creek Valley, then acquired more vineyards and a site for what is planned as a French country-style winery. The design, which includes several acres of formal gardens and guest sites, is slated for completion by the 1986 crush.

J. Carey Cellars
SANTA BARBARA COUNTY

1711 Alamo Pintado Road, Solvang, California 93463 (805-688-8554). FOUNDED: 1978. ACREAGE: 46 acres. PRODUCTION: 6,000 cases. DISTRIBUTION: California, Missouri, New York, Texas, and Washington. OWNERS: Drs. J. Campbell Carey, Sr., James Carey, Jr., Joseph Carey; Richard Longoria, general manager. WINEMAKER: Richard Longoria. Tours and tasting daily 10 A.M.–4 P.M.

A successful obstetrician and gynecologist, Dr. J. Campbell Carey moved from Illinois in 1977 with his wife, Mary Louise, and purchased 25 acres of vineyard in the Santa Ynez Valley that was planted to Cabernet Sauvignon and Merlot. The Careys' two doctor sons, James and Joseph, convinced their parents to convert an old hay barn into a winery, and it was ready for the 1978 crush. The family handmade their wines that year. They have since expanded the winery and the vineyard, and have hired a full-time winemaker.

WHITE

☆☆☆   1982 CHARDONNAY ($9.50) Estate, Santa Ynez Valley. *Lovely oak, crisp fruit, very Burgundian.*

☆☆☆   1983 CHARDONNAY ($10.50) Santa Barbara. *Big, oaky and rich with lovely crisp fruit and depth.*

☆☆   1983 CHARDONNAY ($12.00) Adobe Canyon, Santa Ynez Valley.

O   1982 GEWURZTRAMINER ($5.50) Estate, Santa Maria Valley. *Sour and unattractive.*

☆☆☆   1981 SAUVIGNON BLANC ($8.50) Santa Maria Valley.

☆☆   1982 SAUVIGNON BLANC ($8.50) Central Coast.

☆☆   1983 SAUVIGNON BLANC ($7.75) Santa Barbara. *Grassy, assertive, clean, fresh.*

BLANC DE NOIR

☆☆   1983 CABERNET BLANC ($5.75) Santa Ynez Valley. *Crisp, dry, clean.*

☆☆☆   1984 CABERNET BLANC ($5.75) Alamo Pintado, Santa Ynez Valley. *1% residual sugar. Crisp, tangy fruit, varietal, delightful.*

RED

☆☆   1979 CABERNET SAUVIGNON ($10.50) Estate, Santa Ynez Valley. *Brambly, herbal, dense, raisiny; power, but no finesse.*

☆   1981 CABERNET SAUVIGNON ($8.75) Alamo Pintado, Santa Ynez Valley. *Nicely made, very vegetative.*

1981 CABERNET SAUVIGNON ($8.75) Estate, Santa Ynez Valley. *Weedy, thick, lacking structure.*

☆☆   1979 MERLOT ($6.75) Santa Ynez Valley.

☆☆   1980 MERLOT ($11.00) Reserve, Santa Ynez Valley.

☆☆   1981 MERLOT ($11.50) Santa Ynez Valley. *Richly varietal, tannic and angular. Drink 1986 and beyond.*

RICHARD CAREY *see* R. Montali and Associates

Carmel Bay Winery
MONTEREY COUNTY

P.O. Box 2496, Carmel, California 93921 (408-375-2292). FOUNDED: 1977. ACREAGE: None. PRODUCTION: 1,000 cases. DISTRIBUTION: California. OWNERS: Fred and Karen Crummey, and Bob and Kathy Eyerman. WINEMAKERS: Bob Eyerman and Fred Crummey. Tours by appointment only.

Karen Crummey and Kathy Eyerman, good friends and teaching partners, got tired of making pies and preserves and decided to try their hand at making fruit wine. From there, they advanced to generic "Burgundy" wine. Once their husbands joined in, the enterprise outgrew the two couples' garages, and they turned an old airplane hangar into a winery. Growing steadily, Carmel Bay Winery invaded one hanger after another, until it had to move to a roomy Quonset hut on the north side of the Monterey Peninsula Airport.

WHITE

☆   1982 CHARDONNAY ($9.00) Monterey. *Dull, unpleasant.*

RED

☆☆☆   1979 ZINFANDEL ($5.00) Shandon Valley, San Luis Obispo. *Berried and appealing with nice oak and fruit.*

Carmenet Vineyard
SONOMA COUNTY

1700 Moon Mountain Drive, Sonoma, California 95476 (707-996-5870). FOUNDED: 1980. ACREAGE: 51 acres. PRODUCTION: 30,000 cases. DISTRIBUTION: Nationwide. OWNER: Chalone, Inc. W. Philip Woodward, president. WINEMAKERS: Jeff Baker and Rob McBryde. Tours by appointment on weekdays. See also Chalone Vineyard.

A major shareholder in Chalone Vineyard, "Mac" McQuown, had always wanted to get into the Cabernet business. When the well-known Glen Ellen Vineyard in Sonoma came up for sale, Mac put together a group of five investors to buy the property, plant it over to Bordeaux varieties, and plan a winery. The planting and winery construction took two years and was completed in 1982. The winery is unusual in that its aging cellars are located in underground caves. Winemaker Jeff Baker makes a proprietary wine called "Carmenet" from the three red varieties grown in the vineyards.

WHITE

☆   1982 SAUVIGNON BLANC ($9.00) Edna Valley. *10% Semillon. Grassy, intense, odd.*

☆☆☆   1983 SAUVIGNON BLANC ($9.00) Edna Valley. *Heavy, barrel fermented, varietal, intense, oaky.*

RED

☆☆☆☆   1982 CARMENET RED ($16.00) Sonoma Valley. *85% Cabernet, 10% Merlot, 5% Cabernet Franc. Great structure, fruit. Drink 1988.*

Carneros Creek Winery
NAPA COUNTY

1285 Dealy Lane, Napa, California 94558 (707-253-WINE). FOUNDED: 1971. ACREAGE: 10 acres. PRODUCTION: 25,000 cases. DISTRIBUTION: Nationwide. OWNERS: Balfour and Anita Gibson, and Francis and Kathleen Mahoney. WINEMAKER: Francis Mahoney. Tours by appointment only, Monday–Friday. Retail sales available.

When the history of Pinot Noir in California is recorded, this winery will certainly figure prominently. Francis Mahoney believed that great Pinots—and Chardonnays—could be made in the cool Carneros region of Napa. With care and attention to detail, winemaker Mahoney and partner Balfour Gibson have proved their point. Carneros Creek has worked hard to develop long-standing relationships with growers and recognizes their contributions with vineyard designations on the winery's labels.

WHITE

☆   1981 CHARDONNAY ($13.50) Napa Valley. *Decent but dull and lacking finesse.*

    1981 CHARDONNAY ($13.50) Sonoma.

☆☆   1982 CHARDONNAY ($13.00) Napa Valley. *Rich, heavy, clean, some nice fruit acid. Bottle variation.*

☆☆   1982 FUME BLANC ($7.50) California. *40% Semillon.*

☆☆☆   1982 FUME BLANC ($7.50) Napa Valley. *Fresh, clean, nice varietal character.*

☆   1982 FUME BLANC ($8.30) California.

☆☆   1983 FUME BLANC ($7.50) Napa Valley. *Tart, dry, clean, good depth.*

    1981 SAUVIGNON BLANC ($7.50) California. *10% Semillon. Tired and dull.*

☆☆☆   1982 SAUVIGNON BLANC ($7.50) California. *10% Semillon.*

RED

☆☆☆   1979 CABERNET SAUVIGNON ($12.00) Napa Valley.

☆☆   1980 CABERNET SAUVIGNON ($10.00) Amador. *Atypical. Big, jammy and Zinfandel-like. Should mellow by 1986.*

☆☆☆ 1980 CABERNET SAUVIGNON ($10.00) Fay, Napa Valley. *12% Merlot. Herbal, fresh and youthful. Drink 1986.*

☆☆☆ 1980 CABERNET SAUVIGNON ($12.00) Napa Valley. *Oaky and jammy but with firm structure. Good aging potential.*

☆☆ 1980 CABERNET SAUVIGNON ($13.50) Napa Valley. *Earthy, dense, a bit coarse. Drink now.*

☆☆☆ 1980 CABERNET SAUVIGNON ($13.50) Truchard, Napa Valley. *30% Merlot, 10% Cabernet Franc. Crisp, fresh, lively. Drink now.*

☆ 1980 CABERNET SAUVIGNON ($15.00) Fay-Turnbull, Napa Valley. *Weedy, intense, deep, rough. Drink 1987.*

☆☆ 1981 CABERNET SAUVIGNON ($12.00) 91% Fay, 9% Amador, Napa Valley. *Crisp, clean, full, intense. Drink 1987.*

☆☆ 1981 CABERNET SAUVIGNON ($15.00) Fay, Napa Valley. *Rich, deep, concentrated. Drink 1987.*

☆☆ 1982 MERLOT ($10.00) Napa Valley. *Clean, varietal, a bit thin, pleasant. Drink now.*

☆☆☆☆ 1977 PINOT NOIR ($12.50) Napa Valley. *Lush, superb, rich, velvety. We can make great Pinot Noir!!*

☆☆☆ 1978 PINOT NOIR ($12.00) Carneros District-Napa Valley. *Rich, fruited and complex; cherries and oak, lovely.*

☆☆ 1979 PINOT NOIR ($15.00) Carneros District-Napa Valley.

☆☆☆ 1980 PINOT NOIR ($15.00) Carneros District, Napa Valley. *Earthy and green with good aging potential.*

☆☆ 1981 PINOT NOIR ($16.00) Napa Valley. *Cherry-berry, earthy, rich and full. Drink 1987.*

☆☆☆☆ 1983 PINOT NOIR ($16.00) Napa Valley. *Soft, rich fruit flavors, delicate, superb. Drink 1987.*

☆☆☆ 1980 ZINFANDEL ($6.00) Yolo. *Fresh, snappy and very attractive.*

Cartlidge & Browne
NAPA COUNTY

1472 Railroad Avenue, St. Helena, California 94574 (707-963-3200). FOUNDED: 1980. ACREAGE: None. PRODUCTION: 2,400 cases. DISTRIBUTION: Major market areas. OWNERS: Tony Cartlidge and Glenn Browne. WINEMAKER: Paul Moser. OTHER LABEL: Stratford. No tours or tasting.

Wine broker Tony Cartlidge and retired banker Glenn Browne started their own label in 1980. Tony, who also sells Rutherford Hill and Freemark Abbey wines under the name Associated Wine Brokers, buys grapes and has them custom-crushed at Rombauer Vineyards. In 1982 winemaker Paul Moser was hired.

WHITE

☆ 1982 STRATFORD CHARDONNAY ($8.50) California. *Decent but dull.*

☆☆ 1983 STRATFORD CHARDONNAY ($8.50) California. *Heavy, vinous, rich.*

☆☆ 1983 CHARDONNAY ($11.50) Napa Valley. *Vinous, rich, varietal.*

☆☆☆ 1983 STRATFORD SAUVIGNON BLANC ($6.00) Napa Valley. *Varietal, simple, attractive.*

RED

☆☆☆ 1982 STRATFORD ZINFANDEL ($7.75) Napa Valley. *Crisp, fruity, fresh, tangy, superb. The way Zinfandel should taste.*

Carver Wine Cellars
MISSOURI

P.O. Box 1316, Rolla, Missouri 65401 (314-364-4335). FOUNDED: 1978. ACREAGE: 10 acres. PRODUCTION: 1,700 cases. DISTRIBUTION: Missouri. OWNERS: Larry and Mary Carver. WINEMAKER: Larry Carver. Tours and tasting summer daily 12–5 P.M.; winter weekends 12–5 P.M.

Larry and Mary Carver were making specialty vinegars in Santa Ana, California, when they determined they'd rather make wine. "The average price for potential vineyard land in California was simply more than we could afford at that time," explains Larry. "So we moved back to my home state of Missouri." Larry is a physicist and Mary is a medical technologist, and their first priority upon arrival was to find jobs. Next, on a piece of property fairly close to both of their jobs, they planted Cabernet, Chardonnay, Riesling, and some French-American hybrids. Then they built a Tudor-style wooden winery on their vineyard property.

Casa de Fruta
SANTA CLARA COUNTY

6680 Pacheco Pass Highway, Hollister, California 95023 (408-637-0051). FOUNDED: 1973. ACREAGE: 20 acres. PRODUCTION: 14,000 cases. DISTRIBUTION: At winery. OWNERS: Joseph and Eugene Zanger. WINEMAKER: Joseph C. Zanger. Tasting daily 9 A.M.–6 P.M.

This roadside operation started as a tasting room only, where wines bought from selected wineries were poured. Later, in 1976, vineyards were purchased, and the winery began having wines made for them using only their own grapes. Fruit wines are made at Bargetto Winery.

Casa Larga Vineyards
NEW YORK

2287 Turk Hill Road, Fairport, New York 14450 (716-223-4210). FOUNDED: 1974. ACREAGE: 17 acres. PRODUCTION: 6,000 cases. DISTRIBUTION: At winery and local outlets. OWNER: Colaruotolo family. Andrew and John Colaruotolo, managers. WINEMAKERS: Andrew and John Colaruotolo. Tours and tasting Tuesday–Sunday, 10 A.M.–5 P.M. Tours hourly 1 P.M.–4 P.M.

Casa Larga, Italian for "large house," was the name of the Colaruotolos' vineyards in Italy. Andrew Colaruotolo grew up there on his grandmother's farm, where he learned to make wine. Now, as owner of Anco Builders, he has built his own Casa Larga winery on a 98-acre site originally planned for a housing development. Sitting at one of the highest elevations in Monroe County, the winery has a wide view of Rochester's skyline as well as rolling farmlands. Andrew has used the grafting and nursery facilities at Casa Larga to replace his Concord and Delaware grapes with vinifera and French-American hybrid vines.

WHITE

☆☆   1982 CHARDONNAY ($7.50) Finger Lakes Region. *Lemony crisp, fresh but lacking varietal character.*

Casa Nuestra
NAPA COUNTY

3451 Silverado Trail, St. Helena, California 94574 (707-944-8444). FOUNDED: 1979. ACREAGE: 10 acres. PRODUCTION: 1,500 cases. DISTRIBUTION: By mailing list. OWNERS: Eugene and

Cody G. Kirkham. WINEMAKER: Allen Price. Tours Saturday–Sunday 10 A.M.–5 P.M. Weekdays by appointment.

Gene and Cody Kirkham are a young couple whose tiny winery specializes in Chenin Blanc, Cabernet Sauvignon, and a blend of Gamay and Zinfandel. The Spanish name means "our house." The production is sold mostly by mailing list and to Bay Area restaurants. Plans are to expand volume from 1,500 to 2,500 cases.

WHITE

☆☆ 1981 CHENIN BLANC ($6.25) Napa Valley. *Intense, dry, varietal.*
☆☆☆ 1982 CHENIN BLANC ($5.75) Napa Valley. *Dry. Fruity, crisp and nicely rounded.*
☆ 1983 CHENIN BLANC ($6.00) Napa Valley. *Varietal but a bit vegetal.*

RED

☆☆ NV TINTO ($5.00) Napa Valley. *72% Gamay, 20% Zinfandel, Petite Sirah 4%, Cabernet 4%. Simple, nice.*
☆☆ 1980 TINTO ($6.25) Napa Valley. *75% Gamay, 25% Zinfandel. Fresh, ripe, clean and snappy.*

Cascade Mountain Vineyards
NEW YORK

Flinthill Road, Amenia, New York 12501 (914-373-9021). FOUNDED: 1977. ACREAGE: 14 acres. PRODUCTION: 6,000 cases. DISTRIBUTION: Eastern states. OWNERS: William and Margaret Wetmore. WINEMAKER: Peter Monteforte. Tours and tasting daily 10 A.M.–6 P.M. Restaurant 10 A.M.–4 P.M.

In order to secure a steady source of good but cheap wine, Bill Wetmore, a freelance writer and novelist, started to make his own. The idea of planting a vineyard was partly inspired by the need to fund his children's education. "You can't borrow money to write a book, but you can borrow money to start a farm," explains Bill. The winery also served as a high school senior project for his son, Charles. Father and son designed the winery and Charles completed the construction. "He [Charles] will pop in every now and then when we need a little construction work," says Bill.

WHITE

☆ 1982 RAVAT VIGNOLES ($7.00) New York State. *Dry, fruity and clean.*

RED

O 1982 RESERVED RED ($7.00) Hudson River Region. *Weedy and astringent.*

Cassayre-Forni Cellars
NAPA COUNTY

1271 Manley Lane, Rutherford, California 94573 (707-944-2165). FOUNDED: 1976. ACREAGE: None. PRODUCTION: 7,500 cases. DISTRIBUTION: Major market states. OWNERS: Paul M. Cassayre and Michael J. Forni. James L. Cassayre, president. WINEMAKER: Michael J. Forni. Tours and tasting by appointment only.

Jim and Paul Cassayre are consulting engineers who, with winemaker Mike Forni, have been operating this small winery since 1976. All grapes are purchased with four varieties being emphasized: Chenin Blanc, Chardonnay, Cabernet Sauvignon, and Zinfandel.

WHITE

☆☆ 1981 CHARDONNAY ($12.00) Napa Valley. *Fresh, clean and a bit short.*
☆☆ 1982 CHARDONNAY ($10.75) Alexander Valley. *Crisp, clean and fruity. Quite lovely.*
☆☆☆ 1981 CHENIN BLANC ($6.00) Napa Valley.
☆ 1982 CHENIN BLANC ($6.00) Lot 1, Napa Valley.
☆☆ 1982 CHENIN BLANC ($6.00) Very Dry, Napa Valley. *1.4% residual sugar. Tangy, good
        acid, a touch of sweetness.*
☆☆ 1983 CHENIN BLANC ($6.00) Dry, Napa Valley.

RED

☆☆☆ 1978 CABERNET SAUVIGNON ($9.00) Napa Valley. *Rich, thick, complex. Should age
        well.*
☆☆ 1979 CABERNET SAUVIGNON ($10.75) Napa. *Intense, berried.*
☆ 1980 CABERNET SAUVIGNON ($12.00) Napa Valley. *Weedy, lush, fat, lacks structure.
        Drink now.*
☆☆ 1981 CABERNET SAUVIGNON ($10.25) Napa Valley. *Big, lush, tannic. Drink 1986.*
☆☆ 1979 ZINFANDEL ($7.50) Sonoma. *Fruity and crisp with good depth.*
☆☆☆ 1980 ZINFANDEL ($8.00) Sonoma. *Lush, berried, balanced.*
O 1981 ZINFANDEL ($7.50) Sonoma.
☆ 1982 ZINFANDEL ($7.00) Sonoma. *Dull and soft but acceptable.*

Caswell Vineyards
SONOMA COUNTY

13207 Dupont Road, Sebastopol, California 95472 (707-874-2517). FOUNDED: 1982. ACREAGE: 20 acres. PRODUCTION: 2,000 cases. DISTRIBUTION: California. OWNERS: Dwight and Helen Caswell. WINEMAKER: Dwight Caswell, Jr. Tours and tasting weekends 10 A.M.–5 P.M. Weekdays by appointment. Seasonal wine-tasting festivals.

Dwight Caswell, Jr., became fascinated with wine when he worked as a photographer for some wineries in the Santa Clara Valley. Fortunately for him, his parents happened to move to a ranch full of old vineyards and orchards just outside Sebastopol. Dwight jumped at this opportunity to get involved in the wine business. Since then, the Caswell family has worked together, building homes, planting vineyards, tearing down old buildings, and setting up the new winery in their two-car garage. The plans for a new winery building will accommodate a 10,000-case production.

Catoctin Vineyards
MARYLAND

805 Greenbridge Road, Brookeville, Maryland 20833 (301-774-2310). FOUNDED: 1983. ACREAGE: 24 acres. PRODUCTION: 3,000 cases. DISTRIBUTION: Maryland and Washington D.C. OWNERS: Partnership. Robert Lyon, manager. WINEMAKER: Robert Lyon. Tours and tasting weekends 10 A.M.–6 P.M. Weekdays by appointment.

After having worked in six wineries, both in the East and in California, Robert Lyon wanted one of his own. He formed a partnership with several grape growers whose vineyards are in the Catoctin Mountains, hence the winery's name. When they learned that the Provenza Winery was for sale, none of the partners had the funds to purchase the winery outright, so they leased the building in 1983. Robert, who manages the winery, has refurbished the facility and purchased new equipment.

CAVISTE *see* Acacia Winery

Caymus Vineyards
NAPA COUNTY

Box 268, Rutherford, California 94573 (707-963-4204). FOUNDED: 1971. ACREAGE: 64 acres. PRODUCTION: 35,000 cases. DISTRIBUTION: Nationwide. OWNER: Charles Wagner. WINE-MAKERS: Charles Wagner and Randy Dunn. OTHER LABEL: Liberty School. Tours by appointment.

Charlie Wagner is one of the Napa Valley's most delightful fixtures. A grower and former orchardist, he started making wine in the early 1970s and immediately dazzled the world with his elegant Cabernet. His son Chuck works in the winery; Charlie can usually be found behind the counter in the winery's small tasting room dispensing wine and his personal style of gruff and cynical humor. The winery has a second label, Liberty School, named after the tiny school on the property that Charlie attended when he was growing up in Napa.

WHITE

☆ NV CHARDONNAY ($6.00) Napa Valley. *Snappy, crisp, decent.*

☆☆☆ 1980 CHARDONNAY ($12.00) Napa Valley.

☆☆ 1981 CHARDONNAY ($9.50) Estate, Napa Valley. *Crisp, clean, appealing, simple.*

☆☆ 1982 CHARDONNAY ($9.00) Estate, Napa Valley. *Toasty, good fruit, solid, medium weight.*

1982 LIBERTY SCHOOL CHARDONNAY ($9.25) Napa Valley. *Minty, herbal, no varietal character, odd.*

☆ 1984 LIBERTY SCHOOL CHARDONNAY ($6.00) Lot 4, Napa Valley. *Decent, drinkable but dirty.*

☆☆☆ 1981 FUME BLANC ($8.50) Napa Valley. *Full, rounded, clean and complex.*

☆☆ 1982 JOHANNISBERG RIESLING ($9.00) Special Select, Napa Valley. *70% botrytis, 7% residual sugar. Snappy, balanced, likable.*

☆☆ 1982 SAUVIGNON BLANC ($6.50) Napa Valley. *Crisp, assertively grassy, lacks stuffing.*

☆ 1983 SAUVIGNON BLANC ($7.50) Napa Valley. *Floral, lacking structure.*

☆☆☆ 1984 LIBERTY SCHOOL SAUVIGNON BLANC ($5.00) Lot 1, Napa Valley. *Lush, fresh, fruity, varietal, very attractive.*

BLANC DE NOIR

○ 1981 OEIL DE PERDRIX ($5.00) Estate, Napa Valley. *Made from Pinot Noir grapes.*

☆☆ 1982 OEIL DE PERDRIX ($5.00) Napa Valley. *Made from Pinot Noir grapes. Earthy, clean, crisp, dry.*

1983 OEIL DE PERDRIX ($6.50) Napa Valley. *Made from Pinot Noir grapes. Dry, dull, lacking fruit.*

☆☆ NV LIBERTY SCHOOL GAMAY BLANC ($4.00) Napa Valley. *Clean, crisp and appealing.*

RED

☆ NV LIBERTY SCHOOL CABERNET SAUVIGNON ($6.00) Lot 10, Napa Valley. *Soft, weedy, attractive, simple.*

☆☆ 1974 CABERNET SAUVIGNON Napa Valley. *Herbal, still fruity, good structure. Drink now.*

☆☆ 1976 CABERNET SAUVIGNON Estate, Napa Valley. *Nicely structured and well made. Finishes with raisins.*

☆☆☆☆ 1976 CABERNET SAUVIGNON ($35.00) Special Selection, Estate, Napa Valley. *Re-markable balance and complexity, assertive and classic.*
☆☆☆ 1978 CABERNET SAUVIGNON ($12.50) Napa Valley. *Snappy, oaky, attractive.*
☆☆☆ 1978 CABERNET SAUVIGNON ($30.00) Special Selection, Estate, Napa Valley. *Crisp, balanced, elegant, fruity, lovely structure. Will age.*
☆☆☆ 1979 CABERNET SAUVIGNON ($12.50) Napa Valley. *Fresh, clean, snappy and delight-ful. Will age nicely.*
☆☆☆☆ 1979 CABERNET SAUVIGNON ($30.00) Special Selection, Estate, Napa Valley. *Superb. Crisp, clean, classic, Bordeaux-like. Drink 1986.*
☆☆☆☆ 1980 CABERNET SAUVIGNON ($12.50) Estate, Napa Valley. *Lean, elegant, herbal and intense. Good now, better in 1987.*
☆☆☆☆ 1981 CABERNET SAUVIGNON ($12.50) Estate, Napa Valley. *Elegant, firm, complex, fruity, great acidity. Drink 1986.*
☆☆ 1982 LIBERTY SCHOOL CABERNET SAUVIGNON ($6.00) Lot 11, Alexander Valley. *Fresh, clean, attractive. Drink now.*
☆☆ NV PETITE SIRAH ($7.50) Napa Valley.
☆☆ 1978 PINOT NOIR ($8.00) Napa Valley.
☆ 1980 PINOT NOIR ($6.50) Estate, Napa Valley. *Balanced but a bit underripe. Beginning to show some age.*
☆☆☆ 1981 PINOT NOIR ($7.50) Estate, Napa Valley. *Fresh, clean, balanced, complex.*
☆☆ 1981 PINOT NOIR ($12.50) Special Selection, Napa Valley. *Rich, balanced, nicely structured.*
☆☆☆ 1977 ZINFANDEL ($5.50) California. *Spicy, balanced, clean.*
☆☆☆ 1978 ZINFANDEL ($6.50) California. *Complex, rich, balanced, varietal.*
☆☆ 1979 ZINFANDEL ($7.50) California (Amador and Napa). *Big, rich, intense, lacks finesse.*
☆☆☆ 1980 ZINFANDEL ($6.50) Napa Valley. *Firmly structured and well balanced. Drink now or hold.*
☆ 1981 ZINFANDEL ($6.50) Napa Valley. *Clean, good fruit, hard tannin.*

CBC *see* Cordtz Brothers Cellars

Cedar Hill Wine Company
OHIO

2195 Lee Road, Cleveland Heights, Ohio 44118 (216-321-9511). FOUNDED: 1974. ACREAGE: None. PRODUCTION: 2,000 cases. DISTRIBUTION: At winery, restaurants, and other local outlets. OWNER: Au Provence, Inc. Dr. Thomas W. Wykoff, president; Jack Foster, cellarmaster. WINEMAKER: Dr. Thomas W. Wykoff. OTHER LABEL: Château Lagniappe. Tours and tasting from the Wine Shop. Restaurant open Monday–Saturday 11 A.M.–7 P.M.

Physician Thomas Wycoff, surgeon and head of the ear, nose, and throat department of Cleveland's St. Luke Hospital, developed a passion for food and wine on a visit to New Orleans. When he returned home, with dreams of restaurants and wineries dancing in his head, he noticed for the first time that there were vineyards in his neighborhood—vineyards that could, he believed, produce European-style wines. Into his fertile mind was born the idea for a combination winery-restaurant. Renting a rundown beauty parlor in a suburban business district, Tom started the Au Provence restaurant upstairs and the Cedar Hill Winery downstairs. As if that were not enough, he also opened a retail wine shop next door. Tom, who manages all three businesses, makes wines that complement the restaurant's food which, he says, is prepared in the tradition of "cuisine classique" with a little New Orleans spice thrown in.

WHITE

☆☆☆ 1982 CHATEAU LAGNIAPPE CHARDONNAY ($12.00) Lake Erie.
  ☆ 1981 CHATEAU LAGNIAPPE SPECIAL SEYVAL BLANC ($7.50) Lake Erie. *Off-dry, a bit strange.*
  ☆ 1982 CHATEAU LAGNIAPPE SEYVAL BLANC ($5.50) Lake Erie.
 ☆☆ 1982 CHATEAU LAGNIAPPE VIDAL BLANC ($5.50) Lake Erie. *Dry, fruity, pleasant.*

SPARKLING

 ☆☆ 1982 CHATEAU LAGNIAPPE ($10.00) Lake Erie, Ohio.

ROSE

 ☆☆ 1983 CHATEAU LAGNIAPPE ($5.50) Lake Erie.

RED

1981 CHATEAU LAGNIAPPE TERMINAL ($8.50) Red, Lake Erie.
1982 CHATEAU LAGNIAPPE ORCHESTRA ($8.50) Lake Erie.
1983 CHATEAU LAGNIAPPE FRAMBOISE ($8.50) Lake Erie.
1980 CHATEAU LAGNIAPPE CABERNET SAUVIGNON ($12.00) Lake Erie. *Highly acidic.*
  ☆ 1982 CHATEAU LAGNIAPPE CHELOIS ($5.50) Ohio.
 ☆☆ 1981 CHATEAU LAGNIAPPE CHAMBOURSIN ($5.50) Lake Erie.

Chaddsford Winery
PENNSYLVANIA

Route 1, Box 229, Chadds Ford, Pennsylvania 19317 (215-388-6221). FOUNDED: 1982. ACREAGE: None. PRODUCTION: 10,400 cases. DISTRIBUTION: At winery and 3 winery-owned retail outlets. OWNERS: Eric and Lee Miller. WINEMAKER: Eric Miller. Tours and tasting Tuesday–Saturday 10 A.M.–5:30 P.M., Sunday 12–5:00 P.M.

Eric Miller is the son of Mark Miller, who owns Benmarl Wine Company in New York (see). From 1970 to 1980 Eric worked for his father as vineyard manager and winemaker. After some father-son disagreements, Eric went looking for his own wine domain in 1982. He settled on five acres in the colonial area of Chadds Ford, Pennsylvania. The property had a house, a guest house, and an old barn which was modernized and converted into a winery.

WHITE

 ☆☆ 1982 CHARDONNAY ($12.00) Pennsylvania.
☆☆☆ 1983 JOHANNISBERG RIESLING ($7.00) Pennsylvania. *Rich yet delicate, lovely and fresh.*

Chadwick Bay Wine Company
NEW YORK

10001 Route 60, Fredonia, New York 14063 (716-672-5000). FOUNDED: 1980. ACREAGE: None. PRODUCTION: 14,000 cases. DISTRIBUTION: New York. OWNERS: Partnership. George Borzilleri, Jr., president. WINEMAKER: Carmen K. Jugovich. Tours and tasting daily 10 A.M.–5 P.M., Sunday 12–5 P.M.

Grape growing is an affront to one's common sense, according to George Borzilleri. A long-time grape grower, George describes his decision to start a winery as "a mental lapse." His original idea was to have better control over the marketing of his grapes. He purchased property on the Fredonia shores of Lake Erie and built a winery of rough-cut wood siding, and an A-frame tasting room. He hired a winemaker who specializes in barrel-aged red wines from both French-American hybrids and Labrusca varieties.

ॐ

Chalet DeBonne Vineyards
OHIO

7743 Doty Road, Madison, Ohio 44057 (216-466-3485). FOUNDED: 1971. ACREAGE: 60 acres. PRODUCTION: 20,000 cases. DISTRIBUTION: At winery and local outlets. OWNER: Corporation. Anthony P. Debevec, president and manager. WINEMAKER: Tony Carlucci. Tours and tasting Tuesday–Saturday 1 P.M.–8 P.M. Gift shop.

The Chalet DeBonne looks more like Heidi's house than a winery. The tasting room chalet was built on top of the underground winery and cellar after longtime grape grower Tony Debevec, Sr., decided to offer his homemade wines to more than just his friends and neighbors. The impetus for all this came from Tony Jr. who, after graduating with a degree in pomology, became interested in starting a commercial winery with his father. Joined by their wives, the older and younger Debevecs expanded their vineyards and built the cozy mountain chalet.

ॐ

CHALK HILL *see* Donna Maria Vineyards

Chalone Vineyard
MONTEREY COUNTY

P.O. Box 855, Soledad, California 93960 (415-441-8975). FOUNDED: 1960. ACREAGE: 110 acres. PRODUCTION: 12,000 cases. DISTRIBUTION: Major market states. OWNER: Corporation. Richard H. Graff, chairman; Phil Woodward, president. WINEMAKER: Michael Michaud. OTHER LABEL: Gavilan. Tours, tasting and retail sales by appointment only. See also Edna Valley Vineyard and Carmenet Vineyard.

Two thousand feet up in the moonscape of the Pinnacles National Monument is a strange place to plant a vineyard, but grapes were first planted here in 1919 by Will Silvear. In 1960 a group of investors revived the vineyard and built a rudimentary winery. Dick Graff, his brother Peter Watson-Graff, and Phil Woodward formed a management corporation in the early 1970s and with help from 150 investors built a new winery. They have established Chalone as one of the premier labels in California. The corporation owns a piece of Edna Valley Vineyard, producer of Chardonnay and Pinot Noir in San Luis Obispo County, and wholly owns Carmenet Vineyard, a Sauvignon Blanc and Cabernet Sauvignon maker in Sonoma Valley. All wines are barrel fermented. Recently the entire Chalone complex of wineries was brought public by the investment banking house of Hambrecht and Quist.

WHITE

☆☆☆☆ 1981 CHARDONNAY ($17.50) Estate, Gavilan Mountains. *Toasty, superbly balanced, elegant and assertive.*

☆☆☆☆ 1982 CHARDONNAY ($17.00) Estate, Monterey. *More finesse and elegance than the '81, the same depth.*

☆☆☆ 1983 CHARDONNAY ($18.75) Estate, Monterey. *Earthy, rich, deep, big.*

☆☆   1981 GAVILAN CHENIN BLANC ($5.00) Napa Valley. *Crisp, dry, vinous.*

☆☆   1982 PINOT BLANC ($12.00) Estate, Monterey. *Crisp, complex and earthy.*

☆☆   1982 PINOT BLANC ($15.00) Reserve, Estate, California. *Earthy, rich, clean, fat. Old vines.*

☆☆☆ 1983 PINOT BLANC ($12.50) California. *Lovely, soft, clean, lively and oaky.*

RED

☆☆☆ 1976 PINOT NOIR Estate, Monterey. *Rich and Burgundian, complex and fruity. Drink now.*

☆☆   1979 PINOT NOIR ($15.00) Estate, Monterey. *Complex and stemmy, aging potential.*

☆☆☆ 1980 PINOT NOIR ($20.00) California.

☆☆☆ 1981 PINOT NOIR ($15.00) Estate, Monterey. *Clean, rich with oak, earth, fruit and some stems.*

☆☆   1982 PINOT NOIR ($15.00) Estate, Monterey. *Earthy, rich, deep. Drink 1987.*

Chamisal Vineyard
SAN LUIS OBISPO COUNTY

7525 Orcult Road, San Luis Obispo, California 93401 (805-544-3576). FOUNDED: 1980. ACREAGE: 60 acres. PRODUCTION: 3,000 cases. DISTRIBUTION: Selected states. OWNER: Norman L. Goss. WINEMAKER: Scott C. Boyd; Thomas Goss, vineyard manager. Tours and tasting Wednesday–Sunday 11 A.M.–5 P.M.

This first vineyard planted in the Edna Valley is mostly Chardonnay grown from Burgundian cuttings. The winery is a family operation owned by Norman Goss, a symphony cellist and former proprietor of the Stuffed Shirt Restaurant in Southern California. Norman is accompanied in this venture by his son Thomas, his son-in-law Scott Boyd, who is the winemaker, and his daughter Allyn Goss Boyd, who is the sales manager.

WHITE

☆☆ 1980 CHARDONNAY ($11.75) Edna Valley.

    1982 CHARDONNAY ($8.00) Estate, Edna Valley. *Dull, vinous, thin and unappealing.*

O   1981 SAUVIGNON BLANC ($7.75) California. *Weedy.*

Champs de Brionne Winery
WASHINGTON

Star Route 1, 98 Road W, NW, Quincy, Washington 98848 (509-785-6685). FOUNDED: 1984. ACREAGE: 124 acres. PRODUCTION: 12,000 cases. DISTRIBUTION: 4 states. OWNERS: Partnership. Dr. Vincent and Carol Bryan. WINEMAKER: Michael Hoffman. Tours and tasting daily 11 A.M.–5 P.M. Picnic facilities.

"We were normal people before all of this," says Carol Bryan. "It started with the vineyard and soon became an all-consuming way of life." In 1980, Dr. Vincent Bryan, after an in-depth study of eastern Washington's climate and soil conditions, founded a winery on a wheat and alfalfa farm situated on a bluff above the Colombia River. Seeing similarities between the gravely soil of this parcel and the Bordeaux and Burgundy areas of France, Dr. Bryan begin by planting eight or nine experimental varieties. "Vince has always been interested in agriculture and has always appreciated wine, so after the vineyard, we were ready to put a winery together," says Carol. The Bryans hired Michael Hoffman, former winemaker of California's HMR Vineyards. Mike crushed the 1983 vintage at another winery, but the Bryans' own winery was ready just in time for the 1984 crush. They are now planning to triple production.

WHITE

☆☆ 1983 A NICE LITTLE WINE ($5.00) Washington. *Crisp, snappy, fresh, attractive.*
☆☆ 1983 JOHANNISBERG RIESLING ($6.00) Washington. *Sweet, good fruit acid, balanced.*
☆☆ 1983 SEMILLON ($7.00) Washington State. *Crisp, clean, charming.*

Chanticleer Vineyards
SONOMA COUNTY

816 Healdsburg Avenue, Healdsburg, California 95448 (707-431-7288). FOUNDED: 1980. ACREAGE: 5 acres. PRODUCTION: 2,000 cases. DISTRIBUTION: California. OWNER: Dennis Hill. WINEMAKER: Dennis Hill. No tours or tasting.

While he was the winemaker at Alexander Valley Vineyards, Dennis Hill also advised other wineries. "As a consultant, I discovered some very attractive wines that were simply not being blended, bottled, or marketed successfully," says Dennis. "I decided to take advantage of this by purchasing these wines in bulk and blending, aging, and bottling them myself under my own label." The Chanticleer wines have been finished at various wineries, including Alexander Valley Vineyards, from 1980 to 1984. In the near future Dennis plans to build his own winery.

WHITE

☆☆☆ 1983 SAUVIGNON BLANC ($6.75) Lake. *Fruity, rich, oaky, charming.*

RED

☆☆ 1979 ZINFANDEL ($6.25) Sonoma.

Chappellet Winery
NAPA COUNTY

1581 Sage Canyon Road, St. Helena, California 94574 (707-963-7136). FOUNDED: 1967. ACREAGE: 110 acres. PRODUCTION: 27,500 cases. DISTRIBUTION: 44 states and 6 foreign countries. OWNER: Donn Chappellet, owner and president. WINEMAKER: Cathy Corison. Tours Friday at 1 P.M. by appointment.

Donn Chappellet is a mountain of a man, a gentle giant who has carved a winery out of the rough terrain 1,700 feet above the floor of the Napa Valley. Back in 1965, at the age of 34, Donn left his successful food service business in Los Angeles and set out to establish his own winery. With his wife, Molly, Donn built his home and his winery on Pritchard Hill in the rough high country on the eastern side of the Napa Valley. There the Chappellets have raised their six children and produced some of the United States' finest Cabernet Sauvignons. Although several winemakers have made the wines—Philip Togni, Joe Cafaro, Tony Soter, and, currently, Cathy Corison—there is an unmistakable Chappellet character, which can be attributed in large part to the gravelly, well-drained hillside soil.

WHITE

☆☆ 1980 CHARDONNAY ($14.00) Napa Valley.
☆☆ 1981 CHENIN BLANC ($7.50) Napa Valley.
☆☆☆ 1983 CHENIN BLANC ($7.50) Napa Valley. *Dry, fresh, fruity, clean, lemony.*

RED

☆☆☆ 1968 CABERNET SAUVIGNON Napa Valley. *Clean, crisp, tart, elegant.*
☆☆☆☆ 1969 CABERNET SAUVIGNON Napa Valley. *Clean, tannic and ripe, lush, complex, with years to go.*

☆☆☆ 1970 CABERNET SAUVIGNON Napa Valley. *Earthy, fresh, fruity and firmly structured.*
☆☆ 1971 CABERNET SAUVIGNON Napa Valley. *Short, lacks firmness, nice however.*
☆☆ 1972 CABERNET SAUVIGNON Napa Valley. *Slightly green, quite good for this difficult year.*
☆☆☆ 1973 CABERNET SAUVIGNON Napa Valley. *Snappy, clean and complex. Great aging potential.*
☆☆ 1974 CABERNET SAUVIGNON Napa Valley. *Raisiny, hard, intense, lacks elegance.*
☆☆☆ 1975 CABERNET SAUVIGNON ($35.00) Napa Valley. *Edgy, tannic, elegant, hard. Long aging potential.*
☆☆☆ 1976 CABERNET SAUVIGNON ($40.00) Napa Valley. *Great fruit and depth; hard edge with a long life ahead.*
☆☆☆ 1977 CABERNET SAUVIGNON ($18.00) Napa Valley. *Big, lush, ripe and round. Good aging potential.*
☆☆ 1978 CABERNET SAUVIGNON ($15.00) Napa Valley. *Cherry nose, vegetal, crisp, clean but not elegant.*
☆☆☆ 1979 CABERNET SAUVIGNON ($12.50) Napa Valley. *Gorgeous depth, fresh, tannic. Great aging potential.*
☆☆☆☆ 1980 CABERNET SAUVIGNON ($18.00) Napa Valley. *Graceful, firm and intense. Earthy, complex and superb.*
☆☆☆ 1982 CABERNET SAUVIGNON ($18.00) Napa Valley. *Rich, firm, complex, great structure. Drink 1990 and beyond.*

Château Benoit Winery
OREGON

Route 1, Box 29B-1, Carlton, Oregon 97111 (503-864-3666). FOUNDED: 1979. ACREAGE: 50 acres. PRODUCTION: 10,000 cases. DISTRIBUTION: California, Oregon, Idaho, Montana, and Washington. OWNERS: Fred and Mary Benoit. Mark Benoit, vineyard manager. WINEMAKER: Rich Cushman. Tours and tasting weekdays 11 A.M.–5 P.M., weekends 12–5 P.M.

This small winery is owned by Fred Benoit, a physician, and his wife, Mary. Their first winemaker was a Swiss, Max Zellweger, who has since moved on to the big Langguth winery in Washington. He was replaced by Rich Cushman, a U.C. Davis graduate who did his on-the-job training at the great European vineyard Dr. Bürklin-Wolf in the Rheingau. Château Benoit specializes in white wines, particularly Sauvignon Blanc and sparkling wines.

WHITE

☆ 1981 WHITE RIESLING ($7.00) Washington. *Spritzy, clean, good balance, a hint of bitterness in back.*

SPARKLING

☆ NV BRUT ($12.00) Oregon. *Grapey, simple, clean.*

RED

☆ 1981 PINOT NOIR ($5.00) Oregon.
☆☆ 1982 PINOT NOIR ($8.95) Oregon.

Château Boswell
NAPA COUNTY

3468 Silverado Trail, St. Helena, California 94574 (707-963-5472). FOUNDED: 1982. ACREAGE: 1 acre. PRODUCTION: 2,000 cases. DISTRIBUTION: At winery. OWNER: Robert Thornton

Boswell. Sue FaGalde, general manager. WINEMAKER: André Tchelistcheff, consultant. Tours and tasting daily 10 A.M.–5 P.M. Picnic facilities.

Dr. R. Thornton Boswell has become a fixture on Air California. Every week he travels back and forth from his home in Laguna Beach to his "château" in the Napa Valley. Attracted by the romance of winemaking, he bought a land parcel and designed an elaborate castle winery. But Dr. Boswell was so caught up in the outward appearance of his fairy tale structure that he neglected to outfit it with winemaking equipment. Since the château has neither machinery nor storage space, the wine is being made at another winery under the watchful eye of André Tchelistcheff.

RED

☆☆ 1979 CABERNET SAUVIGNON ($12.00) Napa Valley. *Dark, lush and raisiny.*

Château Bouchaine
NAPA COUNTY

1075 Buchli Station Road, Napa, California 94558 (707-252-9065). FOUNDED: 1980. ACREAGE: 31 acres. PRODUCTION: 25,000 cases. DISTRIBUTION: Major U.S. markets. OWNERS: Partnership. David Pollak, Jr., president and general partner. WINEMAKER: Jerry Luper; Bo Martinelli, cellarmaster. OTHER LABEL: Poplar. Tasting by appointment Monday–Saturday 9 A.M.–5 P.M.

This much-touted new venture—headed by David Pollak—is the brainchild of a group of wealthy partners, and includes investors such as Gerret Copeland, a Dupont heir from Wilmington. They bought and renovated an old winery property in the Carneros district and brought in renowned winemaker Jerry Luper (see Château Montelena) as a partner. The winery specializes in Pinot Noir and Chardonnay, but other varieties are also offered.

WHITE

☆☆ 1981 POPLAR CHARDONNAY ($7.50) Sonoma. *Fruity, simple, clean and attractive.*

☆☆☆ 1982 POPLAR CHARDONNAY ($7.50) Sonoma. *Crisp and soft with good oak and nice balance.*

☆☆☆ 1982 CHARDONNAY ($12.50) Alexander Valley. *Clean, fresh, fruity, complex, good acidity.*

☆☆☆ 1982 CHARDONNAY ($14.00) 50% Keith, 50% Black Mountain, Alexander Valley. *Ripe, fruity, classy, very likable.*

☆☆ 1982 CHARDONNAY ($14.50) Napa Valley. *Heavy, decent, a bit coarse.*

☆☆ 1982 POPLAR RIESLING ($4.75) Sonoma. *Fragrant, balanced and lovely. Almost dry.*

☆☆☆ 1982 SAUVIGNON BLANC ($8.50) Sonoma. *Beautifully crisp and elegant, Graves style.*

☆☆☆ 1983 SAUVIGNON BLANC ($8.50) Napa Valley. *Crisp, high acidity, fruity, good varietal character.*

RED

☆☆☆ 1982 CABERNET SAUVIGNON ($15.00) Jerry Luper Reserve, Rutherford. *Rich, elegant, great structure. Drink 1988.*

☆☆☆ 1981 PINOT NOIR ($8.50) Winery Lake, Carneros District-Napa Valley. *Tart, fruity, cherry flavors, lovely varietal character.*

☆☆ 1981 PINOT NOIR ($15.00) Winery Lake, Carneros District-Napa Valley. *Clean, earthy, light, lovely.*

☆☆ 1982 PINOT NOIR ($12.50) Los Carneros, Napa Valley. *Cherry flavors, clean, attractive, short.*

☆☆☆ 1982 PINOT NOIR ($15.00) Winery Lake, Carneros District-Napa Valley. *Fruity, complex flavors, a bit fuller than the '81.*

Château Chevalier Winery
NAPA COUNTY

3101 Spring Mountain Road, St. Helena, California 94574 (707-963-2342). FOUNDED: 1884. ACREAGE: 59 acres. PRODUCTION: 12,000 cases. DISTRIBUTION: Nationwide. OWNERS: John and Gil Nickel. John Nickel, general manager. WINEMAKER: Dirk Hampson. Tours by appointment. See Far Niente Winery.

This fantastic castle winery, modeled after a French château, was built in 1891 by George Chevalier, whose father, Fortune, started the estate's winemaking tradition. A family misfortune caused George to sell the estate, and it went from owner to owner for over 50 years. Greg and Kathy Bissonette bought the property in 1969 and undertook the grueling task of bringing the winery and the vineyards back into production. By 1982 they had had enough of the charm and challenge of winemaking and, once again, Château Chevalier was put up for sale. In 1984 Gil and John Nickel of Far Niente Winery bought the château and immediately began a complete renovation program, including plans to increase production to 25,000 cases.

WHITE

☆ 1981 CHARDONNAY ($14.00) Edna Valley. *Big, vinous, oaky, good acidity but a bit vegetal.*

☆☆☆ 1982 CHARDONNAY ($12.50) Edna Valley. *Fresh, lively, attractive. A good food wine.*

RED

☆☆ 1978 CABERNET SAUVIGNON ($25.00) Private Reserve, Napa Valley. *Big, fat, lush and tannic. Lacks structure.*

☆ 1979 CABERNET SAUVIGNON ($10.00) Napa Valley.

   1980 CABERNET SAUVIGNON ($11.25) Napa Valley. *Fat, big, lacking finesse. Some bottles are spoiled.*

☆☆ 1981 CABERNET SAUVIGNON ($10.00) Napa Valley.

☆☆ 1982 CABERNET SAUVIGNON ($12.00) Napa Valley. *15% Merlot. Dense, raisined, tannic. Drink 1986 and beyond.*

☆☆ 1981 MERLOT ($10.50) Napa Valley. *Fruity and varietal, some light herbaceousness.*

☆ 1979 PINOT NOIR ($15.00) Stanton's Pinot Patch, Napa Valley.

O 1980 PINOT NOIR ($10.50) Stanton's Pinot Patch, Napa Valley. *Asparagus flavors. Lacking in varietal character.*

☆☆☆ 1981 PINOT NOIR ($11.50) Stanton's Pinot Patch, Napa Valley. *Toasty, earthy, with some stems and earth. Very nice.*

Château Chèvre Winery
NAPA COUNTY

2040 Hoffman Lane, Yountville, California 94599 (707-944-2184). FOUNDED: 1979. ACREAGE: 21 acres. PRODUCTION: 4,000 cases. DISTRIBUTION: Major market states. OWNERS: Gerald P. Hazen and Robert Mueller. WINEMAKER: Gerald P. Hazen. Tours and tasting by appointment.

This ten-acre property used to be a goat farm—thus the name, which means "goat castle." The winery, in fact, is in the goat barn. Retired airplane pilot Gerald Hazen planted grapes here in 1973 and contracted to sell them to Franciscan Winery. His timing was terrible; the next year Franciscan went bankrupt. Gerald's neighbor Bob Mueller, an enologist at Robert Mondavi Winery, helped him make some experimental wines. Encouraged by the quality of his Merlot and Bob's enthusiasm, Gerald started his own winery in 1979. The Merlot's success prompted Gerald to plant an additional eleven acres, this time of Sauvignon Blanc.

RED

☆☆☆ 1979 MERLOT ($10.50) Napa Valley. *Meaty, rich, velvety, clean and oaky.*

☆☆ 1980 MERLOT ($10.50) Napa Valley. *Slightly vegetal, clean, tannic.*
☆☆ 1980 PINOT NOIR ($10.00) Napa Valley.

Château de Leu Winery
SOLANO COUNTY

1635 West Mason Road, Suisun City, California 94585 (707-864-1517). FOUNDED: 1982. ACREAGE: 80 acres. PRODUCTION: 10,000 cases. DISTRIBUTION: Major market states and Japan. OWNERS: Ben Volkhardt, Jr., and Ben Volkhardt III. WINEMAKER: Ben Volkhardt III. OTHER LABEL: Green Valley Vineyards. Tours, tasting, and retail sales daily 11 A.M.–4:30 P.M. Gift shop.

Just over the Napa County border, in Solano County's Green Valley, Ben Volkhardt has been growing quality grapes since 1954 in a vineyard originally planted in the 1880s. Green Valley is a cool microclimate where Chardonnay, Sauvignon Blanc, and other premium varieties flourish. In 1981 the Volkhardts decided to build their own winery on a knoll overlooking their 75 acres of vineyard. They make their wines from both estate and purchased grapes and have plans to triple the current volume of production.

WHITE

☆☆ 1982 DE LEU BLANC ($3.75) Lake. *Dry, crisp and apple flavored.*
    1981 CHARDONNAY ($9.50) Russian River Valley, Sonoma.
O   1982 CHARDONNAY ($9.50) Jimtown Ranch, Alexander Valley. *Dull, no varietal char-
        acter, unattractive.*
☆☆ 1982 CHARDONNAY ($10.00) Estate, Green Valley, Solano. *Crisp, fruity, simple, fresh
        and appealing.*
☆☆ 1981 FRENCH COLOMBARD ($5.95) Estate, Solano.
☆☆ 1982 FUME BLANC ($7.50) Estate, Lake. *Lemony, varietal, nice.*
☆☆ 1983 FUME BLANC ($3.50) Estate, Green Valley, Solano. *Clean, fresh, fruity, good.*
 ☆ 1982 SAUVIGNON BLANC ($7.00) Estate, Green Valley, Solano.

Château du Lac
LAKE COUNTY

600 Mathews Road, Lakeport, California 95453 (707-263-9333). FOUNDED: 1978. ACREAGE: 100 acres. PRODUCTION: 100,000 cases. DISTRIBUTION: Nationwide. OWNER: Jess Jackson. WINEMAKER: Jed Steele. OTHER LABELS: Kendall-Jackson, Jackson Vineyards, Chevriot du Lac. Tours by appointment on Fridays. Tasting daily 11 A.M.–6 P.M.

Jess Jackson started growing grapes in Lake County in 1974. He had been involved with farming all his life, and the vineyard was a welcome diversion from his San Francisco law practice. At first his grapes were sold to Fetzer Vineyards, but the wines made from them won so many awards that Jess decided to try winemaking himself. Today, the winery has grown to a size that will enable it to be a successful business, not just a tax shelter or a hobby. Winemaker Jed Steele, formerly at Edmeades Vineyards, has won plenty of awards already for the winery's new Kendall-Jackson label. Jess continues his practice as a trial lawyer, involving himself mainly with consti-tutional cases. He is also partners with Dennis Canning in a brokerage-import venture called "Winestates." They import a few wines and represent two or three California wineries, including Château du Lac.

WHITE

☆☆ 1982 KENDALL-JACKSON VINEYARDS & WINERY CHARDONNAY ($7.00) Cali-
        fornia. *Pleasant, slightly vegetal, clean.*
☆☆☆ 1982 CHARDONNAY ($9.50) Clear Lake. *A lovely wine. Rich, balanced, clean, complex.*

☆☆ 1983 KENDALL-JACKSON VINEYARDS & WINERY CHARDONNAY ($9.50) Reserve, Santa Barbara 23%, Napa 21%, Monterey 20%, Sonoma 19%, Lake 17%, California. *Simple, fruity, lacking varietal definition, decent.*

☆☆☆ 1982 KENDALL-JACKSON VINEYARDS & WINERY JOHANNISBERG RIESLING ($6.00) Clear Lake. 2.7% residual sugar. *Soft, clean and fruity.*

☆☆☆ 1983 KENDALL-JACKSON VINEYARDS & WINERY JOHANNISBERG RIESLING ($7.00) Lake. *Crisp, clean, lots of varietal fruit, lovely.*

☆☆☆☆ 1984 JOHANNISBERG RIESLING ($7.00) Monterey. *Stunning. Luscious apple fruit, clean, balanced. Off-dry.*

☆☆☆☆ 1984 KENDALL-JACKSON VINEYARDS & WINERY JOHANNISBERG RIESLING ($7.00) Monterey. *Stunning. Fresh, delicate, crisp apple fruit. Off-dry, charming.*

☆☆☆ 1984 MUSCAT CANELLI ($7.50) Lake. 4.8% residual sugar. *Spritzy, peachy, fruity, balanced.*

☆ 1982 KENDALL-JACKSON VINEYARDS & WINERY SAUVIGNON BLANC ($7.00) Lake.

☆☆ 1983 CHEVRIOT DU LAC SAUVIGNON BLANC ($6.25) Lake. 5% Semillon. *Fruity, dense, clean, some unusual flavors.*

☆☆☆ 1983 KENDALL-JACKSON VINEYARDS & WINERY SAUVIGNON BLANC ($7.25) Clear Lake. *Fruity, rich, soft, great acidity, varietal.*

BLANC DE NOIR

☆☆☆ 1983 KENDALL-JACKSON VINEYARDS & WINERY CABERNET SAUVIGNON ($6.00) Cabernet Blanc, Lake. 0.9% residual sugar. *Fresh, varietal, crisp, superb.*

RED

1980 CABERNET SAUVIGNON ($8.00) Lake.

☆☆ 1982 KENDALL-JACKSON VINEYARDS & WINERY CABERNET SAUVIGNON ($7.00) Clear Lake. *Ripe, balanced, some weediness, pleasant, clean. Drink now.*

☆☆☆ 1983 KENDALL-JACKSON VINEYARDS & WINERY ZINFANDEL ($7.00) Viña-Los Lomas, Clear Lake. *Fresh, light and fruity; very good.*

☆☆☆ 1983 KENDALL-JACKSON VINEYARDS & WINERY ZINFANDEL ($7.00) Vina-Las Lomas, Clear Lake. *Light, fruity, fresh, Beaujolais style.*

☆☆☆ 1983 KENDALL-JACKSON VINEYARDS & WINERY ZINFANDEL ($7.00) Zeni, Mendocino. *Stunning, rich, lovely fruit, balanced, new oak, wonderful.*

Château Esperanza
NEW YORK

Route 54A, Box 76, Bluff Point, New York 14478 (315-536-7481). FOUNDED: 1979. ACREAGE: None. PRODUCTION: 8,000 cases. DISTRIBUTION: New York. OWNER: Mrs. Angela Lombardi. WINEMAKER: Jeff Sully. Tours and tasting May–November: Monday–Saturday 10 A.M–5 P.M., Sunday 12–5 P.M. Sales only November–April: Monday–Friday 10 A.M.–5 P.M., or by appointment.

Angela Lombardi and her husband had dreamed of buying a château in France until they found a deserted Greek Revival stone mansion sitting on a knoll above Keuka Lake. The house was built in 1838 by the Rose family, who had vineyards and made wine prior to Prohibition; later it was used as a home for the aged and then as an art gallery. Forgetting about France, Angela bought the estate, gave it the name "hope" in Spanish and renewed its winemaking history.

WHITE

○ NV CHATEAU WHITE ($4.50) American. *1.5 liter. Vinous, oxidized, ugly.*
☆ 1982 JOHANNISBERG RIESLING ($8.00) New York State.
☆ 1982 JOHANNISBERG RIESLING ($8.00) Individual Bunch Selection, Martini, Finger
        Lakes. *375ml. 8% residual sugar. Nice fruit, funny nose.*
    1982 RAVAT ($8.00) Individual Bunch Selection, Martini, Finger Lakes Region. *375ml.*
        8% residual sugar.

RED

☆☆ 1979 CHANCELLOR ($5.00) Planes, New York State.
    1981 PINOT NOIR ($9.00) New York State.

Château Grand Traverse
MICHIGAN

12239 Center Road, Traverse City, Michigan 49684 (616-223-7355). FOUNDED: 1975. ACREAGE: 100 acres. PRODUCTION: 8,000 cases. DISTRIBUTION: 7 states. OWNER: O'Keefe Centre, Ltd. Edward O'Keefe, president. WINEMAKER: Roland Pfleger. Tours and tasting daily 10 A.M.–5 P.M.

When Ed O'Keefe wants something he goes after it with a passion. A former Green Beret colonel and FBI agent, Ed was operating nursing homes, among other things, when he became interested in wine. Determined to start his own winery, he went to Germany and studied at Geisenheim University. He even persuaded Dr. Helmut Becker, Germany's top viticulturist, to come to Michigan for a consultation. On the highest point of the Old Mission Peninsula, they found the ideal climate for Johannisberg Riesling and Chardonnay. To date, Grand Traverse is still the only winery in Michigan to grow 100 percent vinifera.

WHITE

☆ 1981 CHARDONNAY ($10.00) Michigan. *Herbal, vinous, richly varietal.*
☆☆ 1981 JOHANNISBERG RIESLING ($7.00) Michigan. *3.2% residual sugar. Full, rich,*
        clean, balanced.
☆ 1981 JOHANNISBERG RIESLING ($9.50) Late Harvest, Michigan. *7% residual sugar.*
        Candied, clean, vinous. Made with "sweet reserve."
☆☆ 1982 JOHANNISBERG RIESLING ($35.00) Botrytised Berry Select, Michigan. *12.3%*
        residual sugar. Sweet but nicely balanced; clean.

Château Julien
MONTEREY COUNTY

8940 Carmel Valley Road, P.O. Box 221775, Carmel Valley, California 93922 (408-624-2600). FOUNDED: 1982. ACREAGE: 7 acres. PRODUCTION: 20,000 cases. DISTRIBUTION: Nationwide. OWNER: Great American Wineries, Inc. Robert S. Brower, president; William Anderson, winery manager. WINEMAKER: William Anderson. Tours by appointment.

Great American Wineries has built a huge château, modeled after the grand Bordeaux estates, and named it Julien after the Saint-Julien district in France. From the esthetics to the winery equipment, cooperage, and promotion, the winery is "state of the art."

WHITE

○ 1982 CHARDONNAY ($12.25) Monterey. *Awful.*
☆☆☆ 1982 CHARDONNAY ($17.00) Private Reserve, Monterey. *Sweet oak, lovely complexity,*
        rich and loaded with finesse.

1983 CHARDONNAY ($8.75) Rancho Tierra Rejada, San Luis Obispo. *Heavy and overdone.*

☆☆ 1983 CHARDONNAY ($15.00) Paraiso Springs, Monterey.

1983 CHARDONNAY ($20.00) Private Reserve, Cobblestone, Monterey. *Strange.*

☆☆ 1983 FUME BLANC ($5.75) Rancho Tierra Rejada, San Luis Obispo. *Soft, grassy, fresh, clean.*

1983 FUME BLANC ($6.75) French Camp, San Luis Obispo. *Oxidized, unattractive.*

RED

☆ 1982 MERLOT ($12.00) Sonoma. *Berried, a bit thin, lacking varietal character.*

CHÂTEAU LAGNIAPPE *see* Cedar Hill Wine Company

CHÂTEAU M *see* Monticello Cellars

Château Montelena Winery
NAPA COUNTY

1429 Tubbs Lane, Calistoga, California 95415 (707-942-5105). FOUNDED: 1882. ACREAGE: 110 acres. PRODUCTION: 25,000 cases. DISTRIBUTION: Nationwide and Great Britain. OWNER: Montelena Associates. James L. Barrett, managing partner. WINEMAKER: James P. "Bo" Barrett; Gary Galleron, cellarmaster. OTHER LABEL: Silverado Cellars. Tasting daily 10 A.M.–4 P.M. Picnic facilities by appointment only. Closed holidays.

This 103-year-old winery in northern Napa County has been known, since its startling victory in the renowned 1976 "Paris Tasting," as one of America's finest producers of Chardonnay. The current management took over in 1972. Their first winemaker was Mike Grgich (see Grgich-Hills Cellars), who was followed by Jerry Luper (see Château Bouchaine). The wine is now made by Bo Barrett, son of the managing partner, Jim Barrett. In the past decade Château Montelena has built a splendid reputation for Cabernet Sauvignon and Zinfandel as well as Chardonnay and Johannisberg Riesling.

WHITE

☆☆ 1976 CHARDONNAY Napa and Alexander valleys. *Big, vinous and earthy, intense, toasty; a period piece.*

☆ 1980 CHARDONNAY ($16.00) Centennial, Napa Valley. *Dank, grassy, very disappointing.*

☆☆☆ 1981 CHARDONNAY ($14.00) Alexander Valley. *Fresh apple flavors with lovely balance.*

☆☆☆ 1981 CHARDONNAY ($16.00) Napa Valley. *Big but nicely balanced. Citrus, pineapple and toasty oak.*

☆☆☆ 1982 CHARDONNAY ($14.00) Alexander Valley. *Ripe, clean, fresh, deep. A lovely and serious wine.*

☆☆ 1982 CHARDONNAY ($16.00) Napa Valley. *Heavy, rich, vinous.*

☆☆☆ 1982 CHARDONNAY ($16.00) Estate, Napa Valley. *Rich, vinous, deep, lush, balanced.*

☆☆☆ 1983 CHARDONNAY ($14.00) Alexander Valley. *Big, lush, balanced, oaky, rich, lovely fruit.*

RED

☆☆☆ 1977 CABERNET SAUVIGNON ($14.00) Napa Valley. *Intense and richly structured. Deep, will improve for years.*

☆☆☆ 1978 CABERNET SAUVIGNON ($12.00) Sonoma. *Herbal and intense with nice oak and a long future.*

☆☆ 1978 CABERNET SAUVIGNON ($16.00) Centennial Bottling, Estate, Napa Valley.

☆☆☆ 1979 CABERNET SAUVIGNON ($14.00) Sonoma. *Rich and balanced, fruity and complex. Will improve further.*

☆☆☆ 1979 CABERNET SAUVIGNON ($16.00) Estate, Napa Valley. *Rich, clean, nicely structured. Drink 1986 and beyond.*

☆☆☆ 1980 CABERNET SAUVIGNON ($16.00) Estate, Napa Valley. *Intense, complex, rich, dark, lovely structure. Drink 1988.*

☆ 1982 SILVERADO CELLARS CABERNET SAUVIGNON ($8.00) Estate, Napa Valley. *Dark, heavy, bitter, intense. Drink 1987.*

☆☆ 1977 ZINFANDEL ($6.50) California. *Dense but well bred. Clean and varietal, ready to drink.*

☆☆ 1979 ZINFANDEL ($7.00) California. *Big and rich but with some finesse.*

☆☆ 1980 ZINFANDEL ($7.00) Napa Valley.

☆☆ 1981 ZINFANDEL ($8.00) Napa Valley. *Clean, tangy, fruity and rich.*

☆☆☆ 1982 ZINFANDEL ($10.00) Estate, Napa Valley. *Rich, dense, berry flavors. Clean and complex. Drink 1987.*

Château Montgolfier Vineyards
TEXAS

P.O. Box 12423, Fort Worth, Texas 76116 (817-448-8479). FOUNDED: 1982. ACREAGE: 7 acres. PRODUCTION: 2,500 cases. DISTRIBUTION: Texas. OWNERS: Dr. Henry C. McDonald, Bill and Mike McDonald. WINEMAKER: Dr. Henry C. McDonald. Tours and tasting weekends 12–5:30 P.M., or by appointment.

Besides running his winery and working as an orthopedic surgeon, Dr. Henry McDonald likes to fly. So do his two sons, Mike and Bill, who share their father's fascination with hot air ballooning. The winery, a complex of log buildings, is named after the Montgolfier brothers, who in 1783 invented and flew the first hot air balloon. "We scheduled our first release of Nouveau Barbera on the anniversary of the first Montgolfier balloon flight, which took place on November 21, 1783," says Dr. McDonald. Having built a balloon port on the winery grounds, the McDonalds sponsor a number of events that result in hoards of multicolored balloons cruising the sky above the vineyards. Even the logo on their label is a flying balloon decorated with a bunch of Cabernet Sauvignon grapes.

Château Morrisette Winery
VIRGINIA

P.O. Box 766, Meadows of Dan, Virginia 24120 (703-593-2865). FOUNDED: 1982. ACREAGE: 30 acres. PRODUCTION: 17,000 cases. DISTRIBUTION: Virginia and North Carolina. OWNERS: W.|F. and David Morrisette. WINEMAKER: David Morrisette. Tours and tasting Wednesday–Sunday 10 A.M.–4 P.M.

William Morrisette started a winery named Woolwine, but he never got around to making any wine. Meanwhile his son David was studying enology and viticulture at Mississippi State University. When David graduated, he and his dad started again. They found a new location, built a brand new stone and wood winery, and gave it the name Château Morrisette. David is basically running the winery, since his father works at a paper distribution company in North Carolina. "He is kind of a silent partner," says David. The chief advantage of the new winery is its proximity to the Morrisette vineyards and to a fairly large population center. The Morrisettes still own the Woolwine facility, which they use for case storage.

Château Natural Vineyard
VIRGINIA

Rocky Mount, Virginia 24151 (703-483-0758). FOUNDED: 1976. ACREAGE: 10 acres. PRO-
DUCTION: 400 cases. DISTRIBUTION: Virginia. OWNERS: Arthur C. and Ercelle Hodges.
WINEMAKERS: Arthur C. and Michael W. Hodges. Tours and tasting Monday–Saturday 10 A.M.–
6 P.M., Sunday 1 P.M.–5 P.M.

    "Making wine is as natural as picking blackberries here in Rocky Mount," says Arthur Hodges,
who used to be a carpenter ("and a good one, too," says Ercelle, his wife). Arthur has always been
fascinated with wine, having read virtually every good book written on the subject. Both Hodgeses
are longtime home winemakers. Ercelle has made wine every year since she was thirteen years old.
"We're just country people and have always made wine," she says. After planting vineyards in
1976, Arthur used his carpentry talents to build his own winery at home. The Hodgeses make only
four wines, the most popular of which is their blackberry wine. "We sell out of blackberry faster
than we can make it," says Ercelle.

Château Nouveau
NAPA COUNTY

377 McCormick, St. Helena, California 94574 (707-944-8863). FOUNDED: 1980. ACREAGE:
None. PRODUCTION: 600 cases. DISTRIBUTION: Nationwide. OWNER: Jack Clark. WINE-
MAKER: None at present. Tours by appointment.

    This label was an experimental enterprise of three partners who wanted to see if Beaujolais,
made in the traditional French nouveau style, would sell in the United States. For their first two
years, the partners leased space at the Shown and Sons winery in the Napa Valley, where their
wine was made by Tom Cotrell. Complications arose. The winemaker moved out of the state, the
winery lease expired, the vineyard from which they had been buying grapes was pulled out, and
the plummeting value of the French franc made imported Beaujolais nouveau a more attractive
buy. Faced with these problems, two of the partners sold their interests to the third, Jack Clark,
who wants to continue Château Nouveau once he finds a winemaker and a winery. Wine has been
made at Monticello Cellars, but no wine was made in 1983.

RED

1982 GAMAY BEAUJOLAIS ($5.00) Napa Valley.

CHATEAU RUTHERFORD *see* Rutherford Vintners

Château St. Jean
SONOMA COUNTY

8555 Sonoma Highway, Kenwood, California 95452 (707-833-4134). FOUNDED: 1973. ACREAGE:
77 acres. PRODUCTION: 120,000 cases. DISTRIBUTION: Nationwide and 5 foreign countries.
OWNER: Suntory International. Allan J. Hemphill, president. WINEMAKERS: Richard L. Arrowood and Edgar B. "Pete" Downs. Self-guided tours daily 10:30 A.M–4 P.M. Tasting daily 10
A.M.–4 P.M. Retail sales daily 10 A.M.–4:30 P.M. Newsletter.

    One of California's most celebrated producers of white wines, Château St. Jean has grown
from a boutique winery to a producer of over 100,000 cases per year. The picturesque, state-of-

the-art winery is nestled in the hills on the east side of Sonoma County. Dick Arrowood, who has been the winemaker from the beginning, specializes in assertive, vineyard-designated wines. As many as nine different Chardonnays have been released in one year. Arrowood, a local Santa Rosa native, is also a master at botrytized late harvest wines. The founders of this very successful winery were W. Kenneth Sheffield and Robert and Edward Merzoian, who come from a family that is an important factor in the Central Valley table grape business. Merzoian and the Sheffields have also built a new winery near the Sonoma coast that produces only sparkling wine. The winemaker there is Pete Downs. In the fall of 1984 Château St. Jean was sold to Suntory, the large Japanese wine and spirits company that also owns a piece of The Firestone Vineyard (see).

WHITE

☆☆ 1982 VIN BLANC ($5.00) Sonoma. *Fresh, fruity and very attractive.*

☆☆☆ 1982 SAUVIGNON D'OR ($15.00) Sonoma. *12.8% residual sugar. 59% Sauvignon Blanc, 41% Semillon. Superb.*

☆☆☆ 1983 VIN BLANC ($5.25) Sonoma. *Mostly Sauvignon Blanc with five other varieties. A delight.*

☆ 1984 VIN BLANC ($4.75) Sonoma. *Vinous, clean, a bit hard, decent.*

☆☆ 1979 CHARDONNAY ($12.00) Belle Terre, Alexander Valley. *Big, rich, oaky, intense, heavy.*

☆☆ 1980 CHARDONNAY ($13.00) Wildwood, Sonoma Valley. *Earthy, vinous, no middle. Very intense.*

☆☆ 1980 CHARDONNAY ($13.50) Frank Johnson, Sonoma. *Big, fat, vinous. Lacking finesse and balance.*

☆☆ 1980 CHARDONNAY ($14.00) Gauer Ranch, Alexander Valley. *Vinous, earthy, very high extract.*

☆ 1980 CHARDONNAY ($14.00) Hunter Ranch, Sonoma Valley. *Decent but dull—lacks fruit.*

☆☆☆ 1980 CHARDONNAY ($14.00) Jimtown Ranch, Alexander Valley. *Vinous but also with fine acidity, rich and balanced.*

☆☆ 1980 CHARDONNAY ($14.00) McCrea Vineyards, Sonoma Valley. *Rich and pleasant with good crisp acid and soft oak.*

☆☆ 1980 CHARDONNAY ($14.50) St. Jean, Sonoma. *Vinous, decent but a bit flat.*

☆ 1980 CHARDONNAY ($15.00) Belle Terre, Alexander Valley. *Fat, lush, heavy and clumsy.*

☆☆☆ 1980 CHARDONNAY ($18.00) Robert Young, Alexander Valley. *Assertive and toasty, with some crisp fruit. Should age well.*

☆☆☆ 1981 CHARDONNAY ($13.50) Frank Johnson, Sonoma. *Rich, soft, good acidity, high alcohol (14.2%).*

☆☆☆ 1981 CHARDONNAY ($14.00) McCrea Vineyards, Sonoma Valley. *Stunning: rich, varietal, crisp, fresh oak.*

☆☆☆ 1981 CHARDONNAY ($14.75) Hunter Ranch, Sonoma Valley. *Lush, fat, fruity, intense, super.*

☆☆☆ 1981 CHARDONNAY ($14.75) Jimtown Ranch, Alexander Valley. *Crisp and bright with fine varietal complexity.*

☆ 1981 CHARDONNAY ($15.00) Belle Terre, Alexander Valley. *Acidic and fresh, but lacking varietal character.*

☆☆☆☆ 1981 CHARDONNAY ($18.00) Robert Young, Alexander Valley. *Exquisite and complex. Rich and deep, yet very elegant.*

☆☆ 1982 CHARDONNAY ($11.00) Sonoma. *Earthy, decent, lacks finesse.*

☆☆ 1982 CHARDONNAY ($15.50) Belle Terre, Alexander Valley. *Fresh, clean, attractive. Nicely balanced.*

☆ 1982 CHARDONNAY ($15.50) St. Jean, Sonoma. *Off aromas and off flavors.*

☆☆☆ 1982 CHARDONNAY ($18.00) Robert Young, Alexander Valley. *Lush, clean, big, intense.*

☆ 1983 CHARDONNAY ($12.00) Sonoma. *Dull, lacking finesse.*

☆☆☆ 1983 CHARDONNAY ($16.00) Jimtown Ranch, Alexander Valley. *Rich, firm, varietal, clean, complex.*

☆☆☆ 1983 CHARDONNAY ($16.75) Belle Terre, Alexander Valley. *Balanced, rich, oaky, elegant, very stylish.*

☆☆☆ 1983 CHARDONNAY ($18.00) Robert Young, Alexander Valley. *Crisp and balanced, good acidity and complexity.*

☆☆ 1984 CHARDONNAY ($12.00) Sonoma. *Crisp, clean, simple, well made.*

☆☆☆ 1980 FUME BLANC ($9.00) La Petite Etoile, Sonoma. *Lush, fruity, smooth, balanced, holding well.*

☆ 1981 FUME BLANC ($10.00) Sonoma.

☆☆☆ 1982 FUME BLANC ($9.50) St. Jean, Sonoma. *Varietal, clean, ripe and round.*

☆☆☆ 1982 FUME BLANC ($9.75) Sonoma. *Crisp, varietal, clean and very good.*

☆☆ 1982 FUME BLANC ($10.25) St. Jean, Sonoma Valley. *Soft, earthy, decent.*

☆☆☆☆ 1982 FUME BLANC ($10.50) La Petite Etoile, Sonoma. *Rich, rounded, varietal, superb.*

☆☆☆ 1983 FUME BLANC ($9.50) Murphy Ranch, Alexander Valley. *Grassy, intensely varietal, well made and attractive.*

☆☆☆ 1983 FUME BLANC ($10.00) St. Jean, Sonoma Valley. *Rich, clean, balanced, lovely.*

☆☆☆☆ 1983 FUME BLANC ($10.50) La Petite Etoile, Sonoma. *Fresh, clean, balanced, rounded, complex, superb.*

☆☆☆☆ 1984 FUME BLANC ($10.50) La Petite Etoile, Sonoma. *Crisp, tangy, with varietal fruit; lovely balance.*

☆☆☆ 1981 GEWURZTRAMINER ($7.50) Belle Terre, Sonoma.

☆☆☆ 1981 GEWURZTRAMINER ($7.75) Robert Young, Alexander Valley.

☆☆☆☆ 1981 GEWURZTRAMINER ($13.00) Select Late Harvest, Belle Terre, Alexander Valley. *375ml. 18.7% residual sugar. Varietal, honied, unctuous, superb.*

1982 GEWURZTRAMINER ($8.00) Alexander Valley. *Off aromas, some odd flavors but decent fruit.*

☆☆☆ 1982 GEWURZTRAMINER ($8.00) Frank Johnson, Alexander Valley. *1.9% residual sugar. Crisp, snappy, clean and lovely.*

☆☆ 1983 GEWURZTRAMINER ($8.00) Alexander Valley. *0.5% residual sugar. Varietal character, crisp, clean, decent.*

☆☆☆ 1983 GEWURZTRAMINER ($8.00) Frank Johnson, Alexander Valley. *0.7% residual sugar. Lovely varietal character, tart, super.*

☆☆☆ 1983 GEWURZTRAMINER ($14.00) Select Late Harvest, Robert Young, Alexander Valley. *12.5% residual sugar. Varietal, fruity, balanced.*

☆☆☆☆ 1983 GEWURZTRAMINER ($16.00) Selected Late Harvest, Belle Terre, Sonoma. *375ml. 13% residual sugar. Lush, varietal, balanced.*

☆☆☆ 1984 GEWURZTRAMINER ($8.00) Alexander Valley. *0.72% residual sugar. Fresh, crisp, snappy, charming.*

☆☆ 1984 GEWURZTRAMINER ($8.00) 86% Belle Terre, 14% Robert Young, Alexander Valley. *0.73% residual sugar. Crisp, intense, clean, with good fruit.*

☆☆☆ 1984 GEWURZTRAMINER ($8.00) Frank Johnson, Sonoma. *Dry, crisp, clean, tight, varietal.*

☆☆ 1980 JOHANNISBERG RIESLING ($7.00) Belle Terre, Alexander Valley. *3% residual sugar. Crisp, clean, fruity. Showing no signs of age.*

☆☆☆ 1980 JOHANNISBERG RIESLING ($25.00) Individual Dried Bunch Selected Late Harvest, Robert Young, Alexander Valley. *375ml. 23% residual sugar. Lush, clean, balanced, superb.*

☆☆ 1981 JOHANNISBERG RIESLING ($15.00) Select Late Harvest, Belle Terre, Alexander Valley. *14.5% residual sugar. Clean, lush and lovely.*

☆☆☆ 1981 JOHANNISBERG RIESLING ($15.00) Selected Late Harvest, Robert Young, Alexander Valley. *375ml. 15.1% residual sugar. Honied, lush, rich, lovely.*

☆☆☆ 1982 JOHANNISBERG RIESLING ($7.50) Sonoma. *1.7% sugar. Melony and crisp—a good food wine.*

☆☆ 1982 JOHANNISBERG RIESLING ($7.75) Robert Young, Alexander Valley. *1.7% residual sugar. Fleshy, crisp and clean.*

☆☆☆☆ 1982 JOHANNISBERG RIESLING ($12.00) Late Harvest, Robert Young, Alexander Valley. *11% sugar. Balanced and fruity, lush.*

☆☆ 1982 JOHANNISBERG RIESLING ($15.00) Selected Late Harvest, St. Jean, Sonoma Valley. *375ml. 14% residual sugar. Rich, fruity, harsh finish*

☆☆ 1982 JOHANNISBERG RIESLING ($22.50) Select Late Harvest, Robert Young, Alexander Valley. *375ml. 29.5% residual sugar. Thick, syrupy, rich.*

☆☆☆☆ 1982 JOHANNISBERG RIESLING ($22.50) Special Select Late Harvest, Robert Young, Alexander Valley, Sonoma. *375ml. 29.5% residual sugar! Botrytis, rich, crisp, splendid.*

☆☆ 1983 JOHANNISBERG RIESLING ($8.00) Robert Young, Alexander Valley. *2.3% residual sugar. Rich fruit, clean, a bit heavy.*

☆☆☆ 1983 JOHANNISBERG RIESLING ($8.00) Sonoma. *1.6% residual sugar. Fresh, crisp, varietal, delightful.*

☆☆ 1983 JOHANNISBERG RIESLING ($10.00) Late Harvest, Alexander Valley. *7.2% residual sugar. Lush, sweet, balanced, lovely.*

☆☆ 1984 JOHANNISBERG RIESLING ($8.00) Sonoma. *1.4% residual sugar. Varietal, vinous, hard.*

☆☆☆ 1981 PINOT BLANC ($11.00) Robert Young, Alexander Valley. *Firm and fruity with lovely structure.*

☆☆☆ 1982 PINOT BLANC ($11.00) Robert Young, Alexander Valley. *Clean, crisp, lovely fruit and perfect balance.*

☆☆☆ 1983 SAUVIGNON BLANC ($9.75) Sonoma. *Crisp, snappy, varietal, charming.*

SPARKLING

☆☆ 1981 BLANC DE NOIRS ($15.00) Sonoma. *Heavy nose, crisp, tart acidity.*

☆☆☆ 1981 BLANC DE BLANC BRUT ($17.00) Sonoma. *Yeasty, crisp, richly fruity, delicious.*

☆☆☆ 1980 BRUT ($19.00) Sonoma. *Grapey and crisp, with great acidity. Méthode champenoise.*

☆☆☆☆ 1981 BRUT ($17.00) Sonoma. *Yeasty, rich, complex, clean, tangy fruit acid, stunning.*

☆☆☆ 1980 CHARDONNAY ($19.00) Blanc de Blanc, Sonoma. *Fruity, deep, great acidity.*

RED

☆☆☆ 1978 CABERNET SAUVIGNON ($17.00) Glen Ellen, Sonoma. *Rich, fruity, clean and lovely. Will continue to improve.*

☆☆☆☆ 1979 CABERNET SAUVIGNON ($17.00) Wildwood, Sonoma Valley. *Rich, deep, fruity, complicated and superb. Drink 1987.*

Château Ste. Michelle
WASHINGTON

One Stimson Lane, Woodinville, Washington 98072 (206-488-1133). FOUNDED: 1967. ACREAGE: 2,900 acres. DISTRIBUTION: Nationwide and some international markets. OWNER: U.S. Tobacco Company. Allen C. Shoup, president. WINEMAKERS: Peter Bachman, winemaster; Cheryl Barber, winemaker, white and rosé; Doug Gore, winemaker, red wine. OTHER LABEL: Farron Ridge Cellars. Tours and tasting daily 10 A.M.–4:30 P.M. Gift shop.

The largest winery in all of the Pacific Northwest, this burgeoning company just opened a $26-million winery, its third, and expects to grow into one of the United States' most prolific and respected operations. Right now, four out of five bottles of wine made in Washington are made by Château Ste. Michelle. The winery's 2,900 acres of vineyard are on the east side of the Cascade Mountains, where the soil is light, rainfall is minimal, and temperatures are similar to southern Napa Valley. All grape vines are planted on their own rootstock. Consultant André Tchelistcheff, former winemaker Joel Klein, and current winemaster Peter Bachman have all contributed to the remarkable success of this winery, which is owned by the United States Tobacco Company, a leading producer of snuff.

WHITE

☆☆ NV FARRON RIDGE CELLARS WHITE TABLE WINE ($3.10) Washington. *Crisp,*
clean, fresh, attractive.

☆☆ 1981 CHARDONNAY ($9.50) Washington. *Fruity and clean.*

☆☆ 1982 CHARDONNAY ($9.75) Washington. *Fresh, clean, varietal, simple.*

☆☆☆ 1981 CHENIN BLANC ($5.50) Washington. *Crisp, fruity and clean with a nice sugar-*
acid balance.

☆☆☆ 1982 CHENIN BLANC ($5.50) Washington. *Tangy, fresh and delightful. Lush, off-dry.*

☆ 1983 CHENIN BLANC ($5.50) Washington.

☆☆ 1981 FUME BLANC ($6.75) Washington.

1983 FUME BLANC ($7.50) Washington State. *Dirty, varnishy, unattractive.*

1982 GEWURZTRAMINER ($6.00) Washington. *Dull, lacking varietal character.*

1983 GEWURZTRAMINER ($5.60) Washington. *Some oxidation, lacking fruit.*

1981 JOHANNISBERG RIESLING ($5.50) Washington.

☆ 1982 JOHANNISBERG RIESLING ($5.50) Washington.

☆☆ 1983 JOHANNISBERG RIESLING ($6.00) Washington. *Dry, crisp, clean, richly varietal.*
Excellent.

☆☆☆ 1982 SEMILLON BLANC ($5.00) Washington. *Crisp, yet soft and rounded.*

O 1982 WHITE RIESLING ($6.90) Limited Bottling, Washington. *Musty, oxidized.*

SPARKLING

☆☆ 1978 BLANC DE NOIRS BRUT ($22.50) Washington. *Spicy, clean, balanced, dense,*
lovely.

RED

☆☆ 1976 CABERNET SAUVIGNON Washington.

O 1978 CABERNET SAUVIGNON ($9.00) Washington State. *Skunky, vegetal.*

☆ 1978 CABERNET SAUVIGNON ($17.00) Château Reserve, Cold Creek, Benton County,
Washington. *Meaty, clean, decent. Drink now.*

☆ 1979 CABERNET SAUVIGNON ($17.00) Cold Creek, Benton County, Washington. *Rai-*
siny, clean and lacking in fresh fruit.

☆ 1980 CABERNET SAUVIGNON ($9.00) Washington. *Dull, dreary, lacking fruit.*

☆☆ 1980 CABERNET SAUVIGNON ($16.00) Reserve, Cole Ranch, Washington. *Minty, in-*
tense, clean and very well made. Attractive.

☆☆ 1978 MERLOT ($7.00) Washington State. *Light, clean and pleasant.*

☆☆ 1980 MERLOT ($7.25) Washington. *Varietal, clean, light and attractive.*

Chehalen Mountain Winery
OREGON

Route 1, Box 99C, Newberg, Oregon 97132 (503-628-2417). FOUNDED: 1979. ACREAGE: 35
acres. PRODUCTION: 8,500 cases. DISTRIBUTION: Oregon and Washington. OWNERS: Pat
and Zane Mulhausen. WINEMAKER: Zane Mulhausen. OTHER LABEL: Mulhausen. Tours by
appointment. Tasting weekends 12–5 P.M.

Zane Mulhausen is a former mechanical engineer who began planting his hillside vineyard in 1973. He and his wife, Pat, built their winery-home overlooking the Tualatin Valley and were bonded in 1979. Mulhausen, who is very much a loner, produces wines from his own grapes and from purchased fruit.

WHITE

☆☆☆   1982 MULHAUSEN WHITE RIESLING ($6.40) Willamette Valley, Oregon. *Very crisp and elegant, snappy with lovely fruit.*

RED

1982 MULHAUSEN PINOT NOIR ($9.00) Maresh, Oregon. *Flabby, dull, lacking structure.*

Chermont Winery
VIRGINIA

Route 1, Box 59, Esmont, Virginia 22937 (804-286-2639). FOUNDED: 1981. ACREAGE: 10 acres. PRODUCTION: 2,000 cases. DISTRIBUTION: Local. OWNER: Corporation. John O. Sherman, Jr., president and manager. WINEMAKER: John O. Sherman, Jr.; Nick Hammer, assistant winemaker. Tours by appointment.

Navy captain John O. Sherman, Jr., became interested in wine while he was stationed in Los Altos, California, in the early 1950s. His interest increased during a tour of duty in Europe. Upon retirement in 1977, after 33 years of service, he found a home in Virginia with a basement, a detached garage, and enough plantable acreage to stake his first vines of Chardonnay and Cabernet Sauvignon. Over the next four years, he filled out his ten-acre vineyard with Riesling.

WHITE

O   1981 CHARDONNAY ($6.00) Albemarle County, Virginia. *Fat, oxidized, earthy, not much fruit.*

RED

☆   1981 CABERNET SAUVIGNON ($7.50) Albemarle County, Virginia. *Toasty nose, rich, complex, clean, varietal, a bit simple.*

CHEVRIOT DU LAC *see* Château du Lac

Chicama Vineyards
MASSACHUSETTS

Stoney Hill Road, West Tisbury, Massachusetts 02575 (617-693-0309). FOUNDED: 1971. ACREAGE: 35 acres. PRODUCTION: 10,000 cases. DISTRIBUTION: Massachusetts and New Hampshire. OWNERS: George and Catherine Mathiesen. WINEMAKERS: George and Catherine Mathiesen, Lynn Hoeft, and Timothy Mathiesen. Tours and tasting April–September. Call winery for more information. Christmas shop open November 24–December 24 11 A.M.–5 P.M.

If they had stayed in California a while longer, George and Catherine Mathiesen would probably be making California wine today. But George's job with Westinghouse Broadcasting Company moved them first to the Midwest and finally to New England. They didn't seriously consider starting a vineyard there until Dr. Konstantin Frank convinced them that it was possible to grow vinifera on the East Coast. Scouting weather charts and reports, the Mathiesens found an ideal 58-acre parcel. With vine cuttings supplied by Dr. Frank, they planted the first commercial vinifera vineyard in Massachusetts and started the first commercial winery on the island of Martha's Vineyard.

SPARKLING

☆ NV SEA MIST ($10.00) Massachusetts. *Fruity, clean, some bitterness.*

RED

1980 CABERNET SAUVIGNON ($12.50) Massachusetts. *Grapey, clumsy, tannic, decent.*

Chispa Cellars
CALAVERAS COUNTY

P.O. Box 255, Murphys, California 95247 (209-728-2106). FOUNDED: 1976. ACREAGE: None. PRODUCTION: 400 cases. DISTRIBUTION: California. OWNER: Robert J. Bliss. WINEMAKER: Robert J. Bliss. Tours and tasting by appointment.

"Chispa" is a term that was used in Calaveras and Tulare counties during the Gold Rush. It meant "nugget." Robert Bliss, a friendly if somewhat shy mountain man, began his winery in a low-ceilinged, cramped basement with the help of a winemaking friend. Too many stiff backs prompted Robert to move the winery into a larger building—a vaulted barn that had once served as a feed store.

RED

☆☆☆ 1980 ZINFANDEL ($6.00) Amador. *Ripe and varietal but very soft and attractive.*

John Christ Winery
OHIO

32421 Walker Road, Avon Lake, Ohio 44012 (216-933-3046). FOUNDED: 1946. ACREAGE: 20 acres. PRODUCTION: 2,000 cases. DISTRIBUTION: Local. OWNER: Alex Christ. WINE-MAKER: Alex Christ. Tours by appointment. Tasting and sales Monday–Friday 9 A.M.–8 P.M.

His original plan was to grow grapes and live off the profits, but when that didn't pan out, John Christ started making wine in his cellar. The winery grew from there—out the back door, into a new building and a new cellar. After John retired in 1962, his son Alex took over. Alex worked for B. F. Goodrich for 29 years before he resigned in 1984 to devote his full time to the vineyards and the winery.

The Christian Brothers
NAPA COUNTY

4411 Redwood Road, Napa, California 94558 (707-226-5566). FOUNDED: 1882. ACREAGE: 1,200 acres. PRODUCTION: 1 million cases. DISTRIBUTION: Worldwide. OWNER: The Christian Brothers of California. Brother David Brennan F.S.C., president. OTHER LABELS: Mont La Salle, Altar Wines. Tours and tasting daily 10:30 A.M.–4 P.M. at Greystone Cellars, 2555 Main Street, St. Helena. Gift shop.

The Christian Brothers is an order of the Catholic church dedicated to education. The brothers operate schools all over the world, which their winemaking activities help to support. Originally located in Martinez, wine activities were moved to the Napa Valley in 1950 with the purchase of the historic Greystone Cellars. Headquarters are presently at the picturesque Mont La Salle winery located in the hills on the west side of the valley, but most wines are made at a modern facility just south of St. Helena. Christian Brothers is the largest winery in the Napa Valley, producing wines made from estate-grown grapes as well as grapes purchased from independent growers.

WHITE

☆ NV   CHARDONNAY ($7.50) Napa Valley. *Underripe, clean and decent.*
☆ 1981 CHARDONNAY ($9.00) Napa Valley. *Simple and crisp.*
☆☆ NV   CHENIN BLANC ($4.50) Napa Valley. *Crisp, clean, quite decent.*
☆ NV   FUME BLANC, CUVEE 811 ($5.00) Napa Valley.
☆☆ NV   FUME BLANC, CUVEE 812 ($5.00) Napa Valley. *Snappy, grassy, fresh, attractive.*
  NV   FUME BLANC ($6.00) Napa Valley. *Dull, no freshness.*
  NV   GREY RIESLING ($5.00) Napa Valley.
☆☆ NV   JOHANNISBERG RIESLING ($4.75) Napa Valley. *0.7% residual sugar. Round, varietal, crisp.*

SPARKLING

☆ NV   ROSE CHAMPAGNE ($1.75) California. *Lush, sweet and drinkable.*
  NV   BRUT ($4.50) California. *A bit flabby. Charmat.*
☆ NV   EXTRA DRY ($5.75) California.
  NV   EXTRA COLD DUCK ($6.50) California. *Sweet and syrupy.*

RED

☆☆ 1975 CABERNET SAUVIGNON ($7.00) Napa Valley. *Soft, elegant, a bit thin.*
☆☆ 1977 CABERNET SAUVIGNON ($7.50) Napa Valley. *Herbal, lean and nicely made. Lacks power. Drink now.*
☆ 1978 CABERNET SAUVIGNON ($8.00) Napa Valley. *Soft, elegant, ready to drink now.*
  NV   GAMAY NOIR ($4.00) Napa Valley.
☆ NV   ZINFANDEL ($4.50) Napa.
☆ 1978 ZINFANDEL ($8.00) Special Harvest, Napa Valley.
☆☆ 1979 ZINFANDEL ($5.00) Napa Valley. *Lush, soft and clean. Showing some age.*

Christina Wine Cellars
WISCONSIN

109 Vine Street, LaCrosse, Wisconsin 54601 (608-785-2210). FOUNDED: 1979. ACREAGE: None. PRODUCTION: 4,000 cases. DISTRIBUTION: At winery. OWNER: Lawlor family. Robert Lawlor, manager. WINEMAKERS: Christina and Tim Lawlor. Tours May–October: Monday–Saturday 1 P.M.–3 P.M. Tasting Monday–Saturday 10 A.M.–8 P.M., Sunday 12–5 P.M.

Robert Lawlor was so interested in winemaking that he urged his daughter Christina to go to Fresno State College in California and study enology. Upon her graduation, the Lawlor family started their first winery in McGregor, Iowa. Since then, the family has opened a new winery in LaCrosse, in the old Milwaukee depot alongside the Freight House Restaurant. Christina and her brother Scott opened yet another winery in Galena, Illinois. Each of the Lawlor kids now has a winery to run, with Christina splitting her time between all three.

Cilurzo Vineyard and Winery
RIVERSIDE COUNTY

41220 Calle Contento, Temecula, California 92390 (714-676-5250). FOUNDED: 1978. ACREAGE: 10 acres. PRODUCTION: 8,500 cases. DISTRIBUTION: Western U.S. OWNERS: Vincenzo and Audrey Cilurzo. WINEMAKER: Vincenzo Cilurzo. Tours and tasting daily 9 A.M.–5 P.M. Small gift shop.

Vincenzo Cilurzo still does the lighting on the Merv Griffin Show, but he is spending more and more time at his winery with his wife, Audrey, and their children, Chenin and Vinnie. An Emmy award–winning lighting director, Vincenzo planted the first vineyard in the Temecula area in 1968. According to him, this area is exactly like the middle to northern sections of the Napa Valley. "Wine is in my blood and I can't do anything about it," Vincenzo explains. If the vicissitudes of making wine in Temecula's climate don't stop him, nothing will.

WHITE

☆ 1982 CHARDONNAY ($6.95) Temecula. *Fresh, some oxidation, some depth.*
  1982 CHENIN BLANC ($4.95) Temecula. *Thin and watery.*
  1983 CHENIN BLANC ($5.00) Temecula. *Dry, dull, unappealing. 0.45% residual sugar.*
☆ 1982 FUME BLANC ($5.00) Temecula. *Soft, slightly sweet, clean.*

RED

☆☆ NV VINCHENO ($4.00)
○ 1980 CABERNET SAUVIGNON ($5.00) La Cresta and Long Valley, Temecula. *Vegetal, unattractive.*
☆ 1980 PETITE SIRAH ($6.95) Temecula. *Intense, cooked, dull.*

Cimmaron Cellars
OKLAHOMA

Route 1, Box 79, Caney, Oklahoma 74533 (405-889-6312). FOUNDED: 1983. ACREAGE: 40 acres. PRODUCTION: 2,000 cases. DISTRIBUTION: Oklahoma. OWNERS: Dwayne and Linda Pool. WINEMAKER: Dwayne Pool. Tours by appointment only.

When the Pools moved to Oklahoma from Napa, California, they discovered an abandoned 40-acre vineyard. For some reason, the idea of growing grapes in Oklahoma, and perhaps starting a winery someday, did not seem farfetched. They purchased the property, brought vigor back to vines that had not been touched in years, and sold most of their crop to a winery in Texas. Their own winery was a dream scheduled for much later, but in 1983 the crop was so large that they had to quickly build a winery and plunge head first into the wine business.

RED

1983 MARECHAL FOCH ($4.50) Oklahoma.

Claiborne & Churchill Vintners
SAN LUIS OBISPO COUNTY

2585 Biddle Ranch Road, San Luis Obispo, California 93401 (805-544-9594). FOUNDED: 1983. ACREAGE: None. PRODUCTION: 1,100 cases. DISTRIBUTION: California and other markets.

OWNERS: Claiborne Thompson and Fredrika Churchill. WINEMAKER: Claiborne Thompson. Tours by appointment only. No tasting.

Claiborne Thompson left his position as professor of Scandinavian languages in Ann Arbor, Michigan, to move to California. He started working at Edna Valley Vineyards, where he learned the basics of winemaking and sales. After three years at Edna Valley, Claiborne and his wife, Fredrika Churchill, started their own label. Using the facilities at Edna Valley "for a small fee," Claiborne started making Riesling and Gewürztraminer in a dry, Alsatian style. "They are meant to be dinner wines, not sweet sipping wines," says Claiborne.

WHITE

☆☆ NV EDELZWICKER ($4.75) Edna Valley. *50% Riesling, 50% Gewürztraminer. Fresh, tangy, clean.*

☆☆☆ 1983 GEWURZTRAMINER ($8.50) Edna Valley. *Dry. Floral, varietal, crisp, elegant.*

Clarke Vineyard
CONNECTICUT

Route 2, Box 151 C, Taugwonk Road, Stonington, Connecticut 06378 (203-535-0235). FOUNDED: 1983. ACREAGE: 12 acres. PRODUCTION: 2,000 cases. DISTRIBUTION: Connecticut. OWNER: Barbara Clarke. WINEMAKER: Tom Clarke. Tours and tasting Tuesday–Sunday 10 A.M.–5 P.M.

Since boyhood, Tom Clarke had been fascinated with grape growing and winemaking. Everywhere he lived, from Chicago to Baton Rouge, he planted vines. After meeting Dr. Konstantine Frank, Tom planted his first vinifera vineyard in Marlboro, New York, using the grafted vines from Dr. Frank's own vineyard. Then Connecticut passed the Farm Winery Act, so Tom, who sells construction equipment when he's not planting vineyards, and his wife bought 58 acres in Stonington in 1979. The vineyards were planted in 1979, and in 1983 the winery was built. Barbara became keeper of the vineyards while Tom delved deeply into the mysteries of winemaking. Since the winery is located right next to the Mystic Seaport, the Clarkes chose a nautical logo for their label.

CLEVELAND *see* Dover Vineyards

Cline Cellars
CONTRA COSTA COUNTY

Route 2, Box 175 C, Oakeley, California 94561 (415-754-0652). FOUNDED: 1933. ACREAGE: 5 acres. PRODUCTION: 3,000 cases. DISTRIBUTION: California. OWNER: Fred Cline. WINEMAKER: Fred Cline. Tours and tasting summer: daily 9 A.M.–6 P.M.; winter: daily 9 A.M.–5 P.M.

Fred Cline bought the old Firpo Winery when the original owners died. It had to be completely renovated into a producing winery because the Firpos hadn't made wine at the facility for over twenty years—they had been using it just as a retail outlet. Fred is a farmer; he raises grain and almonds on his grandparents' farm. His grandfather was the one who introduced Fred to the wonderful world of winemaking. "I learned from him and then I went to U.C. Davis," says Fred. On the grounds of the winery is Cline Nursery, owned and managed by Fred's brother Mike.

WHITE

☆ 1983 SAUVIGNON BLANC ($5.00) North Coast. *Chalky, simple, decent.*

Clinton Vineyards
NEW YORK

Schultzville Road, Clinton Corners, New York 12514 (914-266-5372). FOUNDED: 1975. ACREAGE: 15 acres. PRODUCTION: 4,000 cases. DISTRIBUTION: New York. OWNERS: Ben and Kathy Feder. WINEMAKER: Ben Feder. Tours by appointment.

For their part in the revival of the Hudson River region's wine tradition, Ben and Kathy Feder shooed the cattle off their ranch in the early 1970s and planted Seyval Blanc. Clinton Vineyards became the first eastern winery to specialize in one wine. Now that the champagne cellar is finished, the winery makes one wine and one sparkling wine, a méthode champenoise sparkling Seyval.

WHITE

☆☆   1982 SEYVAL BLANC ($6.00) Estate, Hudson River region. *Snappy and dry.*

Clos du Bois Winery
SONOMA COUNTY

5 Fitch Street, Healdsburg, California 95448 (707-433-5576). FOUNDED: 1964. ACREAGE: 650 acres. PRODUCTION: 85,000 cases. DISTRIBUTION: Nationwide, Canada, England, and Puerto Rico. OWNER: Frank M. Woods. Tom Hobart, manager. WINEMAKER: John Hawley. OTHER LABEL: River Oaks. Tours and tasting weekdays 12–4 P.M.; weekends and holidays 10 A.M.– 4 P.M.

Frank Woods, president of Clos du Bois, is a keen marketing man. A graduate of Cornell University's hotel management school, Frank worked in the advertising department of Proctor and Gamble, then started his own marketing firm before he put together his successful winery business, which also includes River Oaks Vineyards. Clos du Bois is the premium line, produced from estate-grown grapes and given careful oak aging. River Oaks wines, also made from owned vineyards in the Alexander Valley, tend to be less expensive, made more simply, and released younger. Wines from both lines are vinified at the same facility in Healdsburg.

WHITE

☆   NV RIVER OAKS VINEYARDS PREMIUM DRY WHITE ($3.25) Alexander Valley. *55% French Colombard, 32% Sauvignon Vert, 13% Gewürztraminer. Fresh, simple, dull.*

☆   1982 RIVER OAKS VINEYARDS ($3.25) Sonoma. *54% French Colombard, 33% Sauvignon Vert, 13% Gewürztraminer.*

☆☆   1980 CHARDONNAY ($18.00) Proprietor's Reserve, Alexander Valley. *Fresh, bright, snappy and attractive.*

☆☆☆   1980 CHARDONNAY ($21.00) Flintwood, Dry Creek Valley. *Snappy, lovely balance between oak and fruit, elegant.*

☆   1981 RIVER OAKS VINEYARDS CHARDONNAY ($7.00) Alexander Valley.

☆☆☆   1981 CHARDONNAY ($9.75) Alexander Valley. *Apples and fresh fruit in the nose with a clean, lemony taste.*

☆☆☆   1981 CHARDONNAY ($12.00) Calcaire, Alexander Valley.

☆☆☆   1981 CHARDONNAY ($21.00) Flintwood, Dry Creek Valley. *Lovely fruit and oak, nicely rounded.*

☆☆   1982 RIVER OAKS VINEYARDS CHARDONNAY ($6.25) Sonoma. *Nice, rich, clean, well made.*

☆☆☆   1982 CHARDONNAY ($9.00) Barrel Fermented, Alexander Valley. *Rich, toasty, intense, with good, crisp fruit.*

☆☆☆   1982 CHARDONNAY ($11.25) Calcaire, Alexander Valley. *Crisp, clean, tangy, very good.*

☆☆ 1982 CHARDONNAY ($11.25) Flintwood, Dry Creek Valley. *Toasty, earthy, nice fruit.*

☆☆ 1983 RIVER OAKS VINEYARDS CHARDONNAY ($6.00) Sonoma. *Fresh, clean, varietal, low-key, attractive.*

☆☆ 1984 CHARDONNAY ($6.00) Alexander Valley. *Woody, clean, appealing.*

☆☆ 1984 RIVER OAKS VINEYARDS CHARDONNAY ($6.00) Alexander Valley. *Fresh, fruity, simple but quite attractive.*

☆☆ 1981 RIVER OAKS VINEYARDS FRENCH COLOMBARD ($4.50) Alexander Valley. *Big and rich with some oak complexity.*

☆☆ 1979 GEWURZTRAMINER ($6.50) Late Harvest, Sonoma. 6.2% residual sugar. *Crisp, clean and pleasant. A bit short.*

☆☆ 1981 GEWURZTRAMINER ($7.00) Early Harvest, Alexander Valley. 1.6% residual sugar. *Fruity, clean, soft and attractive.*

☆ 1981 GEWURZTRAMINER ($40.00) Individual Bunch Selected, Late Harvest, Sonoma. 19.48% residual sugar. *Rich but spoiled by vegetal flavors.*

☆☆ 1982 GEWURZTRAMINER ($7.50) Early Harvest, Alexander Valley. 1.5% residual sugar. *Soft, crisp, fruity, not varietal.*

☆☆☆ 1983 GEWURZTRAMINER ($7.50) Early Harvest, Alexander Valley. 1.4% residual sugar. *Varietal, rich, fruity, crisp, superb.*

☆ 1981 JOHANNISBERG RIESLING ($12.50) Late Harvest, Individual Bunch, Sonoma. 375ml. 13.8% residual sugar. *Volatile acidity, rich.*

☆☆ 1982 JOHANNISBERG RIESLING ($6.50) Early Harvest, Alexander Valley. 1.7% residual sugar. *Crisp lemon and green apple flavors.*

☆☆☆ 1982 JOHANNISBERG RIESLING ($20.00) Individual Bunch Late Harvest, Alexander Valley. 13.5% residual sugar. *Exquisite, fruity, deep and honied.*

1983 RIVER OAKS VINEYARDS JOHANNISBERG RIESLING ($5.50) Alexander Valley. 1.67% residual sugar. *Lacking varietal character, dull.*

1983 JOHANNISBERG RIESLING ($6.50) Early Harvest, Sonoma. *Strange nose, not up to standard.*

☆☆☆ 1983 JOHANNISBERG RIESLING ($12.50) Late Harvest, Alexander Valley. 15.7% residual sugar. *Fresh, lovely, botrytized, lush.*

☆☆☆ 1982 SAUVIGNON BLANC ($8.00) Alexander Valley. *Richly varietal, controlled grassiness, great fruit, lovely.*

☆☆☆ 1983 SAUVIGNON BLANC ($7.00) Sonoma. 19% Semillon. *Lush, attractive, clean, fat and rounded.*

RED

☆☆ NV RED WINE–VIN ROUGE ($4.35) Sonoma. *Simple but fruity and appealing.*

☆☆ NV RIVER OAKS VINEYARDS PREMIUM RED ($4.00) Sonoma. *Crisp, fresh and tangy.*

☆☆☆ 1977 RIVER OAKS VINEYARDS PREMIUM RED ($3.25) Alexander Valley. 54% Zinfandel, 23% Pinot Noir, 23% Estate. *Crisp, berries, depth; lovely.*

☆☆ 1979 MARLSTONE ($15.00) Sonoma.

☆☆ 1978 CABERNET SAUVIGNON ($12.00) Briarcrest, Alexander Valley. *Soft, herbal, lovely.*

O 1978 CABERNET SAUVIGNON ($12.50) Woodleaf, Sonoma. *Tanky, dull, nothing much.*

☆ 1978 CABERNET SAUVIGNON ($19.25) Proprietor's Reserve, Dry Creek Valley. *A bit weedy, but clean. Beginning to fade.*

☆☆☆ 1979 RIVER OAKS VINEYARDS CABERNET SAUVIGNON ($5.95) Alexander Valley. *Simple, herbal, clean and fruity. Drink now.*

☆☆ 1979 CABERNET SAUVIGNON ($9.00) Dry Creek Valley. *Simple and very nice.*

1980 CABERNET SAUVIGNON ($9.50) Sonoma. *Weedy and dull, lacking fruit.*

☆☆☆ 1980 CABERNET SAUVIGNON ($15.00) Marlstone, Alexander Valley. 55% Cabernet, 45% Merlot. *Rich and herbal, velvety and super.*

☆☆☆ 1981 RIVER OAKS VINEYARDS CABERNET SAUVIGNON ($6.25) Healdsburg area, Sonoma. *Rich, deep, great fruit, lovely balance. Drink now.*

☆☆☆ 1982 CABERNET SAUVIGNON ($6.00) Alexander Valley. *Rich, soft, varietal, deep, charming. Drink now.*

☆☆ 1982 RIVER OAKS VINEYARDS CABERNET SAUVIGNON ($6.50) Sonoma. *Lush, clean and simple, but very attractive. Drink now.*

☆☆ 1979 MERLOT ($8.00) Napa Valley. *25% Cabernet. Balanced, clean and decent.*

☆☆☆ 1981 MERLOT ($8.50) Alexander Valley. *Fragrant, firm, rich and balanced.*

☆☆ 1982 MERLOT ($8.50) Alexander Valley. *20% Cabernet. Ripe, lush, balanced. Drink now.*

1978 PINOT NOIR ($6.20) Cherry Hill, Dry Creek Valley.

O 1979 PINOT NOIR ($6.00) Alexander Valley. *Thin and stinky.*

☆☆ 1979 PINOT NOIR ($6.00) Dry Creek.

☆☆☆ 1979 PINOT NOIR ($8.50) Cherry Hill, Dry Creek Valley. *Richly varietal, crisp and tangy.*

☆☆ 1980 PINOT NOIR ($6.50) Alexander Valley. *Crisp, clean, fresh, modestly attractive.*

☆ 1980 PINOT NOIR ($10.75) Proprietor's Reserve, Dry Creek Valley. *Rich, dense, with some bitterness, decent. Drink 1986.*

☆☆ 1981 PINOT NOIR ($7.00) Dry Creek Valley. *Crisp, clean, attractive, simple but nice. Drink now.*

☆☆ 1978 ZINFANDEL ($8.50) Napa Valley.

☆☆☆ 1980 RIVER OAKS VINEYARDS ZINFANDEL ($7.00) Private Reserve, Alexander Valley. *Rich and balanced with lovely varietal character. Drink now.*

Clos du Val
NAPA COUNTY

5330 Silverado Trail, Napa, California 94558 (707-252-6711). FOUNDED: 1972. ACREAGE: 300 acres. PRODUCTION: 45,000 cases. DISTRIBUTION: Major national and international markets. OWNER: John Goelet. WINEMAKER: Bernard M. Portet. OTHER LABEL: Gran Val. Tours and tasting Monday–Saturday 10 A.M.–4 P.M.

Bernard Portet came to California by way of France, where his father was cellarmaster at Château Lafite-Rothschild, and Chile, where he met his wife. The winery, built on the Silverado Trail in the eastern Napa Valley, set out to make long-lived, Bordeaux-style Cabernet Sauvignon, softened with a dose of Merlot. Wines are made from 120 acres of vineyard planted near the winery and a new 180-acre piece in the Carneros region, which grows mostly Chardonnay and Pinot Noir. Some additional fruit is purchased from selected growers.

WHITE

☆☆☆ 1981 CHARDONNAY ($12.50) Napa Valley. *Refined and lovely. Clean, rich, mature.*

☆☆ 1982 CHARDONNAY ($12.50) Napa Valley. *Lemony, fresh and appealing.*

1982 GRAN VAL CHARDONNAY ($12.50) Napa Valley.

☆ 1983 GRAN VAL CHARDONNAY ($8.00) California. *Snappy, clean, simple.*

☆☆ 1983 CHARDONNAY ($11.50) Napa Valley. *Spicy, nice oak, decent.*

☆ 1982 SAUVIGNON BLANC ($7.00) Napa Valley. *Odd minty nose, lemony and tart, with a twinge of bitterness.*

☆☆☆ 1983 SEMILLON ($7.50) California. *20% Sauvignon Blanc. Lovely, clean, fresh, floral.*

RED

☆☆ NV RED TABLE WINE ($4.50) Napa Valley. *Fresh, clean, moderately complex, quite pleasant.*

☆☆☆☆ 1974 CABERNET SAUVIGNON ($12.50) Napa Valley. *At its peak: complex, rich, silky, superb.*

☆☆ 1975 CABERNET SAUVIGNON Napa Valley. *15% Merlot. Light, a bit thin in middle, good structure.*

☆☆ 1976 CABERNET SAUVIGNON ($9.00) Napa Valley.

☆☆ 1977 CABERNET SAUVIGNON ($10.00) Napa Valley. *Herbal, clean, drink now.*

☆☆ 1977 CABERNET SAUVIGNON ($20.00) Reserve, Napa Valley. *Well made but disappointing. Lacking fruit and depth.*

☆☆☆ 1978 CABERNET SAUVIGNON ($12.00) Napa Valley. *Varietal, ripe, crisp and aristocratic. Drink 1986.*

☆☆☆ 1978 CABERNET SAUVIGNON ($25.00) Reserve, Napa Valley. *Silky and elegant, fruity and complex. Drink 1986 and beyond.*

☆☆☆ 1979 CABERNET SAUVIGNON ($12.50) Napa Valley. *Elegant, varietal, long finish. Drink 1989 and beyond.*

☆☆☆ 1979 CABERNET SAUVIGNON ($25.00) Reserve, Napa Valley. *Fat and rich with lovely structure and depth. Drink 1987.*

☆☆☆☆ 1980 CABERNET SAUVIGNON ($12.50) Napa Valley. *Stunning, rich, deep, velvety. Will age beautifully.*

☆☆☆☆ 1981 CABERNET SAUVIGNON ($12.50) Napa Valley. *Soft, rich, complex, elegant, superb. Drink 1988 and beyond.*

☆☆ 1982 GRAN VAL CABERNET SAUVIGNON ($7.50) Napa Valley. *Fresh, fruity, clean, delightful for present drinking.*

☆☆☆ 1982 CABERNET SAUVIGNON ($13.00) Napa Valley. *10% Merlot. Rich, soft, intense, complex, superb. Drink 1986.*

☆☆☆ 1978 MERLOT ($10.00) Napa Valley. *Structured and attractive. Drink now.*

☆☆ 1979 MERLOT ($12.00) Napa Valley. *Snappy, fruity, tannic. Drink 1986 and beyond.*

☆☆☆ 1980 MERLOT ($12.50) Napa Valley. *Dense, rich, complex and stylish. Should age gracefully.*

☆☆☆ 1981 MERLOT ($13.50) Napa Valley. *Soft and herbal; clean, rich and lovely. Great structure.*

☆☆☆ 1982 MERLOT ($12.50) Napa Valley. *Deeply colored, plummy, ripe, structured. Drink 1986.*

☆☆☆ 1984 MERLOT ($12.50) Napa Valley. *Ripe, fruity, clean and elegant. Drink 1988.*

☆☆☆ 1980 PINOT NOIR ($10.00) Napa Valley. *From the Madonna Vineyard used by Acacia. Rich and superb.*

☆ 1981 PINOT NOIR ($9.75) Napa Valley. *O.K. structure and stemmy flavors.*

☆☆ 1981 PINOT NOIR ($10.75) Proprietor's Reserve, Sonoma. *Spicy, varietal, decent, some green flavors.*

☆ 1982 PINOT NOIR ($10.75) Napa Valley. *Odd, off aromas, meaty, decent acid, good balance.*

☆☆ 1973 ZINFANDEL Napa Valley. *Rich, elegant, clean, nice.*

☆☆☆ 1977 ZINFANDEL ($7.50) Napa Valley. *Peppery, rich, berried. Drink now.*

☆☆☆ 1979 ZINFANDEL ($10.00) Napa Valley. *Elegant, well-bred, delightful. Should mature gracefully.*

☆☆☆ 1980 ZINFANDEL ($9.00) Napa Valley. *Berried but beautifully structured, clean and snappy.*

☆☆ 1981 ZINFANDEL ($9.00) Napa Valley. *Elegant and well built but lacking fruit.*

☆☆☆ 1983 ZINFANDEL ($9.00) Napa Valley. *Rich, fresh, elegant and clean; firm structure. Drink 1986.*

Cloudstone Vineyards
SANTA CLARA COUNTY

27345 Deer Springs Way, Los Altos Hills, California 94022 (415-948-8621). FOUNDED: 1980. ACREAGE: 0.25 acre. PRODUCTION: 600 cases. DISTRIBUTION: California. OWNERS: Peter L. and Judith Wolken. WINEMAKER: Peter L. Wolken. Tours and tasting by appointment.

Peter and Judith Wolken planted a Zinfandel vineyard on the hillside behind their Los Altos home. When the vines began to produce, Peter, who had lived in Europe for seven years, made a few experimental batches of wine. The results were encouraging enough to convince the Wolkens to build and bond their own winery in 1981. Plans are to keep the winery small

RED

☆☆   1981 CABERNET SAUVIGNON ($12.00) Santa Cruz.

Colonial Vineyards
OHIO

6222 N.S.R. 48, Lebanon, Ohio 45036 (513-932-3842). FOUNDED: 1978. ACREAGE: 20 acres. PRODUCTION: 1,500 cases. DISTRIBUTION: Ohio. OWNERS: Norman and Marion Greene. WINEMAKER: Norman Greene. Tours and tasting Monday–Saturday 11 A.M.–8 P.M. Summer pig roasts, winter potluck dinners.

It was not an urge to grow grapes so much as a desire to live on a farm that motivated Norman Greene to buy twenty acres of land in 1973. While working as a systems analyst for National Cash Register Corporation, Norman, led by his keen interest in wine, started his own winery business. He began by planting some French-American hybrids in 1974 and made his first commercial wines in 1977. He revamped three barns on his property, one for processing, one for bottling and storage, and one, which dates back to 1857, for a tasting room. Norman has computerized all winery records, sales, inventory, and projections, which affords him a complete overview of his business. According to Norman, the computer allows him to keep the winery at a hobby size. He and his wife are the only employees.

Colony
SONOMA COUNTY

26150 Asti Road, Asti, California 95413 (707-894-2541). FOUNDED: 1881. ACREAGE: None. PRODUCTION: 500,000 cases. DISTRIBUTION: Nationwide. OWNER: ISC Wines of California. Richard McCombs, chief executive officer. WINEMAKER: Edmund A. Rossi, Jr. OTHER LABELS: Italian Swiss Colony, Petri, Lejon, Jacques Bonet, Gambarelli & Davitto. Tours and tasting daily 10 A.M.–5 P.M.

The "little old winemaker" has been reinstated at Italian Swiss Colony, thanks to the quick formation of ISC Wines. The oldest winery in Sonoma County was about to be shut down forever by its owner, the Heublein Corporation. This prospect terrified North Coast grape growers, who had relied heavily on this winery as a grape buyer. Colony had been part of the United Vintners package deal bought from Allied Grape Growers by Heublein in 1968. When Heublein threatened to shut down the winemaking facility in 1983 after closing the Asti tasting room—one of the oldest in California—Allied, the principal grape supplier of the winery, quickly established ISC Wines in order to buy back Italian Swiss Colony, three other winemaking facilities, and several brands. Plans call for restoring the historic Colony winery, upgrading the winemaking facilities, and emphasizing premium varietal wines.

WHITE

1981 CHARDONNAY ($5.25) Centennial Vintage, Sonoma.

☆☆ NV CHENIN BLANC ($4.30) California. *1.5 liter. Lush, sweet, fruity, varietal.*

BLANC DE NOIR

☆☆ 1984 WHITE ZINFANDEL ($3.00) California. *Fresh, sweet, tangy.*

ROSE

☆ 1983 GRENACHE ROSE ($4.00) Mendocino. *1.1% residual sugar.*
☆☆ 1983 PINOT NOIR ROSE ($5.00) Sonoma. *1.8% residual sugar.*

RED

☆ NV CABERNET SAUVIGNON ($2.98) California. *Lush, fat, cherry tones, very nice.*
☆☆ NV ZINFANDEL ($3.00) Classic, California.
☆☆ 1982 ZINFANDEL ($5.00) Sonoma. *Balanced, clean, rounded and quite attractive.*

Colorado Mountain Vineyards
COLORADO

3553 E Road, Palisade, Colorado 81526 (303-464-7948). FOUNDED: 1978. ACREAGE: None. PRODUCTION: 5,000 cases. DISTRIBUTION: Colorado. OWNER: Colorado Corporation. James E. Seewald, president. WINEMAKER: James E. Seewald. OTHER LABEL: Puesta del Sol. Tours and tasting June–August: Tuesday–Saturday 12–4 P.M.; September–May: Friday–Saturday 12–4 P.M., or by appointment.

James Seewald, who owned two wine- and beermaking supply stores, became intrigued by the wine grape feasibility studies being done for western Colorado. For twenty years he had been importing California grapes for home winemaking, but he was now convinced that wine grapes could be grown successfully in Colorado. Local farmers were willing to try a grape vine or two but would not commit to a sizable crop without a buyer. So James sold his businesses and started a winery with the announced purpose of using 100 percent Colorado grapes. "Presently, one out of every four bottles is from Colorado fruit," says James, "but in two or three years, we should be making 100 percent Colorado wine."

WHITE

☆ 1982 CHARDONNAY ($8.00) Colorado. *Decent, clean, varietal.*

RED

O 1981 CABERNET SAUVIGNON Colorado.

Columbia Winery
WASHINGTON

1445 120th Northeast, Bellevue, Washington 98005 (206-453-1977). FOUNDED: 1962. ACREAGE: None. PRODUCTION: 40,000 cases. DISTRIBUTION: Major market states. OWNER: Corporation. Dan Baty, president; David Adir, sales and general manager. WINEMAKER: David L. Lake. OTHER LABEL: Associated Vintners (AV). Tours and tasting Wednesday–Saturday 11 A.M.–4 P.M.

The state's oldest premium winery began in the garage of Professor Lloyd Woodbourne. He and a few colleagues from the University of Washington were having such a great time making wine at home that they pooled their interest and their resources, bought a crusher, and set up a cooperative winery called Associated Vintners in Woodbourne's garage. They have moved three times since then and have expanded their production four or five fold. In the process, they sold their vineyards, brought in more partners, and brought in marketing and administrative expertise. They hired the "Master of Wine," enologist David Lake, and built a new winery. The new 20,000-square-foot facility in Bellevue, full of the most modern equipment and oak cooperage, is a far cry from the Woodbourne garage. David Lake's philosophy is to make wines that don't attempt to imitate French or California styles; they emphasize the honest character and style of Washington State. Deciding that "Associated Vintners" lacked charm, the winery started labeling its wines "Columbia" in 1984.

WHITE

☆ 1982 CHARDONNAY ($8.50) Yakima Valley, Washington. *Lush, vinous and dirty.*
☆☆ 1982 ASSOCIATED VINTNERS (AV) GEWURZTRAMINER ($6.00) Yakima Valley. *Clean, nice, a bit short.*

RED

☆☆ 1980 ASSOCIATED VINTNERS (AV) CABERNET SAUVIGNON ($9.00) Yakima Valley, Washington. *Dusty, varietal, nicely structured, appealing.*
☆ 1981 CABERNET SAUVIGNON ($8.00) Yakima Valley. *Deep, berried, fat. This one just misses.*
☆☆☆ 1981 MERLOT ($8.50) 76% Bacchus, 24% Cabernet Sauvignon, Otis, Washington. *Lush and elegant, with complexity and grace. Drink now.*
☆☆☆ 1979 ASSOCIATED VINTNERS (AV) PINOT NOIR ($9.00) Yakima Valley. *Great color, intense and angular, splendid fruit and acid.*
☆ 1981 PINOT NOIR ($7.00) Yakima County, Washington.

Commonwealth Winery
MASSACHUSETTS

22 Lothrop Street, Plymouth, Massachusetts 02360 (617-746-4940). FOUNDED: 1978. ACREAGE: None. PRODUCTION: 15,000 cases. DISTRIBUTION: Massachusetts. OWNER: Corporation. David S. Tower, president; Bill Dendor, marketing director. WINEMAKER: David S. Tower. Tours and tasting Monday–Saturday 10 A.M.–5 P.M., Sunday 12–5 P.M.

Faced with a crisis in 1978 (he had ordered 50 tons of grapes from New York without provisions for processing them), David Tower quickly rented an abandoned library building in Plymouth and ordered fermenting tanks. The tanks arrived a week before the grapes, and Federal approval came two days before the start of the crush. Before this frenetic introduction to winemaking, David had previously been a teacher at a girls' school. His studies in wine began in California at U.C. Davis, then took him to Germany. Upon his return, David considered eastern Long Island, but after passage of the Massachusetts Farm Winery Act he settled in the Bay State.

WHITE

1980 CAYUGA ($6.95) Massachusetts.
☆☆ NV CHARDONNAY ($10.95) Winemaker's Reserve, Quail Hill, Long Island, New York. *Lovely, clean, varietal, dry, excellent acidity.*
☆ 1983 CHARDONNAY ($7.95) Dana, Massachusetts. *Clean, decent, soft.*
☆☆ NV GEWURZTRAMINER ($7.00) American. *Varietal, soft, balanced, clean.*

☆☆ NV GEWURZTRAMINER ($7.95) American. *Crisp, fruity, tangy, varietal.*
☆☆ 1983 RIESLING ($7.95) Massachusetts. *Soft, lush, fruity.*
 ☆ 1979 VIDAL BLANC ($6.95) Massachusetts.

ROSE

 ☆ NV PLYMOUTH ROCK ROSE ($5.00) American. *DeChaunac rosé. Simple, clean, dry, balanced.*

RED

NV DECHAUNAC ($6.45) Massachusetts.
NV DECHAUNAC ($6.45) Massachusetts. *"Bottled in 1981." Vegetal, deep, rich, ripe.*
 ☆ NV DECHAUNAC ($7.95) Massachusetts. *"Bottled in 1980." Snappy, decent fruit, vegetative.*

Concannon Vineyard
ALAMEDA COUNTY

4590 Tesla Road, Livermore, California 94550 (415-447-3760). FOUNDED: 1883. ACREAGE: 180 acres. PRODUCTION: 110,000 cases. DISTRIBUTION: Nationwide. OWNER: Distillers Company, Ltd. James J. Concannon, president; Sergio Traverso, vice president and general manager. WINEMAKER: Sergio Traverso. Tours and tasting Monday–Saturday 10 A.M.–4:30 P.M., Sunday 12–4:30 P.M.

Over 100 years ago James Concannon founded this operation 50 miles east of San Francisco. Jim Concannon, third-generation president of the winery, sold control a few years ago to Agustin Huneeus, former president of Paul Masson. "Cucho" Huneeus, a Chilean, modernized the winery and upgraded quality; he also hired Chilean winemaker Sergio Traverso away from Sterling Vineyards. In 1983 Concannon was sold to the Distillers Company, producer of Johnny Walker Scotch. Throughout this period of change, Jim Concannon has remained as president, giving the management of the winery continuity as well as a rare Irish personality.

WHITE

☆☆ 1982 CHABLIS ($3.88) California. *Clean, decent, pleasant and unremarkable.*
☆☆ 1983 CHABLIS ($4.00) California. *Fresh, round, some sweetness and a lot of crispness.*
 ☆ 1981 CHARDONNAY ($8.00) Monterey.
    1982 CHARDONNAY ($8.00) Santa Maria Valley. *Crisp but strange, with some volatile acidity.*
☆☆ 1983 CHARDONNAY ($8.00) 62% Tepusquet, Santa Maria; 38% Santa Clara, California. *Decent varietal character, dense, clean.*
☆☆☆ 1983 CHARDONNAY ($8.00) Selected Vineyards, 38% Mistral; 62% Tepusquet, California. *Rich, fruity, clean, beautifully balanced. Concannon's best yet.*
☆☆ 1982 CHENIN BLANC ($5.00) Noble, California. *Great fruit, clean, soft, very attractive.*
    1983 CHENIN BLANC ($4.75) California. *Tired, dirty.*
 ☆ 1982 JOHANNISBERG RIESLING ($6.00) Livermore Valley.
☆☆ 1982 SAUVIGNON BLANC ($7.00) California. *24% Livermore, 76% San Luis Obispo.*

☆☆☆ 1982 SAUVIGNON BLANC ($7.00) Estate, Livermore Valley. *Fresh, fruity, clean, complex, balanced, delicious.*

☆☆ 1983 SAUVIGNON BLANC ($8.00) California. *Crisp, snappy, fresh, appealing.*

☆☆☆ 1983 SAUVIGNON BLANC ($8.25) Estate, Livermore. *Rich, clean, fruity, nicely balanced.*

ROSE

☆☆ 1983 ZINFANDEL ROSE ($4.75) California.

RED

☆☆ 1971 CABERNET SAUVIGNON Estate, Livermore Valley. *Balanced and still fruity.*

☆☆ 1975 CABERNET SAUVIGNON Estate, Livermore Valley. *Light but well made, balanced and clean.*

☆ 1977 CABERNET SAUVIGNON ($7.50) Estate, Livermore Valley. *Meaty, rich, toasty, nice. Drink now.*

☆ 1978 CABERNET SAUVIGNON ($9.00) Estate, Livermore Valley. *Raisiny and earthy.*

1978 100 YEAR ANNIVERSARY CABERNET SAUVIGNON ($9.75) Livermore Valley. *Lacking fruit, rich, complex, not delicious.*

☆ 1979 CABERNET SAUVIGNON ($7.25) Livermore Valley. *Vegetal, lacking depth.*

☆ 1981 CABERNET SAUVIGNON ($9.00) Estate, Livermore Valley. *Thin, vegetal.*

☆☆ 1974 PETITE SIRAH ($20.00) Limited Bottling, Estate, Livermore Valley. *Jammy and intense but nicely balanced. Drink now.*

☆ 1977 PETITE SIRAH ($13.50) Estate, Livermore Valley. *Berries and oak, nicely balanced but limited appeal.*

☆ 1978 PETITE SIRAH ($8.00) Estate, Livermore Valley. *Bigger and more aggressive than usual. Chewy, intense, mature.*

☆☆☆ 1979 PETITE SIRAH ($6.50) California. *Clean, balanced and rich, with nice complexity. Drink now.*

☆☆ 1979 PETITE SIRAH ($15.00) Centennial, Estate, Livermore Valley. *Grapey, rich, intense but short.*

☆☆☆ 1980 PETITE SIRAH ($5.75) 54% Wilson, Clarksburg; 46% Estate, California. *Rich, clean, balanced, well made. Drink now or hold.*

☆☆☆ 1981 PETITE SIRAH ($6.50) Estate, Livermore. *Clean, well made, rich, attractive. Drink now or hold.*

Conestoga Vineyards
PENNSYLVANIA

415 South Queen Street, Lancaster, Pennsylvania 17603 (717-393-0141). FOUNDED: 1963. ACREAGE: None. PRODUCTION: 3,000 cases. DISTRIBUTION: Pennsylvania. OWNERS: R. Martin and Arthur H. Keen. WINEMAKER: R. Martin Keen. Tours by appointment. Tasting at 2323 Lincoln Highway East, Lancaster. Call for information.

The founder of the original Conestoga Vineyards, Melvin S. Gordon was one of the first to use French-American hybrid grapes in commercial winemaking in Pennsylvania. That was in 1963. Today, the winery is owned by two grape-growing brothers, Martin and Arthur Keen. Martin did his thesis in wine research at Pennsylvania State University to obtain his master's degree in food science. Arthur also majored in food science but got his master's in business. They bought part of the Conestoga Vineyards in 1976 from David Fondots, who is currently vice president of the winery. When the lease on the land ran out, the winery was moved to the Keens' "Queen Dairy Plant" in the city of Lancaster, and the original winery was closed. The wine is sold locally through a tasting room in Lancaster.

Congress Springs Vineyard
SANTA CLARA COUNTY

23600 Congress Springs Road, Saratoga, California 95070 (408-867-1409). FOUNDED: 1976. ACREAGE: 15 acres. PRODUCTION: 5,000 cases. DISTRIBUTION: California. OWNERS: Vic Erickson and Dan Gehrs. WINEMAKER: Dan Gehrs. Tours and tasting weekends 11 A.M.–5 P.M.

In 1975 Robin and Dan Gehrs convinced Vic Erickson to revive the old vineyard and winery on his property. Established by Frenchman Pierre Pourroy in 1892, the winery had been out of operation since 1952. The Gehrs' total experience with wine at that point was Dan's non-winemaking job at Paul Masson and some home winemaking experiments. Nevertheless, they forged ahead and bought into the Erickson property. Part of the old Zinfandel vineyard was grafted over to Gewürztraminer and Chardonnay, and a vineyard in Los Gatos was acquired. The wine business has been difficult, but the small winery has always been infused with Robin's infectious enthusiasm.

WHITE

○ 1982 MONT BLANC ($5.00) San Luis Obispo. *Made from Sauvignon Blanc grapes.*

☆☆☆ 1982 CHARDONNAY ($10.00) Santa Clara. *Balanced, attractive, good fruit, low alcohol (12.7%).*

☆☆☆ 1982 CHARDONNAY ($20.00) Private Reserve, Monmartre, Santa Cruz. *Big, rich, toasty oak. A monster in the old style.*

☆ 1982 CHARDONNAY ($25.00) Private Reserve, Santa Cruz Mountains. *An old-style monster: big, fat and intense.*

☆☆☆ 1983 CHARDONNAY ($11.50) Santa Clara. *Barrel fermented. Clean, fresh, oaky, crisp fruit.*

☆☆ 1983 CHENIN BLANC ($7.00) Santa Cruz Mountains. *0.5% residual sugar. Snappy, crisp, clean, delightful.*

☆☆ 1984 CHENIN BLANC ($7.00) Santa Cruz Mountains. *Sweet, fruity, fresh, attractive.*

☆ 1982 FUME BLANC ($8.50) Santa Clara 56%, San Luis Obispo 44%.

☆ 1983 PINOT BLANC ($9.00) Santa Cruz. *Clean but dull.*

☆☆ 1983 SEMILLON ($8.00) Santa Cruz.

RED

☆ 1979 CABERNET SAUVIGNON ($7.00) Santa Clara Valley. *Crisp, light and without much varietal character.*

☆ 1980 CABERNET SAUVIGNON ($10.00) Santa Cruz. *10% Merlot. Oaky, earthy, decent.*

1981 CABERNET SAUVIGNON ($8.50) California. *Thin, tart, unattractive.*

☆☆ 1983 CABERNET SAUVIGNON ($8.00) 80% Santa Clara, 20% San Luis Obispo. *Soft, clean, crisp, fresh, simple. Drink now.*

☆☆ 1978 PINOT NOIR ($12.00) St. Charles, Santa Cruz.

☆☆☆ 1981 PINOT NOIR ($15.00) Private Reserve, Santa Cruz Mountains. *Varietal, fruity, lovely, crisp.*

☆☆☆ 1982 PINOT NOIR ($15.00) Private Reserve, Santa Cruz Mountains. *Intense, tannic, ripe, complex, woody.*

☆ 1980 ZINFANDEL ($9.00)

☆☆☆ 1981 ZINFANDEL ($9.00) Santa Cruz Mountains. *Lush, soft, fruity.*

Conn Creek Winery
NAPA COUNTY

8711 Silverado Trail, St. Helena, California 94574 (707-963-5133). FOUNDED: 1974. ACREAGE: 120 acres. PRODUCTION: 20,000 cases. DISTRIBUTION: Nationwide, England, France, and

Belgium. OWNERS: Partnership. Bill and Kathy Collins, Ropner P.L.C. WINEMAKER: Daryl Eklund. OTHER LABEL: Château Maja. Tours and tasting by appointment only.

Bill and Kathy Collins are a charming couple who have been Napa Valley growers for years. Bill, an ex-Navy man with an electronics background, started his winery in partnership with Stanford professor Bill Beaver and his wife, Mary. For a while Conn Creek wines were made in a rented winery (see Ehlers Lane Winery). Now the wines are made by young winemaker Daryl Eklund in a handsome, modern facility that uses Styrofoam in its walls for insulation. About 150 acres of vineyard are controlled by the partners.

WHITE

☆☆ 1979 CHARDONNAY ($11.00) Napa Valley.

☆☆ 1980 CHARDONNAY ($12.00) Napa Valley. *Vinous, rich, lacks finesse.*

☆☆ 1981 CHARDONNAY ($12.50) Napa Valley. *Soft, vinous, oily, nice oak.*

☆☆ 1983 CHATEAU MAJA CHARDONNAY ($5.00) Napa Valley. *Simple, pleasant.*

RED

☆☆☆ 1977 CABERNET SAUVIGNON ($13.75) Napa Valley. *Rich and big, structured, firm, lovely. Drink now.*

☆☆☆ 1978 CABERNET SAUVIGNON ($12.50) Lot 1, Napa Valley. *Rich, herbal, velvety, aristocratic. Drink now.*

☆☆☆ 1978 CABERNET SAUVIGNON ($12.50) Lot 2, Napa Valley. *Lush and deep. Drink 1986.*

☆☆☆ 1979 CABERNET SAUVIGNON ($13.00) Napa Valley. *Rich and plummy with excellent depth. Drink 1987.*

☆☆☆ 1980 CABERNET SAUVIGNON ($13.00) Napa Valley. *Herbed, fat, classic. Drink 1988.*

☆☆☆ 1981 CABERNET SAUVIGNON ($13.50) Napa Valley. *Rich, crisp, hard, with a lovely future. Drink 1989.*

☆☆☆ 1978 ZINFANDEL ($7.50) Napa Valley. *Big but well under control. Complex, clean and good fruit.*

☆☆☆ 1979 ZINFANDEL ($7.50) Napa Valley. *Clean, rich, balanced, lovely.*

☆☆ 1980 ZINFANDEL ($7.50) Estate, Napa Valley. *Tannic and intense. Drink 1987.*

Conneaut Cellars Winery
PENNSYLVANIA

Route 322, Conneaut Lake, Pennsylvania 16316 (814-382-3999). FOUNDED: 1982. ACREAGE: None. PRODUCTION: 4,000 cases. DISTRIBUTION: Local. OWNERS: Partnership. Dr. Alan Wolf, general manager. WINEMAKER: Dr. Alan Wolf. Tours and tasting daily 1 P.M.–5 P.M., sales Monday–Saturday 10 A.M.–6 P.M., Sunday 12–6 P.M.

The dream began long ago and far away for Dr. Alan Wolf, when he visited numerous European wineries while serving in the foreign service. The idea of owning a winery simmered silently until Pennsylvania farm winery legislation in 1968 made it possible for Alan and his wife, Phyllis, to realize their dream. They located their winery in the heart of a thriving tourist region. "The theme of this area is turn-of-the-century, so we built a winery in that style," says Alan. "We even make our wines in a fruity, full, old-fashioned style." Phyllis, director of hospitality and marketing, makes certain that visitors receive a warm welcome.

A. Conrotto Winery
SANTA CLARA COUNTY

1690 Hecker Pass Highway, Gilroy, California 95020 (408-842-3053). FOUNDED: 1926. ACREAGE: 5 acres. PRODUCTION: 9,000 cases. DISTRIBUTION: California. OWNERS: James and Jean

Burr, and Gerald and Jermaine Case. WINEMAKERS: James Burr and Gerald Case. No tours. Tasting summer: weekends 11 A.M.–6 P.M.; winter: weekends 12–5 P.M.

Anselmo Conrotto, an Italian immigrant, built this old-style, gravity-flow winery in 1926. First it was passed down to his son Chinto, and then the winery was bought by Chinto's daughters and their husbands, James Burr and Gerald Case, who now own and manage the property. The wine is sold mainly to San Francisco–area restaurants as house wine.

TONIO CONTI *see* Adelaida Cellars

R. & J. Cook
YOLO COUNTY

Netherlands Road, Clarksburg, California 95612 (916-775-1234). FOUNDED: 1979. ACREAGE: 130 acres. PRODUCTION: 62,000 cases. DISTRIBUTION: 21 states and 2 foreign countries. OWNERS: Roger and Joanne Cook. WINEMAKER: Janos Radvanyi, Jr. Tours by appointment. Tasting weekdays 10 A.M.–4:30 P.M.; weekends by appointment.

The "R & J" stands for Roger and Joanne Cook, a husband-and-wife team that knows it's way around a vineyard. Roger, a fourth-generation grape grower in the Clarksburg area, had bought and planted his own vineyard in 1971 because of a disagreement with his father over viticultural practices. As newlyweds in 1978, the Cooks quickly realized that the only way they could make a living growing grapes was to make wine as well. They moved the winery into any and every available building on their property. They have recently consolidated the winery in a new facility.

WHITE

☆   NV   VARIETAL WHITE ($3.40) California. *90% Chenin Blanc, 10% Sauvignon Blanc. Crisp, clean and pleasant.*
    1982 CHENIN BLANC ($5.50) Very Dry, Estate, Clarksburg. *Weedy.*
    1983 CHENIN BLANC ($5.50) Semi Dry, Clarksburg. *2.3% residual sugar. Sappy, sweet, vegetal.*
☆   1983 CHENIN BLANC ($5.75) Very Dry, Estate, Clarksburg. *Earthy, vinous.*
O   1981 FUME BLANC ($9.00) Clarksburg. *Sweet and dull.*
    1983 FUME BLANC ($7.00) Estate, Clarksburg. *14% Semillon. Sweet, dull.*
O   1982 SAUVIGNON BLANC ($7.00) Reggeli Harmat, Clarksburg. *Vinous, flat.*

BLANC DE NOIR

☆☆   1981 MERLOT BLANC ($5.50) Estate, Clarksburg.
    1982 MERLOT BLANC ($5.25) Clarksburg. *Oily, heavy.*
☆☆   1983 MERLOT BLANC ($5.25) Estate, Clarksburg. *1% residual sugar. Balanced, varietal, attractive.*

RED

☆   NV   VARIETAL RED ($4.75) California.
☆☆   1979 CABERNET SAUVIGNON ($6.50) Northern California.
    1980 CABERNET SAUVIGNON ($6.00) Estate, Clarksburg.
☆   1980 MERLOT ($7.00) Estate, Clarksburg.
☆   1979 PETITE SIRAH ($5.50) Northern California.

Cook-Ellis Winery
SANTA CRUZ COUNTY

2900 Buzzard Lagoon Road, Corraltos, California 95076 (408-688-7208). FOUNDED: 1981. ACREAGE: None. PRODUCTION: 700 cases. DISTRIBUTION: California. OWNER: Cook-Ellis

Winery, Inc. Jim Ellis and Ken Wassner, managing partners. WINEMAKER: Jim Ellis. OTHER LABEL: Buzzard Lagoon Vineyards. Tours and tasting by appointment.

On a small piece of property tucked into the Santa Cruz Mountains, Jim Ellis and his wife, Rebecca Cook, cleared their land, built a geodesic-dome home, and put a winery in the basement. Both the house and the winery run on alternative energy sources and are without gas or electric power. There isn't even a phone in the house. In this mountain oasis, Jim Ellis makes small amounts of wine but is planning to double production each year until he reaches 6,000 gallons.

WHITE

NV BUZZARD LAGOON WHITE ($4.00) California. *Vinous, heavy, pine flavors, unappealing.*

☆ 1983 CHARDONNAY ($10.00) Monterey. *Lush, fat, vinous.*

○ 1983 FUME BLANC ($6.00) Monterey. *Burnt, unattractive.*

Copenhagen Cellars
SANTA BARBARA COUNTY

448 Alisal Road, Solvang, California 93463 (805-688-4218). FOUNDED: 1965. ACREAGE: None. PRODUCTION: 15,000 cases. DISTRIBUTION: California and Midwest. OWNERS: Doug and Candace Scott. WINEMAKER: Doug Scott. OTHER LABELS: Stearns Wharf Vintners, Warner West. No tours. Tasting daily 10 A.M.–6 P.M. at winery, and 10 A.M.–9 P.M. at Stearns Wharf Vintners, Stearns Wharf, Santa Barbara. Picnic area.

Copenhagen Cellars began as a tasting room in the tourist town of Solvang. Foreign and domestic wines were bought to be sold under the Copenhagen label. After Doug and Candace Scott bought the business in 1979, they began making their own wines in addition to continuing the tasting room—import business. They still buy the wines for their Copenhagen Cellars label, but they make their own wine for the Stearns Wharf Vintners label. The Scotts, who have been using space leased from another winery, are completing their own facility in Santa Barbara County.

WHITE

☆☆ 1983 CHENIN BLANC ($5.95) La Presa, Santa Ynez Valley. *1.97% residual sugar. Crisp, balanced, clean.*

Corbett Canyon Vineyards
SAN LUIS OBISPO COUNTY

Corbett Canyon Road, P.O. Box 315, San Luis Obispo, California 93403 (805-544-5800). FOUNDED: 1979. ACREAGE: None. PRODUCTION: 100,000 cases. DISTRIBUTION: Nationwide. OWNER: Glenmore Distilleries Company. James Thompson, president. WINEMAKER: Cary Gott. Tasting Monday–Saturday 10 A.M.–4 P.M., Sunday 12–4 P.M. Gift shop. Newsletter.

In hopes of eradicating the memory of the disastrous Lawrence Winery, Glenmore Distilleries replaced the staff and the management and changed the name to Corbett Canyon in 1982. One of the smartest things new boss Jeffrey Maiken did was hire Cary Gott, the former winemaker at Monteviña. Arriving at harvest time in June 1983, Cary had two months to acclimate himself to a new viticultural area and a new winery—a winery filled with flawed and unreleasable wines. Glenmore gave Cary $1.5 million to redesign the winery, fill it with the best modern equipment, and buy quality Central Coast grapes.

WHITE

☆☆ 1983 COASTAL CLASSIC ($4.50) California. *1.5 liter. Fresh, clean, with some interesting complexity.*

1982 LAWRENCE WINERY CHARDONNAY ($7.50) Bien Nacido, California. *Soft, dull, not much fruit.*

☆ 1983 CHARDONNAY ($8.00) Central Coast. *Earthy, clean, crisp, some oiliness.*
☆☆ 1984 CHARDONNAY ($6.00) Coastal Classic, Central Coast. *1 liter. Round, lush, clean, attractive.*
☆☆ 1983 CHENIN BLANC ($5.00) Paragon, San Luis Obispo. *Dry, fresh, clean and quite lovely.*
☆☆ 1984 CHENIN BLANC ($5.00) Central Coast. *0.93% residual sugar. Clean, varietal, attractive.*
○ NV LAWRENCE WINERY FUME BLANC ($6.50) California.
○ 1980 LAWRENCE WINERY SAUVIGNON BLANC ($6.50) California.
1983 SAUVIGNON BLANC ($6.00) San Luis Obispo. *Fruity, decent, some redwood flavor.*

BLANC DE NOIR

☆☆ 1983 PINOT NOIR–BLANC ($5.00) Santa Barbara. *Fresh, clean and attractive.*
☆☆ 1984 WHITE ZINFANDEL ($5.00) Central Coast. *1 liter. 2.57% residual sugar. Dull but clean and fresh.*

RED

☆ 1983 COASTAL CLASSIC ($4.50) Central Coast. *1 liter. Clean, rich, snappy, nice fruit, some veggies.*
○ 1979 LAWRENCE WINERY CABERNET SAUVIGNON California.
○ 1980 LAWRENCE WINERY CABERNET SAUVIGNON ($6.00) California.
1980 LAWRENCE WINERY MERLOT ($10.00) California.
1981 LAWRENCE WINERY MERLOT ($6.50) Bien Nacido, Santa Barbara.
1981 LAWRENCE WINERY ZINFANDEL ($7.00) San Luis Obispo.

Cordtz Brothers Cellars
SONOMA COUNTY

28237 River Road, Cloverdale, California 95425 (707-894-5245). FOUNDED: 1980. ACREAGE: None. PRODUCTION: 13,500 cases. DISTRIBUTION: California and 7 other states. OWNER: Vintage Wine Cellars. David Cordtz, general manager. WINEMAKER: David Cordtz; Jay Vesco, assistant winemaker. Tours, tasting, and retail sales daily 10 A.M.–4 P.M. Gift shop. Other tasting at 210 N. Cloverdale Boulevard, Cloverdale.

When the Cordtz family leased the Hollis Black winery, they made the old concrete tanks into storage and barrel rooms by cutting doors into their sides. The thickness of the concrete walls provides excellent insulation, and the tanks give the winery an odd, beehive look. The operation has experienced financial troubles and was recently recapitalized and reorganized.

WHITE

☆ 1982 CHARDONNAY ($8.75) Dry Creek Valley. *Decent but with dull flavors and lacking depth.*
☆ 1981 GEWURZTRAMINER ($5.75) Alexander Valley. *Overripe, varietal, lush, a touch of oxidation.*
1981 SAUVIGNON BLANC ($7.00) Alexander Valley, Sonoma.
1982 SAUVIGNON BLANC ($8.00) Alexander Valley, Sonoma.

RED

☆ 1980 CBC RED WINE ($3.95) North Coast. *Big, hot and slightly sweet.*
☆ 1980 CABERNET SAUVIGNON ($8.00) Upper Alexander Valley.
1981 CABERNET SAUVIGNON ($10.00) Alexander Valley.

☆   1981 ZINFANDEL ($4.50) North Coast.
☆☆☆   1982 ZINFANDEL ($6.00) Upper Alexander Valley. *Fruity, rich, smooth, clean, lovely.*

ૐ

Cosentino Wine Company
STANISLAUS COUNTY

417 Hosmer, Box 4751, Modesto, California 95352 (209-577-0556). FOUNDED: 1982. ACREAGE: None. PRODUCTION: 15,000 cases. DISTRIBUTION: 7 states. OWNER: Mitch Cosentino. WINEMAKER: Mitch Cosentino. OTHER LABELS: Crystal Valley Cellars, Cosentino Select. Tours and tasting Monday–Friday 10 A.M.–5 P.M., Saturday 10 A.M.–4 P.M.

In his work as a wine distributor, Mitch Cosentino had been complimented more than once by winemakers on having a "winemaker's palate." Spotting what he thought was a big gap between jug wines and premium wines, Mitch jumped in to bridge it. His good relationships with growers and wineries made it fairly easy for him to contract for grapes and rent winery space. With a low overhead and a busy mind swarming with new marketing ideas, Mitch has made a splash with his Crystal Valley sparkling wines and selected varietals.

WHITE

NV   CRYSTAL VALLEY CELLARS VIN BLANC ($3.75) California.
☆   1982 CRYSTAL VALLEY CELLARS VIN BLANC ($3.75) California. *92% Chardonnay, 8% Sauvignon Blanc. Clean, crisp and simple.*
☆☆   1982 CRYSTAL VALLEY CELLARS CHARDONNAY ($4.50) Deer Creek, California. *Balanced and well made.*
1982 CRYSTAL VALLEY CELLARS CHARDONNAY ($5.50) Deer Creek, Napa Valley.
1982 CHARDONNAY ($8.00) The Sculptor, California. *Not at all varietal, peculiar.*
1983 CRYSTAL VALLEY CELLARS CHARDONNAY ($8.00) Deer Creek, California. *Strange nose, decent but thin fruit flavors.*
1982 CRYSTAL VALLEY CELLARS SAUVIGNON BLANC ($7.00) Limited Reserve, 25% Napa, 50% Lake, 25% Sacramento. *25% Chardonnay. Grassy, intense, overdone.*
☆☆   1982 SAUVIGNON BLANC ($8.00) The Novelist, Napa Valley. *12% Chardonnay. Attractive and varietal, clean and crisp.*
1983 SAUVIGNON BLANC ($8.00) The Novelist, Napa Valley. *Dull, lacking fruit.*

SPARKLING

NV   CRYSTAL VALLEY CELLARS ROSE ($4.95) California. *"Extra dry." Dull, unpleasant.*
☆☆☆   NV   CRYSTAL VALLEY CELLARS ROBINS GLOW ($5.75) California. *Blanc de Noirs. Yeasty, soft, sweet and lovely.*
☆☆   NV   CRYSTAL VALLEY CELLARS SPUMANTE ($5.75) California. *Muscat. Sweet, lush, very appealing.*
☆☆   NV   CRYSTAL VALLEY CELLARS EXTRA DRY ($6.50) California. *Snappy, fresh, crisp and simple.*

RED

☆   1980 CRYSTAL VALLEY CELLARS CABERNET SAUVIGNON ($5.50) Lake.
1980 CABERNET SAUVIGNON ($6.00) Lake. *18% Merlot.*
☆   1982 CRYSTAL VALLEY CELLARS CABERNET SAUVIGNON ($7.00) North Coast. *Earthy, decent fruit, tannic. Drink 1986.*
1978 CRYSTAL VALLEY CELLARS MERLOT ($7.00) Napa Valley. *Nicely made but a bit tired.*
1980 CRYSTAL VALLEY CELLARS MERLOT ($7.00) California. *15% Cabernet. Dull and tired.*

ૐ

Costello Vineyards
NAPA COUNTY

1200 Orchard Avenue, Napa, California 94558 (707-252-8483). FOUNDED: 1982. ACREAGE: 40 acres. PRODUCTION: 9,000 cases. DISTRIBUTION: Nationwide. OWNER: Costello family. John, Maria, and son Greg. WINEMAKER: John Costello. Tours and tasting by appointment.

John and Maria Costello farmed avocados and citrus in Southern California before they planted a 40-acre vineyard in the Napa Valley. When their vines produced their first commercial crop, John, who had worked in the farming and packaging business for many years, determined (once he found out how difficult it was to sell Gewürztraminer grapes) that they could market their own wine. They set up shop behind their house, slapping together a board and bat barn-style winery. John, who still works in farm packaging, makes the wine himself.

WHITE

☆☆   1982 CHARDONNAY ($9.00) Estate, Napa Valley. *Charming, crisp, well made, an impressive first wine.*

☆☆   1983 CHARDONNAY ($9.75) Estate, Napa Valley. *Quite dark. Big, balanced, clean and intense.*

☆   1982 GEWURZTRAMINER ($6.00) Estate, Napa Valley. *Oily, dry, lemony, Alsatian style.*

☆☆☆   1983 GEWURZTRAMINER ($10.75) Select Late Harvest, Napa Valley. *375ml. 10.8% residual sugar. Varietal, lush, fruity, lovely.*

Côte des Colombes Vineyard
OREGON

Route 1, Box 22A, P.O. Box 266, Banks, Oregon 97106 (503-646-1223). FOUNDED: 1977. ACREAGE: 5 acres. PRODUCTION: 8,000 cases. DISTRIBUTION: Oregon and Washington. OWNER: Corporation. Joseph R. P. Coulombe, president. WINEMAKER: Joseph R. P. Coulombe. Tours and tasting weekends 1 P.M.–5 P.M.

Joe Coulombe ran two shops catering to the home winemaker and worked for Tektronix before starting the winery. His background as a weather specialist in the Air Force helped him to identify the microclimate on his property as ideal for Cabernet Sauvignon. The vineyard name translates as "hill of the doves" and, appropriately enough, the winery sits on a hillside northwest of Portland. Joe got his Cabernet cuttings from Concannon Vineyard, his Pinot Noir from Eyrie Vineyards, and his Grey Riesling from Wente Brothers. Expansion plans call for growth in capacity from 8,000 to 20,000 cases. Joe and Betty Coulombe also operate a small tasting room at the winery.

Cottage Vineyards
NEW YORK

Old Post Road, P.O. Box 608, Marlboro, New York 12542 (914-236-4870). FOUNDED: 1981. ACREAGE: 4 acres. PRODUCTION: 400 cases. DISTRIBUTION: Local. OWNER: Allan

MacKinnon. WINEMAKER: Allan MacKinnon. Tours and tasting weekends 1 P.M.–5 P.M. Closed January–February.

An economic advisor with Merrill Lynch, Allan MacKinnon was reliving his boyhood joys when he bought a little farm in Marlboro. Allan had grown up on a farm in Maine and still had fond memories of the farmer's life. "Once I planted grapes, the temptation to make a little wine was too great," says Allan. The winery is named for Allan's small cottage that used to sit next to the winery.

꿿

H. Coturri and Sons
SONOMA COUNTY

6725 Enterprise Road, Glen Ellen, California 95442 (707-996-6247). FOUNDED: 1979. ACREAGE: 10 acres. PRODUCTION: 2,500 cases. DISTRIBUTION: California only. OWNERS: Harry, Fern, Philip, and Tony Coturri and Dan Parun. WINEMAKER: Tony Coturri. Tours by appointment. No tasting. Sales through mailing list subscription.

Winemaker Tony Coturri claims his wines are "pure, hand-crafted wines, made in the same manner as old-world French wines." Natural yeasts, basket presses, open-top fermenters, and no use of chemicals are among his winemaking rules. Tony always warns his customers that due to the "naturalness" of his wines, they can, and usually do, drop a heavy sediment. The backyard winery is in an out-building behind the Coturri house, just off the patio.

WHITE

O 1982 CHARDONNAY ($9.00) Gordon, Sonoma Valley. *Oxidized, hazy, horrible.*
O 1982 CHARDONNAY ($12.50) Freiberg, Sonoma Valley. *"Burnt match" nose, overdone. Process flavors spoil good fruit.*

RED

1979 CABERNET SAUVIGNON ($20.00) Sonoma. *Raisiny, concentrated, overpowering—lacks finesse.*

1980 CABERNET SAUVIGNON ($13.00) Sonoma Valley. *Raisiny, hot, no varietal character.*

☆☆ 1980 CABERNET SAUVIGNON ($25.00) Old Vines, Glen Ellen, Sonoma Valley. *Intense, dark, concentrated, complex. Drink 1990.*

☆☆ 1981 CABERNET SAUVIGNON ($11.25) Horne, Sonoma Valley. *Lush, complex, fruity, some dirty flavors. Drink 1986.*

1979 PINOT NOIR ($15.75) Glen Ellen, Sonoma Valley. *Weird, sweet, not clean.*

☆☆☆ 1980 PINOT NOIR ($15.00) Sonoma Valley. *Lush, rich, earthy, aggressive.*

☆☆☆ 1981 PINOT NOIR ($10.00) Miller Ranch, Sonoma. *Soft, fruity, clean and quite lovely.*

☆ 1981 PINOT NOIR ($10.00) Sangiacoma, Sonoma Valley. *Smoky, intense, earthy, heavy, a bit overdone.*

☆ 1980 ZINFANDEL ($10.00) Les Vignerons, Sonoma Valley. *Berries and jam, intense, no finesse.*

1980 ZINFANDEL ($12.00) Sonoma Valley. *Dense, clumsy and unappealing.*

☆☆ 1980 ZINFANDEL ($13.00) Glen Ellen, Sonoma Valley. *Big, rich, berried, late harvest style.*

☆☆ 1981 ZINFANDEL ($8.50) Sonoma Valley. *Dark, dense, crisp acidity, earthy and a bit heavy.*

꿿

Country Creek Winery
PENNSYLVANIA

133 Cressman Road, Telford, Pennsylvania 18969 (215-723-6516). FOUNDED: 1977. ACREAGE: 5 acres. PRODUCTION: 4,500 cases. DISTRIBUTION: At winery. OWNER: Bill Scheidell. WINE-MAKER: Bill Scheidell. Tours and tasting May–December: daily 9 A.M.–6 P.M.; January–April: weekends 9 A.M.–6 P.M.

The Scheidell family had a successful pick-your-own fruit orchard on their farm before Bill decided to start a winery. "I had been making wine for thirty years. I thought a winery would fit our orchard business, and darned if it didn't," says Bill. In a 150-year-old barn that had been part of a dairy, Bill started making both grape and fruit wines, selling them only at the winery. He is growing French-American hybrids only, having had troubles with vinifera. Bill keeps both the orchard and the winery going strong with the help of his wife and son.

Cowie Wine Cellars
ARKANSAS

Route 2, Box 110 A, Paris, Arkansas 72855 (501-963-3990). FOUNDED: 1967. ACREAGE: 1 acre. PRODUCTION: 2,000 cases. DISTRIBUTION: Arkansas. OWNERS: Robert G. and Bette Kay Cowie. WINEMAKER: Robert G. Cowie. OTHER LABEL: River Valley Winery. Tours and tasting Monday–Saturday 9 A.M.–6 P.M. Gift shop.

While growing up in Paris, Robert Cowie became fascinated with winemaking. He considered the process nothing short of a miracle. When he was older, he began making wine with the seriousness of a student. Today, the Cowie Winery, built by Robert's sons, John, George, and Louis, is an organized family operation. Robert's wife, Bette Kay Cowie, participates by painting winemaking scenes on the heads of wine barrels. Robert is still just as serious about making wine. "If I had to choose between making wine and drinking wine," says Robert, "I would make wine."

WHITE
O NV DRY MUSCADINE ($3.75) Arkansas.

RED
NV CYNTHIANA ($12.95) Arkansas.

CRANBROOK CELLARS *see* Monticello Cellars

Crescini Wines
SANTA CRUZ COUNTY

2621 Old San Jose Road, P.O. Box 216, Soquel, California 95073 (408-462-1466). FOUNDED: 1980. ACREAGE: None. PRODUCTION: 650 cases. DISTRIBUTION: California. OWNERS: Richard and Paulé Crescini. WINEMAKER: Richard Crescini. Tours by appointment.

Richard and Paulé Crescini both work full time in the field of radiology and have discovered the joys of making wine part time. Graduating quickly from amateur status, the Crescinis built a small winery on their home property which they intend to keep at the hobby level. Richard and Paulé are the only winery employees.

WHITE

○ 1981 CHENIN BLANC ($5.50) Monterey. *Strange, unattractive.*

RED

☆☆☆ 1981 CABERNET SAUVIGNON ($7.50) Napa Valley. *Minty, berried, deep, very good. Drink 1987.*

☆☆ 1981 MERLOT ($6.50) Napa Valley. *Ripe, fruity, oaky, charming.*

CRESTA BLANCA WINERY *see* Guild Wineries

Creston Manor Vineyards & Winery
SAN LUIS OBISPO COUNTY

17 mile post, Highway 58, Creston, California 93432 (805-238-7398). FOUNDED: 1982. ACREAGE: 95 acres. PRODUCTION: 8,000 cases. DISTRIBUTION: Major market states. OWNERS: Koontz and Rosenbloom families. David and Christina Crawford Koontz; Lawrence and Stephanie Rosenbloom. WINEMAKER: Victor Hugo Roberts. Tours by appointment.

David and Christina Crawford Koontz found the Indian Creek Ranch in San Luis Obispo while searching the California coast for a vineyard-winery site. The ranch consisted of 479 acres of pastureland with a good 150 acres suitable for vineyard. For financial as well as moral support, Christina invited her old high school chum Stephanie Rosenbloom and her husband, Lawrence, to join in this winemaking adventure. With 95 acres of Sauvignon Blanc, Chardonnay, and Cabernet Sauvignon in production, they will continue to buy a portion of their total tonnage from other growers in San Luis Obispo County. Both couples live and work in Los Angeles, leaving winemaker Victor Hugo Roberts to manage the winery operations. Christina Crawford Koontz is the author of the best-selling book *Mommie, Dearest.*

WHITE

○ 1982 CHARDONNAY ($11.50) San Luis Obispo. *Oxidized, unattractive.*

☆ 1983 CHARDONNAY ($6.00) Chamisal, Edna Valley.

1982 SAUVIGNON BLANC ($9.00) San Luis Obispo. *15% Semillon.*

☆☆☆ 1983 SAUVIGNON BLANC ($9.00) San Luis Obispo. *Clean, balanced, nice fruit.*

CRIBARI *see* Guild Wineries

Cronin Vineyards
SAN MATEO COUNTY

11 Old La Honda Road, Woodside, California 94062 (415-851-1452). FOUNDED: 1980. ACREAGE: 1 acre. PRODUCTION: 500 cases. DISTRIBUTION: California. OWNER: Duane Mansell Cronin. WINEMAKER: Duane Mansell Cronin. Tours and tasting by appointment.

Duane Cronin is an engineering and computer programming professional who was also an avid home winemaker. When his hobby grew beyond the 200-gallon limit, he had his winery bonded. "Making wine balances out the rest of my life," says Duane. "The rewards of working with computers cannot compare with the gratification that comes from making a quality wine." Because the winery is more a pleasure than a business, Cronin Vineyards will expand just to the point where each step of work can still be personally supervised by Duane.

WHITE

☆☆☆ 1982 CHARDONNAY ($12.00) Alexander Valley, Sonoma. *Deep, lush, rich, balanced.*
☆☆☆ 1982 CHARDONNAY ($12.00) Ventana, Monterey. *Deep, lush, lovely depth and balance.*
☆☆☆ 1982 CHARDONNAY ($14.00) Napa Valley. *Lush, deep, clean, lovely.*
  ☆☆ 1983 CHARDONNAY ($13.50) Napa Valley. *Earthy, rich, intense, ripe.*

RED

  ☆☆ 1980 CABERNET SAUVIGNON ($14.00) Napa Valley. *Earthy and intense but with a lovely fruitiness. Drink 1986.*
  ☆☆ 1981 CABERNET SAUVIGNON ($12.00) Napa Valley. *Berry fruit, balanced, tangy, attractive. Drink now.*
         1980 PINOT NOIR ($15.00) Ventana, Monterey. *Overly stemmy.*
  ☆☆ 1981 PINOT NOIR ($8.50) Ventana, Monterey. *Crisp, clean, complex, nicely made.*
    ☆ 1981 PINOT NOIR ($10.00) Winery Lake, Napa Valley. *Pale, thin but nice. Good flavors.*
         1982 PINOT NOIR ($9.00) Ventana, Monterey. *Soapy, vegetal, unpleasant.*
    ☆ 1980 ZINFANDEL ($7.50) Santa Clara.

CROSS CANYON *see* Ranchita Oaks Winery

Crosswoods Vineyards
CONNECTICUT

75 Chester Mane Road, North Stonington, Connecticut 06359 (203-535-2205). FOUNDED: 1984. ACREAGE: 30 acres. PRODUCTION: 3,800 cases. DISTRIBUTION: Connecticut, New York, Vermont, and Massachusetts. OWNERS: Susan and Hugh Connell. WINEMAKER: George Sulick, Jr. Tours by appointment.

The Connell family is surprised and delighted at how its innocent family project has become a spectacular new winery complex. They also have 30 acres of vines. When Susan Connell started planting vines, she was apprenticing at Benmarl Vineyards in New York while her husband, Hugh, worked as an international lawyer. Then the Connells bought an old dairy farm in Connecticut with the express purpose of planting vinifera and building a winery. They tore down the nineteenth-century dairy barn and carefully reconstructed it according to its original design. Inside, the winery is paneled in mahogany and gray ceramic tiles. There is an enormous barrel-aging cellar and a silo office tower. The Connells' first vintage was 1984.

Crown Regal Wine Cellars
NEW YORK

657 Montgomery Street, Brooklyn, New York 11225 (212-604-1430). FOUNDED: 1981. ACREAGE: None. PRODUCTION: 4,000 cases. DISTRIBUTION: Nationwide. OWNER: Joseph Zakon. WINEMAKER: Joseph Zakon. OTHER LABEL: Kesser. No tours or tasting.

"The only way I could drink good kosher wine was to make it myself," says Joseph Zakon, "but once I began making it, my friends all wanted to buy it. They kept bothering me. So I bonded my hobby, and that's just what Crown Regal Wine Cellars is—a 'bonded hobby'." Since being bonded meant that Joseph had to move the winery out of his house and onto separate premises, he rented some space from a friend. For Joseph, who started as one of the youngest winery owners in the country, winemaking is still just fun—something he does for himself and his friends.

WHITE

☆☆ NV CHARDONNAY ($10.00) Kosher, Long Island, New York. *Fresh, clean, varietal, quite lovely.*

ROSE

☆☆ NV KESSER KOSHER CONCORD ($3.00) New York State. *Fruity, sweet, clean and quite lovely.*

RED

☆ NV KESSER KOSHER MELLOW ($3.00) New York State. *French-American hybrids. Sweet, attractive, balanced.*

☆☆ NV DECHAUNAC ($5.00) Finger Lakes Region. *Kosher. Tart, dry, fresh, clean, with good fruit and complexity.*

CRYSTAL VALLEY *see* Cosentino Wine Company

John Culbertson Winery
SAN DIEGO COUNTY

2608 Via Rancheros, Fallbrook, California 92028 (619-728-0156). FOUNDED: 1981. ACREAGE: 14 acres. PRODUCTION: 8,000 cases. DISTRIBUTION: California. OWNERS: John and Martha Culbertson. WINEMAKER: Ron McClendon. Tours and tasting by appointment.

As a home winemaker, John Culbertson seemed to have a special talent for making sparkling wines. He won top awards in practically every amateur competition he entered. But the main reason he chose to make a career out of producing sparkling wine was that it's the kind of wine his wife likes best. Once John decided to start a real winery, he couldn't settle on whether to locate it in Texas or in California, since he owned a deep-sea diving company in Houston and an 80-acre avocado ranch in San Diego. He opted for San Diego, but he still commutes to Houston to keep an eye on all three businesses.

SPARKLING

☆☆☆ NV DEMI-SEC, CUVEE FRONTIGNAN ($12.00) California. *Muscat. Crisp, fresh, balanced, some sweetness, delightful.*

☆☆ 1981 BRUT ($14.00) California. *Rich, ripe, flavorful, heavy.*

☆☆ 1981 NATURAL ($16.50) California. *Toasty, rich, a bit heavy.*

☆☆☆ 1981 NATURAL, RECENT DISGORGE ($19.50) California. *Austere, toasty, clean, attractive.*

ঽ৯

Cuvaison Vineyard
NAPA COUNTY

4550 Silverado Trail, Calistoga, California 95415 (707-942-6266). FOUNDED: 1970. ACREAGE: 200 acres. PRODUCTION: 30,000 cases. DISTRIBUTION: Nationwide and 7 foreign countries. OWNER: Isenhold, Inc. Dr. Robert Logan, president and general manager. WINEMAKER: John Thacher. OTHER LABEL: Calistoga Vineyards. Tours by appointment. Tasting and retail sales daily 10 A.M.–4 P.M. Picnic area.

This winery, which has gone through quite a few changes in its short history, was started by scientists from Silicon Valley who eventually sold it to Commerce Clearinghouse, a publisher of research books. It was in turn acquired by its present owner, Isenhold, Inc., also proprietor of a Swiss vineyard. For six years this winery was home to talented but difficult winemaker Philip Togni. Before his departure in 1981, a large vineyard was acquired in the Carneros district of southern Napa Valley and planted to Chardonnay. John Thacher, who had been cellarmaster during Togni's reign, has assumed winemaking duties. *Cuvaison* is the French word for the fermentation of red wines in contact with the skins of grapes.

WHITE

☆☆ 1975 CHARDONNAY Napa Valley. *Fresh, clean, balanced. Attractive but beginning to fade.*

☆☆☆ 1980 CHARDONNAY ($12.50) Napa Valley. *Subtle and elegant, with ripe fruitiness and finesse.*

☆☆☆ 1981 CHARDONNAY ($12.00) Napa Valley. *Elegant and austere, crisp, fruity and very classy.*

☆☆☆ 1982 CHARDONNAY ($12.50) Napa Valley. *Youthful, hard, partly from new Carneros vines, nice.*

☆☆ 1983 CALISTOGA VINEYARDS CHARDONNAY ($7.00) Napa Valley. *Fresh, simple, clean—good everyday wine.*

RED

☆☆ 1976 CABERNET SAUVIGNON ($10.00) Napa Valley. *Intense, well made but lacking structure.*

☆☆ 1977 CABERNET SAUVIGNON ($10.00) Napa Valley. *Rich and intense, lacking grace but showing aging potential.*

☆☆☆ 1978 CABERNET SAUVIGNON ($12.00) Napa Valley. *Tannic, clean, intense, balanced. Age for at least two years.*

1979 CABERNET SAUVIGNON ($10.00) Napa Valley. *Very disappointing—off flavors, odd aromas.*

☆☆☆ 1980 CABERNET SAUVIGNON ($10.00) Napa Valley. *Lush, rich, clean and well made. Drink 1987 and beyond.*

☆☆ 1980 CABERNET SAUVIGNON ($11.00) Napa Valley. *Spicy, rich, peppery, very good structure. Drink 1988.*

☆☆☆ 1978 ZINFANDEL ($8.50) Napa Valley. *Peppery, rich and complex. Good aging potential.*

Cygnet Cellars
SANTA CLARA COUNTY

1020 Lupine Drive, Sunnyvale, California 94806 (408-733-4276). FOUNDED: 1977. ACREAGE: None. PRODUCTION: 2,000 cases. DISTRIBUTION: California. OWNERS: Partnership. Jim Johnson and Bob Lane, general partners. WINEMAKER: Jim Johnson. Tours by appointment on weekends.

"It is kind of a hobby gone mad," says winemaker-owner Jim Johnson. He started by making fruit wines in his garage while designing computers as a profession. But once he began making grape wine, the hobby quickly outgrew the garage, so Jim and his partners bought ten acres of land and built a winery. As for style, Cygnet Cellars is proud of the fact that while everyone else is talking "light and fruity," it is making rich and robust wines with high alcohol and big flavors.

CYNTHIANA *see* Cowie Wine Cellars

Cypress Valley Vineyards
TEXAS

Goeth Ranch, Cypress Mill, Texas 78654 (512-825-3333). FOUNDED: 1982. ACREAGE: 50 acres. PRODUCTION: 5,000 cases. DISTRIBUTION: Texas. OWNERS: Dale and Penny Bettis. WINE-MAKER: Penny Bettis. Tours and tasting weekends 12–5 P.M. Weekdays by appointment.

Dale Bettis became interested in wine in Switzerland, where he was finishing his post-doctorate work in engineering. He and his wife, Penny, a horticulturist-turned-viticulturist, bought a large piece of property with a 101-year-old house in a German-settled community in Texas. They began planting their own vineyards while managing the first vineyard in the state to be used for wine production. "When we began planting, we really had no idea it would lead to a winery," says Penny. But in 1982 the tool shed was insulated, and the Bettises started making wine. Penny has been the winemaker for the most part, since Dale works full time as a professor of engineering at the University of Texas. Now that her small son is demanding more attention Penny plans to hire a full-time winemaker.

D'Agostini Winery
AMADOR COUNTY

14430 Shenandoah Road, Plymouth, California 95669 (209-245-6612). FOUNDED: 1856. ACREAGE: 125 acres. PRODUCTION: 40,000 cases. DISTRIBUTION: California and western states. OWNER: Armagan Ozdiker. WINEMAKER: Charlie Tsegeletos. Tours and tasting daily 10 A.M.–5 P.M.

Since 1911, the D'Agostini Winery had been a tight family operation. It had established a reputation for making big, rich, red wines, fermented with natural yeast. In 1983, however, the D'Agostini brothers and sisters decided to retire. Armagan Ozdiker, owner of Wine Merchants of Sacramento, purchased the old cement-block winery and began rebuilding, replanting, and redesigning the package. "We are adding a few new wines to the line," says Charlie Tsegeletos, the new winemaker, "like Sauvignon Blanc and Muscat Canelli, but we will still be making D'Agostini Zinfandel and Burgundy." The D'Agostini brothers, who live four miles away, act as consultants for the winery.

BLANC DE NOIR

☆ 1984 WHITE ZINFANDEL, RESERVE ($4.50) Amador County. *1.3% residual sugar.*

Daquila Wines
WASHINGTON

1434 Western Avenue, Seattle, Washington 98181 (206-343-9521). FOUNDED: 1981. ACREAGE: None. PRODUCTION: 2,400 cases. DISTRIBUTION: Washington. OWNER: Corporation. Billie Hardin, general manager. WINEMAKER: Billie Hardin. Tours by appointment.

Musician Frank Daquila first made wine in his native Italy when he was twelve. In 1981, at age sixty-five, he opened his own winery right in the heart of Seattle. Located next to the bustling and historic Pike Place Market, the operation is small but efficient. Frank Daquila was so delighted to have finally realized a lifelong dream that his label bears a drawing of his smiling face. Three years later, in 1984, Frank died, leaving the future of the winery to his partners Billie Hardin and Bob Bune.

Daughters Wine Cellar
OHIO

5573 North Ridge Road, Madison, Ohio 44057 (216-428-7545). FOUNDED: 1980. ACREAGE: None. PRODUCTION: 3,000 cases. DISTRIBUTION: Local. OWNER: Daughters family. Dana Daughters, president. WINEMAKER: Dana Daughters. Tours and tasting Tuesday, Thursday 12–9 P.M. Wednesday, Friday, Saturday 12–1 A.M. Live entertainment on Wednesday, Friday, and Saturday. Picnic area.

Dana Daughters, the member of the family with the drive and winemaking experience, got this winery started on his own before bringing his father and brother in on the deal. Once a partnership was formed, the family bought property that contained a two-story house and a florist shop. They renovated the house, polished up the oak wood floors, and furnished the place appropriately. The florist shop is now run by Mrs. Daughters. For two years before the winery was officially opened, the family made wine from vinifera and French-American hybrids.

The Daume Winery
VENTURA COUNTY

270 Aviador, Camarillo, California 93010 (805-484-0597). FOUNDED: 1982. ACREAGE: None. PRODUCTION: 2,000 cases. DISTRIBUTION: California. OWNER: John Daume. WINE-MAKER: John Daume. Tours by appointment.

John Daume, a winemaker for fifteen years, owns a winemaking shop in Woodland Hills—home of the famous "Cellarmasters Club," a home-winemakers club that has produced 25 professional winemakers. "I figured it was my turn," says John. In 1982 he rented space in an industrial park and started "what we politely call a suburban winery, meaning the romance is in the barrel, not in the building." John, a true lover of Burgundy, makes only Burgundian varieties. He emphasizes that his wines are not for sipping by the poolside. "They are dinner wines," he says, "that need to be taken seriously."

WHITE

☆☆ 1982 CHARDONNAY ($10.00) Central Coast. *Rich, fat, clean, spicy.*

𝔢𝔟

De Loach Vineyards
SONOMA COUNTY

1791 Olivet Road, Santa Rosa, California 95401 (707-526-9111). FOUNDED: 1975. ACREAGE: 150 acres. PRODUCTION: 30,000 cases. DISTRIBUTION: Major market states. OWNER: Cecil De Loach. WINEMAKER: Cecil De Loach. Tours by appointment. Tasting daily 10 A.M.–4:30 P.M. except on major holidays.

Cecil De Loach was a fireman in San Francisco when he started growing grapes in the Russian River Valley in 1970. After five years of commuting to the city, he quit the fire fighting business in order to start a small winery. He used rented space to make his first 1,200 cases of Zinfandel. In 1979 he built a winery in his vineyard and began to expand his varietal line, adding Pinot Noir, Gewürztraminer, Chardonnay, and Fume Blanc. He has just finished a new addition to the winery, "with a real tasting room and everything."

WHITE

☆☆☆ 1980 CHARDONNAY ($10.00) Russian River Valley. *Oaky and rich with finesse and balance.*
☆☆☆ 1981 CHARDONNAY ($12.00) Russian River Valley–Sonoma. *Rich, oily, deep, lovely.*
☆☆☆ 1982 CHARDONNAY ($12.00) Russian River Valley. *Ripe, sweetish, rich and fruity.*
☆☆☆ 1983 CHARDONNAY ($12.50) Sonoma. *Big, ripe, rich, clean and crisp.*
☆☆☆ 1981 FUME BLANC ($8.50) Alexander Valley.
☆☆☆ 1982 FUME BLANC ($8.50) Sonoma. *Barrel fermented. Complex and fruity.*
☆☆☆ 1983 FUME BLANC ($9.00) Russian River Valley, Sonoma. *Fresh, clean, lovely, varietal.*
☆☆ 1982 GEWURZTRAMINER ($7.00) Russian River Valley. *2.5% residual sugar.*
☆☆☆ 1983 GEWURZTRAMINER ($7.00) Estate, Russian River Valley. *0.8% residual sugar. Spritzy, crisp, clean, lean and likable.*
☆☆☆ 1984 GEWURZTRAMINER ($7.00) Estate, Russian River Valley. *1% residual sugar. Clean, spritzy, varietal, balanced.*

BLANC DE NOIR

☆☆☆ 1982 ZINFANDEL ($5.75) Sonoma. *1.1% residual sugar. Fresh, crisp and delicious.*
☆☆☆ 1983 WHITE ZINFANDEL ($5.75) Russian River Valley, Sonoma. *1.1% residual sugar. Superb, crisp, fruity, varietal, pink.*
☆☆☆ 1984 WHITE ZINFANDEL ($5.75) Sonoma. *1.1% residual sugar. A classic—crisp, fruity, an absolute delight.*

RED

☆☆ 1981 CABERNET SAUVIGNON ($11.00) Dry Creek Valley. *Rich, lush, fruity, balanced, structured. Drink 1987.*
☆☆☆ 1981 PINOT NOIR ($9.00) Estate, Sonoma. *Velvety and lush, with great fruit. A stunner.*
☆☆☆ 1981 PINOT NOIR ($12.00) Reserve, Estate, Sonoma. *Rich, clean, cherry fruit, sturdy, complex.*
☆☆ 1982 PINOT NOIR ($10.00) Estate, Russian River Valley. *Some depth and youthful tannin. Drink 1986.*
☆☆☆ 1980 ZINFANDEL ($7.50) Estate, Russian River Valley.
☆☆☆ 1981 ZINFANDEL ($7.50) Estate, Russian River Valley. *Rich, velvety, complex, balanced, fruity, varietal, super.*

𝔢𝔟

Paul De Martini
ALAMEDA COUNTY

5919 Clayton Road, Clayton, California 94517 (415-846-2133). FOUNDED: 1983. ACREAGE: None. PRODUCTION: 5,000 cases. DISTRIBUTION: California. OWNER: Historic Properties, Inc. Lessor, Gloria Forni Patton. WINEMAKER: Sam Balderas. Tours and tasting daily 11 A.M.– 5 P.M.

The old, weather-beaten De Martini winery, built in 1885, is being completely restored and put back into operation for the first time since Prohibition. Owner Gloria Forni Patton had lived in the third floor of the old sandstone building until 1975. After she left, the winery became the victim of vandals, neglect, and time. The surrounding open land areas were quickly being overrun by large residential and commercial developments. The winery was destined to become a shopping center until Historic Properties of Pleasanton offered to lease the facility for champagne processing. Under this agreement, the winery was completely restored and modernized while keeping the original design intact.

De May Wine Cellars
NEW YORK

R.D. 88, Hammondsport, New York 14840 (607-569-2040). FOUNDED: 1977. ACREAGE: 30 acres. PRODUCTION: 10,000 cases. DISTRIBUTION: At winery. OWNER: Patrice S. De May; Serge J. De May, manager. WINEMAKER: Serge J. De May. Tours and tasting daily 10 A.M.–5 P.M. Closed Sundays November–June. Gift shop.

The De May family moved from the Loire Valley of France to Hammondsport, New York, in 1974. They immediately began looking for land and found 30 acres of vineyards near Keuka Lake. The De Mays had arranged to sell their grapes to a major wine company, but found it became more difficult each year to get a respectable price. Old hands at the winery business, having owned and operated their family winery in Vouvray (which is currently being run by grandparents De May), the De Mays bought and restored a run-down three-story building that is located approximately fifteen minutes from the vineyards. Serge De May and his son, Patrice, make table wine and have added méthode champenoise sparkling wine, which they prefer to call "Champagne."

Deer Park Winery
NAPA COUNTY

1000 Deer Park Road, Deer Park, California 94576 (707-963-5411). FOUNDED: 1979. ACREAGE: 6 acres. PRODUCTION: 5,000 cases. DISTRIBUTION: Major market states. OWNERS: David and Kinta Clark, and Lila and Robert Knapp. WINEMAKER: David S. Clark. Tours by appointment. Picnic area by appointment.

The old stone Deer Park Winery had been totally abandoned until it was purchased in 1979 by Lila and Robert Knapp and Kinta and David Clark. David, the winemaker, worked at both Cuvaison and Clos du Val wineries for several years. Since there are only six acres planted on the rocky 48-acre estate, most of the winery's grapes are purchased.

WHITE

      1981 CHARDONNAY ($7.50) Napa Valley.
☆☆☆ 1982 CHARDONNAY ($9.50) Napa Valley. *Big, intense, with fresh fruit acidity and elegant bearing.*

☆☆   1983 CHARDONNAY ($12.00) Summit Lake, Howell Mountain, Napa Valley. *Rich, intense.*
○   1981 SAUVIGNON BLANC ($7.50) Napa Valley.
☆   1982 SAUVIGNON BLANC ($6.75) Napa Valley. *Soft, fruity, undistinguished.*

RED

☆☆   1979 ZINFANDEL ($6.75) Napa Valley. *Soft, grapey, intense.*
☆☆   1980 ZINFANDEL ($6.75) Napa. *Varietal and fresh, with good fruit. Needs age.*

Dehlinger Winery
SONOMA COUNTY

6300 Guerneville Road, Sebastopol, California 95472 (707-823-2378). FOUNDED: 1976. ACREAGE: 31 acres. PRODUCTION: 7,000 cases. DISTRIBUTION: California and major market states. OWNER: Tom Dehlinger. WINEMAKER: Tom Dehlinger. Tours Monday–Friday 1 P.M.– 4:30 P.M., weekends 10 A.M.–5 P.M.

Studious in appearance and expression, Tom Dehlinger is a man deeply devoted to his vineyards, to his winery, and to his agricultural life. His involvement is total. He built his own winery, a small efficient redwood building, as well as a two-story octagonal house that sits atop a neatly groomed vineyard knoll.

WHITE

☆   1980 CHARDONNAY ($9.00) Sonoma. *Vinous, rich, lacking grace.*
☆☆   1981 CHARDONNAY ($9.00) 80% Estate, Sonoma.
☆☆   1982 CHARDONNAY ($9.00) Russian River Valley. *Earthy, deep, oily, vegetal.*
☆   1982 CHARDONNAY ($9.00) Russian River Valley. *Soapy, vegetal, unappealing.*

RED

☆☆   1979 CABERNET SAUVIGNON ($8.75) Sonoma. *Assertive and Zinfandel-like. Should mellow with age.*
☆☆☆ 1980 CABERNET SAUVIGNON ($9.00) Sonoma. *Rich, full, berry-style with plummy, lush flavors. Drink 1987.*
☆☆   1981 CABERNET SAUVIGNON ($10.00) Sonoma. *Peppers, rich, lush, clean. Drink 1986.*
☆☆   NV   PINOT NOIR ($8.00) Russian River Valley. *Earthy, rich, intense, heavy.*
☆   1979 PINOT NOIR ($7.50) Sonoma. *Varietal, earthy. Some good fruit but lacking richness.*
☆☆   1980 PINOT NOIR ($10.00) Sonoma. *Varietal, rich, earthy and lean. Nice structure.*
☆   1981 PINOT NOIR ($10.00) Sonoma. *Earthy, raisiny, varietal.*
☆☆☆ 1982 PINOT NOIR ($10.00) Sonoma. *Lush, oaky but delicate, varietal, charming.*
☆☆☆ 1979 ZINFANDEL ($7.00) Sonoma. *13% Petite Sirah. Ripe, fruity, balanced.*
☆☆   1980 ZINFANDEL ($7.50) Sonoma. *21% Petite Sirah. Jammy, peppery, ripe and fruity.*
☆☆   1981 ZINFANDEL ($7.50) Sonoma. *14% Petite Sirah. Snappy fruit, rich, varietal.*

Del Vista Vineyards
NEW JERSEY

R.D. 1, Box 84, Frenchtown, New Jersey 08825 (201-996-2849). FOUNDED: 1982. ACREAGE: 11 acres. PRODUCTION: 625 cases. DISTRIBUTION: New Jersey. OWNERS: Jim and Jonetta Williams. WINEMAKER: Jim Williams. Tours and tasting Wednesday and Friday 2 P.M.–4 P.M., weekends 1 P.M.–5 P.M.

Winemaking was a relaxing hobby for Jim Williams, who works for the telephone company. But in 1977 things got serious. Jim and his wife, Jonetta, purchased a piece of property and began planting vines. In 1982 they turned an empty chicken hatchery into a winery, and the hobby had become a business.

Delicato Vineyards
SAN JOAQUIN COUNTY

12001 South Highway 99, Manteca, California 95336 (209-239-1215). FOUNDED: 1935. ACREAGE: 365 acres. PRODUCTION: 825,000 cases. DISTRIBUTION: 14 major market states; Japan, Germany, and England. OWNER: Corporation. Anthony, Frank, and Vincent Indelicato. WINEMAKER: Bill Nakata. OTHER LABEL: Delicato Medallion. Tours on Friday 10 A.M., 2 P.M., and 4 P.M. Tasting daily 9 A.M.–5:30 P.M. Gift shop. Newsletter.

In 1925, during Prohibition, Gaspare Indelicato, an Italian immigrant, developed a thriving business shipping grapes to home winemakers in the Midwest and East. After Repeal, the family remained content to be growers until the boom year of 1968 encouraged them to plunge into winemaking. Three of Gaspare's sons, Frank, Anthony, and Vincent, run the winery, which is known for producing bulk wines for other wineries, private labels, and restaurant house wines. The winery has also participated in the recent rush to sell wine in boxes, bags, and cardboard barrels.

WHITE

☆　1982 CHENIN BLANC ($3.45) California. *Light and slightly sweet.*
○　1980 SAUVIGNON BLANC ($4.30) Northern California. *Oxidized.*

RED

☆☆　NV　BURGUNDY ($2.40) Northern California. *Brambly, decent fruit, rich and soft.*
○　1980 CABERNET SAUVIGNON ($5.00) Northern California. *Weedy, sweet and a bit oxidized.*
　　1982 CABERNET SAUVIGNON ($3.75) California. *Clean and decent but a bit sweet and very strange.*

Delmonico's
NEW YORK

182 15th Street, Brooklyn, New York 11215 (212-768-7020). FOUNDED: 1912. ACREAGE: None. PRODUCTION: 50 cases. DISTRIBUTION: New York. OWNER: Corporation. Joseph Della Monica, president. WINEMAKER: Gerald Della Monica. No tours or tasting.

After Repeal, Joseph Della Monica wasted no time in converting his grocery warehouse into a winery. He purchased grapes, made and bottled the wine, and sold every drop he made. Today, the winery is still in that same warehouse but very little appears under the Delmonico label—99 percent of the wine is sold in bulk to other wineries. Joseph's son Gerald runs the winery in a relaxed manner, having been born into a family where winemaking is as normal as eating breakfast.

Desantis Vineyards
SANTA CLARA COUNTY

2825 Day Road, Gilroy, California 95020 (408-847-2060). FOUNDED: 1981. ACREAGE: 2 acres. PRODUCTION: 700 cases. DISTRIBUTION: California. OWNERS: John and Carol Desantis. WINEMAKER: John Desantis. Tours by appointment.

Encouraged by friends at a local home winemaking club, John Desantis started making wine in Los Angeles. After relocating to the Santa Clara Valley for a job in computer manufacturing, he and his wife, Carol, bought a three-acre parcel in Morgan Hill. They planted a small Cabernet vineyard and turned the three-car garage into a winery.

Devlin Wine Cellars
SANTA CRUZ COUNTY

P.O. Box 728, Soquel, California 95073 (408-476-7288). FOUNDED: 1978. ACREAGE: None. PRODUCTION: 3,000 cases. DISTRIBUTION: Major market states. OWNERS: Charles and Cheryl Devlin. WINEMAKER: Charles Devlin. Tasting daily 12–5 P.M. at 2815 Porter Street, Soquel (408-476-9300).

Chuck Devlin, an earnest young man with a black belt in judo, believes strongly in the concept of the "mid-range" winery that makes good moderately-priced wines year after year. Chuck studied at U.C. Davis and served his apprenticeship at Wiederkehr Wine Cellars in Arkansas and at Louis M. Martini in the Napa Valley. To Chuck, good grapes are the most important aspect of making good wine. In his search for exceptional fruit he has sought out older hillside vineyards in the coastal counties of California. Chuck changes the varieties of wine he makes each year, depending on what looks good for that vintage.

WHITE

1981 CHARDONNAY ($10.00) Edna Valley. *Minty, vinous, short.*
☆ 1981 CHARDONNAY ($10.00) Sonoma. *Earthy, some dirty flavors, decent.*
1982 CHARDONNAY ($8.00) Sonoma. *Some oxidation, lacks varietal character and fruit.*
O 1982 CHENIN BLANC ($5.00) 67% San Luis Obispo, 33% Santa Clara. *Dull and oxidized.*
☆ 1980 SAUVIGNON BLANC ($6.50) Monterey.

RED

☆☆ 1980 CABERNET SAUVIGNON ($6.00) Sonoma. *Herbal, balanced, clean and attractive. Drink now.*
☆☆ 1981 MERLOT ($9.00) Sonoma. *Lush, rich, clean; a very nice wine.*
☆☆ 1982 MERLOT ($8.00) Central Coast. *Lush, varietal, clean and attractive.*
☆ 1979 ZINFANDEL ($10.00) Paso Robles.
☆☆☆ 1980 ZINFANDEL ($7.50) Paso Robles.

DIABLO *see* Lake Sonoma Winery

Diamond Creek Vineyards
NAPA COUNTY

1500 Diamond Mountain Road, Calistoga, California 94515 (707-942-6926). FOUNDED: 1972. ACREAGE: 20 acres. PRODUCTION: 3,200 cases. DISTRIBUTION: Major market states. OWNER: Al Brounstein. WINEMAKER: Al Brounstein. No tours or tasting.

Al and Boots Brounstein moved to the Napa Valley from Los Angeles, where Al had owned a pharmaceutical distribution company. They bought property on Diamond Mountain near Calistoga and planted twenty acres of vines, mainly Cabernet Sauvignon with a little Merlot for blending. After soil studies were made, Al decided he actually had three distinct vineyards. He bottles them separately, and they do display quite disparate qualities. Besides making some of California's most sought-after wines, Al is one of the Napa Valley's true originals, somehow feisty and charming at the same time.

RED

☆☆☆ 1977 CABERNET SAUVIGNON ($10.00) Gravelly Meadow, Napa Valley. *Delicate, soft, clean and very nice. Drink now.*

☆☆☆ 1977 CABERNET SAUVIGNON ($10.00) Red Rock Terrace, Napa Valley. *Tart, tannic, good. Drink now or hold a few more years.*

☆☆☆ 1977 CABERNET SAUVIGNON ($10.00) Volcanic Hill, Napa Valley. *Rich, fruited, clean and full. Drink 1986 and beyond.*

☆☆☆ 1978 CABERNET SAUVIGNON ($12.50) Gravelly Meadow, Napa Valley. *Deep, complex and aristocratic. Great potential. Drink 1986.*

☆☆☆ 1978 CABERNET SAUVIGNON ($12.50) Red Rock Terrace, Napa Valley. *Tight, rich and showing great aging potential. Drink 1988.*

☆☆☆ 1978 CABERNET SAUVIGNON ($12.50) Volcanic Hill, Napa Valley. *Perhaps the best of the three—firm yet very supple. Superb.*

☆☆☆ 1979 CABERNET SAUVIGNON ($15.00) Gravelly Meadow, Napa Valley. *Concentrated, complex and gracefully structured. Drink 1987.*

☆☆☆ 1979 CABERNET SAUVIGNON ($15.00) Red Rock Terrace, Napa Valley. *Slightly lighter and more delicate. Complex. Drink now.*

☆☆☆ 1979 CABERNET SAUVIGNON ($15.00) Volcanic Hill, Napa Valley. *Austere, hard-edged, rich and complex. Needs time. Drink 1988.*

☆☆☆ 1980 CABERNET SAUVIGNON ($20.00) Gravelly Meadow, Napa Valley. *Softer, richer, more herbal than Red Rock. Drink 1987.*

☆☆☆ 1980 CABERNET SAUVIGNON ($20.00) Red Rock Terrace, Napa Valley. *Tight and austere but showing great promise. Drink 1990.*

☆☆☆ 1980 CABERNET SAUVIGNON ($20.00) Volcanic Hill, Napa Valley. *Austerely structured but deep and rich. Drink 1989 or beyond.*

☆☆☆ 1982 CABERNET SAUVIGNON ($18.75) Special Selection, Volcanic Hill, Napa Valley. *Clean, crisp, lovely, but not as complex as the regular Volcanic Hill below.*

☆☆☆ 1982 CABERNET SAUVIGNON ($20.00) Gravelly Meadow, Napa Valley. *Rich, complex, lovely structure. Drink 1988.*

☆☆☆ 1982 CABERNET SAUVIGNON ($20.00) Red Rock Terrace, Napa Valley. *Dark, intense, rich, a bit coarse. Drink 1989.*

☆☆☆☆ 1982 CABERNET SAUVIGNON ($20.00) Volcanic Hill, Napa Valley. *Rich, clean, soft, lovely, balanced. Drink 1988.*

Diamond Oaks Vineyard
SONOMA COUNTY

26700 Dutcher Creek Road, Cloverdale, California 95425 (415-873-9463). FOUNDED: 1980. ACREAGE: 300 acres. PRODUCTION: 10,000 cases. DISTRIBUTION: 8 states. OWNERS: Dinesh Maniar. WINEMAKER: Jeff Libarle. No tours or tasting.

Dinesh Maniar is a real estate developer whose passion for renovating antique buildings got him involved in the wine business. Maniar is the founder of one of the largest real estate companies in the San Francisco Bay Area, Northwest Equity Corporation. Diamond Oak's first vineyard parcel was a 53-acre ranch that Maniar acquired because it holds the Kelsey Hearthstone, a historical landmark considered to be one of the oldest structures in northern Napa Valley. Fortunately, this plot of land had the soil and the climate to produce good yields of Sauvignon Blanc. Then Wild Horse Valley Vineyard in Napa was purchased for Chardonnay production. In 1982, Diamond Oaks Vineyard was permanently established in Cloverdale in Sonoma County.

WHITE

☆ 1983 SAUVIGNON BLANC ($4.50) Thomas Knight, Napa Valley.

RED

☆ 1980 CABERNET SAUVIGNON ($9.95) North Coast.

J. E. Digardi Winery
CONTRA COSTA COUNTY

3785 Pacheco Boulevard, Martinez, California 94553 (415-228-2638). FOUNDED: 1886. ACREAGE: None. PRODUCTION: 30,000 cases. DISTRIBUTION: At winery. OWNER: Francis Digardi. WINEMAKER: Francis Digardi. Tours by appointment.

Francis Digardi, sole proprietor of J. E. Digardi Winery, knows the harsh side of the wine business. His winery, family owned since 1912, used to win medals during the 1940s, but that was before the vineyards were "taxed away," as Francis puts it. "Confiscation by taxation," he sighs. "We had thirty-six vineyard acres ourselves and were leasing two hundred and fifty more. Then the leased property was split into sub-divisions. Now Contra Costa County is growing houses instead of grapes. They call that progress." Due to the loss of the vineyards and fierce industry competition, the winery is now used mainly for storage of sparkling wine stock for Weibel Vineyards.

Doerflinger Wine Cellars
PENNSYLVANIA

3248 Old Berwick Road, Bloomsburg, Pennsylvania 17815 (717-784-2112). FOUNDED: 1975. ACREAGE: None. PRODUCTION: 8,000 cases. DISTRIBUTION: Local. OWNERS: Ludwig and Virginia Doerflinger. WINEMAKER: Ludwig Doerflinger. Tours and tasting Monday–Friday 10 A.M.–6 P.M.

Ludwig Doerflinger retired many years ago, but he won't stop working. Now in his eighties, he may talk about retiring, "but the next day he will change his mind," says his wife Virginia. Although Ludwig came from a winemaking family in Baden, Germany, his first job in America was as a chef, before getting a job with a Brooklyn winery. The first time he retired, he and his wife moved to their present home in Pennsylvania. But when the Small Winery Act was passed, Ludwig started a winery in their cellar. The Doerflingers don't grow or crush grapes because "Ludwig doesn't want all that dirt and mess around," so they purchase juice from Pennsylvania producers. They presently make both fruit and grape wines, but Ludwig is once again starting to talk about semi-retirement or, at least, going to Florida during the winters.

Dolan Vineyards
MENDOCINO COUNTY

1482 Inez Way, Redwood Valley, California 95470 (707-485-7250). FOUNDED: 1980. ACREAGE: 5 acres. PRODUCTION: 3,000 cases. DISTRIBUTION: California and 7 other states. OWNER:

Paul Dolan. WINEMAKER: Paul Dolan; Raymond Willmers, assistant winemaker-marketing director. Tours by appointment.

Paul Dolan was accused of being a workaholic when he built his own winery on the hill in back of his house. Full-time winemaker at burgeoning Fetzer Vineyards, Paul didn't need more wine to make. He's still up to his elbows in wine at Fetzer, but the wine he makes at Dolan Vineyards reflects his own personal style.

WHITE

☆☆☆ 1980 CHARDONNAY ($10.00) Mendocino. *Tasty and dark. Good acid balances it.*
☆☆ 1981 CHARDONNAY ($12.00) Mendocino. *Toasty nose; rich, snappy flavor, lacking a middle.*
☆☆ 1982 CHARDONNAY ($13.00) Lolonis, Mendocino. *Fresh, crisp, attractive.*

RED

☆☆ 1981 CABERNET SAUVIGNON ($12.00) Mendocino. *Herbal, big, fat, deep.*

Domaine Chandon
NAPA COUNTY

California Drive, Yountville, California 94599 (707-944-8844). FOUNDED: 1973. ACREAGE: 850 acres. PRODUCTION: 378,000 cases. DISTRIBUTION: Nationwide; Canada and Puerto Rico. OWNER: Moet-Hennessy, Inc. John Wright, president; Gino Zepponi, vice president operations; Michaela Rodeno, vice president marketing; Will Nord, vice president viticulture. WINEMAKER: Dawnine Sample Dyer. Tours daily 11 A.M.–5:30 P.M. Tasting daily May–October: 11 A.M.–5:30 P.M.; November–April: Wednesday–Sunday 11 A.M.–5:30 P.M. Restaurant.

Moet-Hennessy's investment in the Napa Valley was a turning point for American sparkling wine production. This modern facility with its curved concrete forms started a boom that has yet to subside. Under the watchful and twinkling eye of Edmund Maudière, Moet et Chandon's champagne master, a new sparkling wine was created that represented a merger of American grapes and French know-how. It was a sensation. The winery, big to begin with, has been enlarged twice already. The winery complex also houses a rather extraordinary restaurant.

SPARKLING

☆☆ NV BLANC DE NOIRS ($13.50) Napa Valley. *Fruity and pleasant with some weight and Pinot Noir flavors.*
☆☆ NV BRUT ($13.25) Napa Valley. *Fresh, clean and attractive with plenty of rich fruit.*
☆☆☆ NV BRUT SPECIAL RESERVE ($40.00) Napa Valley. *Magnums only. 1979 vintage. Clean, graceful and delicious.*
☆☆☆ NV 10TH ANNIVERSARY RESERVE ($16.95) Napa Valley. *16% Pinot Blanc gives this wine complexity and roundness.*

Domaine Laurier
SONOMA COUNTY

8075 Martinelli Road, P.O. Box 550, Forestville, California 95436 (707-887-2176). FOUNDED: 1978. ACREAGE: 30 acres. PRODUCTION: 10,000 cases. DISTRIBUTION: California, East Coast, and a few other states. OWNERS: Jacob and Barbara Shilo. WINEMAKER: Stephen Test. Tours by appointment. No tasting room. Retail sales.

Barbara and Jacob Shilo were looking for an escape from urban life, but they wanted to be close enough to San Francisco to partake of the city's cultural delights. They chose a farm in Sonoma that happened to have eighteen acres of grapevines, an old barn full of farming equipment, and a flourishing population of bay laurel trees. Once the Shilos tasted a few of the homegrown wines made by the previous owner, they began to flirt with the idea of starting their own winery. They filled the barn with equipment, replanted some of the older vineyards, and added twenty additional acres. Then they hired Mary Ann Graf, former Simi winemaker, as a consultant. The Shilos named their winery in honor of a huge 150-year-old bay laurel tree that overlooks the vineyards.

WHITE

☆☆ 1981 CHARDONNAY ($13.00) Sonoma. *Lean, snappy, vinous, with good fruit.*

☆☆☆ 1982 CHARDONNAY ($15.00) Sonoma. *Soft, carefully constructed, a lovely wine.*

☆☆☆ 1983 CHARDONNAY ($13.00) Sonoma. *Oaky, austere, crisp and lovely structure; delightful.*

☆☆☆☆ 1982 SAUVIGNON BLANC ($9.00) Sonoma-Green Valley. *Firm fruit, crisp and superb. A virtually perfect wine.*

☆ 1983 SAUVIGNON BLANC ($9.50) Sonoma. *Simple, snappy, fruity but dull.*

RED

☆ 1978 CABERNET SAUVIGNON ($10.00) Estate, Sonoma. *Weedy, crisp and balanced. Drink now.*

☆☆☆ 1979 CABERNET SAUVIGNON ($12.50) Sonoma. *Elegant, varietal, fruity. Will improve with age.*

1980 CABERNET SAUVIGNON ($12.00) Green Valley. *Intense, raisiny and marred by off odors.*

☆☆ 1982 CABERNET SAUVIGNON ($12.00) Estate, Sonoma–Green Valley. *Dark, rich, velvety, intense. Drink 1987.*

☆☆ 1978 PINOT NOIR ($10.00) Estate, Russian River Valley, Sonoma. *Good fruit and varietal character.*

☆ 1979 PINOT NOIR ($10.00) Estate, Russian River Valley, Sonoma. *Meaty, balanced, decent.*

☆☆ 1980 PINOT NOIR ($10.00) Estate, Sonoma.

☆ 1981 PINOT NOIR ($10.00) Estate, Sonoma–Green Valley. *Thin, pale, vegetal, earthy.*

Donatoni Winery
LOS ANGELES COUNTY

10604 South La Cienega Boulevard, Inglewood, California 90304 (213-645-5445). FOUNDED: 1980. ACREAGE: None. PRODUCTION: 1,200 cases. DISTRIBUTION: California. OWNERS: Hank and Judy Donatoni. WINEMAKER: Hank Donatoni. Tours by appointment.

Hank Donatoni is a pilot for United Airlines who planted a few vines at his Topanga Canyon home and then bought a book about winemaking. After this first step, Hank began buying grapes from the Paso Robles area and taking classes in enology at U.C. Davis. He has kept his winery close to his work by renting space two blocks from the Los Angeles airport.

RED

☆ 1979 CABERNET SAUVIGNON ($8.50) Lot 2, Nepenthe, California (San Luis Obispo). *A bit overdone—vegetal, earthy and lush.*

Donna Maria Vineyards
SONOMA COUNTY

10286 Chalk Hill Road, Healdsburg, California 95448 (707-838-4306). FOUNDED: 1980. ACREAGE: 175 acres. PRODUCTION: 24,000 cases. DISTRIBUTION: California and 24 states. OWNER: Frederick P. Furth, owner; Gary Chesak, general manager; Elizabeth Pressler, marketing director. WINEMAKER: Larry Wara. OTHER LABEL: Chalk Hill Winery. Tours and tasting by appointment.

When Fred Furth purchased the Donna Maria Ranch, he wasn't quite sure what to do with it. Gary Chesak, the ranch's caretaker, knew that grapes had been cultivated and that a winery had existed on the property before Prohibition. Historically, wine grapes had always done well in the Chalk Hill area, so with the blessing of the experts at U.C. Davis, 130 acres were planted. A large, barn-shaped winery, designed and equipped for expansion, was built on the property, and wine consultant Larry Wara was hired to oversee wine production. The wines made under the Donna Maria label are made only from estate-grown grapes; the second label, Chalk Hill Winery, features wines made from purchased Chalk Hill appellation grapes.

WHITE

☆☆☆ 1981 CHARDONNAY ($10.00) Sonoma. *Crisp, oaky and well balanced.*

☆☆☆ 1982 CHALK HILL CHARDONNAY ($6.00) Sonoma. *Crisp, well made, fresh and quite lovely.*

☆☆☆ 1982 CHARDONNAY ($10.00) Estate, Sonoma. *Toasty, rich, complex, very good.*

☆☆ 1983 CHALK HILL CHARDONNAY ($7.00) Sonoma. *Crisp, snappy, balanced, very nice.*

☆☆ 1983 CHALK HILL CHARDONNAY ($10.00) Proprietor's Reserve, Sonoma. *Clean, varietal, smoky, attractive.*

☆ 1982 GEWURZTRAMINER ($6.00) Estate, Chalk Hill, Sonoma. *1.2% residual sugar. Good fruit but dull and not varietal.*

☆☆☆ 1983 GEWURZTRAMINER ($6.00) Estate, Chalk Hill, Sonoma. *Spritzy, clean, dry, varietal.*

☆☆☆ 1984 GEWURZTRAMINER ($6.00) Estate, Chalk Hill, Sonoma. *Crisp, spritzy, clean, varietal, charming.*

☆☆ 1982 CHALK HILL SAUVIGNON BLANC ($6.00) Sonoma. *Crisp and lemony, low on varietal character.*

☆☆☆ 1983 CHALK HILL SAUVIGNON BLANC ($6.00) Sonoma. *Fresh, fruity, clean, charming.*

☆☆ 1982 CHALK HILL SEMILLON ($15.00) Late Harvest, Chalk Hill, Sonoma. *14% residual sugar. Rich and grassy, botrytis.*

RED

☆☆☆ 1981 CHALK HILL CABERNET SAUVIGNON ($8.00) Sonoma. *Rich, beautifully structured, fruity. Drink now.*

☆☆ 1981 PINOT NOIR ($6.00) Estate, Chalk Hill, Sonoma. *Pleasant cherry nose, lush fruit, varietal, very nice. Drink now.*

J. Patrick Dore Selections
MARIN COUNTY

42 Miller Avenue, Mill Valley, California 94941 (415-388-9082). FOUNDED: 1982. ACREAGE: None. PRODUCTION: 250,000 cases. DISTRIBUTION: Nationwide. OWNER: Coastal Wines, Ltd. J. Patrick Dore, president. WINEMAKER: Kurt Lorenzi. No tours or tasting.

J. Patrick Dore, a marketing specialist and commodities trader, saw an ad for a French negociant label in a magazine. "Why not be a negociant of California wines?" he thought. He had the money, the contacts, and the marketing skill, so he created his own label, bought wines in bulk, and produced some inexpensive blends. With Patrick's marketing talent behind them, the wines were a hit. Eventually his production began to include custom crushing at several wineries, and Patrick realized that he needed a winemaker. He hired Kurt Lorenzi, previously with Estrella River Winery and Los Vineros Winery, to work with the wineries and grape growers. Dore's goal is to reach a half-million-case production and to buy a winery by 1989.

WHITE

☆☆ 1982 CHARDONNAY ($6.50) Napa Valley. *Dense, rich, earthy, varietal.*
☆ 1983 CHARDONNAY ($4.75) California. *Simple, clean, varietal, decent but dull.*
☆☆ 1983 SAUVIGNON BLANC San Luis Obispo.

BLANC DE NOIR

1983 BLANC OF CABERNET ($4.50) San Luis Obispo. *Weedy and sweet.*

RED

☆ 1980 MERLOT ($4.00) Napa Valley. *Smoky, light, nice flavors.*
☆ 1979 ZINFANDEL Napa Valley.

Dover Vineyards
OHIO

24945 Detroit Road, Westlake, Ohio 44145 (216-871-0700). FOUNDED: 1932. ACREAGE: None. PRODUCTION: 60,000 cases. DISTRIBUTION: Ohio. OWNER: Dover Vineyards, Inc. WINE-MAKER: Donald Bower. Tours and tasting Monday–Saturday 11 A.M.–5 P.M. Wine and beer-making supply shop.

Not much is known about the mysterious Hungarian immigrant, Zoltan Wolovits, who purchased Dover Vineyards in 1932. When Zoltan bought the winery, then a cooperative of eighteen growers, he brought a little Hungarian tradition to the winemaking practices of Westlake, Ohio. The grapes, however, have remained American. The winery is an ambitious facility with a chalet restaurant and a home wine- and beer-making supply store. The store is just a small part of the winery's larger business, which is the importation and national wholesaling of home wine- and beer-making equipment.

WHITE

☆ NV CREAM NIAGARA ($2.50) New York State. *Lush, Labrusca flavor, good balance.*

ROSE

NV HALF & HALF ($2.50) Ohio. *Concord-Niagara blend, sweet and foxy. Volatile acidity.*
☆ NV PINK CATAWBA ($2.50) Ohio. *Sweet, fresh, balanced, good.*
☆ NV VIN ROSE ($2.50) Ohio. *Foxy, clean, off-dry.*

RED

☆ NV LABRUSCA Ohio. *Labrusca character, crisp, sweet, fresh, some volatile acid.*

FLAVORED

☆☆ CLEVELAND PLUM DELIGHT ($2.90) Ohio. *Grape wine flavored with plum.*

Dry Creek Vineyard
SONOMA COUNTY

3770 Lambert Bridge Road, Healdsburg, California 95448 (707-433-1000). FOUNDED: 1972. ACREAGE: 75 acres. PRODUCTION: 50,000 cases. DISTRIBUTION: 30 states nationwide. OWNER: David Stare. WINEMAKER: Larry Levin. Tours by appointment. Tasting daily 10:30 A.M.–4:30 P.M. Picnic area. Newsletter.

David Stare, a Bostonian schooled at Massachusetts Institute of Technology, is a jolly, outspoken fellow who has found a comfortable lifestyle in the wilds of Sonoma County. After becoming extremely interested in wine, he went to U.C. Davis to study enology and viticulture. When he had located a promising vineyard site in the Healdsburg area of Sonoma County, he had a winery built to resemble the smaller country wineries he had seen in France. Now, more than a decade later, David has been around Sonoma long enough to be considered "establishment."

WHITE

☆☆ 1978 CHARDONNAY ($12.00) Robert Young, Sonoma. *Intense, rich, vinous.*

☆☆ 1980 CHARDONNAY ($10.00) Sonoma.

☆ 1980 CHARDONNAY ($14.00) Vintner's Reserve, 50% Robert Young, 50% Dry Creek, Sonoma. *Vinous and vegetal.*

☆☆ 1981 CHARDONNAY ($10.00) Sonoma County. *Clean, rich and slightly earthy.*

☆☆ 1981 CHARDONNAY ($14.00) Vintner's Reserve, 50% Robert Young, 50% Estate, Sonoma. *Lush and complex, with nicely balanced fruitiness.*

☆ 1982 CHARDONNAY ($10.00) 62% Estate, 30% Robert Young, 8% others, Sonoma. *Crisp and clean but lacking varietal character and depth.*

☆☆☆ 1982 CHARDONNAY ($10.00) Sonoma. *Good acidity and varietal character. Should age gracefully.*

☆☆☆ 1983 CHARDONNAY ($10.00) Sonoma. *Crisp, fruity, clean, nicely made.*

☆☆ 1982 CHENIN BLANC ($6.00) Dry, California. *57% Mandeville Island, San Joaquin River Delta; 43% Sonoma.*

☆☆ 1983 CHENIN BLANC ($6.00) 60% Northern Sonoma, 40% Mandeville, California. *0.8% residual sugar. Crisp, fresh, rounded, charming.*

☆☆☆ 1984 CHENIN BLANC ($6.00) Sonoma. *0.7% residual sugar. Fresh, clean, crisp, balanced.*

☆☆ 1984 DRY CHENIN BLANC ($6.00) Sonoma. *Crisp, dry, green, pleasant.*

☆ 1980 FUME BLANC ($8.50) Sonoma. *Highly vegetal.*

☆☆☆ 1982 FUME BLANC ($8.50) Sonoma. *Varietal herbaceousness, crisp fruit and a touch of oak.*

☆☆ 1983 FUME BLANC ($8.50) Sonoma. *Grassy, oaky, good fruit.*

☆☆☆ 1983 GEWURZTRAMINER ($4.50) Larson, Sonoma. *375ml. 4.3% residual sugar. Lush, crisp, varietal.*

☆☆ 1983 GEWURZTRAMINER ($4.50) Late Harvest, Sonoma. *375ml. 4.8% residual sugar. Varietal, soft, balanced, clean.*

☆☆ 1981 SAUVIGNON BLANC ($8.50) Dry Creek Valley. *Fresh and snappy, with a touch of sweetness.*

RED

☆ NV IDLEWOOD CABERNET ($6.00) Sonoma. *Herbal, soft, balanced. Drink now.*

☆☆☆ 1975 CABERNET SAUVIGNON Dry Creek Valley. *23% Merlot. Earthy and still fruity.*

☆☆ 1976 CABERNET SAUVIGNON ($7.50) Sonoma. *Clean, fresh, appealing. Drink now.*

1977 CABERNET SAUVIGNON ($7.50) Vintner's Selection, Sonoma. *Considerably past its prime.*

☆☆ 1978 CABERNET SAUVIGNON ($8.00) Sonoma. *Clean, well structured, nice acidity. Drink now.*

☆ 1979 CABERNET SAUVIGNON ($8.00) Sonoma. *Weedy, dense, raisiny.*

☆☆ 1980 CABERNET SAUVIGNON ($9.50) Sonoma. *40% Merlot. Herbal, rich, smooth textured. Drink now or hold.*

☆ 1981 CABERNET SAUVIGNON ($8.00) Sonoma. *15% Merlot, 9% Petite Sirah. Vegetative and soft.*

☆ 1981 CABERNET SAUVIGNON ($9.00) Sonoma. *Herbal and fruity, some off aromas.*

☆ 1982 CABERNET SAUVIGNON ($9.50) Sonoma. *Herbal, toasty, dull fruit, thin.*

☆☆ 1980 MERLOT ($12.00) Estate, Dry Creek Valley. *18% Cabernet Sauvignon. Spicy, clean and rich.*

☆ 1981 MERLOT ($12.00) Sonoma. *Nice velvety texture, a bit weedy.*

☆☆ 1982 PETITE SIRAH ($9.00) Dry Creek Valley. *Dark, intense, raisiny, clean, attractive.*

☆☆ 1977 ZINFANDEL ($7.50) Sonoma. *Rich, powerful but the fruit is fading fast.*

☆ 1978 ZINFANDEL ($6.00) Late Harvest Style, Sonoma. *Vegetal, slightly sweet, a silly style.*

☆☆☆ 1978 ZINFANDEL ($6.50) Sonoma. *Rich, berried, earthy and well structured. Drink now.*

1979 ZINFANDEL ($7.50) Dry Creek Area, Sonoma.

☆☆ 1980 ZINFANDEL ($7.00) Sonoma. *Clean and fresh, with appealing flavors and fruit. Drink now.*

☆☆☆ 1981 ZINFANDEL ($7.50) Dry Creek Valley. *Fragrant, snappy, attractively varietal.*

Georges Duboeuf & Son
SONOMA COUNTY

476 Moore Lane, Unit V, Healdsburg, California 95448 (707-433-8619). FOUNDED: 1981. ACREAGE: None. PRODUCTION: 7,000 cases. DISTRIBUTION: 35 states. OWNER: Corporation. Georges Duboeuf and Jack Nelson. WINEMAKER: Patrick Leon. No tours or tasting.

Renowned Beaujolais shipper-producer Georges Duboeuf wanted to expand his operation into the United States by setting up a negociant-type winery in California that would produce Beaujolais in the French style. Originally, he had planned just to buy bulk wine from California producers and make his own blend, but he soon found that very few winemakers make Gamay Beaujolais in the quantity—or quality—he wanted. After changing the game plan in 1981, the winery now buys grapes and trucks them to a Sonoma winery, where the traditional Beaujolais carbonic maceration technique is used. The finished wine is stored and bottled at Georges Duboeuf & Son.

WHITE

☆☆ 1982 FRENCH COLOMBARD ($5.00) North Coast.

RED

☆☆ 1984 GAMAY ($4.50) North Coast.

☆☆ 1984 GAMAY ($6.00) North Coast. *Cherry fruit, fresh, attractive.*

☆☆ 1983 GAMAY BEAUJOLAIS ($5.00) Sonoma. *Snappy, fresh, clean, very simple.*

Duckhorn Vineyards
NAPA COUNTY

3027 Silverado Trail, St. Helena, California 94574 (707-963-7108). FOUNDED: 1976. ACREAGE: 6.5 acres. PRODUCTION: 10,000 cases. DISTRIBUTION: California and 20 other states. OWNER: Corporation. Daniel J. Duckhorn, president; Margaret L. Duckhorn, secretary. WINEMAKER: Tom Rinaldi. Tours by appointment. Retail sales Monday–Friday 9 A.M.–4 P.M. Newsletter.

Dan and Margaret Duckhorn's new winery burst on the scene in the fall of 1980 and the spring of 1981 with 800 cases of Cabernet and 800 cases of Merlot. These wines were so well received that demand has far outpaced supply ever since. The Duckhorns have also planted a small vineyard of Sauvignon Blanc and Semillon. Other grapes are purchased.

WHITE

☆☆ 1982 SAUVIGNON BLANC ($9.00) Napa Valley. *Decent but a bit off. Austere and oaky.*

☆☆☆☆ 1983 SAUVIGNON BLANC ($9.00) Napa Valley. *Lush fruit, intensely varietal, lovely oak. A great one.*

RED

☆☆☆ 1978 CABERNET SAUVIGNON ($10.50) Napa Valley. *Rich, firmly structured, complex. Drink over next three years.*

☆☆☆ 1980 CABERNET SAUVIGNON ($14.00) Napa Valley. *Austere and angular with great depth. Age several years.*

☆☆☆ 1981 CABERNET SAUVIGNON ($15.00) Napa Valley. *Rich and structured, lovely. Drink 1987 and beyond.*

☆☆ 1978 MERLOT ($12.50) Three Palms, Napa Valley. *Crisp and fruity, with a touch of vegetal character.*

☆☆☆ 1979 MERLOT ($12.50) Napa Valley. *Meaty, open, clean and rich.*

☆☆☆ 1980 MERLOT ($12.50) Napa Valley. *Deep, cherry flavor, supple, exquisite. Will age ten years.*

☆☆☆☆ 1981 MERLOT ($12.50) Three Palms, Napa Valley. *Tart and deep, with great fruit. Drink now and for many years.*

☆☆☆☆ 1981 MERLOT ($13.00) Napa Valley. *11% Cabernet Franc. Rich, lush, remarkably complex and deep.*

☆☆☆☆ 1982 MERLOT ($13.00) Napa Valley. *Deep, lush, balanced, structured, berried. Drink 1987.*

Dunn Vineyards
NAPA COUNTY

805 White Cottage Road, Angwin, California 94508 (707-965-3642). FOUNDED: 1979. ACREAGE: 6 acres. PRODUCTION: 1,000 cases. DISTRIBUTION: California and a few major market states. OWNERS: Randy and Lori Dunn. WINEMAKER: Randy Dunn. No tours or tasting.

Although Randy Dunn is the full-time winemaker at Caymus Vineyards, he bonded the cellar of his home and has made his own wine from his six-acre vineyard of Cabernet Sauvignon. His wife and college-age son are the work force. "I'm a city girl from Iowa," says Lori Dunn, "but I've learned a lot about winemaking, from plowing fields to pumping wine and labeling by hand."

RED

☆☆☆☆ 1979 CABERNET SAUVIGNON ($12.00) Napa Valley. *Elegant, complex, refined, lovely. Drink 1986.*

☆☆☆☆ 1980 CABERNET SAUVIGNON ($12.50) Napa Valley. *Lovely, crisp, tannic, elegant. Great structure. Drink 1986.*

☆☆☆☆ 1981 CABERNET SAUVIGNON ($12.50) Howell Mountain-Napa Valley. *Deep, rich, structured, very complex. Drink 1988.*

Duplin Wine Cellars
NORTH CAROLINA

Highway 117, Box 756, Rose Hill, North Carolina 28458 (919-289-3888). FOUNDED: 1976. ACREAGE: None. PRODUCTION: 52,000 cases. DISTRIBUTION: North Carolina and Washington D.C. OWNER: Cooperative. 95 stockholders. David Fussell, president. WINEMAKER: Jeff Randall. Tours and tasting Monday–Saturday 9 A.M.–5 P.M.

Duplin Wine Cellars was started by two brothers, David and Dan Fussell. After tiring of selling grapes out of state and at low prices, the Fussells took on two partners and built a small winery in their vineyard. It quickly became too small as more local grapes became available and as more local grape growers bought into the business. The winery was turned into a cooperative, and increases its membership every year.

SPARKLING

O   1983 CHAMPAGNE ($7.50) North Carolina.
NV SCUPPERNONG ($7.50) North Carolina.

Durney Vineyard
MONTEREY COUNTY

P.O. Box 1146, Carmel Valley, California 93924 (408-625-5433). FOUNDED: 1977. ACREAGE: 142 acres. PRODUCTION: 15,000 cases. DISTRIBUTION: 22 states. OWNER: William W. Durney; David Armanasco, general manager. WINEMAKER: Dan Lee; David Sharp, assistant winemaker. Tours by appointment.

Bill Durney owns the Carnation Seafood Company; his wife (under her professional name, Dorothy Kingsley) has written numerous screenplays, including "Seven Brides for Seven Brothers." In the wilds of the Carmel Valley, in the Santa Lucia Mountains, the Durneys carved out a meticulous 142-acre wine estate complete with its own chapel. The wines produced here are quite different from Monterey wines grown in the big Salinas Valley. The Durneys live mostly in Pebble Beach and Los Angeles, while the winery is ably managed by their son-in-law, David Armanasco.

WHITE

☆☆ 1982 CHENIN BLANC ($6.00) Estate, Carmel Valley, Monterey. *1% residual sugar. Snappy, clean and fruity.*
☆☆ 1983 CHENIN BLANC ($6.50) Estate, Carmel Valley. *Apple flavors, clean, charming.*
O   1981 JOHANNISBERG RIESLING ($6.00) Estate, Carmel Valley.
☆☆ 1982 JOHANNISBERG RIESLING ($6.00) Estate, Carmel Valley, Monterey. *1.5% residual sugar. Crisp, fruity and appealing.*
☆☆☆ 1983 JOHANNISBERG RIESLING ($6.50) Estate, Carmel Valley. *2.3% residual sugar. Lush, rich, clean, lovely.*

RED

☆☆☆ 1977 CABERNET SAUVIGNON ($12.00) Carmel Valley. *Mellow, mature, fruity, complex, Bordeaux-like. Drink now.*
☆☆☆ 1978 CABERNET SAUVIGNON ($12.00) Estate, Carmel Valley. *Lovely fruit, clean, delightful. Drink now or age up to five years.*
☆☆☆ 1978 CABERNET SAUVIGNON ($15.00) Private Reserve, Estate, Carmel Valley. *Rich, dense but nicely structured. Drink now and next two years.*
☆☆ 1979 CABERNET SAUVIGNON ($12.50) Estate, Carmel Valley.
☆   1980 CABERNET SAUVIGNON ($12.50) Estate, Carmel Valley, Monterey. *Grapey and berried like a Zinfandel.*
☆☆☆ 1981 CABERNET SAUVIGNON ($12.50) Carmel Valley, Monterey. *Rich and tannic, lush and beautifully balanced.*
☆☆☆ 1982 CABERNET SAUVIGNON ($12.50) Carmel Valley. *Lovely, elegant, firmly structured. Drink 1987.*
1982 GAMAY BEAUJOLAIS ($7.00) Estate, Carmel Valley, Monterey. *Soft and dull. Acceptable red table wine.*

Duxoup Wine Works
SONOMA COUNTY

9611 West Dry Creek Road, Healdsburg, California 95448 (707-433-5195). FOUNDED: 1981. ACREAGE: None. PRODUCTION: 2,000 cases. DISTRIBUTION: California. OWNERS: Robert Andrew and Deborah Ann Cutter. WINEMAKER: Robert Andrew Cutter. No tours or tasting.

Andy and Deborah Cutter used to work at Field Stone Winery together, he in the cellars and she as winemaker. Both Marx Brothers fans, they named their tiny winery after one of their favorite movies. The specialty of the house is Rhone-like Syrah made from Lou Preston's grapes. Andy, a big, black-bearded fellow with a zany sense of humor, works at the winery full time. Deborah is an enologist at Franciscan Vineyards in Napa.

RED

☆☆☆ 1980 NAPA GAMAY ($6.00) Sonoma. *Lush, rich and much more like a Pinot Noir than a Gamay.*

☆☆☆ 1981 NAPA GAMAY ($6.00) Sonoma. *Velvety, rich, like a Moulin à Vent.*

☆☆☆ 1983 NAPA GAMAY ($6.00) Sonoma. *Rich, deep, clean, complex, amazing.*

☆☆☆ 1980 SYRAH ($9.00) Preston, Sonoma. *Splendid. Rich, berried, very Rhone-like.*

☆☆☆ 1981 SYRAH ($9.00) Preston, Sonoma. *California's best Syrah—rich, firm and complex.*

☆☆ 1982 SYRAH ($9.00) Sonoma. *Rich, structured, some off quality in nose, aging potential.*

☆☆☆ 1983 SYRAH ($10.00) Sonoma. *Rich, deep, lush, peppery, clean, superb. Drink now or hold.*

☆☆☆ 1980 ZINFANDEL ($7.50) Sonoma. *Lush but elegant and well structured.*

EAGLEPOINT *see* Scharffenberger Cellars

Easley Winery
INDIANA

205 North College Avenue, Indianapolis, Indiana 46202 (317-636-4516). FOUNDED: 1974. ACREAGE: 57 acres. DISTRIBUTION: Indiana. OWNER: Easley Enterprises, Inc. John Easley, president. WINEMAKER: John Easley. Tours by appointment. Tasting Monday–Saturday 12–6 P.M.

The Easley family has owned vineyards near the Ohio River in Indiana since 1963. Selling all his grapes each year, save for a few small lots used for home winemaking, John Easley was frustrated by being financially at the mercy of other wineries. As a solution, the Easley family members pooled their resources, bought an ice cream plant in downtown Indianapolis some 155 miles away from the vineyards, scoured away years of sugar and milk residue, and started their own urban winery.

EAST SIDE *see* Oak Ridge Vineyards

Eaton Vineyards
NEW YORK

P.O. Box 284, Pine Plains, New York 12567 (518-398-7791). FOUNDED: 1981. ACREAGE: 10 acres. PRODUCTION: 2,000 cases. DISTRIBUTION: New York. OWNERS: Jerome and Shirley Eaton. WINEMAKER: Jerome Eaton. No tours or tasting.

In the tiny village of Gallatin, a town without a post office, the Eatons have been growing grapes and making wine for over 25 years. Jerome, a botanist and horticulturist, applied his inquisitive mind to grape growing, planting various vines in order to discover the varieties that could best survive the winter cold of that particular area. Seyval Blanc seemed to respond most favorably in Jerome's meticulously kept vineyards.

WHITE

☆☆   1982 SEYVAL BLANC ($4.75) Hudson River Region. *Deep, dry, apple flavors. Balanced, clean and attractive.*

Eberle Winery
SAN LUIS OBISPO COUNTY

P.O. Box 2459, Paso Robles, California 93446 (805-238-9607). FOUNDED: 1982. ACREAGE: None. PRODUCTION: 8,000 cases. DISTRIBUTION: 10 states. OWNER: Gary Eberle, general partner. WINEMAKER: Gary Eberle. Tours summer: daily 10 A.M.–6 P.M.; winter: daily 10 A.M.– 5 P.M. Closed major holidays.

Gary Eberle was the winemaker at Estrella River Winery until it got too big—there were just too many tanks and too many wines. Gary knew he needed his own small winery. There were certainly no hard feelings when he left because his own first wines were made at Estrella River from Estrella Vineyard's grapes.

WHITE

    1980 CHARDONNAY ($10.00) San Luis Obispo. *Well made but dominated by a musty quality.*
☆☆☆   1981 CHARDONNAY ($10.00) Paso Robles. *Rich, oily, crisp, clean, attractive.*
☆☆   1982 CHARDONNAY ($10.00) Paso Robles. *Woody, herbal. Rich and balanced, but a bit short in the finish.*

RED

☆☆☆   1979 CABERNET SAUVIGNON ($10.00) San Luis Obispo. *Crisply fruity and lean in structure. Will age well.*
☆☆☆   1980 CABERNET SAUVIGNON ($10.00) Paso Robles. *Rich, meaty, ripe, intense, with great depth. Drink 1987.*
☆☆☆   1981 CABERNET SAUVIGNON ($10.00) Paso Robles. *Earthy but nicely structured, clean, attractive. Drink 1986.*

Edmeades Vineyards
MENDOCINO COUNTY

5500 Highway 128, Philo, California 95466 (707-895-3232). FOUNDED: 1972. ACREAGE: 37 acres. PRODUCTION: 17,000 cases. DISTRIBUTION: 25 states. OWNER: Corporation. Deron Edmeades, president. WINEMAKER: Tex Sawyer. Tours by appointment. Tasting May–October: daily 10 A.M.–6 P.M.; November–April: daily 11 A.M.–5 P.M.

This rustic winery, located on an Anderson Valley hillside, was converted from an apple dryer by Deron Edmeades in 1972. Deron's father, Dr. Donald Edmeades, had purchased the 108-acre ranch in 1964 and planted fifteen acres of grapes. The fruit was sold to Parducci Wine Cellars until Dr. Edmeades died. In 1974 a new winery building was constructed. The winery has produced some remarkable vineyard-designated Zinfandels from Anderson Valley grapes and has also gained some attention for its colorful labels and unusual proprietary names such as Whale Wine, Rain Wine, and Opal.

WHITE

☆ 1980 CHARDONNAY ($9.50) Mendocino.

☆☆☆ 1980 CHARDONNAY ($12.50) Reserve, Mendocino. *Vinous, rich and balanced. Drink now.*

☆☆ 1981 CHARDONNAY ($8.00) Anderson Valley. *Clean, crisp and varietal.*

☆☆☆ 1981 CHARDONNAY ($12.50) Reserve Bottling, Anderson Valley, Mendocino. *Delicate, clean and lovely, with balanced varietal character.*

☆☆☆ 1982 CHARDONNAY ($8.00) Anderson Valley. *Fruity and clean, lovely acidity and structure.*

1982 CHARDONNAY ($10.00) Anderson Valley. *Crisp, bitter, dull.*

1979 JOHANNISBERG RIESLING ($25.00) Late Harvest, B. J. Carney, Anderson Valley, Mendocino. *10.4% residual sugar. Grapey, fruity but strange.*

RED

☆☆☆ 1978 CABERNET SAUVIGNON ($9.00) Estate, Anderson Valley, Mendocino. *Light and classy, angular and complex.*

☆☆☆ 1979 CABERNET SAUVIGNON ($8.00) Anderson Valley, Mendocino. *Snappy, fresh, with tangy fruit. Very appealing.*

☆ 1980 CABERNET SAUVIGNON ($9.00) Anderson Valley, Mendocino.

☆☆ 1980 CABERNET SAUVIGNON ($9.00) Mendocino. *Meaty, with good structure and complexity.*

☆☆ 1981 CABERNET SAUVIGNON ($7.50) Anderson Valley. *25% Merlot. Lovely, rich, clean, supple. Drink now.*

☆ 1980 PINOT NOIR ($9.50) Anderson Valley, Mendocino. *Fruity but lacking finesse.*

☆☆☆ 1982 PINOT NOIR ($10.00) B. J. Carney, Anderson Valley, Mendocino. *Rich black cherry, velvety texture, fruity, elegant.*

☆☆☆☆ 1979 ZINFANDEL ($9.00) Du Pratt, Mendocino. *Deep but elegant, fruity and complex. Remarkable.*

☆☆ 1980 ZINFANDEL ($8.00) Pacini, Mendocino. *Brambly, rich, big.*

☆ 1980 ZINFANDEL ($9.00) Ciapusci, Mendocino. *Peppery, big and coarse.*

☆☆ 1980 ZINFANDEL ($9.00) Zeni, Mendocino. *80-year-old vines. Rich and intense.*

☆☆ 1980 ZINFANDEL ($10.00) Du Pratt, Mendocino. *A bit clumsy and quite disappointing.*

☆☆☆ 1981 ZINFANDEL ($7.50) Anzilotti, Mendocino. *Balanced, clean, soft and fruity.*

☆☆☆ 1981 ZINFANDEL ($9.00) Ciapusci, Mendocino. *Berried, tannic, lovely fruit, balanced. Drink 1986.*

☆☆☆ 1981 ZINFANDEL ($12.00) Du Pratt, Mendocino. *Rich, deep, fruity, elegant, charming. Drink now.*

☆ 1982 ZINFANDEL ($7.00) Mendocino. *Light, decent, a bit dirty.*

Edna Valley Vineyard
SAN LUIS OBISPO COUNTY

2585 Biddle Ranch Road, San Luis Obispo, California 93401 (805-544-9594). FOUNDED: 1980. ACREAGE: 600 acres at Paragon Vineyard. PRODUCTION: 25,000 cases. DISTRIBUTION: Nationwide; Great Britain and British Columbia. OWNERS: Partnership. Chalone Vineyard, Inc. and Paragon Vineyard Co.; Chalone Vineyard, managing partner. WINEMAKER: Gary Mosby; Clay Thompson, assistant winemaker. OTHER LABEL: Gavilan. Tours and retail sales by appointment.

This successful Central Coast winery is a joint venture between Chalone Vineyard (see) and Paragon Vineyard. The wines are made from grapes grown at Paragon but winemaking is directed by Chalone. The style here, as at Chalone, favors complex, barrel-fermented wines—in particular Pinot Noirs and Chardonnays.

WHITE

☆☆☆ 1981 CHARDONNAY ($12.00) Estate, San Luis Obispo. *Toasty, rich, beautifully balanced.*

☆☆ 1982 CHARDONNAY ($12.00) Edna Valley. *Toasty, rich, oaky, earthy, with a touch of vegetation.*

☆ 1983 CHARDONNAY ($12.00) Edna Valley. *Heavy, oily, barrel-fermented, vinous.*

☆☆ 1983 CHENIN BLANC ($6.00) Edna Valley. *Crisp, fruity, round, complex.*

BLANC DE NOIR

☆☆☆ 1984 PINOT NOIR ($5.00) Vin Gris, Estate, Edna Valley. *Fresh, complex, off-dry, rich, attractive.*

RED

☆☆ 1981 GAVILAN CABERNET SAUVIGNON ($6.75) Sonoma. *Fruity, oaky, fresh and attractive. Drink now.*

O 1980 PINOT NOIR ($14.00) San Luis Obispo. *Overpoweringly weedy, with volatile acidity too.*

☆☆ 1981 PINOT NOIR ($14.00) Estate, Edna Valley. *Less weedy than the '80; rich, fruited, with nice structure.*

☆☆ 1982 PINOT NOIR ($12.50) Edna Valley. *Earthy, some veggies, well built, should age well. Drink 1986.*

Ehlers Lane Winery
NAPA COUNTY

3222 Ehlers Lane, St. Helena, California 94574 (707-963-0144). FOUNDED: 1983. ACREAGE: None. PRODUCTION: 15,000 cases. DISTRIBUTION: 4 states. OWNERS: Partnership. John R. Jensen, managing general partner. WINEMAKER: Robert Moeckley. Tours by appointment.

The old, stone winery building on Ehlers Lane has been bought, sold, and leased a great number of times since it was built in 1886. In 1968, after being empty for eleven years, the winery was bought by Mike Casey, who leased the facility to wineries wanting only to rent space. The building has been the home of Conn Creek, Vichon, and Saintsbury wineries. Mike watched these tenants come and go, then took a serious look into starting his own winery. Mike and partner John Jensen put together a prospectus, raised enough capital, and hired Robert Moeckley away from Robert Mondavi Winery in Woodbridge.

WHITE

☆☆ 1983 CHARDONNAY ($13.75) Napa Valley. *Woody, ripe, decent fruit, nice but lacking finesse.*

☆☆☆ 1983 SAUVIGNON BLANC ($8.95) Napa Valley. *Varietal, fresh, rounded, lovely.*

Ehrle Brothers Winery
IOWA

Homestead, Iowa 52236 (319-622-3241). FOUNDED: 1934. ACREAGE: None. PRODUCTION: 4,000 cases. DISTRIBUTION: At winery. OWNER: Corporation. Arthur Miller, president. WINE-

MAKER: Arthur Miller. Tours and tasting Monday–Saturday 9 A.M.–6 P.M.; summer: Sunday 12–5 P.M.

In the German-American town of Amana, winemaking is more of a tradition than an industry. In fact, before Prohibition there had been a community winery, but when that closed the Ehrle family made wine in their basement. Today, upholding community tradition, rhubarb wine is their specialty and still the favorite at the Ehrle Brothers Winery. Other favorites are cherry and berry wines. The winery is still in the basement of the Ehrle house and remains a family operation.

૨&

E & K Wine Company
OHIO

220 East Water Street, Sandusky, Ohio 44870 (419-627-9622). FOUNDED: 1863. ACREAGE: None. PRODUCTION: 5,800 cases. DISTRIBUTION: Local. OWNER: Corporation. Edward Feick, president. WINEMAKER: Clifford Gregory. OTHER LABEL: Mellow Monk. Tours and tasting daily 10 A.M.–5 P.M.

Founded in 1863 by two German brothers, Engel and Krugwig, this winery was built by digging out a cellar and then using the excavated limestone to construct the winery walls. The limestone keeps the wines from freezing in the winter. Every year the Engel family pumped 500,000 gallons out of their winery until 1970 when Edward Feick bought it. Feick cut back production, disposed of the old, rotting cooperage and worked hard to get the winery back on its feet. Today the winery does not crush grapes but buys juice from local grower cooperatives.

૨&

El Dorado Vineyards
EL DORADO COUNTY

3551 Carson Road, Camino, California 95709 (916-644-3773). FOUNDED: 1975. ACREAGE: None. PRODUCTION: 600 cases. DISTRIBUTION: California. OWNERS: Earl and JoAnne McGuire, and John and Margaret Mirande. Tours and tasting September–December: daily 12–5 P.M.; January–August: weekends 12–5 P.M.

Earl McGuire left his job as city manager of Placerville to make a family dream come true. He bought an old ranch and converted it into a working winery. The winery sells 80 percent of its wine right out the door to passing summer tourists.

WHITE

☆☆   1981 CHARDONNAY ($6.50) El Dorado.

RED

☆   1980 ZINFANDEL ($4.50) El Dorado.

૨&

El Paso de Robles Winery
SAN LUIS OBISPO COUNTY

Route 1, Box 101, Willow Creek Road, Paso Robles, California 93446 (805-238-6986). FOUNDED: 1981. ACREAGE: 18 acres. PRODUCTION: 4,000 cases. DISTRIBUTION: California. OWNERS: Partnership. George Mulder, president; Stan Hall, vice president. WINEMAKERS: George and

Tahoma Mulder, and Stan Hall. Tasting summer: daily 10 A.M.–6 P.M.; winter: 10 A.M.–5 P.M.

Tomme and George Mulder have demanding professional careers; George is a psychologist at California Polytechnic and Tomme is a learning specialist. "Winemaking is just something we do for fun when we get home from work," says Tomme. They live on an 80-acre ranch, a fairy tale farm with a converted Victorian house and barn that is now the winery.

RED

☆☆ 1982 MERLOT ($7.50) Radike, Paso Robles. *Fat, lush, rich, fruity. Drink 1987.*

El Paso Winery
NEW YORK

R.D. No. 1, Box 170, Ulster Park, New York 12487 (914-331-8642). FOUNDED: 1977. ACREAGE: None. PRODUCTION: 1,200 cases. DISTRIBUTION: At winery. OWNER: Publio Felipe Beltra. WINEMAKER: Publio Felipe Beltra. Tasting Monday–Friday 12–6 P.M., weekends 10 A.M.–6 P.M.

When Publio Beltra came to the land of plenty from South America, there was but one profession he felt confident about pursuing: winemaking, which he had learned from his father. Once in New York, Publio began looking for a place to begin his own winery. He purchased an old barn and obtained his winery license in 1977.

Elk Cove Vineyards
OREGON

Route 3, Box 23, Gaston, Oregon 97119 (503-985-7760). FOUNDED: 1977. ACREAGE: 24 acres. PRODUCTION: 8,000 cases. DISTRIBUTION: Oregon, Washington, and 15 other states. OWNERS: Pat and Joe Campbell. WINEMAKERS: Pat and Joe Campbell. Tours and tasting daily 12–5 P.M.

Pat and Joe Campbell's winery is located northwest of Portland in the Tualatin Valley. Joe, a practicing physician, is quite serious about winemaking, and Elk Cove's Burgundian-style Pinot Noirs demonstrate the Campbells' admiration for European techniques. Success during their first few years of production led to construction of a new winery in 1981, but the Campbells are committed to producing handmade wines in small lots.

WHITE

1981 CHARDONNAY ($7.50) Estate, Willamette Valley, Oregon. *Toasty and lemony, with a touch of oxidation.*

1982 CHARDONNAY ($12.00) Dundee Hills, Willamette Valley, Oregon. *Dull, with a touch of oxidation.*

1983 GEWURZTRAMINER ($10.00) Dry, Estate, Willamette Valley, Oregon. *An impressive wine but some bottles have aldehyde spoilage.*

☆ 1982 RIESLING ($6.75) Willamette Valley, Oregon. *6% residual sugar. Sweet, rich, with some off flavors.*

☆☆☆ 1983 RIESLING ($5.40) Willamette Valley, Oregon. *Off-dry, crisp, fresh, rich, delicious.*

RED

1977 PINOT NOIR Willamette Valley, Oregon. *Smoky, stemmy, showing its age.*

1978 PINOT NOIR Willamette Valley, Oregon. *Earthy, toasty; past its prime.*

☆   1979 PINOT NOIR ($9.00) Wind Hill, Willamette Valley, Oregon. *Peppery, berried, fruity and appealing.*
☆☆ 1979 PINOT NOIR ($12.00) Reserve, Estate, Willamette Valley, Oregon. *Soft, varietal, violets and earth. Very nice.*
    1980 PINOT NOIR ($9.00) Estate, Willamette Valley, Oregon.
☆☆ 1982 PINOT NOIR ($12.00) Reserve, 50% Dundee Hills, 50% Estate, Willamette Valley, Oregon. *Earthy, firm, good fruit, nice structure.*

Ellendale Vineyards
OREGON

300 Reuben Boise Road, Dallas, Oregon 97338 (503-623-5617). FOUNDED: 1981. ACREAGE: 13 acres. PRODUCTION: 20,000 cases. DISTRIBUTION: At winery and specialty shops. OWNERS: Robert and Ella Mae Hudson, officers and major shareholders. WINEMAKERS: Robert and Ella Mae Hudson. Tours and tasting Wednesday–Sunday 12–6 P.M. Art gallery.

Retired Air Force officer Robert Hudson and his wife, Ella Mae, bought a fruit farm in 1968. Robert, still in the Air Force at the time, cleared out all but 100 apple trees and started planting vines, but each year the deer would eat the vineyard clean. It wasn't until Robert retired in 1975 that he was able to build a fortress of impenetrable fencing. The winery was built in 1980 and the Hudsons started by selling fruit and berry wines "just so we would have something to offer in the tasting room," says Robert. "The Willamette Valley is one of the finest producers of strawberries and apples, so we figured we might as well take advantage of that." Today three-quarters of the Hudsons' production is fruit and berry wine.

Elliston Vineyards
ALAMEDA COUNTY

463 Kilkare Road, P.O. Box 163, Sunol, California 94586 (415-862-2377). FOUNDED: 1983. ACREAGE: 3 acres. PRODUCTION: 1,000 cases. DISTRIBUTION: California. OWNERS: Ramon and Amy Awtrey. WINEMAKER: Ramon Awtrey. Tours and tasting Sunday 1 P.M.–4 P.M., or by appointment.

In 1969 teachers Ramon and Amy Awtrey bought a historic three-story stone house that dates back to the 1800s. "It looked like a winery," says Ramon, "so we decided that the best way to use the property was to start a winery in the remodeled carriage house." Ramon, who had never made wine before, took enology courses at U.C. Davis and the Napa Valley School of Cellaring. The historic house is now the Awtrys' home, but they have opened it to the public for tours.

Henry Endress Winery
OREGON

13300 South Clackamas River Drive, Oregon City, Oregon 97045 (503-656-7239). FOUNDED: 1935. ACREAGE: 2 acres. PRODUCTION: 4,200 cases. DISTRIBUTION: Oregon. OWNER: Henry Endress. WINEMAKER: Henry Endress. Tours and tasting Monday–Saturday 10 A.M.– 7 P.M.

The third Henry Endress is currently running the historic family winery started by his grandfather, Henry Endress, Sr., a native of Germany. Henry's father, Henry Jr., took over the winery in

1951 after working for Clackamus County. Now Henry II is about ready to let his son, Henry III, take over. The split-level, river-view winery and the winemaking have remained as constant as the Endress surname, although production has been cut back in the last few years. Fruit wines are the winery's specialty.

Enz Vineyards
SAN BENITO COUNTY

Lime Kiln Valley, P.O. Box 1435, Hollister, California 95023 (408-637-3956). FOUNDED: 1973. ACREAGE: 30 acres. PRODUCTION: 10,000 cases. DISTRIBUTION: 5 states. OWNERS: Robert and Susan Enz. WINEMAKER: Robert Enz. Tours and tasting by appointment.

The vineyards date back to 1895, and Robert Enz has had a friendly tiff with the Christian Brothers over who has the oldest plantings of Pinot St. George. "I know we have the oldest plantings of Orange Muscat in California," says Robert. Once an engineer in San Francisco, Robert quit his job to start the winery in a converted barn on the vineyard property. With the help of his wife and four children, he runs a real working farm winery—not a flashy showplace. The only outdoor sights are insulated winery tanks and a few tractors.

WHITE

     1981 FUME BLANC ($6.30) Estate, San Benito. *Dry, dull, no depth.*

☆☆ 1982 DRY ORANGE MUSCAT ($5.00) Estate, San Benito. *0.5% residual sugar. Orangy, spicy, clean and interesting.*

☆☆ 1983 DRY ORANGE MUSCAT ($5.60) San Benito. *Delicate, floral, clean, attractive.*

☆ 1984 SAUVIGNON BLANC ($6.30) Rancho dos Amigos, San Luis Obispo.

RED

☆☆ 1979 PINOT ST. GEORGE ($7.90) San Benito. *Rich, chocolatey, clean, quite attractive.*

☆ 1979 ZINFANDEL ($6.30) Estate, San Benito. *Intense, tannic, decent.*

FLAVORED

☆☆ LIMESTONE ($5.30) Estate, San Benito. *Flavored with herbs. Sweet and spicy.*

Estrella River Winery
SAN LUIS OBISPO COUNTY

Shandon Star Route, Highway 46 East, Paso Robles, California 93446 (805-238-6300). FOUNDED: 1972. ACREAGE: 875 acres. PRODUCTION: 70,000 cases. DISTRIBUTION: Nationwide and 4 foreign countries. OWNERS: Sally and Clifford R. Giacobine. WINEMAKER: Tom Myers. Tours and tasting daily 10 A.M.–5 P.M.

Cliff Giacobine was looking for cattle grazing– and farmland in Paso Robles when his agricultural consultant told him that wine grapes were the best new crop. Cliff, a retired space industry employee, had no previous experience with either grapes or wine. After some sketchy viticultural research, he convinced his brothers to form a partnership and plant over 500 acres of grapes. The winery started in 1977 after Cliff's brother, Gary Eberle, agreed to give up his doctoral studies in cytology to become the winemaker. In 1981 Gary left Estrella (which means "star" in Spanish) to start his own winery (see Eberle Winery). His assistant, Tom Myers, became Estrella's winemaker.

WHITE

☆☆ NV CHARDONNAY ($4.70) San Luis Obispo. *Fruity, clean and decent.*

☆☆ 1980 CHARDONNAY ($9.25) Estate, San Luis Obispo. *Sweet oak, intense fruit, showing its age but interesting.*

☆☆☆ 1980 CHARDONNAY ($12.00) Star Reserve, San Luis Obispo. *Toasty, rich, intense, rounded.*

☆☆ 1981 CHARDONNAY ($9.25) Estate, San Luis Obispo. *Clean, soft and fresh, with a snappy finish.*

☆☆ 1982 CHARDONNAY ($9.00) Estate, Paso Robles. *Simple, clean, decent.*

☆☆ 1982 CHENIN BLANC ($5.20) Estate, Paso Robles. *1% residual sugar. Crisp, soft, clean and lovely.*

☆☆ 1983 CHENIN BLANC ($5.00) Estate, Paso Robles. *1% residual sugar. Crisp, snappy, good acidity.*

1984 CHENIN BLANC ($5.00) Estate, Paso Robles. *1.1% residual sugar. Skunky.*

1980 FUME BLANC ($6.00) Estate, San Luis Obispo.

1981 FUME BLANC ($6.00) Estate, San Luis Obispo. *Oily and lacking freshness.*

1982 FUME BLANC ($6.00) Estate, Paso Robles. *Oxidized, vinous, unattractive.*

☆☆ 1983 FUME BLANC ($6.00) San Luis Obispo. *Crisp, clean, decent.*

O 1982 JOHANNISBERG RIESLING ($5.63) Estate, Paso Robles. *2.1% residual sugar. Sweet and candy-like, low acid.*

☆ 1983 JOHANNISBERG RIESLING ($6.00) Estate, Paso Robles. *1.9% residual sugar. Fruity, clean but dull.*

☆ 1984 JOHANNISBERG RIESLING ($6.00) Paso Robles. *Heavy, vinous, coarse.*

☆☆ 1979 MUSCAT ($15.00) Late Harvest, San Luis Obispo. *17.8% residual sugar. Lush, balanced, varietal.*

☆☆☆☆ 1981 MUSCAT ($7.50) San Luis Obispo. *Lush, spicy, off-dry, clean, complex, delicious.*

☆☆☆ 1981 MUSCAT ($14.00) Late Harvest, Paso Robles. *13.8% residual sugar. Richly varietal, balanced, lovely.*

SPARKLING

☆☆☆ 1982 BLANC DE BLANCS ($15.00) Paso Robles. *Clean, fresh, very attractive.*

BLANC DE NOIR

☆☆ NV WHITE ZINFANDEL ($3.62) San Luis Obispo. *Off-dry, fresh flavors.*

☆☆ NV WHITE ZINFANDEL ($3.75) Estate, Paso Robles. *2% residual sugar. Fruity, crisp, balanced, pretty color.*

☆☆ 1984 WHITE ZINFANDEL ($5.00) Estate, Paso Robles. *1.9% residual sugar. Crisp, fruity, lush, short.*

RED

☆ 1979 BARBERA ($4.75) Estate, San Luis Obispo. *Snappy and crisp.*

☆ NV CABERNET SAUVIGNON ($6.00) San Luis Obispo. *Meaty, intense, simple, decent.*

☆☆ 1978 CABERNET SAUVIGNON ($10.00) Estate, San Luis Obispo. *Fat, rich, concentrated. Drink now.*

☆ 1979 CABERNET SAUVIGNON ($8.50) Estate, San Luis Obispo. *Nice, lighter weight, attractive.*

☆☆ 1980 CABERNET SAUVIGNON ($10.00) Paso Robles. *Rich, lush, fruity. Drink now.*

☆ 1981 CABERNET SAUVIGNON ($9.00) Paso Robles. *Big and clumsy.*

☆☆☆ NV ZINFANDEL ($3.50) San Luis Obispo. *Clean and well balanced.*

☆☆ 1979 ZINFANDEL ($4.70) Estate, San Luis Obispo. *Soft and raisiny.*

☆☆ 1980 ZINFANDEL ($5.00) San Luis Obispo. *Lush, deep, heavy, decent.*

ETOWAH RIDGES *see* Habersham Vintners

Evensen Vineyards and Winery
NAPA COUNTY

8254 St. Helena Highway, Oakville, California 94562 (707-944-2396). FOUNDED: 1979. ACREAGE: 6 acres. PRODUCTION: 800 cases. DISTRIBUTION: Major market states. OWNERS: Richard and Sharon Evensen. WINEMAKER: Richard Evensen. No tours or tasting.

The Evensens learned how to make wine from "an old family friend, Michael Chelini, the winemaker at Stony Hill Winery," says Sharon Evensen. Sharon was born and raised in the Napa Valley and her husband, Richard, is from Healdsburg. They have been growing grapes for over sixteen years, selling the crop to Allied Grape Growers. When Richard was not working in his TV appliance store, he was making wine in the Evensen basement. "In fact, we made our first four vintages in the basement," says Sharon. "We have now moved the winery to a new building in back of the house." Both the house and the new winery are designed in an English Tudor style. The only wine made is estate-bottled Gewürztraminer.

WHITE

☆☆ 1981 GEWURZTRAMINER ($6.50) Napa Valley. *Dry, intensely varietal, rich but slightly bitter.*

Evilsizer Cellar
NAPA COUNTY

P.O. Box 2445, Yountville, California 94599 (707-944-8568). FOUNDED: 1980. ACREAGE: None. PRODUCTION: 350 cases. DISTRIBUTION: Local and by mailing list. OWNERS: Larry and Beth Evilsizer. WINEMAKER: Larry Evilsizer. No tours or tasting.

When Larry Evilsizer lived in Colorado, he made wine from imported California grapes. After moving to the Napa Valley, he and his wife, Beth, waited until their children had left home, then channeled all their loving care into winemaking. The winery is presently a part-time venture; each fall they make wines from bought grapes by hauling a portable crusher to local wineries that have a little extra tank space. They hope one day to expand their own facilities and make their winery a full-time job for both of them.

The Eyrie Vineyards
OREGON

935 East 10th Street, McMinnville, Oregon 97128 (503-472-6315). FOUNDED: 1970. ACREAGE: 26 acres. PRODUCTION: 5,000 cases. DISTRIBUTION: 10 states; England and Australia. OWNERS: David and Diana Lett. WINEMAKER: David Lett. Tours by appointment only.

David Lett was sure he was going to be a dentist. But after graduating from the University of Utah with a degree in philosophy, he took a short trip to the Napa Valley, visited a few wineries, and realized that there was more to life than gold inlays and root canals. Against the advice of his enology professor at the U.C. Davis, where he went to get a degree in viticulture, David chose the Willamette Valley as the site for his vineyard because he believed the area had the best potential for making "great American Pinot Noir." He liked its "marginal climate," which is just warm enough to ripen the fruit by the end of the harvest season. While Pinot Noir is David's first love, he is also one of the few commercial producers of estate-grown Pinot Gris, Muscat Ottonel, and Pinot Meunier. The winery and vineyards were named for the red-tailed hawks (seen on the label) that have made their "eyrie" in the huge fir tree that stands near the vineyard.

WHITE

☆☆☆ 1983 PINOT GRIS ($8.75) Willamette Valley, Yamhill, Oregon. *Rich, fruity, clean, balanced, delightful.*

RED

☆☆ 1982 PINOT NOIR ($12.50) Willamette Valley, Yamhill County. *Smoky, toasty, a bit green, pretty fruit. Drink 1986.*

Louis Facelli Vineyards
IDAHO

Highway 95, P.O. Box 39, Wilder, Idaho 83676 (208-482-7719). FOUNDED: 1982. ACREAGE: 160 acres. PRODUCTION: 40,000 cases. DISTRIBUTION: 7 western states. OWNERS: Fred and Norm Batt. Louis Facelli, president. WINEMAKER: Louis Facelli. Tours and tasting Sunday–Thursday 12–5 P.M.; Friday–Saturday 12–6 P.M.

An Italian-Portuguese Californian, Lou Facelli moved to Idaho in 1973. After trying his hand at various jobs, Lou decided to return to his family heritage of winemaking. Since there were no producing grapevines in Idaho worth the trouble at that time, Lou had been making only fruit wines at home. But he was serious about becoming an honest-to-goodness winemaker; he mortgaged his house, planted vineyards, and built a winery in 1981. One year later, his two partners joined him and the winery was incorporated. New facilities were built and production was increased from 1,400 gallons to 40,000 cases.

WHITE

   1983 GEWURZTRAMINER ($5.50) Semi-Dry, Washington. *Dull, lacking fruit and freshness.*

☆☆ 1983 JOHANNISBERG RIESLING ($6.00) Dry, Washington. *Crisp, snappy, clean, short on fruit.*

☆☆☆ 1983 JOHANNISBERG RIESLING ($6.00) Idaho. *Fresh, clean, lovely fruit and acidity.*

☆☆☆ 1983 JOHANNISBERG RIESLING ($7.00) Reserve, Washington. *Lush, deep, clean fruit, with lovely complexity.*

☆ 1982 WHITE RIESLING ($5.50) Washington. *Toasty, overdone.*

Fair Haven Winery
NEW YORK

4001 Searsburg Road, R.D. 1, Valois, New York 14888 (607-546-9861). FOUNDED: 1981. ACREAGE: 20 acres. PRODUCTION: 1,000 cases. DISTRIBUTION: New York. OWNER: John Marmora. WINEMAKER: John Marmora. Tours and tasting by appointment.

John Marmora has been a grape grower for fifteen years. He also has a shoe repair business and works part time as a librarian at Cornell University. John used to sell grapes to Taylor Wine Company when it was owned by Coca-Cola, but "the price of grapes got too low," he says, "so I started a winery." The wines are processed in John's barn and cellared underneath his house.

Fairmont Cellars
NAPA COUNTY

P.O. Box 3218, Yountville, California 94599 (707-944-8373). FOUNDED: 1982. ACREAGE: None. PRODUCTION: 7,000 cases. DISTRIBUTION: Western United States and Australia. OWNER: George Kolarovich. WINEMAKER: George Kolarovich. Tours by appointment.

George Kolarovich made wine professionally for 35 years in Europe and Australia before he came to the Napa Valley. George owns vineyards in Yugoslavia that have been in his family since 1796, and he and his wife travel to Australia for the spring crush. When George first moved to Napa, he worked for the California Wine Association, but in 1982, after a few years of making his own wine at a friend's winery, George decided it was time to start his own business. By that time he had gained experience in both the marketing and the production of wine. He developed the Fairmont label for his 100-percent Napa Valley varietal wines and the Claridge label for the wines he makes in Australia.

WHITE

☆☆☆ 1981 CHARDONNAY ($12.00) Sonoma. *Very Burgundian, high acidity, crisp fruit.*

RED

☆☆ 1978 CABERNET SAUVIGNON ($12.00) Napa Valley.

☆☆ 1982 CABERNET SAUVIGNON ($9.50) Private Selection, Napa Valley. *Fruity, clean, round, pleasant.*

FALCON CREST *see* Spring Mountain Vineyards

Fall Creek Vineyards
TEXAS

Tow, Texas 78672 (915-379-5361). FOUNDED: 1979. ACREAGE: 40 acres. PRODUCTION: 7,000 cases. DISTRIBUTION: Texas. OWNERS: Ed and Susan Auler. WINEMAKER: Ed Auler. Tours and tasting by appointment and on the last Saturday of each month 1 P.M.–5 P.M.

A lawyer, cattle rancher, and Texas oil man, Ed Auler went to France to educate himself on breeds of French cattle, but he and his wife, Susan, found themselves spending most of their time exploring the wine country. Returning home with a new appreciation for winemaking, Ed noticed similarities in soil and topography between his Fall Creek ranch and the vineyard areas he had visited in France. Then, in 1974, the cattle market took a nose dive. Searching for a cash crop to cushion himself against such disasters, Ed researched the possibility of growing wine grapes. In 1975, he planted the first vineyard of vinifera and French-American hybrids on his ranch, and now a new 10,000-square-foot, two-story winery—designed in the style of an elegant ranch house— stands in the neatly kept vineyards.

WHITE

☆ 1983 BLANC DE BLANCS ($6.00) Llano County, Texas. *61% Villard Blanc, 31% Aurora, 8% Verdelet. Dry, heavy, decent.*

☆☆ 1983 CHENIN BLANC ($6.00) Texas. *Lovely, rich, sweet, clean.*

☆ 1983 EMERALD RIESLING ($5.00) Llano County, Texas. *Clean, decent, lacking fruit.*

☆ 1983 SAUVIGNON BLANC Texas.

Far Niente Winery
NAPA COUNTY

One Acacia Drive, Oakville, California 94562 (707-944-2861). FOUNDED: 1979. ACREAGE: None. PRODUCTION: 12,500 cases. DISTRIBUTION: Worldwide. OWNERS: Gil and John Nickel, and Doug Stelling. WINEMAKER: Dirk Hampson; Charles Ortman, consultant. Tours by appointment only.

Gil Nickel is a slow-talking country boy from Oklahoma with lots of style. After getting a degree in physics, he ran his family's nursery business—one of the nation's largest. He dabbled in restaurants and oil and gas before heading west. With his brother, John, and Doug Stelling, he undertook a lavish, three-year restoration of the old 1885 Far Niente Winery, turning it into one of the valley's most beautiful estates. In 1984 Gil and John bought the Château Chevalier Winery (see), which will undoubtedly get the same stylish treatment.

WHITE

☆☆ 1979 CHARDONNAY ($15.00) Napa Valley. *Rich and complex, holding well.*

☆☆ 1980 CHARDONNAY ($16.50) Napa Valley. *Toasty oak and crisp fruit. Good, but not as good as the '81.*

☆☆☆ 1981 CHARDONNAY ($18.00) Estate, Napa Valley. *Rich and well balanced, lovely ripe fruit.*

☆☆ 1982 CHARDONNAY ($18.00) Napa Valley. *Rich, full, forward, well made, with lovely ripe qualities.*

☆☆☆ 1982 CHARDONNAY ($20.00) Estate, Napa Valley. *Outstanding—rich, oaky, lush, fruity, complex.*

☆☆☆☆ 1983 CHARDONNAY ($18.00) Napa Valley. *Toasty, rich, heavy, oaky.*

Farfelu Vineyard
VIRGINIA

Flint Hill, Virginia 22627 (703-364-2930). FOUNDED: 1975. ACREAGE: 12 acres. PRODUCTION: 1,500 cases. DISTRIBUTION: Virginia. OWNER: C. J. Raney. WINEMAKER: C. J. Raney. Tours and tasting Monday–Friday 9 A.M.–5 P.M., weekends 12–4 P.M., and by appointment.

When C. J. Raney was in the Mediterranean as a navy pilot, he developed an interest in wine that has stayed with him ever since. He visited wineries and read anything he could find on the subject of winemaking. When he began working as a commercial pilot, C. J. moved to Virginia to start a vineyard. "Virginia is still in the process of learning where the right sites are and which varieties to plant where, but we are definitely making progress," says C. J. His own experiments have included the cultivation of forty different varieties planted on his fifteen acres, which he feels is ridiculous. "Now I have narrowed it down to fifteen or fewer varieties," he says. C. J. hopes that some day he will find the perfect variety to make the perfect wine.

FARRON RIDGE CELLARS *see* Château Ste. Michelle

Farview Farm Vineyard
SAN LUIS OBISPO COUNTY

Route 2, Box 40, Templeton, California 93465 (805-434-1247). FOUNDED: 1979. ACREAGE: 51 acres. PRODUCTION: 7,000 cases. DISTRIBUTION: 22 states. OWNERS: Dan Roy and Ray Krause. WINEMAKER: Ray Krause. Tours and tasting by appointment.

Dan Roy, a board member for Western Financial Printing in Los Angeles, had been growing grapes in Templeton for seven years when he met dapper Ray Krause, who asked him if he would be interested in making a profit from his grapes by making his own wine. Ray, who had worked at both Papagni and Mirassou vineyards, generated a five-year plan of production and sales growth, and in 1979 Farview Farms began crushing in a rented facility. Currently crushing at Estrella River Winery, Ray and Dan have plans and a place in the vineyard for construction of a gravity-flow winery once their production reaches 10,000 cases.

RED

1980 MERLOT ($7.25) Templeton. *Weedy.*
☆ 1980 ZINFANDEL ($4.85) First Release, Reserve, San Luis Obispo.
O 1980 ZINFANDEL ($7.25) San Luis Obispo. *Very strange.*

FELTA SPRINGS *see* Mill Creek Vineyards

Felton-Empire Vineyards
SANTA CRUZ COUNTY

379 Felton-Empire Road, Felton, California 95018 (408-335-3939). FOUNDED: 1976. ACREAGE: 11 acres. PRODUCTION: 20,000 cases. DISTRIBUTION: Major market states. OWNER: Corporation. Leo P. McCloskey, president; Glenn Luque, general manager; Bill Gibbs, vice president. WINEMAKERS: Leo P. McCloskey; Steve Storrs and Brooks Painter, assistants. Tours and tasting weekends 11 A.M.–4:30 P.M. Open most holidays.

Tucked in the pines just west of Felton is this small property that was founded by San Francisco attorney Chaffee Hall in the early 1940s. Known then as Hallcrest, the winery developed a reputation for Cabernet Sauvignon. Hall closed up shop in 1964 and died a few years later. In 1976 three young men decided to revive Hallcrest. They renamed it Felton-Empire and decided to specialize in white wines—especially Riesling and Gewürztraminer. Leo McCloskey, a Ph.D. in microbiology (see Ridge Vineyards), is the guiding creative force. The winery also makes excellent non-alcoholic grape juice.

WHITE

1981 CHARDONNAY ($9.00) Maritime Series, California.
1982 CHARDONNAY ($9.50) Maritime, 50% Fort Ross, 50% Tepusquet, California. *Heavy, vinous, vegetal.*
☆ 1983 CHARDONNAY ($11.00) Santa Barbara. *Crisp, earthy, odd.*
☆☆ 1983 CHARDONNAY ($11.00) Tonneaux Francais, Tepusquet, Santa Barbara. *Rich, woody, fat, lush; lacks finesse.*
1982 CHENIN BLANC ($6.75) Maritime Series, California. *Decent, fruity, dull.*
☆ 1980 GEWURZTRAMINER ($9.00) Late Harvest, Russian River. *375ml. Honey and some fruit and flowers.*
1981 GEWURZTRAMINER ($10.00) Select Late Harvest, Russian River Valley, Sonoma. *375ml. 15% residual sugar. Oxidized, syrupy, dull.*
☆☆☆ 1982 GEWURZTRAMINER ($6.50) Maritime Series, California. *1.4% residual sugar. Lovely, clean, soft and very good.*
O 1982 GEWURZTRAMINER ($6.75) Talmadge Town, California. *1.05% residual sugar. Oxidized, strange flavors, no fruit.*
☆☆☆ 1983 GEWURZTRAMINER ($6.75) Maritime Series, California. *Varietal, tangy, crisp; Alsatian in style.*
☆☆☆ 1983 GEWURZTRAMINER ($6.75) Talmadge Town, Mendocino. *Clean, varietal; great fruit and balance.*
☆☆☆ 1981 WHITE RIESLING ($10.00) Select Late Harvest, Tepusquet, Santa Barbara. *375ml. Rich botrytis, elegant fruit, crisp and lush.*
☆ 1982 WHITE RIESLING ($6.50) Maritime Series, California. *Varietal but essentially dull.*
☆☆ 1982 WHITE RIESLING ($6.75) Santa Cruz Mountains. *Good fruit and varietal character, a bit thin.*
☆☆ 1982 WHITE RIESLING ($7.50) Fort Ross. *2.25% residual sugar. Sweet, soft, smooth, fruity and crisp.*
☆☆ 1982 WHITE RIESLING ($10.00) Select Late Harvest, Tepusquet, Santa Barbara. *375ml. 16.5% residual sugar. Lovely, lush, fruity.*

☆☆   1983 WHITE RIESLING ($6.75) Santa Cruz Mountains. *1.75% residual sugar. Snappy, fresh, clean, attractive.*

☆☆☆   1983 WHITE RIESLING ($6.75) Santa Cruz Mountains. *2.2% residual sugar.*

1983 WHITE RIESLING ($9.00) Hallcrest, Santa Cruz Mountains. *Some oxidation and dirtiness mar this one.*

☆☆☆   1983 WHITE RIESLING ($12.00) Fort Ross. *375ml. 20% residual sugar. Lush, sweet, botrytis, super.*

RED

1979 CABERNET SAUVIGNON ($12.00) Beauregard Ranch, Santa Cruz Mountains. *Big and crude, lacking fruit.*

1980 CABERNET SAUVIGNON ($12.00) Napa Valley. *Herbal and simple, without much appeal.*

☆☆   1980 CABERNET SAUVIGNON ($12.00) Santa Cruz Mountains. *Cherry-berry fruit, clean, snappy. Drink 1986.*

☆☆   1980 PETITE SIRAH ($7.00) Bergstrom Ranch, San Miguel, Santa Cruz. *Big, dense, with some late harvest character. Drink 1986.*

☆   1980 PETITE SIRAH ($7.38) Maritime Series, Santa Cruz. *Jammy, intense, chocolatey, late harvest style.*

☆   1981 PETITE SIRAH ($7.50) Bergstrom Ranch, San Miguel, Santa Cruz. *Decent, clean, intense. Should improve with age. Drink 1986.*

☆☆☆   1979 PINOT NOIR ($7.50) Maritime Series, Reserve, Chaparral, San Luis Obispo. *Lovely, rich, Burgundian, fleshy and showing great promise.*

O   1980 PINOT NOIR ($10.00) Maritime Series, Sonoma Mountain, Sonoma. *Weedy and unappealing.*

☆☆   1981 PINOT NOIR ($7.50) Fort Ross, Sonoma. *Firm, varietal, attractive.*

1981 PINOT NOIR ($10.00) Maritime Series, California. *Chocolate, intensely leathery, vegetal.*

☆☆   1981 PINOT NOIR ($10.00) Tonneaux Americains, California. *Dense, fruity, fresh flavors, attractive. Drink now.*

☆☆   1981 PINOT NOIR ($11.00) Tonneaux Francais, California. *Nicely structured, French oak, Burgundian. Drink 1986.*

☆☆☆   1982 PINOT NOIR ($11.00) Tonneaux Francais, California. *Super varietal and balanced. Rich, complex, charming.*

Fenestra Winery
ALAMEDA COUNTY

83 East Vallecitos Road, Livermore, California 94550 (415-447-5246). FOUNDED: 1976. ACREAGE: None. PRODUCTION: 2,500 cases. DISTRIBUTION: Arizona, California, New Mexico, Utah, and Wyoming. OWNERS: Lanny and Fran Replogle. WINEMAKER: Lanny Replogle. Tours by invitation only.

Lanny Replogle was working for his chemistry degree at the University of Washington when he met Fran. They got married, moved to California, and while Lanny was teaching chemistry at San Jose State College, pursued winemaking as a hobby at home. For Lanny, winemaking expressed the artistic side of his scientific self. Like so many other wine hobbyists, Lanny and Fran wanted to turn their avocation into a profession. In order to increase their wine production they rented space and moved into an old Livermore Valley winery that had been built in 1889. Lanny still teaches chemistry, but his winery, Fenestra, gives him a "new view of life."

WHITE

☆☆   1979 CHARDONNAY ($10.00) La Reina, Monterey. *Rich oak and subdued fruit.*

☆☆   1981 CHARDONNAY ($12.00) La Reina, Monterey. *Vinous, earthy, fruity but lacking finesse.*

☆☆　1982 CHARDONNAY ($9.50) La Reina, Monterey. *Crisp, oaky, varietal, pleasant.*
☆☆☆　1982 SAUVIGNON BLANC ($7.50) San Luis Obispo. *Rich fruit, clean and bright.*
☆☆　1983 SAUVIGNON BLANC ($7.50) San Luis Obispo. *Herbaceous, fresh and fruity, very nice.*

RED

☆　1979 CABERNET SAUVIGNON ($6.25) Monterey. *A bit weedy, with dense, big flavors and low fruit.*
☆☆　1982 MERLOT ($11.00) Napa Valley. *Herbal, clean, well made. Drink 1986.*
☆　1980 ZINFANDEL ($5.25) Livermore Valley. *16.5% alcohol. Port-like late harvest.*
　1981 ZINFANDEL ($7.00) Livermore Valley. O.K. *fruit but tired and thin.*

Fenn Valley Vineyards
MICHIGAN

6130 122nd Avenue, Fennville, Michigan 49408 (616-561-2396). FOUNDED: 1973. ACREAGE: 55 acres. PRODUCTION: 16,000 cases. DISTRIBUTION: 3 states. OWNER: Welsch family. Douglas Welsch, vineyard manager. WINEMAKER: Douglas Welsch; Vince Boreczky, cellarmaster. OTHER LABEL: Briarwood. Tours and tasting Monday–Saturday 10 A.M.–5 P.M., Sunday 1 P.M.–5 P.M.

Around 1970, William Welsch, owner of a lumber company in Illinois, was looking for a tax shelter. Convinced of the advantages of winemaking by his son Douglas, and after a cautious three-year search for a viable parcel of land, they found an old fruit farm four miles from Lake Michigan. It took them two more years to pull out the old orchards, clear and fumigate the soil, plant the first vineyards, and build a simple wooden winery. Fenn Valley is very much a family operation; William still runs his lumber business, but Douglas works full time in the winery while his sister Diana handles all the office work.

WHITE

☆　1982 JOHANNISBERG RIESLING ($6.50) Fennville. *Pleasant, lacking definition.*
☆　1982 SEYVAL BLANC ($4.00) Estate, Fennville, Michigan. *Clean, decent.*
☆☆　1982 VIDAL BLANC ($4.50) Reserve, Fennville, Michigan.

FENTON ACRES *see* J. Rochioli Vineyards

Ferrara Winery
SAN DIEGO COUNTY

1120 West 15th Avenue, Escondido, California 92025 (619-745-7632). FOUNDED: 1932. ACREAGE: 3 acres. PRODUCTION: 45,000 cases. DISTRIBUTION: At winery. OWNER: Gasper Ferrara, Sr. WINEMAKER: George Ferrara. Self-guided tours weekdays 9 A.M.–5:30 P.M., weekends 10 A.M.–5:30 P.M. Museum.

Grandfather Ferrara believed Teddy Roosevelt's promise that Prohibition was coming to an end enough to begin farming 1,000 acres of grapes in the Escondido area at a time when every other winery was closing down. With each generation, the Ferraras have expanded and modernized the winery. The three brothers now in charge have replaced equipment, enlarged the storage capacity, and created a new winery within a winery: Ferrara Wine Cellars.

Ferrigno Vineyards and Winery
MISSOURI

Box 227, Route 2, St. James, Missouri 65559 (314-265-7742). FOUNDED: 1982. ACREAGE: 25 acres. PRODUCTION: 2,100 cases. DISTRIBUTION: Missouri. OWNERS: Richard and Susan Ferrigno. WINEMAKER: Richard Ferrigno. Tours and tasting daily 10 A.M.–6 P.M. Wine garden.

Richard Ferrigno, a sociologist at the University of Missouri, and his wife Susan, a teacher, decided to leave St. Louis and buy a farm north of St. James. They learned farming and viticulture thanks to thirteen acres of Concord grapevines on the property. By selling their fruit to Welch's Grape Juice, the Ferrignos were able to finance the planting of French-American hybrids. When the vines were mature, the dairy barn was cleared out and converted into a winery, complete with a hayloft tasting room.

Fetzer Vineyards
MENDOCINO COUNTY

1150 Bel Arbres Road, P.O. Box 227, Redwood Valley, California 95470 (707-485-7634). FOUNDED: 1968. ACREAGE: 700 acres. PRODUCTION: 500,000 cases. DISTRIBUTION: Nationwide and 5 foreign markets. OWNER: Fetzer family. John Fetzer, president and general manager. WINE-MAKER: Paul Dolan. OTHER LABEL: Bel Arbres Vineyards. Tours by appointment. Tasting room in Hopland, Hwy 101. Tasting daily 9 A.M.–5 P.M. Picnic facilities, delicatessen, gift shop. Newsletter.

Barnie Fetzer was working for the Masonite Corporation when he bought his Redwood Valley ranch in the mid-1950s. He replanted the vineyards and sold the fruit to home winemakers all over the country. In 1968 Fetzer Vineyards produced its first 2,500 cases. Based on a philosophy of selling youthful wines at very reasonable prices, Fetzer grew to be one of the most successful operations in California. Red wines had been Fetzer's forte, until Paul Dolan came on board and brought the whites up to standard. Since Barnie's sudden death, the winery has been ably run by ten of his eleven children.

WHITE

☆☆☆ NV PREMIUM WHITE ($3.25) Mendocino. *Fruity, clean, very attractive. Consistently one of the best.*

☆☆ 1982 BLANC DE BLANCS ($4.25) Mendocino. *Fresh, crisp, dry and lemony.*

☆ 1981 CHARDONNAY ($7.50) Early Bottling, Mendocino. *Underripe, heavily vinous, dull.*

☆☆ 1981 CHARDONNAY ($8.00) Barrel Select, Mendocino.

☆ 1981 BEL ARBRES CHARDONNAY ($8.50) Puente del Monte, Monterey. *Clean, simple and decent.*

☆☆☆ 1981 CHARDONNAY ($10.00) Special Reserve, California. *Complex and snappy with ripe fruit and elegance.*

1982 CHARDONNAY ($6.50) Sundial, Mendocino. *Grassy; more like a Sauvignon Blanc than a Chardonnay.*

☆☆☆ 1982 CHARDONNAY ($8.50) Barrel Select, Mendocino. *Fresh, clean and simple but very nicely made.*

☆ 1982 BEL ARBRES CHARDONNAY ($8.50) California. *Simple, decent fruit and modest charms.*

☆☆ 1982 CHARDONNAY ($10.00) Special Reserve, California (Monterey-Mendocino). *Toasty, rich, smooth and intensely varietal.*

1982 CHARDONNAY ($12.00) Tasting Room Select, Mendocino. *Rather unpleasant.*

☆☆ 1983 CHARDONNAY ($6.50) Sundial, Mendocino. *Apple nose; crisp and fruity, very pleasant.*

☆ 1983 CHARDONNAY ($8.50) Barrel Select, California. *Simple, clean, not much.*

☆☆☆ 1983 CHARDONNAY ($10.00) Special Reserve, California. *Rich, silky, smooth, fruity, delightful.*

☆☆ 1984 CHARDONNAY ($6.50) Sundial, Mendocino. *Fresh, simple, attractive.*

☆ 1984 CHARDONNAY ($6.50) Sundial Chardonnay, Mendocino. *Clean, decent, simple.*

☆ 1982 BEL ARBRES CHENIN BLANC ($5.50) 47% Mendocino, 53% Monterey. *Toasty and decent but dulled fruit.*

☆☆ 1982 CHENIN BLANC ($5.50) North Coast. *Fresh, clean and sweet, with lovely fruit.*

☆☆ 1983 CHENIN BLANC ($4.75) North Coast. *Fresh, sweet, charming.*

☆☆ 1984 CHENIN BLANC ($5.50) Mendocino. *Lush floral nose; varietal, crisp, sweet, snappy, clean.*

☆☆☆ 1982 FRENCH COLOMBARD ($4.25) Mendocino. *Snappy, clean, delightful. Just a touch of sugar rounds it.*

☆ 1981 FUME BLANC ($7.00) Mendocino.

☆☆ 1982 FUME BLANC ($7.00) Mendocino. *Lemony and crisp.*

☆ 1983 FUME BLANC ($7.00) 63% Lake, 37% Mendocino. *Simple, heavy, sweetish, decent.*

☆☆☆ 1984 FUME BLANC ($6.50) Valley Oaks Fume, California. *Round, fresh, varietal, very nice.*

☆☆☆ 1982 GEWURZTRAMINER ($6.00) Mendocino. *3.4% residual sugar. Crisp and fruity, balanced, varietal.*

☆☆☆ 1983 GEWURZTRAMINER ($6.00) North Coast. *2.5% residual sugar. Some botrytis, rich, intense, lush.*

☆☆☆ 1984 GEWURZTRAMINER ($6.00) California. *2.8% residual sugar. Charming, intensely varietal, lush.*

☆☆ 1981 JOHANNISBERG RIESLING ($6.00) Cole Ranch, Mendocino. *Elegant and fruity, with nice complexity.*

1981 JOHANNISBERG RIESLING ($6.00) Lake.

☆☆☆ 1982 JOHANNISBERG RIESLING ($6.00) Mendocino. *Varietal and clean. Off-dry, with delicate fruit.*

☆☆☆ 1983 JOHANNISBERG RIESLING ($6.00) Mendocino. *2.5% residual sugar. Melony, spritzy, clean and delicious.*

☆☆☆ 1984 JOHANNISBERG RIESLING ($6.00) California. *2.7% residual sugar. Floral, lush, fruity, lovely.*

☆☆☆ 1981 MUSCAT ($6.50) Lake. *Fresh and spicy, off-dry.*

☆☆☆ 1984 MUSCAT CANELLI ($6.00) Bartolucci, Lake. *3.7% residual sugar. Spritzy, clean, spicy, varietal, lovely.*

☆☆☆ 1981 PINOT BLANC ($8.50) Redwood Valley, Mendocino. *Crisp, clean, very attractive. Complex.*

☆☆ 1982 PINOT BLANC ($8.50) Redwood Valley, Mendocino. *Creamy, balanced, very good. A bit simpler than the '81.*

☆ 1981 BEL ARBRES SAUVIGNON BLANC ($4.25) Lake.

O 1982 SAUVIGNON BLANC ($8.00) Tasting Room Selection, Mendocino. *Very weedy.*

☆ 1983 SAUVIGNON BLANC ($10.00) Tasting Room Select, Sonoma-Cutrer Shilo, Sonoma. *Grassy, toasty, intense, decent.*

BLANC DE NOIR

☆☆☆ 1984 BEL ARBRES WHITE CABERNET ($4.50) Mendocino. *Varietal, spritzy, charming.*

☆☆☆ 1983 BEL ARBRES WHITE ZINFANDEL ($4.40) Mendocino. *Charming, bright and fruity.*

☆☆☆ 1984 BEL ARBRES WHITE ZINFANDEL ($4.50) Mendocino. *1.5% residual sugar. Crisp, tart, fresh and charming.*

RED

☆ NV PREMIUM RED ($3.25) Mendocino.

☆☆ 1976 CABERNET SAUVIGNON Estate, Mendocino. *Simple, clean, varietal, still fresh.*

☆☆ 1979 CABERNET SAUVIGNON ($8.50) Home, Mendocino. *Crisp and fruity, good varietal character.*

☆☆ 1979 CABERNET SAUVIGNON ($10.00) Cole Ranch, Mendocino. *Fragrant, clean, herbal. Good structure but a trifle simple.*

☆ 1980 CABERNET SAUVIGNON ($5.50) Lake. *Fresh, fruity, some weediness, nicely balanced.*

☆ 1980 BEL ARBRES CABERNET SAUVIGNON ($6.32) Alexander Valley, Sonoma. *Fruity, berried, a bit sweet, simple.*

☆☆ 1980 CABERNET SAUVIGNON ($7.00) Mendocino. *Rich, velvety, nice.*

☆☆ 1981 CABERNET SAUVIGNON ($5.50) Lake. *Simple but fresh, soft and appealing.*

☆ 1981 CABERNET SAUVIGNON ($7.00) Mendocino. *Soft, fruity, clean and simple.*

☆ 1982 CABERNET SAUVIGNON ($5.50) Lake. *Simple, clean, a bit dull.*

☆ 1982 CABERNET SAUVIGNON ($6.50) Barrel Select, Mendocino. *Soft, clean, a bit strange.*

☆☆ 1982 CABERNET SAUVIGNON ($7.00) Barrel Select, Mendocino. *Fruity, oaky, balanced, clean. Drink now.*

☆ NV GAMAY ($4.25) Mendocino.

☆☆ 1984 GAMAY ($4.00) Nouveau, Mendocino. *Carbonic maceration. Fresh, clean, snappy.*

☆☆ 1983 GAMAY BEAUJOLAIS ($4.25) Mendocino. *Fruity, fresh, clean, tart, very attractive.*

☆☆ 1983 GAMAY BEAUJOLAIS ($4.25) Mendocino. *Fresh, fruity, clean, tart. Serve slightly chilled.*

☆ 1981 BEL ARBRES MERLOT ($7.00) Sonoma. *Intense, lacking finesse.*

☆☆ 1980 PETITE SIRAH ($5.50) Mendocino. *Decent, clean, a bit off target.*

☆☆☆ 1980 PETITE SIRAH ($8.50) Special Reserve, Redwood Valley, Mendocino. *Peppery, dark, rich, clean and tannic. Drink 1987 or later.*

☆☆ 1981 PETITE SIRAH ($5.50) Mendocino. *Fresh, attractive and relatively light.*

☆☆ 1982 PETITE SIRAH ($5.50) Mendocino. *Fresh, dense, spicy, pleasant, forward, nice.*

☆ 1970 PINOT NOIR Redwood Valley, Mendocino. *Lush, complex, raisined, showing its age.*

☆ 1979 PINOT NOIR ($8.50) Special Reserve, Mendocino.

☆ 1980 PINOT NOIR ($5.50) Mendocino.

1980 PINOT NOIR ($10.00) Special Reserve, Mendocino. *Vinous, green, medicinal, vegetal, unattractive.*

☆☆ 1981 PINOT NOIR ($5.50) Mendocino. *Beaujolais-like—snappy, clean, simple; good red wine.*

☆ 1979 ZINFANDEL ($3.50) Lake.

☆☆ 1979 ZINFANDEL ($5.50) Mendocino. *Rich and raisiny.*

☆☆☆ 1979 ZINFANDEL ($7.50) Lolonis, Mendocino. *Snappy, clean and peppery.*

☆ 1979 ZINFANDEL ($7.50) Scharffenberger, Mendocino.

1979 ZINFANDEL ($8.50) Ricetti, Mendocino. *Hard and raisiny. May benefit from aging.*

☆☆☆ 1980 ZINFANDEL ($3.00) Lake. *Crisp, clean and lovely, with great balance.*

1980 ZINFANDEL ($5.50) Mendocino.

☆☆ 1980 ZINFANDEL ($8.00) Scharffenberger, Mendocino. *Good structure, snappy fruit.*

☆☆ 1980 ZINFANDEL ($9.00) Ricetti, Mendocino. *15.7% alcohol.*

☆ 1980 ZINFANDEL ($10.00) Commemorative, Home, Mendocino.

☆ 1981 ZINFANDEL ($4.50) Lake.

○ 1981 ZINFANDEL ($8.00) Home, Mendocino.

☆☆☆ 1981 ZINFANDEL ($8.00) Lolonis, Mendocino. *Balanced, Bordeaux-style.*

1981 ZINFANDEL ($9.00) Ricetti, Mendocino.

☆ 1982 ZINFANDEL ($4.50) Lake. *Vegetal nose, tart, crisp, some muddiness, decent.*

☆☆ 1982 ZINFANDEL ($5.50) Mendocino. *Light, balanced, clean, varietal, charming.*

☆☆☆ 1982 ZINFANDEL ($8.00) Home, Mendocino. *Fruity, soft, clean, rich, balanced. Drink now.*

☆☆☆ 1982 ZINFANDEL ($8.00) Lolonis, Mendocino. *Soft, rich, velvety, clean and balanced. Drink now.*

☆☆☆ 1982 ZINFANDEL ($8.00) Ricetti, Mendocino. *Rich, deep, balanced. Drink 1986.*

☆☆ 1982 ZINFANDEL ($8.00) Scharffenberger, Mendocino. *Soft, brambly, clean, tart, pleasant. Drink 1986.*

Ficklin Vineyards
MADERA COUNTY

30246 Avenue 7 1/2, Madera, California 93637 (209-674-4598). FOUNDED: 1948. ACREAGE: 200 acres. PRODUCTION: 10,000 cases. DISTRIBUTION: Nationwide. OWNER: Ficklin family. David Ficklin and Walter Ficklin, Jr., founders. WINEMAKER: Peter Ficklin; Steve Ficklin, vineyard manager. Tours by appointment.

After working on a degree in chemistry at UCLA, David Ficklin attended U.C. Davis to study enology. While at Davis, he brought five port grape varieties home to his brother Walter, who planted them in the family vineyard. Once out of school, David constructed his own adobe-brick winery. The idea was to produce California ports in the style of fine Portuguese ports. David's son, Peter, who grew up in the winery, became the winemaker in 1978 after his graduation from U.C. Davis. Walter's son, Steve, is now the vineyard manager.

FORTIFIED

☆☆☆   PORT ($6.00) California. *Rich, deep, sweet, complex.*

Field Stone Winery
SONOMA COUNTY

10075 Highway 128, Healdsburg, California 95448 (707-433-7266). FOUNDED: 1977. ACREAGE: 140 acres. PRODUCTION: 14,000 cases. DISTRIBUTION: 15 states. OWNER: Johnson family. John Staten, general manager. WINEMAKER: Jim Thomson. Tours by appointment. Tasting daily 10 A.M.–5 P.M.

Wallace Johnson bought this magnificent Alexander Valley ranch in 1955. After trying cattle for a while, he noticed that many of his neighbors were planting vineyards in the deep valley soil. In the mid-1960s he turned 130 acres into a model vineyard. After selling his grapes for several years, he decided they were of high enough quality to warrant building his own winery. He built it underground, in the side of a hill, and it was ready for the 1977 harvest. Since Wally Johnson's death in 1979, his son-in-law, John Staten, has managed both the ranch and the winery. André Tchelistcheff has served as an advisor.

WHITE

☆☆   1983 FUME BLANC ($7.00) Alexander Valley. *Grassy, oaky, slim fruit, decent.*
☆☆   1983 GEWURZTRAMINER ($6.00) Estate, Alexander Valley. *Dry, fresh, fruity, varietal.*
☆☆   1982 JOHANNISBERG RIESLING ($6.50) Alexander Valley. *2% residual sugar. Soft, fruity, clean and delicious.*
☆☆   1983 JOHANNISBERG RIESLING ($6.50) Alexander Valley. *1.6% residual sugar. Varietal, fresh, crisp, attractive.*

ROSE

☆☆   1982 SPRING-CABERNET ($5.00) Sonoma. *1.5% residual sugar. Crisp, pink and clean.*
☆☆   1983 SPRING-CABERNET ($5.25) Alexander Valley. *0.8% residual sugar. Herbal, rich, varietal.*
☆☆☆ 1982 PETITE SIRAH ($6.00) Estate, Alexander Valley. *2% residual sugar. Snappy, crisp and off-dry. Delightful.*
☆☆   1983 ROSE OF PETITE SIRAH ($6.00) Sonoma. *1.9% residual sugar. Spritzy, varietal, fruity, nice.*

RED

☆   1978 CABERNET SAUVIGNON ($7.50) Alexander Valley. *Dense and earthy; soft and lacking structure.*
    1979 CABERNET SAUVIGNON ($10.00) Estate, Alexander Valley. *Weedy and clumsy.*

☆☆   1980 CABERNET SAUVIGNON ($10.00) Estate, Alexander Valley. *Berried, clean, tannic, soft and mellow. Drink 1986.*

☆☆☆   1979 PETITE SIRAH ($7.50) Estate, Alexander Valley. *Rich, fruity and clean. Very good.*

☆☆☆   1981 PETITE SIRAH ($8.50) Alexander Valley. *Rich, fruity, graceful, lovely.*

Fieldbrook Valley Winery
HUMBOLDT COUNTY

4241 Fieldbrook Road, Fieldbrook, California 95521 (707-839-4140). FOUNDED: 1976. ACREAGE: None. PRODUCTION: 1,000 cases. DISTRIBUTION: Local. OWNERS: Robert and Judy Hodgson; Judy Hodgson, general manager. WINEMAKER: Robert Hodgson. Tours by appointment. Annual open house.

High in the hills of Humboldt County, Robert Hodgson makes wine from local grapes. While working as a professor of oceanography, Robert made wine at home for several years. He and his wife, Judy, decided to start a little business on the side, so they bonded their home winery. They intend to keep their winery comfortably small.

RED

☆   1981 MERLOT ($7.25) Humboldt. *Dense, berried, like a Zinfandel.*

☆☆   1980 PETITE SIRAH ($7.00) Special Reserve, Humboldt. *Rich, deep, clean, attractive. Drink 1986 or later.*

J. Filippi Vintage Company
SAN BERNARDINO COUNTY

13052 Jurupa Avenue, Fontana, California 92335 (714-984-4514). FOUNDED: 1934. ACREAGE: 400 acres. PRODUCTION: 150,000 cases. DISTRIBUTION: East Coast and California. OWNER: Corporation. Filippi family. Joseph A. Filippi, president; William W. Nix, vice president and general manager. WINEMAKER: Joseph Filippi. OTHER LABELS: Joseph Filippi, Château Filippi, Pride of California. Tasting daily 9 A.M.–6 P.M. Five other retail outlets.

The Filippis got an early start in the 1920s when they planted vineyards in the Cucamonga Valley. Prohibition slowed them down a bit, but in 1934, Joseph and Mary Filippi began making wine in a small room of their house. Joseph sold the wine from the barrel, filling up bottles brought in by his customers. Now Joseph is chairman of the board and his son Joseph Jr. is the winemaker, enologist, and president of the J. Filippi Vintage Company. While they no longer sell wine from the barrel, their major distribution outlets are their own six retail stores. The company also owns and makes the wine for Thomas Vineyards Winery (see), one of the oldest wineries in California.

Filsinger Vineyards and Winery
RIVERSIDE COUNTY

39050 De Portola Road, Temecula, California 92390 (714-676-4594). FOUNDED: 1980. ACREAGE: 65 acres. PRODUCTION: 10,000 cases. DISTRIBUTION: California. OWNERS: William and Katherine Filsinger. WINEMAKER: Gregory Hahn. Tours and tasting weekends 11 A.M.–5 P.M.

Perhaps Dr. Filsinger purchased his vineyards in Temecula as a tax shelter, but he quickly became interested in viticulture. He began by selling grapes to various wineries and then built his own winery and began making estate wines in 1980.

WHITE

☆ 1980 CHARDONNAY ($7.50) Temecula. *Simple but crisp and clean; moderately appealing at the price.*

☆ 1982 CHARDONNAY ($8.50) Temecula.

☆ 1983 EMERALD RIESLING ($4.00) Temecula. *1.5% residual sugar.*

1981 FUME BLANC ($4.50) Temecula.

1983 SAUVIGNON BLANC ($5.50) Temecula. *0.4% residual sugar. Dull, no fruit or acid.*

Finger Lakes Wine Cellars
NEW YORK

R.D. 1, Italy Hill Road, P.O. Box 13, Branchport, New York 14418 (315-595-2812). FOUNDED: 1981. ACREAGE: 75 acres. PRODUCTION: 4,000 cases. DISTRIBUTION: New Jersey, New York, and Virginia. OWNERS: Arthur C. and Joyce Hunt. WINEMAKER: Derek Wilber. Tours and tasting May–October: Tuesday–Saturday 10 A.M.–4 P.M. Gift shop.

When Arthur and Joyce Hunt moved onto their family property in 1973, it seemed that grape growing was a sure road to financial success. Encouraged by local wineries and economic forecasts, the Hunts started planting more and more vines. Three years later, before the first saleable crop had been harvested, the market turned sour. Grape prices fell and the economic climate turned nasty. It became obvious to Arthur, who had even more grapevines on order, that if he was going to survive in the wine business, he would have to start a winery. Taking it slowly this time, the Hunts started small but have increased their production each year.

Fink Winery
MICHIGAN

208 Main, Dundee, Michigan 48131 (313-529-3296). FOUNDED: 1975. ACREAGE: 5 acres. PRODUCTION: 4,000 cases. DISTRIBUTION: Michigan. OWNERS: Gary and Carl Fink. WINEMAKERS: Gary and Carl Fink. OTHER LABEL: Crest. Tours and tasting Monday–Saturday 9 A.M.–5 P.M.

Gary and Carl Fink own a winemaking supply store, and after selling equipment and grape concentrate for almost twenty years, the brothers decided to expand their business by starting a winery. An area in back of the store was bonded, and they began making wine from fruits and California grape concentrate. Their specialty is mead.

The Firestone Vineyard
SANTA BARBARA COUNTY

P.O. Box 244, Los Olivos, California 93441 (805-688-3940). FOUNDED: 1973. ACREAGE: 253 acres. PRODUCTION: 75,000 cases. DISTRIBUTION: Nationwide and 6 foreign countries. OWNERS: Brooks Firestone, Leonard Firestone, Suntory of Japan. Allen Russell, general manager. WINEMAKER: Alison Green. Tours and tasting Monday–Saturday 10 A.M.–4 P.M.

After twelve years of working in the family tire company, Brooks Firestone moved to the Santa Ynez Valley to grow grapes. Soon it was time to build a winery, so a partnership was formed between Brooks; his father, a former ambassador to Belgium, Leonard Firestone; and Keiso Saji, chairman of Suntory, Japan's biggest wine and spirits company. A lovely, modern winery was built, and Sonoma-born Tony Austin was brought in to make the wine (Tony has since left to open Austin Cellars). The tall and patrician Mr. Firestone and his delightful English wife, Kate, are thriving in California.

WHITE

☆☆ 1980 CHARDONNAY ($9.50) Santa Ynez Valley. *Good balance and fruit, nice varietal character.*

☆☆ 1981 CHARDONNAY ($9.50) Santa Ynez Valley. *Rich and balanced but lacking finesse.*

☆ 1982 CHARDONNAY ($10.00) Santa Ynez Valley. *Pineapple and oak; good fruit but lacking finesse.*

☆☆☆ 1981 JOHANNISBERG RIESLING ($12.00) Select Harvest, Estate, Santa Ynez Valley. *375ml. 23.5% residual sugar. Syrupy yet balanced, great.*

☆☆☆ 1982 JOHANNISBERG RIESLING ($12.00) Selected Harvest, Ambassador's, Santa Ynez Valley. *12.2% residual sugar. Crisp, fruity, botrytis, lovely.*

☆ 1982 SAUVIGNON BLANC ($7.50) Santa Ynez Valley. *Lacks freshness and varietal character.*

☆ 1983 SAUVIGNON BLANC ($7.00) Santa Ynez Valley. *Clean and decent but lacking varietal character and fruit.*

ROSE

☆☆ 1982 ROSE OF CABERNET SAUVIGNON ($4.50) Santa Ynez Valley. *A bit veggie but clean and crisp.*

☆☆ 1983 ROSE OF CABERNET SAUVIGNON ($4.50) Santa Ynez Valley. *Crisp, herbal, clean, attractive.*

RED

☆☆ 1977 CABERNET SAUVIGNON ($9.50) Santa Ynez Valley. *Cherry fruit, clean, pleasant but lacks depth.*

☆ 1977 CABERNET SAUVIGNON ($15.00) Vintage Reserve, Estate, Santa Ynez Valley. *Dense and complex, with some weediness and earth.*

☆☆ 1978 CABERNET SAUVIGNON ($9.75) Arroyo Perdido, Santa Ynez Valley. *Rich, velvety and perfumy, with a hint of mushrooms. Drink now.*

☆☆☆ 1978 CABERNET SAUVIGNON ($12.00) Vintage Reserve, Estate, Santa Ynez Valley. *Rich, full and appealing. Should age gracefully.*

☆☆ 1979 CABERNET SAUVIGNON ($8.00) Arroyo Perdido, Santa Ynez Valley. *Rich, full, clean and velvety.*

☆ 1981 CABERNET SAUVIGNON ($8.00) Estate, Santa Ynez Valley. *Fat, dull, earthy, vegetal.*

☆☆ 1982 CABERNET SAUVIGNON ($8.00) Estate, Santa Ynez Valley. *Clean, medium weight; pleasant. Drink now.*

☆ 1981 CABERNET SAUVIGNON ($8.00) Santa Ynez Valley. *Vegetal.*

☆ 1978 MERLOT ($7.50) Ambassador's, Santa Ynez Valley.

☆☆ 1979 MERLOT ($7.50) Ambassador's, Santa Ynez Valley. *Stylish, with good wood and varietal richness; elegant.*

1979 PINOT NOIR ($8.25) Estate, Santa Ynez Valley. *Thin, vegetal, slightly oxidized.*

☆ 1980 PINOT NOIR ($6.20) Santa Ynez Valley.

Fisher Ridge Wine Company
WEST VIRGINIA

Liberty, West Virginia 25124 (304-342-8702). FOUNDED: 1979. ACREAGE: 7 acres. PRODUCTION: 2,500 cases. DISTRIBUTION: West Virginia. OWNER: Fisher Ridge Wine Company, Inc.

Dr. Wilson Ward and Louise Pearson, managers. WINEMAKER: Dr. Wilson Ward. Tours by appointment.

It seems — Dentist-winemaker Dr. Wilson Ward became a wine lover while stationed near San Francisco in a mobile dental unit. When he returned to West Virginia, he was dismayed by the poor selection of available wines, so he began making wines at home. Eight years later, in 1977, he and his wife, Louise Pearson, purchased land and planted grapes. In 1979 they started a winery. The vineyards are Louise's domaine; Wilson runs the winery while maintaining his dental practice.

Fisher Vineyards
SONOMA COUNTY

6200 St. Helena Road, Santa Rosa, California 95404 (707-539-7511). FOUNDED: 1979. ACREAGE: 75 acres. PRODUCTION: 7,000 cases. DISTRIBUTION: 20 states. OWNERS: Fred J. and Juelle Fisher. WINEMAKER: Fred Fisher; Charles Ortman, consultant. Tours and tasting by appointment.

It seems that everything Fred Fisher does has style. Fred, a member of the "Body by Fisher" family, and his wife, Juelle, found a sloping hillside property on the Sonoma side of the Mayacamas Mountains. He planted Chardonnay and Cabernet Sauvignon in the shallow, well-drained soil and built a dramatic winery that has won awards for its beauty. But the wine is what matters most, and Fred's wines are carefully made and elegantly proportioned. Like Fred, they have style.

WHITE

☆☆☆ 1980 CHARDONNAY ($14.00) Sonoma. *Crisp and well built, with citrusy flavors and good depth.*

☆☆☆ 1981 CHARDONNAY ($14.00) Sonoma. *Fresh, clean, graceful and elegant.*

☆☆☆ 1982 CHARDONNAY ($14.00) Sonoma.

☆☆ 1983 EVERYDAY CHARDONNAY ($8.50) Sonoma. *Varietal, clean, some volatile acidity—a decent everyday wine.*

☆☆☆ 1983 CHARDONNAY ($14.00) Napa-Sonoma. *Elegant, clean, complex, delicate oak, lovely.*

☆☆☆ 1983 CHARDONNAY ($14.00) 65% Sonoma, 35% Napa. *Elegant, balanced, lovely oak, charming varietal character, a classic.*

☆☆☆ 1984 EVERYDAY CHARDONNAY ($8.50) Sonoma. *Simple, clean, oaky, charming.*

RED

☆☆☆ 1979 CABERNET SAUVIGNON ($12.00) Sonoma. *Lovely fruit, varietal intensity and balance.*

☆☆☆ 1980 CABERNET SAUVIGNON ($12.00) Sonoma. *Balanced, soft and quite Bordeaux-like. Drink 1986 and beyond.*

☆☆☆ 1981 CABERNET SAUVIGNON ($12.00) Sonoma. *Tart, clean, varietal, lean. Drink 1986.*

Fitzpatrick Winery
EL DORADO COUNTY

6881 Fairplay Road, Somerset, California 95684 (209-245-3248). FOUNDED: 1980. ACREAGE: 15 acres. PRODUCTION: 4,000 cases. DISTRIBUTION: Alaska, California, New Jersey, and New York. OWNERS: Brian and Michael Fitzpatrick. WINEMAKER: Brian Fitzpatrick. Tours and tasting weekends 11 A.M.–5 P.M.

Winemaking duties at this winery have bounced back and forth between the three founding partners, Brian and Michael Fitzpatrick and Bill Bertram. It was originally named FBF Winery

(Fitzpatrick, Bertram, and Fitzpatrick), and Bill and Brian shared the early winemaking responsibilities. Then Bill carried the ball alone for three years, from 1981 to 1984. In 1984 Bill left the winery and the partnership to be the assistant winemaker at D'Agostini Winery. Since his departure, the winery has undergone numerous changes, and is now under the Fitzpatrick name. Brian, a U.C. Davis graduate in soil and water sciences, is the winemaker.

WHITE

☆ 1982 SAUVIGNON BLANC ($7.00) Clockspring, Shenandoah Valley, Amador.

☆ 1983 SAUVIGNON BLANC ($6.00) Erie Ban, Turn Run, Lateham, Gold Hill, El Dorado. *20% Chenin Blanc. Lush, rich, clean and decent but lacks snap.*

RED

☆ 1980 CABERNET SAUVIGNON ($7.00) El Dorado. *Earthy and big without much finesse. Not typically varietal.*

☆☆ 1981 CABERNET SAUVIGNON ($7.50) Mount Lassen, Tehama. *Dense, rich, tannic, fruity. Drink 1988 and beyond.*

☆☆ 1981 ZINFANDEL ($6.50) Clockspring, Shenandoah Valley, California. *Tangy, rich, clean.*

☆☆ 1982 ZINFANDEL ($5.50) Jehling, Shenandoah Valley, California. *Crisp, fruity, clean, good.*

Flora Springs Wine Company
NAPA COUNTY

1978 West Zinfandel Lane, St. Helena, California 94574 (707-963-5711). FOUNDED: 1978. ACREAGE: 300 acres. PRODUCTION: 15,000 cases. OWNER: Komes family. Jerry, Flora, Mike, Rose, John and Carrie Komes; Pat and Julie Garvey. WINEMAKER: Ken Deis. Tours by appointment.

Jerry Komes had no idea when he purchased the old Louis Martini property that his children would become so attached to it. The land held two old, abandoned wineries and 50 acres of vines. Julie, Jerry's daughter, and her husband, Pat, were the first to leave their white-collar livelihoods in San Jose to take care of the vineyard. Later, Julie's brother John, a contractor in Berkeley, converted one of the old wineries into his home. The idea to start a winery came from John, who wished to escape his daily commute to the city. So the other winery was modernized and put into operation. Some grapes are still sold to other wineries and some are made into wine under the family label.

WHITE

☆☆ 1980 CHARDONNAY ($11.00) Napa Valley. *Balanced and restrained, clean and attractive.*

☆☆☆ 1980 CHARDONNAY ($16.00) Special Select, Napa Valley. *Crisp and clean, with nicely controlled oak flavors.*

☆☆ 1981 CHARDONNAY ($12.00) Napa Valley. *Crisp, fruity, angular, richly rounded.*

☆☆☆ 1981 CHARDONNAY ($13.50) Barrel Fermented, Napa Valley. *Toasty, rich and plump.*

☆☆☆ 1982 CHARDONNAY ($12.00) Napa Valley. *Rich, fruity, clean and lush.*

☆☆ 1983 CHARDONNAY ($13.50) Barrel Fermented, Napa Valley. *Rich, deep, soft, fruity, lush.*

☆☆☆ 1982 SAUVIGNON BLANC ($8.00) Napa Valley. *Steely and crisp, nice fruit, clean.*

☆☆ 1983 SAUVIGNON BLANC ($8.00) Napa Valley. *Snappy fruit, clean, varietal.*

RED

☆☆ 1980 CABERNET SAUVIGNON ($12.00) Napa Valley. *Oaky and forward, nice complexity. Drink 1986 and beyond.*

☆☆ 1981 CABERNET SAUVIGNON ($12.00) Napa Valley. *12% Merlot, 3% Cabernet Franc. Oaky, ripe and clean. Drink 1986.*

Florida Heritage Winery
FLORIDA

P.O. Box 116, Anthony, Florida 32617 (904-732-3427). FOUNDED: 1981. ACREAGE: 65 acres. PRODUCTION: 5,000 cases. DISTRIBUTION: Florida. OWNERS: Dr. and Mrs. Robert C. Price, Jr.; Witold Rossochacki, general manager. WINEMAKER: Witold Rossochacki. Tours and tasting daily 9 A.M.–5 P.M.

Dr. Price inherited a large plot of land smack in the middle of Florida's peninsula. Since he was neither a rancher nor a farmer, he felt it would be impractical for him to start raising cattle or growing corn. But his wife, coming from Germany's Rheingau, convinced him to consider growing grapes. Before getting too serious, however, the Prices contacted the University of Florida, then traveled to Europe to learn more about growing grapes and making wine. After this research, the doctor planted Muscadine vines.

Thomas Fogarty Winery
SAN MATEO COUNTY

5937 Alpine Road, Portola Valley, California 94025 (415-851-1946). FOUNDED: 1982. ACREAGE: 20 acres. PRODUCTION: 6,000 cases. DISTRIBUTION: California and Washington D.C. OWNER: Thomas Fogarty. WINEMAKER: Michael Martella. Tours by appointment.

Thomas Fogarty is a cardiovascular surgeon and the inventor of the "Fogarty catheter," which is quite well known in medical circles. When Dr. Fogarty moved to the Portola Valley, he planted a few experimental grapevines on the property he had purchased near the Portola Valley Skyline. By 1981 he had expanded his vineyard to twelve acres. He then started a winery and hired winemaker Michael Martella, who lives in a house built on top of the winery.

WHITE

☆☆☆ 1981 CHARDONNAY ($12.50) Ventana, Monterey. *Rich, deep, clean, elegant and very French.*
☆☆ 1982 CHARDONNAY ($14.50) Ventana, Monterey. *Crisp, well made, lacking finesse.*
1983 CHARDONNAY ($14.50) Ventana, Monterey.
☆ 1983 CHARDONNAY ($15.00) Winery Lake, Napa Valley. *Very oaky, big, earthy, a bit unbalanced.*

RED

☆☆☆ 1981 PINOT NOIR ($15.00) Winery Lake, Napa Valley. *Rich, soft, complex—a dazzling first effort.*
☆☆ 1982 PINOT NOIR ($12.00) Ventana, Monterey. *Herbal, clean, nice fruit.*

Folie à Deux Winery
NAPA COUNTY

3070 St. Helena Highway, St. Helena, California 94574 (707-963-1160). FOUNDED: 1981. ACREAGE: 13 acres. PRODUCTION: 2,700 cases. DISTRIBUTION: Major market states. OWNERS: Evie and Larry Dizmang. WINEMAKER: Larry Dizmang. Tours and tasting Wednesday–Sunday 11:30 A.M.–4:30 P.M.

Roughly translated, *folie à deux* means "a shared foolishness," which is in this case shared by Larry and Evie Dizmang. Larry, a psychiatrist, is the head of the Mental Health Department at St.

Helena Hospital, and Evie works as a psychological counselor and social worker. After being urged on by several winemaker friends in the Napa Valley, the Dizmangs decided to start a small winery and vineyard on their home property.

WHITE

☆☆   1982 CHARDONNAY ($12.00) Napa Valley. *Lovely, crisp and fruity but lacks depth in middle.*

RED

☆☆   1982 CABERNET SAUVIGNON ($10.00) Robert Egan, State Lane, Napa Valley. *Leafy, dense, good structure, balanced. Drink 1986.*

E. B. Foote Winery
WASHINGTON

9354 Fourth Avenue South, Seattle, Washington 98108 (206-763-9928). FOUNDED: 1978. ACREAGE: None. PRODUCTION: 1,500 cases. DISTRIBUTION: Washington. OWNERS: Eugene and Mary Foote. WINEMAKER: Eugene Foote. Tours by appointment. Tasting Tuesday–Thursday 6:30 P.M.–9:30 P.M., Saturday 9:30 A.M.–3:30 P.M.

After twenty years of working as an engineer for Boeing, Gene Foote wanted "something else," so he turned to winemaking. His first attempts were with berry wine, which led to experiments with grape wine. He then established a commercial winery in an industrial park in south Seattle. Despite its location, the winery is surrounded on all sides by gardens. Gene's sole interest is winemaking; he has no desire to grow grapes and is very satisfied with the fruit he buys from the Yakima and Grandview areas. He still works full time as an engineer, a job he enjoys a great deal and "cannot afford to give up"; and he very much appreciates the help he gets in the winery from his four sons.

Louis Foppiano Wine Company
SONOMA COUNTY

12707 Old Redwood Highway, Healdsburg, California 95448 (707-433-7272). FOUNDED: 1896. ACREAGE: 200 acres. PRODUCTION: 150,000 cases. DISTRIBUTION: Major market states. OWNER: Foppiano family. Louis J. Foppiano, president; Louis M. Foppiano, general manager. WINEMAKER: Bill Regan. OTHER LABEL: Riverside Farm. Tasting daily 10 A.M.–4:30 P.M.

Gold Rush–dropout John Foppiano of Genoa, Italy, knew his voyage to America wasn't a mistake when he discovered the enormous agricultural potential of the Russian River Valley. After trying vegetables, he switched to prunes, then grapes, and by 1896 he owned a winery. John was succeeded by son Louis Andrew, who was in turn succeeded by his son, Louis Joseph. In 1984 the winery was stunned by the untimely death of Louis's son, viticulturist Rod Foppiano. The winery, however, continues to thrive under the able leadership of young Lou, a delightful fellow with a wry sense of humor and a keen marketing sense.

WHITE

☆☆   NV   RIVERSIDE FARM MEDIUM DRY ($2.50) California. *Off-dry, soft, clean and attractive.*
☆☆   NV   RIVERSIDE FARM PREMIUM ($3.90) California. *Snappy, fruity, crisp, some Gewürztraminer character.*

1982 SONOMA WHITE BURGUNDY ($5.50) Sonoma. *78% French Colombard, 22% Chardonnay. Dull, not clean.*

☆ 1980 CHARDONNAY ($8.50) Sonoma. *Earthy and intense, with no finesse but some power.*

☆ 1981 CHARDONNAY ($8.75) Sonoma.

☆☆ 1982 CHARDONNAY ($9.25) Sonoma. *Fresh, lemony fruit, decent varietal character.*

☆☆ 1983 CHARDONNAY ($10.00) Sonoma.

☆ 1983 CHENIN BLANC ($3.10) California.

1983 RIVERSIDE FARM CHENIN BLANC ($3.70) California. *Tart, varietal, flabby on finish.*

☆☆ 1983 CHENIN BLANC ($5.00) Sonoma. *0.85% residual sugar. Fruity, clean and fresh.*

☆ 1982 RIVERSIDE FARM FRENCH COLOMBARD ($3.00) California.

☆☆☆ 1982 SAUVIGNON BLANC ($7.00) Sonoma. *Crisp, clean, lovely fruit, well made.*

☆☆☆ 1983 SAUVIGNON BLANC ($7.50) Russian River Valley. *Fruity, clean, snappy, nicely balanced.*

BLANC DE NOIR

☆☆ 1984 RIVERSIDE FARM WHITE ZINFANDEL ($3.75) California. *Clean, fruity, off-dry, charming.*

ROSE

☆☆ NV RIVERSIDE FARM DRY ROSE ($2.75) California. *Fresh and clean, with soft, attractive fruitiness.*

RED

☆☆ NV RIVERSIDE FARM PREMIUM RED ($2.75) California. *Open, soft, fruity and good.*

☆ 1978 CABERNET SAUVIGNON ($6.00) Sonoma. *Simple and direct, somewhat heavy-handed.*

☆ 1979 CABERNET SAUVIGNON ($6.00) Sonoma. *Another very drinkable and simple Cabernet; pleasant, decent.*

☆☆ 1980 CABERNET SAUVIGNON ($6.50) Sonoma. *Some vegetal quality, nice fruit, clean. Drink now.*

☆☆ 1981 RIVERSIDE FARM CABERNET SAUVIGNON ($3.75) 50% Sonoma, 50% Lake. *Fresh, fruity, attractive.*

☆☆☆ 1981 CABERNET SAUVIGNON ($7.75) Russian River Valley. *15% Merlot, 5% Cabernet Franc. Lush, lovely. Drink now.*

☆☆ 1979 PETITE SIRAH ($5.50) Sonoma. *Balanced and fresh tasting.*

☆☆ 1980 PETITE SIRAH ($6.25) Sonoma. *Berries, well structured, clean and rich. Drink now.*

☆ 1980 PINOT NOIR ($5.00) Russian River Valley.

1978 ZINFANDEL ($7.50) Sonoma.

☆ 1979 ZINFANDEL ($5.75) Sonoma.

☆☆☆ 1980 RIVERSIDE FARM ZINFANDEL ($3.10) California. *Fruity and attractive.*

☆☆ 1982 RIVERSIDE FARM WINERY ZINFANDEL ($3.70) Sonoma. *Rich, soft, good balance, clean.*

Forgeron Vineyard
OREGON

89697 Sheffler Road, Elmira, Oregon 97437 (503-935-1117). FOUNDED: 1978. ACREAGE: 20 acres. PRODUCTION: 5,000 cases. DISTRIBUTION: East Coast and Oregon. OWNERS: George "Lee" and Linda C. Smith. WINEMAKER: George "Lee" Smith; Dr. William Nelson, consultant.

Tours and tasting May–September: daily 12–5 P.M.; October–April: weekends 12–5 P.M.; closed January.

After three years of hobnobbing with French winemakers, Lee Smith came back to the U.S. to scour the West Coast for a vineyard site. A Burgundy lover, he was hoping to find an area that approximated Burgundy's climate. He studied a scientific evaluation of weather patterns in a 30-square-mile area east of Eugene and found five promising vineyard sites, though none for sale. After persistent efforts, Lee convinced one of the landowners to sell. While planting the vineyards on this secluded estate of fir and oak trees, Lee worked in a local plywood mill and drove trucks. He saved enough money for his winery, and moved the winemaking equipment from his basement into a brand-new winery in 1981. Still a Francophile, Lee named the winery *Forgeron*, which means "Smith" in French.

WHITE

1983 CHENIN BLANC ($7.50) Oregon. *Vegetal, sweet.*
☆ 1981 PINOT GRIS ($7.50) Lane County, Oregon.
☆☆ 1981 WHITE RIESLING ($6.75) Lane County, Oregon.
1982 WHITE RIESLING Oregon. *Cardboard flavors, but fruity and decent.*

RED

1979 CABERNET SAUVIGNON ($8.00) Lane County, Oregon.
☆☆☆ 1979 PINOT NOIR ($8.00) Lane County, Oregon.
☆☆ 1980 PINOT NOIR ($7.50) Lane County, Oregon. *Perfumy, with a candied nose; earthy, thin, nice flavors. Drink 1986.*

Fortino Winery
SANTA CLARA COUNTY

4525 Hecker Pass Highway, Gilroy, California 95020 (408-842-3305). FOUNDED: 1970. ACREAGE: 60 acres. PRODUCTION: 20,000 cases. DISTRIBUTION: California, 5 other states; Switzerland. OWNER: Ernest Fortino, president; Marie Fortino, secretary. WINEMAKER: Ernest Fortino. Tours and tasting daily 9 A.M.–6 P.M.

The Fortino family made wine in Calabria, southern Italy, before emigrating to California. They rebuilt the old Cassa Brothers winery and began where their forefathers left off, making generics and varietals in the Italian style. In 1983, the winery lost 90 percent of its bottled inventory in a warehouse fire. But Ernie Fortino, an accomplished accordionist, doesn't let such things get him down. His smiling face and warm handshake are still a main attraction at the small winery.

BLANC DE NOIR

☆ 1981 PINOT NOIR BLANC ($5.50) San Benito. *Soft, dull and lacking varietal identity.*
1981 ZINFANDEL BLANC ($4.50) Central Coast. *Dull.*

RED

☆ 1977 CABERNET SAUVIGNON ($18.50) Central Coast. *Big, earthy, not varietal.*
☆☆ 1980 CABERNET SAUVIGNON ($7.50) San Benito. *Good, clean and attractive; simple but decent.*
☆ 1979 CHARBONO ($7.50) San Benito. *Lush, clean, showing some age.*
☆☆ 1980 CHARBONO ($7.50) Santa Clara. *Rich, clean, intense.*
☆ 1978 PETITE SIRAH ($6.50) San Benito. *Intense and somewhat overdone.*
☆ 1981 PINOT NOIR ($6.50) Santa Clara.

Four Chimneys Farm Winery
NEW YORK

R.D. 1, Hall Road, Himrod, New York 14842 (607-243-7502). FOUNDED: 1980. ACREAGE: 15 acres. PRODUCTION: 2,500 cases. DISTRIBUTION: New York. OWNERS: Walter G. and Dale Pedersen; Scott and Dongmee Smith, managers. WINEMAKER: Scott Smith. Tours and tasting May–October: Monday–Saturday 10 A.M.–6 P.M., Sunday 1 P.M.–6 P.M.

Walter Pedersen, a former editor for Macmillan Publishing Company in New York City, moved his family of eight to an old Italian-style villa, Four Chimneys Farm, located near beautiful Lake Seneca. The grapevines on the property held no special fascination for the Pedersons until Walter began making some wine. As he became more interested in farming, he demonstrated his belief in the natural way of life by researching and practicing organic grape growing. He uses only natural substances, such as manure, compost, and seaweed for fertilizer, and herbal and vegetable sprays as pesticides. The winery also produces and sells organic grape juice.

WHITE

☆☆ 1982 DELAWARE ($8.25) Late Harvest-Organic, Estate, Finger Lakes. *Labrusca nose, rich, thick, fruity, clean, nice.*

☆ 1982 JOHANNISBERG RIESLING ($7.65) Finger Lakes. *Varietal and fruity, but overwhelmed by sulfur dioxide in the nose.*

☆☆ 1982 JOHANNISBERG RIESLING ($8.75) Special Selection, Finger Lakes. *Soft, melony nose; rich, sweet, with good fruit and botrytis.*

RED

☆☆ 1981 CABERNET SAUVIGNON ($12.00) Finger Lakes. *Chocolate nose, smooth, varietal, good acidity. Drink 1986.*

Foxwood Wine Cellars
SOUTH CAROLINA

Route 3, Woodruff, South Carolina 29388 (803-476-3153). FOUNDED: 1979. ACREAGE: 240 acres. PRODUCTION: 5,000 cases. DISTRIBUTION: North and South Carolina. OWNER: Capitol Funds of South Carolina. Patti Simmons, general manager. WINEMAKER: Patti Simmons. Tours by appointment.

When the original owners of the winery went bankrupt, Capitol Funds took charge. They changed the name, the label, and the management but kept the red and white prefabricated winery building. Winemaker Patti Simmons started as the winery's secretary, and picked up her winemaking skills by working with the winery manager, filling out forms, and working in the lab. Now she is making the wine and managing the entire operation. She and her husband, the winery foreman, live on the winery property.

Franciscan Vineyards
NAPA COUNTY

1178 Galleron Road, Rutherford, California 94573 (707-963-7111). FOUNDED: 1973. ACREAGE: 500 acres. PRODUCTION: 100,000 cases. DISTRIBUTION: Nationwide. OWNER: Peter Eckes; Harry Ellis, general manager. WINEMAKER: Deborah Cutter, enologist. Self-guided tours daily 10 A.M.–5 P.M.; special tours by appointment. Tasting daily at 2 P.M. Gift shop.

This winery has had a hard time getting on track. Rescued from bankruptcy in 1975 by former Christian Brother Justin Meyer and Colorado businessman Ray Duncan (see Silver Oak Wine Cellars), Franciscan was subsequently sold to the German wine company Peter Eckes in 1979. The quality of the wines was inconsistent until 1982, when Tom Ferrell left his winemaking position at Inglenook to become Franciscan's winemaker. The wines of the "Ferrell era" were a great improvement over the winery's past efforts, and it looked as though Franciscan was finally on the right track. But in 1984, Tom left Franciscan to become the president of Sterling Vineyards.

WHITE

NV CASK 321 CHABLIS ($3.25) California. *Slight mothball nose, not clean.*

O   1980 CHARDONNAY ($6.33) Oakwood Ranch, Napa Valley. *Soapy.*

☆☆   1981 CHARDONNAY ($9.50) Alexander Valley. *Lean and clean, nice fruit and freshness.*

☆   1981 CHARDONNAY ($9.50) Napa Valley. *Ripe fruit and oak, likable.*

☆☆☆   1982 CHARDONNAY ($10.50) Vintner Grown, Alexander Valley. *A stunner. Delicate, balanced, with lush fruit and oak—superb.*

☆☆☆   1982 CHARDONNAY ($12.00) Carneros Reserve, Napa Valley. *Crisp, snappy, very lovely.*

☆☆☆   1982 CHARDONNAY ($12.00) Reserve, Oakville Estate, Napa Valley. *Soft, woody, elegant, complex; quite lovely.*

☆☆   1983 CHARDONNAY ($10.50) Alexander Valley. *Toasty, oaky, crisp, fruity and lush.*

1982 FUME BLANC ($7.00) Red River, Vintner Grown, Alexander Valley. *Dull, soft, no fruit.*

1983 FUME BLANC ($6.00) Alexander Valley. *Dull, composty, oily, lacking fruit.*

1981 JOHANNISBERG RIESLING ($6.00) Duncan (Estate), Napa Valley. *Oily and dull, with a short finish.*

1982 JOHANNISBERG RIESLING ($6.50) Estate, Napa Valley. *Lush nose but dull and lifeless flavors.*

☆   1982 JOHANNISBERG RIESLING ($25.00) Select Late Harvest, Estate, Napa Valley. *19% residual sugar. Sweet and soft but some cardboard taste.*

☆☆   1983 JOHANNISBERG RIESLING ($6.00) Oakville Estate, Napa Valley. *2.17% residual sugar. Fresh, varietal, crisp, attractive.*

1981 SAUVIGNON BLANC ($6.00) California (Temecula).

☆☆   1982 SAUVIGNON BLANC ($10.00) Reserve, Alexander Valley. *Lovely fruit and balance, clean, with just a touch of oxidation.*

RED

NV BURGUNDY ($2.16) North Coast.

NV RED DINNER WINE, CASK 320 ($2.50) California.

☆   1977 CABERNET SAUVIGNON ($12.50) Private Reserve, Duncan, Napa Valley. *Heavy, clumsy, some complexity and interesting age nuances.*

☆   1978 CABERNET SAUVIGNON ($8.00) Napa Valley. *Vegetal and ungainly.*

1978 CABERNET SAUVIGNON ($12.00) Estate, Napa Valley. *Weedy, unpleasant.*

☆   1978 CABERNET SAUVIGNON ($12.50) Private Reserve, Napa. *A well made wine that is spoiled by excessive weediness.*

1979 CABERNET SAUVIGNON ($6.50) Alexander Valley. *21% Merlot. Dull and weedy.*

1979 CABERNET SAUVIGNON ($8.50) Estate, Napa Valley. *Not holding well, flabby, over the hill.*

☆☆☆   1980 CABERNET SAUVIGNON ($7.50) Alexander Valley. *Round, fresh, deep, charming. Drink 1987 and beyond.*

☆☆   1979 CHARBONO ($9.50) Napa Valley. *Rich, lush and attractive.*

☆☆   1984 CHARBONO ($6.00) Harvest Nouveau, Napa Valley. *Lively, fresh and fruity. Serve chilled.*

☆☆   1978 MERLOT ($6.88) Napa Valley. *20% Cabernet. Soft, lovely and rich; finishes short.*

☆☆   1979 MERLOT ($8.50) Oakville, Napa Valley. *25% Cabernet. Lightly vegetal and nicely oaked.*

1980 MERLOT ($9.00) Napa Valley. *Oxidized, off flavors.*
1979 ZINFANDEL ($6.50) Oakville, Napa. *Weedy and tired.*
1980 ZINFANDEL ($6.48) Estate, Napa. *Weedy.*

KONSTANTIN FRANK *see* Vinifera Wine Cellars

Franzia Winery
SAN JOAQUIN COUNTY

Highway 120, Ripon, California 95366 (209-599-4111). FOUNDED: 1906. ACREAGE: 4,500 acres. DISTRIBUTION: Nationwide. OWNER: Arthur Ciocca, president. WINEMAKER: Louis Quaccia. Tasting daily 10 A.M.–7 P.M.

Started by the Franzia family in the early 1900s, this winery has come a long way from its modest roots. The Coca-Cola Company of New York (not Atlanta) purchased the winery in 1973. They completely revamped the facility, adding new equipment, a cooperage, a lab, and a bottling line. In 1981, Coca-Cola sold all its wine holdings to a group of private investors, many of whom had been running the winery all along. "It was just a case of changing banks," says president Arthur Ciocca.

SPARKLING

☆☆ NV ALMOND FLAVORED CHAMPAGNE ($3.50) California. *Clean and sweet, with a strong amaretto flavor.*
NV LIGHT CHAMPAGNE ($3.50) California. *Dull.*

RED

NV CABERNET SAUVIGNON ($2.60) California.

Frasinetti Winery
SACRAMENTO COUNTY

7395 Frasinetti Road, Sacramento, California 95828 (916-383-2444). FOUNDED: 1897. ACREAGE: None. PRODUCTION: 20,000 cases. DISTRIBUTION: Northern California. OWNERS: Howard and Gary Frasinetti; John Czech, general manager. WINEMAKERS: Howard and Gary Frasinetti. Tours by appointment. Tasting Monday–Friday 9 A.M.–6 P.M, Saturday 11 A.M.–6 P.M. Restaurant.

The Frasinetti Winery is a well-kept community secret. Nearly all of this winery's business is done with longtime local customers. It is the oldest family winery in the Sacramento area, having been founded in 1897 by James Frasinetti.

Freemark Abbey Winery
NAPA COUNTY

3022 St. Helena Highway North, St. Helena, California 94574 (707-963-9694). FOUNDED: 1967. ACREAGE: 130 acres. PRODUCTION: 28,000 cases. DISTRIBUTION: Nationwide. OWNERS: Partnership. Charles Carpy and William Jaeger, Jr., managing partners. WINEMAKER: Larry Langbehn. Tours daily at 2 P.M. Tasting daily 10 A.M.–4:30 P.M.

This 1895 stone winery was acquired by a partnership of seven people, most of whom are old-guard Napa Valley residents, and several of whom are growers. The winery has been a success from the beginning and has served as a training ground for many who went on to run their own wineries. Six of the partners are also partners in Rutherford Hill Winery, an operation that was meant to produce a lower-priced, less prestigious line, but that has developed into one of Napa Valley's better wineries.

WHITE

☆☆ 1982 EDELWEIN GOLD ($17.50) Napa Valley. *375ml. 21.9% residual sugar. Johannisberg Riesling.*

☆ 1976 CHARDONNAY Napa Valley. *Dull, faded.*

☆ 1977 CHARDONNAY Napa Valley. *Decent but faded.*

☆☆☆ 1980 CHARDONNAY ($13.50) Napa Valley. *Earthy, clean and intense. Will age well.*

☆☆ 1981 CHARDONNAY ($13.50) Napa Valley. *Earthy and toasty, rich, with shy fruitiness.*

☆☆ 1982 CHARDONNAY ($12.00) Napa Valley. *Initial off aromas give way to a richly oaked, good wine.*

☆☆☆ 1983 CHARDONNAY ($14.00) Napa Valley. *Lovely fruit and acid, good oak.*

☆☆ 1983 JOHANNISBERG RIESLING ($6.75) Napa Valley. *2.2% residual sugar. A bit overripe but rich, clean and nice.*

☆☆ 1984 JOHANNISBERG RIESLING ($7.00) Napa Valley. *Fresh, clean, vinous, varietal.*

RED

☆☆☆ 1975 CABERNET BOSCHE Napa Valley. *Smooth and rich, fulfills its early promise.*

☆☆ 1977 CABERNET SAUVIGNON ($10.50) Napa Valley. *Decent, clean and varietal; complex but not lovable.*

☆☆☆ 1978 CABERNET SAUVIGNON ($11.50) Napa Valley. *Intense, rich fruit, lovely structure, deep. Drink now.*

☆☆ 1979 CABERNET SAUVIGNON ($11.50) Napa Valley. *Herbal and a bit muddy but firm, with good aging potential.*

☆ 1979 CABERNET BOSCHE ($12.50) Napa Valley. *Nicely structured, but some off flavors intrude.*

☆ 1980 CABERNET SAUVIGNON ($14.00) Napa Valley. *Intense, chocolatey, vegetal, deep, composty, oily.*

☆☆☆ 1980 CABERNET BOSCHE ($14.50) Napa Valley. *Crisp, balanced, clean, complex, lovely. Drink 1986.*

☆☆☆ 1981 CABERNET BOCHE ($14.00) Napa Valley. *Lovely fruit and structure. Earthy, complex. Drink 1987.*

☆☆☆ 1980 PETITE SIRAH ($8.50) Yale Creek Vineyards, Napa Valley. *Peppery, fresh, soft and very attractive. Drink now.*

French Creek Cellars
WASHINGTON

15372 Northeast 96th Place, Redmond, Washington 98052 (206-883-0757). FOUNDED: 1983. ACREAGE: None. PRODUCTION: 5,500 cases. DISTRIBUTION: Washington. OWNER: Corporation. Hans and Trudel Doerr, and Arthur and Leah Grossman. WINEMAKER: Hans Doerr. Tours and tasting summer: Thursday–Saturday 11 A.M.–5 P.M.; winter: Saturday 11 A.M.–5 P.M.

Hans Doerr had been making wine at home for years; there had been talk about starting a commercial venture, but it just never seemed to happen. Finally, Hans and his wife, Trudie, teamed up with their long-time friends Arthur and Leah Grossman. Arthur and Hans both teach at the University of Washington and Leah owns a bakery. "We originally planned the winery so the work load could be handled by just us four," says Arthur. "We all share the work and the winemaking and we all have outside jobs as well." Trudi adds, "We are now moving toward a more professional organization and have hired a full-time cellarmaster."

Fretter Wine Cellars
ALAMEDA COUNTY

805 Camelia Street, Berkeley, California 94710 (415-525-3232). FOUNDED: 1977. ACREAGE: None. PRODUCTION: 1,000 cases. DISTRIBUTION: California and Pennsylvania. OWNER: Travis D. Fretter, president; W. B. Fretter, vice president; Robert H. Powles, treasurer. WINE-MAKER: Travis D. Fretter. OTHER LABELS: Leaky Lake, Mountain Glen Vineyard. Tours by appointment. Newsletter.

Berkeley born and raised, Travis Fretter has a quiet, studious mellowness about him. His winery, a funky, narrow room of barrels and demijohns, is located in a semi-residential, semi-industrial part of Berkeley. While working as a wine salesman, Travis was inspired to start his winery when his father didn't want to sell the Cabernet grapes on his three-and-a-half-acre vineyard in the Napa Valley. Travis bases his winemaking philosophy on individual vineyards. Written on his labels is the slogan, "Single vineyard wines." "That's because I believe the wine is made in the vineyard," explains Travis. "I want the vineyard to speak for itself."

WHITE

NV   MOUNTAIN GLEN VINEYARD CHARDONNAY ($7.50) Mendocino. *Intensely oaky, dark, old and lacking fruit.*

O   1981 CHARDONNAY ($6.50) Eisele, Napa Valley. *Musty, dirty.*

☆   1981 CHARDONNAY ($10.00) Leaky Lake, Napa Valley. *Dull.*

1982 MOUNTAIN GLEN VINEYARD CHARDONNAY ($8.50) Mendocino. *Dark, intense, oxidized.*

RED

☆☆☆   1979 LEAKY LAKE CABERNET SAUVIGNON ($7.50) Napa Valley.

☆☆☆   1980 LEAKY LAKE CABERNET SAUVIGNON ($12.00) Napa Valley. *Berried, oaky, clean, balanced. Drink 1987 and beyond.*

1981 LEAKY LAKE CABERNET SAUVIGNON ($9.00) Napa Valley. *Raisiny, dense, bitter, not much fruit.*

☆☆☆   1980 MERLOT ($10.00) Narsai David, Napa Valley. *Snappy, rich, tannic, oaky and big. Should age well.*

☆☆   1981 MERLOT ($10.00) Narsai David, Napa Valley. *Clean, appealing but some off characteristics.*

☆☆☆   1982 MERLOT ($10.00) Narsai David, Napa Valley. *Oaky and big, with rich, deep fruit. Drink 1989.*

Frey Vineyards
MENDOCINO COUNTY

14000 Tomki Road, Redwood Valley, California 95470 (707-485-8551). FOUNDED: 1980. ACREAGE: 30 acres. PRODUCTION: 5,500 cases. DISTRIBUTION: California and 4 other states. OWNER: Frey family. Dr. and Mrs. Paul Frey and their twelve children. WINEMAKER: Jonathan Frey. Tours by appointment. Tasting and retail sales daily 9 A.M.–5 P.M. Tasting room on Highway 101 north of Ukiah.

A family of lanky, towheaded boys and their retired father tore down the old Garret Winery, where a famous wine called "Virginia Dare" was once made. That was when the Freys began thinking about starting a winery. Paul Frey, the father, had been growing grapes in the Redwood Valley since 1967. His sons, Matthew and Jonathan, who had worked at neighboring wineries, used some of the wood from the Garret Winery to make their own winery, a board-and-nail cowbarn building that sits among a rusty clutter of farming equipment. Paul raises only "certified organic grapes." He claims he uses "no pesticides, herbicides, or fungicides."

WHITE

1982 CHARDONNAY ($8.00) Mendocino. *Not clean, low varietal character.*

☆☆ 1982 FRENCH COLOMBARD ($4.00) Mendocino. *Crisp, dry and snappy.*

1982 GEWURZTRAMINER ($4.50) Guntly, Mendocino. *Odd and low in varietal character.*

☆ 1982 GREY RIESLING ($4.00) Mendocino. *Dry, snappy and appealing.*

☆ 1982 SAUVIGNON BLANC ($8.00) Mendocino. *3.3% residual sugar. Weird, grapey and crisp—rather attractive.*

RED

☆ 1980 CABERNET SAUVIGNON ($6.00) Mendocino. *Light, herbal, nice.*

☆ 1980 CABERNET SAUVIGNON ($7.00) Esterbrook, Mendocino.

☆ 1980 CABERNET SAUVIGNON ($9.00) Special Reserve, Mendocino. *Rich, intense but lacking in fruit.*

Frick Winery
SANTA CRUZ COUNTY

303 Potrero Street #39, Santa Cruz, California 95060 (408-426-8623). FOUNDED: 1976. ACREAGE: None. PRODUCTION: 3,500 cases. DISTRIBUTION: California and other markets. OWNERS: Bill and Judith Frick. WINEMAKER: Bill Frick. Tours and tasting Saturday 1 P.M.–4 P.M., or by appointment during the week.

Bill and Judith Frick traveled up and down the California coast for ten years, searching for the perfect place to produce distinctive Pinot Noir. "We settled in Santa Cruz for two reasons," says Bill. "There are a number of well-established microclimates with small vineyards surrounding the area. These, as well as older vineyards of the Santa Clara Valley and Monterey County, consistently produce quality grapes on a large scale. The other reason is that it's a nice place to live." Bill and Judith are basically self-taught winemakers who want nothing more than a lifetime of making wine together.

WHITE

☆☆☆☆ 1981 CHARDONNAY ($10.00) Ventana, Monterey. *Toasty, clean, complex and quite lovely.*

☆ 1982 CHARDONNAY ($11.00) Monterey. *Off flavors, ripe, heavy, oaky.*

RED

1980 PETITE SIRAH ($7.00) Monterey. *Very vegetal. Decent structure underneath but it's wasted.*

1981 PETITE SIRAH ($7.00) Monterey. *Weedy, unpleasant.*

☆ 1979 PINOT NOIR ($10.00) Monterey.

1980 PINOT NOIR ($10.00) Monterey. *Earthy, peppery; overdone and lacking freshness but decent.*

☆☆☆ 1981 ZINFANDEL ($6.00) Santa Clara. *Sweet oak, rich varietal fruit, buttery, nice. Drink now.*

Fritz Cellars
SONOMA COUNTY

24691 Dutcher Creek Road, Cloverdale, California 95425 (707-433-7268). FOUNDED: 1979. ACREAGE: 90 acres. PRODUCTION: 15,000 cases. DISTRIBUTION: California and 14 other states. OWNER: Arthur Jay Fritz, Jr.; Christopher Stone, general manager. WINEMAKER: David Hastings. OTHER LABEL: Quail Hill. No tours or tasting.

The Fritz family owns a very successful international freight forwarding company. Jay and his wife, Barbara, have been avid wine lovers for years, and they had been itching to start their own winery on their property in Sonoma. After planting vineyards and selling their fruit to others, they built a small winery, most of which is underground.

WHITE

☆☆☆ 1981 CHARDONNAY ($9.00) Fritz, Dry Creek Valley. *Clean, snappy, good depth.*
☆☆☆ 1981 CHARDONNAY ($10.00) Gauer Ranch, Alexander Valley. *A bit more complex than the other '81. Lovely fruit and oak.*
☆☆ 1982 CHARDONNAY ($9.00) Sonoma. *Rich, clean, hard-edged, complex and woody.*
☆☆ 1982 FUME BLANC ($7.50) Sonoma. 5% Semillon. *Grassy, varietal, clean and pleasant.*

BLANC DE NOIR

☆☆☆ 1984 WHITE ZINFANDEL ($5.80) Alexander Valley. 1.6% residual sugar. *Fruity, clean, balanced, charming.*

RED

☆☆☆ 1981 CABERNET SAUVIGNON ($7.00) North Coast. *Complex, rich, fruity and very attractive.*
☆☆ 1980 GAMAY ($4.50) Sonoma. *Light and attractive.*
☆☆☆ 1979 PINOT NOIR ($6.50) Sonoma. *Delicate but complex and very attractive.*
☆☆ 1981 PINOT NOIR ($4.50) Dry Creek Valley.
☆☆ 1981 QUAIL HILL PINOT NOIR ($16.00) Estate, Sonoma. *Dark, rich, Burgundian, should age well.*
☆☆☆ 1982 QUAIL HILL PINOT NOIR ($10.00) Reserve, Sonoma. *Rich, lush, soft and balanced, with lovely varietal character.*
1981 ZINFANDEL ($6.00) Dry Creek Valley, Sonoma.

Frog's Leap Winery
NAPA COUNTY

3358 St. Helena Highway, St. Helena, California 94574 (707-963-4704). FOUNDED: 1981. ACREAGE: 1 acre. PRODUCTION: 6,500 cases. DISTRIBUTION: Major market states. OWNERS: Dr. Larry and Jeannine Turley, and John and Julie Williams. WINEMAKER: John Williams. Tours and retail sales by appointment. Open house first weekend in June.

Jeannine Yeomans, a newscaster for KRON in San Francisco, has always loved wine. When she married lanky, bearded Larry Turley, a Napa Valley physician, a winery seemed like a good idea. Together with Julie and John Williams (the winemaker at Spring Mountain Vineyards), they bought an old frog farm and, much to the chagrin of the Stag's Leap people, named their winery Frog's Leap. They created a handsome logo and have leapt at every opportunity to make a pun on the name. In 1984 they made a "Leap Year Cuvée." The winery's slogan is "Time's fun when you're having flies."

WHITE

☆☆☆ 1982 CHARDONNAY ($11.00) Napa Valley. *Delightfully crisp and fruity, angular and graceful.*
1983 CHARDONNAY ($11.00) Napa Valley. *Dull, flabby.*

NV   SAUVIGNON BLANC ($10.00) Leap Year Cuvée, Napa Valley. *Good varietal character but marred by oxidation.*

☆☆   1982 SAUVIGNON BLANC ($8.00) Napa Valley. *Crisp and attractive.*

1983 SAUVIGNON BLANC ($8.50) Napa Valley. *Crisp and varietal but with a touch of oxidation.*

RED

☆☆   1982 CABERNET SAUVIGNON ($9.00) Napa Valley. *Balanced, oaky and fruity, with good lean structure. Drink 1987.*

☆☆☆   1981 ZINFANDEL ($6.50) Spottswoode, Napa Valley. *15% Cabernet. Fruity, crisp, spicy and charming.*

Frontenac Point Vineyard
NEW YORK

Road 3, Box 112, Route 89, Trumansburg, New York 14886 (607-387-9619). FOUNDED: 1982. ACREAGE: 16 acres. PRODUCTION: 800 cases. DISTRIBUTION: New York. OWNER: James Doolittle. WINEMAKER: James Doolittle. No tours or tasting.

Carol and Jim Doolittle became interested in growing vinifera grapes in New York while working for the New York State Department of Agriculture. They had backgrounds in marketing and public relations and Jim had a degree in agriculture from Cornell University. "With our work experience and Jim's education, you would think we would know better than to become farmers," says Carol. But in 1978, they purchased property in the Finger Lakes region, planted vinifera, and set up a winery in the cellar of their home. Today, the care of the vineyards and the winery is a full-time job for both Doolittles.

Frontenac Vineyard
MICHIGAN

39149 Red Arrow Highway, P.O. Box 215, Paw Paw, Michigan 49079 (616-657-5531). FOUNDED: 1933. ACREAGE: None. PRODUCTION: 10,000 cases. DISTRIBUTION: Michigan, Ohio, Illinois, Indiana, and Wisconsin. OWNER: International Wine and Liquor. Richard Tupper, general manager. WINEMAKER: Tony Podkol. Tours and tasting Monday–Saturday 9 A.M.–4 P.M., Sunday 12–4 P.M.

One of the pioneers of winemaking in Michigan, John Corsi started his Frontenac winery in Detroit in 1933. Moving in 1952 to an area more conducive to grape growing, he built a large stone-block winery. In 1967, John retired, selling the winery to the American Distilling Company, which more than doubled the production, making mostly fruit wines. In the early 1970s, the winery was sold to International Wine and Liquor.

Fruit Wines of Florida
FLORIDA

513 South Florida Avenue, Tampa, Florida 33602 (813-223-1222). FOUNDED: 1972. ACREAGE: 60 acres. PRODUCTION: 9,500 cases. DISTRIBUTION: Florida. OWNER: Joseph Midulla, Sr.; Frank Garafalo, general manager. WINEMAKER: Greg Williams. OTHER LABELS: Midulla Vineyards, Mr. Dude 44, Manukai, Floriana, Plantation Paradise. Tours and tasting by appointment.

The first winery in Florida to produce commercial wines, Fruit Wines of Florida was started by Joseph Midulla of the Tampa Wholesale Liquor Company. After Repeal, Joe thought wine might be a profitable item for his company to sell. The winery, established in 1972, first produced citrus and other oddly flavored wines. It wasn't until 1979 that he planted 60 acres of hybrids; he then hired an enologist from California and began making grape wines. The winery has a variety of labels and has continued to produce a line of fruit wines, plus some with almond, coffee, and tropical flavors.

WHITE

O NV MIDULLA LORENZ ($4.00) Florida. *Dull, oxidized. Made from Stover grapes.*

RED

☆ 1983 MIDULLA JEAN DE NOIR ($4.00) Florida. *Sweet, tart, clean; odd but attractive.*

GABRIEL Y CAROLINE *see* Smith & Hook Vineyard

Gainey Vineyards
SANTA BARBARA COUNTY

P.O. Box 910, Santa Ynez, California 93460 (805-688-0558). FOUNDED: 1984. ACREAGE: 54 acres. PRODUCTION: 10,000 cases. DISTRIBUTION: At winery, by mailing list, and in restaurants. OWNER: Daniel J. Gainey; Barry Johnson, general manager. WINEMAKER: Rick Longoria. Tours and tasting daily 10 A.M.–5 P.M.

Before they started planting grapes, the Gaineys were farming various crops and breeding Arabian horses on their 1,800-acre ranch. Having lived in the Santa Ynez Valley for twenty years, Daniel Gainey could not help noticing the grape-wine boom during the late 1970s and early 1980s. He planted six different premium grape varieties on 54 acres of his ranch and built a winery, all in the belief that his ranch could produce "something of significant value." The Spanish-style winery, completed in 1984, is designed to show visitors every phase of winemaking, from the vineyard to bottling line. It also has a professional kitchen for gourmet cooking classes.

Galleano Winery
RIVERSIDE COUNTY

4231 Wineville Road, Mira Loma, California 91752 (714-685-5376). FOUNDED: 1933. ACREAGE: 400 acres. PRODUCTION: 13,000 cases. DISTRIBUTION: At winery. OWNER: Galleano family. Donald Galleano. WINEMAKER: Donald Galleano. Tours by appointment. Tasting Monday–Saturday 8 A.M.–6 P.M. Picnic facilities.

Domenico Galleano bought his ranch in 1926 from Estaban Cantu, former governor of Baja California. The winery was started after Prohibition ended in 1933 and has remained in the Galleano family ever since. The family sells grapes and wine in bulk to other wineries. Don Galleano, Domenico's grandson, is a bit disheartened as he watches urban sprawl creeping into the vineyards, but he is determined to continue growing grapes in the traditional way.

E. & J. Gallo Winery
STANISLAUS COUNTY

600 Yosemite Boulevard, Modesto, California 95353 (209-579-3111). FOUNDED: 1933. ACREAGE: 2,000 acres. PRODUCTION: 250,000 cases a day, 60 million cases a year. DISTRIBUTION:

Nationwide and international. OWNER: Gallo family. Ernest Gallo, chairman; Julio R. Gallo, president. WINEMAKER: Julio R. Gallo. OTHER LABELS: Andre, Carlo Rossi, Boone's Farm, Polo Brindisi, Thunderbird, Tyrolia, Night Train Express, Wine Cellars of Ernest and Julio Gallo, and several others. No tours or tasting.

In 1933, when Prohibition ended, Ernest and Julio Gallo were struggling grape growers in Modesto. They scraped some money together and bought a crusher—without knowing much about making wine. Through hard work and marketing savvy, they now own the world's largest wine business. The Gallos produce about 60 million wine cases each year and purchase more California North Coast grapes than any other winery. The winery has recently entered the premium market with considerable success, and it also recently acquired Frei Bros. in Sonoma after a relationship with the former owners that lasted more than two decades. The Gallo winery complex includes a warehouse that covers 27 acres and a glass plant that turns out two million bottles each day.

WHITE

☆☆☆ NV POLO BRINDISI BIANCO ($2.50) California. *Sweet, great acidity, crisp, clean, very attractive.*

☆☆ NV POLO BRINDISI BIANCO SECCO ($2.50) California. *Crisp, clean, snappy, off-dry.*

☆ NV CHABLIS BLANC ($1.75) California. *Fresh, fruity, clean and pleasant. America's best seller.*

☆ NV CARLO ROSSI CHABLIS ($2.30) California. *1.5 liters. Sweet, fresh, fruity, decent.*

☆☆☆ NV RESERVE CHABLIS ($2.60) California. *Dry, clean, fruity and very attractive.*

☆☆ NV RHINE WINE ($1.75) California. *Clean, spritzy, sweet, great acidity, balanced.*

NV CARLO ROSSI RHINE ($2.30) California. *1.5 liters. Vegetal, sweet, clean.*

☆☆ NV CHARDONNAY ($4.00) California. *Restrained but clean and pleasant, with some oak complexity.*

☆ NV CHENIN BLANC ($2.30) California. *Crisp, fresh, but dull and lacking character.*

☆☆ NV FRENCH COLOMBARD ($2.30) California. *Crisp, off-dry, not varietal but attractive.*

☆☆ NV GEWURZTRAMINER ($2.60) California. *Spicy, varietal, rich, fresh.*

NV JOHANNISBERG RIESLING ($2.60) California. *Off-dry, clean, lacking character.*

☆☆ NV SAUVIGNON BLANC ($2.60) California. *Varietal, clean, very nice, although a bit laid back.*

SPARKLING

☆☆ NV DRY CHAMPAGNE ($3.75) California.

NV PINK CHAMPAGNE ($3.75) California. *Clean, sweet and syrupy.*

☆☆ NV ANDRE PINK CHAMPAGNE ($4.00) California. *Fresh, surprisingly rich in flavor, clean, pleasant.*

NV ANDRE "VERY DRY" ($3.81) California. *Candy-like flavor. Charmat.*

☆ NV ANDRE COLD DUCK ($4.00) California. *Clean, sweet, strawberry flavors, simple.*

☆☆☆ NV BALLATORE SPUMANTE ($4.50) California. *Spicy, sweet, fruity, clean, delightful.*

ROSE

☆☆ NV PINK CHABLIS ($1.75) California. *Fruity, crisp, off-dry, very attractive.*

☆ NV CARLO ROSSI PINK CHABLIS ($2.30) California. *1.5 liters. Off-dry, lively, fresh, attractive.*

☆ NV VIN ROSE ($1.75) California. *Crisp, simple, decent.*

NV RED ROSE ($1.75) California. *Oily, sweet, vegetal.*

☆☆ NV CARLO ROSSI VIN ROSE ($2.30) California. *1.5 liters. Fresh, clean, pleasant.*

☆ NV ROSE OF CALIFORNIA ($2.30) California. *Crisp, somewhat sweet, clean, decent.*

RED

☆ NV BURGUNDY ($1.75) California. *Clean, balanced, pleasant.*

☆☆ NV HEARTY BURGUNDY ($1.75) California. *A classic—herbal, clean, fresh and deep. Amazing.*

        NV CARLO ROSSI BURGUNDY ($2.30) California. *1.5 liters. Sweet and vegetal.*

☆ NV RESERVE BURGUNDY ($2.60) California. *Good fruit, clean but heavy; lacking depth.*

O NV CARLO ROSSI LIGHT CHIANTI ($2.30) California. *1.5 liters. Sweet and vegetal.*

☆ NV CARLO ROSSI PAISANO ($2.30) California. *1.5 liters. Crisp, sweet, decent.*

☆ NV POLO BRINDISI ROSSO ($2.50) California. *Sweet, snappy, clean, a good imitation of Labrusca.*

☆ NV BOONE'S FARM WILD MOUNTAIN ($1.30) California. *Concord grape. Fresh, sweet, fruity.*

☆ NV CABERNET SAUVIGNON ($5.00) California. *Herbal, clean, somewhat simple but nice.*

☆☆ 1978 CABERNET SAUVIGNON ($8.00) Limited Release, California. *Gallo's first vintage wine. Soft, ripe and lovely. Drink 1986.*

☆ NV ZINFANDEL ($2.60) California. *Husky, raisiny, intense, low varietal character.*

FORTIFIED

      NIGHT TRAIN EXPRESS ($2.00) California. *Concord grape, very sweet, like grape jelly. 19% alcohol.*

      PORT ($1.50) California. *Vegetal, sweet, unappealing.*

      WHITE PORT ($1.50) California. *Odd, not pleasant, quite sweet.*

☆ LIVINGSTON CELLARS TAWNY PORT ($2.00) California. *Sweet, rich, decent.*

☆ COCKTAIL PALE DRY SHERRY ($1.50) California. *Simple, clean, attractive.*

☆☆ CREAM SHERRY ($1.50) California. *Sweet, fruity, clean.*

☆ SHERRY ($1.50) California. *Sweet, clean, pleasant.*

☆☆ LIVINGSTON CELLARS CREAM SHERRY ($2.00) California. *Rich, sweet, deep, lovely.*

☆☆ LIVINGSTON CELLARS VERY DRY SHERRY ($2.00) California. *Lush, nutty, clean, complex.*

☆ THUNDERBIRD ($2.00) California. *Spicy, very sweet, ginger flavors. 19% alcohol.*

      EXTRA DRY VERMOUTH ($1.65) California. *Unpleasant.*

      SWEET VERMOUTH ($1.65) California. *Sweet, decent.*

FLAVORED

      CARLO ROSSI SANGRIA ($2.30) California. *1.5 liters. Vegetal, clean, fruit flavors, sweet.*

      SPANADA ($1.50) California. *Heavy, dull, sweet.*

☆☆ TYROLIA ($1.50) California. *Spicy, fresh, sweet.*

Gardiner Vineyard & Farm Corporation
NEW YORK

714 Albany Post Road, Gardiner, New York 12525 (914-255-0892). FOUNDED: 1982. ACREAGE: 30 acres. PRODUCTION: 3,000 cases. DISTRIBUTION: New York. OWNER: George Nutman. WINEMAKER: Jim Moss. OTHER LABEL: Château Georges. Tours and tasting daily 12–5 P.M.

    George Nutman, a successful contractor, thoroughly examined all the options. What should he do with his piece of land in the Hudson Valley? He had a sincere interest in horticulture, so he leaned toward the possibility of growing something on the property. When he decided on grapes, he didn't plant a few acres here, a few acres there, but started with 30,000 vines of French hybrids.

Not too much later George was building a winery, cellar, and tasting room. The winery sits high, overlooking the vineyards with a view of the Shawangunk Mountains.

ఇ⋒

GARRISON FOREST *see* St. Clement Vineyards

GAVILAN *see* Chalone Vineyard

Gem City Vineland Company
ILLINOIS

South Parley Street, Nauvoo, Illinois 62354 (217-453-2218). FOUNDED: 1857. ACREAGE: 45 acres. PRODUCTION: 8,500 cases. DISTRIBUTION: Illinois. OWNER: Corporation. Baxter family. WINEMAKER: Fred Baxter. OTHER LABEL: Old Nauvoo. Tours and tasting April–November: weekdays 8 A.M.–5 P.M., weekends 10 A.M.–5 P.M.; December–March: Monday–Friday 8 A.M.– 5 P.M.

Growing fruit is the mainstay of the Baxters' business; the winery is just a sideline, although it has been active since 1857. Fred Baxter's great grandfather, a French immigrant, built the company's large cement-block building with its small, arched wine cellars. During Prohibition, the winery produced pasteurized grape juice. All the while, the Baxters continued to grow grapes, mostly Concord, for both wine and table use. Today the fifth generation of Baxters, Fred and Dorothy's sons, are becoming part of the family business.

ఇ⋒

Gemello Winery
SANTA CLARA COUNTY

2003 El Camino Real, Mountain View, California 94040 (415-948-7723). FOUNDED: 1934. ACREAGE: None. PRODUCTION: 5,000 cases. DISTRIBUTION: California and 30 other states. OWNERS: Paul and Sandy Obester. WINEMAKER: Sandy Obester. Tours and tasting by appointment.

John Gemello started his family winery in 1934, making good Italian-style red wines in a big, assertive manner. He set a stylistic example for his son Mario, who became the winemaker and owner during the mid-1940s. Mario stayed with the winery through some pretty shaky times, including when it was almost sold to another family. Finally, in 1982, he decided to bottle every wine in the winery. He then sold the whole operation to his niece, Sandy Obester, who had been making wine with her husband, Paul, at their own winery in Half Moon Bay. "My grandfather was the one who inspired us to make wine," says Sandy. Keeping the family tradition, Sandy maintains Gemello as a red-wine winery.

BLANC DE NOIR

☆   1983 WHITE ZINFANDEL ($5.25) Amador. *Soft, dull, sweet.*

RED

☆   1975 CABERNET SAUVIGNON ($8.00) Scott Knight Smith, Santa Clara Valley. *Raisiny, past its prime.*

☆☆   1978 MERLOT ($9.00) Templeton. *Showing some age but leathery, rich and complex.*

☆☆   1977 PETITE SIRAH ($7.00) California. *Complex, fruity and showing its age well.*
　　　1978 PINOT NOIR ($7.50)

☆☆☆   NV ZINFANDEL ($6.25) Reminiscence, Lot 75A, Amador. *Lush, rich, deep, intense, lovely.*

ఇ⋒

J. H. Gentili Wines
SAN MATEO COUNTY

60 Lowell Street, Redwood City, California 94062 (415-368-4740). FOUNDED: 1981. ACREAGE: 1 acre. PRODUCTION: 1,000 cases. DISTRIBUTION: At winery and local outlets. OWNER: Jim Anderson. WINEMAKER: Jim Anderson. No tours or tasting. Retail sales by appointment. Newsletter.

Tennis teacher Jim Anderson started making wine as a hobby, but he soon had his winery bonded. The winery, part of Jim's house, is basically a one-man operation, though Jim has some fair-weather assistance. "My brother-in-law and my father like to help out now and then, picking grapes or bottling, but when something needs to be done at 2:00 A.M., everyone disappears," says Jim.

WHITE

1982 CHARDONNAY ($12.00) Napa Valley. *Good varietal character but flabby.*

Germanton Vineyard and Winery
NORTH CAROLINA

R.F.D. 1, Box G, Germanton, North Carolina 27019 (919-969-5745). FOUNDED: 1981. ACREAGE: 13 acres. PRODUCTION: 2,000 cases. DISTRIBUTION: Local. OWNER: Partnership. William H. McGee, president. WINEMAKER: J. B. Pegram. Tours and tasting weekends 8 A.M.–5 P.M.

Six friends, all members of the Piedmont Grape Growers Association, pooled their resources and rudimentary knowledge of winemaking techniques and started their own winery. They leased a dairy farm, set up a modest facility, and began cautiously, making only one wine at first and slowly adding others. Their relaxed pace and slow growth has had a dramatic effect on demand among their fans. "We simply cannot make it fast enough," says William H. McGee, winery president.

Gerwer Winery
EL DORADO COUNTY

8221 Stony Creek Road, Somerset, California 95684 (209-245-3467). FOUNDED: 1982. ACREAGE: 12 acres. PRODUCTION: 3,000 cases. DISTRIBUTION: Alaska, California, and Nevada. OWNERS: Vernon and Marcia Gerwer. WINEMAKER: Vernon Gerwer. Tours and tasting weekends 11 A.M.–5 P.M., weekdays by appointment. Picnic facilities.

Born and raised on a large ranch north of Sacramento, Vernon Gerwer has always been involved in land development and agriculture. He has worked for the California Department of Fish and Game, sold farm supplies, and traveled around the state and beyond in the real estate business. In 1977 he and his wife, Marcia, settled in the Sierra foothills. They purchased 40 acres of land from Marcia's father with the intention of planting grapes and making wine. In 1981 they bought grapes and made their first wine at a neighboring winery. Now crushing in their own small winery, which they have outgrown, they have plans for more vineyards and up to 6,000 cases of wine a year.

Geyser Peak Winery
SONOMA COUNTY

22280 Chianti Road, Geyserville, California 95441 (707-433-6585). FOUNDED: 1880. ACREAGE: 1,000 acres. PRODUCTION: 1.5 million cases. DISTRIBUTION: Nationwide and 5 foreign countries. OWNER: Vimark, Inc. Trione family. John McClelland, chairman. WINEMAKER: Armand Bussone. OTHER LABELS: Summit, Trione. No tours. Tasting daily 10 A.M.–5 P.M. Gift shop.

In the ten years it was owned by the Joseph Schlitz Brewing Company, which had purchased the property from the Bagnani family, Geyser Peak experienced considerable growth in both vineyard holdings and wine production. In addition, the winery became known as a packaging innovator— putting wine in cans, boxes, and even plastic bottles. But the big beer company never really understood the subtleties of the wine business. In 1982 new life was pumped into this large operation when it was purchased by the Trione family, which was able to add some 500 vineyard acres of its own to an already large holding. Henry Trione is a wealthy Santa Rosa businessman, a self-made multimillionaire with a passion for good wine and polo. In fact, Geyser Peak is the only American winery that fields its own polo team; two of the players are Henry Trione and Vic Trione, one of Henry's two sons.

WHITE

NV SUMMIT CHABLIS ($2.90) California. *Vinous and dirty.*

O NV SUMMIT RHINE ($3.00) California.

☆☆ NV SUMMIT WINTERCHILL WHITE ($3.00) California. *1.5 liter. Off-dry, fruity, pleasant.*

☆ 1982 SONOMA WHITE ($4.00) Sonoma. *Some herbaceousness, clean and crisp.*

1983 SONOMA VINTAGE WHITE ($4.00) Sonoma.

☆☆ 1980 CHARDONNAY ($6.00) Sonoma. *Fresh, clean and very nice.*

☆☆ 1981 CHARDONNAY ($7.50) Sonoma. *Vinous, decent. A nice wine with modest charms.*

☆ 1982 CHARDONNAY ($6.50) Los Carneros-Sonoma.

☆ 1982 CHARDONNAY ($7.00) Sonoma. *Crisp, clean, uncomplicated.*

☆☆ 1982 CHARDONNAY ($8.00) Kiser Ranch, Los Carneros-Sonoma. *Decent, clean, attractive.*

☆ 1982 TRIONE CHARDONNAY ($9.00) Alexander Valley. *Earthy, decent, lacking fruit.*

☆ 1982 CHENIN BLANC ($3.70) Soft, Nervo Ranch, Alexander Valley. *Simple but snappy and fresh.*

☆ 1982 CHENIN BLANC ($4.00) Nervo Ranch, Sonoma. *0.8% residual sugar. Celery flavor, decent.*

1983 CHENIN BLANC ($4.00) Alexander Valley, Sonoma. *Overripe, sappy, dull.*

☆☆ 1984 CHENIN BLANC ($4.50) Nervo Ranch, Alexander Valley. *Varietal, clean, quite nice.*

☆ 1982 FUME BLANC ($6.00) Kiser Ranch, Sonoma.

☆ 1983 FUME BLANC ($6.00) Sonoma. *Decent varietal character, clean, but a bit thin and watery.*

☆☆ 1983 GEWURZTRAMINER ($5.00) Sonoma. *1.9% residual sugar. Minty, crisp, clean, charming.*

1981 JOHANNISBERG RIESLING ($6.00) Soft, Kiser Ranch (Estate), Sonoma Valley. *Odd; the nose is overripe and the flavor is underripe.*

☆☆ 1983 JOHANNISBERG RIESLING ($5.00) Sonoma. *2.9% residual sugar. Flowery, fruity, decent, balanced.*

SPARKLING

NV BRUT CHAMPAGNE ($9.00) California.

NV BLANC DE NOIRS AU NATUREL ($16.70) California. *Dull, lifeless.*

BLANC DE NOIR

☆☆☆ 1982 PINOT NOIR BLANC ($5.00) Kiser Ranch, Sonoma Valley. *Dry, crisp and very appealing.*

☆ 1983 PINOT NOIR BLANC ($4.50) Kiser Ranch, Los Carneros, Sonoma. *Odd nose, decent fruit.*

O NV SUMMIT WHITE ZINFANDEL ($3.00) California. *1.5 liter. 2% residual sugar. Dull and vegetal.*

☆☆ 1984 WHITE ZINFANDEL ($4.00) Russian River Valley, Sonoma. *Fresh, sweet, clean, pleasant.*

ROSE

  NV SUMMIT VIN ROSE ($2.50) California.
 ☆ 1982 ROSE OF CABERNET ($4.00) Sonoma. *Varietal, heavy, lacking finesse.*
☆☆ 1983 ROSE OF CABERNET ($4.00) Alexander Valley. *Fresh, herbal, clean and crisp.*

RED

☆☆ NV SUMMIT BURGUNDY ($4.00) California.
 ☆ 1980 SONOMA VINTAGE RED ($3.25) Sonoma. *Odd nose, decent fruit and flavors.*
 ☆ 1981 SONOMA VINTAGE RED ($4.00) Sonoma.
 ☆ 1978 CABERNET SAUVIGNON ($7.25) California. *Herbaceous but decent.*
 ☆ 1979 CABERNET SAUVIGNON ($7.25) Estate, Hoffman Ranch, Alexander Valley. *Lush and weedy, balanced, decent.*
 ☆ 1980 CABERNET SAUVIGNON ($6.00) Sonoma.
☆☆☆ 1981 CABERNET SAUVIGNON ($7.00) Sonoma. *Rich, round, berried, attractive. Drink 1986.*
☆☆ NV SUMMIT MERLOT ($3.50) Sonoma. *1.5 liter. Lush, varietal, very pleasant.*
☆☆ 1980 TRIONE MERLOT ($11.00) Alexander Valley. *Lush, raisiny, deep, clean.*
  1974 PINOT NOIR Limited Bottling, Sonoma.
 ☆ 1977 PINOT NOIR Sonoma.
 ☆ 1978 PINOT NOIR ($5.85) Kiser Ranch, Sonoma.
 O 1979 PINOT NOIR ($5.75) Sonoma Valley. *Musty.*
 ☆ 1980 TRIONE PINOT NOIR ($10.00) Los Carneros. *Decent but lacking varietal character and fruit.*
 ☆ 1978 ZINFANDEL ($6.00) California. *Spicy nose, intense, lacking fruit.*

Giasi Vineyard
NEW YORK

Route 414, Box 72 B, Burdett, New York 14818 (607-546-4601). FOUNDED: 1984. ACREAGE: 20 acres. PRODUCTION: 1,666 cases. DISTRIBUTION: Local. OWNERS: Michael and Vera Giasi. WINEMAKER: Michael Giasi. Tours and tasting spring and summer: daily 9 A.M.–5 P.M.

 Michael Giasi retired from his job as a patent coordinator in 1976 to start intensive work on two vineyard sites and to design his own winery. The Giasis have been making wine each year since 1980, but the long, slow process of converting a large barn into a winery delayed the actual opening until spring of 1984. Using just their own grapes, they make mainly red wines from French hybrids.

Gibson Wine Company
FRESNO COUNTY

1720 Academy Avenue, Sanger, California 93657 (209-875-2505). FOUNDED: 1939. ACREAGE: None. PRODUCTION: 7,500 cases a day, 1.5 million cases a year. DISTRIBUTION: Nationwide. OWNER: Cooperative. William J. Boos, president. WINEMAKER: Gerald Homolka, Sanger; Alex Farafontoff, Elk Grove. OTHER LABELS: Das Guten, Cresta Bella, Cardo Brothers, Gibson Vineyards, Silverstone Cellars, California Villages, Ramano. No tours or tasting.

 What was once the Sanger Winery got its new name from Robert Gibson, who also owned the Elk Grove Winery, a producer of fruit wines. In 1961, Gibson sold the Gibson Wine Company to the Sanger Winery Association, a cooperative of grape growers that used the facility for bottling and fruit wine production. The winery is still owned by 135 growers in Fresno, Tulare, Madera, and Kings counties.

Girard Winery
NAPA COUNTY

7717 Silverado Trail, Oakville, California 94562 (707-944-8577). FOUNDED: 1980. ACREAGE: 53 acres. PRODUCTION: 14,000 cases. DISTRIBUTION: Nationwide. OWNER: Girard family. Stephen Girard, Jr., president. WINEMAKER: Fred Payne. OTHER LABEL: Stephens. Tours and tasting by appointment. Retail sales weekdays 9 A.M.–5 P.M., weekends 1 P.M.–5 P.M.

When wineries started bidding higher and higher for the Girard vineyard grapes, Steve Girard, Jr., convinced his family that having their own winery just might be profitable. Steve and his dad, Steve Sr., had been absentee growers for years, with Steve Sr. working in San Francisco and Steve Jr. in San Diego. Steve Jr. moved up to the Napa Valley once construction of the split-stone winery began in 1980. "Originally, the winery was going to be a retirement project for my father," says Steve Jr., "but he never retired!" Young Steve is now the president and manager of the winery. He has been expanding the vineyard holdings with the goal of making Girard wines 100-percent estate bottled.

WHITE

☆☆   1980 STEPHENS CHARDONNAY ($9.50) Alexander Valley. *Pleasant but simple.*
☆☆☆   1980 CHARDONNAY ($11.00) Napa Valley.
☆☆☆   1981 CHARDONNAY ($12.50) Napa Valley. *Bright, clean, great acidity, good.*
☆☆☆   1982 CHARDONNAY ($12.50) Estate, Napa Valley. *Snappy, clean, lean.*
☆☆   1982 CHENIN BLANC ($6.50) Dry, Estate, Napa Valley. *Clean, rounded, appealing.*
        1983 CHENIN BLANC ($6.50) Estate, Napa Valley. *Strange flavors, lacking varietal character.*
☆☆☆   1981 STEPHENS SAUVIGNON BLANC ($8.00) North Coast.
☆☆   1982 SAUVIGNON BLANC ($8.00) North Coast. *Grassy, intensely vegetal, fat, with good acidity.*
☆   1983 SAUVIGNON BLANC ($8.00) North Coast. *Assertively varietal, lacking finesse.*

RED

☆☆   1980 CABERNET SAUVIGNON ($12.00) Napa. *Dark, raisiny and big.*
☆☆☆   1981 STEPHENS CABERNET SAUVIGNON ($8.00) Napa Valley. *10% Merlot. Herbal, supple, Bordeaux-like.*
☆☆☆   1981 CABERNET SAUVIGNON ($14.00) Estate, Napa Valley. *Lush, velvety, firm, complex, superb. Will age very well.*

Giumarra Vineyards
KERN COUNTY

Edison Road and Edison Highway, Edison, California 93303 (805-395-7000). FOUNDED: 1946. ACREAGE: 4,000 acres. PRODUCTION: 4.2 million cases. DISTRIBUTION: Nationwide; 4 foreign countries. OWNER: Sal, John, and George Giumarra, and Joe Giumarra, president. WINEMAKER: Dale Anderson. OTHER LABELS: Breckenridge, Ridgecrest, Golden Vineyards. Tours by appointment. Tasting daily 9 A.M.–4:30 P.M. Gift shop.

An outgoing Italian family, the Giumarras have been making wine from their own vineyards in the southern San Joaquin Valley since 1946, but they didn't begin bottling under their own label until 1974. "We were the winemaker's winemaker," quips John Giumarra, Jr., referring to their history of selling wine in bulk to other wineries. Although much of the Giumarra production is still sold to others, John is very proud of his own label wines, some of which are sold internationally.

WHITE

1982 CHARDONNAY ($5.00) Tulare. *0.4% residual sugar. Pleasant but low in varietal identity.*

☆ 1983 CHARDONNAY ($6.00) California. *0.3% residual sugar. Lush, fat, clean, but lacking fruit.*

NV CHENIN BLANC ($3.25) California. *Flabby.*

1982 GREEN HUNGARIAN ($3.75) California. *2% residual sugar. Sweet, dull, decent.*

○ 1982 JOHANNISBERG RIESLING ($3.75) California.

ROSE

☆☆ 1983 GEWURZTRAMINER ($4.25) Blush of Gewürztraminer, California. *2.5% residual sugar. Crisp, varietal, attractive.*

RED

1977 CABERNET SAUVIGNON ($4.43) California. *Vegetal and unattractive.*

☆ 1977 CABERNET SAUVIGNON ($8.00) Founder's Selection, California. *Herbal, rich, soft, quite nice.*

☆ 1979 PETITE SIRAH ($5.00) California. *Fruity, nice flavors, a bit watery.*

☆ 1980 PETITE SIRAH ($6.00) California. *Berried, sweet, clean, odd.*

☆☆ 1981 PETITE SIRAH ($6.00) California. *Berried, lush, late-harvest style.*

☆ 1980 ZINFANDEL ($4.40) California.

Glen Creek Winery
OREGON

6057 Orchard Heights Road NW, Salem, Oregon 97304 (503-581-7510). FOUNDED: 1982. ACREAGE: 10 acres. PRODUCTION: 2,400 cases. DISTRIBUTION: California, Oregon, and Washington. OWNERS: Sylvia and Thomas Dumm. WINEMAKER: Thomas Dumm. Tours and tasting summer: weekends 12–5 P.M.; other times by appointment.

Thomas and Sylvia Dumm owned a wine shop in Long Beach, California, for several years before they decided to escape Orange County's urban sprawl and move to a healthier, more rural setting. "We wanted our kids to grow up in an open, nature-filled place," says Tom. After selling the wine shop, they built a house on a fifteen-acre parcel of meadow and forest in Oregon. The Dumms, who had made wine at home for many years, have moved their home operation into a newly constructed building next to their house and "have gone commercial." The wines are sold in Oregon and Washington as well as at their old wine shop in Long Beach.

WHITE

○ 1983 SAUVIGNON BLANC ($6.50) Washington.

Glen Ellen Winery
SONOMA COUNTY

1883 London Ranch Road, Glen Ellen, California 95442 (707-996-1066). FOUNDED: 1981. ACREAGE: 80 acres. PRODUCTION: 30,000 cases. DISTRIBUTION: California and other states.

OWNER: Benziger family. Bruno Benziger and his five children. WINEMAKER: Mike Benziger. Tours by appointment. Tasting daily 10 A.M.–4 P.M.

Mike Benziger had been looking for a vineyard-winery site for two years when he came upon the secluded ranch in Glen Ellen. He persuaded his father, Bruno Benziger, a founder of the wine and spirits distributor Park, Benziger, and Company, to move to California from New York. The Benzigers, Bruno and five of his seven children, now live and work on their 80-acre ranch. The property, with its gently rolling vineyards, has two handsome old homes and a functional warehouse-style winery, which is guarded by fifteen strutting, screaming peacocks.

WHITE

☆ NV PROPRIETOR'S RESERVE WHITE ($3.50) California. *Riesling, Chenin Blanc, French Colombard. Sweet, decent, clean.*

☆☆ 1982 PROPRIETOR'S RESERVE ($3.50) Sonoma. *Off-dry, fruity, with some complexity.*

☆☆ NV CHARDONNAY ($4.50) Proprietor's Reserve, California. *Simple, attractive, clean.*

☆☆ 1981 CHARDONNAY ($9.50) Les Pierres, Sonoma Valley. *Snappy, bright, oaky, very nice.*

☆☆ 1982 CHARDONNAY ($10.00) Les Pierres, Sonoma Valley. *Fruity, clean and attractive.*

☆☆ 1983 CHARDONNAY ($12.00) Sonoma Valley. *Fat, intense, heavy, pleasant, clean.*

☆☆ 1983 FUME BLANC ($7.50) Sonoma Valley. *Soft, attractive, simple.*

☆☆☆ 1984 FUME BLANC ($7.50) Sonoma Valley. *Fresh, rich, balanced and attractive.*

☆☆☆ 1981 SAUVIGNON BLANC ($8.00) Estate, Sonoma. *Grassy, intense, fruity and round.*

☆☆ 1982 SAUVIGNON BLANC ($8.50) Sonoma.

☆☆☆ 1982 SAUVIGNON BLANC ($9.00) Estate, Sonoma. *Grassy, intense, round and balanced. Not quite up to the '81.*

☆☆☆ 1983 SAUVIGNON BLANC ($8.50) Sonoma. *Very grassy. Clean, lemony, oaky and fresh.*

RED

☆☆ NV PROPRIETOR'S RESERVE RED ($3.50) California. *Clean, fresh, attractive.*

☆☆ 1981 PROPRIETOR'S RESERVE RED ($3.50) Sonoma. *Mostly Cabernet. Varietal, clean, crisp, well made.*

☆☆ 1979 CABERNET SAUVIGNON ($8.00) Sonoma. *Big, rich, uncomplicated.*

☆☆ 1981 CABERNET SAUVIGNON ($9.75) Sonoma Valley. *Rich, intense. Good aging potential.*

☆☆ 1982 CABERNET SAUVIGNON ($4.00) Proprietor's Reserve, Sonoma. *15% Zinfandel. Lush and charming. Drink now.*

☆☆☆ 1982 CABERNET SAUVIGNON ($10.00) Estate, Sonoma Valley. *Peppery, lush, deep and beautifully structured. Drink 1986.*

☆☆☆ 1982 BENZIGER FAMILY WINERY & VINEYARDS ZINFANDEL ($4.50) Geyserville, Sonoma. *Rich, lush, deep, complex, balanced.*

Glenora Wine Cellars
NEW YORK

R.D. 4, Glenora-on-Seneca, Dundee, New York 14837 (607-243-5511). FOUNDED: 1977. ACREAGE: 500 acres. PRODUCTION: 15,000 cases. DISTRIBUTION: Nationwide. OWNER: Partnership. Ray Spencer, general manager. WINEMAKER: Ray Spencer. Tours and tasting May–November: Monday–Saturday 10 A.M.–5 P.M., Sunday 12–5 P.M.; December–April: Tuesday–Saturday 10 A.M.–4 P.M.

Glenora Wine Cellars is taking part in the "renaissance of eastern winemaking" by making vinifera grape wines while continuing with the more traditional French-American hybrids. Four established grape growers in the Finger Lakes Region took advantage of the Farm Winery Act in 1976 to form their own co-op winery. They constructed and bonded Glenora Wine Cellars in 1977 and started with a complete menu of varieties, including Labrusca, French-American hybrids, and vinifera grapes. They have since narrowed the line to five white vinifera and hybrid varieties plus a 100-percent Chardonnay cuvée sparkling wine.

WHITE

☆ 1982 CAYUGA ($5.00) Finger Lakes District. *Crisp, dry and clean, but lacking character.*
☆ 1982 CHARDONNAY ($10.00) Finger Lakes Region. *Light, in the French Chablis style.*
☆☆☆ 1981 JOHANNISBERG RIESLING ($9.00) Springledge, New York. *Lovely botrytis nose, Auslese-type, complex and dry.*
☆☆☆ 1982 JOHANNISBERG RIESLING ($7.00) Finger Lakes Region. *Clean, superb and varietal.*
☆☆☆ 1982 JOHANNISBERG RIESLING ($9.00) Select Late Harvest, Finger Lakes District. *9.6% residual sugar. Toasty, botrytized, nutty, lovely.*
☆☆☆ 1983 JOHANNISBERG RIESLING ($6.00) New York.
☆☆ 1982 RAVAT ($5.00) Finger Lakes District. *Clean, crisp, vinous.*
☆☆ 1982 SEYVAL BLANC ($4.00) Finger Lakes District. *Fresh, crisp and clean, with apple flavors.*

Louis Glunz
ILLINOIS

7100 Capitol Drive, Lincolnwood, Illinois 60645 (312-262-6400). FOUNDED: 1888. ACREAGE: None. DISTRIBUTION: 22 states. OWNER: Louis Glunz, Inc. Louis Glunz III, president. WINE-MAKER: Joseph Glunz, vice president. OTHER LABEL: Coastal Valley. No tours or tasting.

A third-generation family business, Louis Glunz Incorporated has made its name as a distributor of California and imported wines and beers. The company has had a bottling license since 1888 that has been used occasionally, mostly for the blending and bottling of bulk wines. In 1976 it introduced wine on tap for restaurants, under the name "Coastal Valley" wines.

WHITE

☆ NV CHABLIS California. *Sold in kegs to bars. Clean, vinous, off-dry, crisp.*

RED

NV RED TABLE WINE California. *Sold in kegs to bars. Off-dry, vegetal, clean, decent.*

Gold Seal Vineyards
NEW YORK

The Taylor Wine Company, Inc., Route 54A, Hammondsport, New York 14840 (607-569-2111). FOUNDED: 1865. ACREAGE: 1,700 acres. DISTRIBUTION: Eastern states. OWNER: Joseph E. Seagram & Sons, Inc. WINEMAKER: Domenic Carisetti. OTHER LABELS: Henri Marchant, Charles Fournier. Tours and tasting November–April: Monday–Saturday 11 A.M.–3 P.M.; May–October: Monday–Saturday 10 A.M.–4 P.M.

Built by the Urbana Wine Company in 1865, Gold Seal has hired only French Champagne winemakers. The winery took the name Gold Seal during Prohibition when it applied for a license to make sacramental wines. Charles Fournier, who came to the winery from Veuve Clicquot Pon-sardin in Reims, France, brought nationwide attention to the winery with his sparkling "Charles Fournier Brut." Then he started experimental vineyards of vinifera in 1953 with Dr. Konstantin Frank, an unabashed believer in vinifera. Their work together brought about the first vinifera wines from an eastern winery. Charles Fournier retired in 1967 as the Honorary Lifetime President of Gold Seal Vineyards. He died in 1983. The 120-year-old winery, a large complex of multistoried stone buildings and champagne cellars, continues to make champagnes and wines under the Fournier name.

WHITE

☆ NV CHABLIS SUPERIEUR ($3.85) American. *Slightly foxy, pleasant, balanced, off-dry, dull finish.*

☆☆ 1981 CHARDONNAY ($10.50) Estate, New York State. *Oaky, vinous, intense, very interesting.*

☆ 1982 CHARDONNAY ($11.00) Charles Fournier, Estate, Finger Lakes. *Buttery, rich nose, nice oak, fruity, simple and shallow.*

☆☆ 1980 JOHANNISBERG RIESLING ($8.90) Charles Fournier Selection, Estate, New York State. *2% residual sugar, light botrytis. Clean, balanced, lovely.*

☆☆☆ 1980 JOHANNISBERG RIESLING ($10.90) Select Late Harvest, Estate, New York State. *6.2% residual sugar. Fragrant, clean and fruity. Lovely.*

☆☆☆☆ 1981 JOHANNISBERG RIESLING ($8.00) Harvested Late, Estate, New York State. *7.3% residual sugar, high acid. Complex, botrytized, superb.*

☆ 1981 JOHANNISBERG RIESLING ($8.70) Charles Fournier Selection, New York State. *Dry.*

☆ 1982 JOHANNISBERG RIESLING ($8.00) Charles Fournier Selection, New York State. *Fruity and clean but essentially dull.*

☆☆ 1982 JOHANNISBERG RIESLING ($12.00) Bunch Selected, Estate, Finger Lakes Region. *375ml. 11.8% residual sugar. Soft, simple, clean, fruity.*

☆ 1982 RIESLING ($8.00) Charles Fournier, New York State. *Odd nose, dull flavors, decent fruit.*

SPARKLING

NV BRUT ($7.70) American. *Sweet, low fruit.*

O NV EXTRA DRY ($7.70) New York State. *Sweet, fat, awful.*

O NV PINK CHAMPAGNE ($7.70) New York State. *Oily and sweet.*

O NV SPARKLING BURGUNDY ($7.70) New York State.

O NV NATUREL ($8.00) New York State.

NV BLANC DE BLANCS ($10.50) Fournier, New York State. *Sweet, dull, lacking fruit.*

☆☆ NV BLANC DE NOIRS ($10.50) Fournier, American. *Nice, crisp, sweet, clean and likable.*

ROSE

NV ROSE SUPERIEUR ($3.85) Fournier, American. *Sweet nose, simple, clean, lacking fruit.*

RED

O NV BURGUNDY SUPERIEUR ($3.85) American. *Foxy, sweet nose, thin, unattractive.*

Golden Creek Vineyard
SONOMA COUNTY

4480 Wallace Road, Santa Rosa, California 95404 (707-538-2350). FOUNDED: 1983. ACREAGE: 12 acres. PRODUCTION: 1,800 cases. DISTRIBUTION: Local. OWNER: Ladi Danielik. WINE-MAKER: Ladi Danielik. No tours or tasting.

Ladi Danielik's grandfather and father in Czechoslovakia both grew grapes and made wine. Ladi, on the other hand, worked in New Jersey as a dental technician. In 1980 he and his wife moved to California, bought some land, and planted vineyards. While continuing his dental work, Ladi makes wine in the basement of his house and sells most of it in Santa Rosa.

GOLDEN RAIN TREE *see* St. Wendel Cellars

Good Harbor Vineyards
MICHIGAN

R.D. 1, Box 888, Lake Leelanau, Michigan 49653 (616-256-7165). FOUNDED: 1980. ACREAGE: 18 acres. PRODUCTION: 5,000 cases. DISTRIBUTION: Michigan. OWNER: Bruce Simpson. WINEMAKER: Bruce Simpson. Tours and tasting Monday–Saturday 11 A.M.–6 P.M., Sunday 12–6 P.M. Farmers' market, bakery, and delicatessen open May–November: daily 9 A.M.–6 P.M.

Although he came from a family of fruit growers, Bruce Simpson was more interested in the once-a-year harvesting of grapes than in the constant pruning of fruit trees. After graduating from Michigan State University, he left the orchards to his family and went to U.C. Davis to study winemaking and viticulture. When Bruce returned to Michigan, he built a winery in back of his family's farm market.

WHITE

☆☆ 1982 WHITE TABLE WINE ($5.00) Leelanau Peninsula, Michigan. *Made with Seyval Blanc. Fresh, spritzy, attractive.*

☆☆☆ 1982 RAVAT VIGNOLES ($6.00) Leelanau Peninsula, Michigan. *Complex oak, full fruit.*

☆☆ NV JOHANNISBERG RIESLING ($6.00) Yakima Valley. *Grapes shipped from Washington State. Fruity, pleasant.*

☆☆ 1982 SEYVAL BLANC ($6.00) Lot 2, Leelanau Peninsula, Michigan.

RED

☆ NV BACO NOIR ($4.50) Leelanau Peninsula, Michigan. *Pale, some fruit, lacking oomph.*

1982 MARECHAL FOCH ($7.75) Leelanau Peninsula, Michigan. *1.5 liter. Thin, low in fruit.*

Gordon Brothers Cellars
WASHINGTON

1040-D Star Route, Pasco, Washington 99301 (509-547-6224). FOUNDED: 1983. ACREAGE: 80 acres. PRODUCTION: 1,250 cases. DISTRIBUTION: Washington. OWNERS: Jeff and Bill Gordon. WINEMAKER: Steve Philips. No tours or tasting.

Jeff and Bill Gordon are potato farmers who wanted to try their luck with grapes. Alongside 500 acres of potatoes, cherries, asparagus, and walnuts, they planted grapes in 1980. Their plantings were so successful, they produced more fruit than they could sell. Undaunted, they built a small winery. "You can hold on to a bottle of wine for a while, but you can't hold on to a ripe grape," says Jeff. The Gordons brought in their friend Steve Philips to help with the winemaking. "All three of us are just experimenting and testing the waters, which may prove to be too cold—but we are going to give it a try," says Jeff.

Grand Cru Vineyards
SONOMA COUNTY

One Vintage Lane, Glen Ellen, California 95442 (707-996-8100). FOUNDED: 1970. ACREAGE: 30 acres. PRODUCTION: 60,000 cases. DISTRIBUTION: Nationwide. OWNERS: Walter and Bettina Dreyer. WINEMAKER: Robert L. Magnani. Tours by appointment. Tasting daily 10 A.M.– 5 P.M.

Allen Ferrera and winemaker Bob Magnani started this Sonoma Valley winery with the help of a limited partnership. In 1981, when new capital was needed, Walt and Tina Dreyer assumed controlling interest from several other partners. Bob is still the winemaker, but a dramatic new label indicates an aggressive new style for the winery.

WHITE

☆☆   1983 VIN MAISON WHITE ($4.50) California. *Dry, clean, crisp and very pleasant.*
☆☆☆   1982 CHENIN BLANC ($6.75) Clarksburg. *Crisp, fresh, fruity and dry.*
☆☆☆   1983 CHENIN BLANC ($6.50) Perry Cook, Clarksburg. *1% residual sugar. Tangy fruit acid, good balance. A classic.*
☆☆☆   1984 CHENIN BLANC ($6.00) Dry, Perry Cook's Delta, Clarksburg. *1% residual sugar. Fresh, crisp, fruity, lively, delightful.*
☆   1978 GEWURZTRAMINER ($30.00) Induced Botrytis, Garden Creek Ranch, Alexander Valley. *31% residual sugar. Lush and syrupy, fat and flabby.*
☆☆   1981 GEWURZTRAMINER ($8.50) Sonoma Valley.
☆☆☆   1982 GEWURZTRAMINER ($8.50) Alexander Valley. *2% residual sugar. Fresh, ripe, lovely.*
☆☆   1983 GEWURZTRAMINER ($8.50) Sonoma. *1.72% residual sugar. Earthy, clean, varietal, nice.*
☆   NV SAUVIGNON BLANC ($4.50) Vin Maison, California. *Crisp, snappy, decent.*
☆   1981 SAUVIGNON BLANC ($10.00) Northern California.
☆☆☆   1982 SAUVIGNON BLANC ($9.00) California. *Fresh and round.*
☆☆☆   1983 SAUVIGNON BLANC ($9.00) Sonoma. *13% Semillon. Lush, fat, varietal, great fruit.*

BLANC DE NOIR

☆☆☆   1984 VIN MAISON WHITE ZINFANDEL ($4.50) Sonoma. *1.5% residual sugar. Snappy, clean, delightful.*

RED

   NV CABERNET SAUVIGNON ($4.50) Vin Maison, California. *Coffee grounds and vegetal flavors.*
☆☆☆   1979 CABERNET SAUVIGNON ($14.50) Collector Series, Garden Creek Ranch, Alexander Valley. *Earthy and lush, with wonderful structure. Drink 1986.*
☆☆☆   1980 CABERNET SAUVIGNON ($7.65) Cook's Delta, Clarksburg.
☆☆   1980 CABERNET SAUVIGNON ($14.00) Collector Series, Alexander Valley. *Raisiny, fat, lush. Drink 1986.*
☆☆   1981 CABERNET SAUVIGNON ($8.50) California. *Simple, herbed, clean and decent. Drink now.*
☆   1982 CABERNET SAUVIGNON ($4.50) Vin Maison, California. *Decent, weedy, fruity.*
☆☆   1981 ZINFANDEL ($8.50) Sonoma Valley. *Snappy, crisp and light.*

Grand River Wine Company
OHIO

5750 Madison Road, Madison, Ohio 44057 (216-298-9838). FOUNDED: 1976. ACREAGE: 22 acres. PRODUCTION: 4,000 cases. DISTRIBUTION: Ohio. OWNER: Corporation. Bill Worthy, president. WINEMAKERS: Bill Worthy and Rick Kovacic. Tours by appointment. Tasting Monday and Thursday 1 P.M.–8 P.M., Wednesday 1 P.M.–10 P.M., Friday–Saturday 1 P.M–6 P.M.

As it quickly expanded from five gallon jugs in the basement to 22 vineyard acres in Madison, Grand River Wine Company became a full-time job for Bill Worthy. Once he started planting grapes in 1971, it wasn't long until he gave up his job as an investment banker. Taking it slowly, he grew grapes for five years before building a winery in 1976—a concrete, L-shaped structure with an upstairs patio and underground storage cellar. While Bill has planted vinifera (including two varieties rarely grown in Ohio, Merlot and Sauvignon Blanc), he thinks that some French-American hybrids make just as good, if not better, wines.

ᵊ⧫

Granite Springs Winery
EL DORADO COUNTY

6060 Granite Springs Road, Somerset, California 95684 (209-245-6395). FOUNDED: 1981. ACREAGE: 23 acres. PRODUCTION: 6,500 cases. DISTRIBUTION: 7 states. OWNERS: Lester and Lynne Russell. WINEMAKER: Lester Russell. Tours and tasting weekends 11 A.M.–5 P.M., or by appointment. Large groups by appointment.

Lester Russell had lived in various parts of California and Nevada before he returned to his childhood home in the Sierra foothills in 1979. He bought a piece of property and began planting grapes. Having acquired a true appreciation for wines from his friend David Bruce (see David Bruce Winery), Lester got "caught up in the excitement of it all," built a winery, and made his first wines from purchased local grapes.

WHITE

☆☆   1984 CHENIN BLANC ($5.00) El Dorado. *Sweet, crisp, clean, charming.*

BLANC DE NOIR

☆☆   1984 WHITE ZINFANDEL ($5.00) El Dorado. *1.2% residual sugar. Big, lush, complex, delightful.*

RED

☆   1980 CABERNET SAUVIGNON ($8.00) El Dorado.
☆   1980 ZINFANDEL ($6.00) El Dorado.

ᵊ⧫

GRAN VAL *see* Clos du Val

The Grape Vine Winery
IOWA

Box 283, Amana, Iowa 52203 (319-622-3698). FOUNDED: 1982. ACREAGE: None. PRODUCTION: 1,000 cases. DISTRIBUTION: At winery. OWNERS: Debbie and George Schuerer, Jr. WINEMAKER: George Schuerer, Jr. Tasting daily 10 A.M.–6 P.M. Gift shop.

In Amana, winemaking is as commonplace as making dinner—it's simply part of a family's normal activities. George Schuerer's parents, natives of Amana, had been making wine for as long as they could remember, but the wines were made just for family and friends. George and his wife, Debbie, decided to take this tradition one step further. They bonded the basement of their 200-

year-old brick home and opened their doors to Amana's large tourist trade. Lately they have expanded the winery into another basement and have plans to build on top of that.

GREAT WESTERN *see* Taylor Wine Company

Green and Red Vineyards
NAPA COUNTY

3208 Chiles Valley Road, St. Helena, California 94574 (707-965-2346). FOUNDED: 1977. ACREAGE: 17 acres. PRODUCTION: 2,000 cases. DISTRIBUTION: 10 states. OWNER: Jay Heminway. WINEMAKER: Jay Heminway. Tours by appointment.

Jay Heminway was a sculptor and a teacher in Berkeley before moving to the Napa Valley. He bought property in the Chiles Valley area without any intention of getting involved in wine, but once he was settled, planting grapes seemed like the logical thing to do. He sold his first few crops of Zinfandel to Cuvaison before starting his own winery. Recently Jay has increased his plantings to include Chardonnay.

WHITE

☆☆ 1982 CHARDONNAY ($9.50) Napa Valley. *Rich, vinous, deep, varietal. Lacks finesse.*

BLANC DE NOIR

1983 WHITE ZINFANDEL ($4.50) Napa Valley. *Dry, crisp, simple, with some volatile acidity.*

RED

☆ 1977 ZINFANDEL ($7.00) Napa Valley. *Rich, full and complex but lacking finesse.*
1978 ZINFANDEL ($6.50) Napa Valley. *Hard-edged and lacking fruit.*
1979 ZINFANDEL ($6.00) Chiles Canyon, Napa. *Lacking fruit and depth.*
☆☆ 1980 ZINFANDEL ($7.00) Chiles Canyon, Napa. *Vegetal and earthy, with brambly, peppery flavors.*
☆☆☆ 1981 ZINFANDEL ($5.75) Estate, Napa Valley. *Elegant, balanced, fruity, very attractive.*

Green Valley Vineyards
MISSOURI

Highway D, Rural Route, Portland, Missouri 65067 (314-676-5771). FOUNDED: 1972. ACREAGE: 20 acres. PRODUCTION: 2,000 cases. DISTRIBUTION: Missouri. OWNER: Nicholas A. Lamb. WINEMAKER: Nicholas A. Lamb. Tours and tasting Saturday 11 A.M.–4 P.M., or by appointment.

In 1970, while working as a chemical engineer at McDonnell Douglas, Nicholas Lamb planted a test vineyard. He was curious as to which of fifteen different varieties planted would produce the highest quality wine. After learning as much as he could about viticulture, Nicholas took early retirement and started his winery. He built a compact facility and, on the side of the road, a tasting room.

WHITE

☆☆ 1981 CHARDONNAY ($7.50) Edna Valley. *Short but crisp and lively.*

Greenstone Winery
AMADOR COUNTY

Highway 88 at Jackson Valley Road, Ione, California 95640 (209-274-2238). FOUNDED: 1980. ACREAGE: 23 acres. PRODUCTION: 9,000 cases. DISTRIBUTION: California. OWNERS: Durward and Jane Fowler; Stan and Karen Van Spanje, managing partners. WINEMAKER: Stan Van Spanje. Tours and tasting summer: Wednesday–Sunday 10 A.M.–4 P.M; winter: weekends 10 A.M.– 4 P.M.

Stan Van Spanje and Durward Fowler began their wine education in college, drinking Red Mountain mixed with Fresca. By the time the two friends and their wives were teachers in Southern California, they had expanded their wine drinking repertoire considerably. Eager for a change of lifestyle, the two couples found a prime piece of pastureland in the Amador foothills that was ideal for a vineyard and winery. The winery was named for the natural belt of serpentine, a deeply colored green rock, that surrounds the property.

BLANC DE NOIR

☆☆   1981 WHITE ZINFANDEL ($4.50) Amador. *2% residual sugar.*
☆☆   1984 WHITE ZINFANDEL ($4.50) 73% Potter-Cowan, 27% Ferrero, Amador. *Heavy, lush, rich, attractive.*

ROSE

☆☆   1981 ZINFANDEL ($3.25) Amador. *1.7% residual sugar.*

Greenwood Ridge Vineyards
MENDOCINO COUNTY

Box 1090, Star Route, Philo, California 95466 (707-877-3262). FOUNDED: 1980. ACREAGE: 8 acres. PRODUCTION: 2,000 cases. DISTRIBUTION: California. OWNER: Allan Green. WINEMAKER: Allan Green. Tours by appointment.

Allan Green, a free-lance graphic designer, was enthralled by his family's vineyard in Mendocino—his first few batches of homemade Riesling had shown definite promise. Allan immersed himself in winemaking books and enology seminars while absorbing all the advice he could get from neighborly Mendocino vintners. His first wine, a 1980 White Riesling, made a dramatic debut by winning several medals at state and county fair competitions. Now the winery is also making estate-grown Cabernet Sauvignon, and it is the site for the annual California wine tasting championships in July.

WHITE

☆☆☆   1982 JOHANNISBERG RIESLING ($6.75) Estate, Mendocino. *1.7% residual sugar. Crisp, spritzy, ripe and complex. Super.*
☆☆☆☆   1984 JOHANNISBERG RIESLING ($7.00) Mendocino. *1.6% residual sugar. Fresh, clean, varietal, lovely fruit.*

RED

☆☆☆   1982 CABERNET SAUVIGNON ($9.75) Estate, Mendocino. *20% Merlot. Lush, elegant, clean, complex. Drink 1986.*

Grgich Hills Cellars
NAPA COUNTY

1829 St. Helena Highway, Rutherford, California 94573 (707-963-2784). FOUNDED: 1977. ACREAGE: 20 acres. PRODUCTION: 20,000 cases. DISTRIBUTION: California and 25 other states; 3 foreign markets. OWNER: Corporation. Miljenko "Mike" Grgich, president; Austin E. Hills, secretary-treasurer. WINEMAKER: Miljenko "Mike" Grgich. Tours by appointment daily 9:30 A.M.–4:30 P.M. Newsletter.

Mike Grgich is a scrappy Yugoslavian who has become one of America's stellar winemakers. His 1973 Château Montelena Chardonnay won the famous Paris tasting that pitted France's best against California's best. After working at Robert Mondavi Winery, Mike came to Montelena in 1972. He left in 1977 when coffee heir Austin Hills offered him a partnership in this new winery. Grgich Hills was an immediate success and has from the start been considered one of America's top premium labels.

WHITE

☆☆☆ 1978 CHARDONNAY ($18.00) Napa Valley. *Soft, rich and mellow.*
☆☆☆ 1979 CHARDONNAY ($16.00) Napa Valley. *Rich, oily, complex and buttery. A monster.*
☆☆☆ 1980 CHARDONNAY ($17.00) Napa Valley. *Full, round, oaky, fresh fruit. A stunning wine.*
☆☆ 1981 CHARDONNAY ($17.00) Napa Valley. *A bit more two-dimensional than previous efforts; should age.*
☆☆☆ 1982 CHARDONNAY ($17.00) Napa Valley. *Rich, oaky, clean, lush.*
☆☆☆ 1982 CHARDONNAY ($18.00) Napa Valley. *A later release. Rich, oaky, intense, balanced, clean, handsome.*
☆☆☆ 1981 FUME BLANC ($9.00) Napa Valley. *Lemony, crisp, clean, varietal and nice.*
☆☆☆ 1982 FUME BLANC ($9.00) Napa. *Fresh, balanced, slightly grassy, attractive.*
☆ 1983 FUME BLANC ($9.00) Napa Valley. *Dull, lacking fruit.*
☆☆☆ 1983 FUME BLANC ($9.50) Napa Valley. *Lush, varietal, complex, lovely.*
O 1981 JOHANNISBERG RIESLING ($7.50) Napa Valley.
☆☆☆ 1982 JOHANNISBERG RIESLING ($8.00) Napa Valley. *Fragrant, soft and snappy. Off-dry.*
☆☆☆ 1983 JOHANNISBERG RIESLING ($7.50) Napa Valley. *Perfumed and lemony crisp. Fruity, clean and delightful.*
☆☆☆ 1984 JOHANNISBERG RIESLING ($7.50) Napa Valley. *1.5% residual sugar. Crisp, tangy, lively fruit, delightful.*

RED

☆☆☆ 1980 CABERNET SAUVIGNON ($16.00) 34% Napa, 66% Sonoma. *Rich, ripe, complex, velvety and lovely. Drink now or 1986.*
☆☆☆ 1978 ZINFANDEL ($9.00) Alexander Valley. *Velvety, rich, complex, deep.*
☆☆☆ 1979 ZINFANDEL ($10.00) Alexander Valley. *Tart, fruity, deep and rich.*
☆☆☆ 1980 ZINFANDEL ($10.00) Alexander Valley. *Rich, deep, brambly and supple, with great aging potential.*
☆☆☆ 1981 ZINFANDEL ($10.00) Sonoma. *Rich, fresh, deeply fruity and balanced. Delicious.*
☆☆☆☆ 1982 ZINFANDEL ($10.00) Alexander Valley. *Lush, clean flavors, rich fruit, complex, superb, classic.*

ও

Gross Highland Winery
NEW JERSEY

212 Jim Leeds Road, Absecon, New Jersey 08201 (609-652-1187). FOUNDED: 1934. ACREAGE: 80 acres. PRODUCTION: 32,000 cases. DISTRIBUTION: At winery and local outlets. OWNER: Bernard D'Arcy. WINEMAKER: Nathan Stackhouse. Tours and tasting Monday–Saturday 10 A.M.– 6 P.M., Sunday 12–5 P.M.

Long ago, at the end of Prohibition, German immigrant John Gross bought a bit of acreage in New Jersey, planted a few vines, and built a small chalet-style winery. Like generations before him, John passed his skills on to his son Bernard J. D'Arcy, who in turn passed them down to his son Bernard S. D'Arcy. (Bernard S. doubts he will be passing this family tradition on to his own son, who is currently studying for the priesthood.) With each generation the winery has expanded, but the decor has remained the same. Painted wine casks and other old-world memorabilia set the theme, but in the tasting room one can watch the workings of the modern bottling line.

≥●

Groth Vineyards and Winery
NAPA COUNTY

P.O. Box 412, Oakville, California 94562 (707-255-7466). FOUNDED: 1982. ACREAGE: 164 acres. PRODUCTION: 30,000 cases. DISTRIBUTION: Nationwide. OWNERS: Dennis and Judy Groth and Nils Venge. WINEMAKER: Nils Venge. Tours and tasting by appointment.

Dennis Groth moved from the high-tech world of computers to the simple farming life in the Napa Valley. After Dennis made his fortune at Atari in the Santa Clara Valley, he sought out the guidance of investment counselors and wine experts and began touring, tasting, and looking for land. He and his wife, Judy, bought a parcel in both the Oakville and the Yountville areas of the Napa Valley and hired winemaker Nils Venge away from Villa Mount Eden Vineyards. The first two Groth vintages were made at Château Bouchaine. Some varieties were crushed at the half-finished Groth facility in 1983. The early American–style winery was completed in 1985.

WHITE

☆☆☆ 1982 CHARDONNAY ($12.50) Napa Valley. *Exquisite acidity, great oak and fruit.*
☆☆ 1982 SAUVIGNON BLANC ($8.50) Napa Valley. *Round, fruity, clean and soft.*
☆☆ 1983 SAUVIGNON BLANC ($9.00) Napa Valley. *Simple, toasty, clean.*

RED

☆☆☆☆ 1982 CABERNET SAUVIGNON ($13.00) Napa Valley. *Stunning. Lovely, delicate fruit and great acidity. Drink 1988.*

≥●

Grover Gulch Winery
SANTA CRUZ COUNTY

7880 Glen Haven Road, Soquel, California 95073 (408-475-0568). FOUNDED: 1979. ACREAGE: None. PRODUCTION: 1,000 cases. DISTRIBUTION: At winery only. OWNERS: Dennis Bassano and Reinhold Banek. WINEMAKERS: Dennis Bassano and Reinhold Banek. Tours by appointment on weekends.

Two red-wine lovers, Dennis Bassano and Reinhold Banek, decided to try making their own. The partners admit that their first efforts were "marginal," but the quality improved with every new vintage. Once they felt they had acquired adequate experience, they built and bonded their winery. They make red wines in what they call a "California-Italian" style.

RED

○ 1980 CABERNET SAUVIGNON ($4.75) Late Harvest, Santa Cruz Mountains. *A bad idea, badly executed. Dull, weedy, unattractive.*
☆☆☆ 1981 CABERNET SAUVIGNON ($9.50) Santa Cruz Mountains. *Nice, rich, good depth and fruit. Drink now.*
☆☆ 1980 CARIGNANE ($6.50) Santa Cruz Mountains. *Rich, deep, balanced—a fine example of a little-made wine.*
☆☆ 1980 PETITE SIRAH ($8.50) Santa Cruz Mountains. *Spicy, clean, good fruit. Drink 1986.*

≥●

Guadalupe Valley Winery
TEXAS

1720 Hunter Road, New Braunfels, Texas 78130 (512-629-2351). FOUNDED: 1975. ACREAGE: None. PRODUCTION: 2,500 cases. DISTRIBUTION: Texas. OWNER: Corporation. Larry Lehr, president. WINEMAKER: Larry Lehr. Tours and tasting daily. Call for information.

Larry Lehr felt that with proper management and updated equipment the Guadalupe Valley Winery had potential. The previous owners had lost interest in the old winery and put it up for sale. Larry, his wife, and his father formed a family corporation and bought the winery in 1980. In buying new equipment and remodeling, the Lehrs made the winery more functional and much more practical. By properly managing the tasting room and adding a restaurant on the second-story balcony, the Lehrs turned their winery into a major tourist attraction.

Guenoc Winery
LAKE COUNTY

21000 Butts Canyon Road, Middletown, California 95461 (707-987-2385). FOUNDED: 1981. ACREAGE: 270 acres. PRODUCTION: 36,000 cases. DISTRIBUTION: Nationwide. OWNER: Orville Magoon, proprietor. WINEMAKER: Walter Raymond; Roy Raymond, Jr., viticulturist. Tours Thursday–Sunday 10 A.M.–4:30 P.M. No tours of Langtry House.

This property was owned in the 1880s by British actress Lillie Langtry, who used it as a retreat from her glamorous life. Her Victorian house has been restored and furnished with period antiques by present owners Bob and Orville Magoon. Her portrait also adorns Guenoc's labels. The federal government has granted an appellation of origin to the Guenoc Valley, recognizing its unique character. Roy Raymond, Jr., (see Raymond Vineyards) is the viticulturist, and the wines are made by his brother Walt.

WHITE

☆☆   1983 WHITE TABLE WINE ($4.25) Lake. *Fruity, soft and off-dry.*
☆☆   1980 CHARDONNAY ($8.50) North Coast.
☆   1981 CHARDONNAY ($8.50) California. *Very oaky and heavy.*
☆   1982 CHARDONNAY ($9.15) 67% Lake, 33% Mendocino. *Earthy, dull, lacking fruit.*
☆☆☆   1982 CHENIN BLANC ($5.00) Guenoc Valley. *Rich, complex and rounded, with nice, crisp acid.*
☆☆   1983 CHENIN BLANC ($5.00) Guenoc Valley. *Crisp, clean, pleasant.*
1982 SAUVIGNON BLANC ($6.50) Guenoc Valley.
☆☆   1983 SAUVIGNON BLANC ($6.00) Lake. *Soft, grassy, varietal, nice.*

RED

☆☆   1981 RED TABLE WINE ($4.25) Lake. *Spicy, rich, clean, tarry, good.*
☆☆☆   1980 CABERNET SAUVIGNON ($8.00) 70% Lake, 30% Napa. *Snappy, clean and balanced. Complex and lovely. Drink now.*
☆☆☆   1981 CABERNET SAUVIGNON ($8.00) Lake. *Lovely fruit and balance, nice oak. Drink now or hold a year.*
☆☆   1982 CABERNET SAUVIGNON ($8.25) Guenoc Valley. *Herbaceous, fresh, clean. Drink now.*
☆☆☆   1981 PETITE SIRAH ($6.50) Lake. *Soft, lush, balanced. Drink now.*
☆☆   1981 ZINFANDEL ($5.50) Lake. *Crisp fruit, clean.*

Emilio Guglielmo Winery
SANTA CLARA COUNTY

1480 East Main Avenue, Morgan Hill, California 95037 (408-779-2145). FOUNDED: 1925. ACREAGE: 125 acres. PRODUCTION: 63,000 cases. DISTRIBUTION: 9 states. OWNER: Guglielmo family. George W., George E., Madeleine, and Eugene Guglielmo; George W. Guglielmo, president. WINEMAKER: George E. Guglielmo. Tours by appointment. Tasting daily 9 A.M.–6 P.M. Closed major holidays. Picnic facilities, gift shop.

Emilio Guglielmo started his winery during Prohibition, making wine beneath his house and selling it to family and friends. Emilio's son George remembers driving cases of wine to San Francisco and delivering them door to door just like milk. Now Emilio's grandsons George and Eugene run the family winery. The original cement-block building, with its red-tile roof and thickly ivy-covered facade, is still used, although it has been enlarged four separate times.

WHITE

☆ 1981 CHARDONNAY ($8.50) Central Coast. *Simple, fresh, fruity.*
O 1981 JOHANNISBERG RIESLING ($5.75) Santa Clara Valley. *Horrible.*

RED

1977 ZINFANDEL ($5.25) Mount Madonna, Santa Clara Valley.

Guild Wineries
SAN JOAQUIN COUNTY

One Winemaster's Way, Lodi, California 95240 (209-368-5151). FOUNDED: 1933. PRODUCTION: Approximately 5 million cases. DISTRIBUTION: Nationwide and 12 foreign markets. OWNER: Cooperative. WINEMAKER: Eli C. Skofis, vice president production; Albert Cribari, winemaster. OTHER LABELS: Cresta Blanca (see), Cribari, Roma, Tavola, Winemaster's. Brandies: Ceremony, Cresta Blanca, Cribari, Guild Blue Ribbon. Tours and tasting daily 10 A.M.–5 P.M. at three wineries: Cresta Blanca, Winemaster's Guild Winery and Cribari.

After Repeal, in 1934, two small cooperative wineries sprang up near Lodi: the Del Rio and Bear Creek wineries. As time passed, more grower co-ops were started, until they all joined together in 1946 to form one large cooperative, the "Wine Growers' Guild." The Guild later took over a number of independent co-ops and became the parent winery. It also took over Cribari Winery and bought Cresta Blanca from Schenley, moving it from Fresno to Ukiah. Today, Guild Wineries is still cooperatively owned by growers. There are seven winery facilities, each with its own winery manager and winemaker.

WHITE

1981 CRESTA BLANCA CHARDONNAY ($7.00) Santa Maria Valley. *A bit weird.*
1982 CRESTA BLANCA CHARDONNAY ($6.00) Mendocino. *Dull and lifeless.*
1983 CRESTA BLANCA CHARDONNAY ($8.00) Mendocino. *Dull, lifeless.*
1982 CRESTA BLANCA CHENIN BLANC ($4.50) Estate, Mendocino. *Dull, low acid.*
☆☆ 1983 CRESTA BLANCA CHENIN BLANC ($5.00) Mendocino. *2% residual sugar. Soft, clean, varietal.*
☆☆ 1981 CRESTA BLANCA GEWURZTRAMINER ($5.00) Santa Maria. *2% residual sugar. Lovely varietal fruitiness.*
1981 CRESTA BLANCA JOHANNISBERG RIESLING ($4.60) Santa Maria Valley.

SPARKLING

O NV CRESTA BLANCA BRUT ($8.00) California. *Transfer.*
☆☆ NV CRIBARI EXTRA DRY ($3.75) California. *Fresh, fruity, clean and appealing.*

NV   CRESTA BLANCA EXTRA DRY CHAMPAGNE ($7.75) California.
NV   CRESTA BLANCA CHARDONNAY ($7.75) California.
☆ NV   CRIBARI SPUMANTE ($3.50) California. *Simple, decent, sweet, a bit thin.*

BLANC DE NOIR

☆   1983 CRESTA BLANCA WHITE ZINFANDEL ($5.00) Mendocino. *2% residual sugar.
       Candy-like, not enough acidity. White.*
☆   1984 CRIBARI WHITE ZINFANDEL ($2.50) California. *Fresh and fruity; a bit thin but
       quite pleasant.*

ROSE

☆   1982 CRESTA BLANCA GAMAY ($3.30) Mendocino. *Crisp, clean, simple, quite attractive.*

RED

☆☆   1977 CRESTA BLANCA CABERNET SAUVIGNON ($5.00) Mendocino. *Fresh, fruity,
       clean and simple.*
☆☆   1978 CRESTA BLANCA CABERNET SAUVIGNON ($5.00) Mendocino. *Herbal, clean,
       light and lovely.*
O   NV   CRIBARI ZINFANDEL ($2.50) California. *Weedy and sweet.*
☆   1979 CRESTA BLANCA ZINFANDEL ($4.70) Mendocino.
☆   1980 CRESTA BLANCA ZINFANDEL ($4.00) Mendocino. *Smoky, nice varietal char-
       acter, light, good.*

Gundlach-Bundschu Winery
SONOMA COUNTY

2000 Denmark Street, Vineburg, California 95487 (707-938-5277). FOUNDED: 1858. ACREAGE:
350 acres. PRODUCTION: 30,000 cases. DISTRIBUTION: Nationwide and 2 foreign markets.
OWNER: Jim Bundschu. WINEMAKER: Lance Cutler. Tours and tasting daily 11 A.M.–4:30 P.M.
Newsletter.

Prior to the 1906 earthquake this winery, selling wines under the Bacchus label, was one of
the most important in California. The earthquake changed all that by destroying the large stock
of wine kept in vaults in San Francisco. The Bundschu family, however, was still growing grapes
in its famous Rhinefarm vineyard in 1973. Young Jim Bundschu and his brother-in-law John Merritt
revived the old winery and began producing premium wines, including the only Kleinberger in
America. John, the winemaker, has since left (see California Wine Company).

WHITE

☆☆   1980 CHARDONNAY ($11.25) Special Selection, Sangiacomo, Sonoma. *Toasty and good,
       with a touch of vegetal character.*
☆☆☆   1981 CHARDONNAY ($10.00) Sangiacomo, Sonoma. *Big, fat, oaky, nicely balanced.*
☆☆☆   1981 CHARDONNAY ($12.00) 125th Anniversary, Sangiacomo Ranch, Sonoma Valley.
       Angular and clean; nice varietal character; good balance.
☆   1982 CHARDONNAY ($9.75). *Fruity, rich, overripe, some oxidation.*
       1983 CHARDONNAY ($9.75) Sonoma Valley. *Bitter, dirty.*
☆☆   1982 DRESEL'S SONOMA RIESLING ($5.00) Sonoma Valley. *Soft and clean; balanced
       and off-dry.*
       1982 JOHANNISBERG RIESLING ($11.00) Rhinefarm, Sonoma Valley.

☆☆ 1983 DRESEL'S SONOMA RIESLING ($4.95) Sonoma Valley. *1.2% residual sugar. 80% Johannisberg Riesling, 19% Sylvaner, 2% Kleinberger. Lovely.*

☆☆ 1982 KLEINBERGER ($6.00) Rhinefarm, Sonoma Valley. *1% residual sugar.*

☆☆ 1983 KLEINBERGER ($6.00) Estate, Sonoma Valley. *Fresh, crisp, clean, snappy, very attractive.*

RED

☆☆☆ NV SONOMA RED WINE ($3.90) Sonoma Valley. *Rich, fresh, clean, tannic, good structure. Terrific.*

1978 CABERNET SAUVIGNON ($8.75) Rhinefarm, Sonoma Valley.

☆☆☆ 1979 CABERNET SAUVIGNON ($8.00) Gregory, Sonoma Valley. *Rich, berried and round; good structure and aging potential.*

☆☆☆ 1979 CABERNET SAUVIGNON ($9.00) Batto Ranch, Sonoma Valley. *Lovely. Fruity and firm structure. Great aging potential.*

☆☆ 1979 CABERNET SAUVIGNON ($9.00) Olive Hill, Sonoma Valley. *Fruity, oaky and attractive.*

☆☆ 1979 CABERNET SAUVIGNON ($12.00) 125th Anniversary, Rhinefarm, Sonoma. *It's all here—it just needs some age to come together.*

☆☆☆ 1979 CABERNET SAUVIGNON ($12.50) Special Selection, Rhinefarm, Sonoma Valley. *Earthy, rich and showing great aging potential.*

☆☆ 1980 CABERNET SAUVIGNON ($9.50) Rhinefarm, Estate, Sonoma Valley. *Spicy, herbal, toasty, earthy, attractive. Drink now.*

☆☆☆ 1980 CABERNET SAUVIGNON ($13.50) Batto Ranch, Sonoma Valley. *Complex and nicely structured.*

☆☆☆ 1981 CABERNET SAUVIGNON ($9.95) Sonoma Valley. *Deep, rich, fat, lush. Drink now.*

☆☆☆☆ 1981 CABERNET SAUVIGNON ($12.00) Batto Ranch, Sonoma Valley. *Complex, elegant, rich, magnificently structured. Will age.*

☆☆ 1981 CABERNET SAUVIGNON ($12.00) Rhinefarm, Sonoma Valley. *Soft, rich, elegant and fruity. Good aging potential.*

☆☆☆ 1982 CABERNET SAUVIGNON ($12.00) Batto Ranch, Sonoma Valley. *Clean, fruity, stiff, angular. Drink 1988.*

☆☆ 1976 MERLOT Rhinefarm, Sonoma Valley. *Rich, dense, clean and well knit. Showing its age.*

☆☆☆ 1977 MERLOT Rhinefarm, Sonoma Valley. *Soft, well structured, lovely, clean, mature.*

☆☆☆ 1978 MERLOT ($7.50) Rhinefarm, Sonoma Valley. *Soft, clean, lovely. Will continue to age well.*

☆☆☆ 1979 MERLOT ($9.50) Rhinefarm, Sonoma Valley. *Lovely, clean, complex and rich. Will age well.*

☆☆☆ 1980 MERLOT ($10.00) 125th Anniversary, Rhinefarm, Sonoma Valley. *Big, rich and raisiny.*

☆☆ 1980 MERLOT ($10.15) Rhinefarm, Sonoma Valley. *Tarry, dense and tannic but should smooth out with some age.*

☆☆ 1981 MERLOT ($10.00) Rhinefarm, Sonoma Valley. *Soft, lush, clean.*

1980 PINOT NOIR ($9.00) Sonoma.

☆☆☆ 1982 PINOT NOIR ($9.95) Estate-Rhinefarm, Sonoma Valley. *Medium weight, good fruit and varietal character.*

☆☆ 1979 ZINFANDEL ($9.10) Sonoma Valley.

☆ 1980 ZINFANDEL ($8.00) Rhinefarm, Sonoma Valley. *Deep, berried and oaky but lacking structure and integrity.*

☆☆ 1980 ZINFANDEL ($9.00) Late Harvest, Barricia, Sonoma Valley. *0.6% residual sugar. Peppery, fruity and intense.*

☆☆ 1981 ZINFANDEL ($7.00) Rhinefarm, Sonoma Valley. *Spicy, fresh, clean.*

Habersham Vintners
GEORGIA

P.O. Box 526, Baldwin, Georgia 30511 (404-778-5845). FOUNDED: 1983. ACREAGE: 30 acres. PRODUCTION: 2,500 cases. DISTRIBUTION: Georgia and Florida. OWNERS: Tom and Charles Slick. Russell Jones, general manager. WINEMAKER: Russell Jones. OTHER LABEL: Etowah Ridges. Tours and tasting Monday–Saturday 10 A.M.–4 P.M.

In the 1970s, before the advent of the bag-in-the-box, Tom Slick went to California to research the possibility of packaging wine in boxes. Although he decided the concept wouldn't work, his interest in wine was still so vital that when he returned to Georgia he planted a small vineyard in the Clarksville area. Tom started with four acres of vines; he now has thirty. Before building a winery, he obtained a special temporary permit allowing him to make wine in a dry county, but just as the first vintage was arriving at the winery, the permit was revoked by certain local political-religious groups. "We had to sit on those grapes for two months. We kept them in cold storage until a winery in a wet county let us crush them at its facility," says Russell Jones. Now the winery is located in a wet county, fifteen miles from the vineyards.

WHITE

☆ NV CHABLIS ($5.50) Georgia.
○ NV ETOWAH RIDGES WHITE TABLE WINE ($5.00) Georgia. *Stinky.*
☆ NV JOHANNISBERG RIESLING ($7.50) Georgia. *Melony, clean.*
☆ 1983 SAUVIGNON BLANC ($8.50) Georgia. *Varietal, pleasant.*

RED

☆ NV PINOT NOIR ($8.50) Georgia.

Hacienda del Rio Winery
SONOMA COUNTY

P.O. Box 195, Fulton, California 95539 (707-887-7480). FOUNDED: 1981. ACREAGE: None. PRODUCTION: 600 cases. DISTRIBUTION: California. OWNERS: Williams and Selyem families. WINEMAKER: Burt Williams. Tours by appointment.

Two couples, the Williams and the Selyems, experimented with winemaking at home. When they had produced some good wines, they decided to turn their hobby into a part-time business. They leased a building in Fulton, fixed up its dilapidated garage, and established a red-wine winery. "We may make white wines eventually," says Jane Williams, "but that means more equipment." Burt Williams, a printer with a local newspaper, makes Pinot Noir because it is his favorite wine. The winery also produces Zinfandel from the 80-year-old Martinelli vineyard. Burt's partner, Ed Selyem, is the wine buyer-manager at a local market, which sells a lot of Hacienda del Rio wine.

RED

☆☆ 1983 PINOT NOIR ($7.00) Sonoma. *Great structure and varietal complexity; very good.*

Hacienda Wine Cellars
SONOMA COUNTY

1000 Vineyard Lane, Sonoma, California 95476 (707-938-3220). FOUNDED: 1973. ACREAGE: 50 acres. PRODUCTION: 23,000 cases. DISTRIBUTION: California and 24 other states. OWNER:

Corporation. Crawford Cooley, president; Frank Bartholomew and Steve MacRostie, vice presidents. WINEMAKER: Steve MacRostie. Tours by appointment. Tasting daily 10 A.M.–5 P.M. Newsletter.

In 1941 Frank Bartholomew, a journalist and eventual head of United Press International, bought a piece of property in Sonoma sight unseen. Upon inspecting his purchase, he found two old stone buildings that were, as it turned out, the ruins of Agoston Haraszthy's original Buena Vista winery. Frank restored the estate and revived the winery in one of the buildings. He sold Buena Vista in 1968, but kept the vineyard property, on which there was a Mediterranean-style building that was converted to a winery. By 1976 Hacienda had grown so rapidly that Frank called upon a family friend, grape grower Crawford Cooley, to manage the operation. Frank died in 1985.

WHITE

☆☆ 1980 CHARDONNAY ($10.00) Clair de Lune, Sonoma Valley. *Heavy, oily and dense. Lacking finesse and somewhat crude.*

☆ 1981 CHARDONNAY ($11.00) Clair de Lune, Sonoma. *Soft, faint and decent.*

☆ 1981 CHARDONNAY ($15.00) Selected Reserve, Sonoma Valley. *Heavy and overoaked.*

☆ 1982 CHARDONNAY ($9.00) Clair de Lune, Sonoma Valley. *Strange.*

1982 CHARDONNAY ($9.00) Selected Reserve, Sonoma Valley. *Lacks fruit and depth. Bitter.*

☆☆☆ 1983 CHARDONNAY ($9.00) Clair de Lune, Sonoma. *Crisp, rich, good fruit and oak, the best "Clair de Lune" yet.*

☆☆☆ 1982 CHENIN BLANC ($5.50) Dry, Estate, Sonoma. *Soft, rich and well made.*

☆☆ 1983 CHENIN BLANC ($5.50) California. *0.84% residual sugar. Vinous, varietal, well balanced.*

☆☆☆ 1981 GEWURZTRAMINER ($6.75) Sonoma. *Dry, elegant.*

☆☆☆ 1982 GEWURZTRAMINER ($6.75) Dry, Sonoma Valley. *0.7% sugar rounds it. Spicy, rich, varietal—great food wine.*

☆☆ 1983 GEWURZTRAMINER ($6.75) Sonoma Valley. *0.75% residual sugar. Dry, fruity, clean, attractive.*

☆☆☆ 1983 GEWURZTRAMINER ($7.00) Sonoma. *0.75% residual sugar. Tart, clean, charming and varietal.*

☆☆☆ 1984 GEWURZTRAMINER ($6.75) Sonoma. *0.75% residual sugar. Snappy, clean, varietal, balanced.*

☆☆ 1982 JOHANNISBERG RIESLING ($6.75) Sonoma Valley. *2.6% residual sugar. Spicy and soft, with good acid balance.*

☆ 1983 SAUVIGNON BLANC ($8.00) Sonoma. *23% Semillon. Fruity, with some volatile acidity. Odd.*

RED

☆☆☆ 1978 CABERNET SAUVIGNON ($10.00) Sonoma Valley. *Rich but nicely structured. Good aging potential.*

☆☆☆ 1979 CABERNET SAUVIGNON ($11.00) Sonoma. *Balanced, graceful, attractive. Drink now.*

☆☆☆ 1980 CABERNET SAUVIGNON ($11.00) Sonoma. *Lush and rich; great depth and complexity. Drink 1987 and later.*

☆☆☆ 1981 CABERNET SAUVIGNON ($11.00) 76% Jansen, 24% Buena Vista, Sonoma Valley. *Minty, clean and velvety.*

☆☆☆ 1982 CABERNET SAUVIGNON ($10.75) Sonoma Valley. *Lush, fruity, varietal, balanced, charming. Drink 1986.*

O 1980 PINOT NOIR ($12.00) Buena Vista, Sonoma Valley. *Raisiny and flabby.*

☆☆ 1981 PINOT NOIR ($12.00) Sonoma Valley. *Leathery, with some stem character but well made.*

☆☆ 1982 PINOT NOIR ($12.00) Sonoma. *Crisp, jammy, decent.*

☆☆ 1982 PINOT NOIR ($12.00) Sonoma Valley.

☆☆ 1979 ZINFANDEL ($7.00) Sonoma.

☆☆   1980 ZINFANDEL ($6.00) Sonoma Valley. *Good varietal fruit but a little harsh on the
        finish.*
☆☆   1982 ZINFANDEL ($6.50) 44% Cooley, 52% D'Agostini, 4% Buena Vista, Sonoma.

Hafle Vineyards
OHIO

2369 Upper Valley Pike, Springfield, Ohio 45502 (513-399-2334). FOUNDED: 1974. ACREAGE:
9 acres. PRODUCTION: 2,000 cases. DISTRIBUTION: Local. OWNER: Daniel D. Hafle. WINE-
MAKER: Daniel D. Hafle. Tours by appointment. Tasting Monday–Thursday 11 A.M.–8 P.M.,
Friday–Saturday 11 A.M.–10 P.M.

A farmboy from southern Ohio, Dan Hafle grew all kinds of vegetables and fruits on his Clark
County spread before he planted French-American hybrid vines. In a 60-year-old barn built of
hardwoods grown and cut on the farm, he started the Hafle winery in 1974, preserving the building's
rustic ambiance by installing the tasting room in the former horse stalls. Generously sponsoring
festivals throughout the year—on the Fourth of July, Decoration Day, and Labor Day—complete
with German bands, barbecued bratwurst, and roasted home-grown sweet corn, the Hafle family
may seem carefree and good natured. They have had to fight hard, however, to secure their way
of life. For two years, Dan battled the hard-nosed trustees of this German-American town, who
claimed the winery violated zoning regulations; during this time he had to crush his Clark County
grapes in Franklin County. He won the battle in 1980, finally getting his winery approved as an
"on-farm" operation.

Hafner Vineyard
SONOMA COUNTY

P.O. Box 1038, Healdsburg, California 95448 (707-433-4675). FOUNDED: 1982. ACREAGE: 95
acres. PRODUCTION: 10,000 cases. DISTRIBUTION: By California mailing list. OWNERS: Richard and Mary Hafner. WINEMAKER: Parke Hafner. Tours by appointment.

During the summer months, Parke Hafner worked in his parents' Alexander Valley vineyard.
After inhaling a lot of dust, he decided it wasn't what he wanted to do for a living. When he entered
U.C. Davis, however, he majored in enology—mostly for the chemistry and science, he says—and
discovered that he really enjoyed winemaking. The Hafners built a two-story winery overlooking
the vineyard, and Parke manages all winery operations. His brother Scott is in charge of marketing.
The Hafners still sell most of their fruit to other wineries, such as Davis Bynum, Matrose, and
Château Montelena.

WHITE

☆☆☆   1982 CHARDONNAY ($12.00) Estate, Alexander Valley. *Rich, intense, balanced and
          oaky. A stunner.*

RED

☆☆☆   1982 CABERNET SAUVIGNON ($15.00) Estate, Alexander Valley. *Crisp, structured, rich
          and complex, with loads of finesse. Drink 1987.*

Hagafen Cellars
NAPA COUNTY

P.O. Box 3035, Napa, California 94558 (707-252-0781). FOUNDED: 1980. ACREAGE: None.
PRODUCTION: 5,000 cases. DISTRIBUTION: 12 states and Canada. OWNER: Corporation.

Ernie Weir, president; Norman Miller and René di Rosa, vice presidents; Zach Berkowitz. WINE-MAKERS: Zach Berkowitz and Ernie Weir. No tours or tasting.

Ernie Weir, Norman Miller, and Zach Berkowitz—all of whom work for different wineries in the Napa Valley—were attracted to the idea of producing premium varietal kosher wines there. They formed a corporation with René di Rosa, owner of the renowned Winery Lake Vineyard in the Carneros district, and most Hagafen grapes come from there. The wines are certified kosher by the Orthodox Rabbinical Council of San Francisco.

WHITE

☆☆   1982 CHARDONNAY ($13.50) Kosher, Winery Lake, Napa Valley. *Lush, fruity, varietal.*

☆☆   1983 CHARDONNAY ($13.50) Napa Valley. *Kosher. Crisp, decent, clean.*

☆   1982 JOHANNISBERG RIESLING ($8.50) Kosher, Winery Lake, Napa Valley.

☆☆☆   1984 JOHANNISBERG RIESLING ($8.95) Winery Lake, Napa Valley. *Kosher. 2% residual sugar. Spritzy, crisp, fruity, excellent.*

BLANC DE NOIR

☆☆☆   1984 PINOT NOIR BLANC ($5.75) Napa Valley. *Kosher. Crisp, fresh, varietal, lovely.*

RED

☆☆☆   1982 CABERNET SAUVIGNON ($12.00) Yountville Selection, Napa Valley. *Kosher. Rich, clean, complex, charming, excellent. Drink 1986.*

Haight Vineyard
CONNECTICUT

Chestnut Hill, Litchfield, Connecticut 06759 (203-567-4045). FOUNDED: 1975. ACREAGE: 45 acres. PRODUCTION: 6,000 cases. DISTRIBUTION: Connecticut and New England states. OWNER: Sherman P. Haight, Jr. WINEMAKER: Shorn Mills. Tours and tasting summer: Monday–Saturday 10:30 A.M.–5 P.M., Sunday 12–5 P.M. Closed for major holidays.

Tired and frustrated by the series of less-than-successful crops he had planted, Sherman Haight was looking for something new to grow on his 165 acres of Connecticut farmland. Although he loved wine, he was sure vinifera could not grow in Connecticut, and he had no desire to experiment with Labrusca or French-American hybrids. But his thinking was changed by an article on cultivating vinifera in New York written by Dr. Konstantin Frank. He contacted the doctor, who advised him on which varieties might produce well in his particular region. Sherman planted three quarters of an acre of experimental vines, and in a short time he was producing quite creditable fruit. Convinced, Sherman converted his hay barn into a winery, planted more vineyards, and began to make vinifera wines in earnest.

WHITE

☆   NV   COVERTSIDE ($5.00) Connecticut.

   NV   CHARDONNAY ($8.00) Connecticut. *Acidic nose; intensely earthy and vinous.*

☆   NV   RIESLING ($8.00) American. *Spicy, fruity, rich and short, with a flabby finish.*

RED

☆   NV   MARECHAL FOCH ($4.98) Connecticut. *Oak nose, rich, slightly sweet and heavy.*

Hale Cellars
SANTA BARBARA COUNTY

P.O. Box 5, Los Alamos, California 93440 (805-344-2391). FOUNDED: 1974. ACREAGE: 325 acres. PRODUCTION: 5,000 cases. DISTRIBUTION: California. OWNERS: Sam and Dona Hale.

WINEMAKER: Mary Vigoroso. OTHER LABEL: Los Alamos Vineyard. Tours and tasting by appointment Tuesday–Sunday 10 A.M.–5 P.M.

Sam Hale, a Los Angeles attorney, gave his mother-in-law, Mary Vigoroso, a new career when he bought 680 acres as a tax shelter. Since Sam was busy in Los Angeles, he put Mary in charge of the winery. "At first, I was only going to make a barrel of each variety, but I ended up making four tons of each," says Mary. Mary runs the winery single-handedly, making batches of "natural wines" in the dairy barn.

è🙚

Hamlet Hill Vineyards
CONNECTICUT

Route 101, Pomfret, Connecticut 06258 (203-928-5550). FOUNDED: 1975. ACREAGE: 28 acres. PRODUCTION: 6,000 cases. DISTRIBUTION: 3 states. OWNER: A. W. Loos. WINEMAKER: Dr. Howard Bursen. Several other labels. Tours and tasting daily 10 A.M.–6 P.M.

Sunlight beams in through the center skylight and bounces off the stainless steel tanks and polished wood catwalks of this state-of-the-art showplace winery. Hamlet Hill was built by A. W. Loos, a modern renaissance man who was confident that his mountain property had a special microclimate. He was right; the growing season at Hamlet Hill is normally quite a bit longer than that experienced by other vineyards as close as one-half mile away. Loos hired Dr. Howard Bursen as consultant and winemaker, and together they designed the twelve-sided superstructure, sparing no expense in outfitting it with the latest winemaking equipment.

è🙚

Handley Cellars
MENDOCINO COUNTY

2160 Guntley Road, Philo, California 95466 (707-895-3876). FOUNDED: 1982. ACREAGE: None. PRODUCTION: 1,000 cases. DISTRIBUTION: California. OWNERS: Rex McCallan and Milla Handley. WINEMAKER: Milla Handley. Tours and tasting by appointment.

After graduating from U.C. Davis with a degree in enology, Milla Handley, a pleasant, soft-spoken woman, moved to Sonoma County, where she worked for Fritz Cellars. She then worked at Château St. Jean for a short time before settling into the relaxed lifestyle of the Mendocino hills. She lived in Philo and worked with Jed Steele (see Château du Lac) at Edmeades Winery for three years before finally committing to her own winery. She plans to keep the winery small and use the Chardonnay grapes grown on her father's vineyard in Healdsburg. "Nevertheless, the winery which began in our basement is beginning to creep into my husband's garage," says Milla.

WHITE

☆☆ 1982 CHARDONNAY ($12.00) 55% Handley, 45% Carney, North Coast. *Oaky and ripe, with good, firm acidity.*

☆☆☆☆ 1983 CHARDONNAY ($12.50) Dry Creek Valley. *Elegant, balanced and clean; richly varietal with good oak. Lovely.*

è🙚

Hanzell Vineyards
SONOMA COUNTY

18596 Lomita Avenue, Sonoma, California 95476 (707-996-3860). FOUNDED: 1957. ACREAGE: 31 acres. PRODUCTION: 1,500 cases. DISTRIBUTION: California, New York, and by mailing list. OWNER: Barbara de Brye; Robert Sessions, general manager. WINEMAKER: Robert Sessions; Jeffrey Pueh, vineyard manager. Tours by appointment.

James D. Zellerbach, former ambassador to Italy and heir to a large paper fortune, brought Burgundy to the Sonoma Valley in 1957 when he built a two-story winery with a stone facade modeled after the château of Clos de Vougeot in France. Five years before, he had planted Pinot Noir and Chardonnay vines on a terraced hillside. Zellerbach, a stickler for authenticity, inadvertently caused a winemaking revolution when he imported a boatload of French oak barrels. Founding winemaker Brad Webb soon discovered that the Burgundian barrels' effect on the wine was much more than cosmetic, and American wineries have been aging their Chardonnays and Pinot Noirs in French oak ever since. After Zellerbach's death, Hanzell was bought by Douglas and Mary Day, who then sold it in 1975 to an Australian heiress, Barbara de Brye. Robert Sessions, who succeeded consultant Brad Webb in 1973, is the winemaker and general manager.

WHITE

1979 CHARDONNAY ($16.00) Sonoma Valley. *Heavy, clumsy and oaky.*
☆ 1981 CHARDONNAY ($18.00) Sonoma Valley. *Vinous and somewhat weedy but not bad.*
☆☆ 1982 CHARDONNAY ($19.00) Sonoma Valley. *Rich oak, vinous, lacking fruit.*

RED

☆ 1976 PINOT NOIR Sonoma Valley.
☆☆ 1977 PINOT NOIR ($14.00) Sonoma Valley. *Rich and complex but just not very likable. Maybe age will help.*
☆☆ 1978 PINOT NOIR ($15.00) Sonoma Valley. *Clean, varietal and nicely structured.*
☆☆ 1980 PINOT NOIR ($16.00) Sonoma Valley. *Hard, austere and dense. Drink 1987.*

Happy B Farm Winery
GEORGIA

Route 4, Bunn Road, Forsyth, Georgia 31029 (912-994-6549). FOUNDED: 1979. ACREAGE: 1 acre. PRODUCTION: 800 cases. DISTRIBUTION: Local. OWNER: Vernelle Bunn. WINEMAKER: Vernelle Bunn. Tours and tasting on weekends.

The Bunns had an abundance of tomatoes growing on their farm, and so did every other local produce farmer. One day, as the tomatoes sat on the ground, slowly rotting, the Bunns were visited by a young man who asked them what they were going to do with all those tomatoes. "Why, I'm just going to let them sit there," said Vernelle Bunn. "What else can I do?" "Put them in a barrel," replied the young man, "and make wine out of them." Not a bad idea. After conquering tomato wine, the Bunns started making fruit wines and grape wines from Scuppernong.

Harbor Winery
YOLO COUNTY

610 Harbor Boulevard, West Sacramento, California 95691 (916-371-6776). FOUNDED: 1972. ACREAGE: None. PRODUCTION: 1,700 cases. DISTRIBUTION: California and 4 other states; England. OWNER: Charles H. Myers. WINEMAKER: Charles H. Myers. Tours by appointment.

As a home winemaker, Charles Myers had once made a white wine from Mission grapes harvested from vines planted in the 1880s. He called the wine "Mission del Sol." When Charles started making wine commercially, he planned to make Chardonnay. "But in 1972, the weather was so horrible that the Chardonnay I had contracted to buy was not worth picking," says Charles.

"I needed a white wine, so I bought Mission grapes from the same grower who had sold it to me years before, and made the first commercial Mission del Sol." Since then Charles has been able to make Chardonnay and other, more modern varieties, but Mission is still in his line.

WHITE

☆☆☆ 1980 CHARDONNAY ($8.50) Reserve, Napa Valley. *Rich, varietal, lush, smooth.*

RED

○ 1978 COUNTRY STYLE ZINFANDEL ($3.75) Shenandoah Valley, California. *4% residual sugar. A travesty.*
☆ 1979 CABERNET SAUVIGNON ($9.00) Napa Valley. *Ripe, soft and pleasant.*

Hargrave Vineyard
NEW YORK

Route 48, Cutchogue, New York 11935 (516-734-5158). FOUNDED: 1973. ACREAGE: 84 acres. PRODUCTION: 7,000 cases. DISTRIBUTION: New York. OWNERS: Alexander, Louisa, and Charles Hargrave. WINEMAKER: Alexander Hargrave. Tours and tasting May–December: weekends 10 A.M.–5 P.M.

Summers in Bordeaux and a love of cooking cultivated the Hargraves' deep interest in wine. When Alex, a Harvard graduate in Chinese, and his wife, Louisa, a Harvard graduate in education, began looking for vineyard land in 1972, they considered California, Oregon, Washington, and even Alex's hometown of Rochester. Discouraged by their unsuccessful search, they found new hope on Thanksgiving day 1972, when the strong arguments and firsthand experience of a Cornell professor convinced them that vinifera would grow well on Long Island. So the Hargraves bought a 66-acre potato farm and began planting in 1973. The vines took several years to mature before they began producing fruit that could meet the Hargraves' European winemaking standards. "By 1980, we were finally producing the wines we had hoped we could," says Alex.

WHITE

☆☆ 1981 CHARDONNAY ($7.50) North Fork, Long Island, New York.
☆☆☆ 1982 CHARDONNAY ($12.00) Collector Series, Estate, Long Island. *Rich fruit and buttery complexity.*
☆☆ 1982 JOHANNISBERG RIESLING ($9.75) Estate, Long Island. *Varietal, clean and fresh.*
☆ 1983 SAUVIGNON BLANC ($8.00) Long Island, North Fork. *Clean, decent, balanced.*

RED

☆ 1980 CABERNET SAUVIGNON ($5.50) North Fork, New York. *Vegetal but decently structured.*
☆☆ 1980 CABERNET SAUVIGNON ($10.00) North Fork, Long Island, New York. *Peppery and deep but a bit overoaked.*
☆ 1981 CABERNET SAUVIGNON ($11.00) Estate, North Fork, Long Island, New York. *Lush, green, weedy, rich and heavy. Drink 1987.*
○ 1979 PINOT NOIR ($5.00) Whole Berry, Estate, North Fork, Long Island, New York.

Hart Winery
RIVERSIDE COUNTY

41300 Avenue Biona, Temecula, California 92390 (714-676-6300). FOUNDED: 1980. ACREAGE: 11 acres. PRODUCTION: 7,000 cases. DISTRIBUTION: California. OWNERS: Travis and Nancy Hart. WINEMAKER: Travis Hart. Tours and tasting Saturday 11 A.M.–4 P.M.

"You have to be compulsive and obsessed to start a winery on a small scale," claims Travis "Joe" Hart. The more wine he drank and the more wine he made at home, the more Joe knew he would not rest until he had a real commercial winery and vineyard. He quit his teaching job and bought property in Temecula ("It was the closest legitimate grape-growing area to my home in Carlsbad"). Making a full-time commitment to winemaking, he started growing grapes and built a barn-style winery.

WHITE

☆☆ 1982 CHENIN BLANC ($5.00) Temecula. *Dry, fruity, and quite attractive.*
☆☆ 1982 SAUVIGNON BLANC ($7.50) Temecula. *Nice, clean and snappy.*

RED

☆☆ 1981 CABERNET SAUVIGNON ($8.00) Temecula. *6% Merlot. Rich, balanced and intense, with good varietal character.*

Haviland Vintners
WASHINGTON

19029 36th Avenue West, Lynnwood, Washington 98036 (206-771-6933). FOUNDED: 1981. ACREAGE: 12 acres. PRODUCTION: 14,000 cases. DISTRIBUTION: 5 states. OWNER: Corporation. George DeJarnatt, president. WINEMAKER: George DeJarnatt. Tours at 2 P.M. Tasting Thursday–Saturday 11 A.M.–3 P.M., Sunday 12–4 P.M.

George DeJarnatt, a CPA who didn't like accounting, became interested in the state's oldest Cabernet Sauvignon vineyard, first as a tax shelter and later as a new career. When he and six partners bought the neglected vineyard, they sold its fruit to Château Ste. Michelle and Ste. Chapelle Winery. George became upset when he learned that his lovely Cabernet grapes were being used to make "Rosé de Cabernet," so he rounded up a few more shareholders and opened his winery in an industrial park. "During the first year we made 6,000 gallons just to prove we could make good wine," says George. "The next year we made 16,000 to prove we could make good wine commercially, and in 1984 we will make more than 30,000 gallons to see if we can make wine and make money."

WHITE

O 1983 TRAMINER ($5.95) Ciel du Cheval, Yakima Valley, Washington. *Dry. My bottle had a violent secondary fermentation going on.*
☆☆ 1982 CHARDONNAY ($8.95) Dionysis, Columbia Valley, Washington. *Soft and complex.*
O 1982 SAUVIGNON BLANC ($5.25) Washington. *Oxidized, sweet, unappealing.*
☆ 1982 WHITE RIESLING ($5.00) Washington. *Dry, varnishy, clean and decent.*

BLANC DE NOIR

1983 PINOT NOIR BLANC ($4.75) Yakima Valley, Washington. *Dull and lacking fruit.*

RED

☆ 1982 MERLOT ($5.95) Washington. *Vegetal nose and grapey flavors. Decent.*

HAWK CREST *see* Stag's Leap Wine Cellars

Haywood Winery
SONOMA COUNTY

18701 Gehricke Road, Sonoma, California 95476 (707-996-4298). FOUNDED: 1980. ACREAGE: 100 acres. PRODUCTION: 9,000 cases. DISTRIBUTION: California and major market states.

OWNER: Peter Haywood, president; Dennis Bowker, vineyard manager. WINEMAKER: Charles Tolbert. Tasting daily 11 A.M.–5 P.M.

Peter Haywood had been cultivating his Sonoma Valley vineyards since 1974, selling his crop to various wineries. But then his neighbor lost interest in the small, functional winery he had just built down the road, and Peter bought it. A man of quiet confidence, Peter knows that the key to making excellent wines is skillful and fastidious grape growing. He has expanded the winery little by little in the hope of eventually being able to use the vineyard's total production. As it stands now, one half of the Haywood grapes are sold to other wineries.

WHITE

☆☆   1982 ESTATE WHITE ($5.75) Chamizal, Sonoma. *Blend of Chardonnay, Riesling and Gewürztraminer. Crisp, fruity, dry.*

☆☆   1980 CHARDONNAY ($11.00) Second Lot, Sonoma Valley. *Well structured, tangy fruit, high alcohol, complex.*

☆☆   1980 CHARDONNAY ($11.50) First Lot, Sonoma Valley. *Nice, with fresh fruit and oak complexity. Well made.*

☆☆   1981 CHARDONNAY ($9.75) Sonoma Valley. *Balanced, with good fruit and oak; modest.*

☆   1982 CHARDONNAY ($10.00) Napa Valley.

☆☆☆   1983 CHARDONNAY ($11.00) Sonoma Valley. *Fresh, fruity, crisp; very attractive.*

☆☆   1981 JOHANNISBERG RIESLING ($8.00) Sonoma Valley.

☆☆   1982 JOHANNISBERG RIESLING ($6.75) Early Harvest, Sonoma Valley. *Off-dry.*

☆☆☆   1983 WHITE RIESLING ($6.75) Sonoma Valley. *0.5% residual sugar. Crisp, dry, lovely, varietal.*

☆☆   1984 WHITE RIESLING ($7.00) Estate, Sonoma Valley. *Clean, fresh, hard-edged, good.*

RED

☆   NV SPAGHETTI RED ($4.25) Sonoma Valley.

☆   1980 CABERNET SAUVIGNON ($9.75) Sonoma Valley. *Dark, intense, lacking fruit.*

    1980 MERLOT ($25.00) Late Harvest, Chamizal, Sonoma Valley. *17.8% alcohol. Raisiny and port-like. A bad idea all around.*

☆☆   1981 ZINFANDEL ($7.50) Estate, Sonoma Valley.

☆☆   1982 ZINFANDEL ($7.50) Estate, Sonoma Valley. *Clean, fresh, snappy.*

Hecker Pass Winery
SANTA CLARA COUNTY

4605 Hecker Pass Highway, Gilroy, California 95020 (408-842-1755). FOUNDED: 1972. ACREAGE: 14 acres. PRODUCTION: 5,000 cases. DISTRIBUTION: California. OWNERS: Mario and Francis Fortino. WINEMAKER: Mario Fortino. No tours. Tasting daily 9 A.M.–5 P.M. Picnic facilities.

Mario Fortino, whose family owns the winery that bears their name, decided to go out on his own in 1972. He had learned the wine business from two generations of family winemakers in Italy and from work in California at San Martin Winery and Almadén Vineyards. His own wines, made in the traditional Italian-American style, are fermented in open-top redwood tanks and aged anywhere from two to five years in either redwood or oak cooperage. New vines have been planted on the Gilroy property over the years, but many are more than 30 years old.

Heineman Winery
OHIO

Put-in-Bay, Ohio 43456 (419-285-2811). FOUNDED: 1888. ACREAGE: 20 acres. PRODUCTION: 10,000 cases. DISTRIBUTION: At winery and local outlets. OWNER: Heineman family. WINE-MAKERS: Edward Heineman and Gerald Bane. Tours and tasting summer: daily 11 A.M.–5 P.M.

Grapes have been growing on the island of Put-in-Bay in Lake Erie since the 1850s. Louis Heineman's grandfather worked in those vineyards until he planted his own and built a winery in 1888. Now the fourth generation of Heinemans are working in the family winery. For Louis, who grew up and always worked there, the winery is all he knows. The changes over the years have been simple and practical—some machinery has been added and the original cellar has been expanded. Louis is waiting for his son, now the winemaker, to provide the fifth generation of Heineman family management.

WHITE

NV   CATAWBA ($3.25) Lake Erie. *Sweet.*

RED

NV   BURGUNDY ($3.25) Lake Erie.

Heinrichshaus Vineyards
MISSOURI

Route 2, Box 139, St. James, Missouri 65559 (314-265-5000). FOUNDED: 1978. ACREAGE: 10 acres. PRODUCTION: 2,000 cases. DISTRIBUTION: Missouri. OWNERS: Heinrich and Lois Grohe. WINEMAKER: Heinrich Grohe. Tours and tasting Monday–Saturday 9 A.M.–6 P.M., Sunday 12–6 P.M.

Heinrich Grohe came to the United States as an exchange student. Since he grew up in a viticultural region of Germany, winemaking and grape growing were second nature to him. While working as an engineer, Heinrich made wine at home just for his wife, Lois, and himself. Finally, with the encouragement of the winery-owning Bardenheirs in St. Louis, he bought a farm and started planting grapes. He continued his engineering career, and Lois worked as an artist and teacher. They sold their grapes to other wineries until 1978, when they had accumulated enough money to build their own winery. In 1982 the Grohes left their jobs to work full time at the winery.

Heitz Wine Cellars
NAPA COUNTY

500 Taplin Road, St. Helena, California 94574 (707-963-3542). FOUNDED: 1961. ACREAGE: 130 acres. PRODUCTION: 37,000 cases. DISTRIBUTION: Nationwide and 10 foreign markets. OWNER: Joe Heitz, president; Alice Heitz, vice president; Kathleen and Rollie Heitz. WINEMAKERS: Joe and David Heitz. Tours by appointment. Tasting daily 11 A.M.–4:30 P.M. at 436 St. Helena Highway South, St. Helena, California. Newsletter.

Following Air Force duty during World War II, Joe Heitz got a master's degree at U.C. Davis and worked at Beaulieu Vineyards for about seven years. He started his own business in 1961 after buying a plot of old Grignolino vines. He also often bought wine from other wineries and sold it under his own label. In 1964 he reconditioned an old winery in the hills on the east side of the Napa Valley, and with the help of his wife, Alice, made the old house on the property livable. Heitz, a true maverick, has made some of California's best Cabernets from Tom and Martha May's Oakville vineyard.

WHITE

☆ 1980 CHARDONNAY ($10.00) Napa Valley. *Perfumy and a bit strange.*
☆☆ 1981 JOHANNISBERG RIESLING ($6.50) Napa Valley.

RED

☆☆☆☆ 1968 CABERNET SAUVIGNON Martha's, Napa Valley. *Mint and chocolate. Firm, rich, assertive and big. Should live on.*
☆☆☆ 1968 CABERNET SAUVIGNON Napa Valley. *Elegant, refined, charming and balanced. At its peak now.*
☆☆☆☆ 1970 CABERNET SAUVIGNON Napa Valley. *Minty, rich, round, ripe, mouth filling.*
☆☆☆☆ 1973 CABERNET SAUVIGNON ($40.00) Martha's, Napa Valley. *Mint-eucalyptus character along with fruit and oak—stunning.*
☆☆☆☆ 1974 CABERNET SAUVIGNON ($55.00) Martha's, Napa Valley. *The best Martha's of the '70s. Stylish, deep, rich and magical.*
☆☆☆ 1975 CABERNET SAUVIGNON ($15.00) Fay, Napa Valley. *Less complicated than the '75 Martha's but quite enchanting.*
☆☆☆ 1975 CABERNET SAUVIGNON ($25.00) Martha's, Napa Valley. *Minty, soft and firm, with a velvety texture and great depth.*
☆☆ 1976 CABERNET SAUVIGNON ($20.00) Fay, Napa Valley. *Big, rich and concentrated from the drought. Ready now.*
☆☆☆ 1976 CABERNET SAUVIGNON ($25.00) Bella Oaks, Napa Valley. *The first Bella Oaks shows depth, richness and aging potential.*
☆☆ 1976 CABERNET SAUVIGNON ($35.00) Martha's, Napa Valley. *A bit disjointed. Blustery and big, lacking finesse.*
☆ 1977 CABERNET SAUVIGNON ($11.00) Napa Valley. *Damp, off-flavors mar this effort.*
☆☆ 1977 CABERNET SAUVIGNON ($17.50) Fay, Napa Valley. *Spicy fruit and oak, with good aging potential.*
☆☆☆☆ 1977 CABERNET SAUVIGNON ($35.00) Bella Oaks, Napa Valley. *Earthy, soft and velvety. Superb—better than Martha's '77.*
☆☆☆ 1977 CABERNET SAUVIGNON ($35.00) Martha's, Napa Valley. *Rich and intense but a bit short on fruit and somewhat weedy.*
☆☆ 1978 CABERNET SAUVIGNON ($11.00) Napa Valley.
☆☆ 1978 CABERNET SAUVIGNON ($12.75) Fay, Napa Valley.
☆☆☆☆ 1978 CABERNET SAUVIGNON ($20.00) Bella Oaks, Napa Valley.
☆ 1978 CABERNET SAUVIGNON ($27.00) Martha's, Napa Valley. *Very disappointing. Gluey, dull and lacking structure.*
☆☆☆☆ 1979 CABERNET SAUVIGNON ($30.00) Martha's, Napa Valley. *Mint and eucalyptus in nose, with fruit, oak, depth and richness. Age it.*
☆☆ 1980 CABERNET SAUVIGNON ($11.75) Napa Valley.
☆☆ 1980 CABERNET SAUVIGNON ($11.75) Napa Valley. *Lean, herbal, clean, with good structure. Drink 1986.*
☆☆☆ 1980 CABERNET SAUVIGNON ($25.00) Bella Oaks, Napa Valley.
☆☆☆ 1980 CABERNET SAUVIGNON ($35.00) Martha's, Napa Valley. *Minty, rich, complex, with wonderful structure and intensity. Drink 1988.*
☆ 1979 PINOT NOIR ($7.50) Napa Valley. *Tart, simple and clean.*
☆ 1981 ZINFANDEL ($6.25) Napa Valley. *Clean, decent.*

Henry Winery
OREGON

Hubbard Creek Road, Umpqua, Oregon 97486 (503-459-5120). FOUNDED: 1978. ACREAGE: 31 acres. PRODUCTION: 6,000 cases. DISTRIBUTION: 8 states. OWNER: Scott Henry. WINEMAKER: Scott Henry. Tours and tasting daily 11 A.M.–5 P.M.

Scott Henry is a native of the Umpqua Valley; his family started a homestead there 110 years ago. But although he had a background in farming, Scott was intent upon pursuing a career in aerospace, which eventually took him to California where he met Gino Zepponi of ZD Wines. Together they developed several new design ideas for winemaking equipment, and Scott gradually became engrossed in the whole enological process. Once he was back on the family farm, he planted some Napa vine cuttings. Then, after a class in winemaking and some consultation with Gino, Scott started making wine in 1978. Since then, Scott has been very active in the Oregon Winegrowers Association, trying to bring more public attention to the quality of Oregon wines and to forge a feeling of unity between the individual winegrowers of the state.

WHITE

☆　1979 CHARDONNAY ($9.00) Oregon. *Lacks depth.*

RED

☆☆　1979 PINOT NOIR ($9.00) Oregon. *Soft and complex, with good fruit and firm structure.*

Herbert Vineyards
EL DORADO COUNTY

P.O. Box 438, Somerset, California 95684 (916-626-0548). FOUNDED: 1980. ACREAGE: 12 acres. PRODUCTION: 800 cases. DISTRIBUTION: Northern California and Washington. OWNER: Frank Herbert. WINEMAKER: John MacCready. Tours and tasting by appointment.

Although wine is sold under its label, Herbert Vineyards is not a winery; it is a vineyard of Zinfandel and Sauvignon Blanc that Frank Herbert planted in 1974 on his family's vacation property in the Sierra foothills. At first, the Zinfandel was sold to nearby Sierra Vista Winery, where it was blended with wines from other vineyards. The Herbert Vineyards label was born when winemaker John MacCready decided to keep the Herbert vineyard lot separate. So Frank continues to grow his grapes and John makes the wine at Sierra Vista.

BLANC DE NOIR

☆☆　1984 WHITE ZINFANDEL ($5.00) El Dorado.

RED

☆☆　1980 ZINFANDEL ($6.00) Amador.
☆☆　1982 ZINFANDEL ($6.00) Herbert, El Dorado. *Rich, deep, clean, intense, quite nice.*

Heritage Vineyards
OHIO

6020 Wheelock Road, West Milton, Ohio 45383 (513-698-5369). FOUNDED: 1978. ACREAGE: 20 acres. PRODUCTION: 5,000 cases. DISTRIBUTION: Local. OWNERS: Edward Stefanko and John Feltz. WINEMAKER: Edward Stefanko. Tours and tasting Saturday 1 P.M.–9 P.M.

At the time the Stefanko family bought their farm, there was a rising demand for French-American hybrid grapes in Ohio. Planting twenty acres of hybrids, Edward Stefanko, who works for an electronics research company, figured his vineyard would bring in extra cash. But as fate would have it, Edward's vines came into production just as the market was reeling from a glut of wine grapes. There were no buyers for the Stefanko grapes. Taking the practical approach, Edward remodeled his 100-year-old barn, read winemaking textbooks, talked to winemakers, and dredged up every last bit of college chemistry he could remember. In record time he became a professional winemaker. With the help of his wife, who runs the tasting room, and his four children, Edward sees the winery as a possible early retirement project, but he's taking things one year at a time.

ᐧᐧᐧ

Heritage Wine Cellars
PENNSYLVANIA

12162 East Main Road, North East, Pennsylvania 16428 (814-725-8015). FOUNDED: 1977. ACREAGE: 400 acres. PRODUCTION: 15,000 cases. DISTRIBUTION: At winery-owned retail outlets. OWNER: Corporation. Kenneth Bostwick, president; Julia Bostwick, vice president. WINE-MAKER: Robert C. Bostwick. Tours and tasting Monday–Saturday 10 A.M.–6 P.M., Sunday 12–6 P.M.

It was Robert Bostwick's idea to start the winery. His family had been growing grapes in the Lake Erie wine region since 1833 on grandfather D. C. Bostwick's fruit farm. Robert's father, Kenneth, tore out the fruit trees to plant vineyards and start the family in the business of selling grapes and pressed juice. Meanwhile, Robert had been making wine as a hobby with his two brothers, Bill and Mike. The brothers started the family winery in a converted nineteenth-century barn, naming it "Heritage" in honor of the family's long tradition of grape growing. Today, the winery is owned by Robert and his parents.

ᐧᐧᐧ

Hermannhof
MISSOURI

330 East 1st Street, Hermann, Missouri 65041 (314-486-5959). FOUNDED: 1852. ACREAGE: 50 acres. PRODUCTION: 10,000 cases. DISTRIBUTION: Illinois and Missouri. OWNER: Dierberg family. James Dierberg, president. WINEMAKERS: Doug Lawton and Otto Klein. Tours and tasting Monday–Saturday 9:30 A.M.–5 P.M., Sunday 12–5:30 P.M.

This old pre-Prohibition brewery was being used as an apartment building when James Dierberg, a wealthy banker, bought it. He restored the building completely, clearing out the eight arched, underground caves and filling what was to be his new winery with German antiques. He added a sausage and cheese factory as well as a pottery shop to the facility. In the midst of all this, Mr. Dierberg did not fail to provide newly planted vineyards and modern equipment for the winery. He has also provided funding, equipment, and personnel for viticultural and enological research in the area.

WHITE

NV   WHITE LADY ($5.30) Missouri.
☆ NV   SEYVAL BLANC ($5.30) Missouri.

ᐧᐧᐧ

Heron Hill Vineyards
NEW YORK

Road 2, County Route 76, Hammondsport, New York 14840 (607-868-4241). FOUNDED: 1977. ACREAGE: 50 acres. PRODUCTION: 8,000 cases. DISTRIBUTION: New York. OWNER: Corporation. John Ingle, Jr., chairman; Peter Johnstone, president. WINEMAKER: Peter Johnstone. OTHER LABEL: Otter Spring. Tours and tasting May–November: Monday–Saturday 10 A.M.–5 P.M., Sunday 12–5 P.M. Gift shop.

There is no Heron Hill. There are vineyards and a winery, but there is no hill named "Heron." Peter Johnstone, with a background in advertising, and his partner, grape-grower John Ingle, Jr., decided on the name after extensive research on the visual appeal of certain animal-related names and label graphics. The final choice was between otters and herons. (The otter appears on the second label.) The winery, a stucco-and-timber building, is on top of a vine-covered hill overlooking Keuka Lake.

WHITE

☆☆ 1980 CAYUGA ($4.70) New York State. *Dry, crisp yet rounded; fruity, clean and attractive.*

☆☆ 1981 OTTER SPRING CAYUGA ($5.30) New York State. *Clean, fresh and dry, with great acidity. Very nice.*

1980 CHARDONNAY Special Reserve, Estate, New York State. *Vinous, green and thin.*

O 1980 OTTER SPRING FREE RUN CHARDONNAY ($7.00) Estate, New York State. *Odd, green nose. Oxidized and unattractive.*

☆ 1980 OTTER SPRING FREE RUN JOHANNISBERG RIESLING ($8.00) Estate, New York State. *Varietal, melony, off-dry, clean and a bit faint. Nice.*

☆ 1981 JOHANNISBERG RIESLING ($9.50) Estate, New York State. *Melony and sweet.*

☆☆☆ 1982 JOHANNISBERG RIESLING ($7.00) Estate, Ingle Vineyard, Finger Lakes. *Clean and fresh, with great fruit and long, rich flavors.*

☆☆ 1983 JOHANNISBERG RIESLING ($8.00) Estate, Ingle Vineyard, Finger Lakes. *1.8% residual sugar. Crisp, varietal and rich, with good acidity. Lovely.*

☆☆ 1982 RAVAT ($6.00) Finger Lakes Region. *Very appealing and fruity.*

☆ 1981 SEYVAL BLANC ($5.00) New York State. *Crisp, fresh, off-dry and decent.*

Hidden Cellars
MENDOCINO COUNTY

1500 Cunningham Road, Talmage, California 95481 (707-462-0301). FOUNDED: 1981. ACREAGE: None. PRODUCTION: 9,000 cases. DISTRIBUTION: California and 12 other states. OWNERS: Dennis Patton and Jim Salzman. WINEMAKER: Dennis Patton. Tours and tasting by appointment daily in summer 10 A.M.–5 P.M.

This operation was started by two young wine devotées, Dennis Patton and Joe Rawitzer, who were quite serious about Mendocino County as a premium grape-growing area. All their grapes are purchased from Mendocino County vineyards. Joe has since left, and Dennis Patton, also the winemaker, carries on with his slanted wine label (designed by Adler Fels's David Coleman) and new winery building.

WHITE

☆☆ 1982 CHARDONNAY ($9.50) Keith, Alexander Valley.

☆☆ 1983 CHARDONNAY ($10.00) Matheu, Mendocino. *Fruity, crisp, varietal, complex, attractive.*

☆☆ 1981 GEWURZTRAMINER ($7.50) Anderson Valley. *0.96% residual sugar. Clean, snappy, pleasant.*

☆☆ 1982 GEWURZTRAMINER ($8.00) Mendocino. *Crisp, dry and clean, with lots of zippy acidity.*

☆ 1983 GEWURZTRAMINER ($7.50) Anderson Valley, Mendocino. *Dry. Varietal, balanced, slightly bitter, decent.*

☆☆ 1982 JOHANNISBERG RIESLING ($7.50) Mendocino. *Botrytis, 5.8% residual sugar. Interesting and unusual.*

☆☆☆☆ 1982 JOHANNISBERG RIESLING ($10.00) Late Harvest, Bailey J. Lovin, Mendocino. *375ml. Botrytized, rich, sweet (8.1% residual sugar) and balanced.*

☆☆☆ 1983 JOHANNISBERG RIESLING ($7.50) Potter Valley, Mendocino. *Rich botrytis flavor. Deep, fruity and complex.*

☆   1981 SAUVIGNON BLANC ($8.00) Mendocino.
☆☆   1982 SAUVIGNON BLANC ($8.00) Mendocino. *20% barrel fermented. Clean and snappy,
        with some complexity.*
☆   1983 SAUVIGNON BLANC ($6.75) Turula, Mendocino. *Weird, thin, with strange flavors.*
O   1983 SAUVIGNON BLANC ($7.95) Turula, Mendocino. *Dirty and moldy.*

RED

☆☆   1981 ZINFANDEL ($7.75) Mendocino. *Rich but not overbearing.*
☆☆   1982 ZINFANDEL ($7.50) Mendocino. *Tangy, clean, decent.*

Hidden Springs Winery
OREGON

Route 1, Box 252-B, Amity, Oregon 97101 (503-835-2782). FOUNDED: 1980. ACREAGE: 25
acres. PRODUCTION: 3,300 cases. DISTRIBUTION: Oregon, Washington, and some midwestern
markets. OWNER: Corporation. Alvin Alexanderson, chairman; Don Byard, president; Mary Jo
Alexander and Carolyn Byard, vice presidents. WINEMAKERS: Al Alexanderson and Don Byard;
Rodrigue Deschenes, cellarmaster. Tours and tasting daily 12–5 P.M.; large groups by appointment.

Hidden Springs Winery is a joint venture between Don Byard, an urban planner, and Alvin
Alexanderson, an attorney for Portland General Electric. Since both men had some experience in
making wine on a small scale, they decided to combine their vineyard holdings and start a winery.
Their goal is to produce the finest Pinot Noir and Chardonnay in the world, and they feel Oregon
is the place to do it. All they need is a little more time and more clonal experimentation. Don, who
still works as a transportation planner for the State of Oregon, has become involved at Oregon
State University, where he is learning more about Oregon's microclimates.

RED

O   1981 PINOT NOIR Reserve, Oregon. *Stinky and unattractive.*

High Tor Vineyards
NEW YORK

High Tor Road, Box 641, New City, New York 10956 (914-634-7960). FOUNDED: 1950. ACRE-
AGE: 10 acres. PRODUCTION: 2,500 cases. DISTRIBUTION: Eastern states. OWNER: Christopher Wells. WINEMAKER: Alberto Giacomini. Tours and tasting weekends 12–5 P.M., weekdays
by appointment.

Long before the other New York wineries, High Tor Winery was making wines from strictly
New York–grown, French-American hybrids. Founder Everett Crosby, determined to make wines
that could compete with European imports, established a tradition that has been carried on by the
present owner, Christopher Wells. Christopher makes natural wines—without fining agents, sta-
bilizers, or chemicals of any sort—and uses mainly wood for storage and aging. He renovated the
original one-story winery building and added a farmhouse restaurant.

Highland Manor Winery
TENNESSEE

Highway 127 South, P.O. Box 203, Jamestown, Tennessee 38556 (615-879-9519). FOUNDED:
1979. ACREAGE: 8 acres. PRODUCTION: 2,000 cases. DISTRIBUTION: At winery. OWNER:

Corporation. Fay W. Wheeler, president. WINEMAKER: Fay W. Wheeler. Tours and tasting Monday–Saturday 10 A.M.–6 P.M.

"We're still in the dark ages in Tennessee as far as the wine laws are concerned, but we're working on it," says Fay Wheeler, vineyard and winery manager for the first licensed winery in Tennessee. "We have a saying: 'When the moon comes up in Tennessee, it's in gallon jugs.' Well, I wanted to change that image of Tennessee 'moonshine' by putting my wine in little green bottles." After twenty years in the Air Force, Fay retired to start his "glorified hobby" of growing grapes and making wine. He bemoans the fact that grape production in his state is not really sufficient to meet the demands of would-be winemakers, and yet the state law allows wineries to import only 15 percent of their grapes from other states. Regardless of these obstacles, Highland captured international gold medals for quality in 1983 and in 1984.

❧

William Hill Winery
NAPA COUNTY

P.O. Box 3989, Napa, California 94558 (707-224-6565). FOUNDED: 1976. ACREAGE: 1,400 acres. PRODUCTION: 25,000 cases. DISTRIBUTION: 42 states. OWNERS: Partnership. William Hill, president. WINEMAKER: William Hill; Mike Fallow, consultant. Tours by appointment.

An Oklahoman with a yen for hillside vineyards, Bill Hill got into winemaking by way of investment counseling. A group of clients had hired Bill to research agricultural properties, some of which included vineyard land. Although up to that point Bill hadn't had any opinions or thoughts about the wine industry, by the time he finished his research he was ready for a career in it. In 1974 he established a company for buying and developing vineyard land, and in 1976 started the winery in an old fruit juice plant. In ten years' time, William Hill Winery acquired over 1,200 acres of first-rate vineyard property in the Mount Veeder and Atlas Peak areas.

WHITE

☆☆☆ 1980 CHARDONNAY ($16.50) Napa Valley. *Enormous oak balanced by rich fruit and delicacy.*

☆☆ 1981 CHARDONNAY ($16.50) Mount Veeder-Napa Valley. *Big, earthy, oaky and complex.*

☆☆ 1982 CHARDONNAY ($10.50) Silver Label, California. *Clean, crisp and varietal.*

☆☆ 1982 CHARDONNAY ($16.50) Gold Label, Napa Valley. *Rich, varietal, vinous, oaky; very good.*

☆☆☆ 1982 CHARDONNAY ($25.00) Reserve, Napa Valley. *Rich and oaky yet crisp and fruity. Should age well.*

☆☆ 1983 CHARDONNAY ($10.50) Silver Label, Napa Valley. *Crisp, fresh, clean, balanced.*

RED

☆☆☆ 1978 CABERNET SAUVIGNON ($15.00) Mount Veeder-Napa Valley. *Great fruit in a classy package—intense, firm and beautiful.*

☆☆☆ 1979 CABERNET SAUVIGNON ($17.00) Mount Veeder-Napa Valley. *Rich, firmly structured and elegant. Will age 10 years or more.*

☆☆☆☆ 1980 CABERNET SAUVIGNON ($18.00) Napa Valley. *Rich, smooth, lean and elegant. Superb. Drink 1986 and later.*

☆☆☆ 1981 CABERNET SAUVIGNON ($16.00) Mount Veeder-Napa Valley. *Rich, angular, deep and stunning. Drink 1987.*

☆☆ 1982 CABERNET SAUVIGNON ($10.50) Silver Label, California. *50% Monterey. Fruity, simple, soft, earthy. Drink now.*

❧

Hillcrest Vineyard
OREGON

240 Vineyard Lane, Roseburg, Oregon 97470 (503-673-3709). FOUNDED: 1963. ACREAGE: 30 acres. PRODUCTION: 10,000 cases. DISTRIBUTION: Oregon. OWNER: Richard H. Sommer. WINEMAKER: Bill Nelson, enologist. Tours and tasting daily 10 A.M.–5 P.M.

Richard Sommer, a native San Franciscan, moved to Oregon from Davis, California, in search of the ideal climate in which to grow White Riesling. His studies in agriculture at U.C. Davis had led him to believe that the cooler climates in some parts of Oregon could be just right for certain vinifera varieties. In 1961, to test his theory, he planted some Napa Valley vine cuttings on his 40-acre farm, ten miles west of Roseberg. The dramatic success of these first plantings was the start of a serious wine industry in Oregon. In 1963 Richard built a rustic board-and-bat winery, and has expanded his vineyard planting to include Cabernet Sauvignon and Pinot Noir.

WHITE

1982 GEWURZTRAMINER ($7.00) Oregon. *Musty, dry and earthy; low in fruit.*
1981 WHITE RIESLING ($7.00) Oregon. *2.5% residual sugar. Musty, old and unattractive.*

RED

☆ 1979 CABERNET SAUVIGNON ($12.00) Oregon. *Rich, woody, decent.*
1980 CABERNET SAUVIGNON ($8.00) Oregon. *Peppery and crisp, with some volatile acidity. Odd.*
1979 PINOT NOIR ($11.00) Oregon. *Dull.*

HINEY BROTHERS *see* LaMont Winery

Hinman Vineyards
OREGON

27012 Briggs Hill Road, Eugene, Oregon 97405 (503-345-1945). FOUNDED: 1979. ACREAGE: 25 acres. PRODUCTION: 13,000 cases. DISTRIBUTION: Oregon, Washington, and California. OWNERS: Doyle W. and Betty Lou Hinman, Annette and David E. Smith, Richard and Jean Smith. WINEMAKERS: Doyle Hinman and David Smith. Tours and tasting weekends 12–5 P.M., or by appointment. Concert series during summer.

A schoolteacher, Doyle Hinman got started in the wine business after taking a seminar on grape growing and winemaking. He bought a piece of property, planted his first vines, and then took off for the Geisenheim Institute in Germany to study winemaking for six months. Upon his return, he joined with David Smith, who had helped Doyle with his vineyard and had also planted one of his own. Together, they started the winery in a small building on the Hinman property. Each year since then, the winery has doubled its production. Both David and Doyle work full time in the winery, which is now housed in a handsome building separated into three sections built around a sunny, grass amphitheater, where summer concerts are held.

WHITE

☆☆ 1983 TIOR ($4.50) Washington. *Spicy nose, fresh and fruity. Some heaviness but crisp and lovely.*
☆☆ 1981 CHARDONNAY ($6.00) Oregon. *Simple, clean and crisp.*

☆☆☆ 1981 GEWURZTRAMINER ($7.00) Oregon. *1.1% residual sugar. Lovely, varietal and clean.*

☆☆☆ 1982 GEWURZTRAMINER ($7.00) Willamette Valley, Oregon. *1.5% residual sugar. Fresh, fruity, varietal, balanced.*

☆☆ 1982 WHITE RIESLING ($7.00) Oregon. *3% residual sugar. Decent but dull and lacking fruit.*

BLANC DE NOIR

☆☆ 1981 PINOT NOIR ($6.00) Oregon. *Crisp, dry, clean, attractive.*

☆ 1982 WHITE PINOT NOIR ($4.50) Oregon.

RED

1980 CABERNET SAUVIGNON ($10.00) Washington. *Earthy, weedy and heavy.*

☆☆ 1980 PINOT NOIR ($9.00) Oregon.

Hinzerling Vineyards
WASHINGTON

1520 Sheridan Avenue, Prosser, Washington 99350 (509-786-2163). FOUNDED: 1976. ACREAGE: 23 acres. PRODUCTION: 6,000 cases. DISTRIBUTION: 5 states. OWNER: Wallace family. Mike Wallace, general manager. WINEMAKER: Mike Wallace. Tours and tasting April–December. Call for information.

While involved in medical research, Mike Wallace read about the studies on grape growing in Washington that were being conducted at Washington State University. His increasing interest in Washington's viticultural potential and his own home winemaking eventually led Mike to quit his research job and enroll at U.C. Davis to learn viticulture and winemaking. In 1972 he returned to Washington to start his Yakima Valley vineyard, also taking a job at Washington State University in grape and wine research. Six miles from his vineyards, Mike bought and transformed a huge cement-block produce garage into a winery.

WHITE

○ 1979 CHARDONNAY ($7.75) Estate, Yakima Valley. *Oily, oxidized and unattractive.*

○ 1980 CHARDONNAY ($8.75) Estate, Yakima Valley, Washington. *Intensely oxidized. Horrible.*

1981 CHARDONNAY ($7.75) Yakima Valley, Washington. *Bitter and strange; a bit oxidized.*

☆☆ 1981 GEWURZTRAMINER ($6.00) Estate, Yakima Valley. *0.25% residual sugar. Fresh and clean but a bit soft.*

○ 1981 WHITE RIESLING ($6.00) Yakima Valley. *Varnishy and odd.*

☆☆☆ 1982 WHITE RIESLING ($6.00) Yakima Valley, Washington. *1.5% residual sugar. Floral nose and crisp fruit. Lovely.*

RED

☆☆ 1978 CABERNET SAUVIGNON ($11.00) Yakima Valley. *Tart, crisp and cherry flavored.*

☆☆☆ 1979 CABERNET SAUVIGNON ($13.00) Yakima Valley. *Rich, tart and tannic. Lovely fruit. Drink 1986.*

☆☆ 1980 CABERNET SAUVIGNON ($12.00) Yakima Valley, Washington. *Lush and raisiny; attractive but on the heavy side.*

☆☆ 1981 CABERNET SAUVIGNON ($8.00) Yakima Valley. *16% Merlot, 2% Malbec. Grassy, unusual, decent. Drink now.*

HMR Estate Winery
SAN LUIS OBISPO COUNTY

Adelaide Road, Paso Robles, California 93446 (805-238-7143). FOUNDED: 1972. ACREAGE: 58 acres. PRODUCTION: 30,000 cases. DISTRIBUTION: 30 states. OWNER: Intra-Leisure, Inc. Ray Krause, general manager. WINEMAKER: Chris Johnson. OTHER LABEL: Santa Lucia Cellars. Tours by appointment. Tasting daily 11 A.M.–6 P.M. at 1145 24th Street, Paso Robles.

Tall and lanky cardiologist Dr. Stanley Hoffman planted the first French grape varieties in San Luis Obispo County in 1965. He chose an area that consultant André Tchelistcheff called a "jewel of ecological elements." The first wines were made in the doctor's garage, but a beautiful, modern winery was completed in 1975. The wines were made by Dr. Hoffman's son Michael (see Champs de Brionne Winery) and overseen by Tchelistcheff. Despite producing several good wines and achieving some critical attention, Hoffman Mountain Ranch was undercapitalized and went bankrupt in 1980. It was then purchased by a group of land developers in Redondo Beach. A new winemaker was hired, more acreage was planted, and HMR was financially revived with the help of some creative land development ideas.

WHITE

☆☆☆ 1979 CHARDONNAY ($15.00) Estate, Paso Robles. *Toasty and very elegant; good fruit and finesse.*

☆☆ 1980 CHARDONNAY ($10.00) Tepusquet, Central Coast.

1981 CHARDONNAY ($7.00) Vintner's Reserve, Paso Robles. *Thin and dull.*

1981 CHARDONNAY ($9.25) Central Coast Counties. *Lemony, low in varietal character.*

☆☆ 1982 CHARDONNAY ($8.00) Paso Robles. *Vinous, oaky, heavy, rich, attractive.*

☆☆ 1983 CHARDONNAY ($8.00) Paso Robles. *Soft, round, decent varietal character.*

☆ 1983 CHARDONNAY ($8.00) Paso Robles. *Woody, varietal, not clean.*

☆☆☆ 1982 CHENIN BLANC ($6.25) Paso Robles. *1.4% residual sugar. Snappy, fruity, clean; very appealing.*

1983 CHENIN BLANC ($5.50) Paso Robles. *Sweet, unattractive, lacking acidity.*

O 1982 PASO ROBLES RIESLING ($5.00) Estate, Paso Robles. *Sour and unpleasant.*

☆ 1983 SANTA LUCIA CELLARS SAUVIGNON BLANC ($5.25) Paso Robles. *Crisp and varietal, grassy, coarse.*

1983 SAUVIGNON BLANC ($8.00) Paso Robles. *Heavy, vinous, unattractive.*

BLANC DE NOIR

☆☆ 1983 PINOT NOIR BLANC ($6.00) Estate, Paso Robles. *0.7% residual sugar. Crisp, fresh, well made, charming.*

☆☆ 1984 PINOT NOIR BLANC ($5.25) Paso Robles. *0.8% residual sugar. Soft, clean, fresh, fruity.*

RED

☆☆☆ 1981 SANTA LUCIA CELLARS ($2.95) San Luis Obispo. *This "Burgundy" is clean and fresh and so is the label.*

☆☆☆ 1975 CABERNET SAUVIGNON ($25.00) Doctor's Reserve, Estate, Paso Robles. *Herbal, edgy, tangy, clean. It's aging well.*

☆ 1977 CABERNET SAUVIGNON ($26.00) Doctor's Reserve, Estate, Paso Robles. *Complex and well made but coarse and heavy.*

☆ 1979 CABERNET SAUVIGNON ($8.50) Central Coast. *Some vegetal quality and lots of oak seem to block the fruit.*

☆☆☆ 1979 CABERNET SAUVIGNON ($8.75) Hoffman, Paso Robles. *Cherries and full fruit. Lovely varietal character. Drink now.*

☆ 1979 CABERNET SAUVIGNON ($12.50) Paso Robles. *Well built but rather weedy.*

1980 CABERNET SAUVIGNON ($4.50) Santa Maria Valley. *Weedy.*

☆☆ 1978 PINOT NOIR ($10.00) Paso Robles. *Charming but without much depth.*

☆☆☆ 1980 PINOT NOIR ($15.00) Doctor's Reserve, Paso Robles. *Crisp cherry flavors, great structure; superb.*

☆☆ 1981 PINOT NOIR ($25.00) Doctor's Reserve, Estate, Paso Robles. *Rich, intense, earthy, herbaceous. Drink 1986.*

☆☆ 1982 PINOT NOIR ($4.50) Paso Robles. *Stemmy but solid and clean; a bit underripe but charming.*

☆☆ 1982 SANTA LUCIA CELLARS PINOT NOIR ($4.50) Paso Robles. *A bit stemmy but clean and varietal; somewhat underripe.*

☆☆ 1978 ZINFANDEL ($3.50) Sauret, Paso Robles. *Fresh and appealing; simple but very good.*

1979 ZINFANDEL ($6.00) San Luis Obispo.

☆ 1980 ZINFANDEL ($4.50) Paso Robles. *Simple but pleasant and fruity.*

HNW VINEYARDS *see* Louis Honig Cellars

The Hogue Cellars
WASHINGTON

Route 2, Box 2898, Prosser, Washington 99350 (509-786-4557). FOUNDED: 1982. ACREAGE: 250 acres. PRODUCTION: 25,000 cases. DISTRIBUTION: 7 states. OWNER: Hogue family. Mike Hogue, president and general manager. WINEMAKER: Rob Griffin; Mike Conway, consultant. Tours and tasting summer: Monday–Friday 10 A.M.–5 P.M., Saturday and Sunday 1 P.M.–5 P.M.; winter: Monday–Friday 12–5 P.M., Saturday and Sunday 1 P.M.–5 P.M.

Third generation farmer Mike Hogue started out with a huge family ranch that had been a successful producer of hops, Concord grapes, asparagus, and Scotch spearmint. Mike's first vinifera vineyard was planted in 1979; by 1982 he was ready to start a winery. The first 2,000 cases of Hogue wine were made in a rented warehouse with the help of Mike Conway (see Latah Creek Winery). The entire first year's production was sold to customers over a card table at the winery's new location in Prosser Industrial Park. Mike Conway continued to make the wine until 1984 when Rob Griffin from Preston Wine Cellars was hired as full-time winemaker.

WHITE

☆☆☆ 1983 CHENIN BLANC ($5.00) Yakima Valley. *1.9% residual sugar. Crisp, clean, snappy, super.*

☆☆☆ 1983 FUME BLANC ($7.50) Yakima Valley, Washington. *Rich, fragrant, round, varietal. Delightful.*

☆☆ 1982 WHITE RIESLING ($4.75) Schwartzman, Yakima Valley. *1.9% residual sugar. Fruity, fresh, well made.*

☆☆☆ 1983 WHITE RIESLING ($5.50) Washington State. *Crisp, tart, clean, delicate.*

☆☆☆ 1983 WHITE RIESLING ($6.00) Schwartzman, Yakima Valley. *1.8% residual sugar. Melony, clean, delicate, lovely.*

☆☆☆ 1983 WHITE RIESLING ($6.50) Markin, Estate, Yakima Valley. *4.5% residual sugar. Lush, fruity, complex, extraordinary.*

Louis Honig Cellars
NAPA COUNTY

850 Rutherford Road, P.O. Box 406, Rutherford, California 94573 (707-963-5618). FOUNDED: 1980. ACREAGE: 54 acres. PRODUCTION: 10,000 cases. DISTRIBUTION: California and other

states. OWNERS: Partnership. Bill Honig, Daniel Weinstein, and Rick Tracy, general managers. WINEMAKER: Rick Tracy. OTHER LABEL: HNW. No tours or tasting.

In 1966 Louis Honig and his family founded HNW Vineyards on land that was part of the Caymus Land Grant. In 1980 the family decided to make some wine from their own grapes and use the name HNW Vineyards. They tested the market with 500 cases of Sauvignon Blanc made at another winery. The following year, the family brought in the help of Rick Tracy, winemaker and vineyard manager, who became a partner in the winery. Rick, who holds a master's degree in viticulture from U.C. Davis and an undergraduate degree in science, worked for Austin Hills of Grgich Hills Cellars before he came to HNW. The winery name was changed to that of the founder, Louis Honig, in 1983.

WHITE

☆☆☆   1981 HNW SAUVIGNON BLANC ($8.00) Napa Valley. *Crisp and varietal, with nicely rounded edges.*
☆   1982 SAUVIGNON BLANC ($8.00) Napa Valley. *Odd, sulfurous odors mar this one.*
☆☆☆   1983 SAUVIGNON BLANC ($8.00) Estate, Napa Valley. *Round, fresh, clean, balanced.*

Hood River Vineyards
OREGON

4693 Westwood Drive, Hood River, Oregon 97031 (503-386-3772). FOUNDED: 1981. ACREAGE: 12 acres. PRODUCTION: 3,000 cases. DISTRIBUTION: Oregon and Washington. OWNER: Cliff Blanchette. WINEMAKER: Cliff Blanchette. Tours and tasting daily May–December 1 P.M.–5 P.M. Closed Friday.

One of the few eastern Oregon wineries making grape wines, Hood River was started by Cliff Blanchette and his wife when their home wine production began to exceed their own needs. Owners of a small fruit farm, the Blanchettes made fruit wine at home until they visited some friends in California who were growing grapes. "We figured if they could do it, we could too," says Cliff. They planted grapes and began to include grape wines in their home production. At the same time, Cliff, who owns a commercial glass business, was beginning to think about retiring. Since one of his five sons was showing an interest in farming, Cliff cleaned up the old cattle barn and started a winery to provide a retirement fund for himself and a salary for his son Tom.

WHITE

☆☆☆   1982 WHITE RIESLING ($6.50) Oregon. *Lush, varietal, crisply fruity, delicious.*

RED

   1981 PINOT NOIR ($7.50) Washington.
☆☆   1981 ZINFANDEL ($5.95) Washington. *Beaujolais-style. Pale, snappy, fruity, crisp.*

Hoodsport Winery
WASHINGTON

Star Route 1, Box 5, Hoodsport, Washington 98548 (206-877-9894). FOUNDED: 1980. ACREAGE: None. PRODUCTION: 8,000 cases. DISTRIBUTION: Washington and Idaho. OWNER: Hoodsport Winery, Inc. Dick and Peggy Patterson, general managers. WINEMAKER: Dick Patterson. Tasting daily 10 A.M.–6 P.M. on Hood Canal, 15 miles north of Shelton. Group tours by appointment.

In the small town of Hoodsport, Dick and Peggy Patterson had been running a small gift shop for four years before they started their own winery. Making both grape and fruit wines, the

Pattersons keep themselves busy all year long by buying both fresh and frozen fruit. Dick still works part time as a counselor and teacher, while Peggy helps run the winery. In 1983 the Pattersons enlarged the winery, giving themselves room to spread out, expand their production, and even hire some help.

✒

Hop Kiln Winery
SONOMA COUNTY

6050 Westside Road, Healdsburg, California 95448 (707-433-6491). FOUNDED: 1975. ACREAGE: 70 acres. PRODUCTION: 8,400 cases. DISTRIBUTION: California and 8 other states. OWNER: L. M. Griffin, Jr. WINEMAKER: Steve Strobl. Tours by appointment. Tasting daily 10 A.M.–5 P.M.

Dr. Martin Griffin, public health officer, internist, and wildlife conservationist, added vineyardist to his list of occupations when he bought an old hop farm and sheep ranch near Healdsburg. Discovering that wine grapes were a marketable commodity in the area, he planted vines and sold the fruit to neighboring wineries. The next project, which lasted fifteen years, was the careful restoration of the 1905 hop-drying barn and its conversion into a winery. In 1974 Dr. Griffin moved an abandoned Victorian house onto the property and started making wine in his renovated hop kiln.

WHITE

☆☆ 1982 A THOUSAND FLOWERS ($4.75) Russian River Valley. *Nice Riesling flavors, dry, clean.*

☆ 1983 A THOUSAND FLOWERS ($5.00) Sonoma. *Vinous, dry, decent blend of four premium varieties.*

O 1981 CHARDONNAY ($10.00) Russian River Valley. *What happened here? Oxidized and dead before its time.*

☆ 1982 CHARDONNAY ($9.00) Russian River Valley. *Nice, simple, low varietal character.*

☆ 1982 JOHANNISBERG RIESLING ($6.50) Russian River Valley. *1.5% residual sugar. Soft and a trifle flabby.*

☆☆ 1982 JOHANNISBERG RIESLING ($15.00) Late Harvest, Botrytis, Russian River Valley. *9% residual sugar. Intense, rich, deep, appealing.*

RED

☆☆ 1979 PRIMITIVO ($12.50) Sonoma. *Zinfandel. Snappy, intense, very good.*

☆☆☆ 1981 MARTY GRIFFIN'S BIG RED ($6.00) Russian River Valley. *Lovely, dense, forward, dark and delightful.*

☆☆☆ 1981 CABERNET SAUVIGNON ($9.00) Alexander Valley. *Earthy, big, concentrated. Fine aging potential.*

☆☆☆ 1976 PETITE SIRAH ($8.00) Russian River Valley. *Lovely balance, great fruit, intense without being heavy.*

☆☆☆ 1979 PETITE SIRAH ($8.50) Russian River Valley.

☆☆☆ 1981 PETITE SIRAH ($8.50) Russian River Valley. *Dark, lush and plummy, with great fruit. Drink now through 1988.*

☆☆ 1982 PETITE SIRAH ($10.00) Russian River Valley. *Clean, vinous, complex, fruity.*

☆ 1981 PINOT NOIR ($10.00) Russian River Valley.

☆ 1978 ZINFANDEL ($8.00) Russian River Valley. *This award-winning wine hasn't aged well.*

☆☆ 1980 ZINFANDEL ($8.00) Russian River Valley, Sonoma.

☆☆☆ 1981 ZINFANDEL ($8.50) Russian River Valley. *Crisp, clean, great fruit.*

✒

Hopkins Vineyard
CONNECTICUT

Hopkins Road, New Preston, Connecticut 06777 (203-868-7954). FOUNDED: 1979. ACREAGE: 20 acres. PRODUCTION: 3,500 cases. DISTRIBUTION: Connecticut. OWNERS: William and Judy Hopkins. WINEMAKER: William Hopkins. Tours and tasting weekends 11 A.M.–5 P.M.; May–December: daily 11 A.M.–5 P.M.

The Berkshire property overlooking Lake Waramaug had been farmed by the Hopkins family for nearly 200 years before Bill and Judy Hopkins began planting grapevines on the south-facing slopes. They planted French-American hybrids, adding more each year. In addition, they converted an ancient barn into a modern winery with a tasting room, whose large windows look down on the lake. The Hopkins have also created the Master Winemaker Society, which offers special wine prices, limited edition wines, and personalized labels to its members.

WHITE

☆ NV LAKESIDE WHITE ($4.75) American. *Semisweet, minty, with decent fruit.*
☆ NV WARAMAUG WHITE ($5.00) American. *Neutral nose, decent balance, clean, acceptable.*
☆ NV SEYVAL BLANC ($6.00) American. *Crisp, clean, not much else.*

RED

☆☆ NV BARN RED ($5.00) American. *Rich nose, crisp, fruity and tart flavors.*
☆☆ NV SACHEM'S PICNIC RED ($5.00) American. *Semisweet but clean, fresh and attractive.*

Hopper Creek Winery
NAPA COUNTY

6200 St. Helena Highway, P.O. Box 2785, Napa, California 94558 (707-252-8444). FOUNDED: 1980. ACREAGE: 7 acres. PRODUCTION: 8,400 cases. DISTRIBUTION: California. OWNER: Brad Terrill. Tours by appointment.

Through his management consulting business, Brad Terrill got to know quite a few winemakers. Being a true oenophile himself, he quietly slipped into the wine business. He bought property in 1979 and was the first to build a new winery under Napa County's "small winery ordinance," allowing him to make up to 20,000 gallons of wine. While still very much involved in his consulting business, Brad is by no means an absentee winery owner. He spends the majority of his time "totally buried in and committed to the winery."

Horizon Winery
SONOMA COUNTY

P.O. Box 191, Santa Rosa, California 95401 (707-544-2961). FOUNDED: 1977. ACREAGE: None. PRODUCTION: 5,500 cases. DISTRIBUTION: California. OWNER: Paul Gardner. WINE-MAKER: Paul Gardner. Tours by appointment on weekends.

It's hard to avoid the wine business when you live in the Russian River area of Sonoma County. Since many of Paul Gardner's friends were winemakers, grape growers, or home winemakers, he decided to get involved by turning his basement into a winery. Paul and his wife enjoy big, heavy-bodied red wines, so they seek out grapes from the older vineyards in the Dry Creek and Russian River areas, focusing most of their attention on Zinfandel.

RED

1979 ZINFANDEL ($7.50) Teldeschi Ranch, Sonoma.

☆☆☆   1980 ZINFANDEL ($8.00) Sonoma. *Rich, intense, with great fruit and good structure. Needs age.*

Houtz Vineyards
SANTA BARBARA COUNTY

P.O. Box 542, Los Olivos, California 93441 (805-688-8664). FOUNDED: 1984. ACREAGE: 16 acres. PRODUCTION: 4,500 cases. DISTRIBUTION: California. OWNERS: Dave and Margaret Houtz. WINEMAKER: Richard Longoria. Tours by appointment.

David and Margaret Houtz lived for years in Santa Monica, but their lifelong ambition was to have a farm, grow grapes, and make wine. To fullfill this dream, they moved from the city in 1980 to Los Olivos in the peaceful Santa Ynez Valley. David, who had been working in real estate in Los Angeles, designed a beautiful redwood-barn winery. While their house was being built, the Houtzes lived in a winery annex, which has since been converted into a cozy tasting room. David is in charge of the winery, and Margaret takes care of their full-fledged goat and chicken farm.

HS *see* Hultgren Samperton Winery

Huber Orchard Winery
INDIANA

Route 1, Box 202, Borden, Indiana 47106 (812-923-9463). FOUNDED: 1978. ACREAGE: 12 acres. PRODUCTION: 8,000 cases. DISTRIBUTION: At winery. OWNERS: Gerald and Carl Huber. WINEMAKER: Gerald Huber; Jim Duffy, assistant. Tours and tasting. Call for information.

The Huber family U-Pick Farm has over 100 acres of fruit trees, strawberries, vegetables, and even Christmas trees. The farm has been run by the family for five generations. Wanting to start a separate business in which their children could become involved, the Hubers decided to add a winery to the property. "Since we had made wine at home, the winery seemed to fit right in with our plans," Gerald Huber explains. The family transformed the dairy barn into a tasting-sales room and built the winery underground. The first vineyard was planted in 1983.

Hudson Valley Winery
NEW YORK

Blue Point Road, Highland, New York 12528 (914-691-7296). FOUNDED: 1907. ACREAGE: 80 acres. PRODUCTION: 20,000 cases. DISTRIBUTION: New York. OWNER: Herbert Feinberg. WINEMAKER: Sam Williams. Tours and tasting April–December: daily 10 A.M.–5 P.M.

In 1907 Alexander Bolognesi retired from a prosperous banking career in New York to start his own little Italian village on a high crest of land overlooking the Hudson. Planting vineyards, Alexander started with several stone winery buildings, a large family home, and spacious gardens surrounded by Italian-style villas. When Alexander died, his wife maintained the winery until 1972, when she sold it to Herbert Feinberg. Herbert kept the winery exactly the same, except for introducing the tourist trade to the village.

Hultgren Samperton Winery
SONOMA COUNTY

P.O. Box 1026, Healdsburg, California 95448 (707-433-5102). FOUNDED: 1978. ACREAGE: None. PRODUCTION: 10,000 cases. DISTRIBUTION: 12 states and 3 foreign markets. OWNERS: Leonard Hultgren and Gloria Samperton; Kathleen Mooney, general manager. WINEMAKER: Geoffrey Fischer. OTHER LABEL: HS. Tours and tasting by appointment only.

Ed Samperton's longtime friend, J. Leonard Hultgren, decided that if Ed couldn't be happy working in another man's winery then the two cronies should start their own operation. Their winery, located on a Dry Creek Valley hillside, is an unusual complex of energy-efficient geodesic domes in four parts. Ed Samperton left the partnership in 1984 and Kathleen Mooney became general manager.

RED

      1979 HS CABERNET SAUVIGNON ($11.25) Sonoma.
☆☆ 1979 CABERNET SAUVIGNON ($12.00) Sonoma. *Rich and firm, with lovely structure. Needs some age.*

Robert Hunter
NAPA COUNTY

3027 Silverado Trail, St. Helena, California 94574 (707-963-7108). FOUNDED: 1979. ACREAGE: 40 acres. PRODUCTION: 8,000 cases. DISTRIBUTION: California and 20 other states. OWNER: Sonoma Valley Cellars. Robert Hunter, general partner; Dan Duckhorn, general manager. WINE-MAKER: Dimitri Tchelistcheff, technical consultant. Sparkling wine is made at Château St. Jean's champagne facility in Graton, although the business offices are at Duckhorn Vineyards in St. Helena.

Robert Hunter has a top-quality vineyard of Chardonnay, Pinot Noir, and Pinot Blanc in Glen Ellen. Although content selling his white varieties to premium wineries, he became concerned about the future of his Pinot Noir since, at the time, there was little demand for the variety. He consulted his friend Dan Duckhorn, who suggested making sparkling wine from it. As it turned out, Château St. Jean's new sparkling wine facility had excess space, and the winemaker, Pete Downs, agreed to oversee production on the Hunter cuvée. The winery has just purchased land and plans to build a separate winemaking facility.

SPARKLING

☆☆ 1982 BRUT DE NOIRS ($20.25) Sonoma Valley. *Crisp, clean, balanced, attractive.*

Husch Vineyards
MENDOCINO COUNTY

4900 Star Route, Philo, California 95466 (707-895-3216). FOUNDED: 1971. ACREAGE: 200 acres. PRODUCTION: 12,000 cases. DISTRIBUTION: 5 states. OWNER: H. A. Oswald family. WINEMAKER: Mark Theis. Tours by appointment. Tasting daily summer: 10 A.M.–6 P.M.; winter 10 A.M.–5 P.M. Picnic facilities.

The Oswald family bought the Husch winery from Tony and Gretchen Husch in 1978, chosing to keep the winery's name. Hugo Oswald, Sr., and his family are vineyardists and fruit growers who own two grape-growing ranches in the Anderson Valley and one in the Ukiah Valley. For several years, Hugo's son Hugo, Jr., a quiet young man, was making the wine in this rustic, old barn winery. Now Hugo Sr. oversees the day-to-day operations; Rich Robinson, his son-in-law, is general manager; and Mark Theis makes the wine.

WHITE

☆☆ 1981 CHARDONNAY ($9.00) Mendocino. *Nicely built, with good structure and snappy fruit.*

☆☆ 1982 CHARDONNAY ($9.00) Estate, Anderson Valley. *Rich, vinous, smooth, ripe and lush.*

☆☆☆ 1982 CHARDONNAY ($9.00) La Ribera Ranch, Mendocino. *Crisp and bright, with good structure and great fruit acidity.*

☆☆ 1983 CHARDONNAY ($10.00) Mendocino. *Crisp, fresh, not much depth.*

☆☆☆ 1984 CHENIN BLANC ($6.00) La Ribera, Estate, Mendocino. *Crisp, clean, some spritz, attractive.*

☆☆☆ 1984 GEWURZTRAMINER ($6.00) Estate, Anderson Valley. *1.2% residual sugar. Crisp, fresh, snappy, charming food wine.*

☆ 1981 SAUVIGNON BLANC ($7.00) Estate, La Ribera Ranch, Mendocino.

1982 SAUVIGNON BLANC ($7.00) Estate, La Ribera Ranch, Mendocino.

☆☆☆ 1983 SAUVIGNON BLANC ($7.50) La Ribera, Estate, Mendocino. *Fresh, clean, varietal, lovely.*

☆☆☆ 1984 SAUVIGNON BLANC ($7.00) La Ribera Ranch, Estate, Mendocino. *Fresh, round, fruity, complex, very appealing.*

RED

☆☆☆ 1981 CABERNET SAUVIGNON ($10.00) La Ribera, Mendocino. *Fruity, oaky, balanced, structured. Drink 1986 and beyond.*

☆ 1982 CABERNET SAUVIGNON ($10.00) La Ribera Ranch, Estate, Mendocino. *Varietal, bitter, lacking fruit.*

☆ 1981 PINOT NOIR ($8.00) Anderson Valley.

Inglenook Vineyards
NAPA COUNTY

1991 St. Helena Highway South, Rutherford, California 94573 (707-963-2616). FOUNDED: 1879. ACREAGE: 1,200 acres. PRODUCTION: 150,000 cases premium varietals, 7 million cases Navelle jug wines. DISTRIBUTION: Nationwide. OWNER: Hueblein, Inc. Dennis Fife, general manager. WINEMAKER: John Richburg and Michael Weis. Tours and tasting daily 10 A.M.–5 P.M.

In 1879 fur-trading sea captain Gustave Niebaum bought the Inglenook vineyard and built a large Gothic winery, which thrived until Prohibition. In 1933 the winery was reopened by Carl Bundschu (of the Gundlach-Bundschu family) and John Daniel, the grandnephew of Niebaum's widow, Suzanne. For the next 30 years Inglenook produced some of California's finest wines, many of which are still excellent today. Then in 1964 the winery was sold to Heublein, which expanded production and lowered quality. Inglenook seems to have reached bottom in the 1970s and is now staging a comeback under new management.

WHITE

☆ NV NAVALLE CHABLIS ($2.80) California. *Fresh, fat, off-dry, decent.*

☆ 1982 CHARDONNAY ($7.00) Cabinet Selection, Napa Valley. *Simple, clean, decent.*

☆☆ 1982 CHARDONNAY ($9.00) Estate, Napa Valley. *Simple, crisp, clean, fruity.*

☆ 1982 CHARDONNAY ($14.00) Special Reserve, Estate, Napa Valley. *Small lot. Overdone, vinous and oaky.*

☆☆ 1983 CHARDONNAY ($9.50) Estate, Napa Valley. *Crisp, fresh, varietal and well balanced.*

☆☆ 1983 CHARDONNAY ($16.00) Limited Reserve Select, Napa Valley. *Heavy flavors, low fruit, not altogether pleasant.*

☆☆ 1982 CHENIN BLANC ($5.50) Estate, Napa Valley. *1% residual sugar. Fruity and clean but a bit thin.*

☆☆ 1983 CHENIN BLANC ($5.75) Napa Valley.

☆ 1981 FUME BLANC ($6.75) Estate, Napa Valley.

☆☆ 1982 FUME BLANC ($7.00) Estate, Napa Valley. *Clean, smoky, crisp; nicely made.*

☆ 1982 FUME BLANC ($10.00) Special Reserve, Estate, Napa Valley. *Big, oaky and clean but heavy and dull.*

☆☆ 1981 GEWURZTRAMINER ($5.50) Estate, Napa Valley.

☆☆ 1982 JOHANNISBERG RIESLING ($6.87) Napa Valley. *1.5% residual sugar. Dry, crisp and appealing.*

☆☆ 1981 MUSCAT ($8.00) Napa Valley. *Dry, crisp and appealingly varietal.*

☆☆☆ 1983 SAUVIGNON BLANC ($7.50) Estate, Napa Valley. *18% Semillon. Lush, fresh, round, varietal.*

☆☆☆ 1983 SAUVIGNON BLANC ($10.00) Reserve, Estate, Napa Valley. *Fruity and crisp, with great depth and style.*

RED

☆☆☆ 1955 CABERNET SAUVIGNON Napa Valley. *Remarkably youthful and richly complex. A lovely wine.*

☆☆ 1974 CABERNET SAUVIGNON ($40.00) Cask, Estate, Napa Valley. *Ripe, intense and good but lacking some complexity.*

☆☆ 1976 CABERNET SAUVIGNON Cask 59, Napa Valley.

☆☆☆ 1977 CABERNET SAUVIGNON ($10.00) Limited Cask, Napa Valley. *Rich, earthy, elegant and very French. Will age for years.*

☆☆ 1977 CABERNET SAUVIGNON ($13.00) Napa Valley. *Nice but short.*

☆☆ 1978 CABERNET SAUVIGNON ($6.00) Napa Valley. *Simple but charming and easy-going.*

☆☆ 1978 CABERNET SAUVIGNON ($8.50) Cask 14, Estate, Napa Valley.

☆☆☆ 1978 CABERNET SAUVIGNON ($14.00) Limited Cask, Estate, Napa Valley. *Soft, elegant, clean and firm. Good aging potential.*

☆☆☆ 1979 CABERNET SAUVIGNON ($7.00) Centennial, Napa. *Clean and nice; herbal and delightful. Drink now.*

☆☆ 1979 CABERNET SAUVIGNON ($14.00) Limited Cask, Centennial, Napa Valley. *Herbal, clean and attractive but slight. Drink now.*

☆ 1980 CABERNET SAUVIGNON ($5.00) Cabinet Selection, Napa Valley. *Herbal, dense, clean, a bit short.*

☆☆ 1980 CABERNET SAUVIGNON ($8.00) Estate, Napa Valley. *12% Merlot. Soft, clean, simple but nice. Drink now.*

☆☆☆ 1980 CABERNET SAUVIGNON ($9.00) Lot 2, Estate, Napa Valley. *Bright, lush, clean, fruity. Drink 1986.*

☆☆☆ 1980 CABERNET SAUVIGNON ($19.00) Limited Cask Reserve, Napa Valley. *Stunning. Crisp, clean, elegant, complex. Drink 1986.*

☆ 1981 CABERNET SAUVIGNON ($5.00) Cabinet, Napa Valley. *Lacking varietal definition and depth.*

☆ 1977 CHARBONO ($6.50) Napa Valley.

☆ 1980 CHARBONO ($8.50) Napa Valley.

☆☆ 1983 CHARBONO ($7.00) Napa Valley.

☆☆ 1980 MERLOT ($10.00) Limited Bottling, Napa Valley. *Soft, lush, clean, well made.*

☆☆ 1981 MERLOT ($12.00) Limited Cask, Estate, Napa Valley. *Rich, deep, clean and varietal.*

☆☆☆ 1980 PETITE SIRAH ($6.90) Estate, Napa Valley. *Rich, fruity and very lovely.*

☆☆☆ 1981 PETITE SIRAH ($6.00) Napa Valley. *Varietal, lush, balanced.*

☆☆ 1980 PINOT NOIR ($6.00) Napa Valley. *Soft, complex and well balanced.*

☆☆ 1981 PINOT NOIR ($7.50) Napa Valley. *Clean, simple.*

1978 ZINFANDEL ($6.50) Napa Valley. *Dreary, non-varietal, dull.*

☆ 1980 ZINFANDEL ($5.50) Napa Valley. *Tannic; decent but low in fruit.*

☆☆ 1981 ZINFANDEL ($7.00) Napa Valley. *Claret style. Clean and balanced.*

Ingleside Plantation Winery
VIRGINIA

P.O. Box 1038, Oak Grove, Virginia 22443 (804-224-7111). FOUNDED: 1980. ACREAGE: 35 acres. PRODUCTION: 10,000 cases. DISTRIBUTION: 4 states. OWNER: Ingleside Plantation, Inc. Douglas Flemer, general manager. WINEMAKER: Jacques Recht. Tours and tasting Thursday–Sunday 1 P.M.–5 P.M., or by appointment.

Carl Flemer, owner of Ingleside Plantation Nursery—a large wholesale nursery, had a notion that Virginia's climate and soils were similar to Bordeaux. Planting a few grapevines on what was once the family's dairy farm, Carl made wines at home. These wines were such a success with friends and family that Carl began thinking about the commercial possibilities. He built a winery out of his old barn and hired Jacques Recht, a retired Belgian enologist, to become the winery's winemaker. Now the winery is run by Carl's son Douglas, who learned about the wine business on trips to California and France.

WHITE

☆ 1983 CHARDONNAY ($10.00) Virginia. *Soft, simple.*
☆ 1983 RIESLING ($6.50) Virginia. *Good nose; decent but watery, with some off flavors.*
☆ 1983 SEYVAL BLANC ($4.75) Virginia. *Varietal, decent but a bit watery and slight.*

SPARKLING

☆ NV CHAMPAGNE ($10.00) Virginia. *Yeasty nose; crisp, clean and nice. Méthode champenoise.*

RED

☆☆ 1983 NOUVEAU RED ($4.00) Virginia. *Snappy, fresh, clean, quite good.*
O 1980 CABERNET SAUVIGNON ($7.00) Virginia. *Gluey, weird.*

Iron Horse Vineyards
SONOMA COUNTY

9786 Ross Station Road, Sebastopol, California 95472 (707-887-2913). FOUNDED: 1979. ACREAGE: 145 acres. PRODUCTION: 25,000 cases. DISTRIBUTION: Nationwide. OWNERS: Barry and Audrey Sterling, and Forrest Tancer. WINEMAKER: Forrest Tancer. OTHER LABEL: Tin Pony. Tours, tasting, and retail sales by appointment.

Native San Franciscan Forrest Tancer had managed the Iron Horse Vineyards for several years before it was put up for sale. Fearful that the property might be plowed under to make room for a housing development, Forrest was relieved when Barry Sterling, an American attorney who had practiced in Paris for eight years, bought the property to fulfill a longtime dream of owning a winery. The Sterlings and Forrest formed a partnership, and Barry and Audrey Sterling set about turning the rundown main house into one of Sonoma's true showplaces, which they surrounded with magnificent gardens. Forrest began replanting the vineyards and making wines that were, from their first release, very well received. With the 1980 vintage, the winery began to produce a high-quality line of sparkling wines. Iron Horse Vineyards is one of the California wine country's most dramatic success stories.

WHITE

☆☆ 1980 CHARDONNAY ($11.00) Barrel Fermented, Sonoma. *A bit heavy and low in fruit.*
☆☆ 1981 CHARDONNAY ($12.00) Green Valley, Sonoma. *Complex, clean, apple-fruity, attractive.*

☆☆ 1982 TIN PONY CHARDONNAY ($6.00) Green Valley, Sonoma. *Vinous, simple, a little bitter.*

☆☆ 1982 CHARDONNAY ($13.00) Estate, Green Valley, Sonoma. *Tight and hard. Should improve with age.*

☆☆ 1983 CHARDONNAY ($12.00) Green Valley, Sonoma. *Clean, fresh, tangy, nice oak, pleasant but lacking varietal intensity.*

☆☆☆ 1984 CHARDONNAY ($12.00) Estate, Green Valley, Sonoma. *Lush, clean, rich, fruity, firm.*

☆☆ 1982 FUME BLANC ($11.00) Proprietor Grown, Alexander Valley, Sonoma. *Balanced and fruity, low varietal character.*

☆☆☆ 1983 FUME BLANC ($8.75) Alexander Valley. *Fresh, soft, crisp, round and fruity.*

SPARKLING

☆☆ 1980 BLANC DE BLANCS ($16.50) Green Valley, Sonoma. *Made from Chardonnay grapes. Crisp and dry, with good acid.*

☆☆ 1981 BLANC DE BLANCS ($18.00) Estate, Green Valley, Sonoma. *Dense, lush, clean, charming.*

☆☆☆ 1982 BLANC DE BLANCS ($16.50) Estate, Green Valley, Sonoma. *Crisp, angular, tangy, with Chardonnay varietal character.*

☆☆☆ 1981 BLANC DE NOIR ($16.50) Estate, Green Valley, Sonoma. *Rich, deep, complex, clean and lovely.*

☆☆☆ 1982 WEDDING BLANC DE NOIR ($16.50) Cuvée, Estate, Green Valley, Sonoma. *Deep, round, good Pinot Noir character, charming.*

☆☆☆ 1980 BRUT ($16.50) Estate, Green Valley, Sonoma. *Pinot Noir. Richly flavored, complex and elegant. Superb.*

☆☆ 1981 BRUT ($19.00) Estate, Green Valley, Sonoma.

☆☆☆ 1982 BRUT ($16.50) Estate, Green Valley, Sonoma. *Lush, round, rich, fruity and clean.*

BLANC DE NOIR

☆☆☆ 1982 BLANC DE PINOT NOIR ($6.75) Estate, Green Valley, Sonoma. *Dry, snappy, delicious.*

☆☆ 1983 BLANC DE PINOT NOIR ($6.50) Green Valley, Sonoma. *Dry, clean, crisp.*

RED

☆ NV TIN PONY RED ($4.00) Sonoma. *95% Pinot Noir. Decent.*

☆☆☆ 1978 CABERNET SAUVIGNON ($12.00) Sonoma. *Herbal and elegant, with plenty of time left. Drink now.*

☆☆☆ 1979 CABERNET SAUVIGNON ($12.00) Alexander Valley. *Soft, balanced, lovely fruit, delightful.*

☆☆☆ 1980 CABERNET SAUVIGNON ($12.00) Estate, Alexander Valley. *Sleek, clean and richly flavored. Drink now.*

☆☆☆☆ 1981 CABERNET SAUVIGNON ($13.50) Estate, Green Valley, Sonoma. *Crisp, beautifully structured, clean and elegant. Drink 1986.*

☆☆ 1979 PINOT NOIR ($10.75) Sonoma.

☆☆ 1980 PINOT NOIR ($13.50) Estate, Sonoma.

☆☆ 1982 PINOT NOIR ($13.50) Estate, Green Valley, Sonoma. *Clean, elegant, varietal.*

☆☆ 1981 ZINFANDEL ($6.50) Alexander Valley. *Varietal and clean; fruity and attractive.*

☆☆ 1982 ZINFANDEL ($7.00) Alexander Valley. *Spicy, rich, hard, intense. Needs a year or two to mellow.*

ॐ

ITALIAN SWISS COLONY *see* Colony

Jaeger Family Wine Company
NAPA COUNTY

P.O. Box 322, St. Helena, California 94574 (707-963-9694). FOUNDED: 1979. ACREAGE: 40 acres. PRODUCTION: 4,000 cases. DISTRIBUTION: California, Colorado, and Ohio. OWNER:

Jaeger family. William, Sr., William, Jr., Jeff, and Jack Jaeger. WINEMAKER: Phil Baxter. No tours or tasting.

Bill Jaeger, general manager of Rutherford Hill and Freemark Abbey wineries, lives on a 100-year-old ranch known as the Inglewood estate. With 40 acres of Merlot vines on the property, Bill decided to start a family label using only the Jaeger family grapes, the expertise of winemaker Phil Baxter, and the crushing facilities at Rutherford Hill. The wine is aged and stored in a new stone building and cave at the estate. "At one time there was a winery on the Inglewood property," says Bill Jaeger, Jr., who manages the Jaeger vineyards. "Dad wanted to revive the estate's history of winemaking."

RED

☆☆   1979 MERLOT ($12.00) Inglewood, Napa Valley. *Mellow, complex, rich. Drink now.*
☆☆   1980 MERLOT ($12.00) Inglewood, Napa Valley. *Rich, berried, clean, good. Drink 1987.*
☆☆   1981 MERLOT ($12.00) Inglewood, Napa Valley. *Fruity, varietal, attractive.*

JEFFERSON CELLARS *see* Monticello Cellars

Jekel Vineyard
MONTEREY COUNTY

40155 Walnut Avenue, Greenfield, California 93927 (408-674-5522). FOUNDED: 1978. ACREAGE: 140 acres. PRODUCTION: 50,000 cases. DISTRIBUTION: Nationwide; Canada and the United Kingdom. OWNERS: Bill and Gus Jekel. WINEMAKER: Rick Jekel. Tours and tasting Thursday–Monday 10 A.M.–5 P.M.

In 1972 twins Bill and Gus Jekel, both Hollywood movie producers, established this vineyard in the lower Salinas Valley. Their first release of Johannisberg Riesling in 1978 caused a sensation. The combination of cool, foggy days, a long growing season, and skillful winemaking by Dan Lee (see Durney Vineyards and Morgan Winery) had created a California classic. Since then, Jekel has also been quite successful with Chardonnay and Cabernet Sauvignon.

WHITE

☆☆☆   1980 CHARDONNAY ($10.00) Monterey. *Clean and well balanced.*
☆☆   1980 CHARDONNAY ($14.50) Private Reserve, Estate, Monterey. *Big, rich and assertive. Lots of flavor but lacking grace.*
☆☆☆   1981 CHARDONNAY ($10.00) Monterey. *Clean, snappy, very appealing.*
☆☆☆   1981 CHARDONNAY ($14.50) Private Reserve, Estate, Monterey. *Crisp, clean and very angular.*
         1982 CHARDONNAY ($10.00) Monterey. *Nice fruit and oak but marred by volatile acidity.*
☆☆   1982 CHARDONNAY ($10.50) Home, Arroyo Seco.
☆☆   1982 CHARDONNAY ($14.50) Private Reserve, Estate, Monterey. *Clean, fresh, simple. Should improve with age.*
☆☆☆☆   1979 JOHANNISBERG RIESLING ($20.00) Late Harvest, Estate, Monterey. *10% residual sugar. Rich, complex, botrytized, superb.*
         1980 JOHANNISBERG RIESLING ($10.00) Late Harvest, Estate, Monterey. *375ml. 16% residual sugar. Soft, flabby.*
☆☆☆   1981 JOHANNISBERG RIESLING ($6.50) Home, Monterey. *Pretty, crisp and fresh.*
☆☆☆☆   1981 JOHANNISBERG RIESLING ($6.50) Ventana, Monterey. *Rich fruit, crisp acidity, lovely, intense, a classic.*
☆☆☆   1981 JOHANNISBERG RIESLING ($12.00) Late Harvest, Estate, Monterey. *12.8% residual sugar. Lush, somewhat simple, clean, good.*
☆☆   1982 JOHANNISBERG RIESLING ($6.50) Arroyo Seco, Monterey. *2.2% residual sugar. Melony and attractive.*

1982 JOHANNISBERG RIESLING ($6.75) Home, Monterey. *Surprisingly dull and tired.*

☆☆ 1983 JOHANNISBERG RIESLING ($6.75) Monterey. *Ripe, fat, a bit softer than usual.*

☆   1981 PINOT BLANC ($7.50) Home, Monterey. *Clean and nicely balanced but a bit dull.*

☆☆☆ 1982 PINOT BLANC ($7.50) Home, Monterey. *Fat, clean and attractive.*

RED

NV CABERNET SAUVIGNON ($4.90) California.

☆   1977 CABERNET SAUVIGNON ($12.50) Monterey. *Nicely built, some weediness, fat, dense. Initial release.*

1978 CABERNET SAUVIGNON ($12.00) Private Reserve, Estate, Monterey. *Overwhelmed by weediness.*

☆☆☆ 1979 CABERNET SAUVIGNON ($10.00) Estate, Monterey.

☆   1979 CABERNET SAUVIGNON ($16.50) Private Reserve, Estate, Monterey. *Weedy, raisiny, oaky, heavy.*

☆   1981 CABERNET SAUVIGNON ($10.00) 65% Monterey, 35% San Luis Obispo. *Lush, raisiny but a bit weedy. Drink 1987.*

☆☆ 1979 PINOT NOIR ($8.50) Estate, Monterey. *Toasty and clean.*

☆☆ 1980 PINOT NOIR ($9.00) Home, Monterey. *Stemmy but nicely made. Good fruit.*

☆☆ 1981 PINOT NOIR ($9.00) Home, Monterey. *Burgundian but a bit underripe.*

Louis Jindra Winery
OHIO

2701 Camba Road, C.R. 15, Jackson, Ohio 45640 (614-286-6578). FOUNDED: 1980. ACREAGE: 20 acres. PRODUCTION: 2,000 cases. DISTRIBUTION: Ohio. OWNERS: Dr. Louis J. and Louis V. Jindra. WINEMAKER: Louis V. Jindra. Tours and tasting Tuesday–Saturday 12–8 P.M.

When Dr. Louis Jindra asked his son Louis V. what he wanted to do when he finished school, the young man replied without hesitation that he wanted to start a winery. Although nonplussed, the doctor said "why not?" and the two set out to find vineyard land. The doctor was working at the local hospital at the time, and Louis V. supported his new vineyard by working as a state investigator. The Jindras sold their grapes to other wineries until they finally decided to convert their apple barn into a winery and construct a tasting room, the walls of which are lined with timber from seven different local barns. Situated in Ohio's southeastern hills, the winery makes only estate wines, which are sold mainly at the winery.

Johlin Century
OHIO

3935 Corduroy Road, Oregon, Ohio 43616 (419-693-6288). FOUNDED: 1870. ACREAGE: 1 acre. PRODUCTION: 3,500 cases. DISTRIBUTION: Local. OWNER: Richard Johlin. WINEMAKER: Richard Johlin. Tours and tasting Monday–Saturday 11 A.M.–6 P.M.

Richard Johlin, a somewhat gruff, reticent fellow, runs the family winery that was started by his German grandfather. At that time, the winery was underneath the family house, but it is now located in a concrete building next door. Richard has always worked in the winery, first with his uncle and now as sole proprietor. After his uncle died three years ago, the name of the winery was changed from Edward W. Johlin to Johlin Century. Over the years changes have come slowly, but Richard has just started his first experimental vineyard.

Johnson Estate
NEW YORK

Box 52, Westfield, New York 14787 (716-326-2191). FOUNDED: 1961. ACREAGE: 125 acres. PRODUCTION: 10,000 cases. DISTRIBUTION: 3 states. OWNER: Fredrick S. Johnson. WINE-MAKER: William A. Gulvin. Tours daily July–August 10 A.M.–5:30 P.M. Tasting daily 10 A.M.–6 P.M.

Traveling the world over as a tropical agricultural consultant, Fredrick Johnson had seen grapevines grow in some pretty bizarre places. When he returned home and bought his father's farm in 1961, he saw no reason why quality grapes could not be produced in his own front yard. Fredrick's father had been an entomologist and had planted a mixed fruit farm on the property. Fred converted the farm into a vineyard and used the cold storage room for a winery. Located in the center of Lake Erie's viticultural area, the Johnson Estate is the oldest family-owned winery in the state.

Johnson Turnbull Vineyards
NAPA COUNTY

8210 St. Helena Highway, P.O. Box 41, Oakville, California 94562 (707-963-5839). FOUNDED: 1979. ACREAGE: 20 acres. PRODUCTION: 2,500 cases. DISTRIBUTION: 12 states. OWNERS: Reverdy and Marta S. Johnson, and William Turnbull, Jr. WINEMAKER: Lawrence Wara, consulting enologist. Tours and tasting by appointment.

Architect William Turnbull, lawyer Reverdy Johnson, and his wife, Marta, purchased twenty acres of Cabernet vineyard plus an old house and barn right across the highway from Robert Mondavi Winery. In 1977 William sold the grapes to Charles Krug, "but in 1978, the grapes didn't have a home and we began to realize that grape growing on its own can be hazardous." They believed in the quality of the grapes, since Cakebread Cellars had made a fine 1978 Cabernet from them. So in 1979 they bonded the barn. While the small winery is only making Cabernet at present, William says they may be making Chardonnay by 1988.

RED

☆☆ 1979 CABERNET SAUVIGNON ($10.50) Estate, Napa Valley. *Good structure and fruit. Underripe but pleasant. Drink now.*

☆☆☆ 1980 CABERNET SAUVIGNON ($12.00) Napa Valley. *Balanced and charming now, will improve for years.*

☆☆☆ 1981 CABERNET SAUVIGNON ($12.00) Napa Valley. *Lovely nose, lush, fruity. Not as elegant as the '80. Drink 1987.*

Johnson's Alexander Valley Winery
SONOMA COUNTY

8333 State Highway 128, Healdsburg, California 95448 (707-433-2319). FOUNDED: 1975. ACREAGE: 45 acres. PRODUCTION: 10,500 cases. DISTRIBUTION: California and 13 other states. OWNER: Johnson family. Jay Johnson, president; Will Johnson, vice president; Tom Johnson, manager. WINEMAKER: Tom Johnson. OTHER LABEL: J. D. Martin. Tours and tasting daily 10 A.M.–5 P.M. Organ concerts monthly in summer. Picnic areas.

In 1952 James Johnson tore out most of the vines on the old Whitten Ranch in Healdsburg and kept the acres of prune and pear trees. "There's no money in grapes," he said. In 1975 his three sons replanted the property with grapes and began the family winery. Tom Johnson, the prime mover in this new venture, got his brothers Jay and Will interested in the wine business after he had made some homemade wine, taken a few enology courses, and worked for a time at a winery nearby. In the Johnson's tasting room, there is a 1924 Marr-Colton theater pipe organ on which frequent concerts are given.

WHITE

☆☆ NV CHARDONNAY ($6.50) Alexander Valley. *Modest but decent.*
 ☆ 1982 CHENIN BLANC ($6.00) Alexander Valley. *1.5% residual sugar. Decent but a bit flabby.*
 O 1983 CHENIN BLANC ($6.00) Alexander Valley. *Varnishy.*
☆☆ 1981 JOHANNISBERG RIESLING ($5.00) Sonoma.

BLANC DE NOIR

1982 PINOT NOIR ($5.00) Alexander Valley. *Dull, flat and unappealing.*
1982 WHITE ZINFANDEL ($5.00) Alexander Valley.
1983 WHITE ZINFANDEL ($5.00) Alexander Valley. *Watery, unattractive.*

RED

1978 PINOT NOIR ($6.00) Sonoma.
☆☆ 1979 PINOT NOIR ($6.00) Alexander Valley. *Rich, deep, balanced, attractive.*
 ☆ 1979 ZINFANDEL ($6.50) Alexander Valley. *Thick, jammy, overdone.*
 ☆ 1980 ZINFANDEL ($4.50) Late Harvest, Sauers, Sonoma.
 ☆ 1980 ZINFANDEL ($12.00) Late Harvest, Sauers, Alexander Valley. *2.85% residual sugar.*

JONATHAN VINTNERS *see* R. Montali and Associates

Jonicole Vineyards
OREGON

491 Winery Lane, Roseburg, Oregon 97470 (503-679-5771). FOUNDED: 1975. ACREAGE: 5 acres. PRODUCTION: 4,100 cases. DISTRIBUTION: Oregon. OWNER: Jon Marker. WINE-MAKER: Jon Marker. Tours and tasting summer: daily 11 A.M.–5 P.M.; winter: Friday–Monday 12–5 P.M.

Los Angeles–born and –raised Jon Marker went to Napa College to study agriculture and viticulture while working for a few wineries. Eventually, the pioneer spirit took hold and he went off to Oregon. After scouting about, he bought property in the Umpqua Valley where, according to Jon, there are "microclimates galore!" Starting fast, the winery rapidly outgrew its small capital investment, which forced Jon and his partners to shut down temporarily. But after a few adept financial moves, the winery is now back operating at full steam.

Jordan Vineyard and Winery
SONOMA COUNTY

1474 Alexander Valley Road, Healdsburg, California 95448 (707-433-6955). FOUNDED: 1972. ACREAGE: 240 acres. PRODUCTION: 70,000 cases. DISTRIBUTION: Nationwide; 3 foreign markets. OWNER: Thomas N. Jordan, Jr. WINEMAKER: Robert H. Davis. Tours by appointment.

Tom Jordan, a Denver oil man, and his wife, Sally, wanted to buy a Bordeaux château. One night, however, in a San Francisco restaurant they tasted a Beaulieu Reserve Cabernet and were convinced that great wines could be made in California. They found a large piece of property in Sonoma's Alexander Valley and built a lavish French-style château. Consultant Mike Rowan helped plan the vineyard, which was planted in 1972 with Cabernet Sauvignon and some Merlot for blending. Later, Chardonnay was added. All wines are made from estate-grown fruit.

WHITE

☆☆ 1981 CHARDONNAY ($15.75) Alexander Valley.

☆☆☆ 1982 CHARDONNAY ($15.75) Alexander Valley. *Crisp, balanced, stylish, elegant.*

RED

☆☆☆ 1976 CABERNET SAUVIGNON ($13.00) Alexander Valley. *The first release still holds up. Fruity, earthy and rich.*

☆☆ 1977 CABERNET SAUVIGNON ($14.00) Alexander Valley.

☆☆☆ 1978 CABERNET SAUVIGNON ($16.00) Estate, Alexander Valley. *Rich, earthy, lush and complex, with very elegant structure.*

☆☆☆ 1979 CABERNET SAUVIGNON ($16.00) Alexander Valley. *8% Merlot. Earthy, well structured, elegant. Will age well.*

☆☆☆ 1980 CABERNET SAUVIGNON ($18.00) Estate, Alexander Valley. *Sweet oak and clean flavors, earthy, rich. Drink 1987.*

☆☆ 1981 CABERNET SAUVIGNON ($18.00) Estate, Alexander Valley. *Elegant, silky, lovely structure, herbaceous. Drink 1988.*

Kalin Cellars
MARIN COUNTY

61 Galli Drive, Suite F and G, Novato, California 94947 (415-883-3543). FOUNDED: 1977. ACREAGE: None. PRODUCTION: 5,000 cases. DISTRIBUTION: California and 13 other states; Canada. OWNER: Corporation. Terrance Leighton, president; Francis Leighton, secretary-treasurer. WINEMAKER: Terrance Leighton. No tours or tasting.

Terry and Frances Leighton approach winemaking from a scientific point of view; the winery is their laboratory and wine is their subject of study. Both are professional microbiologists—Terry is a university professor and Frances, a research assistant. Their interest is in advancing the evolution of enology by learning how to control the microbiological processes that take place in winemaking. Although the Leightons' approach is highly scientific, they use small, wood fermenters and barrels in the traditional European style.

WHITE

☆☆ 1980 CHARDONNAY ($14.00) Cuvée W, Sonoma. *Toasty oak and fresh fruit.*

☆☆ 1981 CHARDONNAY ($15.00) Cuvée L, Sonoma. *Big, oaky and a bit clumsy, but should mellow with age.*

☆☆☆ 1982 CHARDONNAY ($15.00) Cuvée D, Dutton Ranch, Sonoma. *Unfiltered, rich, lush, heavy, intense; old style.*

☆☆☆ 1982 CHARDONNAY ($16.00) Cuvée L, Sonoma. *Toasty, rich, good fruit.*

☆☆☆ 1980 JOHANNISBERG RIESLING ($15.00) Mendocino. *A rich, complex, botrytis wine. Like a fine Auslese.*

1980 SEMILLON ($9.00) Livermore Valley.

☆☆ 1982 SEMILLON ($10.00) Livermore. *Lush, clean, very attractive.*

RED

☆ 1979 CABERNET SAUVIGNON ($15.00) Santa Barbara. *Clean and well made but very weedy. Drink 1987.*

1980 CABERNET SAUVIGNON ($17.95) Tepusquet, Santa Barbara. *Vegetal, asparagus flavor, rich fruit, balanced.*

☆☆   1979 PINOT NOIR ($12.50) Santa Barbara. *Varietal and rich, with some vegetal notes.*
☆☆   1981 PINOT NOIR ($15.00) Cuvée WD, Dutton Ranch, Sonoma. *Rich, intense, deep,*
        earthy; quite lovely.
      1979 ZINFANDEL ($7.50) Livermore Valley.
○   1980 ZINFANDEL ($8.00) Livermore Valley. *Vegetal and harsh.*

Karly Wines
AMADOR COUNTY

11076 Bell Road, Plymouth, California 95669 (209-245-3922). FOUNDED: 1979. ACREAGE: 18 acres. PRODUCTION: 5,000 cases. DISTRIBUTION: California and 5 other states; Canada. OWNERS: Partnership. Lawrence L. "Buck" Cobb, general partner. WINEMAKER: Lawrence L. Cobb. Tours by appointment.

Karly Cobb doesn't have a lawn or a swimming pool at her home in the Mother Lode country; instead, she has tanks in the front yard and barrels in the garage. Her husband, Lawrence "Buck" Cobb, a research engineer for the California State Energy Commission in Sacramento, took his gold medals for homemade wine seriously, very seriously. Karly now drives tractors, tops barrels, and carries out routine cellar work as if she had done it all her life. She knows she should find some romantic consolation in the fact that her husband named the winery after her, but when Karly stares out over the patio at the stainless steel tanks, she just shakes her head.

WHITE

☆   1981 CHARDONNAY ($11.50) Tepusquet, Santa Maria Valley. *Heavy, somewhat weedy.*
○   1982 CHARDONNAY ($12.00) Tepusquet, Santa Maria Valley.
☆☆☆ 1983 CHARDONNAY ($12.00) Tepusquet, Santa Maria Valley. *Lovely, rich, deep, clean.*
☆   1982 FUME BLANC ($7.50) Amador. *Dirty flavors, low varietal character.*

RED

☆☆   1980 ZINFANDEL ($7.50) Amador. *Big, spicy, brambly.*
☆☆   1981 ZINFANDEL ($7.50) Amador. *Berried, rich and clean.*
☆☆   1982 ZINFANDEL ($7.50) Amador. *Raisiny, intense, with some sweetness.*

Robert Keenan Winery
NAPA COUNTY

3660 Spring Mountain Road, St. Helena, California 94574 (707-963-9177). FOUNDED: 1977. ACREAGE: 45 acres. PRODUCTION: 8,000 cases. DISTRIBUTION: Nationwide. OWNER: Robert H. Keenan. WINEMAKER: Rex Geitmer. Tours by appointment.

When Robert Keenan bought his steep hillside property on the east side of Spring Mountain, the old vineyards had been completely overgrown. Robert had the vineyards replanted and remodeled the old winery on the property, using the four stone walls that still stood. The renewed facility sits back on the hillside, overlooking the vineyards. Keenan's winery, under former winemaker Joe Cafaro, who departed in 1984 for Acacia Winery, had established a reputation—which it has maintained—for making tight, hard red wines that benefit from long-term aging.

WHITE

☆ 1981 CHARDONNAY ($14.50) Napa Valley.
☆☆ 1982 CHARDONNAY ($14.50) Napa Valley. *Clean, crisp, attractive but lacking complexity.*
☆☆ 1982 CHARDONNAY ($15.00) Estate, Napa Valley.
☆☆ 1983 CHARDONNAY ($15.00) Estate, Napa Valley. *Heavy, ripe, intense, hard-edged.*

RED

☆☆☆ 1979 CABERNET SAUVIGNON ($12.00) Napa Valley. *Big and lumbering but complex, structured and promising.*
☆☆☆ 1980 CABERNET SAUVIGNON ($12.00) Napa Valley. *Dark, dense, berried, with good acidity. Lovely. Drink 1987.*
☆☆☆ 1981 CABERNET SAUVIGNON ($12.00) Napa Valley. *Lovely, crisp, clean, varietal, balanced. Drink 1988.*
☆☆ 1978 MERLOT ($9.00) Napa Valley. *Peppery, clean and rich. Drink now or hold.*
☆☆☆ 1979 MERLOT ($11.00) Napa Valley. *Rich, fruity, lush, cherry-flavored. Lovely. Drink now or hold.*
☆☆☆☆ 1982 MERLOT ($12.50) Napa Valley. *Lush, fresh, complex, with beautiful fruit flavors. Drink 1986.*

KENDALL-JACKSON *see* Château du Lac

Kathryn Kennedy Winery
SANTA CLARA COUNTY

13180 Pierce Road, Saratoga, California 95070 (408-867-4170). FOUNDED: 1979. ACREAGE: 8 acres. PRODUCTION: 1,000 cases. DISTRIBUTION: California. OWNER: Kathryn Kennedy. Martin Mathis, vineyard manager. WINEMAKER: Bill Anderson. OTHER LABEL: Saratoga Cellars. Tasting by appointment.

Kathryn Kennedy had to choose between planting Christmas trees or grapes on her eight-acre property. Observing that the Cabernet Sauvignon vineyards across the way looked fairly easy to care for, she chose grapes. Soon enough Kathryn learned that what looks easy usually isn't. When ready, the grapes were sold to local wineries, one of which was Mount Eden Vineyards. Bill Anderson, who worked at Mount Eden, supplied Kathryn with the encouragement and know-how needed to start a winery. The Kathryn Kennedy label is used for the estate-grown Cabernet, while wine made from purchased grapes is bottled under the Saratoga Cellars label.

RED

☆ 1979 CABERNET SAUVIGNON ($12.00) Estate, Santa Cruz Mountains. *Spicy, intense, lacking structure, with plum and tobacco flavors.*
☆ 1981 CABERNET SAUVIGNON ($12.00) Estate, Santa Cruz Mountains. *Aging quickly, losing its freshness. Drink now.*

Kenwood Vineyards
SONOMA COUNTY

9592 Sonoma Highway, Kenwood, California 95452 (707-833-5891). FOUNDED: 1970. ACREAGE: 1 acre. PRODUCTION: 100,000 cases. OWNERS: Partnership. John Sheela, president; Martin M.

Lee, Jr., vice president. Other partners: Neil Knott, Martin M. Lee, Sr., and Michael Lee. WINE-MAKER: Michael Lee. Bob Kozlowski, consultant. Tasting daily 10 A.M.–4:30 P.M.

The Lee brothers and their brother-in-law, John Sheela, started Kenwood Vineyards in the mid-1970s because they liked the idea of going into business together. Besides having come from diverse business backgrounds, the partners didn't know a thing about making wine. They learned fast. Mike enlisted the help of Chevron chemist Bob Kozlowski, who became a partner and consultant. Marty, a photography fanatic, originated some creative marketing ideas, such as the "Artist Series" Cabernets, with labels that carry a painting by a different artist each year. John Sheela specializes in finding the best grape sources.

WHITE

☆☆ 1982 VINTAGE WHITE ($4.75) California. *0.5% residual sugar. Crisp, fruity and very good.*

☆☆ 1980 CHARDONNAY ($15.00) Beltane Ranch, Sonoma Valley. *Vinous, lush and pleasant.*

☆☆ 1981 CHARDONNAY ($12.00) Sonoma Valley. *High acidity, fruity, yet nicely balanced.*

☆☆ 1981 CHARDONNAY ($15.00) Beltane, Sonoma Valley. *Rich, oaky, vinous, complex.*

☆☆☆ 1982 CHARDONNAY ($11.00) Sonoma Valley.

☆☆ 1982 CHARDONNAY ($14.00) Beltane Ranch, Sonoma Valley. *Balanced, fruity and rich, with lovely oak and depth.*

☆☆☆ 1982 CHENIN BLANC ($6.00) California. *Crisp, fruity and delicious.*

☆☆☆ 1983 CHENIN BLANC ($6.00) California. *0.89% residual sugar. Fresh, crisp, delightful.*

☆☆☆ 1983 GEWURZTRAMINER ($6.50) Sonoma Valley. *3.01% residual sugar. Lovely, rich, balanced. Super.*

☆ 1983 JOHANNISBERG RIESLING ($6.50) Estate, Sonoma Valley. *1.4% residual sugar. Ripe, heavy, with nice fruit.*

☆☆☆ 1983 JOHANNISBERG RIESLING ($8.50) Late Harvest, Estate, Sonoma Valley. *10% residual sugar. Apples and honey; lush, rich yet balanced.*

☆☆☆ 1984 JOHANNISBERG RIESLING ($7.50) Sonoma. *1.5% residual sugar. Lush, lovely, fruity, rich.*

☆☆☆ 1982 SAUVIGNON BLANC ($8.50) Sonoma. *Richly varietal. Fruity and clean.*

☆☆☆ 1983 SAUVIGNON BLANC ($8.50) Sonoma. *Assertive, charming, intensely fruity, delightful.*

☆☆☆ 1984 SAUVIGNON BLANC ($8.50) Sonoma. *Charming, melony, rich, delightful.*

BLANC DE NOIR

☆☆ 1983 PINOT NOIR BLANC ($5.50) Sonoma Valley. *Clean, decent, fruity.*

☆☆ 1984 PINOT NOIR BLANC ($5.50) Sonoma Valley. *Soft, fruity, clean, varietal, balanced.*

☆☆ 1984 WHITE ZINFANDEL ($5.50) Sonoma Valley. *1.4% residual sugar. Crisp, tangy, charming, fruity.*

RED

☆ 1981 VINTAGE RED WINE ($4.50) California.

☆☆ 1978 CABERNET SAUVIGNON ($8.50) Sonoma Valley. *37% Merlot. Deep and lush. Drink 1986 and beyond.*

☆ 1978 CABERNET SAUVIGNON ($10.00) Jack London, Sonoma Valley. *Supple, ripe but short and lacking depth. Drink now.*

☆☆☆ 1978 CABERNET SAUVIGNON ($20.00) Artist Series, Laurel Glen & Steiner, Sonoma Valley. *Intense fruit and rich flavors. Drink 1986 and beyond.*

☆☆☆ 1979 CABERNET SAUVIGNON ($20.00) Artist Series, Sonoma Valley. *Rich, rounded and fruity. Drink 1987 and beyond.*

1980 CABERNET SAUVIGNON ($12.00) Jack London, Sonoma Valley. *Dense and vegetal, tannic, clean but unattractive.*

☆ 1980 CABERNET SAUVIGNON ($12.00) Sonoma Valley. *Heavy, vegetal, clean but unpleasant. Drink 1986.*

☆☆ 1980 CABERNET SAUVIGNON ($25.00) Artist Series, Sonoma Valley. *Some weeds, some depth, good fruit and structure. Drink 1988.*

☆ 1981 CABERNET SAUVIGNON ($8.50) Sonoma. *16% Merlot. Earthy, simple, decent.*

   1981 CABERNET SAUVIGNON ($12.50) Jack London, Sonoma Valley. *Skunky, very unattractive.*

☆☆ 1981 CABERNET SAUVIGNON ($25.00) Artist Series, Sonoma Valley. *Herbed, rich, dense, big, lush. Drink 1988.*

O 1980 PINOT NOIR ($12.00) Jack London, Sonoma Valley. *Off flavors.*

☆☆ 1979 ZINFANDEL ($7.75) Sonoma Valley.

Kenworthy Vineyards
AMADOR COUNTY

P.O. Box 361, Plymouth, California 95669 (209-245-3198). FOUNDED: 1979. ACREAGE: 8 acres. PRODUCTION: 1,800 cases. DISTRIBUTION: California. OWNERS: John and Pat Kenworthy. WINEMAKER: John Kenworthy. Tours by appointment. Tasting weekends 12–5 P.M.

Weary of his engineering job in Los Angeles, John Kenworthy and his wife, Pat, decided to look for vineyard property. True Zinfandel lovers, they purchased 30 acres in Amador County, an area famous for its untamed Zinfandels. In addition to Zinfandel, the Kenworthys have made some Chardonnay and Cabernet Sauvignon, but their future plans are to specialize in Zinfandel.

RED

   1979 CABERNET SAUVIGNON ($8.00) Stonebarn, El Dorado.

   1980 CABERNET SAUVIGNON ($8.50) Stonebarn, El Dorado. *Heavy, unbalanced and strange.*

☆ 1979 ZINFANDEL ($7.00) Potter-Cowan, Amador.

☆☆ 1980 ZINFANDEL ($7.00) Potter-Cowan, Amador.

Kiona Vineyards and Winery
WASHINGTON

Route 2, P.O. Box 2169E, Benton City, Washington 99320 (509-967-3212). FOUNDED: 1979. ACREAGE: 30 acres. PRODUCTION: 2,000 cases. DISTRIBUTION: Idaho, Oregon, and Washington. OWNERS: J. J. Holmes and J. A. Williams. WINEMAKER: J. J. Holmes. Tours and tasting April–October: daily 12–5 P.M.

The Holmes and Williams families bought an 86-acre piece of land near the Yakima River as an investment. Jim Holmes, a native of San Francisco who had made wine at home for several years, got the idea of planting vines on the jointly owned property. The result was Kiona Vineyards, which produced high-quality wine grapes from the start. Selling their first crops to Oregon and Washington wineries, the Kiona couples finally field-crushed their first wines in 1980 and finished them in the Holmes' garage. Since then, the winery has been split into two parts: fermentation and lab work takes place in the garage; storage of barrels and bottles is in the cellar of the Williams' new house near the vineyards.

WHITE

☆☆ 1983 CHENIN BLANC ($5.00) Estate, Yakima Valley. *1.4% residual sugar.*

1982 LEMBERGER ($8.75) Washington. *Syrupy, sweet, strange.*

☆☆ 1983 WHITE RIESLING ($5.70) Estate, Yakima Valley. *1.4% residual sugar.*

☆☆ 1983 WHITE RIESLING ($5.70) Late Harvest, Estate, Yakima Valley. *2% residual sugar.
      Lush, rich, fruity, simple, clean.*

ROSE

☆☆ 1983 MERLOT ROSE ($4.70) Estate, Yakima Valley. *1.1% residual sugar. Varietal, soft,
      lovely.*

Kirigin Cellars
SANTA CLARA COUNTY

11500 Watsonville Road, Gilroy, California 95020 (408-847-8827). FOUNDED: 1976. ACREAGE:
50 acres. PRODUCTION: 10,000 cases. DISTRIBUTION: At winery and local outlets. OWNER:
Nikola Kirigin Chargin. WINEMAKER: Nikola Kirigin Chargin. Tasting locations: 11550 Watsonville Road, Gilroy and 19500 Monterey Road, Morgan Hill. Both are open daily 9 A.M.–6 P.M.

After years of working for many of California's big wineries, Nikola Kirigin Chargin wanted
his own winery, just as he had had in his homeland of Croatia. He bought the Bonesio family
winery and made it into what he proudly calls "the most modern small winery in California."

WHITE

1981 PINOT CHARDONNAY ($7.50) California. *Dull, no varietal character.*

☆☆ 1982 GEWURZTRAMINER ($5.50) California. *1.5% residual sugar. Varietal, lush, with
      good fruit.*

☆☆ NV MALVASIA ($5.50) San Benito. *Soft and varietal, lacking acidity but clean and
      sweet.*

1981 SAUVIGNON VERT ($5.00) California. *Fat, flabby, no fruit.*

☆   1982 SAUVIGNON VERT ($5.00) California.

ROSE

☆   NV OPOL ROSE ($5.00) California. *Pinot Noir, Zinfandel, Cabernet. Crisp, clean,
      simple.*

RED

1977 PINOT NOIR ($6.00) California. *Soft, toasty, brown and old.*

Kistler Vineyards
SONOMA COUNTY

997 Madrone Road, Glen Ellen, California 95442 (707-996-5117). FOUNDED: 1978. ACREAGE:
35 acres. PRODUCTION: 7,000 cases. DISTRIBUTION: California. OWNER: Corporation.
WINEMAKER: Stephen Kistler. OTHER LABEL: Mearen Lake. No tours or tasting.

After attending Stanford University, Steve Kistler headed to U.C. Davis, then to Fresno State,
taking every enology class available. He also became friends with Mark Bixler, a young and energetic
chemistry teacher. The two wine-loving buddies took off in separate winemaking directions, always

with the intention of eventually starting a winery together. In 1979, when the Kistler family bought property—2,000 feet above the Sonoma Valley floor—Steve, Mark, and Steve's brother John started Kistler Vineyards. From the winery building to the cooperage, the technique, and even the label, Steve and Mark have attempted to recreate a true Burgundian winery on North American soil.

WHITE

○ 1980 CHARDONNAY ($16.00) Dutton Ranch, California. *Seriously flawed.*

○ 1980 CHARDONNAY ($16.00) Sonoma-Cutrer, Sonoma. *Serious sulfur dioxide problems here. Avoid.*

  1980 CHARDONNAY ($18.00) Winery Lake, Napa Valley. *Big problems here too.*

☆☆ 1981 MEAREN LAKE CHARDONNAY ($12.00) Sonoma. *Very toasty, crisp. A bit hot but to be taken seriously.*

☆☆☆☆ 1981 CHARDONNAY ($15.00) Dutton Ranch, California. *Lovely, delicate, richly varietal, elegant and oaky. Superb.*

☆☆ 1981 CHARDONNAY ($15.00) Winery Lake, California. *Rich and oaky; some off smells and hotness.*

☆☆☆ 1982 CHARDONNAY ($12.50) Sonoma-Cutrer, California. *Rich and toasty yet exquisitely balanced. A classic.*

☆☆☆ 1982 CHARDONNAY ($15.00) Dutton Ranch, Sonoma. *Rich and vinous, with good acid and fruit; high alcohol.*

☆☆☆ 1983 CHARDONNAY ($9.75) Sonoma Valley. *Lush, round, clean, lovely oak, delightfully complex.*

☆ 1983 CHARDONNAY ($10.50) Sonoma Valley. *Oaky but short on fruit.*

☆☆☆ 1983 CHARDONNAY ($12.00) Napa Valley. *Crisp, clean, balanced, lovely oak.*

☆☆☆ 1983 CHARDONNAY ($14.00) Winery Lake, California. *Big, rich, toasty, fruity, intense.*

☆☆☆ 1983 CHARDONNAY ($15.00) Dutton Ranch, Sonoma. *Clean, crisp, balanced, oaky.*

RED

☆☆ 1979 CABERNET SAUVIGNON ($18.00) Glen Ellen, California. *Big and somewhat awkward; obviously good but not likable.*

☆ 1979 CABERNET SAUVIGNON ($20.00) Veeder Hills-Veeder Peak, California. *Complex but essentially strange.*

☆☆☆ 1980 CABERNET SAUVIGNON ($16.00) Veeder Hills-Veeder Peak, Napa. *Herbal, rich and snappy; clean. Drink 1987 and beyond.*

☆☆☆ 1980 CABERNET SAUVIGNON ($20.00) Glen Ellen, California. *Big, rich, complex, with delicacy and finesse. Drink 1987.*

☆☆☆ 1981 CABERNET SAUVIGNON ($12.00) Veeder Hills-Veeder Peak, California. *Rich and dense, with excellent structure and aging potential.*

☆☆☆ 1982 CABERNET SAUVIGNON ($11.00) Veeder Hills-Napa Valley. *Lush, deep, dense, with good fruit and oak. Drink 1987.*

☆☆ NV MEAREN LAKE PINOT NOIR ($7.50) Carneros District, Napa Valley. *Rich, oaky and berried, with some raw qualities. Drink 1986.*

☆☆ 1979 PINOT NOIR ($16.00) Winery Lake, California. *Powerful but still awkward. Further aging may help.*

Klingshirn Winery
OHIO

33050 Webber Road, Avon Lake, Ohio 44012 (216-933-6666). FOUNDED: 1935. ACREAGE: 12 acres. PRODUCTION: 4,000 cases. DISTRIBUTION: Ohio. OWNER: Corporation. Allan A. Klingshirn, president. WINEMAKER: Allan A. Klingshirn. Tours and tasting Monday–Friday 12– 6 P.M., Saturday 9 A.M.–6 P.M.

Making profitable use of their excess grapes during Prohibition, grape growers Albert Kling-shirn, his two brothers, and a friend sold juice to home winemakers. After Repeal they began some fermentation of their own in twenty oak barrels stored in the basement of the family farmhouse. Since the Klingshirn family's primary interest had always been farming, the winery was mostly ignored. Expansion began slowly when Albert's son Allan bought the winery in 1955. Allan, waiting to see which way the wine industry would go, prepared for growth by buying equipment at auctions and storing it in the farm's outbuildings. When the wine boom hit in the 1970s, Allan was ready. He built a big, new winery facility in 1978 and put all the equipment to use.

Knapp Farms
NEW YORK

2770 Country Road, Romulus, New York 14541 (607-869-9271). FOUNDED: 1982. ACREAGE: 65 acres. PRODUCTION: 1,666 cases. DISTRIBUTION: Local. OWNER: Douglas Knapp. WINE-MAKER: Douglas Knapp. Tasting and sales at the junction of Route 5 and Route 20, Seneca Falls. Call for information.

Douglas Knapp was working in electronics when he bought his 65-acre "grape farm." Before long, he became so involved with grape growing that he became a full-time farmer and the president of the state growers' association. Winemaking was the natural next step. Aware of the difficulties facing the small winery, Douglas tried a different approach to selling his wines. "A winery with a small production cannot survive the three-tier distribution system," says Douglas. "So I decided to sell all my wine out of my own retail outlet. Besides, I enjoy the direct feedback I get from my customers."

Knudsen-Erath Winery
OREGON

Worden Hill Road, Dundee, Oregon 97115 (503-538-3318). FOUNDED: 1972. ACREAGE: 111 acres. PRODUCTION: 42,000 cases. DISTRIBUTION: Nationwide. OWNER: Partnership. Rich-ard Erath and C. Calvert Knudsen. WINEMAKER: Richard Erath. OTHER LABELS: Dundee Villages, Willamette Cellars. Tours by appointment. Tasting at winery weekdays 10 A.M.–3 P.M., weekends 11 A.M.–5 P.M. Tasting also at 641 Highway 99W, Dundee, daily 10 A.M.–6 P.M.

Dick Erath, who moved to Oregon from California to be an electrical engineer, was a pioneer in planting vinifera in the Northwest. Richard Sommer of Hillcrest Vineyard convinced him that Oregon had potential as a great grape-growing region. Dick and his wife, Kina, started their vineyard in 1968 in the Red Hills near Dundee. Three years later Cal Knudsen, a successful lumber executive, entered into a partnership with the Eraths, bringing his Knudsen Vineyard with him. Together they founded the winery in 1972. As winemaker, Dick learned that the U.C. Davis enology textbook can be tossed out the window when it comes to Oregon grapes. Convinced that the climate and soil conditions of his vineyards are ideal, Dick has aimed to prove that truly great Pinot Noir, Chardonnay, and White Riesling can be produced in this relatively new viticultural area.

WHITE

☆ 1980 CHARDONNAY ($7.50) Willamette Valley, Oregon. *Lemony and quite decent.*
☆☆ 1981 CHARDONNAY ($8.00) Willamette Valley, Oregon. *Crisp, clean, with good fruit but little depth.*
☆☆ 1982 WHITE RIESLING ($6.00) Willamette Valley, Oregon. *Crisp, fruity, clean and tart.*

RED

1979 MERLOT ($7.00) 81% Sagemoor (Washington), 19% Chehalem (Oregon), Wash-ington-Oregon.
☆ 1981 MERLOT ($6.50) 82% Washington, 18% Oregon. *Herbal, snappy, crisp, underripe.*

☆☆ 1979 PINOT NOIR ($10.00) Maresh, Oregon.
☆☆ 1979 PINOT NOIR ($10.75) Vintage Select, Yamhill County, Oregon. *Earthy, with ap-
     pealing, smooth flavors. Lacks structure.*
  ☆ 1980 PINOT NOIR ($7.50) Willamette Valley, Oregon. *Pale, stemmy, underripe, but with
     some nice berry character.*

🍇

Kolln Vineyards
PENNSYLVANIA

R.D. 1, P.O. Box 439, Bellefonte, Pennsylvania 16823 (814-355-4666). FOUNDED: 1978. ACREAGE:
5 acres. PRODUCTION: 2,000 cases. DISTRIBUTION: Local. OWNERS: John and Martha Kolln.
WINEMAKER: John Kolln. Tours and tasting except in January. Call for information. Monthly
concerts in summer.

John Kolln, a technical drawing teacher at Pennsylvania State University, regularly made wine
in his spare time until 1971, when he and his wife, an English teacher, bought a little farm and
planted vines. Once the vineyards were under way, John and his son built a winery, which now
keeps John working full time.

🍇

Konocti Winery
LAKE COUNTY

4350 Thomas Drive, Kelseyville, California 95451 (707-279-8861). FOUNDED: 1974. ACREAGE:
500 acres. PRODUCTION: 30,000 cases. DISTRIBUTION: California and some other states;
England. OWNER: Partnership. Walter Lyon, president; Al Moorhead, vice president. WINE-
MAKER: William T. Pease. Tours and tasting daily 10 A.M.–5 P.M. Small gift shop.

This small cooperative winery is owned by twenty-seven small growers whose Lake County
vineyards range from two to fifty acres. Named after nearby Mount Konocti, an inactive volcano,
the winery was completed in 1979. In 1983 John and George Parducci acquired a 50-percent interest
in the operation.

WHITE

☆☆☆ 1982 FUME BLANC ($5.50) Lake. *Clean, soft, balanced, elegant.*
☆☆☆ 1983 FUME BLANC ($5.50) Lake. *12% Semillon. Fruity, snappy, varietal, clean.*
 ☆☆ 1981 JOHANNISBERG RIESLING ($5.60) Lake. *Decent, off-dry, clean.*
 ☆☆ 1983 JOHANNISBERG RIESLING ($5.00) Lake. *Fresh, soft, fruity, clean, very nice.*
  ☆ 1981 SAUVIGNON BLANC ($6.11) Lake.
 ☆☆ 1982 WHITE RIESLING ($3.80) Lake. *Clean, fruity, snappy and appealing.*
 ☆☆ 1982 WHITE RIESLING ($4.00) Lake. *Fresh, soft, crisp, fruity, somewhat subdued.*

BLANC DE NOIR

 ☆☆ 1982 CABERNET SAUVIGNON BLANC ($4.50) Lake. *Clear, fresh, clean and delicious.*
 ☆☆ 1983 CABERNET BLANC ($4.50) Lake. *Herbal, clean, dry, attractive.*

RED

 ☆☆ 1979 CABERNET SAUVIGNON ($6.00) Estate, Lake. *Herbaceous, balanced, well made.
      Drink now.*
 ☆☆ 1979 CABERNET SAUVIGNON ($6.00) Lot II, Lake. *Earthy, varietal, clean and ap-
      pealing. Drink now.*

☆☆   1980 CABERNET SAUVIGNON ($6.50) Lake. *5% Cabernet Franc. Fruity, oaky, attractive. Drink 1986.*
     NV   ZINFANDEL ($4.00) Lake. *Weedy.*
     1980 ZINFANDEL ($5.00) Primitivo, Late Harvest, Lake. *375ml. 8.5% residual sugar. Peppery, odd, decent.*
☆☆   1981 ZINFANDEL ($4.75) Lake. *Fruity, clean and attractive in a simple style.*

F. Korbel and Brothers
SONOMA COUNTY

13250 River Road, Guerneville, California 95446 (707-887-2294). FOUNDED: 1882. ACREAGE: 640 acres. PRODUCTION: 650,000 cases. DISTRIBUTION: Nationwide. OWNER: Gary B. Heck, president. William Botkin, vice president. WINEMAKER: Robert M. Stashak. Tours and tasting daily 9:45 A.M.–3:45 P.M. Gift shop. Picnic facilities.

Korbel winery, founded by the three Korbel brothers who emigrated from Czechoslovakia, began making "Champagne" around the turn of the century. In 1954 the Hecks—descendants of an Alsatian family—bought the winery, which specializes in "méthode champenoise" sparkling wine. Currently run by Gary Heck, son of Adolf Heck (one of the original Heck brothers), Korbel makes fresh and fruity wines that avoid the yeasty and oaky qualities for which some other sparkling winemakers strive.

WHITE

☆☆   1982 JOHANNISBERG RIESLING ($5.00) Sonoma. *1.5% residual sugar.*

SPARKLING

☆   NV   BLANC DE BLANCS ($15.75) California. *Soft, sweet, simple.*
☆☆☆   NV   BLANC DE BLANCS ($16.00) California. *100% Chardonnay. Disgorged 9/84. Crisp, clean, complex.*
☆☆   NV   BLANC DE NOIRS ($12.00) California. *Pinot Noir. Raspberry nose; crisp, clean and appealing.*
☆☆   NV   BRUT ($9.80) California. *Fresh, clean and appealing. Méthode champenoise.*
☆   NV   EXTRA DRY CHAMPAGNE ($9.75) California. *Decent but dull.*
☆☆   NV   NATURAL CHAMPAGNE ($12.00) California. *Floral, sweet, attractive.*
☆   NV   ROSE-PINK CHAMPAGNE ($9.00) California. *Fresh berry flavors.*

Hanns Kornell Champagne Cellar
NAPA COUNTY

1091 Larkmead Lane, St. Helena, California 94574 (707-963-9333). FOUNDED: 1952. ACREAGE: None. PRODUCTION: 170,000 cases. DISTRIBUTION: Nationwide; 9 foreign markets. OWNER: Hanns Kornell family. WINEMAKER: Hanns Kornell. Tours and tasting daily 10 A.M.–4 P.M. Gift shop. Newsletter.

Son of a German winemaker, Hanns Kornell had a struggle leaving Germany during World War II. Because of his Jewish heritage, Hanns spent a year in a concentration camp before managing to get to the United States in 1939. He hitchhiked from New York to California, where he worked in wineries, often helping to make sparkling wines. When he had accumulated enough money, he started his own champagne cellars in the 114-year-old stone Larkmead winery building in St. Helena. About the same time, Hanns met and married Marielouise Rossini, who has been his right hand in the winery ever since. A jolly, white-haired man with a thick accent, Hanns also gets plenty of help from their two children, Paula and Peter. All still wines for the sparkling wine cuvées are purchased. Several of the varietal wines used, such as Johannisberg Reisling, Chenin Blanc, and Semillon, are uncommon in traditional "Champagne" production.

SPARKLING

1980 BLANC DE BLANCS ($19.00) California. *Chenin Blanc. Sweet, unappealing.*

O NV BRUT ($10.75) California. *Méthode champenoise.*

   NV EXTRA DRY CHAMPAGNE ($11.25) California.

O NV ROSE ($9.75) Dry, California. *Off odors and flavors.*

   NV ROSE CHAMPAGNE ($10.00) California. *1.5% residual sugar. Oily, unattractive, bitter.*

   NV SEHR TROCKEN ($14.00) California. *Strange, off flavors, clean.*

1979 SEHR TROCKEN ($12.25) California. *Bitter, unattractive.*

   NV MUSCAT ALEXANDRIA ($11.00) California. *Bitter, unpleasant.*

Charles Krug Winery
NAPA COUNTY

2800 St. Helena Highway, St. Helena, California 94574 (707-963-2761). FOUNDED: 1861. ACREAGE: 1,200 acres. PRODUCTION: 1.2 million cases. DISTRIBUTION: Nationwide. OWNERS: Peter Mondavi, president; Mary Westbrook, vice president; Marc Mondavi and Peter Mondavi, Jr., managers. WINEMAKER: Barry Douglas. OTHER LABEL: C. K. Mondavi. Tours and tasting daily 10 A.M.– 4:30 P.M. Newsletter.

Prussian emigré Charles Krug, one of Napa's pioneers, opened his winery in 1861. He was one of the first to popularize California wines, both at home and abroad. The Krugs ran the winery until Prohibition, when the new owners, the Moffitt family, closed it down. In 1943 it was purchased by Italian immigrant Cesare Mondavi, a self-made millionaire who ran the winery until his death in 1959. His widow, Rosa, became president and, in traditional Italian fashion, gave more authority to older son Peter than to younger son Robert. After numerous disagreements, Robert left to start his own winery in 1966 (see Robert Mondavi Winery). A nasty court battle ensued, and the two still don't speak.

WHITE

1981 CHARDONNAY ($10.00) Napa Valley. *A bit of oxidation mars this one.*

1982 CHARDONNAY ($10.00) Sonoma. *Oxidized, candied, not much.*

1983 C. K. MONDAVI CHENIN BLANC ($4.00) California. *1.5 liter. Dull, no depth, no fruit.*

O 1983 CHENIN BLANC ($4.50) Napa Valley. *Oxidized, unattractive.*

1980 FUME BLANC ($6.50) Napa Valley.

1982 GEWURZTRAMINER ($6.50) Napa Valley. *1.5% residual sugar. Dull, lifeless.*

☆☆ 1981 JOHANNISBERG RIESLING ($7.25) Napa Valley. *Dry, crisp and clean.*

 ☆ 1982 JOHANNISBERG RIESLING ($6.50) Napa Valley. *Rich, vinous, varietal and slightly bitter.*

☆☆ 1979 MUSCAT ($10.00) Napa Valley. *4.5% residual sugar. Clean, varietal, balanced.*

1983 SAUVIGNON BLANC ($6.50) Napa Valley. *Flabby, dull, lacking interest.*

RED

☆☆ 1977 CABERNET SAUVIGNON ($14.00) Vintage Selection, Napa Valley. *Somewhat faint and dried out but soft and elegant.*

☆☆ 1978 CABERNET SAUVIGNON ($12.50) Vintage Selection, Napa Valley. *Rich, oaky and beginning to show some age.*

☆☆ 1979 CABERNET SAUVIGNON ($6.50) Napa Valley. *Earthy, grapey, pleasant. Drink 1987.*
☆☆ 1982 C. K. MONDAVI CABERNET SAUVIGNON ($7.00) California. *1.5 liter. Snappy, clean, fruity, attractive. Drink now.*
☆☆ 1978 MERLOT ($7.00) Napa Valley. *Leathery and older in style.*
☆☆ 1979 PINOT NOIR ($5.50) Napa Valley. *Clean, balanced, pleasant.*
 O   1980 PINOT NOIR ($5.50) Napa Valley, Carneros Region.
☆☆ 1979 ZINFANDEL ($4.80) Napa. *Jammy and intense.*

Kruger's Winery & Vineyards
MISSOURI

Route 1, Nelson, Missouri 65347 (816-761-4311). FOUNDED: 1977. ACREAGE: 6 acres. PRODUCTION: 830 cases. DISTRIBUTION: Local. OWNER: Corporation. Lawrence C. Kruger, president; Leana F. Kruger, vice president and secretary. WINEMAKER: Lawrence C. Kruger. Tours and tasting weekends 12–6 P.M. Closed January–May.

"My family has made wine for as long as I can remember," says Lawrence Kruger. While working for the U.S. Post Office in Kansas City, he purchased a corner of his father's property near Arrowrock, a historic little town where Larry was born and raised. There he burrowed a hole into a hillside and built a concrete winery.

Thomas Kruse Winery
SANTA CLARA COUNTY

4390 Hecker Pass Road, Gilroy, California 95020 (408-842-7016). FOUNDED: 1971. ACREAGE: None. PRODUCTION: 3,800 cases. DISTRIBUTION: At winery. OWNER: Thomas Kruse. WINEMAKER: Thomas Kruse. OTHER LABEL: Aptos. Tours and tasting daily 12–5 P.M.

Buying an old wine press may not be the best reason to become a winemaker, but Thomas Kruse felt he should justify his impulsive purchase by making at least one barrel of wine. One was not enough; with a hand-cranked crusher and a basket press, Tom got his winery off the ground. His lighthearted, satirical humor is displayed on the winery's hand-lettered labels.

WHITE

1983 CHARDONNAY ($8.00) Santa Clara.

SPARKLING

☆ NV BLANC DE BLANCS ($10.00) San Benito. *Méthode champenoise. Clean, simple and attractive.*

RED

 NV GILROY RED ($4.50) Santa Clara. *100% Cabernet. Quite vegetal.*
☆ 1982 GRIGNOLINO ($5.00) Santa Clara. *Floral, astringent, snappy.*
☆ 1981 CABERNET SAUVIGNON ($7.00) Santa Clara. *Grapey, simple, decent.*
    1980 APTOS PINOT NOIR ($6.00) Santa Cruz. *Vegetal, stinky, unappealing.*
☆ 1981 ZINFANDEL ($6.00) Santa Clara.
☆☆ 1982 ZINFANDEL ($6.00) Santa Clara.

La Abra Farm & Winery
VIRGINIA

Route 1, Box 139, Lovingston, Virginia 22949 (804-263-5392). FOUNDED: 1973. ACREAGE: 12 acres. PRODUCTION: 2,000 cases. DISTRIBUTION: Local. OWNER: Corporation. A. C. Weed, general manager. WINEMAKER: A. C. Weed. OTHER LABEL: Mountain Cove Vineyards. Tours and tasting daily 11 A.M.–5 P.M.

Former investment banker A. C. Weed wanted to farm and harvest, then make and market his own product. Grape growing and winemaking fit these back-to-the-soil, entrepreneurial goals perfectly. After he quit his job at the bank, A. C. and his wife sold their house, bought an abandoned farm, and moved to the country. Most of the buildings on the property were in wretched condition, so the Weeds built a brand new, 70-foot-long winery topped with a tin roof. A. C. is pleased (and relieved) with the way his wines and winery have been progressing, "except that my wife keeps asking me when we are going to make some money."

La Buena Vida Vineyards
TEXAS

Weatherford Star Route Box 18-3, Springtown, Texas 76082 (817-523-4366). FOUNDED: 1978. ACREAGE: 12 acres. PRODUCTION: 8,000 cases. DISTRIBUTION: California, Texas, and New York. OWNERS: Bobby G. and Steve Smith. WINEMAKER: Steve Smith. Tours and tasting daily 12–6 P.M. at Route 2, Box 927, Fort Worth.

When Bobby G. Smith was just a boy, he helped his parents grow Scuppernong grapes in Alabama, "for jams and jellies mostly, since my parents were teetotalers," explains Bobby. "But looking back on it now, I figure we sold plenty of grapes that were used for something other than making jelly." Bobby purchased an abandoned dairy farm in 1972 and started his own vineyards in 1974, this time with the intention of making wine. As he was preparing to start his winery, he ran into one major obstacle: His vineyards were planted in a dry county where wine production was forbidden by law. "I wasn't about to convince a dry county to become wet, so instead I somehow persuaded the state legislative offices that Texas's best vineyard land was located in dry counties, and certain provisions ought to be made for the would-be winemaker," says Bobby. Maybe it was Bobby's impassioned testimony, or maybe it was the shine on his hand-tooled, snakeskin boots that did the trick. In any case, a Farm Winery Act was passed in 1977 and La Buena Vida had its first crush the next year in its corrugated-steel winery. The tasting room, which required a separate bond and permit, is located in a wet county about eighteen miles from the winery.

La Chiripada Winery
NEW MEXICO

P.O. Box 191, Dixon, New Mexico 87527 (505-579-4675). FOUNDED: 1982. ACREAGE: 5 acres. PRODUCTION: 1,450 cases. DISTRIBUTION: New Mexico. OWNER: Partnership. Michael and Patrick Johnson. WINEMAKERS: Michael and Patrick Johnson. Tours and tasting Monday–Saturday 10 A.M.–5 P.M.

In 1977 the Johnson brothers decided to plant some grapes on their seven unused acres in northern New Mexico. Patrick, a potter by trade, and Michael, a community organizer, started with successive plantings of French-American hybrids just to see what would and would not grow. "We knew the Spaniards had planted grapes all along the Rio Grande and had made their own wine," says Michael. Once the grapes came into production, the brothers built an adobe winery in the vineyard. "We will always keep it small," says Michael. "We just want to make a good, drinkable New Mexico wine."

WHITE

1983 VIDAL BLANC ($5.75) New Mexico.

RED

☆ NV LA NUEVA SUERTE ($5.50) New Mexico.
☆ 1983 MARECHAL FOCH ($6.75) New Mexico. *Deep, clean, decent.*

La Crema Vinera
SONOMA COUNTY

P.O. Box 976, Petaluma, California 94953 (707-762-0393). FOUNDED: 1979. ACREAGE: None. PRODUCTION: 10,000 cases. DISTRIBUTION: Major market states. OWNERS: 4 principal partners—Rick Burmeiscer, John Bessey, Rod Berglund, Bob Goyette—and limited partners. Hartley Katlick, public relations and marketing. WINEMAKER: Rod Berglund; Bob Goyette, assistant. OTHER LABEL: Petaluma Cellars. Tours by appointment. Newsletter.

Four partners, with backgrounds in art, business, biology, and physics, began planning this winery in 1978. They became the first post-Prohibition winery in Petaluma when they set up shop in an old warehouse. The goal of winemaker Rod Berglund is to produce wine in traditional Burgundian styles. He has also experimented with winemaking techniques, using procedures based on his conception of natural European methods. Grapes are purchased from cool, Burgundy-like growing areas in California, especially the Carneros district.

WHITE

1981 CHARDONNAY ($13.50) Arrendell, Sonoma. *Oxidation and oak dominate this fruitless effort.*
☆☆ 1981 CHARDONNAY ($13.50) California. *Toasty, rich, crisp, fruity—all in one wine. Charming.*
☆ 1981 CHARDONNAY ($13.50) Dutton Ranch, Sonoma.
☆☆☆ 1981 CHARDONNAY ($14.50) Ventana, Monterey. *Big, rich, statuesque—a monster but wonderful.*
☆☆ 1981 CHARDONNAY ($16.50) Winery Lake, Carneros District, Napa. *Rich and woody. Needs more depth but a lovely effort.*
O 1982 CHARDONNAY ($12.75) Arrendell, Sonoma County-Green Valley. *Sour, intense, unpleasant.*
☆ 1982 CHARDONNAY ($13.50) California.
1982 CHARDONNAY ($13.50) Winery Lake, Napa Valley. *Lush, intense, oxidized, very oaky.*
☆☆☆ 1982 CHARDONNAY ($14.50) Dutton, Sonoma-Green Valley.
☆ 1982 CHARDONNAY ($16.00) Ventana, Monterey. *Very oaky and big, awkward and heavy.*

BLANC DE NOIR

☆☆ 1983 VIN GRIS DE PINOT NOIR ($5.00) Carneros, Sonoma. *Rich, lush, complex, clean.*

RED

☆ 1979 PINOT NOIR ($14.50) Ventana, Monterey.
☆☆☆ 1979 PINOT NOIR ($14.50) Winery Lake, Carneros District. *Earthy and fresh, with good fruit and considerable complexity.*

☆☆   1980 PINOT NOIR ($15.00) Ventana, Monterey. *Rich, appealingly varietal, needs age. Lots of sediment.*

☆☆   1982 PINOT NOIR ($9.00) Vineburg, Carneros District, Sonoma. *Big and earthy, with great depth.*

☆☆☆☆ 1982 PINOT NOIR ($10.00) Porter Creek, Russian River Valley. *Violets, rich, lovely, complex, elegant, superb.*

ফ্ল

La Jota Vineyard Company
NAPA COUNTY

1102 Las Posadas Road, Angwin, California 94508 (707-965-2878). FOUNDED: 1898. ACREAGE: 30 acres. PRODUCTION: 5,000 cases. DISTRIBUTION: At winery and local outlets, and by mailing list. OWNERS: Bill and Joan Smith. WINEMAKER: Randy Dunn, consultant. Tours by appointment.

Bill Smith was scanning a topographical map when he saw a little black dot in the Howell Mountain area. At first he thought it was another new winery until he drove up to the location and discovered a pre-Prohibition winery that had never been reopened. Bill, who works in the oil and gas business, and his wife, Joan, bought the property, intending to plant one or two acres of grapes. "Two acres grew to thirty acres, and with that many grapes, we figured we might as well reopen the winery," says Joan. The first crush was in 1982; the first wines will be released in 1986.

ফ্ল

La Vina Winery
NEW MEXICO

P.O. Box 121, Chamberino, New Mexico 88027 (505-882-2092). FOUNDED: 1977. ACREAGE: 20 acres. PRODUCTION: 3,750 cases. DISTRIBUTION: New Mexico and Texas. OWNER: Clarence Cooper. WINEMAKER: Clarence Cooper. Tours and tasting Monday–Friday 12–4 P.M., Saturday 9 A.M.–6 P.M. September wine festival.

Clarence Cooper began his enological career by making wine in the bathtub, much to the dismay of his wife, Martha, a microbiologist. She gave him her grateful blessing when he began building a Mexican adobe winery with an old stagecoach-stop facade. Clarence, a physics professor, had been growing just enough grapes to supply his bathtub hobby, but once he turned professional, he planted more acreage. At first he imported California grapes, but now he makes wines only from his own grapes.

ফ্ল

Lafayette Vineyards
FLORIDA

Route 7, Box 481, 6505 Mahan Drive, Tallahassee, Florida 32308 (904-878-9041). FOUNDED: 1983. ACREAGE: 38 acres. PRODUCTION: 7,500 cases. DISTRIBUTION: Florida. OWNER: Partnership. Gary Cox and Robert Ketchum. WINEMAKER: Jeanne Burgess. Tours and tasting Tuesday–Saturday 10 A.M.–6 P.M., Sunday 12–6 P.M.

Gary Cox, a former accountant, and Robert Ketchum, a former lawyer, started their winery and vineyards in 1982 because they "decided that it would be a real good thing to do." They put together a limited partnership, began planting vineyards, and, after retiring from their respective professions, built a stucco, chalet-style winery in 1983, just in time for that year's crush.

WHITE

☆ NV STOVER ($6.50) Florida.

ð

Laird Vineyards
NAPA COUNTY

1010 Sir Francis Drake Boulevard, Kentfield, California 94904 (415-459-2620). FOUNDED: 1980. ACREAGE: 250 acres. PRODUCTION: 5,000 cases. DISTRIBUTION: California and some other states. OWNERS: Ken and Gail Laird, and John and Sheryl Richburg. WINEMAKER: John Richburg. No tours or tasting.

Ken Laird sold his original vineyard in Calistoga in 1970 and moved to Arizona, where he bought an industrial gas and welding equipment business. In 1980 he moved back to California and returned to grape growing with the purchase of a vineyard in the Carneros region of the Napa Valley. He started making wine at Rombauer Vineyards with the help of his winemaking neighbor, John Richburg, the winemaker at Inglenook. For the first two years they bought grapes, but by 1982 Ken's own vineyards were producing enough to supply all their winemaking needs. Today Ken has thirteen different vineyard parcels in the Napa Valley and enough surplus grapes to sell to other wineries.

WHITE

☆☆ 1980 CHARDONNAY ($15.00) Napa Valley. *Crisp, fresh and somewhat simple.*

RED

☆☆☆ 1980 CABERNET SAUVIGNON ($11.00) Napa Valley. *Clean, balanced, elegant. Drink 1987.*

ð

Lake Sonoma Winery
SONOMA COUNTY

P.O. Box 263, Healdsburg, California 95448 (707-433-8534). FOUNDED: 1977. ACREAGE: 3 acres. PRODUCTION: 1,200 cases. DISTRIBUTION: California and Nevada. OWNER: Robert Polson. WINEMAKER: Robert Polson; Donald Polson, vineyard manager. OTHER LABEL: Diablo Vista. No tours or tasting.

According to an aptitude test he took at Stanford University, there were a number of potential career areas in which Bob Polson could excel, among them engineering and agriculture. He tried engineering at Dow Chemical Company in Michigan, but by 1971 he was itching to work with the soil. He and his wife, Mary Lou, moved to California and bought a vineyard of aged Zinfandel vines in Sonoma's Dry Creek Valley. In 1978, living in the San Francisco Bay area and still working for Dow Chemical, Bob began making wine in a former cafeteria. That was the deciding step; in 1982 he quit his job and moved his family to Healdsburg.

WHITE

O 1981 DIABLO VISTA CHARDONNAY ($9.50) Vail Vista, Sonoma. *Brown and oxidized.*
☆☆ 1982 DIABLO VISTA CHENIN BLANC ($6.90) Alexander Valley. *Woody, vinous, rich, intense, Chardonnay-like.*

RED

☆☆☆ 1978 DIABLO VISTA CABERNET SAUVIGNON ($9.00) North Coast. *3% Merlot. Earthy, rich, delightful for current drinking.*
☆ 1978 DIABLO VISTA MERLOT ($9.00) Polson, Dry Creek Valley. *Dried-out fruit, decent but dirty.*

☆☆   1980 DIABLO VISTA MERLOT ($8.50) Polson, Dry Creek Valley. *Grapey and simple; good texture, rich and forward.*

☆☆   1981 DIABLO VISTA MERLOT ($7.50) Sonoma. *Big, berried, Zinfandel-like. Not varietal but still interesting.*

○   1979 DIABLO VISTA ZINFANDEL ($9.00) Late Harvest, Sonoma. *Dense, ugly.*

☆☆☆ 1980 DIABLO VISTA ZINFANDEL ($6.90) Polson, Dry Creek Valley, Sonoma. *Earthy, complex, big.*

☆☆☆ 1981 DIABLO VISTA ZINFANDEL ($6.90) Dry Creek Valley. *Grapey, rich, fruity, clean, with great acidity. Super.*

Lakeside Vineyard
MICHIGAN

13581 Red Arrow Highway, Harbert, Michigan 49115 (616-469-0700). FOUNDED: 1948. ACREAGE: None. PRODUCTION: 35,000 cases. DISTRIBUTION: 5 Midwestern states. OWNER: Leonard Olson. William Voss, vice president research and quality control; Art Sandtveit, production manager. WINEMAKER: Leonard Olson. OTHER LABELS: Old Family Wine Cellars, Molly Pitcher, Leonardo da Vino. Tours and tasting April–October: daily 10 A.M.–6 P.M.; November–March: tasting only. Call for information.

In 1982 the founder of Tabor Hill Winery, Leonard Olson, bought the Lakeside Winery for a song from Cecil Pond. Olson, known as one of the pioneers of the premium wine industry in the mid-United States, started with nothing but old inventory and a pre-Prohibition building. He revived the winery as economically as possible, demolishing the old cement tanks in favor of barrel storage and training his staff in a special, frugal style of winery management. There are no vineyards, but Olson works with local growers, giving them instruction and a reliable place to sell their grapes. Still in its infancy, the winery produced its first vinifera wine in 1984.

Lakespring Winery
NAPA COUNTY

2055 Hoffman Lane, Napa, California 94558 (707-944-2475). FOUNDED: 1980. ACREAGE: 7 acres. PRODUCTION: 16,000 cases. DISTRIBUTION: Nationwide. OWNERS: Frank, Harry, and Ralph Battat. WINEMAKER: Randy W. C. Mason; Kristin Anderson, assistant. OTHER LABEL: Trois Frères. Tours by appointment only.

This modern winery was built by the three Battat brothers, Frank, Harry, and Ralph, who made their fortune in the wholesale food business. They hired young winemaker Randy Mason and have used their marketing expertise to carve a niche for Lakespring wines in the already crowded premium wine market.

WHITE

☆☆☆ 1981 CHARDONNAY ($10.00) Napa. *Rich and clean. Toasty and very good.*

○   1982 TROIS FRERES CHARDONNAY ($6.00) Napa Valley. *Vegetal and unattractive.*

☆☆   1983 CHARDONNAY ($11.50) Napa Valley. *Heavy, rich, oaky.*

☆☆   1982 CHENIN BLANC ($6.50) Napa Valley. *Lively, fruity, almost dry; quite nice.*

☆   1981 SAUVIGNON BLANC ($7.50) California.

☆☆☆   1982 SAUVIGNON BLANC ($7.50) California. *Varietal, crisp and fruity.*

☆☆   1983 SAUVIGNON BLANC ($8.50) California. *Grassy, vegetal, crisp, clean, attractive.*

RED

☆☆   1980 CABERNET SAUVIGNON ($11.00) Napa Valley. *Ripe, clean, raisiny, with some vegetal qualities.*

☆☆☆   1981 CABERNET SAUVIGNON ($11.00) Napa Valley. *Lovely, with hints of cherry. Great structure. Drink now.*

☆☆   1980 MERLOT ($9.00) Napa Valley. *Lush and well structured but just a bit vegetal.*

☆☆☆   1981 MERLOT ($10.00) Napa Valley. *Rich, varietal, attractive. Drink now.*

Ronald Lamb Winery
SANTA CLARA COUNTY

17785 Casa Lane, Morgan Hill, California 95037 (408-779-4268). FOUNDED: 1976. ACREAGE: None. PRODUCTION: 750 cases. DISTRIBUTION: California. OWNERS: Ronald and Aldrene Lamb. WINEMAKER: Ronald Lamb. Tours by appointment on weekends.

After touring Europe, visiting wineries, and talking with vintners, Ronald Lamb felt encouraged to make his home winemaking practice into a small sideline business. He and his wife began with a 400-square-foot garage. The winery has since more than doubled its production, and a second building has been added. Ron began making primarily red wines but later added white wines to his line.

RED

☆   1979 ZINFANDEL ($5.50) Friends Dedication, Santa Clara.

☆   1979 ZINFANDEL ($6.50) Upton Ranch, Amador. *Clumsy and harsh.*

Lambert Bridge
SONOMA COUNTY

4085 West Dry Creek Road, Healdsburg, California 95448 (707-433-5855). FOUNDED: 1975. ACREAGE: 78 acres. PRODUCTION: 13,000 cases. DISTRIBUTION: Nationwide and foreign markets. OWNERS: Gerard and Margaret Lambert. Dave Rafanelli, vineyard and general manager. WINEMAKER: Ed Killian. Tours by appointment.

Jerry Lambert, an heir to the Warner-Lambert pharmaceutical fortune, and his wife, Margaret, live in San Francisco and have created a lovely winery estate in the Dry Creek area. All the wines are made from estate-grown grapes.

WHITE

☆   1980 CHARDONNAY ($10.00) Sonoma. *Weedy, strange.*

    1981 CHARDONNAY ($13.75) Sonoma. *Heavy, vinous, vegetal, intense, unpleasant.*

☆☆☆   1982 CHARDONNAY ($13.00) Sonoma. *Crisp, balanced, clean, complex, lovely, vinous.*

RED

O   1979 CABERNET SAUVIGNON ($9.00) Sonoma. *Weedy and cooked.*

    1980 CABERNET SAUVIGNON ($8.00) Sonoma. *Simple, weedy.*

☆   1981 CABERNET SAUVIGNON ($11.00) Sonoma. *Clean, snappy, balanced but very vegetal. Drink 1986.*

☆   1981 MERLOT ($11.50) Sonoma. *Weedy, lush and complex. Drink now.*
☆☆ 1982 MERLOT ($11.50) Sonoma. *Soft and rich but vegetal.*

LaMont Winery
KERN COUNTY

1 Bear Mountain Winery Road, DiGiorgio, California 93217 (805-327-2200). FOUNDED: 1940. ACREAGE: None. PRODUCTION: 1.5 million cases. DISTRIBUTION: Nationwide. OWNER: John Labatt, Ltd. of Canada. Ed Bradley, president; John McCray, vice president; Ken Ford, vice president production; Bill Hill, vice president sales and marketing. WINEMAKER: Charles Feaver, chief winemaker. OTHER LABELS: Di Giorgio Fresh-Pak, Ambassador, A. R. Morrow Brandy, Aristocrat Brandy, and others. No tours or tasting.

When the old DiGiorgio winery became a Kern County growers' cooperative in the 1960s, it was renamed "Bear Mountain Winery." Then Labatt Breweries of Canada bought it and renamed it LaMont Winery. The winery still purchases grapes from the growers who originally owned the cooperative. A long line of varietal, generic, and fortified wines are being produced and sold under several brand labels, private labels, and in bulk.

RED

NV HINEY BROTHERS ($3.00) California. *A combination of de-alcoholized wine and grape juice. Tastes like thin, dry grape juice.*

Lancaster County Winery
PENNSYLVANIA

R.D. 1, Box 329, Willow Street, Pennsylvania 17584 (717-464-3555). FOUNDED: 1979. ACREAGE: 28 acres. PRODUCTION: 4,000 cases. DISTRIBUTION: At winery. OWNERS: Todd and Suzanne Dickel. WINEMAKER: Todd Dickel. Tours and tasting Monday–Saturday 10 A.M.–4 P.M.

Sick of New York and tired of the retail oil business and of living in the confines of an apartment, Todd Dickel said "to heck with this" and moved to Willow Street. He and his wife, a Lancaster County native, bought a 60-acre farm with a defunct winery and an 1819 stone house. "Every building and piece of equipment was run down and useless," says Todd, "and now it's in tip-top condition." He completely restored the house and rebuilt the barn winery by himself.

Landmark Vineyards
SONOMA COUNTY

9150 Los Amigos Road, Windsor, California 95492 (707-838-9466). FOUNDED: 1974. ACREAGE: 126 acres. PRODUCTION: 22,000 cases. DISTRIBUTION: Nationwide. OWNER: Mabry family. Bill Mabry III, president; Maxine Mabry, marketing; Marcia Mabry, sales. WINEMAKER: Bill Mabry III. Tours weekends 10 A.M.–5 P.M., or by appointment. Tasting Saturday and Sunday 10 A.M.–5 P.M.

When the Mabrys started planting vineyards in Sonoma County, the plan was to sell the grapes and make a little homemade wine in the garage. Bill Mabry, just out of high school, helped plant his family's vineyards in the Sonoma and Alexander valleys, all the while becoming more interested in winemaking. By 1972, after taking enology courses at U.C. Davis, he was making Landmark's first wines in rented space at another winery. Then the Mabrys bought a large parcel of land in the Russian River area with a two-story, Spanish-style house and a long driveway lined with cypress trees. They built the winery behind the house and planted the ranch with vines. During the first years of production, Bill made several different varieties, experimenting while waiting for his own Chardonnay and Cabernet Sauvignon vineyards to come into production. Now the winery is making only three wines: Chardonnay, Cabernet Sauvignon, and a proprietary white wine, Petit Blanc.

WHITE

☆☆ 1983 PETIT BLANC ($5.00) Sonoma. *Chenin Blanc, Sauvignon Blanc, and Chardonnay. Fresh and appealing.*

☆☆ 1980 CHARDONNAY ($10.50) Alexander Valley. *Toasty and well balanced.*

☆☆ 1981 CHARDONNAY ($9.00) Sonoma. *Balanced and likable.*

☆☆ 1981 CHARDONNAY ($10.00) Alexander Valley.

☆☆ 1981 CHARDONNAY ($14.00) Proprietor's Reserve, Sonoma. *Vinous, rich and heavy— perhaps too intense.*

☆☆☆ 1982 CHARDONNAY ($9.50) Sonoma. *Fresh and clean, with crisp acid and good balance.*

☆☆ 1982 CHARDONNAY ($10.00) Proprietor Grown, Alexander Valley. *Vinous, intense, lacking finesse.*

☆☆☆ 1983 CHARDONNAY ($9.00) Proprietor Grown, Sonoma Valley. *Rich, clean, with great fruit.*

RED

☆☆☆ 1978 CABERNET SAUVIGNON ($7.00) 75% Sonoma, 25% Napa. *Fragrant, soft and deep; delicious. Drink now or hold.*

O 1979 CABERNET SAUVIGNON ($8.50) Dry Creek Valley. *Bitter, dirty.*

☆☆☆ 1980 CABERNET SAUVIGNON ($8.50) Estate, Alexander Valley. *Lovely, crisp and complex, with wonderful fruit and earth.*

☆☆ 1980 CABERNET SAUVIGNON ($11.00) Estate, Alexander Valley. *Fruity, intense and balanced. Drink 1986.*

☆ 1981 CABERNET SAUVIGNON ($8.50) Robert Young, Alexander Valley. *Decent but a trifle bitter.*

☆☆ 1978 PINOT NOIR Sonoma-Cutrer, Sonoma.

Franz Wilhelm Langguth Winery
WASHINGTON

2340 Southwest Road F-5, Mattawa, Washington 99344 (509-932-4943). FOUNDED: 1982. ACREAGE: 265 acres. PRODUCTION: 100,000 cases. DISTRIBUTION: 7 states. OWNER: Partnership. WINEMAKER: Max Zellweger. OTHER LABEL: Saddle Mountain. Tours and tasting Friday–Sunday 10 A.M.–5 P.M.

A large winemaking firm from the Mosel region of Germany started this Washington winery. They chose a location similar in geography and soil to their own region and hired Max Zellweger, a German-speaking Swiss winemaker who acts as liaison with the parent company. The vineyards, owned by a partnership and called "Weinbau," were planted in 1981; the winery was built nearby during the following year.

WHITE

☆ 1983 SADDLE MOUNTAIN CHARDONNAY ($5.00) Washington. *Decent, simple, clean.*

☆ 1982 SADDLE MOUNTAIN GEWURZTRAMINER ($4.00) Washington. *Attractive but lacking freshness.*

O 1982 JOHANNISBERG RIESLING ($5.50) Extra Dry, Washington. *Muddy, dry, ordinary.*

☆☆ 1983 SADDLE MOUNTAIN JOHANNISBERG RIESLING ($4.00) Washington. *Fresh, crisp, clean, attractive.*

☆ 1983 JOHANNISBERG RIESLING ($6.70) Anders Gyving, Washington. *Hard, a bit strange but with good varietal character.*

☆☆ 1982 WHITE RIESLING ($6.00) Late Harvest, Washington. *4.1% residual sugar. Fruity, simple, fresh and attractive.*

RED

1982 CABERNET SAUVIGNON ($9.00) Washington. *Thin, dull.*

Lapic Winery
PENNSYLVANIA

682 Tulip Drive, New Brighton, Pennsylvania 15066 (412-846-2031). FOUNDED: 1977. ACREAGE: 2 acres. PRODUCTION: 4,000 cases. DISTRIBUTION: At winery and local outlets. OWNERS: Paul and Josephine Lapic. WINEMAKER: Paul Lapic. OTHER LABEL: Château La Pic. Tours Sunday 1 P.M.–5 P.M. Tasting Monday–Saturday 12–9 P.M.

When his homemade wine hobby grew past the 200-gallon limit, Paul Lapic considered starting a small winery as a retirement project. While still working with a utility company, Paul, a member of the American Wine Society and the Society of Enologists, met and questioned many winemakers about their experiences. Feeling somewhat secure about the possibilities, Paul built a rustic, rough-cut lumber winery on a four-acre parcel near his home. Since Paul and his wife have only two acres in vines, they buy grapes from other growers, including Paul's brother Walter. The winery has recently been expanded, and a new tasting room was built to accommodate large tour groups.

LaRocca Wine Company
NORTH CAROLINA

408 Buie Court, Fayetteville, North Carolina 28304 (919-484-8865). FOUNDED: 1968. ACREAGE: None. PRODUCTION: 2,500 cases. DISTRIBUTION: Local. OWNER: Sam LaRocca. WINE-MAKER: Sam LaRocca. OTHER LABEL: Carolina Pines. Tours by appointment.

Discharged from the army in North Carolina, Sam LaRocca decided that he might as well just stay there. He went back to work, then back to school, since his education had been cut short by his army stint. About the same time, Sam also became interested in home winemaking. After graduation, he constructed a few buildings near his house and started a small winery business. Under a different label, "Carolina Pines," Sam makes two Muscadine wines, one red and one white.

LAS COCHES CELLARS *see* Ventana Vineyards Winery

Las Montanas
SONOMA COUNTY

4400 Cavedale, Glen Ellen, California 95442 (707-996-2448). FOUNDED: 1982. ACREAGE: None. PRODUCTION: 750 cases. DISTRIBUTION: California and Virginia. OWNER: Aleta Olds. WINEMAKER: Aleta Olds. Tours and tasting by appointment.

Aleta Olds and her husband had worked in many wineries before they started Sky Vineyards. They made only Zinfandel and bottled it all under the "Las Montanas" label. Aleta took that name with her after she and Lore were divorced and began her own winery about one mile down the road from Sky Vineyards. Her wines are made without the use of chemicals of any sort in the cellar of her house.

RED

1983 GAMAY BEAUJOLAIS ($6.00) Naturel, Padilla, Napa Valley. *Simple, strange.*
1983 ZINFANDEL ($8.00) Naturel, Sonoma. *Strange nose, not much varietal character.*

Latah Creek Winery
WASHINGTON

Indiana Road, Spokane, Washington 99216 (509-448-0102). FOUNDED: 1982. ACREAGE: 50 acres. PRODUCTION: 12,000 cases. DISTRIBUTION: Alaska, Idaho, Montana, Oregon, and Washington. OWNERS: Mike Hogue and Mike Conway. WINEMAKER: Mike Conway. Tours and tasting daily 10 A.M.–4 P.M.

Mike Conway was the winemaker at Worden's Washington Winery when he met grower Mike Hogue, who had been selling his grapes to Worden's for some time. Conway, having established an impressive reputation as a Washington State winemaker, was ready to start his own winery. Likewise, Hogue had established a reputation for growing fine wine grapes and was ready to start his own winery; so the two made a deal. Mike Hogue agreed to be Mike Conway's partner in Latah Creek, and Mike Conway agreed to be Mike Hogue's consultant-winemaker for Hogue Cellars. Thus far, it has been an ideal arrangement.

WHITE

☆☆☆   1983 CHENIN BLANC ($5.00) Washington. *2% residual sugar. Fresh, clean, crisp, balanced, lovely.*

CAVES LAURENT PERRIER *see* Almadén Vineyards

Laurel Glen Vineyard
SONOMA COUNTY

P.O. Box 548, Glen Ellen, California 95442 (707-526-3914). FOUNDED: 1980. ACREAGE: 30 acres. PRODUCTION: 5,000 cases. DISTRIBUTION: Nationwide; Australia. OWNER: Patrick Campbell. WINEMAKER: Patrick Campbell. No tours or tasting.

Patrick Campbell purchased a 30-acre vineyard parcel of Cabernet on Sonoma Mountain in 1976. For a while he played the viola "semiprofessionally," made some wine at home, and sold his fruit to other wineries. In 1981 he built a wood-frame winery and began making his own Cabernet. "I am making only Cabernet and Merlot because I prefer to do one thing well," says Patrick. "Since I am only making 5,000 cases, the wine must be excellent."

RED

☆☆☆☆   1981 CABERNET SAUVIGNON ($12.50) Estate, Sonoma Mountain. *Firm, rich, deep, beautifully made. Drink 1986 and beyond.*

☆☆☆   1982 CABERNET SAUVIGNON ($12.50) Sonoma. *Structured, complex, clean. Not quite as rich as the '81 but lovely.*

☆☆☆   1982 MERLOT ($9.00) Sonoma. *Cherry fruit, good clean oak, fresh flavors. Drink 1987.*

LAWRENCE WINERY *see* Corbett Canyon Vineyards

Lazy Creek Winery
MENDOCINO COUNTY

4610 Highway 128, Philo, California 95466 (707-895-3623). FOUNDED: 1979. ACREAGE: 20 acres. PRODUCTION: 1,500 cases. DISTRIBUTION: California. OWNER: Johann Kobler. WINE-MAKERS: Johann and Theresa Kobler. Tours by appointment.

A soft-spoken Swiss-German couple, Johann and Theresa Kobler were looking to escape their restaurant careers in San Francisco. They found a cozy piece of property in Mendocino's Anderson Valley, where they planted vineyards. Johann quit his city job, built a small winery, and settled happily into the life of a farmer-winemaker.

LEAKY LAKE *see* Fretter Wine Cellars

LE DOMAINE *see* Almadén Vineyards

Leelanau Wine Cellars
MICHIGAN

12683 County Road 626, Omena, Michigan 49674 (616-386-5201). FOUNDED: 1975. ACREAGE: 25 acres. PRODUCTION: 12,000 cases. DISTRIBUTION: Michigan. OWNER: Michael Jacobson. WINEMAKER: Edward Van Dyne. Tasting at two locations: Omena—at the winery: Monday–Saturday 10:30 A.M.–6 P.M., Sunday 12–6 P.M.; tours in summer only. Frankenmuth—975 South Main: Monday–Saturday 10:30 A.M.–6 P.M., Sunday 12–6 P.M.

Farmer Charles Kalchek had grown many different kinds of fruit in his orchards for years before he thought about planting wine grapes. He started with experimental vineyards, after which he planted 22 acres of French-American hybrids and formed a partnership with lawyer Michael Jacobson. They started the winery in what used to be a cherry processing building on Charles' farm. Eventually Charles tired of the wine business and went back to what he loved best, farming, and Michael, the silent partner, became the sole owner of the winery.

Leeward Winery
VENTURA COUNTY

2784 Johnson Drive, Ventura, California 93003 (805-656-5054). FOUNDED: 1978. ACREAGE: None. PRODUCTION: 10,000 cases. DISTRIBUTION: California and 35 other states. OWNERS:

Chuck Brigham and Chuck Gardner. WINEMAKERS: Chuck Brigham and Chuck Gardner. Tours and tasting by appointment. Newsletter.

Chuck Brigham was selling clothes and Chuck Gardner was working for Safeway when they started making wine together at Chuck B.'s house in the "Leeward Estates." They went commercial in 1979 with 900 cases of wine. "We really see advantages to being small; there is better control over the wine, and it gives us a chance to learn about our vineyard sources," explains Chuck B. Leeward specializes in vineyard-designated wines and has stuck with those same vineyards year after year. In 1982, after moving to their new location in Ventura—"in a building that was actually designed to be a winery"—both Chucks began working full time in their winery.

WHITE

☆☆ 1981 CHARDONNAY ($13.00) Santa Maria Valley. *Varietal, clean and very pleasant.*

☆☆☆ 1981 CHARDONNAY ($14.00) MacGregor, San Luis Obispo. *Lemony, crisp and deep, with fresh oak and fruit nuances.*

☆☆☆ 1981 CHARDONNAY ($15.00) Ventana, Monterey. *Rich and clean, with hints of earth. Fat and varietal.*

☆☆☆ 1982 CHARDONNAY ($12.00) Bien Nacido, Santa Maria Valley. *Lush and oaky; fragrant and nicely balanced. The best of the '82s.*

☆☆☆ 1982 CHARDONNAY ($14.00) Central Coast. *Toasty nose and crisp, lemony flavor.*

☆☆ 1982 CHARDONNAY ($14.00) MacGregor, Edna Valley. *Buttery nose and crisp, tangy fruit. Complex and delicious.*

☆ 1982 CHARDONNAY ($14.00) Ventana, Monterey. *Earthy nose, crisp, snappy fruit but unbalanced.*

☆ 1983 CHARDONNAY ($8.00) 54% Edna Valley, 46% Santa Maria Valley, Central Coast. *Heavy, clumsy, oaky, intense.*

☆☆☆ 1983 CHARDONNAY ($14.00) MacGregor, Edna Valley. *Crisp and angular, with nice oak and plenty of fruit.*

☆☆ 1983 CHARDONNAY ($15.00) Ventana, Monterey. *Lush, clean, fruity, a bit heavy.*

1983 SAUVIGNON BLANC ($6.00) California. *Lush, oxidized, very strange.*

BLANC DE NOIR

☆☆ 1984 CORAL—PINOT NOIR BLANC ($5.25) Santa Maria. *Crisp, fresh, lively.*

RED

☆ 1980 CABERNET SAUVIGNON ($9.50) Jensen, San Luis Obispo. *Clumsy and unbalanced.*

☆ 1981 CABERNET SAUVIGNON ($9.00) Nepenthe, San Luis Obispo.

☆☆☆ 1981 ZINFANDEL ($7.50) Shenandoah Valley, Amador. *Lovely oak and fruit; elegant and superb.*

CHARLES LEFRANC CELLARS *see* Almadén Vineyards

Lenz Vineyards
NEW YORK

Main Road, Peconic, Long Island, New York 11958 (516-734-7499). FOUNDED: 1978. ACREAGE: 30 acres. PRODUCTION: 5,000 cases. DISTRIBUTION: New York. OWNER: Corporation. Patricia and Peter Lenz. WINEMAKER: Gary Patzwald. Retail sales daily 11 A.M.–4 P.M.

Owners of a restaurant in Westhampton Beach, Patricia and Peter Lenz were expert wine consumers. Since the restaurant had an exemplary American wine list, they had already met many people in the wine industry. When it came time to retire from the restaurant business, the Lenzes thought owning a vineyard and winery would provide a very attractive lifestyle. They looked all over the United States for land but decided to stay right in Long Island. They purchased a potato farm with a 90-foot-long barn. The potato barn, artfully remodeled in the style of a Bordeaux *chai*, has won several awards for its architecture.

WHITE

☆☆ 1983 CHARDONNAY ($9.00) Long Island, North Fork. *Crisp, firm, varietal, clean, attractive.*

☆☆☆ 1983 GEWURZTRAMINER ($7.00) Long Island, North Fork. *Delicate, fresh, varietal, beautifully structured.*

RED

☆☆☆ 1983 RESERVE ($12.00) Long Island, North Fork. *Cabernet, Merlot and Cabernet Franc. Rich and complex. Drink 1986.*

☆☆☆ 1983 MERLOT ($8.00) Long Island, North Fork. *Herbal, rich, soft, balanced, charming. Drink now.*

Leonetti Cellars
WASHINGTON

1321 School Avenue, Walla Walla, Washington 99362 (509-525-1428). FOUNDED: 1977. ACREAGE: 2.5 acres. PRODUCTION: 1,500 cases. DISTRIBUTION: Washington. OWNERS: Gary and Nancy Figgins. WINEMAKER: Gary Figgins. Tours by appointment.

Gary chose his mother's maiden name, Leonetti, over his own, Figgins, when he named his winery. This was because Gary learned about wine from his maternal grandfather, Frank Leonetti, an Italian immigrant who regularly made wine for his family. By the time he was twenty, Gary had been sufficiently inspired by the growth of the California wine industry to begin reading enology texts from U.C. Davis. After trying to grow grapes on the windowsill of an apartment, Gary and his wife, Nancy, bought a house with a couple of acres of land and planted a vineyard of Cabernet and Merlot. Gary has plans for a winery built from native stone that will enable him to expand his production to 6,000 gallons. "And we will continue to limit our production to red wines only," he says.

RED

☆ 1981 MERLOT ($10.00) Washington. *Crisp and clean, with some vegetal qualities.*

LIBERTY SCHOOL *see* Caymus Vineyards

Live Oaks Winery
SANTA CLARA COUNTY

3875 Hecker Pass Highway, Gilroy, California 95020 (408-842-2401). FOUNDED: 1912. ACREAGE: 10 acres. PRODUCTION: 30,000 cases. DISTRIBUTION: California. OWNER: Peter Scagliotti. WINEMAKER: Mitsuo Takemoto. Tasting daily 8 A.M.–5 P.M. Picnic and barbecue facilities.

Peter Scagliotti opens his tasting room early in the morning to catch commuters on their way to work. Most of his wine is sold out of his tasting room to families and friends who have bought the wines for years. "I was studying to be a doctor when my father died in 1938, so I came back to keep the winery going," says Peter, who never really wanted the winemaker's life. The winery was built before the advent of electricity, in the traditional gravity-flow design, with one building directly under the other.

Livermore Valley Cellars
ALAMEDA COUNTY

1508 Wetmore Road, Livermore, California 94550 (415-447-1751). FOUNDED: 1978. ACREAGE: 34 acres. PRODUCTION: 3,000 cases. DISTRIBUTION: California, Colorado, Massachusetts, and Texas. OWNERS: Chris and Beverly Lagiss. WINEMAKER: Chris Lagiss. Tours and tasting daily 11 A.M.–5 P.M.

If Wente can make wine, Chris Lagiss thought, then so can I. Chris had been growing grapes and selling them to Wente Brothers winery since 1953. "But being a farmer just doesn't pay," says Chris. So as a semi-retirement project, he built a small winery behind his house on the vineyard and made estate wines, all of them white. His daughter and her husband live in one of the homes on the property, and Chris hopes that someday they will run the winery.

WHITE

1981 CHARDONNAY ($8.00) Estate, Livermore Valley. *Fruity and slightly sweet; heavy and quite odd.*

O   1981 FUME BLANC ($4.95) Estate, Livermore Valley. *Heavy, dull, oxidized, sweet.*

LIVINGSTON CELLARS *see* E. & J. Gallo Winery

Llano Estacado Winery
TEXAS

P.O. Box 3487, Lubbock, Texas 79452 (806-745-2258). FOUNDED: 1976. ACREAGE: 11 acres. PRODUCTION: 15,000 cases. DISTRIBUTION: Texas. OWNER: Corporation. John Lowey, president. WINEMAKER: Kim McPherson. Tours and tasting Saturday 12–6 P.M., Sunday 1:30 P.M.– 6 P.M.

In the mid-1950s Robert Reed, a professor of viticulture at Texas Tech University, took home some vine cuttings that had been discarded by the university. He planted them in his backyard and was surprised by their vigorous growth. Robert then teamed up with Clinton McPherson to start a fifteen-acre vineyard of 75 different varieties. In 1973 they received permission to establish a wine lab at Texas Tech, and in 1975 they organized their own winery. Clinton and Robert are still involved with the winery and have been joined by Clinton's son Kim, who is the enologist, and John Lowey, who acts as president. While it has quadrupled in size since its start, the cement-block winery has kept its practical and unpretentious design. The winery's Spanish name, *Llano Estacado*, translates as "Staked Plains." As the story goes, the explorer Coronado planted stakes on this flat, desert-like part of Texas to mark a trail, and hence the name.

WHITE

☆☆   1983 CHENIN BLANC ($6.25) Texas. *0.5% residual sugar. Dry, fresh, clean, good acidity.*

Llords and Elwood Winery
NAPA COUNTY

6525 Washington Street, P.O. Box 2500, Yountville, California 94599 (707-944-8863). FOUNDED: 1955. ACREAGE: None. PRODUCTION: 15,000 cases. DISTRIBUTION: California and 8 other states. OWNERS: Llords and Elwood, Inc. Richard H. Elwood, president. WINEMAKER: Richard H. Elwood. Tours and tasting by appointment.

Mike Elwood, founder of this winery, thought that one type of wine made in California just couldn't compare with its European equivalent: sherry. A retailer in Beverly Hills, Mike believed high-quality sherry could be made in California, and he was going to be the one to make it. He quit the retail business and opened the Llords and Elwood Winery. His son Richard is now owner and winemaker.

WHITE

1981 JOHANNISBERG RIESLING ($7.25) Castle Magic, California.
☆ 1982 JOHANNISBERG RIESLING ($7.25) Castle Magic, California. *2.5% residual sugar. Herbaceous, soft and sweet, with nice fruit.*

J. Lohr Winery
SANTA CLARA COUNTY

1000 Lenzen Avenue, San Jose, California 95126 (408-288-5057). FOUNDED: 1974. ACREAGE: 500 acres. PRODUCTION: 225,000 cases. DISTRIBUTION: Nationwide. OWNER: Limited partnership. Jerry Lohr, general partner. WINEMAKER: Barry Gnekow. Tours and tasting daily 10 A.M.–5 P.M. Special winery events.

Jerry Lohr divides his time between the winery and the construction business. Most of the wines are made from grapes grown on winery-owned acreage near Greenfield in Monterey. The winery, once a brewery, underwent a name change in 1984 from Turgeon and Lohr Winery to J. Lohr Winery.

WHITE

☆ NV WHITE WINE SELECTION ($3.50) California. *Decent, clean, lacking character. Sold only at Hyatt Hotels.*
☆☆ 1981 CHARDONNAY ($9.00) Monterey. *The fruit and oak are nice, but the other flavors are strange.*
☆☆ 1981 CHARDONNAY ($12.50) Reserve, Monterey. *Rich, toasty and earthy, with nice oak.*
☆☆ 1981 CHARDONNAY ($14.00) Monterey Reserve, Monterey. *Attractive.*
☆ 1982 CHARDONNAY ($9.00) Greenfield, Monterey. *Fruity and clean but without much depth.*
☆☆ 1982 CHARDONNAY ($12.50) Reserve, Monterey.
1983 CHARDONNAY ($12.00) Reserve, Monterey. *Minty and quite bizarre.*
☆☆☆ 1982 CHENIN BLANC ($6.25) Rosebud, Sacramento. *1.3% residual sugar. Fresh flavored, fruity, delightful.*
☆ 1983 CHENIN BLANC ($5.50) Rosebud, Sacramento. *Clean but flabby and dull.*
☆ 1981 FUME BLANC ($8.00) Greenfield, Monterey. *29% Pinot Blanc, 18% Chardonnay.*
☆☆ 1982 FUME BLANC ($7.50) Greenfield, Monterey. *Smoky, richly varietal, nice.*
☆☆☆ 1981 JOHANNISBERG RIESLING ($7.80) Late Harvest, Monterey. *Herbal, crisp and clean, with honest fruit.*
☆☆ 1982 JOHANNISBERG RIESLING ($6.50) Greenfield, Monterey. *2.4% residual sugar. Ripe fruit and good acidity; fresh.*
☆☆☆ 1983 JOHANNISBERG RIESLING ($6.00) Greenfield, Monterey. *2.4% residual sugar. Lush, rich and intense. Lovely.*

☆☆   1982 PINOT BLANC ($7.00) Monterey. *Decent fruit, barrel fermented, clean.*
     1981 SAUVIGNON BLANC ($10.00) Late Harvest, Monterey. *11% residual sugar. Grassy
       and unappealing.*
☆   1982 SAUVIGNON BLANC ($10.00) Late Harvest, Monterey. *375ml. 9.25% residual
       sugar. Soft, sweet, lacking acid.*

RED

☆   NV   RED WINE SELECTION ($3.50) California.
O   NV   CABERNET SAUVIGNON ($4.00) Trois Cuvées, Northern California.
☆☆   NV   CABERNET SAUVIGNON ($5.75) California. *"12% alcohol." Cherry-berry, sim-
       ple, lovely. Drink now.*
☆   NV   CABERNET SAUVIGNON ($5.75) California. *"12.5% alcohol." Weedy, dense,
       with good fruit and depth. Drink now.*
     1978 CABERNET SAUVIGNON ($7.00) Greenfield, Monterey.
O   1980 CABERNET SAUVIGNON ($4.70) Keig, Napa Valley. *Not fresh, dull, no varietal
       character.*
     1980 CABERNET SAUVIGNON ($10.50) Keig, Napa Valley. *Decent fruit and varietal
       character, but tanky and not clean.*
☆☆☆ 1981 CABERNET SAUVIGNON ($9.00) St. Regis, Napa. *Crisp, clean and lively, with
       attractive floral notes. Drink 1986.*
☆☆   1982 GAMAY ($4.50) Greenfield, Monterey. *Surprising depth and clean, fresh fruitiness.*
☆☆☆ 1984 MONTEREY GAMAY ($4.50) Greenfield, Monterey. *Purple; ripe, spicey, lush and
       attractive.*
O   1979 PETITE SIRAH ($7.50) Northern California. *Overcome by weediness.*
☆   1978 PINOT NOIR ($7.00) Monterey.
☆☆   1978 ZINFANDEL ($4.00) Northern California.

Lolonis Winery
MENDOCINO COUNTY

2901 Road B, Redwood Valley, California 95470 (707-485-8027). FOUNDED: 1983. ACREAGE:
300 acres. PRODUCTION: 4,000 cases. DISTRIBUTION: California and some other states. OWN-
ERS: Petros and Ulysses Lolonis and family. WINEMAKER: James Milone. No tours or tasting.
   The Lolonis brothers had been growing grapes since 1920 on their Redwood Valley vineyards.
Ulysses Lolonis, a schoolteacher, managed the vineyards while his brother, Petros, worked as an
executive of Roos-Atkins. The Lolonis Vineyards became known to the wine world when wineries
such as Fetzer, Milano, and Dolan consistently named the vineyard on the labels of some of their
best wines. Once the vineyards' fame was established, Ulysses and Petros felt the time was right to
start their own winery. Their first vintage, 1982, was made by Jim Milone at Milano Winery, while
their own winery was being designed by architects specializing in classical Greek architecture.

WHITE

☆☆   1982 CHARDONNAY ($12.50) Estate, Mendocino. *Crisp, intense, vinous, lacking finesse
       and depth.*

Long Vineyards
NAPA COUNTY

P.O. Box 50, St. Helena, California 94574 (707-963-2496). FOUNDED: 1977. ACREAGE: 16
acres. PRODUCTION: 1,500 cases. DISTRIBUTION: California and by mailing list. OWNERS:

Bob and Zelma Long. Bob Long, general manager. WINEMAKER: Zelma Long. Tours by appointment.

This tiny winery in the eastern hills of the Napa Valley was founded by Zelma and Bob Long when Zelma was making wine at the Robert Mondavi Winery. Zelma, who is now winemaker at Simi Winery (see), makes the wine, and Bob takes care of the vines and manages the winery. The Longs have since divorced, but their professional relationship has endured.

WHITE

☆☆☆ 1980 CHARDONNAY ($24.00) Napa Valley. *Big, oaky, intense, quite remarkable. A monster.*

☆☆☆ 1982 CHARDONNAY ($24.00) Napa Valley. *Barrel fermented. Rich, deep, toasty, complex.*

☆☆☆ 1981 JOHANNISBERG RIESLING ($14.00) Late Harvest, Napa Valley. *9% residual sugar. Super—rich, deep, clean, balanced.*

☆☆☆ 1983 SAUVIGNON BLANC ($10.00) Sonoma. *20% Chardonnay. Rich, complex, rounded, fruity, oaky.*

Longoria Winery
SANTA BARBARA COUNTY

2670 Ontiveros Road, Los Olivos, California 93441 (805-688-8664). FOUNDED: 1982. ACREAGE: None. PRODUCTION: 1,000 cases. DISTRIBUTION: California, Arizona, and Texas. OWNERS: Jules W. Longoria, Jr., and Richard Longoria. WINEMAKER: Richard Longoria. Tours and tasting Saturday 10 A.M.–4 P.M., or by appointment.

Rick Longoria is the winemaker at J. Carey Winery. "Like so many people involved in the wine business, I always envisioned myself with my own winery," says Rick. "I just didn't have the financial means." But with the help of his father, Jules, Rick made their first vintage in 1982 at J. Carey Winery. Since then he has leased space at the new Houtz winery. Eventually Rick hopes to have his own land and winery building, but for now he's content to have his own label and to continue to work for J. Carey.

WHITE

☆ 1982 CHARDONNAY ($8.75) Santa Maria Valley. *Vinous, heavy, with good acidity but not likable.*

RED

1982 PINOT NOIR ($11.00) Santa Maria Valley. *Vegetal, nice fruit, clean but unappealing.*

Lonz Winery
OHIO

Middle Bass Island, Ohio 43446 (419-285-5411). FOUNDED: 1884. ACREAGE: 70 acres. DISTRIBUTION: Ohio. OWNER: Paramount Distillers. Robert Gottesman, president. WINEMAKER: Ted Moulton. Tours and tasting Monday–Thursday 12–8 P.M., Friday 12–10 P.M., Saturday 12–12 A.M. Large nautical gift shop.

Located on Middle Bass Island in Lake Erie, Lonz Winery was once a "party place" for boaters who would come out to the island, dock in the 150-boat marina, and spend the day drinking wine and picnicking. That was back in the 1950s when the winery was run by George Lonz. His father, Peter, had bought the winery from founder Andrew Wehrle in 1884, but it was George who managed the winery through its best times. After George died in 1969, the castle-like winery and vineyards went to ruin in the hands of inexperienced owners. When it was finally sold at an auction in 1976, Meiers Wine Cellars bought it, brought in new management, and began to restore the winery's property, vineyards, and reputation.

FORTIFIED

☆   3 ISLANDS MADEIRA Ohio.

❧

LOS HERMANOS *see* Beringer Vineyards

Los Vineros Winery
SANTA BARBARA COUNTY

618 Hanson Way, P.O. Box 334, Santa Maria, California 93454 (805-928-5917). FOUNDED: 1980. ACREAGE: None. PRODUCTION: 20,000 cases. DISTRIBUTION: California and some other states. OWNER: Cooperative. E. N. Woods, president. WINEMAKER: Andrew Starr. Tours and tasting Monday–Saturday 10 A.M.–4 P.M.

In 1980 eight grape growers in the Santa Ynez and Santa Maria valleys banded together to build this gray brick winery with its Spanish facade. They called it *Los Vineros*, "the vineyard owners." The winery was founded as a cooperative—a home for their grapes. Some of the partners continue to sell grapes to other wineries, and the winery purchases other grapes as well, mostly Sauvignon Blanc. Only one of these growers works actively in the winery—E. N. Woods, the president. Since 1980 the winery has gone through three winemakers, ending up with Andy Starr, a U.C. Davis graduate who used to be the assistant winemaker at HMR Estate Winery.

WHITE

☆☆☆   1981 CHARDONNAY ($9.00) Santa Barbara. *Charming and fresh.*
          1982 CHARDONNAY ($9.25) Santa Barbara. *Intense, sour and somewhat oxidized.*
☆   1981 SAUVIGNON BLANC ($7.50) Santa Maria Valley.
☆☆   1982 SAUVIGNON BLANC ($7.50) Santa Maria Valley. *Grassy and attractive.*
☆☆☆   1983 SAUVIGNON BLANC ($7.50) Central Coast. *Crisp, fresh, clean and varietal.*

RED

1981 CABERNET SAUVIGNON ($7.50) Santa Barbara. *Vegetal, unattractive.*
1981 PINOT NOIR ($9.50) Santa Maria Valley. *Bitter, unappealing.*

❧

Lost Hills Vineyards
SAN JOAQUIN COUNTY

3125 East Orange, Acampo, California 95220 (209-369-2746). FOUNDED: 1868. ACREAGE: 12 acres. PRODUCTION: 450,000 cases. DISTRIBUTION: Nationwide; 3 foreign markets. OWNER: Herbert Benham, Jr., president. Albert Luongo, general manager. WINEMAKER: Phil Loechler. OTHER LABELS: Lost Hills, Barengo, Dudenhoefer. Tours and tasting daily 9 A.M.–6 P.M. Gift shop.

The old Barengo Winery and vineyards were bought by Verdugo Vineyards in 1981 to be a home for its Lost Hills Winery brand. The winery building itself is a century old. The new managers, who call their facility the Lost Hills/Barengo Winery, have done their best to keep the late-1800s look of the old, double-brick winery while sprucing it up a bit with landscaping and new equipment. The Lost Hills label is used on table wines and generics; the Barengo label identifies dessert wines.

WHITE

○ 1981 FRENCH COLOMBARD ($4.00) California. *Dirty and oxidized.*

Lost Mountain Winery
WASHINGTON

730 Lost Mountain Road, Sequim, Washington 98382 (206-683-5229). FOUNDED: 1981. ACREAGE: 1 acre. PRODUCTION: 350 cases. DISTRIBUTION: At winery. OWNER: Romeo J. Conca. WINEMAKER: Romeo J. Conca. Tours and tasting by appointment.

You can follow the aroma of spicy sausages and rich sauces to the door of Romeo Conca, winemaker and cook. While working for International Telephone and Telegraph as a research scientist, Romeo's passion for food and wine inspired him to become a home winemaker. His wines are all red and full-bodied to match his homemade sausages, cured meats, and hearty home cooking. His tiny winery is in the foothills of the Olympic Mountains. "I hope the winery will augment my modest retirement income," says Romeo, "and allow me to keep up with inflation and the taxman—and still have fun." If Romeo has his way, he plans to have even more fun by opening his own Italian restaurant.

Lowden Schoolhouse Winery
WASHINGTON

41 Lowden School Road, Lowden, Washington 99360 (509-525-0940). FOUNDED: 1983. ACREAGE: None. PRODUCTION: 4,000 cases. DISTRIBUTION: Washington. OWNERS: Jean and Baker Ferguson. WINEMAKER: Jean Ferguson. Tours by appointment.

Baker Ferguson had driven past the old Lowden schoolhouse for years, never dreaming that one day he would make it into a winery. While working as chief executive officer of the Baker Boyer National Bank, he had dreamed about going into the wine business someday. When he finally started looking for a vineyard site, he heard the schoolhouse was for sale. "Whoever built schoolhouses must have had winemaking in mind," says Baker. "They convert into wineries very nicely." A three-level structure, the schoolhouse has the tasting room and entertainment facilities on the ground level, the winery below, and the Fergusons' living quarters above. Baker is the cellar assistant to his wife, Jean, the winemaker, when he is not being chairman of the board at the bank.

Lower Lake Winery
LAKE COUNTY

Highway 29, P.O. Box 950, Lower Lake, California 95457 (707-994-4069). FOUNDED: 1977. ACREAGE: None. PRODUCTION: 7,000 cases. DISTRIBUTION: England. OWNER: Partnership. Harry W. Stuermer, Marjorie E. and Daniel H. Stuermer, Elizabeth A. Stuermer, Thomas S. and Harriet E. Scavone. WINEMAKER: Daniel H. Stuermer, Ph.D. Tours and tasting Sunday 10 A.M.–5 P.M., or by appointment.

The Stuermer family, who lived in Los Angeles, owned 53 acres in Lake County on which they intended to raise either Black Angus cattle or Clydesdale horses. Then Dan Stuermer read an article in the *Los Angeles Times* about the Charles Krug Winery. He called his dad, Harry, an orthopedic surgeon, and suggested that they build a winery on the property instead. So in 1977 Dan, who had been working as a researcher in oceanography, moved up to Lake County and began building a redwood winery while moonlighting as a scientist in Berkeley and Livermore labs. Although Dan does have some horses and cattle on the property, they're there just for appearances and to keep the grass mowed.

WHITE

☆ 1981 FUME BLANC ($6.50) Oldham (66%), Hartshorn (34%), Lake.
O 1982 FUME BLANC ($7.00) Lake.
☆☆ 1979 SAUVIGNON BLANC ($7.50) 41% Stromberg, 40% Holdenreid, 16% Lovisone, Lake. *Interesting—crisp acid and rich fruit; Italianate.*

RED

☆☆ 1979 CABERNET SAUVIGNON ($7.50) 41% Stromberg, 40% Holdenreid, 19% Lovisone, Lake. *Good oak and fruit; clean but not likable.*
☆☆☆☆ 1979 CABERNET SAUVIGNON ($12.00) Devoto, Lake. *Lush, deep, balanced, superb. Drink 1986.*
☆ 1979 CABERNET SAUVIGNON ($12.00) Reserve, Devoto, Lake. *Raisiny, intense and a trifle weedy.*
☆☆ 1980 CABERNET SAUVIGNON ($8.50) 52% Holdenreid, 32% Devoto, 19% Lovisone, Lake. *Good, open, rich, fresh, balanced. Charming fruit.*
☆☆ 1981 CABERNET SAUVIGNON ($8.50) Lake. *Herbal, nicely made, easygoing. Drink now.*

Lucas Vineyards
NEW YORK

R.D. 2, County Road 150, Interlaken, New York 14847 (607-532-4825). FOUNDED: 1980. ACREAGE: 25 acres. PRODUCTION: 3,000 cases. DISTRIBUTION: New York. OWNERS: William and Ruth Lucas. WINEMAKERS: William and Ruth Lucas. Tours and tasting June–October: weekends 11 A.M.–5 P.M.; July–August: daily 11 A.M.–5 P.M.

William and Ruth Lucas had wanted to make their own grapes into wine for some time. Although they had been slowly expanding their vineyard acreage nine acres at a time, they were still selling their grapes to local wineries. When the Farm Winery Act passed in 1976, they gave into the temptation and built their own winery in the dairy barn. Since William is often away, working on a tugboat in New York harbor, Ruth and the three Lucas children are the full-time winery workers.

The Lucas Winery
SAN JOAQUIN COUNTY

18196 North Davis Road, Lodi, California 95240 (209-368-2006). FOUNDED: 1978. ACREAGE: 30 acres. PRODUCTION: 1,000 cases. DISTRIBUTION: California and Chicago. OWNERS: David and Tamara Lucas. WINEMAKERS: David and Tamara Lucas. Tours by appointment.

Tamara and David Lucas bought a 30-acre vineyard with 55-year-old vines near their home in Lodi. David, who was working for California Canners and Growers at the time, rebuilt the 100-year-old white farmhouse and redwood barn on the property. The Lucases made their first Zinfandel from their vineyard in 1977. "It was so good that we decided to bond the winery in 1978," says Tamara. By this time David had started working for his current employer, the Robert Mondavi Winery in Lodi. The Lucases make only Zinfandel, using only the grapes from the old vines on their vineyard.

RED

☆   1979 ZINFANDEL ($5.00) Estate, Lodi.
☆   1981 ZINFANDEL ($5.00) Lodi.

JERRY LUPER *see* Château Bouchaine

Lyeth Vineyard and Winery
SONOMA COUNTY

24625 Chianti Road, Geyserville, California 95441 (707-857-3562). FOUNDED: 1981. ACREAGE: 100 acres. PRODUCTION: 30,000 cases. DISTRIBUTION: 5 major market states. OWNER: Lyeth family. Munro Lyeth, Jr., general partner. WINEMAKER: William Arbios, enologist; Munro Lyeth, Jr., winemaster. Tours by appointment.

The name of the wine is not Cabernet Sauvignon or Sauvignon Blanc, but Lyeth. It's a family name, silk-screened in fourteen-karat gold on the bottle. The wines are varietal blends, emulating those of Bordeaux. They are intentionally without varietal designation. Munro "Chip" Lyeth (Lyeth rhymes with "teeth") explains: "We are emphasizing the winery and the name Lyeth, not any one varietal." Chip had been growing grapes in the Alexander Valley for twelve years when his father, a Colorado banker, asked him if he would like to have a winery. With dad paying all the bills, Chip could hardly say no. The winery is designed to look like an affluent European estate rather than a winery. There are guest rooms, dining salons, galleries, libraries, and a wing for the winery.

WHITE

☆☆☆   1982 WHITE TABLE WINE ($9.00) Alexander Valley. *75% Sauvignon Blanc, 20% Sem-illon, 5% Muscat. Rich, clean, fruity, soft.*

RED

☆☆☆   1981 RED TABLE WINE ($15.00) Alexander Valley. *65% Cabernet, 30% Cabernet Franc, 5% Merlot. Clean, rich, structured. Drink 1986.*
☆☆☆   1982 RED TABLE WINE ($15.00) Alexander Valley. *Same blend as the '81. Rich and deep, with a lovely violet flavor. Drink 1988.*

Lynfred Winery
ILLINOIS

15 South Roselle Road, Roselle, Illinois 60172 (312-529-WINE). FOUNDED: 1977. ACREAGE: None. PRODUCTION: 4,000 cases. DISTRIBUTION: At winery and local outlets. OWNER: Corporation. Fred E. Koehler, president. WINEMAKER: Fred E. Koehler. Tours and tasting daily 11 A.M.–7 P.M. Gift shop.

The Koehlers spent close to two years reworking a grossly overdecorated 1912 Victorian house. (It took a full year to strip the woodwork.) One of the house's best features is its thick-walled cellar, which provides ideal wine storage temperatures. The Koehlers' next project is digging underground caverns. The winery is Fred's hobby; he manages a nearby country club full time.

WHITE

☆☆   NV   JOHANNISBERG RIESLING ($9.00) Washington State. *Lush, delightful.*

Lytton Springs Winery
SONOMA COUNTY

650 Lytton Springs Road, Healdsburg, California 95448 (707-433-7721). FOUNDED: 1977. ACREAGE: 50 acres. PRODUCTION: 10,000 cases. DISTRIBUTION: Nationwide; England. OWNER: Walt Walters, president; Dee Sindt, vice president. WINEMAKER: Walt Walters. Tours and tasting Monday–Friday 9 A.M.–4:30 P.M., weekends 10 A.M.–4:30 P.M.

This winery is located on an old dry-farmed hillside vineyard that was planted before the turn of the century with Zinfandel and Petite Sirah. Before the winery was established, the grapes were sold to Ridge Vineyards, and the resulting wine was bottled separately, with a vineyard designation. The popularity of the Ridge wines persuaded B. W. "Walt" Walters to make his own wine from the vineyard. Walt believes in letting the quality of the grapes make the wine; he offers assistance, not interference.

BLANC DE NOIR

☆ 1983 WHITE ZINFANDEL ($6.00) Cuvée Andrea, Sonoma. *1.3% residual sugar. Heavy and vinous; they missed the point of what a "blush" wine is supposed to be.*

RED

☆☆ NV ZINFANDEL ($5.00) Wineburger, Sonoma. *Snappy, fresh, clean. A good everyday red wine.*

☆☆☆☆ 1977 ZINFANDEL ($6.50) Sonoma. *Lush, smooth, complex, superb—still their best.*

☆☆ 1978 ZINFANDEL ($7.50) Sonoma. *Rich, clean and mellow. A classic aged Zinfandel.*

☆☆ 1979 ZINFANDEL ($7.50) Sonoma. *Intense, big, rich, berried—the Lytton Springs style.*

☆ 1980 ZINFANDEL ($7.50) Special Select, Sonoma. *Low on fruit and musty to boot!*

☆☆☆ 1980 ZINFANDEL ($8.00) Sonoma. *Rich, briary, velvety, concentrated but likable.*

☆☆☆ 1981 ZINFANDEL ($8.00) Sonoma. *Rich, intense and balanced, with nice, fresh berry flavors. Will age.*

Madrona Vineyards
EL DORADO COUNTY

Gatlin Road, P.O. Box 454, Camino, California 95709 (916-644-5948). FOUNDED: 1980. ACREAGE: 35 acres. PRODUCTION: 10,000 cases. DISTRIBUTION: Major markets. OWNERS: Richard and Leslie Bush. WINEMAKER: Paul Wofford. Tours and tasting Monday–Friday 8 A.M.– 5 P.M.; Saturday 10 A.M.–5 P.M.; Sunday 1 P.M.–5 P.M.

Engineering consultant Richard Bush wanted a vineyard—not for investment or tax purposes, but simply because he wanted to grow grapes. "It was an emotional decision," says Richard. The winery, on the other hand, was more of a business decision. A few difficult years of trying to sell grapes were the impetus. In 1980 Richard built a two-story rectangular winery on a ridge over-looking his vineyards and began making 100 percent estate-grown wines.

WHITE

☆☆ 1981 CHARDONNAY ($8.50) Estate, El Dorado. *Fresh, clean and richly varietal.*

☆☆☆ 1982 CHARDONNAY Château d'Or, Select Harvest, Estate, El Dorado. *375ml. 13.2% residual sugar. Nutty, rich botrytis.*

☆☆☆ 1982 CHARDONNAY ($8.50) El Dorado. *Crisp, snappy and fresh, with good oak and fruit flavors.*

1981 WHITE RIESLING ($5.00) Estate.

BLANC DE NOIR

1983 WHITE ZINFANDEL ($5.00) Estate, El Dorado. *Dull, lifeless.*

☆☆ 1984 WHITE ZINFANDEL ($5.00) Estate, El Dorado. *1.2% residual sugar. Crisp, varietal, clean, attractive.*

RED

☆☆☆ 1979 CABERNET SAUVIGNON ($6.50) El Dorado. *5% Merlot. Beautiful structure, nice fruit, complex.*

☆☆☆ 1980 CABERNET SAUVIGNON ($8.75) El Dorado. *Structured and richly varietal, with good oak and fruit. Drink 1987.*

1979 ZINFANDEL ($6.00) El Dorado. *2.6% Merlot.*

☆☆☆ 1980 ZINFANDEL ($6.00) Estate, El Dorado. *Elegant and nicely structured.*

☆☆ 1981 ZINFANDEL ($6.00) Estate, El Dorado. *Raisiny, intense, tannic, rich. Drink 1986.*

MAGNOLIA *see* Perdido Vineyards

MANISCHEWITZ *see* Monarch Wine Company

Mantey Vineyards
OHIO

917 Bardshar Road, Sandusky, Ohio 44870 (419-625-5474). FOUNDED: 1880. ACREAGE: 40 acres. PRODUCTION: 20,000 cases. DISTRIBUTION: Ohio. OWNER: Paramount Distillers. Robert Gottesman, president. WINEMAKER: Claudio Salvador. Tours in summer: daily 10 A.M.– 3 P.M. Tasting and sales daily 9 A.M.–5 P.M. See also Meier's Wine Cellars, Lonz Cellars, Mon Ami Wine Company.

Started by the Mantey family in 1880, this winery remained in the family until 1980, when it was purchased by Paramount Distillers of Cleveland. The change of ownership brought about a modernization, a substantial increase in production, and a new, progressive management. Nevertheless, much of the original Mantey staff stayed on. The line of wines has also remained basically the same, though some vinifera varieties have been added. The old Mantey house and winery cellars are still standing near the original winery, which now houses the tasting room.

Manzanita
NAPA COUNTY

P.O. Box 1014, St. Helena, California 94574 (707-253-8698). FOUNDED: 1980. ACREAGE: None. PRODUCTION: 1,500 cases. DISTRIBUTION: California. OWNERS: Steve Koster, Bob Holder, and Richard Wolff. WINEMAKER: Steve Koster. No tours or tasting.

Steve Koster sells winery equipment, but his first love is making wine. After working with a number of wineries, Steve eventually began buying grapes and making his own wine at Monticello Cellars. This has been an amiable and very successful arrangement, and even if Manzanita grows large enough to be Steve's main source of income, he will probably lease storage space and continue to crush at Monticello.

WHITE

☆☆☆   1981 CHARDONNAY ($14.00) Napa Valley. *Clean, fresh and well made; good fruit-oak balance.*

☆☆☆   1982 CHARDONNAY ($14.00) Napa Valley. *Nice fruit and oak, well made and nicely balanced.*

ફ્⚭

Marietta Cellars
SONOMA COUNTY

P.O. Box 1260, Healdsburg, California 95448 (707-433-2747). FOUNDED: 1980. ACREAGE: None. PRODUCTION: 8,000 cases. DISTRIBUTION: 7 states and Washington D.C. OWNER: Chris Bilbro. WINEMAKER: Chris Bilbro. No tours or tasting.

Chris Bilbro was working as a hospital administrator when he and a friend bought Chris's family's winery, the Bandiera Winery. He tried to continue his hospital work while running the winery part time, but it wasn't long before he wanted to be on his own. A low-key fellow, Chris wants only to make enough wine to make a living and to give him the free time to be with his three children, so he sold his interest in the Bandiera Winery (see California Wine Company). He then quit his hospital job, insulated a storage building near his home, and began Marietta Cellars.

RED

☆☆   1981 CABERNET SAUVIGNON ($9.75) Sonoma. *Ripe, forward, attractive fruit. Drink 1988 and beyond.*

ફ્⚭

M. Marion & Company
SANTA CLARA COUNTY

14573 2B Big Basin Way, P.O. Box 265, Saratoga, California 95071 (408-867-6055). FOUNDED: 1979. ACREAGE: None. PRODUCTION: 80,000 cases. DISTRIBUTION: Nationwide. OWNERS: Dennis and Eunice Marion. WINEMAKER: Dennis Marion, blendmaster. No tours or tasting.

If you see Dennis Marion standing still, it must be an illusion. Running three different businesses keeps him constantly moving. An experienced wine retailer, wholesaler, and marketer, he started his own negociant label, M. Marion, in 1979 with an "Artist Series" of floral labels. He is also the president of David Bruce Winery and part owner of a racing yacht. As a negociant, Dennis buys varietal wines in bulk from different wineries throughout California, blends them to his taste, and bottles them with his own label.

WHITE

NV CHARDONNAY ($4.50) California.
☆ 1981 CHARDONNAY ($4.50) North Coast. *Simple and slightly oxidized.*
☆ 1982 CHARDONNAY ($4.50) California. *Soft, herbal, clean.*
1983 CHARDONNAY ($4.50) California. *Dull, flabby.*

BLANC DE NOIR

NV WHITE ZINFANDEL ($4.00) California. *Snappy and clean but lacking depth of fruit.*

RED

1980 CABERNET SAUVIGNON ($4.00) California. *Good structure but marred by dirty flavors.*
1982 CABERNET SAUVIGNON ($5.00) California. *Odd, off aromas. Decent fruit.*

❧

Mark West Vineyards
SONOMA COUNTY

7000 Trenton-Healdsburg Road, Forestville, California 95436 (707-544-4813). FOUNDED: 1976. ACREAGE: 62 acres. PRODUCTION: 20,000 cases. DISTRIBUTION: Nationwide; Hong Kong, Singapore, and England. OWNERS: Bob and Joan Ellis. WINEMAKER: Joan Ellis; Robert Iantasco, assistant. Tours and tasting daily 10 A.M.–5 P.M.

In love with the view and the seclusion of their new Russian River Valley property, Bob and Joan Ellis decided to build a winery estate. After planting Pinot Noir and Chardonnay, Joan took some enology courses while Bob, a pilot for Pan American, plied the air lanes. Two years after the vineyards were planted, they established the winery in a garage-sized redwood building. Bob still flies about half the time, while Joan splits her days between winemaking and cooking.

WHITE

☆☆☆ 1980 CHARDONNAY ($10.00) Wasson Ranch, Alexander Valley. *Crisp and nicely oaked. A classically structured wine.*
☆☆ 1981 CHARDONNAY ($12.00) Barrel Fermented, Estate, Sonoma. *Lemony.*
☆☆☆ 1983 GEWURZTRAMINER ($7.00) Sonoma. *0.9% residual sugar. Crisp, clean, melony, spicy, varietal.*
☆☆☆ 1981 JOHANNISBERG RIESLING ($6.00) Estate, Russian River Valley. *Crisp, fruity and off-dry.*
☆☆☆ 1982 JOHANNISBERG RIESLING ($6.00) Russian River Valley. *1% residual sugar. Crisp, fragrant, clean and appealing.*
☆☆☆ 1982 JOHANNISBERG RIESLING ($12.50) Late Harvest, Sonoma. *375ml. 9.4% residual sugar. Crisp, fruity and lovely.*

SPARKLING

☆☆ 1981 BLANC DE NOIRS ($12.00) Russian River Valley. *Clean, fresh, balanced. Mostly Pinot Noir.*

BLANC DE NOIR

☆☆☆ 1983 PINOT NOIR BLANC ($5.75) Estate, Russian River Valley. *Crisp, dry, fruity and clean.*

RED

1980 RUSSIAN RIVER RED ($4.00) Russian River Valley.
☆ 1981 RUSSIAN RIVER RED ($4.00) Russian River Valley. *Made from Pinot Noir grapes.*

☆☆ 1979 PINOT NOIR ($8.50) Estate, Russian River Valley. *Tart, crisp, clean and snappy.*
☆☆☆ 1980 ZINFANDEL ($8.50) Sonoma. *Big berry nose and snappy fruit flavors; crisp.*

Markham Winery
NAPA COUNTY

2812 North Street, Helena Highway, St. Helena, California 94574 (707-963-5292). FOUNDED: 1978. ACREAGE: 300 acres. PRODUCTION: 18,000 cases. DISTRIBUTION: 28 states. OWNER: Markham Advertising Company, Inc. H. Bruce Markham, president; Kate F. Markham, vice president; Bryan Del Bondio, general manager. WINEMAKER: Robert Foley, Jr. OTHER LABEL: Vin Mark. Tours by appointment. Tasting daily 11 A.M.–4 P.M.

Bruce Markham made his fortune in the outdoor advertising business. He began acquiring Napa Valley acreage in 1975 and bought an old stone winery built in 1876. Two thirds of the Markham-grown grapes are still sold to other wineries; the other third is made into Markham estate-bottled wines.

WHITE

☆☆☆ 1981 CHARDONNAY ($11.00) Napa Valley. *Snappy, clean and very classy. Stunning.*
☆☆☆ 1982 CHARDONNAY ($10.35) Napa Valley. *Crisp, clean, toasty, superb.*
☆☆☆ 1982 CHARDONNAY ($12.00) Markham Estate, Napa Valley. *Soft, round, clean and fresh, with lush fruitiness.*
☆☆ 1982 CHENIN BLANC ($6.85) Markham-Stelzner, Napa Valley. *Dry, intense, rich, round and interesting.*
☆☆ 1981 JOHANNISBERG RIESLING ($6.65) Estate-Yountville, Napa Valley. *Nice fruit but a trifle bitter on the finish.*
1982 JOHANNISBERG RIESLING ($6.50) Estate, Napa Valley. *1.3% residual sugar. Piney, unpleasant.*
☆☆ 1982 SAUVIGNON BLANC ($7.85) Napa Valley.
☆☆☆ 1983 SAUVIGNON BLANC ($7.85) Napa Valley. *Crisp, clean, fresh, varietal, lovely.*

BLANC DE NOIR

☆☆☆ 1983 GAMAY BLANC ($5.25) Estate, Napa Valley. *5% Chenin Blanc. Dry, crisp, pretty, very appealing.*

RED

☆☆☆ 1978 CABERNET SAUVIGNON ($12.00) Estate (Yountville), Napa Valley. *Lovely, well balanced, nicely structured.*
☆☆☆ 1979 CABERNET SAUVIGNON ($12.85) Yountville, Napa. *Austere, tannic, fruity. Will age well for many years.*
☆☆☆ 1982 CABERNET SAUVIGNON ($13.00) Napa Valley. *Crisp, clean, nice structure, earthy finish. Drink 1988.*
☆☆☆ 1980 MERLOT ($8.75) Stag's Leap District, Napa Valley. *Crisp and snappy, with nice cherry fruit.*
☆☆☆ 1981 MERLOT ($8.75) Napa Valley. *Rich, fruity, velvety. Drink now.*

Markko Vineyard
OHIO

R.D. 2, South Ridge Road, Conneaut, Ohio 44030 (216-593-3197). FOUNDED: 1968. ACREAGE: 14 acres. PRODUCTION: 2,000 cases. DISTRIBUTION: At winery. OWNERS: Arnulf Esterer and Thomas H. Hubbard. WINEMAKER: Arnulf Esterer. Tours and tasting Monday–Saturday 11 A.M.–6 P.M.

In 1968 two wine-loving friends teamed up and, with the guidance of Dr. Konstantin Frank, started planting vinifera vineyards. The winery, a low, concrete building nestled in a deeply wooded area of their property, was built in 1972. Over the years Arnulf Esterer and his family have worried through some pretty gruesome winters, wondering if the tender vinifera could survive. Their biggest reward has been the farming life—working together while developing a deep respect for wine and the earth. While they are proud of what has been achieved so far, they realize that it is just a beginning. "We are still experimenting," says Arnulf. "We need to discover if and where vinifera can produce wines of consistent quality, where they develop their most distinctive character. We are just beginning to get an idea."

WHITE

☆☆☆ 1978 CHARDONNAY Reserve, Ohio. *Lovely, complex and extremely elegant.*
☆☆ 1980 CHARDONNAY ($8.00) Ohio. *Varietal, oily, deep.*
☆ 1981 CHARDONNAY ($7.00) Ohio.
☆☆☆ 1982 CHARDONNAY ($9.00) Ohio. *Lovely balance and varietal character.*
☆ 1981 JOHANNISBERG RIESLING ($7.00) Reserve, Ohio. *Well made but dull.*

RED

☆ 1980 CABERNET SAUVIGNON ($9.00) Ohio. *10% Chamboursin. Crisp, tart, attractive.*

Marlo Winery
OHIO

Route 47, 3636 Street, Fort Laramie, Ohio 45845 (513-295-3232). FOUNDED: 1979. ACREAGE: 7 acres. PRODUCTION: 1,250 cases. DISTRIBUTION: At winery. OWNERS: Milo and Margaret Strozensky. WINEMAKER: Milo Strozensky. Tours and tasting winter: Friday 6 A.M.–10 P.M., Saturday 2 P.M.–10 P.M.; summer: Wednesday–Friday 2 P.M.–9 P.M., Saturday 2 P.M.–10 P.M.

Clergyman, salesman, and winemaker Milo Strozensky bought a farm in 1970, which allowed him to expand his home winemaking operation into a small but serious commercial venture. He first made wine in 1953, while working as an automobile industry salesman; his first commercial wines were released in 1979. Strictly a family enterprise, the winery and farm are staffed by Milo, his wife, his parents, and his two children.

Martin Brothers Winery
SAN LUIS OBISPO COUNTY

North Buena Vista Drive, Paso Robles, California 93446 (805-238-2520). FOUNDED: 1981. ACREAGE: 60 acres. PRODUCTION: 7,000 cases. DISTRIBUTION: Major markets in 10 western states. OWNER: Martin & MacFarlane, Inc. Edward Martin, chairman; Thomas Martin, president; Dominic Martin and David Weyrich, vice presidents. WINEMAKER: Dominic Martin. Tours by appointment. Tasting Wednesday–Sunday 11 A.M.–5 P.M.

Dominic Martin left his position as winemaker at Lambert Bridge to join his family in their own winery on California's central coast. The Martins—Dominic's father, wife, brothers, and sisters—bought an old dairy farm near Paso Robles, began planting vineyards, and converted the hay barn into a winery and the milk barn into a warehouse and tasting room. The winery has experimented with Nebbiolo, a noble variety rarely encountered outside the Piedmont region of Italy. If Dominic could have his way, he would make nothing but Nebbiolo and Muscat, but the rest of his family won't allow it.

WHITE

☆☆☆ 1982 CHARDONNAY ($10.00) Edna Valley. *Crisp, clean, fresh and snappy.*

☆ 1982 CHENIN BLANC ($5.50) Central Coast. *Lemony and crisp but a bit thin.*

☆☆ 1983 CHENIN BLANC ($5.00) Smoot and Perata, Paso Robles. *Dry, lemony, crisp, clean.*

☆☆☆ 1984 DRY CHENIN BLANC ($5.50) Smoot and Perata, Paso Robles. *Dry, crisp, fruity, rounded, delightful. A classic Chenin Blanc.*

☆☆ 1982 SAUVIGNON BLANC ($7.50) Paso Robles. *Attractive, varietal, good fruit.*

☆☆☆ 1983 SAUVIGNON BLANC ($7.50) Paso Robles.

RED

☆☆ 1982 NEBBIOLO ($7.00) California. *Fresh, intense and youthful—should develop nicely.*

☆☆ 1981 ZINFANDEL ($5.50) Paso Robles. *Tart, fruity, somewhat simple.*

☆☆☆ 1983 ZINFANDEL ($6.00) Paso Robles. *Light, tangy, fruity, fresh, charming.*

☆☆ 1983 ZINFANDEL ($7.50) 49% Venturini, 26% Obermayer, 25% Sauret, Paso Robles. *Lush, clean, varietal, nice.*

Martin Winery
LOS ANGELES COUNTY

11800 West Jefferson Boulevard, Culver City, California 90230 (213-390-5736). FOUNDED: 1917. ACREAGE: None. PRODUCTION: 2,000 cases. DISTRIBUTION: At winery only. OWNER: Charles Martin. Jim Umphries, general manager. WINEMAKER: Jim Umphries. Tasting and retail sales daily 11 A.M.–7 P.M. Cafe open Monday–Saturday 11 A.M.–6 P.M., Sunday 11 A.M.–5 P.M.

The tasting room at Martin Winery is a wine taster's supermarket. Under what is called a "Grand Daddy" tasting room license, the winery offers not only its own wines for tasting and sales, but other domestic and imported wines as well. "People who came to the tasting room would ask for other wines, so I figured, heck, why not?" Chuck Martin explains. His own winery produces limited amounts of wine that are sold only in the tasting room. Only rarely are grapes actually crushed at the facility; Chuck prefers to buy the juice already crushed.

Louis M. Martini
NAPA COUNTY

St. Helena Highway South, St. Helena, California 94574 (707-963-2736). FOUNDED: 1922. ACREAGE: 1,500 acres. PRODUCTION: 325,000 cases. DISTRIBUTION: Nationwide; 8 foreign markets. OWNER: Martini family. Louis P. Martini, president; Carolyn Martini, marketing; Patricia Martini, controller. WINEMAKERS: Louis P. and Michael Martini. Tours and tasting daily 10 A.M.–4:30 P.M.

Louis Michael Martini came to America in 1900 at the age of thirteen to work in his father's San Francisco fish business. After the 1906 earthquake he returned to Italy to learn winemaking. He came back to California and made grape concentrate during Prohibition. After Repeal in 1934, Louis built the St. Helena winery and began acquiring vineyards. His winery became one of the most celebrated and most important in California. Louis M. turned management of this booming wine operation over to his son Louis Peter in 1960, but he remained active in the business until his death in 1974 at age 87. Today Louis P.'s son Michael is the winemaker, daughter Carolyn works in marketing, and daughter Patricia is the controller.

WHITE

1981 VINEYARD SELECTION ($5.56) Monte Rosso, Sonoma. *Dull.*
1978 CHARDONNAY ($4.85) Special Lot, California.

○   1979 CHARDONNAY ($9.00) Private Reserve, Los Vinedos del Rio, California. *Horrifying; dead, oxidized, brown.*

☆   1981 CHARDONNAY ($7.00) California. *Dull.*

☆   1982 CHARDONNAY ($7.00) Napa Valley. *Snappy, crisp, decent but not completely clean.*

    1982 CHARDONNAY ($10.00) Vineyard Selection, Los Vinedos del Rio, Russian River Valley. *Lacking fruit, dull.*

    1982 CHARDONNAY ($12.00) Vineyard Selection, Napa Valley. *Musty wood, lacking fruit, thin flavors.*

    1983 CHENIN BLANC ($4.90) Napa. *Tanky, dry, varietal.*

☆☆ 1981 FOLLE BLANCHE ($5.50) Sonoma Valley. *Fresh, clean, fruity, balanced, very nice.*

☆☆ 1983 FOLLE BLANCHE ($4.75) Sonoma Valley.

☆   1982 GEWURZTRAMINER ($5.45) Sonoma. *Crisp but dull; no varietal character or fruit.*

○   1981 JOHANNISBERG RIESLING ($5.45) Monte Rosso, Sonoma. *Dull, dry, dreary.*

○   1982 SAUVIGNON BLANC ($6.80) North Coast. *35% Semillon. Musty, unpleasant.*

    1983 SAUVIGNON BLANC-SEMILLON ($6.50) Napa Valley.

RED

☆☆☆ 1979 BARBERA ($4.50) California. *Fruity, snappy and smooth.*

     1980 BARBERA ($4.90) California. *The taste of redwood overwhelms the charms of this wine.*

     1974 CABERNET SAUVIGNON ($12.00) Special Selection, California (60% Sonoma, 40% Napa). *Soft, earthy, lacking fruit and depth.*

☆   1975 CABERNET SAUVIGNON ($10.00) Special Selection, Napa Valley. *Varietal but dull at this point.*

☆   1976 CABERNET SAUVIGNON ($10.00) Special Selection, California. *Raisiny and a bit musty.*

     1977 CABERNET SAUVIGNON ($9.50) Private Reserve, California Mountain. *Vegetal, astringent, thin.*

☆☆   1978 CABERNET SAUVIGNON ($5.75) California.

☆   1978 CABERNET SAUVIGNON ($9.00) Special Selection, California. *Clean, lacking fruit.*

     1979 CABERNET SAUVIGNON ($4.75) North Coast. *Thin, dull, lacking varietal character.*

☆☆☆ 1979 CABERNET SAUVIGNON ($12.00) Vineyard Selection, Lot 2, Monte Rosso, Sonoma. *Rich fruit, mint and varietal character. Complex. Drink 1986.*

☆☆☆ 1979 CABERNET SAUVIGNON ($15.00) Vineyard Selection, Lot 1, Monte Rosso, Sonoma. *Classic structure, richly varietal, fruity. Drink 1987.*

     1980 CABERNET SAUVIGNON ($6.00) North Coast. *Dull, lacking fruit, tired.*

     1980 CABERNET SAUVIGNON ($6.50) Monte Rosso, Sonoma. *A pleasant wine that is overridden by dirty, moldy flavors.*

☆☆   1981 CABERNET SAUVIGNON ($15.00) La Loma, Napa Valley. *Clean, lithe, lovely, a bit short.*

○   1983 GAMAY NOUVEAU ($4.50) Sonoma. *Simple, oxidized, unpleasant.*

☆☆   1975 MERLOT California.

☆☆   1976 MERLOT California.

☆   1977 MERLOT California.

☆☆   1978 MERLOT ($5.00) California.

     1979 MERLOT ($5.00) California.

☆   1980 MERLOT ($5.00) North Coast. *Earthy and dull.*

☆   1981 MERLOT ($5.50) Napa. *Musty, decent fruit.*

☆☆☆ 1981 MERLOT ($10.00) Russian River Valley. *Elegant, balanced, lovely, a very graceful wine.*

☆☆   1981 MERLOT ($10.00) Vineyard Selection, Los Vinedos del Rio, Russian River Valley. *Light and pleasant, with attractive fruit and some oak.*

1981 PETITE SIRAH ($4.90) Napa Valley. *Redwood flavors mar the potential appeal here.*

☆☆   1975 PINOT NOIR ($8.50) Special Selection, California. *Earthy, varietal, very appealing.*

☆☆☆ 1976 PINOT NOIR ($4.00) California. *Smoky, balanced, smooth and Burgundian.*

☆☆☆ 1976 PINOT NOIR ($11.00) Special Selection, California. *Smoky, fresh, crisp, clean and varietal, with fresh fruitiness.*

☆   1977 PINOT NOIR ($9.00) Special Selection, La Loma, Napa Valley. *Good structure but very earthy, with dirty flavors.*

☆☆   1979 PINOT NOIR ($3.40) Napa Valley. *Nice structure; clean, simple and pleasant.*

O   1979 PINOT NOIR ($10.00) Vineyard Selection, La Loma, Napa Valley. *Oxidized.*

☆☆   1979 PINOT NOIR ($10.00) Vineyard Selection, Las Amigas, Napa Valley. *Soft, rich and earthy. Should age well.*

☆☆   1981 PINOT NOIR ($5.57) La Loma and Las Amigas, Napa Valley. *Round, fruity, clean, attractive.*

☆   1982 PINOT NOIR ($8.00) Los Carneros. *Fat, overripe.*

☆☆☆ 1968 ZINFANDEL Monte Rosso, Sonoma. *Lush, smooth, complex, mellow.*

☆☆   1974 ZINFANDEL ($10.00) Special Selection, California. *Nice, rich, clean and decent.*

☆   1977 ZINFANDEL ($10.00) Monte Rosso, Sonoma.

O   1977 ZINFANDEL ($10.00) Special Selection, Monte Rosso (Sonoma), California. *Dried fruit, bitter, unpleasant.*

☆☆   1978 ZINFANDEL ($10.00) Special Selection, Monte Rosso (Sonoma), California. *15.3% alcohol. Bramble and fruit; earthy and hot.*

☆☆   1980 ZINFANDEL ($4.45) North Coast. *Clean, with nice, snappy fruit.*

☆☆   1981 ZINFANDEL ($4.90) North Coast. *Fresh, clean, snappy, charming.*

Martini and Prati
SONOMA COUNTY

2191 Laguna Road, Santa Rosa, California 95401 (707-823-2404). FOUNDED: 1870. ACREAGE: 450 acres. PRODUCTION: 1 million cases. DISTRIBUTION: California. OWNER: Corporation. Elmo Martini, president. WINEMAKER: Frank Vannucci. OTHER LABEL: Fountain Grove. No tours. Tasting weekends 8 A.M.–5 P.M.

For many years the majority of this winery's production was bulk wine for Paul Masson. Founded by the Martini and Prati families and owned for many years by the Hiram Walker corporation, the winery has always been managed by Elmo Martini and his sons. In the early 1980s the Martini and Prati families bought back their winery. It still looks and operates like a pre-Prohibition bulk winery, using huge cement vats for fermentation, rebuilt machinery, and a variety of historic redwood tanks. If asked, Elmo will tell the story of every redwood tank and each scrap of equipment.

WHITE

O   NV CHABLIS ($1.80) Sonoma. *0.75% residual sugar. Seriously flawed.*

Paul Masson Vineyards
SANTA CLARA COUNTY

13150 Saratoga Avenue, Saratoga, California 95070 (408-257-7800). FOUNDED: 1852. ACREAGE: 4,535 acres. PRODUCTION: 9 million cases. DISTRIBUTION: Nationwide; 60 foreign markets.

OWNER: Seagram Wine Company. Dick Maher, president. WINEMAKER: Larry Brink. OTHER LABEL: St. Regis. Tours and tasting weekends 10 A.M.–4 P.M. Gift shop.

Frenchman Paul Masson, Charles Lefranc's son-in-law (see Almadén Vineyards), came to work at the Lefranc winery in the early 1880s. In short order the savvy Masson had put his own name over the door, and by 1892 he was producing creditable champagne. Masson retired in 1936 and sold the winery to the controversial Martin Ray, who sold it to Seagram in 1943. The new owner expanded plantings into Monterey County in 1960 and built a new winery there in 1967. Paul Masson is now one of California's largest wineries, and the Seagram wine stable, which also includes Taylor, is now second in size only to Gallo.

WHITE

☆ NV ST. REGIS BLANC ($3.00) California. *Nonalcoholic. Strange but drinkable; off-dry and fruity.*

☆ NV LIGHT CHABLIS ($3.15) California. *Heavy nose; soft, light flavors; acceptable.*

NV PREMIUM CHABLIS ($3.25) California. *Clean but dull.*

☆☆☆ 1982 EMERALD DRY ($3.25) California. *Some residual sugar. Spritzy, clean and lovely.*

☆☆ 1983 EMERALD DRY ($3.25) California. *Crisp, fresh, clean, off-dry, charming.*

☆ NV RHINE California. *Fresh, sweet, crisp; fruity, clean and nice.*

☆☆ NV LIGHT RHINE ($3.50) California. *Soft, decent, clean, pleasant.*

☆ 1982 RHINE CASTLE ($3.00) California. *Very sweet, almost syrupy. Fruity, clean, simple flavors.*

1980 CHARDONNAY ($8.50) Pinnacles Selection, Monterey. *Vinous, heavy, lacking fruit.*

☆☆ 1980 CHARDONNAY ($9.75) California. *1.5 liter.*

☆☆ 1981 CHARDONNAY ($6.50) Monterey. *Clean and snappy; not much varietal character.*

1981 CHARDONNAY ($8.50) Pinnacles Selection, Estate, Monterey. *Unattractive nose, rich, vinous, not pleasant.*

☆ 1983 CHARDONNAY ($6.00) Monterey. *Coarse, lacking varietal character, thin.*

☆ 1983 CHARDONNAY ($8.50) Estate, Monterey.

☆☆ 1983 CHARDONNAY ($12.00) Monterey.

☆☆ 1982 CHENIN BLANC ($3.75) California. *Nice, clean, fresh and appealing.*

1982 CHENIN BLANC ($6.50) California. *Varietal but quite dull.*

☆ 1983 CHENIN BLANC ($3.35) California. *Decent fruit, dull, watery.*

1982 FRENCH COLOMBARD ($3.25) California. *Crisp and somewhat sweet. Decent.*

☆ 1983 FRENCH COLOMBARD ($3.50) California. *Flabby, dull, clean, decent.*

O 1980 FUME BLANC ($7.15) Pinnacles, Monterey. *Weedy.*

☆ 1983 FUME BLANC ($8.00) Estate, Monterey. *Watery, decent flavors.*

☆ 1981 GEWURZTRAMINER ($6.50) Estate, Monterey. *Simple, fruity, melony.*

☆☆☆ 1982 GEWURZTRAMINER ($7.00) Estate, Monterey. *Soft, varietal, clean and fresh.*

1982 JOHANNISBERG RIESLING ($5.50) California. *Oily, dry, rather dull.*

☆ 1983 JOHANNISBERG RIESLING ($5.50) Monterey. *Decent, clean, some varietal character. A touch of oxidation.*

☆ 1982 RIESLING ($3.25) California. *1.7% residual sugar. Decent fruit, simple, no depth.*

☆☆ 1983 RIESLING ($3.75) California. *Soft, ripe, off-dry and attractive.*

☆ 1981 SAUVIGNON BLANC ($5.25) Monterey.

☆ 1982 SAUVIGNON BLANC ($5.50) Pinnacles Selection, Estate, Monterey. *Grassy, decent fruit, clean, a bit thin.*

SPARKLING

☆ 1982 BRUT ($8.00) California. *Sweet, heavy, decent but not very interesting.*

☆ NV CRACKLING CHABLIS ($5.15) California. *Crisp, clean, Muscat nose, not bad.*

NV PINK CHAMPAGNE ($8.00) California.

☆ 1981 EXTRA DRY CHAMPAGNE ($8.00) California. *Soft, sweet, fruity, decent.*
☆ 1982 EXTRA DRY CHAMPAGNE ($8.00) California. *Simple, lush, fat, fruity.*
   NV CRACKLING ROSE ($5.15) California. *Sweet.*

BLANC DE NOIR

☆☆ 1984 WHITE ZINFANDEL ($3.25) California. *Fresh, sweet, fruity, delightful.*

RED

☆☆ NV PREMIUM BURGUNDY ($3.25) California. *Rich, lush, good balance.*
   1979 CABERNET SAUVIGNON ($6.00) California.
☆ 1980 CABERNET SAUVIGNON ($5.75) California.
☆ 1981 CABERNET SAUVIGNON ($5.50) California.
☆☆ 1982 CABERNET SAUVIGNON ($6.20) Sonoma County. *Simple and a bit thin but pleasant.*
☆☆ 1982 PINOT NOIR ($5.40) Sonoma. *Decent, clean, fruity, pleasant.*
☆☆☆ 1979 ZINFANDEL ($3.75) California. *Fruity, clean and appealing.*
☆ 1982 ZINFANDEL ($3.25) California. *Crisp and vegetal; decent.*

Mastantuono Winery
SAN LUIS OBISPO COUNTY

Route 1, Willow Creek Road, Paso Robles, California 93446 (805-238-1078). FOUNDED: 1977. ACREAGE: 15 acres. PRODUCTION: 8,000 cases. DISTRIBUTION: California and 8 other states. OWNERS: Pasquale Mastantuono, president; and Leona Mastantuono, secretary-treasurer. WINE-MAKER: Pasquale Mastantuono. Tours by appointment.

As a home winemaker, Pasquale "Pat" Mastantuono bought Zinfandel grapes from vineyards up and down the California coast. He preferred the grapes grown in the Templeton–Paso Robles area, so when he and his wife began looking for winery property, Paso Robles was his first choice. The Mastantuonos bought a barley field, built the winery, the barn, and finally their house. Zinfandel is still Pat's greatest love, although he experiments with other varieties from several different viticultural areas.

WHITE

   1982 CHARDONNAY ($9.25) San Luis Obispo.
O 1983 CHENIN BLANC ($3.75) California. *Skunky, vegetal.*

RED

☆☆ 1982 PINOT NOIR ($15.00) Paso Robles. *Earthy, clean, rich, intense.*
☆☆ 1980 ZINFANDEL ($8.25) Dusi, Templeton, San Luis Obispo. *Lush, big, peppery, berried.*
☆ 1981 ZINFANDEL ($9.25) Dusi, Templeton, San Luis Obispo. *Heavy and simple; decent but not lovable.*
O 1981 ZINFANDEL ($20.00) Centennial, San Luis Obispo. *Raisiny, late harvest, grotesque.*

Matanzas Creek Winery
SONOMA COUNTY

6097 Bennett Valley Road, Santa Rosa, California 95401 (707-542-8242). FOUNDED: 1978. ACREAGE: 58 acres. PRODUCTION: 5,000 cases. DISTRIBUTION: California and 11 other states; England. OWNERS: Bill and Sandra McIver. WINEMAKER: David Ramey. Tours by appointment.

Bill and Sandra McIver met Merry Edwards while she was making wine at Mount Eden Vineyards. The McIvers, who owned vineyard property in the Bennett Valley area of Sonoma, asked Merry to help them design a small winery and then become their winemaker. Matanzas Creek quickly established an extraordinary reputation for its Chardonnay (winning the sweepstakes award at the Sonoma Harvest Fair wine judging didn't hurt). Efforts in Cabernet, Merlot, and Sauvignon Blanc are also becoming impressive as the estate vineyards mature. In 1984 Merry Edwards left Matanzas Creek to make wine for her parents' new winery, Merry Vintners (see). She was replaced by David Ramey, who had been Zelma Long's assistant at Simi Winery.

WHITE

☆☆ 1980 CHARDONNAY ($15.00) Sonoma. *Big, oily, vinous and forward.*

☆☆☆☆ 1981 CHARDONNAY ($14.50) Sonoma. *Toasty and elegant; rich, yet fruity and balanced.*

☆☆ 1982 CHARDONNAY ($15.00) Sonoma. *Toasty, soft, clean, lacking depth of fruit.*

☆☆☆☆ 1982 CHARDONNAY ($18.00) Estate, Sonoma Valley. *Rich and oaky, with lovely balance and finesse. A classic.*

☆☆☆☆ 1983 CHARDONNAY ($18.00) Estate, Sonoma Valley. *Crisp, clean, angular, elegant.*

☆☆ 1982 SAUVIGNON BLANC ($10.50) Sonoma.

☆☆☆ 1983 SAUVIGNON BLANC ($10.50) Sonoma. *Crisp fruit, great acidity, lovely fruit. Subtle and rich.*

RED

☆☆☆ 1979 CABERNET SAUVIGNON ($16.00) Sonoma. *Velvety and rich, with lovely complexity. Will be great with age.*

1980 CABERNET SAUVIGNON ($16.00) Sonoma. *Hard and weedy. Maybe time will help, but I'm not optimistic.*

☆☆☆ 1982 CABERNET SAUVIGNON ($14.00) Sonoma. *Lovely balance, rich fruit, nice wood. Drink 1988.*

☆ 1978 MERLOT ($18.00) Estate, Sonoma.

☆☆ 1979 MERLOT ($12.00) Sonoma. *Intense and complicated but basically unsatisfying. Needs time.*

☆☆☆ 1980 MERLOT ($12.50) Sonoma Valley. *Lush, lovely, ripe and earthy.*

1981 MERLOT ($12.50) Sonoma Valley. *Marred by off aromas and flavors.*

☆☆ NV PINOT NOIR ($10.50) Assemblage de Deux Vins, Quail Hill Ranch, Sonoma. *Lithe, clean and a bit stemmy.*

Matrose Wines
SONOMA COUNTY

1061 Moody Lane, Geyserville, California 95441 (707-857-3335). FOUNDED: 1982. ACREAGE: None. PRODUCTION: 1,400 cases. DISTRIBUTION: California, Utah, and Wisconsin. OWNERS: Jamie and Ann Meves. WINEMAKER: Jamie Meves. No tours or tasting.

"Matrose is a cross between a custom crush and a negociant label," says winemaker Jamie Meves. "Most people consider it an extension of the Pat Paulsen line." Jamie, who is the winemaker at Pat Paulsen Vineyards (see) and his family's winery, Pacheco Ranch (see), started his own label because of his love for Gewürztraminer. Since this variety is not part of the Paulsen line, he asked the winery if he could make it under his own label. "I wanted to do something different with Gewürztraminer—make it almost dry, with some barrel aging and malolactic fermentation," says Jamie. He has also produced the first commercial bottling of a new U.C. Davis variety called "Symphony."

WHITE

☆☆   1983 GEWURZTRAMINER ($7.00) Dry, Alexander Valley. *0.61% residual sugar. Varietal, serious, clean, well made.*

☆☆☆☆   1984 GEWURZTRAMINER ($7.50) Hafner, Alexander Valley. *0.67% residual sugar. Varietal, dry, crisp, round, complex, elegant.*

☆☆☆   1984 SYMPHONY ($5.50) Sonoma. *375ml. 5.37% residual sugar. A lovely new variety.*

☆☆☆   1982 TRAMINER ($7.00) Hafner, Alexander Valley. *Dry, richly varietal, clean, masterful.*

L. Mawby Vineyards
MICHIGAN

4519 Elm Valley Road, Suttons Bay, Michigan 49682 (616-271-3522). FOUNDED: 1978. ACREAGE: 10 acres. PRODUCTION: 1,000 cases. DISTRIBUTION: Michigan. OWNER: Lawrence Mawby. WINEMAKER: Lawrence Mawby. OTHER LABEL: Elm Valley Vineyards. Tours and tasting May– October: Saturday and Sunday 1 P.M.–6 P.M., or by appointment.

The son of a fruit farmer, Lawrence Mawby had developed a keen interest in wine by the time he graduated from college. He hoped there was potential for grape growing in his orchard-covered county. He bought thirty acres, planted ten in grapevines, and built a combination winery-residence. By 1977 there was sufficient crop from Larry's vineyards to supply the winery's entire needs. Meanwhile, Larry also operates his family's orchard business, which, he admits, "maintains my livelihood."

WHITE

☆   1982 WHITE TABLE WINE ($4.38) Leelanau. *55% Ravat Vignoles, 45% Seyval Blanc. Tart, fresh, snappy.*

☆☆☆   1982 RAVAT VIGNOLES ($6.25) Lot FR, Leelanau Peninsula. *Complex, balanced, delightful.*

RED

    1981 MARECHAL FOCH ($7.50) Red, Leelanau Peninsula.

☆☆   1983 MARECHAL FOCH ($5.50) Red, Leelanau Peninsula.

Mayacamas Vineyards
NAPA COUNTY

1155 Lokoya Road, Napa, California 94558 (707-224-4030). FOUNDED: 1889. ACREAGE: 55 acres. PRODUCTION: 5,000 cases. DISTRIBUTION: 28 major market states. OWNERS: Robert and Nonie Travers, and other investors. Robert Travers, president. WINEMAKER: Robert Travers; Lore Olds, assistant. Tours by appointment. Newsletter twice a year.

Jack and Mary Taylor bought the 1889 Fisher winery high up on Mount Veeder in 1941. They spent years reconditioning it and replanting the old vineyards to Chardonnay and Cabernet Sauvignon. With the financial backing of some limited partners, Bob Travers, a stockbroker turned winemaker, purchased the operation in 1968. Bob had taken courses at U.C. Davis and trained at Heitz. Now he and his wife, Nonie, live in the Taylor house and make a small number of wines. Most compelling is the intense Cabernet. Made from sparsely yielding mountain vines, it takes many years to mature.

WHITE

☆☆☆   1975 CHARDONNAY Napa Valley. *Remarkable fruit and fresh flavors. Complex and charming.*

☆☆   1976 CHARDONNAY Napa Valley. *Rich yet crisp; clean and fruity.*

☆ 1979 CHARDONNAY ($13.50) California. *Pleasant but not much more.*

☆☆ 1980 CHARDONNAY ($16.00) Napa Valley. *Nice, light, clean.*

☆☆☆ 1981 CHARDONNAY ($16.00) California. *Spicy, oaky, fruity, rich, intense.*

☆☆ 1980 SAUVIGNON BLANC ($8.50) California. *Clean, decent but unremarkable.*

☆☆☆ 1982 SAUVIGNON BLANC ($10.00) California. *Toasty and varietal, with decent fruit, good balance and complexity.*

RED

☆ 1962 CABERNET SAUVIGNON Napa Valley. *Minty, dull, flat in the finish.*

☆☆☆ 1965 CABERNET SAUVIGNON Napa Valley. *Lovely, clean, rich, quite lively.*

☆☆ 1968 CABERNET SAUVIGNON Napa Valley. *Rich, mature, earthy.*

☆☆ 1969 CABERNET SAUVIGNON Napa Valley. *Herbal, rich, clean, short.*

☆☆☆ 1970 CABERNET SAUVIGNON Napa Mountain. *Amazing intensity and tannin. Still needs time. (Is it worth it?)*

☆☆ 1972 CABERNET SAUVIGNON Napa Valley. *Slim, simple, clean, lacking depth.*

☆☆☆ 1973 CABERNET SAUVIGNON Napa Valley. *Fragrant, crisp, fruity, lovely. Drink now.*

☆☆☆ 1974 CABERNET SAUVIGNON Napa Valley. *Big and hard, with great structure. Actually needs more time.*

☆☆☆ 1975 CABERNET SAUVIGNON ($12.00) Napa Mountain. *Dark, rich, intense. Needs two to five years to smooth out.*

☆☆☆ 1976 CABERNET SAUVIGNON ($15.00) California. *Another monster—needs at least five years to be drinkable.*

☆☆☆ 1977 CABERNET SAUVIGNON ($15.00) Napa Valley. *Hard-edged and concentrated. Needs four or five more years.*

☆☆ 1978 CABERNET SAUVIGNON ($18.00) Napa Valley. *Big and hulking, lacking the fruit needed to carry it through.*

☆☆ 1980 CABERNET SAUVIGNON ($18.00) California. *Herbaceous, big, heavy—maybe time will help. Drink 1990.*

☆☆☆ 1982 CABERNET SAUVIGNON ($18.00) Napa Valley. *Beautiful, rich, dense, lush, big. Drink 1992 and beyond.*

1977 PINOT NOIR ($9.00) Napa Valley. *Muddy, stemmy, unpleasant.*

Mazza Vineyards
PENNSYLVANIA

11815 East Lake Road, North East, Pennsylvania 16428 (814-725-8695). FOUNDED: 1972. ACREAGE: 2 acres. PRODUCTION: 10,000 cases. DISTRIBUTION: Pennsylvania. OWNER: Robert Mazza. WINEMAKER: Gary Mosier. Tours and tasting summer: Monday–Saturday 9 A.M.– 8 P.M., Sunday 12–4:30 P.M.; October–June: Monday–Saturday 9 A.M.–5 P.M., Sunday 12– 4:30 P.M.

Two ambitious grape-growing brothers, Frank and Robert Mazza, sold over 25 acres of their family vineyards to finance their winery. Construction was just under way when winemaker Frank left for Germany with the U.S. Army Corps of Engineers. Once Frank returned, the Mazzas decided to merge with the Mount Hope Estate (see). At first the wines were made at the Mazza winery and then shipped to the Mount Hope facility. Then Frank started working at Mount Hope, taking most of the winery equipment with him. Robert stayed behind, and in 1982 he bought back the original Mazza winery and started making wine on his own. Gary Mosier, Frank's assistant at Mount Hope, became the winemaker at Mazza Vineyards.

WHITE

☆☆ 1980 SEYVAL BLANC ($5.50) Pennsylvania.

McCarthy & Spaulding Negociants
NAPA COUNTY

1216 B Church Street, St. Helena, California 94574 (707-963-0219). FOUNDED: 1984. ACREAGE: None. PRODUCTION: 4,000 cases. DISTRIBUTION: Major markets. OWNER: Partnership. Ann Spaulding and Dan McCarthy. WINEMAKER: Duane DeBoer. Tours and tasting by appointment.

Ann Spaulding and Dan McCarthy started planning their own wine company while working at Ernie's, a St. Helena wine retail store. Dan was the import buyer and manager for the store; Ann, whose family owns Stonegate Winery, was the assistant manager and California wine buyer. In 1984 Ann and Dan formed a partnership and started a diversified wine business. For their own label, they buy wines that are stored and bottled at Girard Winery. They also import a selection of French wines, manage retail sales out of their warehouse (a former brandy distillery), and run a private label program. "We are still a baby company," says Ann, "but we have lots of ideas."

WHITE

☆   1983 CHARDONNAY ($6.00) Napa Valley. *Tart, crisp but simple and dull.*

McDowell Valley Vineyards
MENDOCINO COUNTY

3811 Highway 175, Hopland, California 95449 (707-744-1053). FOUNDED: 1978. ACREAGE: 400 acres. PRODUCTION: 66,000 cases. DISTRIBUTION: California and 35 other states; Canada, Japan, the Netherlands, and England. OWNERS: Richard and Karen Keehn, managers. WINE-MAKER: George Bursick. Tours by appointment. Tasting daily 10 A.M.–5 P.M. Gift shop. Concerts, fashion shows, cooking classes. Wine education seminars. Also tasting room on Highway 101 in Hopland.

In 1852 unsuccessful Forty-niner Paxton McDowell found and settled this Mendocino valley that bears his name. In 1970 Richard and Karen Keehn bought a large estate in the valley and planted vineyards. Nine years later they built California's first comprehensive solar winery. They also petitioned the federal government for a separate appellation for their cool, high-altitude valley, and succeeded. Now McDowell Valley is an appellation with only one winery. The Keehns expect to increase production to 100,000 cases in the near future.

WHITE

☆   1981 CHARDONNAY ($8.50) Estate, McDowell Valley. *Earthy, simple, decent.*
☆☆   1982 CHARDONNAY ($9.50) McDowell Valley. *Soft, round, oaky, pleasant.*
☆☆   1983 CHARDONNAY ($11.00) McDowell Valley. *Fat, buttery, oily, rich, good.*
☆   1982 CHENIN BLANC ($6.75) Estate, McDowell Valley. *Apple aroma; flowery fruit on palate, lacking depth.*
○   1983 CHENIN BLANC ($5.75) McDowell Valley. *Heavy, unattractive, moldy.*
    1983 FRENCH COLOMBARD ($4.50) McDowell Valley. *Sweet, oxidized, unattractive.*
☆☆   1982 FUME BLANC ($7.50) Estate, McDowell Valley. *Soft and smoky, rounded and elegant.*
☆☆☆   1983 FUME BLANC ($7.50) Estate, McDowell Valley. *Charming, round and fruity. A delightful rendition.*

BLANC DE NOIR

☆☆   1983 ZINFANDEL BLANC ($4.50) Estate, McDowell Valley. *13.5% French Colombard, 5.5% Sylvaner. Crisp and attractive.*
☆☆☆   1984 ZINFANDEL BLANC ($5.00) Estate, McDowell Valley. *2% residual sugar. Fresh, crisp, balanced, delicious.*

RED

☆☆   1979 CABERNET SAUVIGNON ($8.50) McDowell Valley. *A pleasant, well-made wine, with modest charms.*
☆☆☆   1980 CABERNET SAUVIGNON ($9.00) Estate, McDowell Valley. *Crisp, tart, nice varietal character, delightful. Drink now.*

☆☆☆ 1981 CABERNET SAUVIGNON ($9.50) Estate, McDowell Valley. *Spicy, balanced, graceful, medium weight, charming. Drink now.*

☆☆☆ 1979 PETITE SIRAH ($7.50) McDowell Valley. *Elegant, restrained, attractive.*

☆ 1980 PETITE SIRAH ($9.00) Estate, McDowell Valley, Mendocino. *Heavy and rich. Good but not quite up to the '79.*

☆☆☆ 1980 SYRAH ($7.50) Estate, McDowell Valley. *Soft and rich, with great charm and balance.*

☆☆ 1981 SYRAH ($9.50) Estate, McDowell Valley. *Tart and clean, with great fruit and good balance. Drink 1986.*

☆ 1980 ZINFANDEL ($6.25) McDowell Valley.

☆ 1981 ZINFANDEL ($6.25) Estate, McDowell Valley.

McFarland Wine Company
MONTEREY COUNTY

P.O. Box 1010, Gonzales, California 93926 (408-675-2315). FOUNDED: 1982. ACREAGE: 5,000 acres. PRODUCTION: 15,000 cases. DISTRIBUTION: Nationwide. OWNER: McFarland family. WINEMAKER: Various. OTHER LABEL: Wolfe Vintners and Gabriel y Caroline. Vineyard tours by appointment.

Brothers Jerry and Myron McFarland and viticulturist Jerry Decoto started planting vineyards in the Salinas Valley in 1972. Today, McFarland Farms owns and/or manages over 10,000 acres of vineyard in the area. It co-founded The Monterey Vineyard (see), started Smith & Hook Vineyard (see), and now specializes in vineyard investment, management consultation, and wine marketing. After Smith & Hook, a producer of Cabernet Sauvignon, was sold, the McFarlands' next enterprise was Wolfe Vintners. A Johannisberg Riesling estate, it consists of a 240-acre vineyard located on the alluvial plains of the Salinas Valley. The 1983 wine was made at Château du Lac by Linda O'Brien, who had previously worked for The Monterey Vineyard. Another recent project is a Chardonnay made under the direction of Brian Pendleton (see Pendleton Winery). The McFarlands plan to build their own winery soon.

WHITE

☆☆ 1983 WOLFE VINTNERS JOHANNISBERG RIESLING ($6.50) Monterey County. *Soft, lush, varietal, delightful.*

McGregor Vineyard Winery
NEW YORK

5503 Dutch Street, Dundee, New York 14837 (607-292-3999). FOUNDED: 1980. ACREAGE: 20 acres. PRODUCTION: 2,900 cases. DISTRIBUTION: New York. OWNER: East Branch Winery. Bob McGregor, president. WINEMAKER: Jim Moss; Bob McGregor, consultant. Tours and tasting April–November: daily 11 A.M.–5 P.M., except Mondays and holidays.

Before the McGregors started their winery, they were selling grapes to established wineries in New York. "When these wineries, such as Glenora, started winning awards for the wines made from our grapes, we decided to start making the wine ourselves," says Marge McGregor. They have been growing grapes on their property, which overlooks Keuka Lake, since 1973, although they live some 50 miles away. Marge's husband, Bob, still works for Eastman Kodak in Rochester, which means the vineyards and the winery do not get his full attention. "Once we get our three daughters through college, we will move out to the vineyard, and Bob will work in the winery full time," says Marge.

RED

☆☆ 1982 PINOT NOIR ($11.95) Finger Lakes, New York. *Simple but clean, varietal and attractive.*

McHenry Vineyards
SANTA CRUZ COUNTY

6821 Bonny Doon Road, Santa Cruz, California 95060 (916-756-3202). FOUNDED: 1980. ACREAGE: 4 acres. PRODUCTION: 300 cases. DISTRIBUTION: California. OWNER: Partnership. Henry, Linda, Dean, and Jane McHenry. WINEMAKER: Henry McHenry. No tours or tasting.

The McHenrys planted vineyards in Santa Cruz in the hope of selling their grapes to other wineries. They also intended to make a little wine for themselves. From their small homemade batches they could see the great potential of their Pinot Noir grapes. They were also consistently disappointed when other wineries used their grapes in anonymous blends. Although they live in Davis (Henry is a professor of anthropology at U.C. Davis), the McHenrys built a winery on their vineyard property, dedicating it to making exceptional Pinot Noir in the Santa Cruz area.

WHITE

O   1981 CHARDONNAY ($10.00) Santa Cruz Mountains. *Bitter, unattractive, a mistake.*
☆☆   1981 PINOT BLANC ($4.00) Santa Cruz Mountains. *Lovely, clean, fresh, varietal.*

RED

☆☆☆   1980 PINOT NOIR ($17.50) Santa Cruz Mountains. *Lush, deep, graceful, complex, superb. Only 42 cases made.*
☆☆☆   1981 PINOT NOIR ($14.50) Santa Cruz Mountains. *Rich, deep, complex, lovely.*

McIntosh's Ohio Valley Wines
OHIO

2033 Bethel New Hope Road, Bethel, Ohio 45106 (513-379-1159). FOUNDED: 1972. ACREAGE: 25 acres. PRODUCTION: 10,000 cases. DISTRIBUTION: Ohio. OWNER: Charles McIntosh. WINEMAKER: Charles McIntosh. Tours and tasting Tuesday–Thursday 1 P.M.–11 P.M., Friday and Saturday 1 P.M.–12 A.M.

Charles McIntosh was farming grain and running an active trucking business when he started planting grapes in 1965, attracted to the idea of a crop that only needed harvesting once a year. Then, in his spare time, he started experimenting with winemaking, turning his garage and workshop into a rudimentary winery. Soon he sold his trucking business and built a new white winery building with an attractive porch and a huge concrete slab to one side that is used for square dancing when it isn't harvest time.

McLester Winery
LOS ANGELES COUNTY

10670-D South La Cienega, Inglewood, California 90304 (213-641-9686). FOUNDED: 1979. ACREAGE: None. PRODUCTION: 2,500 cases. DISTRIBUTION: California, Arizona, and Texas; Canada. OWNERS: Cecil McLester and Marcella Mattson-McLester. WINEMAKER: Cecil McLester. Tours by appointment weekends 12–5 P.M.

Cecil McLester got a home winemaking kit for Christmas in 1970. From then on he made increasing amounts of wine every year. In 1978, when he moved to Los Angeles with eleven 50-gallon oak barrels, he realized his hobby had outgrown his garage. A year later his 1975 Cabernet Sauvignon won the Best of Show in the World Home Winemakers Competition. Following the lead of several other local home-winemakers-gone-commercial, he rented space in a 2,000-square-foot, air-conditioned industrial building located directly under the Los Angeles airport flight pattern. The same building houses six other small winery operations.

WHITE

1983 SAUVIGNON BLANC ($7.50) Nepenthe, San Luis Obispo. *Spicy, lacking freshness.*

RED

☆☆☆ 1980 ZINFANDEL ($7.50) Cowan, Shenandoah Valley, Amador. *A bit crude but balanced and appealing. Should age nicely.*

1980 ZINFANDEL ($7.50) Radike, Templeton, San Luis Obispo. *Heavy, dirty, bitter.*

☆☆☆ 1981 ZINFANDEL ($6.00) Radike, San Luis Obispo. *Rich, lush, clean, deep, lovely.*

DOUGLAS MEADOR *see* Ventana Vineyards Winery

MEAREN LAKE *see* Kistler Vineyards

Meier's Wine Cellars
OHIO

6955 Plain Field Pike, Silverton, Ohio 45236 (513-891-2900). FOUNDED: 1895. ACREAGE: 300 acres. DISTRIBUTION: Nationwide. OWNER: Paramount Distillers. Robert Gottesman, president. WINEMAKER: Ted Moulton. Tours and tasting May–October: Monday–Saturday 10 A.M.–3 P.M. Gift shop. Garden.

In 1928 Henry Sonneman bought the 70-year-old Meier's Grape Juice Company, where he had once worked as a bottle washer, and started a successful business selling Catawba grape juice in champagne bottles. After Repeal, he made wine. Changing the plant's name to Meier's Wine Cellars, Henry bought half of the Isle of St. George for vineyard land, and the winery was on its way to becoming one of the largest, most successful wine and juice production facilities in the East. After Sonneman died in 1974, Meier's was purchased by Robert Gottesman of Paramount Distillers in Cleveland. He also bought the Isle of St. George and three other Ohio wineries, Lonz Winery, Mon Ami Wine Company, and Mantey Vineyards (see).

WHITE

NV RHINE ($3.50) American. *Sweet but sappy and odd.*

RED

NV ISLAND RED ($3.50) American. *Off-dry, heavy, lacking fruit.*

1984 NOUVEAU ROUGE ($4.00) Lake Erie.

FORTIFIED

☆☆ CREAM SHERRY NUMBER 44 ($6.00) American.

Menghini Winery
SAN DIEGO COUNTY

150 Julian Orchards Drive, Julian, California 92036 (619-765-2072). FOUNDED: 1982. ACREAGE: 10 acres. PRODUCTION: 2,000 cases. DISTRIBUTION: California. OWNERS: Mike and Toni Menghini. WINEMAKER: Mike Menghini. Tours and tasting Friday–Sunday 10 A.M.–4 P.M.

Mike Menghini worked for San Pasqual Vineyards, Callaway Vineyards and Winery, and Filsinger Wineries before he and his wife decided to start their own winery venture. Although the Menghinis live in Escondido, their winery is in Julian. "I always thought Julian would be a dandy spot for a winery; it's a well-traveled area, and I think we can grow some good grapes up here," says Mike. The winery is located in a renovated apple-packing shed on the property, and Mike and Toni plan a full-fledged tasting room.

Meredyth Vineyard
VIRGINIA

P.O. Box 347, Middleburg, Virginia 22117 (703-687-6277). FOUNDED: 1972. ACREAGE: 55 acres. PRODUCTION: 10,000 cases. DISTRIBUTION: 19 states. OWNERS: Archie M. Smith, Jr., and family. WINEMAKER: Archie M. Smith III. Tours and tasting daily 10 A.M.–4 P.M.

Cattle rancher Archie Smith, Jr., and his wife, Dody, began planting grapes in 1972 in order to free themselves from the fluctuating price of hamburger. "A farmer is always at the mercy of the market for raw product unless he can process that product himself and sell it not only to the wholesaler but to the retail customer as well," says Archie. Starting in 1975, armed with a five-year grape-growing and winemaking plan, the family built a winery out of a three-stall stable, adding one story above and a cellar below. While the vineyards were maturing and the first wines were being made, Archie's son, Archie III, lent a hand by flying back and forth between terms at Oxford, England, where he was teaching philosophy. Finally the young Archie had to choose between academics and viticulture; he elected to stay and help with the winery. Archie's daughter, Susan Meredyth Smith, handles marketing. "We have our own jobs, yet we all do a little bit of everything," says Archie.

WHITE

☆☆   1981 CHARDONNAY ($9.50) Virginia.
☆☆   1982 CHARDONNAY ($9.50) Virginia. *Crisp, clean and European in style.*
☆☆   1983 CHARDONNAY ($9.00) Virginia. *Balanced, clean, varietal.*
 O   1982 JOHANNISBERG RIESLING ($7.00) Virginia.
☆☆☆ 1983 JOHANNISBERG RIESLING ($9.00) Virginia. *3.2% residual sugar. Crisp, fresh.*
☆☆   1982 SEYVAL BLANC ($6.50) Estate, Virginia. *Soft, clean and appealing.*

RED

☆☆   1980 CABERNET SAUVIGNON ($8.00) Virginia. *Herbal and elegant. Very French in style. Only 95 cases made.*
☆☆   1981 CABERNET SAUVIGNON ($8.00) Virginia. *Balanced and attractive. Drink 1986.*
 ☆   1980 DE CHAUNAC ($6.25) Estate, Virginia.
 ☆   1980 MARECHAL FOCH ($6.25) Estate, Virginia.
☆☆☆ 1980 MERLOT ($9.00) Virginia. *25% Cabernet. Soft, clean and elegant. Only 30 cases made.*

JOHN B. MERRITT *see* California Wine Company

Merritt Estate Winery
NEW YORK

2264 King Road, Forestville, New York 14062 (716-965-4800). FOUNDED: 1976. ACREAGE: 100 acres. PRODUCTION: 7,000 cases. DISTRIBUTION: New York. OWNERS: William Merritt and family. WINEMAKER: William Merritt. OTHER LABEL: Sheridan Wine Cellars. Tours and tasting Monday–Saturday 10 A.M.–5 P.M., Sunday 1 P.M.–5 P.M.

The Merritt family had been growing wine and table grapes for years when in 1976 their biggest grape customer calmly mentioned that it would be taking only 70 percent of its normal order. William Merritt, having toyed with the idea of starting a winery over the previous few years, decided it was the time to take action. "People usually start a winery for one of two reasons, to take care of grapes they can't sell or to make a superior wine," says William. "Our reason would have to be more of the former than the latter."

Merry Vintners
SONOMA COUNTY

3339 Hartman Road, Santa Rosa, California 95401 (707-526-4441). FOUNDED: 1984. ACREAGE: None. PRODUCTION: 3,000 cases. DISTRIBUTION: Nationwide. OWNERS: Merry Edwards, Bill Miller, and Charles and D. J. Edwards. WINEMAKER: Merry Edwards. Tours by appointment.

Merry Edwards gained stardom as winemaker for Matanzas Creek Winery and Mount Eden Vineyards. Then she left Matanzas Creek in 1984 and joined her parents and her husband in a family winery. "I think every winemaker dreams of having his or her own winery. My husband, Bill, and I have wanted our own winery since the time we were working at Mount Eden," says Merry. When her father retired as an electronics executive, the family decided to combine their talents and start their own winery. The plans began in 1983, and the foundations were laid in July 1984, a month before the first crush. Because Merry has earned a reputation for award-winning Chardonnays, she plans to make this variety the mainstay of her new winery.

Mesa Verde Vineyards
RIVERSIDE COUNTY

34567 Rancho California Road, Temecula, California 92390 (714-676-2370). FOUNDED: 1980. ACREAGE: 89 acres. PRODUCTION: 25,000 cases. DISTRIBUTION: California and major market states. OWNER: Lynne Kaarup. WINEMAKER: Jack Ryno. Tours by appointment. Tasting and sales weekends 10 A.M.–5 P.M.

After selling their grapes for four years, the Kaarups felt there would be a better financial return if they made their own grapes into wine. They met their winemaker, Jack Ryno, who was previously with Quady Winery (see), at a wine tasting. The winery is a complex of small buildings that sit atop a knoll overlooking the vineyards.

Messina Hof Wine Cellars
TEXAS

Route 7, Box 905, Bryan, Texas 77802 (409-779-2411). FOUNDED: 1977. ACREAGE: 30 acres. PRODUCTION: 7,500 cases. DISTRIBUTION: Texas. OWNERS: Paul V. and Merrill Bonarrigo. WINEMAKER: Paul V. Bonarrigo. Tasting Monday–Friday 8 A.M.–5 P.M. Tours on the third Sunday of each month, or by appointment.

Paul Bonarrigo's family had a winery and vineyards in the sunny town of Messina, Sicily. When Paul moved to Texas from New York by way of the Navy, he started planting his own little Messina. Professionally, Paul works as a physical therapist; he owns his own clinic and works in a hospital.

With his busy schedule, he depends upon the help of his wife, Merrill, to oversee winery production. Their first crush was in a metal building with a small tasting room, but they are presently in the process of reassembling a turn-of-the-century Gothic building that was once a Catholic girls' school. This remarkable edifice, which they had dismantled and moved to the vineyard site, will be their winery and should be complete by April 1986.

WHITE

☆☆☆   1984 CHENIN BLANC ($6.00) Texas. *Fresh, crisp, clean, very attractive.*

MICHAEL'S *see* Artisan Wines

Michtom Vineyards
SONOMA COUNTY

602 Limerick Lane, Healdsburg, California 95448 (707-433-3118). FOUNDED: 1982. ACREAGE: 130 acres. PRODUCTION: 9,000 cases. DISTRIBUTION: 7 states. OWNERS: James Wolner and Mark Michtom. WINEMAKER: James Wolner. Tours and tasting Wednesday–Sunday 10 A.M.– 4 P.M.

Mark Michtom, whose family founded the Ideal Toy Company, met his partner, James Wolner, at Sonoma Vineyards. James was working as the winemaker, and Mark, who owns vineyards in the Alexander Valley, was selling his grapes to the winery at that time. After knowing each other for several years, the two men formed a partnership in 1982. They leased the Sodini Winery, a 50-year-old bulk wine facility, and began making Chardonnay and Cabernet Sauvignon, all from grapes grown in Mark's vineyard.

WHITE

☆☆   1981 CHARDONNAY ($6.00) Alexander Valley. *Medium weight, clean and varietal.*

RED

☆☆   1978 CABERNET SAUVIGNON ($6.00) Alexander Valley. *Lush, earthy and well structured.*

Midi Vineyards
MISSOURI

Route 1, Lone Jack, Missouri 64070 (816-566-2119). FOUNDED: 1977. ACREAGE: 13 acres. PRODUCTION: 3,000 cases. DISTRIBUTION: Local. OWNERS: Dutton Biggs and George Gale. WINEMAKERS: George Gale and Dutton Biggs. Tours and tasting Monday–Saturday 10 A.M.–6 P.M., Sunday 12–6 P.M.

While studying for his doctorate in philosophy at U.C. Davis, George Gale made beer. It was not until he had graduated and secured a professorship at the University of Missouri in Kansas City that he began making wine out of grape concentrate. Then he met Dutton Biggs, an architectural engineer interested in starting a vineyard. Doing all the dirty work themselves, the two men planted each and every one of their vines with their own hands. In 1976 Dutton designed one of the strangest winery structures in the United States. Built in just five weeks, the winery started as a huge crater, which was then covered with an egg-shaped dome sprayed with concrete. Half the dome is covered with earth to insulate this underground igloo even further.

RED

○ 1981 LEON MILLOT ROUGE ($6.25) Jackson City, Missouri. *Weedy, sour, rich but strange.*

○ 1981 LEON MILLOT NOIR ($7.25) Missouri. *Weird, dark, thick, weedy.*

MIDULLA VINEYARDS *see* Fruit Wines of Florida

Louis K. Mihaly
NAPA COUNTY

3103 Silverado Trail, Napa, California 94558 (707-253-9306). FOUNDED: 1979. ACREAGE: 34 acres. PRODUCTION: 10,000 cases. DISTRIBUTION: Hotels and restaurants; East and West Coast states. OWNER: Louis K. Mihaly. WINEMAKER: John D. Nemeth. Tours by invitation only.

It was at a Middle European reunion that Louis Mihaly, a wealthy international businessman of Hungarian descent, met John Nemeth, a winemaker who had worked in Hungary, Italy, and Germany before getting involved in the wine import business. Louis had retired to the Napa Valley to buy a vineyard, build a winery, and play golf. John, a jolly, red-faced man who is never without a cigarette, had tired of "the business" of wine and wanted to get back into wine production. His first attempt, Panonnia Winery, had been unsuccessful, but Louis Mihaly pumped enough capital into the failed facility to turn it into a showplace. The Mihaly winery sells its wines only to restaurants.

WHITE

○ 1979 CHARDONNAY ($18.75) Special Reserve, Estate, Napa Valley. *Decent but marred by off flavors from faulty filtration.*

☆ 1980 CHARDONNAY ($18.70) Special Reserve, Estate, Napa Valley. *Crisp, clean but lacking varietal character.*

☆☆ 1982 CHARDONNAY ($19.00) Napa Valley. *Crisp, clean, attractive, simple.*

☆ 1979 SAUVIGNON BLANC ($17.50) Special Reserve, Estate, Napa Valley. *Grassy, decent.*

☆☆ 1980 SAUVIGNON BLANC ($15.00) Napa Valley. *Grassy, round, good fruit.*

☆☆ 1981 SAUVIGNON BLANC ($12.50) Napa Valley. *Perfumed and decent.*

☆☆ 1982 SAUVIGNON BLANC ($18.00) Special Reserve, Estate, Napa Valley. *Snappy, quite decent.*

RED

1980 PINOT NOIR ($18.00) Estate, Napa Valley. *Thin, dull.*

☆☆ 1982 PINOT NOIR ($18.00) Special Release, Estate, Napa Valley. *Spicy, clean, decent.*

Milano Winery
MENDOCINO COUNTY

14594 South Highway 101, Hopland, California 95449 (707-744-1396). FOUNDED: 1977. ACREAGE: None. PRODUCTION: 10,000 cases. DISTRIBUTION: 6 states. OWNER: Milano Winery, Inc. James Milone, president. WINEMAKER: James Milone. Tours by appointment. Tasting daily 10 A.M.–5 P.M.

After college, bushy-haired Jim Milone and his friend Greg Graziano rebuilt the old Milone hop kiln into a winery. The name they chose was a blend of their two last names: MIL-one and

Grazi-ANO. The hop kiln had been built by Jim's grandfather and his father in the 1940s and had been left unused for over twenty years. Both Greg and Jim, having come from families with a long history of grape growing in Mendocino County, were opinionated, self-taught winemakers who wanted to produce wines that would proclaim the glories of Mendocino grapes. Their partnership has since dissolved, and Jim Milone now manages the winery with the help of family and friends.

WHITE

☆☆   1981 CHARDONNAY ($14.00) Lolonis, Mendocino. *Soft, richly varietal, clean and fresh.*

☆☆   1982 CHARDONNAY ($10.00) 29% San Luis Obispo, 71% Mendocino, California. *Clean, attractive, fruity, yet soft.*

☆☆☆   1982 CHARDONNAY ($12.00) Oakgrove, Sonoma. *Clean, lush, balanced.*

☆☆   1982 CHARDONNAY ($14.00) Lolonis, Mendocino. *Rich, clean, soft, very lush.*

☆   1983 CHARDONNAY ($7.50) Sonoma-Mendocino. *Heavy, oily, oaky.*

☆☆☆☆   1981 JOHANNISBERG RIESLING ($20.00) Individual Dried Bunch Select, Mendocino. *375ml. 17.4% residual sugar. Honey and firm acidity.*

☆☆☆☆   1982 JOHANNISBERG RIESLING ($25.00) Individual Bunch Select Late Harvest, Ordway's Valley Foothills, Mendocino. *375ml. 17.2% residual sugar. Apples and botrytis; super.*

☆   1982 SAUVIGNON BLANC ($8.75) 20% Mendocino, 80% San Luis Obispo.

RED

☆☆   1978 CABERNET SAUVIGNON ($15.00) Sanel, Mendocino. *Plummy, intense, unusual but attractive. Give it time.*

☆   1980 CABERNET SAUVIGNON ($18.00) Sanel Valley, Mendocino. *Intense, overdone.*

☆   1977 PETITE SIRAH ($6.00) Mendocino.

O   1981 PINOT NOIR ($10.50) Hunter, Potter Valley, Mendocino. *Fermenting in the bottle. Horrible.*

☆☆   1979 ZINFANDEL ($10.00) Pacini, Mendocino.

☆☆   1981 ZINFANDEL ($6.00) Mendocino. *Lush, soft, clean.*

Mill Creek Vineyards
SONOMA COUNTY

1401 Westside Road, Healdsburg, California 95448 (707-433-5098). FOUNDED: 1974. ACREAGE: 65 acres. PRODUCTION: 14,000 cases. DISTRIBUTION: California and other major market states. OWNERS: Charles W. Kreck, president; William C. and James Kreck, vice presidents. WINEMAKER: James R. Kreck. OTHER LABELS: Claus Vineyards, Felta Springs. Tasting daily 10:30 A.M.–5 P.M. Picnic facilities.

Mill Creek Vineyards, owned and operated by the Kreck family, started with a few vineyard parcels in the Dry Creek Valley. Some years after moving onto the Mill Creek ranch, the Krecks planted Cabernet Sauvignon. In 1969, they bought an orchard, pulled out the plum trees, and planted a new vineyard of four different varieties. Once the Kreck boys, Bob and Bill, were old enough to contribute some serious work, the family converted a cement-block barn into a winery. Added to the winery in 1982 was a two-story, redwood tasting room with a water mill and a patio area that overlooks the Dry Creek Valley.

WHITE

1981 CHARDONNAY ($11.00) Estate, Dry Creek Valley, Sonoma. *Dull, lacking fruit.*
☆ 1983 FELTA SPRINGS CHARDONNAY ($5.00) Sonoma. *Clean, simple, short.*
1983 SAUVIGNON BLANC ($8.00) Estate, Dry Creek Valley. *Extremely grassy, not clean, intense, overpowering.*

ROSE

O 1982 CABERNET BLUSH ($5.00) Estate, Sonoma. *Sweet and oxidized; dull.*
☆ 1983 CABERNET BLUSH ($5.00) Estate, Dry Creek Valley. *1% residual sugar. Grapey, clumsy.*

RED

☆ 1978 CABERNET SAUVIGNON ($8.50) Estate, Sonoma. *Simple and a bit weedy.*
☆☆☆ 1979 CABERNET SAUVIGNON ($8.50) Estate, Sonoma. *10% Merlot. Earthy and herbal. Complex and balanced. Drink now.*
☆ 1980 CABERNET SAUVIGNON ($9.00) Sonoma. *Vegetative.*
1982 FELTA SPRINGS CABERNET SAUVIGNON ($5.00) Sonoma. *Extremely vegetal.*
☆☆☆ 1982 GAMAY BEAUJOLAIS ($5.00) Sonoma. *Fresh, clean, snappy, beautifully made.*
☆ 1983 GAMAY BEAUJOLAIS ($5.00) Estate, Dry Creek Valley. *Fruity but quite vegetal.*
☆☆ 1979 MERLOT ($7.50) Sonoma.
☆☆☆ 1980 MERLOT ($8.50) Estate, Sonoma. *Raisiny and intense; good acid and aging potential.*
☆☆ 1981 MERLOT ($9.00) Sonoma. *Lush, simple and a bit vegetal.*
☆☆ 1982 MERLOT ($8.50) Estate, Dry Creek Valley. *Good texture, some vegetal off notes.*
☆ 1980 PINOT NOIR ($6.50) Estate, Dry Creek Valley.
☆ 1981 PINOT NOIR ($7.00) Sonoma.

Minnesota Winegrowers Co-op
MINNESOTA

402 North Main Street, Stillwater, Minnesota 55082 (507-288-5510). FOUNDED: 1983. ACREAGE: None. PRODUCTION: 1,500 cases. DISTRIBUTION: Minnesota. OWNER: Cooperative. Dick Williams, general manager. WINEMAKER: David McGregor.

When grape growers in Minnesota were just getting started, they sold their grapes for a pretty decent price to local wineries. But once these established vineyards began to expand and more vineyards were planted, the surplus of grapes cut the price in half. Eleven growers decided to rectify this situation by starting their own winery. Grower Charles Knox came up with the idea to start a cooperative winery from which the proceeds could be returned to the growers themselves. "We hope to bring more grape growers into the cooperative," says Charlie, "but I think many are waiting to see if we'll survive or not."

Mirassou Vineyards
SANTA CLARA COUNTY

3000 Aborn Road, San Jose, California 95135 (408-274-4000). FOUNDED: 1854. ACREAGE: 1,300 acres. PRODUCTION: 300,000 cases. DISTRIBUTION: Nationwide. OWNER: Partnership. Mirassou family. Daniel Mirassou, president; Jim and Peter Mirassou, vice presidents-managers. WINEMAKERS: Peter Mirassou and Tom Stutz. Tasting Monday–Saturday 10 A.M.–5 P.M., Sunday 12–4 P.M. Tours Monday–Saturday at 10 A.M., 12:30 P.M., 2:30 P.M., 3:30 P.M.; Sunday at 12:30 P.M. and 2:30 P.M.

The fifth generation of this family is now growing grapes and making wine near San Jose. Until the current management took over, the winery made only bulk wines that were sold to other wineries. In the 1960s the Mirassous began selling wines under their own label, and they expanded their plantings into Monterey County. The winery specializes in moderately priced varietals and has developed a good reputation for sparkling wines.

WHITE

☆ 1980 AU NATURAL ($12.75) Monterey. *Decent, simple, clean, attractive.*

☆ 1982 DRY CHABLIS ($3.95) Monterey. *Dry, clean and attractive.*

☆ 1979 FLEURI BLANC ($6.50) California. *Soft, overripe, candy-like.*

☆ 1982 WHITE BURGUNDY ($5.75) Monterey. *Made with Pinot Blanc grapes. Soft, fruity and dull.*

☆ 1983 WHITE BURGUNDY ($5.75) Monterey. *Pinot Blanc. Heavy, with a touch of sweetness; clean but lacking depth.*

☆ 1983 WHITE BURGUNDY ($6.00) Monterey. *Mostly Pinot Blanc. 0.58% residual sugar. Clean, soft, simple.*

○ 1980 CHARDONNAY ($10.00) Harvest Reserve, Monterey. *Dull and weedy.*

☆ 1981 CHARDONNAY ($7.50) Monterey. *Nice, simple, acceptable.*

☆☆ 1981 CHARDONNAY ($9.00) Harvest Reserve, Monterey. *Rich and buttery, with earthy fruit and lovely structure.*

☆ 1982 CHARDONNAY ($7.50) Monterey. *Decent, dull, clean.*

☆☆ 1983 CHARDONNAY ($7.00) Monterey. *Fresh, crisp, balanced.*

☆☆☆ 1983 CHARDONNAY ($8.00) Monterey. *Clean, fresh, lovely food wine, simple.*

☆☆ 1983 CHARDONNAY ($11.00) Harvest Reserve, Monterey. *Fresh, clean, good varietal character.*

☆☆ 1984 CHARDONNAY ($8.00) Monterey. *Crisp, clean, simple, decent.*

☆☆ 1982 CHENIN BLANC ($5.50) Monterey. *1.79% residual sugar. Grapey and slightly sweet.*

☆ 1983 CHENIN BLANC ($4.75) Monterey.

○ 1982 FUME BLANC ($6.00) Harvest Reserve, Fume, Monterey.

1982 JOHANNISBERG RIESLING ($6.50) Monterey.

☆☆☆ 1982 JOHANNISBERG RIESLING ($8.50) Late Harvest, Monterey. *10% residual sugar. Sweet, yet crisp and elegant.*

☆☆☆ 1983 JOHANNISBERG RIESLING ($8.50) Late Harvest, Monterey. *Fresh, sweet, fruity, delicious. Serve with fruit desserts.*

☆ 1981 MONTEREY RIESLING ($5.75) Monterey. *Dry, crisp, decent.*

SPARKLING

☆ 1979 BLANC DE NOIRS ($15.50) Monterey. *Clean and well made but lacking character.*

☆☆☆ 1980 BLANC DE NOIRS ($15.00) Monterey. *Great richness, clean, deep, complex, elegant.*

☆☆ NV BRUT ROSE ($12.00) Monterey. *Rich, deep, herbal, dry, pink.*

☆ 1979 BRUT ($12.50) Monterey. *Méthode champenoise.*

1979 BRUT ($15.50) Late Disgorged, Monterey. *Oily, leathery, not much charm.*

1980 BRUT ($12.50) Monterey. *Fat, dull, volatile.*

1981 BRUT ($12.00) Monterey. *Dull, uninteresting.*

☆☆☆ 1982 BRUT ($12.00) Monterey. *Round, rich, lush, fruity, appealing.*

○ 1979 AU NATURAL CHAMPAGNE ($14.00) California.

☆☆ 1982 NATURAL ($12.00) Monterey. *Snappy, crisp, rich, dry.*

BLANC DE NOIR

☆ 1984 WHITE ZINFANDEL ($5.50) Monterey. *2.3% residual sugar. Soft, lush, clean, varietal.*

RED

☆ NV CABERNET SAUVIGNON ($8.00) Cuvée, Central Coast. *Heavy but attractive flavors.*

☆ 1973 CABERNET SAUVIGNON Harvest Selection, Monterey. *Showing its age.*

☆   1974 CABERNET SAUVIGNON Monterey.
☆☆ 1974 CABERNET SAUVIGNON ($7.50) Harvest Selection, Monterey. *Rich, mature but still loaded with fruit. Drink now.*
    1975 CABERNET SAUVIGNON Harvest Selection, Monterey. *Weedy but well made.*
☆   1975 CABERNET SAUVIGNON Nonfiltered, California.
    1977 CABERNET SAUVIGNON Harvest Selection, Monterey. *Weedy and short.*
O   1977 CABERNET SAUVIGNON ($6.50) Lot 1, Home, Santa Clara.
O   1978 CABERNET SAUVIGNON ($9.00) Harvest Reserve, Monterey. *Intense and vegetal; good texture but overwhelmed by weeds.*
☆   1979 CABERNET SAUVIGNON ($6.50) Monterey. *Vegetal but crisp and quite presentable.*
☆   1979 CABERNET SAUVIGNON ($9.00) Harvest Reserve, Monterey. *Raisiny and lacking structure.*
    1981 CABERNET SAUVIGNON ($6.50) Cuvée, Central Coast, California. *Vegetal, musty.*
☆☆ 1982 CABERNET SAUVIGNON ($12.00) Napa Valley. *Rich, deep, soft, velvety, cherry fruit. Drink 1987.*
    1979 PETITE SIRAH ($7.45) Monterey. *Showing too much age and not enough fruit.*
O   1978 PINOT NOIR ($8.00) Harvest Selection, Monterey. *Harsh and overpoweringly vegetal.*
☆   1981 PINOT NOIR ($7.00) Monterey. *Green, thin, decent.*
☆☆ 1980 ZINFANDEL ($5.00) Monterey. *Fruity, clean and berried.*
☆   1981 ZINFANDEL ($8.00) Harvest Reserve, Monterey. *Lush, rich texture, soft, decent.*

MJC Vineyards
VIRGINIA

Route 1, Box 293, Blacksburg, Virginia 24060 (703-552-9083). FOUNDED: 1981. ACREAGE: 14.5 acres. PRODUCTION: 3,800 cases. DISTRIBUTION: Virginia. OWNER: Dr. Karl Hereford. Maury and Eric Israelson, managers. WINEMAKER: Dr. Karl Hereford. Tours and tasting Monday–Saturday 10 A.M.–5 P.M. For groups of eight or more, there is a charge of $1.50 per person, which includes wine and cheese.

Wine collector and educator Dr. Karl Hereford bought a small farm in the valley to be his homestead and experimental vineyard site. While teaching "wine production" at Virginia Polytechnic Institute and working with winemakers during the summer, the doctor became more and more involved with his own vineyards. He even began a business of custom grafting vinifera vines. Eventually, after experimental batches of wine proved to be of commercial quality, Dr. Hereford started a winery in his large, redesigned two-car garage. A storage cellar was dug out of the foundation of the old farmhouse, and the doctor began to make wine. He has since been joined in this endeavor by his daughter, Maury, and her husband, Eric.

WHITE

☆☆ 1983 CHARDONNAY ($7.95) Virginia. *Rich, deep, varietal.*

Mon Ami Wine Company
OHIO

325 West Catawba Road, Port Clinton, Ohio 43452 (419-797-4481). FOUNDED: 1872. ACREAGE: None. PRODUCTION: 30,000 cases. DISTRIBUTION: Ohio. OWNER: Paramount Distillers. Robert Gottesman, president. WINEMAKER: Claudio Salvadore. OTHER LABEL: Catawba Island Wine Company. Tours and tasting Monday–Saturday 11 A.M.–2 P.M., Sunday 1 P.M.–8 P.M. Restaurant. See also Lonz Winery, Mantey Vineyards, and Meier's Wine Cellars.

This historic winery was started as a co-op in 1870 by local growers. In the woods of Catawba Island, they built a five-level limestone winery, using native stone and walnut. The champagne cellars, large limestone caves of European design, have an Old World charm. For many years the facility was operated as the sister winery of Mantey Vineyards in Sandusky by Norman Mantey, a third-generation grape grower. When Mantey Vineyards was sold to Paramount Distillers in 1980, Mon Ami was sold with it. The restaurant, started by Norman, is now run by the Buckantz family.

ટે

Monarch Wine Company
GEORGIA

451 Sawtell Avenue Southeast, Atlanta, Georgia 30315 (404-622-4661). FOUNDED: 1936. ACREAGE: None. PRODUCTION: 360,000 cases. DISTRIBUTION: East of the Mississippi. OWNER: Kane-Miller Corporation. WINEMAKER: Mr. Viet. No tours or tasting.

In the late 1930s there was a surplus of peaches in Georgia. To remedy the situation the mayor of Atlanta granted a tax break to all processing plants that could do something quickly with this abundance of fruit. Charles Gilsten, not one to pass up a creative opportunity, built a winery and, with the help of his family, started making peach wine. He even created a baked peach wine that was reminiscent of sherry. When the novelty wore off and the demand for peach wine began to slip, the winery started making grape wines from concentrate. But Charles lost interest in the business and in 1968 sold the winery to the Kane-Miller Corporation, which has developed it into a bulk wine-producing facility.

ટે

Monarch Wine Company
NEW YORK

4500 Second Avenue, Brooklyn, New York 11232 (212-965-8800). FOUNDED: 1933. ACREAGE: None. PRODUCTION: 4 million cases. DISTRIBUTION: Worldwide. OWNERS: Robinson and Star families. Leo Star, president; Marshall Goldberg, chairman. WINEMAKERS: Carlos Pato and Henry Charney. OTHER LABEL: Manischewitz. No tours or tasting.

If the name Monarch Wine Company doesn't sound familiar, perhaps the name Manischewitz does. When Monarch introduced its line of kosher wines, it wanted to use a name that would be trusted by Jewish households. Since Jews had been munching on Manischewitz matzohs for over 50 years, Monarch leased the name for use on wine and continues to pay royalties for the privilege. Everything about the four-block-long winery is kosher. The 400-plus employees are observant Jews, the entire winemaking process is supervised by a rabbi, and only kosher food is allowed to enter the winery. Wine is made year round by freezing juice and using it as needed. In addition to making its own grape wines, fruit wines, and vermouth, the winery is one of the largest producers of champagne in America, though much of it is for private labels. It also imports wines under the Tytell label.

WHITE

○ NV MANISCHEWITZ DRY CHABLIS ($2.50) American. *Varnishy nose, tanky, oxidized. Kosher.*

☆ NV MANISCHEWITZ CONCORD ($3.00) Cream White Concord, American. *Clean but lacking flavor. Kosher.*

ROSE

☆ NV MANISCHEWITZ CREAM PINK CONCORD ($3.00) American. *Pink, sweet, fairly attractive. Kosher.*

RED

NV MANISCHEWITZ DRY BURGUNDY ($2.50) American. *Fruity, lush, a little sweet, drinkable. Kosher.*

NV MANISCHEWITZ CONCORD ($2.90) American. *Clean, foxy, some fruit, a little bitter on the finish. Kosher.*

☆ NV MANISCHEWITZ HEAVY CONCORD ($2.90) American. *Candied, sweet, clean. Like liquid grape jelly. Kosher.*

☆ NV MANISCHEWITZ CREAM RED CONCORD ($3.00) American. *Foxy, candied, very sweet, clean. Kosher.*

☆ NV MANISCHEWITZ MALAGA ($2.90) Extra Heavy Malaga, American. *18% residual sugar. Buttery, sweet, syrupy, clean, attractive. Kosher.*

FLAVORED

☆ MANISCHEWITZ ($3.50) Cream Almonetta, American. *Natural almond flavor. Sweet, candied, decent. Kosher.*

MANISCHEWITZ ($3.50) Pina Coconetta, American. *Syrupy, artificial flavors, clean. Kosher.*

MANISCHEWITZ ($3.50) Strawberry Coconetta, American. *Strawberry jam, fruity, some bitterness. Kosher.*

❧

Robert Mondavi Winery
NAPA COUNTY

7801 St. Helena Highway, Oakville, California 94562 (707-963-9611). FOUNDED: 1966. ACREAGE: 1,250 acres. PRODUCTION: 300,000 cases in Oakville; 1 million cases at Woodbridge. DISTRIBUTION: Nationwide; 14 foreign markets. OWNER: Robert Mondavi family. Robert Mondavi, chairman; Michael Mondavi, president. WINEMAKER: Tim Mondavi. OTHER LABEL: Opus One. Tours and tasting summer and fall: daily 9 A.M.–5 P.M; winter and spring: daily 10 A.M.–4:30 P.M. Summer concerts. Cooking classes and seminars.

Robert Mondavi, the younger son of Cesare Mondavi, who owned Charles Krug Winery (see), went out on his own in 1966 and built a magnificent mission-style winery that has become one of the most influential in California. It has assumed stature both as a research center and as a training ground. Its state-of-the-art, computerized winemaking has had a profound effect on American winemakers. Bob has turned the day-to-day operation of the winery over to his children Mike (management), Tim (winemaking), and Marcy (marketing), but he is still the American wine industry's most effective worldwide ambassador. The large California Central Valley facility at Woodbridge produces one million cases of generic table wines, while the well-known Mondavi premium varietals are made at the Napa Valley winery in Oakville. Production in the Napa Valley also includes Opus One, the Cabernet Sauvignon made as a joint venture with Baron Philippe de Rothschild of Château Mouton-Rothschild in Bordeaux.

WHITE

☆☆ 1982 ROBERT MONDAVI WHITE ($3.50) California. *Fresh, clean, fruity, with a definite Sauvignon Blanc style.*

☆☆ 1980 CHARDONNAY ($14.00) Napa Valley. *Crisp and appealing; lacks depth.*

☆☆☆ 1980 CHARDONNAY ($20.00) Reserve, Napa Valley. *Big and heavy, with rich oak and complex varietal character.*

☆☆ 1981 CHARDONNAY ($14.00) Napa Valley. *Lush, full, quite pleasant but lacking finesse.*

☆☆☆☆ 1981 CHARDONNAY ($20.00) Reserve, Napa Valley. *Crisp, delicate, elegant. The best Mondavi Chardonnay of all.*

☆☆☆ 1982 CHARDONNAY ($14.00) Napa Valley. *Balanced, clean, varietal, rich.*

☆☆☆ 1982 CHARDONNAY ($20.00) Reserve, Napa Valley. *Lush, rich, oaky, intense, complex.*

☆☆ 1983 CHARDONNAY ($10.00) Napa Valley. *Fresh, decent, clean, somewhat simple.*

☆☆☆ 1981 CHENIN BLANC ($7.00) Napa Valley. *Clean and sweet, with fresh fruit and tangy acidity.*

☆☆☆ 1982 CHENIN BLANC ($7.75) Napa Valley. *Sunny apples; clean, soft and lush, with sweet fruitiness.*

☆☆ 1983 CHENIN BLANC ($6.75) Napa Valley. *Fruity, clean, balanced, attractive.*

☆☆☆ 1974 FUME BLANC Reserve, Napa Valley. *Fresh, open, clean, varietal, soft, complex.*

☆☆ 1976 FUME BLANC Napa Valley. *Clean, fruity, mellow. Beginning to fade but still very good.*

☆☆ 1980 FUME BLANC ($10.25) Napa Valley. *Varietal, clean and well made.*

☆ 1980 FUME BLANC ($15.00) Reserve, Napa. *Grassy and vegetal; oaky.*

☆☆☆ 1981 FUME BLANC ($9.00) Napa. *Smoky, rich flavors; smooth, complex, elegant.*

☆☆☆ 1981 FUME BLANC ($13.00) Reserve, Napa Valley. *Smoky, complex and fat, with plenty of French oak.*

☆☆☆ 1982 FUME BLANC ($9.00) Napa Valley. *4% Semillon. Varietal, deep, lush.*

☆☆☆ 1982 FUME BLANC ($15.00) Reserve, Napa Valley. *Big, rich, oaky, varietal, lovely.*

☆☆☆ 1983 FUME BLANC ($9.00) Napa Valley. *Grassy, rich, deep, intense. A very attractive departure.*

☆☆☆ 1984 FUME BLANC ($7.00) Napa Valley. *10% Semillon. Crisp, fruity, clean and fresh.*

☆ 1982 JOHANNISBERG RIESLING ($7.75) Napa Valley. *Dull nose, decent fruit, not great.*

☆☆ 1982 JOHANNISBERG RIESLING ($8.50) Special Selection, Napa Valley. *4.3% residual sugar. Apples, sweet fruit, unusual, pleasant.*

☆☆☆ 1982 JOHANNISBERG RIESLING ($9.00) Special Selection, Napa Valley. *Botrytis; sweet, rich fruit; lush but balanced.*

☆☆☆ 1983 JOHANNISBERG RIESLING ($7.50) Napa Valley. *1.65% residual sugar. Crisp, clean, varietal, spritzy.*

☆☆ 1983 JOHANNISBERG RIESLING ($7.75) Napa Valley. *1.4% residual sugar. Crisp, clean, fresh, lively.*

☆☆☆ 1984 JOHANNISBERG RIESLING ($9.50) Special Selection, Napa Valley. *4.3% residual sugar. Lush and balanced, with crisp apple flavors; delightful.*

☆☆☆ 1982 MUSCATO D'ORO ($8.00) Napa Valley. *5.6% residual sugar. Spicy, floral, delicious.*

☆ 1983 MUSCATO D'ORO ($8.75) Napa Valley. *5.2% residual sugar. Varietal but coarse and heavy.*

ROSE

☆☆ 1981 ROBERT MONDAVI ROSE ($3.75) California. *Fresh, crisp and slightly sweet.*

☆☆ 1983 ROBERT MONDAVI ROSE ($3.75) California. *Decent, dry, clean.*

☆☆ 1984 ROBERT MONDAVI ROSE ($3.75) California. *1% residual sugar. Snappy, fresh, fruity, with a lovely color.*

RED

☆☆ 1981 ROBERT MONDAVI RED ($4.14) California. *Vegetal, balanced and quite decent.*

☆☆ 1983 RED TABLE WINE ($3.75) California. *83.5% Cabernet. Lush, round, fruity, very attractive.*

☆☆ 1973 CABERNET SAUVIGNON Napa Valley. *Lush, clean but lacking structure.*

☆☆ 1973 CABERNET SAUVIGNON ($35.00) Reserve, Napa Valley. *Beginning to fade and lose balance and fruit.*

☆ 1974 CABERNET SAUVIGNON Napa Valley. *Earthy, concentrated, meaty, lacking depth.*

☆☆ 1974 CABERNET SAUVIGNON ($45.00) Reserve, Napa Valley. *The biggest Robert Mondavi Reserve—rich, heavy and not aging well.*

☆☆☆ 1975 CABERNET SAUVIGNON ($35.00) Reserve, Napa Valley. *Elegant, complex, spicy, soft and well bred. Still improving.*

☆☆☆ 1976 CABERNET SAUVIGNON ($25.00) Reserve, Napa Valley. *Lush, intense, concentrated, deep; very good but not great.*

☆☆☆ 1977 CABERNET SAUVIGNON ($35.00) Reserve, Napa Valley. *Rich, balanced, complex, elegant and ready to drink.*

☆☆ 1978 CABERNET SAUVIGNON ($13.00) Napa Valley.

☆☆☆☆ 1978 CABERNET SAUVIGNON ($40.00) Reserve, Napa Valley. *Lush, elegant, deep; a great wine with pinpoint balance.*

☆☆ 1979 CABERNET SAUVIGNON ($12.00) Napa Valley. *Soft and fruity, with a subdued spiciness. Clean and appealing.*

☆☆☆ 1979 CABERNET SAUVIGNON ($25.00) Reserve, Napa Valley. *Balanced, rich, deep, fuller than the '78 Reserve. Drink 1987.*

☆☆☆ 1979 OPUS ONE CABERNET SAUVIGNON ($50.00) Napa Valley. *Complex, rich, balanced. Good medium-term aging potential.*

☆☆ 1980 CABERNET SAUVIGNON ($12.00) Napa Valley. *Angular and herbal, with good aging potential. Drink 1986.*

☆☆ 1980 CABERNET SAUVIGNON ($30.00) Reserve, Napa Valley. *Crisp, thin, attractive, lacking the depth of the '79. Drink 1986.*

☆☆☆☆ 1980 OPUS ONE CABERNET SAUVIGNON ($50.00) Napa Valley. *Sweet oak and fruit; elegance, structure and intensity. Super.*

☆☆ 1981 CABERNET SAUVIGNON ($12.00) Napa Valley. *Herbal, balanced, clean, attractive. Drink now.*

☆☆☆☆ 1981 OPUS ONE CABERNET SAUVIGNON ($50.00) Napa Valley. *Dense, complicated, superb flavors, stunning. Drink 1988.*

☆☆☆ 1982 CABERNET SAUVIGNON ($9.50) Napa Valley. *Rich, velvety, plummy, oaky—the best in years. Drink now.*

☆☆☆☆ 1983 CABERNET SAUVIGNON ($35.00) Reserve, Napa Valley. *Complex, elegant, lush, fresh oak, lovely. Drink 1989.*

☆☆ 1975 PINOT NOIR Reserve, Napa Valley.

1977 PINOT NOIR ($9.75) Reserve, Napa Valley.

☆☆ 1978 PINOT NOIR ($7.50) Napa Valley. *Soft and lush; very appealing.*

☆☆☆ 1978 PINOT NOIR ($15.00) Reserve, Napa Valley. *Lush, clean and complex. Very Burgundian.*

☆☆ 1979 PINOT NOIR ($8.00) Napa Valley. *Spicy and fruity.*

☆☆☆ 1979 PINOT NOIR ($15.00) Reserve, Napa Valley. *Earthy and lush, with rich flavors.*

☆ 1980 PINOT NOIR ($7.50) Napa Valley. *Thin, underripe, decent, clean but essentially dull.*

☆☆☆ 1980 PINOT NOIR ($15.00) Reserve, Napa Valley. *Dark, lush, complex, toasty, superb; delightful cherry tones.*

☆☆ 1981 PINOT NOIR ($8.00) Napa Valley. *Varietal, balanced; nice texture and structure.*

☆☆☆ 1981 PINOT NOIR ($14.00) Reserve, Napa Valley. *The best Mondavi Pinot yet. Delicate, complex, rich, lovely.*

☆ 1980 ZINFANDEL ($5.50) Napa. *The last Mondavi Zinfandel.*

ﾠﾠﾠﾠﾠﾠﾠﾠﾠﾠﾠﾠﾠﾠﾠﾠﾠﾠﾠﾠﾠﾠﾠﾠﾠ ❧

C. K. MONDAVI *see* Charles Krug Winery

Mont Elise Vineyards
WASHINGTON

315 West Steuben, Box 28, Bingen, Washington 98605 (509-493-3001). FOUNDED: 1975. ACREAGE: 30 acres. PRODUCTION: 6,000 cases. DISTRIBUTION: Alaska, Illinois, Oregon, and Washington. OWNERS: Charles Henderson and family. WINEMAKER: Charles Henderson. Tasting summer: daily 12–5 P.M.; other months: Monday–Saturday 12–5 P.M.

In the German-American community of Bingen, cherry grower Charles Henderson was looking for an alternative crop for his 300-acre cherry orchard. In 1964 he planted a few grape varieties in his orchard just to see how they would do. Gewürztraminer and Pinot Noir showed the best results, and he expanded his plantings of these two varieties in 1972. The winery, once the apple-pear warehouse, was bonded in 1975 under the name Bingen Wine Cellars, but Charles later changed it to Mont Elise, in honor of his daughter Elise.

Mont St. John Cellars
NAPA COUNTY

5400 Old Sonoma Road, Napa, California 94558 (707-255-8864). FOUNDED: 1979. ACREAGE: 160 acres. PRODUCTION: 25,000 cases. DISTRIBUTION: 15 states. OWNER: Louis Bartolucci. WINEMAKER: Andrea Bartolucci. Tours by appointment. Tasting daily 10 A.M.–4:30 P.M. Gift shop.

Louis Bartolucci's family winery, known as the Oakville Vineyards in Oakville, was sold well before Louis was ready to retire, so he built Mont St. John Cellars, named for the mountain just beyond the winery. (Oakville subsequently went bankrupt.) With the help of his son Andrea he started making wine using the grapes from Andrea's Madonna Vineyard (see Acacia Winery), located in the Carneros region of the Napa Valley.

WHITE

☆ 1981 CHARDONNAY ($9.50) Carneros Region, Napa. *Snappy, lemony, simple.*
☆☆ 1983 CHARDONNAY ($11.00) Carneros-Napa Valley. *Round, varietal, oaky, pleasant.*

RED

☆☆ 1979 PINOT NOIR ($10.00) Carneros Region, Napa.
☆☆ 1981 PINOT NOIR ($10.00) Carneros-Napa Valley. *Rich, clean, deep.*

R. Montali and Associates
ALAMEDA COUNTY

600 Addison Street, Berkeley, California 94710 (415-540-5384). FOUNDED: 1982. ACREAGE: None. PRODUCTION: 60,000 cases. DISTRIBUTION: Nationwide; some foreign markets. OWNER: Corporation. Ralph Montali, president; Dieter Tede, secretary-treasurer; Robert Sciaqua, vice president. WINEMAKER: Chuck Grushkowitz. OTHER LABELS: Sonoma Mission Winery, Jonathan Vintners, Lombard Hills. Tasting daily 12–5 P.M. Tours by appointment.

Ralph Montali has been in the wine and spirits wholesale business for 50 years. At the age of 71 he met Richard Carey, whose winery was in financial trouble. He came in as a consultant and eventually bought the winery himself with a group of investors. Their new winery in Berkeley was completed in 1983. Richard Carey left the winery in April of 1985.

WHITE

☆ 1982 SONOMA MISSION WINERY ($3.00) California. *Crisp, clean, fruity.*
1980 CHARDONNAY ($8.50) Santa Maria Valley. *Dark, heavy, vinous.*

☆ 1982 SONOMA MISSION WINERY CHARDONNAY ($6.00) California. *Oily, odd, weedy; not varietal or fruity.*

1982 CHARDONNAY ($9.00) Bien Nacido, Santa Maria Valley. *Perfumy, odd.*

1983 CHARDONNAY ($8.50) Santa Maria Valley. *Dull, oxidized.*

☆☆ 1984 CHARDONNAY ($8.00) Bien Nacido, Santa Maria Valley. *Rich, clean, ripe, attractive.*

☆☆☆ 1984 CHARDONNAY ($10.00) Hopkins River, Sonoma. *Rich, varietal, with lovely oak and clean fruit; balanced.*

☆☆ 1982 SONOMA MISSION WINERY CHENIN BLANC ($3.50) California (Temecula). *Slight vegetative quality. Great fruit and clean acidity.*

1980 FUME BLANC ($7.50) French Camp, Peck, San Luis Obispo.

☆ 1982 GEWURZTRAMINER ($6.50) Santa Maria. *1.8% residual sugar. Decent varietal character and fruit.*

☆☆☆ 1983 GEWURZTRAMINER ($6.50) Santa Maria Valley. *1.8% residual sugar. Fresh, clean, lush, with great fruit.*

☆☆ 1984 GEWURZTRAMINER ($6.50) Bien Nacido, Santa Maria Valley. *1.12% residual sugar. Spritzy, fresh, varietal, clean.*

1982 SONOMA MISSION WINERY SAUVIGNON BLANC ($5.50) California. *Vinous, lacking fruit, strange.*

1982 SAUVIGNON BLANC ($7.50) Paso Robles. *Dull, heavy, lacking fruit.*

1982 SAUVIGNON BLANC ($7.50) San Luis Obispo.

BLANC DE NOIR

☆ 1983 SONOMA MISSION WINERY "CAPRICE" ZINFANDEL ($4.50) California. *Off-dry. Rich, clean, varietal.*

☆☆ 1983 ZINFANDEL ($4.95) Bel Blanc, California. *1.19% residual sugar. Fresh, clean, varietal.*

1984 SONOMA MISSION WINERY WHITE ZINFANDEL ($3.00) California. *0.9% residual sugar. Dull, flabby.*

RED

NV SONOMA MISSION WINERY ($3.00) California. *Spicy, peculiar.*

1977 CABERNET SAUVIGNON ($8.25) 48% Tepusquet, 48% Santa Ynez, 4% Merlot, Santa Maria Valley. *Odd flavors, simple and dull.*

☆☆ 1982 SONOMA MISSION WINERY CABERNET SAUVIGNON ($5.00) Paso Robles. *Fat, lush, balanced.*

☆ 1982 SONOMA MISSION WINERY CABERNET SAUVIGNON ($5.50) California. *Berried, clean, decent.*

☆ 1982 CABERNET SAUVIGNON ($6.50) Alexander Valley, Sonoma.

1982 CABERNET SAUVIGNON ($8.50) Paso Robles. *Grapey, strange.*

☆☆ 1983 CABERNET SAUVIGNON ($8.50) Napa Valley. *Herbal, rich, smooth. Drink 1987 and beyond.*

1980 GAMAY BEAUJOLAIS ($4.50) Santa Maria. *Vegetal, thick, dull.*

☆ NV JONATHAN VINTNERS MERLOT ($3.00) California. *Weedy.*

☆☆ 1980 SONOMA MISSION WINERY PETITE SIRAH ($4.50) California. *Big, fat, rich, round, attractive. Drink now.*

☆ 1982 PINOT NOIR ($7.50) Proprietor's Series, Santa Maria Valley. *Vegetal.*

☆ 1983 PINOT NOIR ($7.00) Napa Valley. *Soft and rich, with a hard vegetal edge.*

☆ 1979 ZINFANDEL Paso Robles. *Raisiny, heavy, some nice flavors.*

☆ 1979 RICHARD CAREY ZINFANDEL Paso Robles.

1979 SONOMA MISSION WINERY ZINFANDEL San Luis Obispo. *Raisiny, hot, not much.*

☆ 1980 ZINFANDEL ($7.50) Shenandoah Valley, Amador. *Tannic, rich, hot, earthy. Drink 1986.*

1981 SONOMA MISSION WINERY ZINFANDEL ($4.50) Reserve, Amador. *Raisiny, sweet, unattractive.*

☆☆   1982 LOMBARD HILL CELLARS ZINFANDEL ($4.50) Amador. *Tannic, rich, fruity,*
       attractive.
☆☆   1982 ZINFANDEL ($7.50) Alexander Valley. *Rich, complex, varietal. Drink now.*

Montbray Wine Cellars
MARYLAND

818 Silver Run Valley Road, Westminster, Maryland 21157 (301-346-7878). FOUNDED: 1966.
ACREAGE: 30 acres. PRODUCTION: 2,900 cases. DISTRIBUTION: Maryland and Washington
D.C. OWNER: Mowbray family. G. H. Mowbray, president. WINEMAKER: Hamilton Mowbray.
Tours and tasting Monday–Saturday 10 A.M.–6 P.M., Sunday 1 P.M.–6 P.M.

   "A hobby that turned into a passion and is now a madness"—that's how psychologist G. H.
Mowbray describes his seduction by wine. G. H. was working full time at Johns Hopkins University,
doing research in experimental psychology while making wine at home. "Making wine soon began
to demand more time, so of course I had to quit working at the university," he explains. The
Mowbray family bought some property and planted their first vineyards in 1964. An old German-
style bank barn became the winery, and the Mowbrays went to work, sharing responsibilities in
the vineyards and the winery.

Montclair Winery
ALAMEDA COUNTY

910 81st Avenue, Oakland, California 94609 (415-658-1014). FOUNDED: 1975. ACREAGE:
None. PRODUCTION: 1,500 cases. DISTRIBUTION: California and 4 other states. OWNERS:
R. K. Dove, president; J. H. Burkhard, L. A. Dove, and C. Dove, vice presidents. WINEMAKER:
R. K. Dove. No tours or tasting.

   Rick Dove had to start making wine. "I married an Italian lady and since I wasn't Catholic
and I wasn't Italian, the only way I could gain acceptance in the family was to make wine." Rick
lives in Piedmont and makes wine in a concrete-block warehouse near the Oakland Coliseum.
Particular about his grape sources, he purchases Zinfandel from the Dry Creek area of Sonoma.
"I believe that Dry Creek Valley is the best place in the world for Zinfandel," says Rick, who
prefers heavy, rich, high-alcohol red wines.

WHITE

O   1981 FRENCH COLOMBARD ($5.00)

RED

☆☆☆   1979 PETITE SIRAH ($6.50) Sonoma.
☆☆☆   1980 ZINFANDEL ($8.50) Kelley Creek, Sonoma. *Lovely—fresh fruit, balance and com-*
         plexity. It's all here.
☆☆☆   1981 ZINFANDEL ($6.50) Teldeschi, Sonoma. *Big and assertive but with charming fruit*
         and great depth.
☆☆☆   1981 ZINFANDEL ($8.50) Kelley Creek, Sonoma. *Lush, fruity, jammy—charming. Will*
         improve with some age.

Montdomaine Cellars
VIRGINIA

Route 6, Box 168A, Charlottesville, Virginia 22901 (804-971-8947). FOUNDED: 1979. ACREAGE:
32 acres. PRODUCTION: 9,000 cases. DISTRIBUTION: Virginia and Washington D.C. OWNER:

Corporation. Michael Bowles, president. WINEMAKER: Steven Warner. OTHER LABEL: Monticello Wine Company. Tours by appointment.

Michael Bowles, a pilot for Pan American World Airways, read an article in the *New York Times* about Virginia's new wine industry. He was living in Manhattan at the time with his wife, Lynn, who is a flight attendant. Mike decided to look at a vineyard in Barboursville. The Bowleses were fascinated by the history of Virginia's early wine industry and were especially enchanted by the story of how Philip Mazzi was sent from Italy to research the area's grape-growing potential during the 1770s. Mazzi's assessment, stated in a letter to George Washington, was that "the best wines in the world will be made here." Without any previous wine production experience, the Bowleses started a small 2.2-acre vineyard. Two and a half years later, in 1979, they had their first crush. Now with 32 acres of vineyard and a brand-new, 27,000-gallon winery, Mike and Lynn are determined to make Mazzi's prediction come true.

WHITE

☆☆ 1983 MONTICELLO WINE COMPANY CHARDONNAY Virginia. *Rich, varietal, balanced, clean, vinous.*

RED

☆☆ 1983 MONTICELLO WINE COMPANY MERLOT ($8.00) Cuvée Bernard Chamberlain, Albemarle County, Virginia. *Lush, soft, balanced, fruity and charming.*
1983 MONTICELLO WINE COMPANY CABERNET SAUVIGNON Albemarle County, Virginia.

Montelle Vineyards
MISSOURI

Route 1, Box 94, Augusta, Missouri 63332 (314-228-4464). FOUNDED: 1970. ACREAGE: 5 acres. PRODUCTION: 3,000 cases. DISTRIBUTION: Missouri. OWNER: Partnership. Clayton and Nissel Byers, and Robert and Judith Silfer. WINEMAKER: Clayton Byers. Tours and tasting Monday–Saturday 10 A.M.–6 P.M., Sunday 12–6 P.M.

Clayton Byers feels he made a big mistake when he attended Alexis Lichine's tasting of 24 first-growth Bordeaux. "I fell head over heels in love," says Clayton. "I knew I would never be happy until I contributed my two drops' worth to the wine world." Limited financially, he began looking at land in many different parts of the United States and found a plot in Augusta, where French-American hybrids had been grown. With the help of his sons, Clayton converted a smokehouse and a garage on the property into a winery and then planted five acres of French-American hybrids. So far the winery has had greater success with blends than with straight varietal wines.

Monterey Peninsula Winery
MONTEREY COUNTY

2999 Monterey-Salinas Highway, Monterey, California 93940 (408-372-4949). FOUNDED: 1974. ACREAGE: None. PRODUCTION: 15,000 cases. DISTRIBUTION: Nationwide. OWNERS: Roy L. Thomas D.D.S. and Deryck Nuckton D.D.S. WINEMAKER: Peter Watson-Graff. OTHER LABELS: Monterey Cellars, Big Sur Wines. Tasting daily 10 A.M.–6 P.M. Gift shop. Newsletter.

This rather eclectic winery is owned by dentist Roy Thomas and retired orthodontist Dick Nuckton. At first they indulged in such hyperbole as Late Harvest Grenache and Zinfandel Champagne, but things seem to have calmed down a bit. Emphasis is still on reds, particularly Zinfandel and Cabernet Sauvignon. The label notes, written by Dr. Thomas and Mr. Watson-Graff, are among the most complete and amusing in the wine industry.

WHITE

☆ 1979 CHARDONNAY ($12.00) Junction, Monterey. *Dark, toasty, clean, rich, low in fruit.*

O 1979 CHARDONNAY ($19.00) Late Harvest, Hacienda, Monterey. *375ml. Oxidized, weird, unattractive.*

1980 CHARDONNAY ($12.00) Arroyo Seco, Monterey. *Clumsy, heavy, overcooked.*

☆☆ 1981 CHARDONNAY ($14.00) Arroyo Seco, Monterey. *A big bruiser: oaky, rich, vinous, intense, rather good.*

☆ 1981 CHARDONNAY ($15.00) Cobblestone, Monterey. *Oily, rich, oaky, fat. Good but a bit overdone.*

☆☆ 1982 CHARDONNAY ($15.00) Cobblestone, Monterey. *Big, fat, rich, oily, balanced.*

☆☆ 1982 PINOT BLANC ($9.50) Cobblestone, Monterey. *Clean, balanced, crisp, earthy.*

☆☆☆ 1981 WHITE RIESLING ($18.50) Late Harvest, Monterey. *15% residual sugar. Lovely botrytis, crisp acid, stunning.*

BLANC DE NOIR

O 1983 WHITE ZINFANDEL ($6.50) Willow Creek, California. *Dirty, dull, unpleasant.*

RED

☆ 1977 CABERNET SAUVIGNON ($8.50) Arroyo Seco, Monterey.

☆ 1978 MONTEREY CABERNET ($6.50) Monterey. *5% Zinfandel.*

☆☆ 1978 CABERNET SAUVIGNON ($9.00) Shell Creek, San Luis Obispo. *Rich, intensely fruity. Deeply colored. Drink 1986.*

☆☆ 1979 CABERNET SAUVIGNON ($13.00) Santa Lucia Mountains-Monterey. *Lovely, complex, a bit vegetal.*

☆☆☆ 1979 CABERNET SAUVIGNON ($18.00) Arroyo Seco, Monterey. *Herbal, fruity, fresh and attractive, with crisp acid. Drink now.*

☆☆☆☆ 1980 CABERNET SAUVIGNON ($25.00) Monterey. *Lush, beautifully structured, complex, superb.*

☆☆ 1981 CABERNET SAUVIGNON ($12.00) Smith & Hook, Monterey. *Lush, balanced, clean, rich, round. Drink 1986.*

☆☆☆ 1981 CABERNET SAUVIGNON ($14.00) Doctor's Reserve, Monterey. *Rich, deep, lush and lovely.*

☆☆☆ 1981 MERLOT ($12.00) Monterey. *20% Cabernet. Rich, deep, clean and complex. Will age well.*

O 1978 PINOT NOIR ($10.00) D.M. Junction, Monterey. *Heavy vegetation plus spoilage.*

1981 PINOT NOIR ($7.00) D.M. Junction, Monterey. *Meaty, some oxidation.*

☆☆ 1981 PINOT NOIR ($12.00) Junction, Monterey. *Tart, crisp, varietal.*

☆ 1977 ZINFANDEL ($12.00) Late Harvest, Amador. *Intense, dark, tannic, deep.*

☆☆☆ 1978 ZINFANDEL ($6.50) 29% Amador, 45% Templeton, 20% Paso Robles, California. *Clean, rich and fruity. An ideal Zinfandel.*

☆ 1978 ZINFANDEL ($6.50) Late Harvest, Hilltop, Monterey. *Decent—lush and clean, with some volatile acidity.*

☆☆ 1978 ZINFANDEL ($9.00) Late Harvest, Oak Flat, San Luis Obispo. *6.5% residual sugar. Big, lush, berried, clean and good.*

☆☆ 1978 ZINFANDEL ($9.00) Late Harvest, Willow Creek, San Luis Obispo. *6% residual sugar. Intense, coffee-like, rich, good fruit.*

☆☆ 1978 ZINFANDEL ($13.50) Late Harvest, Ferrero Old Ranch, Amador. *3.5% residual sugar. Port-like, rich, lush.*

☆☆ 1978 ZINFANDEL ($15.00) Late Harvest, Dusi, Templeton. *18% residual sugar. Port-like, lush and lovely.*

☆ 1978 ZINFANDEL ($18.00) Sweet, Late Harvest, Amador. *16% residual sugar. Crisp acid and syrupy sweetness; jammy.*

☆ 1979 ZINFANDEL ($6.25) California.

☆☆☆ 1979 ZINFANDEL ($7.50) California. *Clean, fresh, fruity, fairly simple but very attractive.*

☆☆ 1979 ZINFANDEL ($7.50) 47% Miller, 50% Ferrero, 3% Petite Sirah, Shenandoah Valley, Amador.

☆☆ 1979 ZINFANDEL ($7.50) Wilpete Farms, Willow Creek, San Luis Obispo. *Jammy and big.*

☆ 1979 ZINFANDEL ($8.00) 31% Dusi, 26% Brown, 20% Farview, 16% Willow Creek, San Luis Obispo, 7% Petite Sirah, Shell Creek Vineyard. *Fat, lush, berried, heavy.*

☆ 1979 ZINFANDEL ($8.00) Ferrero Ranch, Amador. *Soft, dull, lacking fruit.*

☆ 1979 ZINFANDEL ($8.50) Dusi, San Luis Obispo. *Raisiny, intense, deep.*

The Monterey Vineyards
MONTEREY COUNTY

800 South Alta Street, Gonzales, California 93926 (408-675-2481). FOUNDED: 1974. ACREAGE: None. PRODUCTION: 150,000 cases. DISTRIBUTION: Nationwide. OWNER: Seagram Classics Wine Company. Dr. Richard Peterson, president. WINEMAKER: Richard Peterson. Tours and tasting daily 11 A.M.–4 P.M. Newsletter.

In 1973 the McFarland Land Company (see), which controlled thousands of acres of Monterey vineyards, made winemaker Richard Peterson, then with Beaulieu Vineyards, an offer he couldn't refuse. They would let him design his own winery and run it. The winery, a handsome structure, went through various financial problems and managements until it was sold to Coca-Cola in 1977. In 1983 the winery was acquired by Seagram as part of its Wine Spectrum purchase. Through all this, Dick Peterson has remained as winemaker.

WHITE

☆☆☆ 1982 CLASSIC CALIFORNIA WHITE ($4.00) California. *Lemony crisp, with clean and dry flavors. Delightful.*

☆☆ 1983 CLASSIC CALIFORNIA WHITE ($4.00) California. *Nice fruit; dry, clean. Five-variety blend.*

1979 CHARDONNAY ($6.00) Monterey. *Dull, tired.*

1981 CHARDONNAY ($6.00) California. *Dull, weak fruit.*

☆ 1982 CHARDONNAY ($6.00) California. *Simple, clean, balanced, with some off flavors.*

☆☆ 1982 CHENIN BLANC ($4.50) Monterey. *Clean, fresh, simple and very nice.*

☆☆ 1983 CHENIN BLANC ($4.00) Monterey. *Varietal, snappy, clean and charming.*

O 1980 FUME BLANC ($4.95) San Luis Obispo.

O 1980 FUME BLANC ($5.00) Monterey.

1981 FUME BLANC ($5.50) San Luis Obispo. *Sweet, oxidized.*

☆ 1982 GEWURZTRAMINER ($5.00) Monterey. *Fat, ripe, sappy.*

☆☆ 1983 GEWURZTRAMINER ($5.00) Monterey. *1.8% residual sugar. Crisp, varietal, charming.*

☆☆☆ 1978 JOHANNISBERG RIESLING ($5.00) Thanksgiving Harvest, Monterey. *Crisp and richly fruity, with good depth.*

1981 JOHANNISBERG RIESLING ($5.50) Monterey.

O 1982 JOHANNISBERG RIESLING ($5.00) Monterey. *Sour, unattractive, dry.*

☆ 1980 PINOT BLANC ($4.25) Monterey. *Vinous, tired.*
☆☆ 1983 PINOT BLANC ($4.00) Monterey. *Fresh, clean, snappy, balanced.*
1978 SAUVIGNON BLANC ($10.00) Special Selection, San Luis Obispo. *7.6% residual sugar. Viscous, dull flavors.*

SPARKLING

☆ 1979 BRUT ($12.00) Monterey. *Soft, crisp and fruity, but with some heavy vegetal notes.*

ROSE

☆☆ 1983 CLASSIC CALIFORNIA ROSE ($4.00) Monterey. *42% Gamay, 29% Grenache, 23% Cabernet. Off-dry, charming.*

BLANC DE NOIR

☆☆☆ 1984 WHITE ZINFANDEL ($4.50) Monterey. *2.25% residual sugar. Soft, fruity, clean, very attractive.*

RED

○ 1978 TAWNY DESSERT WINE ($10.00) Monterey County. *9.85% residual sugar. Pinot Noir. Sweet asparagus, unattractive.*
☆☆ 1979 CLASSIC CALIFORNIA RED ($4.00) Central Coast Counties. *65% Cabernet, 20% Zinfandel, 15% Pinot Noir. Rich, fresh, good.*
☆☆ 1980 CLASSIC CALIFORNIA RED ($4.00) California. *75% Cabernet, 14% Zinfandel, 11% Pinot Noir. Fruity, clean.*
☆☆ 1979 CABERNET SAUVIGNON ($8.00) French Camp, San Luis Obispo. *Clean, slight and pleasant.*
○ 1976 ZINFANDEL Monterey.

Monteviña Wines
AMADOR COUNTY

20680 Shenandoah School Road, Plymouth, California 95669 (209-245-6942). FOUNDED: 1973. ACREAGE: 100 acres. PRODUCTION: 35,000 cases. DISTRIBUTION: Nationwide; England. OWNER: Walter H. Field, president. WINEMAKERS: Jeffrey Runquist and Jeffrey Meyers. Tasting daily 11 A.M.–4 P.M.

The Monteviña estate was established when Walter Field bought two Amador County land parcels, the Massoni Ranch and the Brown Homestead. The estate had 60 acres of vines at that time. Walter's son-in-law Cary Gott made Monteviña wines in the basement of the Massoni ranch house until 1974, when a large winery building was built on the estate. By specializing in Zinfandel in both a heavy, Amador style and a fresh, carbonic maceration style, Monteviña helped to bring recognition to Amador County and the Shenandoah Valley as a serious wine-producing area. Over the years the winery has concentrated on expanding its vineyard plantings of both red and white varieties. Cary has since left the winery (see Corbett Canyon Vineyards), but winemaker Jeff Runquist, who had worked with Cary since 1979, continues to specialize in both Zinfandel and Sauvignon Blanc.

WHITE

☆☆ 1981 CHARDONNAY ($10.00) Santa Barbara. *Vinous, crisp and clean.*
☆ 1982 CHARDONNAY ($9.00) 83% Tepusquet, 17% Robert Young, California. *Ripe, vinous, lush.*
☆☆ 1983 CHARDONNAY ($9.00) California. *Crisp, balanced, clean, complex, attractive.*
☆☆ 1983 FUME BLANC ($5.00) Estate, Shenandoah Valley, California. *Ripe fruit, rich, clean, pleasant.*

☆☆   1981 SAUVIGNON BLANC ($8.00) Estate, Amador.
☆☆   1982 SAUVIGNON BLANC ($6.50) Estate, Amador.
      1982 SEMILLON ($5.75) Estate, Shenandoah Valley, Amador.

BLANC DE NOIR

☆☆☆   1983 WHITE ZINFANDEL ($4.75) Amador. *Charming, crisp, fruity, coral-colored, varietal.*
☆☆   **1984 WHITE ZINFANDEL ($4.95) Estate, Shenandoah Valley, California.** *1% residual sugar. Varietal, fresh, attractive.*

RED

☆☆   NV   PREMIUM RED ($3.75) Amador. *Fruity and tangy; tannic, clean, berried. Very nice.*
☆☆   **1980 BARBERA ($7.00) Amador.**
☆   1981 BARBERA ($6.00) Estate, Shenandoah Valley, California. *Raisiny, berried, overdone.*
☆☆   **1976 CABERNET SAUVIGNON Amador.** *Lush and earthy, with some bitterness but adequate structure.*
☆   **1980 CABERNET SAUVIGNON ($6.75) Estate, Shenandoah Valley, Amador.**
☆☆   1981 CABERNET SAUVIGNON ($7.50) Shenandoah Valley, California. *Lush, round, clean, varietal, charming. Drink now.*
☆☆   **1979 ZINFANDEL ($6.50) Shenandoah Valley, Amador.** *Berried, oaky, balanced, a bit coarse.*
O   1980 ZINFANDEL ($5.00) Montino, Amador. *Unattractive, off flavors mar this one.*
☆☆   **1980 ZINFANDEL ($6.50) Amador.** *Big, thick, overpowering.*
☆   **1980 ZINFANDEL ($9.00) Winemaker's Choice, Estate, Shenandoah Valley, California.** *Big, syrupy, late-harvest style; awkward and overdone.*
☆☆☆   1981 ZINFANDEL ($5.00) Montino, Estate, Shenandoah Valley, California. *Fruity and pleasant.*

Monticello Cellars
NAPA COUNTY

4242 Big Ranch Road, Napa, California 94558 (707-253-2802). FOUNDED: 1980. ACREAGE: 225 acres. PRODUCTION: 15,000 cases. DISTRIBUTION: 20 states. OWNER: Jay Corley. WINE-MAKER: Alan Phillips. OTHER LABELS: Château M, Cranbrook Cellars, Jefferson Cellars. Tours and tasting by appointment.

Jay Corley, an Italian linguist and Southern California investor and venture capitalist, moved to the Napa Valley and became a grape grower in 1970. He is fascinated by enophile Thomas Jefferson, partly because the Corley family was once involved in Virginia agriculture. A replica of Jefferson's home, Monticello, has been built on the property. The winery, started in 1980, has been a success. Winemaker Alan Phillips, a U.C. Davis honors graduate, worked at Lamont and was assistant to Phil Baxter at Rutherford Hill.

WHITE

☆☆   NV   JEFFERSON CELLARS VIN BLANC ($4.95) Napa Valley. *Fresh, attractive, clean.*
☆☆   1982 WHITE DINNER WINE ($5.50) Napa Valley. *65% Chardonnay, 30% Gewürztra-miner, 5% Semillon. Crisp and fresh.*
☆☆☆   **1981 CHARDONNAY ($11.00) Napa Valley.** *Classic structure, toasty oak nose, firm fruit.*
☆☆☆   **1982 CHARDONNAY ($13.50) Napa Valley.** *Crisp, clean, snappy, fresh, lovely.*
☆☆☆   **1982 CHARDONNAY ($14.00) Barrel Fermented, Estate, Napa Valley.** *Toasty, rich, va-rietal, fruity. More complex than the regular '82.*
☆☆☆   1983 CRANBROOK CELLARS CHARDONNAY ($8.00) Napa Valley. *Crisp, fresh, va-rietal, with a round and soft finish.*

☆☆ 1983 CRANBROOK CELLARS CHEVRIER ($5.75) Napa Valley. *Varietal, attractive, simple and round.*

☆☆☆ 1982 GEWURZTRAMINER ($6.50) Napa Valley. *0.75% residual sugar. Crisp, fruity and rounded.*

☆☆☆ 1983 CRANBROOK CELLARS GEWURZTRAMINER ($5.50) Napa Valley. *Fresh, fruity, varietal.*

☆☆☆ 1983 GEWURZTRAMINER ($8.50) Estate, Napa Valley. *0.6% residual sugar. Crisp, fresh, varietal, clean, super.*

☆☆☆ 1982 SAUVIGNON BLANC ($8.50) Napa Valley. *Fresh and grassy.*

☆☆☆ 1982 CHATEAU M SAUVIGNON BLANC ($17.50) Late Harvest, Napa Valley. *375ml. 10% residual sugar. 94% Sauvignon Blanc, 6% Semillon.*

☆☆☆ 1983 SAUVIGNON BLANC ($9.00) Estate, Napa Valley. *Subdued grass, crisp fruit, lovely.*

RED

☆☆ NV JEFFERSON CELLARS CLARET ($4.95) Napa Valley. *Delightful. Same wine as Cranbrook Cellars Zinfandel Nouveau.*

☆☆ 1983 JEFFERSON CELLARS CLARET ($4.95) Napa Valley. *Same wine as Cranbrook Cellars Zinfandel.*

☆☆☆☆ 1980 CABERNET SAUVIGNON ($9.75) Napa Valley. *22% Merlot. Fruity, structured, superb. Drink now or hold.*

☆☆ 1981 CABERNET SAUVIGNON ($10.00) Napa Valley. *Nice structure, complex, a bit weedy. Drink 1987.*

☆☆ NV CRANBROOK CELLARS ZINFANDEL ($4.95) Napa Valley. *Fresh, fruity, snappy, clean, delightful. Serve chilled.*

☆☆ 1983 CRANBROOK CELLARS PREMIER ZINFANDEL ($4.95) Napa Valley. *Grapey, rich, deep, clean, attractive.*

MONTICELLO WINE COMPANY *see* Montdomaine Cellars

Moon Vineyards
NAPA COUNTY

3315 Sonoma Highway, Napa, California 94559 (707-226-2642). FOUNDED: 1982. ACREAGE: 60 acres. PRODUCTION: 600 cases. DISTRIBUTION: California. OWNERS: Doyle and Kathy Moon. WINEMAKER: Jerry Luper. No tours or tasting.

Doyle and Kathy Moon were looking for a country retreat when they found their nineteenth-century house and ranch in Napa. At the time Doyle, the owner of three renowned Bay Area restaurants, had no intention of getting into the wine business. But after buying the ranch in 1980, he and Kathy began ripping out all but the 30-year-old Zinfandel vines and planting Chardonnay. "The first year (1982) we had our Zinfandel custom-crushed at Acacia Winery," says Kathy. "That was the last wine to be made from those old vines; we ripped them out the following year." In 1983 the new Chardonnay vines produced 450 cases of wine, made at Château Bouchaine by Jerry Luper. Needless to say, the wines are available at Doyle's three restaurants: the Balboa Cafe, the Santa Fe Bar & Grill, and Stars.

RED

☆☆☆ 1982 ZINFANDEL ($4.00) Estate, Napa Valley-Carneros. *Crisp, fruity and superb. Fresh and charming. Made at Acacia.*

Moore-Dupont Winery
MISSOURI

Interstate 55, Route 77, Benton, Missouri 63736 (314-545-4141). FOUNDED: 1982. ACREAGE: 175 acres. PRODUCTION: 2,000 cases. DISTRIBUTION: Missouri. OWNERS: J. Handy Moore and Jean René Dupont. WINEMAKER: Bill Camberton. Tours and tasting daily. Call for information.

One day while playing tennis, Handy Moore and Jean René Dupont hit on the subject of wine and discovered they both were interested in something besides a better backhand. Moore had been growing grapes since 1972 as part of his larger agricultural business, and Dupont, a surgeon, had just started growing grapes and making wine at home. After forming a partnership, they started and quickly outgrew their first facility and in 1984 moved to their new and much larger winery.

Morgan Winery
MONTEREY COUNTY

526 East Brunken Avenue, Salinas, California 93901 (408-455-1382). FOUNDED: 1982. ACREAGE: None. PRODUCTION: 5,000 cases. DISTRIBUTION: Major market states. OWNERS: Mr. and Mrs. L. D. Lee; Donna, George, David, and Dan Lee. WINEMAKER: Dan Lee. OTHER LABEL: St. Vrain. Tours and tasting by appointment.

This tiny operation is run by Dan Lee, former winemaker at Jekel Vineyards and current winemaker at Durney Vineyard. Morgan is Dan's middle name. He hopes to be able to turn to his winery full time within a few years. At that time the winery will be expanded to its projected production of 10,000 cases annually.

WHITE

☆☆☆☆ 1982 CHARDONNAY ($12.00) Cobblestone, Hillside, Monterey. *Extraordinary Burgundian effort: balanced, elegant, delicious.*

☆☆☆ 1983 CHARDONNAY ($12.50) Monterey. *Rich and balanced. Lovely.*

☆☆☆ 1983 ST. VRAIN SAUVIGNON BLANC ($7.50) Alexander Valley. *Fresh, lush, clean, very attractive.*

James Moroney Winery
PENNSYLVANIA

243-247 North 63rd Street, Philadelphia, Pennsylvania 19139 (215-471-5300). FOUNDED: 1845. ACREAGE: None. PRODUCTION: 10,000 cases. DISTRIBUTION: Pennsylvania. OWNER: James Moroney. No tours or tasting.

Not a single grape has ever been crushed at James Moroney Winery. Established in 1845, the winery is one of the nation's oldest bottlers of sacramental wines. After selling Scotch and whiskey in downtown Philadelphia, the family turned to making sacramental wines during Prohibition in a larger facility west of town. After Repeal, they expanded their distribution business, adding California and European wines to their list. The stock may have changed over the years, but the staff is still the Moroney family.

J. W. Morris Wineries
SONOMA COUNTY

101 Grant Avenue, P.O. Box 921, Healdsburg, California 95448 (707-431-7015). FOUNDED: 1975. ACREAGE: 275 acres. PRODUCTION: 30,000 cases. DISTRIBUTION: 25 states. OWNERS: Ken and Beatrice Toth. WINEMAKER: Richard J. Mafit. Tours by appointment.

Originally, J. W. Morris Winery made only fortified wines. Owned by J. W. Morris and James Olsen, the winery established quite a respectable reputation for quality California ports. Problems began in 1977, when they began making table wines that were less than warmly received in the marketplace. In 1983 the winery was sold to Ken Toth, owner of Black Mountain Vineyards in Sonoma County, a leading source of grapes for J. W. Morris. Ken, who at one time was the president of Sonoma Vineyards, wanted a winery closer to Black Mountain, so he moved his new purchase to a functional metal building in Healdsburg. The specialty of the winery is still port, all of which is estate bottled.

WHITE

☆☆ 1981 WHITE PRIVATE RESERVE ($3.95) California.

1983 WHITE PRIVATE RESERVE ($3.00) California. *Sour, unpleasant, oxidized.*

1981 CHARDONNAY ($7.50) California Select, 80% Monterey, 20% Sonoma. *Vinous, fat and clumsy.*

1981 CHARDONNAY ($7.50) California Select, Healdsburg, California.

1983 CHARDONNAY ($7.50) Alexander Valley, Sonoma. *Dirty, unattractive.*

☆ 1983 CHARDONNAY ($8.75) Alexander Valley. *Heavy and somewhat dull.*

☆ 1981 SAUVIGNON BLANC ($6.00) California Select, California.

1982 SAUVIGNON BLANC ($6.00) California Select, California. *Vinous, heavy.*

O 1983 SAUVIGNON BLANC ($5.00) Alexander Valley, Sonoma. *Musty, dirty.*

☆☆☆ 1984 SAUVIGNON BLANC ($6.25) Alexander Valley. *Clean, peppery, varietal, with wonderful acidity.*

RED

1979 RED PRIVATE RESERVE ($3.95) California.

☆ 1981 RED PRIVATE RESERVE ($3.00) California. *Decent, weedy, balanced.*

O 1979 CABERNET SAUVIGNON ($9.50) Sonoma. *Weedy, volatile acidity, really ugly.*

☆☆☆ 1981 CABERNET SAUVIGNON ($7.50) Alexander Valley. *22% Merlot. Lovely balance; clean, lean. Drink 1986.*

☆☆☆ 1981 CABERNET SAUVIGNON ($8.00) California Selection. *Lovely fruit, deep oak; smooth and clean. Drink 1987.*

☆ 1979 PINOT NOIR ($9.50) Monterey.

☆ 1980 PINOT NOIR ($6.00) Monterey.

☆ 1980 ZINFANDEL ($8.50) Sonoma. *Oak, fruit and a touch of volatile acidity.*

O 1981 ZINFANDEL ($5.00) California. *Overripe, harsh and unappealing.*

FORTIFIED

☆☆☆ 1979 PORT ($10.00) Black Mountain, Sonoma.

Mount Baker Vineyards
WASHINGTON

4298 Mount Baker Highway, Everson, Washington 98247 (206-592-2300). FOUNDED: 1981. ACREAGE: 25 acres. PRODUCTION: 6,700 cases. DISTRIBUTION: California, Oregon, and Washington. OWNERS: Al Stratton and family, and Jim Hildt. WINEMAKER: Al Stratton; Brent Charnley, assistant. Tours and tasting by appointment.

Colonel Al Stratton, a retired army surgeon, started with a home winemaking kit, and before long he was making "research" wine for Washington State University. While working at the university extension service, Al started his own experimental vineyard to identify which varieties grow best in certain environments. He chose a site west of the Cascades, in a valley below Mount Baker. Planting cool-climate varieties, including the unusual Madeleine Angevine and Madeleine Sylvaner, kept Al busy in the vineyard, but when his son Charlie showed interest in winemaking, Al decided a winery might be fun. Jim Hildt, a former dairy farmer and horticulture student at the university, joined the project. Jim, who helped Al plant his vineyards, now works full time as the winery's financial advisor, marketing director, vineyard and winery assistant, and carpenter. Al's wife, Marjorie, helps her husband with the vineyard, along with Brent Charnley, a newly hired enologist from U.C. Davis.

WHITE

☆ 1983 CHARDONNAY ($9.00) Washington. *Vinous, oily, with some fruit and nice oak.*
☆☆ 1983 GEWURZTRAMINER ($5.85) Washington. *1.3% residual sugar. Varietal, rich, decent.*
☆ 1983 MADELEINE ANGEVINE ($5.85) Washington. *0.75% residual sugar. Vinous, dry, clean, heavy.*
1982 MULLER-THURGAU ($5.85) Washington. *1.1% residual sugar. Earthy, musty, acceptable.*
1983 PRECOCE DE MALINGRE ($5.85) Washington. *Grassy, heavy, oily, vinous.*

Mount Bethel Winery
ARKANSAS

U.S. Highway 64, Altus, Arkansas 72821 (501-468-2444). FOUNDED: 1956. ACREAGE: 22 acres. PRODUCTION: 8,500 cases. DISTRIBUTION: Arkansas. OWNER: Eugene Post. WINEMAKER: Eugene Post. Tours and tasting daily 7 A.M.–11 A.M.

The original Post Winery, founded by Bavarian immigrant Jacob Post in 1880, was left empty when the family moved the operation to a nearby location. The land and buildings remained in the family when James Post sold them to his son Eugene in 1956. Eugene kept the original turn-of-the-century winery, using the old cellar as a sales room. He has added a modern building directly behind it and works hard to keep the vineyards in first-rate condition. He uses only his own estate grapes, mostly Delaware and Niagara.

Mount Eden Vineyards
SANTA CLARA COUNTY

22020 Mount Eden Road, Saratoga, California 95070 (408-867-5832). FOUNDED: 1961. ACREAGE: 32 acres. PRODUCTION: 3,500 cases. DISTRIBUTION: 6 states. OWNER: MEV. WINEMAKER: F. Jeffrey Patterson. OTHER LABEL: MEV. Tours by appointment. MEV tasting by appointment (no estate tasting).

This operation, owned by a group of investors, many of whom are doctors, is the larger portion of Martin Ray's (see) winery that was partitioned by a 1971 court settlement. Dick Graff and Phil Woodward of Chalone Vineyard (see) were hired to manage the winery, and one of the first winemakers they employed was Merry Edwards (see Matanzas Creek Winery and Merry Vintners). She was followed by Bill Anderson, Rick White, Fred Peterson, and now Jeffrey Patterson. Graff and Woodward left in 1982, and some of the partners took over. Mary Ann Graff (see Simi and Ste. Chapelle wineries) was brought in as a consultant.

WHITE

☆☆☆ 1973 CHARDONNAY ($16.00) Estate, Santa Cruz Mountains. *Oaky, with buttery flavor and mellow varietal character.*
☆☆☆ 1979 CHARDONNAY Estate, Santa Cruz Mountains. *Crisp, tart, lovely oak.*

☆☆☆☆ 1980 CHARDONNAY ($15.00) Estate, Santa Cruz Mountains. *Exquisite, toasty, varietal, mellow. Will age for years.*
        1982 MEV CHARDONNAY ($12.50) Ventana, Monterey. *Vinous, earthy and oxidized.*
☆☆☆   1982 CHARDONNAY ($18.00) Santa Cruz Mountains. *Rich, big, yet elegant and beautifully structured.*

RED

☆☆☆   1973 CABERNET SAUVIGNON ($14.00) Estate, Santa Cruz Mountains. *Fresh, berried, rich and crisply fruity. Will age for years.*
☆☆   1974 CABERNET SAUVIGNON ($12.00) Estate, Santa Cruz Mountains. *Rich extract, deep and still tannic.*
☆☆   1975 CABERNET SAUVIGNON ($20.00) Estate, Santa Cruz Mountains. *Lovely, earthy, deep, varietal and oaky.*
☆☆   1976 CABERNET SAUVIGNON ($30.00) Estate, Santa Cruz Mountains. *Rich herbs, raisiny, nice structure but low fruit.*
☆☆   1978 CABERNET SAUVIGNON ($25.00) Estate, Santa Cruz Mountains. *Big, simple, earthy, dense.*
☆☆   1979 CABERNET SAUVIGNON ($25.00) Estate, Santa Cruz Mountains. *Rich, deep, tastes like Zinfandel. Clean and jammy.*
☆   1980 CABERNET SAUVIGNON ($30.00) Estate, Santa Cruz Mountains. *Weedy, green beans, balanced but a bit weak.*
☆☆   1981 CABERNET SAUVIGNON ($18.00) Santa Cruz Mountains.
☆☆   1981 CABERNET SAUVIGNON ($30.00) Estate, Santa Cruz Mountains. *Big, rich, dense, with lovely earth and chocolate. Drink 1987.*
☆☆   1976 PINOT NOIR ($10.00) Estate, Santa Cruz Mountains. *Leathery and a bit tired, with some hotness.*
☆☆☆   1977 PINOT NOIR ($18.00) Estate, Santa Cruz Mountains. *Earthy, rich, clean and super.*
☆☆   1978 PINOT NOIR ($10.00) Estate, Santa Cruz Mountains. *Fat, lush, meaty, with good fruit acid.*
☆☆☆   1979 PINOT NOIR ($15.00) Estate, Santa Cruz Mountains. *Peppery, elegant, lovely.*
☆☆☆   1980 PINOT NOIR ($15.00) Estate, Santa Cruz Mountains. *Superb, rich and complex, with cherry flavors and some stems.*
☆☆☆   1981 PINOT NOIR ($15.00) Estate, Santa Cruz Mountains. *Cherry, clean, complex, with fruit and floral aromas.*

Mount Hope Estate & Winery
PENNSYLVANIA

P.O. Box 685, Cornwall, Pennsylvania 17016 (717-665-7021). FOUNDED: 1972. ACREAGE: 10 acres. PRODUCTION: 20,000 cases. DISTRIBUTION: Pennsylvania. OWNER: Mazza Vineyards, Inc. Charles J. Romito, president; Frank Mazza, vice president. WINEMAKER: Frank Mazza. Tours and tasting Monday–Saturday 10 A.M.–5 P.M., Sunday 12–5 P.M.

Lawyer Chuck Romito put together a group of investors who wanted to get into the wine business. At the time, they had no idea that they were about to become renowned historical preservationists. For their vineyard-winery location, they chose the 180-year-old Daisy Grubb estate. The partners provided substantial capital and creative labor to bring the 32-room mansion and surrounding outbuildings back to dazzling Victorian elegance. "We have our own Falcon Crest right here in Lancaster, Pennsylvania," says Chuck. The turreted sandstone mansion, with eighteen-foot ceilings, Egyptian marble fireplaces, winding walnut staircase, greenhouse, and surrounding gardens, is the showplace for many events, including the Pennsylvania Renaissance Fair. The winery is located in one of the reconstructed outbuildings, while the tasting room is in the mansion's Billiard Room (see Mazza Vineyards).

WHITE

☆☆ 1980 JOHANNISBERG RIESLING ($8.00) Pennsylvania.
  ☆ 1980 SEYVAL BLANC ($6.00) Pennsylvania.

Mount Palomar Winery
RIVERSIDE COUNTY

33820 Rancho California Road, Temecula, California 92390 (714-676-5047). FOUNDED: 1975. ACREAGE: 115 acres. PRODUCTION: 12,500 cases. DISTRIBUTION: Southern California. OWNER: John H. Poole, president. Joseph Cherpin, Peter Poole, vice presidents; Richard Alguire, secretary. WINEMAKER: Joseph Cherpin. Tours and tasting daily 9 A.M.–5 P.M. Gift shop.

John Poole, the owner of a radio station, was looking for a way out of urban life and into the peace of farming. He began by planting vineyards in Temecula, an area just beginning to be developed for agriculture. Unfortunately, there were so few wineries in the region that John had a difficult time selling his grapes for a decent price. This frustrating situation motivated him to start his own winery—a simple steel structure built against a hillside. John and his son Peter run the winery with Joe Cherpin, their winemaker.

WHITE

☆ 1983 CHARDONNAY ($6.95) Temecula. *Simple, decent.*
  1983 CHENIN BLANC ($4.50) Temecula. *0.99% residual sugar. Vegetal.*
  1983 FUME BLANC ($5.50) Estate, Temecula. *Dull, lacking fruit.*

Mount Pleasant Vineyard
MISSOURI

101 Webster, Augusta, Missouri 63332 (314-228-4419). FOUNDED: 1881. ACREAGE: 35 acres. PRODUCTION: 10,000 cases. DISTRIBUTION: Missouri. OWNERS: Lucian and Eva B. Dressel. WINEMAKER: Lucian Dressel. OTHER LABEL: The Abbey. Tours and tasting Monday–Saturday 10 A.M.–5:30 P.M., Sunday 12–5:30 P.M.

Lucian Dressel was 26 years old when he and his wife decided to make wine. A disciple of Philip Wagner, who championed the use of French-American hybrids in the United States, Lucian had always been fascinated by grapes—especially French-American hybrids. He prefers to think, however, that his decision to buy the old Munch winery was based on practicality rather than passion. Since the previous owner was a historical preservationist, the winery was in excellent condition and today looks very much the way it did in 1881. The vineyards have been replanted to hybrids and some experimental vinifera. Lucian is serious about making quality wine. "I got rid of the homespun winemaker—me—and hired a professional from California," he explains. Lucian Dressel also owns The Winery of the Abbey in Cuba, Missouri.

Mount Veeder Winery
NAPA COUNTY

1999 Mount Veeder Road, Napa, California 94558 (707-224-4039). FOUNDED: 1973. ACREAGE: 20 acres. PRODUCTION: 5,500 cases. DISTRIBUTION: Nationwide; 6 foreign markets. OWNERS: Henry and Lisille Matheson. WINEMAKER: Peter Franus. Tours and retail sales by appointment.

In 1963 attorney Michael Bernstein and his wife, Arlene, bought the old Moyer place as a country home. The property contained an ancient prune orchard. In 1965 they began planting grapes, and by 1968 they were pulling out prune trees and replacing them with vines. The vineyard scales the slopes of Mount Veeder, with some of the vines planted at 1,400 feet above sea level. Yields are small, and the wines are intense and concentrated. In December 1982 the Bernsteins, through an ad in *The Wall Street Journal*, sold the winery to Henry and Lisille Matheson, a young couple from Florida.

WHITE

☆☆☆ 1983 CHARDONNAY ($13.50) Napa. *Rich oak, crisp, lemony fruit, good depth, long finish.*

☆☆ 1981 CHENIN BLANC ($8.00) Napa Valley. *Dry, crisp and complex.*

☆☆☆ 1981 PINOT BLANC ($9.75) Napa Valley.

RED

☆☆☆ 1973 CABERNET SAUVIGNON Bernstein, Napa. *Rich, chocolatey and soft.*

☆☆☆ 1974 CABERNET SAUVIGNON Bernstein, Napa. *Raisiny, big and tannic.*

☆☆ 1975 CABERNET SAUVIGNON Bernstein, Napa.

☆☆ 1976 CABERNET SAUVIGNON ($11.00) Bernstein, Napa.

☆☆ 1977 CABERNET SAUVIGNON ($11.00) Bernstein, Napa.

☆☆ 1978 CABERNET SAUVIGNON ($12.75) Bernstein, Napa.

☆☆☆ 1979 CABERNET SAUVIGNON ($13.50) Bernstein, Napa. *Rich, fat, with a nice eucalyptus note.*

☆☆ 1980 CABERNET SAUVIGNON ($13.50) Bernstein, Napa. *Big and nicely structured.*

☆☆ 1980 ZINFANDEL ($8.00) Late Harvest, Napa Valley. *0.5% residual sugar.*

☆☆ 1981 ZINFANDEL ($8.50) Bernstein, Mount Veeder-Napa. *Ripe and intense.*

☆☆☆ 1981 ZINFANDEL ($8.50) Napa Valley. *Spicy, rich, clean and concentrated.*

☆☆☆ 1982 ZINFANDEL ($8.50) Napa Valley. *Balanced, clean, complex, elegant, lovely.*

MOUNTAIN GLEN VINEYARD *see* Fretter Wine Cellars

Mountain House Winery
SONOMA COUNTY

38999 Highway 128, Cloverdale, California 95425 (707-894-3074). FOUNDED: 1980. ACREAGE: 5 acres. PRODUCTION: 2,500 cases. DISTRIBUTION: Major market states. OWNER: Ronald Lipp. WINEMAKER: Ronald Lipp. Tours by appointment. Tasting May–November: weekends 10 A.M.–5 P.M. Newsletter.

Noticing how many doctors, lawyers, and businessmen were getting into the wine industry, Ronald Lipp, an antitrust lawyer in Chicago, decided to join the throng. Ron had no real winemaking experience until he went to work at Mayacamus Vineyards for the crush of 1974. This initiation subverted his best lawyer-like intentions to the point that Ron "traded in his briefcase for a pair of cellar boots." After a master's program in enology and viticulture at U.C. Davis, he was off looking for a winery location. In 1979 he found the spooky old McDonald Mountain House, which had been a stagecoach stop and inn during the late 1800s. Although Ron may have settled back into the life of a country winemaker, his intelligent prose surfaces in the winery newsletter.

WHITE

1980 CHARDONNAY ($12.00) Sonoma. *Weedy.*

☆☆☆ 1981 CHARDONNAY ($9.90) Sonoma. *Fresh, clean, balanced, with a lovely sweet oak finish.*

☆☆ 1983 CHARDONNAY ($8.00) Sonoma. *Heavy, rich, oaky, intense.*

The Mountain View Winery
SANTA CLARA COUNTY

2402 Thadeus Drive, Mountain View, California 94043 (415-964-5398). FOUNDED: 1980. ACREAGE: None. PRODUCTION: 1,000 cases. DISTRIBUTION: At winery and local outlets. OWNER: Patrick Ferguson. WINEMAKER: Patrick Ferguson. Tours and tasting by appointment only.

Patrick Ferguson is an independent aerospace consultant. He started his winery for tax reasons, but he also hopes that this side business will give him a clever way to ease into retirement. A home winemaker of long standing, Pat makes wine in a bonded garage.

WHITE

☆☆ 1981 CHARDONNAY ($5.00) Sonoma. *Small and simple but very pleasant.*
☆☆ 1982 CHARDONNAY ($6.25) Sonoma.
☆☆ 1982 CHARDONNAY ($7.50) Special Selection, Napa Valley. *Crisp, clean, simple, quite nice.*
☆☆☆ 1983 CHARDONNAY ($12.00) Dutton Ranch, Sonoma. *Varietal, charming, with rich fruit.*

RED

1979 CABERNET SAUVIGNON ($4.50) Sonoma. *Dull, lacking freshness.*
O 1979 CABERNET SAUVIGNON ($6.25) Sonoma. *Weedy, stinky.*
☆☆ 1980 CABERNET SAUVIGNON ($5.00) North Coast. *Fruity, attractive and varietal.*
☆☆ 1981 CABERNET SAUVIGNON ($7.50) Special Selection, Napa Valley. *Rich, full and fruity. Not elegant but very drinkable.*
☆ 1981 MV SPECIAL SELECTION CABERNET SAUVIGNON ($7.50) Napa Valley.
☆ 1980 ZINFANDEL ($6.00) Fall Creek Ranch, Sonoma Valley. *Big, harsh, 16% alcohol.*
☆☆ 1983 ZINFANDEL ($7.50) Dutton Ranch, Sonoma. *Berried, dense but attractive.*

Moyer Texas Champagne Company
TEXAS

1941 Interstate Highway 35E, New Braunfels, Texas 78130 (512-625-5181). FOUNDED: 1981. ACREAGE: None. PRODUCTION: 5,000 cases. DISTRIBUTION: Texas and Ohio. OWNER: Ken Moyer. WINEMAKER: Ken Moyer. Tours and tasting Monday–Saturday 10 A.M.–5 P.M. See Moyer Vineyards.

SPARKLING

☆ NV MOYER TEXAS BRUT ESPECIAL ($9.95) Texas. *Decent; a bit thin and simple.*

Moyer Vineyards
OHIO

U.S. Highway 52, Manchester, Ohio 45144 (513-549-2957). FOUNDED: 1972. ACREAGE: 10 acres. PRODUCTION: 6,250 cases. DISTRIBUTION: Local. OWNERS: Kenneth and Mary Moyer. WINEMAKERS: Roger Applegate and Kenneth Moyer. OTHER LABEL: River Valley. Limited self-guided tours daily 11 A.M.–4 P.M. See Moyer Texas Champagne Company.

Ken Moyer thought he wanted to expand his winery in Ohio, but what he really wanted was to move back to Texas. So instead of putting more energy and money into the Ohio winery, he and his wife moved their sparkling-wine operation to Texas while keeping the Ohio winery for still-wine production. At first, they imported their still wines from Ohio to make their Texas champagne, but now they are crushing California and Texas grapes for that purpose. Ken travels back and forth from Ohio to Texas, but eventually the Moyers hope to retire to Texas.

MULHAUSEN *see* Chehalen Mountain Winery

Naked Mountain Vineyard
VIRGINIA

Route 688, P.O. Box 131, Markham, Virginia 22643 (703-364-1609). FOUNDED: 1981. ACREAGE: 12 acres. PRODUCTION: 1,600 cases. DISTRIBUTION: Virginia. OWNERS: Robert P. and Phoebe G. Harper. WINEMAKER: Robert Harper. Tours and tasting March–December: weekends and holidays 12–5 P.M.

Robert Harper bought a fifteen-dollar wine kit in the hope that he could make 25 bottles of wine comparable to Château Lafite-Rothschild. "It didn't take me long to learn that there is no substitute for first-class grapes," says Robert. So he started planting a few vines—just enough to support his hobby—on some property he and his wife, Phoebe, had purchased some 50 miles due west of Washington D.C. Soon Robert was planting more and more vines. "It got to the point where I either had to quit my job or hire somebody to take care of the vineyard," says Robert. "So I quit my job as a salesman for Texaco." In order to make a living growing grapes, Robert knew his hobby would have to become a serious winemaking business. In 1981 the Harpers converted one of the farm buildings into a winery and set a goal for themselves: to make good wines and sell them at a profit. They now have a new building with a wine bar.

WHITE

☆☆   1983 CHARDONNAY ($8.00) Virginia. *Rich, balanced and charming.*

☆☆   1982 JOHANNISBERG RIESLING ($7.50) Virginia. *1.9% residual sugar. Clean, simple.*

O   1982 RIESLING ($7.50) Virginia.

Napa Cellars
NAPA COUNTY

7481 St. Helena Highway, Oakville, California 94562 (707-944-2565). FOUNDED: 1976. ACREAGE: 3 acres. PRODUCTION: 10,400 cases. DISTRIBUTION: California and other major market states. OWNER: DeSchepper family. Aaron Mosley, vice president. WINEMAKER: Aaron Mosley. Limited self-guided tours and tasting daily 10 A.M.–5 P.M.

Members of the DeSchepper family, from Belgium, were looking for a Napa Valley investment when they stumbled upon Napa Cellars. They liked the location, the small, quality production, and especially the winemaker and manager, Aaron Mosley. "Since the DeScheppers were not planning on running the winery themselves, it was important for them to find someone they could trust with the day-to-day management," says Aaron. After purchasing the winery in 1983, the DeScheppers' first project was the remodeling of the tour, tasting, and picnic areas. In 1985 they began to remodel the processing facilities.

WHITE

☆☆   1980 CHARDONNAY ($11.50) Alexander Valley.

☆☆   1981 CHARDONNAY ($12.00) Black Mountain, Alexander Valley. *Oaky and intense.*

☆ 1982 CHARDONNAY ($11.50) Alexander Valley. *Vinous, earthy, a touch of oxidation, varietal.*

☆ 1982 CHARDONNAY ($11.50) Black Mountain, Alexander Valley. *Decent, clean, lacking varietal character and charm.*

☆ 1981 SAUVIGNON BLANC ($8.00) Napa Valley.

☆☆ 1982 SAUVIGNON BLANC ($8.00) Napa Valley. *Fresh, clean, fruity, simple.*

☆☆☆ 1983 SAUVIGNON BLANC ($7.50) Napa Valley. *Fresh, balanced, lovely.*

RED

☆☆☆ 1978 CABERNET SAUVIGNON ($12.00) Napa Valley. *Lush, intense, herbal. Should age for several more years.*

☆☆☆ 1979 CABERNET SAUVIGNON ($12.00) Napa Valley. *Chocolatey nose; well bred and delicate.*

☆☆☆ 1980 CABERNET SAUVIGNON ($16.00) Alexander Valley. *Big, rich and earthy. Needs time. Drink 1986.*

☆☆ 1981 CABERNET SAUVIGNON ($12.00) Napa Valley. *Big, fat, lush, well made. Drink 1988 and beyond.*

☆ 1981 ZINFANDEL ($8.00) Alexander Valley.

Napa Creek Winery
NAPA COUNTY

1001 Silverado Trail, St. Helena, California 94574 (707-963-9456). FOUNDED: 1980. ACREAGE: None. PRODUCTION: 12,000 cases. DISTRIBUTION: 11 states. OWNER: Jack Schulze. WINEMAKER: Gordon Madley. Tours and tasting daily 9 A.M.–5 P.M.

Jack Shultze's family owned the old Gibson Wine Company in Elk Grove. After they sold their interest, Jack became a salesman for Beringer in Chicago and then a marketer for Estrella River Winery. Just when Jack's tolerance for office memos and corporate clutter was wearing thin, he and his wife, Judy, found and bought the Sunshine Meat Packing Company in St. Helena. Fully equipped with refrigeration and insulation, the building was easily converted into a winery. Jack contracts for all his grapes and has hired Gordon Madley, previously with Christian Brothers Winery, to do all the cellar work. "My wife and I are more involved in sales and marketing; I never saw lab work as all that exciting," says Jack.

WHITE

  1981 CHARDONNAY ($13.50) Napa Valley.

O 1981 FUME BLANC ($8.00) Napa Valley. *Oxidized.*

☆☆ 1981 GEWURZTRAMINER ($7.50) Napa Valley.

☆☆ 1981 JOHANNISBERG RIESLING ($7.00) Napa Valley. *1.4% residual sugar.*

RED

☆☆ 1980 CABERNET SAUVIGNON ($12.00) Napa Valley. *Fat, good, with nice rich fruitiness but some weediness. Drink 1986.*

Napa Mountain Winery
NAPA COUNTY

1701 Mount Veeder Road, P.O. Box 3107, Napa, California 94558 (707-253-2131). FOUNDED: 1982. ACREAGE: 250 acres. PRODUCTION: 1,000 cases. DISTRIBUTION: California. OWN-

ERS: Donald Hess and Valser Mineral Water Company. Bob Craig, general manager. WINE-MAKER: Randall Johnson. No tours or tasting.

Donald Hess, owner of a mineral water company in Switzerland called Valser, traveled to the Napa Valley hoping to purchase a California mineral-water plant. Instead he bought 120 acres of vineyard on Mount Veeder from an investment group. One of the investors, Bob Craig, a financial consultant, joined Don in his grape-growing venture. They bought two more vineyard parcels on Mount Veeder, one of which was the old Veedercrest vineyard. They knew that eventually they would start a winery, but first they wanted to get to know their grapes and define a style. The experimental years of 1982 and 1983 were devoted to understanding their Cabernet; in 1984 they experimented with Chardonnay. Their winemaking has taken place at J. Mathews Winery, but they plan to have their own winery by 1986.

ح

Navarro Vineyards and Winery
MENDOCINO COUNTY

5601 Highway 128, Philo, California 95466 (707-895-3686). FOUNDED: 1974. ACREAGE: 50 acres. PRODUCTION: 10,000 cases. DISTRIBUTION: California and other major market states. OWNERS: Edward Ted Bennett and Deborah S. Cahn. WINEMAKERS: Edward Ted Bennett and John Montero. Tours by appointment. Tasting summer and fall: daily 10 A.M.–6 P.M.; winter: daily 10 A.M.–5 P.M.

Ted Bennett and Deborah Cahn wanted to specialize in Gewürztraminer, a varietal they felt hadn't gotten its fair due in California. While picnicking in the Anderson Valley, they found a piece of land that had the exact climate and soil conditions they wanted. They planted vineyards, built a winery from trees felled on the property, and converted the barn into a house. The tasting room, also built from the trees on the property, has a porch that overlooks a colorful landscape of flowers in the spring. Eighty percent of Navarro's wine is sold at the tasting room.

WHITE

☆☆☆ 1981 CHARDONNAY ($8.75) Mendocino. *Snappy and well balanced. Clean and attractive.*

☆☆☆ 1981 CHARDONNAY ($11.60) Premiere Reserve, Mendocino. *Toasty, delicate, clean and balanced. Very lovely.*

☆☆ 1982 CHARDONNAY ($8.75) Mendocino.

☆☆ 1981 GEWÜRZTRAMINER ($7.50) Mendocino. *0.6% residual sugar. Varietal and pleasant.*

☆☆☆ 1982 GEWÜRZTRAMINER ($9.75) Late Sweet Harvest, Anderson Valley. *7.9% residual sugar. Gorgeous—lush, rich, fruity, toasty.*

☆☆☆ 1982 JOHANNISBERG RIESLING ($18.50) Cluster Selected, Late Harvest, Anderson Valley, Mendocino. *12.3% residual sugar. Viscous, rich, great fruit, lovely.*

☆ 1982 SAUVIGNON BLANC ($8.50) Anderson Valley, Mendocino. *Slightly volatile, with good fruit.*

RED

☆☆ 1977 CABERNET SAUVIGNON ($8.75) Mendocino. *Soft, floral, with good balance and some elegance.*

1978 CABERNET SAUVIGNON ($9.50) Mendocino. *Disjointed and a bit off.*

☆ 1980 PINOT NOIR ($8.75) Estate, Anderson Valley, Mendocino. *Decent but lacking depth.*

☆ 1981 PINOT NOIR ($8.00) Estate, Anderson Valley, Mendocino. *Dense, lacking character.*

ح

Naylor Wine Cellars
PENNSYLVANIA

R.D. 3, Box 424, Ebaugh Road, Stewartstown, Pennsylvania 17403 (717-993-2431). FOUNDED: 1978. ACREAGE: 22 acres. PRODUCTION: 10,400 cases. DISTRIBUTION: Pennsylvania. OWNERS: Richard and Audrey Naylor. WINEMAKER: Robert Byloff. OTHER LABELS: Golden Grenadier, Ruby Grenadier. Tours and tasting Monday–Saturday 11 A.M.–6 P.M., Sunday 12–5 P.M.

Dick Naylor's first commitment to grape growing came in 1967 when he agreed to care for a neglected three-acre Labrusca vineyard. He was given the crop as payment for his efforts. In 1974 Dick and his wife, Audrey, bought a 52-acre farm at a 1,000-foot elevation in southeastern Pennsylvania. Starting with a batch of dandelion wine, followed by a selection of fruit wines, Dick learned his trade. As luck would have it, the location proved to be a productive area for grapevines. The Naylors converted a potato barn and bought used dairy and winery equipment, trying to keep the overhead as low as possible. They planted both vinifera and French-American hybrids, but Dick feels that vinifera "is not going to keep anybody in business. The difficulty in growing these varieties puts too high a price on the finished wine." Fruit wines are among the winery's best sellers.

RED

☆ 1982 CHAMBOURSIN ($6.85) Pennsylvania. *Dry, decent, clean.*

Nehalem Bay Wine Company
OREGON

34965 Highway 53, Box 440, Nehalem, Oregon 97131 (503-368-5300). FOUNDED: 1973. ACREAGE: None. PRODUCTION: 4,600 cases. DISTRIBUTION: At winery. OWNER: Pat McCoy. WINEMAKER: Dawn Schmidt. Self-guided tours and tasting daily 10 A.M.–5 P.M. Another tasting room is located in Seaside, Oregon.

Pat McCoy got hooked on the idea of being a wine baron after studying grape-growing possibilities at Oregon State University in the early 1960s. He found the perfect building for his winery, one of the original Tillamook cheese factories, built in 1907. He cleaned it up, put up an English Tudor facade, and set up a tasting room in the old boiler room. Continuing to work as a radio station manager in Medford, he started making wine and "making a lot of mistakes." He also started the first French cheese company in Oregon, which he subsequently sold. His next project is a vineyard near the coast, but Pat hopes someone else will try it before he does.

RED

○ NV PINOT NOIR ($7.00) Oregon.

Neri's Wine Cellar
PENNSYLVANIA

373 Bridgetown Pike, Langhorne, Pennsylvania 19047 (215-355-9567). FOUNDED: 1980. ACREAGE: 7 acres. PRODUCTION: 1,500 cases. DISTRIBUTION: At winery. OWNERS: Thomas Broccardi and George Iannacone, Jr. WINEMAKER: Thomas Broccardi. Tours and tasting by appointment only.

To grandfather Neri, making wine was a hobby, but grandsons Thomas and George wanted to make it a business. The two cousins didn't have much winemaking experience, but Tom figured he could count on the talents of his grandfather. On the family farm, which had been producing grapes for many years, they built a large, underground winery with a tasting room above. George and Tom work together, learning from other winemakers and from their grandfather.

Nervo Winery
SONOMA COUNTY

19550 Geyserville Avenue, Geyserville, California 95441 (707-857-3417). FOUNDED: 1908. ACREAGE: 164 acres. PRODUCTION: 20,000 cases. DISTRIBUTION: At winery. OWNER: Geyser Peak Winery. WINEMAKER: Armand Bussone. No tours. Tasting daily 10 A.M.–5 P.M. Picnic facilities.

This old, family winery, started by Frank Nervo, is now owned by Geyser Peak. In 1973 Frank Nervo's children sold the winery to Schlitz Brewing Company, which subsequently sold its wine operation to the Trione family (see Geyser Peak Winery). The wines are made at Geyser Peak but are sold under the Nervo label at the original family winery.

WHITE

☆ 1982 WINTERCHILL WHITE ($2.00) Sonoma. *French Colombard and Chenin Blanc. Pleasant and fresh.*

ROSE

☆ 1983 PINOT NOIR ROSE ($1.90) Sonoma. *2% residual sugar. Dull, sweet, clean.*
1982 PINOT NOIR ($1.90) Sonoma.

RED

☆ 1979 COUNTRY CABERNET ($3.00) California.

Neuharth Winery
WASHINGTON

Still Road, P.O. Box 1457, Sequim, Washington 98382 (206-683-9652). FOUNDED: 1979. ACREAGE: 0.5 acre. PRODUCTION: 1,875 cases. DISTRIBUTION: Washington. OWNERS: Eugene and Maria Neuharth. WINEMAKER: Eugene Neuharth. Tours and tasting Wednesday–Sunday 12–5 P.M.

When Eugene Neuharth retired to the quiet town of Sequim, he had absolutely no intention of starting a winery. He had already spent a lifetime growing grapes near Lodi in California, which had been more than enough. But to relieve the boredom of retirement, he started making wine at home. He then took a few courses at U.C. Davis, asked a million questions of winemakers, and finally decided that it might be fun to start a real winery. He and his wife, Maria, found a 50-year-old dairy barn and, retaining the log-pole construction and 1930s' decor, converted it to a small winery. Gene limits his grape growing to a half-acre of experimental vineyard that grows about 34 different varieties.

RED

1980 CABERNET SAUVIGNON ($9.00) Washington. *Spicy and lacking in fruit.*

Nevada City Winery
NEVADA COUNTY

321 Spring Street, Nevada City, California 95959 (916-265-WINE). FOUNDED: 1980. ACREAGE: None. PRODUCTION: 6,200 cases. DISTRIBUTION: Local and northern California. OWNER: Partnership. Allan S. Haley, president. WINEMAKER: Tony Norskog. Tours and tasting daily 12–5 P.M.

Because Tony Norskog is a skier, Nevada City was the perfect place for his winery. "It's much closer to the slopes than Napa," he says. He was working as the editor of a small wine-industry magazine when he heard that a vineyard in the Sierra foothills was about to be ripped out unless the owners could find a buyer for the grapes. Quickly, Tony and his friend Alan Haley formed a "kitchen-table partnership" and started their winery in a rented building in Davis. The winery has since moved to downtown Nevada City.

WHITE

☆☆ 1982 CHARDONNAY ($9.00) California. *Earthy, rich, pleasant.*
☆ 1983 JOHANNISBERG RIESLING ($5.00) El Dorado.
O 1983 SAUVIGNON BLANC ($6.00) Nevada-Shasta. *Oxidized, sulfurous, dirty.*
O 1982 WHITE RIESLING ($6.00) Mendocino.

BLANC DE NOIR

☆ 1984 ALPENGLOW-WHITE ZINFANDEL ($4.50) Placer, Nevada. *Fruity and dull.*

RED

☆ 1982 DOUCE NOIR ($9.00) Nevada County. *Intense, lush, fat, decent.*
☆☆☆ 1981 CABERNET SAUVIGNON ($6.50) California. *Soft, herbal, supple, appealing. Drink 1986 and beyond.*
☆☆ 1981 CHARBONO ($8.00) Nevada County. *Rich, deep, clean.*
☆☆☆ 1980 PETITE SIRAH ($7.00) Nevada County. *Tart, fruity, clean, snappy and superb.*
☆☆ 1981 PINOT NOIR ($12.00) Nevada County. *Rich, deep, a bit overdone, with good fruit flavors.*
☆☆ 1981 ZINFANDEL ($7.50) Nevada County. *Slight but attractive.*
☆☆ 1982 ZINFANDEL-MERLOT ($5.00) California. *Rich, clean, lush, deep, with lovely fruit.*
☆☆ 1982 ZINFANDEL ($7.00) Nevada. *Rich, fruity, dark, clean.*

Newlan Vineyards and Winery
NAPA COUNTY

1305 Carrell Lane, Napa, California 94558 (707-944-2914). FOUNDED: 1981. ACREAGE: 58 acres. PRODUCTION: 5,000 cases. DISTRIBUTION: Arizona, California, Oregon, Washington, and Hawaii. OWNER: Bruce M. Newlan. WINEMAKER: Bruce Newlan; Larry Wara, consultant. Tours and tasting by appointment.

It didn't take long for Bruce Newlan to become impatient with his partners at Alatera Vineyards. They seemed to see the winery as a hobby while Bruce, who had been growing all the grapes, making the wine, and taking responsibility for the finances and management of the winery, saw it as a serious commercial venture. In frustration, he took his grapes and his land and established his own winery. Now Bruce still has all the responsibility but at least the name over the door is his own. Primarily a farmer and a grape grower, he crushes the best of what he grows for his own winery and sells the rest. He expects his winery to eventually expand to its 18,000-case capacity.

WHITE

☆☆☆   1981 CHARDONNAY ($11.00) Saunders, Napa Valley. *Crisp, lemony and clean.*

RED

☆☆   1980 PINOT NOIR ($7.50) Estate, Napa Valley. *Ripe, clean, simple, attractive.*

Newton Winery
NAPA COUNTY

2555 Madrona Avenue, St. Helena, California 94574 (707-963-4613). FOUNDED: 1978. ACREAGE: 62 acres. PRODUCTION: 14,000 cases. DISTRIBUTION: Nationwide and by mailing list. OWNERS: Peter and Dr. Su Hua Newton. WINEMAKER: John Kongsgaard. Tours by appointment.

Englishman Peter Newton and his wife, Dr. Su Hua Newton, were no strangers to the wine business. Peter was one of the founding partners of nearby Sterling Vineyards, which, after being bought by Coca-Cola, is now owned by Seagram. In association with Sterling's brilliant former winemaker Ric Forman, the Newtons began their new winery estate by taming a promising but difficult land parcel. Vineyards were terraced at elevations of 500 to 1,300 feet on the side of Spring Mountain to enable planting Bordeaux grape varieties, plus Chardonnay. The pagoda-shaped winery was designed to accommodate a traditional Bordeaux style of winemaking, with the cellars buried underground and fermentation facilities above. The Newtons' dramatic home and garden add to the unique character of the estate. In 1983, as a result of the clash of two strong personalities, Ric Forman left (see Charles F. Shaw Vineyard). He was replaced by John Kongsgaard, who shows great promise.

WHITE

☆☆☆   1980 CHARDONNAY ($16.00) Napa Valley. *Complex, elegant and graceful. A delight.*
☆☆☆   1981 CHARDONNAY ($16.00) Napa Valley. *Toasty and very lemony; very attractive.*
☆☆☆   1982 CHARDONNAY ($16.00) Napa Valley. *Toasty oak, lush, clean fruit. A magnificent wine.*
☆☆   1982 SAUVIGNON BLANC ($9.50) Napa Valley. *Decent fruit, delicate, unusual, clean, complex.*

RED

☆☆☆   1980 CABERNET SAUVIGNON ($12.50) Estate, Napa Valley. *Tart, firm, assertive, with lovely fruit. Needs time. Drink 1986.*
☆☆☆☆   1981 CABERNET SAUVIGNON ($12.50) Estate, Napa Valley. *Super—crisp, deep, elegant, with great potential. Drink 1987.*
☆   1979 MERLOT ($10.50) Napa Valley.
☆☆☆   1980 MERLOT ($10.50) Napa Valley. *Snappy, high acid, clean, beautifully structured.*

Neyers Winery
NAPA COUNTY

P.O. Box 1028, St. Helena, California 94574 (707-963-2654). FOUNDED: 1980. ACREAGE: None. PRODUCTION: 4,000 cases. DISTRIBUTION: 10 states. OWNERS: Joseph Phelps, and Bruce and Barbara Neyers. WINEMAKER: Bruce Neyers. No tours or tasting.

Bruce Neyers works for Joseph Phelps Vineyards in administration and marketing, but his first interest and training is in wine production. Wanting to get back to winemaking yet still hold on to his well-paying job, Bruce confided in Joe Phelps. A savvy businessman, Joe saw a way for Bruce to have the best of both worlds. They formed a partnership called Neyers Winery, installing Bruce and his wife, Barbara, as winemaker and assistant, respectively. Bruce happily continues his work at Joseph Phelps while making Neyers wine in his free time.

WHITE

☆☆   1981 CHARDONNAY ($12.00) Napa Valley. *Oaky and varietal; a bit heavy-handed.*
☆☆   1982 CHARDONNAY ($11.00) Napa Valley. *Oaky, buttery, rich, clean, attractive.*

RED

☆☆   1980 CABERNET SAUVIGNON ($10.00) Napa.
☆☆☆ 1982 CABERNET SAUVIGNON ($11.00) Napa Valley. *Rich, velvety, complex, balanced. Drink 1987.*

Nicasio Vineyards
SANTA CRUZ COUNTY

483 Nicasio Way, Soquel, California 95073 (408-423-1073). FOUNDED: 1955. ACREAGE: None. PRODUCTION: 200 cases. DISTRIBUTION: California. OWNER: Dan Wheeler. WINEMAKER: Dan Wheeler. Tours and tasting on Saturday by appointment.

Dan Wheeler, an electrical engineer, is anxiously awaiting his retirement so he can expand his winery and plant vines on his new Lake County property. He started the winery as both a hobby and a retirement plan. Most of the winery work takes place in his house, but the wines are aged and stored in nearby sandstone caves. Once his new vineyard in Lake County starts producing, Dan will move the winery to the vineyard property.

Nichelini Vineyard
NAPA COUNTY

2349 Lower Chiles Road, St. Helena, California 94574 (707-963-3357). FOUNDED: 1890. ACREAGE: 200 acres. PRODUCTION: 10,000 cases. DISTRIBUTION: California. OWNER: Joanne Nichelini Meyer. WINEMAKER: Joanne Nichelini Meyer. Tours and tasting weekends 10 A.M.–6 P.M., weekends by appointment.

Anton Nichelini, a Swiss-Italian, began clearing 160 acres in the Napa Valley for homesteading in 1889. He had no intention of building a winery, but his wife, Catrina, loved the idea, and one was built in 1890. Anton, who worked the mines, made wine, and Catrina made homemade bread, which they also sold to Anton's fellow mineworkers. One hundred years later, the winery continues to make wines in the same local style.

RED

1981 CABERNET SAUVIGNON ($5.00) Napa Valley. *Burnt, odd, with no fruit or varietal character.*
☆   1981 CABERNET SAUVIGNON ($10.00) Private Reserve, Napa Valley.
1980 ZINFANDEL ($5.00) Private Reserve, Napa Valley.

Niebaum-Coppola Estate
NAPA COUNTY

1460 Niebaum Lane, Rutherford, California 94573 (707-963-9435). FOUNDED: 1978. ACREAGE: 85 acres. PRODUCTION: 3,500 cases. DISTRIBUTION: California and some other states. OWNER: Francis Ford Coppola. WINEMAKER: Steven Beresini; André Tchelistcheff, consultant. No tours or tasting.

Gustave Niebaum's mansion (see Inglenook Vineyards) was purchased by producer-director Francis Ford Coppola, who also acquired a large vineyard nearby. The red wines are being made in a Bordeaux style, with Cabernet Sauvignon, Cabernet Franc, and Merlot in the formula. There have been difficulties here; one winemaker has already departed due to stylistic disagreements.

RED

☆☆☆   1978 CABERNET SAUVIGNON ($25.00) Napa Valley. *60% Cabernet, 38% Cabernet Franc, 2% Merlot. Rich and deep.*

☆☆☆   1979 CABERNET SAUVIGNON ($25.00) Napa Valley. *20% Cabernet Franc. Lovely but with less depth than the '78.*

☆☆☆   1980 CABERNET SAUVIGNON ($25.00) Napa Valley. *23% Cabernet Franc, 6% Merlot. Crisp, intense, fruity.*

NIGHT TRAIN EXPRESS *see* E. & J. Gallo Winery

Nissley Vineyards
PENNSYLVANIA

R.D. 1, Bainbridge, Pennsylvania 17502 (717-426-3514). FOUNDED: 1976. ACREAGE: 52 acres. PRODUCTION: 12,500 cases. DISTRIBUTION: Pennsylvania and Washington D.C. OWNER: Corporation. Nissley family. J. Richard Nissley, founder. WINEMAKER: J. Richard Nissley. Tours and tasting April–December: Monday–Saturday 12–6 P.M. Tasting only Sunday 1 P.M.–4 P.M.; January–March: Monday–Saturday 12–6 P.M.

J. Richard Nissley, a retired bridge contractor, started his family winery on a secluded piece of property in northwest Lancaster County. When he bought this piece of rolling farmland, there was an empty eighteenth-century stone mill, a house, and what used to be a tobacco barn. Mr. Nissley and his son planted vines in 1972 and, using an architectural design drawn by a friend, built a Mediterranean-style winery out of the dilapidated tobacco barn. Today, three of the four Nissley children work in the winery full time; the fourth provides holiday help. Concerts are held in this quiet country atmosphere, as well as a Harvest Festival and May Wine Festival.

WHITE

☆   1983 SEYVAL BLANC ($4.50) Pennsylvania.

Nittany Valley Winery
PENNSYLVANIA

724 South Atherton, State College, Pennsylvania 16801 (814-238-7562). FOUNDED: 1980. ACREAGE: None. PRODUCTION: 2,000 cases. DISTRIBUTION: At winery. OWNER: Little Rainbow, Inc. Marina Mebane and Frank Johns. WINEMAKER: Frank Johns. Tours by appoint-

ment. Tasting Tuesday and Wednesday 11 A.M.–6 P.M., Thursday and Friday 11 A.M.–8 P.M., Saturday 10 A.M.–6 P.M., Sunday 12–6 P.M.

One mile from Pennsylvania State University, in what was once an old ice cream plant, a group known as "Little Rainbows" started a winery. One of the partners, Elizabeth Little, ran the winery for more than two years until two other winery partners, Marina Mebane and her father, Frank Johns, took control after a bitter legal battle. Frank, a retired aerospace engineer, is making the wine while Marina, a part-time student in hotel and restaurant management, runs the winery. With the university so close, the winery makes four novelty wines named with reference to the lion, Penn State's mascot.

ε∂

Noble Creek Vineyards
RIVERSIDE COUNTY

39707 Orchard Street, Cherry Valley, California 92223 (714-849-4811). FOUNDED: 1982. ACREAGE: 2 acres. PRODUCTION: 500 cases. DISTRIBUTION: Local and by mailing list. OWNERS: Jan and Tom Tetzlaff. WINEMAKER: Tom Tetzlaff. Tours and tasting by appointment.

Tom Tetzlaff is in the security and fire alarm business. A home winemaker for twelve years, Tom met other wine hobbyists in his neighborhood, several of whom—Jim Ahern and Hank Donatoni, for example—went on to set up their own commercial wineries. "As a home winemaker, your enthusiasm grows to a point where you not only hope others will enjoy what you are making, but you hope to reap some revenue as well," says Tom. In the name of revenue reaping, Tom converted the 100-year-old barn behind his house and joined the ranks of the home-winemakers-turned-pro.

ε∂

A. Nonini Winery
FRESNO COUNTY

2640 North Dickenson Avenue, Fresno, California 93711 (209-275-1936). FOUNDED: 1936. ACREAGE: 190 acres. PRODUCTION: 20,000 cases. DISTRIBUTION: California. OWNERS: Reno, Gildo, and Geno Nonini. WINEMAKER: Reno Nonini. Tours and tasting daily 9 A.M.–4 P.M., except holidays.

Antonio Nonini, who owned 80 acres of vineyard, was never very excited about starting a winery, but he did it so his son Reno would have a place to work. Both Reno and his mother coaxed Antonio to give winemaking a try. Now Reno and his son Thomas work in the winery, which was enlarged once in 1972.

ε∂

NORTH COAST CELLARS *see* Souverain Cellars

North Salem Vineyard
NEW YORK

Rural Route 2, Hardscrabble and Delancy Roads, North Salem, New York 10560 (914-669-5518). FOUNDED: 1979. ACREAGE: 18 acres. PRODUCTION: 900 cases. DISTRIBUTION: New York. OWNER: Corporation. Dr. George W. Naumburg, Jr., president; Peter McMillan, vineyard manager; Michelle Naumburg. WINEMAKER: Dr. George W. Naumburg, Jr. Tours by appointment. Tasting weekends 1 P.M.–5 P.M.

Dr. George Naumburg, a psychiatrist, has taken a calm and practical approach to grape growing and winemaking. When he first planted vineyards on his dairy farm in 1965, he experimented with 41 different grape varieties. He discovered that vinifera vines did not grow well at all, and that he didn't like Aurore. Left with Seyval, Foch, De Chaunac, Chancellor, and small amounts of Chelois and Cascade, the doctor and his wife, Michelle, sold grapes and juice to home winemakers for a number of years. Using his chemistry and bacteriological knowledge, the doctor slowly and carefully developed his winemaking skills. His first commercial wines were bottled in 1980. He has determined that his blended wines are the most successful, especially "Preview," a mixture of De Chaunac and Chancellor.

WHITE

☆   1981 SEYVAL BLANC ($4.00) Estate, Hudson River Region. *Dry, fresh, bright.*

RED

1982 MARECHAL FOCH ($5.00) Estate, Hudson River Region.

Northeast Vineyard
NEW YORK

R.D. 1, Box 115, Millerton, New York 12546 (518-789-3645). FOUNDED: 1975. ACREAGE: 2 acres. PRODUCTION: 250 cases. DISTRIBUTION: At winery. OWNER: Dr. George Green. WINE-MAKER: Dr. George Green. Tours by appointment.

At an elevation of 1,350 feet, the highest point in Duchess County, George Green planted fifteen grape varieties on treacherous, rocky slopes. This land parcel, though somewhat limited in its potential for vineyard expansion, offers a spectacular view that reaches 50 miles across the Hudson River. George and his wife could not resist the panorama. A cardiac surgeon, George became interested in winemaking after attending a wine tasting where he was impressed by the quality of wines produced by local amateurs and professionals. Starting small and experimenting as he went, he carefully established which varieties would grow well at high altitudes, and then built his winery.

Novitiate Wines
SANTA CLARA COUNTY

College and Prospect Avenues, Los Gatos, California 95030 (408-354-6471). FOUNDED: 1888. ACREAGE: None. PRODUCTION: 31,000 cases. DISTRIBUTION: California and 8 other states. OWNER: California Province of the Society of Jesus. WINEMAKER: Brother Lee Williams, S.J. Tours twice daily; call for information. Tasting daily 10 A.M.–5 P.M., except major holidays.

In 1888, in a small, wood-frame building at the new Jesuit seminary in Los Gatos, Brother Constantine Valducci, S.J., made altar wines. By selling the excess wines not required for sacramental purposes, the Jesuits found a way to support the seminary. The winery continued to expand through the 1906 earthquake, through Prohibition, and despite a fire in 1934. The role of winemaker has been passed down from brother to brother. Novitiate is no longer a Jesuit training facility; it serves as a provincial office for the Jesuits and a residence for retired Jesuits. The winery's current spokesman is the very jolly and quite portly Brother Korte.

SPARKLING

☆ NV BLACK ROSE ($6.00) California. *Black Muscat. Like sparkling port.*

RED

☆ NV BLACK ROSE TABLE WINE ($3.75) California. *Black Muscat. Decent, clean and fresh, with some spice.*
☆ 1978 CABERNET SAUVIGNON ($5.00) Monterey. *Vegetal, decent.*

Oak Barrel
ALAMEDA COUNTY

1201 University Avenue, Berkeley, California 94702 (415-849-0400). FOUNDED: 1959. ACREAGE: None. PRODUCTION: 2,000 cases. DISTRIBUTION: Local. OWNER: John Bank. WINEMAKER: John Bank. Retail sales Monday–Saturday 10 A.M.–6:30 P.M. No tasting. Wine- and beer-making retail store.

John Bank found that it is difficult to run a winery in downtown Berkeley. Having made wine in Hungary before working in several Napa Valley wineries, John thought a winery in Berkeley might capture tourist interest. He started by buying juice and half-finished wines from other wineries, but John's Oak Barrel winery slowly evolved into a winemaking and brewing equipment supply store. The store is quite successful, and limited amounts of wine are still made for private labels.

Oak Knoll Winery
OREGON

Route 6, Box 184, Hillsboro, Oregon 97123 (503-648-8198). FOUNDED: 1970. ACREAGE: None. PRODUCTION: 19,000 cases. DISTRIBUTION: Major western market states. OWNERS: Ronald G. and Marjorie M. Vuylsteke and John R. Kobbe. WINEMAKER: Ronald G. Vuylsteke. Tours by appointment. Tasting Wednesday–Sunday 12–5 P.M. Second tasting location on Highway 101 in Lincoln City.

Former electronics engineer Ron Vuylsteke quit his job at Tektronix to move his wife and six children into the world of farming and winemaking. They bought a five-acre farm with a house and large dairy barn that once housed 108 cows. Harnessing the youthful energy of his five sons, Ron converted the barn into a winery in time for the crush of 1970. Production grew rapidly during the first years, going from 4,000 gallons in 1970 to 50,000 by 1980. Making fruit and berry wines in addition to varietal grape wines, Oak Knoll Winery wants to produce a wine for every occasion. In 1983 the Vuylstekes opened a new tasting room in Lincoln City, which they call Shipwreck Cellars, where visitors can taste not only Oak Knoll wines but wines from many other Oregon wineries. The family also hosts the annual "Bacchus Goes Bluegrass" festival every May.

WHITE

1982 CHARDONNAY ($9.00) Oregon. *Some weeds and oxidation mar this one.*
☆ 1982 WHITE RIESLING ($6.50) Oregon.

RED

1978 PINOT NOIR ($7.50) Oregon.
☆☆☆ 1980 PINOT NOIR ($20.00) Dion, Oregon. *Great color, fruit harmony and complexity. Burgundian and superb.*

1982 PINOT NOIR ($14.00) Vintage Select, Dion, Oregon. *Composty, dank.*
☆ 1983 PINOT NOIR ($9.10) 70% Dion, 30% Casper, Oregon. *Intense, berried, Zinfandel-like, decent.*

Oak Ridge Vineyards
SAN JOAQUIN COUNTY

6100 East Highway 12, Lodi, California 95240 (209-369-4768). FOUNDED: 1934. ACREAGE: None. PRODUCTION: 300,000 cases. DISTRIBUTION: 8 states. OWNER: Cooperative. Lodi Grape Growers. Leroy Mitler, president; Ron Kent, marketing and sales. WINEMAKER: Lee Eichele. OTHER LABELS: Royal Host, Conti Royale, Gold Bell, Mission Host. Tours and tasting daily 8 A.M.–5 P.M.

This winery was formed in 1934 by a group of growers who wanted to control their own destiny by assuring a market for their grapes. The operation is still a cooperative of 120 to 130 growers in the Lodi area. Two major labels are produced: Oak Ridge, which features varietal, cork-finished wines; and Royal Host, a generic line.

Oakencroft Vineyards
VIRGINIA

Route 5, Charlottesville, Virginia 22901 (804-295-8175). FOUNDED: 1983. ACREAGE: 12 acres. PRODUCTION: 2,000 cases. DISTRIBUTION: Virginia. OWNER: Mrs. John B. Rogan. WINE-MAKER: Debra Welsh. Tours, tasting, and retail sales by appointment.

The Rogans raise registered cattle on their polled Hereford farm. On top of this, Felicia Rogan is a freelance writer and photographer. Nevertheless, she managed to get her husband and a few friends enthused about planting some vines and making wine just for fun. But when the first wines were a success, Felicia quickly became serious about her hobby. Wine consultant Jacques Recht, winemaker at Ingleside Vineyards, was hired to set up a winery in a converted smokehouse. Though Jacques still assists from time to time, the day-to-day work is handled by Debra Welsh, a self-taught winemaker who began helping the Rogans when they were making wine in their garage.

WHITE

○ 1983 CHARDONNAY ($7.00) Virginia. *Odd, sweet nose; oxidized, weird, dull, flabby.*
☆☆ 1983 SEYVAL BLANC ($6.00) Virginia. *Fresh, vinous nose; soft, sweet and round.*

Oasis Vineyard
VIRGINIA

Route 1, Hume, Virginia 22639 (703-635-7627). FOUNDED: 1980. ACREAGE: 42 acres. PRODUCTION: 6,200 cases. DISTRIBUTION: Virginia. OWNER: David Salahi. WINEMAKER: David Salahi. Tours and tasting daily 10 A.M.–4 P.M.

The Salahis have lived in Virginia for some time, yet they still have melodic French accents that certainly didn't come from a classroom. David Salahi, a consulting scientist, and his wife planted vinifera on their property in 1976 and began making wine in their basement. Now they have one of the largest wineries in the state: a 20,000-square-foot, two-story building capable of producing 100,000 gallons of wine. "The vineyards were producing so beautifully that it would have been a shame not to start a winery," explains Mrs. Salahi. "We have just recently completed the champagne cellar downstairs." The Salahis make wine only from their own grapes.

ಆ

Oberhellmann Vineyards
TEXAS

Llano Route, Box 22, Fredericksburg, Texas 78624 (512-685-3297). FOUNDED: 1982. ACREAGE: 30 acres. PRODUCTION: 5,000 cases. DISTRIBUTION: Texas. OWNERS: Robert and Evelyn Oberhellmann. WINEMAKER: Robert Oberhellmann. Tours and tasting May–December: Saturday 10 A.M.–5 P.M.

A food technologist, Bob Oberhellmann thought that the principles of food processing could be easily adapted to winemaking. Normally a practical man, he figures he must have been "struck by a bolt of lightning" to start planting vineyards and making wine in Texas. His vineyards are 2,000 feet above sea level, in what Texans consider hill country. The first plantings were made in 1976; after four years of making experimental wine and selling grapes to home winemakers, the Oberhellmanns constructed their Swiss chalet–style winery. They are using just their own grapes and making all vinifera wines.

ಆ

Obester Winery
SAN MATEO COUNTY

Route 1, Box 2Q, Half Moon Bay, California 94109 (415-726-9463). FOUNDED: 1977. ACREAGE: None. PRODUCTION: 7,000 cases. DISTRIBUTION: California and other major market states. OWNERS: Paul and Sandy Obester. WINEMAKER: Paul Obester. Tours by appointment. Tasting and sales Friday–Sunday 10 A.M.–5 P.M.

Paul Obester, a man with friendly blue eyes and a devilish, bearded smile, learned how to make wine from his wife's grandfather, John Gemello (see Gemello Winery). It started when John, at the age of 93, came to live with the Obesters. At the time Paul was working in electronics in Palo Alto. After a few years of making wine with grandfather Gemello, Paul decided it was time to go into business for himself, doing something he really liked. He and Sandy found a great location in Half Moon Bay. The winery is right next door to the Obester home, which houses the tasting room.

WHITE

☆☆☆ 1981 CHARDONNAY ($12.00) Potter Valley, Mendocino.
☆☆☆ 1981 JOHANNISBERG RIESLING ($6.25) Ventana, Monterey. *1.4% residual sugar. Lovely, fruity, rounded.*
 ☆ 1982 JOHANNISBERG RIESLING ($6.95) Ventana, Monterey. *1.4% residual sugar. Spicy, balanced, off-dry, a bit odd.*
☆☆☆ 1983 JOHANNISBERG RIESLING ($7.50) Ventana, Monterey. *2.4% residual sugar. Melony, spritzy, floral, super.*
 ☆☆ 1981 SAUVIGNON BLANC ($8.00) Potter Valley, Mendocino.
☆☆☆ 1982 SAUVIGNON BLANC ($9.50) Mendocino. *Unusual, crisp yet rich and complex, with a touch of sugar.*
☆☆☆ 1983 SAUVIGNON BLANC ($8.50) Mendocino. *Soft, round, fruity, varietal, charming.*

RED

 ☆☆ 1979 CABERNET SAUVIGNON ($9.50) Batto Ranch, Sonoma.
☆☆☆ 1977 PETITE SIRAH ($12.00) John Gemello Tribute, Sonoma. *Rich and full but with grace and complexity. Stunning.*
 O 1979 ZINFANDEL ($6.00) Dry Creek Valley, Sonoma.

ಆ

Okoboji Winery
IOWA

Box 449, Arnolds Park, Iowa 51331 (712-332-2674). FOUNDED: 1977. ACREAGE: None. PRO-
DUCTION: 2,500 cases. DISTRIBUTION: At winery. OWNER: Corporation. L. A. Becker, Jr.,
president. WINEMAKER: L. A. Becker. Tours and tasting summer: Monday–Saturday 10 A.M.–5
P.M., Sunday 12–5 P.M.; winter by appointment.

After eighteen years, L. A. Becker had had it with banking. In fact, he figures that it was
banking that drove him crazy. "One day, I turned to my wife and said, 'We ought to start a
winery'—and anyone who would start a winery in the Midwest has to be crazy," says Becker.
Nonetheless, he researched the financial and legal angles, formed a corporation, and started making
wine in a leased facility. A one-man operation, the winery has started to make more grape wines,
though fruit wines are still the top moneymakers.

The Old Creek Ranch Winery
VENTURA COUNTY

10024 Old Creek Road, Oakview, California 93022 (805-649-4132). FOUNDED: 1981. ACREAGE:
4.5 acres. PRODUCTION: 1,500 cases. DISTRIBUTION: Ventura County. OWNER: Corporation.
Charles Branham, president; John Maitland, vice president; Carmel Maitland, financial officer.
WINEMAKER: Charles Branham; Paul Belgum, cellarmaster. Tours, tasting, and sales Friday–
Sunday 10 A.M.–5 P.M., or by appointment.

The old winery on the Old Creek Ranch had to go, since it was beyond repair, having been
totally neglected since 1945. This came as no surprise to Carmel and John Maitland, who had
bought the property with the idea of building a brand-new winery facility. While replanting the
vineyards, they made wine in a new warehouse-type building that they planned to use for case
storage once the new winery was finished. But now everyone at Old Creek has became so attached
to the poor old winery that they hope to find a safe way to preserve as much of it as possible,
perhaps by incorporating it into the design of the new winery.

WHITE

☆☆   1981 JOHANNISBERG RIESLING ($6.50) Rancho Sisquoc, Santa Maria.

Old South Winery
MISSISSIPPI

507 Concord Street, Natchez, Mississippi 39120 (601-445-9924). FOUNDED: 1979. ACREAGE:
20 acres. PRODUCTION: 4,000 cases. DISTRIBUTION: Local. OWNER: Scott Galbreath, Jr.
WINEMAKER: Scott Galbreath, Jr. Tours and tasting daily 10 A.M.–6 P.M.

Scott Galbreath, Jr., has three professional interests: farming, veterinary medicine, and cattle
ranching; but what he really loves is making wine. When he was fifteen years old he enjoyed helping
his parents make home brew, and this family hobby developed into a lifelong passion. Scott planted
vineyards in 1977, and one year later decided to make his production commercially available. "This
is the most fun I have ever had in my life," he says, beaming. "People called me a fool for getting
into this business, but I love it." Scott still has his veterinary practice but keeps the winery close
to home—right across the street from his house.

Old Wine Cellar Winery
IOWA

319 Main, Amana, Iowa 52203 (319-622-3116). FOUNDED: 1961. ACREAGE: None. PRO-
DUCTION: 4,000 cases. DISTRIBUTION: Iowa. OWNER: Ray Goerler. WINEMAKER: Robert
Henry. Tours and tasting summer: daily 9 A.M.–8 P.M.; winter: daily 10 A.M.–5 P.M. Owners also
make fruit wines at Colony Wines, Inc.

Ray Goerler owned another winery in Iowa until he had irreconcilable differences with his
partner. Using his grandfather's winemaking techniques, Ray started another winery in his basement.
He hired Robert Henry to help, teaching him the secrets of his family's winemaking methods. In
1983 the winery was moved to a new location on Main Street, and Ray's basement was remodeled
into a cellar and sales room. They make rhubarb, fruit, and grape wines; the grape wines are always
the best-sellers.

Oliver Winery
INDIANA

8024 North Highway 37, Bloomington, Indiana 47401 (812-876-5800). FOUNDED: 1972.
ACREAGE: 30 acres. PRODUCTION: 10,000 cases. DISTRIBUTION: 6 states. OWNERS: William
and Mary Oliver. WINEMAKER: Dave Schrodt. Tours Saturday 11 A.M.–6 P.M. Tasting Monday–
Saturday 11 A.M.–6 P.M., Sunday 12:30 P.M.–5:30 P.M.

Bill Oliver, a law professor at Indiana University, became interested in grape growing after
appearing as a guest lecturer at Cornell University. A hobby winemaker, Bill was intrigued by the
studies being done at Cornell on grape cultivation. He began his own experimental plantings and
found himself with so much juice that starting a real winery became almost a necessity. Located
just outside Bloomington, the winery took over the production of a honey wine, called Camelot
Mead, that was originally made by Ernie Lane, a wine consultant in California. The mead has
since become its biggest seller.

Olson Vineyards Winery
MENDOCINO COUNTY

3620 Road B, Redwood Valley, California 95470 (707-485-7523). FOUNDED: 1982. ACREAGE:
58 acres. PRODUCTION: 6,200 cases. DISTRIBUTION: California, Oregon, Washington, Montana, Texas, and Idaho. OWNERS: Donald R. and Nancy A. Olson. WINEMAKER: Roger Matson.
OTHER LABEL: Vista Mendocino. Tours and tasting daily 10 A.M.–5 P.M. Picnic facilities. Bed
and breakfast inn on premises.

The Olsons have been growing grapes on their high, secluded property for well over a decade.
They sold their grapes to nearby Fetzer Vineyards, which always seemed to win medals with wines
made from Olson grapes. The Olsons figured that if the Fetzers could make wine, they could too.
They set up a rudimentary winery in their carport until they finished building a large, two-story
facility. Their location gives the winery a 360-degree view of the entire Redwood Valley and much
of Lake Mendocino.

WHITE

☆☆   1983 CHARDONNAY ($8.75) Mendocino. *Soft, lush, decent.*

☆☆   1984 FRENCH COLOMBARD ($4.00) Mendocino. *1.2% residual sugar. Decent, clean and snappy.*

☆   1983 SAUVIGNON BLANC ($7.50) Mendocino. *Dull, fat, lush.*

BLANC DE NOIR

☆☆☆   1984 GAMAY BLANC ($4.00) Napa-Mendocino. *1.5% residual sugar. Strawberry fruit; clean, lush, attractive.*

☆☆☆   1984 WHITE ZINFANDEL ($4.50) Mendocino. *1.2% residual sugar. Soft, rich, clean, charming.*

RED

☆☆   1982 GAMAY ($4.50) Mendocino. *Fresh, crisp, varietal, attractive.*

☆   1982 ZINFANDEL ($8.00) Special Reserve, Mendocino. *0.8% residual sugar. 16% alcohol. Intense, chocolatey, heavy.*

☆☆   1983 ZINFANDEL ($8.00) Special Reserve, Mendocino. *Dry, clean, intense, rich, good.*

Opici Winery
RIVERSIDE COUNTY

Highland and Hermosa Avenue, Alta Loma, California 91701 (714-987-2710). FOUNDED: 1933. ACREAGE: 200 acres. PRODUCTION: 100,000 cases. DISTRIBUTION: East Coast states. OWNERS: Hubert and Rosemarie Opici. WINEMAKER: Consulting winemakers. No tours. Tasting and retail sales daily 10 A.M.–6 P.M.

The Opicis were wine distributors in New Jersey. Old Mr. Opici sent his wife and daughter, Mary, out to rent a California winery, where they would make Opici wine that would then be shipped back to New Jersey. When the elder Opicis died, the Opici children split the operation in true Italian style: Mary kept the winery in California and her brother kept the distributorship in New Jersey. Eventually the winery ceased making wine. It is now a tasting room and retail outlet for Opici imports and domestic Opici wines, which are made and bottled in the San Joaquin Valley.

OPUS ONE *see* Robert Mondavi Winery

Orleans Hill Vinicultural Corporation
YOLO COUNTY

P.O. Box 1254, Woodland, California 95695 (916-661-6538). FOUNDED: 1980. ACREAGE: None. PRODUCTION: 6,000 cases. DISTRIBUTION: California. OWNER: Orleans Hill Vinicultural Corporation. WINEMAKER: James Lapley. Tours and tasting Friday 1 P.M.–4 P.M., Saturday 9 A.M.–12 P.M., or by appointment.

James Lapley became interested in small wineries through his work in the Agriculture Department at U.C. Davis. He, his wife, and their old school chums had been home winemakers since 1973, making mostly Amador County Zinfandel. In 1980 they rented space in an olive processing plant, and the Orleans Hill Vinicultural Corporation began making wines from the Reiff Vineyard, north of Woodland, as well as continuing to turn out that Amador Zinfandel.

WHITE

☆ 1984 ORLEANS BLANC ($4.25) Reiff, Yolo. *0.6% residual sugar. 50% Chenin Blanc, 50% French Colombard. Spritzy, clean and simple.*

☆☆ 1984 CHARDONNAY ($6.75) Clarksburg. *Soft, fruity, clean. A charming everyday white wine.*

☆☆ 1984 SAUVIGNON BLANC ($5.00) Reiff, Yolo. *Soft, clean, varietal, pleasant but a bit short.*

BLANC DE NOIR

☆☆☆ 1984 WHITE ZINFANDEL ($4.50) Reiff, Yolo. *0.9% residual sugar. Crisp, clean, varietal, charming.*

RED

☆☆ 1984 RED TABLE WINE ($4.00) California. *60% Zinfandel, 40% Cabernet Sauvignon. Spicy, soft, attractive.*

Charles Ortman Wines
NAPA COUNTY

1680 Silverado Trail, St. Helena, California 94574 (707-963-4094). FOUNDED: 1979. ACREAGE: 10 acres. PRODUCTION: 4,000 cases. DISTRIBUTION: Nationwide. OWNERS: Charles Ortman and Bruce Rogers. WINEMAKER: Charles Ortman. Tours by appointment.

Charles Ortman started as the winemaker for Spring Mountain Vineyards and then became famous as a winemaking consultant for many of the best California wineries. While consulting at St. Andrews Winery in 1979, he started his own "Charles Ortman" label and a negociant label, "Ortman-Rogers," with a friend, Bruce Rogers. The Ortman wines were made at St. Andrews until Charles and Bruce started planning their own winery on the Silverado Trail. After two years of financial problems, the winery is still a maybe. The partners plan to have a 6,000-case facility that produces mostly Chardonnay, with capacity for custom crushing.

OTTER SPRING *see* Heron Hill Vineyards

Ozark Vineyards
MISSOURI

Highway 65, Chestnut Ridge, Missouri 65630 (417-587-3555). FOUNDED: 1976. ACREAGE: None. PRODUCTION: 5,000 cases. DISTRIBUTION: Local. OWNER: Corporation. Hershel Gray, president. WINEMAKER: L. James Held. Tours by appointment. Tasting summer: daily 9 A.M.–7 P.M.; winter: Monday–Saturday 9 A.M.–4:30 P.M., Sunday 12–6 P.M.

Hershel was just a laid-back grape grower who raised a little cattle and made a little wine. Then he began thinking about having his own winery, and the thought became an obsession. Determined to turn this idea into reality, Hershel rounded up financial assistance from his friends. Utilizing the winemaking know-how of one of the partners, James Held of Stone Hill Winery, Ozark Vineyards began making wine in a dairy barn. Later, the partners bought some property and built a modest metal winery and a spacious tasting room.

Pacheco Ranch Winery
MARIN COUNTY

5495 Redwood Highway, Ignacio, California 94947 (415-456-4099). FOUNDED: 1979. ACREAGE: 10 acres. PRODUCTION: 500 cases. DISTRIBUTION: 4 states. OWNER: Rowland family. Herbert M. Rowland, Jr., vineyard manager. WINEMAKER: T. James Meves. Tours and tasting by appointment.

The ranch, part of a Spanish land grant, has been in the Pacheco-Rowland family since 1836. When the Rowlands began growing grapes in one of Marin County's only vineyards, they sold them to a winery in the Napa Valley. While the possibility of a winery had often been discussed, it wasn't until Ann Rowland's husband, Jamie Meves (see Pat Paulsen Vineyards, Matrose), got his enology degree that the horses were removed from the carriage house so the building could be converted to a winery. With Jamie as winemaker, the entire family is now involved and enjoying it immensely.

WHITE

☆   1982 CHARDONNAY ($8.50) Mettler, Meeker, Sonoma.
☆☆ 1983 CHARDONNAY ($8.50) Marin. *Earthy, rich, varietal, oaky, quite decent.*

RED

☆☆☆ 1979 CABERNET SAUVIGNON ($9.00) Marin. *Full and cherry-toned; rich and herbal. Drink now.*
☆☆ 1980 CABERNET SAUVIGNON ($9.50) Marin. *Lush, varietal, earthy, big. Drink 1986.*

Page Mill Winery
SANTA CLARA COUNTY

13686 Page Mill Road, Los Altos Hills, California 94022 (415-948-0958). FOUNDED: 1976. ACREAGE: None. PRODUCTION: 2,500 cases. DISTRIBUTION: California, Colorado, Texas, and the East Coast, and by mailing list. OWNERS: Dick and Ome Stark. WINEMAKER: Dick Stark. Tours and tasting by appointment.

While flying back from a European tour in the mid-1970s, Dick Stark mused about how much fun it would be to make wine. Taking some time off from his job as marketing manager for an electronics firm, Spectra-Physics, he set up shop in his basement and made 70 gallons of wine. Since then, growth has been limited by the size of his basement, which is now crammed to the rafters with barrels and other winemaking equipment. Dick uses the scientific approach to winemaking, and his primary concern is getting excellent grapes and doing as little as possible to detract from their quality.

WHITE

☆   1981 CHARDONNAY ($13.00) Keene Dimick, Napa Valley. *Decent varietal flavors, with some off flavors.*
☆   1982 CHARDONNAY ($12.50) Keene Dimick, Santa Clara. *Crisp, snappy, decent.*
☆☆ 1983 CHARDONNAY ($12.50) Elizabeth Garbett, Santa Clara. *Oaky, rich, smooth.*

☆☆ 1983 CHARDONNAY ($12.50) Keene Dimick, Napa Valley. *Rich, heavy.*
☆☆☆ 1982 SAUVIGNON BLANC ($8.75) Santa Barbara. *Soft, fragrant and crisp.*
☆☆ 1983 SAUVIGNON BLANC ($9.00) Miller's French Camp, San Luis Obispo. *Grassy, oaky, rich, pleasant.*

RED

☆☆ 1980 CABERNET SAUVIGNON ($11.50) Volker Eisele, Napa Valley. *Herbal, soft, attractive.*
☆ 1981 CABERNET SAUVIGNON ($11.50) Napa Valley.
☆☆ 1980 ZINFANDEL ($8.00) Eisele, Chiles Valley, Napa. *Intense and raisiny.*

Palos Verdes Winery
LOS ANGELES COUNTY

10620-D South La Cienega Boulevard, Inglewood, California 90304 (213-645-3273). FOUNDED: 1982. ACREAGE: None. PRODUCTION: 1,000 cases. DISTRIBUTION: California. OWNER: Brook Harris. WINEMAKER: Brook Harris. Tours and tasting weekends 10 A.M.–5 P.M., or by appointment.

This winery is one of three located on a small strip of county land near the Los Angeles International Airport. "The city of Los Angeles won't allow wineries within the city limits," says Brook Harris, owner and winemaker, "so we leased this facility, which sits just outside the city." The winery is a 1,000-square-foot section of an industrial complex. Donatoni Winery, McLester Winery, a cabinetmaker, and a welder all share this urban artisans' center. Brook, a veteran of the home winemaking club, Cellarmasters, sells all of his wine in Orange and Los Angeles counties.

Papagni Vineyards
MADERA COUNTY

31754 Avenue 9, Madera, California 93638 (209-485-2760). FOUNDED: 1973. DISTRIBUTION: 40 states; Canada. OWNER: Angelo Papagni. WINEMAKER: John Daddino; Bert Marlow, assistant. Tours by appointment. No tasting.

A third-generation winemaker, Demetrio Papagni emigrated to California from Bari, Italy, in 1912. In 1920 he planted the first Papagni vineyard in the San Joaquin Valley. At first, the family's main business was selling grapes, juice, and wine to home winemakers and eastern wineries. In 1973 Demetrio's son Angelo built a state-of-the-art winery near Madera, and the Papagnis began to produce a line of premium varietal wines. The business is now divided between selling grapes and making wines. It has remained a family business, and Angelo's children are already working for the winery.

WHITE

○ 1981 CHARDONNAY ($6.00) Bonita, Madera. *Rich and leathery, without any fruit freshness.*
☆ 1982 CHARDONNAY ($6.50) Bonita, Estate, Madera.
☆ 1981 SAUVIGNON BLANC ($7.00) Madera. *Clean, celery-like flavors.*

SPARKLING

☆☆ NV SPUMANTE D'ANGELO ($7.00) Madera. *Muscat. Fresh, spicy, sweet and appealing.*
☆ 1980 CHARDONNAY AU NATUREL ($7.50) Madera. *Decent and clean but odd flavors.*
○ 1980 SPARKLING CHENIN BLANC ($9.00) Madera. *Weedy.*

RED

☆ 1978 ALICANTE-BOUSCHET ($7.00) Madera. *Crisp, simple, fruity, decent.*
☆ 1978 BARBERA ($4.75) Madera.

1975 ZINFANDEL ($4.70) Estate, California.
O   1978 ZINFANDEL ($5.00) Estate, California.
☆   1979 ZINFANDEL ($4.75) Madera.

Paradise Vintners
BUTTE COUNTY

1656 Nunneley Road, Paradise, California 95969 (916-872-1004). FOUNDED: 1982. ACREAGE: 6 acres. PRODUCTION: 3,000 cases. DISTRIBUTION: Local. OWNERS: Wilson and Phyllis Bruce. WINEMAKER: Wilson Bruce. Tours and tasting by appointment.

Wilson Bruce planted a vineyard in Paradise and, following the family tradition, began making wine. His father had had a winery in Mariposa, and his grandfather reportedly made wine for Lafite-Rothschild in France. But Wilson was just making wine at home. "When you start making a lot of wine, you start making a lot of friends," says Wilson. To supply his friends sufficiently, Wilson bonded and built a wood-frame winery out back, including an underground cellar with a bar and dance floor. "You can have one heck of a party down there, and not a soul will hear a sound," Wilson says.

Parducci Wine Cellars
MENDOCINO COUNTY

501 Parducci Road, Ukiah, California 95482 (707-462-3828). FOUNDED: 1932. ACREAGE: 450 acres. PRODUCTION: 350,000 cases. DISTRIBUTION: Nationwide. OWNER: TMI Corporation. John Parducci, general manager; George Parducci, finance. WINEMAKERS: John Parducci, Joe and Tom Monostori. Tours and tasting daily 9 A.M.–5:30 P.M.

Adolph Parducci was born in California, but when his father, John, became homesick for Tuscany he moved back with him to Italy in 1907. Adolph returned ten years later and built his first winery in Sonoma County. After it burned down in the late 1920s, he moved his operation north to Mendocino. In 1931 Adolph began construction on a new winery and was ready for Repeal in 1933. Adolph retired in 1948; his sons, John and George, took over. John, a frank, no-nonsense fellow, makes honest, no-nonsense, medium-priced wines. In 1983 the Parduccis acquired half interest in Konocti (see), a Lake County winery.

WHITE

☆   1982 CHABLIS ($3.50) Mendocino.
☆   1983 CHABLIS ($3.95) Mendocino. *Soft, fruity, clean, sweetish, decent.*
☆   1983 VINTAGE WHITE ($5.75) California. *1.5 liter. Good—fruity, clean and grapey.*
    1980 CHARDONNAY ($12.00) Cellermaster's Selection, Mendocino. *Lacking fruit, past its prime.*
☆   1982 CHARDONNAY ($7.75) Mendocino. *Vinous, herbal, dull.*
☆☆ 1983 CHARDONNAY ($7.50) Mendocino. *Lovely. Clean, balanced and attractive.*
☆☆☆ 1982 CHENIN BLANC ($4.95) 50th Anniversary, Mendocino. *Crisp, clean and fruity, with a touch of sweetness. Well made.*
☆☆ 1983 CHENIN BLANC ($5.25) Mendocino. *Fresh, clean, decent.*
☆☆ 1981 FRENCH COLOMBARD ($4.60) Mendocino. *Spritzy, crisp, fruity.*
☆   1983 FRENCH COLOMBARD ($4.50) Mendocino. *Crisp, fresh, clean, decent.*
☆   1981 GEWURZTRAMINER ($6.75) Mendocino. *Earthy, varietal, lacking fruit.*
☆☆☆ 1982 MENDOCINO RIESLING ($4.63) Mendocino. *Dry, angular, clean, with nicely balanced fruit and acid.*

☆☆   1982 SAUVIGNON BLANC ($6.35) Mendocino. *0.8% residual sugar. Soft, varietal, sim-ple, attractive.*

☆☆   1983 SAUVIGNON BLANC ($6.00) North Coast. *Snappy, grassy, clean. A touch of sweetness rounds it.*

☆☆   1983 SAUVIGNON BLANC ($6.00) Olympic Commemorative, California. *Clean, grassy, fruity, charming.*

RED

☆   1972 CABERNET SAUVIGNON Cellarmaster's Selection, Mendocino. *Soft, earthy and mature. Lacking structure but very nice.*

☆   1978 CABERNET SAUVIGNON ($7.20) Mendocino.

☆☆   1978 CABERNET SAUVIGNON ($12.00) Cellarmaster's Selection, Mendocino. *Cabernet-Merlot. Lush, tannic, attractive. Drink 1987.*

☆   1979 CABERNET SAUVIGNON ($7.50) Mendocino. *Simple, with very little varietal character.*

☆☆   1979 CABERNET SAUVIGNON ($10.00) Vintage Selection, Mendocino. *Earthy, clean and ripe.*

☆☆   1980 CABERNET SAUVIGNON ($8.50) 50th Anniversary, Estate, Mendocino. *Rich, grapey, intense, tannic.*

☆   1980 CABERNET SAUVIGNON ($8.50) Olympic Bottling, Mendocino. *Vegetative, nicely structured, a bit thin.*

☆   1983 CABERNET SAUVIGNON ($7.25) Mendocino. *Tannic, intense, decent.*

☆☆   1978 MERLOT Special, Cellar Selection, Mendocino. *Rich and deep, with good varietal character. A bit short.*

☆☆   1978 PETITE SIRAH ($7.50) Cellarmaster's Selection, Mendocino. *Rich, clean and varietal but a bit short on the finish.*

☆☆   1979 PETITE SIRAH ($5.75) Mendocino. *Dense, clean, tannic, nicely made. Drink 1986.*

☆   1980 PETITE SIRAH ($5.25) Mendocino.

☆☆   1969 PINOT NOIR Ukiah Valley. *Remarkably good. Aging very gracefully.*

☆   1980 PINOT NOIR ($5.00) Mendocino. *Toasty, light, simple.*

☆   1981 PINOT NOIR ($5.00) Mendocino.

☆☆   1979 ZINFANDEL ($7.75) Cellarmaster's, Mendocino.

☆   1980 ZINFANDEL ($5.00) Mendocino.

O   1981 ZINFANDEL ($4.50) Mendocino. *Oxidized.*

PARELLI-MINETTI WINERY *see* LaMont Winery

Parsons Creek Winery
MENDOCINO COUNTY

3001 South State Street, Ukiah, California 95482 (707-462-8900). FOUNDED: 1979. ACREAGE: None. PRODUCTION: 10,000 cases. DISTRIBUTION: California and other major market states. OWNER: Jesse Tidwell and Hal Doran. WINEMAKER: Jesse Tidwell. Tours and tasting by appointment.

From the name Parsons Creek Winery, one imagines a simple, rustic winery sitting alongside a peaceful, winding creek. But the winery is part of a long, rectangular industrial building near the freeway in the southern part of Ukiah. Jesse Tidwell, a man with a long, thin, Rumplestiltskin beard, and his husky partner, Hal Doran, first met at college in Humboldt. Many years later, they became reacquainted at a neighborhood party in Ukiah. Jesse had his own laboratory business, called Multi-Tech, and Hal was getting bored with his success in the contracting business. At that fateful party, they decided to start a winery. Jesse makes wine like a chemist, carefully checking every component and taking every precaution. He ends up with wines that almost always have some residual sugar.

WHITE

☆ 1981 CHARDONNAY ($10.00) 66% Philo Foothills, 34% Lolonis, Mendocino. *O.K. but heavy and sweetish.*

☆☆ 1982 CHARDONNAY ($11.00) Sonoma. *Lush, deep.*

☆☆ 1983 CHARDONNAY ($9.50) Mendocino. *Crisp yet lush and somewhat deep.*

1981 JOHANNISBERG RIESLING ($7.00) Mendocino. *1% residual sugar.*

☆☆ 1983 JOHANNISBERG RIESLING ($6.50) Mendocino. *Spicy, clean, attractive.*

SPARKLING

☆☆☆ NV BRUT ($13.50) Mendocino. *Rich, balanced, remarkable.*

RED

☆ 1981 ZINFANDEL ($6.00) Mendocino. *Earthy. Good structure but not lovable.*

Pastori Winery
SONOMA COUNTY

23189 Geyserville Avenue, Cloverdale, California 95425 (707-857-3418). FOUNDED: 1972. ACREAGE: 60 acres. PRODUCTION: 3,000 cases. DISTRIBUTION: California. OWNER: Frank Pastori. WINEMAKER: Frank Pastori. No tours. Tasting daily 9 A.M.–5 P.M.

The first Pastori winery, founded in 1914, closed during Prohibition, never to reopen. But in 1975 Frank Pastori, who was growing pears, prunes, and some grapes, decided to get back into the wine business. Farming is still the main Pastori business—winemaking is a small sideline. Most of the wine produced is sold in the tasting room.

Pat Paulsen Vineyards
SONOMA COUNTY

25510 River Road, Cloverdale, California 95425 (707-894-3197). FOUNDED: 1980. ACREAGE: 38 acres. PRODUCTION: 14,000 cases. DISTRIBUTION: Major market states. OWNERS: Patrick and Betty Jane Paulsen. WINEMAKER: T. James Meves. Tasting room in Asti, California. Open daily 10 A.M.–6 P.M.

Straight-faced comic Pat Paulsen, a Sonoma native, has had vineyards in the Cloverdale area since 1970. He first sold his grapes to Château St. Jean but then decided to convert his barn into a winery. Expertly operated by winemaker Jamie Meves (see Matrose, Pacheco Ranch Winery), the winery uses estate-grown grapes and buys some from local growers. While Pat is on the road his wife, Jane, runs the winery.

WHITE

☆☆ 1982 CHARDONNAY ($10.50) Sonoma. *Rich, vinous, oily, with good fruit.*

☆ 1983 CHARDONNAY ($11.00) Sonoma. *Tight, lean, hard, some off qualities.*

☆☆☆ 1984 GEWURZTRAMINER ($6.50) Sonoma. *0.64% residual sugar. Dry, crisp, varietal, delicate, with lovely fruit.*

☆☆☆ 1982 MUSCAT CANELLI ($6.50) Preston, Dry Creek Valley. *Melony, clean, crisp, off-dry. A charming wine.*

☆☆☆ 1983 MUSCAT CANELLI ($7.50) Sonoma. *0.81% residual sugar. Varietal, crisp, delightful. A food wine.*

☆☆☆ 1984 MUSCAT CANELLI ($7.50) Preston, Sonoma. *0.97% residual sugar. Dry, clean, varietal, lovely with food.*

☆ 1981 SAUVIGNON BLANC ($8.50) Estate, Sonoma.

☆☆☆ 1982 SAUVIGNON BLANC ($8.50) Estate, Alexander Valley. *Nice varietal nose; crisp, lemony flavor.*

☆☆☆ 1983 SAUVIGNON BLANC ($9.00) Estate, Sonoma. *Round, rich, lovely acidity, varietal, charming.*

RED

1980 CABERNET SAUVIGNON ($8.00) Sonoma. *Heavy, weedy, unappealing.*

☆☆ 1981 CABERNET SAUVIGNON ($8.00) Sonoma. *Herbal, soft, attractive. Nicely structured.*

☆☆☆ 1982 CABERNET SAUVIGNON ($10.00) Estate, Sonoma. *Lush, soft, herbal, balanced, complex, varietal. Drink now.*

ॐ

Peaceful Bend Vineyard
MISSOURI

Route 2, Steelville, Missouri 65565 (314-775-2578). FOUNDED: 1972. ACREAGE: 13 acres. PRODUCTION: 750 cases. DISTRIBUTION: Local. OWNER: Dr. Axel N. Arneson. WINE-MAKER: Dr. Axel N. Arneson. Tours and tasting Monday–Saturday 9 A.M.–5 P.M., Sunday 12–5 P.M.

Dr. Axel Arneson and his son Norman had a little spot of land on their farm that seemed perfect for a few grapevines. The doctor had been taught how to make wine by his father during Prohibition, and, after visiting the European wine country, he started digging into the history of Missouri's viticulture. Then Axel and Norman bought vine cuttings from Philip Wagner and began filling in their land with grapevines. They sold most of their grapes to home winemakers but saved a part of the crop for their own winemaking enjoyment. It provided so much enjoyment that the father-and-son team built a wooden Dutch-barn winery, ringed with a bank of insulating earth, and turned their hobby into a business.

ॐ

Robert Pecota Winery
NAPA COUNTY

3299 Bennett Lane, P.O. Box 303, Calistoga, California 94515 (707-942-6625). FOUNDED: 1978. ACREAGE: 45 acres. PRODUCTION: 8,500 cases. DISTRIBUTION: Major market states. OWNER: Robert Pecota. WINEMAKER: Robert Pecota. OTHER LABEL: San Micaire. Tours and tasting by appointment.

Bob Pecota is a former coffee-company executive who decided to enter the wine business in the late 1970s. He bought a ranch and built his winery in the northern end of the Napa Valley. Although he started with some rather arcane varieties, such as Flora, his vineyards are now producing more conventional varieties. Bob expects to eventually expand to a production level of 15,000 cases per year.

WHITE

☆☆ 1983 SAN MICAIRE CHARDONNAY ($12.50) Napa Valley. *Crisp, balanced, clean. Made in conjunction with Long Vineyards.*

☆☆☆ 1983 CHARDONNAY ($13.50) Canepa, Alexander Valley. *Rich, heavy, toasty, ripe, dominated by oak.*

☆☆ 1981 FLORA ($6.25) Napa Valley.

☆☆☆ 1983 FRENCH COLOMBARD ($5.25) Napa Valley. *Crisp, fresh, fruity, charming.*

☆☆   1983 GREY RIESLING ($4.75) Napa Valley. *Crisp, fruity, clean. California's best Grey Riesling.*

☆☆   1984 GREY RIESLING ($4.75) Napa Valley. *Fresh, clean, crisp, very attractive.*

☆☆☆   1982 MUSCATO DI ANDREA ($8.50) Napa Valley. *9% residual sugar. Lovely fruit and crisp acid. Delightful.*

☆☆☆☆   1983 MUSCATO DI ANDREA ($7.50) Napa Valley. *8.8% residual sugar. Spicy, fruity, charming, superb.*

☆☆☆   1984 MUSCATO DI ANDREA ($8.00) Napa Valley. *9.8% residual sugar. Rich, grapey, fruity, lush, varietal.*

☆☆   1981 SAUVIGNON BLANC ($9.50) Dedication Series, Napa Valley.

☆   1982 SAUVIGNON BLANC ($8.50) Napa Valley.

☆   1983 SAUVIGNON BLANC ($8.75) Napa Valley. *Oaky, clean but lacking fruit.*

RED

☆☆☆   1982 CABERNET SAUVIGNON ($12.00) Napa Valley. *Rich, deep, lush, structured, lovely. Drink 1987.*

☆☆   1983 CABERNET SAUVIGNON ($10.00) Estate, Napa Valley. *Rich, soft, lush, attractive. Drink 1986.*

☆☆   1983 GAMAY BEAUJOLAIS ($5.50) Nouveau, Napa Valley. *Crisp, peppery and simple.*

☆☆☆   1984 GAMAY BEAUJOLAIS ($5.50) Nouveau, Napa Valley. *Great color. Clean, rich, round, snappy, super.*

PEDREGAL *see* Stags' Leap Winery

Pedrizzetti Winery
SANTA CLARA COUNTY

1645 San Pedro Avenue, Morgan Hill, California 95037 (408-779-7389). FOUNDED: 1945. ACREAGE: None. PRODUCTION: 150,000 cases. DISTRIBUTION: California, Colorado, Florida, Texas, and Illinois. OWNER: Ed Pedrizzetti. WINEMAKER: Allen Kreutzer. Tours by appointment. Tasting daily 9 A.M.–4 P.M. Gift shop.

In 1913 Camillo Colombano discovered a place in California that reminded him so much of his old home in Asti, Italy, that he built a winery there. In 1919 he planted Barbera cuttings he had brought over from Italy. The Colombano family made wine and sold grapes until 1945, when John Pedrizzetti bought the winery and the 65-acre vineyard. At first he and his son Ed made wine for other wineries; they then made big jugs of wine that Ed hand-delivered to San Francisco. In 1963 Ed and his wife, Phyllis, took over the winery, opened a tasting room, and started bottling varietal wines. They tried to sell the winery and retire in 1973, but the deal was never consummated. By 1975 they had expanded the facility and put their three children to work. They now have three grandchildren who are eager to be a part of the business.

ROSE

1982 ZINFANDEL ($4.25) Santa Clara.

J. Pedroncelli Winery
SONOMA COUNTY

1220 Canyon Road, Geyserville, California 95441 (707-857-3531). FOUNDED: 1904. ACREAGE: 135 acres. PRODUCTION: 125,000 cases. DISTRIBUTION: Nationwide. OWNERS: John and

James Pedroncelli. WINEMAKER: John Pedroncelli. Tours by appointment. Tasting daily 10 A.M.–
5 P.M.

John Pedroncelli bought grocer J. Canata's Sonoma winery in 1927. After Repeal he made
generic red and white wines and sold grapes to home winemakers. Today, under the management
of his sons James and John, almost half the winery's production is still jug wines; the rest is
moderately priced varietals. A majority of the grapes the winery uses are purchased.

WHITE

☆ 1980 CHARDONNAY ($7.00) Sonoma.
☆☆ 1981 CHARDONNAY ($7.50) Sonoma. *Toasty, crisp and appealing.*
☆☆ 1982 CHARDONNAY ($7.75) Sonoma. *Crisp, clean, simple but attractive.*
1983 CHARDONNAY ($7.75) Sonoma. *Off flavors, unattractive.*
☆☆☆ 1983 CHENIN BLANC ($4.50) Sonoma. *1.8% residual sugar. Clean, tart, fresh, fruity,
        appealing.*
☆☆ 1982 FRENCH COLOMBARD ($4.00) Sonoma. *1% residual sugar. Snappy and crisp.*
☆☆☆ 1981 GEWURZTRAMINER ($5.00) Sonoma. *1% residual sugar. Attractive, clean, fresh,
        snappy.*
☆ 1982 GEWURZTRAMINER ($5.00) Sonoma. *1.05% residual sugar. Fruity, varietal but
        essentially dull.*
☆☆ 1983 GEWURZTRAMINER ($5.00) Sonoma. *Snappy and fruity; not varietal but fresh
        and good.*
☆☆ 1982 JOHANNISBERG RIESLING ($5.75) Sonoma. *Lemony and crisp.*
☆☆☆ 1983 JOHANNISBERG RIESLING ($5.25) Sonoma. *Dry, fruity, clean, crisp, lovely.*
1984 JOHANNISBERG RIESLING ($4.50) Sonoma. *Lacking freshness.*
1982 SAUVIGNON BLANC ($6.00) Sonoma.
☆☆☆ 1983 SAUVIGNON BLANC ($6.00) Sonoma. *Lovely, smooth, rich, clean, fruity.*

BLANC DE NOIR

☆☆ 1984 WHITE ZINFANDEL ($4.75) Sonoma. *Sweet, fruity.*

ROSE

☆☆☆ 1982 ZINFANDEL ($4.00) Sonoma. *Balanced and fruity. A delicious picnic wine.*
☆☆☆ 1983 ZINFANDEL ($4.00) Sonoma. *Crisp, slightly spritzy, a touch of sweetness. Lovely.*

RED

1978 CABERNET SAUVIGNON ($5.50) Vintage Selection, Sonoma. *Not much here—
        showing some age and off-dry.*
☆ 1978 CABERNET SAUVIGNON ($10.00) Sonoma.
☆ 1979 CABERNET SAUVIGNON ($5.50) Sonoma. *Decent, simple and clean.*
☆ 1980 CABERNET SAUVIGNON ($6.00) Sonoma. *Berried, rich and decent.*
1981 CABERNET SAUVIGNON ($6.00) Dry Creek and Alexander Valleys. *Stinky.*
☆ 1970 PINOT NOIR Sonoma.
☆ 1979 PINOT NOIR ($4.50) Sonoma.
☆ 1980 PINOT NOIR ($7.50) Sonoma. *10% Petite Sirah. Vegetal nose, earthy, rich, no
        depth.*
☆☆ 1981 PINOT NOIR ($5.00) Sonoma. *Dark, intense, woody, with decent fruit.*
☆☆ 1977 ZINFANDEL ($6.50) Vintage Select, Sonoma. *Rich, fruity and fresh.*
☆☆ 1978 ZINFANDEL ($6.50) Vintage Select, Sonoma. *Nice, soft, complex and mature.*
☆☆ 1979 ZINFANDEL ($4.50) Sonoma. *Simple and decent.*
☆☆ 1980 ZINFANDEL ($4.50) Sonoma. *Spicy and clean, with great fruit.*
☆ 1981 ZINFANDEL ($4.50) Dry Creek Valley, Sonoma. *Clean, tangy, decent.*

Peju Province
NAPA COUNTY

8466 St. Helena Highway, Rutherford, California 94573 (707-963-3600). FOUNDED: 1983. ACREAGE: 30 acres. PRODUCTION: 4,000 cases. DISTRIBUTION: California, Texas, and Colorado. OWNER: Tony Peju. WINEMAKER: Walter Schug, consultant. No tours. Tasting winter: Wednesday–Sunday 10 A.M.–5 P.M.; summer: daily 10 A.M.–6 P.M.

"This is the place to be," thought Tony Peju during a visit to the Napa Valley in 1979. At that time, he wanted to buy a winery, "but none of them made sense financially," says Tony. "It would have taken me twice as long to break even with an existing winery than it would to start my own." So Tony bought a vineyard instead. When it came time to crush his first vintage, he talked to all the winemaking consultants he could find and decided Walter Schug, the former winemaker at Joseph Phelps Winery, was his man. The first two vintages were custom crushed at other facilities, but in the spring of 1985 Tony broke ground on his own winery. When not in Napa, Tony takes care of his nursery business in Los Angeles.

WHITE

☆☆☆   1983 SAUVIGNON BLANC ($7.00) Napa Valley. *Fresh, varietal, clean, fruity.*

Pellegrini Brothers Winery
SONOMA COUNTY

4055 West Olivet Road, Santa Rosa, California 95401 (415-761-2811). FOUNDED: 1933. ACREAGE: 100 acres. PRODUCTION: 48,000 cases. DISTRIBUTION: California. OWNER: Partnership. Robert Pellegrini, production manager. WINEMAKER: Bob Fredson. No tours or tasting.

The founding date for this winery is registered as 1933, "but we were cooking long before that!" says Bob Pellegrini. Bob's grandfather started making wine in a rented Geyserville facility, hauling the barrels down to San Francisco for blending and bottling. "I think we were the last winery to bottle within the San Francisco city limits," says Bob. In 1956 the Pellegrinis got out of winemaking and into wine wholesaling, which is still the mainstay of their business. It wasn't until the mid-1970s that they planted grapes in Sonoma County and began making wine again under their own label.

WHITE

☆   1981 CHARDONNAY ($7.00) Russian River Valley. *Very oaky and clumsy.*
O   1982 CHARDONNAY ($8.50) Russian River Valley. *Tanky, dirty and oxidized.*
☆☆   1983 CHARDONNAY ($8.50) Russian River Valley. *Varietal, crisp, clean, attractive.*
☆☆☆ 1983 CHENIN BLANC ($4.00) California. *Fruity, clean, attractive.*
     1982 FRENCH COLOMBARD ($3.00) California.
☆   1981 FUME BLANC ($7.00) Sonoma.

RED

☆   1980 CLOS DE MERLE ($4.50) Russian River Valley, Sonoma. *Mostly Zinfandel. Deep, dense, decent. A field blend.*
     1979 CABERNET SAUVIGNON ($7.50) Russian River Valley.
☆☆   1980 CABERNET SAUVIGNON ($7.50) Russian River Valley. *Big berry style; soft and rich.*
☆☆   1980 ZINFANDEL ($5.00) Sonoma.

Pendleton Winery
SANTA CLARA COUNTY

499 Aldo Avenue, Santa Clara, California 95054 (408-980-9463). FOUNDED: 1977. ACREAGE: None. PRODUCTION: 5,000 cases. DISTRIBUTION: 3 states. OWNER: R. Brian Pendleton. WINEMAKER: R. Brian Pendleton. Tours and tasting by appointment. Retail sales daily 9 A.M.– 5 P.M.

When Brian Pendleton was making wine at home, he was sure his wines could compete head-to-head with the best wines on the commercial market. "Starting with that arrogant attitude, I quickly got whipped into shape," chuckles Brian. Formerly a teacher of physiology at California State University at San Jose, Brian has always been intrigued by the relationship of the brain and the senses. His winemaking and his cooking hobby are closely related to his intellectual pursuits. "I have always made wine for my own palate," says Brian. "I want to extract the utmost from the grape to make a rich, luscious wine."

WHITE

☆☆☆ 1981 CHARDONNAY ($12.50) Private Reserve, Monterey. *Rich and oaky, with good, crisp acidity.*

O 1982 CHARDONNAY ($12.50) Continental, San Luis Obispo. *Dark, heavy and clumsy, with some oxidation.*

RED

☆☆ NV CABERNET SAUVIGNON Lot 7879, 50% 1978 Ventana-Monterey, 50% 1979 Ventana-Napa, California. *Raisiny and rich; lush and full-bodied.*

☆☆☆ 1979 CABERNET SAUVIGNON ($11.00) Adamson-Tupper, Napa Valley. *Clean and bright; lean and very attractive. Aging nicely.*

☆☆ 1980 CABERNET SAUVIGNON ($12.00) Napa Valley. *Big, dense, fruity. Drink 1986.*

1979 ZINFANDEL ($7.00) San Luis Obispo. *Weedy, thick and heavy.*

Penn Shore Vineyards
PENNSYLVANIA

10225 East Lake Road, North East, Pennsylvania 16428 (814-725-8688). FOUNDED: 1969. ACREAGE: None. PRODUCTION: 15,000 cases. DISTRIBUTION: Pennsylvania. OWNERS: P. Blair McCord, George Sceiford, and George Luke. WINEMAKER: Steven Reeder. OTHER LABEL: Free Spirit Wines. Tours and tasting Monday–Saturday 10 A.M.–6 P.M., Sunday 12–6 P.M.

Three ambitious grape growers got the notion to make wine, and the state of Pennsylvania was the first to hear about it. These growers had been growing fruit, table grapes, and modest amounts of wine grapes, along with cultivating hybrids. Their notion sparked legislative action to get a state Farm Winery Act passed so small wineries could sell their wares on their own premises. Penn Shore Vineyards was the first winery to be issued a commercial winemaking license under the act. With the state's go-ahead, the three growers erected a functional pole-barn winery with aluminum siding on a prime lakeshore location off Route 5, easily accessible to tourist traffic. After twelve years of producing jug-style blends, they hired winemaker Steven Reeder, who has directed the winery toward premium varietal white wines.

Penn Yan Wine Cellars
NEW YORK

150 Water Street, Penn Yan, New York 14527 (315-536-2361). FOUNDED: 1943. ACREAGE: None. PRODUCTION: 50,000 cases. DISTRIBUTION: Eastern states. OWNER: Partnership. Stanley Levenson, Maurice Isner, and Julian Lee. WINEMAKER: Squire Osborn. No tours or tasting.

Burt Latz sold his winery to the three men who ran the Stanmore Liquor Company, a wholesale liquor business. Stanmore was distributing Burt's wine at the time his winery came up for sale; Stanley, Julian, and Maurice felt the least they could do was buy the winery that was producing one of their best-selling wines. Julian is the managing partner, concerning himself with everything from finances to winemaking. The original two-story winery building has been expanded, and an extension building has also been added. The wines continue to be sold by Stanmore Liquor Company.

Robert Pepi Winery
NAPA COUNTY

7585 St. Helena Highway, Oakville, California 94562 (707-944-2807). FOUNDED: 1981. ACREAGE: 60 acres. PRODUCTION: 15,000 cases. DISTRIBUTION: Nationwide. OWNERS: Robert A. and Robert L. Pepi. WINEMAKER: Robert L. Pepi; Tony Soter, consultant. Tours by appointment. No tasting. Retail sales weekdays. Call for information.

The Pepi family began making wine in Lucca, Italy. This tradition was revived in 1966 when the family moved to the Napa Valley and once again began growing grapes. Carefully testing many different grape varieties, Robert A. Pepi and his son Robert L. Pepi found that Sauvignon Blanc was well suited to their rolling Oakville property. Fifteen years later the family began drawing plans for a winery with the help of winemaking consultant Tony Soter.

WHITE

  O   1982 CHARDONNAY ($11.00) Napa Valley. *Minty, peculiar.*
  ☆☆ 1982 SAUVIGNON BLANC ($8.00) Napa.
  ☆☆☆ 1982 SEMILLON ($7.00) Napa Valley. *Soft, fresh and appealing.*
  ☆☆ 1983 SEMILLON ($8.00) Napa Valley. *Snappy, fruity, clean.*

Pepperwood Springs Vineyards
MENDOCINO COUNTY

P.O. Box 11, Philo, California 95466 (707-895-2250). FOUNDED: 1981. ACREAGE: 5 acres. PRODUCTION: 700 cases. DISTRIBUTION: California and by mailing list. OWNER: Parsons family. Larry and Nicki Parsons, managers. WINEMAKER: Larry D. Parsons. Tours by appointment. No tasting.

Larry Parsons, blind from birth, became intrigued with laboratory sciences while at California State School of the Blind in Berkeley. Educational facilities at the time could not handle teaching such subjects to blind people, so Larry, disappointed, turned to a more conventional blind person's career—he managed snack bars and cafeterias in federal and state buildings. Larry switched to winemaking after he and his family purchased vineyard property in Mendocino County's Anderson Valley. With his love of science and the outdoors, Larry began cultivating vines and making wine. He is assisted by his wife and two children. Larry has originated the only wine label that is written in Braille.

WHITE

  ☆ 1982 CHARDONNAY ($9.00) Potter Valley, Mendocino. *Dull, simple, decent.*

Perdido Vineyards
ALABAMA

Route 1, Box 20-A, Perdido, Alabama 36562 (205-937-9463). FOUNDED: 1979. ACREAGE: 50 acres. PRODUCTION: 12,500 cases. DISTRIBUTION: Alabama, Florida, Georgia, Louisiana, and

Tennessee. OWNERS: Jim and Marianne Eddins. WINEMAKER: Marianne Eddins. Tours and tasting Monday–Saturday 10 A.M.–5 P.M. Gift shop.

Jim Eddins had to fight the state and the forces of Prohibition to establish the first winery in Alabama since Repeal. He and his wife, Marianne, having planted vineyards in 1972, pushed for the Alabama Farm Winery Act, which stipulated that a winery could operate in the state as long as at least 75 percent of the grapes used came from the winery's own vineyard estate. After Perdido Vineyards received the first permit under this law, Jim faced the opposition of religious groups and loan officials. "People just did not want a winery in this state," says Jim. "What has held Alabama back as a grape-growing, winemaking state is not our viticulture, our soil, or our sun, but our politics," he explains.

WHITE

NV   MAGNOLIA MUSCADINE ($4.50) Alabama.

ROSE

NV   ROSE COU ROUGE ($4.50) Alabama.

Perret Vineyards
NAPA COUNTY

1177 Johnson Street, Suite 200, Menlo Park, California 94025 (415-324-9463). FOUNDED: 1983. ACREAGE: 20 acres. PRODUCTION: 2,000 cases. DISTRIBUTION: 7 states and Washington D.C. OWNERS: Paul Perret and Mary Ann Hurlimann. WINEMAKER: Chuck Ortman, consultant. No tours or tasting.

Paul Perret and his wife, Mary Ann Hurlimann, own twenty acres of Chardonnay vines in the Carneros region. Their wine was originally made at Acacia, but it is now being vinified at Monticello, with Chuck Ortman as consultant.

WHITE

☆☆☆   1980 CHARDONNAY ($13.50) Estate, Napa Valley-Carneros District. *Rich, balanced, clean, complex, super.*

☆☆☆   1981 CHARDONNAY ($13.50) Estate, Napa Valley-Carneros District. *Crisp, fruity, clean, complex, masterful. Made at Acacia.*

☆☆☆   1982 CHARDONNAY ($14.50) Estate, Napa Valley-Carneros. *Toasty, rich, lush, fruity, lovely.*

☆☆☆   1983 CHARDONNAY ($13.50) Estate, Carneros-Napa Valley. *Lush, tangy, fresh, clean oak, superb. Made at Acacia.*

Pesenti Winery
SAN LUIS OBISPO COUNTY

2900 Vineyard Drive, Templeton, California 93465 (805-434-1030). FOUNDED: 1934. ACREAGE: 75 acres. PRODUCTION: 50,000 cases. DISTRIBUTION: California. OWNER: Victor Pesenti. WINEMAKER: Pesenti family. Self-guided tours and tasting Monday–Saturday 8 A.M.–5:30 P.M., Sunday 9 A.M.–5:30 P.M. Gift shop.

With vineyards dating back to 1923, this winery was established by Frank Pesenti right after Repeal. At first Frank ran the winery alone, making mostly Zinfandel from his own grapes. Then his son Victor returned from the service after World War II to help out. Still family operated, the original concrete-block and stucco winery has been expanded little by little over the years. Despite increases in production, most of the wine is still sold only in the local area.

Pheasant Ridge Winery
TEXAS

Route 3, Lubbock, Texas 79401 (806-746-6033). FOUNDED: 1982. ACREAGE: 32 acres. PRODUCTION: 3,000 cases. DISTRIBUTION: Texas. OWNER: Cox family. Charles Robert Cox, Jr., and Charles Robert Cox III. WINEMAKER: Charles Robert Cox III. Tours and tasting by appointment.

Charles Robert Cox III learned about vineyards while working in the fruit and vegetable department of Texas A & M University Experimental Station. His interest in wine was closely tied to his appreciation of French cuisine. After a gastronomic tour of Europe, he set out to learn all he could from winemaking neighbors and universities about growing grapes in Texas. With the help of his father, he bought a 130-acre, Bible-belt cotton field and began planting vinifera. The winery, a plain steel structure, sits in the middle of the long, flat, dusty vineyard. "This area may not be pretty, but it grows the best grapes in Texas," says Robert.

WHITE

☆☆   1983 CHARDONNAY ($10.00) Lubbock, Texas. *Varietal, heavy oak, clean.*

Joseph Phelps Vineyards
NAPA COUNTY

200 Taplin Road, St. Helena, California 94574 (707-963-2745). FOUNDED: 1972. ACREAGE: 288 acres. PRODUCTION: 60,000 cases. DISTRIBUTION: Nationwide; 5 foreign markets. OWNER: Joseph Phelps; Bruce Neyers, vice president. WINEMAKER: Craig Williams. OTHER LABELS: Le Fleuron, Neyers. Tours by appointment Monday–Saturday. Tasting after tours. Retail sales Monday–Saturday 9 A.M.–4 P.M.

Entrepreneur Joe Phelps is the successful head of a Colorado construction firm. When he was hired to build the Souverain wineries in Sonoma and Rutherford Hill, he fell in love with the wine business. In 1973 he began building his own very striking winery. He hired German-born and Geisenheim-trained Walter Schug as winemaker and became best known for Rieslings, although Phelps Cabernets have also made quite a name for the winery. Schug left in 1982 to start his own winery (see Schug Cellars) and Joe Phelps invested in marketing man Bruce Neyers's winery (see). Joe is also part owner of the Oakville Grocery.

WHITE

☆☆   NV   VIN BLANC ($4.75) Napa Valley. *Vinous, heavy, clean and good.*
  ☆   1983 VIN BLANC ($4.75) Napa Valley. *Mostly Chardonnay. Heavy, vinous, fresh but lacking charm.*
  ☆☆   1984 VIN BLANC ($4.75) Napa Valley. *92% Chardonnay. Fresh, soft, clean, appealing.*
        1980 CHARDONNAY ($13.00) Napa Valley. *Dirty and coarse.*
  ☆   1981 CHARDONNAY ($12.75) Napa Valley. *Oaky, decent.*
☆☆☆   1981 CHARDONNAY ($12.75) Schellville, Sonoma. *Balanced and crisp, with a nice oakiness.*
☆☆☆   1981 CHARDONNAY ($16.00) Sangiacomo, Napa. *Rich, toasty and oily, with clean fruitiness. Barrel fermented.*
☆☆☆   1982 CHARDONNAY ($14.00) Sangiacomo, Sonoma. *Rich, oaky, barrel fermented, complex.*

☆ 1982 CHARDONNAY ($14.00) Schellville, Sonoma Valley. *Oily, heavy, vinous, overdone.*

☆☆☆ 1983 CHARDONNAY ($12.50) Napa Valley. *Lush, rich, lovely balance; complex and very attractive.*

☆ 1982 GEWURZTRAMINER ($8.00) Napa Valley. 0.7% residual sugar. *Decent but essentially dull.*

☆☆☆ 1983 GEWURZTRAMINER ($8.00) Napa Valley. 0.9% residual sugar. *Great varietal character, clean, balanced.*

☆☆ 1984 GEWURZTRAMINER ($8.00) Napa Valley. *Spicy, clean, varietal; a bit heavy.*

☆☆☆☆ 1976 JOHANNISBERG RIESLING Selected Late Harvest, Napa Valley. 23.1% residual sugar. *Dark amber, rich and toasty. Superb.*

☆☆☆ 1979 JOHANNISBERG RIESLING ($10.75) Late Harvest, Napa Valley. 8.8% residual sugar.

☆☆☆ 1980 JOHANNISBERG RIESLING ($6.75) Late Harvest, Napa Valley. 8.1% residual sugar.

☆☆☆ 1980 JOHANNISBERG RIESLING ($30.00) Selected Late Harvest, Napa Valley. 16.3% residual sugar. *Lush, botrytized and lovely.*

☆☆ 1981 JOHANNISBERG RIESLING ($7.25) Early Harvest, Napa Valley.

☆☆☆ 1981 JOHANNISBERG RIESLING ($25.00) Selected Late Harvest, Napa Valley. 375ml. 28% residual sugar. *Intensely fruity, lovely.*

☆☆☆ 1982 JOHANNISBERG RIESLING ($7.50) Early Harvest, Napa Valley. 1.2% residual sugar. *Floral, soft and round. Snappy finish.*

☆☆☆ 1982 JOHANNISBERG RIESLING ($8.50) Napa Valley. 2.1% residual sugar. *Ripe fruit, lovely balance. A classic.*

☆☆☆ 1982 JOHANNISBERG RIESLING ($11.25) Late Harvest, Napa Valley. 10.5% residual sugar. *Lovely, elegant and rich, with great fruit.*

☆☆☆ 1982 JOHANNISBERG RIESLING ($25.00) Special Select Late Harvest, Napa Valley. 375ml. 25.4% residual sugar. *Big, fruity, balanced.*

☆☆ 1983 JOHANNISBERG RIESLING ($8.00) Napa Valley. 2% residual sugar. *Soft, lush, fruity, ripe, lovely.*

☆☆☆ 1984 JOHANNISBERG RIESLING ($7.50) Early Harvest, Napa Valley. *Snappy, fresh, floral, lovely balance, clean, appealing.*

☆☆☆ 1984 JOHANNISBERG RIESLING ($8.00) Napa Valley. 2.2% residual sugar. *Fresh, melony, clean, varietal.*

☆☆☆ 1982 SAUVIGNON BLANC ($9.00) Napa Valley. *Soft and fruity.*

☆☆☆ 1983 SAUVIGNON BLANC ($8.50) California. *Crisp, varietal, balanced, clean.*

☆☆☆ 1979 SCHEUREBE ($15.00) Late Harvest, Napa Valley. 7.9% residual sugar. *Perfumed, lushly fruited, lovely.*

☆☆☆ 1981 SCHEUREBE ($15.00) Late Harvest, Napa Valley. 7.9% residual sugar. *Soft, fruity and lush. Lovely and delicate.*

☆☆☆☆ 1982 SCHEUREBE ($15.00) Special Select Late Harvest, Napa Valley. 375ml. 18% residual sugar. *Lush, floral, complex, super.*

☆☆☆☆ 1983 SCHEUREBE ($15.00) Late Harvest, Napa Valley. 12.2% residual sugar. *Floral, rich, deep, fruity, clean, super.*

RED

☆☆ NV VIN ROUGE ($4.75) California. *Remarkably elegant. Pinot Noir–like flavors.*

☆☆ 1982 CLARET ($6.00) Napa Valley. 92% *Cabernet Sauvignon, 8% Cabernet Franc. Lush, clean, attractive.*

☆☆☆ 1974 CABERNET SAUVIGNON ($60.00) Insignia, Napa Valley. *Lush, complex, balanced, wonderful. Drink now.*

☆☆☆ 1975 CABERNET SAUVIGNON ($35.00) Napa Valley. 5% Merlot. *Subtle oak and fruit; well balanced. Drink now.*

☆☆☆ 1976 CABERNET SAUVIGNON ($20.00) Insignia, 94% Eisele, 6% Oakville Merlot, Napa Valley. *Full, rich, fruity, oaky and complex. Drink now through 1990.*

☆ 1976 CABERNET SAUVIGNON ($25.00) Napa Valley. *11% Merlot. Dense, lacking structure; big and concentrated. Dull.*

☆☆☆ 1977 CABERNET SAUVIGNON ($15.00) Backus, Napa Valley. *Dense, rich, massive— a classic California biggie.*

☆☆☆ 1977 CABERNET SAUVIGNON ($25.00) Insignia, Napa Valley. *30% Merlot, 20% Cabernet Franc. Herbal, rich, complex. Drink 1986.*

☆☆ 1977 CABERNET SAUVIGNON ($25.00) Napa Valley. *8% Merlot. Mint and eucalyptus; dense, attractive. Drink now.*

☆☆ 1978 CABERNET SAUVIGNON ($10.75) Napa Valley. *Pleasant, medium weight; nice herbs and fruit.*

☆☆☆ 1978 CABERNET SAUVIGNON ($16.50) Backus, Napa Valley. *Dark, ripe, concentrated and powerful. Drink 1987.*

☆☆☆ 1978 CABERNET SAUVIGNON ($25.00) Insignia, Napa Valley. *30% Merlot, 20% Cabernet Franc. Minty, elegant, lovely. Drink 1986.*

☆☆☆ 1978 CABERNET SAUVIGNON ($30.00) Eisele, Napa Valley. *Spicy, rich and complex, with great aging potential. Drink 1987.*

 1979 CABERNET SAUVIGNON ($11.50) Napa Valley.

☆☆☆ 1979 CABERNET SAUVIGNON ($25.00) Insignia, Napa Valley. *30% Merlot. Deep, assertive, complex, minty. Drink 1986.*

☆☆☆ 1979 CABERNET SAUVIGNON ($30.00) Eisele, Napa Valley. *Dark, rich and delicious— now and for years. Drink 1987.*

 1980 CABERNET SAUVIGNON ($10.75) Napa Valley. *Herbaceous. Well made but too vegetal.*

☆☆☆ 1980 CABERNET SAUVIGNON ($25.00) Insignia, Napa Valley. *15% Merlot. Balanced, rich, intense, lovely. Drink 1988.*

☆☆ 1981 CABERNET SAUVIGNON ($11.00) Napa Valley. *Herbal, clean, soft, attractive. Drink now.*

☆☆☆ 1981 CABERNET SAUVIGNON ($15.00) Backus, Napa Valley. *Lush, rich, deep, structured. Drink 1987 and beyond.*

☆☆☆ 1981 CABERNET SAUVIGNON ($25.00) Insignia, Napa Valley. *28% Merlot, 12% Cabernet Franc. Minty, clean, complex, firmly structured, attractive, with fruit and oak flavors. Drink 1989.*

☆☆☆ 1983 CABERNET SAUVIGNON ($25.00) Insignia, Napa Valley. *50% Cabernet Sauvignon, 40% Merlot, 10% Cabernet Franc. Minty, big, dense. Drink 1990.*

☆☆☆ 1975 MERLOT ($35.00) Insignia, Napa Valley. *86% Merlot, 14% Cabernet. Minty, complex and rich.*

☆ 1977 SYRAH ($6.00) Napa Valley.

☆☆ 1979 SYRAH ($10.50) Napa Valley. *Spicy, clean, complex, very Rhone-like.*

☆☆ 1982 SYRAH ($7.50) Napa Valley. *Meaty, light, attractive. Not Rhone-like.*

☆ 1979 ZINFANDEL ($6.75) Napa Valley. *A bit tired, lacking fresh fruitiness.*

☆☆ 1979 ZINFANDEL ($9.00) Alexander Valley.

☆☆ 1980 ZINFANDEL ($6.75) Alexander Valley. *Lush, deep, attractive.*

☆☆☆ 1981 ZINFANDEL ($6.75) Alexander Valley. *Rich, balanced, fruity, charming, with some finesse.*

☆☆ 1982 ZINFANDEL ($5.75) Napa Valley. *Light, crisp, clean Beaujolais-style.*

☆☆ 1983 ZINFANDEL ($5.75) Napa Valley. *Lovely, fresh.*

☆☆☆ 1984 ZINFANDEL ($5.75) Napa Valley. *Crisp, fruity, Beaujolais-style, charming. Served chilled.*

The R. H. Phillips Vineyards
YOLO COUNTY

Route 1, Box 855, Esparto, California 95627 (916-662-5783). FOUNDED: 1983. ACREAGE: 250 acres. PRODUCTION: 28,000 cases. DISTRIBUTION: California. OWNER: Partnership. John Giguiere, general manager. WINEMAKER: Clark Smith. Tours and tasting by appointment.

Members of the Giguiere family started planting grapes in 1980 for a very practical reason: Water was expensive and they needed to plant a crop that required little or no irrigation. Three years later, when the vines came to bear, the Giguieres realized they had to market the grapes somewhere. To promote the wine-grape potential of the area they decided to make some demonstration wines. They made the first vintage at another winery and later, in 1983, built a large metal building and filled it full of tanks and barrels. Both John and Carl Giguiere are farmers, not winemakers, so they hired John's college friend Clark Smith to be their enologist.

WHITE

☆☆   1983 CHENIN BLANC ($5.00) Dry, Dunnigan Hills, Yolo. *Varietal, clean, balanced, well made.*
☆☆   1984 CHENIN BLANC ($4.50) Estate, Yolo. *0.9% residual sugar. Vegetal, soft, sweet, nice.*
☆☆☆   1984 CHENIN BLANC ($5.25) Dry, Yolo. *Varietal, lush, crisp; very fruity and attractive.*
☆☆   1983 SAUVIGNON BLANC ($5.50) Dunnigan Hills, Yolo. *Lemony, tart, clean, varietal.*
☆☆☆   1983 SAUVIGNON BLANC ($6.00) California. *Grassy, clean, rich.*

Piconi Winery
RIVERSIDE COUNTY

33410 Rancho California Road, Temecula, California 92390 (714-676-5400). FOUNDED: 1981. ACREAGE: 5 acres. PRODUCTION: 6,000 cases. DISTRIBUTION: California and other major market states. OWNERS: John and Gloria Piconi. WINEMAKER: John Piconi. Tours, tasting, and sales weekdays by appointment. Tasting and sales weekends 11 A.M.–4:30 P.M.

Dr. John Piconi came to California to establish a practice in urology. When the best opportunity presented itself in Southern California, he moved to Fallbrook and immediately set out for the nearest grape-growing region, Temecula. He formed a partnership with vineyard owner Vincenzo Cilurzo (see Cilurzo Vineyard and Winery) and made wines under the Cilurzo-Piconi label. The partnership dissolved after two years, and John constructed his own three-level, energy-efficient winery, built into the side of a hill. Piconi Winery is run by John and his six children. "I owe my love of wine to my parents, who used to make wine at home in Pittsburgh," says John. In fact, at harvest time his parents fly out from Pittsburgh to help.

WHITE

1982 CHARDONNAY ($8.00) Temecula. *Decent but not particularly interesting.*

Piedmont Cellars
ALAMEDA COUNTY

468 66th Street, Oakland, California 94609 (415-654-5549). FOUNDED: 1981. ACREAGE: None. PRODUCTION: 500 cases. DISTRIBUTION: Local and by mailing list. OWNER: Corporation. Jerry Miller, general manager. WINEMAKER: Ed Noonan. Tours and tasting by appointment.

Piedmont Cellars was started by four enterprising businessmen, two of whom were home winemakers. Ed Noonan and Jerry Miller had been making wine in Jerry's Oakland basement for several years when they decided in 1981 to get bonded. Jerry, a consultant in advanced technology, and Ed, a high school teacher, are hoping that the winery will provide them with a retirement income. As for grapes, "We have long-term contracts with specific vineyards," says Jerry, who buys Pinot Noir from the Carneros area of Napa Valley and Chardonnay from the Sonoma Valley. Piedmont Cellars barrel ferments all wines and uses only naturally occurring yeast.

Piña Cellars
NAPA COUNTY

8060 Silverado Trail, Rutherford, California 94573 (707-944-2229). FOUNDED: 1979. ACREAGE: 5 acres. PRODUCTION: 3,000 cases. DISTRIBUTION: California. OWNER: Piña family. David Piña, general manager. WINEMAKER: David Piña. Tours and tasting by appointment.

Fourth-generation Napans, the Piña family began making wine after many years in the vineyard management business. (Their father, John Piña, managed vineyards in the area for over 35 years.) In 1979 the Piñas formed a partnership and built a winery on their property in Rutherford. Since the death of their father, the Piña brothers are the labor force of the winery. Several of them have worked in various Napa Valley wineries or continue to work in vineyard management, except for Randy, a carpenter by trade, who built the winery.

WHITE

☆   1980 CHARDONNAY ($13.00) Napa Valley. *Rich, vinous, intense, hot.*

Pindar Vineyards
NEW YORK

P.O. Box 332, Peconic, Long Island, New York 11958 (516-734-6200). FOUNDED: 1979. ACREAGE: 120 acres. PRODUCTION: 20,000 cases. DISTRIBUTION: New York. OWNER: Dr. Herodotus Damiamos. WINEMAKER: Alan LeBlanc-Kinne. Tours Saturday and Sunday 11 A.M.–5 P.M. Tasting daily 11 A.M.–5 P.M.

Dr. Herodotus Damiamos watched as the potato land on Long Island was slowly being converted to vineyards. He was fascinated by the way the stubborn vines battled the elements. In 1980 he bought a potato field and planted his own vineyard of vinifera grapevines. His only goal was to sell grapes, but, once the vines began to bear, the doctor decided to push ahead with a winery. It was completed in six weeks, just in time for the 1982 crush.

Pine Ridge Winery
NAPA COUNTY

5901 Silverado Trail, Napa, California 94558 (707-253-7500). FOUNDED: 1978. ACREAGE: 139 acres. PRODUCTION: 20,000 cases. DISTRIBUTION: Nationwide; England. OWNER: Pine Ridge Realty and Investments, Inc. R. Gary Andrus. WINEMAKER: R. Gary Andrus. Tours and tasting Wednesday–Sunday 11 A.M.–3:30 P.M. Newsletter.

Gary and Nancy Andrus began acquiring vineyard land on the eastern slopes of the Napa Valley in the mid-1970s. In 1980 they moved to the valley and built their winery. The winery's name comes from a stand of pine trees on the top of a knoll terraced with vineyards.

WHITE

☆☆   1980 CHARDONNAY ($12.00) Stag's Leap District, Napa.
☆☆   1981 CHARDONNAY ($10.25) Oak Knoll District, Napa Valley. *Toasty, with nice, firm fruit.*
☆☆☆   1982 CHARDONNAY ($15.00) Oak Knoll District-Napa Valley. *Soft and lush; complex and snappy. Will age well.*
☆☆☆   1982 CHARDONNAY ($16.00) Stag's Leap Cuvée, Napa Valley. *Ripe, fresh, complex, with great fruit.*

☆☆☆ 1983 CHARDONNAY ($13.00) Oak Knoll Cuvée, Napa Valley. *Big, rich, vinous, oaky and fruity.*

☆☆☆ 1982 CHENIN BLANC ($6.50) Napa Valley. *Fresh, crisp and clean, with lovely ripe fruit.*

☆☆☆ 1983 CHENIN BLANC ($6.50) Yountville. *1.5% residual sugar. Crisp, fruity, balanced, attractive.*

☆☆☆ 1984 CHENIN BLANC ($6.75) Yountville Cuvée, Napa Valley. *1.4% residual sugar. Crisp, fruity, stunning. A classic.*

☆☆ 1983 SAUVIGNON BLANC ($8.00) Yountville Cuvée, Napa Valley. *24% Semillon. Rich, fat, dense, attractive.*

RED

☆☆ 1978 CABERNET SAUVIGNON ($7.50) Rutherford District, Napa Valley. *Balanced and well made. Clean, fruity, complex. Drink now.*

☆☆ 1979 CABERNET SAUVIGNON ($9.00) Rutherford District, Napa Valley. *Attractive, with a touch of weediness. Drink now.*

☆☆ 1980 CABERNET SAUVIGNON ($12.00) Rutherford District, Napa Valley. *Meaty, varietal, decent.*

☆☆☆ 1980 CABERNET SAUVIGNON ($17.00) Stag's Leap District, Napa. *Crisp yet remarkably deep, with complexity and style.*

☆☆☆ 1981 CABERNET SAUVIGNON ($13.00) Rutherford, Napa. *Elegant, deep, crisp, beautifully built. Drink 1986 and beyond.*

☆☆☆ 1981 CABERNET SAUVIGNON ($20.00) Stag's Leap Cuvée, Napa Valley. *Dense, rich, soft, complex, concentrated. Drink 1988.*

☆☆☆ 1982 CABERNET SAUVIGNON ($13.00) Rutherford Cuvée, Napa Valley. *10% Merlot, 5% Cabernet Franc. Clean, rich, structured, lovely. Drink 1988.*

☆☆ 1980 MERLOT ($10.00) Napa Valley. *15% Cabernet, 9% Malbec. Complex, clean, vegetal, well made.*

☆☆☆ 1981 MERLOT ($12.50) Napa Valley. *9% Cabernet, 5% Malbec. Fruity, clean, superb. Will age well.*

☆☆☆ 1982 MERLOT ($12.50) Napa Valley. *Lush, varietal, elegant.*

☆☆☆ 1982 MERLOT ($13.00) Selected Cuvée, Napa Valley. *Richly varietal, great structure. Drink 1987.*

Piper-Sonoma
SONOMA COUNTY

11447 Old Redwood Highway, Healdsburg, California 95448 (707-433-8843). FOUNDED: 1981. ACREAGE: None. PRODUCTION: 70,000 cases. DISTRIBUTION: Nationwide. OWNERS: Piper-Heidsieck and Renfield Importers of New York. WINEMAKER: Rodney Strong, winemaster; Michel LaCroix, chef du caves; Chris Markell, sparkling wine manager. Tours and tasting daily 10 A.M.– 5 P.M.

This modern sparkling wine facility is a joint venture between French Champagne maker Piper-Heidsieck and Renfield Importers of New York. The winery was built on the property of Sonoma Vineyards (see), another Renfield-controlled winery. The wine is made by a collaboration of Sonoma's winemaster, Rod Strong, and Piper's chef du caves, Michel LaCroix.

SPARKLING

☆☆☆ 1980 BLANC DE NOIR ($13.50) Sonoma. *All Pinot Noir. Classic—rich, full, deep, clean, with good acid.*

☆☆ 1981 BLANC DE NOIR ($15.25) Sonoma. *Fresh, fruity, clean, attractive.*

☆☆☆ 1980 BRUT ($14.00) Sonoma. *Crisp, elegant and rounded. Good fruit and finesse.*

☆☆☆ 1981 BRUT ($14.00) Sonoma. *Lovely, crisp and well balanced; elegant and well bred.*

☆☆☆   1982 BRUT ($14.00) Sonoma. *Balanced, elegant, fruity and refined. Very lovely.*
☆☆☆   1980 TETE DE CUVEE ($30.00) Sonoma County. *Intense and complex; a bit heavy.*

Pirtle's Weston Vineyards
MISSOURI

502 Spring, Weston, Missouri 64098 (816-386-5588). FOUNDED: 1977. ACREAGE: 13 acres. PRODUCTION: 4,000 cases. DISTRIBUTION: At winery. OWNERS: Dr. Elbert M. Pirtle; Patricia Pirtle, manager. WINEMAKERS: Dr. Elbert and Patricia Pirtle. Tours by appointment. Tasting summer: Monday–Saturday 10 A.M.–6 P.M., Sunday 12–6 P.M.; winter: Monday–Saturday 10 A.M.– 5 P.M., Sunday 12–5 P.M.

One day long ago Dr. Pirtle made some cherry wine. "It was so good! I just knew that he had talent as a winemaker," explains Mrs. Pirtle. Motivated by his wife's enthusiasm, Dr. Pirtle, a professor at the University of Missouri in Kansas City, began researching the wine history of Missouri. He was further encouraged when he learned that Missouri had been one of the largest wine-producing states before Prohibition. Buoyed by this discovery, Dr. Pirtle planted a vineyard and started a winery in what had once been an underground brewery. Before long, however, it became clear that the tired old cavern was about to cave in, so the Pirtles bought a nineteenth-century church. To add to the beauty and ecclesiastical atmosphere of the new winery, Dr. Pirtle filled the windows with stained glass of his own design.

Plane's Cayuga Vineyard
NEW YORK

Route 89, R.D. 2, Ovid, New York 14521 (607-869-5158). FOUNDED: 1980. ACREAGE: 47 acres. PRODUCTION: 4,500 cases. DISTRIBUTION: New York. OWNER: Plane family. Robert and Mary Plane, managers. WINEMAKER: Robert Plane; Christopher Stance, associate winemaker. Tours and tasting summer: daily 12–5 P.M.; September–May: weekends 12–4 P.M.

With the thoroughness and objectivity of scientists, the Planes charted and probed their vineyard site, trying to discover which varieties should be planted where. They now grow eight varieties, six white and two red. Their grapes reached mini-stardom among local wineries, and the name "Robert Plane Vineyard" began to appear on wine labels. The Planes turned the spotlight in their own direction when they started their own winery. Mary is the viticulturist, and Robert, having worked as the chairman of the Chemistry Department at Cornell University and as president of Clarkson University, is involved with the enological side of things.

WHITE

☆☆   1983 DUET ($4.00) 50% Ravat, 50% Cayuga, Finger Lakes. *1.8% residual sugar. Smoky, clean, fresh, fruity, lovely.*
☆☆   1982 CAYUGA ($4.00) Finger Lakes. *Grapey nose, fresh, off-dry, attractive.*
☆☆☆   1982 CHARDONNAY ($9.50) Finger Lakes. *Fragrant, varietal, subtle, clean, balanced.*

RED

1982 CHANCELLOR ($4.00) Estate, Finger Lakes. *Muddy and weedy but dry, decent, balanced.*

Planet of the Grapes
NAPA COUNTY

P.O. Box 11, St. Helena, California 94574 (707-963-8466). FOUNDED: 1981. ACREAGE: None. PRODUCTION: 400 cases. DISTRIBUTION: California. OWNERS: Bob Levy and Beverly Kinney. WINEMAKER: Bob Levy. No tours or tasting.

This "Planet" was formed at the home of Tom Rinaldi, winemaker at Duckhorn Vineyards. Tom, his wife, Beverly, and Bob Levy, winemaker at Rombauer Vineyards, started this project for fun, but "We just got carried away," says Tom. In 1981 the first Planet of the Grapes wine was made at Rombauer Vineyards. "We just want to make a small amount to sell to family and friends," says Bob Levy.

Point Loma Winery
SAN DIEGO COUNTY

3655 Poe Street, San Diego, California 92106 (619-224-1674). FOUNDED: 1980. ACREAGE: None. PRODUCTION: 200 cases. DISTRIBUTION: California. OWNERS: Kurt Mengel and Ron McClendon. WINEMAKERS: Kurt Mengel and Ron McClendon. No tours or tasting.

Kurt Mengel and Ron McClendon became home winemaking friends while they both worked for the City of San Diego. In 1980 they bonded Kurt's garage, and Ron sold his house to finance an enology degree at U.C. Davis, a decision that "went over real big with his wife and two kids," says Kurt. During Ron's two-year study, Kurt handled the winemaking while continuing to work for the local utilities. Ron graduated from Davis, resumed his winemaking responsibilities at Point Loma, and also became the winemaker for John Culbertson Winery (see).

POLO BRINDISI *see* E. & J. Gallo Winery

Pommeraie Vineyards
SONOMA COUNTY

10541 Cherry Ridge Road, Sebastopol, California 95472 (707-823-WINE). FOUNDED: 1979. ACREAGE: 5 acres. PRODUCTION: 2,000 cases. DISTRIBUTION: California and Hawaii. OWNERS: Ken and Arlene Dalton, and Bob and Norma Wiltermood. WINEMAKER: Ken Dalton. Tours and tasting on weekends by appointment.

Ken Dalton and Bob Wiltermood had been making wine at home together for years. At the same time they were both working in what Ken refers to as "middle management in the communication industry." Then Ken found a piece of property that had once been an apple orchard. It was a perfect place to build a small winery, "one that we could run by ourselves and for ourselves." Ken still works for the telephone company, and says "I wish I could quit, but they pay me too much." The winery is located in the heart of apple-growing country—thus the name "Pommeraie," which comes from the French word for apple orchard.

WHITE

☆ 1982 CHARDONNAY ($9.00) Alexander Valley. *Flabby, simple and slightly oxidized.*

RED

☆ 1979 CABERNET SAUVIGNON ($8.25) Sonoma. *Berried, thick and raisiny.*
☆☆ 1980 CABERNET SAUVIGNON ($9.00) Sonoma. *Raisiny, crisp, varietal, good fruit.*

Ponzi Vineyards
OREGON

Route 1, Box 842, Beaverton, Oregon 97007 (503-628-1227). FOUNDED: 1974. ACREAGE: 11 acres. PRODUCTION: 5,000 cases. DISTRIBUTION: Major market states. OWNERS: Richard and Nancy Ponzi. WINEMAKER: Richard Ponzi. Tours by appointment. Tasting weekends 12–5 P.M.

Not everyone finds amusement-park rides amusing. Before Dick Ponzi moved to Oregon in 1969, he designed rides for Disneyland. But after spinning tea cups and Matterhorn bobsleds, what else is there? Since Dick had come from a family of winemakers, all it took were a few enology courses at U.C. Davis and a tour of France and Italy to start him looking for a vineyard site. In 1969, the Ponzis settled in Portland, Oregon, where Dick taught engineering at the community college while he and Nancy planted vinifera on their lowland site. Despite the local belief that only Concord could grow in this area, the vineyards did nicely, and in 1974 Dick and Nancy opened a winery. Nancy, who focuses most of her attention on marketing, has inspired greater wine appreciation throughout the state with seminars, written articles, and organizations.

WHITE
O   1982 CHARDONNAY ($9.00) Willamette Valley, Oregon. *Very unattractive.*
O   1982 CHARDONNAY ($11.00) Reserve, Willamette Valley, Oregon. *The smells and flavors of spoiled apples.*

RED
   1981 PINOT NOIR ($10.00) Willamette Valley, Oregon. *Simple, thin.*
☆   1982 PINOT NOIR ($8.93) Willamette Valley, Oregon. *Clean, varietal, a trifle thin.*
   1982 PINOT NOIR ($12.00) Reserve, Oregon. *Odd flavors, dense.*

POPLAR *see* Château Bouchaine

Poplar Ridge Vineyards
NEW YORK

R.D. 1, Route 414, Valois, New York 14888 (607-582-6421). FOUNDED: 1981. ACREAGE: 22 acres. PRODUCTION: 5,000 cases. DISTRIBUTION: New York. OWNER: David Bagley, president. WINEMAKER: David Bagley. Tours and tasting May–November: daily 10 A.M.–5 P.M., Sunday 12–5 P.M.

Dave Bagley has made wine professionally for five different New York wineries. While working at Wagner Vineyards, he and his father started planting French-American hybrids on a farm near Lake Seneca. David left Wagner Vineyards in 1980 to begin construction of his own winery on the vineyard property. He and his dad designed a long, rectangular winery. Dave believes his white French hybrids rival vinifera wines in quality, but his style is not to make comparisons—he prefers to promote wine as an unpretentious pleasure.

WHITE
☆   1982 CAYUGA ($5.00) New York State.
☆   1982 VIDAL BLANC ($6.00) New York State. *3% residual sugar. Lush and fruity.*

Possum Trot Vineyards
INDIANA

8310 North Possum Trot Road, Unionville, Indiana 47468 (812-988-2694). FOUNDED: 1978. ACREAGE: 6 acres. PRODUCTION: 2,000 cases. DISTRIBUTION: At winery and local outlets.

OWNERS: Lee and Ben Sparks. WINEMAKER: Ben Sparks. Tours and tasting March—December: daily 10 A.M.—6 P.M.; January—February by appointment.

Lee and Ben Sparks seem to gain more energy each year. Now in their mid-60s, they thoroughly enjoy running their "mom and pop" operation and are involved in just about every wine organization around. Ben Sparks, past president of the Indiana Winegrowers' Guild, began experimenting with vineyards and winemaking after he retired from the Navy in 1968. Then, having learned from experiments and mistakes, Lee and Ben started making wine in the restored utility barn behind their home. They never tire of showing their winery to anyone who finds them, tucked away in the hills of Possum Trot Hollow. "Most of the people who drop by are surprised to find a good wine made in Indiana," says Lee.

ॐ

Post Winery
ARKANSAS

Route 1, Box 1, Altus, Arkansas 72821 (501-468-2741). FOUNDED: 1880. ACREAGE: 150 acres. PRODUCTION: 45,000 cases. DISTRIBUTION: Arkansas. OWNER: Post family. Matthew Post, president. WINEMAKER: Andrew Post. Tours summer: Monday—Saturday 9 A.M.—5 P.M.; winter by appointment. Tasting Monday—Saturday 9 A.M.—5 P.M.

This winery was born in the late nineteenth century when Jacob Post, a German immigrant, moved to Altus, where he began farming and making wine. His son and daughter-in-law, Joseph and Catherine, were dedicated winemakers as well. In fact Catherine "Grandma" Post was carted off to jail for making wine and serving it in her restaurant during Prohibition. The Post family had dealings with the law once again when James, Catherine's son, fought successfully for the Arkansas Native Wine Act, which excluded Arkansas wineries and growers from the tax imposed on out-of-state wines and fruit. Today the Post Winery is run by James's son Matthew, a deacon at St. Mary's parish in Altus, and his twelve children.

ॐ

Prager Winery and Port Works
NAPA COUNTY

1281 Lewelling Lane, St. Helena, California 94574 (707-963-3720). FOUNDED: 1979. ACREAGE: 0.33 acre. PRODUCTION: 4,000 cases. DISTRIBUTION: Major western market states. OWNERS: James and Imogene Prager. WINEMAKER: James Prager. Tours, tasting, and sales by appointment.

Like so many others, Jim Prager, an avid wine collector and wine lover, fell in love with the Napa Valley when he visited as a tourist. The idea of a winery and a home in this idyllic county became a preoccupation from his first visit in 1974 until his dream became a reality in 1977. Jim sold his insurance brokerage firm in Orange County and moved to the Napa Valley to start Prager Port Works. The winery specializes in ports mainly because Jim really enjoys them, although he feels that most ports are too sweet and too high in alcohol.

RED

1980 CABERNET SAUVIGNON ($10.00) Gamble Ranch, Napa Valley. *Overripe, volatile acidity, unappealing.*

FORTIFIED

1981 NOBLE COMPANION PORT ($10.50) Lot 1, Napa Valley. *Hot, rough, unpleasant.*

ॐ

Presque Isle Wine Cellars
PENNSYLVANIA

9440 Buffalo Road (U.S. Route 20), North East, Pennsylvania 16428 (814-725-1314). FOUNDED: 1964. ACREAGE: 20 acres. PRODUCTION: 1,200 cases. DISTRIBUTION: At winery and Pennsylvania. OWNERS: Doug and Marlene Moorhead. WINEMAKERS: Doug and Marlene Moorhead. Tours and tasting Tuesday–Saturday 8 A.M.–5 P.M.

Presque Isle Wine Cellars was founded by William Conners, a cabinetmaker who had made wine with his grandfather, and by Doug Moorhead, a pomologist and grape grower. They bought an old cow pasture and built a small winery. In addition, Doug started a retail mail-order winery supply business in Erie. The Moorheads sell their own bottled wine through this outlet, as well as supply home winemakers with juice, grapes, winemaking equipment, and chemicals.

RED

☆ 1980 CABERNET SAUVIGNON ($6.60) Pennsylvania. *15% Merlot, 10% Cabernet Franc. Light, vegetal, nicely structured.*

Preston Vineyards
SONOMA COUNTY

9282 West Dry Creek Road, Healdsburg, California 95448 (707-433-3372). FOUNDED: 1975. ACREAGE: 120 acres. PRODUCTION: 12,000 cases. DISTRIBUTION: California and other major market states. OWNER: Louis Preston. WINEMAKER: Thomas Farella. Tours, tasting, and retail sales by appointment.

Lou Preston, a San Franciscan with a master's degree in business from Stanford University, has one of the best vineyards in the Dry Creek Valley. He and his wife, Susan, have a number of varieties planted on their meticulously kept ranch, all of which are in demand among other wineries. The Prestons built their own winery in the late 1970s.

WHITE

☆☆☆ 1982 CHENIN BLANC ($6.00) Estate, Dry Creek Valley. *Fresh, snappy, clean and very nice.*

1983 CHENIN BLANC ($6.00) Estate, Dry Creek Valley. *Musty.*

☆☆☆ 1984 CHENIN BLANC ($6.00) Dry, Estate, Dry Creek Valley. *Crisp, balanced—what a Chenin Blanc should taste like.*

☆☆☆ 1982 FUME BLANC ($6.50) Cuvée de Fumé, Estate, Dry Creek Valley. *18% Chenin Blanc, 7% Semillon. Soft, fruity and round.*

☆☆ 1981 SAUVIGNON BLANC ($8.25) Sonoma.

☆☆☆ 1982 SAUVIGNON BLANC ($8.50) Estate, Dry Creek Valley. *Varietal and assertive, with great fruit and balance.*

☆☆ 1983 SAUVIGNON BLANC ($9.00) Estate, Dry Creek Valley. *Crisp, fresh, rounded, charming, but not as good as the '82.*

☆☆☆ 1984 SAUVIGNON BLANC ($6.75) Cuvée de Fumé, Estate, Dry Creek Valley. *19% Chenin Blanc, 6% Semillon. Charming, soft, round, fruity, varietal, clean, delightful.*

RED

☆☆☆ 1983 GAMAY BEAUJOLAIS ($5.00) Dry Creek Valley. *Fresh, snappy and simple. Charming.*

☆☆ 1984 GAMAY BEAUJOLAIS ($5.00) Estate, Dry Creek Valley. *Grapey, clean, fruity. Serve chilled.*

☆☆ 1981 PETITE SIRAH ($9.50) Estate, Petite Sirah-Syrah, Dry Creek Valley. *Spicy, lush and Rhone-like.*

1979 ZINFANDEL ($7.25) Estate, Dry Creek Valley, Sonoma.

☆☆☆ 1980 ZINFANDEL ($7.50) Estate, Dry Creek Valley, Sonoma. *Jammy, with great fruit.*

☆☆ 1980 ZINFANDEL ($8.00) Late Harvest, Dry Creek Valley. *2% residual sugar. Sweet, grapey and snappy. Interesting.*

☆☆ 1981 ZINFANDEL ($6.50) Dry Creek Valley. *Rich and berried, with good, firm acidity.*

☆☆ 1982 ZINFANDEL ($7.00) Dry Creek Valley. *Rich, berried, robust, balanced, attractive.*

☆☆☆ 1983 ZINFANDEL ($7.00) Sonoma. *Rich, full, berried, fruity, dense. Drink 1987.*

Preston Wine Cellars
WASHINGTON

502 East Vineyard Drive, Pasco, Washington 99301 (509-545-1990). FOUNDED: 1976. ACREAGE: 180 acres. PRODUCTION: 80,000 cases. DISTRIBUTION: Major market states. OWNERS: Bill and Joann Preston. WINEMAKER: Tomas Sans Souci. Tours and tasting daily 10 A.M.–5:30 P.M. Gift shop. Picnic facilities.

A one-time tractor dealer, Bill Preston bought 190 acres of desert-like land in the Columbia Valley as an investment and potential retirement home. He outfitted 50 acres with an effective sprinkler system and planted grapevines in hopes of increasing the value of his investment. In 1976, the year of his first crush, Bill's winemaker quit unexpectedly, leaving him with a winery full of fermenting wine. He high-tailed it to California to hire a replacement and came back with Rob Griffin, a U.C. Davis graduate who had worked at Buena Vista Winery. The combination of Bill's grapes and Rob's talent established Preston Wine Cellars as the state's largest, most successful family-run winery. In 1984 Rob left Preston Wine Cellars to become the winemaker at Hogue Cellars (see).

WHITE

1980 CHARDONNAY ($8.00) Washington. *Dull, lacking fruit.*

☆☆ 1983 CHENIN BLANC ($4.50) Washington. *2.2% residual sugar. Floral, varietal, balanced, fruity.*

O 1982 FUME BLANC ($6.95) Washington. *Oxidized.*

☆☆ 1983 COLUMBIA RIVER SAUVIGNON BLANC ($4.25) Washington. *Fruity, crisp.*

RED

☆ 1978 CABERNET SAUVIGNON ($7.50) Washington. *Clumsy and simple.*

Prince Michel Vineyards
VIRGINIA

200 Lovers Lane, Culpeper, Virginia 22701 (703-547-3707). FOUNDED: 1983. ACREAGE: 90 acres. PRODUCTION: 1,600 cases. DISTRIBUTION: Virginia and Washington D.C. OWNER: Partnership. Jean Leduca and Norman Martin. WINEMAKER: Yakim Hollerith. Tours available after December 1985. Call for information.

A Parisian and an American who worked for the same company decided to start a Virginia vineyard and winery. Before buying land and planting vines, they consulted Yakim Hollerith of Rapidan River Vineyards. They found a promising location at a 650-foot elevation in the foothills of the Blue Ridge Mountains—a site, they decided, that would be good for attracting customers as well as for growing grapes. While the winery was being built in 1983, they crushed their first vintage in a temporary building.

Private Stock Winery
IOWA

706 Allen, Boone, Iowa 50036 (515-432-8348). FOUNDED: 1977. ACREAGE: 10 acres. PRO-
DUCTION: 3,300 cases. DISTRIBUTION: Iowa. OWNERS: Thomas H. and Rose M. Larson.
WINEMAKER: Thomas H. Larson. Tours and tasting Monday–Saturday 10 A.M.–8 P.M. Gift shop.
Wine- and beermaking supplies. Seminars on winemaking and wine appreciation.

    Tom and Rose Larson were happy producing homemade wine for just their friends. Since both
had steady jobs—Tom was a plumber and Rose worked in a bookstore—they hardly needed the
extra work or worry, but, heeding their wine-loving friends, they became professional winemakers
anyway. They rented a facility for the first five years until they could buy their own winery building.
They now have the largest winery in Iowa, one of the very few using vinifera grapes. Big promoters
of wine appreciation, Rose and Tom give seminars and sell wine- and beermaking supplies in their
retail store.

Prudence Island Vineyards
RHODE ISLAND

Sunset Hill Farm, Prudence Island, Rhode Island 02872 (401-683-2452). FOUNDED: 1973.
ACREAGE: 17 acres. PRODUCTION: 1,000 cases. DISTRIBUTION: Rhode Island and Massa-
chusetts. OWNERS: William, Natalie C., and Nathanael Bacon. WINEMAKER: William Bacon.
Tours and tasting daily June–October: 10 A.M.–12, 2 P.M.–4 P.M., or by appointment.

    Once the kids had grown, Natalie and William Bacon moved from Connecticut to a large farm
in Rhode Island that had belonged to Natalie's family. William, who worked in industry most of
his life, wanted to be a farmer and grow grapes. It wasn't too long before William, at the urging
of local winemakers and grape growers, built an underground winery. William makes the wine,
Natalie "charms the customers," and their son Nathanael is the vineyard manager.

WHITE

  ☆☆   1982 CHARDONNAY ($9.75) Rhode Island. *Clean, fresh, lively.*

Pucci Winery
IDAHO

HCR 66, Box 812, Sandpoint, Idaho 83864 (208-263-5807). FOUNDED: 1982. ACREAGE: None.
PRODUCTION: 3,400 cases. DISTRIBUTION: Idaho and Washington. OWNERS: Eugene and
Nancy Pucci. WINEMAKER: Eugene Pucci. Tours and tasting Tuesday–Sunday 12–5 P.M.

    Construction superintendent Eugene "Skip" Pucci is a sixth-generation winemaker; his family
made wine in Italy before coming to the United States. While living in Idaho, Skip and his wife,
Nancy, would order a ton of grapes from California every year and make wine at home. Their
friends and family loved the wine and encouraged Skip to make more, and he finally decided to
build a winery. Still buying Zinfandel from California and other varieties from Washington, Skip
and Nancy have established a small family winery.

Quady Winery
MADERA COUNTY

13181 Road 24, Madera, California 93637 (209-673-8068). FOUNDED: 1977. ACREAGE: None.
PRODUCTION: 7,500 cases. DISTRIBUTION: Nationwide; Canada. OWNER: Andrew Quady.
WINEMAKER: Andrew Quady. Tours by appointment. Tasting and sales daily 8 A.M.–5 P.M.

Andrew Quady was working for Lodi Vintners (now Turner Winery) when a wine retailer asked him to make a few cases of port for his store. Happy to oblige, Andy made 600 cases of port from Amador County Zinfandel grapes. The retailer took 100 cases and Andy quickly sold the remaining 500 to other customers, who then came running back for more. To supply the demand, Andy built and bonded a 1,600-square-foot stucco winery in back of his home and began making Amador Zinfandel ports on the weekends. In 1981 Andy left his job with United Vintners to work full time in his own winery. A new and much expanded winery and tasting room was completed in early 1985.

FORTIFIED

☆☆☆ 1984 ELYSIUM ($11.00) California. *Spicy red fortified wine with lots of fruit and richness.*
☆☆☆ 1984 ESSENSIA ($11.00) California. *White aperitif fortified wine. Orange and apricot; fresh, clean, very attractive.*
 ☆☆ 1979 PORT ($9.00) California.
 ☆☆ 1982 PORT ($9.00) California. *Lush, smooth, attractive.*

QUAIL HILL *see* Fritz Cellars

Quail Ridge
NAPA COUNTY

1055 Atlas Peak Road, Napa, California 94558 (707-226-2278; 707-944-8128). FOUNDED: 1978. ACREAGE: 20 acres. PRODUCTION: 7,500 cases. DISTRIBUTION: Major market states. OWNERS: Elaine Wellesley and Leon Santoro. WINEMAKERS: Elaine Wellesley and Leon Santoro. Tours by appointment. Tasting summer: weekends 11 A.M.–3 P.M.

English-born Elaine Wellesley began making wine when she was a student at U.C. Davis (from which she was graduated with a degree in enology). She started Quail Ridge in 1978 with her late husband, Jesse Corallo, who handled the sales and marketing. When he died, Elaine brought in the valuable assistance of Leon Santoro, whose winemaking background includes Louis Martini and Stag's Leap Wine Cellars.

WHITE

  ☆ 1981 CHARDONNAY ($13.50) Sonoma.
☆☆☆ 1981 CHARDONNAY ($16.00) Napa Valley. *Vinous, complex, with good fruit and acidity. Drink now.*
☆☆☆ 1982 CHARDONNAY ($9.00) Sonoma. *Lemony, lush, clean, quite attractive.*
 ☆☆ 1982 CHARDONNAY ($14.00) Napa Valley. *Toasty, clean, pleasant.*
    1983 CHARDONNAY ($14.00) Napa Valley. *Dull, heavy, lacking fruit.*
 ☆☆ 1983 FRENCH COLOMBARD ($5.00) Napa Valley. *Dry, crisp, clean, lively.*

RED

☆☆☆ 1982 CABERNET SAUVIGNON ($13.00) Napa Valley. *Richly textured, ripe, well structured, lovely. Drink 1987.*

Quail Run Vintners
WASHINGTON

Morris Road, Route 2, Box 2287, Zillah, Washington 98953 (509-829-6235). FOUNDED: 1982. ACREAGE: 175 acres. PRODUCTION: 35,000 cases. DISTRIBUTION: Northwest states. OWNER:

Partnership. Stan Clarke, general manager. WINEMAKER: Wayne Marcil. Tours and tasting Monday–Saturday 10 A.M.–5 P.M., Sunday 12–5 P.M.

This ambitious, fast-growing winery was started by a friendly challenge. When Stan Clarke was a viticulturist at Château Ste. Michelle, he worked closely with growers in the area, helping them manage their vineyards. Four of these growers asked Stan if he could put together a convincing proposal and prospectus for a winery business. Stan's projections and cost analyses convinced eighteen investors, and Quail Run broke ground in 1982. Stan hired a college friend, Wayne Marcil, who used to work at Monterey Peninsula Winery, to be the winemaker. During the winery's first year, Wayne made 30,000 gallons of eight different wines; Stan expects production to increase to 100,000 gallons in the next two years.

WHITE

☆☆ 1982 WHITE TABLE WINE ($4.00) Washington. *60% Morio Muscat, 20% Gewürztraminer, 20% press wine. Soft and sweet.*

☆☆ 1983 WHITE TABLE WINE ($4.00) Yakima Valley. *66% Riesling, 33% Gewürztraminer. Fresh, clean, charming.*

☆☆ 1982 ALIGOTE ($5.50) Yakima. *Crisp, dry and attractive.*

1983 ALIGOTE ($5.50) Washington. *Dull, sour.*

☆☆ 1983 CHARDONNAY ($8.00) Yakima Valley. *Ripe, fresh, oaky, clean.*

☆☆ 1983 CHENIN BLANC ($6.00) Yakima Valley. *1.6% residual sugar. Fresh, fruity, attractive.*

☆☆☆ 1983 FUME BLANC ($6.30) La Caille de Fumé, Yakima Valley. *40% Sauvignon Blanc, 60% Semillon. Crisp, clean, fresh, super.*

☆ 1983 GEWURZTRAMINER ($4.75) Yakima Valley. *Soft, low varietal flavor.*

☆☆☆☆ 1982 JOHANNISBERG RIESLING ($6.00) Washington. *1.4% residual sugar. Ripe, fruity and amazingly delicate.*

☆☆☆ 1982 JOHANNISBERG RIESLING ($8.00) Limited Bottling, Yakima Valley, Washington. *2.1% residual sugar. Lush, sweet and clean, with a long finish.*

☆☆☆ 1983 JOHANNISBERG RIESLING ($5.00) Washington. *Super. Crisp, fruity, clean.*

☆☆☆ 1982 MORIO MUSCAT ($5.50) Yakima. *3% residual sugar. Spicy and fresh.*

☆☆ 1983 MORIO MUSCAT ($5.30) Yakima Valley. *3% residual sugar.*

☆ 1983 SAUVIGNON BLANC ($7.00) Reserve, Lot 2, Yakima Valley. *Lemony, acidic.*

☆☆☆ 1982 WHITE RIESLING ($5.00) Mahre, Yakima Valley. *3.2% residual sugar. Botrytis. Tart, fruity, lovely.*

RED

☆ 1982 LEMBERGER ($5.50) Yakima. *Snappy, clean and fruity.*

Quarry Hill
PENNSYLVANIA

R.D. 2, Box 168, Shippenburg, Pennsylvania 17257 (717-776-3411). FOUNDED: 1981. ACREAGE: 4 acres. PRODUCTION: 1,000 cases. DISTRIBUTION: Pennsylvania. OWNER: Gene Cromer. WINEMAKER: Gene Cromer. Tours and tasting at winery Wednesday–Sunday 1 P.M.–6 P.M., or at 133 High Street, Carlisle, Wednesday–Sunday 12–6 P.M.

Gene Cromer retired from the U.S. Department of Defense and moved back to his farm in Pennsylvania to grow grapes and make wine. He planted French-American hybrids and native American varieties, using the large cement-block building on the farm for his winery. Since he grows fruit as well as grapes, Gene also makes fruit wines.

Quilceda Creek Vintners
WASHINGTON

5226 Machias Road, Snohomish, Washington 98290 (206-568-2389). FOUNDED: 1978. ACREAGE: None. PRODUCTION: 400 cases. DISTRIBUTION: At winery. OWNERS: Alex P. and Jeanette P. Golitzen. WINEMAKERS: Alex P. Golitzen and André Tchelistcheff. Tours by appointment.

Alex Golitzin, a chemical engineer, is devoted to Cabernet Sauvignon. In the early 1970s his uncle, legendary winemaker André Tchelistcheff, suggested that he might try making a little wine at home. When a little became a lot, André continued to help Alex by giving him leads on good sources for Cabernet grapes. After a few years of production in Alex's garage, the winery moved into a new wooden building across from his house. Alex makes only Cabernet and intends to keep it that way. He is the winery's sole employee.

RED

☆☆☆ 1979 CABERNET SAUVIGNON ($12.50) Washington. *Fresh and crisp, with new oak and good fruit. Drink 1986.*

☆ 1980 CABERNET SAUVIGNON ($12.50) Washington. *Somewhat weedy but lush and quite decent.*

Qupe
SANTA BARBARA COUNTY

Los Olivos, California 93441 (805-688-2477). FOUNDED: 1982. ACREAGE: None. PRODUCTION: 3,100 cases. DISTRIBUTION: California. OWNER: Partnership. Bob Lindquist, general manager. WINEMAKER: Bob Lindquist. No tours or tasting.

Bob Lindquist learned how to make wine when he was a salesman at Zaca Mesa Winery, where he had the opportunity to do some cellar work as well. After a few vintages, he leased space at Zaca Mesa, bought his own barrels, and made his own wine in 1982 and 1983. He has since moved his winemaking to Los Vineros Winery, but he hopes to have his own facility by 1986. A lover of French Rhone wines, Bob hopes to produce similar wines in California.

WHITE

☆☆ 1984 VIN BLANC ($6.00) Santa Barbara. *Nearly equal amounts of Chardonnay, Pinot Blanc and Chenin Blanc.*

☆☆ 1983 CHARDONNAY ($10.00) Sierra Madre, Santa Barbara. *Crisp, clean, lush, richly balanced but heavy.*

BLANC DE NOIR

☆☆ 1983 PINOT NOIR ($6.00) Vin Gris, Santa Barbara. *70% Pinot Noir, 30% Chardonnay. Tangy, with rich oak and clean fruit.*

RED

☆ 1982 SYRAH ($7.00) Paso Robles. *Spicy; balanced but vegetal.*

☆☆☆ 1983 SYRAH ($7.50) Central Coast. *Crisp, clean, fresh, Rhone-like, fruity and very charming.*

A. Rafanelli Winery
SONOMA COUNTY

4685 West Dry Creek Road, Healdsburg, California 95448 (707-433-1385). FOUNDED: 1972. ACREAGE: 30 acres. PRODUCTION: 4,000 cases. DISTRIBUTION: California, Massachusetts,

New York, Texas, and Washington. OWNER: Americo Rafanelli. WINEMAKER: Americo Rafanelli. Tours and tasting by appointment.

Behind the white house sits a tidy redwood barn where Americo Rafanelli makes red wines like they "used to in the old days": fermenting it in small redwood tanks, using only the natural yeast of his vineyards, pressing in a small basket press, and leaving his wines unfiltered and unfined.

RED

☆☆☆   1980 ZINFANDEL ($6.25) Dry Creek Valley, Sonoma. *Clean and crisply fruity.*

Ranchita Oaks Winery
SAN LUIS OBISPO COUNTY

Box 4790, Estrella Route, San Miguel, California 93451 (209-369-0900). FOUNDED: 1979. ACREAGE: 50 acres. PRODUCTION: 6,000 cases. DISTRIBUTION: California and Nebraska. OWNER: Ronald F. Bergstrom. WINEMAKER: Ronald F. Bergstrom. OTHER LABEL: Cross Canyon. Tours by appointment.

Ron Bergstrom, a salesman for Kaiser Steel, wanted to try his hand at farming. He and his wife, Mae, bought a barley field and, with the help of their six daughters, worked weekends to plant their first twenty acres of grapes. Three years and fifty planted acres later, they began to sell grapes to local wineries. "We started the winery in 1979 simply because we didn't want to be at the mercy of other wineries," says Mae. Ron, who also owns his own industrial supply business in Lodi, shares the vineyard work with his son-in-law, Michael Morris. "We also hope that our daughters will become more involved," says Mae.

BLANC DE NOIR

☆☆   1982 CROSS CANYON WHITE ZINFANDEL ($4.25) San Luis Obispo. *Crisp, clean, pleasant.*

RED

       1979 CABERNET SAUVIGNON ($8.50) Estate, San Luis Obispo. *Dull, lifeless.*
☆   1979 PETITE SIRAH San Luis Obispo. *Rich, earthy, lacking finesse.*
☆   1979 ZINFANDEL ($7.00) San Miguel.
☆   1980 CROSS CANYON ZINFANDEL ($4.25) San Luis Obispo.
       1980 ZINFANDEL ($6.50) San Luis Obispo. *Vegetal, earthy, clumsy.*

Rancho de Philo
SAN BERNARDINO COUNTY

10050 Wilson Avenue, Alta Loma, California 91701 (714-987-4208). FOUNDED: 1975. ACREAGE: 16 acres. PRODUCTION: 200 cases. DISTRIBUTION: Local. OWNER: Philo Biane. WINEMAKER: Philo Biane. Tours by appointment.

Philo Biane, the chairman of the board of Brookside Vineyard, had always wanted to develop a sherry solera, but he knew such a venture was economically unsound. After retirement, however, he started twelve soleras of fifteen barrels each—18,000 gallons in all. Each year, new wine is added to the top of the solera and mature sherry is removed from the bottom barrels. The average age of these cream sherries is eighteen years.

Rancho Sisquoc Winery
SANTA BARBARA COUNTY

Foxen Canyon Road, Santa Maria, California 93454 (805-937-3616). FOUNDED: 1977. ACREAGE: 220 acres. PRODUCTION: 3,000 cases. DISTRIBUTION: At winery and local outlets. OWNER: Flood Ranch Company. Harold G. Pfeiffer, general manager. WINEMAKER: Harold G. Pfeiffer. Tours Monday–Saturday 10 A.M.–4 P.M. Picnic facilities.

The 36,000-acre Flood Ranch in Santa Maria was home to cattle, wheat, alfalfa, and beans, but manager Harold G. Pfeiffer needed to diversify his crops even further. "Around 1968, Christian Brothers and Almadén were beginning to snoop around this area, looking for grape-growing sites," says Pfeiffer. "So we planted a test plot and in 1970 were one of the first to plant a vineyard in the Santa Maria Valley." Pfeiffer began attending winemaking classes at U.C. Davis, and in 1972 he made the first experimental wines from Rancho Sisquoc grapes. Now the winery grows and sells all the major premium varietals. "We are really a very small winery with a very large vineyard," says Pfeiffer.

Rapazzini Winery
SANTA CLARA COUNTY

Highway 101, Box 247, Gilroy, California 95021 (408-842-5649). FOUNDED: 1962. ACREAGE: None. PRODUCTION: 25,000 cases. DISTRIBUTION: California and other markets. OWNERS: Jon P. and Sandra K. Rapazzini. WINEMAKERS: Jon and Sandra Rapazzini. Tours and tasting daily 9 A.M.–6 P.M.

The late Angelo Rapazzini, an immigrant from Milan who had run a bakery in San Jose, and his sons Jon and Vic, started making fruit, dessert, and varietal wines in the old Perelli-Minetti Winery near Gilroy. The original winery was completely destroyed by fire in 1980; the losses were so extensive that the Rapazzinis hesitated to start again, but after almost three years of rebuilding the new winery opened in 1982. Jon and his partner, Sandra, are the courageous ones who have kept the winery going.

WHITE

☆☆ 1982 CHARDONNAY ($8.00) Special Reserve, Santa Clara. *Decent. Good fruit, clean and attractive.*

ROSE

1982 GEWURZTRAMINER ($6.50) Santa Clara. *Dull.*

RED

☆☆ 1980 CABERNET SAUVIGNON ($8.00) Special Reserve, Sonoma. *Coarse and raisiny but attractive.*

FLAVORED

☆ NV GARLIC WINE ($4.25) Santa Clara. *Fresh garlic flavor mixed with Chenin Blanc. Weird.*

Rapidan River Vineyards
VIRGINIA

Route 4, Box 199, Culpeper, Virginia 22701 (703-399-1855). FOUNDED: 1978. ACREAGE: 50 acres. PRODUCTION: 5,000 cases. DISTRIBUTION: Virginia and Washington D.C. OWNER: Dr. Gerhard Guth. WINEMAKER: Johannes Haeussleng. Tours and tasting daily 10 A.M.–5 P.M.

Dr. Gerhard Guth, a surgeon who owns 2,500 acres of land southwest of Washington D.C., brought an enologist over from Germany in 1976 to inspect and evaluate the grape-growing potential of his Island View Farm. At this point, the doctor was interested in winemaking only as a hobby, but by the time his first five acres were planted in 1978 he had decided to build a winery as well. For the first few years of production the doctor brought over consultants from Germany or France to oversee the crushes. In 1984 he managed to convince Johannes Haeussleng to stay on as the full-time winemaker.

WHITE

☆☆   1983 WHITE RIESLING ($7.00) Semi-Dry, Virginia.
☆   1983 WHITE RIESLING ($7.00) Virginia.

Ravenswood
SONOMA COUNTY

21415 Broadway, Sonoma, California 95476 (707-938-1960). FOUNDED: 1976. ACREAGE: None. PRODUCTION: 5,000 cases. DISTRIBUTION: 8 states. OWNER: Ravenswood Limited. Joel Peterson and W. Reed Foster. WINEMAKERS: Joel Peterson and John Kemble, Jr. Tours, tasting, and retail sales by appointment.

Joel Peterson works as a medical technologist at Sonoma Valley Hospital when he isn't making wine at Ravenswood; his medical background includes cancer research at Mt. Zion Hospital in San Francisco. His interest in winemaking was inspired by his wine-loving father and a trip to Europe after graduation. Through his father, Joel met Reed Foster, a retired real estate broker and longtime president of the San Francisco Vintners Club. After working with Joseph Swan Winery in 1974, Joel began talking about starting his own winery, and Reed was anxious to listen. Confident in Joel's ability, Reed formed the Ravenswood partnership.

RED

☆☆☆   1978 CABERNET SAUVIGNON ($9.00) California. *Rich, varietal, clean, intense, lovely. Drink 1986 and beyond.*
☆☆   1978 CABERNET SAUVIGNON ($10.50) Madrona, El Dorado. *Spicy, sweet oak, varietal. Awkward now; drink 1986.*
☆   1979 CABERNET SAUVIGNON ($8.50) California. *Coarse and disjointed. Aging probably won't help.*
      1980 CABERNET SAUVIGNON ($10.00) Sonoma. *Awkward, vegetal, heavy and unattractive.*
☆☆   1982 CABERNET SAUVIGNON ($11.00) Sonoma. *Balanced, varietal, pleasant.*
☆   1978 ZINFANDEL ($8.00) Madrona, El Dorado. *Intense, sweet, late harvest style.*
      1978 ZINFANDEL ($8.50) California. *Late harvest style. Woody, hot, overbearing.*
☆☆   1979 ZINFANDEL ($6.75) Sonoma. *Agressive, big and intense. Clean but powerful. Drink 1986.*
☆☆   1979 ZINFANDEL ($8.00) California. *Intense, rich, berried, late harvest style. Drink 1986.*
☆☆   1980 ZINFANDEL ($9.00) Sonoma. *Intense, high extract, tannic, heavy.*
☆☆☆   1981 ZINFANDEL ($6.50) Dry Creek Benchland, Sonoma. *Rich raspberry, deep, woody. Intense but very likable.*
☆☆   1981 ZINFANDEL ($8.50) Bogensen Vineyard, Sonoma. *Concentrated, berried, dark and rich. Drink 1986.*
☆☆☆   1982 ZINFANDEL ($10.00) Limited Edition, Vickerson, Napa Valley. *Big, lush, concentrated, spicy. Drink now.*
☆☆☆   1982 ZINFANDEL ($11.00) Etched Bottle, Dickerson, Napa Valley. *Lush, rich, complex and lovely.*

Martin Ray Vineyards
SANTA CLARA COUNTY

22000 Mount Eden Road, Saratoga, California 95070 (408-867-7118). FOUNDED: 1946. ACREAGE: 4 acres. PRODUCTION: 4,000 cases. DISTRIBUTION: Nationwide. OWNER: Martin Ray Vineyards, Inc. Kenston E. Brooks, president; Douglas C. Fletcher, Sr., vice president. WINEMAKER: Paul Wofford. Tours and tasting by appointment.

Martin Ray was called devil by some, genius by others. After he sold Paul Masson Vineyards (see) in 1943, he bought two plots on Mount Eden. In 1960 he became involved in a strident court battle over the new winery with a group of investors, most of whom were doctors. The conflict ended with the property being split in two; Martin Ray retained his part and the Mount Eden (see) group retained theirs. Ray died in 1976, and after a brief hiatus stepson Peter Martin Ray revived the winery. Young, efficient Ken Brooks is now in charge, producing wines from both estate and purchased grapes.

WHITE

☆☆   NV CHARDONNAY ($8.50) Napa Valley. *Decent, earthy, barrel fermented, pleasant.*

☆☆☆   1981 CHARDONNAY ($16.00) Winery Lake, Carneros District-Napa. *Big, fat, toasty and intense.*

☆☆☆   1981 CHARDONNAY ($18.00) Dutton, Sonoma. *Toasty and rich, with a hint of vanillin and age complexity.*

☆☆☆☆   1982 CHARDONNAY ($14.00) Dutton Ranch, Sonoma. *Big yet elegant, balanced, aristocratic, stunning.*

☆☆☆   1982 CHARDONNAY ($15.00) Santa Cruz Mountains. *Fat, rich fruit and oak, with a lovely firm acidity.*

☆   1983 CHARDONNAY ($14.50) Dutton Ranch, Sonoma. *Earthy, austere, lacking fruit. A big disappointment after the '82.*

SPARKLING

☆☆   NV SPECIAL RESERVE CUVEE 80 ($25.00) California. *Heavy, rich, intense.*

RED

☆   NV CABERNET/MERLOT ($8.00) Napa Valley. *39% Merlot. Oaky, hot, decent.*

☆☆   1978 CABERNET SAUVIGNON ($9.00) Stelzner, Napa Valley.

☆   1979 CABERNET SAUVIGNON ($14.00) Saratoga District, Santa Cruz Mountains. *Intense, dark and deep, with several off flavors. Not much future.*

☆☆   1980 CABERNET SAUVIGNON ($18.00) Stelzner, Napa Valley. *Jammy, grapey and rich, with nice fruit.*

☆☆☆☆   1981 CABERNET SAUVIGNON ($16.50) Steltzner, Napa Valley. *5% Merlot. Rich, clean flavors; extraordinary. Drink 1987.*

☆☆☆   1979 MERLOT ($16.50) Winery Lake, Napa Valley. *Earthy, toasty, intense, big. Will age well.*

☆   1980 MERLOT ($10.00) Winery Lake, Napa Valley. *Odd, weedy, overbearing.*

☆☆☆   1981 MERLOT ($16.00) Winery Lake, Napa Valley. *Rich, deep, clean and complex. Should age gracefully.*

☆☆☆   1982 MERLOT ($18.00) Winery Lake, Napa Valley. *Rich, minty, clean, complex, lovely. Drink 1988.*

☆☆☆   1976 PINOT NOIR ($35.00) Winery Lake, Napa Valley. *Heavy and raisiny; deep and balanced.*

☆   1979 PINOT NOIR ($9.00) Winery Lake, Napa Valley. *Meaty, decent but lacking finesse.*

☆☆   1980 PINOT NOIR ($9.00) Winery Lake, Napa Valley. *Lush, deep, complex, super.*

☆☆☆   1981 PINOT NOIR ($14.00) Winery Lake, Carneros District-Napa. *Rich, intense, toasty and good. Fine aging potential.*

Raymond Vineyard & Cellar
NAPA COUNTY

849 Zinfandel Lane, St. Helena, California 94574 (707-963-3141). FOUNDED: 1970. ACREAGE: 80 acres. PRODUCTION: 50,000 cases. DISTRIBUTION: Nationwide. OWNER: Corporation. Roy Raymond, Sr., Roy Raymond, Jr., and Walter Raymond. WINEMAKER: Walter Raymond. Tours and tasting by appointment Monday–Friday 10 A.M.–4 P.M.

Roy Raymond, Sr., was the winemaker at Beringer until it was sold in 1970 to a division of Nestlé. He then bought 90 acres south of St. Helena and began growing grapes with his sons Roy Jr., who had been vineyard manager at Beringer, and Walter, who had been assistant winemaker there. In 1980 a permanent winery structure was built on the property. Now Walt makes the wine, the younger Roy manages the vineyards, and their father keeps an eye on it all.

WHITE

☆ 1983 VINTAGE SELECT WHITE ($4.25) California. *Grassy, heavy, decent.*
☆ 1980 CHARDONNAY ($12.00) Estate, Napa Valley. *Vinous nose, crisp but flabby in the middle.*
☆ 1981 CHARDONNAY ($12.00) Napa Valley. *Lush, simple, a trifle sweet.*
☆ 1982 CHARDONNAY ($8.50) California. *Earthy, soft, a bit dull. O.K.*
☆ 1982 CHARDONNAY ($12.00) Napa Valley. *Soft, decent. Not enough acidity or fruit.*
☆☆ 1983 CHARDONNAY ($8.50) California. *Clean, simple, fresh, decent.*
☆☆ 1983 CHARDONNAY ($12.00) Napa Valley. *Toasty, rich, heavy, clean, fleshy, with nice oak and some fruit.*
☆☆ 1982 CHENIN BLANC ($6.00) Napa Valley. *Fresh, clean, dry and appealing.*
☆☆ 1983 CHENIN BLANC ($6.00) Napa Valley. *Crisp, oily, clean.*
☆☆☆ 1983 FUME BLANC ($7.50) Napa Valley. *Crisp, rich, balanced, lovely.*
☆☆ 1983 JOHANNISBERG RIESLING ($5.50) Napa Valley. *1% residual sugar. Varietal, fresh, attractive.*

RED

☆☆☆ 1977 CABERNET SAUVIGNON ($18.00) Estate, Napa Valley. *10% Merlot. Herbal, rich, fruity, quite lovely. Aging nicely.*
☆☆ 1978 CABERNET SAUVIGNON ($8.50) Napa Valley. *20% Merlot. Balanced, attractive. Drink now.*
☆☆ 1979 CABERNET SAUVIGNON ($11.00) Estate, Napa Valley. *Rich and berried; raisiny and ripe.*
☆☆ 1980 CABERNET SAUVIGNON ($11.00) Estate, Napa Valley. *Herbal, soft, charming. A delightful wine for drinking now.*
☆☆ 1981 CABERNET SAUVIGNON ($8.25) Napa Valley. *Clean, attractive. Drink now.*
☆☆☆ 1981 CABERNET SAUVIGNON ($12.00) Napa Valley. *18% Merlot. Soft, rich, balanced—Raymond's best yet. Drink now.*
☆☆ 1979 ZINFANDEL ($6.00) Napa Valley. *Good structure, clean fruit, aging possibilities. Drink 1986.*

REDFORD CELLARS *see* Amity Vineyards

Reis Winery
MISSOURI

Route 4, Box 133, Licking, Missouri 65542 (314-674-3763). FOUNDED: 1978. ACREAGE: 7 acres. PRODUCTION: 900 cases. DISTRIBUTION: Missouri. OWNER: Val Reis. WINEMAKER:

Val Reis. Tours and tasting summer: Monday–Saturday 9:30 A.M.–dusk, Sunday 12–6 P.M.; winter: daily 10 A.M.–5 P.M.

Val Reis grows grapes and makes wine in a small winery next to his house. This all began as a hobby; Val says his inclination toward grapes and wine comes partially from his German heritage. He produces twelve wines—varietals and blends—selling most of them right at the winery. Val never wants to make more than 9,000 gallons of wine a year.

ॐ

Renault Winery
NEW JERSEY

Road 3, Box 21B, Egg Harbor City, New Jersey 08215 (609-965-2111). FOUNDED: 1864. ACREAGE: 100 acres. PRODUCTION: 50,000 cases. DISTRIBUTION: New Jersey, Pennsylvania, and Iowa. OWNER: Joseph P. Milza. WINEMAKER: William Bacon; Tien Lee, enologist. Tours and tasting Monday–Saturday 10 A.M.–5 P.M., Sunday 12–5 P.M. Restaurant.

This winery is named after Louis Renault, the Frenchman who built it in 1864. In 1977, after a winemaking family sold it to a corporation, the winery was bought by Joseph Milza, a newspaper publisher. While working at the *Daily Observer*, Joe had written a little about wine, which is how he found out about the Renault Winery. He turned its buildings into a tourist attraction, converting the old cellars and building a maze of shops and rooms for entertaining. But Joe's pride and joy is the restaurant, where customers can sip wine and dine while sitting in what used to be a redwood wine tank.

ॐ

Renick Winery
WISCONSIN

5600 Gordon Road, Sturgeon Bay, Wisconsin 54235 (414-743-7329). FOUNDED: 1982. ACREAGE: 80 acres of fruit, 2 acres of vines. PRODUCTION: 5,000 cases. DISTRIBUTION: Wisconsin. OWNER: Roger Louer. WINEMAKER: Roger Louer. Tours and tasting summer: daily 10 A.M.– 4 P.M.

Roger Louer was running his own wine distributorship in Oakland, California, while trying to find an affordable piece of land in Napa. Discouraged by high real estate prices, he moved to Wisconsin and bought an orchard. After three years of cherries and apples, he planted a few acres of vines and started making wines in a rented building on the highway. Roger makes apple and cherry wines, blends of fruit and grape wines, and non-alcoholic sparkling fruit and grape wines. One of his biggest sellers is a blend of cherry wine and California Thompson grape juice. Although he uses all the grapes from his own little vineyard, most of his grapes are shipped from California.

ॐ

Richardson Vineyards
SONOMA COUNTY

2711 Knob Hill Road, Sonoma, California 95476 FOUNDED: 1980. PRODUCTION: 2,500 cases. DISTRIBUTION: 5 states. OWNER: Partnership. Richardson family, Al Wighton, and Robert Weishit. WINEMAKER: Dennis Richardson. No tours or tasting.

After working for several years as a "peon" in large wineries, Dennis Richardson decided that he could work just as hard and make just as little money if he had his own winery. A partnership was formed between Dennis's family, his old school chum Bob Weishit, and Bob's college buddy

Al Wighton. The winery, a small building near the Richardson home, produced 1,000 gallons of wine the first year. Now Bob and Dennis work overtime and make very little money, but at least they are working for themselves.

WHITE

☆ 1983 CHARDONNAY ($12.00) Sonoma Valley.
   NV SAUVIGNON BLANC ($7.50) Lot 812, Sonoma Valley.
O 1983 SAUVIGNON BLANC ($6.75) Sonoma Valley. *Awful.*

RED

☆ 1980 CABERNET SAUVIGNON ($10.00) Sonoma Valley. *Dull, lacking fruit.*
☆☆☆ 1981 CABERNET SAUVIGNON ($7.50) Sonoma Valley. *Crisp, attractive, clean, well made. Drink now through 1988.*
☆☆ 1982 CABERNET SAUVIGNON ($10.00) Sonoma Valley. *Intense, fruity, attractive. Drink 1986.*
☆☆ 1981 PINOT NOIR ($10.00) Sonoma Valley, Carneros. *Crisp, clean, varietal, attractive.*
☆☆ 1983 PINOT NOIR ($11.75) Sonoma Valley-Los Carneros. *Pleasant, clean, attractive.*
☆☆☆ 1981 ZINFANDEL ($8.50) Sonoma Valley. *Solid, clean and dense. Drink now.*
☆☆ 1982 ZINFANDEL ($6.75) Napa Valley. *Snappy, clean, varietal, attractive. Drink 1986.*

Ridge Vineyards
SANTA CLARA COUNTY

17100 Monte Bello Road, Cupertino, California 95014 (408-867-3233). FOUNDED: 1959. ACREAGE: 50 acres. PRODUCTION: 40,000 cases. DISTRIBUTION: Nationwide; 7 foreign markets. OWNERS: Dave Bennion, Paul Draper, Hew Crane, and Charles Rosen. WINEMAKER: Paul Draper. No tours. Tasting Saturday 11 A.M.–3 P.M.. Retail sales Wednesday 11 A.M.–3 P.M.

Dave Bennion and three Stanford Research Institute associates founded this mountaintop winery in 1959. The idea was to make wines in as natural a way as possible. Winemaker Paul Draper, who came on board in 1969, uses wild yeasts and very little fining or filtration. Ridge's wines are nearly all red, with an emphasis on Zinfandel and Cabernet Sauvignon. Microbiologist Leo McCloskey (see Felton-Empire Vineyards) monitors the winemaking so that, despite the "natural" techniques employed, Ridge wines are very rarely anything less than clean and fresh.

WHITE

1980 CHARDONNAY ($12.00) Monte Bello, Santa Cruz Mountains. *Clumsy, fat and ugly. They should stick to red wines.*

BLANC DE NOIR

☆☆ 1983 WHITE ZINFANDEL ($5.75) California. *Crisp, fresh, varietal.*
☆ 1984 WHITE ZINFANDEL ($5.75) California. *Off-dry, rich, varietal, earthy.*

RED

☆☆ 1980 CLARET ($8.50) Langtry Road, Spring Mountain, Napa Valley, California. *57% Zinfandel, 33% Petite Sirah, 10% Carignane. Brambly, interesting.*
☆☆☆ NV CABERNET SAUVIGNON ($9.50) Jimsomare, Santa Cruz Mountains. *Blend of 1979 and 1982. Fruity, clean and snappy. Drink now.*
☆☆☆ 1968 CABERNET SAUVIGNON ($70.00) Monte Bello, Santa Cruz. *Remarkable. Complex, beautifully structured, with years to go.*
☆☆☆☆ 1971 CABERNET SAUVIGNON ($75.00) Monte Bello, Santa Cruz Mountains. *Rich, earthy, complex bottle bouquet; gentle, great fruit.*

☆☆☆ 1972 CABERNET SAUVIGNON ($60.00) Monte Bello, Santa Cruz Mountains. *Soft and rich, with less structure than the '71.*

☆☆ 1976 CABERNET SAUVIGNON ($45.00) Monte Bello, Santa Cruz Mountains. *Crisp, high acid, lacking depth.*

☆ 1977 CABERNET SAUVIGNON ($24.00) York Creek, Napa Valley. *Lush, fat, deep but no finesse or varietal distinction.*

☆☆ 1977 CABERNET SAUVIGNON ($40.00) Monte Bello, Santa Cruz Mountains. *Earthy, brittle; dried fruit and hard edged. Drink 1987.*

☆☆☆ 1978 CABERNET SAUVIGNON ($30.00) Monte Bello, Santa Cruz Mountains. *Smooth, intense yet soft and earthy, very complex. Drink 1988.*

☆☆ 1979 CABERNET SAUVIGNON ($15.00) York Creek, Spring Mountain, Napa Valley. *12% Merlot. Full, herbal, oaky and rich. Drink 1987.*

☆☆ 1980 CABERNET SAUVIGNON ($12.00) York Creek, Napa. *15% Merlot. Rich, lush, tannic. Drink 1986 and beyond.*

☆☆ 1980 CABERNET SAUVIGNON ($27.50) Monte Bello, Santa Cruz Mountains. *Great fruit and structure. Stunning but muddy. Drink 1988.*

☆☆ 1981 CABERNET SAUVIGNON ($7.50) Mendocino. *Decent, clean but nothing special. Drink now.*

☆ 1981 CABERNET SAUVIGNON ($10.50) Tepusquet, Santa Maria Valley. *Earthy, vegetal, a bit dirty.*

☆☆ 1981 CABERNET SAUVIGNON ($12.00) Spring House, Napa. *8% Merlot. Toasty, crisp, lovely fruit. Drink now through 1988.*

☆☆ 1981 CABERNET SAUVIGNON ($12.00) 28% Monte Bello, 72% Jimsomare, Santa Cruz Mountains. *Clean, rich, decent.*

☆☆☆ 1981 CABERNET SAUVIGNON ($12.00) York Creek, Napa Valley. *Crisp, clean, lovely structure. Drink 1987.*

☆☆☆ 1981 CABERNET SAUVIGNON ($27.50) Monte Bello, Santa Cruz Mountains. *Rich, complex and lush, with enormous aging potential. Drink 1988.*

☆☆☆ 1982 CABERNET SAUVIGNON ($12.00) Beatty, Howell Mountain. *Earthy, rich, tangy, structured. Drink 1988.*

☆☆ 1979 PETITE SIRAH ($9.00) Devil's Hill, York Creek, Napa Valley. *Deep, dark, rich and tannic. Drink 1986.*

☆☆ 1980 PETITE SIRAH ($7.50) Devil's Hill, York Creek, Napa. *Astringent, clean, fruity. Drink 1986.*

☆☆☆ 1980 PETITE SIRAH ($9.00) California. *Peppery, crisp, astringent, clean and rich. Drink 1986.*

☆☆ 1981 PETITE SIRAH ($8.50) York Creek, California. *15% Zinfandel. Dark, round, fruity, attractive.*

☆☆ 1981 PETITE SIRAH ($9.00) California. *15% Zinfandel. Round, deep, intense, fresh. Drink 1987.*

☆ 1975 ZINFANDEL ($20.00) Geyserville. *Past its prime.*

☆ 1978 ZINFANDEL ($7.50) Late Harvest, Esola, Amador.

☆ 1978 ZINFANDEL ($7.50) Paso Robles, Dusi Ranch, San Luis Obispo.

☆ 1978 ZINFANDEL ($8.50) York Creek, Napa County. *15% Petite Sirah. Intense, jammy, ripe.*

☆ 1978 ZINFANDEL ($12.00) Late Harvest, Paso Robles, San Luis Obispo. *O.K. if you like this style. Overripe, heavy, high alcohol.*

☆ 1978 ZINFANDEL ($15.00) Late Picked, Fiddletown, Eschen, Amador. *Overdone, awkward, raisiny.*

☆☆ 1979 ZINFANDEL ($6.00) Dusi, San Luis Obispo. *Berried, rich, intense, a bit hot.*

☆☆ 1979 ZINFANDEL ($6.00) Early Bottling, Esola, Amador. *Pleasant, clean, attractive. Drink now.*

☆ 1979 ZINFANDEL ($7.50) Fiddletown, Eschen, Amador. *A bit disjointed. Drink now.*

1979 ZINFANDEL ($7.50) Jimsomare, Santa Cruz Mountains. *Definite off qualities.*

1979 ZINFANDEL ($8.00) Langtry Road, Spring Mountain, Napa Valley.

☆☆☆ 1979 ZINFANDEL ($9.00) Geyserville, Trentadue Ranch, Sonoma. *5% Petite Sirah. Ripe, berried, oaky, deep. Drink 1985.*

☆ 1979 ZINFANDEL ($9.00) Glen Ellen, Sonoma. *Thin and disjointed; oaky and lacking fruit.*

☆☆ 1979 ZINFANDEL ($9.00) York Creek, Napa Valley. *12% Petite Sirah. Rich, clean, intense, balanced. Drink now.*

☆☆ 1980 ZINFANDEL ($6.00) Amador Foothills, Amador. *Berried, fresh-faced and charming. Drink now.*

☆ 1980 ZINFANDEL ($7.50) Dusi Ranch, Paso Robles.

☆☆☆ 1980 ZINFANDEL ($7.50) Esola, Shenandoah Valley, Amador. *5% Petite Sirah. Crisp fruit and varietal character.*

☆☆☆ 1980 ZINFANDEL ($7.50) Fiddletown, Amador. *Richly varietal yet snappy and fresh.*

☆☆☆ 1980 ZINFANDEL ($9.00) Geyserville, Trentadue Ranch, California. *Intense, concentrated, rich, mouth-filling. Drink 1986.*

☆☆ 1980 ZINFANDEL ($9.00) Jimsomare, Santa Cruz Mountains. *Big and berried. 15.9% alcohol.*

1980 ZINFANDEL ($9.00) Pichetti Ranch, Santa Cruz.

☆ 1980 ZINFANDEL ($9.00) York Creek, Napa. *10% Petite Sirah. Big but lacking depth.*

1980 ZINFANDEL ($10.00) Park-Muscatine, Howell Mountain, Napa. *28% Petite Sirah, 7% Carignane. 14.8% alcohol.*

☆☆ 1981 ZINFANDEL ($6.00) Hillside, California. *20% Petite Sirah. Fresh, simple, direct, attractive. Drink 1986.*

☆☆ 1981 ZINFANDEL ($8.00) Dry Late Picked, Angeli, Alexander Valley. *A monster; big, tannic and hot but not bad. Drink 1987.*

☆☆☆ 1981 ZINFANDEL ($9.00) 85% Trentadue, 15% Angeli, Geyserville, Alexander Valley. *Crisp and snappy, with good varietal character. Deep, rich.*

☆☆ 1982 ZINFANDEL ($6.75) California. *Lush, berried, rich.*

☆☆☆ 1982 ZINFANDEL ($8.00) Dusi, Paso Robles. *5% Petite Sirah. Balanced, round, fruity, delicious.*

☆☆☆ 1982 ZINFANDEL ($9.00) Beatty, Howell Mountain. *Jammy, peppery, intense, rich, superb. Drink 1988.*

☆☆☆ 1982 ZINFANDEL ($9.50) 20th Anniversary, Geyserville, California. *Fruity, clean and nicely structured. Shows restraint and depth.*

☆☆☆ 1982 ZINFANDEL ($10.50) York Creek, California. *14% Petite Sirah. Structured, rich, clean, balanced, superb. Drink 1986.*

Ritchie Creek Vineyards
NAPA COUNTY

4024 Spring Mountain Road, St. Helena, California 94574 (707-963-4661). FOUNDED: 1974. ACREAGE: 8 acres. PRODUCTION: 800 cases. DISTRIBUTION: 6 states. OWNER: Richard P. Minor. WINEMAKER: Richard P. Minor. Tours by appointment.

Dr. Richard Minor, a wine-loving dentist, bought some vineyard property in 1965 and, having a special fondness for Bordeaux, planted Cabernet Sauvignon. As the vineyards grew and matured, so did Dr. Minor's interest. He began allocating more working hours to his vineyard and less to his dental practice. Eventually dentistry became his weekend project and the vineyard became a full-time job. "The winery was just a dream that sort of worked itself out," says Minor. "Our first real crop was in 1974, and that was the year I sold my practice and built a winery."

RED

☆☆☆   1980 CABERNET SAUVIGNON ($12.50) Napa Valley. *Herbal, very Bordeaux-like, classy.*
☆☆☆   1981 CABERNET SAUVIGNON ($12.50) Napa Valley. *Herbal, attractive, clean, rich.*

RIVER OAKS *see* Clos du Bois Winery

River Road Vineyards
SONOMA COUNTY

7145 River Road, Forestville, California 95436 (707-887-7890). FOUNDED: 1978. ACREAGE: 120 acres. PRODUCTION: 4,800 cases. DISTRIBUTION: Nationwide. OWNER: Gary Mills. WINEMAKER: Gary Mills; Larry Wara, consultant. No tours or tasting.

"Basically, we are wine sellers, rather than winemakers," says Gary Mills, owner and chief salesman of River Road wines. "We started the River Road label in order to have a better market position for our grapes," says Gary. In 1978 he started having his grapes custom crushed at Souverain, using his own cooperage for aging. Now winemaking is overseen by enological consultant Larry Wara, and the wine is being made at Fritz Cellars.

WHITE

O   1982 CHARDONNAY Ventana, Monterey. *Melony, overripe, with some spoilage and oxidation.*
☆   1981 JOHANNISBERG RIESLING ($5.00) North Coast. *1.5% residual sugar. Flabby.*

RED

1980 CABERNET SAUVIGNON Shandon, San Luis Obispo. *Bitter, vegetal.*
O   NV ZINFANDEL Shandon, San Luis Obispo. *Vegetal, green, very unattractive.*
☆   1979 ZINFANDEL ($4.50) Sonoma Valley. *Soft, smooth, decent.*
1979 ZINFANDEL ($5.00) Lot 2, Shandon Valley, California. *Big, fat and very weedy. Essentially unappealing.*

River Run Vintners
SANTA CRUZ COUNTY

65 Rogge Lane, Watsonville, California 95076 (408-726-3112). FOUNDED: 1978. ACREAGE: None. PRODUCTION: 1,300 cases. DISTRIBUTION: California. OWNER: Christine Arneson. WINEMAKER: J. P. Pawloski. Tours and tasting by appointment.

J. P. Pawloski and his wife found what they considered to be the perfect piece of property. It had four acres of apple trees and a winery. Since J. P. had been making wine at home for fifteen years, it was only natural to put the winery to good use. "We have been sinking money into this place ever since," he says. The winery had previously been used for red-wine production, so most of J. P.'s renovation involved adding refrigeration for the fermentation and storage of white wines.

RED

1979 CABERNET SAUVIGNON ($4.00) San Luis Obispo.
1979 ZINFANDEL ($4.00) San Luis Obispo.

RIVERSIDE FARM *see* Louis Foppiano Wine Company

J. Rochioli Vineyards
SONOMA COUNTY

6192 Westside Road, Healdsburg, California 95448 (707-433-2305). FOUNDED: 1983. ACREAGE: 80 acres. PRODUCTION: 5,000 cases. DISTRIBUTION: California. OWNERS: Joe and Tom Rochioli. WINEMAKER: Gary Farrel. Tours by appointment.

The J. Rochioli Winery is a spin-off of what once was Fenton Acres. Joe Rochioli and his son Tom have been growing grapes on Westside Road for years. In 1976, with a few partners, they formed Fenton Acres Winery. They bought barrels and equipment, set them up in the nearby Davis Bynum winery, and had the winemaker there make the wine for them. In 1984 Joe and Tom dissolved the Fenton Acres partnership to start their own label. They grow the grapes, and the wine is made at Davis Bynum by winemaker Gary Farrel. This will change again when Joe and Tom complete their own winery on the vineyard property.

WHITE

☆☆ 1983 CHARDONNAY ($10.00) Sonoma. *Soft, ripe, with good, lean fruit; clean and short.*
 ☆ 1983 FUME BLANC ($7.50) Russian River Valley, Sonoma. *Grassy, oily, decent.*

RED

☆☆ 1982 PINOT NOIR ($13.50) Russian River Valley, Sonoma. *Balanced, varietal, very nice.*

Roddis Cellar
NAPA COUNTY

1510 Diamond Mountain Road, Calistoga, California 95415 (707-942-5868). FOUNDED: 1979. ACREAGE: 5 acres. PRODUCTION: 500 cases. DISTRIBUTION: Major market states. OWNER: W. H. Roddis. WINEMAKER: W. H. Roddis. Tours Monday–Friday 9 A.M.–4:30 P.M. Tasting daily by appointment.

William Roddis was persuaded by his wine-drinking friends to put his Cabernet Sauvignon on the market. When William bought his five-acre vineyard adjacent to Diamond Creek Vineyards, his sole interest was to quietly care for the vineyards and make a little homemade wine. William is a quadriplegic who manages both his winery—a vintage 1890 building—and his vineyards by himself. With only 500 cases of estate-grown Cabernet Sauvignon produced each year, William runs one of the smallest, if not *the* smallest, wineries in the Napa Valley.

RED

☆☆☆ 1980 CABERNET SAUVIGNON ($12.00) Estate, Diamond Mountain, Napa Valley. *Deep, nicely structured, well made. Drink 1986 and beyond.*
 ☆☆ 1981 CABERNET SAUVIGNON ($12.50) Estate, Diamond Mountain, Napa Valley.
      1982 CABERNET SAUVIGNON ($12.50) Estate, Diamond Mountain, Napa Valley. *Unattractive, off flavors.*

ॐ

J. ROGET *see* Canandaigua Wine Company

Rolling Hills Vineyard
VENTURA COUNTY

167-L Aviador, Camarillo, California 93010 (805-484-8100). FOUNDED: 1980. ACREAGE: 5 acres. PRODUCTION: 1,000 cases. DISTRIBUTION: California. OWNERS: Edward and Eve Pragor. WINEMAKER: Edward Pragor. Tours by appointment.

Ed Pragor, while working as a regional manager for a metal company, established his winery in a warehouse-type building that is located right off the Ventura freeway. Like many of his winemaking friends, his winery is an outgrowth of a much-loved hobby. He belonged to a home winemaking club that has inspired several other members to start commercial winemaking ventures. Ed plans to keep winery production at about 1,000 cases, limiting the labor force required to the members of his family.

WHITE

 ☆☆ 1983 CHARDONNAY ($11.00) Santa Maria Valley. *Ripe, rich, fat, fruity.*

RED

 ☆☆ 1981 CABERNET SAUVIGNON ($8.00) Temescal. *Lush, rich, attractive. Drink 1986.*
☆☆☆ 1981 MERLOT ($8.00) San Luis Obispo. *Lush, open and fat, with lovely, buttery oak. Splendid.*
      1982 MERLOT ($9.00) San Luis Obispo. *Dull.*

ॐ

The Rolling Vineyards Farm
NEW YORK

P.O. Box 37, Route 414, Hector, New York 14841 (607-546-9302). FOUNDED: 1981. ACREAGE: 50 acres. PRODUCTION: 2,000 cases. DISTRIBUTION: New York. OWNERS: Edwin J. Grow, president; Jo Anne Grow, general manager. WINEMAKER: Edwin J. Grow. Tours and tasting May–October: Monday–Saturday 10 A.M.–5 P.M.; November–December: weekends 10 A.M.–4 P.M., or by appointment.

Edwin and Jo Anne Grow wanted to make wine. They bought a vineyard property in 1976, increased the acreage planted, and began selling grapes to various wineries. Eventually, they got down to the business of winemaking, since that had been the idea all along. The barn was remodeled into a winery, and another farm building was converted into a tasting room.

ॐ

Rombauer Vineyards
NAPA COUNTY

3522 Silverado Trail, St. Helena, California 94574 (707-963-5170). FOUNDED: 1980. ACREAGE: None. PRODUCTION: 4,000 cases. DISTRIBUTION: Major market states. OWNERS: Koerner

Rombauer, Jr., and Joan Rombauer. WINEMAKER: Bob Levy. No tours or tasting. Retail sales daily 8:30 A.M.–5 P.M.

Koerner Rombauer, Jr., and his wife, Joan, were partners and planners in Conn Creek Winery before they decided to build a winery on their own land. Koerner, an airplane pilot, had always possessed a talent for design and construction. He drew the plans for his large, state-of-the-art winery and broke ground in 1982. While Koerner was giving his Cabernet Sauvignon time in the bottle before release, he generated cash flow by leasing his winery as a custom-crush facility. Some of the most promising smaller wineries in Napa have gotten their starts at Rombauer, where 90 percent of the business is still in custom crushing.

WHITE

☆☆☆   1982 CHARDONNAY ($12.50) St. Andrews, Napa Valley. *Crisp, clean, intense, balanced.*
☆☆☆   1983 CHARDONNAY ($13.50) Napa Valley. *Lush, rich, smooth, complex, clean and very lovely.*

RED

☆☆☆   1983 RED TABLE WINE ($12.50) Napa Valley. *61% Cabernet, 31% Cabernet Franc, 8% Merlot. Rich, hard, lovely. Drink 1990.*
☆☆   1980 CABERNET SAUVIGNON ($12.50) Napa Valley. *Intense, complex and lush; some raisiny notes, well built.*
☆☆   1981 CABERNET SAUVIGNON ($12.50) Napa Valley. *Rich, elegant, clean, complex. Drink 1986.*

Rosati Winery
MISSOURI

Route 1, Box 55, St. James, Missouri 65559 (314-265-8629). FOUNDED: 1933. ACREAGE: None. PRODUCTION: 8,000 cases. DISTRIBUTION: Missouri and Illinois. OWNER: Rosati Winery, Inc. Ron Moreland, general manager. WINEMAKER: Ron Moreland. Tours and tasting daily 8 A.M.–6 P.M.; Sunday 12–6 P.M.

Built in 1933, this winery was originally used as a grape juice processing plant before it was abandoned. In 1969 it burned down. The Ashby Vineyard Company, a large owner of vineyards and orchards, bought what was left of it in 1972. A few stone walls and old cellars were still standing, but the rest had to be entirely rebuilt. Actually, it was Ron Moreland, son-in-law of head man Robert Ashby, who wanted to save the old winery. Ron had had winery experience in both Missouri and Ohio and was eager to run his own operation. The latest addition is a new cold-storage room filled with stainless steel tanks.

Rose Bower Vineyard & Winery
VIRGINIA

P.O. Box 126, Hampden-Sydney, Virginia 23943 (804-223-8209). FOUNDED: 1973. ACREAGE: 10 acres. PRODUCTION: 2,000 cases. DISTRIBUTION: Virginia. OWNER: Tom O'Grady. WINE-MAKER: Tom O'Grady. Tours and tasting November–December, April–May, July–August: Friday–Sunday 1 P.M.–5 P.M., or by appointment.

A resident poet and writer for Hampden-Sydney College, Tom O'Grady thought he could supplement his income by growing grapes. He planted two acres of vinifera and French-American hybrids on his country property, hoping to sell the fruit to home winemakers and perhaps make some wine of his own on the side. Once it became evident that he was not going to get rich selling grapes, Tom expanded his winemaking activities to the commercial level by adding a winery onto his eighteenth-century Colonial house. "By keeping it small and expanding slowly, we have been able to experiment with varieties, blends and oaks, late-harvest wines, and nouveau," says Tom. "We are still discovering which varieties grow best and what type of wine we will be able to make."

Rose Family Winery
SONOMA COUNTY

427 Allan Court, Healdsburg, California 95448 (707-433-8170). FOUNDED: 1981. ACREAGE: None. PRODUCTION: 3,000 cases. DISTRIBUTION: California. OWNERS: Bill and Ronette Rose. WINEMAKER: Bill Rose. No tours or tasting.

While planning his own winery, Bill Rose worked for a number of wineries and studied for his degree in chemistry. "It was extremely valuable experience for Bill to work in wineries, gaining practical knowledge while he was getting his degree," says his wife, Ronette. After twelve years of planning, Bill's first wines were released in 1981. The wines are made in a rented space in an industrial park in Healdsburg.

WHITE

☆☆ 1981 CHARDONNAY ($10.00) Sonoma. *Vinous, oaky, rich, moderately attractive.*
 ☆ 1982 CHARDONNAY ($9.25) Cameron, Sonoma. *Vinous and intense; lacks grace and charm.*
☆☆ 1983 CHARDONNAY ($9.75) Western Russian River, Sonoma. *Oily, ripe, oaky, intense.*

RED

☆☆ 1981 PINOT NOIR ($8.00) Sonoma. *A bit stemmy but some nice varietal character too.*
☆☆ 1982 PINOT NOIR ($8.00) Cameron, Sonoma. *Varietal, clean, simple.*

Rosenblum Cellars
ALAMEDA COUNTY

1401 Standford Avenue, Emeryville, California 94608 (415-653-2355). FOUNDED: 1978. ACREAGE: None. PRODUCTION: 5,000 cases. DISTRIBUTION: Major market states. OWNERS: Kent and Kathleen Rosenblum, Roger Rosenblum, Susan Rupert, Cynthia Rice, Mike Sirna, and Bill Gage. WINEMAKERS: Kent and Roger Rosenblum. Tours, tasting, and sales by appointment.

Kent Rosenblum, full-time veterinarian, started making wine in his basement with friends in the early 1970s. By 1978 Kent was ready to advance into professional winemaking. He renovated an old Oakland saloon and set up barrels and tanks. To secure a little extra help, he brought in his winemaking friends as partners. Fortunately, all the partners have other means of financial support. The winery has since moved to Emeryville, where it occupies part of what used to be the Veedercrest Winery. Rosenblum Cellars shares this facility with two other businesses: Bay Cellars, a new winery, and St. George Spirits, a producer of eau de vie (brandy and spirits).

WHITE

☆ **1981 CHARDONNAY ($12.00)** Vintner's Reserve, Napa Valley. *Big, vinous, fat, intense.*
   1983 CHARDONNAY ($10.00) Los Carneros-Napa. *Oily, dull, bitter.*
☆☆ **1982 JOHANNISBERG RIESLING ($6.00)** Late Harvest, Napa Valley. *6.6% residual sugar. Toasty, crisp and clean.*
   1982 MUSCAT OF ALEXANDRIA ($7.50) Dragon, Contra Costa.

SPARKLING

☆ **1983 GEWURZTRAMINER ($11.00)** California. *Grapey, varietal, fresh.*

RED

☆☆☆ 1982 ROSENBLUM RED ($4.00) Napa Valley. *58% Pinot Noir. Character, fruity, structured, superb.*
☆☆ 1978 CABERNET SAUVIGNON ($4.50) Hoffman Ranch, Geyserville, Sonoma. *Round and balanced; quite attractive. Drink now.*
☆☆☆ **1980 CABERNET SAUVIGNON ($9.00)** Cohn & Balfour, Napa Valley.
☆☆☆ **1981 CABERNET SAUVIGNON ($10.00)** Cohn, Napa Valley. *Rich, fruity, clean, lovely. Drink 1986.*
☆☆☆ **1982 CABERNET SAUVIGNON ($10.00)** 62% Napa Valley, 38% Sonoma. *Spicy, rich, intense, complex, superb. Drink 1987.*
☆☆ **1982 CABERNET SAUVIGNON ($12.00)** Vintner's Reserve, McGilvery Vineyard, Sonoma County. *Big, earthy and rich; herbal and fruity. Drink 1987.*
☆☆ 1982 GAMAY ($5.00) Napa. *Fresh, snappy, good.*
☆☆☆ 1980 PETITE SIRAH ($5.50) St. George & Rich Vineyards, Napa Valley. *Lovely, elegant, richly fruity, great balance.*
☆☆☆ **1981 PETITE SIRAH ($6.50)** Napa Valley. *Rich, fruity, purple, clean, intense, terrific. Drink 1986.*
☆☆☆ **1982 PETITE SIRAH ($7.00)** Napa Valley. *Fresh, rich, dark and fruity. Drink 1987 and beyond.*
☆☆☆ **1978 ZINFANDEL ($5.50)** Napa Valley. *Lush, fruity, peppery, big, round and lovely. Drink now.*
☆☆ **1980 ZINFANDEL ($8.00)** Napa-Sonoma. *20% Petite Sirah. Berried, rich, fruity, nicely balanced.*
☆☆☆ 1981 ZINFANDEL ($6.00) Mauritson, Sonoma Valley. *Lovely, berried wine with depth and charm. Drink now.*
☆☆☆ 1981 ZINFANDEL ($6.00) Napa Valley. *Berries and oak; clean fruit and depth. Drink 1987.*
☆☆ **1983 ZINFANDEL ($7.50)** Cullinan, Sonoma. *Fresh, fruity, clean, attractive.*
☆☆ **1983 ZINFANDEL ($7.50)** Napa Valley. *Lush, round, deep. Drink 1987.*
☆☆☆ **1983 ZINFANDEL ($7.50)** Napa Valley. *11% Petite Sirah. Lush, spicy, rich, very attractive.*
☆☆☆ **1983 ZINFANDEL ($7.50)** Sonoma. *Rich, clean, fruity, balanced, charming.*

ε∂

Don Charles Ross Winery
NAPA COUNTY

1721-C Action Avenue, Napa, California 94558 (707-255-9463). FOUNDED: 1976. ACREAGE: None. PRODUCTION: 4,000 cases. DISTRIBUTION: Nationwide. OWNER: Don Charles Ross. WINEMAKER: Don Charles Ross. OTHER LABELS: Napa Vintners, Napa Valley Winery. Tours and tasting by appointment.

Don Charles Ross called his winery Napa Vintners and labeled his wines as Napa Valley Wines until some confusion arose. When he began producing wines from grapes grown in other counties, retailers and customers felt it was misleading to have the "Napa Vintners" title on a wine from Sonoma or Lake County. So he gave the winery his own name. Don Charles, whose father and grandfather were winemakers at Inglenook Vineyards, used to fix cars and repair sprinkler systems for a living. "Winemaking was the one field where I could produce something of quality that would be appreciated," says Don. The wine is made in a leased industrial building in the town of Napa.

RED

☆ 1979 ZINFANDEL ($7.50) Napa Valley. *Intense and tannic; too big for its own fruit.*

Ross-Keller Winery
SAN LUIS OBISPO COUNTY

805 Orchard Avenue, Nipomo, California 93444 (805-929-3627). FOUNDED: 1980. ACREAGE: None. PRODUCTION: 3,000 cases. DISTRIBUTION: California. OWNERS: Howard and Jacqueline Tanner. WINEMAKER: Jim Ryan. Tours and tasting by appointment. Picnic facilities.

Harness horse racing was the Tanners' first hobby-business, but once they broke even they turned to winemaking. Howard, an oral surgeon in Santa Maria, and his wife, Jackie, became friends with Dr. Mosby of Vega Vineyards, who encouraged them to try winemaking. The Tanners rented a facility in Buellton's industrial area to house their winery. In 1983 they moved the winery to what was once their horse-breeding farm and training track in Nipomo. Appropriately, the Tanners use an equestrian motif on their label, "and we still race horses," says Jackie.

B & B Rosser Winery
GEORGIA

547 Ray's Church Road, High Shoals, Georgia 30645 (404-548-8222). FOUNDED: 1983. ACREAGE: 22 acres. PRODUCTION: 3,000 cases. DISTRIBUTION: Georgia. OWNERS: Bill and Barbara Rosser. WINEMAKER: Bill Rosser. Tours by appointment. Tasting Monday–Friday 12–5 P.M., Saturday 9 A.M.–5 P.M.

As secretary for a wine-buying club, Bill Rosser became frustrated when French wines became so expensive in the early 1970s. "I stopped buying French wines, but I still had expensive taste," says Bill. He tried a few California wines and, unimpressed, decided it was the right time to plant a vineyard. In June of 1977 he purchased a well-forested parcel, cleared it, and, after a long spell of studying the climatology, planted Bordeaux varieties. Unfortunately, the year he planned to construct his own winery there was a total crop failure. "That's when the bank asked me if I still wanted to build the winery, and I told them, 'Might as well, since I sure don't have any vineyard work to keep me busy this year.'"

WHITE

O NV MAGNOLIA ($5.00) Georgia. *Volatile acidity.*

RED

1983 CABERNET-MERLOT ($6.00) Georgia.

CARLO ROSSI *see* E. & J. Gallo Winery

Rotolo & Romero Wine Cellars
NEW YORK

234 Rochester Street, Avon, New York 14414 (716-451-2905). FOUNDED: 1980. ACREAGE: None. PRODUCTION: 700 cases. DISTRIBUTION: At winery only. OWNERS: Thomas and Barbara Rotolo. WINEMAKERS: Tom, Barbara, and Ruth Rotolo. Tours and tasting by appointment.

A would-be restaurateur, Tom Rotolo became intrigued by the history and personalities of the wine world while working as wine steward on a cruise ship. Once on land, Tom was tempted to go to California and start a winery there, but he was reluctant to leave Rochester, his hometown. Teaming up with his buddy Paul Romeo, a merchandising scientist, he bought a macaroni factory and converted it into a small winery. In a state where the most successful varieties are white, Tom and Paul are endeavoring to make good red wines.

Roudon-Smith Vineyards
SANTA CRUZ COUNTY

2364 Bean Creek Road, Santa Cruz, California 95066 (408-438-1244). FOUNDED: 1972. ACREAGE: 3 acres. PRODUCTION: 10,000 cases. DISTRIBUTION: Major market states. OWN-ERS: Annamaria and Robert Roudon; June and James Smith, managing partners. WINEMAKER: Bob Roudon. Tours and tasting Saturday by appointment.

Texan Bob Roudon and Wisconsinite Jim Smith are mechanical engineers who met while working for the same California company. They both loved wine, and, with the help of their wives, Annamaria and June, they started a small winery in the Roudon's basement. Bob, a self-taught winemaker, tends toward intense, "natural" wines. They built a new winery in 1978, allowing for a big increase in production—yet this small operation is still a very personal, family winery.

WHITE

☆☆☆ 1980 CHARDONNAY ($11.00) Wasson, Sonoma. *Toasty and deep.*

☆ 1981 CHARDONNAY ($9.00) Estate, Santa Cruz Mountains.

☆☆ 1981 CHARDONNAY ($10.00) Sonoma. *Rich, oily, clean and intense.*

O 1981 CHARDONNAY ($12.00) Mendocino. *Flabby, tired.*

☆☆☆ 1981 CHARDONNAY ($12.00) 10th Anniversary, Edna Valley. *Lovely, rich and balanced.*

☆☆ 1982 CHARDONNAY ($6.00) Sequoia Coast, California. *Fruity and fresh, with some oak complexity.*

☆ 1982 CHARDONNAY ($11.00) Nelson Ranch, Mendocino. *Overdone, too much oak.*

☆☆☆ 1984 PINOT BLANC ($6.50) Santa Maria Valley. *11% Chardonnay. Lush and tangy, fruity, clean. Quite lovely.*

BLANC DE NOIR

☆ 1984 WHITE ZINFANDEL ($5.00) California. *1.1% residual sugar. 25% Pinot Noir. Fruity but heavy. Decent.*

RED

☆☆ NV CLARET ($3.50) California. *61% Cabernet. Some volatile acidity. Clean, snappy, decent.*

☆ 1978 CABERNET SAUVIGNON ($20.00) Steiner, Sonoma. *Drink now.*

☆☆☆ 1978 CABERNET SAUVIGNON ($25.00) 10th Anniversary, Steiner, Sonoma. *Ripe, intense and attractively complex.*

O 1979 CABERNET SAUVIGNON ($7.50) Edna Valley. *Weedy, overdone, unattractive.*

☆☆ 1979 CABERNET SAUVIGNON ($13.00) Steiner, Sonoma. *Dark, lush, berried, ripe. Drink 1985 and beyond.*

1980 CABERNET SAUVIGNON ($8.50) Alexander Valley, Sonoma. *Quite weedy. Simple and clumsy.*

☆☆☆ 1981 CABERNET SAUVIGNON ($12.00) Steiner, Sonoma. *Herbal, rich, balanced, super. Drink 1988 and beyond.*

☆☆☆ 1982 CABERNET SAUVIGNON ($7.50) Nelson Ranch, Mendocino. *Buttery oak, crisp, clean, delightful. Drink 1986 and beyond.*

☆   1981 PETITE SIRAH ($6.50) San Luis Obispo. *5% Chardonnay. Jammy, clean, intense. Drink 1987.*

☆☆   1982 PETITE SIRAH ($6.50) San Luis Obispo. *Deep, clean, attractive. Drink now.*

☆   1981 PINOT NOIR ($14.00) Edna Valley. *Earthy and a bit green; vegetal.*

☆   1982 PINOT NOIR ($13.00) Edna Valley. *Clean, balanced but vegetal.*

☆   1978 ZINFANDEL ($6.00) Late Harvest Dry, Central Coast. *Intense, overripe, berried, raisiny.*

☆☆   1979 ZINFANDEL ($10.00) Old Hill Ranch, Sonoma, California. *Berries and sweet oak; tannic. Drink 1987 and beyond.*

☆☆   1979 ZINFANDEL ($10.00) 10th Anniversary, Chauvet, Sonoma. *Rich, jammy and intense.*

☆☆☆   1980 ZINFANDEL ($7.50) 10th Anniversary, Chauvet, Sonoma. *Snappy, clean, fresh, delightful. Drink now.*

☆☆☆   1980 ZINFANDEL ($9.00) 10th Anniversary, Old Hill Ranch, Sonoma. *Spicy nose and rich varietal character; crisp and snappy. Drink now.*

☆☆   1982 ZINFANDEL ($7.50) Chauvet, Sonoma. *Berried, balanced, intensely varietal, tannic. Drink 1987.*

Round Hill Cellars
NAPA COUNTY

1097 Lodi Lane, St. Helena, California 94574 (707-963-5251). FOUNDED: 1977. ACREAGE: None. PRODUCTION: 100,000 cases. DISTRIBUTION: Nationwide; 6 foreign markets. OWNER: Corporation. Charles A. Abela, president. WINEMAKER: Jim Yerkes. OTHER LABEL: Rutherford Ranch Brand. Tours weekdays by appointment 9 A.M.–5 P.M.; weekends 11 A.M.–5 P.M.

This winery, known for its reasonably priced wines, started as a packager of bulk wines. Many Round Hill wines are still purchased already made, but quite a few of them are now made from scratch in the stone St. Helena winery. A second label, Rutherford Ranch Brand, has been added to the line.

WHITE

  NV   HOUSE CHARDONNAY ($4.50) California.

☆☆   NV   HOUSE CHARDONNAY ($4.65) Lot 4, California. *Clean, simple and decent.*

☆☆   1981 CHARDONNAY ($6.50) Northern California. *Nice—lemony, clean and fresh.*

☆☆   1981 CHARDONNAY ($10.00) Napa Valley. *Fresh, fruity, lacking complexity.*

☆   1981 RUTHERFORD RANCH BRAND CHARDONNAY ($12.00) Napa Valley. *Lacks complexity and charm.*

☆☆☆   1982 CHARDONNAY ($9.00) Napa Valley. *Lovely, varietal, clean, very nice.*

☆☆   1984 CHARDONNAY ($4.65) California. *Crisp, fresh, clean, attractive.*

☆   1982 CHENIN BLANC ($4.50) California.

☆☆☆   NV   HOUSE FUME BLANC ($5.00) Mendocino.

  1981 FUME BLANC ($7.00) Napa Valley.

☆☆   1982 FUME BLANC ($6.00) Napa Valley. *Nice varietal character and freshness.*

☆   1983 FUME BLANC ($6.00) Napa Valley. *Dull, lacking varietal character. Decent.*

  1983 GEWURZTRAMINER ($5.00) Napa Valley. *1% residual sugar. Cardboardy flavors, a bit off but decent.*

☆☆☆   1984 GEWURZTRAMINER ($5.00) Napa Valley. *0.9% residual sugar. Fresh, crisp, clean, varietal, lovely.*

☆   1982 JOHANNISBERG RIESLING ($4.50) Sonoma. *Appealing but dull flavors.*

☆☆   1983 JOHANNISBERG RIESLING ($5.50) Napa Valley. *Dry, crisp, clean, nice.*

☆☆   NV   HOUSE SAUVIGNON BLANC ($4.65) Lot 4, North Coast. *Heavy, round, fruity, intensely varietal, quite pleasant.*

  1981 RUTHERFORD RANCH BRAND SAUVIGNON BLANC ($7.50) Napa Valley.

☆ 1982 SAUVIGNON BLANC ($7.50) Napa Valley. *Dull, not much fruit, vinous.*
☆☆ 1982 RUTHERFORD RANCH BRAND SAUVIGNON BLANC ($7.50) Napa Valley. *Lovely nose. Crisp, fresh, attractive.*
☆☆ 1983 RUTHERFORD RANCH BRAND SAUVIGNON BLANC ($6.50) Napa Valley. *Woody, crisp, varietal, with slightly thin flavors.*

ROSE

☆ 1983 GAMAY ROSE ($5.00) Gamay Acres, Napa Valley. *Dry, dull, with some fruit.*

RED

☆ NV HOUSE CABERNET ($4.50) California. *Weedy, clean, balanced, decent.*
☆☆ NV HOUSE CABERNET SAUVIGNON ($4.65) Lot 4, North Coast. *Varietal, clean, attractive.*
☆☆ 1978 RUTHERFORD RANCH BRAND CABERNET SAUVIGNON ($8.50) Napa Valley. *Big, ripe, tannic, fruity. Needs time; drink 1987.*
☆ 1979 CABERNET SAUVIGNON ($8.00) Napa Valley. *Showing some age already. Earthy, decent. Drink now.*
☆ 1979 CABERNET SAUVIGNON ($8.00) North Coast.
☆☆☆ 1979 RUTHERFORD RANCH BRAND CABERNET SAUVIGNON ($9.00) Napa Valley. *Big and fleshy; full and rich. Drink 1986 and beyond.*
☆ 1980 CABERNET SAUVIGNON ($7.50) Napa Valley. *Nice, varietal, clean but a bit heavy and lacking structure.*
☆☆ 1980 RUTHERFORD RANCH BRAND CABERNET SAUVIGNON ($9.00) Napa Valley. *Intense and varietal; clean and complex. Drink 1988.*
☆☆ 1981 CABERNET SAUVIGNON ($9.00) Napa Valley. *Lush, soft, attractive, clean, varietal. Drink now.*
☆☆☆ 1980 PETITE SIRAH ($6.00) Napa Valley. *Spicy, clean, crisp, tangy, delightful.*
☆☆☆ 1981 RUTHERFORD RANCH BRAND PETITE SIRAH ($7.50) Napa Valley. *Lush, clean, spicy, tannic. Drink 1986.*
☆☆ 1979 PINOT NOIR ($6.00) Gamay Acres, Napa Valley. *Fruity, clean and berried.*
☆ 1981 PINOT NOIR ($6.00) Gamay Acres, Napa Valley. *Clean, fruity, simple.*
☆ 1978 RUTHERFORD RANCH BRAND ZINFANDEL ($7.50) Late Harvest, Napa Valley. *Clean and fruity but with 16.3% alcohol. Sweet, strange.*
☆☆☆ 1979 RUTHERFORD RANCH BRAND ZINFANDEL ($5.00) Napa. *Peppery and fresh, with lovely aging potential. Drink 1987.*
☆☆ 1979 ZINFANDEL ($5.00) Napa Valley. *Harsh and awkward but showing aging potential. Drink 1988.*
☆☆ 1980 ZINFANDEL ($4.50) Napa. *Crisp and bright.*
☆☆ 1980 RUTHERFORD RANCH BRAND ZINFANDEL ($6.00) Napa Valley. *Tart, fruity, good.*
☆☆ 1981 ZINFANDEL ($5.00) Napa Valley. *Underripe but nicely structured. A pleasant wine.*
☆ 1981 RUTHERFORD RANCH BRAND ZINFANDEL ($6.00) Napa Valley. *Clean, decent, a bit dull.*
☆☆ 1982 ZINFANDEL ($5.00) Napa Valley. *Tangy, rich fruit, clean and fresh.*
☆☆ 1982 RUTHERFORD RANCH BRAND ZINFANDEL ($6.00) Napa Valley. *Spicy, lush, richly tannic. Drink 1986.*

Royal Kedem Wine Corporation
NEW YORK

P.O. Box 811, Dock Road, Milton, New York 12547 (914-795-2240). FOUNDED: 1824. ACREAGE: 148 acres. PRODUCTION: 500,000 cases. DISTRIBUTION: Nationwide; South Africa and Australia. OWNERS: Herman, Ernest, Philip, and David Herzog. WINEMAKER: Ernest Herzog. Tours and tasting May–December: Sunday–Friday 10 A.M.–5 P.M.

The four Herzog brothers came from Czechoslovakia after the Second World War and continued their family wine business in a tiny Manhattan storefront. The brothers, representing the seventh generation of winemakers in the family, made sweet kosher wines from native American grapes. When they moved to a cold-storage warehouse in the Hudson Valley, they bought some vinifera acreage and began using French-American hybrids and vinifera from California. Now 70 percent of their wines are dry.

WHITE

☆☆   1983 CHENIN BLANC ($3.50) Monterey. *Clean, off-dry, appealing. Crushed at Giumarra.*

Channing Rudd Cellars
LAKE COUNTY

P.O. Box 426, Middletown, California 95461 (707-987-2209). FOUNDED: 1976. ACREAGE: 10 acres. PRODUCTION: 1,000 cases. DISTRIBUTION: California. OWNERS: Channing and Mary Claire Rudd. WINEMAKER: Channing Rudd. Tours and tasting by appointment only.

Channing Rudd, an award-winning graphic designer, spent six years as Paul Masson's art director before going off to do freelance work for several wineries. Meanwhile (rumor has it) he was making wine at home in his hot tub. In 1976 he bonded his residence in Alameda, designed a wine label, and opened Channing Rudd Cellars. But Alameda was confining for an artistic winemaker, so Channing bought a rugged piece of land on a 1,500-foot rocky slope in Lake County. Once he cleared his wildly overgrown land, he planted vines and moved his winery. He expects to eventually expand plantings to 25 acres.

RED

☆☆   1979 CABERNET SAUVIGNON ($7.00) Cary Gott, Amador. *15% Zinfandel. Ripe, berried, intense. Drink 1986.*
☆☆   1979 CABERNET SAUVIGNON ($7.00) Guenoc Ranch, Lake. *15% Petite Sirah, 10% Zinfandel. Clean, balanced, very pleasant.*
☆☆☆   1980 CABERNET SAUVIGNON ($14.00) Bella Oaks, Napa Valley. *Rich, deep, concentrated, oaky, lovely. Drink 1988.*
☆☆   1979 MERLOT ($9.00) Guenoc Valley. *Lush and velvety.*
☆   1978 ZINFANDEL ($10.00) Sonoma. *Too alcoholic and disjointed; some fruit. Drink now.*

Rutherford Hill Winery
NAPA COUNTY

End of Rutherford Hill Road, Rutherford, California 94573 (707-963-9694). FOUNDED: 1976. ACREAGE: 800 acres. PRODUCTION: 140,000 cases. DISTRIBUTION: Nationwide; 15 foreign markets. OWNER: Partnership. Bill Jaeger, Phil Baxter, Chuck Carpy, and others. WINEMAKER: Phil Baxter. Tours daily 11:30 A.M.–2:30 P.M. Tasting and sales daily 10:30 A.M.–4:30 P.M.

This modern winery (constructed by Joe Phelps) was meant to be Pillsbury's Souverain of Rutherford. When the big flour company opted out of the wine business, the plant was bought by the partners of Freemark Abbey Winery (see). Bill Jaeger, Phil Baxter, and Chuck Carpy are managing general partners, and a large portion of the winery's grapes come from the vineyards of Jaeger and Carpy. Rutherford Hill was first perceived as Freemark's "cheaper" second label, but Phil Baxter's wines have created a constituency and a strong reputation all their own.

WHITE

☆☆ 1980 CHARDONNAY ($11.00) Napa Valley. *Vinous, oily, intense, meaty.*

☆☆☆ 1980 CHARDONNAY ($16.00) Cellar Reserve, Jaeger, Napa Valley. *Rich and beautifully balanced; intense yet very fruity.*

☆☆ 1981 CHARDONNAY ($11.50) Jaeger, Napa Valley. *Vinous, rich, well made.*

☆☆☆ 1982 CHARDONNAY ($10.00) Jaeger, Napa Valley. *Fruity, crisp, charming, with lovely oak.*

☆☆☆ 1983 CHARDONNAY ($10.75) Jaeger, Napa Valley. *Fresh, fruity, clean, balanced.*

☆☆☆ 1978 GEWURZTRAMINER ($5.00) Napa Valley. *Fresh, varietal, balanced, still charming.*

☆☆☆ 1981 GEWURZTRAMINER ($5.00) Napa Valley. *0.74% residual sugar. Solid, crisp, clean, well made.*

☆☆☆ 1982 GEWURZTRAMINER ($5.75) Napa Valley. *0.67% residual sugar. Nearly dry, varietal, fresh, clean.*

☆☆☆ 1983 GEWURZTRAMINER ($6.25) Napa Valley. *0.72% residual sugar. Lush, varietal, charming, crisp.*

1981 JOHANNISBERG RIESLING ($6.75) Napa Valley.

☆☆ 1982 JOHANNISBERG RIESLING ($6.75) Napa Valley. *Crisp and fruity, with a hint of green pepper.*

☆ 1981 SAUVIGNON BLANC ($7.00) Napa Valley.

☆ 1982 SAUVIGNON BLANC ($7.50) Napa Valley. *Varietal but dull.*

☆☆ 1983 SAUVIGNON BLANC ($7.50) Napa Valley. *Clean, fresh, with good acidity.*

1983 SAUVIGNON BLANC ($8.00) Napa Valley. *Bitter, sour, unappealing.*

RED

☆☆☆☆ 1977 CABERNET SAUVIGNON ($9.00) Napa Valley. *Full, rich and complex, with finesse and structure. Drink now.*

☆☆ 1978 CABERNET SAUVIGNON ($10.50) Napa Valley. *Good fruit, varietal, a nice wine. Drink now.*

☆☆☆ 1979 CABERNET SAUVIGNON ($10.50) Napa Valley. *Subtle, balanced, lush, superb. Drink now and the next four years.*

☆☆ 1980 CABERNET SAUVIGNON ($12.00) Napa Valley. *24% Merlot. Rich, clean, herbal. Drink 1986.*

☆☆☆ 1982 CABERNET SAUVIGNON ($11.00) Napa Valley. *15% Merlot. Lush, structured, lovely. Drink 1987.*

☆☆☆☆ 1979 MERLOT ($9.25) Napa Valley. *Toasty, rich, supple, structured and classic. Drink now.*

☆☆ 1980 MERLOT ($10.00) Napa Valley. *Good fruit and varietal aroma but lacking the depth of the '79.*

☆☆ 1981 MERLOT ($10.00) Napa Valley. *Weedy, heavy, with earthy flavors and decent fruit.*

☆☆☆ 1982 MERLOT ($10.00) Napa Valley. *Soft, rich, varietal, excellent.*

☆☆ 1979 PINOT NOIR ($7.50) Napa Valley. *Toasty, earthy and attractive.*

☆ 1981 PINOT NOIR ($7.50) Napa Valley.

☆☆ 1977 ZINFANDEL ($7.00) Mead Ranch, Atlas Peak, Napa Valley. *Marred by high alcohol. Drink now.*

☆☆ 1978 ZINFANDEL ($6.00) Mead Ranch, Atlas Peak, Napa Valley.

☆ 1979 ZINFANDEL ($7.75) Mead Ranch, Atlas Peak, Napa Valley.

RUTHERFORD RANCH BRAND *see* Round Hill Cellars

Rutherford Vintners
NAPA COUNTY

1673 St. Helena Highway, Rutherford, California 94573 (707-963-4117). FOUNDED: 1976. ACREAGE: 30 acres. PRODUCTION: 15,000 cases. DISTRIBUTION: Nationwide; England and

Japan. OWNER: Corporation. Bernard L. Skoda, president. WINEMAKER: Bernard L. Skoda. OTHER LABEL: Château Rutherford. Tasting and retail sales daily 10 A.M.–4:30 P.M.

Bernard Skoda, who came to California from Alsace-Lorraine in eastern France, retired in 1976 after fifteen years as vice president of Louis M. Martini. During that time, in 1967, he and his wife, Evelyn, and a friend purchased a 25-acre parcel of land in Rutherford, which they planted with Cabernet Sauvignon. Some years later they bought another piece of land on Highway 29 for their winery, painstakingly landscaping the grounds to preserve a grove of eucalyptus trees. With Bernard as winemaker and salesman, and Evelyn in charge of the tasting room, they run the winery together with occasional help from their two children, Louis and Jacqueline.

WHITE

1982 CHARDONNAY ($12.00) Napa Valley. *Overoaked and lacking fruit.*

☆☆ 1983 CHARDONNAY ($12.00) Napa Valley. *Pineapple, oak, varietal character. Nicely made.*

☆☆ 1981 MUSCAT OF ALEXANDRIA ($7.00) Napa Valley. *Nearly 6% residual sugar. Lush and clean; coarse but very appealing.*

RED

☆☆ 1977 CABERNET SAUVIGNON ($8.00) Napa Valley. *14% Merlot. Soft, herbaceous, elegant. Drink now.*

☆ 1978 CABERNET SAUVIGNON ($9.00) Napa Valley. *Clean and simple; pleasant but not much else.*

☆☆ 1978 CHATEAU RUTHERFORD CABERNET SAUVIGNON ($13.50) Napa Valley. *Balanced, herbal, a bit low in fruit but attractive.*

1979 CHATEAU RUTHERFORD CABERNET SAUVIGNON ($9.00) Reserve, Napa Valley. *Unpleasant, skunky.*

SADDLE MOUNTAIN *see* Franz Wilhelm Langguth Winery

Saddleback Cellars
NAPA COUNTY

7802 Money Road, Oakville, California 94562 (707-255-7466). FOUNDED: 1983. ACREAGE: 17 acres. PRODUCTION: 2,500 cases. DISTRIBUTION: Western states. OWNERS: Nils Venge and Robert Call. WINEMAKER: Nils Venge. Tours by appointment.

While Nils Venge was the winemaker at Villa Mount Eden, he used to make a Cabernet rosé from the grapes grown on his own Oakville vineyard. When he left Villa Mount Eden to become the winemaker at Groth Winery (see), he and his partner Robert Call (his father-in-law) decided to continue making wine from their own grapes. They turned a concrete storage warehouse into a bonded winery in 1983 but crushed their first vintage at Groth Winery. Along with the Cabernet rosé, they produce Chardonnay, Cabernet Sauvignon, and one of the very few Napa Valley Pinot Blancs.

WHITE

☆☆ 1983 CHARDONNAY ($9.00) Napa Valley. *Crisp, fruity, clean.*

Sage Canyon Winery
NAPA COUNTY

P.O. Box 458, Rutherford, California 94573 (707-963-1491). FOUNDED: 1981. ACREAGE: None. PRODUCTION: 1,200 cases. DISTRIBUTION: Illinois, California, Alaska, and Florida. OWNERS: Gordon and Eugenia Millar. WINEMAKER: Charles Ortman, consultant. Tours by appointment.

Gordon and Eugenia Millar thought that starting a winery might be an amusing way to shelter some of their money. Once they found an appropriate site, they asked Paul Cassayre of Cassayre-Forni Winery to design the winery building. They then brought in Charles Ortman (see Charles Ortman Wines, St. Andrews Winery, St. Clement Vineyards, Perret Vineyards, and Cain Cellars) as winemaker-consultant. At the first crush they were almost grapeless when their expected supply of Chardonnay didn't materialize. Acting quickly they found some Chenin Blanc that Chuck Ortman felt would make a nice dry wine. They were pleased with the results, and the winery has kept Chenin Blanc as its specialty, making only one other wine, White Zinfandel.

WHITE

☆☆☆   1981 CHENIN BLANC ($6.75) Napa Valley. *Rich, clean, oaky, good.*

SAGE CREEK *see* California Wine Company

St. Andrews Winery
NAPA COUNTY

2921 Silverado Trail, Napa, California 94558 (707-252-6748). FOUNDED: 1979. ACREAGE: 63 acres. PRODUCTION: 5,000 cases. DISTRIBUTION: California and other states. OWNER: Imre Vizkelety. WINEMAKER: Robert Britton. OTHER LABEL: Charles Ortman. No tours or tasting.

Imre Vizkelety, a native Swiss with a sophisticated English vocabulary and continental accent, bought a 63-acre Chardonnay vineyard in 1976 and started a winery two years later. "I feel that in order to be truly successful, one cannot run the vineyard separately from the winery or the winery from the vineyard; there must be one manager, an estate manager, who both cultivates and makes the wine," says Vizkelety, who still lives in Switzerland. Robert Britton is Vizkelety's estate manager. St. Andrews crushes only half of its vineyard production, the rest is sold to Domaine Chandon for sparkling wine production.

WHITE

☆   1981 HOUSE CHARDONNAY ($5.00) Napa Valley. *Crisp, clean, simple but attractive.*
☆☆☆   1981 CHARDONNAY ($12.50) Napa Valley. *Firm, clean and elegant.*
☆☆   1982 CHARDONNAY ($7.00) House Chardonnay, Edna Valley. *Fruity, clean, balanced, attractive.*
☆   1982 CHARDONNAY ($7.50) House Chardonnay, Napa Valley. *Rich, decent, simple.*
☆☆☆   1982 CHARDONNAY ($12.50) Napa Valley. *Crisp, clean, fresh, lush, lovely.*
☆☆☆   1983 CHARDONNAY ($12.50) Napa Valley. *Lovely, elegant, balanced.*
☆☆   1983 SAUVIGNON BLANC ($7.00) Napa Valley. *Fresh, earthy, rounded, some oak complexity.*

RED

☆☆☆   1981 CABERNET SAUVIGNON ($9.00) Napa Valley. *Rich, deep, great structure, elegant. Drink 1987.*

ST. CARL *see* The Brander Vineyard

Ste. Chapelle Winery
IDAHO

Route 4, Box 775, Caldwell, Idaho 83605 (208-888-9463). FOUNDED: 1976. ACREAGE: None. PRODUCTION: 110,000 cases. DISTRIBUTION: Nationwide. OWNER: Corporation. Bill Broich,

general manager. WINEMAKER: Bill Broich. Tours and tasting November–March: Monday–
Saturday 10 A.M.–5 P.M.; April–November: Monday–Saturday 10 A.M.–6 P.M, Sunday 12–5 P.M.

In the early 1970s, when Idaho apple growers were diversifying their plantings, a few idealistic
winemakers encouraged growers to plant wine grapes. One of these enthusiasts was Bill Broich,
who had been making wine at home from his own experimental vineyards near Emmett. He bonded
his garage-sized winery, calling it Ste. Chapelle, and then struggled through two tough years of
hard work with little to show for it except experience. Next Bill formed a partnership with two
grape-growing associates, Steve Symms and Jim Mertz. A beautiful new winery, modeled after the
Ste. Chapelle chapel in Paris, was built on Symms's vineyard property, and more vines were planted
locally. While waiting for their Idaho grapes to mature, the partners gained considerable recognition—and cash flow—with wines made from Washington State grapes. As soon as their own
vineyards can supply the winery's entire production requirements, Ste. Chapelle plans to open a
new facility in Washington to make wines just from Washington grapes.

WHITE

☆ 1980 CHARDONNAY ($10.00) Washington.

☆☆☆ 1980 CHARDONNAY ($10.50) Symms Family, Washington. *Rich and deep, with lovely
fruitiness.*

☆ 1981 CHARDONNAY ($10.25) Symms Family, Idaho. *Pleasant, simple, dull.*

☆☆ 1982 CHARDONNAY ($10.00) Symms Family, Idaho.

☆☆ 1983 CHENIN BLANC Symms Family, Idaho. *2.4% residual sugar. Bright, fresh, attractive.*

☆☆☆ 1984 SOFT CHENIN BLANC ($3.00) Washington. *Sweet and tangy; balanced, fresh,
lovely. Only 7.5% alcohol.*

☆☆ 1981 JOHANNISBERG RIESLING ($6.00) Idaho. *Soft and lush.*

☆ 1982 JOHANNISBERG RIESLING ($6.70) Symms Family, Idaho. *2.2% residual sugar.
Meaty and a bit overripe; decent.*

☆☆ 1982 JOHANNISBERG RIESLING ($8.50) Special Harvest, Idaho. *8.9% residual sugar.
Spritzy, fresh, delightful, fruity.*

☆☆☆ 1983 JOHANNISBERG RIESLING ($5.25) Symms Family, Idaho. *Super, fresh, varietal,
lovely.*

☆☆☆ 1984 JOHANNISBERG RIESLING ($10.00) Special Harvest, Idaho. *11.2% residual sugar.
Spritzy, fresh, clean, fragrant; delightful.*

BLANC DE NOIR

☆☆ 1982 BLANC DE NOIR ($6.00) Symms Family, Idaho. *Pinot Noir varietal, clean, appealing.*

RED

☆ 1979 CABERNET SAUVIGNON ($15.00) Reserve, Mercer Ranch, Washington. *Weedy
and lacking in structure; young vines.*

☆ 1980 CABERNET SAUVIGNON Mercer Ranch, Idaho. *Herbal and berried.*

1980 MERLOT ($5.50) Washington. *Weedy, unappealing.*

St. Clement Vineyards
NAPA COUNTY

2867 St. Helena Highway North, St. Helena, California 94574 (707-963-7221). FOUNDED: 1975.
ACREAGE: 3 acres. PRODUCTION: 10,000 cases. DISTRIBUTION: Nationwide; 3 foreign mar-
kets. OWNER: Dr. William J. Casey. WINEMAKER: Dennis Johns. OTHER LABEL: Garrison
Forest. No tours or tasting. Case sales by appointment.

In 1975 Bill Casey, a San Francisco ophthalmologist, heard that the old Spring Mountain
Winery was for sale. He bought the picturesque Victorian house and renamed it St. Clement after
the island in Maryland where his ancestors had landed. Bill and his wife, Alexandra, made a strong

impression with their wines almost immediately. Their first winemaker was Jon Axhelm, followed by Chuck Ortman, who now acts as consultant to current winemaker Dennis Johns.

WHITE

☆☆ 1982 GARRISON FOREST CHARDONNAY ($8.00) Napa (64%) Sonoma (36%). *Clean, hard edged, well made, varietal.*

☆☆☆ 1982 CHARDONNAY ($14.50) Napa Valley. *Crisp, fruity, delicate and lovely.*

☆☆☆ 1983 CHARDONNAY ($14.50) Napa Valley. *Fragrant, clean, crisp, tangy, complex.*

☆☆☆ 1982 SAUVIGNON BLANC ($9.00) Napa Valley. *Fresh, crisp, varietal, beautifully rounded.*

☆☆☆ 1983 SAUVIGNON BLANC ($9.00) Napa Valley. *Rich, clean, balanced, classic.*

RED

☆☆☆☆ 1980 CABERNET SAUVIGNON ($12.50) Napa Valley. *Perfectly built, richly structured, fruity. Drink 1987.*

☆☆☆☆ 1981 CABERNET SAUVIGNON ($12.50) Napa Valley. *Wow! Crisp fruit matched with depth and style. Drink 1987.*

☆☆☆ 1982 CABERNET SAUVIGNON ($13.50) Napa Valley. *Clean, structured, elegant, varietal, stunning. Drink 1986.*

☆☆☆ 1982 GARRISON FOREST MERLOT ($7.75) Napa Valley. *Big, oaky, intense, good fruit. Drink 1987.*

St. Croix Winery
WISCONSIN

214 Front Street, Prescott, Wisconsin 54021 (715-262-3484). FOUNDED: 1981. ACREAGE: None. PRODUCTION: 2,500 cases. DISTRIBUTION: At winery. OWNER: Corporation. Mel and Lori Copeland, managers. WINEMAKERS: Mel and Lori Copeland. Tours and tasting April–November daily 11 A.M.–6 P.M.

A salesman for California's Sebastiani Vineyards, Mel Copeland was transferred to Wisconsin. After starting his own wine brokerage company there in 1976, he got the crazy idea that a winery might be a smart business venture. He leased a warehouse with a beautiful view of the St. Croix River and began making wines from locally grown grapes. Besides wine, Mel makes sauces and spice mixes that are sold nationally. The success he has had with the food products and fruit wines is encouraging him to focus on those areas of his business. "We started out by making grape and fruit wines," says Mel, "but the fruit wines are much more popular so we have cut out grape wines, except for those we make for our food products."

St. Francis Vineyards
SONOMA COUNTY

8450 Sonoma Highway, Kenwood, California 95452 (707-833-4666). FOUNDED: 1979. ACREAGE: 100 acres. PRODUCTION: 24,000 cases. DISTRIBUTION: Nationwide. OWNER: Joe Martin, managing partner. WINEMAKER: Tom Mackey. Tours by appointment. Tasting daily 10 A.M.–4:30 P.M.

Big Joe Martin bought Will Behler's old Kenwood vineyard in 1972. He replanted the vineyards and started selling his grapes to neighboring wineries such as Château St. Jean and Buena Vista. Then in 1979, with the help of consultant Brad Webb and Mike Richmond (see Acacia Winery), Joe built a handsome redwood winery. In addition to St. Francis's wines, the first Acacia wines were made in the new winery.

WHITE

☆☆ 1981 CHARDONNAY ($10.75) Sonoma. *Crisp, fruity and appealing.*

☆ 1982 CHARDONNAY ($9.00) Potter Valley, Mendocino and Estate, North Coast. *Heavy, rich and over-oaky. Clumsy and coarse.*

☆☆☆☆ 1982 CHARDONNAY ($14.00) Jacobs, Carneros District, Napa. *Stunningly elegant blend of oak and crisp fruit. Superb.*

☆☆☆ 1983 CHARDONNAY ($10.75) Estate, Sonoma Valley. *Crisp and bright, with beautifully balanced fruit and oak.*

☆☆☆ 1983 CHARDONNAY ($14.00) Estate, Sonoma Valley. *Crisp, clean, fruity, very attractive.*

☆☆ 1982 GEWURZTRAMINER ($6.35) Estate, Sonoma Valley. *1.95% residual sugar. Caramel, crisp, fruity and clean.*

☆☆☆ 1983 GEWURZTRAMINER ($6.40) Estate, Sonoma Valley. *Crisp, tangy, apple flavors, lovely.*

☆☆☆ 1984 GEWURZTRAMINER ($6.00) Sonoma Valley. *1.98% residual sugar. Spicy, floral, fresh, lovely fruit.*

☆☆ 1981 JOHANNISBERG RIESLING ($5.00) Estate, Sonoma Valley. *1.25% residual sugar. Dry, crisp, low in varietal character.*

☆☆☆ 1982 JOHANNISBERG RIESLING ($5.40) Estate, Sonoma Valley. *1.65% residual sugar. Dry, crisp and varietal.*

1983 JOHANNISBERG RIESLING ($5.40) Sonoma Valley. *2.31% residual sugar. Lacks freshness.*

☆☆☆ 1984 JOHANNISBERG RIESLING ($6.00) Estate, Sonoma Valley. *2% residual sugar. Apple flavors, fresh, fruity, lovely.*

BLANC DE NOIR

☆☆ 1984 PINOT NOIR BLANC ($5.50) Sonoma Valley. *0.9% residual sugar. Clean, fresh and crisp.*

RED

☆ NV POVERELLO ($4.75) Estate, Sonoma Valley. *72% 1983 Pinot Noir, 28% 1982 Pinot Noir. Decent, snappy.*

☆☆ NV SONOMA VALLEY RED ($3.50) Sonoma Valley. *72% Merlot, 16% Pinot Noir, 12% Zinfandel. Rich and balanced.*

☆☆☆ 1981 MERLOT ($10.75) Estate, Sonoma Valley. *Dark, herbal, intense, complex, superb.*

☆☆☆ 1982 MERLOT ($10.75) Estate, Sonoma Valley. *Earthy, fruity, balanced, lovely. Drink now or hold until 1986.*

☆☆ 1980 PINOT NOIR ($12.00) Estate, Sonoma.

☆☆ 1981 PINOT NOIR ($10.75) Estate, Sonoma Valley. *Nice berry ripeness; some stems but attractive and light.*

St. Hilary's Vineyards
CONNECTICUT

Route 12, Webster Road, North Grovenordale, Connecticut 06255 (203-935-5377). FOUNDED: 1977. ACREAGE: 7 acres. PRODUCTION: 170 cases. DISTRIBUTION: At winery. OWNER: Mary Kerensky. WINEMAKER: Peter Kerensky. Tours and tasting daily 10 A.M.–5 P.M.

Peter Kerensky knew he wanted to have something to do with wine when he retired as executive chef at Brown University. He started as a home winemaker, but soon began to exceed the 200-gallon limit. Peter turned his attention to lobbying for the Connecticut Farm Winery Bill, which would make it financially possible for small wineries to survive. Once the bill passed, Peter and his wife, Mary, converted an old barn and opened Connecticut's first winery since Prohibition.

St. James Winery
MISSOURI

540 Sidney Street, St. James, Missouri 65559 (314-265-7912). FOUNDED: 1970. ACREAGE: 70 acres. PRODUCTION: 20,000 cases. DISTRIBUTION: Missouri. OWNERS: Mr. and Mrs. James R. Hofherr. WINEMAKERS: Mr. and Mrs. James R. Hofherr. Tours and tasting summer: Monday–Saturday 8 A.M.–8 P.M., Sunday 12–6 P.M.; winter: Monday–Saturday 8 A.M.–6 P.M., Sunday 12–6 P.M. Gift shop.

Before starting his own champagne cellar, James Hofherr used his knowledge of microbiology in making wine for a number of Missouri wineries. At Post Winery in Altus, he was able to learn a great deal about making sparkling wine. When he was ready, he built a new winery in the heart of Missouri's grape-growing region, right off Highway 44. His first vintages were made from purchased Labrusca grapes. Four years after his first crush, James began planting his own vineyard three miles up the road.

St. Julian Wine Company
MICHIGAN

716 South Kalamazoo Street, Paw Paw, Michigan 49079 (616-657-5568). FOUNDED: 1921. ACREAGE: None. PRODUCTION: 120,000 cases. DISTRIBUTION: 7 states. OWNER: Corporation. Paul R. Braganini, chairman; David Braganini, president. WINEMAKER: Charles W. Catherman. OTHER LABELS: San Giuliano, Château St. Julian. Tours and tasting at Paw Paw and Frankenmuth. Call for information. Delicatessen. Picnic facilities. Gift shop.

This winery was called the "Italian Wine Company" until Mariano Meconi changed the name to honor the patron saint of his Italian birthplace, Faleria. During the 1950s and 1960s, Mariano's sons and his son-in-law, Paul Braganini, took over and expanded the winery, changing the style of wines to meet popular tastes. Paul's son David has worked hard to keep the winery in the family. Recently he started a new facility in Frankenmuth for méthode champenoise sparkling wine, while continuing to make still table wines at the original winery.

WHITE

☆ 1983 RAVAT VIGNOLES RESERVE ($6.50) Lake Michigan Shore. *Overly sweet, some off odors.*

SPARKLING

☆ NV BRUT ($6.60) Michigan.

RED

☆☆ 1981 CHANCELLOR ($8.50) Lake Michigan Shore. *Deep, complex, woody. Drink 1986.*

FORTIFIED

☆☆☆ SOLERA CREAM SHERRY ($6.75) Michigan. *Smooth and rich.*

ST. REGIS VINEYARDS *see* Paul Masson Vineyards

ST. VRAIN *see* Morgan Winery

St. Wendel Cellars
INDIANA

10501 Winery Road, Wadesville, Indiana 47638 (812-963-6441). FOUNDED: 1975. ACREAGE: 30 acres. PRODUCTION: 10,000 cases. DISTRIBUTION: Indiana. OWNER: Corporation. Murli

Dharmadhikari, vice president. WINEMAKER: Murli Dharmadhikari. OTHER LABEL: Golden Raintree. Tours Tuesday–Sunday 11 A.M., 2 P.M., and 4 P.M. Tasting Tuesday–Sunday 11 A.M.– 6 P.M.

After Indiana passed a small winery bill in 1971, a group of ten investors decided to revive viticulture in the southern part of the state. The winery was built into the side of a hill, partially underground, behind a chalet-style, A-frame tasting room. A staff was hired and the winery became functional. The winery's name, previously Golden Raintree Cellars, was changed to St. Wendel in the fall of 1984.

ᶘ

Saintsbury Winery
NAPA COUNTY

1500 Los Carneros Avenue, Napa, California 94558 (707-252-0592). FOUNDED: 1981. ACREAGE: None. PRODUCTION: 15,000 cases. DISTRIBUTION: 34 states. OWNERS: Limited partnership. David W. Graves and Richard A. Ward, managing general partners. WINEMAKERS: Richard A. Ward and David W. Graves. Tours, tasting, and retail sales by appointment.

The two young principals of Saintsbury, Richard Ward and David Graves, met while studying enology at U.C. Davis in 1977. After graduation, both went to work for different wineries, only to meet again a few years later and establish their own winery. Their major concern is to find the right grapes, grown in cool areas, that can produce a certain style of Pinot Noir and Chardonnay. After renting space in an old winery (see Ehlers Lane Winery), they built their own small, efficient facility in the Carneros region, close to where all of their grapes are grown.

WHITE

★★★ 1981 CHARDONNAY ($10.00) Sonoma. *Lovely, soft and toasty. Clean, tart and varietal.*
★★ 1982 CHARDONNAY ($11.00) Sonoma. *Crisp and earthy, with nice varietal flavors. Decent.*
★★★ 1983 CHARDONNAY ($11.00) Napa Valley. *Fresh, balanced, lovely.*

RED

★ 1981 PINOT NOIR ($7.50) Rancho Carneros, Napa Valley.
★★ 1982 PINOT NOIR ($8.00) Sonoma. *Nicely structured, good fruit and aging potential.*
★★★ 1982 PINOT NOIR ($11.00) Carneros District, Napa Valley. *Lush, fruity, clean, with great depth. Drink now.*
★★ 1983 PINOT NOIR ($8.00) Garnet, Carneros. *Varietal, clean, fresh, attractive.*
★★★ 1983 PINOT NOIR ($12.00) Carneros District, Napa Valley. *Spicy, cherry flavored, clean. Drink 1986 and beyond.*

ᶘ

Sakonnet Vineyards
RHODE ISLAND

West Main Road, Little Compton, Rhode Island 02837 (401-635-4356). FOUNDED: 1975. ACREAGE: 50 acres. PRODUCTION: 10,000 cases. DISTRIBUTION: New England states. OWNERS: James A. and Lloyd A. Mitchell. WINEMAKER: Blair Tatman. Tours May–October: Wednesday and Saturday 10 A.M.–5 P.M. Tasting May–December: Tuesday–Saturday 10 A.M.–5 P.M. Picnic facilities.

While working as a consultant in energy and petrochemicals, Jim Mitchell found himself stationed in Libya with very little to do. He found making wine was a very pleasant diversion. Back in the United States, Jim and his wife, Lolly, decided to start a business. They first considered a cheese-making operation, but they decided a winery could be more challenging and much more rewarding. They chose a site not far from Rhode Island Sound (where the America's Cup race takes place), planted French-American hybrids, and later added vinifera. The winery has one section, built in 1980, that is heated and cooled by solar energy. Now that Jim has had experience with French hybrids, Chardonnay, and Riesling, his goal is to make outstanding Pinot Noir.

WHITE

☆   1983 CHARDONNAY ($8.50) Rhode Island. *Clean, attractive.*

RED

1979 RED TABLE WINE ($5.00) Rhode Island. *80% Chancellor.*
☆   1982 RHODE ISLAND RED ($5.00) Newport County. *Clean, fruity.*
☆   NV PINOT NOIR ($9.00) Estate, Southeast New England. *Vegetal, decent.*

Salishan Vineyards
WASHINGTON

Route 2, La Center North Fork Road, La Center, Washington 98629 (206-263-2713). FOUNDED: 1982. ACREAGE: 12 acres. PRODUCTION: 3,000 cases. DISTRIBUTION: Washington and Oregon. OWNER: Corporation. Joan and Lincoln Wolverton, principals. WINEMAKER: Joan Wolverton. Tours and tasting May–December: weekends 1 P.M.–5 P.M., or by appointment.

For eight years the Wolvertons commuted from their home in Seattle to their vineyard in the Columbia Gorge, just over the state line from Portland. Lincoln was working as an economist in Seattle, and Joan was a reporter for the Seattle *Times.* They farmed on the weekends until the vineyard became too important and the desire to start a winery too irresistible. Joan moved to the vineyard with their two sons first, and Lincoln followed later. Joan became the winemaker; her journalistic skills were a great help in getting started. "Reporters are great note-takers," she explains. "My winemaking training came from running down to U.C. Davis for quick courses and taking fourteen years' worth of notes." Lincoln still works as an economist with the Portland Public Power Council.

Salter Winery
EL DORADO COUNTY

7700 Silent Pass, Somerset, California 95684 (209-245-3726). FOUNDED: 1982. ACREAGE: None. PRODUCTION: 2,000 cases. DISTRIBUTION: Local. OWNERS: David and Mary Salter. WINEMAKER: David Salter. Tours by appointment.

David Salter makes carrot wine, beet wine, zucchini wine, parsnip wine, and, for the first time this year, pumpkin wine. To the average American wine drinker, vegetable wines may sound bizarre if not repulsive, but according to English-born David, vegetable wines are an old Anglo-Saxon tradition. "They are usually stronger, around 13 to 17 percent alcohol," David says. Before he and his wife moved to the United States and settled in the Sierra foothills, David made some of these wines in England. Once arrived, they added grape wines to their vegetable and fruit repertoire. Presently, the Salters do not have any vineyards, but they do grow their own vegetables.

San Antonio Winery
LOS ANGELES COUNTY

737 Lamar Street, Los Angeles, California 90031 (213-223-2236). FOUNDED: 1917. ACREAGE: None. PRODUCTION: 400,000 cases. DISTRIBUTION: Southern California. OWNER: Riboli

family. Steve Riboli, president. WINEMAKER: Jon Alexander. Tours daily 10 A.M.–4 P.M.; self-guided tours during the week, guided tours on the weekends. Tasting Monday–Saturday 8 A.M.–7 P.M., Sunday 10 A.M.–6 P.M. Gift shop. Restaurant.

In the smog and industrial innards of downtown Los Angeles, next to the Southern Pacific railroad tracks, stands the last producing winery within the city limits, San Antonio Winery. Listed as Historical Landmark No. 42, the winery is run by the third generation of the founding Cambianica family. More than a winery, it is also a cafeteria that is more like a huge Italian family room—full of spicy smells and the din of happy voices. The winery and the cafeteria draws a steady, loyal band of wine-drinking customers. Like most traditional Italian-American wineries, San Antonio made its reputation from four-liter jug wines. Varietal wine was only added in the 1970s. The family philosophy: "To make wines people enjoy drinking at a price they enjoy paying."

San Martin Winery
SANTA CLARA COUNTY

13000 Depot Street, San Martin, California 95046 (408-683-4000). FOUNDED: 1906. ACREAGE: None. PRODUCTION: 400,000 cases. DISTRIBUTION: Nationwide. OWNER: Somerset Wine Company (DLC Corporation). WINEMAKER: Ronald S. Niino, winemaster; Mark Caporale. No tours. Tasting daily 9 A.M.–5:30 P.M.

This historic Santa Clara winery was originally founded as a cooperative. Later, when owned by the Filice family, the winery made only fruit and berry wines. San Martin was one of the first wineries to popularize the tasting-room concept. In 1973 the facility was modernized when it was purchased by a New York company, Southdown, which added new processing equipment, new management, and a German-American winemaker, Ed Friedrich, who made low-alcohol "soft" wines long before they became stylish. In 1977, the winery was purchased by Norton Simon's Somerset Wine Company, which was subsequently absorbed by the English company that makes Johnnie Walker Scotch whisky.

WHITE

☆ 1982 CHABLIS ($4.00) California. *Clean and fresh, simple, decent.*

☆ 1984 CHABLIS ($3.95) California. *Off-dry, clean, fresh.*

O 1982 RHINE ($4.00) California. *Sweet, oxidized and unattractive.*

☆☆ 1984 RHINE ($3.95) California. *Greenish tint, fruity, off-dry, clean, attractive.*

☆☆ NV CHARDONNAY ($7.00) California. *1.5 liter. Assertive flavors, clean and amazingly complex.*

1980 CHARDONNAY ($11.00) Special Reserve, Santa Barbara.

☆ 1981 CHARDONNAY ($7.15) San Luis Obispo.

☆ 1982 CHARDONNAY ($7.00) San Luis Obispo. *Nice, clean, pleasant but not much depth.*

☆☆ 1983 CHARDONNAY ($7.25) San Luis Obispo. *Decent, clean, buttery oak; attractive.*

☆☆ NV CHENIN BLANC ($6.00) California. *1.5 liter. Off-dry, nice, clean and apple fruity.*

☆☆ 1982 SOFT CHENIN BLANC ($5.25) California. *Sweet, rich, clean and snappy.*

☆ 1983 CHENIN BLANC ($5.25) California. *Soft, sweet, sappy, with some overripe flavors.*

☆ 1983 SOFT CHENIN BLANC ($5.25) California.

☆☆ NV FUME BLANC ($6.00) California. *1.5 liter. Herbal and clean, very good—and what a price!*

1980 FUME BLANC ($7.25) Special Reserve, San Luis Obispo.

☆ 1981 FUME BLANC ($5.50) San Luis Obispo.

☆ 1982 FUME BLANC ($6.50) San Luis Obispo. *Watery but varietal.*

☆☆ NV JOHANNISBERG RIESLING ($6.00) California. *1.5 liter. Off-dry, clean and delicious. A bargain.*

1979 JOHANNISBERG RIESLING ($8.00) Late Harvest, Santa Clara. *15.8% residual sugar. Mushroomy, flat.*

☆☆☆ 1980 JOHANNISBERG RIESLING ($8.00) Late Harvest, Santa Clara. *15% residual sugar. Lovely, soft and lush; fruity, deep.*

☆☆☆ 1981 JOHANNISBERG RIESLING ($8.00) Late Harvest, Santa Clara. *8.6% residual sugar. Unctuous and soft, with lovely fruit.*

☆ 1982 SOFT JOHANNISBERG RIESLING ($6.00) California. *4.58% residual sugar; 8% alcohol.*

☆☆ 1983 JOHANNISBERG RIESLING ($5.50) Central Coast. *0.8% residual sugar. 20% Gewürztraminer. Tangy, crisp, clean.*

☆☆ 1983 SOFT JOHANNISBERG RIESLING ($6.00) California.

☆☆ 1984 SOFT JOHANNISBERG RIESLING ($4.00) Central Coast. *Soft, varietal, elegant, gentle fruit, quite pleasant.*

☆☆ 1983 SAUVIGNON BLANC ($6.50) Central Coast. *Grassy, fruity.*

BLANC DE NOIR

NV WHITE ZINFANDEL ($5.00) California. *Dull.*

☆☆ 1984 SOFT WHITE ZINFANDEL ($4.00) Central Coast. *Crisp, lemony, clean; pleasant.*

ROSE

☆ 1984 ROSE ($3.95) California. *Off-dry, clean, with attractive strawberry flavors.*

RED

☆ 1980 BURGUNDY ($3.95) California. *Clean, balanced but vegetal.*

☆☆ NV CABERNET SAUVIGNON ($6.00) California. *Varietal, oaky, clean, rich; very attractive.*

☆ 1978 CABERNET SAUVIGNON ($12.25) Special Reserve, San Luis Obispo. *Big and fat; grapey, intense. Lacks finesse.*

☆ 1979 CABERNET SAUVIGNON ($6.80) San Luis Obispo. *Soft, sweetish, simple.*

☆ 1981 CABERNET SAUVIGNON ($7.75) Central Coast. *Clean, varietal, simple, decent.*

☆ 1981 CABERNET SAUVIGNON ($8.00) San Luis Obispo. *Thin, simple, decent, balanced and soft.*

☆ 1984 SOFT GAMAY BEAUJOLAIS ($4.00) Central Coast. *Pale, off-dry, crisp, fruity, pleasant.*

☆☆ NV ZINFANDEL ($6.00) California. *1.5 liter. Nice, rich fruit, clean and very likable.*

1980 ZINFANDEL ($4.50) Amador. *Sweet, lush, a bit hot.*

☆ 1982 ZINFANDEL ($6.00) Amador. *Fruity, crisp, clean but lacking varietal character.*

SAN MICAIRE *see* Robert Pecota Winery

San Pasqual Vineyards
SAN DIEGO COUNTY

13455 San Pasqual Road, Escondido, California 92025 (619-741-0855). FOUNDED: 1973. ACREAGE: 120 acres. PRODUCTION: 23,000 cases. DISTRIBUTION: 8 states, West and East Coast. OWNER: Milton Fredman, chairman; Kerry Damskey, president; Charles Froehlich, vice president. WINEMAKER: Kerry Damskey. Tours weekends 1:30 P.M. and 3:30 P.M. OTHER LABEL: Aeolus. Tasting and retail sales daily 11 A.M.–5 P.M.

Before Kerry Damskey came to San Pasqual Vineyards, he was very skeptical about the prospects for wine production in San Diego County. A northern California boy at heart, he had graduated from U.C. Davis and had worked three years for Guild wineries before he heard that the winemaking position at San Pasqual was open. When Kerry saw how well-designed the winery was and how carefully the vineyards were being maintained by a U.C. Davis viticulturalist, he was tantalized by the potential. He took the job and is glad he did.

WHITE

☆ 1981 CHENIN BLANC ($6.25) San Pasqual Valley.
☆ 1983 CHENIN BLANC ($5.00) California. *Fruity, clean, simple, coarse.*
  1981 FUME BLANC ($6.75) San Diego.
☆☆ 1980 MUSCAT ($7.50) San Pasqual Valley.
☆☆☆ 1983 MUSCAT ($8.00) Estrella River, Paso Robles. *4% residual sugar. Soft, clean, fruity, varietal, with good acidity.*
O 1982 SAUVIGNON BLANC ($7.25) San Pasqual Valley. *8% Semillon. Heavy, clumsy, oxidized.*
☆☆ 1983 SAUVIGNON BLANC ($7.25) California. *Grassy, fresh and fruity.*

RED

  1981 GAMAY ($5.75) Highland Valley, San Pasqual Valley. *Dark, intense but overripe.*
☆☆ 1984 GAMAY ($5.00) California. *Grapey, snappy, clean and attractive.*
☆ 1982 GAMAY BEAUJOLAIS ($5.00) San Pasqual Valley.
O 1982 AEOLUS PINOT NOIR ($10.00) Sierra Madre, Santa Maria. *Intensely vegetal.*

Sanchez-Gill-Richter-Cordier
TEXAS

400 West 15th Street, Suite 505, Austin, Texas 78701 (512-454-3333). FOUNDED: 1984. ACREAGE: 1,000 acres. PRODUCTION: 75,000 cases. DISTRIBUTION: Texas. OWNER: Limited partnership. Richardson Gill, president; Paul Merrigan, general manager. WINEMAKERS: Lucien Viaud and Jean-Louis Haberer.

In the early 1970s, the University of Texas began a grape feasibility program, headed by Dr. Charles O. McKinney, on two of its two million acres of flatland. This project grew to include plantings throughout the state. One of the university's experiments, the Escondido Vineyards, was leased to Richardson Gill, principal of Gill Savings and Loan, wine lover, and board chairman of the Llano Estacado Winery. He formed a partnership with two French firms, Richter S.A., a leader in viticultural techniques, and the famous Bordeaux house, Cordier. In 1984, the same year that the huge winery was completed, the Toni Sanchez family joined the partnership. The Sanchezes are affiliated with oil companies and savings and loans.

RED

1981 CABERNET SAUVIGNON ($9.00) Texas. *Smoky, thin, lacking fruit.*

Sandstone Winery
IOWA

P.O. Box 7, Amana, Iowa 52203 (319-622-3081). FOUNDED: 1960. ACREAGE: None. PRODUCTION: 3,300 cases. DISTRIBUTION: At winery. OWNER: Corporation. Elsie Mattes, president. WINEMAKER: Joseph Mattes. No tours. Tasting Monday–Saturday 9 A.M.–8 P.M.; Sundays and holidays 12–5 P.M.

Joseph Mattes learned the winemaking art from his wife's family. Using all he knew, Joe started his own basement winery. Since that time the winery has expanded into the garage above the basement. Despite the expansion Sandstone is still a family operation involving just Joe, Elsie, and their children.

Sanford & Benedict
SANTA BARBARA COUNTY

5500 Santa Rosa Road, Lompoc, California 93436 (805-688-8314). FOUNDED: 1972. ACREAGE: 114 acres. PRODUCTION: 8,000 cases. DISTRIBUTION: Nationwide; England. OWNER: Michael Benedict. WINEMAKER: Michael Benedict. Tours and tasting Monday–Saturday by appointment.

Michael Benedict and Richard Sanford took a very rational, scientific approach to growing grapes, carefully studying the relationship between microclimates and plant response. Prepared to go anywhere to find the right piece of land, they found a 700-acre ranch that, according to Mike's calculations, had an excellent climate for Pinot Noir. An experimental wine made from the grapes in 1975 convinced the partners to start a commercial winery. Although other varieties are produced, Pinot Noir is still Mike's passion. In 1980 Richard Sanford left to start his own winery in Buellton (see Sanford Winery).

WHITE

☆ 1981 CHARDONNAY ($9.00) Estate, Santa Ynez Valley. *Toasty, intense, with some muddy flavors.*

RED

1979 CABERNET SAUVIGNON ($10.00) Santa Maria Valley.
O 1979 PINOT NOIR ($9.00) Estate, Santa Ynez Valley. *Weedy and unpleasant.*

Sanford Winery
SANTA BARBARA COUNTY

7250 Santa Rosa Road, Buellton, California 93427 (805-688-3300). FOUNDED: 1981. ACREAGE: None. PRODUCTION: 18,000 cases. DISTRIBUTION: California and worldwide. OWNERS: Richard and Thekla Sanford. WINEMAKERS: Richard Sanford and Bruno D'Alfonso. Tours by appointment.

The original Sanford of the Sanford & Benedict winery, Richard Sanford broke away from his first winery venture in 1980 because he no longer wanted to make wine by committee. He was also becoming too involved with the administrative rather than the creative side of winemaking. Richard and his wife, Thekla, produced their first crush at Edna Valley Vineyards before they moved their operation to a concrete warehouse in Buellton. In 1982 they bought a 760-acre ranch and began constructing their own adobe-style winery.

WHITE

☆☆☆ 1981 CHARDONNAY ($12.00) Santa Maria Valley. *Oaky, clean, rich, complex.*
☆☆☆ 1982 CHARDONNAY ($12.00) Santa Maria Valley. *Very toasty, with ripe, tart fruitiness.*
☆☆ 1983 CHARDONNAY ($12.50) Central Coast. *Toasty, fat, big, luscious but lacking structure.*
☆☆☆ 1981 SAUVIGNON BLANC ($8.50) Santa Maria Valley. *Grassy, varietal, clean, attractive.*
☆☆ 1982 SAUVIGNON BLANC ($8.50) Santa Maria Valley. *Oaky, rich, vinous; very stylish.*
☆☆☆ 1983 SAUVIGNON BLANC ($8.00) Central Coast. *Deep, grassy, rich, clean, charming.*

BLANC DE NOIR

☆☆☆ 1982 PINOT NOIR ($6.50) Vin Gris, Santa Barbara. *Pinot Noir. Crisp, oaky, clean, rich and flavorful.*

RED

☆☆ 1981 PINOT NOIR ($10.50) Santa Maria Valley. *Earthy, rich, intense. Drink 1986.*
O 1982 PINOT NOIR ($10.50) Santa Maria Valley. *Earthy, vegetal, unattractive.*

Sangre de Cristo Wines
NEW MEXICO

Route 2, Box 20-A, Sapello, New Mexico 87745 (505-425-5077). FOUNDED: 1983. ACREAGE: None. PRODUCTION: 40 cases. DISTRIBUTION: New Mexico. OWNER: Richard Jones. WINE-MAKER: Richard Jones. Tours by appointment.

When Richard Jones began making more homemade wine than he could possibly consume, he started giving it away. "I thought to myself, 'Now that's not very smart,'" says Richard. "Why should I be giving it away instead of selling it?" Consequently, in between freelance writing and other odd jobs, Richard set up a bonded winery in the back of his garage. He is making one wine from an exclusive variety called Luci Kuhlmann.

Santa Barbara Winery
SANTA BARBARA COUNTY

202 Anacapa Street, Santa Barbara, California 93101 (805-963-8924). FOUNDED: 1962. ACREAGE: 50 acres. PRODUCTION: 10,000 cases. DISTRIBUTION: California. OWNER: Pierre Lafond. WINEMAKER: Bruce McGuire; Bill Dubois, consultant. Tours and tasting weekdays 9:30 A.M.– 5 P.M., weekends 10 A.M.–5 P.M. Gift shop.

Pierre Lafond is the owner of two gourmet food and wine shops in Santa Barbara. When he began his winery, there were very few vineyards in the Santa Barbara area, and grapes had to be purchased from the San Luis Obispo region. Most of the production was low-priced generic wine, dessert wine, and fruit wine. After Pierre planted a Santa Ynez Valley vineyard in 1972, the winery began to move towards premium varietal wine production. Located in downtown Santa Barbara, near the beach, the winery is said to be the oldest in Santa Barbara County.

WHITE

☆ 1982 CHARDONNAY ($9.00) Santa Ynez Valley. *Clean and crisp but lacking depth.*
☆☆ 1982 CHENIN BLANC ($5.50) Santa Ynez Valley. *0.6% residual sugar. Good intensity, nice, clean, vinous.*
　　1983 CHENIN BLANC ($5.50) Santa Ynez Valley. *Dull, vegetal.*
　　1981 JOHANNISBERG RIESLING ($6.50) Late Harvest, Santa Barbara. *1.7% residual sugar. Varnishy but decent flavors.*
☆☆☆ 1984 JOHANNISBERG RIESLING ($6.50) Santa Barbara. *2.2% residual sugar. Stunning, varietal, delicious.*
○ 1982 SAUVIGNON BLANC ($7.50) Santa Barbara.

BLANC DE NOIR

☆☆ 1984 WHITE CABERNET ($5.50) Santa Barbara. *1% residual sugar. Snappy, clean, with good varietal flavors.*
☆ 1982 WHITE ZINFANDEL ($5.00) Santa Ynez Valley. *Crisp, clean, decent.*
☆ 1984 WHITE ZINFANDEL ($5.50) Central Coast. *Decent but with some off flavors.*

RED

　　1979 CABERNET SAUVIGNON ($7.50) Reserve, Estate, Santa Ynez Valley. *Weedy and lush, with simple, unappealing flavors.*
☆ 1981 CABERNET SAUVIGNON ($12.00) Reserve, Estate, Santa Ynez Valley. *Vegetal, heavy.*
○ 1980 ZINFANDEL ($5.00) Santa Ynez Valley. *Weedy.*
　　1980 ZINFANDEL ($7.50) Late Harvest, Estate, Santa Ynez Valley.

☆☆   1981 ZINFANDEL ($7.00) Santa Ynez Valley. *Clean and varietal but lacking charm and grace.*
     1981 ZINFANDEL ($7.50) Late Harvest, Santa Ynez Valley. *2% residual sugar. Oxidized, unappealing.*

Santa Cruz Mountain Vineyard
SANTA CRUZ COUNTY

2300 Jarvis Road, Santa Cruz, California 95065 (408-426-6209). FOUNDED: 1974. ACREAGE: 15 acres. PRODUCTION: 3,000 cases. DISTRIBUTION: 13 states. OWNER: Ken Burnap. WINE-MAKER: Ken Burnap; Bill Craig, cellarmaster. Tours, tasting, and sales by appointment.

Ken Burnap is a big, raw-boned, mustachioed fellow who used to run a restaurant in Los Angeles. He is obsessed with the idea of making great Pinot Noir. In 1974 he bought a Pinot Noir vineyard high in the Santa Cruz Mountains that had been planted by David Bruce. The results of his endeavor so far have been rather startling; Ken is well on the way to becoming a legend in his own time.

RED

☆☆   1978 CABERNET SAUVIGNON ($12.00) Bates Ranch, Santa Cruz Mountains. *Rich, berried, tannic. Drink 1986 and beyond.*
☆☆☆ 1979 CABERNET SAUVIGNON ($14.00) Bates Ranch, Santa Cruz Mountains. *Balanced, clean, oaky, varietal, lovely. Drink 1986.*
     1980 CABERNET SAUVIGNON ($14.00) Gamble Ranch, Napa Valley. *Weird; rich, sweet and chocolatey.*
☆☆   1981 CABERNET SAUVIGNON ($12.50) Bates Ranch, Santa Cruz Mountains. *Rough, rich, varietal. Drink 1987.*
☆☆   1978 DURIF ($7.50) Jones Ranch, California. *Big, fat, lush, tannic.*
☆☆   1982 DURIF ($9.00) Santa Cruz Mountains. *Smoky, fruity, clean.*
☆☆   NV 1978/1979 PINOT NOIR ($15.00) 70% 1978 Rider Ridge, 30% Sleepy Hollow, 70% Santa Cruz Mountains, 30% Monterey. *Big, leathery, tart, tannic.*
☆☆☆ 1977 PINOT NOIR ($8.00) Estate, Rider Ridge, Santa Cruz. *Deep, rich and complex.*
☆☆   1979 PINOT NOIR ($15.00) Estate, Rider Ridge, Santa Cruz. *Toasty, clean, with long aging potential.*
☆☆☆ 1981 PINOT NOIR ($15.00) Santa Cruz Mountains. *Rich, balanced, deep; delightful.*

SANTA LUCIA CELLARS *see* HMR Estate Winery

Santa Ynez Valley Winery
SANTA BARBARA COUNTY

365 North Refugio Road, Santa Ynez, California 93460 (805-688-8381). FOUNDED: 1976. ACREAGE: None. PRODUCTION: 12,000 cases. DISTRIBUTION: 10 states. OWNERS: Davidge, Bettencourt, and Brander families. WINEMAKER: Michael Brown. Tours and tasting daily 10 A.M.–4 P.M.

The Davidge and Bettencourt families planted the first vineyard in the Santa Ynez Valley in 1969 on the Bettencourt dairy farm. For a while, they produced milk and farmed grapes, selling most of them to Paul Masson Vineyards. When they tried making a few wines themselves, they enlisted the help of Fred Brander, who was starting his own vineyard and winery nearby (see

Brander Vineyard). Taking advantage of Fred's winemaking skills, the two families closed down the dairy and, with Fred as partner, opened a winery in the dairy barn. Fred made the wine until 1983, when Mike Brown took over as winemaker.

WHITE

☆☆ 1981 CHARDONNAY ($12.00) Reserve, Santa Ynez Valley.

1982 CHARDONNAY ($8.00) Santa Ynez Valley. *Toasty and vegetal; earthy, vinous and clumsy.*

○ 1982 GEWURZTRAMINER ($6.50) Santa Ynez Valley. *0.43% residual sugar. Dry and unpleasant, with volatile acidity.*

1983 GEWURZTRAMINER ($6.50) California. *Odd, unattractive.*

☆☆☆ 1983 JOHANNISBERG RIESLING ($6.00) Santa Ynez Valley. *1.5% residual sugar. Crisp, fresh, clean and varietal.*

☆ 1981 SAUVIGNON BLANC ($8.00) Santa Barbara.

1981 SAUVIGNON BLANC ($9.00) Reserve de Cave, Santa Ynez Valley.

☆ 1982 SAUVIGNON BLANC ($7.50) California.

☆☆ 1983 SAUVIGNON BLANC ($7.00) Santa Ynez Valley. *20% Semillon. Crisp, snappy, varietal.*

☆☆ 1981 WHITE RIESLING ($6.00) Santa Ynez Valley. *2% residual sugar. Oily, lush, clean and melony.*

1982 WHITE RIESLING ($6.00) Santa Ynez Valley. *2.17% residual sugar. Dull, lacking freshness.*

BLANC DE NOIR

☆☆☆ 1983 BLANC DE CABERNET ($5.00) Santa Ynez Valley. *1.8% residual sugar. Lush, clean, fruity, balanced, lovely.*

RED

1980 CABERNET SAUVIGNON ($5.00) Santa Ynez Valley. *Ripe and crisp, with a bell pepper nose and vegetal flavors.*

1980 MERLOT ($6.00) Bien Nacido, Santa Maria Valley.

☆☆ 1982 MERLOT ($7.50) Santa Ynez Valley.

☆ 1983 MERLOT ($4.25) L'Enfant, Santa Ynez Valley. *Vegetal but fresh; fruity and nicely made.*

Santee Valley Winery
SAN DIEGO COUNTY

8665 Mission Gorge Road, Santee, California 92071 (619-448-5089). FOUNDED: 1983. ACREAGE: None. PRODUCTION: 800 cases. DISTRIBUTION: At winery. OWNERS: John R. and Connie Flickinger. WINEMAKER: John "Bob" Flickinger. Tours and tasting by appointment.

Hobby winemaking was good to John Flickinger. While living in Seattle he won prizes for homemade wines, and when he moved to Southern California in 1979 he continued to win awards for his amateur creations. Kerry Damsky, winemaker at San Pasqual, and Joe Hart of Hart Winery encouraged John to expand his production and become a professional winemaker. Heeding their advice, John leased warehouse space next to "Aluminum City," his mobile home accessory business, to set up his winery.

Santino Wines
AMADOR COUNTY

1225 Steiner Road, Plymouth, California 95669 (209-245-6979). FOUNDED: 1979. ACREAGE: None. PRODUCTION: 20,000 cases. DISTRIBUTION: Major market states; Canada. OWNER:

Nancy Santino. WINEMAKER: Scott Harvey. Tours and tasting weekdays 9 A.M.–4 P.M., weekends 12–4 P.M.

Nancy and Mathew Santino were the owners of a liquor store in the San Francisco Bay area when they decided to move to the country. They were attracted to the Sierra foothills because of the area's beauty, and because Nancy "knew this area was a sleeper as far as grape growing and winemaking were concerned." Making wine at home was the extent of their enological background, so Scott Harvey, who had worked at Monteviña and Story wineries, was hired to make the wine.

WHITE

☆ 1983 FUME BLANC ($4.00) Shenandoah Valley.
   1982 SAUVIGNON BLANC ($4.00) HFH Ranch, Shenandoah Valley, Amador.

BLANC DE NOIR

☆☆ 1983 WHITE ZINFANDEL ($4.75) Amador. *2.8% residual sugar.*
☆☆☆ 1984 WHITE HARVEST ZINFANDEL ($4.75) Amador. *Rich, complex, off-dry, with charming acidity.*

RED

☆☆ 1980 CABERNET SAUVIGNON ($8.00) Stone Barn, El Dorado. *Tart, oaky, astringent but quite likable.*
☆ 1980 ZINFANDEL ($6.50) Shenandoah Valley, Amador.
☆☆☆ 1980 ZINFANDEL ($7.50) Special Selection, Eschen Vineyards, Fiddletown, Amador. *Great fruit and character.*
☆☆ 1981 ZINFANDEL ($5.75) Shenandoah Valley. *Tannic, crisp, fruity.*
☆☆ 1981 ZINFANDEL ($7.50) Special Selection, Eschen Vineyards, Fiddletown, Amador. *Rich, berried, varietal.*

Sarah's Vineyard
SANTA CLARA COUNTY

4005 Hecker Pass Highway, Gilroy, California 95020 (408-842-4278). FOUNDED: 1978. ACREAGE: 7 acres. PRODUCTION: 1,800 cases. DISTRIBUTION: Major market states. OWNERS: Marilyn and John Otteman, Steve and Donna Hicks, and Debbie and Craig McManigal. WINEMAKER: Marilyn Otteman. Tours by appointment.

The divorced mother of five children, Marilyn Otteman was trying to decide what to do with her life. Her dream was to make wine. One day she met a "Prince Charming," John Otteman, who found a "castle" on a hilltop and offered to buy it for her to make her dream come true. Six months later, she and John moved in. That was in 1977, and their first crush was in 1978. Marilyn, who learned winemaking on the job, firmly believes that dreams really can come true.

WHITE

☆ 1981 CHARDONNAY ($10.50) California.
☆☆☆ 1981 CHARDONNAY ($14.00) Paragon, Edna Valley. *Beautifully balanced, crisp and complex. A classic.*
☆☆☆ 1982 CHARDONNAY ($14.00) Monterey. *Crisp, clean and lovely. Great varietal character.*
☆☆☆ 1982 CHARDONNAY ($16.00) Ventana, Monterey. *Crisp, clean and varietal. Drink 1986.*

☆☆☆ 1983 CHARDONNAY ($16.00) Ventana, Monterey. *Snappy, clean, lively.*
☆☆☆ 1983 CHARDONNAY ($17.00) Estate, Santa Clara. *Crisp, deep, rich, clean, super.*
 ☆☆☆ 1983 JOHANNISBERG RIESLING ($8.50) Victor Matheu. *6% residual sugar. Clean, sweet, very good.*

RED

☆☆ 1980 CABERNET SAUVIGNON ($12.00) San Luis Obispo. *Mellow and fruity. Drink now.*
☆☆ 1980 ZINFANDEL ($9.00) Lime Kiln Valley, San Benito. *Big and somewhat harsh. Clean and powerful.*
☆☆ 1980 ZINFANDEL ($10.00) Les Vignerons Vignoble, Sonoma. *Big, late-harvest style. Clean, rich and concentrated.*
☆☆☆ 1981 ZINFANDEL ($9.00) Dry Creek Valley. *Rich, ripe and fruity, with great balance.*
☆☆ 1981 ZINFANDEL ($9.00) Peterson, Sonoma. *Lush, rich, fruity and very appealing.*

Satiety
YOLO COUNTY

1027 Maple Lane, Davis, California 95616 (916-757-2699). FOUNDED: 1981. ACREAGE: 29 acres. PRODUCTION: 7,000 cases. DISTRIBUTION: California; Japan. OWNERS: Sterling and Elaine Chaykin. WINEMAKERS: Sterling Chaykin and David Crippen. Tours, sales, and tasting at winery weekends 1 P.M.–4 P.M. Winery is located at the southeast corner of State Highway 113 and County Road 25A, Woodland.

This winery is only a small part of what is supposedly yet to come: a complete country food and wine complex. Sterling Chaykin feels that a vineyard and winery are elemental parts of his concept. The winery, first set up on the Chaykins' side patio, was originally used to make wine vinegar. But in the summer of 1983 Sterling built a fully equipped winery on his vineyard site and began to sell the wine locally. A restaurant is the next step. Sterling has called his operation Satiety, since it is his wish that his customers be satiated with food and wine and life in general.

V. Sattui Winery
NAPA COUNTY

White Lane at Highway 29 South, St. Helena, California 94574 (707-963-7774). FOUNDED: 1885. ACREAGE: None. PRODUCTION: 15,000 cases. DISTRIBUTION: At winery and by mail order. OWNER: Daryl Sattui. WINEMAKERS: Daryl Sattui and Rick Rosenbrand. Tours and tasting daily 9 A.M.–6 P.M. Newsletter. Gift shop. Delicatessen. Picnic facilities.

Daryl Sattui had no money, no previous winemaking experience, and no reputation when he revived his great-grandfather's winery. "When we signed the partnership papers, I was literally broke," says Daryl. Both the winery and the property were leased, and the equipment—except for a few barrels—was rented. Everyone expected a quick and dramatic failure. Daryl knew that if the project was going to work, it had to work fast. One thing the winery had going for it was its location right on heavily traveled Highway 29 in the center of Napa Valley. Daryl devised an ingenious way to get people to stop and try his wine: He opened a large cheese shop in front of the winery and surrounded it with picnic tables. Now a quarter of a million people visit the winery each year, and Daryl can sell all the wine he makes right in his tasting room. He has recently expanded into a 18,000-square-foot building with an underground stone cellar.

WHITE

1981 CHARDONNAY ($9.75) Napa Valley. *Maderized.*
☆☆ 1982 CHARDONNAY ($9.75) Napa Valley. *Simple, clean, with nice varietal character.*
1982 JOHANNISBERG RIESLING ($6.25) Napa Valley. *Very strange; mushroomy.*
☆ 1983 SAUVIGNON BLANC ($7.75) Napa Valley. *25% Semillon. Decent, dense, some bitterness.*

RED

☆☆☆ 1979 CABERNET SAUVIGNON ($9.75) Preston, Napa Valley.
☆☆☆ 1980 CABERNET SAUVIGNON ($9.75) Preston, Napa Valley. *Rich and chocolatey; complex and forceful. Drink 1986.*
☆☆ 1980 ZINFANDEL ($8.75) Napa Valley.
☆☆ 1981 ZINFANDEL ($7.25) Napa Valley. *Clean, tangy, attractive.*

Saucelito Canyon Vineyard
SAN LUIS OBISPO COUNTY

600 Saucelito Creek Road, Arroyo Grande, California 93420 (805-489-8762). FOUNDED: 1982. ACREAGE: 10 acres. PRODUCTION: 1,000 cases. DISTRIBUTION: Local. OWNER: Bill Greenough. WINEMAKER: Bill Greenough. Tours and tasting by appointment.

Bill Greenough brought a 100-year-old Zinfandel vineyard back into production when he bought his remote property behind Lopez Lake in 1974. At first he sold his grapes to other winemakers while making his own wine at home. He then began taking winemaking courses at U.C. Davis and the Napa Valley School of Cellaring and receiving friendly advice from other winemakers. The winery was built in what Bill calls "California barn style" and is located on the vineyard property, not far from the Greenough home.

RED

☆☆ 1982 CABERNET SAUVIGNON ($10.00) San Luis Obispo. *Soft, pleasant, attractive. Drink now.*

Sausal Winery
SONOMA COUNTY

7370 Highway 128, Healdsburg, California 95448 (707-433-2285). FOUNDED: 1973. ACREAGE: 100 acres. PRODUCTION: 8,000 cases. DISTRIBUTION: California, Nevada, and Texas. OWNERS: David, Edward, and Roselee Demostene, and Lucinda Nelson. WINEMAKER: David Demostene. Tours by appointment.

Leo Demostene had always wanted a vineyard and, eventually, a winery. So he pulled out the prunes and apples on his 125-acre ranch in the Alexander Valley, planted grapes, and made plans for a winery. But before he could turn his dreams into reality, Leo died. His children, Dave, Ed, Roselee, and Lucinda, fulfilled their father's wishes and finished his winery. They opened for business in 1973 and have made Zinfandel their specialty.

WHITE

☆ 1982 SAUSAL BLANC ($4.00) Sonoma. *Simple and attractive.*

☆☆ 1983 SAUSAL BLANC ($4.00) Alexander Valley. *French Colombard and Chardonnay. Dry, clean, attractive.*

☆ 1981 CHARDONNAY ($8.50) Alexander Valley.

BLANC DE NOIR

☆☆ 1984 WHITE ZINFANDEL ($5.00) Alexander Valley. *Clean, dry, hard-edged, decent.*

RED

☆☆ 1978 CABERNET SAUVIGNON ($7.50) Alexander Valley. *Fruity, varietal, snappy.*

☆ 1979 CABERNET SAUVIGNON ($7.50) Alexander Valley. *Simple, velvety. Drink now.*

☆ 1978 ZINFANDEL ($5.60) Sonoma. *Overdone: ripe, jammy, almost sweet.*

☆☆ 1979 ZINFANDEL ($5.60) Sonoma. *Grapey and lush.*

☆☆ 1981 ZINFANDEL ($5.60) Alexander Valley. *Rich, varietal, good fruit, a bit heavy.*

☆☆ 1981 ZINFANDEL ($10.00) Private Reserve, Alexander Valley. *Heavy, berried, late-harvest style.*

Sax's Winery
ARKANSAS

Route 1, Altus, Arkansas 72821 (501-468-2534). FOUNDED: 1934. ACREAGE: 13 acres. PRODUCTION: 600 cases. DISTRIBUTION: At winery. OWNER: Henry J. Sax. Charles E. Sax, general manager. WINEMAKER: Charles E. Sax. Tours and tasting daily 8 A.M.–5 P.M.

Apple grower Alfred Sax and his son Henry started in the wine business by making apple wine. Just as they were beginning to produce grape wines, Prohibition came along. Undaunted, they managed to operate a vat or two beneath the house, quietly selling it to the coalminers who worked nearby. After Repeal, Al brought the winery aboveground, Al and Henry planted vineyards of American grapes, and Henry taught the wine business to his son Charles. Now the third generation at the winery, Charles planted French-American hybrids and takes care of the day-to-day affairs.

Schapiro Kosher Wine Company
NEW YORK

126 Rivington Street, New York, New York 10002 (212-674-4404). FOUNDED: 1899. ACREAGE: None. PRODUCTION: 100,000 cases. DISTRIBUTION: Nationwide. OWNER: Schapiro family. Norman Schapiro. WINEMAKER: Nathan Schwartz. Tours and tasting Sundays 10 A.M.–5 P.M.

The oldest kosher winery in the country and the only winery still functioning in New York City, this facility is run by the third generation of the Schapiro family. "Every generation has left its stamp on this winery," says Norman Schapiro, whose grandfather, Samuel Schapiro, a Polish immigrant, started the business by making mead and malaga for restaurants in the early 1900s. The family has increased its business to include berry wines, Concord wines, and "cream" wines. All are faithfully made under strict supervision.

Scharffenberger Cellars
MENDOCINO COUNTY

307 Talmadge Road, Ukiah, California 95482 (707-462-8996). FOUNDED: 1981. ACREAGE: 70 acres. PRODUCTION: 15,000 cases. DISTRIBUTION: Major market states. OWNER: John

Scharffenberger, general manager; Eaglepoint Ranar, partner. WINEMAKER: Robert Porter; Paul Dolan, consultant. OTHER LABEL: Eaglepoint. Tours by appointment. No tasting.

A young man with ambition and a supportive family, John Scharffenberger established himself as a top-quality grower in Mendocino County in 1973. The grapes from his Eaglepoint Ranch, located far above the Ukiah Valley on the slopes of the Mayacamas Mountains, have produced prize-winning wines at several wineries, including Fetzer Vineyards. John became interested in sparkling wine after making several trips to France, during which he discovered the similarities between the climate of the Champagne region and the Anderson Valley. Since he already had a reliable grape source, John rented space in an industrial building, hired winemaker Bob Porter and consultant Paul Dolan (see Fetzer Vineyards), and made his first sparkling wine cuvées.

WHITE

☆☆   1981 EAGLEPOINT CHARDONNAY ($9.50) Mendocino.
☆☆   1982 EAGLEPOINT CHARDONNAY ($9.50) Mendocino. *Fresh, crisp and simple but quite clean and appealing.*
☆☆   1983 EAGLEPOINT SAUVIGNON BLANC ($7.00) Mendocino. *Spritzy, crisp, clean but lacking depth.*

SPARKLING

☆☆   1981 BRUT ($13.50) Mendocino. *Méthode champenoise.*
☆☆   1981 BRUT ($13.50) Cuvée 2, Mendocino. *Nice but not as good as the first cuvée.*

Schloss Doepken Winery
NEW YORK

East Main Road, R.D. 2, Ripley, New York 14775 (716-326-3636). FOUNDED: 1980. ACREAGE: 67 acres. PRODUCTION: 4,000 cases. DISTRIBUTION: New York. OWNER: John S. Watso. WINEMAKER: John S. Watso. No tours. Tasting summer: daily 12–5 P.M.; winter: weekends 12– 5 P.M.

John Watso, a metallurgist for a steel mill, learned that making wine is fine but growing grapes is no picnic when he purchased mountaintop property with the intention of growing vinifera and making world-class wines. He discovered that his Riesling was the only variety that could consistently survive the harsh winters. Discouraged but not broken, John continues to make wine. "Anyone who raises grapes," says John, "when they can just as easily buy them from someone else, is an idiot." The name "Schloss" means castle, and Doepken is John's wife's maiden name.

WHITE

NV   CHARDONNAY ($11.50) First Release, New York State. *Off-dry, fruity, strange.*
1981 JOHANNISBERG RIESLING ($8.00) New York State. *Odd, cheesy nose and some spoilage. Crisp, fruity, not varietal.*

Schramsberg Vineyards
NAPA COUNTY

Schramsberg Road, Calistoga, California 95415 (707-942-4558). FOUNDED: 1862. ACREAGE: 40 acres. PRODUCTION: 50,000 cases. DISTRIBUTION: Nationwide; 8 foreign markets. OWNERS: Jack and Jamie L. Davies. WINEMAKER: Gregory Fowler. Tours and retail sales by appointment. No tasting.

Jacob Schram's winery, which had been visited by Robert Louis Stevenson in 1880, was purchased in 1965 by Jack Davies, a Los Angeles businessman. He and his wife, Jamie, were convinced that quality sparkling wine could be made in the Napa Valley using the méthode champenoise. Thanks to their own hard work and the advice of experienced Napa winemakers, the Davies proved their point. The winery gained national attention in 1972 when President Nixon brought thirteen cases to China on his first visit. The latest Davies project is a joint venture with Remy Martin to produce fine cognac-style brandy in California under the RMS label.

SPARKLING

☆☆ 1979 BLANC DE NOIRS ($23.00) Napa Valley. *Toasty, yeasty and attractive.*

☆☆☆ 1980 BLANC DE BLANCS ($14.00) Napa Valley. *Rich and toasty Chardonnay flavors; crisp and elegant.*

☆☆☆ 1980 BLANC DE NOIRS ($19.85) Napa Valley. *Toasty, yeasty, rich, complex, balanced, superb.*

☆☆ 1981 BLANC DE BLANCS ($19.00) Napa Valley. *Clean, simple and attractive. Made from Chardonnay grapes.*

☆ 1982 BLANC DE BLANCS ($16.00) Napa Valley.

☆☆ 1981 CREMANT ($18.00) Napa Valley. *Fresh, simple and a bit syrupy.*

1981 CUVEE DE PINOT ($18.00) Napa Valley.

☆ 1982 CUVEE DE PINOT ($15.40) Napa Valley. *Some bottle variation.*

☆☆☆ 1977 RESERVE ($25.00) Napa Valley. *Rich, complex, very attractive.*

☆☆ 1978 RESERVE ($25.00) Napa Valley. *Fruity, complex, rich but a bit heavy and lacking finesse.*

Schug Cellars
NAPA COUNTY

3835 Highway 128, Calistoga, California 95415 (707-963-3169). FOUNDED: 1980. ACREAGE: None. PRODUCTION: 8,000 cases. DISTRIBUTION: California and eastern United States. OWNERS: Walter and Gertrude Schug, and Dr. Jerry B. Seps. WINEMAKER: Walter Schug. Tours, tasting, and sales by appointment. See also Storybook Mountain Vineyards.

German-born Walter Schug, the original winemaker for Joseph Phelps winery, started his own venture in winemaking by teaming up with Jerry Seps of Storybook Mountain Vineyards. Their partnership includes joint ownership of the winery building and its equipment. Schug Cellars and Storybook Mountain Vineyards are separate but are housed under one roof. Walter has left Phelps and now consults (see Costello Vineyards) and makes Pinot Noir and Chardonnay at Schug Cellars.

RED

☆☆ 1980 PINOT NOIR ($12.00) Heinemann, Napa Valley. *Rich, minty, and intense, with some bitterness.*

☆☆ 1981 PINOT NOIR ($12.00) Heinemann, Sonoma. *Earthy, raisiny, intense and rich.*

Pete Schwartz Winery
OKLAHOMA

Route 4, Box 95A, Okarche, Oklahoma 73762 (405-263-7664). FOUNDED: 1970. ACREAGE: None. PRODUCTION: 1,200 cases. DISTRIBUTION: At winery. OWNERS: Pete and Clara Schwartz. WINEMAKER: Pete Schwartz. Tours, tasting, and sales Monday–Saturday 10 A.M.– 10 P.M.

All Pete Schwartz wanted was to make wine to sell to his friends. Neither he nor his wife had any idea just how complicated that simple desire would become. Struggling through the time-consuming mess of red tape, they finally built and bonded a concrete, galvanized steel winery on their property. Pete had made wine since he was a child, with his father, a German immigrant. He and his family have kept the same homespun attitude toward winemaking.

Scotella Vineyards Winery
INDIANA

Dugan Hollow Road, Rural Route 2, Madison, Indiana 47250 (812-265-6035). FOUNDED: 1972. ACREAGE: 15 acres. PRODUCTION: 2,500 cases. DISTRIBUTION: Indiana. OWNER: Scott Edward Conboy; Don Conboy, general manager. WINEMAKER: Scott Edward Conboy. Tours and tasting daily 11 A.M.–11 P.M. Restaurant. Gift shop.

Don Conboy and his wife were living in North Africa when they got a call from their son Scott, telling them about a 76-acre winery estate that was for sale in Madison. "He said it had a lot of potential, so I told him to go ahead and buy it, and we would see it when we got there," says Don. "When we saw it, we loved it." For two years, Don and Scott worked to get the winery and the vineyards in shape before producing their first vintage in 1985. Scott, a nuclear power plant inspector, returned in 1984 from his job in Massachusetts to help his father build a restaurant in one of the two New England barns on the property. "The other barn will be remodeled to be our home," says Don. Because Madison receives so many visitors during its regattas and art festivals, the Conboys hope to sell most of their wine at the winery.

Sea Ridge Winery
SONOMA COUNTY

P.O. Box 433, Cazadero, California 95421 (707-847-3469). FOUNDED: 1979. ACREAGE: 7 acres. PRODUCTION: 5,000 cases. DISTRIBUTION: California and other major market states. OWNERS: Timothy Schmidt and Daniel Wickham. WINEMAKER: Daniel Wickham. Tours by appointment.

Some laughed when Tim Schmidt and Dan Wickham planted vineyards in the untried land close to the Sonoma coast near Cazadero. Farm advisors and other growers assured them that the area was too cold for grapes. But Tim and Dan, whose backgrounds are in marine biology and oceanography, respectively, feel the coastal ridges have been misjudged. They are convinced that these areas have great potential for producing Pinot Noir and Chardonnay, varieties that have always grown best in cooler climates. The winery and fifteen acres of Pinot Noir are located on a mountain ridge near the sea, hence the name. While waiting for their own vineyards to come into production, Tim and Dan are purchasing grapes from vineyards located closest to the coast.

WHITE

☆☆ 1981 CHARDONNAY ($10.50) Dutton Ranch, Sonoma. *Big, with intense oak, vanillin, and ripe fruit.*

☆☆ 1981 CHARDONNAY ($11.50) Mill Station, Sonoma. *Intense oak and butter; assertive.*

☆ 1981 CHARDONNAY ($11.50) Searby, Sonoma. *Intense, heavy, slight oxidation.*

○　1982 CHARDONNAY ($10.00) Sonoma. *Dominated by mercaptans and other off smells and tastes.*

☆☆☆　1983 CHARDONNAY ($10.00) Mill Station, Sonoma. *Clean and lush, with toasty oak and rich texture.*

○　1983 SAUVIGNON BLANC ($8.00) Scalabrini, Sonoma. *Seriously flawed with mercaptans.*

RED

☆☆　1981 PINOT NOIR ($8.60) Sonoma.

☆☆☆　1981 PINOT NOIR ($10.50) Bohan, Sonoma. *Rich, toasty, sweet oak, lush, clean, mature.*

☆☆　1981 ZINFANDEL ($8.00) Porter-Bass, Sonoma. *Rich, oaky, good.*

　1982 ZINFANDEL ($8.00) Porter-Bass, Sonoma. *Green, dull.*

Sebastiani Vineyards
SONOMA COUNTY

389 4th Street, East, Sonoma, California 95476 (707-938-5532). FOUNDED: 1904. ACREAGE: 500 acres. PRODUCTION: 2 million cases. DISTRIBUTION: Nationwide. OWNER: Sylvia Sebastiani, chairperson; Sam Sebastiani, president. WINEMAKER: Jim Carter; Doug Davis, winemaster. OTHER LABELS: August Sebastiani, Country. Tours and tasting daily 10 A.M.–4:20 P.M.

Samuele Sebastiani came to California in 1893 and almost immediately began making wine in Sonoma. His son August, famous for his bibbed overalls, expanded the family winery to the point where it was one of the ten largest in America. The wines were dense and simple, a style common to older winemakers of Italian heritage. When August died in 1980, his son Sam took over and has been working hard to update the winemaking style. So far he has spent $6 million modernizing the winery. One of the main winery attractions is a collection of wood casks hand-carved by the late Earle Brown.

WHITE

　1981 CHARDONNAY ($7.50) North Coast. *Flabby, dull.*

　1981 CHARDONNAY ($9.25) Proprietor's Reserve, Sonoma Valley. *Crisp, simple, some oxidation.*

☆☆　1982 CHARDONNAY ($6.25) Sonoma Valley. *Rich, earthy, clean, quite nice.*

☆☆　1982 CHARDONNAY ($10.00) Proprietor's Reserve, Sonoma Valley. *Crisp and clean, with lovely fresh fruit. Delightful.*

☆　1983 CHARDONNAY ($7.25) Sonoma Valley.

☆☆　1983 CHARDONNAY ($10.00) Proprietor's Reserve, Sonoma Valley. *Spicy, clean, fresh, simple.*

☆☆　1984 CHARDONNAY ($10.00) Proprietor's Reserve, Sonoma Valley. *Pretty, clean, floral, light.*

　1983 CHENIN BLANC ($4.70) Sonoma. *1.5% residual sugar. Vinous, oily, heavy.*

　1983 AUGUST SEBASTIANI CHENIN BLANC ($5.75) California. *1.5 liter. Vegetal, sweet.*

☆　1982 COUNTRY FUME BLANC ($7.00) California. *1.5 liter. Fresh and varietal.*

○　1983 COUNTRY FUME BLANC ($8.00) California. *1.5 liter. Flabby, lacking freshness.*

☆☆☆　1983 GEWURZTRAMINER ($7.00) Kellerschatz, Sonoma Valley. *Dry, clean, varietal, soft, delicate, lovely.*

☆　1982 GREEN HUNGARIAN ($4.50) North Coast.

○　1983 GREEN HUNGARIAN ($4.70) North Coast. *1% residual sugar. Moldy tasting, unappealing.*

☆☆　1982 JOHANNISBERG RIESLING ($5.80) Sonoma County. *Delicate and lemony.*

☆☆ 1983 JOHANNISBERG RIESLING ($5.90) Sonoma. *1% residual sugar. Rich fruit, nicely balanced; somewhat coarse in texture.*

☆☆☆ 1983 JOHANNISBERG RIESLING ($12.00) Late Harvest, Sonoma. *375 ml. 8.9% residual sugar. Lush, deep, clean, fruity, lovely.*

☆☆ 1982 MUSCAT ($7.00) Wildwood, Sonoma Valley. *2% residual sugar.*

☆ 1983 MUSCAT ($7.00) Elizabeth Ann, Wildwood, Sonoma Valley. *2.5% residual sugar. Floral, snappy, heavy.*

○ 1982 SAUVIGNON BLANC ($10.00) Proprietor's Reserve, Sonoma Valley. *Oxidized, dirty, unpleasant.*

SPARKLING

☆☆☆ NV BRUT PROPRIETOR'S RESERVE ($10.00) Sonoma. *Méthode champenoise. Clean, richly fruity.*

☆☆☆ NV BRUT THREE STAR ($12.00) Sonoma. *Crisp and tart, with good fruit and depth.*

BLANC DE NOIR

1982 EYE OF THE SWAN ($5.00) North Coast. *Pinot Noir Blanc. Dull, thin.*

☆ 1983 PINOT NOIR ($4.85) Eye of the Swan, Sonoma. *Dry, vinous, decent but lacking acidity.*

1984 COUNTRY WHITE ZINFANDEL ($5.75) California. *1.5 liter. Sweet, dull, unpleasant.*

ROSE

☆ 1982 VIN ROSE ($3.00) California. *2% residual sugar.*

☆ 1982 COUNTRY GAMAY ROSE ($2.50) California.

☆☆☆ 1982 ROSA GEWURZTRAMINER ($4.85) Sonoma Valley. *1% residual sugar. Spicy, fresh, varietal and attractive.*

☆☆ 1983 ROSA GEWURZTRAMINER ($4.85) Sonoma Valley. *1% residual sugar. Crisp, spicy, varietal. Red wine added.*

RED

☆☆ 1978 BARBERA ($8.00) Sonoma. *Tart, fresh, clean, a bit volatile, attractive.*

☆☆ 1979 BARBERA ($8.00) Sonoma. *Rich, deep, clean, lush, good fruit, lovely.*

☆☆ 1975 CABERNET SAUVIGNON Sonoma. *Deep, intense, rich, with good balance and barrel bouquet.*

1977 CABERNET SAUVIGNON ($10.00) Proprietor's Reserve, North Coast. *Dull, lacking fruit, older than its years.*

☆ 1978 CABERNET SAUVIGNON ($5.00) North Coast Counties. *Woody, balanced but lacking fruit. Showing its age.*

☆ 1978 CABERNET SAUVIGNON ($12.00) Proprietor's Reserve, Sonoma. *Earthy, oaky, pleasant but not showing much varietal style.*

☆☆ 1979 CABERNET SAUVIGNON ($5.00) North Coast. *Decent, balanced, clean, unexciting. Drink now.*

1979 CABERNET SAUVIGNON ($11.25) Proprietor's Reserve, North Coast. *Earthy, dirty, not much promise.*

1980 CABERNET SAUVIGNON ($6.35) Estate, Sonoma Valley. *Weedy.*

☆☆ 1980 CABERNET SAUVIGNON ($10.00) Proprietor's Reserve, Sonoma Valley. *Tangy, rich, deep, clean, earthy, fruity, attractive.*

☆ 1980 CABERNET SAUVIGNON ($20.00) Eagle, Sonoma. *Thick and rich; vegetal, dense, somewhat dull. Drink 1987.*

☆☆ 1981 CABERNET SAUVIGNON ($5.00) Sonoma. *Simple but attractive.*

☆☆☆ 1981 CABERNET SAUVIGNON ($20.00) Eagle, Sonoma Valley. *Lush, deep, well made, oaky, super. Drink 1987.*

☆☆☆ 1983 CABERNET SAUVIGNON ($20.00) Eagle, Sonoma Valley. *Rich, deep, well structured, complex. Drink 1989.*

☆☆ 1984 GAMAY ($5.00) Nouveau, Sonoma.
    NV   AUGUST SEBASTIANI PINOT NOIR ($5.60) California. *1.5 liter.*
  ☆ 1978 PINOT NOIR ($4.85) Très Rouge, Tailfeathers, Sonoma.
  ☆ 1980 PINOT NOIR ($4.85) Très Rouge, Tailfeathers, Sonoma. *Raisiny, dense.*
  ☆ 1981 PINOT NOIR ($4.85) Rouge, Sonoma. *Raisiny, lacking fruit.*
☆☆ 1981 PINOT NOIR ($6.00) Sonoma. *Fruity, clean, balanced.*
    1982 PINOT NOIR ($4.85) Rouge, Tailfeathers, Sonoma Valley. *Inky, meaty, metallic.*
☆☆ 1976 ZINFANDEL Proprietor's Reserve, Sonoma. *Rich, aging nicely, clean, good.*
  O 1977 ZINFANDEL ($7.00) Proprietor's Reserve, Northern California. *Raisiny and oxidized.*
    1978 ZINFANDEL ($7.00) Proprietor's Reserve, Northern California. *Vegetal.*
☆☆ 1978 ZINFANDEL ($8.00) Proprietor's Reserve, Sonoma Valley. *Lush, deep, rich, clean, attractive.*
☆☆ 1979 ZINFANDEL ($4.00) California. *Clean, varietal, berried, quite decent.*
    1980 ZINFANDEL ($5.00) California.
☆☆ 1980 ZINFANDEL ($10.00) Proprietor's Reserve, Sonoma Valley. *Intense, dark and balanced.*

Seghesio Winery
SONOMA COUNTY

24035 Chianti Road, Cloverdale, California 95425 (707-857-3581) and 14730 Grove Street, Healdsburg, California (707-433-3579). FOUNDED: 1902. ACREAGE: 400 acres. PRODUCTION: 50,000 cases. DISTRIBUTION: California, Florida, Nevada, Oregon, and Texas. OWNERS: Seghesio Farms and Seghesio Winery. Eugene Seghesio, president; Edward Seghesio, secretary-treasurer. WINEMAKER: Ted Seghesio. No tours or tasting.

The Seghesio family has made wine in bulk and for other labels for seven decades; it was not until 1983 that a wine was released under their own name. This long history began with Edoardo Seghesio, an Italian immigrant, who worked for Italian Swiss Colony until he bought a ranch, planted vineyards, and built a winery. He thrived in the bulk-wine business until 1918. The fourth generation, headed by Eugene and Edward Seghesio, is phasing out bulk production and promoting its own label.

WHITE

☆☆ 1982 CHENIN BLANC ($3.50) Estate, Northern Sonoma. *Dry, crisp, clean and a little dull.*
    1983 CHENIN BLANC ($4.00) 50% Sonoma, 50% Napa. *Musty.*
☆☆ 1981 FRENCH COLOMBARD ($3.00) Sonoma.

BLANC DE NOIR

☆☆ 1984 WHITE ZINFANDEL ($4.50) Northern Sonoma. *Spritzy, off-dry, appealing.*

RED

☆☆☆ 1975 MARIAN'S RESERVE ($4.50) Sonoma. *Complex and rich, with Pinot Noir character.*
  ☆ 1976 CABERNET SAUVIGNON ($4.50) Estate, Northern Sonoma. *Decent fruit; simple, soft and round.*
☆☆ 1975 ZINFANDEL ($5.00) Estate, Sonoma. *Meaty, Italian-style.*

Thomas Sellards Winery
SONOMA COUNTY

6400 Sequoia Circle, Sebastopol, California 95472 (707-823-8293). FOUNDED: 1980. ACREAGE: None. PRODUCTION: 1,000 cases. DISTRIBUTION: At winery and local outlets. OWNER: Tom Sellards. WINEMAKER: Tom Sellards. Tours, tasting, and sales by appointment.

Bonded in 1980, the Thomas Sellards Winery released its first commercial wine in 1983. Tom started out as a home winemaker, attended enology classes, and soon bonded his fast-growing hobby as production quickly approached legal limits. The winery is still next to his home and, even though he is making tiny amounts of wine, running the winery is a full-time job.

WHITE

☆☆☆   1982 CHARDONNAY ($10.50) Sonoma. *Fresh, snappy, with good oak and fruit richness.*

Sequoia Grove Vineyards
NAPA COUNTY

8338 St. Helena Highway, Napa, California 94558 (707-944-2945). FOUNDED: 1979. ACREAGE: 22 acres. PRODUCTION: 8,000 cases. DISTRIBUTION: Nationwide. OWNER: Partnership. James W. Allen, manager. WINEMAKER: James W. Allen; Steve Allen, vineyard manager. Tours daily 11 A.M.–5 P.M.

Jim Allen researched the possibilities of growing vinifera grapes in states such as Utah, Arizona, and New Mexico, but discouraged by the nasty winters in those areas, he and his wife moved to the Napa Valley. They bought a 22-acre vineyard with a nineteenth-century barn, surrounded by ancient Sequoia trees. They were joined by Jim's brother Steve, who took charge of the vineyard. The barn was quickly converted into a winery for the first crush in 1980. The vineyards, some of which already contained ten-year-old Chardonnay vines, have been replanted to more Chardonnay and red Bordeaux varieties.

WHITE

☆   1981 CHARDONNAY ($9.50) Napa Valley.

☆☆   1981 CHARDONNAY ($10.50) Sonoma-Cutrer, Sonoma. *Earthy, vinous, decent but unexciting.*

☆☆   1981 CHARDONNAY ($12.00) Estate, Napa Valley. *Lovely oak and fruit; a bit heavy. Should age well, but can be drunk now.*

☆   1982 CHARDONNAY ($9.50) Napa Valley.

☆☆   1982 CHARDONNAY ($10.50) Sonoma. *Fresh, clean, attractive, balanced.*

☆☆☆   1982 CHARDONNAY ($12.00) Estate, Napa Valley. *Lovely—deep, complex, fruity, balanced.*

RED

☆☆   1980 CABERNET SAUVIGNON ($12.00) Cask One, Napa Valley. *Jammy, ripe but lacking structure.*

☆☆☆   1980 CABERNET SAUVIGNON ($12.00) Cask Two, 90% Fay, Napa Valley. *Rich, intense, ripe, herbal. Good aging potential.*

☆☆☆   1981 CABERNET SAUVIGNON ($12.00) Napa Valley. *Lush, clean, balanced, lovely. Drink 1986.*

☆☆   1981 CABERNET SAUVIGNON ($12.00) Terra Rosa, Alexander Valley, Sonoma. *Varietal, clean, pleasant but fat and clumsy. Drink 1986.*

☆☆☆   1982 CABERNET SAUVIGNON ($12.00) 67% Napa, 33% Alexander Valley. *Lush, complex, clean, structured, varietal. Drink 1987.*

Serendipity Cellars Winery
OREGON

15275 Dunn Forest Road, Monmouth, Oregon 97361 (503-838-4284). FOUNDED: 1981. ACREAGE: 3 acres. PRODUCTION: 1,250 cases. DISTRIBUTION: Oregon. OWNERS: Glen and

Cheryl Longshore. WINEMAKER: Glen Longshore. Tours and tasting May–December: Friday–Sunday 12–6 P.M. January–April: weekends 12–6 P.M., and selected holidays.

After touring Oregon wineries and watching the action at harvest time, Glen and Cheryl Longshore decided to go into the wine business. Both worked in education, but they had often thought of starting a small business of their own. Intrigued by winemaking, they helped out at local wineries and made wine at home. Then the Longshores found a forested parcel in a serene valley near Salem, planted vineyards in 1979, and built a large combination winery-second home. The winery is built into a hill and insulated by earth on three sides; the Longshore's living quarters are above at ground level. Glen and Cheryl are the only full-time employees in their small business.

WHITE

☆☆☆ 1983 CHENIN BLANC ($7.25) 68% Bethel Heights, 32% McCorquodale, Oregon. *Fresh, fruity, slightly spritzy; a delight.*

The Seven Lakes Vineyard
MICHIGAN

1111 Tinsman Road, Fenton, Michigan 48430 (313-629-5686). FOUNDED: 1982. ACREAGE: 20 acres. PRODUCTION: 1,500 cases. DISTRIBUTION: At winery and local restaurants. OWNERS: Harry and Christian Guest. WINEMAKER: Christian Guest. Tours and tasting daily 9 A.M.–5 P.M.

After 50 years in sales, Harry Guest retired to become a farmer and winemaker. He bought 100 acres of land, started planting vines, and drew up plans for a winery. His son Christian took an active interest in his father's retirement project. After taking enology courses and learning as much as he could from other winemakers, Christian became the winemaker.

Shadow Creek Champagne Cellars
SAN LUIS OBISPO COUNTY

P.O. Box 3159, San Luis Obispo, California 93403 (805-544-5800). FOUNDED: 1978. ACREAGE: None. PRODUCTION: 25,000 cases. DISTRIBUTION: Nationwide. OWNER: Glenmore Distilleries. WINEMAKER: Pete Downs. No tours or tasting.

The Shadow Creek label got its start when Château St. Jean had a champagne cuvée they didn't need for their own sparkling wine production. The wine was purchased by George Vare, former president of Geyser Peak. In 1981 George sold Shadow Creek to Glenmore Distilleries of Kentucky. The brand is marketed out of Corbett Canyon Vineyards, another Glenmore property, although the champagne is still made at Château St. Jean's Graton facility under the supervision of Pete Downs.

SPARKLING

☆☆☆ 1981 BLANC DE BLANCS ($13.75) Cuvée 1, Sonoma. *Yeasty, rich, complex, clean, impressive.*

☆☆ NV BRUT ($10.00) Sonoma. *Sweetish, floral, pleasant.*

Shafer Vineyard Cellars
OREGON

Star Route, Box 269, Forest Grove, Oregon 97116 (503-357-6604). FOUNDED: 1980. ACREAGE: 20 acres. PRODUCTION: 6,000 cases. DISTRIBUTION: Oregon and Washington. OWNERS:

Harvey and Sophia Shafer. WINEMAKER: Harvey Shafer. Tours by appointment. Tasting and retail sales weekends 12–5 P.M., except in January.

In 1973, at a time when new Oregon winemakers were eager for good vinifera grapes, Harvey Shafer planted his vineyard. A meticulous farmer, Harvey gained a reputation for producing high-quality fruit, and for some time he made a living selling his grapes. But by 1978 his twenty acres could not produce enough income to carry the farm, and Harvey was ready to make his own wine. He made his first two vintages at other wineries. By 1981 his own new winery, with its skylighted roof and large windows, was finished in time for the crush. Harvey acquired his winemaking skills on the job. He started back in the early 1970s, making wine at home and patiently learning the idiosyncrasies and potential of his own grapes.

WHITE

☆   1981 CHARDONNAY ($10.50) Willamette Valley, Oregon. *Sweet, new oak; rich and decent.*

☆☆☆   1982 CHARDONNAY ($10.50) Willamette Valley, Oregon. *Light, charming, and delicate, with lovely fruit.*

☆☆   1983 RIESLING ($6.75) Estate, Willamette Valley, Oregon. *Crisp, dry, clean, pleasant.*

☆☆   1982 SAUVIGNON BLANC ($8.50) Estate, Willamette Valley, Oregon. *Fresh, fruity, clean, appealing.*

RED

☆   1979 PINOT NOIR ($9.00) Willamette Valley, Oregon. *Berry nose, spicy, clean; decent but lacking charm.*

Shafer Vineyards
NAPA COUNTY

6154 Silverado Trail, Napa, California 94558 (707-944-2877). FOUNDED: 1979. ACREAGE: 65 acres. PRODUCTION: 14,000 cases. DISTRIBUTION: California and 14 other states. OWNER: Partnership. Shafer family. John R. Shafer, general manager. WINEMAKER: Nikko Schoch. Tours and retail sales weekdays by appointment.

John Shafer, an executive with a Chicago publishing firm, decided in 1972 to move his family to the Napa Valley. He bought a neglected old vineyard on the western slopes of the valley and the whole family—John, Bett, and their four children—cleared and replanted it. The first Shafer wines were made at Round Hill, the next wines at Rutherford Hill. By 1980 Shafer wines were being made in the family's own winery.

WHITE

☆☆☆   1981 CHARDONNAY ($11.00) Napa Valley. *Crisp, lemony, and clean, with nice oak and varietal style.*

☆☆   1982 CHARDONNAY ($11.00) Napa Valley. *Soft, lush, fruity.*

☆☆   1983 CHARDONNAY ($12.00) Napa Valley. *Clean, angular, well made, attractive.*

RED

☆☆   1982 RED TABLE WINE ($8.50) Napa Valley. *Fresh, crisp, light, clean and attractive.*

☆☆☆   1978 CABERNET SAUVIGNON ($11.00) Estate, Napa Valley. *Deep, lush, Stag's Leap style. Well structured and supple. Drink now.*

☆☆☆   1979 CABERNET SAUVIGNON ($13.00) Napa Valley. *Crisp and fruity, with a lovely, velvety texture. Drink now.*

☆☆   1980 CABERNET SAUVIGNON ($11.00) Napa Valley. *Meaty, soft, very nice.*

☆☆☆   1982 CABERNET SAUVIGNON ($12.00) Napa Valley. *Lush, big, rich, very nicely balanced. Drink 1987.*

☆☆☆ 1982 CABERNET SAUVIGNON ($16.00) Reserve, Napa Valley. *Deep, rich, mature. Drink 1986.*
 ☆☆ 1980 ZINFANDEL ($6.50) Stag's Leap Area, Napa.
  ☆ 1981 ZINFANDEL ($6.50) Napa Valley. *Tangy, fresh, good.*

❧

Charles F. Shaw Vineyard
NAPA COUNTY

1010 Big Tree Road, St. Helena, California 94574 (707-963-5459). FOUNDED: 1979. ACREAGE: 40 acres. PRODUCTION: 12,000 cases. DISTRIBUTION: Nationwide; 8 foreign markets. OWNER: Charles F. Shaw. WINEMAKER: Ric Forman. OTHER LABEL: Bale Mill Cellars. Tours, tasting, and retail sales by appointment.

Chuck Shaw was a banker in Paris when he fell in love with Beaujolais. He bought a ranch on the west bank of the Napa River and set up his winery to use the carbonic maceration (whole-cluster fermentation) techniques used in Beaujolais. He and his wife, Lucy, now live at the estate and, with the help of winemaker Ric Forman (see Newton Winery, Sterling Vineyards, and Château du Lac), have expanded their line to include other varieties.

WHITE

☆☆☆ 1983 CHARDONNAY ($12.50) Napa Valley. *Toasty, clean, smooth, well balanced, medium weight.*
☆☆☆ 1982 FUME BLANC ($8.00) Flora Springs, Napa Valley. *Crisp and varietal but short in the middle range.*
 ☆☆ 1983 FUME BLANC ($8.75) Napa Valley. *Crisp, clean, and attractive, with lush fruit.*

RED

 ☆☆ 1982 GAMAY ($4.00) Domaine Elucia, Napa Valley. *Snappy, fresh and simple.*
 ☆☆ 1984 GAMAY NOUVEAU ($4.50) Napa Valley. *Snappy, round, clean. Serve chilled.*

❧

Shenandoah Vineyards
AMADOR COUNTY

12300 Steiner Road, Plymouth, California 95669 (209-245-3698). FOUNDED: 1977. ACREAGE: 18 acres. PRODUCTION: 14,000 cases. DISTRIBUTION: Major market states. OWNERS: Leon and Shirley Sobon. WINEMAKER: Leon E. Sobon. Tours and tasting summer: daily 10 A.M.–5 P.M.; fall, winter, and spring: weekends or by appointment.

While working as an engineer in Palo Alto, Leon Sobon became an avid wine hobbyist, making wine at home and working at wineries on weekends. In 1977 Leon, his wife Shirley, and their six children decided to alter their lives drastically. They sold their home and vacation cabin to buy land for a family winery. Shirley went back to work as a nurse to help support the winery through the first four years, and free labor was provided by the children. Two of the older boys continue to work at the winery, and during college vacations the other children bottle wine and prune vines.

WHITE

1982 SAUVIGNON BLANC ($7.50) Amador.

☆ 1983 SAUVIGNON BLANC ($8.00) Amador. *Intensely varietal, grassy, weedy.*

BLANC DE NOIR

1984 WHITE ZINFANDEL ($5.00) Amador. *Dull, lacking fruit.*

RED

1980 CABERNET SAUVIGNON ($12.00) Amador. *Too much oak, not enough fruit. Tannic and dense.*

☆☆ 1981 CABERNET SAUVIGNON ($12.00) Amador. *Earthy, fresh, fruity, oaky, attractive. Drink 1986.*

☆ 1980 ZINFANDEL ($6.50) Dal Porto, Amador. *Big, hard, intense. Might come around by 1988.*

☆☆ 1980 ZINFANDEL ($8.00) Special Reserve, Eschen, Fiddletown, Amador. *A monster. Heavy, concentrated, tannic. Drink 1990.*

Shenandoah Vineyards
VIRGINIA

Route 2, Box 323, Edinburg, Virginia 22824 (703-984-8699). FOUNDED: 1977. ACREAGE: 40 acres. PRODUCTION: 10,000 cases. DISTRIBUTION: Virginia. OWNERS: James and Emma Randel. Mary Fuller, manager. WINEMAKER: Alan LeBlanc-Kinne; Doug Ewalt, assistant winemaker. Tours and tasting daily 10 A.M.–6 P.M.

When they were living in New Jersey, the Randels bought an old fruit farm in Virginia and remodeled the farmhouse to use as a vacation home. After reading a magazine article on Virginia's sudden winery boom, they were inspired to start their own winery. They hired a consultant to plant the vineyards while they worked on transforming the old fruit barn into a winery. Because their first vintages, 1977 and 1978, were made from purchased grapes, the Randels consider that the winery really opened in July 1979, the year their vineyard yielded its first crop.

WHITE

☆☆ 1982 JOHANNISBERG RIESLING ($8.00) Shenandoah Valley, Virginia. *1.75% residual sugar. Snappy, fresh, balanced, ripe.*

☆☆ 1983 VIDAL ($5.00) Semi Dry, Virginia. *Ripe, fruity and lush.*

RED

☆☆ 1982 CABERNET SAUVIGNON ($12.00) Virginia. *Structured, clean; pleasantly complex.*

Sherrill Cellars
SANTA CLARA COUNTY

1185 Skyline Boulevard, Woodside, California 94062 (415-851-1932). FOUNDED: 1973. ACREAGE: None. PRODUCTION: 3,000 cases. DISTRIBUTION: 7 states. OWNERS: Nat and Jan Sherrill. WINEMAKER: Nat Sherrill. Tours, tasting, and retail sales March–September by appointment.

The first crush at Sherrill Cellars took place underneath the Woodside Post Office. That was before Nat Sherrill, an electronics engineer, and his wife, Jan, bought their 24 acres of wide-open space on Skyline Boulevard in 1977. The new winery building was literally put together by 60 or so of the Sherrills' friends on a single day in August 1979.

RED

☆ 1979 CABERNET SAUVIGNON ($9.50) Shell Creek, California. *Tart, fruity, decent. Drink 1986 and beyond.*

☆ 1979 ZINFANDEL ($7.00) Vineyard Hill, Woodside, California. *Thin, simple, tart. Drink now.*

☆☆ 1980 ZINFANDEL ($7.00) Vineyard Hill. *Rich, intense and nicely complex.*

☆ 1984 ZINFANDEL ($5.75) Nouveau, Santa Clara.

Shown and Sons Vineyards
NAPA COUNTY

8514 St. Helena Highway, Rutherford, California 94573 (707-963-9004). FOUNDED: 1977. ACREAGE: 27 acres. PRODUCTION: 12,000 cases. DISTRIBUTION: Nationwide. OWNER: Richard Shown. WINEMAKERS: Chris Shown, vineyard manager, and James Vahl, enologist. Tours and retail sales by appointment. Tasting daily 11 A.M.–4 P.M. Picnic facilities.

Estate planner Dick Shown moved from the Santa Clara Valley to a Cabernet Sauvignon vineyard in the Napa Valley. He made a little homemade wine for himself and sold the rest of his grapes. He soon found out, as most grape growers do, that there is little money to be made growing grapes, so he built a prefabricated winery on the property. After losing Tom Cotrell, his first winemaker, who went to teach enology at Cornell University, he hired a consultant, Jim Vahl. But in 1983 management problems and the consumer's taste for white wines led the winery into Chapter 11 bankruptcy, and the vineyard property was sold to Joe Heitz. Now Shown and Sons is starting afresh at a new location in Rutherford.

WHITE

☆☆ 1983 CHARDONNAY ($13.50) Napa Valley. *Lush, oaky, big, with good fruit.*

☆ 1983 CHENIN BLANC ($7.00) Dry, Napa Valley.

☆ 1981 JOHANNISBERG RIESLING ($7.00) Napa Valley.

RED

O 1982 RUTHERFORD RED BLEND ($4.75) Napa Valley. *Dirty and skunky.*

O 1978 CABERNET SAUVIGNON ($12.00) Las Aguacitas, Napa Valley.

☆ 1979 CABERNET SAUVIGNON ($12.00) Napa Valley.

☆ 1980 CABERNET SAUVIGNON ($12.00) Los Aquacitas, Napa Valley. *A bit vegetal.*

1982 ZINFANDEL ($6.75) Shown Family, Napa Valley. *Green, vegetal, oily.*

Sierra Vista Winery
EL DORADO COUNTY

4560 Cabernet Way, Placerville, California 95667 (916-622-7221). FOUNDED: 1977. ACREAGE: 17 acres. PRODUCTION: 5,000 cases. DISTRIBUTION: California. OWNERS: John and Barbara MacCready. WINEMAKER: John MacCready. Tours and tasting weekends 12–5 P.M.

John MacCready has made wine from almost everything, from potatoes to French-American hybrids. Working as an electrical engineer in Ohio, John was less than enthusiastic about hybrids and even less so about Labrusca varieties. He decided to buy vineyard land in California, and in

1972 he purchased a parcel on a Sierra mountain ridge at an elevation of 2,800 feet. While those who thought they knew better shook their heads, he cleared six acres and planted grapes. Five years later the winery was established.

WHITE

☆☆☆ 1983 FUME BLANC ($6.00) El Dorado. *Rich, fruity, round, balanced, super.*

BLANC DE NOIR

☆   1984 WHITE ZINFANDEL ($5.00) El Dorado.

RED

☆☆   1979 CABERNET SAUVIGNON ($6.75) El Dorado. *Forward, fruity, tannic. Drink 1988 and beyond.*
☆   1980 CABERNET SAUVIGNON ($8.50) Estate, El Dorado. *Ripe, intense, Zinfandel-like. Drink 1986 and beyond.*
☆☆   1981 CABERNET SAUVIGNON ($7.75) Estate, El Dorado. *Fruity, fresh, clean and very lovely. Drink 1986.*
☆☆   NV ZINFANDEL ($4.00) El Dorado. *Ripe, fresh, intense, berried, quite attractive.*
☆☆   1979 ZINFANDEL ($5.00) El Dorado. *Lush, spicy, attractive. Drink 1986.*
☆☆   1980 ZINFANDEL ($6.00) El Dorado. *10% Petite Sirah. Soft, raisiny, lush. Drink now.*
☆☆   1981 ZINFANDEL ($6.00) El Dorado. *Big, ripe, fruity, appealing. Drink 1987 and beyond.*
☆☆   1982 ZINFANDEL ($6.00) Estate, El Dorado. *Rich, deep, fruity, attractive.*

Sierra Wine Corporation
TULARE COUNTY

1887 North Mooney Boulevard, Tulare, California 93274 (209-688-1766). FOUNDED: 1895. ACREAGE: None. PRODUCTION: 10 million cases (bulk). DISTRIBUTION: Bulk sales. OWNER: Early California Industries. WINEMAKERS: Phil Posson, Dave Foster, Dean Cox, and Andy Litwack. No tours. Tasting daily at Tulare plant 10 A.M.–6 P.M. There are three bonded premises: one in Tulare, one in McFarland, and one in Delano.

This historic pre-Prohibition winery, founded by Italian immigrant Frank Giannini and his family in 1895, is now a bulk producer, bottler, and packager of wines. It was purchased in 1979 by Early California Industries, which preserved the winery's turn-of-the-century atmosphere by maintaining the old Giannini house as its offices and tasting room. The focus of the winery today is packaging, with special attention paid to devising innovative wine containers. A historic feature of the winery is the Franklin Delano Roosevelt tank, one of the largest wooden wine barrels in the world. It was built to commemorate the repeal of Prohibition.

Silver Mountain Vineyards
SANTA CRUZ COUNTY

P.O. Box 1695, Los Gatos, California 95031 (408-353-2278). FOUNDED: 1979. ACREAGE: 10 acres. PRODUCTION: 2,000 cases. DISTRIBUTION: California and other states; Australia. OWNER: Jerold O'Brien. WINEMAKER: Jerold O'Brien. Tours and retail sales by appointment. Tasting by invitation from mailing list.

Jerry O'Brien was desperate to get out of the city and move to the country, where he could work outdoors as a grape grower and winemaker. He found a beautiful piece of property, planted his vineyards, and built a simple, sloped-roof wooden winery. While waiting for his own vineyards to come into production, Jerry bought Chardonnay and Zinfandel grapes from other growers.

WHITE

☆☆ 1981 CHARDONNAY ($12.00) Ventana, Monterey. *Oaky, nicely balanced, clean, fruity.*
☆☆☆ 1982 CHARDONNAY ($11.00) Ventana, Monterey. *Rich, clean, snappy, very well made.*

RED

☆☆ 1979 ZINFANDEL ($6.00) 40% Ventana, 60% Butte County, California. *Good, fresh, intense, snappy. Drink now.*
☆☆☆ 1980 ZINFANDEL ($6.50) Paso Robles. *Chocolatey, fruity, clean and fresh. Drink now.*
☆ 1980 ZINFANDEL ($8.00) Glen Ellen, Sonoma Valley. *Intense, concentrated, a bit muddy.*
☆☆ 1982 ZINFANDEL ($6.50) El Dorado. *Fruity, clean, quite attractive.*
☆ 1983 ZINFANDEL ($6.50) Sonoma. *Decent, varietal, clean.*

Silver Oak Wine Cellars
NAPA COUNTY

915 Oakville Crossroad, Oakville, California 94562 (707-944-8808). FOUNDED: 1972. ACREAGE: 15 acres. PRODUCTION: 15,000 cases. DISTRIBUTION: Nationwide. OWNERS: Justin Meyer and Raymond Duncan. David Nickerson, winery manager. WINEMAKER: Justin Meyer. Tours by appointment Monday–Friday. Tasting and retail sales Monday–Friday 9 A.M.–4:30 P.M., Saturday 11 A.M–4 P.M

When they owned Franciscan Vineyards (see), Justin Meyer and Ray Duncan started Silver Oak Wine Cellars as a producer of a single wine, Cabernet Sauvignon. Since selling Franciscan, they have invested more time and effort at Silver Oak. All their grapes came from the Las Amigas Vineyard in the Alexander Valley until the 1979 vintage, when some Napa Valley wine was made, as well as a small lot from Justin's home vineyard. The winery was expanded in 1982.

RED

☆ 1976 CABERNET SAUVIGNON ($14.00) Alexander Valley. *Thin and a bit vegetal.*
☆☆☆ 1977 CABERNET SAUVIGNON ($16.00) Alexander Valley. *Lush but firm; very elegant and balanced. Lovely.*
☆☆☆ 1978 CABERNET SAUVIGNON ($16.00) Alexander Valley. *Elegant but rich and intensely fruity; oaky and earthy.*
☆☆☆ 1979 CABERNET SAUVIGNON ($16.00) Alexander Valley. *Nice, rich, deep and earthy, with some light vegetation. Drink 1987.*
☆☆☆ 1979 CABERNET SAUVIGNON ($16.00) Napa Valley. *Rich, ripe, clean and classic. Gorgeous. Drink 1986.*
☆☆☆ 1979 CABERNET SAUVIGNON ($32.00) Bonny's, Napa Valley. *Complex and extraordinary, with French oak sweetness. Drink 1987.*
☆☆☆ 1980 CABERNET SAUVIGNON ($18.00) Alexander Valley. *Big, earthy, fat, berried, clean. Drink 1986.*
☆ 1980 CABERNET SAUVIGNON ($18.00) Napa Valley. *Raisiny, berried, overdone.*

Silverado Vineyards
NAPA COUNTY

6121 Silverado Trail, Napa, California 94558 (707-257-1770). FOUNDED: 1981. ACREAGE: 180 acres. PRODUCTION: 40,000 cases. DISTRIBUTION: Nationwide; some foreign markets. OWNERS: Lillian Disney and Ronald and Diane Miller. WINEMAKER: John S. Stuart. Retail sales by appointment.

This winery, perched dramatically on a knoll overlooking the Silverado Trail, is the realization of a dream for Lillian Disney, Walt's widow. No expense has been spared, but there aren't many frills either. This is a serious winery with a serious and talented young winemaker, Jack Stuart, who trained at Mondavi and was the winemaker at Durney Vineyard for several years.

WHITE

☆☆☆ 1981 CHARDONNAY ($10.00) Estate, Napa Valley. *Soft, rich and clean, with subtle oak.*
☆☆☆ 1982 CHARDONNAY ($10.00) Estate, Napa Valley. *Complex yet crisp and very attractive.*
☆☆☆ 1983 CHARDONNAY ($10.00) Napa Valley. *Fat, fruity, rich yet balanced, lovely.*
☆☆☆ 1981 SAUVIGNON BLANC ($8.00) Napa Valley. *Varietal, round and elegant, with light oak.*
☆☆☆ 1982 SAUVIGNON BLANC ($8.00) Napa Valley. *Soft, round, clean, fruity and varietal.*
☆☆☆ 1983 SAUVIGNON BLANC ($8.00) Napa Valley. *Varietal but restrained and elegant.*

RED

☆☆☆ 1981 CABERNET SAUVIGNON ($11.00) Napa Valley. *Herbal, fresh, and fruity, with lovely structure. Drink 1986.*
☆☆☆ 1982 CABERNET SAUVIGNON ($11.00) Napa Valley. *Angular, supple yet austere. Should improve with age. Drink 1987.*
☆☆☆ 1983 CABERNET SAUVIGNON ($12.00) Napa Valley. *Angular, clean and beautifully structured. Drink 1988.*
☆☆☆ 1983 MERLOT Napa Valley. *Lush, balanced, cherry-fruity, superb.*

Simi Winery
SONOMA COUNTY

16275 Healdsburg Avenue, Healdsburg, California 95448 (707-433-6981). FOUNDED: 1876. ACREAGE: 200 acres. PRODUCTION: 145,000 cases. DISTRIBUTION: Nationwide; 4 limited foreign markets. OWNER: Moet-Hennessy U.S. Corporation. Michael G. Dacres Dixon, president; Zelma Long, vice president. WINEMAKER: Zelma Long. Tours at 11 A.M., 1 P.M., and 3 P.M. Tasting daily 10 A.M.–5 P.M. Picnic facilities. Newsletter.

The Simi brothers founded this winery in 1876 and called it Montepulciano. It was revived in 1969 by Southern California oilman Russell Green, who revamped the winery and installed Mary Ann Graf as winemaker. In 1974 Green sold it to Michael Dacres Dixon, a dapper Englishman, who two years later sold Simi to Schieffelin and Company, a New York importer. Dixon stayed on as president and in 1979 hired Zelma Long away from Robert Mondavi Winery as winemaker (see Long Vineyards). In 1981 Simi and Schieffelin were acquired by French Champagne and Cognac giant Moet-Hennessy.

WHITE

☆☆☆ 1980 CHARDONNAY ($9.00) Mendocino. *Rich oak and fruity flavors; balanced and very lovely.*
☆☆☆☆ 1980 CHARDONNAY ($20.00) Reserve, Mendocino. *Opulent and toasty, with sweet oak. Complex yet fruity and fresh.*
☆☆☆ 1981 CHARDONNAY ($11.00) Mendocino. *Richly varietal, balanced, fruity and delightful.*
☆☆☆ 1981 CHARDONNAY ($20.00) Reserve, Sonoma County. *Big, rich, oaky and intense. Excellent.*
☆☆☆ 1982 CHARDONNAY ($11.00) Sonoma. *Rich, clean, delightful.*
☆☆☆ 1983 CHARDONNAY ($12.00) 59% Mendocino, 41% Sonoma. *Fresh, varietal, balanced, crisp, lovely.*
☆☆☆ 1982 CHENIN BLANC ($6.25) 53% Sonoma, 47% Mendocino, North Coast. *1.1% residual sugar. Intense, fresh and varietal, with great acidity and fruit.*

☆☆☆ 1983 CHENIN BLANC ($6.50) Mendocino. *Crisp, clean and snappy, with just a touch of residual sugar (0.9%).*

☆☆☆ 1984 CHENIN BLANC ($6.50) Mendocino. *0.8% residual sugar. Fresh, crisp and charming; a classic.*

☆☆☆ 1982 SAUVIGNON BLANC ($9.00) Sonoma. *Subtly varietal and rounded, with a nice lemony finish.*

☆☆ 1983 SAUVIGNON BLANC ($9.50) Sonoma. *Grassy, rich, varietal.*

ROSE

☆☆☆ 1982 CABERNET SAUVIGNON ($5.25) Sonoma. *Spritzy, fresh, varietal, fruity and off-dry (1% residual sugar).*

☆☆☆ 1983 ROSE OF CABERNET ($6.00) Sonoma. *Crisp, varietal, fruity, rounded with 0.9% residual sugar; pretty.*

☆☆☆☆ 1984 ROSE OF CABERNET ($6.50) North Coast. *1% residual sugar. Crisp, varietal, slightly spritzy, superb. America's best rosé.*

RED

☆☆ 1974 CABERNET SAUVIGNON ($25.00) Reserve Vintage, Alexander Valley. *Soft and earthy; clean and tea-like.*

☆☆☆ 1977 CABERNET SAUVIGNON ($15.00) Special Selection, Alexander Valley. *Lovely, angular and well made. Should continue to age well.*

☆☆ 1978 CABERNET SAUVIGNON ($8.00) Alexander Valley. *Soft, lush; lacks stuffing.*

☆☆☆ 1979 CABERNET SAUVIGNON ($9.00) Alexander Valley. *Varietal and meaty, with lean structure and good fruit. Drink 1986.*

☆☆☆☆ 1979 CABERNET SAUVIGNON ($19.00) Reserve, Alexander Valley. *Rich, beautifully structured, with firm fruit and supple textures. Drink 1986.*

☆☆☆ 1980 CABERNET SAUVIGNON ($10.00) Alexander Valley. *Herbal, lush, soft and concentrated. Drink 1986.*

☆☆ 1981 CABERNET SAUVIGNON ($11.00) Alexander Valley. *Herbal, lean, fruity and well structured. Drink 1987.*

☆ 1979 PINOT NOIR ($7.95) Alexander Valley.

☆ 1980 PINOT NOIR ($7.00) Alexander Valley. *Tart, stemmy, crisp.*

☆☆ 1981 PINOT NOIR ($8.00) North Coast. *Fresh, snappy, earthy, with good fruit.*

☆☆ 1978 ZINFANDEL ($7.00) Alexander Valley. *Soft, herbal and appealing.*

☆☆ 1980 ZINFANDEL ($6.25) Alexander Valley. *Peppery, rich, clean, varietal.*

☆☆ 1981 ZINFANDEL ($7.00) Alexander Valley. *Lush, clean, fat, rich.*

Siskiyou Vineyards
OREGON

6220 The Oregon Caves Highway, Cave Junction, Oregon 97523 (503-592-3727). FOUNDED: 1978. ACREAGE: 12 acres. PRODUCTION: 6,000 cases. DISTRIBUTION: Oregon, California, Colorado, and Washington. OWNER: Carol J. "Suzi" David. WINEMAKER: Donna Devine. Tours and tasting daily 11 A.M.–5 P.M. Tasting at 800 Chetco Avenue, Brooking, Monday–Saturday 9 A.M.–5 P.M.

Suzi David felt she had finally found her home when she saw the large ranch of woodlands, hay fields, and forests. She purchased the property in 1974 and moved there from her home in Pacific Palisades, near Los Angeles. After putting in a two-acre trout lake, she planted the first vinifera vineyard in the southwestern part of Oregon. The winery was started in the basement in 1978 and moved in 1982 to a newly constructed redwood winery with an upstairs balcony overlooking the vineyard. Suzi continues to run the winery with all the enthusiasm of a woman who loves her work. Her biggest joy is working among her vines, "but now I have to deal with so much paper work, working in the vineyard has become a luxury," says Suzi.

WHITE

☆   1982 CHARDONNAY ($8.25) Oregon.
☆☆ 1983 WHITE RIESLING ($6.60) Oregon.

ROSE

☆   1982 ROSE OF CABERNET ($5.00) Oregon.

RED

☆   1981 PINOT NOIR ($9.00) Oregon. *Lush, fat, sweetish.*
☆   1982 ZINFANDEL ($7.00) Oregon. *Earthy, intense and fruity, with some muddiness.*

Smith & Hook Vineyard
MONTEREY COUNTY

37700 Foothill Boulevard, Soledad, California 93960 (408-678-2132). FOUNDED: 1980. ACREAGE: 250 acres. PRODUCTION: 10,000 cases. DISTRIBUTION: California and major market states. OWNERS: Partnership, McFarland Management Company. Jerry DeCoto, vineyard manager. WINEMAKER: Duane DeBoer. OTHER LABEL: Gabriel y Caroline. Tours by appointment. No tasting or sales.

Gerald McFarland, part owner-manager of McFarland Land Company which owns and manages several thousand vineyard acres in Monterey County, created Smith & Hook as a one-wine winery estate. He bought a 642-acre parcel that had been a horse ranch and planted 250 acres in the traditional red Bordeaux varieties. Winemaker Duane DeBoer set up the winery in what used to be a stable. Duane, a chemical engineer, devoted twenty years to the Air Force before getting his degree from U.C. Davis in enology and viticulture. Gerald is not above creating new labels on the spur of the moment such as Gabriel y Caroline which was used for a special batch of botrytized Johannisberg Riesling.

WHITE

☆☆ 1982 GABRIEL Y CAROLINE JOHANNISBERG RIESLING ($26.34) Selected Late Harvest, Monterey. *12.2% residual sugar. Crisp, botrytis, rich, balanced.*

RED

1979 CABERNET SAUVIGNON ($9.00) Monterey. *Vegetal and atypical.*
1980 CABERNET SAUVIGNON ($9.50) Monterey. *Weedy; nice texture but not likable.*
☆☆ 1981 CABERNET SAUVIGNON ($13.50) Estate, Monterey. *Soft, lush, fruity, clean, very nice. Drink 1986.*

Smith-Madrone
NAPA COUNTY

4022 Spring Mountain Road, St. Helena, California 94574 (707-963-2283). FOUNDED: 1971. ACREAGE: 40 acres. PRODUCTION: 7,000 cases. DISTRIBUTION: Nationwide. OWNER: Smith family. Stuart Smith, general manager. WINEMAKERS: Charley and Stuart Smith. Tours, tasting, and retail sales by appointment.

Stu Smith built his winery 1,700 feet up the side of Spring Mountain. With the help of his wife Susan and his brother Charley, he cleared and planted a twenty-acre vineyard. The sod-roofed winery was completed in time for the first crush in 1977, and additional facilities are planned.

WHITE

☆☆ 1981 CHARDONNAY ($12.50) Napa Valley. *Fresh, spritzy, light.*

☆☆ 1982 CHARDONNAY ($12.50) Napa Valley. *Toasty, rich, vinous. Nice but lacking freshness.*

☆☆ 1982 JOHANNISBERG RIESLING ($7.00) Napa Valley. *1.5% residual sugar. Solid, clean, well structured.*

☆☆☆ 1983 JOHANNISBERG RIESLING ($7.00) Napa Valley. *1.7% residual sugar. Crisp, clean, varietal, very pleasant.*

RED

☆☆☆☆ 1979 CABERNET SAUVIGNON ($14.00) Estate, Napa Valley. *Rich and intense; velvety and complex. Drink now.*

☆☆☆ 1980 CABERNET SAUVIGNON ($14.00) Estate, Napa Valley. *Soft, rich, balanced. More conventional than the '79. Drink 1988.*

☆ 1980 PINOT NOIR ($14.00) Estate, Napa Valley.

1982 PINOT NOIR ($10.00) Napa Valley. *Undergoing malolactic fermentation. Decent flavors, clean.*

Smokey Mountain Winery
TENNESSEE

Brookside Village, Gatlinburg, Tennessee 37738 (615-436-7551). FOUNDED: 1981. ACREAGE: None. PRODUCTION: 5,000 cases. DISTRIBUTION: At winery. OWNERS: Everett and Miriam Brock. WINEMAKER: Mike Mancuso. Tours and tasting daily 10 A.M.–5 P.M.

Everett Brock, who makes handmade toys, and his wife Miriam, who makes all kinds of notions and cornflowers, became interested in the wine business through winemaking friends in Iowa. They rented space in a new shopping mall in Gatlinburg and, among the gift shops and restaurants, began making both grape and fruit wines. Curious shoppers come by, watch the winemaking process, and taste some wine.

Smothers-Vine Hill Wines
SANTA CRUZ COUNTY

2317 Vine Hill Road, Santa Cruz, California 95060 (408-438-1260). FOUNDED: 1977. ACREAGE: 43 acres. PRODUCTION: 3,000 cases. DISTRIBUTION: California and other markets. OWNER: Richard R. Smothers. Helen Ullrich, manager. WINEMAKER: William Arnold. No tours or tasting.

Dick Smothers, of television fame, and his wife, Linda, bought the eleven-acre Vine Hill Vineyard, not far from their Santa Cruz home, and built a small winery in their garage. Meanwhile, Tom Smothers (the one their mother didn't like as much) was becoming a grape grower in Sonoma. Since 1983 the brothers have been thinking about moving the winery to the Sonoma property or at least nearby.

WHITE

☆ 1982 CHARDONNAY ($11.00) California. *Toasty and richly varietal. Some bottle variation.*

☆☆☆ 1982 CHARDONNAY ($12.50) Remick Ridge Ranch, Sonoma. *Classically balanced, richly fruited, nice oak.*

☆☆ 1983 CHARDONNAY ($12.50) Remick Ridge Ranch, Sonoma Valley. *Rich oak and clean fruit; quite appealing.*

☆☆☆   1981 GEWURZTRAMINER ($9.75) Late Harvest, Alexander Valley. *7.5% residual sugar. Varietal and graceful; great fruit and balance.*

☆☆   1983 GEWURZTRAMINER ($7.00) Sonoma. *0.6% residual sugar. Dry, varietal, clean, attractive.*

☆☆☆   1983 JOHANNISBERG RIESLING ($12.00) Late Harvest, Sonoma. *375ml. 10.8% residual sugar. Soft, lush, fruity, botrytis.*

O   1982 SAUVIGNON BLANC ($8.00) Remick Ridge Ranch, Sonoma. *Overoaked and oxidized.*

☆   1983 SAUVIGNON BLANC ($8.00) Remick Ridge Ranch, Sonoma Valley. *Odd, woody.*

☆☆☆   1981 WHITE RIESLING ($9.00) Vine Hill, Santa Cruz. *4.2% residual sugar. Sweet, fresh, very lovely.*

RED

☆☆☆   1979 CABERNET SAUVIGNON ($12.50) Alexander Valley. *Very fresh and crisp; ripe and structured. Drink 1986.*

☆☆☆   1980 CABERNET SAUVIGNON ($12.50) Alexander Valley. *Fruity, clean, superbly balanced. Drink 1986.*

☆☆   1980 ZINFANDEL ($7.50) Sonoma. *Earthy, crisp and fruity. Drink now.*

Snoqualmie Falls Winery
WASHINGTON

545 Rainier Boulevard North, Issaquah, Washington 98027 (206-392-4000). FOUNDED: 1983. ACREAGE: None. PRODUCTION: 35,000 cases. DISTRIBUTION: Major market states. OWNERS: Joel Klein and David Wyckoff. WINEMAKER: Joel Klein. Tours daily 10 A.M.–4:30 P.M.

After working at United Vintners and at Geyser Peak Winery in California, Joel Klein moved to Château Ste. Michelle, where he helped to design the winery's first facility at Woodinville. After its completion, he became principal winemaker. He was working on the design of Ste. Michelle's second château in Patterson when it struck him that he should be designing his own winery. At about that time, Joel got a telephone call from David Wyckoff, a hard-working eastern Washington farmer and grape grower who was also interested in starting a wine operation. The two men met, became friends, and started a partnership. Their first crush in 1983 yielded 12,000 cases of wine, made at Wyckoff's Coventry Vale winery in Prosser. The following year Joel found the perfect winery site in the well-touristed area of Snoqualmie Falls, and the dramatic new building was opened in early 1985.

WHITE

1983 CHENIN BLANC ($5.50) Washington. *Candied, oxidized, dull.*

1983 SEMILLON ($6.00) Yakima Valley. *Strange, with a candied pineapple flavor.*

Soda Rock Winery
SONOMA COUNTY

8015 Highway 128, Healdsburg, California 95448 (707-433-1830). FOUNDED: 1978. ACREAGE: 2 acres. PRODUCTION: 5,000–7,000 cases. DISTRIBUTION: At winery and local outlets. OWNER: Tomka family. Charles Tomka, Sr., and Charles Jr. WINEMAKER: Charles Tomka, Sr. Tasting daily 10 A.M.–5 P.M.

Charles Tomka, Sr., and his son Charles Jr. have recycled every stone, board, and piece of equipment in the old Ferrari winery, a facility dating from 1880, which the Tomka family purchased in 1978. Charlie Sr. believes in never buying anything new if he can get a deal on it used. All the winery equipment, from the basket press to the hose fittings to the electrical wiring, was used by Ferrari himself. Charlie Sr., who loves to tell tales about making wine for the nobility of Hungary, sold his business in Missouri to help his son restore the old winery. He uses no chemicals and gives his wines lengthy aging in redwood and oak barrels. According to Charlie, if the wine doesn't give you a headache the next morning, it's a good wine.

WHITE

1983 GEWURZTRAMINER ($6.75) DeBaun, Sonoma. *Odd.*

RED

O 1980 CABERNET SAUVIGNON ($8.50) Alexander Valley.
☆ 1979 PINOT NOIR ($14.00) Sonoma. *Tannic, varietal, clean, decent.*

Sokol Blosser Winery
OREGON

Blanchard Lane, Dundee, Oregon 97115 (503-864-3342). FOUNDED: 1977. ACREAGE: 45 acres. PRODUCTION: 25,000 cases. DISTRIBUTION: 30 states; some foreign markets. OWNERS: Sokol and Blosser families. William Blosser, president. WINEMAKER: Robert McRitchie. Tours and tasting daily 11 A.M.–5 P.M.

Originally a weekend vineyard, Sokol Blosser has become one of the largest, most successful wineries in Oregon. Bill Blosser, an urban planner, and Susan Sokol Blosser, a history professor, planted a small vineyard among their fruit trees in 1971. They were impressed with the results. Approaching winemaking in a practical, businesslike way, the Blossers put a winery plan into effect as soon as they felt sure they could make a commercial success of their project. They hired a winemaker, Robert McRitchie, and a well-known architect, John Storrs, who designed a tasting room and banquet hall that would dazzle winery visitors.

WHITE

☆☆☆ 1981 CHARDONNAY ($9.95) Yamhill County, Oregon. *Crisp, fresh, clean and very attractive.*
 O 1982 CHARDONNAY ($9.85) Reserve, Yamhill County, Oregon. *Ruined by high volatile acidity.*
 ☆ 1982 CHARDONNAY ($9.95) Yamhill County, Oregon. *Crisp and snappy but lacking depth.*
 1982 SAUVIGNON BLANC ($6.80) Sagemoor Farms, Washington. *Soapy, tired, thin.*
 O 1983 SAUVIGNON BLANC ($6.00) Washington. *Dirty, seriously flawed, highly unattractive.*
 ☆☆ 1981 WHITE RIESLING ($5.00) Washington. *Crisp, dry, very nice.*
 ☆☆☆ 1982 WHITE RIESLING ($6.60) Yamhill County, Willamette Valley. *Snappy, and clean, with great acidity. Angular and exceptional.*
 ☆ 1983 WHITE RIESLING ($6.95) Yamhill County, Oregon. *Heavy, coarse, unpleasant.*

ROSE

☆☆☆ 1982 BOUQUET ROSE ($4.50) American. *Pinot Noir. Crisp, fruity, varietal, light, slightly off-dry.*

RED

1979 MERLOT ($6.95) Washington. *Meaty and unappealing.*
1980 MERLOT ($6.95) Sagemoor Farms, Washington. *10% Cabernet Sauvignon. Weedy, fat.*

☆   1978 PINOT NOIR ($8.25) Yamhill County, Oregon.

☆☆☆ 1979 PINOT NOIR ($8.95) Hyland, Yamhill County, Oregon. *Intense, rich and toasty. Balanced and clean.*

☆☆   1979 PINOT NOIR ($10.00) 83% Estate, 17% Durant, Yamhill County, Oregon. *Toasty, clean and subtle. Quite elegant.*

☆☆   1980 PINOT NOIR ($7.00) Yamhill.

☆   1982 PINOT NOIR ($8.95) Yamhill County, Oregon. *Peppery, thin, underripe, woody.*

☆☆☆ 1983 PINOT NOIR ($9.95) Hyland, Yamhill County, Oregon. *Varietal, balanced, clean, lovely.*

☆☆   1983 PINOT NOIR ($9.95) Red Hills, Yamhill County, Oregon. *Fat, rich, clean.*

Soleterra
NAPA COUNTY

3027 Silverado Trail, St. Helena, California 94574 (707-924-5251). FOUNDED: 1982. ACREAGE: 83 acres. PRODUCTION: 1,400 cases. DISTRIBUTION: California. OWNERS: Partnership. Sloan and John Upton, and John Thoreen. WINEMAKER: John Thoreen. No tours or tasting.

John and Sloan Upton planted one of Napa's most celebrated vineyards, Three Palms, in 1967. "If we had been more accurate, we would have called it the Three Thousand Rock Vineyard," says Sloan. At first the Uptons sold most of their Merlot and Pinot Noir grapes to Sterling Vineyards. Then Sterling stopped making Pinot Noir. "According to our contract, we could have made them take the grapes anyway," says Sloan, "but rather than be hard-nosed about it, we decided to start our own label." This idea came from John Thoreen, the Upton's good friend and partner, who is also a consultant to Sterling Vineyards. The wine is currently being made at Rombauer Vineyards.

RED

☆☆☆ 1982 PINOT NOIR ($12.00) Three Palms, Napa Valley. *Rich, lush, varietal; very lovely. Drink now.*

Soñoito Vineyards
ARIZONA

6550 North First Street, Tucson, Arizona 85718 (602-297-2850). FOUNDED: 1983. ACREAGE: 55 acres. PRODUCTION: 1,500 cases. DISTRIBUTION: Arizona. OWNER: Corporation. John Harvey, president; Gordon Dutt, vice president and manager. WINEMAKER: Gordon Dutt. Tours and tasting weekends 9 A.M.–5 P.M.

Soil scientist and professor of water and engineering at the University of Arizona, Gordon Dutt was required to make wine for grape studies at the university. In 1979 he became one of the co-directors of the special program on the wine grape feasibility of the Four Corners area. The results of this research compelled him to plant the very first commercial vineyard in the state of Arizona, Vina Soñoita. Other growers followed Gordon's lead, and soon there were enough grapes around to warrant a winery. Established as a cooperative, the winery is funded and managed by partner-growers, all of whom have other jobs. "Every one of the partners works in the winery," says Gordon, "that is, every one except my son. He is finishing up his studies at U.C. Davis."

WHITE

☆   1983 FUME BLANC ($7.35) Arizona.

Sonoma-Cutrer Vineyards
SONOMA COUNTY

4401 Slusser Road, Windsor, California 95492 (707-528-1181). FOUNDED: 1981. ACREAGE: 700 acres. PRODUCTION: 40,000 cases. DISTRIBUTION: California and other major market states. OWNER: Corporation. Bruce Jones, president. WINEMAKER: Bill Bonetti. Tours, tasting, and retail sales by appointment.

Bruce Jones, an Air Force fighter pilot in Vietnam, resigned his commission in 1970 and went to Harvard Business School. In 1972 he formed a partnership with Kent Klineman and 25 limited partners with the express purpose of buying vineyard land. The partners developed more than 700 acres in Sonoma. Grapes were sold to others until a winery was built in time for the 1981 harvest. Bill Bonetti, who spent nearly ten years at Souverain, was hired as winemaker. The winery makes only one wine, Chardonnay, and is expected to reach a production of 85,000 cases.

WHITE

☆☆☆ 1981 CHARDONNAY ($9.50) Estate, Russian River Valley. *Powerful, rich, oaky and complex.*

☆☆☆ 1981 CHARDONNAY ($12.75) Cutrer, Russian River Valley. *Soft and round, with complexity and fruit.*

☆☆☆☆ 1981 CHARDONNAY ($14.50) Les Pierres, Sonoma Valley. *Crisp and rich; complex and remarkably elegant.*

☆☆ 1982 CHARDONNAY ($10.00) Russian River Ranches, Russian River Valley.

☆☆ 1982 CHARDONNAY ($13.00) Cutrer, Russian River Valley.

☆☆☆ 1982 CHARDONNAY ($15.50) Les Pierres, Sonoma Valley. *Crisp and lovely at its best— but there is considerable bottle variation.*

Sonoma Hills Winery
SONOMA COUNTY

4850 Pecacca Road, Santa Rosa, California 95404 (707-523-3415). FOUNDED: 1983. ACREAGE: None. PRODUCTION: 1,000 cases. DISTRIBUTION: California. OWNERS: Terry and John Votruba. WINEMAKER: Terry Votruba. No tours or tasting.

Home winemaker, homemaker, and schoolteacher, Terry Votruba felt that since she and her lawyer husband were living in Sonoma County, right next to Matanzas Creek Winery, she should start her own winery. Besides, she was disenchanted with teaching. The winery, which is located beneath the Votruba's house, will specialize in Chardonnays made from grapes grown in the Bennett Valley area.

SONOMA MISSION WINERY *see* R. Montali and Associates

Sonoma Vineyards
SONOMA COUNTY

11455 Old Redwood Highway, Windsor, California 95492 (707-433-6511). FOUNDED: 1961. ACREAGE: 1,200 acres. PRODUCTION: 500,000 cases. DISTRIBUTION: Nationwide. OWNER: Publicly owned company. WINEMAKER: Rodney Strong. OTHER LABELS: Windsor Vineyards, Rodney Strong. Tours and tasting daily 10 A.M.–5 P.M.

Rod Strong, a former Broadway dancer and choreographer, began by selling wines out of a tasting room in Tiburon, across the bay from San Francisco. Rod pioneered selling wine by mail and with personalized labels, but when he moved to Sonoma, he expanded too fast and much too expensively. Rod's New York distributor, Renfield, bailed the winery out and acquired a big chunk of the action in the bargain. After a number of financial jolts, the company has trimmed its production, started to sell its vineyards, and rededicated itself to making premium wines under the Rodney Strong label.

WHITE

O   1981 WINDSOR VINEYARDS AURORA ($5.00) Great River, New York State. *Weird and heavy.*

☆☆   1981 RODNEY STRONG CHARDONNAY ($9.00) Sonoma. *Clean and rich.*

☆☆☆   1981 CHARDONNAY ($10.00) River West, Sonoma. *Nice balance between richness and fresh fruitiness.*

☆☆   1982 RODNEY STRONG CHARDONNAY ($10.00) Chalk Hill, Sonoma. *Simple, clean, decent.*

☆   1982 RODNEY STRONG CHARDONNAY ($10.00) River West, Russian River Valley.

1983 RODNEY STRONG CHENIN BLANC ($5.50) California.

☆   1983 WINDSOR VINEYARDS CHENIN BLANC ($5.50) California. *1.15% residual sugar. Musty, dull, vinous.*

☆☆   1982 WINDSOR VINEYARDS FRENCH COLOMBARD ($5.50) California.

1981 FUME BLANC ($6.75) Sonoma.

☆☆   1982 WINDSOR VINEYARDS GEWURZTRAMINER ($7.00) Sonoma. *2.33% residual sugar.*

☆☆   1983 WINDSOR VINEYARDS GEWURZTRAMINER ($7.00) Sonoma. *2.3% residual sugar. Crisp, snappy, clean, varietal.*

☆☆☆   1978 JOHANNISBERG RIESLING Late Harvest, LeBaron, Sonoma. *7% residual sugar. Rich, nice botrytis, should hold for years.*

☆☆   1980 WINDSOR JOHANNISBERG RIESLING ($8.00) Late Harvest, Estate, Sonoma. *6.3% residual sugar. Toasty, rich and fruity.*

☆☆   1980 JOHANNISBERG RIESLING ($8.00) Northern California.

1982 WINDSOR VINEYARDS JOHANNISBERG RIESLING ($6.75) Select Late Harvest, Estate, Russian River Valley. *14.9% residual sugar. Oxidized in the nose, soft, decent.*

☆☆   1982 WINDSOR VINEYARDS JOHANNISBERG RIESLING ($6.75) Sonoma. *2.65% residual sugar. Lush, fruity and soft, with good acid.*

☆☆☆   1982 JOHANNISBERG RIESLING ($8.00) LeBaron, Estate, Russian River Valley. *3.45% residual sugar. Soft, sweet and crisply fruity.*

☆☆☆   1982 JOHANNISBERG RIESLING ($12.00) Select Late Harvest, Russian River Valley. *14.8% residual sugar. Rich, syrupy, intense.*

☆   1983 JOHANNISBERG RIESLING ($6.50) Sonoma. *Cardboard-like, dense, fruity.*

☆☆☆   1983 WINDSOR VINEYARDS JOHANNISBERG RIESLING ($7.50) River West, Estate, Russian River Valley. *2.6% residual sugar. Tangy and rich, with lovely fruit.*

☆☆☆   1983 RODNEY STRONG JOHANNISBERG RIESLING ($8.00) Le Baron, Estate, Russian River Valley. *2.2% residual sugar. Spicy, clean, fruity.*

O   1983 RODNEY STRONG SAUVIGNON BLANC ($6.50) Charlotte's Home, Alexander Valley. *Vegetal, oily, heavy, unattractive.*

SPARKLING

1981 WINDSOR VINEYARDS AURORA ($7.50) Marlboro Champagne, New York State. *Stinky.*

☆☆   1981 WINDSOR VINEYARDS BLANC DE NOIR ($12.00) Sonoma.

☆☆   1981 WINDSOR VINEYARDS BRUT ($13.00) Sonoma.

BLANC DE NOIR

☆☆   1982 WINDSOR VINEYARDS PINOT NOIR ($5.75) Sonoma.

ROSE

☆☆☆ 1982 CABERNET SAUVIGNON ($6.00) Mendocino. *1.11% residual sugar. Good varietal character, clean.*

1982 WINDSOR VINEYARDS GRENACHE ROSE ($4.50) California. *1.4% residual sugar.*

☆☆ 1983 WINDSOR VINEYARDS ROSE OF CABERNET ($6.00) Mendocino. *1.25% residual sugar. Lush, varietal, lively, nice.*

RED

☆ 1978 CABERNET SAUVIGNON ($11.00) Alexander's Crown, Estate, Sonoma. *This once grand wine is beginning to show its age.*

☆☆☆ 1978 RODNEY STRONG CABERNET SAUVIGNON ($12.00) Alexander's Crown, Sonoma. *Lovely, clean and elegant, with great breeding.*

☆ 1979 WINDSOR VINEYARDS CABERNET SAUVIGNON ($10.00) Mendocino.

☆☆ 1979 CABERNET SAUVIGNON ($12.00) Sonoma. *Soft and herbal, clean and elegant.*

☆☆☆ 1979 RODNEY STRONG CABERNET SAUVIGNON ($12.95) Alexander's Crown, Alexander Valley. *Rich, earthy and dense, with good structure. Drink 1986.*

☆☆ 1980 WINDSOR VINEYARDS CABERNET SAUVIGNON ($9.00) Lot 1, North Coast. *Violets and rich varietal flavors.*

☆☆☆ 1980 RODNEY STRONG CABERNET SAUVIGNON ($11.00) Alexander's Crown, Alexander Valley. *Rich, heavy, herbal, intense, concentrated.*

☆ 1979 PETITE SIRAH ($6.50) Vintage Selection, Northern California. *Clean, nice body but a bit vegetal and lacking fruit.*

1980 RODNEY STRONG PINOT NOIR ($8.50) River East, Russian River Valley. *Musty.*

☆ 1978 ZINFANDEL ($14.00) River West, Old Vines, Estate, Sonoma.

☆ 1979 ZINFANDEL ($4.25) Northern California.

Sotoyome Winery
SONOMA COUNTY

641 Limerick Lane, Healdsburg, California 95448 (707-433-2001). FOUNDED: 1974. ACREAGE: 10 acres. PRODUCTION: 3,000 cases. DISTRIBUTION: 8 states. OWNER: Corporation. Bill Chaikin, general manager. WINEMAKER: Bill Chaikin. Tours, tasting, and retail sales by appointment. Picnic facilities.

The small, metal-and-wood A-frame building of Sotoyome Winery sits alongside the house of Bill Chaikin, its owner and winemaker. Bill took on the entire responsibility of the winery at the death of his partner, winemaker John Stampfl, and has continued to make wine in John's style. Eventually, Bill would like to make only Petite Sirah and Syrah wines from his own vineyards.

WHITE

1982 CHARDONNAY ($6.75) Dry Creek Valley-Sonoma.

RED

☆ 1978 CABERNET SAUVIGNON ($7.50) Sonoma. *Big, forward and pleasant but lacking grace or depth.*

☆☆☆ 1979 CABERNET SAUVIGNON ($5.75) Dry Creek Valley. *Warm, toasty, clean and intense, with some weeds. Drink 1986.*

☆☆ 1980 CABERNET SAUVIGNON ($5.75) Dry Creek Valley. *Lush, rich, intense, forward. Drink now.*

☆ 1978 PETITE SIRAH ($5.25) Sonoma. *Spicy, jammy, clean; a bit overdone.*

1979 PETITE SIRAH ($5.25) Sonoma. *Dirty.*

☆   1980 PETITE SIRAH ($5.25) Russian River Valley. *Big, fat, tannic.*
☆☆   1979 ZINFANDEL ($4.75) Sonoma. *Big, deep, hearty.*

Souverain Cellars
SONOMA COUNTY

Independence Lane at Highway 101, Geyserville, California 95441 (707-433-8281). FOUNDED: 1973. ACREAGE: 20,000 combined acres of partners. PRODUCTION: 500,000 cases. DISTRI- BUTION: Nationwide; France and the United Kingdom. OWNER: North Coast Grape Growers. William Pauli, president. WINEMAKER: Thomas Peterson. OTHER LABEL: North Coast Cellars. Tours and tasting daily 10 A.M.–5 P.M. Gift shop. Restaurant. Seasonal concerts and events.

The original Souverain Winery, founded by J. Leland Stewart, was in the Napa Valley on Howell Mountain. The winery was relocated after it was purchased by the Pillsbury Company in the early 1970s. Pillsbury built a new winery in Rutherford (now the Rutherford Hill Winery) and a second facility in Sonoma County (now Souverain Cellars) near Geyserville. In 1976, when Pillsbury decided to invest in restaurants rather than wine, the Rutherford winery was sold and the Sonoma facility was purchased by grape growers in Napa, Sonoma, and Mendocino counties. Operating as a cooperative—although the owners dislike that term intensely—Souverain is noted for changing administrative directors, winemakers, and presidents more often than harvest help. It is also known for its extraordinary architecture and lovely restaurant, with a patio in the vineyards, overlooking the Alexander Valley.

WHITE

☆   NV   CHABLIS ($3.50) North Coast. *Fresh and clean but seemingly stripped of character.*
☆☆   1982 CHABLIS ($3.50) California. *Good fruit; fresh, clean and rich. Charming.*
☆☆☆   1982 COLOMBARD BLANC ($4.00) North Coast. *Crisp, clean and appealing.*
☆   NV   NORTH COAST CELLARS CHARDONNAY ($4.75) North Coast. *Decent, bal- anced but not much character.*
☆☆   1982 CHARDONNAY ($9.00) North Coast. *Crisp and snappy, with a touch of oiliness.*
☆   NV   CHENIN BLANC ($3.00) North Coast. *1.5% residual sugar. Heavy, vinous, lush.*
☆   NV   NORTH COAST CELLARS CHENIN BLANC ($3.37) North Coast.
☆☆   1982 CHENIN BLANC ($5.00) North Coast. *Fruity and varietal; a bit soft.*
☆   1983 CHENIN BLANC ($5.00) North Coast. *1.3% residual sugar. Balanced, fruity but dirty.*
☆☆   1983 CHENIN BLANC ($5.50) North Coast. *1.3% residual sugar. Crisp, clean, varietal.*
☆☆   NV   NORTH COAST CELLARS FRENCH COLOMBARD ($3.50) North Coast. *1.3% residual sugar. Fruity, clean and appealing.*
☆   1981 FUME BLANC ($6.75) North Coast.
☆☆   1982 FUME BLANC ($6.00) North Coast. *Grassy, clean, attractive.*
☆☆☆   1982 GEWURZTRAMINER ($5.00) North Coast. *1.3% residual sugar. Soft, fresh and appealing.*
☆   1982 GREY RIESLING ($5.00) North Coast. *Dull and lacking character. Off-dry.*
☆   1983 GREY RIESLING ($5.00) North Coast. *1.2% residual sugar. Fruity, fresh, snappy, decent.*
☆☆   NV   NORTH COAST CELLARS JOHANNISBERG RIESLING ($3.50) North Coast.
☆☆   1982 JOHANNISBERG RIESLING ($6.75) North Coast. *1.4% residual sugar. Fruity and clean. O.K. but not lovable.*

☆☆ 1983 JOHANNISBERG RIESLING ($6.75) North Coast. *1.4% residual sugar. Spicy, clean, simple, very nice.*

☆☆☆ 1982 MUSCAT ($6.50) North Coast. *5.2% residual sugar. Spicy, varietal and lush.*

☆☆ 1982 SAUVIGNON BLANC ($8.50) Vintage Selection, North Coast. *Soft, rounded, clean, richly fruity.*

ROSE

☆☆ NV NORTH COAST CELLARS ROSE ($2.50) North Coast. *Fresh, clean and fruity.*

1983 PINOT NOIR ROSE ($4.50) North Coast. *Strange off flavors, varnishy.*

☆☆ 1982 PINOT NOIR ($4.50) North Coast. *1.4% residual sugar. Fresh and simple.*

NV NORTH COAST CELLARS ZINFANDEL ($2.50) North Coast. *2.5% residual sugar.*

RED

☆ 1978 BURGUNDY ($3.50) North Coast. *Clean and decent but no depth or richness.*

☆ NV NORTH COAST CELLARS CABERNET SAUVIGNON ($3.50) North Coast. *Soft and clean, with some odd flavors.*

☆☆ 1978 CABERNET SAUVIGNON ($7.00) North Coast. *Pleasant. Drink now.*

☆☆ 1978 CABERNET SAUVIGNON ($12.00) Vintage Selection, Estate, Sonoma. *Soft and rich, with good fruit and varietal character. Drink now.*

☆☆☆ 1979 CABERNET SAUVIGNON ($7.75) North Coast. *Rich, clean, varietal and charming. Drink now.*

☆ 1980 CABERNET SAUVIGNON ($7.50) North Coast. *Decent, fruity, simple, nice. Drink now.*

NV NORTH COAST CELLARS GAMAY BEAUJOLAIS ($3.15) North Coast.

☆☆ 1980 GAMAY BEAUJOLAIS ($5.00) North Coast. *Fresh, fruity and clean. Thin but very appealing.*

☆☆ 1979 MERLOT ($5.50) North Coast. *Fresh and appealing. Simple but very nice.*

☆ 1981 MERLOT ($6.75) North Coast. *Light, soft, decent.*

☆ 1978 PETITE SIRAH ($5.00) North Coast. *Rich, deep, clean, some off qualities in the nose.*

☆ NV NORTH COAST CELLARS PINOT NOIR ($3.00) North Coast. *Crisp, snappy, fresh, decent, not much varietal character.*

NV NORTH COAST CELLARS PINOT NOIR ($3.15) North Coast.

1980 PINOT NOIR ($6.75) North Coast. *Thin, stripped of character.*

☆☆ NV NORTH COAST CELLARS ZINFANDEL ($3.15) North Coast. *Toasty, fruity; quite pleasant.*

1979 ZINFANDEL ($4.75) North Coast. *Decent but a bit off.*

☆☆ 1980 ZINFANDEL ($5.00) North Coast. *Balanced and quite nice.*

FORTIFIED

☆☆☆ RESERVE SOLERA PORT ($11.00) Dry Creek Valley. *Extraordinary—rich, complex and delicious. Cabernet grapes.*

SPANADA *see* E. & J. Gallo Winery

Spottswoode Winery
NAPA COUNTY

1401 Hudson, St. Helena, California 94574 (707-963-0134). FOUNDED: 1982. ACREAGE: 40 acres. PRODUCTION: 1,500 cases. DISTRIBUTION: California and by mailing list. OWNERS: Harmon and Mary Brown. WINEMAKER: Tony Soter. No tours or tasting.

In 1972 Mary Brown and her husband left San Diego County to grow grapes in St. Helena. "We bought an old vineyard and began replanting in 1973," says Mary. The grapes from their vineyard gained a reputation for quality among prestigious producers such as Duckhorn and St. Clement vineyards. "The grapes were selling so well, and the wineries were making such exceptional wines from our Cabernet Sauvignon, we decided to make some wine ourselves," Mary explains. The wine was made at another winery facility and then taken to the cellar of the Brown's old Victorian house for aging.

Spring Mountain Vineyards
NAPA COUNTY

2805 Spring Mountain Road, St. Helena, California 94574 (707-963-5233). FOUNDED: 1968. ACREAGE: 135 acres. PRODUCTION: 27,000 cases. DISTRIBUTION: Nationwide; Canada and some foreign markets. OWNER: Michael Robbins, president. WINEMAKER: John Williams. OTHER LABEL: Falcon Crest. Tours by appointment daily at 10:30 A.M. and 2:30 P.M. Newsletter.

A man with an eye for classic architecture and a talent for real estate investment, Mike Robbins started his winery in the cellar of a restored 1876 Victorian house. He soon outgrew the house and sold it to Dr. Bill Casey, who started his own winery there (see St. Clement Vineyards). Mike moved his winery to the Tiburcio Parrott estate with its large Victorian home built by the same architect who designed the Beringer Rhine House. The winery, a long, two-story building with a dome-shaped turret and stained glass windows, sits across from the house. While its wines have certainly brought the winery recognition, Spring Mountain has been catapulted to national fame as the primary location for the television series "Falcon Crest."

WHITE

☆☆☆ 1981 CHARDONNAY ($12.50) Napa Valley. *Rich, clean, full and rounded.*
☆☆ 1981 SAUVIGNON BLANC ($10.50) Napa Valley.
1982 SAUVIGNON BLANC ($10.50) Napa Valley. *Decent acidity, odd flavors, not much depth.*
☆ 1983 SAUVIGNON BLANC ($9.50) Napa Valley. *Earthy, odd flavors, good oak and fruit.*

RED

☆ NV CABERNET SAUVIGNON ($8.50) Les Trois Cuvées, Napa Valley. *Earthy, muddy, decent.*
☆ NV FALCON CREST CABERNET SAUVIGNON ($9.50) Napa Valley. *A blend of 1980 and 1981. Decent, simple, clean.*
☆☆ 1979 CABERNET SAUVIGNON ($13.00) Napa Valley. *Tarry and rich, with good fruit and some elegance.*
☆☆ 1980 CABERNET SAUVIGNON ($15.00) Napa Valley.
NV PINOT NOIR ($10.00) Les Trois Cuvées, Napa Valley. *Stinky and thin.*
☆☆ 1981 PINOT NOIR ($12.00) Napa Valley. *Earthy, balanced, decent.*

Spurgeon Vineyards & Winery
WISCONSIN

Rural Route 1, Box 201, Highland, Wisconsin 53543 (608-929-7692). FOUNDED: 1981. ACREAGE: 16 acres. PRODUCTION: 3,000 cases. DISTRIBUTION: Wisconsin. OWNER: Glen H. Spurgeon. Mary L. Spurgeon, general manager. WINEMAKER: Glen Spurgeon. OTHER LABEL: Bountiful Harvest Winery. Tours and tasting April–December: daily 10 A.M.–5 P.M. January–March: weekends 10 A.M.–5 P.M.

Glen Spurgeon, born and raised in St. James, Missouri, had fond memories of watching his neighbors making wine. As a teacher of agriculture in Wisconsin, he decided to start his own small vineyard and make a little wine at home. Glen and his wife bought some remote property and planted vines. While waiting for them to mature, Glen made a number of fruit wines and built a winery into his vine-covered hillside. Because his location is so remote, Glen persuaded his father-in-law to join him in starting another winery near the interstate highway in Lodi. They call the new facility Bountiful Harvest Winery.

ૐ

Stag's Leap Wine Cellars
NAPA COUNTY

5766 Silverado Trail, Napa, California 94558 (707-944-2020). FOUNDED: 1972. ACREAGE: 44 acres. PRODUCTION: 25,000 cases. DISTRIBUTION: Nationwide; 6 foreign markets. OWNERS: Warren and Barbara Winiarski. WINEMAKER: Warren Winiarski, winemaster; Bob Broman. OTHER LABEL: Hawk Crest. Tours by appointment 11 A.M., 1 P.M., and 3 P.M. Retail sales daily 10 A.M.–4 P.M.

Warren Winiarski, a former lecturer in political philosophy at the University of Chicago, arrived in the Napa Valley in 1964. He went to work for Lee Stewart at the original Souverain winery and for Robert Mondavi. In 1972 he founded his own winery and wasted no time gaining national attention. In 1976 his 1973 Cabernet Sauvignon beat a field of French heavyweights, including Château Mouton-Rothschild, in the well-publicized Paris tasting of 1976 (see Introduction, page xiii). Subsequent vintages have shown that this winery is definitely not a flash in the pan since its wines continue to win international competitions.

WHITE

☆☆ 1982 WHITE TABLE WINE ($4.85) Napa Valley. *Rich, clean, Chardonnay-style.*

☆☆ 1980 CHARDONNAY ($13.50) Napa Valley. *Fruity, clean and fresh.*

☆☆☆ 1981 CHARDONNAY ($13.50) Napa Valley. *Toasty, crisp, good fruit and complexity.*

☆☆ 1982 CHARDONNAY ($13.50) Napa Valley. *Angular, crisp, simple and clean, with excellent aging potential.*

☆☆ 1983 HAWK CREST CHARDONNAY ($6.00) *"La Petite Faux Pas." 2.7% Cabernet blended in by mistake. Simple, clean, decent.*

☆ 1982 JOHANNISBERG RIESLING ($6.00) 50% Napa, 50% Sonoma. *Dull, lacking freshness and fruit.*

☆☆ 1982 SAUVIGNON BLANC ($8.00) Napa Valley.

☆☆☆ 1983 SAUVIGNON BLANC ($9.00) Napa Valley. *24% Semillon. Lovely, rich, varietal, clean, complex.*

☆☆☆ 1981 WHITE RIESLING ($6.75) Napa Valley. *1.8% residual sugar. Clean, crisp, lovely, fruity.*

☆☆☆ 1983 WHITE RIESLING ($6.00) Napa Valley. *1.7% residual sugar. Lush, deep, intensely fruity; charming.*

RED

☆☆ NV HAWK CREST CABERNET SAUVIGNON ($5.50) Napa Valley. *Simple, clean, herbal, decent.*

☆☆☆ 1976 CABERNET SAUVIGNON ($25.00) Lot 2, Napa Valley. *Lush, fat, velvety, with good structure. Drink now or hold.*

☆☆☆ 1977 CABERNET SAUVIGNON ($30.00) Cask 23, Estate, Napa Valley. *Velvety and rich, with good firm structure. Drink 1986.*

☆☆☆ 1978 CABERNET SAUVIGNON ($15.00) Lot 2, Napa Valley. *Violets and oak; clean, bright, intense. Drink now through 1992.*

☆☆☆☆ 1978 CABERNET SAUVIGNON ($35.00) Cask 23, Napa Valley. *Bursting with flavor, intense yet well bred. Drink 1989.*

☆☆☆ 1979 CABERNET SAUVIGNON ($12.50) Estate, Napa Valley. *Lush, ripe, fresh and fruity—but not as impressive as the '78 Lot 2.*

☆☆☆☆ 1980 CABERNET SAUVIGNON ($11.00) Napa Valley. *Velvety, rich, complex, superb. Start drinking in 1986.*

☆☆ 1981 HAWK CREST CABERNET SAUVIGNON ($4.95) Mendocino. *Clean, fruity, simple, very attractive. Drink now.*

☆☆☆☆ 1981 CABERNET SAUVIGNON ($15.00) Stag's Leap, Napa Valley. *Lush, deep, beautifully structured. Drink 1987.*

☆☆☆ 1979 MERLOT ($7.50) Estate, Napa Valley. *Rich, balanced, supple, classic. Will age well. Drink 1986.*

☆☆ 1982 MERLOT ($13.50) Napa Valley. *Lush, herbal, clean and nicely structured. Drink 1987.*

☆☆☆ 1978 PETITE SIRAH ($8.50) Napa Valley. *Ripe and full, with lovely, well-defined varietal character.*

☆☆ 1980 PETITE SIRAH ($8.50) North Coast. *Soft, clean, varietal, a bit short.*

Stags' Leap Winery
NAPA COUNTY

6150 Silverado Trail, Napa, California 94558 (707-944-1303). FOUNDED: 1972. ACREAGE: 100 acres. PRODUCTION: 10,000 cases. DISTRIBUTION: California and other major market states. OWNER: Carl Doumani. WINEMAKER: Steve Galvan. OTHER LABEL: Pedregal. No tours or tasting.

The original winery on this property had burned down, leaving just stone walls and a long hillside tunnel once used for aging wines. Nearby stood what had been the Stags' Leap Manor Hotel, a large, stone structure built in 1891. Carl Doumani bought these 400 acres of rundown, historic property in 1970 and moved his family from Los Angeles. For nine years they were all involved in the intense, seemingly endless project of restoring the old hotel and what was left of the winery—trying to preserve as much of the old stonework and architecture as possible. Their first wines were crushed at Rutherford Hill, then blended and aged in the old cave behind the winery. Finally, in 1979, restoration was completed and Stags' Leap Winery crushed its first grapes. A settlement in a court battle between Carl and Warren Winiarski of Stag's Leap Wine Cellars forbids Stags' Leap Winery from bottling Cabernet or Chardonnay under the Stags' Leap name, thus the Pedregal label.

WHITE

☆☆☆ 1981 PEDREGAL CHARDONNAY ($7.75) Napa Valley. *Clean, rich and oaky.*

RED

☆☆ 1979 MERLOT ($12.00) Napa Valley. *Big, heavy and tannic, with good fruit. Drink 1986 and beyond.*

☆ 1980 PEDREGAL MERLOT ($7.50) Napa Valley. *Dense, muddy, oaky.*

☆☆ 1981 MERLOT ($13.50) Napa Valley. *Dense, rich, lacking structure. Drink 1987.*

☆ 1973 PETITE SIRAH ($37.50) Napa Valley. *Deep, intense, overripe.*

☆☆ 1974 PETITE SIRAH ($37.50) Napa Valley. *Intense, deep, low in fruit.*

☆☆ 1978 PETITE SIRAH ($12.00) Napa Valley. *Fruity, clean, nicely structured.*

☆☆☆ 1979 PETITE SIRAH ($8.75) Napa Valley. *Soft, varietal, clean, lush and superb. Drink now.*

☆☆ 1980 PETITE SIRAH ($10.00) Napa Valley. *Leathery, intense, clean and well made.*

☆☆ 1982 PETITE SIRAH ($10.00) Napa Valley.

P and M Staiger
SANTA CRUZ COUNTY

1300 Hopkins Gulch Road, Boulder Creek, California 95006 (408-338-4346). FOUNDED: 1973. ACREAGE: 5 acres. PRODUCTION: 450 cases. DISTRIBUTION: California. OWNERS: Paul and Marjorie Staiger. WINEMAKERS: Paul and Marjorie Staiger. No tours or tasting.

San Jose State University art professor Paul Staiger and his wife, Marjorie, had been making wine at home when they found and leased a small unused vineyard owned by the Novitiate winery. The Staigers farmed it in their spare time until 1973. They then bought property of their own, planted new vines, and harvested their first crop in 1979. They have kept their production small in order to manage all vineyard and winery work themselves.

WHITE

☆☆ 1982 CHARDONNAY ($10.00) Santa Cruz Mountains. *Crisp and fruity, with great acid; very nice.*

☆☆☆ 1982 CHARDONNAY ($10.00) Estate, Santa Cruz Mountains. *Lemony crisp, clean, rich, fruity, with lovely oak.*

STANFORD *see* Weibel Vineyards

Steltzner Vineyards
NAPA COUNTY

5998 Silverado Trail, Napa, California 94558 (707-944-8393). FOUNDED: 1983. ACREAGE: 115 acres. PRODUCTION: 12,000 cases. DISTRIBUTION: Nationwide. OWNER: Richard Steltzner. WINEMAKER: Douglas Fletcher. Tours by appointment.

Richard Steltzner had been growing his own grapes and managing other people's vineyards since 1965. Frustrated at seeing wineries come and go, and with being at the mercy of their financial vicissitudes, Richard felt that the only way he could get the full value for his grapes was to make his own wine. In 1977 he made his first wine at a Napa Valley winery; by 1983 he had converted an old building on his vineyard into a winery. Steltzner Vineyards continues to sell some of its grapes to other wineries.

RED

☆☆☆ 1977 CABERNET SAUVIGNON ($16.00) Estate, Stag's Leap District, Napa. *Deep, rich, stately, complex, superb. Drink 1987.*

☆☆☆ 1978 CABERNET SAUVIGNON ($14.00) Stag's Leap District, Napa. *Lovely ripe fruit flavors and ideal balance. Drink 1988.*

☆☆☆ 1979 CABERNET SAUVIGNON ($14.00) Stag's Leap District, Napa. *Bright, rich and lush, with lovely oak and fruit. Drink 1986.*

☆☆☆ 1980 CABERNET SAUVIGNON ($14.00) Estate, Napa Valley. *Dense, rich, angular, with a scent of violets. Drink 1989.*

☆☆☆ 1981 CABERNET SAUVIGNON ($14.00) Napa Valley. *Fruity, rich, fat and velvety, with great complexity. Drink 1990.*

Robert Stemmler Winery
SONOMA COUNTY

3805 Lambert Bridge Road, Healdsburg, California 95448 (707-433-6334). FOUNDED: 1977. ACREAGE: 4 acres. PRODUCTION: 8,000 cases. DISTRIBUTION: Major market states. OWN-

ERS: Robert Stemmler and Trumbull Kelly. WINEMAKER: Robert Stemmler. OTHER LABEL: Bel Canto. Tours by appointment. Tasting daily 10:30 A.M.–4:30 P.M.

Robert Stemmler's winery sits in the middle of a vineyard behind his modest one-story house. Bob, a soft-spoken German gentleman, worked for Charles Krug, Inglenook, and Simi wineries after coming to the United States in 1960. In 1977, with the help of his friend Trumbull Kelly, he established his own winery.

WHITE

☆ 1980 CHARDONNAY ($9.50) Sonoma.
O 1983 CHARDONNAY ($12.00) Sonoma. *Tanky, unpleasant.*
☆ 1981 SAUVIGNON BLANC ($7.50) Lake County. *Soft, mellow, varietal but a bit tired.*
☆ 1982 SAUVIGNON BLANC ($7.50) Sonoma County. *Heavy, oily, low on fruit.*

RED

      1978 BEL CANTO CABERNET SAUVIGNON ($6.00) Lake County. *Pale, vegetal, bitter.*
☆☆☆ 1978 CABERNET SAUVIGNON ($12.50) Sonoma. *Intense, clean and supple.*
☆☆☆ 1979 CABERNET SAUVIGNON ($12.50) Sonoma. *Soft and balanced, with lovely fruit. Complex. Drink now.*
☆   1982 CABERNET SAUVIGNON ($15.00) Sonoma. *Rich, decent, a bit short. Drink 1987.*
☆☆☆ 1982 PINOT NOIR ($15.00) Forchini, Dry Creek Valley. *Clean, soft, rich, fruity, very lovely.*
      1983 PINOT NOIR ($15.00) Sonoma.

STEPHENS *see* Girard Winery

Sterling Vineyards
NAPA COUNTY

1111 Dunaweal Lane, Calistoga, California 95415 (707-942-5151). FOUNDED: 1969. ACREAGE: 520 acres. PRODUCTION: 75,000 cases. DISTRIBUTION: Nationwide; 5 foreign markets. OWNER: Seagram Classics Wine Company. WINEMAKER: Theo Rosenbrand; William Dyer, assistant. Tours and tasting April–October: daily 10:30 A.M.–4:30 P.M. November–March: Wednesday–Sunday 10:30 A.M.–4:30 P.M. Gift shop. Newsletter.

In 1964 the principals of Sterling International, a San Francisco paper company, decided to bring their business talents to the Napa Valley. They acquired and planted a large block of upper valley land and then hired Martin Waterfield to design a winery. The bleached-white modern structure is perched on a hill surrounded by vineyard and is accessed by an aerial tramway. Ric Forman was the winemaker from the opening in 1973 until 1978, just after Sterling was sold to Coca-Cola. (He then joined Sterling founder Peter Newton in his new winery [see Newton Winery].) Sterling is now owned by Seagram, who brought in Tom Ferrell, former president of Franciscan Vineyards and winemaker at Inglenook Vineyards, to run this highly regarded winery.

WHITE

☆☆ 1981 CHARDONNAY ($14.00) Estate, Napa Valley. *Crisp, clean, pleasant but a trifle thin.*

☆☆☆ 1982 CHARDONNAY ($14.00) Estate, Napa Valley. *Crisp, fruity, elegant, balanced, clean.*

☆☆☆ 1982 SAUVIGNON BLANC ($10.00) Estate, Napa Valley. *Rounded and fruity, clean and fresh. Sancerre style.*

☆☆ 1983 SAUVIGNON BLANC ($10.00) Napa Valley. *Tight, a bit thin, lacking intensity.*

BLANC DE NOIR

☆☆☆ 1982 CABERNET BLANC ($6.50) Napa Valley. *Crisp, clean, dry and varietally recognizable.*

☆☆☆ 1983 CABERNET BLANC ($6.50) Napa Valley. *0.9% residual sugar. Crisp, snappy, varietal; great with food.*

☆☆☆ 1984 CABERNET BLANC ($6.00) Napa Valley. *Fresh, varietal, tangy, delicious.*

RED

☆☆ 1973 CABERNET SAUVIGNON ($10.00) Reserve, Estate, Napa Valley. *Crisp, herbaceous and fruity, with a tarry finish. Drink now.*

☆☆☆ 1974 CABERNET SAUVIGNON ($20.00) Reserve, Estate, Napa Valley. *Lively, velvety, soft and supple. Balanced and complex. Drink now.*

☆☆ 1975 CABERNET SAUVIGNON ($20.00) Reserve, Estate, Napa Valley. *Firm and well structured; good fruit but lacks finesse.*

☆☆ 1976 CABERNET SAUVIGNON ($20.00) Reserve, Estate, Napa Valley. *Tart, edgy, herbal, with angular structure.*

☆☆☆ 1977 CABERNET SAUVIGNON ($27.50) Reserve, Estate, Napa Valley. *Lush but hard-edged; complex and spicy. Lovely.*

☆☆ 1978 CABERNET SAUVIGNON ($12.00) Estate, Napa Valley. *Tangy, fruity, rich and herbaceous. Drink 1986 and beyond.*

☆☆☆ 1978 CABERNET SAUVIGNON ($20.00) Reserve, Estate, Napa Valley. *Meaty, tannic, great fruit. Will age for ten years or more. Drink 1988.*

☆ 1979 CABERNET SAUVIGNON ($10.50) Estate, Napa Valley.

☆☆☆ 1979 CABERNET SAUVIGNON ($27.50) Reserve, Estate, Napa Valley. *Spicy, peppery, berried, tart, lush, superb. Drink 1986.*

☆☆ 1980 CABERNET SAUVIGNON ($12.50) Estate, Napa Valley. *Classy, firm, ripe, smooth, some weediness.*

☆☆☆ 1980 CABERNET SAUVIGNON ($30.00) Reserve, Estate, Napa Valley. *23.9% Merlot. Soft, rich, oaky and deep. Drink 1987.*

☆ 1976 MERLOT Napa Valley. *Fruity but a bit thin now.*

☆☆☆☆ 1979 MERLOT ($12.00) Estate, Napa Valley. *Rich, clean, supple, complex, lovely. Will age well.*

☆☆☆ 1980 MERLOT ($11.00) Napa Valley. *Lovely balance; nice fruit and oak. Drink now.*

☆☆☆ 1981 MERLOT ($11.00) Napa Valley. *Elegant, lush, complex and firmly structured.*

☆☆☆ 1982 MERLOT ($11.00) Estate, Napa Valley. *Lush, rich, structured. Drink 1986.*

☆☆☆ 1982 MERLOT ($11.00) Napa Valley. *Rich, tangy, varietal and fresh. Drink 1987.*

Steuk Wine Company
OHIO

1001 Fremont Avenue, Sandusky, Ohio 44870 (419-625-0803). FOUNDED: 1855. ACREAGE: 4.5 acres. PRODUCTION: 2,900 cases. DISTRIBUTION: Ohio. OWNER: William C. Steuk. WINEMAKER: Tim Parker. Tours and tasting May–October: Saturday afternoons.

The German-American Steuk family has been growing grapes since 1855 and owns a great deal of vineyard property as well as a historic downtown winery. During Prohibition, the Steuks turned their agricultural endeavors to fruit trees, but after Repeal they reopened the winery in an 1895 barn on one of their vineyards. The old downtown winery was kept as a warehouse. Besides making wine, the fifth-generation Steuks have a retail store where they do a big business in produce and other food items.

Stevenot Vineyards
CALAVERAS COUNTY

2690 San Domingo Road, Murphys, California 95247 (209-728-3436). FOUNDED: 1974. ACREAGE: 27 acres. PRODUCTION: 50,000 cases. DISTRIBUTION: Nationwide. OWNER: Barden Stevenot. WINEMAKER: Steve Millier. Tours and tasting daily 10 A.M.–5 P.M.

Barden Stevenot is a fifth-generation Californian who bought and planted his vineyards in the Sierra foothills in 1974. The winery is in the center of the Mother Lode region, where the 1849 gold rush took place. Barden makes estate wines and purchases grapes from the Sierra foothills and other parts of California.

WHITE

☆☆ 1981 CHARDONNAY ($8.00) Mendocino.
☆☆☆ 1981 CHARDONNAY ($8.50) Sonoma. *Clean, crisp and oaky, with nice, soft edges.*
☆ 1982 CHARDONNAY ($6.00) California. *Vinous, dull fruit, decent.*
☆☆ 1982 CHARDONNAY ($8.50) Brutocao, Mendocino. *Fresh, crisp, clean, with lots of lovely fruit.*
☆☆ 1983 CHARDONNAY ($6.00) California. *Fresh, simple, clean. The grapes are from Lodi.*
☆☆☆ 1983 CHARDONNAY ($11.00) Estate, Calaveras. *Its first "estate" Chardonnay. Delicate, soft, with nice oak.*
☆☆ 1981 CHENIN BLANC ($5.00) El Dorado. *Dry and varietal.*
☆☆☆ 1982 CHENIN BLANC ($5.00) El Dorado. *Crisp, fruity, clean, very appealing.*
☆☆☆ 1984 MUSCAT CANELLI ($7.00) San Luis Obispo. *Lush, spicy, clean, off-dry; charming.*
1981 SAUVIGNON BLANC ($6.95) Northern California.

BLANC DE NOIR

☆☆ 1983 ZINFANDEL ($5.00) Calaveras. *Soft, fruity and a bit sweet.*
☆ 1984 ZINFANDEL BLANC ($4.75) Amador. *2% residual sugar. Sweet, dull, varietal.*

RED

☆☆ 1980 CABERNET SAUVIGNON ($8.00) Calaveras. *Lush, smooth, herbal and complex. Drink 1986.*
1981 CABERNET SAUVIGNON ($8.00) Calaveras. *5% Merlot. Berried, heavy and overdone.*
☆☆ 1982 CABERNET SAUVIGNON ($10.00) Calaveras. *Chocolatey, thick, clean.*
☆ 1980 ZINFANDEL ($5.50) 6 Year Old Vineyards, Calaveras.
☆ 1980 ZINFANDEL ($6.25) Calaveras.
☆ 1981 ZINFANDEL ($6.00) Estate, Calaveras.

Stewart Vineyards
WASHINGTON

Route 3, Box 3578, Sunnyside, Washington 98944 (509-854-1882). FOUNDED: 1983. ACREAGE: 45 acres. PRODUCTION: 8,000 cases. DISTRIBUTION: Washington and Montana. OWNER: George Stewart. WINEMAKER: Mike Januik. Tours by appointment.

A surgeon in Sunnyside, George Stewart owns one of the oldest vineyards of Cabernet Sauvignon in the state of Washington. When the grapes became harder and harder to sell, George flew down to U.C. Davis and hired a winemaker, Mike Januik. Fresh out of school, Mike started making wine for the doctor in the red-metal winery on the vineyard property.

WHITE

☆☆ 1983 MUSCAT ($5.00) Estate, Columbia Valley. *1.5% residual sugar. Clean, varietal, balanced.*

☆ 1983 WHITE RIESLING ($6.00) Estate, Columbia Valley. *Fruity, overripe.*

ટ&

Stillwater Winery
OHIO

2311 West State Route 55, Troy, Ohio 45373 (513-339-8346). FOUNDED: 1981. ACREAGE: 26 acres. PRODUCTION: 11,000 cases. DISTRIBUTION: Local. OWNERS: Allan Jones and James Pour. WINEMAKER: James Pour. Tours by appointment on Friday and Saturday evenings. Tasting Tuesday–Friday, 4:30 P.M.–11 P.M., Saturday 1 P.M.–11 P.M.

James Pour and Allan Jones were grower partners who sold grapes to several wineries. After seven years, they discovered that the grape growing business was a slow but sure way to go broke. After deciding to go a step further and become wine producers in 1981, they learned, after two years, that making wine is different—it's a very quick way to go broke. "But we expected that," says Allan. The winery, built partially underground, is located in a curved mound of earth with a glass front.

ટ&

Stone Hill Winery
MISSOURI

Route 1, P.O. Box 26, Hermann, Missouri 65041 (314-486-2221). FOUNDED: 1847. ACREAGE: 60 acres. PRODUCTION: 32,000 cases. DISTRIBUTION: Missouri and Illinois. OWNERS: L. J. and Betty Ann Held. WINEMAKER: David Johnson. Tours and tasting Monday–Saturday 8:30 A.M.–5 P.M., Sunday 12–6 P.M. Restaurant. Gift shop. A national historical site.

During Prohibition, this winery's large, complex maze of underground vaulted cellars were used to propagate mushrooms. In 1965 the facility, which at one time was one of the country's largest, was purchased by the Held family, who got the winery going again with some old and rudimentary winery machinery. Since then, the Helds have completely modernized the equipment and restored the winery building, which is now a national historic site. The winemaking emphasis, according to founder James Held, is on making dry European-style wines that reflect the family's German heritage.

WHITE

☆ 1982 WEINFRAU ($4.00) Missouri. *Clean, well made white table wine; decent.*

RED

☆ 1979 NORTON PRIVATE RESERVE ($14.00) Missouri. *Tannic, with depth and rich color. Drink 1986.*

ટ&

Stone Mill Winery
WISCONSIN

North 70, West 6340 Bridge Road, Cedarburg, Wisconsin 53012 (414-377-8020). FOUNDED: 1971. ACREAGE: None. PRODUCTION: 4,200 cases. DISTRIBUTION: Wisconsin and Illinois. OWNER: James B. Pape. WINEMAKER: James B. Pape. Tours and tasting Monday–Saturday 10 A.M.–5 P.M., Sunday 12–5 P.M.

For James Pape, making wine was a respite from the boredom of his bookkeeping job at Woolworth's. This afterwork hobby became a profession when James bought an old wool mill in 1969 and transformed the three-and-a-half story building into a complex of small shops. The shopping mill was an immediate success, and it is now the third largest tourist attraction in Wisconsin. Jim is making Wisconsin fruit wines and grape wines from California, New York, and Pennsylvania juice.

ેલ

Stonecrop Vineyards
CONNECTICUT

Box 151A, R.D. 2, Stonington, Connecticut 06378 (203-535-2497). FOUNDED: 1979. ACREAGE: 7 acres. PRODUCTION: 400 cases. DISTRIBUTION: Local. OWNER: Thomas Young. WINE-MAKER: Thomas Young. Tours and tasting May–October: Tuesday, Thursday, and Saturday 9 A.M.–5 P.M. October–December by appointment.

A biochemical engineer, Tom Young was particularly interested in the development of micro-organisms in fermentation. His research peaked his interest in the winemaking process and stim-ulated his curiosity about farming. Consequently, Tom planted vineyards and uses a small barn-garage as a winery.

ેલ

Stonegate Winery
NAPA COUNTY

1183 Dunaweal Lane, Calistoga, California 95415 (707-942-6500). FOUNDED: 1973. ACREAGE: 30 acres. PRODUCTION: 15,000 cases. DISTRIBUTION: Nationwide. OWNERS: Barbara G. and James C. Spaulding, David B. Spaulding, general manager; Kathleen Spaulding, marketing. WINEMAKER: David Spaulding; Al Perry, assistant. Tours, tasting, and sales daily 10 A.M.–4 P.M.

Reporter Jim Spaulding went West from Milwaukee in 1969 to teach at the journalism school of the University of California at Berkeley. The Spauldings bought a hillside property west of Calistoga in the Mayacamas Range and planted a vineyard. The winery, situated on the flat below Sterling Vineyards, was built in 1973. Lanky David Spaulding, Jim and Barbara's son, is the winemaker and a very outgoing spokesman.

WHITE

☆☆ 1980 CHARDONNAY ($11.00) Napa Valley. *Clean and fruity but lacking depth.*
☆☆☆ 1981 CHARDONNAY ($9.00) 85% Keith Ranch, Alexander Valley, Sonoma. *Crisp and clean.*
☆☆☆ 1981 CHARDONNAY ($10.25) Sonoma. *Superb—soft, classic, complex, elegant.*
☆ 1982 CHARDONNAY ($9.00) Alexander Valley. *Oily, thick, butterscotch, slightly sweet.*

☆☆ 1982 CHARDONNAY ($10.00) Napa Valley. *Decent fruit; simple, clean and lean—an attractive food wine.*
 ☆ 1982 SAUVIGNON BLANC ($9.50) Napa Valley. *Snappy, fruity but lacking freshness.*
     1983 SAUVIGNON BLANC ($8.00) Napa Valley. *Dull, no fruit, unattractive; nail polish.*

RED

☆☆ 1978 CABERNET SAUVIGNON ($8.50) Vail Vista, Alexander Valley. *Berried, intense, oaky; not appealing.*
☆☆☆ 1978 CABERNET SAUVIGNON ($12.00) Steiner, Sonoma. *Rich fruit and lovely balance. Drink 1986 and beyond.*
☆☆☆ 1979 CABERNET SAUVIGNON ($12.00) Napa Valley. *Full, ripe, good varietal character. Drink now.*
☆☆☆ 1979 CABERNET SAUVIGNON ($12.00) Vail Vista, Alexander Valley. *Herbal, ripe, complex, forward, very attractive. Drink 1986.*
☆☆☆☆ 1980 CABERNET SAUVIGNON ($8.50) Vail Vista, Alexander Valley. *Eucalyptus and berries; complex and superb. Drink now or hold.*
☆☆ 1980 CABERNET SAUVIGNON ($12.00) Napa Valley. *Hard, structured, clean, attractive. Drink 1988.*
☆☆☆ 1982 CABERNET SAUVIGNON ($9.00) Napa Valley. *Clean and firm, with good fruit. Drink 1987.*
☆☆ 1975 MERLOT ($12.00) Spaulding, Napa Valley. *Bordeaux-like, soft and elegant; a bit short.*
☆☆☆ 1977 MERLOT ($12.00) Spaulding, Napa Valley. *Dense, well balanced and clean, with nice violet tones.*
☆☆☆ 1978 MERLOT ($9.00) Spaulding, Napa Valley. *Minty, clean, rich, intense. Lovely balance, aging potential.*
☆☆☆ 1979 MERLOT ($12.00) Spaulding, Napa Valley. *Rich, intense, classic, with lovely oak.*
☆☆☆ 1980 MERLOT ($12.00) Spaulding, Napa Valley. *Crisp and forward; clean and tannic. Needs some age. Drink 1986.*
☆☆☆ 1982 MERLOT ($12.00) Spaulding, Napa Valley. *Lush, clean, balanced. Drink 1986.*

Stoneridge
AMADOR COUNTY

Route 1, Box 36-B, Ridge Road East, Sutter Creek, California 95685 (209-223-1761). FOUNDED: 1975. ACREAGE: 4 acres. PRODUCTION: 1,500 cases. DISTRIBUTION: California. OWNERS: Gary and Loretta Porteous. Gary Porteous, general manager. WINEMAKER: Gary Porteous. Tours by appointment. Tasting Saturday 12–4 P.M., and sometimes on Sunday.

Gary and Loretta Porteous's love of grape growing got them into the world of winemaking. They have two vineyard parcels, one planted to Ruby Cabernet and the other to Zinfandel vines, some of which are 60 years old. The Porteous's basement is used for aging, while fermentation takes place in a separate building. Gary works full time as a lineman for Pacific Gas & Electric, but Loretta devotes her days to the winery. They plan to keep their production small—at a level where it is still fun and can be managed by just the two of them.

RED

 ☆ 1980 ZINFANDEL ($4.75) Amador.
 O 1981 ZINFANDEL ($6.50) Twin Rivers, El Dorado. *Dirty, tanky, unpleasant.*

Stony Hill Vineyards
NAPA COUNTY

P.O. Box 308, St. Helena, California 94574 (707-963-2636). FOUNDED: 1952. ACREAGE: 45 acres. PRODUCTION: 4,000 cases. DISTRIBUTION: California, New York, and by mailing list. OWNER: Eleanor Wheeler McCrea, president. WINEMAKER: Michael A. Chelini. Tours by appointment. No tasting or retail sales.

This historic winery was started by ad man Fred McCrea in 1951, after his steep goat farm was terraced and planted in vines, mainly Chardonnay. Fred obtained his vine cuttings from Herman Wente. The McCreas had acquired the property in 1943 as a weekend retreat, and Fred became intrigued with the idea of making wine. After cautious experiments, he released his first commercial wines, which were widely praised. They became a standard in the early days of the postwar California wine boom. Fred died in 1977 but his widow, Eleanor, has carried on. The wines are sold mainly to a mailing list of longtime customers.

WHITE

☆☆   1980 CHARDONNAY ($12.00) Estate, Napa Valley. *Pleasant, balanced. Should improve with age.*
☆☆☆ 1981 CHARDONNAY ($12.00) Estate, Napa Valley. *Rich and vinous; balanced and elegant. Good aging potential.*
☆☆   1982 CHARDONNAY ($12.00) Estate, Napa Valley. *Pleasant but withdrawn. Balanced, clean. Drink 1987.*
☆☆   1981 JOHANNISBERG RIESLING ($7.50) Estate, Napa Valley.

Stony Ridge Winery
ALAMEDA COUNTY

444 Vineyard Avenue, Pleasanton, California 94566 (415-846-2133; Sales: 415-829-WINE). FOUNDED: 1975. ACREAGE: 300 acres. PRODUCTION: 125,000 cases. DISTRIBUTION: Nationwide. OWNER: Hank Schneider. WINEMAKER: Sam Balderas; Bob Atkinson, co-winemaker. No tours. Tasting daily 11 A.M.–5 P.M. at 200 Ray Street, Pleasanton (415-846-5356).

The Ruby Hill Winery, an old, three-story brick building, had been left desolate and abandoned by the Southern Pacific Land Company. In the early 1970s a group of ambitious wine lovers leased the estate, renamed it, and brought the century-old winery and the vineyards back into operation. In 1975 they bonded the winery and crushed their first vintage. Stony Ridge's president, Hank Schneider, and his associates worked for several years to restore the winery and the vineyards, while striving to bring attention to the winery's historical significance. From the beginning they had to continually fight urban planners, who wanted the land for commercial building sites. They won the first battle but lost the last one to a computer company that purchased their land from Southern Pacific Land Company. The winery vacated the property in 1983, moving to Hagemann Vineyard, which they lease. Recent financial setbacks have made the winery's future uncertain.

WHITE

1981 CHEVRIER ($8.00) Estate, Livermore Valley. *Mostly Semillon. Weedy, gluey.*
1982 CRESCENT GOLD ($4.00) Livermore Valley. *1.5% residual sugar. Sweet, sappy, dull, unattractive.*
1981 CHARDONNAY ($6.00) Santa Maria Valley. *Weedy, oily, heavy.*
○   1981 CHARDONNAY ($8.50) La Reina, Monterey. *Vinous, oxidized, overoaked, bitter.*
1982 CHARDONNAY ($5.50) Santa Maria Valley. *Lacking fruit and varietal character.*
☆   1983 CHARDONNAY ($6.50) Santa Maria Valley.
1982 CHENIN BLANC ($5.50) Santa Maria Valley. *0.65% residual sugar. Off flavors, dull, unattractive, soft, woody.*

NV   JOHANNISBERG RIESLING ($4.00) Pleasanton Series, California.
O   1981 SAUVIGNON BLANC ($4.00) Pleasanton Collection, Santa Barbara. *Oxidized.*
1981 SAUVIGNON BLANC ($4.00) San Luis Obispo.
O   1983 SAUVIGNON BLANC ($7.75) Estate, Livermore Valley. *Unattractive and dull, with a geranium aroma.*

SPARKLING

☆ NV   BLANC DE NOIR ($6.00) California. *1.5% residual sugar. Crisp, vinous, acceptable.*
☆☆ NV   BLANC DE NOIR ($6.25) Cuvée 1, California. *Snappy, fresh, balanced, attractive.*
☆☆ NV   MALVASIA BIANCA ($6.00) California. *4% residual sugar. Snappy and spicy; balanced and delicious.*

BLANC DE NOIR

☆ 1983 WHITE ZINFANDEL ($4.50) California. *Decent, fruity, clean, off-dry.*

RED

☆☆☆ 1975 CABERNET SAUVIGNON ($4.00) North Coast.
1978 CABERNET SAUVIGNON ($6.50) North Coast. *Vegetal, dull.*
☆☆ 1979 CABERNET SAUVIGNON ($12.50) Limited Bottling, Smith & Hook, Monterey. *Jammy, intense, lacking structure.*
O   1980 CABERNET SAUVIGNON ($4.00) Santa Barbara.
O   1981 CABERNET SAUVIGNON ($14.00) Smith & Hook, Monterey. *Vegetal and very unattractive.*
NV   CARIGNANE ($4.50) California. *Heavy, concentrated, off-dry, dull.*
1980 MERLOT ($4.00) Santa Barbara.
O   1980 PETITE SIRAH ($4.00) San Luis Obispo. *Extremely vegetal; quite unattractive.*
☆ NV   PINOT NOIR ($4.00) Pleasanton Collection, California.
☆ 1979 PINOT NOIR ($9.00) Limited Bottling, Vinco, Monterey.
1979 ZINFANDEL ($5.00) Ruby Hill, Livermore Valley.
1980 ZINFANDEL ($4.00) San Luis Obispo.
☆ 1980 ZINFANDEL ($5.00) Estate, Ruby Hill, Livermore Valley. *Big berry nose, crisp and pleasant.*

Story Vineyards
AMADOR COUNTY

10525 Bell Road, Plymouth, California 95669 (209-245-6208). FOUNDED: 1973. ACREAGE: 35 acres. PRODUCTION: 25,000 cases. DISTRIBUTION: Nationwide. OWNERS: Ann C. Story and Kevin Shannon. WINEMAKER: Dave Akin. Tours by appointment.

Dr. Jean Story and his wife, Ann, started their winery with fourteen acres of Zinfandel and nine acres of old Mission vines dating back to the 1930s and 1940s. When her husband died in 1981, Ann, unsure whether she wanted to run the winery by herself, leased the property to Kevin Shannon and his wine brokerage firm, Vinformation, which is located in San Francisco. The winery's production has increased slightly since the Vinformation involvement; estate-grown Zinfandel is Story Vineyards' mainstay.

BLANC DE NOIR

☆ 1984 WHITE ZINFANDEL ($4.00) Amador. *20% Mission. Soft, decent.*

RED

☆☆☆ NV   ZINFANDEL ($4.50) California.
1979 ZINFANDEL ($5.50) Shenandoah Valley, Amador. *Overbearing, raisiny, overwrought.*
☆☆ 1980 ZINFANDEL ($6.00) Estate, Amador. *Brambly and intense.*

Storybook Mountain Vineyards
NAPA COUNTY

3835 Highway 128, Calistoga, California 95415 (707-942-5310). FOUNDED: 1979. ACREAGE: 36 acres. PRODUCTION: 5,000–7,000 cases. DISTRIBUTION: Nationwide. OWNER: Storybook Mountain Vintners. Dr. Jerry B. Seps and Walter Schug. WINEMAKER: Dr. Jerry B. Seps. Tours, tasting, and sales by appointment.

Jerry Seps walked away from his fifteen-year career as a university history professor for his own little piece of history: the old Grimms Brothers Winery, established in 1880. Originally, Jerry just wanted to grow grapes; the winery was an afterthought. After sifting through historical documents and consulting viticultural experts, he decided that the variety best suited to this location was Zinfandel. He began working on the old winery, most of which had been destroyed by fire, and restored the three wine caves, filling them with barrels and ovals. Storage and winery facilities are shared with Schug Cellars (see).

RED

☆☆☆   1980 ZINFANDEL ($7.75) Sonoma. *Rich nose; crisp, high-acid wine. Atypical but nice.*
☆☆☆   1981 ZINFANDEL ($7.75) Napa Valley. *Big but balanced and very attractive. Drink 1986.*
☆☆☆   1981 ZINFANDEL ($9.50) Estate Reserve, Napa Valley. *Rich, intense, fruity and lovely. Extremely Bordeaux-like.*

Stratford
NAPA COUNTY

1472 Railroad Avenue, St. Helena, California 94574 (707-963-3200). FOUNDED: 1982. ACREAGE: None. PRODUCTION: 45,000 cases. DISTRIBUTION: Nationwide. OWNERS: Tony Cartlidge, James Forsyth, David Lawson, and Paul Moser. WINEMAKER: Paul Moser. No tours or tasting.

Stratford, founded by four enterprising Britons, is yet another wine venture for Tony Cartlidge of Cartlidge and Browne (see). The project started when Tony, a broker, negociant, and wine importer, was approached by venture capitalist David Lawson. David, Tony, James Forsyth and winemaker Paul Moser formed a partnership with the goal of making and aggressively marketing quality wines that could sell nationally for under ten dollars a bottle. In 1982 they bought and blended a Chardonnay that established their reputation for affordable quality. "Our dream was to have the wine recognized by the wine community and heralded by the press," says Tony, "and it was." Wines are still bought for blending, although grapes are now custom-crushed at Rombauer Vineyards for all Stratford white wines. The partners plan to build their own winery by 1987.

RODNEY STRONG *see* Sonoma Vineyards

Sullivan Vineyards Winery
NAPA COUNTY

1090 Galleron Road, Rutherford, California 94573 (707-963-9646). FOUNDED: 1972. DISTRIBUTION: Arizona, Idaho, Montana, Oregon, and Washington. OWNERS: James and JoAnn Sullivan. WINEMAKER: James Sullivan. Tours by appointment.

James and JoAnn Sullivan had a beautiful arbor in their Marysville backyard. "You ought to plant grapevines around that arbor!" said Uncle Charlie. Jim ignored the suggestion until he received cuttings from U.C. Davis in the mail, complete with instructions, compliments of Uncle Charlie. "Once you start reading and learning about grape growing and winemaking, it goes on forever," says Jim. In 1972 he bought and planted four acres of Cabernet Sauvignon in the Rutherford area of the Napa Valley. In 1978 he purchased a larger parcel, built a winery, and made a home for his family.

WHITE

1981 CHENIN BLANC ($7.50) *Oxidized and woody.*
☆ 1982 CHENIN BLANC ($9.00) Dry, Napa Valley. *Pineapple and oak—an interesting wine.*

RED

☆☆☆ 1981 CABERNET SAUVIGNON ($14.00) Napa Valley. *Big, meaty and intense, with good complexity. Should age well. Drink 1987.*

Summerhill Vineyards
SANTA CLARA COUNTY

3920 Hecker Pass Highway, Gilroy, California 95020 (408-842-3032). FOUNDED: 1980. ACREAGE: 6 acres. PRODUCTION: 25,000 cases. DISTRIBUTION: 9 states. OWNER: Hilton T. Johnson, CEO; Gary Hada, vice president; Debra A. Dodd, secretary-treasurer. WINEMAKER: Gary Hada. OTHER LABEL: Thigpen Reserve. No tours. Tasting summer: daily 10 A.M.–6 P.M.; winter: daily 10 A.M.–5 P.M.

When Hilton "Red" Johnson and a group of investors took over the old Bertero winery in 1980, all romantic ideas about winemaking were thrown out the cellar door. Red turned the winemaking over to Gary Hada while he formulated a businesslike and thorough marketing plan.

WHITE

O NV RIESLING ($2.70) California. *Horrible.*

RED

O NV ZINFANDEL ($4.00) California.

SUMMIT *see* Geyser Peak Winery

Summum
UTAH

707 Genesee Avenue, Salt Lake City, Utah 84104 (801-355-0137). FOUNDED: 1980. ACREAGE: 5 acres. PRODUCTION: 5,000 cases. DISTRIBUTION: Nationwide. OWNER: Summum. Claude R. Nowell, president. WINEMAKERS: Michael Burdelt and Claude R. Nowell. Tours and tasting Monday and Wednesday 9 A.M.–5 P.M., Saturday 9 A.M.–12 noon.

The only producer of alcohol in the state of Utah is housed in a pyramid, where a philosophical group, the Summum, makes wine for meditative purposes. The idea for the pyramid came from Summum Bonum Amon Ra, who believes that a pyramid creates an environmental space that has a special effect on the wine, making it an excellent aid to one's meditative process. It is suggested that a small amount of the wine be consumed prior to meditation—any kind of meditation. This philosophy, according to Summum, is very ancient, having been written in the Egyptian Book of the Dead. The Summum got past Utah's strict laws because a statute dating back to the 1800s, before Utah was a state, permits wine to be made for sacramental purposes.

ROSE

NV ROSE TABLE WINE Utah. *Odd, lacking depth. Not sold; the church accepts donations.*

Sunrise Winery
SANTA CRUZ COUNTY

13100 Monte Bello Road, Cupertino, California 95014 (408-741-1310). FOUNDED: 1976. ACREAGE: 3 acres. PRODUCTION: 2,500 cases. DISTRIBUTION: 6 states. OWNERS: Ronald and Rolayne Stortz. WINEMAKER: Lanny Replogle. Tours by appointment on weekends.

Sunrise Winery was started by Keith Hohlfeldt, a microbiologist, and Eugene Lokey. In 1977 a new partnership was formed between Keith and accountant Ronald Stortz, and a year later they took on three more partners. At the time, the winery occupied the old Locatelli facility. In 1978 it suffered a substantial equipment and inventory loss in a fire that destroyed the winery's upper story. Sunrise has since moved to a historic ranch above the city of Cupertino. In 1983 Keith Hohlfeldt left to become the winemaker at David Bruce Winery. The Stortzes hope that their winery will eventually reach its 17,000-case capacity.

WHITE

☆☆☆ 1980 CHARDONNAY ($10.00) Sonoma. *Toasty, crisp, clean, delicate.*
　　　1981 CHARDONNAY ($10.00) *No varietal character.*
　☆　1982 CHARDONNAY ($10.00) North Coast. *Some off flavors but good acidity; decent.*
　☆　1983 SAUVIGNON BLANC ($6.50) San Luis Obispo. *Peas and fruit. Quite vegetal.*

RED

　O　1979 PINOT NOIR ($7.50) Edna Valley, San Luis Obispo. *Very vegetal and unattractive.*
☆☆☆ 1980 PINOT NOIR ($8.00) Glen Ellen, Sonoma. *Peppery, rich, rounded, superb.*
　☆　1980 PINOT NOIR ($8.00) Iron Horse, Sonoma. *Earthy, rich and overdone.*

Susine Cellars
SOLANO COUNTY

301 Spring Street, Suisun City, California 94585 (707-425-0833). FOUNDED: 1981. ACREAGE: None. PRODUCTION: 1,000 cases. DISTRIBUTION: Local and Southern California outlets. OWNER: Edward "Chuck" O'Brien, Jr. WINEMAKER: Edward "Chuck" O'Brien, Jr. Tours by appointment. Tasting Friday 4 P.M.–6 P.M., Saturday 10 A.M.–3 P.M. Wine- and beermaking supplies for sale. Gift shop.

Encouraged by his home-winemaking success in New York, Chuck O'Brien moved to California to study at U.C. Davis. After completing his courses, he started his own small winery, intending to make reasonably priced wines from grapes grown in various regions. To support his winery, Chuck sells winemaking and brewing supplies. Additional support is recruited via a mailing list called *The Friends of Susine Cellars*. For a small membership fee one receives a membership card, a ten percent discount on wine or winemaking supplies, and advance notice of special sales.

WHITE

☆☆☆ 1982 JOHANNISBERG RIESLING ($10.00) Special Select Late Harvest, El Dorado. *375ml. Viscous, rich, toasty, caramel, lovely.*

RED

○ 1981 CABERNET SAUVIGNON ($5.00) Suisun Valley. *A disaster—dirty, stinky; a mess.*
☆☆☆ 1980 ZINFANDEL ($5.00) Amador. *Lush, clean and fruity.*

Sutter Home Winery
NAPA COUNTY

277 St. Helena Highway South, St. Helena, California 94574 (707-963-3104). FOUNDED: 1874. ACREAGE: 950 acres. PRODUCTION: 600,000 cases. DISTRIBUTION: Nationwide; Canada, Belgium, and England. OWNER: Partnership. The Trinchero family. Louis "Bob" and Roger Trinchero. WINEMAKER: Steve Bertolucci. No tours. Tasting daily 10 A.M.–4:30 P.M.

When the Trincheros closed their resort hotel in upstate New York, the members of the family went their separate ways. John, who went to California, bought the old Sutter Home Winery in 1946 and convinced his brother Mario to join him. The second generation of brothers took over in 1960, when John retired and Mario's son Louis "Bob" Trinchero became the winemaker. Bob's brother Roger began working with him in 1972. Until 1970 the winery sold bottled wine and wine in bulk to anyone who came to the winery. Its motto was, "If you can carry it or roll it through the front door, we'll fill it with wine." After the release of its first Amador Zinfandel in 1968, the winery became known for that variety. In fact, Sutter Home was one of the first wineries to recognize the enormous potential of Amador County as a grape-growing region. The winery struck gold recently with its White Zinfandel, selling more than half a million cases a year of this semisweet pink wine.

WHITE

☆☆ 1982 MUSCAT AMABILE ($4.50) California. *7% residual sugar. Fruity, fresh, clean.*
☆☆ 1983 MUSCAT AMABILE ($4.75) California. *Clean, off-dry, fresh, spicy and delicious.*
☆☆ 1984 MUSCAT AMABILE ($4.50) California. *Fat, lush, sweet, varietal.*

BLANC DE NOIR

☆ 1983 WHITE ZINFANDEL ($4.00) Napa Valley. *Crisp, sweet, fruity; rather shallow.*
☆☆ 1984 WHITE ZINFANDEL ($4.50) California. *2% residual sugar. The nation's most popular White Zinfandel. Soft, clean, crisp, appealing.*

RED

☆☆ 1979 ZINFANDEL ($5.95) Deaver, Amador. *Rich, jammy, berried.*
☆ 1980 ZINFANDEL ($6.00) Deaver, Amador. *Dense and raisiny, with very little fruit; hot and powerful.*
☆☆ 1980 ZINFANDEL ($8.75) Reserve, Deaver, Amador. *Clean, complex, low fruit, nice.*
1981 ZINFANDEL ($5.95) Deaver, Amador. *Hard, bitter, lacking fruit.*
☆ 1981 ZINFANDEL ($8.75) Reserve, Deaver, Amador. *Rich, deep, raisiny, unattractive.*
☆ 1982 ZINFANDEL ($6.25) Amador. *Decent, dry, fruity, clean.*

Joseph Swan Vineyards
SONOMA COUNTY

2916 Laguna Road, Forestville, California 95436 (707-546-7711). FOUNDED: 1969. ACREAGE: 10.5 acres. PRODUCTION: 1,200 cases. DISTRIBUTION: At restaurants, other local outlets, and by mailing list. OWNERS: Joseph and June Swan. WINEMAKER: Joseph Swan. No tours or tasting.

Joseph Swan became fascinated with wine first by drinking it, then by reading about it, and then by making it at home for 21 years. Joe, who was a pilot for Western Airlines, knew exactly what he was going to do when he retired. While stationed in San Francisco, he and his wife bought a piece of old vineyard land near Forestville. Swan wines have such an avid following that they are almost all sold to a mailing list of longtime customers.

WHITE

☆☆ 1981 CHARDONNAY ($15.00) Sonoma. *Snappy, oaky and intense.*
O 1982 CHARDONNAY ($12.00) Northern Sonoma. *Harsh, off, unattractive.*

RED

☆☆☆ 1978 PINOT NOIR ($20.00) Sonoma. *Nice fruit, good oak, complex, needs time. Drink 1986.*
☆☆☆☆ 1980 ZINFANDEL ($9.00) Sonoma. *Lovely ripe fruit, crisp acidity and spicy, complex flavors.*

Swiss Valley Vineyards
INDIANA

101 Ferry Street, Vevay, Indiana 47043 (513-521-5096). FOUNDED: 1974. ACREAGE: None. PRODUCTION: 420 cases. DISTRIBUTION: Local. OWNER: Alvin Meyer. WINEMAKER: Alvin Meyer. Tours and tasting by appointment.

When Alvin Meyer established Swiss Valley Vineyards, he was also reviving Indiana's oldest viticultural site. In 1810 the first Labrusca vines had been planted by Jean Jacques Dufour on this property in Vevay, a town named after his home in Switzerland. It was here that Dufour wrote one of America's first books on winemaking and made wines that even Thomas Jefferson found enjoyable. The defunct winery was in the old ferryboat camp near the river. Originally, Alvin Meyer, a machinist by trade, had intended only to revive the vineyard, but in 1974, in the name of historical preservation, he restored and reopened the winery as well.

Sycamore Creek Vineyards
SANTA CLARA COUNTY

12775 Uvas Road, Morgan Hill, California 95037 (408-779-4738). FOUNDED: 1976. ACREAGE: 16 acres. PRODUCTION: 4,500 cases. DISTRIBUTION: Major market states. OWNERS: Terry and Mary Kaye Parks. WINEMAKERS: Terry and Mary Kaye Parks. Tours, tasting, and sales weekends 12–5 P.M. Weekdays by appointment.

Former schoolteachers Terry and Mary Kaye Parks took a small inheritance and bought the rundown, pre-Prohibition Marchetti winery in the Uvas Valley. Home winemakers who had had no previous professional winemaking experience, the Parks took a chance and did the extensive construction necessary to make the old winery functional, restoring the three houses on the property as well. They buy most of their grapes and sell a fairly sizable line of wines produced in small lots.

WHITE

☆☆ 1981 CHARDONNAY ($10.00) River Road, Monterey. *Vinous, crisp and clean, with good acid.*

O 1982 SUMMER CHARDONNAY ($7.50) Monterey. *Sweet, oxidized, awful.*

☆ 1982 CHARDONNAY ($12.00) Estate, California. *Vinous, heavy, rich but lacking depth.*

☆☆ 1982 CHARDONNAY ($12.00) La Reina, Monterey. *European in style; decent, acidic, varietal.*

☆☆ 1983 CHARDONNAY ($10.00) Sleepy Hollow, Monterey.

☆☆ 1983 CHARDONNAY ($15.00) Estate, California. *Rich, deep, clean, lacking fruit.*

O 1983 FUME BLANC ($7.50) Paso Robles. *Dull, lifeless.*

RED

O NV RED TABLE WINE ($4.00) California. *Tanky, very unattractive.*

1979 CABERNET SAUVIGNON ($7.00) San Luis Obispo. *Clumsy and dull.*

1980 CABERNET SAUVIGNON ($7.00) California. *Very vegetal; nicely built but unpleasant.*

☆☆ 1981 CABERNET SAUVIGNON ($18.00) Central Coast, California. *Big and intense, with good fruit. Overpriced. Drink 1986.*

☆☆ 1982 CABERNET SAUVIGNON ($9.00) Central Coast. *Rich, round and deep, with nice fruit. Drink 1986.*

1982 CARIGNANE ($6.50) Estate, Santa Clara. *Dark, rich, bitter, tannic, intense. May be drinkable in 1986.*

☆ 1981 PINOT NOIR ($7.50) Monterey. *Green, crisp, clean, decent.*

☆ 1980 ZINFANDEL ($9.00) Morgan Hill, California. *Big, late-harvest style. Intense, concentrated, overdone.*

☆☆ 1981 ZINFANDEL ($9.00) Morgan Hill, California. *A bit better than the '80—rich, spirited and attractive.*

☆☆☆ 1982 ZINFANDEL ($9.00) Estate, Morgan Hill, California. *Crisp, fruity, balanced, delicious. Drink now or hold one year.*

☆☆☆ 1983 ZINFANDEL ($10.00) Proprietor Grown, California. *Crisp, fruity, balanced, lovely.*

Tabor Hill Winery
MICHIGAN

Route 1, Box 720, Buchanan, Michigan 49107 (616-422-1161). FOUNDED: 1970. ACREAGE: 16 acres. PRODUCTION: 20,000 cases. DISTRIBUTION: 5 states. OWNER: Chi Company. David F. Upton, president; Robert L. Lemon II, winery manager. WINEMAKER: Richard Moersch. Tours and tasting Monday–Saturday 11 A.M.–5 P.M., Sunday 12–5 P.M. Restaurant.

The founders of Tabor Hill Vineyards, Leonard Olsen and Carl Bahnholzer, wanted to be sure that grapes would grow on their farm property near Lake Michigan. After studying climate reports and research done by Dr. Konstantin Frank, they began planting in 1968 and built a European-style chalet winery on their lakeview mountain slope. When Carl Bahnholzer left to start his own winery, Leonard Olsen bought out his interest. By 1976 Tabor Hill was bankrupt. The vineyard and winery were sold to David Upton, a businessman who brought in new machinery and storage facilities, a winemaker, and a refreshing tough-mindedness.

Taft Street Winery
SONOMA COUNTY

6450 1st Street, P.O. Box 878, Forestville, California 95436 (707-887-2801). FOUNDED: 1982. ACREAGE: None. PRODUCTION: 7,000 cases. DISTRIBUTION: California and by mailing list.

OWNER: Corporation. Michael Tierney, general manager. WINEMAKER: John Tierney. Tours by appointment.

In back of his brother's home, John Tierney was making his own wines while working as the winemaker for Berkeley Wine Cellars. In this house on Taft Street in Oakland, his two brothers and three family friends formed a partnership, drew up plans, and made projections for their own winery. From winemaking and winery equipment supply to administration and law, the partners have professional expertise in a variety of fields. The winery is now operating out of rented space in the American Wine Building in Forestville. Grapes are purchased from growing areas throughout the state.

WHITE

☆☆ NV WHITE HOUSE WINE ($4.50) California. *Round, rich, attractive.*
☆☆ 1982 CHARDONNAY ($11.00) 77% Tepusquet, Santa Barbara; 23% Iron Horse, California. *Toasty, crisp and nicely made.*
☆☆ 1983 CHARDONNAY ($11.00) 58% Tepusquet, 42% Sonoma-Cutrer, Santa Barbara-Sonoma.
☆☆ 1984 CHARDONNAY ($6.00) Early Cuvée, California. *Simple, fresh and clean.*

RED

☆☆ NV RED HOUSE WINE ($4.50) California. *Soft, clean, lovely, with some depth.*
☆☆☆ 1982 MEDALLION ($9.75) 61% Sonoma Valley, 39% Napa. *61% Merlot, 26% Cabernet, 13% Cabernet Franc. Lovely. Drink 1986.*
☆☆ 1980 MERLOT ($9.00) Fay, Napa Valley.
☆ 1982 PINOT NOIR ($7.50) Monterey.
1983 PINOT NOIR ($7.50) Monterey. *Vegetal, earthy, not attractive.*

Robert Talbott Vineyards
MONTEREY COUNTY

P.O. Box 267, Carmel Valley, California 93924 (408-659-5522). FOUNDED: 1983. ACREAGE: 47 acres. PRODUCTION: 3,000 cases. DISTRIBUTION: California and by mailing list. OWNERS: Robert F. and Robert S. Talbot. WINEMAKER: Ken Wright. Tours by appointment.

After four years as the winemaker for Ventana Vineyards, Ken Wright took off for the Carmel Valley, prospectus in hand, to find financial backers for his own winery. While researching Carmel Valley's grape-growing areas, he met the Talbotts, who own the Talbott Tie Company. Being true wine lovers, Robert F. Talbott and his son Rob decided to help launch Ken's winery project. Fortunately they happened to own two parcels in the Carmel Valley that were ideal for viticulture. One, called the Diamond T Vineyard, is in a very cool area near Carmel, and the other, Chalk Flats, is fifteen miles inland. Planting began in 1982; the winery, a cedar board-and-bat building, was built in 1983. Ken plans to make only barrel-fermented Chardonnay until 1986, when he will introduce Sauvignon Blanc-Semillon and Pinot Noir.

Tarula Farms
OHIO

1786 Creek Road, Clarksville, Ohio 45113 (513-289-2181). FOUNDED: 1964. ACREAGE: 4 acres. PRODUCTION: 1,250 cases. DISTRIBUTION: At winery. OWNER: Greg Hayward. WINEMAKER: Greg Hayward. Tours by appointment. Tasting June–August: Monday–Saturday 12–9 P.M.; winter: Saturday 12–9 P.M.

The Tarula farmhouse had been virtually destroyed through neglect. Tall, wild grass was growing everywhere, and the vineyards had not been touched for three years. In the dilapidated winery, the remaining wines were completely spoiled. Although faced with this disaster, along with complicated legal problems, the Haywards decided they could save this ravaged farm. After more than a year of intense work, they restored the vineyards, the nineteenth-century barn winery, and the house. Greg and his wife both work as schoolteachers to support their winery, which has yet to make a profit. But money is not the reason for all their hard work—it's their passionate commitment to the agricultural life.

Taylor California Cellars
MONTEREY COUNTY

800 South Alta Street, Gonzales, California 93926 (408-257-7800). FOUNDED: 1978. ACREAGE: None. PRODUCTION: 7 million cases. DISTRIBUTION: Nationwide; the Caribbean and Great Britain. OWNER: Seagram Wine Company. Dick Maher, president. WINEMAKER: Phil Franscioni. OTHER LABELS: Wine Spectrum, Great Western.

In 1977 Taylor Wine Company, a well-established New York producer of Labrusca and French-American hybrid wines, decided to make California "jug" generics from vinifera grapes. Needing a facility in California, Taylor made an agreement with its sister winery, The Monterey Vineyard. Both Taylor and The Monterey Vineyard are a part of the Wine Spectrum, which at that time was owned by Coca-Cola and is now owned by Seagram. The facility at Monterey Vineyard was capable of handling much greater volume than had ever been required of it until Taylor created a new brand called Taylor California Cellars. It became so successful that it quickly outgrew the Monterey Vineyard facility and required the construction of an enormous new winery next door.

WHITE

☆ NV CHARDONNAY ($3.50) California. *Acceptable.*
O NV CHENIN BLANC ($3.25) California. *Sweet, dull, oxidized.*
☆ NV FRENCH COLOMBARD ($3.25) California. *Off-dry, clean and acceptable, with a hint of oxidation.*
    NV JOHANNISBERG RIESLING ($1.75) California.
    NV SAUVIGNON BLANC ($4.25) California.

SPARKLING

NV BRUT ($5.90) California. *Charmat.*
NV EXTRA DRY ($6.00) California. *Dull, clumsy.*
NV PINK CHAMPAGNE ($6.00) California. *Syrupy, dull, simple.*

ROSE

☆ NV ROSE TABLE WINE ($4.00) California. *Clean, simple, off-dry, candy-like.*

RED

☆☆ NV BURGUNDY ($3.30) California. *Soft, big and fresh.*
      NV CABERNET SAUVIGNON ($3.60) California. *Vegetal and astringent.*
☆☆ NV ZINFANDEL ($4.30) California. *Nice balance, clean flavors.*

Taylor Wine Company
NEW YORK

County Route 88, Hammondsport, New York 14840 (607-569-2111). FOUNDED: 1880. ACREAGE: 1,570 acres. PRODUCTION: 15 million cases. DISTRIBUTION: Nationwide. OWNER: Seagram

Wine Company. Michael J. Doyle, president. WINEMAKER: Dr. Andrew Rice, vice president, production; Domenic Carisetti, senior winemaker. OTHER LABELS: Great Western Winery, Gold Seal Vineyards. Tours and tasting November–April: Monday–Saturday 11 A.M.–3 P.M.; May–October: daily 10 A.M.–4 P.M.

For a company once known as "the Coca-Cola of the wine business," Taylor Wine Company had very humble beginnings. In the late 1800s carpenter-cooper Walter Taylor made a modest amount of wine that gained some acceptance in New York City. His sons joined Walter and kept the business growing until 1977, when the Coca-Cola company bought it. By that time, Great Western Winery, once known as Pleasant Valley Winery, had already been acquired by Taylor Wine Company. Then, in 1983 when Seagram and Sons bought the winery from Coca-Cola, the wine production of Seagram-owned Gold Seal Vineyards (see) was moved to Taylor. With these several sister companies and their many different types of wine being produced in the same place, Taylor Wine Company employs six winemakers.

WHITE

☆☆ NV LAKE COUNTRY CHABLIS ($3.00) New York State. *Off-dry, Labrusca flavor, fresh, clean and attractive.*

☆☆ 1983 GREAT WESTERN GEWURZTRAMINER ($5.30) Laursen Farm, Finger Lakes. *Varietal, crisp, clean.*

1982 GREAT WESTERN JOHANNISBERG RIESLING ($5.50) Finger Lakes Region, New York.

☆ 1983 GREAT WESTERN JOHANNISBERG RIESLING ($5.30) Laursen Farm, New York. *Delicate, varietal, soapy.*

☆ 1983 GREAT WESTERN SEYVAL BLANC New York State. *Sweet, heavy.*

O 1982 GREAT WESTERN VIDAL BLANC ($5.30) Finger Lakes Region. *Sweet, maderized, awful.*

☆☆ 1982 GREAT WESTERN VIDAL BLANC ($5.50) Late Harvest, Laursen Farm, Finger Lakes Region. *0.95% residual sugar. Honied nose, earthy.*

SPARKLING

O NV BRUT ($7.36) New York State. *Transfer. Sweet.*

O NV GREAT WESTERN BRUT ($9.00) Pleasant Valley, New York State. *Transfer.*

O NV EXTRA DRY ($8.00) New York State. *Off flavors, oily and sweet.*

O NV GREAT WESTERN EXTRA DRY ($9.00) New York State. *Sweet and syrupy, unappealing.*

NV GREAT WESTERN NATUREL ($9.90) New York State. *Foxy but clean.*

O NV PINK CHAMPAGNE ($8.00) New York State. *Sweet, syrupy, awful.*

NV GREAT WESTERN PINK CHAMPAGNE ($9.00) New York State. *Very sweet.*

O NV SPARKLING BURGUNDY ($8.00) New York State.

O NV GREAT WESTERN SPARKLING BURGUNDY ($9.00) New York State.

ROSE

☆ 1982 GREAT WESTERN DE CHAUNAC ($5.50) Finger Lakes Region. *Snappy, fruity.*

RED

☆ NV GREAT WESTERN BURGUNDY ($3.00) New York State. *Ripe, berried, meaty; not very clean tasting.*

☆☆ 1982 GREAT WESTERN BACO NOIR ($4.20) Estate, Finger Lakes Region. *Snappy, fresh, clean and attractive.*

Tedeschi Vineyard and Winery
HAWAII

P.O. Box 953, Ulupalakua, Maui, Hawaii 96790 (808-878-6058). FOUNDED: 1977. ACREAGE: 20 acres. PRODUCTION: 16,000 cases. DISTRIBUTION: 4 states; Japan. OWNER: Emil Tedeschi,

president; C. Pardee Erdman, vice president. WINEMAKER: Bob Henn. Self-guided tours Monday–
Saturday 1 P.M.–5 P.M., Sunday 10 A.M.–5 P.M.

With over 30,000 acres of land on the island of Maui, C. Pardee Erdman could have built
resort condominiums, but instead he chose to grow crops and raise cattle. Mr. Erdman searched
for crops that require very little water, and grapes presented an attractive possibility. After planting
a few experimental acres, he discovered that some wine grape varieties fared much better than table
grapes. With the help of Emil Tedeschi, who leased the land from Mr. Erdman, vinifera was planted
and a winery was built. While waiting for the vines to produce, Emil stimulated a little cash flow
by making a wine called Maui Blanc from pineapples.

WHITE

☆☆ NV MAUI BLANC ($3.50) Maui, Hawaii. *Made from pineapple. Fresh, clean, lovely
fruit.*

SPARKLING

NV ERDMAN-TEDESCHI BLANC DE NOIR ($12.00) Estate, Maui, Hawaii. *Made
from Carnelian grapes. Decent, a bit heavy and dull.*

Tennessee Valley Winery
TENNESSEE

Hotckiss Valley Road, Route 3, Box 307-A, Louden, Tennessee 37774 (615-986-5147). FOUNDED:
1984. ACREAGE: 25 acres. PRODUCTION: 2,500 cases. DISTRIBUTION: At winery. OWNERS:
Tiegs, Rittenhouse, and Reed families. WINEMAKER: Terry Tiegs. Tours and tasting Saturday 11
A.M.–6:00 P.M.

The Tiegs family of Tiegs Vineyard (see) joined forces with two other families to open another
winery in 1984. "The reason we wanted to open a new facility was to get the winery out of the
house," says Sue Tiegs, "and also to make more wine." They built the new winery structure fifteen
minutes from their vineyards.

Tepusquet
SANTA BARBARA COUNTY

Route 1, Box 142, Santa Maria, California 93454 (415-863-2220). FOUNDED: 1982. ACREAGE:
1,300 acres. PRODUCTION: 100,000 cases. DISTRIBUTION: Nationwide. OWNER: Tepusquet
Vineyards. Alfred Gagnon, general manager; Ed Everett, sales manager. WINEMAKER: Various.
No tours or tasting.

Tepusquet Vineyards was a big name in wine long before Al Gagnon decided to make wine.
The vineyards, owned by Al with Louis and George Lucas, have been supplying many California
wineries with grapes since the mid-1970s. (In fact, Tepusquet is the most frequently mentioned
vineyard designation in this book.) As the vineyards began to establish a reputation, Al decided to
make some wine under the Tepusquet label. Knowing how important good marketing could be, he
established an association with New World Wines, a marketing company directed by Ed Everett.
The wines are made at a number of different wineries by various winemakers.

WHITE

☆☆ 1982 VIN BLANC ($4.00) Estate, Santa Maria Valley. *Dry, clean and attractive.*
 ☆ 1983 HOCK ($5.00) Estate, Santa Maria Valley. *65% Johannisberg Riesling, 22% Ge-
        würztraminer, 10% Sauvignon Blanc. Flat, dull.*

RED

     1982 CLARET ($5.00) Tepusquet, Santa Maria Valley. *Weedy.*
☆☆ 1982 CABERNET SAUVIGNON ($8.00) Vineyard Reserve, Santa Maria Valley. *35%
        Merlot. Soft, rich, weedy, pleasant. Drink now.*

Tewksbury Wine Cellars
NEW JERSEY

Burrell Road, Road 2, Lebanon, New Jersey 08833 (201-832-2400). FOUNDED: 1979. ACREAGE:
20 acres. PRODUCTION: 7,500 cases. DISTRIBUTION: New Jersey. OWNERS: Lynn R. and
Daniel F. Vernon, Jr., V.M.D. WINEMAKER: Daniel F. Vernon, Jr., V.M.D. Tours and tasting
Saturday 10 A.M.–5 P.M., Sunday 1 P.M.–5 P.M. Retail sales only weekdays 3 P.M.–5 P.M.

Veterinarian Daniel Vernon lured John Schaller away from Benmarl Wines by showing him
that New Jersey soil could produce premium wine grapes. Dr. Vernon had been growing grapes
since 1979, and he wanted a winery and a winemaker. John Schaller was somewhat skeptical, but
much to his delight, Dr. Vernon had been right. John wants to make wines that show the character
of the region, "but we are always sensitive to what our customers want," he says. For this reason
Tewksbury now makes apple wine.

WHITE

 ☆☆   1983 CHARDONNAY ($9.00) Hunterdon County, New Jersey. *Elegant, fresh, with good
         fruit and complexity.*
☆☆☆ 1983 GEWURZTRAMINER ($6.75) New Jersey. *Dry, lemony, varietal, elegant, super.*
☆☆☆ 1983 WHITE RIESLING ($6.00) Hunterdon County, New Jersey. *1.5% residual sugar.
         Great balance, crisp and elegant; super.*

Thackrey & Company
MARIN COUNTY

P.O. Box 58, Bolinas, California 94924 (415-868-1781). FOUNDED: 1980. ACREAGE: None.
PRODUCTION: 600 cases. DISTRIBUTION: By mailing list. OWNER: Sean H. Thackrey. WINE-
MAKER: Sean H. Thackrey. Tours and tasting by appointment.

Sean Thackrey is an art dealer and principal partner in Thackrey & Robertson of San Francisco.
He became interested in winemaking through his love of French Burgundies. Sean began planting
Pinot Noir on an experimental basis, and his winemaking efforts have been modeled after small
Burgundian winegrowers. Special attention is paid to vine spacing, clonal selection, and the lime
content of the soil. Sean sells his wines, named Orion, Pleiades, and Aquila, by a mailing list.

Thomas Vineyards
SAN BERNARDINO COUNTY

8910 Foothill Boulevard, Cucamonga, California 91730 (714-987-1612). FOUNDED: 1839.
ACREAGE: 10 acres. DISTRIBUTION: 8 private retail outlets in California. OWNER: Filippi

family. Joseph Filippi, president; William Nix, vice president; Reno Morra, manager. WINE-MAKER: Joseph A. Filippi, Jr. No tours. Tasting daily 8 A.M.–6 P.M.

Claiming to be California's oldest winery, Thomas Vineyards was once part of a Cucamonga land grant given to Tiburcio Tapia. In 1839, Tiburcio planted a vineyard and began making wine. In 1967 the Filippi family, well-known vintners in the area, bought the winery and vineyard property and now make their wines at a separate winery. The old winery is no longer used for wine production; it has become a tourist stop, with wine tasting, sales, a museum, and picnic facilities.

WHITE

☆☆ 1983 WHITE RIESLING ($7.50) Washington. *1% residual sugar. Lush, ripe, snappy, balanced, varietal.*

RED

☆ 1981 CABERNET SAUVIGNON ($13.50) 5th Anniversary, Washington. *Meaty; some vegetal qualities but rich and well made. Drink now.*

Paul Thomas Wines
WASHINGTON

1717 136th Place, Northeast, Bellevue, Washington 98005 (206-747-1008). FOUNDED: 1979. ACREAGE: None. PRODUCTION: 24,000 cases. DISTRIBUTION: Washington and 14 other states. OWNERS: Paul and Judy Thomas. WINEMAKER: Brian Carter. Tours and tasting by appointment. Retail sales daily 9 A.M.–5 P.M.

Paul Thomas is a crusader. He makes quite creditable grape wines, but he also makes fruit wines—serious, mostly dry fruit wines. His Bing Cherry, for example, tastes more like Pinot Noir than fruit wine, and his Crimson Rhubarb tastes more like White Zinfandel. Paul, an intense young man, feels that fruit wines deserve as much respect as grape wines. His own wines make a good case for his contention. Paul's winery is one of Washington's largest, and Crimson Rhubarb accounts for more than half his production.

WHITE

☆☆☆ 1984 JOHANNISBERG RIESLING ($7.00) Vintage Reserve, Washington. *1.75% residual sugar. Soft, fresh, varietal, deep, attractive.*
☆☆☆ 1983 MUSCAT CANELLI ($9.00) Washington. *3.3% residual sugar. Fruity, fresh, spicy, delightful.*
1982 SAUVIGNON BLANC ($7.00) Washington. *Dull, unattractive.*
☆☆ 1983 SAUVIGNON BLANC ($7.00) Washington. *Fruity, fresh, intense, varietal.*
☆☆ 1983 WHITE RIESLING ($7.00) Washington. *Crisp, fresh, clean, fruity, and attractive.*

Thompson Winery
ILLINOIS

P.O. Box 127, Monee, Illinois 60449 (312-534-8050). FOUNDED: 1964. ACREAGE: 3 acres. PRODUCTION: 4,000 cases. DISTRIBUTION: Illinois. OWNER: Dr. John E. Thompson. WINE-MAKER: Brian Thompson. Tours and tasting weekends 1 P.M.–4 P.M.

Dr. Thompson was definitely interested when Bern Ramey and Joseph Allen put their vineyards and winery up for sale. He and his son immediately made plans to leave the pork packaging business. Dr. Thompson, a physiology instructor at the Illinois Institute of Technology in addition to his other activities, had heard about Ramey and Allen's success in making sparkling wines from Illinois grapes. He bought the property without hesitation. Thanks to the slightly bizarre imaginations of Ramey and Allen, the winery is constructed out of two railroad stations that were disassembled and merged at the vineyard site. To heighten the effect, the Thompsons added several locomotives.

Thousand Oaks Vineyard
MISSISSIPPI

Route 4, Box 293, Starkville, Mississippi 39759 (601-323-6657). FOUNDED: 1978. ACREAGE: 25 acres. PRODUCTION: 7,500 cases. DISTRIBUTION: Mississippi and Tennessee. OWNER: Robert M. Burgin. WINEMAKER: Robert M. Burgin. Tours and tasting Monday–Saturday 10 A.M.–4 P.M.

William Burgin bought a home winemaking kit in 1971. Since the family had some unused land that was appropriate for grape production, he planted a few vines—just enough to provide grapes for his home winemaking experiments. His son Robert, then in high school, became fascinated with grape growing and winemaking; he studied enology in college and was one of the first graduates from Mississippi State University's enology program. While still in college, Robert bought property and opened his own winery in the cellar of a log cabin. The winery has since expanded into a larger metal building, and the cellar of the cabin is now used as the tasting room.

THUNDERBIRD *see* E. & J. Gallo Winery

Tiegs Vineyard
TENNESSEE

Route 3, Jackson Bend Road, Lenoir City, Tennessee 37771 (615-986-9949). FOUNDED: 1980. ACREAGE: 5 acres. PRODUCTION: 600 cases. DISTRIBUTION: At winery. OWNER: Terry and Peter Tiegs. WINEMAKER: Terry Tiegs. Tours and tasting Saturday 9 A.M.–6 P.M.

After twenty years of home winemaking, ceramics engineer Terry Tiegs started the first commercial winery in Tennessee. He bought a small parcel of vineyard land, built a winery and a two-story, chalet-style home, and produced his first commercial vintage in 1980. In 1984 the Tiegs family formed a partnership with two other families to start a new winery, Tennessee Valley Winery (see). Since then, they have cut back considerably on the Tiegs Vineyard production. "We will still always make some wine here at Tiegs," says Terry's wife, Sue, "since it was the first winery in the state. Eventually we hope to start making champagne here."

TIJSSELING *see* Tyland Vineyards

TIN PONY *see* Iron Horse Vineyards

Tobias Vineyards
SAN LUIS OBISPO COUNTY

P.O. Box 733, Paso Robles, California 93446 (805-238-6380). FOUNDED: 1980. ACREAGE: None. PRODUCTION: 1,000 cases. DISTRIBUTION: California. OWNERS: Pat and Martha Wheeler. WINEMAKER: Pat Wheeler. Tours and tasting by appointment.

Pat and Martha Wheeler were members of the famous home-winemaking group in Los Angeles, the Cellarmasters Club, where so many professional winemakers get their starts. While making homemade wine, they became especially fond of the Zinfandel from San Luis Obispo County, so when it came time to move from the big city, they chose Paso Robles. Pat, a tool-and-dye maker, and Martha purchased a 30-acre ranch and built a chalet-style winery out of a prefabricated barn.

RED

☆☆ 1981 ZINFANDEL ($8.25) Benito Dusi Ranch, Paso Robles. *Big, lush, ripe and forward.*

Tomasello Winery
NEW JERSEY

225 White Horse Pike, Hammonton, New Jersey 08037 (609-561-0567). FOUNDED: 1933. ACREAGE: 88 acres. PRODUCTION: 30,000 cases. DISTRIBUTION: 3 states. OWNER: Corporation. Charles J. Tomasello, Jr., president; John K. Tomasello, vice president. WINEMAKERS: Charles J. Jr. and John K. Tomasello. Tours and tasting Monday–Saturday 9 A.M.–8 P.M., Sunday 11 A.M.–6 P.M. Tours by appointment for groups of five or more.

Frank Tomasello was a farmer who raised a number of crops, including grapes, and he made a barrel or two of wine each year for his family and friends. But once his two sons got involved, the winery expanded from 5,000 gallons to 50,000 gallons. They began producing sparkling wines and planted the state's first French-American hybrids. Today the winery is run by the third generation of Tomasellos, Charlie Jr. and John. They have weeded out the large line of Tomasello wines and champagnes, planted more hybrids, and added another, more visible tasting room in the tourist town of Smithville.

Topolos at Russian River
SONOMA COUNTY

5700 Gravenstein Highway North, Forestville, California 95436 (707-887-2956). FOUNDED: 1978. ACREAGE: 125 acres. PRODUCTION: 8,000 cases. DISTRIBUTION: California and other major market states. OWNERS: Michael, Jerry, and Christine Topolos. WINEMAKER: Michael Topolos. Tours and tasting June–October: daily 11 A.M.–5 P.M.; November–May: Wednesday–Sunday 11 A.M.–5 P.M. Retail sales daily 11 A.M.–5 P.M.

A strange architectural mix of Russian Orthodox and old Sonoma hop kiln, this winery was acquired by Michael Topolos and his brother in 1978. Mike had immersed himself in viticulture and enology at U.C. Davis after traveling in the French wine country. Since planting his vineyards in the Glen Ellen area, he has been involved with almost every aspect of his winery. Mike also teaches classes in wine appreciation, has written books on diverse wine subjects, and recently reopened the winery restaurant.

WHITE

1981 CHARDONNAY ($7.00) Sonoma. *Dreary, lacking varietal character.*
☆☆ 1982 CHARDONNAY ($8.50) Sonoma. *Balanced, clean, oaky, subdued.*
☆ 1982 MUSCAT ($7.50) Sonoma.

BLANC DE NOIR

☆☆ 1983 CABERNET BLANC ($6.00) Russian River Valley. *Crisp, fresh, vinous, intense.*

RED

☆☆ 1980 CABERNET SAUVIGNON ($9.50) Sonoma. *Dark, earthy and intense.*
○ 1979 PINOT NOIR ($15.00) Quail Hill Ranch, Sonoma. *Stinky.*
○ 1980 PINOT NOIR ($8.50) Sonoma. *Moldy.*
☆☆☆ 1980 ZINFANDEL ($7.50) Sonoma. *Spicy, berried and oaky—a lovely wine. Drink 1987 and beyond.*

TOYON *see* Zaca Mesa Winery

Toyon Vineyards
SONOMA COUNTY

9648 Highway 128, Healdsburg, California 95448 (415-461-8528). FOUNDED: 1973. ACREAGE: 6.5 acres. PRODUCTION: 6,000 cases. DISTRIBUTION: Major U.S. coast markets. OWNER: Donald Holm. WINEMAKER: Donald Holm. Tours, tasting, and sales by appointment.

Bordering the Holm vineyards in the Alexander Valley is a green shrub that bears red berries during the winter months. Toyon Vineyards is named for this shrub. Don Holm had been working in a winery and caring for his own vineyard when his wife, Suzanne, suggested that he should have his own winery. "Don is so full of ideas and energy that I felt great things could happen if he started his own winery," says Suzanne. Don and one other partner, who has since been bought out, began the winery in a warehouse in Healdsburg. The winery has since moved to the vineyard location.

WHITE

1982 WHITE TABLE WINE ($3.60) California. *Decent but hopelessly dull.*
☆☆☆ 1983 CHARDONNAY ($8.50) Dry Creek Valley. *Crisp, earthy, lovely fruit.*
☆ 1982 SAUVIGNON BLANC ($7.00) Handly Ranch, Sonoma.
☆ 1982 SAUVIGNON BLANC ($7.50) Vineyard Select, Sonoma. *Overripe, dull.*

RED

NV RED TABLE WINE ($3.60) California. *Old and dull.*
☆ 1979 CABERNET SAUVIGNON ($7.00) Edna Valley. *Weedy but crisp and drinkable.*
☆☆☆ 1982 CABERNET SAUVIGNON ($10.00) Estate, Alexander Valley. *Lush, balanced, clean. Drink 1986.*

Traulsen Vineyards
NAPA COUNTY

2250 Lake County Highway, Calistoga, California 95415 (707-942-0283). FOUNDED: 1980. ACREAGE: 2 acres. PRODUCTION: 800 cases. DISTRIBUTION: California. OWNERS: John and Patricia Traulsen. WINEMAKER: John Traulsen. Tours, tasting, and sales by appointment.

John and Patricia Traulsen had been making wine in their Piedmont basement for years while John ran his pharmacy in Berkeley. One day, while looking at vineyard land in Napa County, they decided the time had come to make a major move. They bought the property, sold the pharmacy and their house, and moved to Calistoga to start a winery. John now owns Smith's Pharmacy in St. Helena, and he spends most of his time there. "The pharmacy helps us to buy French oak barrels," says John.

RED

☆☆☆ 1980 ZINFANDEL ($8.50) Napa Valley. *Rich, snappy, clean and beautifully fruity.*

Trefethen Vineyards Winery
NAPA COUNTY

1160 Oak Knoll Avenue, Napa, California 94558 (707-255-7700). FOUNDED: 1968. ACREAGE: 600 acres. PRODUCTION: 45,800 cases. DISTRIBUTION: Major market states; England, France, and Switzerland. OWNERS: John and Janet Trefethen. WINEMAKER: David C. Whitehouse, Jr. Tours and tasting by appointment.

Kaiser Steel executive Gene Trefethen bought the unused 1886 Eschol winery and its surrounding 600-acre vineyard north of Napa in 1968. The vineyard's first crop was sold to Domaine Chandon for its initial sparkling wine. By 1973 the old winery was completely renovated, and Trefethen quickly became known for its Chardonnay, which was understated at a time when others were seeing how big and heavy theirs could be. Gene has remained the grape grower, but the winery is now run by his son John and John's wife, Janet.

WHITE

☆☆ NV ESCHOL WHITE ($5.25) Napa Valley. *66% Chardonnay, 16% Johannisberg Riesling, 15% Gewürztraminer, 3% Pinot Noir Blanc. Very good.*

☆☆☆ NV ESCHOL WHITE ($5.25) Napa Valley. *75% Chardonnay, 16% Gewürztraminer, 6% Johannisberg Riesling. Rich, balanced, clean.*

☆☆☆ 1979 CHARDONNAY ($11.00) Napa Valley. *Still lively; clean, fresh, attractive.*

☆☆ 1980 CHARDONNAY ($12.00) Napa Valley. *Toasty, clean, apple flavors.*

☆☆☆ 1981 CHARDONNAY ($12.00) Napa Valley. *Tart, snappy, clean and varietal, with subtle oak.*

☆☆ 1982 CHARDONNAY ($13.50) Napa Valley. *Clean, crisp, simple, decent.*

☆☆☆ 1982 WHITE RIESLING ($7.75) Napa Valley. *Fresh and delightful.*

☆ 1983 WHITE RIESLING ($6.75) Napa Valley. *Dry, decent fruit but dull and thin.*

RED

☆☆ NV ESCHOL RED ($4.25) Blend 283, Napa Valley. *Herbal, clean and nice. Drink now.*

☆☆ NV ESCHOL RED ($4.50) Blend 282, Napa Valley. *Good, meaty, balanced.*

☆ 1978 CABERNET SAUVIGNON ($10.00) Estate, Napa Valley. *Pleasant but a rather minor effort.*

☆ 1979 CABERNET SAUVIGNON ($11.00) Napa Valley. *Pleasant but vegetal; simple and lacking depth.*

1980 CABERNET SAUVIGNON ($12.50) Napa Valley. *Overwhelmed by vegetative qualities.*

☆ 1981 CABERNET SAUVIGNON ($12.50) Estate, Napa Valley. *Still vegetal but less obnoxious than previous vintages. Progress is apparent.*

1979 PINOT NOIR ($8.00) Napa Valley. *Dull and tired.*

☆ 1980 PINOT NOIR ($8.00) Napa Valley.

☆ 1981 PINOT NOIR ($8.50) Napa Valley. *Tart, underripe, not much interest here.*

Trentadue Winery
SONOMA COUNTY

19170 Redwood Highway, Geyserville, California 95441 (707-433-3104). FOUNDED: 1969. ACREAGE: 200 acres. PRODUCTION: 23,000 cases. DISTRIBUTION: California OWNERS: Leo and Evelyn Trentadue. WINEMAKER: Nikko Schoch. Tours by appointment. Tasting daily 10 A.M.–5 P.M. Gift shop.

The Trentadues were pioneer grape growers in the Geyserville area during the early 1960s. Developing over 200 acres of vineyard, Leo Trentadue (the name means "32" in Italian) planted premium varietals and some varietals of questionable merit, such as Golden Chasselas and Early Burgundy. The winery was started when Leo's homemade Carignane became popular with his friends. Once Leo's son Victor became active in the winery, a new facility was built and the tasting room was expanded. Victor's mother, Evelyn, took charge of stocking the tasting room and turned it into a gift store full of crystal, china, and wine accessories.

BLANC DE NOIR

O   1982 ZINFANDEL ($2.50) Alexander Valley.

RED

☆☆   1971 CABERNET SAUVIGNON Alexander Valley. *Earthy and showing age but quite pleasant.*
☆   1975 CABERNET SAUVIGNON ($6.50) Sonoma. *Earthy and crisp.*
☆☆☆   1980 GAMAY ($5.00) Alexander Valley. *Grapy and fresh.*
☆   1978 MERLOT ($7.00) Alexander Valley. *Tea-like and tired.*
1980 MERLOT ($7.50) Alexander Valley. *Jammy, rich, intense but not varietal.*
☆   1980 ZINFANDEL ($7.50) Late Harvest, Alexander Valley. *3.2% residual sugar. Jammy and sweet, with good acid balance.*

Tri Mountain Winery
VIRGINIA

Box 254, Route 1, Middletown, Virginia 22645 (703-869-3030). FOUNDED: 1981. ACREAGE: 30 acres. PRODUCTION: 4,000 cases. DISTRIBUTION: Virginia. OWNER: Joseph C. Geraci. WINEMAKER: Steven Cackler. Tours and tasting April–December: Tuesday–Sunday 11 A.M.–5 P.M.; January–March: Friday–Sunday 12–5 P.M

Joseph Geraci planted his vineyards in 1973, mainly as a tax shelter. His primary business is a prehistoric farm that features models of over 34 kinds of dinosaurs and other extinct creatures. Joe built his winery out of necessity when he could no longer sell all of his grapes to other wineries. After constructing a large, L-shaped winery on his 115-acre farm, he hired a succession of winemakers: first Jim Law, then Steve Rigby in 1983, and finally Steve Cackler in 1984.

Michel Tribaut de Romery
ALAMEDA COUNTY

27910 Industrial Avenue, Hayward, California 94545 (415-864-1161). FOUNDED: 1981. ACREAGE: None. PRODUCTION: 4,000 cases. DISTRIBUTION: Major market states. OWNERS: Michel Tribaut and Bertram Devavry. WINEMAKERS: Michel Tribaut and Bertram Devavry. Tours by appointment.

Two French Champagne producers, Michel Tribaut and Bertram Devavry, became partners in a business venture in the United States with the goal of producing mèthode champenoise sparkling wine. Both vintners travel back and forth between their separate family Champagne houses in France and their California operation. The partners' concept is to make a French-style champagne out of Monterey grapes, using the same percentages of Pinot Noir and Chardonnay used in their French Champagnes. The wine is presently made in a rented facility, but there are plans to build a permanent winery near the grape source and increase production to 13,000 cases.

SPARKLING

☆   NV   BRUT ($16.00) Monterey. *Graceless, dull, lacking finesse.*

TRIONE *see* Geyser Peak Winery

TROIS FRERES *see* Lakespring Winery

Truluck Vineyards & Winery
SOUTH CAROLINA

P.O. Drawer 1265, Route 3, Lake City, South Carolina 29560 (803-389-3400). FOUNDED: 1976. ACREAGE: 100 acres. PRODUCTION: 7,500 cases. DISTRIBUTION: South Carolina and Georgia. OWNERS: James P. and James Truluck, Jr. WINEMAKER: James Truluck, Jr. Tours and tasting Monday–Saturday 10:30 A.M.–5:30 P.M.

James Truluck became fascinated with wines and winemaking while in France with the Air Force. Out of the service and working as a dentist in South Carolina, Jim began researching ways to turn his tobacco-soybean farm into a high-quality vineyard. Discouraged at first by the all-too-often-expressed opinion that only Muscadine could grow in South Carolina, he worked with viticulture experts at several universities to find out what other varieties might grow. With the help of his son Jim Jr. he planted over 300 varieties of French-American hybrid and vinifera grapevines. The Trulucks built a Mediterranean-style winery and have plans for a restaurant and inn. The winery complex has received an award as the Most Outstanding Privately Owned Tourist Attraction in the state.

RED

☆   1981 CHAMBOURSIN ($3.85) Estate, Texas.

Tualatin Vineyards
OREGON

Box 339, Route 1, Forest Grove, Oregon 97116 (503-357-5005; California office 415-328-1190). FOUNDED: 1972. ACREAGE: 85 acres. PRODUCTION: 18,000–20,000 cases. DISTRIBUTION: Major market states. OWNERS: William Malkmus, president; William Fuller, vice president. WINEMAKER: William Fuller. Tours and tasting weekdays 10 A.M.–12, 1 P.M.–4 P.M.; weekends 1 P.M.– 5 P.M. Group tours by appointment. Closed in January.

In 1973 Bill Fuller planted vineyards on an old farm overlooking the Tualatin Valley. Bill had been the chief chemist for Louis Martini winery in California before he teamed up with businessman Bill Malkmus of San Francisco to start his own winery. Bill Malkmus, who runs the winery's office in Palo Alto, provided the financial planning and support for the winery; Bill Fuller, in addition to managing the winery and vineyards, renovated and redesigned a strawberry packing shed into a state-of-the-art winery. Meanwhile Bill Malkmus developed one of the most sophisticated national distribution systems for an Oregon winery.

WHITE

☆☆   1980 CHARDONNAY ($9.60) Estate, Willamette Valley, Oregon. *Very toasty and crisp,*
         with good balance.
       1980 SAUVIGNON BLANC ($7.00) Washington. *Dull, tired.*
 O   1982 WHITE RIESLING ($6.50) Estate, Willamette Valley, Oregon. *Mushroomy, strange.*

RED

☆   1980 PINOT NOIR ($9.75) Estate, Willamette Valley. *Soft, earthy, good varietal character.*

Tucker Cellars
WASHINGTON

Highway 12 and Ray Road, Sunnyside, Washington 98944 (509-837-8701). FOUNDED: 1981.
ACREAGE: 30 acres. PRODUCTION: 8,300 cases. DISTRIBUTION: Washington. OWNER: Dean
Tucker. WINEMAKER: Dean Tucker. Tours and tasting summer: daily 9 A.M.–6 P.M.; winter: 11
A.M.–4:30 P.M.

When the U & I sugar refinery pulled out of Washington in 1979 it left behind some very
unhappy sugar beet farmers. One of them, Dean Tucker, a lifelong farmer with a 500-acre spread
of fruits and vegetables, turned from sugar beets to grapes, intending to sell the crop to a Sunnyside
winery. As it turned out, Dean produced more grapes than he could ever sell, so he designed a big,
blue metal winery and had it built right next to his famous Tucker Fruit Stand, just outside Sunnyside.
The first year Dean made wine with the help of Stan Clarke, a partner in Quail Run Vintners. Then
he brought in Craig Winchell, fresh from U.C. Davis. But Craig left to make wine in California
(see Vina Vista Vineyards), and Dean took over as winemaker again.

WHITE

 O   1982 CHARDONNAY ($7.00) Washington. *Thin, off flavors, lacking depth.*

Tucquan Vineyard
PENNSYLVANIA

R.D. 2, Box 1830, Drytown Road, Holtwood, Pennsylvania 17532 (717-284-2221). FOUNDED:
1978. ACREAGE: 10 acres. PRODUCTION: 2,000 cases. DISTRIBUTION: At winery. OWNERS:
Thomas and Lucinda Hampton. WINEMAKER: Thomas Hampton. Tours by appointment. Tasting
April–December: Monday–Saturday 11 A.M.–5 P.M.; January–March: Saturday 11 A.M.–5 P.M.

The Hamptons' vineyard was planted in 1968, but they didn't make their own wine until ten
years later. "We now use our entire grape harvest ourselves," says Lucinda Hampton. They also
make some estate-grown peach wine. The winery consists of a small, rustic tasting room and a
larger barn-like building for fermentation and aging. A concrete deck over two stainless steel tanks
overlooks the vineyards, the orchards, and a trellis of dwarf apple trees.

Tudal Winery
NAPA COUNTY

1015 Big Tree Road, St. Helena, California 94574 (707-963-3947). FOUNDED: 1979. ACREAGE:
10 acres. PRODUCTION: 3,000 cases. DISTRIBUTION: 6 states. OWNERS: Arnold, Alma, and

John Tudal, Marilyn Fidge, and Janet Baltas. WINEMAKER: Arnold Tudal; Charles Ortman, consultant. Tours and tasting by appointment only.

Arnold Tudal used to grow vegetables on Harbor Bay Isle near San Francisco until urban sprawl caused him to move up to the Napa Valley. He bought a walnut orchard, pulled out the trees, planted grapes, and started making wine at home. A little turned into a lot, and Arnold found himself in the wine business. He changed his workshop, "the nicest little workshop in the Valley," into a winery and stepped out of semi-retirement and into winery management.

WHITE

☆☆☆　1982 CHARDONNAY ($9.00) Edna Valley. *Rich oak, ripe fruit, lovely varietal character.*

RED

☆☆☆　1979 CABERNET SAUVIGNON ($10.75) Napa Valley. *Deep, velvety, herbal and impressive.*

☆☆☆　1980 CABERNET SAUVIGNON ($11.50) Napa Valley. *Dense, rich, ripe, nicely structured. Drink 1986 and beyond.*

☆☆☆　1981 CABERNET SAUVIGNON ($11.50) Napa Valley. *Herbal, soft, luxurious, chocolatey, lush.*

Tulocay Winery
NAPA COUNTY

1426 Coombsville Road, Napa, California 94558 (707-255-4064). FOUNDED: 1975. ACREAGE: None. PRODUCTION: 2,000 cases. DISTRIBUTION: 6 states. OWNER: William C. Cadman. WINEMAKER: William C. Cadman. Tours and tasting by appointment only.

Bill Cadman was a stockbroker in San Francisco when he decided to give it all up for the life of grapes and wine. He began with a series of winery jobs in the Napa Valley. He worked at Charles Krug for one crush, moved on to Heitz Cellars for a while, and then to Clos du Val. Finally he and his wife purchased a piece of property complete with two weathered buildings that had at one time been part of a chicken ranch. Bill redesigned the buildings and began making his own wine. When he's not working at his own winery, Bill is a tour guide for Robert Mondavi Winery.

WHITE

☆☆　1981 CHARDONNAY ($10.00) Napa Valley. *Decent and appealing but modest.*

☆☆　1982 CHARDONNAY ($10.00) Napa Valley. *Toasty, meaty, rich, complex; a bit heavy.*

O　1983 CHARDONNAY ($10.00) De Celles, Napa Valley. *Oxidized, oaky, unattractive.*

RED

☆☆☆　1979 CABERNET SAUVIGNON ($9.00) Napa Valley.

☆☆☆　1980 CABERNET SAUVIGNON ($9.00) Napa Valley.

☆　1980 CABERNET SAUVIGNON ($9.00) Stag's Leap Ranch, Napa Valley.

☆☆　1981 CABERNET SAUVIGNON ($9.00) Napa Valley. *Big, ripe, attractive. Drink 1986.*

☆☆　1979 PINOT NOIR ($7.50) Napa Valley. *Simple but very nice.*

☆☆　1980 PINOT NOIR ($9.50) Napa Valley. *Pleasant, soft, varietal.*

☆☆　1981 PINOT NOIR ($9.50) Napa Valley. *Simple, clean, attractive.*

O　1982 PINOT NOIR ($12.50) Haynes, Napa Valley. *Strange, flowery, off flavors.*

☆☆☆　1980 ZINFANDEL ($6.50) Napa Valley. *Charming and restrained. Balanced, clean, bright. Drink now.*

Turner Winery
SAN JOAQUIN COUNTY

3750 East Woodbridge Road, Woodbridge, California 95258 (209-368-5338). FOUNDED: 1935. ACREAGE: 800 acres. PRODUCTION: 100,000 cases. DISTRIBUTION: 25 states. OWNER: Turner family. John Turner, manager. WINEMAKER: John Turner. Tours by appointment. Tasting daily 10 A.M.–5 P.M.

In 1979, a time when few bothered with Lake County as a grape-growing region, the Turner family—Ivan and his sons—purchased 480 acres and planted new vines. The Turners sold their grapes to out-of-county wineries before deciding that the only way to put Lake County on the map was to make wines themselves. Oddly enough, they didn't put their winery in Lake County, but bought an old winery building in the Central Valley near Lodi. The Turners feel that the money saved by not building a new winery has been passed on to the consumer in the modest prices of their wines.

WHITE

O   NV PREMIUM WHITE ($3.00) Lake. *Malolactic taste, awful.*

O   NV CHARDONNAY ($3.20) California. *Dull and too old.*

O   1982 CHARDONNAY ($8.00) Highland Springs District, Lake. *Oxidized and over the hill.*

☆☆☆ 1984 CHENIN BLANC ($5.00) Lake. *Fresh, varietal, crisp, clean, with lovely fruit.*

O   1981 FUME BLANC ($5.75) Lake.

☆ 1982 FUME BLANC ($5.50) Lake. *Decent varietal character but some oxidation.*

   1983 FUME BLANC ($5.75) Lake. *Oily, heavy, unattractive.*

O   1982 JOHANNISBERG RIESLING ($4.90) Family, Highland Springs District, Lake. *Maderized.*

RED

   NV BURGUNDY ($2.95) California. *Raisiny, muddy, unappealing.*

   NV PREMIUM RED ($3.50) Lake. *Dull and odd.*

   NV CABERNET SAUVIGNON ($3.50) California. *Berried but dull and weedy.*

☆☆ 1975 CABERNET SAUVIGNON ($14.00) Lake. *Soft and quite appealing.*

O   1979 CABERNET SAUVIGNON ($4.00) Lake. *Dull, old, unattractive.*

☆ 1980 CABERNET SAUVIGNON ($6.00) Highland Springs District, Lake. *Vegetative but pleasant, with good fruit and clean flavors.*

   1980 MERLOT ($4.50) Lake.

   1981 MERLOT ($5.20) Lake. *Skunky.*

☆ 1981 PETITE SIRAH ($4.40) Limited Bottling, Estate, Lake. *Rich but not heavy; clean and snappy.*

   1980 ZINFANDEL ($4.85) Lake.

Twin Hills Ranch Winery
SAN LUIS OBISPO COUNTY

P.O. Box 2485, Paso Robles, California 93446 (805-239-3060). FOUNDED: 1979. ACREAGE: 45 acres. PRODUCTION: 10,000 cases. DISTRIBUTION: California. OWNER: James Lockshaw. WINEMAKER: James Lockshaw. Tours by appointment. Tasting room. Call for information.

An aerospace executive from Southern California, James Lockshaw yearned for the serenity of a farmer's life. He bought an almond ranch in Paso Robles that had a few grapevines and built a house. He raises nuts and grapes and makes wine while continuing his Southern California businesses. His most recent project was the construction of a new tasting room that features Twin Hills Ranch wines, Twin Hills Ranch nuts, and other Twin Hills farm products. "I'd also like to make some cheese," says James.

WHITE

☆ 1983 CHENIN BLANC ($5.00) Paso Robles. *0.68% residual sugar. Varietal, subdued fruit, lacking vitality.*

Tyland Vineyards
MENDOCINO COUNTY

2200 McNab Ranch Road, Ukiah, California 95482 (707-462-1810). FOUNDED: 1979. ACREAGE: 250 acres. PRODUCTION: 8,000 cases. DISTRIBUTION: California and other major market states. OWNERS: Dick and Judy Tijsseling. Dick Tijsseling, manager. WINEMAKER: Miles Karakasevic. OTHER LABEL: Tijsseling. Tours and tasting by appointment.

With 250 acres of producing vineyard in southern Mendocino County, Dick Tijsseling and his family started a small hobby winery on their ranch in 1979. The attractive redwood winery was designed by Dick, a San Francisco contractor. He says this first winery was an experiment from which he learned his most valuable lesson: how to choose a winemaker. After hiring and firing a few questionable winemakers, he is pleased that everything seems to have come together under enologist Miles Karakasevic. Rather than expand Tyland Vineyards, the Tijsselings decided to start fresh by building a new winery facility under a separate bond. The new winery is owned by Dick's parents, although both Tyland Vineyards and Tijsseling Vineyards share the same vineyards, management, and winemaker. The main difference between the two is the style and varieties of the wines made.

WHITE

☆☆☆ 1981 TIJSSELING CHARDONNAY ($11.75) Mendocino. *Toasty, crisp and very attractive.*
☆☆☆ 1982 CHARDONNAY ($8.75) Estate, Mendocino. *Wonderful fruit and acid; varietal and delightful.*
☆☆ 1982 TIJSSELING CHARDONNAY ($10.00) Mendocino. *Crisp, clean, fresh, attractive.*
☆☆ 1983 TIJSSELING CHARDONNAY ($7.75) Mendocino. *Crisp, fruity, attractive.*
☆☆ 1982 GEWURZTRAMINER ($6.00) Dry, Mendocino. *Spicy, fresh and angular.*
☆☆☆☆ 1982 TIJSSELING SAUVIGNON BLANC ($7.50) Estate, Mendocino. *Fruity, clean, stunning, with softness and charm.*
☆ 1983 TIJSSELING SAUVIGNON BLANC ($7.00) Mendocino. *Decent fruit but strange and slightly oxidized.*

SPARKLING

☆☆ NV BLANC DE BLANC ($9.00) Estate, Mendocino. *100% Chenin Blanc. Complex, rich, a bit coarse but attractive—and at a good price.*
☆☆ 1982 BRUT ($11.50) Estate, Mendocino. *100% Pinot Noir. Rich, fruity, clean, coarse, pleasant.*

BLANC DE NOIR

☆☆☆ 1983 WHITE ZINFANDEL ($4.50) Estate, Mendocino. *1.3% residual sugar. Crisp, pink, snappy, delicious.*
☆ 1984 WHITE ZINFANDEL ($4.50) Estate, Mendocino. *Soft, dull.*

RED

☆☆ 1982 TIJSSELING DRY RED TABLE WINE ($4.00) Estate, Mendocino. *Fresh and charming; a bit tannic.*
☆ 1979 CABERNET SAUVIGNON ($7.75) Mendocino. *A minor effort—lacking balance. Decent flavors.*

☆   1980 CABERNET SAUVIGNON ($6.50) Mendocino.
☆☆ 1981 TIJSSELING CABERNET SAUVIGNON ($7.25) Mendocino. *Oaky, clean, attractive. Drink now.*
☆☆ 1980 ZINFANDEL ($6.00) Mendocino. *Clean and fresh, featuring lush fruitiness.*
☆☆ 1981 ZINFANDEL ($3.50) Estate, Mendocino. *Fresh, balanced.*

TYROLIA *see* E. & J. Gallo Winery

ULTRAVINO *see* Artisan Wines

Val Verde Winery
TEXAS

139 Hudson Drive, Del Rio, Texas 78840 (512-775-9714). FOUNDED: 1883. ACREAGE: 30 acres. PRODUCTION: 2,900 cases. DISTRIBUTION: Texas. OWNER: Thomas M. Qualia. WINEMAKER: Thomas M. Qualia; Dr. Enrique Ferro, consultant. Tours and tasting Monday–Saturday 9 A.M.–5 P.M.

The oldest winery in Texas, Val Verde is operated by Thomas Qualia, a third-generation Texan winemaker. His grandfather, an Italian produce farmer, started the winery in 1883 because he wanted good wine to go with hearty family meals. The old adobe winery doesn't look much different than it did then, although equipment has been modernized and production has grown. Thomas, who gives his full attention to the family winery, has a teenage son, Thomas Michael, Jr., who is likely to be the fourth-generation winemaker at Val Verde.

Valfleur Winery
SONOMA COUNTY

601 University Avenue, Suite 283, Sacramento, California 95825 (916-921-9248). FOUNDED: 1984. ACREAGE: 200 acres. PRODUCTION: 15,000 cases. DISTRIBUTION: 9 states. OWNER: Jones family. Sandy Jones, president; Derek Jones, vice president. WINEMAKER: Janet Pagano. Tours by appointment.

In 1974 the Jones family bought part of one of the premier vineyards in the Alexander Valley, the Jimtown Ranch (see Château St. Jean). Vern Jones had become interested in owning vineyards after he retired from the oil business and opened an investment management office in Sacramento. His children, Sandy and Derek, joined their father's firm, and were particularly interested in the wine business. After a year of feasibility studies, Sandy and Derek decided that the smartest way to start a winery was to have grapes custom crushed. In 1982, following the advice of André Tchelistcheff, they made wine at a rented facility. Their own winery was completed in 1985.

WHITE

☆☆☆ 1982 CHARDONNAY ($10.00) Alexander Valley. *Rich, lush, balanced. Clean and varietal, with good oak.*

Valley of the Moon
SONOMA COUNTY

777 Madrone Road, Glen Ellen, California 95442 (707-996-6941). FOUNDED: 1943. ACREAGE: 200 acres. PRODUCTION: 48,000 cases. DISTRIBUTION: California. OWNER: Harry Parducci, Sr. WINEMAKER: Harry Parducci, Jr. No tours. Tasting daily 10 A.M.–5 P.M. Picnic facilities.

In 1941 Enrico Parducci, founder of the Columbus Sausage and Salami Company, bought 500 acres of vineyard, known at that time as the Madrone Vineyards, and an old winery in the Valley of the Moon near the town of Glen Ellen. The Madrone vineyards were first planted in 1851 by Joseph Hooker, also known as "Fighting Joe Hooker" in the Union Army. Enrico began the Parducci era at Madrone Vineyards by making jug wines with the help of winemaker Otto Toschi. Enrico's son Harry eventually took over winery management, and Harry's son Harry Jr. became the wine-maker in 1982 after Otto retired. The original winery building is still standing; it remains the central attraction of the winery complex.

WHITE

☆ 1983 FRENCH COLOMBARD ($4.25) Estate, Sonoma Valley. *Lush, off-dry, pleasant.*
NV SEMILLON ($2.75) California. *Flabby and dull.*
☆☆ 1984 SEMILLON ($4.00) Estate, Sonoma Valley. *Crisp, clean but short on varietal character.*

BLANC DE NOIR

☆ NV PINOT NOIR ($4.00) Sonoma Valley.
☆☆ 1981 PINOT NOIR BLANC ($4.25) Sonoma Valley. *Varietal, pleasant.*
1982 ZINFANDEL ($4.25) Estate, Sonoma Valley.
O 1983 WHITE ZINFANDEL ($6.00) Sonoma Valley. *Dull, lifeless.*
☆☆ 1984 WHITE ZINFANDEL ($5.00) Sonoma Valley. *Simple, fresh, fruity, medium sweet.*

ROSE

O 1982 ZINFANDEL ($4.25) Estate, Sonoma Valley. *3.2% residual sugar.*
O 1983 DRY ZINFANDEL ROSE ($5.00) Sonoma Valley. *Candied nose, oxidized, no fruit.*

RED

☆ 1980 PINOT NOIR ($6.00) Sonoma Valley. *Leathery, with a touch of sweetness (0.35% residual sugar).*

Valley View Vineyard
OREGON

1000 Applegate Road, Jacksonville, Oregon 97530 (503-899-8468). FOUNDED: 1978. ACREAGE: 26 acres. PRODUCTION: 8,000 cases. DISTRIBUTION: 4 states. OWNER: Anne Wisnousky. WINEMAKER: John Eagle. Tours and tasting daily 11 A.M.–5 P.M.

Frank Wisnousky, a construction engineer, decided that he had had enough of roaming the earth to build bridges. A Cabernet Sauvignon fanatic, he and his wife Anne decided to settle down in Oregon, plant a vineyard and start a winery. In 1972 they established their first experimental vineyard but waited until 1977 and 1978 before expanding the plantings of grape varieties that showed the most promise. Luckily for Frank, Cabernet Sauvignon was one of the varieties that fared well. After making the first few wines at other wineries, Frank converted the old hay barn into a winery. Two years later in 1980, Frank died in an accidental drowning, leaving Anne to keep the winery going with the help of winemaker, John Eagle.

WHITE

☆☆☆ 1982 CHARDONNAY ($7.50) Oregon. *Fresh, clean, snappy, with some depth.*
1982 GEWURZTRAMINER ($6.50) Oregon. *Snappy fruit but oxidized and flawed.*

RED

1980 CABERNET SAUVIGNON ($7.50) Oregon. *Strange off flavors; meaty, unpleasant.*
☆☆☆ 1980 PINOT NOIR Oregon. *Rich, soft, round, fruity, lovely.*
☆ 1982 PINOT NOIR ($8.50) Oregon.

Valley Vineyards
OHIO

2041 East U.S. 22-3, Morrow, Ohio 45152 (513-899-2485). FOUNDED: 1970. ACREAGE: 45 acres. PRODUCTION: 6,000 cases. DISTRIBUTION: Ohio. OWNERS: Kenneth and James Schuchter. WINEMAKER: Greg Pollman; Lou Lynch, assistant winemaker. Tours and tasting Monday–Thursday 11 A.M.–8 P.M., Friday and Saturday 11 A.M.–11 P.M. Closed Sunday.

One night Ken Schuchter was enjoying a glass of wine at a party when a friend suggested that he should grow grapes and make his own wine. Ken loved the idea. He had been running the Schuchter family farm and selling fruits and vegetables at a roadside stand. Ken figured he would plant about two acres and sell the grapes, but having never seen a grapevine in his life, he ordered enough cuttings for twenty acres. He needed a winery and his old barn fit the bill, until it burned down in 1983. "Now we have the newest winery in Ohio," says Ken. The new winery, with two Swiss-style chalets on either side of a large tasting room, opened in March 1985.

Van der Kamp Champagne Cellars
SONOMA COUNTY

P.O. Box 609, Kenwood, California 95452 (707-883-1883). FOUNDED: 1981. ACREAGE: 3 acres. PRODUCTION: 3,500 cases. DISTRIBUTION: California. OWNER: Partnership. Martin Van der Kamp and Jeff Welch. WINEMAKERS: Martin Van der Kamp, Jeff Welch, and André Tchelistcheff, consultant. No tours or tasting.

Martin Van der Kamp developed a taste for sparkling wine when he worked at Schramsberg Vineyards as a young man. "After that, I spent the rest of my life trying to make enough money to start my own sparkling wine business," says Martin. This was eventually accomplished through jewelry—Martin owns a company that specializes in earrings. Meanwhile, he was making small batches of Cabernet Sauvignon with his friend Jeff Welch. When they were finally ready to make wine professionally, they chose to make sparkling wine because "we couldn't see making a profit from small lots of Cabernet," says Martin. In 1981 Martin and Jeff rented space at St. Francis Vineyards. "A large part of our cuvée comes from St. Francis Vineyards," explains Martin.

SPARKLING

☆☆   1981 BLANC DE NOIRS–MIDNIGHT ($14.50) Sonoma Valley.
☆☆   1981 BRUT–ENGLISH CUVEE ($14.50) Sonoma Valley.

Vega Vineyards Winery
SANTA BARBARA COUNTY

9496 Santa Rosa Road, Buellton, California 93427 (805-688-2415). FOUNDED: 1979. ACREAGE: 35 acres. PRODUCTION: 6,000 cases. DISTRIBUTION: 4 states. OWNERS: Bill and Geraldine Mosby. WINEMAKER: Bill Mosby. Tours and tasting daily 11 A.M.–4 P.M. Picnic facilities.

Bill Mosby became the winemaker at his own winery by default. If things had gone as planned, his son Gary would be making the wine—after all Gary was the one with the degree in enology. But in 1979, just before their first crush, Gary was hired by Edna Valley Vineyards. Bill slid into the role of winemaker and has been having a good time ever since. The winery is located in what was once a Victorian carriage house on Rancho de la Vega (*vega* meaning "meadow"). "When the old carriage house blew down in a storm, all the neighbors became so upset that I had no choice but to rebuild it. So I put the winery inside, still preserving the 1860 Victorian look," says Bill.

WHITE

☆ 1982 CHARDONNAY ($9.50) Caldwell, Santa Ynez Valley. *Lemony and vinous; acceptable.*

1982 GEWURZTRAMINER ($5.95) Santa Ynez Valley. *0.1% residual sugar. Dry, soapy, dull, unpleasant.*

1982 JOHANNISBERG RIESLING ($5.50) Estate, Santa Ynez Valley. *Earthy, grassy, atypical.*

1982 JOHANNISBERG RIESLING ($6.75) Special Selection, Estate, Santa Barbara. *6.5% residual sugar. Odd flavors, volatile acidity.*

RED

1980 CABERNET SAUVIGNON ($7.50) Santa Barbara. *Weedy, earthy, unappealing.*

☆ 1982 PINOT NOIR ($8.50) Estate, Santa Ynez Valley. *Raisiny and a bit vegetal.*

Ventana Vineyards Winery
MONTEREY COUNTY

Los Coches Road, Soledad, California 93960 (408-678-2606). FOUNDED: 1978. ACREAGE: 305 acres. PRODUCTION: 10,000 cases. DISTRIBUTION: Major market states. OWNER: Douglas Meador. WINEMAKER: Douglas Meador. OTHER LABELS: Los Coches Cellars, Douglas Meador. Tours by appointment only. Retail sales 9 A.M.–5 P.M. Newsletter.

Doug Meador is an outspoken former Navy pilot who loves the soil. He started growing apples in Washington State and moved to the Salinas Valley in Monterey to grow grapes. Doug is an accomplished winemaker, but viticulture is his real interest. He feels that much attention has been paid to enological techniques and not nearly enough to the nuances of grape growing. Doug runs his vineyard like a laboratory, and, as a result, Ventana grapes are sought after by many wineries. The name appears on the labels of Obester, Roudon-Smith, and many others. Recent legal problems have left the future of Ventana Vineyards somewhat uncertain.

WHITE

☆☆☆ 1979 CHARDONNAY ($9.00) Monterey. *Rich and dense; balanced and complex. Drink now.*

1980 CHARDONNAY ($19.00) Late Harvest, Monterey. *6% residual sugar. Caramel flavors, lacking fruit.*

☆☆ 1981 CHARDONNAY ($12.00) Monterey. *Big, fat, rich, with good fruit and oak. A bit clumsy.*

☆ 1982 CHARDONNAY ($11.75) Monterey.

☆☆ 1982 CHARDONNAY ($12.00) Barrel Fermented, Monterey. *Crisp, clean and quite attractive.*

☆☆ 1982 DOUGLAS MEADOR CHARDONNAY ($14.00) Monterey.

☆☆☆ 1982 DOUGLAS MEADOR CHENIN BLANC ($5.50) Monterey. *1.2% residual sugar. Spritzy, clean and attractive.*

☆☆☆ 1982 CHENIN BLANC ($6.00) Monterey. *1.2% residual sugar. Spritzy, great fruit, superb.*

☆☆☆ 1984 CHENIN BLANC ($5.50) Estate, Monterey. *Fresh, rounded, soft, balanced and bright.*

☆☆ 1984 GEWURZTRAMINER ($6.00) Estate, Monterey. *Crisp, varietal and balanced, with charming fruit.*

O 1981 SAUVIGNON BLANC ($8.00) Monterey. *Weedy.*

☆☆☆ 1982 DOUGLAS MEADOR SAUVIGNON BLANC ($10.00) Monterey. *Varietal, lemony and clean.*

☆☆ 1984 SAUVIGNON BLANC ($7.00) Barrel Fermented, Monterey. *Soft, varietal, clean.*

☆ 1982 WHITE RIESLING ($7.50) Monterey. *2% residual sugar. Pleasant, good fruit but some oxidation.*

☆☆☆ 1984 WHITE RIESLING ($6.00) Estate, Monterey. *Crisp and bright, with intense varietal character and luscious fruit.*

BLANC DE NOIR

☆☆ 1984 BLANC DE NOIR ($4.00) Estate, Monterey. *Mostly Pinot Noir. Dry, clean, attractive.*

RED

○ NV LAS COCHES CELLARS ($3.50) California. *Very weedy.*

1981 RED TABLE WINE ($4.75) Estate, Monterey. *Vegetal, with volatile acidity; light, decent.*

1979 CABERNET SAUVIGNON ($8.25) Estate, Monterey. *Weedy and burnt. Unattractive.*

○ 1981 CABERNET SAUVIGNON ($9.00) Estate, Monterey. *Vegetal, unappealing.*

○ 1980 PINOT NOIR ($13.00) Monterey.

☆☆☆ 1982 PINOT NOIR ($6.25) Estate, Monterey. *Crisp and tangy like a Beaujolais. Charming, varietal character, with clean flavors. Drink now.*

☆ 1979 ZINFANDEL ($5.00) Estate, Monterey.

Vernier Wines
WASHINGTON

430-3 South 96th Street, Seattle, Washington 98108 (206-763-3633). FOUNDED: 1982. ACREAGE: None. PRODUCTION: 6,300 cases. DISTRIBUTION: Washington and California. OWNER: Partnership. Mark Floren, Bruce Crabtree, Ken Rogstad, and Bobby Capps. WINEMAKERS: Mark Floren and Bruce Crabtree. Tours, tasting, and retail sales by appointment.

Victor Rosellini's 410 Restaurant was the catalyst that brought the partners of Vernier Wines together. Bruce Crabtree, wine steward at the restaurant, had been making wine at home for quite some time with his childhood friend Mark Floren. They had often talked about starting a winery, but a wine steward's salary and Mark's job with a truck leasing company were not enough to make it possible. Then Bobby Capps and Ken Rogstad, two faithful patrons of Rosellini's, offered to bankroll the project. The four men formed a partnership and rented space in an industrial park for their winery, which was named after the patron saint of Burgundy and Rhone.

Nicholas G. Verry
FRESNO COUNTY

400 1st Street, Parlier, California 93648 (209-646-2785). FOUNDED: 1933. ACREAGE: None. PRODUCTION: 20,000 cases. DISTRIBUTION: Nationwide. OWNERS: Athena and John Verry. WINEMAKER: John Verry. Tours daily 9 A.M.–6 P.M. No tasting.

After Repeal, as wineries opened and wine began to flow once again, the Verrys still had one more battle to win before they could begin to make Retsina, the wine flavored with resin that is so popular in their native Greece. The convoluted laws at the time forbade the production of Retsina, so Nicholas Verry's father asked for and received special permission from President Franklin D. Roosevelt himself. The first winery was in Glendale, near Los Angeles, but the Verrys moved it further north, nearer their grape supply.

Conrad Viano Winery
CONTRA COSTA COUNTY

150 Morello Avenue, Martinez, California 94553 (415-228-6465). FOUNDED: 1946. ACREAGE: 60 acres. DISTRIBUTION: At winery and local outlets. OWNER: Clement Viano. WINEMAKER: Clement Viano. Tours when there is time and personnel available. Tasting daily 9 A.M.–12, 1 P.M.– 5 P.M.

When the Viano family moved onto their property, there were vines dating back to the 1880s. Conrad Viano continued cultivating these vineyards, selling the grapes, and making wine for his family. Later on, he built a sturdy, basalt-block winery, and his son Clement became the winemaker. Today Conrad claims to have retired, but only to the tasting room, where he is often found talking with winery visitors. Currently the third generation of Vianos, Clement's sons, are studying enology at U.C. Davis.

RED

○   1979 ZINFANDEL ($3.85) Private Stock, Viano, Northern California. *Raisiny, ugly, still fermenting.*

1980 ZINFANDEL ($3.25) Private Stock, Viano, California. *Dense, showing age.*

Vichon Winery
NAPA COUNTY

1595 Oakville Grade, Oakville, California 94562 (707-944-2811). FOUNDED: 1980. ACREAGE: None. PRODUCTION: 45,000 cases. DISTRIBUTION: California, New York, and Nebraska. OWNER: Robert Mondavi Winery. WINEMAKER: George Vierra. Tasting and retail sales daily 10 A.M.–5 P.M.

Vichon Winery was started by a limited partnership made up of restaurateurs and hoteliers from all over the country. The first wines were made by George Vierra—a Krug and Mondavi alumnus—at the old, stone winery that is now Ehlers Lane (see). The new winery, built on the winding Oakville Grade, opened in 1982. A power struggle that began in 1984 between the operating partners resulted in the winery's sale to Robert Mondavi's three children in 1985. Vichon will be operated by the Mondavis as a separate entity; it is the first of several acquisitions planned by this powerful Napa Valley family.

WHITE

☆☆   1983 CHEVRIGNON ($9.60) Napa Valley. *53% Sauvignon Blanc, 47% Semillon. Round, oaky, varietal.*

☆☆☆   1981 CHARDONNAY ($15.00) Napa Valley. *Crisp, clean and lemony. A charming, well-made wine.*

☆☆   1982 CHARDONNAY ($15.00) Napa Valley. *Toasty, crisp and hard-edged. Should improve with age.*

☆☆☆   1983 CHARDONNAY ($15.00) Napa Valley. *Ripe, rich, oaky, with lovely fruit and varietal character.*

RED

☆☆☆   1980 CABERNET SAUVIGNON ($16.00) Fay, Napa Valley. *Lean and elegant, with Bordeaux-like structure. Drink 1986.*

☆☆☆   1980 CABERNET SAUVIGNON ($16.00) Volker Eisele, Napa Valley. *Tangy, well structured, complex. Drink 1986.*

☆☆☆☆   1981 CABERNET SAUVIGNON ($12.75) Fay and Eisle, Napa Valley. *Rich and deep, with super structure, finesse and elegance. Drink 1987.*

Manfred Vierthaler Winery
WASHINGTON

17136 Highway 410 East, Sumner, Washington 98390 (206-863-1633). FOUNDED: 1976.
ACREAGE: 5 acres. PRODUCTION: 5,000 cases. DISTRIBUTION: At winery, restaurants, and
local retail outlets. OWNER: Manfred J. Vierthaler. WINEMAKER: Manfred J. Vierthaler. Tours
daily 11 A.M.–6 P.M. Tasting daily 12–6 P.M. Two restaurants.

   An active and outspoken participant in civic and business events, German-born Manfred
Vierthaler developed an appreciation for food and wine at an early age by helping his parents run
their Bavarian restaurant. After traveling the world, he spent three years studying enology at
Geisenheim in Germany and in 1970 was honored by an invitation to join the "Rheingauer Wein-
convent." On El-Hi Hill in Washington, Manfred built a grand chalet—a five-story Bavarian castle
that houses his winery, a tasting room, a "Royal Bavarian " restaurant, a roof garden and lounge,
a gift shop, and the Vierthaler residence.

Villa Armando Winery
ALAMEDA COUNTY

5500 Greenville Road, Livermore, California 94550 (415-846-5488). FOUNDED: 1902. ACREAGE:
75 acres. PRODUCTION: 1.5 million cases. DISTRIBUTION: Nationwide. OWNERS: Scotta
family and Villa Banfi. WINEMAKER: Anthony Scotta, Sr. Tasting at original location: 553 St.
John Street, Pleasanton, Monday–Friday 12–5 P.M., weekends 12–5:30 P.M. Restaurant at original
location open Wednesday–Sunday for dinner only. Tours and tasting in Livermore. Call for
information.

   The Villa Armando label was started by Anthony Scotta in the early 1930s. The wine was
made by Cesare Mondavi and then shipped to Scotta's wholesale wine business in New York. In
1961 Anthony and his brother purchased the Garatti winery in the Sunol Valley of Alameda County
and began making wine there. Most of Villa Armando's wines are still shipped to New York. In
the old days the winery established a reputation for big, Italian-style red wines that were instantly
aged by a heated fermentation technique. Today Villa Armando, which has expanded to a new
facility in Livermore, is probably known for its bag-in-the-box and wine coolers in cans.

WHITE

   ○ NV OROBIANCO, SEMI-DRY ($3.25) California. *Oxidized, sweet, awful.*

RED

   ○ NV BURGUNDY ($2.00) California. *Tired, oxidized, dreary.*
   ☆☆ 1977 CABERNET SAUVIGNON ($6.00) California. *Subtle, clean, rich, fruity. Drink now.*
   ○ 1980 CABERNET SAUVIGNON ($3.00) California. *Dirty, musty, unpleasant.*
   ○ 1980 CABERNET SAUVIGNON ($3.00) California. *Dirty, weedy; unacceptable at any
       price.*

VILLA BACCALA *see* William Baccala Winery

Villa Bianchi
FRESNO COUNTY

5806 North Modoc Avenue, Kerman, California 93630 (209-846-7356). FOUNDED: 1930.
ACREAGE: 450 acres. PRODUCTION: 1 million cases. DISTRIBUTION: Major market states.

OWNER: Bianchi family. Joseph S. and Glen Bianchi, managers. WINEMAKER: Hector Castro; Rob Lovell, assistant winemaker. No tours. Tasting Monday–Friday 8 A.M.–4 P.M.

The Bianchi family bought an old wine storage facility, built in 1938, took out the antiquated winemaking equipment, and started from scratch. The entire processing line was modernized, cement tanks were replaced with stainless steel tanks, and the production capacity was tripled. Joseph Bianchi, who has 40 years of experience in chemistry, called in a number of winemakers and engineers to design the winery. The Bianchis began with generic table wines for restaurants, but they now specialize in all sorts of packages, such as bag-in-the-box, and wine coolers in cans and bottles.

 è

Villa Mount Eden Winery
NAPA COUNTY

620 Oakville Crossroads, Oakville, California 94562 (707-944-2414). FOUNDED: 1881. ACREAGE: 80 acres. PRODUCTION: 18,000 cases. DISTRIBUTION: Nationwide. OWNER: James K. McWilliams, general manager; Anne G. McWilliams, partner. WINEMAKER: Mike McGrath. Tours by appointment. Tasting Monday–Friday 10 A.M.–4 P.M. Newsletter. Gift shop.

Financier Jim McWilliams and his wife, Anne, granddaughter of A. P. Giannini, the founder of the Bank of America, bought this vineyard estate in 1970. They ripped out old vines, planted a model 80-acre vineyard, modernized the 1881 winery, and installed Nordic Nils Venge as winemaker. Their first Cabernet, the 1974, caused quite a sensation. Nils left in 1982 (see Groth Vineyards) and was replaced by Mike McGrath, who had been Nils's assistant.

WHITE

☆☆ NV RANCH WHITE ($3.95) Estate, Napa Valley. *Lush, balanced, clean and very attractive.*

☆☆ 1981 CHARDONNAY ($13.00) Napa Valley. *Heavy, oaky, with some depth.*

1982 CHARDONNAY ($12.00) Estate, Napa Valley. *Woody, soft and not fresh.*

☆☆ 1983 CHARDONNAY ($10.00) Estate, Napa Valley. *A bit on the oaky, heavy side. Clean fruit in the finish.*

1982 CHENIN BLANC ($6.50) Estate, Napa Valley. *Dry, no fruit, unappealing.*

☆☆ 1983 CHENIN BLANC ($5.00) Napa Valley. *Crisp, clean, dull.*

☆☆☆ 1983 GEWURZTRAMINER ($12.00) Late Harvest, Napa Valley. *10.2% residual sugar. Lush, varietal, lovely, will age nicely.*

RED

NV RANCH RED ($3.95) Napa Valley. *Cooked veggies, weird.*

☆☆☆☆ 1978 CABERNET SAUVIGNON ($12.00) Estate, Napa Valley. *Lovely, clean oak; rich, deep flavors.*

☆☆☆ 1978 CABERNET SAUVIGNON ($25.00) Reserve, Estate, Napa Valley. *Rich, intense, better than the '79 Reserve. Drink 1989 or later.*

☆☆☆ 1979 CABERNET SAUVIGNON ($13.00) Estate, Napa Valley. *Soft, round, very attractive. Drink now.*

☆☆☆ 1979 CABERNET SAUVIGNON ($25.00) Reserve, Estate, Napa Valley. *Big, hard and tannic, with firm fruit; good potential. Drink 1987.*

☆☆ 1980 CABERNET SAUVIGNON ($11.00) Estate, Napa Valley. *Tannic, rich, clean, intense, quite lovely. Drink 1987.*

☆☆☆ 1980 CABERNET SAUVIGNON ($25.00) Reserve, Estate, Napa Valley. *Rich, complex, balanced, super. Drink 1987 and beyond.*

☆☆☆ 1982 CABERNET SAUVIGNON ($25.00) Reserve, Napa Valley. *Firm, clean, dense, rich. Drink 1990 and beyond.*

☆☆ 1978 PINOT NOIR ($10.50) Tres Ninos, Napa Valley. *Crisp, clean, appealing.*

☆ 1980 PINOT NOIR ($9.00) Estate, Tres Ninos, Napa.
☆☆ 1981 PINOT NOIR ($5.00) Estate, Tres Ninos, Napa Valley. *Varietal, with some complexity; clean, attractive.*
☆ 1982 PINOT NOIR ($9.00) Tres Ninos, Napa Valley. *Heavy, raisiny, lacking finesse.*

Villa Paradiso Vineyards
SANTA CLARA COUNTY

1830 West Edmundson Avenue, Morgan Hill, California 95037 (408-778-1555). FOUNDED: 1981. ACREAGE: None. PRODUCTION: 1,000 cases. DISTRIBUTION: At winery. OWNERS: Hank and Judith Bogardus. WINEMAKER: Hank Bogardus. No tours. Tasting weekends 11 A.M.–5 P.M.

Until 1981, the winery and vineyard property owned by Henry Bogardus was being leased to Richert and Sons winery. But when the tenants moved out, Henry and his wife, Judith, longtime home winemakers, decided they would be the next occupants. Filling the winery with their own new equipment, they began making red table wines, which are only sold there.

Village Winery
IOWA

Amana, Iowa 52203 (319-622-3448). FOUNDED: 1973. ACREAGE: None. PRODUCTION: 3,300 cases. DISTRIBUTION: At winery. OWNERS: Don and Eunice Krauss. WINEMAKER: Don Krauss. No tours. Tasting daily. Call for information.

In 1973 there were only two wineries in Amana. Don Krauss, a home-winemaking pharmacist, thought there should be at least one more. Since he was used to making wine in his home basement, he designed a cellar winery with a tasting room directly above. Don still works at the pharmacy while making wine for serious fun.

Viña Madre
NEW MEXICO

P.O. Box 2002, Roswell, New Mexico 88201 (505-622-7070). FOUNDED: 1967. ACREAGE: 40 acres. PRODUCTION: 1,600 cases. DISTRIBUTION: At winery. OWNER: Lillian T. Hinkle. WINEMAKER: Jim Hinkle. Tours and tasting weekends by appointment.

When Jim Hinkle was sent to Germany by his "rich Uncle Sam," he spent a lot of time visiting wineries. Back in New Mexico, he indulged his love of wine by buying a piece of land in an area that promised to support the production of vinifera. The initial plantings were delayed because of weather problems, but in 1967 Jim planted a number of varieties on his *Viña Madre*, or "Mother Vineyard." While the vines were struggling through their first years, Jim developed a number of different businesses. In 1969 he built his winery near the rural highway that runs by his property.

WHITE

O   1982 VIDAL BLANC ($5.25) New Mexico. *Sulfur problem.*

RED

O   NV RUBY CABERNET ($6.25) New Mexico. *Dark, earthy, musty.*
O   NV ZINFANDEL ($6.25) Shaffer, New Mexico. *Sweet, unpleasant.*

Vina Vista Vineyards
SONOMA COUNTY

24401 Chianti Road, Cloverdale, California 95425 (707-857-3722). FOUNDED: 1972. ACREAGE: None. PRODUCTION: 2,000 cases. DISTRIBUTION: California. OWNER: Corporation. Craig Winchell, manager. WINEMAKER: Craig Winchell. Tours by appointment.

While Keith Nelson was flat on his back recovering from a hip operation, he filled his hours by devising winery plans for his 113 acres of dry farmland in Sonoma County. When he got out of bed, he set up a five-man corporation, had the old winery on the property torn down, and built a new, redwood winery. For the first eight years, Keith, who also works as an aerospace engineer, tried to manage the winery himself. By 1981 he realized that the winery needed a full-time winemaker and a few truckloads of updated equipment. He hired Craig Winchell, former winemaker at Tucker Cellars in Washington, and modernized the winery by adding a new refrigeration system, new tanks, cooperage, and a state-of-the-art bottling line.

WHITE

☆ 1983 SAUVIGNON BLANC ($6.00) Napa Valley.

RED

☆ 1978 CABERNET ($6.00) Napa Valley. *Vegetal, fat.*
☆ 1981 CABERNET SAUVIGNON ($6.00) Napa Valley. *Lush, fat, deep, with some vegetal qualities. Drink now.*

The Vineyard
VIRGINIA

Route 5, Box 322, Winchester, Virginia 22601 (703-667-6467). FOUNDED: 1978. ACREAGE: 5 acres. PRODUCTION: 250 cases. DISTRIBUTION: Virginia. OWNER: Robert Viehman. WINEMAKER: Robert Viehman. No tours or tasting.

When planning for his retirement from his job as a government statistician, Robert Viehman bought a farm and started planting grapes in 1970. The inspiration for this change of lifestyle came from a book he read, though he's not sure now just which book it was. Using his old farmhouse as a winery, Robert started making wine, "just to see if I could do it." Now that the mystery is over, he is having as much fun with wine as he did with statistics.

Vinifera Wine Cellars
NEW YORK

R.D. 2, Hammondsport, New York 14840 (607-868-4884). FOUNDED: 1959. ACREAGE: 70 acres. PRODUCTION: 10,400 cases. DISTRIBUTION: Major eastern market states. OWNER: Frank family. Willy K. Frank, president and general manager. WINEMAKER: Michael Elliot. OTHER LABEL: Dr. Konstantin Frank and Sons. Tours and tasting by appointment.

A determined Russian immigrant, Konstantin Frank shook eastern winemakers out of their delusion that only French-American hybrids or native Labruscas could grow in their chilly climate. After coming to America in 1951, speaking no English, Dr. Frank made his way to the Geneva Experimental Station in New York. After two years of trying to convince so-called experts that if vinifera vines could survive fierce Russian winters they could make it in the American Northeast, Dr. Frank was hired by the only man who took him seriously, Charles Fournier of Gold Seal

Vineyards. The work of Fournier and Frank produced the first vinifera wine from the East in 1959. Proving his point, Dr. Frank started his own vinifera vineyards and small winery in 1959. In his thick Russian accent, Dr. Frank explains that he is making the "most excellent American wines from the most excellent European varieties." Dr. Frank, now 85, has retired, and the winery is presently run by his son, Willy K. Frank.

WHITE

☆   1979 KONSTANTIN FRANK AND SONS CHARDONNAY Estate, New York State. *Vinous, varietal, a bit heavy.*

RED

☆   1980 KONSTANTIN FRANK AND SONS PINOT NOIR ($8.00) New York.

Vinterra Farm and Winery
OHIO

6505 Stoker Road, Houston, Ohio 45333 (513-492-2071). FOUNDED: 1976. ACREAGE: 10 acres. PRODUCTION: 1,250 cases. DISTRIBUTION: Local. OWNER: H. K. Monroe. WINE-MAKER: H. K. Monroe. Tours and tasting summer: Tuesday–Saturday 1 P.M.–10 P.M.; winter: Friday 5 P.M.–10 P.M., Saturday 1 P.M.–10 P.M, or by appointment.

Herman Monroe became interested in grape growing and winemaking by taking a series of short courses given at Ohio State University. He turned this interest into a retirement project in 1972, when he bought 40 acres and started planting French-American hybrids. While hand-tending his vineyards, Herman kept his job as an engineer. In 1976 he built a Bavarian-style winery over-looking the valley. "We even put in an apartment upstairs in the hopes that some young person would work and live at the winery," says Herman, "but so far, that hasn't happened." For now, Herman does it all himself.

Vose Vineyards
NAPA COUNTY

4035 Mount Veeder Road, Napa, California 94558 (707-944-2254). FOUNDED: 1977. ACREAGE: 100 acres. PRODUCTION: 10,000 cases. DISTRIBUTION: California and other major market states. OWNER: Hamilton Vose III. WINEMAKER: Hamilton Vose III. No tours. Tasting May–October: daily 11 A.M.–4 P.M.; November–December by appointment. Picnic facilities.

In order to produce world-class wine, Hamilton Vose III, a Chicago businessman, bought a heavily forested, steep mountainside property, 2,000 feet up the slopes of Mount Veeder, and decided to clear it himself. It took three years of clearing, ripping, terracing, and planting, but Hamilton completed the job he set out to do. Proud of his athletic ability, his fluent Spanish, and his knowledge of wines, Hamilton has also been active in every aspect of his winery business. It goes without saying that he is also the winemaker.

WHITE

☆ 1980 CHARDONNAY ($9.75) Estate, Napa Valley.

1981 CHARDONNAY ($10.00) Estate, Mt. Veeder, Napa Valley. *Oxidized, hot, lacking charm.*

☆☆ 1982 FUME BLANC ($5.75) Amador.

1982 GEWURZTRAMINER ($7.50) Napa Valley. *1.5% residual sugar. Dull, oxidized.*

BLANC DE NOIR

○ 1983 ZINBLANCA ($4.50) White Zinfandel, Amador. *1.35% residual sugar. Heavy, candied.*

☆☆☆ 1984 ZINBLANCA ($4.75) White Zinfandel, California. *Lush, fruity, off-dry.*

RED

☆☆☆ 1978 CABERNET SAUVIGNON ($10.00) Special Reserve, Napa Valley. *Big, tart, deep and delicious. Should age well.*

☆☆☆ 1979 CABERNET SAUVIGNON ($12.50) Mt. Veeder, Napa Valley. *Lean and angular structure, tart, lovely. Drink 1986.*

1980 CABERNET SAUVIGNON ($12.50) Estate, Mt. Veeder, Napa Valley. *Big, fat and overdone.*

☆☆☆ 1980 ZINFANDEL ($8.75) Estate, Mt. Veeder, Napa.

☆☆ 1981 ZINFANDEL ($7.50) Napa-Mt. Veeder. *Snappy, ripe, interesting.*

Wagner Vineyards
NEW YORK

Route 414, Lodi, New York 14860 (607-582-6450). FOUNDED: 1976. ACREAGE: 125 acres. PRODUCTION: 22,000 cases. DISTRIBUTION: At winery. OWNER: Bill Wagner. WINE-MAKERS: John Herbert and Ann Raffato. Tours and tasting April–December: daily 10 A.M.–4:30 P.M.; January–March: tours by appointment. Cafe.

Bill Wagner has been growing both wine and table grapes on his farm for over 30 years. Once the Farm Winery Act was passed, Bill, inspired by the wine boom of the early 1970s, began designing his octagonal, pine-and-hemlock winery—a structure admired as one of the most attractive wineries in the state. Approaching winemaking from a grape grower's perspective, the Wagners emphasize the importance of grape quality and consider their own grapes to be of the highest available in the state. The Wagners have fitted out their winery with modern equipment and experienced wine-makers. Next door to the tasting room is the new "Jenny Lee Cafe," named after Bill's granddaughter.

WHITE

☆☆ 1982 JOHANNISBERG RIESLING ($8.30) Estate, Finger Lakes Region. *Rich, flowery and very well made.*

☆☆ 1982 SEYVAL BLANC ($5.50) Estate, Finger Lakes Region. *Complex and delightful.*

Walker Valley Vineyards
NEW YORK

Walker Valley, New York 12588 (914-744-3449). FOUNDED: 1978. ACREAGE: None. PRO-DUCTION: 1,000 cases. DISTRIBUTION: Local. OWNER: Gary Dross. WINEMAKER: Gary Dross. Tours and tasting June–October: daily 10 A.M.–5 P.M.; May, November, and December: weekends 10 A.M.–5 P.M.

A wine drinker while in college and a home winemaker while teaching college, Gary Dross bought grapes from both local and California growers to support his winemaking habit. Preferring to have his own supply of grapes, he purchased a farm and planted white French-American hybrids and vinifera. He then built a moderate-sized wooden winery on the stone foundation of a burned-out dairy barn. He constructed a two-story addition in 1983, which allowed him to double production.

Walker Wines
SANTA CRUZ COUNTY

P.O. Box F-1, Felton, California 95018 (408-335-2591). FOUNDED: 1979. ACREAGE: None. PRODUCTION: 1,000 cases. DISTRIBUTION: California. OWNER: Russ Walker. WINEMAKER: Russ Walker. Tours and tasting by appointment.

Russ and Drizz Walker had been making homemade wine since 1968, when they were living in Bedford, Massachusetts. In 1976 Russ, a Ph.D. in astronomy, was hired by NASA in California. After settling in the Los Altos Hills, the Walkers bonded their garage and started making wine. Russ and Drizz have since moved the winery to larger quarters in Felton in the Santa Cruz Mountains.

WHITE

1980 CHARDONNAY ($7.00) Solano.

BLANC DE NOIR

1982 WHITE ZINFANDEL ($5.00) Amador. *Dry and vinous; unappealing.*

RED

1980 CABERNET SAUVIGNON ($7.00) Santa Clara. *Burnt, unattractive.*
1980 GAMAY ($4.00) San Luis Obispo. *Dull, lacking fruit, composty.*
☆☆ 1979 PETITE SIRAH ($5.50) San Luis Obispo. *Heavy, deep, concentrated. Drink 1988.*

Warnelius Winery
SONOMA COUNTY

24517 Chianti Road, Cloverdale, California 95425 (707-857-3767). FOUNDED: 1982. ACREAGE: 140 acres. PRODUCTION: 3,000 cases. DISTRIBUTION: California. OWNER: Nils Warnelius. WINEMAKER: Nils Warnelius. Tours by appointment.

Nils Warnelius was an agricultural engineer in Sweden before he moved to Sonoma County in 1975. Once there, he started buying and replanting old vineyards as well as cultivating his own rootstock. With the help of Craig Winchell at the Vina Vista Vineyards winery, he began to make his own wine there. Recently, Nils bought another piece of property that includes an old winery, Villa Maria. "It has an incredible history," says Nils in his lilting Swedish accent. Legend has it that there's a cave, stocked with old wines, buried somewhere near the winery. "True or not, I will keep looking for it," says Nils. While he is restoring the winery, Nils will continue to make wine at Vina Vista.

BLANC DE NOIR

1983 WHITE ZINFANDEL ($4.50) Sonoma. *Flabby, dull.*

RED

☆☆☆ 1982 PETITE SIRAH ($4.00) Sonoma. *Cherry-berry, lush, clean, lovely.*
☆☆ 1982 PETITE SIRAH ($4.50) Sonoma. *Fresh, clean, snappy, with buttery oak.*

Warner Vineyards
MICHIGAN

706 South Kalamazoo Street, Paw Paw, Michigan 49079 (616-657-3165). FOUNDED: 1938. ACREAGE: 300 acres. PRODUCTION: 200,000 cases. DISTRIBUTION: Eastern states. OWNER: Warner family. Jim Warner, president. WINEMAKER: Michael Byrne. Tours and tasting daily 9 A.M.–5 P.M. Tasting also at 408 South Main Street.

In 1938 John Turner, a farmer and banker, turned a pre-Prohibition winery into a grape processing plant where he began making both juice and wine from Concord grapes. Later, Turner's son-in-law, James Warner, took over and, with hard work and determination, expanded the operation dramatically. Under the Warner family's administration, the winery has produced an array of table and fruit wines, juices, and sparkling wines, as well as solera ports and sherries dating back to 1946. With another facility in Lawton, the winery continues to expand and maintain its title as Michigan's largest winery.

Wasson Brothers Winery
OREGON

37675 Highway 26, Sandy, Oregon 97055 (503-668-3124). FOUNDED: 1981. ACREAGE: 9 acres. PRODUCTION: 4,000 cases. DISTRIBUTION: Oregon. OWNERS: Jim and John Wasson. WINEMAKERS: Jim and John Wasson. Tours by appointment. Tasting Monday–Thursday 9 A.M.–5 P.M., Friday–Sunday 9 A.M.–6 P.M.

After Jim and John Wasson won some gold medals in state fair competitions for their homemade wines, they decided to augment their full-time careers by establishing a small commercial winery. Starting at home "on a shoestring," Jim and John bartered with other wineries for used equipment. Jim, a plumber, would exchange his services for barrels, labelers, tanks, or anything else the new winery needed. After two years, the brothers moved their operation out of the house and over to Sandy, Oregon. The new wood-frame winery on Highway 26 has a spacious tasting room. Jim has given up plumbing, but John continues to work for the government in the Army Corps of Engineers. "Once a bureaucrat, always a bureaucrat," says Jim.

Waterbrook Winery
WASHINGTON

Route 1, Box 46, McDonald Road, Lowden, Washington 99360 (509-529-4770). FOUNDED: 1983. ACREAGE: None. PRODUCTION: 1,200 cases. DISTRIBUTION: Washington. OWNERS: Eric and Janet Rindal. WINEMAKER: Eric Rindal. Tours by appointment.

Janet and Eric Rindel wanted to try something new on Janet's family farm, where they had been farming wheat, alfalfa, and asparagus. They both liked wine and were attracted by the idea of winemaking. Eric began to read everything he could on the subject and attended winemaking seminars. Meanwhile, he was preparing an empty farm building, located in the middle of a wheat field, to become the future winery.

Watson Vineyards
SAN LUIS OBISPO COUNTY

Adelaide Road, Star Route, Paso Robles, California 93446 (805-238-6091). FOUNDED: 1981. ACREAGE: 15 acres. PRODUCTION: 600 cases. DISTRIBUTION: By mailing list and some retail outlets. OWNERS: Bryan and Jennifer Watson. WINEMAKER: Bryan Watson. OTHER LABEL: Tempe Wick Vineyards. No tours or tasting.

Bryan Watson was looking for just the right location, soil, and climate to grow Chardonnay and Pinot Noir, when he found a sparse piece of land that had once been part of the old Ignace Paderewski estate. It was said that the famous Polish pianist had successfully grown Zinfandel vines on the property. Bryan, while working in Los Angeles, planted the vineyards in 1975. Afterwards, he began construction of the family home and, finally, the winery. Bryan's number one goal as a winemaker is to make a superb Pinot Noir. He also expects the winery to eventually reach an annual production of 20,000 cases.

≈♠

R. W. Webb Winery
ARIZONA

4260 North Sullinger Avenue, Tucson, Arizona 85705 (602-887-1537). FOUNDED: 1980. ACREAGE: 20 acres. PRODUCTION: 3,600 cases. DISTRIBUTION: Local. OWNER: Corporation. Robert W. Webb, general manager. WINEMAKER: Robert W. Webb. Tours by appointment. Tasting every fourth Sunday 12–5 P.M.

While running his winemaking supply store, Robert Webb dreamed of having his own winery. For a time he imported California grapes to sell to local home winemakers. But after reading the wine grape feasibility studies being done at the University of Arizona, Robert was convinced that grapes could be grown in his own state. He encouraged farmers to start planting grapes and, realizing they would only plant a crop they could sell, started his own winery to provide a market.

≈♠

Weibel Vineyards
ALAMEDA/MENDOCINO COUNTY

1250 Stanford Avenue, Mission San Jose, California 94539 (415-656-2340). FOUNDED: 1945. ACREAGE: 610 acres. PRODUCTION: 950,000 cases. DISTRIBUTION: Nationwide; 6 foreign markets. OWNER: Fred Weibel, Sr., president; Fred Weibel, Jr., Peter Wolf, and Ed Russell, vice presidents. WINEMAKER: Richard Casqueiro. OTHER LABELS: Château Napoleon, Château Lafayette, Jacques Reynard, Stanford. No tours. Tasting daily 10 A.M.–6 P.M. in Redwood Valley. Tours weekdays and tasting daily 10 A.M.–5 P.M. at Mission San Jose. Picnic facilities at both locations.

The original Weibel winery and vineyards are in Mission San Jose on property that has a grape-growing and winemaking history extending back to the 1780s. The property underwent its biggest development while owned by Josiah W. Stanford, son of California governor Leland Stanford. The Weibels, a Swiss family experienced in the wine and spirits business, bought the property in 1945. They made sparkling wines to begin with, eventually expanding to table wines. They purchased vineyards in Mendocino County and built another winery and tasting room in the Redwood Valley. Today, all the wine is made at their Redwood Valley facility and is bottled at Mission San Jose.

WHITE

NV CHABLIS ($2.50) California. *Musty, dull, dirty.*
☆ 1982 CHABLIS ($2.50) California. *Dry, crisp, clean, decent.*
☆ 1984 CHABLIS ($4.50) Mendocino. 3.2% *residual sugar. Soft, sweet, spritzy, clean, acceptable.*
1981 CHARDONNAY ($6.00) Estate, Santa Clara Valley. *Vinous and sour, lacking fruit.*
1981 CHARDONNAY ($6.50) Mendocino. *Heavy, vinous, flabby, lacking fruit.*

☆ 1983 CHARDONNAY ($6.00) Mendocino. *Dull, light, decent.*

1983 CHARDONNAY ($6.50) Mendocino. *Dull, not varietal; clean but lacking character.*

☆ 1981 CHENIN BLANC ($4.50) Mendocino. *Oily, sweet and clean, with good fruit.*

☆☆ 1982 CHENIN BLANC ($4.50) Mendocino. *0.5% residual sugar. Crisp, clean, fruity, charming.*

☆☆☆ 1983 CHENIN BLANC ($4.50) Mendocino. *0.5% residual sugar. Super crisp, clean and varietal; yummy.*

1982 FUME BLANC ($6.00) Mendocino. *Dirty, dull, unattractive.*

☆ 1983 FUME BLANC ($6.00) Mendocino. *Grassy, vinous, heavy.*

☆☆ NV GREEN HUNGARIAN ($4.50) California. *3.5% residual sugar. Sweet, crisp, clean and likable.*

1982 GREY RIESLING ($3.50) Mendocino. *Weedy, watery.*

☆ 1981 JOHANNISBERG RIESLING ($5.00) Mendocino. *3.8% residual sugar. Sweet, clean, appealing.*

☆☆☆ 1983 JOHANNISBERG RIESLING ($5.00) Mendocino. *Melony, lush, with great balance. A classic.*

1982 MENDOCINO RIESLING ($5.75) Mendocino. *Sweet, low in fruit.*

☆☆☆ 1983 MENDOCINO RIESLING ($5.00) Mendocino. *Spicy, fresh, fruity, charming.*

☆☆ 1983 SAUVIGNON BLANC ($8.00) Proprietor's Reserve, Mendocino. *Crisp, clean, varietal, balanced.*

SPARKLING

☆ NV BLANC DE BLANC ($6.00) California. *3% residual sugar. Soda pop but nice.*

NV BLANC DE NOIR ($6.50) California. *0.75% residual sugar. Sweetish, dull, unappealing.*

☆☆ NV STANFORD BLANC DE NOIR ($3.50) California. *Simple, clean, fruity, nicely made.*

☆☆☆ NV BLANC DE PINOT NOIR ($7.75) California. *Crisp, dry, good varietal character.*

☆ NV BRUT ($7.50) California. *Transfer. 1.5% residual sugar. Hard, some bitterness, decent.*

NV CHARDONNAY BRUT ($9.50) California. *0.5% residual sugar. Vinous, fat, not much.*

☆ NV CHATEAU NAPOLEON ($3.00) California. *1.8% residual sugar. Odd nose, crisp fruit.*

☆ NV CHENIN BLANC ($6.00) Mendocino.

☆ NV CRACKLING ROSE ($6.00) California. *3% residual sugar. Strawberry flavors, sweet, heavy.*

NV EXTRA DRY ($6.50) California. *2% residual sugar. Weedy, unappealing.*

☆ NV STANFORD GOVERNOR'S CUVEE ($4.00) California. *2.4% residual sugar. Fresh, fruity, simple.*

☆☆ NV LAFAYETTE PINK CHAMPAGNE ($3.00) California. *Vinous, clean, simple.*

NV SPARKLING BURGUNDY ($6.00) California. *Vegetal and weird.*

☆ NV SPARKLING CHENIN BLANC ($6.00) California. *Fruity but dull, lacking acidity.*

☆☆ NV SPARKLING GREEN HUNGARIAN ($6.00) California. *3.5% residual sugar. Grapy and fresh.*

☆☆ NV SPARKLING WHITE ZINFANDEL ($6.00) California. *2.2% residual sugar. Clean, fresh, nice fruit.*

☆☆ NV SPUMANTE ($6.00) California. *4% residual sugar. Sweet, fresh, Muscaty, clean.*

BLANC DE NOIR

☆ 1982 WHITE CABERNET SAUVIGNON ($4.50) Mendocino. *Dry, clean, decent but lacking charm.*

☆ 1983 WHITE CABERNET ($4.50) Mendocino. *Crisp, varietal, decent.*

☆ 1981 PINOT NOIR BLANC ($5.00) Mendocino. *Dry, acceptable but dull.*

☆☆ 1983 WHITE PINOT NOIR ($4.50) Mendocino. *Crisp, clean, fresh fruit; delightful.*

1982 WHITE ZINFANDEL ($4.50) Mendocino. *Dry, rich, not very fresh.*

☆☆ 1983 WHITE ZINFANDEL ($4.50) Mendocino. *Varietal, crisp, clean, off-dry.*

☆☆ 1984 WHITE ZINFANDEL ($4.50) Mendocino. *Dry and clean, with decent flavors.*

ROSE

O   NV   VIN ROSE ($2.50) California. *Overdone; oxidized to sherry.*

RED

☆   NV   BURGUNDY ($2.50) California. *Crisp, fruity, with some Pinot Noir character; nice.*

☆   1973 CABERNET SAUVIGNON ($8.00) California. *Nicely balanced and quite lively for its age.*

☆   1976 CABERNET SAUVIGNON ($7.00) Proprietor's Reserve, Mendocino. *Thin, mature, lacking fruit.*

☆   1978 CABERNET SAUVIGNON ($9.50) Proprietor's Reserve, Mendocino. *Decent, clean, varietal.*

☆   1979 CABERNET SAUVIGNON ($10.00) Proprietor's Reserve, Mendocino. *Varietal, clean but lacks fruit and definition.*

☆☆ 1980 CABERNET SAUVIGNON ($9.00) Proprietor's Reserve, Mendocino. *Tannic, fresh and varietal, with dense fruit. Drink 1986.*

☆   1980 GAMAY BEAUJOLAIS ($3.50) Mendocino. *Crisp, clean, fruity, decent.*

1978 PETITE SIRAH ($4.50) Mendocino. *Thin, minty, lacking fruit.*

☆   1971 PINOT NOIR ($8.00) Estate, California. *Lush, bottle bouquet; mature, leathery, not bad. Drink up.*

☆☆ 1972 PINOT NOIR ($10.00) Santa Clara Valley. *Earthy, complex; holding up nicely.*

☆☆☆ 1974 PINOT NOIR ($12.00) Santa Clara Valley. *Clean, soft, rich, complex.*

☆   1976 PINOT NOIR ($4.50) Monterey. *Varietal, mature, some life still left.*

☆☆☆ 1976 PINOT NOIR ($9.50) Santa Clara Valley. *Rich, round, balanced, very attractive.*

☆☆☆ 1978 PINOT NOIR ($8.00) Proprietor's Reserve, Mendocino. *Lush, deep, clean; nicely made.*

☆   1980 PINOT NOIR ($8.50) Proprietor's Reserve, Mendocino. *Dull, simple.*

☆☆☆ 1981 PINOT NOIR ($8.00) Proprietor's Reserve, Mendocino. *Clean, lovely, somewhat simple but charming.*

☆   1981 PINOT NOIR ($10.00) Fremont 25th Anniversary, Mendocino. *Pleasant, short, simple.*

1978 ZINFANDEL ($4.00) Mendocino. *Thin, clean, with very little varietal character or depth.*

☆☆ 1980 ZINFANDEL ($8.00) Proprietor's Reserve, Mendocino. *Tart, crisp, fruity; nice. Drink now.*

Wente Brothers
ALAMEDA COUNTY

5565 Tesla Road, Livermore, California 94550 (415-447-3603). FOUNDED: 1883. ACREAGE: 1,800 acres. PRODUCTION: 600,000 cases. DISTRIBUTION: Nationwide; 6 foreign markets. OWNER: Wente family. Eric Wente, president; Philip Wente, vice president. WINEMAKER: Eric Wente. Tours and tasting Monday–Saturday 9 A.M.–5 P.M.; tasting only Sunday 11 A.M.–5 P.M.

Carl Wente came from Germany in 1880 and worked his way across the country. He apprenticed himself to fellow countryman Charles Krug and then went out on his own, acquiring land in Livermore in 1883. The winery was continued and expanded by his sons, Ernest and Herman. A third brother, Carl, became president of the Bank of America and helped many growers survive the Depression. Ernest's son Karl took over in 1961 and ran things until his death in 1977. Now this very successful winery is run by his children, Philip, Carolyn, and Eric. The winery has vineyards in both Livermore and Monterey.

WHITE

1980 CHATEAU WENTE ($6.00) California. *57% Sauvignon Blanc, 43% Semillon. 5.1% residual sugar. Vegetal, sweet candy.*

1981 PINOT CHARDONNAY ($5.26) California. *Decent, crisp, fruity, not a bit of depth. No oak used.*

1982 BLANC DE BLANCS ($5.00) California. *1.38% residual sugar. Lush, sweet, unappealing.*

☆ 1983 BLANC DE BLANCS ($3.60) California. *Mostly Chenin Blanc. Sweet, fresh, clean.*

☆☆ 1982 CHARDONNAY ($7.00) California. *Clean, simple, subdued, mildly appealing.*

☆ 1982 GREY RIESLING ($4.00) California. *Simple, dull, decent but nondescript.*

O 1981 JOHANNISBERG RIESLING ($5.45) Monterey.

☆☆ 1982 JOHANNISBERG RIESLING ($5.25) Monterey. *1.5% residual sugar. Varietal, a trifle short.*

☆☆ 1982 JOHANNISBERG RIESLING ($5.50) Monterey. *1.5% residual sugar. Snappy, fruity, some varietal character.*

☆☆ 1981 PINOT BLANC ($5.50) Monterey. *Crisp, clean, nicely made, simple.*

O 1980 SAUVIGNON BLANC ($4.20) Livermore Valley. *Tanky.*

☆☆ 1981 SAUVIGNON BLANC ($6.00) Livermore Valley. *Soft, fruity.*

O 1982 SAUVIGNON BLANC ($5.00) Estate, Livermore Valley. *Oily, heavy, unappealing.*

☆☆ 1984 SAUVIGNON BLANC ($6.00) Estate, Livermore. *Toasty, with apple flavors.*

☆☆☆ 1979 SEMILLON ($9.00) Arroyo Seco, Monterey. *6.8% residual sugar. Botrytis, rich, lush, intense.*

1980 SEMILLON ($4.20) Estate, Livermore.

☆☆ 1981 SEMILLON ($4.92) Estate, Livermore Valley. *Soft, grassy and clean.*

☆☆☆ 1981 SEMILLON ($6.50) Centennial Reserve, Estate, Livermore Valley. *Soft, luscious, clean, lovely fruit and depth.*

SPARKLING

☆☆ 1980 100TH ANNIVERSARY BRUT ($13.00) Monterey. *Méthode champenoise. Heavy but some fruit and complexity.*

☆☆☆ 1981 BRUT ($8.95) Monterey. *Fresh, balanced, elegant, very good.*

ROSE

☆☆ 1983 ROSE WENTE ($3.50) California. *Fresh, pleasant.*

RED

1979 CABERNET SAUVIGNON ($5.75) 100th Anniversary, California. *Soft and dull, lacking depth.*

1980 CABERNET SAUVIGNON ($6.00) California. *Dark, dank, muddy.*

☆ 1980 CABERNET SAUVIGNON ($6.00) Livermore. *Soft and smooth, with some muddiness. No depth.*

☆☆ 1978 PETITE SIRAH ($6.25) Centennial Reserve, Estate, Livermore Valley. *Rich, deep, soft.*

☆☆ 1980 PETITE SIRAH ($5.00) Estate, Livermore Valley. *Jammy, big and tannic. Good fruit. Drink 1986.*

☆ 1981 PETITE SIRAH ($5.00) Livermore Valley. *Lush, raisiny, short finish.*

☆ 1979 PINOT NOIR ($5.00) Monterey. *Leathery and stemmy, with snappy fruit; decent.*

1980 ZINFANDEL ($4.00) California. *Slight and simple, with some dirty notes.*

West Park Vineyards
NEW YORK

Burroughs Drive, West Park, New York 12493 (914-384-6709). FOUNDED: 1979. ACREAGE: 40 acres. PRODUCTION: 2,000 cases. DISTRIBUTION: Local and by mailing list. OWNERS:

Louis J. Fiore and Kevin C. Zraly. WINEMAKER: Tim Biancalana. Tours and tasting Friday–Sunday 10 A.M.–4 P.M. Seminars. Restaurant.

Always thinking big, Lou Fiore, who already owned a computer consulting company, purchased 800 acres of what used to be the Irish Christian Brothers Seminary. Lou had spoken to the brothers about his plan to start a vineyard and a winery, and they liked the idea. Then Lou became partners with Kevin Zraly, wine director of Windows on the World restaurant in New York. With Kevin came all sorts of new ideas on how the 800 acres could become a "university of wine" where people could come for seminars and hands-on winemaking and grape-growing experience. Residence facilities for wine buffs and a gourmet restaurant are planned to be built on the property. The winery, another ongoing project, is presently making only Chardonnay.

West-Whitehill Winery
WEST VIRGINIA

Route 1, Box 247-A, Keyser, West Virginia 26726 (304-788-3066). FOUNDED: 1981. ACREAGE: 9.5 acres. PRODUCTION: 625 cases. DISTRIBUTION: West Virginia. OWNER: Corporation. Stephen D. West, general manager. WINEMAKER: Dr. Charles D. Whitehill. Tours by appointment.

Dr. Charles Whitehill, professor at Potomac State College, discovered early in his winemaking efforts that Labrusca grapes from West Virginia make "pretty terrible wine." He began buying French-American hybrids from Pennsylvania for his homemade wines while working with Dr. Hamilton Mowbray, a well-known Maryland vintner, to learn more about viticulture. In 1980 Dr. Whitehill took the plunge and planted a five-acre parcel with hybrids and a little Chardonnay. About that same time he met Stephen West, a Pennsylvania lawyer who had been growing hybrids since 1973. The two of them formed a corporation and made wine from West Virginia grapes in Dr. Whitehill's basement. Now they are making wine in a simple, functional winery located next to the Whitehill vineyards. Production will increase as more West Virginia grapes become available.

Weston Winery
IDAHO

Route 4, Box 759, Caldwell, Idaho 83605 (208-454-1682). FOUNDED: 1982. ACREAGE: 15 acres. PRODUCTION: 4,000 cases. DISTRIBUTION: Idaho and surrounding states. OWNERS: Cheyne and Murray Weston. WINEMAKER: Cheyne Weston. Tours and tasting Wednesday–Sunday 12–6 P.M., or by appointment.

Cheyne Weston was working as an independent filmmaker when he met Murray in 1975. After working together for a while, they fell in love, got married, and decided to raise a family. Cheyne, who had worked in Oregon and California wineries, felt that making wine was a more suitable career for a family man than making films. Murray was busy raising their three children while Cheyne was working for Bill Broich of Ste. Chappelle Winery. At the same time, Cheyne began planting his own vineyards. In due course, Cheyne and Murray bought a cinderblock building on Highway 55 and turned it into a winery. Their vineyards are located near the Snake River.

Whaler Vineyards
MENDOCINO COUNTY

6200 East Side Road, Ukiah, California 95482 (707-462-6355). FOUNDED: 1981. ACREAGE: 23 acres. PRODUCTION: 4,000 cases. DISTRIBUTION: California. OWNERS: Russ and Ann Nyborg. WINEMAKER: Russ Nyborg. Tours by appointment.

Russ and Annie Nyborg had been selling their Zinfandel grapes to local Mendocino wineries until 1980, when they realized that the only growers who make a profit are the ones who produce their own wine. They added two buildings to a converted tractor-barn on the vineyard to complete a winery. They use only their own grapes and plan to remain a family operation. Since Russ is a full-time San Francisco Bay boat pilot, Annie and her three children are the day-to-day work force in the vineyards and the winery.

BLANC DE NOIR

☆☆☆   1984 WHITE ZINFANDEL ($5.25) Mendocino. *Varietal, fresh, tangy, off-dry.*

RED

☆☆   1981 ZINFANDEL ($5.25) Mendocino. *Fruity, fresh and appealing. Drink now.*

William Wheeler Winery
SONOMA COUNTY

130 Plaza Street, Healdsburg, California 95448 (707-433-8786). FOUNDED: 1981. ACREAGE: 28 acres. PRODUCTION: 14,000 cases. DISTRIBUTION: California and other major market states. OWNERS: William and Ingrid Wheeler. WINEMAKER: Julia Iantosca. Tours and tasting by appointment.

The Wheelers made a major lifestyle change. While living in San Francisco, they planted a vineyard on their property in the Dry Creek Valley. They sold grapes to various wineries and then decided to start their own winery in a Healdsburg storefront. Then they went even further. They took their children out of the city school, sold their house, and moved to their Sonoma ranch to become a full-time farm family.

WHITE

☆   1981 CHARDONNAY ($10.00) Sonoma.
☆☆☆   1981 CHARDONNAY ($10.00) Monterey. *Woody, earthy, complex, beautifully made. Should age well.*
☆☆☆   1982 CHARDONNAY ($10.00) Monterey. *Herbaceous, rich and lovely.*
☆☆☆   1982 CHARDONNAY ($11.00) Sonoma. *Rich, vinous, oaky yet crisp and fruity.*
☆☆☆   1983 CHARDONNAY ($10.00) Monterey. *Rich yet crisp and fruity.*
☆☆☆   1983 CHARDONNAY ($11.00) Sonoma. *Lush, rich, balanced, deep, attractive.*
☆☆☆   1982 SAUVIGNON BLANC ($8.00) Sonoma.
☆☆☆   1983 SAUVIGNON BLANC ($8.00) Sonoma. *Lively, varietal, lovely.*

RED

☆☆☆   1979 CABERNET SAUVIGNON ($7.50) Dry Creek Valley. *40% Merlot. Snappy, balanced, intense, rich. Drink 1990.*
☆☆☆☆   1980 CABERNET SAUVIGNON ($12.00) Special Reserve, Norse, Dry Creek Valley. *Richly varietal, supple, fruity, superbly structured.*
☆   1981 CABERNET SAUVIGNON ($9.00) Dry Creek Valley. *Fat, weedy.*
☆☆   1981 CABERNET SAUVIGNON ($13.50) Private Reserve, Norse, Dry Creek Valley. *Herbal, lush, dense, with good structure. Drink 1986.*
    1982 CABERNET SAUVIGNON ($10.00) Dry Creek Valley. *Overwhelmed by vegetal flavors.*
☆☆   1981 PINOT NOIR ($8.00) Bacigalupi, Sonoma.

White Oak Vineyards
SONOMA COUNTY

208 Haydon Street, Healdsburg, California 95448 (707-433-8429). FOUNDED: 1981. ACREAGE: 6 acres. PRODUCTION: 8,000 cases. DISTRIBUTION: 10 states. OWNERS: William and Barbara Myers. WINEMAKER: Paul Brasset. Tours, tasting, and sales daily 11 A.M.–4 P.M.

A former building contractor and fisherman, Bill Myers moved to Healdsburg from Alaska and immediately began thinking about building a winery. Before taking the plunge, however, Bill employed consultant Mary Ann Graf to analyze the experimental wines Bill had made from different vineyards in Sonoma County. In 1981 Bill began construction on his modern, functional downtown winery. He hired Paul Brasset, previously the winemaker at Fritz Cellars, in 1983. Except for a little freelance fishing—he still owns a fishing boat in Alaska—Bill's only occupation is his winery.

WHITE

☆☆☆   1982 CHARDONNAY ($10.00) Sonoma. *Rich, vinous nose, heavy but well balanced; big but lovely.*

☆☆   1983 CHARDONNAY ($10.00) Sonoma. *Oaky, austere, pleasant, clean.*

☆☆☆   1982 CHENIN BLANC ($5.00) Alexander Valley. *Dry, fresh, clean, with great fruit.*

☆☆   1983 CHENIN BLANC ($5.50) Napa Valley. *0.85% residual sugar. Spritzy, varietal, fresh, attractive.*

☆☆   1984 CHENIN BLANC ($6.00) Dry Creek Valley. *0.94% residual sugar. Clean, vinous, decent, some bitterness on finish.*

O   1981 JOHANNISBERG RIESLING ($6.00) Sonoma.

☆☆☆   1982 JOHANNISBERG RIESLING ($6.00) Russian River Valley. *1.7% residual sugar. Vinous, perfumed and intensely varietal.*

☆☆   1983 JOHANNISBERG RIESLING ($6.50) Alexander Valley. *1.5% residual sugar. Citrusy, fresh, varietal.*

☆   1984 JOHANNISBERG RIESLING ($6.00) Alexander Valley. *Dull, lacking fruit.*

☆☆   1982 SAUVIGNON BLANC ($7.00) Dry Creek Valley. *Clean and snappy—a fine first effort.*

☆☆☆   1983 SAUVIGNON BLANC ($7.50) Sonoma. *Lovely, rich, varietal, balanced.*

RED

☆☆☆   1982 ZINFANDEL ($6.00) Dry Creek Valley. *Fruity, crisp, tannic, balanced.*

Whitehall Lane Winery
NAPA COUNTY

1563 St. Helena Highway, St. Helena, California 94574 (707-963-9454). FOUNDED: 1980. ACREAGE: 23 acres. PRODUCTION: 20,000 cases. DISTRIBUTION: 15 states. OWNERS: Arthur and Bunnie Finklestein, and Alan and Charlene Steen. WINEMAKER: Arthur Finkelstein. Tours by appointment. Tasting daily 11 A.M.–5 P.M.

Two brothers, Alan Steen and Art Finkelstein, and their wives, Charlene and Bunnie, constructed this striking, modern, redwood winery in 1980. Art, an architect, designed a building that was both energy efficient and an attraction to visitors driving through the Napa Valley via Highway 29. The partners have experience in different fields, but they participate in all the winery operations, assisted by their children.

WHITE

1981 WHITE TABLE WINE ($3.40) California. *Oxidized and unattractive.*

☆   1981 CHARDONNAY ($9.75) Cerro Vista, Napa Valley. *Decent, clean but not much.*

☆☆☆ 1981 CHARDONNAY ($11.00) Napa Valley. *Clean and crisp.*
☆ 1982 CHARDONNAY ($11.00) Cerro Vista, Napa Valley.
☆☆ 1984 CHENIN BLANC ($5.25) Napa Valley. *Fresh, sweet, varietal, charming.*
1982 SAUVIGNON BLANC ($8.00) 51% San Luis Obispo, 49% Napa.

BLANC DE NOIR

1984 WHITE PINOT NOIR ($5.75) Blanc de Pinot Noir, Napa Valley. *Candy flavors, sour, unappealing.*

RED

☆ 1981 RED TABLE WINE ($4.70) Napa Valley. *83% Cabernet, 17% Merlot. Tannic, decent; nose is a bit off.*
☆☆ 1980 CABERNET SAUVIGNON ($12.00) Napa Valley. *5% Merlot. Big, intense, tannic, oaky. Drink 1987.*
☆☆☆ 1981 CABERNET SAUVIGNON ($12.00) Napa Valley. *Big, ripe and overdone but great fruit saves it. Drink 1986.*
☆☆☆ 1982 CABERNET SAUVIGNON ($12.00) Napa Valley. *Lush, deep, clean, nicely structured and varietal. Drink 1987.*
☆☆☆ 1982 MERLOT ($10.00) Knights Valley. *Dark, rich, intense, with lovely fruit. Drink 1986.*

Wickham Vineyards
NEW YORK

Box 62, 1 Wine Place, Hector, New York 14841 (607-546-8415). FOUNDED: 1981. ACREAGE: 160 acres. PRODUCTION: 11,000 cases. DISTRIBUTION: New York. OWNERS: Will Wickham, president and manager; Judy Wickham Butterfield and Bill Wickham. WINEMAKERS: Bill Lamberton and David Wickham. Tours and tasting. Call for information.

The Wickhams have been fruit growers since the 1790s, farming peaches for the most part, along with apples, cherries, and grapes. The fourth and current generation of grape-growing Wickhams developed an interest in winemaking during the wine boom of the 1970s. Will Wickham, encouraged by his family, researched the winery business. He and an architect designed a two-story winery and a wedge-shaped tasting room with a glass wall that overlooks the valley. Inside, drawings of vineyards by Fred Wickham, the family artist, are displayed. As with the fruit farm, every member of the Wickham family participates in the operation of the winery.

WHITE

○ 1982 CHARDONNAY ($9.00) Barrel Fermented, Finger Lakes. *Earthy, tanky, dull, not varietal, no finish.*
☆ NV JOHANNISBERG RIESLING ($7.00) Finger Lakes. *Slightly musty, sweet, crisp, clean, not varietal.*
☆ 1982 JOHANNISBERG RIESLING ($6.50) Finger Lakes Region. *3.3% residual sugar. Barrel fermented, soft, fruity.*
1982 RAVAT ($5.00) Finger Lakes. *1.1% residual sugar. Odd nose; sour and unappealing.*
☆ 1982 SEYVAL BLANC ($4.70) Finger Lakes Region. *Nice, simple, decent.*

Wickliffe Winery
OHIO

29555 Euclid Avenue, Wickliffe, Ohio 44092 (216-943-1030). FOUNDED: 1939. ACREAGE: None. PRODUCTION: 4,200 cases. DISTRIBUTION: Local. OWNER: Peter Vitantonio. WINE-

MAKER: Peter Vitantonio. No tours. Tasting in fall: weekdays 8 A.M.–8 P.M., Saturday 8 A.M.–6 P.M., Sunday 8 A.M.–1 P.M.

Peter Vitantonio, who inherited this winery after his father's death, has worked there all his life, but he doesn't seem to be able to muster much enthusiasm for it. Like his father before him, Peter buys all his grapes from both local and California growers. He now has the help of his grandson Louis, who may breathe some life back into the business.

Widmer's Wine Cellars
NEW YORK

West Avenue and Tobey Street, Naples, New York 14512 (716-374-6311). FOUNDED: 1888. ACREAGE: 250 acres. DISTRIBUTION: Northeastern states and Wisconsin. OWNER: Charles Hetterich, president. WINEMAKER: Daniel Robinson. Tours and tasting June–October: Monday–Saturday 10 A.M.–4 P.M., Sunday 11:30 A.M.–4:30 P.M.

John Jacob Widmer and his son Will established this famous winery in the late 1880s. Will, who had attended the Geisenheim "Royal Wine School" in Germany, introduced "Spätlese" and "Auslese" wines to the winery's production. He was also the first winemaker in the state of New York to make unblended varietal and vintage-dated wines. In 1971 the winery was bought by the R. T. French Company, the makers of French's mustard, and underwent considerable expansion and equipment upgrading. The large winery, a composite of old and new buildings, contains solera stacks for aging ports and sherries on top of the roof. In 1983 the winery's present management bought the winery from R. T. French.

Wiederkehr Wine Cellars
ARKANSAS

Route 1, Box 9, Franklin, Arkansas 72536 (501-468-2611). FOUNDED: 1880. ACREAGE: 400 acres. PRODUCTION: 500,000 cases. DISTRIBUTION: 8 states. OWNER: Wiederkehr family. Al Wiederkehr, CEO; Leo Wiederkehr, president; Don Neumeier, operations officer. WINEMAKER: Al Wiederkehr. Tours and tasting Monday–Saturday 9 A.M.–4:30 P.M. Gift shop. Restaurant.

This winery's history began with Johann Wiederkehr, who emigrated with his family from Switzerland to St. Mary's Mountain in 1880. Building a log cabin and digging a rudimentary wine cellar, Johann started by making persimmon, cherry, and apple wine. Brothers Al and Leo Wiederkehr, the current owners, work hard to preserve the winery's Swiss traditions, although they have expanded and modernized the facility considerably. Today's Wiederkehr Village consists of the winery, the Weinkeller Restaurant, which was Johann's original wine cellar, a weingarten, a gift shop, and the new "Die Trauben Stube," a cocktail lounge.

ROSE

☆☆   1982 ROSE OF CABERNET SAUVIGNON ($6.00) Arkansas. *Crisp, clean, varietal.*

Hermann J. Wiemer Vineyard
NEW YORK

Route 14, P.O. Box 4, Dundee, New York 14837 (607-243-7971). FOUNDED: 1979. ACREAGE: 60 acres. PRODUCTION: 7,500 cases. DISTRIBUTION: New York and Pennsylvania. OWNER:

Hermann J. Wiemer. WINEMAKER: Dana Keeler. Tours and tasting May–November: Monday–Saturday 11 A.M.–4:30 P.M., Sunday 12–5 P.M.; December–April: by appointment.

On 140 acres between Lake Seneca and Lake Keuka, Hermann J. Wiemer keeps to himself and to his strong belief in growing vinifera grapes. In 1975, while working as the winemaker at Bully Hill Vineyards, he began planting his own vineyards of Chardonnay and Johannisberg Riesling. Working for Walter Taylor, an enthusiastic champion of French-American hybrids, Hermann did not call attention to his own vineyard work. Vinifera grapes were simply not planted near Lake Seneca at that time. Trained at the enology school at Geisenheim, this quiet viticulturist-winemaker has created his own little Mosel region where he successfully tends fragile vinifera vines through the winters and specializes in Rieslings and Chardonnay.

WHITE

☆ 1982 CHARDONNAY ($10.00) Estate, Finger Lakes Region. *Clean but lacking character.*
☆ 1982 JOHANNISBERG RIESLING ($7.50) Estate, Finger Lakes Region. *Dry, fresh, a bit faint.*
☆ 1982 JOHANNISBERG RIESLING ($9.00) Late Harvest, Estate, Finger Lakes Region. *2% residual sugar. Rounded and fruity.*

WILD IRISH ROSE *see* Canandaigua Wine Company

Willow Creek Vineyards
HUMBOLDT COUNTY

1904 Pickett Road, McKinleyville, California 95521 (707-839-3373). FOUNDED: 1976. ACREAGE: 2.5 acres. PRODUCTION: 625 cases. DISTRIBUTION: California. OWNER: Dean Williams. WINEMAKER: Dean Williams. Tours and tasting by appointment.

Dean Williams had been interested in wine for years, both as a collector and as a home winemaker. As his hobby began to reach commercial proportions, he also became interested in grape growing. In Humboldt County there were few vineyards, so he planted his own. Located 30 miles west of the vineyards, the winery uses Dean's own grapes for 99 percent of its production.

WHITE

☆ 1981 CHARDONNAY ($8.25) North Coast. *Lacking varietal character.*

Wimberley Valley Wines
TEXAS

1110 North Loop 336 West, Conroe, Texas 77301 (409-760-2122). FOUNDED: 1983. ACREAGE: None. PRODUCTION: 8,500 cases. DISTRIBUTION: Texas. OWNER: Corporation. Lee Herford, president. WINEMAKER: Dean Valentine. Tasting at 25210 Grogan's Park, Woodlands. Tuesday–Saturday 11 A.M.–7 P.M.

"When I was working an oil field in Houston, every day I would pass this sign on the road advertising the 'Second Oldest Winery in Texas.' I didn't even know they made wine in Texas!" says Lee Herford. One day, Lee dropped by that winery and met the winemaker, Dean Valentine. After tasting a few wines, Lee asked Dean what was needed to make an even better Texas wine. Dean replied, "Better grapes and modern winemaking facilities." This discussion led to serious winery plans and, eventually, to a limited partnership and a modern winery on Dean's 30-acre farm. Lee became part owner of one of the oldest vinifera vineyards in the state, Blue Mountain

Vineyards, which had been severely neglected. "But hard work and twenty-four-hour attention has brought the old vines back into production," says Lee, "and now this vineyard produces the best Cabernet Sauvignon in the state of Texas."

Windsor Vineyards
NEW YORK

104 Western Avenue, Marlboro, New York 12542 (914-236-4440). FOUNDED: 1944. ACREAGE: None. PRODUCTION: 2,500 cases. DISTRIBUTION: New York and by mail order. OWNER: Sonoma Vineyards. J. B. Winkler, manager. WINEMAKER: J. B. Winkler. OTHER LABEL: Great River Winery. No tours. Tasting daily 10 A.M.–5 P.M.

What was once the "Marlboro Champagne Cellars" is now part of a California-based mail-order winery, Windsor Vineyards. Owned by Sonoma Vineyards (see), Windsor Vineyards bought the cellars from Arnold Kneitel in 1980. It became the bottling and blending facility for their three New York wines and champagne as well as the New York headquarters for wine mail orders. No wine is actually produced at the old, stone, ivy-covered winery; it is only blended, bottled, and stored there.

WINDSOR WINERY *see* Sonoma Vineyards

WINE DISCOVERY *see* Belvedere Wine Company

The Winery of the Abbey
MISSOURI

Cuba, Missouri 65453 (314-885-2168). FOUNDED: 1980. ACREAGE: 10 acres. PRODUCTION: 4,000 cases. DISTRIBUTION: At winery. OWNER: Lucian Dressel. WINEMAKER: Paul Burdick. Tours and tasting Monday–Saturday 9 A.M.–5 P.M., Sunday 12–5 P.M.

In 1980 Lucian Dressel of Mount Pleasant Vineyards bought a former restaurant to serve as an additional winery facility. He named this redwood-and-granite facility "Winery of the Abbey." "We were buying grapes from vineyards in that area for our Mount Pleasant wines, and we felt it would be much easier to process them at that location," says Dressel. Besides, the winery is on a well-traveled road, making it an inviting tourist stop. The management and winemaker for the two wineries are the same, but there is a stylistic difference in the wines. The Abbey wines use a higher percentage of Labrusca varieties and are usually sweeter than those of Mount Pleasant Vineyards.

WINERY LAKE *see* Belvedere Wine Company

Winery of the Little Hills
MISSOURI

1219 South Main Street, St. Charles, Missouri 63301 (314-723-7313). FOUNDED: 1982. ACREAGE: None. PRODUCTION: 5,000 cases. DISTRIBUTION: Missouri. OWNERS: Martha and Tony Kooyumjian. WINEMAKER: Tony Kooyumjian. Tours and tasting Monday–Saturday 10 A.M.–6 P.M.; Sunday 12–6 P.M.

Tony Kooyumjian, an airplane pilot, had always been interested in wine. The idea of starting a winery, however, was just a pipe dream until Tony and his wife, Martha, discovered an old winery, built in 1860, that had been turned into a restaurant. They leased the barn-type building behind the old winery, now the "Vintage House" restaurant, and put in a cement floor, electricity, plumbing, drainage, and everything else needed to make it an operating winery.

The Winery Rushing
MISSISSIPPI

P.O. Drawer F, Old Drew Road, Merigold, Mississippi 38759 (601-748-2731). FOUNDED: 1977. ACREAGE: 25 acres. PRODUCTION: 5,000 cases. DISTRIBUTION: Mississippi and Louisiana. OWNER: Sam Rushing. WINEMAKER: Jim Barbee. Tours and tasting Tuesday–Saturday 10 A.M.– 5 P.M.

Once it was legal, Sam Rushing wasted no time in establishing Mississippi's first post-Prohibition winery. Sam had toured the vineyards of Germany while in the Army and, when he got back, started planting vines on his grandfather's 350-acre farm. "I found out that compared to other fruits I could make more money per acre growing grapes," says Sam. A year later, the Farm Winery Act was passed, and Sam, at 22 years of age, started his winery. The restaurant and tea room next door are run by Sam's wife, Diane.

The Wines of St. Augustine
FLORIDA

1205 Eighth Avenue, Box 75465, Tampa, Florida 33675 (813-273-0070). FOUNDED: 1983. ACREAGE: None. PRODUCTION: 125,000 cases. DISTRIBUTION: 4 states. OWNER: Corporation. Edward V. Gogel, president. WINEMAKER: Edward V. Gogel. Tours and tasting Monday– Saturday 11 A.M.–5 P.M., Sunday 1 P.M.–5 P.M.

Ed Gogel has been back and forth across the United States trying to find his niche in the wine industry. He finally found it in Florida. Starting his wine education with the Wine Group, which runs three different winery plants—Mogen David, Franzia, and Tribuno—Edward worked in New York, Chicago, and Modesto. In 1973 he went to Florida for the first time to manage a distillery and research orange- and grape-wine production. In 1980 he went back to Modesto to head research and development for the Wine Group. Finally, in 1983, Edward moved to Florida to start his own winery. "Why Florida, you ask?" says Ed. "Because it is the third largest wine-consuming state per capita, but it has just a handful of wineries."

Winterbrook Vineyards
AMADOR COUNTY

4851 Lancha Plana Road, Ione, California 95640 (209-274-4627). FOUNDED: 1984. ACREAGE: 60 acres. PRODUCTION: 6,500 cases. DISTRIBUTION: California and Ohio. OWNERS: Bob and Jane Roberts. WINEMAKER: Christina Benz; Charles Ortman, consultant. Tours and tasting weekends 11 A.M.–5 P.M., or by appointment.

While living in Modesto and running an aluminum-processing plant, Bob Roberts became a weekend farmer. He bought a ranch and began planting grapes in 1980. Once he was faced with the difficult job of trying to sell his grapes, Bob decided to turn his 120-year-old horse barn into a winery. Consultant Charles Ortman helped design it, and he continues to consult with Winterbrook's winemaker, Christina Benz. Meanwhile, Bob is happily living in Modesto and still managing the aluminum plant.

BLANC DE NOIR

☆☆☆   1984 WHITE ZINFANDEL ($4.50) Amador. *2.4% residual sugar. Rich, spritzy, with deep fruit; lovely.*

Winters Winery
YOLO COUNTY

15 Main Street, Winters, California 95694 (916-795-3201). FOUNDED: 1980. ACREAGE: None. PRODUCTION: 5,000 cases. DISTRIBUTION: 4 states. OWNERS: David R. Storm, manager, and Joseph P. Mack; Leona Storm, vice president. WINEMAKER: David R. Storm. Tours by appointment. Tasting daily 10 A.M.–5 P.M. Gift shop.

Next door to the John Gere Antique Store and across the street from the famous Buckhorn Restaurant stands an 1876 brick building. David Storm, an environmental engineer and microbiologist, rented this historic, 5,000-square-foot brick building until 1980. For eight months it was without a tenant. "The building had a full cellar, perfect for barrel storage," says David. "Since no one wanted to rent it, I figured it was a sign to jump in, re-rent it, and start a winery."

RED

☆☆☆   1979 PINOT NOIR ($6.00) Napa Valley. *Burgundian, rich, deep; very lovely.*

Wittwer Winery
HUMBOLDT COUNTY

2440 Frank Avenue, Eureka, California 95501 (707-443-8852). FOUNDED: 1969. ACREAGE: None. PRODUCTION: 200 cases. DISTRIBUTION: Local. OWNERS: Dr. J. Roy and Trae Wittwer. WINEMAKER: Dr. J. Roy Wittwer. No tours or tasting.

Winemaking was a regular practice in the Wittwer household when Roy was a child. Roy always helped his Swiss-born parents make the family wine. The tradition stuck, and Roy and his wife made wine in their backyard barn every once in a while. A physician, Roy wanted to make wines that he and his wife could enjoy at home and give to their friends, but it is against the law to give away homemade wine. So they bonded the winery, and now Roy sells all of his wine.

Wollersheim Winery
WISCONSIN

Highway 188, Prairie du Sac, Wisconsin 53578 (608-643-6515). FOUNDED: 1857. ACREAGE: 23 acres. PRODUCTION: 5,000–6,300 cases. DISTRIBUTION: Wisconsin, Illinois, and by mailing list. OWNER: Robert P. Wollersheim. WINEMAKER: Robert P. Wollersheim. OTHER LABEL: River Country. Tours and tasting daily 10 A.M.–5 P.M.

Before heading out to California, Count Agostin Haraszthy started a vineyard in Wisconsin in 1849. Today, that vineyard is owned by the Wollersheim Winery. Peter Kale, a German immigrant, bought the vineyards in 1857 and built a large winery from native pine and limestone, designing it to resemble his fondly remembered estate on the Rhine. Robert P. Wollersheim, ex-electrical engineer, teacher, and project manager for NASA, stopped teaching at the University of Wisconsin in 1972 (he is still Professor Emeritus) in order to devote his full energies to the restoration of this historic winery and vineyard. Sitting on the edge of a large bluff overlooking the Wisconsin River, the winery looks much as it did in Kale's day, with its limestone caves, caverns, and 64-foot pine beams. Now, however, the old carriage house is the tasting room and gift shop, and the upstairs dance hall is used for storage.

RED

1984 RUBY NOUVEAU ($4.50) Wisconsin.

Woodbury Vineyards
NEW YORK

R.D. 1, South Roberts Road, Dunkirk, New York 14048 (716-679-WINE). FOUNDED: 1979. ACREAGE: 45 acres. PRODUCTION: 12,000 cases. DISTRIBUTION: 4 states. OWNER: Partnership. Gary Woodbury, president. WINEMAKER: Andrew Dabrowski. Tours and tasting Monday–Saturday 10 A.M.–5 P.M., Sunday 12–5 P.M.

It was the third generation of Woodburys that added vinifera grapes to their "U-pick" fresh fruit farm. Once the Chardonnay and Johannisberg Riesling began producing nicely, the family extended the farm even further by building a winery. Made of reinforced concrete, the winery has a champagne cellar and a tasting room that overlooks fruit orchards and Lake Erie. The family still operates their U-pick orchards of apples, pears, and grapes.

WHITE

○   1980 CHARDONNAY ($9.00) Estate, New York State.

SPARKLING

○   1980 BLANC DE BLANCS, BRUT ($9.00) New York State. *Mostly Chardonnay. Very unattractive.*

Woodbury Winery
MARIN COUNTY

32 Woodland Avenue, San Rafael, California 94901 (415-454-2355). FOUNDED: 1977. ACREAGE: None. PRODUCTION: 4,000 cases. DISTRIBUTION: Nationwide; United Kingdom and Canada. OWNER: Russell T. Woodbury. WINEMAKER: Russell T. Woodbury. Tours by appointment.

As marketing director of a major California winery, Russ Woodbury could see that the quality of dry table wines was improving every year, while dessert wines, ports in particular, continued to be given short shrift. Russ felt that, as American palates became more sophisticated, the need for high-quality dessert wines would grow. He began making varietal ports from 50-year-old vines, using only his own low-proof, pot-distilled brandy for fortification. In addition to running his winery, Russ is a partner in a mobile bottling line called Château Bottlers.

WHITE

1982 CHARDONNAY ($4.50) Signature Selections, Santa Maria Valley. *Decent, vinous, lacking oomph.*

RED

1981 CABERNET SAUVIGNON ($3.00) Signature Selections, Mendocino. *Tannic, thin, drinkable.*

1980 MERLOT ($3.30) Signature Selections, Napa Valley. *Dull, odd flavors.*

FORTIFIED

☆　　ALEXANDER VALLEY DESSERT ($8.50) Alexander Valley. *9% residual sugar. Vegetal, hot, with some lush, nice flavors.*

☆　　1979 OLD VINES PORT ($9.00)*Weedy, lush, not much.*

☆☆　1980 RESERVE DESSERT WINE ($12.00) Alexander Valley. Zinfandel. *Raisiny, intense, clean, attractive.*

☆☆　1980 RESERVE PORT ($15.00) *15% residual sugar. Zinfandel. Rich, dark, raisiny; nice.*

Wooden Valley Winery
SOLANO COUNTY

4756 Suisun Valley Road, Suisun City, California 94585 (707-864-0730). FOUNDED: 1932. ACREAGE: 160 acres. PRODUCTION: 60,000 cases. DISTRIBUTION: At winery. OWNERS: Mario and Richard Lanza. WINEMAKERS: Richard and Mario Lanza. No tours. Tasting daily 9 A.M.–5 P.M., except Monday.

Started by the Brae brothers in 1932, this winery produces bulk wines. The Brae brothers were partners with the Mario Lanza (not the singer) family until 1944, when one of the Brae brothers died and the other decided to go back to Italy. The Lanzas bought the entire winery and have continued making bulk wines. Three generations of the Lanza family now work in the winery after many years of modernization and growth.

Woodhall Cellars
NEVADA

15115 Wheeler Lane, Sparks, Nevada 89431 (301-467-8438). FOUNDED: 1983. ACREAGE: 6 acres. PRODUCTION: 1,291 cases. DISTRIBUTION: Local. OWNER: Corporation. Woodhall Vineyards and Wine Cellar. Albert M. Copp, president. WINEMAKER: Albert M. Copp. Tours and tasting Sunday 12–5 P.M., or by appointment.

Three amateur winemakers started their own vineyard just so they could guarantee the quality of the grapes they used for home winemaking. Albert Copp, one of the threesome, knew a fellow who owned a farm that would make a perfect vineyard site. Albert approached his friend with the idea, and a four-man partnership was formed. "Then we started making more wine than we could drink," says Albert, "so we decided to share our wines with the rest of the world." An old dairy barn was converted into a winery, and Albert became its winemaker and president. He is also the president of a nonprofit corporation that oversees the planning and growth of the city of Baltimore.

Woodside Vineyards
SANTA CLARA COUNTY

340 Kings Mountain Road, Woodside, California 94062 (415-851-7475). FOUNDED: 1960. ACREAGE: 8 acres. PRODUCTION: 600 cases. DISTRIBUTION: California and New York. OWNER: Bob Mullen. WINEMAKER: Frank Churchill. Tours by appointment.

For a few years, Bob Mullen helped a friend make wine at home. While working for Armstrong World Industries as a western regional salesman, Bob enjoyed this friendly, relaxing hobby. After a few garage vintages, the two friends and their wives decided to bond the carport and the basement and form a partnership with a third couple. For all six partners, the winery is a part-time business. Bob, who still works as a salesman, and his wife, Pauline, are the day-to-day winery workers.

WHITE

☆☆ 1982 CHARDONNAY ($11.00) Santa Cruz Mountains. *Fresh, clean, snappy.*
☆☆☆ 1982 CHARDONNAY ($11.50) Ventana, Monterey. *Lovely fruit, lush, deep; very attractive.*
☆☆ 1983 CHARDONNAY ($12.00) Santa Cruz Mountains. *Lush, rich, fruity, clean, appealing.*

RED

☆☆ 1978 CABERNET SAUVIGNON ($7.50) Fay, Stag's Leap Area, Napa Valley. *Fresh, clean, complex and surprising. Drink now.*
☆☆ 1978 CABERNET SAUVIGNON ($9.00) Santa Cruz Mountains. *Ripe, oaky, forward. Drink 1986 and beyond.*

Woodstock Winery
NEW YORK

HC 01, Box 62-1, West Shoken, New York 12494 (914-657-2018). FOUNDED: 1983. ACREAGE: None. PRODUCTION: 1,000 cases. DISTRIBUTION: New York. OWNERS: George and Judy Boston. WINEMAKER: George Boston. Tours by appointment.

Former systems analyst George Boston got a taste of winemaking by working at Benmarl Wine Company. Eager to go into business for himself, he left his job in computers to build a passive solar house on his upstate property. He and his wife, Judy, started their winery in the large cellar under the house. "It is the only passive solar winery in the East," says Judy, who works as a classical music disc jockey when she isn't in the winery. Similar to Benmarl, Woodstock Winery has its own wine club, which rewards paid-up members with a personalized case of wine, a newsletter, and invitations to wine tastings and special events.

Woodward Canyon Winery
WASHINGTON

Route 1, Box 387, State Highway 12, Lowden, Washington 99360 (509-525-2262). FOUNDED: 1981. ACREAGE: 10 acres. PRODUCTION: 1,500 cases. DISTRIBUTION: Washington, Oregon, and Idaho. OWNER: Ray L. Small, Jr. WINEMAKER: Richard L. Small. Tours by appointment.

The Ray Small family are farmers with 6,000 acres of wheat, livestock, and other money-making crops. When Ray and Jean's son Rick returned home from college with his agriculture degree, he intended to work at his father's grain elevator. But then, with the encouragement of his friend Gary Figgins of Leonetti Cellar, Rick began making homemade wine. Soon his basement was packed to the rafters with wine barrels. He moved the winery into a galvanized tin shed, and, with his father's help, started Woodward Canyon Winery. Rick makes small lots of Cabernet Sauvignon and Chardonnay from grapes purchased from the central part of the state.

WHITE

☆☆☆ 1981 CHARDONNAY ($10.00) Washington. *Toasty, rich, clean, lovely.*

Worden's Washington Winery
WASHINGTON

7217 West 45th, Spokane, Washington 99204 (509-455-7835). FOUNDED: 1980. ACREAGE: None. PRODUCTION: 12,000–13,000 cases. DISTRIBUTION: Washington, Oregon, Montana, Idaho, and Alaska. OWNERS: Jack Worden, manager. WINEMAKER: Cameron Fries. Tours and tasting daily summer: 12–5 P.M.; winter 12–4 P.M.

Rather than expand his apple orchard, Jack Worden decided in 1970 to plant grapes. He envisioned a bright future for the Washington wine industry. But as his vines matured, Jack realized that there were plenty of Washington grapes and very few Washington wineries. He took a few enology seminars and planned his own winery. He hired enologist Mike Conway, who had been working at Parducci Wine Cellars in California, and established Spokane's first winery in a storage shed behind a log-cabin tasting room. Mike's award-winning wines in those first years brought valuable recognition to the winery. Mike has since left to open his own winery, Latah Creek.

WHITE

☆ 1981 CHARDONNAY ($6.50) Washington State. *Varietal and crisp but lacking depth and charm.*

O 1982 CHARDONNAY ($6.50) Washington State. *Oxidized, dark and ugly.*

1981 FUME BLANC ($5.50) Moreman, Washington.

1981 FUME BLANC ($5.65) Sagemoor Winery, Washington.

O 1982 FUME BLANC ($5.65) Washington.

O 1982 FUME BLANC ($5.85) Moreman, Washington.

☆☆ 1983 FUME BLANC ($6.00) Washington. *Fruity, clean, varietal, charming.*

1982 GEWURZTRAMINER ($6.00) Washington. *2% residual sugar. Lush, heavy, overripe.*

☆☆☆ 1982 JOHANNISBERG RIESLING ($5.00) Proprietor's Reserve, Moreman, Washington. *2% residual sugar. Soft, elegant, very grapy and sweet.*

Wyandotte Wine Cellars
OHIO

4640 Wyandotte Drive, Gahanna, Ohio 43230 (614-476-3624). FOUNDED: 1977. ACREAGE: None. PRODUCTION: 4,000 cases. DISTRIBUTION: At winery retail outlet. OWNER: Floyd Jones. WINEMAKER: Floyd Jones. Tours and tasting daily 10 A.M.–6 P.M.

Tired of being transferred from office to office by his insurance company employer, Floyd Jones decided to start his own business—one that would keep him in Ohio. He visited a friend in Iowa and saw how a small-scale winery operation works. Having worked on a farm until he was 45, Floyd was quickly seduced by the idea of a small winery of his own. Above a 3,200-square-foot basement, he built a new house and a retail sales room next door.

Yakima River Winery
WASHINGTON

Route 1, Box 1657, North River Road, Prosser, Washington 99350 (509-786-2805). FOUNDED: 1978. ACREAGE: None. PRODUCTION: 14,000 cases. DISTRIBUTION: Montana, Oregon,

Idaho, and Washington. OWNERS: John and Louise Rauner. WINEMAKER: John Rauner. Tours and tasting daily 10 A.M.–5 P.M.

John and Louise Rauner were living happily in New York's Hudson River Valley when they tasted two wines from the Yakima Valley. "They were the best Chardonnay and Cabernet I had ever tasted," says John. Soon afterwards, the Rauners made their first visit to Washington, where they found a new breed of grape growers, many of whom couldn't find wineries to vinify their new, large crops. The Rauners moved to Washington, and John went to school to study winemaking, chemistry, and microbiology. At the same time, he kept food on the table by working as a welder. In 1978 the Rauner garage became a winery; recently the Rauners built a new facility behind their house. "Everyone tells us it looks like a big, red New England barn," says John, who is now a full-time winemaker.

WHITE

☆☆☆ 1983 CHENIN BLANC ($5.50) Washington. *2% residual sugar. Snappy, round, delightful.*
1982 GEWURZTRAMINER ($5.50) Fairacre Nursery, Yakima Valley.
☆☆ 1982 WHITE RIESLING ($5.50) Ciel du Cheval, Yakima River. *1.8% residual sugar.*

RED

☆ 1980 CABERNET SAUVIGNON ($10.50) Special Selection, Washington State. *Tea-like, soft and fruity.*
1981 MERLOT ($7.50) Ciel du Cheval, Yakima Valley.

Yankee Hill Winery
TUOLUMNE COUNTY

11755 Coarsegold Lane, Columbia, California 95310 (209-532-3015). FOUNDED: 1970. ACREAGE: None. PRODUCTION: 2,200 cases. DISTRIBUTION: At winery. OWNER: Ron Erickson. WINEMAKER: Ron Erickson. Tours and tasting by appointment.

Ron Erickson sold his restaurant in San Francisco to buy the Yankee Hill Winery and to semi-retire. He and his family had a cabin in the Columbia area and were very fond of the region. "You come to a place like this to relax and slow down, but before you know it you are back to the same pace as you were before," says Ron, who is working as director of culinary arts at a nearby college and as a manager for the City Hotel restaurant, as well as being the winemaker and manager of his family winery.

Yerba Buena Winery
SAN FRANCISCO COUNTY

500 Beale Street, San Francisco, California 94105 (415-896-5550). FOUNDED: 1977. ACREAGE: None. PRODUCTION: 500 cases. DISTRIBUTION: California. OWNER: Sean Kearney, manager. WINEMAKER: Sean Kearney. No tours or tasting.

The founder of this winery, Brian Whipple, set up shop in a railroad mail car on Pier 33 in San Francisco. This waterfront location was excellent for keeping winery temperatures cool, but it limited any plans for expansion. With the assistance of Sean Kearney, Brian decided to move operations to a more practical location, and in 1982 the winery moved to the corner of a large warehouse. Sean is now the sole owner of the only winery within the city limits of San Francisco.

YORK CREEK *see* Belvedere Wine Company

York Mountain Winery
SAN LUIS OBISPO COUNTY

Route 2, Box 191, York Mountain Road, Templeton, California 93465 (805-238-3925). FOUNDED: 1882. ACREAGE: 10 acres. PRODUCTION: 5,000 cases. DISTRIBUTION: Local and statewide. OWNER: Max Goldman; Steve Goldman, manager. WINEMAKER: Steve Goldman. Tours and tasting daily 10 A.M.–5 P.M.

Built by Andrew York in 1882, this brick-and-stone winery has been standing for over 100 years. It was here that the grapes of renowned Polish pianist Ignace Paderewski were made into wine. In 1970 Max Goldman, former president of the American Society of Enologists, who had worked in the wine industry both in New York and California, bought the York winery. "I was getting ready to retire," says Max, "but instead I went to work." Renovating certain sections, replanting old vines, but keeping the original look of the winery, Max has indeed worked hard, although his son and daughter are beginning to take over, allowing Max to retire at last.

WHITE

☆   1982 CHARDONNAY ($7.50) MacBride, San Luis Obispo. *Snappy, lemony, lacking depth; decent.*

RED

O   1977 MERLOT ($7.50) California. *Very weedy.*
☆☆   1980 PINOT NOIR ($9.50) San Luis Obispo. *Rich, intense, Burgundian.*
☆   1980 PINOT NOIR ($9.50) San Luis Obispo. *Decent but a trifle tired.*
☆☆☆   1981 ZINFANDEL ($6.95) Estate, San Luis Obispo. *Tart and grapy; with some volatility and great fruit.*

York Springs Winery
PENNSYLVANIA

420 Latimore Road, York Springs, Pennsylvania 17372 (717-528-8490). FOUNDED: 1978. ACREAGE: 12 acres. PRODUCTION: 2,500 cases. DISTRIBUTION: Pennsylvania. OWNERS: Andrew and Betty Campbell, general partners. WINEMAKER: Andrew Campbell. Tours and tasting daily 10 A.M.–6 P.M.

On a whim, Andrew and Betty Campbell started growing grapes in Pennsylvania. "We were looking for something to do," says Andrew. They had been living in Washington D.C., where Andrew was working as a mathematician. They found a vineyard location, felt that the old cow barn on the property would make a nice winery, and, on another whim, started making wine.

ROBERT YOUNG *see* Belvedere Wine Company

Yverdon
NAPA COUNTY

3787 Spring Mountain Road, St. Helena, California 94574 (707-963-4270). FOUNDED: 1970. ACREAGE: 100 acres. PRODUCTION: 5,000 cases. DISTRIBUTION: Nationwide. OWNER: Fred J. Aves. WINEMAKER: Fred J. Aves. No tours or tasting.

Fred Aves, a hermit-like inventor, had a complete education that included foreign languages, electronics, opera, and gourmet cooking. He became an inventor and created automotive accessories for a living until 1969, when he moved to Spring Mountain and built a winery. The building is an imaginative invention in itself: a two-story stone structure with stained glass windows and underground tunnels. Fred made his first wine in 1970. Despite being one of Napa's older wineries, Yverdon wines are still very hard to find—mostly because of Fred's disinterest in the marketing side of the business.

RED

☆ 1977 CABERNET SAUVIGNON ($9.00) Spring Mountain, Napa Valley. *Coarse, dirty; a bit odd.*

☆☆ 1978 CABERNET SAUVIGNON ($8.00) Napa Valley. *Earthy and fat, with nice fruit.*

Zaca Mesa Winery
SANTA BARBARA COUNTY

Foxen Canyon Road, P.O. Box 547, Los Olivos, California 93441 (805-688-9339). FOUNDED: 1972. ACREAGE: 350 acres. PRODUCTION: 85,000 cases. DISTRIBUTION: OWNER: Corporation. Marshall Ream, president. WINEMAKER: Ken Brown. OTHER LABEL: Toyon. Tours and tasting daily 10 A.M.–4 P.M.

Marshall Ream took early retirement from his top management job at Atlantic Richfield in order to pursue his vineyard interests. In 1972 he bought 1,800 acres in the Santa Ynez Valley near Los Olivos and planted some of it to vineyards. A cautious person, Marshall had his first wines made at The Monterey Vineyard—he didn't want to build a winery if his grapes weren't worthy of it. They were. He then hired Ken Brown, a Fresno State University–trained winemaker, and constructed a winery. Marshall also built a chapel on the property. *Zaca* is an Indian word meaning "peace and quiet."

WHITE

☆ 1981 CHARDONNAY ($8.00) Tepusquet, Santa Maria Valley. *Earthy, dense, lacking freshness.*

☆☆☆ 1981 CHARDONNAY ($11.00) American Estate, Chapel, Santa Ynez Valley. *Beautifully balanced, clean and ripe. A lovely wine.*

☆☆ 1982 TOYON CHARDONNAY ($6.00) Santa Barbara.

☆☆☆ 1982 CHARDONNAY ($10.00) Santa Barbara. *Soft and oaky, with finesse.*

☆ 1982 CHARDONNAY ($12.00) American Reserve, Santa Barbara. *Heavy, with some vegetal notes, ripe, fruity.*

☆☆ 1983 CHARDONNAY ($6.00) Toyon, California. *Fruity, oaky, clean, simple.*

1981 JOHANNISBERG RIESLING ($6.50) 92% Zaca Mesa Ranch; 8% Douglas, Santa Ynez Valley. *Not aging well.*

☆☆☆ 1982 JOHANNISBERG RIESLING ($6.50) Santa Barbara County. *Appealingly crisp and fruited.*

☆☆ 1982 JOHANNISBERG RIESLING ($7.75) American Classic, Santa Barbara.

☆☆ 1982 SAUVIGNON BLANC ($8.00) Santa Barbara.

☆☆ 1982 SAUVIGNON BLANC ($10.00) American Reserve, Santa Barbara. *23.6% Semillon. Vegetal nose, crisp but rounded, assertive.*

☆☆ 1983 SAUVIGNON BLANC ($6.25) California. *Weedy, round, varietal, clean.*

BLANC DE NOIR

☆☆ 1983 TOYON BLANC ($4.50) Santa Barbara. *Clean, fresh, pleasant, coral color.*

RED

☆ 1981 TOYON NOIR ($4.00) 95% Estate Zinfandel; 5% Nielson Cabernet, Santa Barbara. *Vegetal and fat, with good varietal character.*

O 1982 TOYON NOIR ($4.50) Santa Barbara. *Overwhelmed by vegetation.*

☆☆☆ 1979 CABERNET SAUVIGNON ($8.00) Santa Ynez Valley. *12% Merlot. Lush, deep, intense. Drink 1986 and beyond.*

☆ 1980 CABERNET SAUVIGNON ($12.50) Santa Ynez Valley. *Vegetal quality dominates.*

1981 CABERNET SAUVIGNON ($6.00) California. *Weedy, unattractive.*

☆ 1981 CABERNET SAUVIGNON ($12.00) American Reserve, Santa Ynez Valley. *Herbal, fruity, concentrated, with some difficult flavors.*

O 1982 CABERNET SAUVIGNON ($5.00) Toyon, California. *Very vegetal.*

☆☆☆ 1978 PINOT NOIR ($10.00) Special Selection, Estate, Santa Ynez Valley. *Vinous, complex and rich, with good acid balance. Should age well.*

☆☆ 1979 PINOT NOIR ($10.00) Special Select, Estate, Chapel, Santa Barbara.

1980 ZINFANDEL ($6.75) American Estate, Toyon, Santa Ynez Valley, Santa Barbara. *Weedy.*

☆☆ 1980 ZINFANDEL ($8.00) Estate, Santa Barbara.

1981 ZINFANDEL ($7.50) California. *Lacking fruit, too much earthiness. A disappointment.*

ZD Wines
NAPA COUNTY

8383 Silverado Trail, Napa, California 94558 (707-963-5188). FOUNDED: 1969. ACREAGE: 4 acres. PRODUCTION: 10,000 cases. DISTRIBUTION: California and 26 other states. OWNERS: Gino Zepponi and Norman De Leuze. WINEMAKERS: Norman and Robert De Leuze. Tours, tasting, and sales by appointment.

Gino Zepponi, who works at Domaine Chandon, and Norman De Leuze have moved their winery from one county to another. They started in a small facility in the Sonoma Valley, buying grapes from nearby vineyards. In 1979 they built a new winery on the Silverado Trail in Napa.

WHITE

☆ 1980 CHARDONNAY ($12.95) Napa Valley. *Oily, vinous, somewhat dirty.*

☆☆ 1981 CHARDONNAY ($12.95) Napa Valley. *Fat, fruity, vinous, lacking finesse.*

☆☆ 1981 CHARDONNAY ($13.00) California. *Clean, earthy, full and rich.*

☆☆ 1982 CHARDONNAY ($14.00) California. *Big, heavy, fat.*

☆☆☆ 1983 GEWURZTRAMINER ($10.00) Select Late Harvest, Napa Valley. *375ml. 18% residual sugar. Rich, ripe, botrytized.*

RED

☆ 1979 CABERNET SAUVIGNON ($15.00) California. *24% Merlot, grapes from Napa and Santa Maria. Fat and clumsy.*

☆☆ 1980 CABERNET SAUVIGNON ($12.00) California. *Dense and raisiny but appealing.*

☆☆ 1980 CABERNET SAUVIGNON ($14.00) Napa Valley. *Toasty nose, deep, with complex flavors.*

☆☆ 1981 CABERNET SAUVIGNON ($10.00) Napa Valley. *Intense, heavy, deep. Drink 1989 and beyond.*

☆☆ 1981 CABERNET SAUVIGNON ($12.00) Napa Valley. *Rich, deep, heavy. Drink 1986.*

☆☆ 1979 MERLOT ($9.50) California (75% Napa, 25% Santa Barbara). *Big berry taste; crude, tannic, appealing.*

☆ 1980 PINOT NOIR ($12.00) Tepusquet, Santa Barbara.

☆☆ 1980 PINOT NOIR ($12.50) 66% Madonna, 33% Toribeth, Carneros, Napa. *Deep and rich. Good fruit and complexity.*

1981 PINOT NOIR ($12.00) Napa Valley-Carneros. *Dull, simple.*

☆   1979 ZINFANDEL ($7.50) Mt. Veeder area, Pickle Canyon, Napa Valley. *Tannic, lacking freshness.*

☆☆ 1980 ZINFANDEL ($7.50) Estate, Napa. *Raisiny and intense.*

Stephen Zellerbach Vineyard
SONOMA COUNTY

14350 Chalk Hill Road, Healdsburg, California 95448 (707-433-9463). FOUNDED: 1982. ACREAGE: 71 acres. PRODUCTION: 20,000 cases. DISTRIBUTION: 30 states. OWNER: Stephen Zellerbach. WINEMAKER: John Jaffray. Tours by appointment. Tasting and sales daily 10 A.M.– 5 P.M.

Stephen Zellerbach had a successful career in the family business, Zellerbach Paper Company, but what he really wanted was his own piece of land. The influence of his uncle James D. Zellerbach, ambassador to Rome and founder of Hanzell Vineyards (see), and teenage memories of working on a farm coaxed Stephen to sell his leasing company and buy a piece of vineyard land in the Alexander Valley. Planting began immediately. Professionals at U.C. Davis and six private consultants approved Stephen's decision to plant Cabernet Sauvignon and Merlot. The first Stephen Zellerbach wine was made from his own grapes at a rented winery facility. Recent vintages have been made at the new Zellerbach winery located at the vineyard site.

WHITE

1982 CHARDONNAY ($10.00) Warnecke Sonoma, Alexander Valley. *Thin and lacking freshness.*

☆☆☆ 1983 CHARDONNAY ($9.95) Alexander Valley. *Toasty, clean, fruity.*

RED

☆   1978 CABERNET SAUVIGNON ($8.50) Alexander Valley. *Decent, simple, attractive.*

☆   1979 CABERNET SAUVIGNON ($9.00) Alexander Valley.

☆☆ 1980 CABERNET SAUVIGNON ($8.00) Alexander Valley. *Rich, deep, clean, attractive. Drink now.*

☆☆ 1979 MERLOT ($9.00) Alexander Valley. *Herbal, complex, tannic. Drink 1988.*

☆☆ 1980 MERLOT ($10.00) Alexander Valley. *5% Cabernet Sauvignon. Fruity, oaky, ripe, attractive.*

☆☆☆ 1982 MERLOT ($8.50) Estate, Alexander Valley. *10% Cabernet Sauvignon. This winery's first estate wine is a real winner. Fruity, complex, rich, clean, lovely. Drink 1986.*

Ziem Vineyards
MARYLAND

Route 1, Fairplay, Maryland 21733 (301-223-8352). FOUNDED: 1977. ACREAGE: 6 acres. PRODUCTION: 840 cases. DISTRIBUTION: Maryland and Washington D.C. OWNERS: Robert W. and Ruth Ziem. WINEMAKER: Robert W. Ziem. Tours and tasting Monday–Friday 11 A.M.– dusk, Saturday 11 A.M.–dusk.

Since he started to make wine from grape concentrate, Robert Ziem has wanted to move to a farm, grow grapes, and start a small winery. He discovered the ideal place in Washington County— a farm with a 200-year-old stone house and an old bank barn surrounded by low, curving stone walls. Besides the charm of this picturesque farm, Robert was attracted by its loamy, well-drained soils. Working as an engineer for NASA and the U.S. Department of Defense, Robert has a long commute to Washington D.C. during the week, but the joys of farming and dreams of retirement make every mile a little easier.

Appendix

Good-Value Wines

WHITE

Non-varietal

☆☆ NV Almadén Vineyards *Mountain Rhine* ($2.88) California
☆☆ 1983 Almadén Vineyards CHARLES LEFRANC *Maison Blanc* ($3.40) San Benito
☆☆☆ 1982 Beaulieu Vineyard *Chablis* ($5.25) Estate, Napa Valley
☆☆ 1983 Beaulieu Vineyard *Hock* ($7.00) Napa Valley 1.5 liter
☆☆ 1983 Boeger Winery *Sierra Blanc* ($4.50) El Dorado
☆☆ 1981 Buena Vista Winery *Chablis* ($4.00) North Coast
☆☆ 1982 Buena Vista Winery *Spiceling* ($5.50) Sonoma Valley
☆☆☆ 1983 Buena Vista Winery *Spiceling* ($5.00) Estate, Sonoma Valley
☆☆☆ 1982 Davis Bynum Winery *Bellefleur* ($4.00) Sonoma
☆☆ 1984 Callaway Vineyards and Winery *Vin Blanc* ($4.75) California
☆☆ 1982 Château St. Jean *Vin Blanc* ($5.00) Sonoma
☆☆☆ 1983 Château St. Jean *Vin Blanc* ($5.25) Sonoma
☆☆ NV Château Ste. Michelle FARRON RIDGE CELLARS *White Table Wine* ($3.10) Washington
☆☆ 1982 Concannon Vineyard *Chablis* ($3.88) California
☆☆ 1983 Concannon Vineyard *Chablis* ($4.00) California
☆☆ 1983 Corbett Canyon Vineyards *Coastal Classic* ($4.50) California
☆☆☆ NV Fetzer Vineyards *Premium White* ($3.25) Mendocino
☆☆ NV Louis Foppiano Wine Company RIVERSIDE FARM *Medium Dry* ($2.50) California
☆☆ NV Louis Foppiano Wine Company RIVERSIDE FARM *Premium* ($3.90) California
☆☆☆ NV E. & J. Gallo Winery POLO BRINDISI *Bianco* ($2.50) California
☆ NV E. & J. Gallo Winery *Chablis Blanc* ($1.75) California
☆ NV E. & J. Gallo Winery CARLO ROSSI *Chablis* ($2.30) California
☆☆☆ NV E. & J. Gallo Winery *Reserve Chablis* ($2.60) California
☆☆ NV E. & J. Gallo Winery *Rhine Wine* ($1.75) California
☆☆ NV Geyser Peak Winery SUMMIT *Winterchill White* ($3.00) California
☆☆ 1982 Glen Ellen Winery *Proprietor's Reserve* ($3.50) Sonoma
☆☆ 1983 Grand Cru Vineyards *Vin Maison White* ($4.50) California
☆☆ 1983 Guenoc Winery *White Table Wine* ($4.25) Lake
☆☆ 1982 Haywood Winery *Estate White* ($5.75) Chamizal, Sonoma
☆☆ 1983 Hinman Vineyards *Tior* ($4.50) Washington
☆☆ 1982 Hop Kiln Winery *A Thousand Flowers* ($4.75) Russian River Valley
☆☆ 1982 Kenwood Vineyards *Vintage White* ($4.75) California
☆☆ 1983 Landmark Vineyards *Petit Blanc* ($5.00) Sonoma
☆ NV Paul Masson Vineyards *Rhine* ($2.50) California
☆☆ NV Paul Masson Vineyards *Light Rhine* ($3.50) California
☆☆☆ 1982 Paul Masson Vineyards *Emerald Dry* ($3.25) California
☆☆ 1983 Paul Masson Vineyards *Emerald Dry* ($3.25) California
☆ 1982 Mirassou Vineyards *Dry Chablis* ($3.95) Monterey
☆☆ 1982 Robert Mondavi Winery *Robert Mondavi White* ($3.50) California
☆☆☆ 1982 The Monterey Vineyards *Classic California White* ($4.00) California
☆☆ NV Monticello Cellars JEFFERSON CELLARS *Vin Blanc* ($4.95) Napa Valley
☆☆ 1982 Monticello Cellars *White Dinner Wine* ($5.50) Napa Valley
☆☆ 1983 Monticello Cellars CRANBROOK *Chevrier* ($5.75) Napa Valley
☆ 1982 Nervo Winery *Winterchill White* ($2.00) Sonoma
☆☆ NV Joseph Phelps Vineyards *Vin Blanc* ($4.75) Napa Valley
☆☆ 1984 Joseph Phelps Vineyards *Vin Blanc* ($4.75) Napa Valley
☆☆ 1983 Plane's Cayuga Vineyard *Duet* ($4.00) 50% Ravat, 50% Cayuga, Finger Lakes
☆☆ 1982 Quail Run Vintners *White Table Wine* ($4.00) Washington

WHITE/*Non-varietal*

☆☆ 1983 Quail Run Vintners *White Table Wine* ($4.00) Yakima Valley
☆☆ 1984 San Martin Winery *Rhine* ($3.95) California
☆☆ 1983 Sausal Winery *Sausal Blanc* ($4.00) Alexander Valley
☆☆ 1982 Souverain Cellars *Chablis* ($3.50) California
☆☆☆ 1982 Souverain Cellars *Colombard Blanc* ($4.00) North Coast
☆☆ 1982 Stag's Leap Wine Cellars *White Table Wine* ($4.85) Napa Valley
☆☆ NV Taft Street Winery *White House Wine* ($4.50) California
☆☆ NV Taylor Wine Company *Lake Country Chablis* ($3.00) New York State
☆☆ NV Tedeschi Vineyard and Winery *Maui Blanc* ($3.50) Maui, Hawaii
☆☆ 1982 Tepusquet *Vin Blanc* ($4.00) Estate, Santa Maria Valley
☆☆ NV Trefethen Vineyards Winery *Eschol White* ($5.25) Napa Valley
☆☆☆ NV Trefethen Vineyards Winery *Eschol White* ($5.25) 75% Chardonnay, Napa Valley
☆☆ NV Villa Mount Eden *Ranch White* ($3.95) Estate, Napa Valley

Chardonnay

☆☆ 1982 Burgess Cellars BELL CANYON CELLARS ($6.75) Sonoma
☆☆ 1983 Byrd Vineyards ($7.50) Estate, Catoctin, Maryland
☆☆ 1981 Château Bouchaine POPLAR ($7.50) Sonoma
☆☆☆ 1982 Château Bouchaine POPLAR ($7.50) Sonoma
☆☆ 1982 Clos du Bois Winery RIVER OAKS VINEYARDS ($6.25) Sonoma
☆☆ 1983 Clos du Bois Winery RIVER OAKS VINEYARDS ($6.00) Sonoma
☆☆ 1984 Clos du Bois Winery ($6.00) Alexander Valley
☆☆ 1984 Clos du Bois Winery RIVER OAKS VINEYARDS ($6.00) Alexander Valley
☆☆☆ 1983 Concannon Vineyard ($8.00) Selected Vineyards, 38% Mistral, 62% Tepusquet, California
☆☆ 1983 Conn Creek Winery CHATEAU MAJA ($5.00) Napa Valley
☆☆ 1984 Corbett Canyon Vineyards ($6.00) Coastal Classic, Central Coast
☆☆ 1982 Cosentino Wine Company CRYSTAL VALLEY CELLARS ($4.50) Deer Creek, California
☆☆ 1983 Cuvaison Vineyard CALISTOGA VINEYARDS ($7.00) Napa Valley
☆☆☆ 1982 Donna Maria Vineyards CHALK HILL ($6.00) Sonoma
☆☆ 1983 Donna Maria Vineyards CHALK HILL ($7.00) Sonoma
☆☆ NV Estrella River Winery ($4.70) San Luis Obispo
☆☆ 1983 Fetzer Vineyards ($6.50) Sundial, Mendocino
☆☆ 1984 Fetzer Vineyards ($6.50) Sundial, Mendocino
☆☆ 1983 Fisher Vineyards *Everyday Chardonnay* ($8.50) Sonoma
☆☆☆ 1984 Fisher Vineyards *Everyday Chardonnay* ($8.50) Sonoma
☆☆ NV E. & J. Gallo Winery ($4.00) California
☆☆ 1980 Geyser Peak Winery ($6.00) Sonoma
☆☆ NV Glen Ellen Winery ($4.50) Proprietor's Reserve, California
☆☆☆ 1982 Madrona Vineyards ($8.50) El Dorado
☆☆ 1980 Paul Masson Vineyards ($9.75) California. 1.5 liter
☆☆ 1981 Michtom Vineyards ($6.00) Alexander Valley
☆☆☆ 1983 Mirassou Vineyards ($8.00) Monterey
☆☆☆ 1983 Monticello Cellars CRANBROOK CELLARS ($8.00) Napa Valley
☆☆ 1981 The Mountain View Winery ($5.00) Sonoma
☆☆ 1982 The Mountain View Winery ($7.50) Special Selection, Napa Valley
☆☆ 1984 Orleans Hill Vinicultural Corporation ($6.75) Clarksburg
☆☆ 1983 Parducci Wine Cellars ($7.50) Mendocino
☆☆ 1981 J. Pedroncelli Winery ($7.50) Sonoma
☆☆ 1982 Roudon-Smith Vineyards ($6.00) Sequoia Coast, California
☆☆ NV Round Hill Cellars *House Chardonnay* ($4.65) Lot 4, California
☆☆ 1984 Round Hill Cellars ($4.65) California
☆ 1981 St. Andrews Winery *House Chardonnay* ($5.00) Napa Valley

☆☆ 1982 St. Andrews Winery *House Chardonnay* ($7.00) Edna Valley
☆☆ NV San Martin Winery ($7.00) California. 1.5 liter
☆☆ 1983 Stag's Leap Wine Cellars HAWK CREST ($6.00) "La Petite Faux Pas"
☆☆☆ 1981 Stags' Leap Winery PEDREGAL ($7.75) Napa Valley
☆☆ 1983 Stevenot Vineyards ($6.00) California
☆☆ 1984 Taft Street Winery ($6.00) Early Cuvée, California
☆ NV Taylor California Cellars ($3.50) California
☆☆☆ 1983 Toyon Vineyards ($8.50) Dry Creek Valley
☆☆☆ 1982 Tyland Vineyards ($8.75) Estate, Mendocino
☆☆☆ 1982 Valley View Vineyard ($7.50) Oregon
☆☆ 1982 Zaca Mesa Winery TOYON ($6.00) Santa Barbara
☆☆ 1983 Zaca Mesa Winery TOYON ($6.00) California

Chenin Blanc

☆☆☆ 1982 Alexander Valley Vineyards *Chenin Blanc Dry* ($6.00) Estate, Alexander Valley
☆☆ 1983 Beringer Vineyards ($4.75) Napa Valley
☆☆☆ 1983 Boeger Winery ($5.50) El Dorado
☆☆☆☆ 1982 Bogle Vineyards ($5.00) Dry, Clarksburg
☆☆☆ 1983 Cambiaso Vineyards ($4.00) Clarksburg
☆☆ NV The Christian Brothers ($4.50) Napa Valley
☆☆ NV Colony ($4.30) California
☆☆☆ 1984 Grand Cru Vineyards ($6.00) Dry, Perry Cook's Delta, Clarksburg
☆☆☆ 1982 Guenoc Winery ($5.00) Guenoc Valley
☆☆ 1983 Guenoc Winery ($5.00) Guenoc Valley
☆☆☆ 1983 The Hogue Cellars ($5.00) Yakima Valley
☆☆☆ 1982 Kenwood Vineyards ($6.00) California
☆☆☆ 1983 Kenwood Vineyards ($6.00) California
☆☆☆ 1984 Martin Brothers Winery *Dry Chenin Blanc* ($5.50) Smoot and Perata, Paso Robles
☆☆ 1982 Paul Masson Vineyards ($3.75) California
☆☆☆ 1982 Parducci Wine Cellars ($4.95) 50th Anniversary, Mendocino
☆☆☆ 1983 J. Pedroncelli Winery ($4.50) Sonoma
☆☆☆ 1983 Pellegrini Brothers Winery ($4.00) California
☆☆☆ 1984 The R. H. Phillips Vineyards ($5.25) Dry, Yolo
☆☆ 1983 Royal Kedem Wine Corporation ($3.50) Monterey
☆☆☆ 1984 Ste. Chapelle Winery *Soft Chenin Blanc* ($3.00) Washington
☆☆ NV San Martin Winery ($6.00) California. l.5 liter
☆☆☆ 1984 Turner Winery ($5.00) Lake
☆☆☆ 1982 Ventana Vineyards Winery DOUGLAS MEADOR ($5.50) Monterey
☆☆☆ 1984 Ventana Vineyards Winery ($5.50) Estate, Monterey
☆☆☆ 1983 Weibel Vineyards ($4.50) Mendocino
☆☆☆ 1983 Yakima River Winery ($5.50) Washington

French Colombard

☆☆ 1981 Clos du Bois Winery RIVER OAKS VINEYARDS ($4.50) Alexander Valley
☆☆ 1982 Georges Duboeuf & Son ($5.00) North Coast
☆☆☆ 1982 Fetzer Vineyards ($4.25) Mendocino
☆☆ NV E. & J. Gallo Winery ($2.30) California
☆☆ 1984 Olson Vineyards Winery ($4.00) Mendocino
☆☆ 1981 Parducci Wine Cellars ($4.60) Mendocino
☆☆☆ 1983 Robert Pecota Winery ($5.25) Napa Valley
☆☆ 1982 J. Pedroncelli Winery ($4.00) Sonoma
☆☆ 1983 Quail Ridge ($5.00) Napa Valley

WHITE/*French Colombard*

☆☆ 1981 Seghesio Winery ($3.00) Sonoma
☆☆ NV Souverain Cellars NORTH COAST CELLARS ($3.50) North Coast

Fume Blanc

☆☆ 1983 Château de Leu Winery ($3.50) Estate, Green Valley, Solano
☆☆ 1983 Château Julien ($5.75) Rancho Tierra Rejada, San Luis Obispo
☆☆ NV The Christian Brothers ($5.00) Cuvée 812, Napa Valley
☆☆☆ 1984 Fetzer Vineyards ($6.50) Valley Oaks Fume, California
☆☆☆ 1982 Konocti Winery ($5.50) Lake
☆☆☆ 1983 Konocti Winery ($5.50) Lake
☆☆ 1983 Monteviña Wines ($5.00) Estate, Shenandoah Valley, California
☆☆☆ 1982 Preston Vineyards ($6.50) Cuvée de Fumé, Estate, Dry Creek Valley
☆☆☆ 1983 Quail Run Vintners ($6.30) La Caille de Fumé, Yakima Valley
☆☆☆ NV Round Hill Cellars *House Fume Blanc* ($5.00) Mendocino
☆☆ NV San Martin Winery ($6.00) California. l.5 liter
☆ 1982 Sebastiani Vineyards COUNTRY ($7.00) California. 1.5 liter
☆☆☆ 1983 Sierra Vista Winery ($6.00) El Dorado
☆☆ 1982 Souverain Cellars ($6.00) North Coast
☆☆ 1982 Vose Vineyards ($5.75) Amador
☆☆ 1983 Worden's Washington Winery ($6.00) Washington

Gewürztraminer

☆☆ 1982 Davis Bynum Winery ($5.00) Sonoma
☆☆☆ 1983 Dry Creek Vineyard ($4.50) Larson, Sonoma
☆☆ NV E. & J. Gallo Winery ($2.60) California
☆☆ 1981 Guild Wineries CRESTA BLANCA ($5.00) Santa Maria
☆☆☆ 1983 Monticello Cellars CRANBROOK CELLARS ($5.50) Napa Valley
☆☆☆ 1981 J. Pedroncelli Winery ($5.00) Sonoma
☆☆ 1984 Round Hill Cellars ($5.00) Napa Valley
☆☆☆ 1978 Rutherford Hill Winery ($5.00) Napa Valley
☆☆☆ 1982 Rutherford Hill Winery ($5.75) Napa Valley
☆☆☆ 1984 St. Francis Vineyards ($6.00) Sonoma Valley
☆☆☆ 1982 Souverain Cellars ($5.00) North Coast

Green Hungarian

☆☆ NV Weibel Vineyards ($4.50) California

Grey Riesling

☆☆ 1984 Robert Pecota Winery ($4.75) Napa Valley

Johannisberg Riesling

☆☆ 1983 Acacia Winery CAVISTE ($4.00) Napa Valley
☆☆ 1981 Almadén Vineyards ($5.35) San Benito
☆☆☆ 1983 Durney Vineyard ($6.50) Estate, Carmel Valley
☆☆☆ 1983 Kenwood Vineyards ($8.50) Late Harvest, Estate, Sonoma Valley
☆☆ 1983 Konocti Winery ($5.00) Lake
☆☆ 1983 Franz Wilhelm Langguth Winery SADDLE MOUNTAIN ($4.00) Washington
☆☆ 1982 J. Pedroncelli Winery ($5.75) Sonoma
☆☆☆ 1983 J. Pedroncelli Winery ($5.25) Sonoma
☆☆☆☆ 1982 Quail Run Vintners ($6.00) Washington
☆☆☆ 1984 St. Francis Vineyards ($6.00) Estate, Sonoma Valley
☆☆ NV San Martin Winery ($6.00) California. l.5 liter
☆☆ 1984 San Martin Winery *Soft Johannisberg Riesling* ($4.00) Central Coast
☆☆☆ 1984 Santa Barbara Winery ($6.50) Santa Barbara

☆☆☆ 1983 Santa Ynez Valley Winery ($6.00) Santa Ynez Valley
☆☆☆ 1983 Weibel Vineyards ($5.00) Mendocino
☆☆☆ 1982 Zaca Mesa Winery ($6.50) Santa Barbara County

Melon

☆☆☆ 1982 Beaulieu Vineyard ($8.50) Estate, Napa Valley

Muscat

☆☆ 1983 Stewart Vineyards ($5.00) Estate, Columbia Valley
☆☆ 1982 Sutter Home Winery *Muscat Amabile* ($4.50) California

Pinot Blanc

☆☆ 1983 The Monterey Vineyards ($4.00) Monterey
☆☆☆ 1984 Roudon-Smith Vineyards ($6.50) Santa Maria Valley

Ravat

☆☆☆ 1982 Good Harbor Vineyards *Ravat Vignoles* ($6.00) Leelanau Peninsula, Michigan
☆☆☆ 1982 L. Mawby Vineyards *Ravat Vignoles* ($6.25) Lot FR, Leelanau Peninsula, Michigan

Riesling

☆☆ NV Almadén Vineyards ($3.75) California
☆☆ 1982 Château Bouchaine POPLAR ($4.75) Sonoma
☆☆☆ 1983 Elk Cove Vineyards ($5.40) Willamette Valley, Oregon
☆☆ 1983 Gundlach-Bundschu Winery *Dresel's Sonoma Riesling* ($4.95) Sonoma Valley
☆☆ 1983 Paul Masson Vineyards ($3.75) California

Sauvignon Blanc

☆☆☆☆ 1982 Boeger Winery ($6.00) 10th Anniversary, El Dorado
☆☆ 1982 California Wine Company BANDIERA ($4.50) Mendocino
☆☆☆ 1984 Caymus Vineyards LIBERTY SCHOOL ($5.00) Lot 1, Napa Valley
☆☆☆ 1983 Donna Maria Vineyards CHALK HILL ($6.00) Sonoma
☆☆ 1983 J. Patrick Dore Selections, San Luis Obispo
☆☆ NV E. & J. Gallo Winery ($2.60) California
☆☆ 1984 Orleans Hill Vinicultural Corporation ($5.00) Reiff, Yolo
☆☆☆ 1983 J. Pedroncelli Winery ($6.00) Sonoma
☆☆ 1983 Preston Wine Cellars COLUMBIA RIVER ($4.25) Washington
☆☆ NV Round Hill Cellars ($4.65) House Sauvignon Blanc, Lot 4, North Coast

Semillon

☆☆☆ 1983 Alderbrook Winery ($6.00) Sonoma
☆☆☆ 1982 Château Ste. Michelle *Semillon Blanc* ($5.00) Washington
☆☆ 1984 Valley of the Moon ($4.00) Estate, Sonoma Valley
☆☆ 1981 Wente Brothers ($4.92) Estate, Livermore Valley

Seyval Blanc

☆☆ 1982 Wagner Vineyards ($5.50) Estate, Finger Lakes Region

White Riesling

☆☆☆ 1984 Callaway Vineyards and Winery ($5.50) Temecula
☆☆ 1982 The Hogue Cellars ($4.75) Schwartzman, Yakima Valley
☆☆☆ 1983 The Hogue Cellars ($5.50) Washington State
☆☆☆ 1983 The Hogue Cellars ($6.00) Schwartzman, Yakima Valley
☆☆ 1982 Konocti Winery ($4.00) Lake

WHITE/*White Riesling*

☆☆☆ 1982 Quail Run Vintners ($5.00) Mahre, Yakima Valley
☆☆☆ 1984 Ventana Vineyards ($6.00) Estate, Monterey

SPARKLING

Non-varietal

☆ NV The Christian Brothers *Rosé Champagne* ($1.75) California
☆☆ NV Cosentino Wine Company CRYSTAL VALLEY CELLARS *Extra Dry* ($6.50) California
☆☆ NV Cosentino Wine Company CRYSTAL VALLEY CELLARS *Spumante* ($5.75) California
☆☆ NV E. & J. Gallo Winery *Dry Champagne* ($3.75) California
☆☆ NV E. & J. Gallo Winery ANDRE *Pink Champagne* ($4.00) California
☆☆☆ NV E. & J. Gallo Winery BALLATORE *Spumante* ($4.50) California
☆☆ NV Guild Wineries CRIBARI *Extra Dry* ($3.75) California
☆ NV Guild Wineries CRIBARI *Spumante* ($3.50) California
☆☆ NV Stony Ridge Winery *Blanc de Noir* ($6.25) Cuvée 1, California
☆☆ NV Weibel Vineyards STANFORD *Blanc de Noir* ($3.50) California
☆☆ NV Weibel Vineyards LAFAYETTE *Pink Champagne* ($3.00) California
☆☆☆ 1981 Wente Brothers *Brut* ($8.95) Monterey

Green Hungarian

☆☆ Weibel Vineyards *Sparkling Green Hungarian* ($6.00) California

BLANC DE NOIR

Cabernet Sauvignon

☆☆ 1984 Beringer Vineyards LOS HERMANOS *White Cabernet* ($2.00) California
☆☆ 1982 Konocti Winery *Cabernet Sauvignon Blanc* ($4.50) Lake
☆☆☆ 1984 Sterling Vineyards *Cabernet Blanc* ($6.00) Napa Valley

Gamay

☆☆ NV Caymus Vineyards LIBERTY SCHOOL *Gamay Blanc* ($4.00) Napa Valley
☆☆☆ 1983 Markham Winery *Gamay Blanc* ($5.25) Estate, Napa Valley
☆☆☆ 1984 Olson Vineyards Winery *Gamay Blanc* ($4.00) Napa, Mendocino

Merlot

☆☆☆ 1983 The Brander Vineyard ST. CARL *Merlot Blanc* ($4.75) Santa Ynez Valley

Pinot Noir

☆☆☆ 1984 Buena Vista Winery *Blanc de Pinot Noir* ($5.50) Sonoma Valley-Carneros
☆☆☆ 1982 Geyser Peak Winery *Pinot Noir Blanc* ($5.00) Kiser Ranch, Sonoma Valley
☆☆ 1983 La Crema Vinera *Vin Gris de Pinot Noir* ($5.00) Carneros, Sonoma
☆☆☆ 1983 Mark West Vineyards *Pinot Noir Blanc* ($5.75) Estate, Russian River Valley
☆☆ 1981 Valley of the Moon *Pinot Noir Blanc* ($4.25) Sonoma Valley

Zinfandel

☆☆ 1984 Almadén Vineyards CHARLES LEFRANC *White Zinfandel* ($4.50) California
☆☆☆ 1982 Amador City Winery *White Zinfandel* ($5.00) Amador
☆☆☆ 1984 Amador Foothill Winery *White Zinfandel* ($5.25) Amador
☆☆ 1984 Braren Pauli Winery *White Zinfandel* ($4.50) Mendocino
☆☆☆ 1983 Buehler Vineyards *White Zinfandel* ($5.50) Estate, Napa Valley
☆☆ 1984 Buehler Vineyards *White Zinfandel* ($5.50) Estate, Napa Valley

☆☆☆ 1984 California Wine Company BANDIERA *White Zinfandel* ($4.25) Sonoma
☆☆ 1984 Corbett Canyon Vineyards *White Zinfandel* ($5.00) Central Coast
☆☆☆ 1982 De Loach Vineyards *White Zinfandel* ($5.75) Sonoma
☆☆☆ 1983 De Loach Vineyards *White Zinfandel* ($5.75) Russian River Valley, Sonoma
☆☆☆ 1984 De Loach Vineyards *White Zinfandel* ($5.75) Sonoma
☆☆ NV Estrella River Winery *White Zinfandel* ($3.62) San Luis Obispo
☆☆ NV Estrella River Winery *White Zinfandel* ($3.75) Estate, Paso Robles
☆☆☆ 1984 Fetzer Vineyards BEL ARBRES *White Zinfandel* ($4.50) Mendocino
☆☆ 1984 Louis Foppiano Wine Company RIVERSIDE FARM *White Zinfandel* ($3.75) California
☆ 1984 Guild Wineries CRIBARI *White Zinfandel* ($2.50) California
☆☆ 1984 Paul Masson Vineyards *White Zinfandel* ($3.25) California
☆☆☆ 1984 McDowell Valley Vineyards *Zinfandel Blanc* ($5.00) Estate, McDowell Valley
☆☆☆ 1984 Monterey Vineyards *White Zinfandel* ($4.50) Monterey
☆☆☆ 1983 Monteviña Wines *White Zinfandel* ($4.75) Amador
☆☆☆ 1984 Olson Vineyards Winery *White Zinfandel* ($4.50) Mendocino
☆☆☆ 1984 Orleans Hill Vinicultural Corporation *White Zinfandel* ($4.50) Reiff, Yolo
☆☆☆ 1984 Vose Vineyards *Zinblanca* ($4.75) California
☆☆☆ 1984 Whaler Vineyards *White Zinfandel* ($5.25) Mendocino

ROSE

Non-varietal

☆☆ 1983 Beaulieu Vineyard *Beaurosé* ($5.00) Estate, Napa Valley
☆☆ NV Crown Regal Wine Cellars KESSER *Kosher Concord* ($3.00) New York State
☆☆ 1982 Field Stone Winery *Spring-Cabernet* ($5.00) Sonoma
☆☆ 1983 Field Stone Winery *Spring-Cabernet* ($5.25) Alexander Valley
☆☆ NV Louis Foppiano Wine Company RIVERSIDE FARM *Dry Rosé* ($2.75) California
☆☆ NV E. & J. Gallo Winery *Pink Chablis* ($1.75) California
☆ NV E. & J. Gallo Winery CARLO ROSSI *Pink Chablis* ($2.30) California
☆☆ NV E. & J. Gallo Winery CARLO ROSSI *Vin Rosé* ($2.30) California
☆☆ 1984 Robert Mondavi Winery ($3.75) California
☆☆ 1983 The Monterey Vineyards *Classic California Rosé* ($4.00) Monterey
☆☆☆ 1982 Sokol Blosser Winery *Bouquet Rosé* ($4.50) American
☆☆ NV Souverain Cellars NORTH COAST CELLARS ($2.50) North Coast
☆☆ 1983 Wente Brothers *Rosé Wente* ($3.50) California

Cabernet Sauvignon

☆☆ 1983 The Firestone Vineyard *Rosé of Cabernet Sauvignon* ($4.50) Santa Ynez Valley
☆☆☆ 1982 Simi Winery *Rosé of Cabernet* ($5.25) Sonoma
☆☆☆ 1982 Sonoma Vineyards ($6.00) Mendocino

Gamay

☆ 1982 Guild Wineries CRESTA BLANCA ($3.30) Mendocino

Gewürztraminer

☆☆ 1983 Giumarra Vineyards *Blush of Gewürztraminer* ($4.25) California
☆☆☆ 1982 Sebastiani Vineyards *Rosa Gewürztraminer* ($4.85) Sonoma Valley

Merlot

☆☆ 1983 Kiona Vineyards and Winery *Merlot Rosé* ($4.70) Estate, Yakima Valley

Petite Sirah

☆☆☆ 1982 Field Stone Winery ($6.00) Estate, Alexander Valley

Pinot Noir

☆☆ 1982 Souverain Cellars ($4.50) North Coast

Zinfandel

☆☆ 1981 Greenstone Winery ($3.25) Amador
☆☆☆ 1982 J. Pedroncelli Winery ($4.00) Sonoma
☆☆☆ 1983 J. Pedroncelli Winery ($4.00) Sonoma

RED

Non-varietal

☆☆ NV Almadén Vineyards *Monterey Burgundy* ($3.52) Monterey
☆   1983 Almadén Vineyards CHARLES LEFRANC *Maison Rouge* ($3.00) San Benito
☆☆ 1980 Baldinelli Vineyards *Red Table Wine* ($3.80) Estate, Shenandoah Valley
☆☆ 1981 Boeger Winery *Hangtown Red* ($3.95) California
☆☆ 1979 Buena Vista Winery *Burgundy* ($4.00) Sonoma Valley
☆☆☆ 1984 Buena Vista Winery *Pinot Jolie* ($5.50) Sonoma Valley
☆☆ NV California Wine Company BANDIERA *Dry Red* ($3.73) North Coast
☆☆ NV Casa Nuestra *Tinto* ($5.00) Napa Valley
☆☆ NV Cilurzo Vineyard and Winery *Vincheno* ($4.00)
☆☆ NV Clos du Bois Winery *Red Wine—Vin Rouge* ($4.35) Sonoma
☆☆ NV Clos du Bois Winery RIVER OAKS VINEYARDS *Premium Red* ($4.00) Sonoma
☆☆☆ 1977 Clos du Bois Winery RIVER OAKS VINEYARDS *Premium Red* ($3.25) Alexander
          Valley
☆☆ NV Clos du Val *Red Table Wine* ($4.50) Napa Valley
☆   NV Crown Regal Wine Cellars KESSER *Kosher Mellow* ($3.00) New York State
☆☆ NV Delicato Vineyards *Burgundy* ($2.40) Northern California
☆   NV Fetzer Vineyards *Premium Red* ($3.25) Mendocino
☆☆ NV Louis Foppiano Wine Company RIVERSIDE FARM *Premium Red* ($2.75) California
☆☆ NV E. & J. Gallo Winery *Hearty Burgundy* ($1.75) California
☆   NV E. & J. Gallo Winery BOONE'S FARM *Wild Mountain* ($1.30) California
☆☆ NV Geyser Peak Winery SUMMIT *Burgundy* ($4.00) California
☆☆ NV Glen Ellen Winery *Proprietor's Reserve Red* ($3.50) California
☆☆ 1981 Glen Ellen Winery *Proprietor's Reserve Red* ($3.50) Sonoma
☆☆ 1981 Guenoc Winery *Red Table Wine* ($4.25) Lake
☆☆☆ NV Gundlach-Bundschu Winery *Sonoma Red Wine* ($3.90) Sonoma Valley
☆   NV Haywood Winery *Spaghetti Red* ($4.25) Sonoma Valley
☆☆☆ 1981 HMR Estate Winery SANTA LUCIA CELLARS ($2.95) San Luis Obispo
☆☆☆ 1981 Hop Kiln Winery *Marty Griffin's Big Red* ($6.00) Russian River Valley
☆☆ NV Hopkins Vineyard *Sachem's Picnic Red* ($5.00) American
☆☆ 1983 Ingleside Plantation Winery *Nouveau Red* ($4.00) Virginia
☆☆ NV Paul Masson Vineyards *Premium Burgundy* ($3.25) California
☆☆ 1983 Robert Mondavi Winery *Red Table Wine* ($3.75) California
☆☆ 1979 The Monterey Vineyards *Classic California Red* ($4.00) Central Coast Counties
☆☆ 1980 The Monterey Vineyards *Classic California Red* ($4.00) California
☆☆ NV Monteviña Wines *Premium Red* ($3.75) Amador
☆☆ NV Monticello Cellars JEFFERSON CELLARS *Claret* ($4.95) Napa Valley
☆☆ 1983 Monticello Cellars JEFFERSON CELLARS *Claret* ($4.95) Napa Valley
☆☆ 1984 Orleans Hill Vinicultural Corporation *Red Table Wine* ($4.00) California
☆☆ NV Joseph Phelps Vineyards *Vin Rouge* ($4.75) California
☆☆ 1982 Joseph Phelps Vineyards *Claret* ($6.00) Napa Valley
☆☆☆ 1982 Rosenblum Cellars *Rosenblum Red* ($4.00) Napa Valley
☆☆ NV Roudon-Smith Vineyards *Claret* ($3.50)
☆☆ NV St. Francis Vineyards *Sonoma Valley Red* ($3.50) Sonoma Valley
☆☆☆ 1975 Seghesio Winery *Marian's Reserve* ($4.50) Sonoma
☆☆ NV Taft Street Winery *Red House Wine* ($4.50) California
☆☆ NV Taylor California Cellars *Burgundy* ($3.30) California
☆☆ NV Trefethen Vineyards Winery *Eschol Red—Blend 283* ($4.25) Napa Valley
☆☆ 1982 Tyland Vineyards TIJSSELING *Dry Red Table Wine* ($4.00) Estate, Mendocino

Baco Noir

☆☆ 1982 Taylor Wine Company GREAT WESTERN ($4.20) Estate, Finger Lakes Region

Cabernet Sauvignon

☆☆ 1977 Almadén Vineyards ($4.50) Monterey
☆☆☆ 1981 Almadén Vineyards ($4.00) Monterey

☆☆☆ 1981 Almadén Vineyards CHARLES LEFRANC ($8.50) Monterey
☆☆☆ 1979 Baldinelli Vineyards ($7.00) Estate, Amador
☆ 1981 Belvedere Wine Company WINE DISCOVERY ($3.75) Napa Valley
☆☆ 1982 Belvedere Wine Company ($4.00) Discovery Series, Lake
☆☆ NV Beringer Vineyards LOS HERMANOS ($2.00) California
☆☆ 1981 Beringer Vineyards ($7.00) Napa Valley
☆☆☆ 1981 California Wine Company JOHN B. MERRITT ($8.00) Sonoma
☆☆ 1981 Cambiaso Vineyards ($4.75) Dry Creek Valley
☆☆ 1982 Caymus Vineyards LIBERTY SCHOOL ($6.00) Lot 11, Alexander Valley
☆☆☆ 1979 Clos du Bois Winery RIVER OAKS VINEYARDS ($5.95) Alexander Valley
☆☆☆ 1981 Clos du Bois Winery RIVER OAKS VINEYARDS ($6.25) Healdsburg Area, Sonoma
☆☆☆ 1982 Clos du Bois Winery ($6.00) Alexander Valley
☆☆ 1982 Clos du Bois Winery RIVER OAKS VINEYARDS ($6.50) Sonoma
☆ NV Colony ($2.98) California
☆☆ 1980 Devlin Wine Cellars ($6.00) Sonoma
☆☆☆ 1981 Donna Maria Vineyards CHALK HILL ($8.00) Sonoma
☆☆ 1981 Edmeades Vineyards ($7.50) Anderson Valley
☆☆ 1981 Edna Valley Vineyard GAVILAN ($6.75) Sonoma
☆☆ 1981 Fetzer Vineyards ($5.50) Lake
☆☆ 1982 Fetzer Vineyards ($7.00) Barrel Select, Mendocino
☆☆ 1980 Louis Foppiano Wine Company ($6.50) Sonoma
☆☆ 1981 Louis Foppiano Wine Company RIVERSIDE FARM ($3.75) 50% Sonoma, 50% Lake
☆☆☆ 1981 Louis Foppiano Wine Company ($7.75) Russian River Valley
☆☆☆ 1980 Franciscan Vineyards ($7.50) Alexander Valley
☆☆☆ 1981 Fritz Cellars ($7.00) North Coast
☆☆ 1982 Glen Ellen Winery ($4.00) Proprietor's Reserve, Sonoma
☆☆☆ 1980 Guenoc Winery ($8.00) 70% Lake, 30% Napa
☆☆☆ 1981 Guenoc Winery ($8.00) Lake
☆☆ 1977 Guild Wineries CRESTA BLANCA ($5.00) Mendocino
☆☆ 1978 Guild Wineries CRESTA BLANCA ($5.00) Mendocino
☆☆ 1978 Inglenook Vineyards ($6.00) Napa Valley
☆☆☆ 1979 Inglenook Vineyards ($7.00) Centennial, Napa
☆☆ 1979 Konocti Winery ($6.00) Estate, Lake
☆☆ 1979 Konocti Winery ($6.00) Lot II, Lake
☆☆ 1980 Konocti Winery ($6.50) Lake
☆☆ 1979 Charles Krug Winery ($6.50) Napa Valley
☆☆ 1982 Charles Krug Winery C. K. MONDAVI ($7.00) California
☆☆☆ 1978 Landmark Vineyards ($7.00) 75% Sonoma, 25% Napa
☆☆☆ 1980 Landmark Vineyards ($8.50) Estate, Alexander Valley
☆☆ NV J. Lohr Winery ($5.75) California
☆☆ 1982 Paul Masson Vineyards ($6.20) Sonoma County
☆☆ 1978 Michtom Vineyards ($6.00) Alexander Valley
☆☆ 1982 R. Montali and Associates SONOMA MISSION WINERY ($5.00) Paso Robles
☆☆ 1981 Monteviña Wines ($7.50) Shenandoah Valley, California
☆☆☆ 1981 J. W. Morris Wineries ($7.50) Alexander Valley
☆☆☆ 1981 J. W. Morris Wineries ($8.00) California Selection
☆☆ 1980 The Mountain View Winery ($5.00) North Coast
☆☆ 1981 The Mountain View Winery ($7.50) Special Selection, Napa Valley
☆☆ 1980 Pellegrini Brothers Winery ($7.50) Russian River Valley
☆☆☆ 1981 Richardson Vineyards ($7.50) Sonoma Valley
☆☆ 1978 Rosenblum Cellars ($4.50) Hoffman Ranch, Geyserville, Sonoma
☆☆ NV Round Hill Cellars *House Cabernet Sauvignon* ($4.65) Lot 4, North Coast
☆☆ NV San Martin Winery ($6.00) California. 1.5 liter

RED/*Cabernet Sauvignon*

☆ 1979 San Martin Winery ($6.80) San Luis Obispo
☆☆ 1979 Sebastiani Vineyards ($5.00) North Coast
☆☆ 1981 Sebastiani Vineyards ($5.00) Sonoma
☆☆ 1981 Sierra Vista Winery ($7.75) Estate, El Dorado
☆☆☆ 1979 Sotoyome Winery ($5.75) Dry Creek Valley
☆☆ 1980 Sotoyome Winery ($5.75) Dry Creek Valley
☆ NV Souverain Cellars NORTH COAST CELLARS ($3.50) North Coast
☆☆☆ 1979 Souverain Cellars ($7.75) North Coast
☆☆ NV Stag's Leap Wine Cellars HAWK CREST ($5.50) Napa Valley
☆☆ 1981 Stag's Leap Wine Cellars HAWK CREST ($4.95) Mendocino
☆☆☆☆ 1980 Stonegate Winery ($8.50) Vail Vista, Alexander Valley
☆☆☆ 1975 Stony Ridge Winery ($4.00) North Coast
☆ 1981 Vina Vista Vineyards ($6.00) Napa Valley
☆☆ 1978 Woodside Vineyards ($7.50) Fay, Stag's Leap Area, Napa Valley
☆☆ 1978 Yverdon ($8.00) Napa Valley
☆☆☆ 1979 Zaca Mesa Winery ($8.00) Santa Ynez Valley

Charbono

☆☆ 1984 Franciscan Vineyards ($6.00) Harvest Nouveau, Napa Valley

DeChaunac

☆☆ NV Crown Regal Wine Cellars ($5.00) Finger Lakes Region

Gamay

☆☆☆ 1983 Duxoup Wine Works *Napa Gamay* ($6.00) Sonoma
☆☆ 1984 Fetzer Vineyards ($4.00) Nouveau, Mendocino
☆☆☆ 1984 J. Lohr *Monterey Gamay* ($4.50) Greenfield, Monterey
☆☆ 1982 Olson Vineyards Winery ($4.50) Mendocino
☆☆ 1982 Rosenblum Cellars ($5.00) Napa
☆☆ 1984 San Pasqual Vineyards ($5.00) California
☆☆ 1984 Sebastiani Vineyards ($5.00) Nouveau, Sonoma
☆☆ 1982 Charles F. Shaw Vineyard ($4.00) Domaine Elucia, Napa Valley
☆☆ 1984 Charles F. Shaw Vineyard *Gamay Nouveau* ($4.50) Napa Valley
☆☆☆ 1980 Trentadue Winery ($5.00) Alexander Valley

Gamay Beaujolais

☆☆ 1983 Fetzer Vineyards ($4.25) Mendocino
☆☆☆ 1982 Mill Creek Vineyards ($5.00) Sonoma
☆☆ 1983 Robert Pecota Winery ($5.50) Nouveau, Napa Valley
☆☆☆ 1984 Robert Pecota Winery ($5.50) Nouveau, Napa Valley
☆☆☆ 1983 Preston Vineyards ($5.00) Dry Creek Valley
☆☆ 1984 Preston Vineyards ($5.00) Estate, Dry Creek Valley

Merlot

☆☆☆ 1981 Clos du Bois Winery ($8.50) Alexander Valley
☆☆ 1981 Crescini Wines ($6.50) Napa Valley
☆ 1980 J. Patrick Dore Selections ($4.00) Napa Valley
☆☆ NV Geyser Peak Winery SUMMIT ($3.50) Sonoma
☆☆☆ 1980 Mill Creek Vineyards ($8.50) Estate, Sonoma
☆☆ 1979 Souverain Cellars ($5.50) North Coast
☆☆☆ 1982 Stephen Zellerbach Vineyard ($8.50) Estate, Alexander Valley

Petite Sirah

☆☆ 1982 Fetzer Vineyards ($5.50) Mendocino
☆☆ 1979 Louis Foppiano Wine Company ($5.50) Sonoma

☆☆☆ 1981 Guenoc Winery ($6.50) Lake
☆☆☆ 1981 Inglenook Vineyards ($6.00) Napa Valley
 ☆☆ 1980 R. Montali and Associates SONOMA MISSION WINERY ($4.50) California
☆☆☆ 1980 Rosenblum Cellars ($5.50) St. George & Rich Vineyards, Napa Valley
☆☆☆ 1980 Round Hill Cellars ($6.00) Napa Valley
 ☆☆ 1982 Warnelius Winery ($4.50) Sonoma
 ☆☆ 1978 Wente Brothers ($6.25) Centennial Reserve, Estate, Livermore Valley

Pinot Noir

 ☆☆ 1980 Burgess Cellars ($6.00) Napa Valley
☆☆☆ 1981 Caymus Vineyards ($7.50) Estate, Napa Valley
 ☆☆ 1979 Clos du Bois Winery ($6.00) Dry Creek
 ☆☆ 1980 Clos du Bois Winery ($6.50) Alexander Valley
 ☆☆ 1981 Donna Maria Vineyards ($6.00) Chalk Hill, Estate, Sonoma
☆☆☆ 1979 Felton-Empire Vineyards ($7.50) Maritime Series, Reserve, Chaparral, San Luis
        Obispo
 ☆☆ 1981 Felton-Empire Vineyards ($7.50) Fort Ross, Sonoma
☆☆☆ 1979 Fritz Cellars ($6.50) Sonoma
 ☆☆ 1983 Hacienda del Rio Winery ($7.00) Sonoma
 ☆☆ 1982 HMR Estate Winery ($4.50) Paso Robles
 ☆☆ 1982 HMR Estate Winery SANTA LUCIA CELLARS ($4.50) Paso Robles
 ☆☆ 1980 Inglenook Vineyards ($6.00) Napa Valley
 ☆☆ NV Kistler Vineyards MEAREN LAKE ($7.50) Carneros District, Napa Valley
☆☆☆ 1976 Louis M. Martini ($4.00) California
 ☆☆ 1979 Louis M. Martini ($3.40) Napa Valley
 ☆☆ 1981 Louis M. Martini ($5.57) La Loma and Las Amigas, Napa Valley
 ☆☆ 1981 J. Pedroncelli Winery ($5.00) Sonoma
 ☆☆ 1979 Round Hill Cellars ($6.00) Gamay Acres, Napa Valley
 ☆☆ 1981 Sebastiani Vineyards ($6.00) Sonoma
☆☆☆ 1982 Ventana Vineyards ($6.25) Estate, Monterey
 ☆☆ 1981 Villa Mt. Eden Winery ($5.00) Estate, Tres Ninos, Napa Valley
☆☆☆ 1979 Winters Winery ($6.00) Napa Valley

Syrah

☆☆☆ 1980 McDowell Valley Vineyards ($7.50) Estate, McDowell Valley
☆☆☆ 1983 Qupe ($7.50) Central Coast

Zinfandel

 ☆☆ 1979 Almadén Vineyards ($3.75) 34% Monterey, 64% San Benito
 ☆☆ 1980 Argonaut Winery ($3.00) Calaveras
 ☆☆ 1980 Argonaut Winery ($5.00) Amador
 ☆☆ 1982 Buehler Vineyards ($6.00) Estate, Napa Valley
 ☆☆ 1981 Buena Vista Winery ($6.00) Sonoma
☆☆☆ 1980 California Wine Company BANDIERA ($4.25) North Coast
☆☆☆ 1979 Carmel Bay Winery ($5.00) Shandon Valley, San Luis Obispo
☆☆☆ 1980 Carneros Creek Winery ($6.00) Yolo
☆☆☆ 1980 Chispa Cellars ($6.00) Amador
 ☆☆ NV Colony ($3.00) Classic, California
 ☆☆ 1982 Colony ($5.00) Sonoma
☆☆☆ 1982 Cordtz Brothers Cellars ($6.00) Upper Alexander Valley
☆☆☆ NV Estrella River Winery ($3.50) San Luis Obispo
 ☆☆ 1979 Estrella River Winery ($4.70) Estate, San Luis Obispo
 ☆☆ 1979 Fetzer Vineyards ($5.50) Mendocino
☆☆☆ 1980 Fetzer Vineyards ($3.00) Lake
 ☆☆ 1982 Fetzer Vineyards ($5.50) Mendocino

RED/*Zinfandel*

☆☆☆ 1980 Louis Foppiano Wine Company RIVERSIDE FARM ($3.10) California
 ☆☆   1982 Louis Foppiano Wine Company RIVERSIDE FARM ($3.70) Sonoma
☆☆☆ 1981 Frog's Leap Winery ($6.50) Spottswoode, Napa Valley
☆☆☆ 1982 Glen Ellen Winery BENZIGER FAMILY WINERY & VINEYARDS ($4.50) Gey-
              serville, Sonoma
☆☆☆ 1981 Green and Red Vineyards ($5.75) Estate, Napa Valley
  ☆   1980 Guild Wineries CRESTA BLANCA ($4.00) Mendocino
 ☆☆   1978 HMR Estate Winery ($3.50) Sauret, Paso Robles
 ☆☆   1981 Konocti Winery ($4.75) Lake
 ☆☆   1979 Charles Krug Winery ($4.80) Napa
☆☆☆ 1980 Lake Sonoma Winery DIABLO VISTA ($6.90) Polson, Dry Creek Valley, Sonoma
 ☆☆   NV Lytton Springs Winery ($5.00) Wineburger, Sonoma
☆☆☆ 1980 Madrona Vineyards ($6.00) Estate, El Dorado
☆☆☆ 1983 Martin Brothers Winery ($6.00) Paso Robles
 ☆☆   1980 Louis M. Martini ($4.45) North Coast
 ☆☆   1981 Louis M. Martini ($4.90) North Coast
☆☆☆ 1979 Paul Masson Vineyards ($3.75) California
☆☆☆ 1981 McLester Winery ($6.00) Radike, San Luis Obispo
 ☆☆   1980 Mirassou Vineyards ($5.00) Monterey
 ☆☆   1982 R. Montali and Associates LOMBARD HILL CELLARS ($4.50) Amador
☆☆☆ 1981 Montclair Winery ($6.50) Teldeschi, Sonoma
☆☆☆ 1978 Monterey Peninsula Winery ($6.50) 29% Amador, 45% Templeton, 20% Paso Ro-
              bles, California
☆☆☆ 1981 Monteviña Wines ($5.00) Montino, Estate, Shenandoah Valley, California
 ☆☆   NV Monticello Cellars CRANBROOK CELLARS ($4.95) Napa Valley
 ☆☆   1983 Monticello Cellars CRANBROOK CELLARS *Premier* ($4.95) Napa Valley
☆☆☆ 1982 Moon Vineyards ($4.00) Estate, Napa Valley-Carneros
 ☆☆   1982 Nevada City Winery *Zinfandel-Merlot* ($5.00) California
 ☆☆   1980 J. Pedroncelli Winery ($4.50) Sonoma
☆☆☆ 1981 Joseph Phelps Vineyards ($6.75) Alexander Valley
 ☆☆   1982 Joseph Phelps Vineyards ($5.75) Napa Valley
☆☆☆ 1984 Joseph Phelps Vineyards ($5.75) Napa Valley
☆☆☆ 1980 Ridge Vineyards ($7.50) Esola, Shenandoah Valley, Amador
☆☆☆ 1981 Rosenblum Cellars ($6.00) Mauritson, Sonoma Valley
☆☆☆ 1981 Rosenblum Cellars ($6.00) Napa Valley
 ☆☆   1979 Round Hill Cellars ($5.00) Napa Valley
☆☆☆ 1979 Round Hill Cellars RUTHERFORD RANCH BRAND ($5.00) Napa
 ☆☆   1980 Round Hill Cellars ($4.50) Napa
 ☆☆   1981 Round Hill Cellars ($5.00) Napa Valley
 ☆☆   1982 Round Hill Cellars ($5.00) Napa Valley
 ☆☆   NV San Martin Winery ($6.00) California. 1.5 liter
 ☆☆   1979 Sebastiani Vineyards ($4.00) California
 ☆☆   1975 Seghesio Winery ($5.00) Estate, Sonoma
 ☆☆   NV Sierra Vista Winery ($4.00) El Dorado
 ☆☆   1979 Sierra Vista Winery ($5.00) El Dorado
 ☆☆   1979 Silver Mountain Vineyards ($6.00) 40% Ventana, 60% Butte County, California
 ☆☆   1980 Simi Winery ($6.25) Alexander Valley
 ☆☆   1979 Sotoyome Winery ($4.75) Sonoma
 ☆☆   1980 Souverain Cellars ($5.00) North Coast
☆☆☆ NV Story Vineyards ($4.50) California
 ☆☆   1980 Story Vineyards ($6.00) Estate, Amador
☆☆☆ 1980 Susine Cellars ($5.00) Amador
 ☆☆   NV Taylor California Cellars ($4.30) California

☆☆☆   1980 Tulocay Winery ($6.50) Napa Valley
☆☆   1981 Whaler Vineyards ($5.25) Mendocino

FORTIFIED

Non-varietal

☆☆   Brotherhood Winery *Fino Sherry* ($7.00) New York State
☆☆☆   Ficklin Vineyards *Port* ($6.00) California
☆   E. & J. Gallo Winery *Cocktail Pale Dry Sherry* ($1.50) California
☆☆   E. & J. Gallo Winery *Cream Sherry* ($1.50) California
☆   E. & J. Gallo Winery *Sherry* ($1.50) California
☆☆   E. & J. Gallo Winery LIVINGSTON CELLARS *Cream Sherry* ($2.00) California
☆☆   E. & J. Gallo Winery LIVINGSTON CELLARS *Very Dry Sherry* ($2.00) California
☆   E. & J. Gallo Winery *Thunderbird* ($2.00) California

Cabernet Sauvignon

☆☆   Beringer Vineyards *Cabernet Sauvignon Port* ($6.00) Estate, Napa Valley

FLAVORED

Non-varietal

☆☆   California Cooler—Citrus ($.75) California. 12 oz.
☆☆   California Cooler—Orange ($.75) California. 12 oz.
☆☆   Canandaigua Wine Company SUN COUNTRY COOLER—Orange ($.75) American. 12 oz.
☆☆   Canandaigua Wine Company SUN COUNTRY COOLER—Tropical Fruit ($.75) American. 12 oz.
☆☆   E. & J. Gallo Winery *Tyrolia* ($1.50) California

Three-Star Wines

WHITE

Non-varietal

1982 Beaulieu Vineyard *Chablis* ($5.25) Estate, Napa Valley
1983 Bonny Doon Vineyard *Vin de Paille* ($12.00) Central Coast
1983 Buena Vista Winery *Spiceling* ($5.00) Estate, Sonoma Valley
1982 Davis Bynum Winery *Bellefleur* ($4.00) Sonoma
1982 Château St. Jean *Sauvignon d'Or* ($15.00) Sonoma
1983 Château St. Jean *Vin Blanc* ($5.25) Sonoma
NV Fetzer Vineyards *Premium White* ($3.25) Mendocino
NV E. & J. Gallo Winery POLO BRINDISI *Bianco* ($2.50) California
NV E. & J. Gallo Winery *Reserve Chablis* ($2.60) California
1982 Lyeth Vineyard and Winery *White Table Wine* ($9.00) Alexander Valley
1982 Paul Masson Vineyards *Emerald Dry* ($3.25) California
1982 The Monterey Vineyards *Classic California White* ($4.00) California
1982 Souverain Cellars *Colombard Blanc* ($4.00) North Coast
NV Trefethen Vineyards Winery *Eschol White* ($5.25) Napa Valley

Chardonnay

1979 Acacia Winery ($14.00) Winery Lake, Napa Valley-Carneros
1980 Acacia Winery ($12.50) Napa Valley
1980 Acacia Winery ($17.50) Winery Lake, Napa Valley-Carneros
1981 Acacia Winery ($14.00) Napa Valley-Carneros
1981 Acacia Winery ($17.50) Winery Lake, Napa Valley-Carneros
1982 Acacia Winery ($12.50) Napa Valley
1982 Acacia Winery ($16.00) Marina, Napa Valley-Carneros
1982 Acacia Winery ($17.50) Winery Lake, Napa Valley-Carneros
1983 Acacia Winery ($12.50) Napa Valley
1983 Acacia Winery ($14.00) Napa Valley-Carneros
1983 Acacia Winery ($15.00) Marina, Napa Valley-Carneros
1983 Acacia Winery ($17.50) Winery Lake, Napa Valley-Carneros
1984 Acacia Winery ($15.00) Marina, Napa Valley-Carneros
1981 Ahern Winery ($11.00) MacGregor, San Luis Obispo
1982 Ahern Winery ($12.00) Paragon, San Luis Obispo
1983 Alderbrook Winery ($8.75) Sonoma
1975 Alexander Valley Vineyards, Alexander Valley
1982 Alexander Valley Vineyards ($10.00) Estate, Alexander Valley
1983 Alexander Valley Vineyards ($10.00) Estate, Alexander Valley
1981 S. Anderson Vineyard ($12.50) Estate, Napa Valley
1982 S. Anderson Vineyard ($12.50) Napa Valley
1982 Arbor Crest ($10.00) Sagemoor, Washington
1982 Artisan Wines MICHAEL'S ($15.00) Napa Valley
1983 Au Bon Climat ($10.00) Los Alamos, Santa Barbara
1983 Au Bon Climat ($10.00) Santa Barbara
1981 Balverne Winery & Vineyards ($13.00) Deerfield, Sonoma
1982 Balverne Winery & Vineyards ($12.00) Deerfield, Sonoma
1982 Bay Cellars ($12.00) Tepusquet, Santa Maria
1982 Beaulieu Vineyard ($14.00) Los Carneros Region, Napa Valley
1983 Belvedere Wine Company BACIGALUPI ($12.00) Sonoma
1983 Belvedere Wine Company WINERY LAKE ($12.00) Napa Valley
1979 Beringer Vineyards ($11.00) Gamble Ranch, Napa Valley
1980 Beringer Vineyards ($11.50) Gamble Ranch, Napa Valley

1980 Beringer Vineyards ($13.50) Private Reserve, Estate, Napa Valley
1981 Beringer Vineyards ($13.00) Private Reserve, Napa Valley
1982 Beringer Vineyards ($9.75) Estate, Napa Valley
1983 Beringer Vineyards ($12.00) Gamble Ranch, Napa Valley
1982 Boeger Winery ($9.00) El Dorado
1983 Bonny Doon Vineyard ($12.00) La Reina, Monterey
1981 David Bruce Winery ($18.00) Estate, Santa Cruz Mountains
1980 Buena Vista Winery ($15.00) Special Selection, Sonoma Valley
1981 Burgess Cellars ($12.75) Napa Valley
1982 Burgess Cellars ($11.75) Vintage Reserve, Napa Valley
1983 Burgess Cellars ($12.00) Vintage Reserve, Napa Valley
1981 Davis Bynum Winery ($10.00) Allen-Hafner Reserve, Allen, Alexander Valley
1983 Davis Bynum Winery ($12.50) Allen-Hafner Reserve, Sonoma
1981 Cache Cellars ($11.00) Ventana, Monterey
1983 Cache Cellars ($11.00) La Reina, Monterey
1981 Cain Cellars ($9.00) Napa Valley
1982 Cakebread Cellars ($13.75) Napa Valley
1982 Callaway Vineyards and Winery ($8.50) Temecula
1982 J. Carey Cellars ($9.50) Estate, Santa Ynez Valley
1983 J. Carey Cellars ($10.50) Santa Barbara
1980 Caymus Vineyards ($12.00) Napa Valley
1982 Cedar Hill Wine Company CHATEAU LAGNIAPPE ($12.00) Lake Erie
1983 Chalone Vineyard ($18.75) Estate, Monterey
1982 Château Bouchaine POPLAR ($7.50) Sonoma
1982 Château Bouchaine ($12.50) Alexander Valley
1982 Château Bouchaine ($14.00) 50% Keith, 50% Black Mountain, Alexander Valley
1982 Château Chevalier Winery ($12.50) Edna Valley
1982 Château du Lac ($9.50) Clear Lake
1982 Château Julien ($17.00) Private Reserve, Monterey
1981 Château Montelena Winery ($14.00) Alexander Valley
1981 Château Montelena Winery ($16.00) Napa Valley
1982 Château Montelena Winery ($14.00) Alexander Valley
1982 Château Montelena Winery ($16.00) Estate, Napa Valley
1983 Château Montelena Winery ($14.00) Alexander Valley
1980 Château St. Jean ($14.00) Jimtown Ranch, Alexander Valley
1980 Château St. Jean ($18.00) Robert Young, Alexander Valley
1981 Château St. Jean ($13.50) Frank Johnson, Sonoma
1981 Château St. Jean ($14.00) McCrea Vineyards, Sonoma Valley
1981 Château St. Jean ($14.75) Hunter Ranch, Sonoma Valley
1981 Château St. Jean ($14.75) Jimtown Ranch, Alexander Valley
1982 Château St. Jean ($18.00) Robert Young, Alexander Valley
1983 Château St. Jean ($16.00) Jimtown Ranch, Alexander Valley
1983 Château St. Jean ($16.75) Belle Terre, Alexander Valley
1983 Château St. Jean ($18.00) Robert Young, Alexander Valley
1980 Clos du Bois Winery ($21.00) Flintwood, Dry Creek Valley
1981 Clos du Bois Winery ($9.75) Alexander Valley
1981 Clos du Bois Winery ($12.00) Calcaire, Alexander Valley
1981 Clos du Bois Winery ($21.00) Flintwood, Dry Creek Valley
1982 Clos du Bois Winery ($9.00) Barrel Fermented, Alexander Valley
1982 Clos du Bois Winery ($11.25) Calcaire, Alexander Valley
1981 Clos du Val ($12.50) Napa Valley
1983 Concannon Vineyard ($8.00) Selected Vineyards, 38% Mistral, 62% Tepusquet, California
1982 Congress Springs Vineyard ($10.00) Santa Clara
1982 Congress Springs Vineyard ($20.00) Private Reserve, Monmartre, Santa Cruz

WHITE/*Chardonnay*
1983 Congress Springs Vineyard ($11.50) Santa Clara
1982 Cronin Vineyards ($12.00) Alexander Valley, Sonoma
1982 Cronin Vineyards ($12.00) Ventana, Monterey
1982 Cronin Vineyards ($14.00) Napa Valley
1980 Cuvaison Vineyard ($12.50) Napa Valley
1981 Cuvaison Vineyard ($12.00) Napa Valley
1982 Cuvaison Vineyard ($12.50) Napa Valley
1980 De Loach Vineyards ($10.00) Russian River Valley
1981 De Loach Vineyards ($12.00) Russian River Valley-Sonoma
1982 De Loach Vineyards ($12.00) Russian River Valley
1983 De Loach Vineyards ($12.50) Sonoma
1982 Deer Park Winery ($9.50) Napa Valley
1980 Dolan Vineyards ($10.00) Mendocino
1982 Domaine Laurier ($15.00) Sonoma
1983 Domaine Laurier ($13.00) Sonoma
1981 Donna Maria Vineyards ($10.00) Sonoma
1982 Donna Maria Vineyards CHALK HILL ($6.00) Sonoma
1982 Donna Maria Vineyards ($10.00) Estate, Sonoma
1982 Dry Creek Vineyard ($10.00) Sonoma
1983 Dry Creek Vineyard ($10.00) Sonoma
1981 Eberle Winery ($10.00) Paso Robles
1980 Edmeades Vineyards ($12.50) Reserve, Mendocino
1981 Edmeades Vineyards ($12.50) Reserve Bottling, Anderson Valley, Mendocino
1982 Edmeades Vineyards ($8.00) Anderson Valley
1981 Edna Valley Vineyard ($12.00) Estate, San Luis Obispo
1980 Estrella River Winery ($12.00) Star Reserve, San Luis Obispo
1981 Fairmont Cellars ($12.00) Sonoma
1981 Far Niente Winery ($18.00) Estate, Napa Valley
1982 Far Niente Winery ($20.00) Estate, Napa Valley
1981 Fetzer Vineyards ($10.00) Special Reserve, California
1982 Fetzer Vineyards ($8.50) Barrel Select, Mendocino
1983 Fetzer Vineyards ($10.00) Special Reserve, California
1980 Fisher Vineyards ($14.00) Sonoma
1981 Fisher Vineyards ($14.00) Sonoma
1982 Fisher Vineyards ($14.00) Sonoma
1983 Fisher Vineyards ($14.00) Napa-Sonoma
1983 Fisher Vineyards ($14.00) 65% Sonoma, 35% Napa
1984 Fisher Vineyards *Everyday Chardonnay* ($8.50) Sonoma
1980 Flora Springs Wine Company ($16.00) Special Select, Napa Valley
1981 Flora Springs Wine Company ($13.50) Barrel Fermented, Napa Valley
1982 Flora Springs Wine Company ($12.00) Napa Valley
1981 Thomas Fogarty Winery ($12.50) Ventana, Monterey
1982 Franciscan Vineyards ($10.50) Vintner Grown, Alexander Valley
1982 Franciscan Vineyards ($12.00) Carneros Reserve, Napa Valley
1982 Franciscan Vineyards ($12.00) Reserve, Oakville Estate, Napa Valley
1980 Freemark Abbey Winery ($13.50) Napa Valley
1983 Freemark Abbey Winery ($14.00) Napa Valley
1981 Fritz Cellars ($9.00) Fritz, Dry Creek Valley
1981 Fritz Cellars ($10.00) Gauer Ranch, Alexander Valley
1982 Frog's Leap Winery ($11.00) Napa Valley
1980 Girard Winery ($11.00) Napa Valley
1981 Girard Winery ($12.50) Napa Valley
1982 Girard Winery ($12.50) Estate, Napa Valley
1978 Grgich Hills Cellars ($18.00) Napa Valley

1979 Grgich Hills Cellars ($16.00) Napa Valley
1980 Grgich Hills Cellars ($17.00) Napa Valley
1982 Grgich Hills Cellars ($17.00) Napa Valley
1982 Grgich Hills Cellars ($18.00) Napa Valley (A later release)
1982 Groth Vineyards and Winery ($12.50) Napa Valley
1981 Gundlach-Bundschu Winery ($10.00) Sangiacomo, Sonoma
1981 Gundlach-Bundschu Winery ($12.00) 125th Anniversary, Sangiacomo Ranch, Sonoma Valley
1983 Hacienda Wine Cellars ($9.00) Clair de Lune, Sonoma
1982 Hafner Vineyard ($12.00) Estate, Alexander Valley
1980 Harbor Winery ($8.50) Reserve, Napa Valley
1982 Hargrave Vineyard ($12.00) Collector Series, Estate, Long Island
1983 Haywood Winery ($11.00) Sonoma Valley
1980 William Hill Winery ($16.50) Napa Valley
1982 William Hill Winery ($25.00) Reserve, Napa Valley
1979 HMR Estate Winery ($15.00) Estate, Paso Robles
1982 Husch Vineyards ($9.00) La Ribera Ranch, Mendocino
1984 Iron Horse Vineyards ($12.00) Estate, Green Valley, Sonoma
1980 Jekel Vineyard ($10.00) Monterey
1981 Jekel Vineyard ($10.00) Monterey
1981 Jekel Vineyard ($14.50) Private Reserve, Estate, Monterey
1982 Jordan Vineyard and Winery ($15.75) Alexander Valley
1982 Kalin Cellars ($15.00) Cuvée D, Dutton Ranch, Sonoma
1982 Kalin Cellars ($16.00) Cuvée L, Sonoma
1983 Karly Wines ($12.00) Tepusquet, Santa Maria Valley
1982 Kenwood Vineyards ($11.00) Sonoma Valley
1982 Kistler Vineyards ($12.50) Sonoma-Cutrer, California
1982 Kistler Vineyards ($15.00) Dutton Ranch, Sonoma
1983 Kistler Vineyards ($9.75) Sonoma Valley
1983 Kistler Vineyards ($12.00) Napa Valley
1983 Kistler Vineyards ($14.00) Winery Lake, California
1983 Kistler Vineyards ($15.00) Dutton Ranch, Sonoma
1981 La Crema Vinera ($14.50) Ventana, Monterey
1982 La Crema Vinera ($14.50) Dutton, Sonoma-Green Valley
1981 Lakespring Winery ($10.00) Napa
1982 Lambert Bridge ($13.00) Sonoma
1982 Landmark Vineyards ($9.50) Sonoma
1983 Landmark Vineyards ($9.00) Proprietor Grown, Sonoma Valley
1981 Leeward Winery ($14.00) MacGregor, San Luis Obispo
1981 Leeward Winery ($15.00) Ventana, Monterey
1982 Leeward Winery ($12.00) Bien Nacido, Santa Maria Valley
1982 Leeward Winery ($14.00) Central Coast
1983 Leeward Winery ($14.00) MacGregor, Edna Valley
1980 Long Vineyards ($24.00) Napa Valley
1982 Long Vineyards ($24.00) Napa Valley
1981 Los Vineros Winery ($9.00) Santa Barbara
1982 Madrona Vineyards, Château d'Or, Select Harvest, Estate, El Dorado
1982 Madrona Vineyards ($8.50) El Dorado
1981 Manzanita ($14.00) Napa Valley
1982 Manzanita ($14.00) Napa Valley
1980 Mark West Vineyards ($10.00) Wasson Ranch, Alexander Valley
1981 Markham Winery ($11.00) Napa Valley
1982 Markham Winery ($10.35) Napa Valley
1982 Markham Winery ($12.00) Markham Estate, Napa Valley
1978 Markko Vineyard, Reserve, Ohio

WHITE/*Chardonnay*

1982 Markko Vineyard ($9.00) Ohio
1982 Martin Brothers Winery ($10.00) Edna Valley
1975 Mayacamas Vineyards, Napa Valley
1981 Mayacamas Vineyards ($16.00) California
1982 Milano Winery ($12.00) Oakgrove, Sonoma
1983 Mirassou Vineyards ($8.00) Monterey
1980 Robert Mondavi Winery ($20.00) Reserve, Napa Valley
1982 Robert Mondavi Winery ($14.00) Napa Valley
1982 Robert Mondavi Winery ($20.00) Reserve, Napa Valley
1984 R. Montali and Associates ($10.00) Hopkins River, Sonoma
1981 Monticello Cellars ($11.00) Napa Valley
1982 Monticello Cellars ($13.50) Napa Valley
1982 Monticello Cellars ($14.00) Barrel Fermented, Estate, Napa Valley
1983 Monticello Cellars CRANBROOK CELLARS ($8.00) Napa Valley
1983 Morgan Winery ($12.50) Monterey
1973 Mount Eden Vineyards ($16.00) Estate, Santa Cruz Mountains
1979 Mount Eden Vineyards, Estate, Santa Cruz Mountains
1982 Mount Eden Vineyards ($18.00) Santa Cruz Mountains
1983 Mount Veeder Winery ($13.50) Napa
1981 Mountain House Winery ($9.90) Sonoma
1983 The Mountain View Winery ($12.00) Dutton Ranch, Sonoma
1981 Navarro Vineyards and Winery ($8.75) Mendocino
1981 Navarro Vineyards and Winery ($11.60) Premiere Reserve, Mendocino
1981 Newlan Vineyards and Winery ($11.00) Saunders, Napa Valley
1980 Newton Winery ($16.00) Napa Valley
1981 Newton Winery ($16.00) Napa Valley
1982 Newton Winery ($16.00) Napa Valley
1981 Obester Winery ($12.00) Potter Valley, Mendocino
1983 Robert Pecota Winery ($13.50) Canepa, Alexander Valley
1981 Pendleton Winery ($12.50) Private Reserve, Monterey
1980 Perret Vineyards ($13.50) Estate, Napa Valley-Carneros District
1981 Perret Vineyards ($13.50) Estate, Napa Valley-Carneros District
1982 Perret Vineyards ($14.50) Estate, Napa Valley-Carneros
1983 Perret Vineyards ($13.50) Estate, Carneros-Napa Valley
1981 Joseph Phelps Vineyards ($12.75) Schellville, Sonoma
1981 Joseph Phelps Vineyards ($16.00) Sangiacomo, Napa
1982 Joseph Phelps Vineyards ($14.00) Sangiacomo, Sonoma
1983 Joseph Phelps Vineyards ($12.50) Napa Valley
1982 Pine Ridge Winery ($15.00) Oak Knoll District-Napa Valley
1982 Pine Ridge Winery ($16.00) Stag's Leap Cuvée, Napa Valley
1983 Pine Ridge Winery ($13.00) Oak Knoll Cuvée, Napa Valley
1982 Plane's Cayuga Vineyard ($9.50) Finger Lakes
1981 Quail Ridge ($16.00) Napa Valley
1982 Quail Ridge ($9.00) Sonoma
1981 Martin Ray Vineyards ($16.00) Winery Lake, Carneros District-Napa
1981 Martin Ray Vineyards ($18.00) Dutton, Sonoma
1982 Martin Ray Vineyards ($15.00) Santa Cruz Mountains
1982 Rombauer Vineyards ($12.50) St. Andrews, Napa Valley
1983 Rombauer Vineyards ($13.50) Napa Valley
1980 Roudon-Smith Vineyards ($11.00) Wasson, Sonoma
1981 Roudon-Smith Vineyards ($12.00) 10th Anniversary, Edna Valley
1982 Round Hill Cellars ($9.00) Napa Valley
1980 Rutherford Hill Winery ($16.00) Cellar Reserve, Jaeger, Napa Valley
1982 Rutherford Hill Winery ($10.00) Jaeger, Napa Valley

1983 Rutherford Hill Winery ($10.75) Jaeger, Napa Valley
1981 St. Andrews Winery ($12.50) Napa Valley
1982 St. Andrews Winery ($12.50) Napa Valley
1983 St. Andrews Winery ($12.50) Napa Valley
1982 St. Clement Vineyards ($14.50) Napa Valley
1983 St. Clement Vineyards ($14.50) Napa Valley
1980 Ste. Chapelle Winery ($10.50) Symms Family, Washington
1983 St. Francis Vineyards ($10.75) Estate, Sonoma Valley
1983 St. Francis Vineyards ($14.00) Estate, Sonoma Valley
1981 Saintsbury Winery ($10.00) Sonoma
1983 Saintsbury Winery ($11.00) Napa Valley
1981 Saintsbury Winery ($10.00) Sonoma
1981 Sanford Winery ($12.00) Santa Maria Valley
1982 Sanford Winery ($12.00) Santa Maria Valley
1981 Sarah's Vineyard ($14.00) Paragon, Edna Valley
1982 Sarah's Vineyard ($14.00) Monterey
1982 Sarah's Vineyard ($16.00) Ventana, Monterey
1983 Sarah's Vineyard ($16.00) Ventana, Monterey
1983 Sarah's Vineyard ($17.00) Estate, Santa Clara
1983 Sea Ridge Winery ($10.00) Mill Station, Sonoma
1982 Thomas Sellards Winery ($10.50) Sonoma
1982 Sequoia Grove Vineyards ($12.00) Estate, Napa Valley
1981 Shafer Vineyards ($11.00) Napa Valley
1982 Shafer Vineyard Cellars ($10.50) Willamette Valley, Oregon
1983 Charles F. Shaw Vineyard ($12.50) Napa Valley
1982 Silver Mountain Vineyards ($11.00) Ventana, Monterey
1981 Silverado Vineyards ($10.00) Estate, Napa Valley
1982 Silverado Vineyards ($10.00) Estate, Napa Valley
1983 Silverado Vineyards ($10.00) Napa Valley
1980 Simi Winery ($9.00) Mendocino
1981 Simi Winery ($11.00) Mendocino
1981 Simi Winery ($20.00) Reserve, Sonoma County
1982 Simi Winery ($11.00) Sonoma
1983 Simi Winery ($12.00) Mendocino 59%, Sonoma 41%
1982 Smothers-Vine Hill Wines ($12.50) Remick Ridge Ranch, Sonoma
1981 Sokol Blosser Winery ($9.95) Yamhill County, Oregon
1981 Sonoma-Cutrer Vineyards ($9.50) Estate, Russian River Valley
1981 Sonoma-Cutrer Vineyards ($12.75) Cutrer, Russian River Valley
1982 Sonoma-Cutrer Vineyards ($15.50) Les Pierres, Sonoma Valley
1981 Sonoma Vineyards ($10.00) River West, Sonoma
1981 Spring Mountain Vineyards ($12.50) Napa Valley
1981 Stag's Leap Wine Cellars ($13.50) Napa Valley
1981 Stags' Leap Winery PEDREGAL ($7.75) Napa Valley
1982 P and M Staiger ($10.00) Estate, Santa Cruz Mountains
1982 Sterling Vineyards ($14.00) Estate, Napa Valley
1981 Stevenot Vineyards ($8.50) Sonoma
1983 Stevenot Vineyards ($11.00) Estate, Calaveras
1981 Stonegate Winery ($9.00) 85% Keith Ranch, Alexander Valley, Sonoma
1981 Stonegate Winery ($10.25) Sonoma
1982 Tudal Winery ($9.00) Edna Valley
1981 Tyland Vineyards TIJSSELING ($11.75) Mendocino
1982 Tyland Vineyards ($8.75) Estate, Mendocino
1982 Valfleur Winery ($10.00) Alexander Valley
1982 Valley View Vineyard ($7.50) Oregon

WHITE/*Chardonnay*

1979 Ventana Vineyards Winery ($9.00) Monterey
1981 Vichon Winery ($15.00) Napa Valley
1983 Vichon Winery ($15.00) Napa Valley
1981 William Wheeler Winery ($10.00) Monterey
1982 William Wheeler Winery ($10.00) Monterey
1982 William Wheeler Winery ($11.00) Sonoma
1983 William Wheeler Winery ($10.00) Monterey
1983 William Wheeler Winery ($11.00) Sonoma
1982 White Oak Vineyards ($10.00) Sonoma
1981 Whitehall Lane Winery ($11.00) Napa Valley
1982 Woodside Vineyards ($11.50) Ventana, Monterey
1981 Woodward Canyon Winery ($10.00) Washington
1981 Zaca Mesa Winery ($11.00) American Estate, Chapel, Santa Ynez Valley
1982 Zaca Mesa Winery ($10.00) Santa Barbara
1983 Stephen Zellerbach Vineyard ($9.95) Alexander Valley

Chenin Blanc

1982 Alexander Valley Vineyards *Chenin Blanc Dry* ($6.00) Estate, Alexander Valley
1983 Alexander Valley Vineyards ($6.00) Estate, Alexander Valley
1983 Boeger Winery ($5.50) El Dorado
1983 Bogle Vineyards ($4.50) Clarksburg
1983 Cambiaso Vineyards ($4.00) Clarksburg
1982 Casa Nuestra ($5.75) Napa Valley
1981 Cassayre-Forni Cellars ($6.00) Napa Valley
1983 Chappellet Winery ($7.50) Napa Valley
1981 Château Ste. Michelle ($5.50) Washington
1982 Château Ste. Michelle ($5.50) Washington
1984 Dry Creek Vineyard ($6.00) Sonoma
1982 Grand Cru Vineyards ($6.75) Clarksburg
1983 Grand Cru Vineyards ($6.50) Perry Cook, Clarksburg
1984 Grand Cru Vineyards ($6.00) Dry, Perry Cook's Delta, Clarksburg
1982 Guenoc Winery ($5.00) Guenoc Valley
1982 Hacienda Wine Cellars ($5.50) Dry, Estate, Sonoma
1982 HMR Estate Winery ($6.25) Paso Robles
1983 The Hogue Cellars ($5.00) Yakima Valley
1984 Husch Vineyards ($6.00) La Ribera, Estate, Mendocino
1982 Kenwood Vineyards ($6.00) California
1983 Kenwood Vineyards ($6.00) California
1983 Latah Creek Winery ($5.00) Washington
1982 J. Lohr Winery ($6.25) Rosebud, Sacramento
1984 Martin Brothers Winery *Dry Chenin Blanc* ($5.50) Smoot and Perata, Paso Robles
1984 Messina Hof Wine Cellars ($6.00) Texas
1981 Robert Mondavi Winery ($7.00) Napa Valley
1982 Robert Mondavi Winery ($7.75) Napa Valley
1982 Parducci Wine Cellars ($4.95) 50th Anniversary, Mendocino
1983 J. Pedroncelli Winery ($4.50) Sonoma
1983 Pellegrini Brothers Winery ($4.00) California
1984 The R. H. Phillips Vineyards ($5.25) Dry, Yolo
1982 Pine Ridge Winery ($6.50) Napa Valley
1983 Pine Ridge Winery ($6.50) Yountville
1984 Pine Ridge Winery ($6.75) Yountville Cuvée, Napa Valley
1982 Preston Vineyards ($6.00) Estate, Dry Creek Valley
1984 Preston Vineyards ($6.00) Dry, Estate, Dry Creek Valley
1981 Sage Canyon Winery ($6.75) Napa Valley
1984 Ste. Chapelle Winery *Soft Chenin Blanc* ($3.00) Washington

1983 Serendipity Cellars Winery ($7.25) 68% Bethel Heights, 32% McCorquodale, Oregon
1982 Simi Winery ($6.25) 53% Sonoma, 47% Mendocino, North Coast
1983 Simi Winery ($6.50) Mendocino
1984 Simi Winery ($6.50) Mendocino
1982 Stevenot Vineyards ($5.00) El Dorado
1984 Turner Winery ($5.00) Lake
1982 Ventana Vineyards Winery DOUGLAS MEADOR ($5.50) Monterey
1982 Ventana Vineyards Winery ($6.00) Monterey
1984 Ventana Vineyards Winery ($5.50) Mendocino
1983 Weibel Vineyards ($4.50) Mendocino
1982 White Oak Vineyards ($5.00) Alexander Valley
1983 Yakima River Winery ($5.50) Washington

French Colombard

1982 Fetzer Vineyards ($4.25) Mendocino
1983 Robert Pecota Winery ($5.25) Napa Valley

Fume Blanc

1983 Adler Fels Winery ($8.50) Salzgeber-Chan, Sonoma
1983 Beringer Vineyards ($7.50) Sonoma
1983 Beringer Vineyards ($12.00) Reserve, Sonoma
1982 Davis Bynum Winery ($8.00) Rochioli-Harrison Reserve, Sonoma
1982 Carneros Creek Winery ($7.50) Napa Valley
1981 Caymus Vineyards ($8.50) Napa Valley
1980 Château St. Jean ($9.00) La Petite Etoile, Sonoma
1982 Château St. Jean ($9.50) St. Jean, Sonoma
1982 Château St. Jean ($9.75) Sonoma
1983 Château St. Jean ($9.50) Murphy Ranch, Alexander Valley
1983 Château St. Jean ($10.00) St. Jean, Sonoma Valley
1981 De Loach Vineyards ($8.50) Alexander Valley
1982 De Loach Vineyards ($8.50) Sonoma
1983 De Loach Vineyards ($9.00) Russian River Valley, Sonoma
1982 Dry Creek Vineyard ($8.50) Sonoma
1984 Fetzer Vineyards ($6.50) Valley Oaks Fume, California
1984 Glen Ellen Winery ($7.50) Sonoma Valley
1981 Grgich Hills Cellars ($9.00) Napa Valley
1982 Grgich Hills Cellars ($9.00) Napa
1983 Grgich Hills Cellars ($9.50) Napa Valley
1983 The Hogue Cellars ($7.50) Yakima Valley, Washington
1983 Iron Horse Vineyards ($8.75) Alexander Valley
1982 Konocti Winery ($5.50) Lake
1983 Konocti Winery ($5.50) Lake
1983 McDowell Valley Vineyards ($7.50) Estate, McDowell Valley
1974 Robert Mondavi Winery, Reserve, Napa Valley
1981 Robert Mondavi Winery ($9.00) Napa
1981 Robert Mondavi Winery ($13.00) Reserve, Napa Valley
1982 Robert Mondavi Winery ($9.00) Napa Valley
1982 Robert Mondavi Winery ($15.00) Reserve, Napa Valley
1983 Robert Mondavi Winery ($9.00) Napa Valley
1984 Robert Mondavi Winery ($7.00) Napa Valley
1982 Preston Vineyards ($6.50) Cuvée de Fumé, Estate, Dry Creek Valley
1983 Quail Run Vintners ($6.30) La Caille de Fumé, Yakima Valley
1983 Raymond Vineyard & Cellar ($7.50) Napa Valley
NV   Round Hill Cellars *House Fume Blanc* ($5.00) Mendocino

WHITE/*Fume Blanc*

1982 Charles F. Shaw Vineyard ($8.00) Flora Springs, Napa Valley
1983 Sierra Vista Winery ($6.00) El Dorado

Gewürztraminer

1983 Alexander Valley Vineyards ($6.50) Estate, Alexander Valley
1982 Almadén Vineyards ($5.85) San Benito
1982 Austin Cellars ($8.00) Bien Nacido, Santa Barbara
1984 Belvedere Wine Company WINERY LAKE ($6.50) Napa Valley
1981 Château St. Jean ($7.50) Belle Terre, Sonoma
1981 Château St. Jean ($7.75) Robert Young, Alexander Valley
1982 Château St. Jean ($8.00) Frank Johnson, Alexander Valley
1983 Château St. Jean ($8.00) Frank Johnson, Alexander Valley
1983 Château St. Jean ($14.00) Select Late Harvest, Robert Young, Alexander Valley
1984 Château St. Jean ($8.00) Alexander Valley
1984 Château St. Jean ($8.00) Frank Johnson, Sonoma
1983 Claiborne & Churchill Vintners ($8.50) Edna Valley
1983 Clos du Bois Winery ($7.50) Early Harvest, Alexander Valley
1983 Costello Vineyards ($10.75) Select Late Harvest, Napa Valley
1983 De Loach Vineyards ($7.00) Estate, Russian River Valley
1984 De Loach Vineyards ($7.00) Estate, Russian River Valley
1983 Donna Maria Vineyards ($6.00) Estate, Chalk Hill, Sonoma
1984 Donna Maria Vineyards ($6.00) Estate, Chalk Hill, Sonoma
1983 Dry Creek Vineyard ($4.50) Larson, Sonoma
1982 Felton-Empire Vineyards ($6.50) Maritime Series, California
1983 Felton-Empire Vineyards ($6.75) Maritime Series, California
1983 Felton-Empire Vineyards ($6.75) Talmage Town, Mendocino
1982 Fetzer Vineyards ($6.00) Mendocino
1983 Fetzer Vineyards ($6.00) North Coast
1984 Fetzer Vineyards ($6.00) California
1982 Grand Cru Vineyards ($8.50) Alexander Valley
1981 Hacienda Wine Cellars ($6.75) Sonoma
1982 Hacienda Wine Cellars ($6.75) Dry, Sonoma Valley
1983 Hacienda Wine Cellars ($7.00) Sonoma
1984 Hacienda Wine Cellars ($6.75) Sonoma
1981 Hinman Vineyards ($7.00) Oregon
1982 Hinman Vineyards ($7.00) Willamette Valley, Oregon
1984 Husch Vineyards ($6.00) Estate, Anderson Valley
1983 Kenwood Vineyards ($6.50) Sonoma Valley
1983 Lenz Vineyards ($7.00) Long Island, North Fork
1983 Mark West Vineyards ($7.00) Sonoma
1982 Paul Masson Vineyards ($7.00) Estate, Monterey
1983 R. Montali and Associates ($6.50) Santa Maria Valley
1982 Monticello Cellars ($6.50) Napa Valley
1983 Monticello Cellars CRANBROOK CELLARS ($5.50) Napa Valley
1983 Monticello Cellars ($8.50) Estate, Napa Valley
1982 Navarro Vineyards and Winery ($9.75) Late Sweet Harvest, Anderson Valley
1984 Pat Paulsen Vineyards ($6.50) Sonoma
1981 J. Pedroncelli Winery ($5.00) Sonoma
1983 Joseph Phelps Vineyards ($8.00) Napa Valley
1984 Round Hill Cellars ($5.00) Napa Valley
1978 Rutherford Hill Winery ($5.00) Napa Valley
1981 Rutherford Hill Winery ($5.00) Napa Valley
1982 Rutherford Hill Winery ($5.75) Napa Valley
1983 Rutherford Hill Winery ($6.25) Napa Valley
1983 St. Francis Vineyards ($6.40) Estate, Sonoma Valley

1984 St. Francis Vineyards ($6.00) Sonoma Valley
1983 Sebastiani Vineyards ($7.00) Kellerschatz, Sonoma Valley
1981 Smothers-Vine Hill Wines ($9.75) Late Harvest, Alexander Valley
1982 Souverain Cellars ($5.00) North Coast
1983 Tewksbury Wine Cellars ($6.75) New Jersey
1983 Villa Mount Eden Winery ($12.00) Late Harvest, Napa Valley
1983 ZD Wines ($10.00) Select Late Harvest, Napa Valley

Johannisberg Riesling

1976 Almadén Vineyards CHARLES LEFRANC ($10.00) Special Harvest, San Benito
1982 Austin Cellars ($6.90) Bien Nacido, Santa Barbara
1981 Ballard Canyon Winery ($6.25) Santa Ynez Valley
1981 Ballard Canyon Winery ($8.25) Reserve, Santa Ynez Valley
1982 Ballard Canyon Winery ($8.75) Reserve, Santa Ynez Valley
1984 Ballard Canyon Winery ($7.50) Estate, Santa Barbara
1982 Beaulieu Vineyard ($7.50) Beauclair, Estate, Napa Valley
1982 Beringer Vineyards ($15.00) Botrytised, Napa Valley
1982 Beringer Vineyards ($15.00) Special Select Late Harvest, Napa Valley
1981 Buena Vista Winery ($8.90) Special Selection, Sonoma Valley, Carneros
1982 California Wine Company JOHN B. MERRITT ($15.00) Potter Valley, Mendocino
1983 Chaddsford Winery ($7.00) Pennsylvania
1982 Château du Lac KENDALL-JACKSON VINEYARDS & WINERY ($6.00) Clear Lake
1983 Château du Lac KENDALL-JACKSON VINEYARDS & WINERY ($7.00) Lake
1980 Château St. Jean ($25.00) Individual Dried Bunch Selected Late Harvest, Robert Young, Alexander Valley
1981 Château St. Jean ($15.00) Selected Late Harvest, Robert Young, Alexander Valley
1982 Château St. Jean ($7.50) Sonoma
1983 Château St. Jean ($8.00) Sonoma
1982 Clos du Bois Winery ($20.00) Individual Bunch Late Harvest, Alexander Valley
1983 Clos du Bois Winery ($12.50) Late Harvest, Alexander Valley
1983 Durney Vineyard ($6.50) Estate, Carmel Valley
1983 Louis Facelli Vineyards ($6.00) Idaho
1983 Louis Facelli Vineyards ($7.00) Reserve, Washington
1982 Fetzer Vineyards ($6.00) Mendocino
1983 Fetzer Vineyards ($6.00) Mendocino
1984 Fetzer Vineyards ($6.00) California
1981 The Firestone Vineyard ($12.00) Select Harvest, Estate, Santa Ynez Valley
1982 The Firestone Vineyard ($12.00) Selected Harvest, Ambassador's, Santa Ynez Valley
1981 Glenora Wine Cellars ($9.00) Springledge, New York
1982 Glenora Wine Cellars ($7.00) Finger Lakes Region
1982 Glenora Wine Cellars ($9.00) Select Late Harvest, Finger Lakes District
1983 Glenora Wine Cellars ($6.00) New York
1980 Gold Seal Vineyards ($10.90) Select Late Harvest, Estate, New York State
1982 Greenwood Ridge Vineyards ($6.75) Estate, Mendocino
1982 Grgich Hills Cellars ($8.00) Napa Valley
1983 Grgich Hills Cellars ($7.50) Napa Valley
1984 Grgich Hills Cellars ($7.50) Napa Valley
1984 Hagafen Cellars ($8.95) Winery Lake, Napa Valley
1982 Heron Hill Vineyards ($7.00) Estate, Ingle Vineyard, Finger Lakes
1983 Hidden Cellars ($7.50) Potter Valley, Mendocino
1981 Jekel Vineyard ($6.50) Home, Monterey
1981 Jekel Vineyard ($12.00) Late Harvest, Estate, Monterey
1980 Kalin Cellars ($15.00) Mendocino
1983 Kenwood Vineyards ($8.50) Late Harvest, Estate, Sonoma Valley
1984 Kenwood Vineyards ($7.50) Sonoma
1981 J. Lohr Winery ($7.81) Late Harvest, Monterey

WHITE/*Johannisberg Riesling*

1983 J. Lohr Winery ($6.00) Greenfield, Monterey
1981 Long Vineyards ($14.00) Late Harvest, Napa Valley
1981 Mark West Vineyards ($6.00) Estate, Russian River Valley
1982 Mark West Vineyards ($6.00) Russian River Valley
1982 Mark West Vineyards ($12.50) Late Harvest, Sonoma
1983 Meredyth Vineyard ($9.00) Virginia
1982 Mirassou Vineyards ($8.50) Late Harvest, Monterey
1983 Mirassou Vineyards ($8.50) Late Harvest, Monterey
1982 Robert Mondavi Winery ($9.00) Special Selection, Napa Valley
1983 Robert Mondavi Winery ($7.50) Napa Valley
1984 Robert Mondavi Winery ($9.50) Special Selection, Napa Valley
1978 The Monterey Vineyards ($5.00) Thanksgiving Harvest, Monterey
1982 Navarro Vineyards and Winery ($18.50) Cluster Selected, Late Harvest, Anderson Valley,
        Mendocino
1981 Obester Winery ($6.25) Ventana, Monterey
1983 Obester Winery ($7.50) Ventana, Monterey
1983 J. Pedroncelli Winery ($5.25) Sonoma
1979 Joseph Phelps Vineyards ($10.75) Late Harvest, Napa Valley
1980 Joseph Phelps Vineyards ($6.75) Late Harvest, Napa Valley
1980 Joseph Phelps Vineyards ($30.00) Selected Late Harvest, Napa Valley
1981 Joseph Phelps Vineyards ($25.00) Selected Late Harvest, Napa Valley
1982 Joseph Phelps Vineyards ($7.50) Early Harvest, Napa Valley
1982 Joseph Phelps Vineyards ($8.50) Napa Valley
1982 Joseph Phelps Vineyards ($11.25) Late Harvest, Napa Valley
1982 Joseph Phelps Vineyards ($25.00) Special Select Late Harvest, Napa Valley
1984 Joseph Phelps Vineyards ($7.50) Early Harvest, Napa Valley
1984 Joseph Phelps Vineyards ($8.00) Napa Valley
1983 Quail Run Vintners ($5.00) Washington
1982 Quail Run Vintners ($8.00) Limited Bottling, Yakima Valley, Washington
1983 Ste. Chapelle Winery ($5.25) Symms Family, Idaho
1984 Ste. Chapelle Winery ($10.00) Special Harvest, Idaho
1982 St. Francis Vineyards ($5.40) Estate, Sonoma Valley
1984 St. Francis Vineyards ($6.00) Estate, Sonoma Valley
1980 San Martin Winery ($8.00) Late Harvest, Santa Clara
1981 San Martin Winery ($8.00) Late Harvest, Santa Clara
1984 Santa Barbara Winery ($6.50) Santa Barbara
1983 Santa Ynez Valley Winery ($6.00) Santa Ynez Valley
1983 Sarah's Vineyard ($8.50) Victor Mathew
1983 Sebastiani Vineyards ($12.00) Late Harvest, Sonoma
1983 Smith-Madrone ($7.00) Napa Valley
1983 Smothers-Vine Hill Wines ($12.00) Late Harvest, Sonoma
1978 Sonoma Vineyards, Late Harvest, LeBaron, Sonoma
1982 Sonoma Vineyards ($8.00) LeBaron, Estate, Russian River Valley
1982 Sonoma Vineyards ($12.00) Select Late Harvest, Russian River Valley
1983 Sonoma Vineyards WINDSOR VINEYARDS ($7.50) River West, Estate, Russian River Valley
1983 Sonoma Vineyards RODNEY STRONG ($8.00) LeBaron, Estate, Russian River Valley
1982 Susine Cellars ($10.00) Special Select Late Harvest, El Dorado
1984 Paul Thomas Wines ($7.00) Vintage Reserve, Washington
1983 Weibel Vineyards ($5.00) Mendocino
1982 White Oak Vineyards ($6.00) Russian River Valley
1982 Worden's Washington Winery ($5.00) Proprietor's Reserve, Moreman, Washington
1982 Zaca Mesa Winery ($6.50) Santa Barbara County

Melon

1982 Beaulieu Vineyard ($8.50) Estate, Napa Valley

Muscat

1984 Château du Lac *Muscat Canelli* ($7.50) Lake
1981 Estrella River Winery ($14.00) Late Harvest, Paso Robles

1981 Fetzer Vineyards ($6.50) Lake
1984 Fetzer Vineyards *Muscat Canelli* ($6.00) Bartolucci, Lake
1982 Robert Mondavi Winery *Muscato d'Oro* ($8.00) Napa Valley
1982 Pat Paulsen Vineyards *Muscat Canelli* ($6.50) Preston, Dry Creek Valley
1983 Pat Paulsen Vineyards ($7.50) Sonoma
1984 Pat Paulsen Vineyards *Muscat Canelli* ($7.50) Preston, Sonoma
1982 Robert Pecota Winery *Muscato di Andrea* ($8.50) Napa Valley
1984 Robert Pecota Winery *Muscato di Andrea* ($8.00) Napa Valley
1982 Quail Run Vintners *Morio Muscat* ($5.50) Yakima
1983 San Pasqual Vineyards ($8.00) Estrella River, Paso Robles
1982 Souverain Cellars ($6.50) North Coast
1984 Stevenot Vineyards *Muscat Canelli* ($7.00) San Luis Obispo
1983 Paul Thomas Wines *Muscat Canelli* ($9.00) Washington

Pinot Blanc

1983 Buehler Vineyards ($8.00) Estate, Napa Valley
1983 Chalone Vineyard ($12.50) California
1981 Château St. Jean ($11.00) Robert Young, Alexander Valley
1982 Château St. Jean ($11.00) Robert Young, Alexander Valley
1981 Fetzer Vineyards ($8.50) Redwood Valley, Mendocino
1982 Jekel Vineyard ($7.50) Home, Monterey
1981 Mount Veeder Winery ($9.75) Napa Valley
1984 Roudon-Smith Vineyards ($6.50) Santa Maria Valley

Pinot Gris

1983 The Eyrie Vineyards ($8.75) Willamette Valley, Yamhill, Oregon

Ravat

1982 Good Harbor Vineyards *Ravat Vignoles* ($6.00) Leelanau Peninsula, Michigan
1982 L. Mawby Vineyards *Ravat Vignoles* ($6.25) Lot FR, Leelanau Peninsula

Riesling

1983 Elk Cove Vineyards ($5.40) Willamette Valley, Oregon
1982 Parducci Wine Cellars *Mendocino Riesling* ($4.63) Mendocino
1983 Weibel Vineyards *Mendocino Riesling* ($5.00) Mendocino

Sauvignon Blanc

1981 Austin Cellars ($8.50) Botrytis, Sierra Madre, Santa Barbara
1983 Beaulieu Vineyard ($8.00) Estate, Napa Valley
1983 Boeger Winery ($7.50) El Dorado
1983 Jean-Claude Boisset ($7.50) Napa Valley
1980 The Brander Vineyard ($7.00) Santa Ynez Valley
1981 The Brander Vineyard ($7.50) Estate, Santa Barbara
1983 The Brander Vineyard ($8.25) Santa Ynez Valley
1983 Byrd Vineyards ($8.00) Maryland
1982 Cain Cellars ($7.50) Napa Valley
1983 Cakebread Cellars ($9.50) Napa Valley
1983 Calafia Cellars ($7.50) Honig, Napa Valley
1981 J. Carey Cellars ($8.50) Santa Maria Valley
1983 Carmenet Vineyard ($9.00) Edna Valley
1982 Carneros Creek Winery ($7.50) California
1983 Cartlidge & Browne STRATFORD ($6.00) Napa Valley
1984 Caymus Vineyards LIBERTY SCHOOL ($5.00) Lot 1, Napa Valley
1983 Chanticleer Vineyards ($6.75) Lake
1982 Château Bouchaine ($8.50) Sonoma
1983 Château Bouchaine ($8.50) Napa Valley
1983 Château du Lac KENDALL-JACKSON VINEYARDS & WINERY ($7.25) Clear Lake

WHITE/*Sauvignon Blanc*

1983 Château St. Jean ($9.75) Sonoma
1982 Clos du Bois Winery ($8.00) Alexander Valley
1983 Clos du Bois Winery ($7.00) Sonoma
1982 Concannon Vineyard ($7.00) Estate, Livermore Valley
1983 Concannon Vineyard ($8.25) Estate, Livermore
1983 Creston Manor Vineyards & Winery ($9.00) San Luis Obispo
1983 Donna Maria Vineyards CHALK HILL ($6.00) Sonoma
1983 Ehlers Lane Winery ($8.95) Napa Valley
1982 Fenestra Winery ($7.50) San Luis Obispo
1982 Flora Springs Wine Company ($8.00) Napa Valley
1982 Louis Foppiano Wine Company ($7.00) Sonoma
1983 Louis Foppiano Wine Company ($7.50) Russian River Valley
1981 Girard Winery STEPHENS ($8.00) North Coast
1981 Glen Ellen Winery ($8.00) Estate, Sonoma
1982 Glen Ellen Winery ($9.00) Estate, Sonoma
1983 Glen Ellen Winery ($8.50) Sonoma
1982 Grand Cru Vineyards ($9.00) California
1983 Grand Cru Vineyards ($9.00) Sonoma
1981 Louis Honig Cellars (HNW Vineyards) HNW ($8.00) Napa Valley
1983 Louis Honig Cellars (HNW Vineyards) ($8.00) Estate, Napa Valley
1983 Husch Vineyards ($7.50) La Ribera, Estate, Mendocino
1984 Husch Vineyards ($7.00) La Ribera Ranch, Estate, Mendocino
1983 Inglenook Vineyards ($7.50) Estate, Napa Valley
1983 Inglenook Vineyards ($10.00) Reserve, Estate, Napa Valley
1982 Kenwood Vineyards ($8.50) Sonoma County
1983 Kenwood Vineyards ($8.50) Sonoma
1984 Kenwood Vineyards ($8.50) Sonoma
1982 Lakespring Winery ($7.50) California
1983 Long Vineyards ($10.00) Sonoma
1983 Los Vineros Winery ($7.50) Central Coast
1983 Markham Winery ($7.85) Napa Valley
1983 Martin Brothers Winery ($7.50) Paso Robles
1983 Matanzas Creek Winery ($10.50) Sonoma
1982 Mayacamas Vineyards ($10.00) California
1982 Monticello Cellars ($8.50) Napa Valley
1982 Monticello Cellars *Château M* ($17.50) Napa Valley
1983 Monticello Cellars ($9.00) Estate, Napa Valley
1983 Morgan Winery ST. VRAIN ($7.50) Alexander Valley
1983 Napa Cellars ($7.50) Napa Valley
1982 Obester Winery ($9.50) Mendocino
1983 Obester Winery ($8.50) Mendocino
1982 Page Mill Winery ($8.75) Santa Barbara
1982 Pat Paulsen Vineyards ($8.50) Estate, Alexander Valley
1983 Pat Paulsen Vineyards ($9.00) Estate, Sonoma
1983 J. Pedroncelli Winery ($6.00) Sonoma
1983 Peju Province ($7.00) Napa Valley
1982 Joseph Phelps Vineyards ($9.00) Napa Valley
1983 Joseph Phelps Vineyards ($8.50) California
1983 The R. H. Phillips Vineyards ($6.00) California
1982 Preston Vineyards ($8.50) Estate, Dry Creek Valley
1984 Preston Vineyards ($6.75) Cuvée de Fumé, Estate, Dry Creek Valley
1982 St. Clement Vineyards ($9.00) Napa Valley
1983 St. Clement Vineyards ($9.00) Napa Valley

1981 Sanford Winery ($8.50) Santa Maria Valley
1983 Sanford Winery ($8.00) Central Coast
1981 Silverado Vineyards ($8.00) Napa Valley
1982 Silverado Vineyards ($8.00) Napa Valley
1983 Silverado Vineyards ($8.00) Napa Valley
1982 Simi Winery ($9.00) Sonoma
1983 Stag's Leap Wine Cellars ($9.00) Napa Valley
1982 Sterling Vineyards ($10.00) Estate, Napa Valley
1982 Ventana Vineyards Winery DOUGLAS MEADOR ($10.00) Monterey
1982 William Wheeler Winery ($8.00) Sonoma
1983 William Wheeler Winery ($8.00) Sonoma
1983 White Oak Vineyards ($7.50) Sonoma

Scheurebe

1979 Joseph Phelps Vineyards ($15.00) Late Harvest, Napa Valley
1981 Joseph Phelps Vineyards ($15.00) Late Harvest, Napa Valley

Semillon

1983 Alderbrook Winery ($6.00) Sonoma
1982 Château Ste. Michelle *Semillon Blanc* ($5.00) Washington
1983 Clos du Val ($7.50) California
1982 Robert Pepi Winery ($7.00) Napa Valley
1979 Wente Brothers ($9.00) Arroyo Seco, Monterey
1981 Wente Brothers ($6.50) Centennial Reserve, Estate, Livermore Valley

Symphony

1984 Matrose Wines ($5.50) Sonoma

Traminer

1982 Matrose Wines ($7.00) Hafner, Alexander Valley

White Riesling

1981 Ahern Winery ($6.00)
1981 Alpine Vineyards ($7.00) Estate, Oregon
1982 Alpine Vineyards ($7.50) Estate, Willamette Valley, Oregon
1983 Callaway Vineyards and Winery ($5.25)Temecula
1984 Callaway Vineyards and Winery ($5.50)Temecula
1982 Chehalen Mountain Winery MULHAUSEN ($6.40) Willamette Valley, Oregon
1981 Felton-Empire Vineyards ($10.00) Select Late Harvest, Tepusquet, Santa Barbara
1983 Felton-Empire Vineyards ($6.75) Santa Cruz Mountains
1983 Felton-Empire Vineyards ($12.00) Fort Ross
1983 Haywood Winery ($6.75) Sonoma Valley
1982 Hinzerling Vineyards ($6.00) Yakima Valley, Washington
1983 The Hogue Cellars ($5.50) Washington State
1983 The Hogue Cellars ($6.00) Schwartzman, Yakima Valley
1983 The Hogue Cellars ($6.50) Markin, Estate, Yakima Valley
1982 Hood River Vineyards ($6.50) Oregon
1981 Monterey Peninsula Winery ($18.50) Late Harvest, Monterey
1982 Quail Run Vintners ($5.00) Mahre, Yakima Valley
1981 Smothers-Vine Hill Wines ($9.00) Vine Hill, Santa Cruz
1982 Sokol Blosser Winery ($6.60) Yamhill County, Willamette Valley
1981 Stag's Leap Wine Cellars ($6.75) Napa Valley
1983 Stag's Leap Wine Cellars ($6.00) Napa Valley
1983 Tewksbury Wine Cellars ($6.00) Hunterdon County, New Jersey

WHITE/*White Riesling*

1982 Trefethen Vineyards Winery ($7.75) Napa Valley
1984 Ventana Vineyards ($6.00) Monterey

SPARKLING

Non-varietal

1982 Adelaida Cellars TONIO CONTI *Blanc de Blancs* ($17.00) Paso Robles
1980 S. Anderson Vineyard *Blanc de Noirs* ($15.50) Estate, Napa Valley
1982 S. Anderson Vineyard *Cuvée de la Cave* ($14.00) Napa Valley
1981 Bargetto Winery *Blanc de Noir* ($12.50) Monterey
1980 Château St. Jean *Brut* ($19.00) Sonoma
1981 Château St. Jean *Blanc de Blanc Brut* ($17.00) Sonoma
NV Cosentino Wine Company CRYSTAL VALLEY CELLARS *Robins Glow* ($5.75) California
NV John Culbertson Winery *Demi-Sec, Cuvée Frontignan* ($12.00) California
1981 John Culbertson Winery *Natural, Recent Disgorge* ($19.50) California
NV Domaine Chandon *Brut Special Reserve* ($40.00) Napa Valley
NV Domaine Chandon *10th Anniversary Reserve* ($16.95) Napa Valley
1982 Estrella River Winery *Blanc de Blancs* ($15.00) Paso Robles
NV E. & J. Gallo Winery BALLATORE *Spumante* ($4.50) California
1980 Iron Horse Vineyards *Brut* ($16.50) Estate, Green Valley, Sonoma
1981 Iron Horse Vineyards *Blanc de Noirs* ($16.50) Estate, Sonoma, Green Valley
1982 Iron Horse Vineyards *Blanc de Blancs* ($16.50) Estate, Green Valley, Sonoma
1982 Iron Horse Vineyards *Wedding Blanc de Noir* ($16.50) Cuvée, Estate, Green Valley, Sonoma
1982 Iron Horse Vineyards *Brut* ($16.50) Estate, Green Valley, Sonoma
NV F. Korbel and Brothers *Blanc de Blancs* ($16.00) California
1980 Mirassou Vineyards *Blanc de Noirs* ($15.00) Monterey
1982 Mirassou Vineyards *Brut* ($12.00) Monterey
NV Parsons Creek Winery *Brut* ($13.50) Mendocino
1980 Piper-Sonoma *Blanc de Noir* ($13.50) Sonoma
1980 Piper-Sonoma *Brut* ($14.00) Sonoma
1980 Piper-Sonoma *Tête de Cuvée* ($30.00) Sonoma County
1981 Piper-Sonoma *Brut* ($14.00) Sonoma
1982 Piper-Sonoma *Brut* ($14.00) Sonoma
1977 Schramsberg Vineyards *Reserve* ($25.00) Napa Valley
1980 Schramsberg Vineyards *Blanc de Blancs* ($14.00) Napa Valley
1980 Schramsberg Vineyards *Blanc de Noirs* ($19.85) Napa Valley
NV Sebastiani Vineyards *Brut Proprietor's Reserve* ($10.00) Sonoma
NV Sebastiani Vineyards *Brut Three Star* ($12.00) Sonoma
1981 Shadow Creek Champagne Cellars *Blanc de Blancs* ($13.75) Cuvée 1, Sonoma
1981 Wente Brothers *Brut* ($8.95) Monterey

Chardonnay

1980 Château St. Jean ($19.00) Blanc de Blanc, Sonoma

Pinot Noir

NV Weibel Vineyards *Blanc de Pinot Noir* ($7.75) California

BLANC DE NOIR

Cabernet Sauvignon

1984 J. Carey Cellars *Cabernet Blanc* ($5.75) Alamo Pintado, Santa Ynez Valley
1983 Château du Lac KENDALL-JACKSON VINEYARDS & WINERY ($6.00) Cabernet Blanc, Lake

1984 Fetzer Vineyards BEL ARBRES *White Cabernet* ($4.50) Mendocino
1983 Santa Ynez Valley Winery *Blanc de Cabernet* ($5.00) Santa Ynez Valley
1982 Sterling Vineyards *Cabernet Blanc* ($6.50) Napa Valley
1983 Sterling Vineyards *Cabernet Blanc* ($6.50) Napa Valley
1984 Sterling Vineyards *Cabernet Blanc* ($6.00) Napa Valley

Merlot

1983 The Brander Vineyard ST. CARL *Merlot Blanc* ($4.75) Santa Ynez Valley

Pinot Noir

1984 Buena Vista Winery *Blanc de Pinot Noir* ($5.50) Sonoma Valley-Carneros
1984 Edna Valley Vineyard ($5.00) Vin Gris, Estate, Edna Valley
1982 Geyser Peak Winery *Pinot Noir Blanc* ($5.00) Kiser Ranch, Sonoma Valley
1984 Hagafen Cellars *Pinot Noir Blanc* ($5.75) Napa Valley
1982 Iron Horse Vineyards *Blanc de Pinot Noir* ($6.75) Estate, Green Valley, Sonoma
1983 Mark West Vineyards *Pinot Noir Blanc* ($5.75) Estate, Russian River Valley
1982 Sanford Winery ($6.50) Vin Gris, Santa Barbara

White Gamay

1983 Markham Winery *Gamay Blanc* ($5.25) Estate, Napa Valley
1984 Olson Vineyards Winery *Gamay Blanc* ($4.00) Napa-Mendocino

Zinfandel

1982 Amador City Winery *White Zinfandel* ($5.00) Amador
1984 Amador Foothill Winery *White Zinfandel* ($5.25) Amador
1984 Bargetto Winery *White Zinfandel* ($5.75) California
1983 Buehler Vineyards *White Zinfandel* ($5.50) Estate, Napa Valley
1983 Davis Bynum Winery *White Zinfandel* ($4.50) Sonoma
1984 California Wine Company BANDIERA *White Zinfandel* ($4.25) Sonoma
1982 De Loach Vineyards ($5.75) Sonoma
1983 De Loach Vineyards *White Zinfandel* ($5.75) Russian River Valley, Sonoma
1984 De Loach Vineyards *White Zinfandel* ($5.75) Sonoma
1983 Fetzer Vineyards BEL ARBRES *White Zinfandel* ($4.40) Mendocino
1984 Fetzer Vineyards BEL ARBRES *White Zinfandel* ($4.50) Mendocino
1984 Fritz Cellars *White Zinfandel* ($5.80) Alexander Valley
1984 Grand Cru Vineyards *Vin Maison White Zinfandel* ($4.50) Sonoma
1984 McDowell Valley Vineyards *Zinfandel Blanc* ($5.00) Estate, McDowell Valley
1984 Monterey Vineyards *White Zinfandel* ($4.50) Monterey
1983 Monteviña Wines *White Zinfandel* ($4.75) Amador
1984 Olson Vineyards Winery *White Zinfandel* ($4.50) Mendocino
1984 Orleans Hill Vinicultural Corporation *White Zinfandel* ($4.50) Reiff, Yolo
1984 Santino Wines *White Harvest Zinfandel* ($4.75) Amador
1983 Tyland Vineyards *White Zinfandel* ($4.50) Estate, Mendocino
1984 Vose Vineyards *Zinblanca* ($4.75) California
1984 Whaler Vineyards *White Zinfandel* ($5.25) Mendocino
1984 Winterbrook Vineyards *White Zinfandel* ($4.50) Amador

ROSE

Non-varietal

1982 Sokol Blosser Winery *Bouquet Rosé* ($4.50) American

Cabernet Sauvignon

1982 Simi Winery ($5.25) Sonoma
1983 Simi Winery *Rosé of Cabernet* ($6.00) Sonoma
1982 Sonoma Vineyards ($6.00) Mendocino

Gewürztraminer

1982 Sebastiani Vineyards *Rosa Gewürztraminer* ($4.85) Sonoma Valley

Petite Sirah

1982 Field Stone Winery ($6.00) Estate, Alexander Valley

Zinfandel

1982 J. Pedroncelli Winery ($4.00) Sonoma
1983 J. Pedroncelli Winery ($4.00) Sonoma

RED

Non-varietal

1968 Beaulieu Vineyard *Burgundy,* Napa Valley
1983 Bonny Doon Vineyard *Claret* ($9.00) Central Coast
1983 Buena Vista Winery *Pinot Jolie* ($5.00) Sonoma Valley
1984 Buena Vista Winery *Pinot Jolie* ($5.50) Sonoma Valley
1977 Clos du Bois Winery RIVER OAKS VINEYARDS *Premium Red* ($3.25) Alexander Valley
NV   Gundlach-Bundschu Winery *Sonoma Red Wine* ($3.90) Sonoma Valley
1981 HMR Estate Winery SANTA LUCIA CELLARS ($2.95) San Luis Obispo
1981 Hop Kiln Winery *Marty Griffin's Big Red* ($6.00) Russian River Valley
1983 Lenz Vineyards *Reserve* ($12.00) Long Island, North Fork
1981 Lyeth Vineyard and Winery *Red Table Wine* ($15.00) Alexander Valley
1982 Lyeth Vineyard and Winery *Red Table Wine* ($15.00) Alexander Valley
1983 Rombauer Vineyards *Red Table Wine* ($12.50) Napa Valley
1982 Rosenblum Cellars *Rosenblum Red* ($4.00) Napa Valley
1975 Seghesio Winery *Marian's Reserve* ($4.50) Sonoma
1982 Taft Street Winery *Medallion* ($9.75) 61% Sonoma Valley, 39% Napa

Barbera

1979 Louis M. Martini ($4.50) California

Cabernet Sauvignon

1978 Ahlgren Vineyard ($12.00) Napa Valley
1978 Alexander Valley Vineyards ($6.50) Estate, Alexander Valley
1981 Alexander Valley Vineyards ($9.00) Estate, Alexander Valley
1980 Almadén Vineyards ($5.50) Monterey
1981 Almadén Vineyards ($4.00) Monterey
1981 Almadén Vineyards CHARLES LEFRANC ($8.50) Monterey
1982 Artisan Wines MICHAEL'S ($12.00) Napa Valley
1979 Baldinelli Vineyards ($7.00) Estate, Amador
1980 Balverne Winery & Vineyards ($25.00) Sonoma
1981 Bargetto Winery ($12.00) Dedication, St. Regis, Sonoma
1958 Beaulieu Vineyard, Private Reserve, Estate, Napa Valley
1973 Beaulieu Vineyard, Private Reserve, Estate, Napa Valley
1974 Beaulieu Vineyard, Private Reserve, Estate, Napa Valley
1976 Beaulieu Vineyard ($18.00) Private Reserve, Estate, Napa Valley
1978 Beaulieu Vineyard ($18.00) Private Reserve, Estate, Napa Valley

1980 Bellerose Vineyard ($12.00) Cuvée Bellerose, Sonoma
1982 Belvedere Wine Company ROBERT YOUNG ($10.00) Alexander Valley
1982 Belvedere Wine Company YORK CREEK ($12.00) Napa Valley
1973 Beringer Vineyards, Centennial Cask Selection, Estate, Napa Valley
1977 Beringer Vineyards ($18.00) Private Reserve, Lemmon Ranch, Napa Valley
1979 Beringer Vineyards ($9.00) State Lane, Napa Valley
1980 Beringer Vineyards ($15.00) State Lane, Napa Valley
1981 Beringer Vineyards ($15.00) Private Reserve, State Lane, Lemmon-Chabot, Napa Valley
1981 David Bruce Winery, California
1982 David Bruce Winery ($12.50) Vintners Select, California
1978 Buehler Vineyards ($9.00) Estate, Napa Valley
1982 Buehler Vineyards ($10.00) Estate, Napa Valley
1978 Buena Vista Winery ($18.00) Special Selection, Estate, Sonoma Valley
1979 Buena Vista Winery ($18.00) Special Selection, Estate, Sonoma Valley
1980 Buena Vista Winery ($18.00) Special Selection, Estate, Sonoma Valley
1981 Buena Vista Winery ($9.00) Sonoma Valley-Carneros
1981 Buena Vista Winery ($11.00) Sonoma-Carneros
1982 Buena Vista Winery ($11.00) Napa Valley-Carneros
1979 Burgess Cellars ($16.95) Vintage Selection, Napa Valley
1980 Burgess Cellars ($15.95) Vintage Selection, Napa Valley
1980 Byrd Vineyards ($12.00) Maryland
1983 Cache Cellars, Napa Valley
1979 Cakebread Cellars ($14.00) Napa Valley
1980 Cakebread Cellars ($14.00) Rutherford Reserve, Napa Valley
1981 Calafia Cellars ($11.00) Kitty Hawk, Napa Valley
1978 California Wine Company ARROYO SONOMA Special Reserve ($12.00) Sonoma
1981 California Wine Company JOHN B. MERRITT ($8.00) Sonoma
1979 Carneros Creek Winery ($12.00) Napa Valley
1980 Carneros Creek Winery ($10.00) Fay, Napa Valley
1980 Carneros Creek Winery ($12.00) Napa Valley
1980 Carneros Creek Winery ($13.50) Truchard, Napa Valley
1978 Cassayre-Forni Cellars ($9.00) Napa Valley
1978 Caymus Vineyards ($12.50) Napa Valley
1978 Caymus Vineyards ($30.00) Special Selection, Estate, Napa Valley
1979 Caymus Vineyards ($12.50) Napa Valley
1968 Chappellet Winery, Napa Valley
1970 Chappellet Winery, Napa Valley
1973 Chappellet Winery, Napa Valley
1975 Chappellet Winery ($35.00) Napa Valley
1976 Chappellet Winery ($40.00) Napa Valley
1977 Chappellet Winery ($18.00) Napa Valley
1979 Chappellet Winery ($12.50) Napa Valley
1982 Chappellet Winery ($18.00) Napa Valley
1982 Château Bouchaine ($15.00) Jerry Luper Reserve, Rutherford
1977 Château Montelena Winery ($14.00) Napa Valley
1978 Château Montelena Winery ($12.00) Sonoma
1979 Château Montelena Winery ($14.00) Sonoma
1979 Château Montelena Winery ($16.00) Estate, Napa Valley
1980 Château Montelena Winery ($16.00) Estate, Napa Valley
1978 Château St. Jean ($17.00) Glen Ellen, Sonoma
1979 Clos du Bois Winery RIVER OAKS VINEYARDS ($5.95) Alexander Valley
1980 Clos du Bois Winery ($15.00) Marlstone, Alexander Valley
1981 Clos du Bois Winery RIVER OAKS VINEYARDS ($6.25) Healdsburg Area, Sonoma
1982 Clos du Bois Winery ($6.00) Alexander Valley

RED/*Cabernet Sauvignon*

1978 Clos du Val ($12.00) Napa Valley
1978 Clos du Val ($25.00) Reserve, Napa Valley
1979 Clos du Val ($12.50) Napa Valley
1979 Clos du Val ($25.00) Reserve, Napa Valley
1982 Clos du Val ($13.00) Napa Valley
1977 Conn Creek Winery ($13.75) Napa Valley
1978 Conn Creek Winery ($12.50) Lot 1, Napa Valley
1978 Conn Creek Winery ($12.50) Lot 2, Napa Valley
1979 Conn Creek Winery ($13.00) Napa Valley
1980 Conn Creek Winery ($13.00) Napa Valley
1981 Conn Creek Winery ($13.50) Napa Valley
1981 Crescini Wines ($7.50) Napa Valley
1978 Cuvaison Vineyard ($12.00) Napa Valley
1980 Cuvaison Vineyard ($10.00) Napa Valley
1980 Dehlinger Winery ($9.00) Sonoma
1977 Diamond Creek Vineyards ($10.00) Gravelly Meadow, Napa Valley
1977 Diamond Creek Vineyards ($10.00) Red Rock Terrace, Napa Valley
1977 Diamond Creek Vineyards ($10.00) Volcanic Hill, Napa Valley
1978 Diamond Creek Vineyards ($12.50) Gravelly Meadow, Napa Valley
1978 Diamond Creek Vineyards ($12.50) Red Rock Terrace, Napa Valley
1978 Diamond Creek Vineyards ($12.50) Volcanic Hill, Napa Valley
1979 Diamond Creek Vineyards ($15.00) Gravelly Meadow, Napa Valley
1979 Diamond Creek Vineyards ($15.00) Red Rock Terrace, Napa Valley
1979 Diamond Creek Vineyards ($15.00) Volcanic Hill, Napa Valley
1980 Diamond Creek Vineyards ($20.00) Gravelly Meadow, Napa Valley
1980 Diamond Creek Vineyards ($20.00) Red Rock Terrace, Napa Valley
1980 Diamond Creek Vineyards ($20.00) Volcanic Hill, Napa Valley
1982 Diamond Creek Vineyards ($18.75) Special Selection, Volcanic Hill, Napa Valley
1982 Diamond Creek Vineyards ($20.00) Gravelly Meadow, Napa Valley
1982 Diamond Creek Vineyards ($20.00) Red Rock Terrace, Napa Valley
1979 Domaine Laurier ($12.50) Sonoma
1981 Donna Maria Vineyards CHALK HILL ($8.00) Sonoma
1975 Dry Creek Vineyard, Dry Creek Valley
1978 Duckhorn Vineyards ($10.50) Napa Valley
1980 Duckhorn Vineyards ($14.00) Napa Valley
1981 Duckhorn Vineyards ($15.00) Napa Valley
1977 Durney Vineyard ($12.00) Carmel Valley
1978 Durney Vineyard ($12.00) Estate, Carmel Valley
1978 Durney Vineyard ($15.00) Private Reserve, Estate, Carmel Valley
1981 Durney Vineyard ($12.50) Carmel Valley, Monterey
1982 Durney Vineyard ($12.50) Carmel Valley
1979 Eberle Winery ($10.00) San Luis Obispo
1980 Eberle Winery ($10.00) Paso Robles
1981 Eberle Winery ($10.00) Paso Robles
1978 Edmeades Vineyards ($9.00) Estate, Anderson Valley, Mendocino
1979 Edmeades Vineyards ($8.00) Anderson Valley, Mendocino
1978 The Firestone Vineyard ($12.00) Vintage Reserve, Estate, Santa Ynez Valley
1979 Fisher Vineyards ($12.00) Sonoma
1980 Fisher Vineyards ($12.00) Sonoma
1981 Fisher Vineyards ($12.00) Sonoma
1981 Louis Foppiano Wine Company ($7.75) Russian River Valley
1980 Franciscan Vineyards ($7.50) Alexander Valley
1975 Freemark Abbey Winery *Cabernet Bosche*, Napa Valley

1978 Freemark Abbey Winery ($11.50) Napa Valley
1980 Freemark Abbey Winery *Cabernet Bosche* ($14.50) Napa Valley
1981 Freemark Abbey Winery *Cabernet Bosche* ($14.00) Napa Valley
1979 Fretter Wine Cellars LEAKY LAKE ($7.50) Napa Valley
1980 Fretter Wine Cellars LEAKY LAKE ($12.00) Napa Valley
1981 Fritz Cellars ($7.00) North Coast
1981 Geyser Peak Winery ($7.00) Sonoma
1981 Girard Winery STEPHENS ($8.00) Napa Valley
1981 Girard Winery ($14.00) Estate, Napa Valley
1982 Glen Ellen Winery ($10.00) Estate, Sonoma Valley
1979 Grand Cru Vineyards ($14.50) Collector Series, Garden Creek Ranch, Alexander Valley
1980 Grand Cru Vineyards ($7.65) Cook's Delta, Clarksburg
1982 Greenwood Ridge Vineyards ($9.75) Estate, Mendocino
1980 Grgich Hills Cellars ($16.00) 34% Napa, 66% Sonoma
1981 Grover Gulch Winery ($9.50) Santa Cruz Mountains
1980 Guenoc Winery ($8.00) 70% Lake, 30% Napa
1981 Guenoc Winery ($8.00) Lake
1979 Gundlach-Bundschu Winery ($8.00) Gregory, Sonoma Valley
1979 Gundlach-Bundschu Winery ($9.00) Batto Ranch, Sonoma Valley
1979 Gundlach-Bundschu Winery ($12.50) Special Selection, Rhinefarm, Sonoma Valley
1980 Gundlach-Bundschu Winery ($13.50) Batto Ranch, Sonoma Valley
1981 Gundlach-Bundschu Winery ($9.95) Sonoma Valley
1982 Gundlach-Bundschu Winery ($12.00) Batto Ranch, Sonoma Valley
1978 Hacienda Wine Cellars ($10.00) Sonoma Valley
1979 Hacienda Wine Cellars ($11.00) Sonoma
1980 Hacienda Wine Cellars ($11.00) Sonoma
1981 Hacienda Wine Cellars ($11.00) 76% Jansen, 24% Buena Vista, Sonoma Valley
1982 Hacienda Wine Cellars ($10.75) Sonoma Valley
1982 Hafner Vineyard ($15.00) Estate, Alexander Valley
1982 Hagafen Cellars ($12.00) Yountville Selection, Napa Valley
1968 Heitz Wine Cellars, Napa Valley
1975 Heitz Wine Cellars ($15.00) Fay, Napa Valley
1975 Heitz Wine Cellars ($25.00) Martha's, Napa Valley
1976 Heitz Wine Cellars ($25.00) Bella Oaks, Napa Valley
1977 Heitz Wine Cellars ($35.00) Martha's, Napa Valley
1980 Heitz Wine Cellars ($25.00) Bella Oaks, Napa Valley
1980 Heitz Wine Cellars ($35.00) Martha's, Napa Valley
1978 William Hill Winery ($15.00) Mt. Veeder-Napa Valley
1979 William Hill Winery ($17.00) Mt. Veeder-Napa Valley
1981 William Hill Winery ($16.00) Mt. Veeder-Napa Valley
1979 Hinzerling Vineyards ($13.00) Yakima Valley
1975 HMR Estate Winery ($25.00) Doctor's Reserve, Estate, Paso Robles
1979 HMR Estate Winery ($8.75) Hoffman, Paso Robles
1981 Hop Kiln Winery ($9.00) Alexander Valley
1981 Husch Vineyards ($10.00) La Ribera, Mendocino
1955 Inglenook Vineyards, Napa Valley
1977 Inglenook Vineyards ($10.00) Limited Cask, Napa Valley
1978 Inglenook Vineyards ($14.00) Limited Cask, Estate, Napa Valley
1979 Inglenook Vineyards ($7.00) Centennial, Napa
1980 Inglenook Vineyards ($9.00) Lot 2, Estate, Napa Valley
1980 Inglenook Vineyards ($19.00) Limited Cask Reserve, Napa Valley
1978 Iron Horse Vineyards ($12.00) Sonoma
1979 Iron Horse Vineyards ($12.00) Alexander Valley
1980 Iron Horse Vineyards ($12.00) Estate, Alexander Valley
1979 Jekel Vineyard ($10.00) Estate, Monterey

RED/*Cabernet Sauvignon*

1980 Johnson Turnbull Vineyards ($12.00) Napa Valley
1981 Johnson Turnbull Vineyards ($12.00) Napa Valley
1976 Jordan Vineyard and Winery ($13.00) Alexander Valley
1978 Jordan Vineyard and Winery ($16.00) Estate, Alexander Valley
1979 Jordan Vineyard and Winery ($16.00) Alexander Valley
1980 Jordan Vineyard and Winery ($18.00) Estate, Alexander Valley
1979 Robert Keenan Winery ($12.00) Napa Valley
1980 Robert Keenan Winery ($12.00) Napa Valley
1981 Robert Keenan Winery ($12.00) Napa Valley
1978 Kenwood Vineyards ($20.00) Artist Series, Laurel Glen & Steiner, Sonoma Valley
1979 Kenwood Vineyards ($20.00) Artist Series, Sonoma Valley
1980 Kistler Vineyards ($16.00) Veeder Hills-Veeder Peak, Napa
1980 Kistler Vineyards ($20.00) Glen Ellen, California
1981 Kistler Vineyards ($12.00) Veeder Hills-Veeder Peak, California
1982 Kistler Vineyards ($11.00) Veeder Hills, Napa Valley
1980 Laird Vineyards ($11.00) Napa Valley
1978 Lake Sonoma Winery DIABLO VISTA ($9.00) North Coast
1981 Lakespring Winery ($11.00) Napa Valley
1978 Landmark Vineyards ($7.00) 75% Sonoma, 25% Napa
1980 Landmark Vineyards ($8.50) Estate, Alexander Valley
1982 Laurel Glen Vineyard ($12.50) Sonoma
1981 J. Lohr Winery ($9.00) St. Regis, Napa
1979 Madrona Vineyards ($6.50) El Dorado
1980 Madrona Vineyards ($8.75) El Dorado
1978 Markham Winery ($12.00) Estate (Yountville), Napa Valley
1979 Markham Winery ($12.85) Yountville, Napa
1982 Markham Winery ($13.00) Napa Valley
1979 Louis M. Martini ($12.00) Vineyard Selection, Lot 2, Monte Rosso, Sonoma
1979 Louis M. Martini ($15.00) Vineyard Selection, Lot 1, Monte Rosso, Sonoma
1979 Matanzas Creek Winery ($16.00) Sonoma
1982 Matanzas Creek Winery ($14.00) Sonoma
1965 Mayacamas Vineyards, Napa Valley
1970 Mayacamas Vineyards, Napa Mountain
1973 Mayacamas Vineyards, Napa Valley
1974 Mayacamas Vineyards, Napa Valley
1975 Mayacamas Vineyards ($12.00) Napa Mountain
1976 Mayacamas Vineyards ($15.00) California
1977 Mayacamas Vineyards ($15.00) Napa Valley
1982 Mayacamas Vineyards ($18.00) Napa Valley
1980 McDowell Valley Vineyards ($9.00) Estate, McDowell Valley
1981 McDowell Valley Vineyards ($9.50) Estate, McDowell Valley
1979 Mill Creek Vineyards ($8.50) Estate, Sonoma
1975 Robert Mondavi Winery ($35.00) Reserve, Napa Valley
1976 Robert Mondavi Winery ($25.00) Reserve, Napa Valley
1977 Robert Mondavi Winery ($35.00) Reserve, Napa Valley
1979 Robert Mondavi Winery ($25.00) Reserve, Napa Valley
1979 Robert Mondavi Winery OPUS ONE ($50.00) Napa Valley
1982 Robert Mondavi Winery ($9.50) Napa Valley
1979 Monterey Peninsula Winery ($18.00) Arroyo Seco, Monterey
1981 Monterey Peninsula Winery ($14.00) Doctor's Reserve, Monterey
1981 J. W. Morris Wineries ($7.50) Alexander Valley
1981 J. W. Morris Wineries ($8.00) California Selection
1973 Mount Eden Vineyards ($14.00) Estate, Santa Cruz Mountains

1973 Mount Veeder Winery, Bernstein, Napa
1974 Mount Veeder Winery, Bernstein, Napa
1979 Mount Veeder Winery ($13.50) Bernstein, Napa
1978 Napa Cellars ($12.00) Napa Valley
1979 Napa Cellars ($12.00) Napa Valley
1980 Napa Cellars ($16.00) Alexander Valley
1981 Nevada City Winery ($6.50) California
1980 Newton Winery ($12.50) Estate, Napa Valley
1982 Neyers Winery ($11.00) Napa Valley
1978 Niebaum-Coppola Estate ($25.00) Napa Valley
1979 Niebaum-Coppola Estate ($25.00) Napa Valley
1980 Niebaum-Coppola Estate ($25.00) Napa Valley
1979 Pacheco Ranch Winery ($9.00) Marin
1982 Pat Paulsen Vineyards ($10.00) Estate, Sonoma
1982 Robert Pecota Winery ($12.00) Napa Valley
1979 Pendleton Winery ($11.00) Adamson-Tupper, Napa Valley
1974 Joseph Phelps Vineyards ($60.00) Insignia, Napa Valley
1975 Joseph Phelps Vineyards ($35.00) Napa Valley
1976 Joseph Phelps Vineyards ($20.00) Insignia, 94% Eisele, 6% Oakville Merlot, Napa Valley
1977 Joseph Phelps Vineyards ($15.00) Backus, Napa Valley
1977 Joseph Phelps Vineyards ($25.00) Insignia, Napa Valley
1978 Joseph Phelps Vineyards ($16.50) Backus, Napa Valley
1978 Joseph Phelps Vineyards ($25.00) Insignia, Napa Valley
1978 Joseph Phelps Vineyards ($30.00) Eisele, Napa Valley
1979 Joseph Phelps Vineyards ($25.00) Insignia, Napa Valley
1979 Joseph Phelps Vineyards ($30.00) Eisele, Napa
1980 Joseph Phelps Vineyards ($25.00) Insignia, Napa Valley
1981 Joseph Phelps Vineyards ($15.00) Backus, Napa Valley
1981 Jospeh Phelps Vineyards ($25.00) Insignia, Napa Valley
1983 Joseph Phelps Vineyards ($25.00) Insignia, Napa Valley
1980 Pine Ridge Winery ($17.00) Stag's Leap District, Napa
1981 Pine Ridge Winery ($13.00) Rutherford, Napa
1981 Pine Ridge Winery ($20.00) Stag's Leap Cuvée, Napa Valley
1982 Pine Ridge Winery ($13.00) Rutherford Cuvée, Napa Valley
1982 Quail Ridge ($13.00) Napa Valley
1979 Quilceda Creek Vintners ($12.50) Washington
1978 Ravenswood ($9.00) California
1977 Raymond Vineyard & Cellar ($18.00) Estate, Napa Valley
1981 Raymond Vineyard & Cellar ($12.00) Napa Valley
1981 Richardson Vineyards ($7.50) Sonoma Valley
NV   Ridge Vineyards ($9.50) Jimsomare, Santa Cruz Mountains
1968 Ridge Vineyards ($70.00) Monte Bello, Santa Cruz
1972 Ridge Vineyards ($60.00) Monte Bello, Santa Cruz Mountains
1978 Ridge Vineyards ($30.00) Monte Bello, Santa Cruz Mountains
1981 Ridge Vineyards ($12.00) York Creek, Napa Valley
1981 Ridge Vineyards ($30.00) Monte Bello, Santa Cruz Mountains
1982 Ridge Vineyards ($12.00) Beatty, Howell Mountain
1980 Ritchie Creek Vineyards ($12.50) Napa Valley
1981 Ritchie Creek Vineyards ($12.50) Napa Valley
1980 Roddis Cellar ($12.00) Estate, Diamond Mountain, Napa Valley
1980 Rosenblum Cellars ($9.00) Cohn & Balfour, Napa Valley
1981 Rosenblum Cellars ($10.00) Cohn, Napa Valley
1982 Rosenblum Cellars ($10.00) 62% Napa Valley, 38% Sonoma
1978 Roudon-Smith Vineyards ($25.00) 10th Anniversary, Steiner, Sonoma
1981 Roudon-Smith Vineyards ($12.00) Steiner, Sonoma

RED/*Cabernet Sauvignon*

1982 Roudon-Smith Vineyards ($7.50) Nelson Ranch, Mendocino
1979 Round Hill Cellars RUTHERFORD RANCH BRAND ($9.00) Napa Valley
1980 Channing Rudd Cellars ($14.00) Bella Oaks, Napa Valley
1979 Rutherford Hill Winery ($10.50) Napa Valley
1982 Rutherford Hill Winery ($11.00) Napa Valley
1981 St. Andrews Winery ($9.00) Napa Valley
1982 St. Clement Vineyards ($13.50) Napa Valley
1979 Santa Cruz Mountain Vineyard ($14.00) Bates Ranch, Santa Cruz Mountains
1979 V. Sattui Winery ($9.75) Preston, Napa Valley
1980 V. Sattui Winery ($9.75) Preston, Napa Valley
1981 Sebastiani Vineyards ($20.00) Eagle, Sonoma Valley
1983 Sebastiani Vineyards ($20.00) Eagle, Sonoma Valley
1980 Sequoia Grove Vineyards ($12.00) Cask Two, 90% Fay, Napa Valley
1981 Sequoia Grove Vineyards ($12.00) Napa Valley
1982 Sequoia Grove Vineyards ($12.00) 67% Napa, 33% Alexander Valley
1978 Shafer Vineyards ($11.00) Estate, Napa Valley
1979 Shafer Vineyards ($13.00) Napa Valley
1982 Shafer Vineyards ($12.00) Napa Valley
1982 Shafer Vineyards ($16.00) Reserve, Napa Valley
1977 Silver Oak Wine Cellars ($16.00) Alexander Valley
1978 Silver Oak Wine Cellars ($16.00) Alexander Valley
1979 Silver Oak Wine Cellars ($16.00) Alexander Valley
1979 Silver Oak Wine Cellars ($16.00) Napa Valley
1979 Silver Oak Wine Cellars ($32.00) Bonny's, Napa Valley
1980 Silver Oak Wine Cellars ($18.00) Alexander Valley
1981 Silverado Vineyards ($11.00) Napa Valley
1982 Silverado Vineyards ($11.00) Napa Valley
1983 Silverado Vineyards ($12.00) Napa Valley
1977 Simi Winery ($15.00) Special Selection, Alexander Valley
1979 Simi Winery ($9.00) Alexander Valley
1980 Simi Winery ($10.00) Alexander Valley
1980 Smith-Madrone ($14.00) Estate, Napa Valley
1979 Smothers-Vine Hill Wines ($12.50) Alexander Valley
1980 Smothers-Vine Hill Wines ($12.50) Alexander Valley
1978 Sonoma Vineyards RODNEY STRONG ($12.00) Alexander's Crown, Sonoma
1979 Sonoma Vineyards RODNEY STRONG ($12.95) Alexander's Crown, Alexander Valley
1980 Sonoma Vineyards RODNEY STRONG ($11.00) Alexander's Crown, Alexander Valley
1979 Sotoyome Winery ($5.75) Dry Creek Valley
1979 Souverain Cellars ($7.75) North Coast
1976 Stag's Leap Wine Cellars ($25.00) Lot 2, Napa Valley
1977 Stag's Leap Wine Cellars ($30.00) Cask 23, Estate, Napa Valley
1978 Stag's Leap Wine Cellars ($15.00) Lot 2, Napa Valley
1979 Stag's Leap Wine Cellars ($12.50) Estate, Napa Valley
1977 Steltzner Vineyards ($16.00) Estate, Stag's Leap District, Napa
1978 Steltzner Vineyards ($14.00) Stag's Leap District, Napa
1979 Steltzner Vineyards ($14.00) Stag's Leap District, Napa
1980 Steltzner Vineyards ($14.00) Estate, Napa Valley
1981 Steltzner Vineyards ($14.00) Napa Valley
1978 Robert Stemmler Winery ($12.50) Sonoma
1979 Robert Stemmler Winery ($12.50) Sonoma
1974 Sterling Vineyards ($20.00) Reserve, Estate, Napa Valley
1977 Sterling Vineyards ($27.50) Reserve, Estate, Napa Valley
1978 Sterling Vineyards ($20.00) Reserve, Estate, Napa Valley

1979 Sterling Vineyards ($27.50) Reserve, Estate, Napa Valley
1980 Sterling Vineyards ($30.00) Reserve, Estate, Napa Valley
1978 Stonegate Winery ($12.00) Steiner, Sonoma
1979 Stonegate Winery ($12.00) Napa Valley
1979 Stonegate Winery ($12.00) Vail Vista, Alexander Valley
1982 Stonegate Winery ($9.00) Napa Valley
1975 Stony Ridge Winery ($4.00) North Coast
1981 Sullivan Vineyards Winery ($14.00) Napa Valley
1982 Toyon Vineyards ($10.00) Estate, Alexander Valley
1979 Tudal Winery ($10.75) Napa Valley
1980 Tudal Winery ($11.50) Napa Valley
1981 Tudal Winery ($11.50) Napa Valley
1979 Tulocay Winery ($9.00) Napa Valley
1980 Tulocay Winery ($9.00) Napa Valley
1980 Vichon Winery ($16.00) Fay, Napa Valley
1980 Vichon Winery ($16.00) Volker Eisele, Napa Valley
1978 Villa Mount Eden Winery ($25.00) Reserve, Estate, Napa Valley
1979 Villa Mount Eden Winery ($13.00) Estate, Napa Valley
1979 Villa Mount Eden Winery ($25.00) Reserve, Estate, Napa Valley
1980 Villa Mount Eden Winery ($25.00) Reserve, Estate, Napa Valley
1982 Villa Mount Eden Winery ($25.00) Reserve, Napa Valley
1978 Vose Vineyards ($10.00) Special Reserve, Napa Valley
1979 Vose Vineyards ($12.50) Mt. Veeder, Napa Valley
1979 William Wheeler Winery ($7.50) Dry Creek Valley
1981 Whitehall Lane Winery ($12.00) Napa Valley
1982 Whitehall Lane Winery ($12.00) Napa Valley
1979 Zaca Mesa Winery ($8.00) Santa Ynez Valley

Gamay

1980 Duxoup Wine Works *Napa Gamay* ($6.00) Sonoma
1981 Duxoup Wine Works *Napa Gamay* ($6.00) Sonoma
1983 Duxoup Wine Works *Napa Gamay* ($6.00) Sonoma
1984 J. Lohr Winery *Monterey Gamay* ($4.50) Greenfield, Monterey
1980 Trentadue Winery ($5.00) Alexander Valley

Gamay Beaujolais

1982 Mill Creek Vineyards ($5.00) Sonoma
1984 Robert Pecota Winery ($5.50) Nouveau, Napa Valley
1983 Preston Vineyards ($5.00) Dry Creek Valley

Merlot

1981 Adelsheim Vineyard ($12.00) Limited Bottling, Sagemoor Farms, Washington
1982 Adelsheim Vineyard ($9.00) 90% Washington, 10% Oregon, 5% Cabernet
1982 Belvedere Wine Company ROBERT YOUNG ($10.00) Alexander Valley
1982 Cain Cellars ($11.00) Napa Valley
1982 Calafia Cellars ($12.00) Pickle Canyon, Napa Valley
1979 Château Chèvre Winery ($10.50) Napa Valley
1981 Clos du Bois Winery ($8.50) Alexander Valley
1978 Clos du Val ($10.00) Napa Valley
1980 Clos du Val ($12.50) Napa Valley
1981 Clos du Val ($13.50) Napa Valley
1982 Clos du Val ($12.50) Napa Valley

RED/*Merlot*

1984 Clos du Val ($12.50) Napa Valley
1981 Columbia Winery ($8.50) 76% Bacchus, 24% Cabernet Sauvignon, Otis, Washington
1979 Duckhorn Vineyards ($12.50) Napa Valley
1980 Duckhorn Vineyards ($12.50) Napa Valley
1980 Fretter Wine Cellars ($10.00) Narsai David, Napa Valley
1982 Fretter Wine Cellars ($10.00) Narsai David, Napa Valley
1977 Gundlach-Bundschu Winery, Rhinefarm, Sonoma Valley
1978 Gundlach-Bundschu Winery ($7.50) Rhinefarm, Sonoma Valley
1979 Gundlach-Bundschu Winery ($9.50) Rhinefarm, Sonoma Valley
1980 Gundlach-Bundschu Winery ($10.00) 125th Anniverary, Rhinefarm, Sonoma Valley
1979 Robert Keenan Winery ($11.00) Napa Valley
1981 Lakespring Winery ($10.00) Napa Valley
1982 Laurel Glen Vineyard ($9.00) Sonoma
1983 Lenz Vineyards ($8.00) Long Island, North Fork
1980 Markham Winery ($8.75) Stag's Leap District, Napa Valley
1981 Markham Winery ($8.75) Napa Valley
1981 Louis M. Martini ($10.00) Russian River Valley
1980 Matanzas Creek Winery ($12.50) Sonoma Valley
1980 Meredyth Vineyard ($9.00) Virginia
1980 Mill Creek Vineyards ($8.50) Estate, Sonoma
1981 Monterey Peninsula Winery ($12.00) Monterey
1980 Newton Winery ($10.50) Napa Valley
1975 Joseph Phelps Vineyards ($35.00) Insignia, Napa Valley
1981 Pine Ridge Winery ($12.50) Napa Valley
1982 Pine Ridge Winery ($12.50) Napa Valley
1982 Pine Ridge Winery ($13.00) Selected Cuvée, Napa Valley
1979 Martin Ray Vineyards ($16.50) Winery Lake, Napa Valley
1981 Martin Ray Vineyards ($16.00) Winery Lake, Napa Valley
1982 Martin Ray Vineyards ($18.00) Winery Lake, Napa Valley
1981 Rolling Hills Vineyard ($8.00) San Luis Obispo
1982 Rutherford Hill Winery ($10.00) Napa Valley
1982 St. Clement Vineyards GARRISON FOREST ($7.75) Napa Valley
1981 St. Francis Vineyards ($10.75) Estate, Sonoma Valley
1982 St. Francis Vineyards ($10.75) Estate, Sonoma Valley
1983 Silverado Vineyards, Napa Valley
1979 Stag's Leap Wine Cellars ($7.50) Estate, Napa Valley
1980 Sterling Vineyards ($11.00) Napa Valley
1981 Sterling Vineyards ($11.00) Napa Valley
1982 Sterling Vineyards ($11.00) Estate, Napa Valley
1982 Sterling Vineyards ($11.00) Napa Valley
1977 Stonegate Winery ($12.00) Spaulding, Napa Valley
1978 Stonegate Winery ($9.00) Spaulding, Napa Valley
1979 Stonegate Winery ($12.00) Spaulding, Napa Valley
1980 Stonegate Winery ($12.00) Spaulding, Napa Valley
1982 Stonegate Winery ($12.00) Spaulding, Napa Valley
1982 Whitehall Lane Winery ($10.00) Knights Valley
1982 Stephen Zellerbach Vineyard ($8.50) Estate, Alexander Valley

Petite Sirah

1979 Concannon Vineyard ($6.50) California
1980 Concannon Vineyard ($5.75) 54% Wilson, Clarksburg; 46% Estate, California
1981 Concannon Vineyard ($6.50) Estate, Livermore
1980 Fetzer Vineyards ($8.50) Special Reserve, Redwood Valley, Mendocino

1979 Field Stone Winery ($7.50) Estate, Alexander Valley
1981 Field Stone Winery ($8.50) Alexander Valley
1980 Freemark Abbey Winery ($8.50) Yale Creek Vineyards, Napa Valley
1981 Guenoc Winery ($6.50) Lake
1976 Hop Kiln Winery ($8.00) Russian River Valley
1979 Hop Kiln Winery ($8.50) Russian River Valley
1981 Hop Kiln Winery ($8.50) Russian River Valley
1980 Inglenook Vineyards ($6.90) Estate, Napa Valley
1981 Inglenook Vineyards ($6.00) Napa Valley
1979 McDowell Valley Vineyards ($7.50) McDowell Valley
1979 Montclair Winery ($6.50) Sonoma
1980 Nevada City Winery ($7.00) Nevada County
1977 Obester Winery ($12.00) John Gemello Tribute, Sonoma
1980 Ridge Vineyards ($9.00) California
1980 Rosenblum Cellars ($5.50) St. George & Rich Vineyards, Napa Valley
1981 Rosenblum Cellars ($6.50) Napa Valley
1982 Rosenblum Cellars ($7.00) Napa Valley
1980 Round Hill Cellars ($6.00) Napa Valley
1981 Round Hill Cellars RUTHERFORD RANCH BRAND ($7.50) Napa Valley
1978 Stag's Leap Wine Cellars ($8.50) Napa Valley
1979 Stags' Leap Winery ($8.75) Napa Valley
1982 Warnelius Winery ($4.00) Sonoma

Pinot Noir

1979 Acacia Winery ($15.00) Iund, Napa Valley-Carneros
1979 Acacia Winery ($15.00) Lee, Napa Valley-Carneros
1979 Acacia Winery ($15.00) St. Clair, Napa Valley-Carneros
1980 Acacia Winery ($15.00) Iund, Napa Valley-Carneros
1981 Acacia Winery ($15.00) Iund, Napa Valley-Carneros
1981 Acacia Winery ($15.00) Lee, Napa Valley-Carneros
1981 Acacia Winery ($15.00) Madonna, Napa Valley-Carneros
1982 Acacia Winery ($15.00) Lee, Napa Valley-Carneros
1982 Acacia Winery ($15.00) Madonna, Napa Valley-Carneros
1983 Acacia Winery ($15.00) Iund, Napa Valley-Carneros
1983 Acacia Winery ($15.00) Lee, Napa Valley-Carneros
1983 Acacia Winery ($15.00) Winery Lake, Napa Valley-Carneros
1981 Adelsheim Vineyard ($10.00) Yamhill, Oregon
1982 Alpine Vineyards ($9.00) Estate, Willamette Valley, Oregon
1978 Amity Vineyards ($20.00) Winemaker's Reserve, 76% Windhill, 24% Estate Gamay, Oregon
1982 Austin Cellars ($10.00) Bien Nacido, Santa Barbara
1982 Austin Cellars ($12.00) Sierra Madre, Santa Barbara
1982 Bay Cellars ($13.50) Buena Vista, Carneros District
1976 Beaulieu Vineyard ($8.00) Los Carneros Region-Napa Valley
1979 Belvedere Wine Company BACIGALUPI ($15.00) Sonoma
1981 Belvedere Wine Company BACIGALUPI ($11.00) Sonoma
1982 Belvedere Wine Company BACIGALUPI ($12.00) Sonoma
1983 Bonny Doon Vineyard ($18.00) Bethel Heights, Willamette Valley, Oregon
1980 David Bruce Winery ($15.00) Estate, Santa Cruz
1981 David Bruce Winery ($12.50) Estate, Santa Cruz Mountains
1982 David Bruce Winery ($12.50) Estate, Santa Cruz Mountains
1983 David Bruce Winery ($12.50) Estate, Santa Cruz Mountains
1981 Buena Vista Winery ($12.00) Special Selection, Sonoma Valley
1982 Davis Bynum Winery ($10.00) Westside Road, Russian River Valley
1982 Davis Bynum Winery ($10.00) Westside Road, Sonoma

RED/*Pinot Noir*

1978 Calera Wine Company ($9.00) Jensen, California
1978 Calera Wine Company ($9.00) Selleck, California
1979 Calera Wine Company ($18.00) Reed, California
1979 Calera Wine Company ($18.00) Selleck, California
1981 Calera Wine Company ($18.00) Jensen, California
1982 Calera Wine Company ($23.00) Jensen, California
1982 Calera Wine Company ($23.00) Reed, California
1983 Calera Wine Company ($23.00) Jensen, California
1983 Calera Wine Company ($23.00) Selleck, California
1978 Carneros Creek Winery ($12.00) Carneros District-Napa Valley
1980 Carneros Creek Winery ($15.00) Carneros District, Napa Valley
1981 Caymus Vineyards ($7.50) Estate, Napa Valley
1976 Chalone Vineyard, Estate, Monterey
1980 Chalone Vineyard ($20.00) California
1981 Chalone Vineyard ($15.00) Estate, Monterey
1981 Château Bouchaine ($8.50) Winery Lake, Carneros District-Napa Valley
1982 Château Bouchaine ($15.00) Winery Lake, Carneros District-Napa Valley
1981 Château Chevalier Winery ($11.50) Stanton's Pinot Patch, Napa Valley
1979 Clos du Bois Winery ($8.50) Cherry Hill, Dry Creek Valley
1980 Clos du Val ($10.00) Napa Valley
1979 Columbia Winery ASSOCIATED VINTNERS (AV) ($9.00) Yakima Valley
1981 Congress Springs Vineyard ($15.00) Private Reserve, Santa Cruz Mountains
1982 Congress Springs Vineyard ($15.00) Private Reserve, Santa Cruz Mountains
1980 H. Coturri and Sons ($15.00) Sonoma Valley
1981 H. Coturri and Sons ($10.00) Miller Ranch, Sonoma
1981 De Loach Vineyards ($9.00) Estate, Sonoma
1981 De Loach Vineyards ($12.00) Reserve, Estate, Sonoma
1982 Dehlinger Winery ($10.00) Sonoma
1982 Edmeades Vineyards ($10.00) B. J. Carney, Anderson Valley, Mendocino
1979 Felton-Empire Vineyards ($7.50) Maritime Series, Reserve, Chaparral, San Luis Obispo
1982 Felton-Empire Vineyards ($11.00) Tonneaux Francais, California
1981 Thomas Fogarty Winery ($15.00) Winery Lake, Napa Valley
1979 Forgeron Vineyard ($8.00) Lane County, Oregon
1979 Fritz Cellars ($6.50) Sonoma
1982 Fritz Cellars QUAIL HILL VINEYARD ($10.00) Reserve, Sonoma
1982 Gundlach-Bundschu Winery ($9.95) Estate-Rhinefarm, Sonoma Valley
1980 HMR Estate Winery ($15.00) Doctor's Reserve, Paso Robles
1979 La Crema Vinera ($14.50) Winery Lake, Carneros District
1976 Louis M. Martini ($4.00) California
1976 Louis M. Martini ($11.00) Special Selection, California
1980 McHenry Vineyards ($17.50) Santa Cruz Mountains
1981 McHenry Vineyards ($14.50) Santa Cruz Mountains
1978 Robert Mondavi Winery ($15.00) Reserve, Napa Valley
1979 Robert Mondavi Winery ($15.00) Reserve, Napa Valley
1980 Robert Mondavi Winery ($15.00) Reserve, Napa Valley
1981 Robert Mondavi Winery ($14.00) Reserve, Napa Valley
1977 Mount Eden Vineyards ($18.00) Estate, Santa Cruz Mountains
1979 Mount Eden Vineyards ($15.00) Estate, Santa Cruz Mountains
1980 Mount Eden Vineyards ($15.00) Estate, Santa Cruz Mountains
1981 Mount Eden Vineyards ($15.00) Estate, Santa Cruz Mountains
1980 Oak Knoll Winery ($20.00) Dion, Oregon
1976 Martin Ray Vineyards ($35.00) Winery Lake, Napa Valley
1981 Martin Ray Vineyards ($14.00) Winery Lake, Carneros District-Napa

1982 Saintsbury Winery ($11.00) Carneros District, Napa Valley
1983 Saintsbury Winery ($12.00) Carneros District, Napa Valley
1977 Santa Cruz Mountain Vineyard ($8.00) Estate, Rider Ridge, Santa Cruz
1981 Santa Cruz Mountain Vineyard ($15.00) Santa Cruz Mountains
1981 Sea Ridge Winery ($10.50) Bohan, Sonoma
1979 Sokol Blosser Winery ($8.95) Hyland, Yamhill County, Oregon
1983 Sokol Blosser Winery ($9.95) Hyland, Yamhill County, Oregon
1982 Soleterra ($12.00) Three Palms, Napa Valley
1982 Robert Stemmler Winery ($15.00) Forchini, Dry Creek Valley
1980 Sunrise Winery ($8.00) Glen Ellen, Sonoma
1978 Joseph Swan Vineyards ($20.00) Sonoma
1980 Valley View Vineyard, Oregon
1982 Ventana Vineyards ($6.25) Estate, Monterey
1974 Weibel Vineyards ($12.00) Santa Clara Valley
1976 Weibel Vineyards ($9.50) Santa Clara Valley
1978 Weibel Vineyards ($8.00) Proprietor's Reserve, Mendocino
1981 Weibel Vineyards ($8.00) Proprietor's Reserve, Mendocino
1979 Winters Winery ($6.00) Napa Valley
1978 Zaca Mesa Winery ($10.00) Special Selection, Estate, Santa Ynez Valley

Syrah

1983 Bonny Doon Vineyard ($10.50) Central Coast
1980 Duxoup Wine Works ($9.00) Preston, Sonoma
1981 Duxoup Wine Works ($9.00) Preston, Sonoma
1983 Duxoup Wine Works ($10.00) Sonoma
1980 McDowell Valley Vineyards ($7.50) Estate, McDowell Valley
1983 Qupe ($7.50) Central Coast

Zinfandel

1980 Almadén Vineyards CHARLES LEFRANC *Royale* ($7.50) San Benito
1980 Amador Foothill Winery ($8.00) Eschen Vineyard, Fiddletown, Amador
1980 Baldinelli Vineyards ($6.00) Lot 1, Shenandoah Valley, Amador
1982 Belli and Sauret Vineyards ($6.75) Paso Robles
1977 Berkeley Wine Cellars, Kelley Creek, Dry Creek Region, Sonoma
1979 Berkeley Wine Cellars ($7.25) Kelley Creek, Dry Creek Region, Sonoma
1979 Buehler Vineyards ($7.00) Estate, Napa Valley
1980 Buehler Vineyards ($8.00) Estate, Napa Valley
1982 Buehler Vineyards ($7.00) Napa Valley
1981 Buena Vista Winery ($12.00) Special Selection, Sonoma Valley
1982 Buena Vista Winery ($10.00) Vineyard Selection, Barricia, Sonoma Valley
1977 Burgess Cellars ($6.75) Napa Valley
1982 Burgess Cellars ($6.50) Napa Valley
1981 Cache Cellars ($6.50) Baldinelli, Amador
1981 Cakebread Cellars ($10.75) Napa Valley
1980 Calafia Cellars ($7.50) Pickle Canyon, Napa Valley
1980 California Wine Company BANDIERA ($4.25) North Coast
1979 Carmel Bay Winery ($5.00) Shandon Valley, San Luis Obispo
1980 Carneros Creek Winery ($6.00) Yolo
1982 Cartlidge & Browne STRATFORD ($7.75) Napa Valley
1980 Cassayre-Forni Cellars ($8.00) Sonoma
1977 Caymus Vineyards ($5.50) California
1978 Caymus Vineyards ($6.50) California
1980 Caymus Vineyards ($6.50) Napa Valley

RED/*Zinfandel*

1983 Château du Lac KENDALL-JACKSON VINEYARDS & WINERY ($7.00) Viña-Los Lomas,
     Clear Lake
1983 Château du Lac KENDALL-JACKSON VINEYARDS & WINERY ($7.00) Zeni, Mendocino
1982 Château Montelena Winery ($10.00) Estate, Napa Valley
1980 Chispa Cellars ($6.00) Amador
1980 Clos du Bois Winery RIVER OAKS VINEYARDS *Private Reserve* ($7.00) Alexander Valley
1977 Clos du Val ($7.50) Napa Valley
1979 Clos du Val ($10.00) Napa Valley
1980 Clos du Val ($9.00) Napa Valley
1983 Clos du Val ($9.00) Napa Valley
1981 Congress Springs Vineyard ($9.00) Santa Cruz Mountains
1978 Conn Creek Winery ($7.50) Napa Valley
1979 Conn Creek Winery ($7.50) Napa Valley
1982 Cordtz Brothers Cellars ($6.00) Upper Alexander Valley
1978 Cuvaison Vineyard ($8.50) Napa Valley
1980 De Loach Vineyards ($7.50) Estate, Russian River Valley
1981 De Loach Vineyards ($7.50) Estate, Russian River Valley
1979 Dehlinger Winery ($7.00) Sonoma
1980 Devlin Wine Cellars ($7.50) Paso Robles
1978 Dry Creek Vineyard ($6.50) Sonoma
1981 Dry Creek Vineyard ($7.50) Dry Creek Valley
1980 Duxoup Wine Works ($7.50) Sonoma
1981 Edmeades Vineyards ($7.50) Anzilotti, Mendocino
1981 Edmeades Vineyards ($9.00) Ciapusci, Mendocino
1981 Edmeades Vineyards ($12.00) Du Pratt, Mendocino
NV Estrella River Winery ($3.50) San Luis Obispo
1979 Fetzer Vineyards ($7.50) Lolonis, Mendocino
1980 Fetzer Vineyards ($3.00) Lake
1981 Fetzer Vineyards ($8.00) Lolonis, Mendocino
1982 Fetzer Vineyards ($8.00) Home, Mendocino
1982 Fetzer Vineyards ($8.00) Lolonis, Mendocino
1982 Fetzer Vineyards ($8.00) Ricetti, Mendocino
1980 Louis Foppiano Wine Company RIVERSIDE FARM ($3.10) California
1981 Frick Winery ($6.00) Santa Clara
1981 Frog's Leap Winery ($6.50) Spottswoode, Napa Valley
NV Gemello Winery ($6.25) Reminiscence, Lot 75A, Amador
1982 Glen Ellen Winery BENZIGER FAMILY WINERY & VINEYARDS ($4.50) Geyserville, Sonoma
1981 Green and Red Vineyards ($5.75) Estate, Napa Valley
1978 Grgich Hills Cellars ($9.00) Alexander Valley
1979 Grgich Hills Cellars ($10.00) Alexander Valley
1980 Grgich Hills Cellars ($10.00) Alexander Valley
1981 Grgich Hills Cellars ($10.00) Sonoma
1981 Hop Kiln Winery ($8.50) Russian River Valley
1980 Horizon Winery ($8.00) Sonoma
1980 Lake Sonoma Winery DIABLO VISTA ($6.90) Polson, Dry Creek Valley, Sonoma
1981 Lake Sonoma Winery DIABLO VISTA ($6.90) Dry Creek Valley
1981 Leeward Winery ($7.50) Shenandoah Valley, Amador
1980 Lytton Springs Winery ($8.00) Sonoma
1981 Lytton Springs Winery ($8.00) Sonoma
1980 Madrona Vineyards ($6.00) Estate, El Dorado
1980 Mark West Vineyards ($8.50) Sonoma
1983 Martin Brothers Winery ($6.00) Paso Robles
1968 Louis M. Martini, Monte Rosso, Sonoma

1979 Paul Masson Vineyards ($3.75) California
1980 McLester Winery ($7.50) Cowan, Shenandoah Valley, Amador
1981 McLester Winery ($6.00) Radike, San Luis Obispo
1980 Montclair Winery ($8.50) Kelley Creek, Sonoma
1981 Montclair Winery ($6.50) Teldeschi, Sonoma
1981 Montclair Winery ($8.50) Kelley Creek, Sonoma
1978 Monterey Peninsula Winery ($6.50) 29% Amador, 45% Templeton, 20% Paso Robles,
       California
1979 Monterey Peninsula Winery ($7.50) California
1981 Monteviña Wines ($5.00) Montino, Estate, Shenandoah Valley, California
1982 Moon Vineyards ($4.00) Estate, Napa Valley-Carneros
1981 Mount Veeder Winery ($8.50) Napa Valley
1982 Mount Veeder Winery ($8.50) Napa Valley
1981 Joseph Phelps Vineyards ($6.75) Alexander Valley
1984 Joseph Phelps Vineyards ($5.75) Napa Valley
1980 Preston Vineyards ($7.50) Estate, Dry Creek Valley, Sonoma
1983 Preston Vineyards ($7.00) Sonoma
1980 A. Rafanelli Winery ($6.25) Dry Creek Valley, Sonoma
1981 Ravenswood ($6.50) Dry Creek Benchland, Sonoma
1982 Ravenswood ($10.00) Limited Edition, Vickerson, Napa Valley
1982 Ravenswood ($11.00) Etched Bottle, Dickerson, Napa Valley
1981 Richardson Vineyards ($8.50) Sonoma Valley
1979 Ridge Vineyards ($9.00) Geyserville, Trentadue Ranch, Sonoma
1980 Ridge Vineyards ($7.50) Esola, Shenandoah Valley, Amador
1980 Ridge Vineyards ($7.50) Fiddletown, Amador
1980 Ridge Vineyards ($9.00) Geyserville, Trentedue Ranch, California
1981 Ridge Vineyards ($9.00) 85% Trentedue, 15% Angeli, Geyserville, Alexander Valley
1982 Ridge Vineyards ($8.00) Dusi, Paso Robles
1982 Ridge Vineyards ($9.00) Beatty, Howell Mountain
1982 Ridge Vineyards ($9.50) 20th Anniversary, Geyserville, California
1982 Ridge Vineyards ($10.50) York Creek, California
1978 Rosenblum Cellars ($5.50) Napa Valley
1981 Rosenblum Cellars ($6.00) Mauritson, Sonoma Valley
1981 Rosenblum Cellars ($6.00) Napa Valley
1983 Rosenblum Cellars ($7.50) Napa Valley
1983 Rosenblum Cellars ($7.50) Sonoma
1980 Roudon-Smith Vineyards ($7.50) 10th Anniversary, Chauvet, Sonoma
1980 Roudon-Smith Vineyards ($9.00) 10th Anniversary, Old Hill Ranch, Sonoma
1979 Round Hill Cellars RUTHERFORD RANCH BRAND ($5.00) Napa
1980 Santino Wines ($7.50) Special Select, Eschen Vineyards, Fiddletown, Amador
1981 Sarah's Vineyard ($9.00) Dry Creek Valley
1980 Silver Mountain Vineyards ($6.50) Paso Robles
NV   Story Vineyards ($4.50) California
1980 Storybook Mountain Vineyards ($7.75) Sonoma
1981 Storybook Mountain Vineyards ($7.75) Napa Valley
1981 Storybook Mountain Vineyards ($9.50) Estate Reserve, Napa Valley
1980 Susine Cellars ($5.00) Amador
1982 Sycamore Creek Vineyards ($9.00) Estate, Morgan Hill, California
1983 Sycamore Creek Vineyards ($10.00) Proprietor Grown, California
1980 Topolos at Russian River ($7.50) Sonoma
1980 Traulsen Vineyards ($8.50) Napa Valley
1980 Tulocay Winery ($6.50) Napa Valley
1980 Vose Vineyards ($8.75) Estate, Mount Veeder, Napa
1982 White Oak Vineyards ($6.00) Dry Creek Valley
1981 York Mountain Winery ($6.95) Estate, San Luis Obispo

FORTIFIED

Non-varietal

Ficklin Vineyards *Port* ($6.00) California
1979 J. W. Morris Wineries *Port* ($10.00) Black Mountain, Sonoma
1984 Quady Winery *Elysium* ($11.00) California
1984 Quady Winery *Essensia* ($11.00) California
St. Julian Wine Company *Solera Cream Sherry* ($6.75) Michigan
Souverain Cellars *Reserve Solera Port* ($11.00) Dry Creek Valley

Four-Star Wines

WHITE

Chardonnay

1980 Acacia Winery ($14.00) Napa Valley-Carneros
1981 Acacia Winery ($12.50) Napa Valley
1983 Au Bon Climat ($20.00) Babcock, Santa Barbara
1983 William Baccala Winery ($11.00) Mendocino
1981 Chalone Vineyard ($17.50) Estate, Gavilan Mountains
1982 Chalone Vineyard ($17.00) Estate, Monterey
1981 Château St. Jean ($18.00) Robert Young, Alexander Valley
1983 Far Niente Winery ($18.00) Napa Valley
1981 Frick Winery ($10.00) Ventana, Monterey
1983 Handley Cellars ($12.50) Dry Creek Valley
1981 Kistler Vineyards ($15.00) Dutton Ranch, California
1981 Matanzas Creek Winery ($14.50) Sonoma
1982 Matanzas Creek Winery ($18.00) Estate, Sonoma Valley
1983 Matanzas Creek Winery ($18.00) Estate, Sonoma Valley
1981 Robert Mondavi Winery ($20.00) Reserve, Napa Valley
1982 Morgan Winery ($12.00) Cobblestone, Hillside, Monterey
1980 Mount Eden Vineyards ($15.00) Estate, Santa Cruz Mountains
1982 Martin Ray Vineyards ($14.00) Dutton Ranch, Sonoma
1982 St. Francis Vineyards ($14.00) Jacobs, Carneros District, Napa
1980 Simi Winery ($20.00) Reserve, Mendocino
1981 Sonoma-Cutrer Vineyards ($14.50) Les Pierres, Sonoma Valley

Chenin Blanc

1982 Bogle Vineyards ($5.00) Dry, Clarksburg

Fume Blanc

1982 Château St. Jean ($10.50) La Petite Etoile, Sonoma
1983 Château St. Jean ($10.50) La Petite Etoile, Sonoma
1984 Château St. Jean ($10.50) La Petite Etoile, Sonoma

Gewürztraminer

1981 Château St. Jean ($13.00) Select Late Harvest, Belle Terre, Alexander Valley
1983 Château St. Jean ($16.00) Selected Late Harvest, Belle Terre, Sonoma
1984 Matrose Wines ($7.50) Hafner, Alexander Valley

Johannisberg Riesling

1984 Château du Lac ($7.00) Monterey
1984 Château du Lac KENDALL-JACKSON VINEYARDS & WINERY ($7.00) Monterey
1982 Château St. Jean ($12.00) Late Harvest, Robert Young, Alexander Valley
1982 Château St. Jean ($22.50) Special Select Late Harvest, Robert Young, Alexander Valley,
          Sonoma. 375 ml
1981 Gold Seal Vineyards ($8.00) Harvested Late, Estate, New York State
1984 Greenwood Ridge Vineyards ($7.00) Mendocino
1982 Hidden Cellars ($10.00) Late Harvest, Bailey J. Lovin, Mendocino
1979 Jekel Vineyard ($20.00) Late Harvest, Estate, Monterey
1981 Jekel Vineyard ($6.50) Ventana, Monterey
1981 Milano Winery ($20.00) Individual Dried Bunch Select, Mendocino
1982 Milano Winery ($25.00) Individual Bunch Select Lake Harvest, Ordway's Valley Foothills,
          Mendocino

WHITE/*Johannisberg Riesling*

1976 Joseph Phelps Vineyards, Selected Late Harvest, Napa Valley
1982 Quail Run Vintners ($6.00) Washington

Muscat

1981 Estrella River Winery ($7.50) San Luis Obispo
1983 Robert Pecota Winery *Muscato di Andrea* ($7.50) Napa Valley

Sauvignon Blanc

1982 Boeger Winery ($6.00) 10th Anniversary, El Dorado
1982 Domaine Laurier ($9.00) Sonoma-Green Valley
1983 Duckhorn Vineyards ($9.00) Napa Valley
1982 Tyland Vineyards TIJSSELING ($7.50) Estate, Mendocino

Scheurebe

1982 Joseph Phelps Vineyards ($15.00) Special Select Late Harvest, Napa Valley
1983 Joseph Phelps Vineyards ($15.00) Late Harvest, Napa Valley

SPARKLING

Non-varietal

1981 Château St. Jean *Brut* ($17.00) Sonoma

ROSE

Cabernet Sauvignon

1984 Simi Winery *Rosé of Cabernet* ($6.50) North Coast

RED

Non-varietal

1982 Carmenet Vineyard *Carmenet Red* ($16.00) Sonoma Valley

Cabernet Sauvignon

1966 Beaulieu Vineyard, Private Reserve, Estate, Napa Valley
1970 Beaulieu Vineyard, Private Reserve, Estate, Napa Valley
1980 Belvedere Wine Company ROBERT YOUNG ($12.00) Sonoma
1978 Beringer Vineyards ($22.00) Private Reserve, Lemmon Ranch, Napa Valley
1980 Beringer Vineyards ($20.00) Private Reserve, Lemmon-Chabot, Napa Valley
1981 Beringer Vineyards ($25.00) Lemmon-Chabot, Napa Valley
1981 Buena Vista Winery ($18.00) Special Selection, Estate, Sonoma Valley-Carneros
1978 Burgess Cellars ($16.00) Vintage Selection, Napa Valley
1976 Caymus Vineyards ($35.00) Special Selection, Estate, Napa Valley
1979 Caymus Vineyards ($30.00) Special Selection, Estate, Napa Valley
1980 Caymus Vineyards ($12.50) Estate, Napa Valley
1981 Caymus Vineyards ($12.50) Estate, Napa Valley
1969 Chappellet Winery, Napa Valley
1980 Chappellet Winery ($18.00) Napa Valley
1979 Château St. Jean ($17.00) Wildwood, Sonoma Valley
1974 Clos du Val ($12.50) Napa Valley
1980 Clos du Val ($12.50) Napa Valley
1981 Clos du Val ($12.50) Napa Valley

1982 Diamond Creek Vineyards ($20.00) Volcanic Hill, Napa Valley
1979 Dunn Vineyards ($12.00) Napa Valley
1980 Dunn Vineyards ($12.50) Napa Valley
1981 Dunn Vineyards ($12.50) Howell Mountain-Napa Valley
1982 Groth Vineyards and Winery ($13.00) Napa Valley
1981 Gundlach-Bundschu Winery ($12.00) Batto Ranch, Sonoma Valley
1968 Heitz Wine Cellars, Martha's, Napa Valley
1970 Heitz Wine Cellars, Napa Valley
1973 Heitz Wine Cellars ($40.00) Martha's, Napa Valley
1974 Heitz Wine Cellars ($55.00) Martha's, Napa Valley
1977 Heitz Wine Cellars ($35.00) Bella Oaks, Napa Valley
1978 Heitz Wine Cellars ($20.00) Bella Oaks, Napa Valley
1979 Heitz Wine Cellars ($30.00) Martha's, Napa Valley
1980 William Hill Winery ($18.00) Napa
1981 Iron Horse Vineyards ($13.50) Estate, Green Valley, Sonoma
1981 Laurel Glen Vineyard ($12.50) Estate, Sonoma Mountain
1979 Lower Lake Winery ($12.00) Devoto, Lake
1978 Robert Mondavi Winery ($40.00) Reserve, Napa Valley
1980 Robert Mondavi Winery OPUS ONE ($50.00) Napa Valley
1981 Robert Mondavi Winery OPUS ONE ($50.00) Napa Valley
1983 Robert Mondavi Winery ($35.00) Reserve, Napa Valley
1980 Monterey Peninsula Winery ($25.00) Monterey
1980 Monticello Cellars ($9.75) Napa Valley
1981 Newton Winery ($12.50) Estate, Napa Valley
1981 Martin Ray Vineyards ($16.50) Steltzner, Napa Valley
1971 Ridge Vineyards ($75.00) Monte Bello, Santa Cruz Mountains
1977 Rutherford Hill Winery ($9.00) Napa Valley
1980 St. Clement Vineyards ($12.50) Napa Valley
1981 St. Clement Vineyards ($12.50) Napa Valley
1979 Simi Winery ($19.00) Reserve, Alexander Valley
1979 Smith-Madrone ($14.00) Estate, Napa Valley
1978 Stag's Leap Wine Cellars ($35.00) Cask 23, Napa Valley
1980 Stag's Leap Wine Cellars ($11.00) Napa Valley
1981 Stag's Leap Wine Cellars ($15.00) Stag's Leap, Napa Valley
1980 Stonegate Winery ($8.50) Vail Vista, Alexander Valley
1981 Vichon Winery ($12.75) Fay and Eisle, Napa Valley
1978 Villa Mt. Eden Winery ($12.00) Estate, Napa Valley
1980 William Wheeler Winery ($12.00) Special Reserve, Norse, Dry Creek Valley

Merlot

1981 Duckhorn Vineyards ($12.50) Three Palms, Napa Valley
1981 Duckhorn Vineyards ($13.00) Napa Valley
1982 Duckhorn Vineyards ($13.00) Napa Valley
1982 Robert Keenan Winery ($12.50) Napa Valley
1979 Rutherford Hill Winery ($9.25) Napa Valley
1979 Sterling Vineyards ($12.00) Estate, Napa Valley

Pinot Noir

1980 Acacia Winery ($15.00) Madonna, Napa Valley-Carneros
1980 Acacia Winery ($15.00) St. Clair, Napa Valley-Carneros
1982 Acacia Winery ($15.00) St. Clair, Napa Valley-Carneros
1982 Acacia Winery ($15.00) Winery Lake, Napa Valley-Carneros
1983 Acacia Winery ($15.00) Madonna, Napa Valley-Carneros
1983 Acacia Winery ($15.00) St. Clair, Napa Valley-Carneros

RED/*Pinot Noir*

1981 Belvedere Wine Company WINERY LAKE ($12.00) Estate, Los Carneros
1977 Carneros Creek Winery ($12.50) Napa Valley
1983 Carneros Creek Winery ($16.00) Napa Valley
1982 La Crema Vinera ($10.00) Porter Creek, Russian River Valley

Zinfandel

1979 Edmeades Vineyards ($9.00) Du Pratt, Mendocino
1982 Grgich Hills Cellars ($10.00) Alexander Valley
1977 Lytton Springs Winery ($6.50) Sonoma
1980 Joseph Swan Vineyards ($9.00) Sonoma

Wineries by Region

Hawaiian Islands

Hawaii

Tedeschi Vineyard and Winery, Ulupalakua, Maui

Mid-Atlantic States

New Jersey

Antuzzi's Winery, Delran
Del Vista Vineyards, Frenchtown
Gross Highland Winery, Absecon
Renault Winery, Egg Harbor City
Tewksbury Wine Cellars, Lebanon
Tomasello Winery, Hammonton

New York

Baldwin Vineyards, Pine Bush
The Barry Wine Company, Conesus
Batavia Wine Cellars, Batavia
Benmarl Wine Company, Marlboro
Bridgehampton Winery, Bridgehampton
Brimstone Hill Vineyards, Pine Bush
Brotherhood Winery, Washingtonville
Bully Hill Vineyards, Hammondsport
Cagnasso Winery, Marlboro
Canandaigua Wine Company, Canandaigua
Casa Larga Vineyards, Fairport
Cascade Mountain Vineyards, Amenia
Chadwick Bay Wine Company, Fredonia
Château Esperanza, Bluff Point
Clinton Vineyards, Clinton Corners
Cottage Vineyards, Marlboro
Crown Regal Wine Cellars, Brooklyn
De May Wine Cellars, Hammondsport
Delmonico's, Brooklyn
Eaton Vineyards, Pine Plains
El Paso Winery, Ulster Park
Fair Haven Winery, Valois
Finger Lakes Wine Cellars, Branchport
Four Chimneys Farm Winery, Himrod
Frontenac Point Vineyard, Trumansburg
Gardiner Vineyard & Farm Corporation, Gardiner
Giasi Vineyard, Burdett
Glenora Wine Cellars, Dundee
Gold Seal Vineyards, Hammondsport
Hargrave Vineyard, Cutchogue
Heron Hill Vineyards, Hammondsport
High Tor Vineyards, New City

Hudson Valley Winery, Highland
Johnson Estate, Westfield
Knapp Farms, Romulus
Lenz Vineyards, Peconic, Long Island
Lucas Vineyards, Interlaken
McGregor Vineyard Winery, Dundee
Merritt Estate Winery, Forestville
Monarch Wine Company, Brooklyn
North Salem Vineyard, North Salem
Northeast Vineyard, Millerton
Penn Yan Wine Cellars, Penn Yan
Pindar Vineyards, Peconic, Long Island
Plane's Cayuga Vineyard, Ovid
Poplar Ridge Vineyards, Valois
The Rolling Vineyards Farm, Hector
Rotolo & Romero Wine Cellars, Avon
Royal Kedem Wine Corporation, Milton
Schapiro Kosher Wine Company, New York
Schloss Doepken Winery, Ripley
Taylor Wine Company, Hammondsport
Vinifera Wine Cellars, Hammondsport
Wagner Vineyards, Lodi
Walker Valley Vineyards, New York
West Park Vineyards, West Park
Wickham Vineyards, Hector
Widmer's Wine Cellars, Naples
Hermann J. Wiemer Vineyard, Dundee
Windsor Vineyards, Marlboro
Woodbury Vineyards, Dunkirk
Woodstock Winery, West Shoken

Pennsylvania

Adams County Winery, Orrtanna
Allegro Vineyards, Brogue
Stephen Bahn Winery, Brogue
Blue Ridge Winery, Carlisle
Brandywine Vineyards, Kemblesville
Buckingham Valley Vineyards, Buckingham
Bucks County Vineyards, New Hope
Buffalo Valley Winery, Lewisburg
Calvaresi Winery, Reading
Chaddsford Winery, Chadds Ford
Conestoga Vineyards, Lancaster
Conneaut Cellars Winery, Conneaut Lake
Country Creek Winery, Telford
Doerflinger Wine Cellars, Bloomsburg
Heritage Wine Cellars, North East
Kolln Vineyards, Bellefonte
Lancaster County Winery, Willow Street
Lapic Winery, New Brighton
Mazza Vineyards, North East

James Moroney Winery, Philadelphia
Mount Hope Estate & Winery, Cornwall
Naylor Wine Cellars, Stewartstown
Neri's Wine Cellar, Langhorne
Nissley Vineyards, Bainbridge
Nittany Valley Winery, State College
Penn Shore Vineyards, North East
Presque Isle Wine Cellars, North East
Quarry Hill, Shippenburg
Tucquan Vineyard, Holtwood
York Springs Winery, York Springs

Midwestern States

Illinois

Gem City Vineland Company, Nauvoo
Louis Glunz, Lincolnwood
Lynfred Winery, Roselle
Thompson Winery, Monee

Indiana

Banholzer Winecellars, Hesston
Easley Winery, Indianapolis
Huber Orchard Winery, Borden
Oliver Winery, Bloomington
Possum Trot Vineyards, Unionville
St. Wendel Cellars, Wadesville
Scotella Vineyards Winery, Madison
Swiss Valley Vineyards, Vevay

Iowa

Ehrle Brothers Winery, Homestead
The Grape Vine Winery, Amana
Okoboji Winery, Arnolds Park
Old Wine Cellar Winery, Amana
Private Stock Winery, Boone
Sandstone Winery, Amana
Village Winery, Amana

Michigan

Boskydel Vineyard, Lake Leelanau
Bronte Champagne & Wine Company, Detroit
Château Grand Traverse, Traverse City
Fenn Valley Vineyards, Fennville
Fink Winery, Dundee
Frontenac Vineyard, Paw Paw
Good Harbor Vineyards, Lake Leelanau
Lakeside Vineyard, Harbert
Leelanau Wine Cellars, Omena
L. Mawby Vineyards, Suttons Bay
St. Julian Wine Company, Paw Paw
The Seven Lakes Vineyard, Fenton
Tabor Hill Winery, Buchanan
Warner Vineyards, Paw Paw

Minnesota

Alexis Bailly Vineyard, Hastings
Minnesota Winegrowers Co-op, Stillwater

Missouri

Bardenheier's Wine Cellar, St. Louis
Bias Vineyards & Winery, Berger
Bristle Ridge Vineyards, Nob Noster
Carver Wine Cellars, Rolla
Ferrigno Vineyards and Winery, St. James
Green Valley Vineyards, Portland
Heinrichshaus Vineyards, St. James
Hermannhof, Hermann
Kruger's Winery & Vineyards, Nelson
Midi Vineyards, Lone Jack
Montelle Vineyards, Augusta
Moore-Dupont Winery, Benton
Mount Pleasant Vineyard, Augusta
Ozark Vineyards, Chestnut Ridge
Peaceful Bend Vineyard, Steelville
Pirtle's Weston Vineyards, Weston
Reis Winery, Licking
Rosati Winery, St. James
St. James Winery, St. James
Stone Hill Winery, Hermann
The Winery of the Abbey, Cuba
Winery of the Little Hills, St. Charles

Ohio

Breitenbach Wine Cellars, Dover
Leslie J. Bretz, Middle Bass
Brushcreek Vineyards, Peebles
Buccia Vineyard, Conneaut
Cedar Hill Wine Company, Cleveland Heights
Chalet DeBonne Vineyards, Madison
John Christ Winery, Avon Lake
Colonial Vineyards, Lebanon
Daughters Wine Cellar, Madison
Dover Vineyards, Westlake
E & K Wine Company, Sandusky
Grand River Wine Company, Madison
Hafle Vineyards, Springfield
Heineman Winery, Put-in-Bay
Heritage Vineyards, West Milton
Louis Jindra Winery, Jackson
Johlin Century, Oregon
Klingshirn Winery, Avon Lake
Lonz Winery, Middle Bass Island
Mantey Vineyards, Sandusky
Markko Vineyard, Conneaut
Marlo Winery, Fort Laramie
McIntosh's Ohio Valley Wines, Bethel
Meier's Wine Cellars, Silverton
Mon Ami Wine Company, Port Clinton
Moyer Vineyards, Manchester

Steuk Wine Company, Sandusky
Stillwater Winery, Troy
Tarula Farms, Clarksville
Valley Vineyards, Morrow
Vinterra Farm and Winery, Houston
Wickliffe Winery, Wickliffe
Wyandotte Wine Cellars, Gahanna

Wisconsin

Christina Wine Cellars, LaCrosse
Renick Winery, Sturgeon Bay
St. Croix Winery, Prescott
Spurgeon Vineyards & Winery, Highland
Stone Mill Winery, Cedarburg
Wollersheim Winery, Prairie du Sac

New England States

Connecticut

Clarke Vineyard, Stonington
Crosswoods Vineyards, North Stonington
Haight Vineyard, Litchfield
Hamlet Hill Vineyards, Pomfret
Hopkins Vineyard, New Preston
St. Hilary's Vineyards, North Grovenordale
Stonecrop Vineyards, Stonington

Massachusetts

Chicama Vineyards, West Tisbury
Commonwealth Winery, Plymouth

Rhode Island

Prudence Island Vineyards, Prudence Island
Sakonnet Vineyards, Little Compton

Pacific Coast States

California

Alameda County

Bay Cellars, Emeryville
Berkeley Wine Cellars, Berkeley
Concannon Vineyard, Livermore
Paul De Martini, Clayton
Elliston Vineyards, Sunol
Fenestra Winery, Livermore
Fretter Wine Cellars, Berkeley
Livermore Valley Cellars, Livermore
R. Montali and Associates, Berkeley
Montclair Winery, Oakland
Oak Barrel, Berkeley
Piedmont Cellars, Oakland
Rosenblum Cellars, Emeryville

Stony Ridge Winery, Pleasanton
Michel Tribaut de Romery, Hayward
Villa Armando Winery, Livermore
Wente Brothers, Livermore

Alameda/Mendocino County

Weibel Vineyards, Mission San Jose

Amador County

Amador City Winery, Amador City
Amador Foothill Winery, Plymouth
Amador Winery, Amador City
Argonaut Winery, Ione
Baldinelli Vineyards, Plymouth
Beau Val Wines, Plymouth
D'Agostini Winery, Plymouth
Greenstone Winery, Ione
Karly Wines, Plymouth
Kenworthy Vineyards, Plymouth
Monteviña Wines, Plymouth
Santino Wines, Plymouth
Shenandoah Vineyards, Plymouth
Stoneridge, Sutter Creek
Story Vineyards, Plymouth
Winterbrook Vineyards, Ione

Butte County

Belle Creek Ranch, Paradise
Paradise Vintners, Paradise

Calaveras County

Chispa Cellars, Murphys
Stevenot Vineyards, Murphys

Contra Costa County

Cline Cellars, Oakeley
J. E. Digardi Winery, Martinez
Conrad Viano Winery, Martinez

El Dorado County

Boeger Winery, Placerville
El Dorado Vineyards, Camino
Fitzpatrick Winery, Somerset
Gerwer Winery, Somerset
Granite Springs Winery, Somerset
Herbert Vineyards, Somerset
Madrona Vineyards, Camino
Salter Winery, Somerset
Sierra Vista Winery, Placerville

Fresno County

Gibson Wine Company, Sanger
A. Nonini Winery, Fresno

Nicholas G. Verry, Parlier
Villa Bianchi, Kerman

Humboldt County
Fieldbrook Valley Winery, Fieldbrook
Willow Creek Vineyards, McKinleyville
Wittwer Winery, Eureka

Kern County
Giumarra Vineyards, Edison
LaMont Winery, DiGiorgio

Lake County
Château du Lac, Lakeport
Guenoc Winery, Middletown
Konocti Winery, Kelseyville
Lower Lake Winery, Lower Lake
Channing Rudd Cellars, Middletown

Los Angeles County
Ahern Winery, San Fernando
Donatoni Winery, Inglewood
Martin Winery, Culver City
McLester Winery, Inglewood
Palos Verdes Winery, Inglewood
San Antonio Winery, Los Angeles

Madera County
Ficklin Vineyards, Madera
Papagni Vineyards, Madera
Quady Winery, Madera

Marin County
J. Patrick Dore Selections, Mill Valley
Kalin Cellars, Novato
Pacheco Ranch Winery, Ignacio
Thackrey & Company, Bolinas
Woodbury Winery, San Rafael

Mendocino County
William Baccala Winery, Ukiah
Blanc Vineyards, Redwood Valley
Braren Pauli Winery, Potter Valley
Dolan Vineyards, Redwood Valley
Edmeades Vineyards, Philo
Fetzer Vineyards, Redwood Valley
Frey Vineyards, Redwood Valley
Greenwood Ridge Vineyards, Philo
Handley Cellars, Philo
Hidden Cellars, Talmage
Husch Vineyards, Philo
Lazy Creek Winery, Philo
Lolonis Winery, Redwood Valley

McDowell Valley Vineyards, Hopland
Milano Winery, Hopland
Navarro Vineyards and Winery, Philo
Olson Vineyards Winery, Redwood Valley
Parducci Wine Cellars, Ukiah
Parsons Creek Winery, Ukiah
Pepperwood Springs Vineyards, Philo
Scharffenberger Cellars, Ukiah
Tyland Vineyards, Ukiah
Whaler Vineyards, Ukiah

Monterey County
Carmel Bay Winery, Carmel
Chalone Vineyard, Soledad
Château Julien, Carmel Valley
Durney Vineyard, Carmel Valley
Jekel Vineyard, Greenfield
McFarland Wine Company, Gonzales
Monterey Peninsula Winery, Monterey
The Monterey Vineyards, Gonzales
Morgan Winery, Salinas
Smith & Hook Vineyards, Soledad
Robert Talbott Vineyards, Carmel Valley
Taylor California Cellars, Gonzales
Ventana Vineyards Winery, Soledad

Napa County
Acacia Winery, Napa
Alta Vineyard Cellar, Calistoga
S. Anderson Vineyard, Napa
Artisan Wines, Napa
Beaulieu Vineyard, Rutherford
Beringer Vineyards, St. Helena
Jean-Claude Boisset, Rutherford
Buehler Vineyards, St. Helena
Burgess Cellars, St. Helena
Cain Cellars, St. Helena
Cakebread Cellars, Rutherford
Calafia Cellars, St. Helena
Carneros Creek Winery, Napa
Cartlidge & Browne, St. Helena
Casa Nuestra, St. Helena
Cassayre-Forni Cellars, Rutherford
Caymus Vineyards, Rutherford
Chappellet Winery, St. Helena
Château Boswell, St. Helena
Château Bouchaine, Napa
Château Chevalier Winery, St. Helena
Château Chèvre Winery, Yountville
Château Montelena Winery, Calistoga
Château Nouveau, St. Helena
The Christian Brothers, Napa
Clos du Val, Napa
Conn Creek Winery, St. Helena
Costello Vineyards, Napa

Cuvaison Vineyard, Calistoga
Deer Park Winery, Deer Park
Diamond Creek Vineyards, Calistoga
Domaine Chandon, Yountville
Duckhorn Vineyards, St. Helena
Dunn Vineyards, Angwin
Ehlers Lane Winery, St. Helena
Evensen Vineyards and Winery, Oakville
Evilsizer Cellar, Yountville
Fairmont Cellars, Yountville
Far Niente Winery, Oakville
Flora Springs Wine Company, St. Helena
Folie à Deux Winery, St. Helena
Franciscan Vineyards, Rutherford
Freemark Abbey Winery, St. Helena
Frog's Leap Winery, St. Helena
Girard Winery, Oakville
Green and Red Vineyards, St. Helena
Grgich Hills Cellars, Rutherford
Groth Vineyards and Winery, Oakville
Hagafen Cellars, Napa
Heitz Wine Cellars, St. Helena
William Hill Winery, Napa
Louis Honig Cellars (HNW Vineyards),
    Rutherford
Hopper Creek Winery, Napa
Robert Hunter, St. Helena
Inglenook Vineyards, Rutherford
Jaeger Family Wine Company, St. Helena
Johnson Turnbull Vineyards, Oakville
Robert Keenan Winery, St. Helena
Hanns Kornell Champagne Cellar, St. Helena
Charles Krug Winery, St. Helena
La Jota Vineyard Company, Angwin
Laird Vineyards, Kentfield
Lakespring Winery, Napa
Llords and Elwood Winery, Yountville
Long Vineyards, St. Helena
Manzanita, St. Helena
Markham Winery, St. Helena
Louis M. Martini, St. Helena
Mayacamas Vineyards, Napa
McCarthy & Spaulding Negociants, St. Helena
Louis K. Mihaly, Napa
Robert Mondavi Winery, Oakville
Mont St. John Cellars, Napa
Monticello Cellars, Napa
Moon Vineyards, Napa
Mount Veeder Winery, Napa
Napa Cellars, Oakville
Napa Creek Winery, St. Helena
Napa Mountain Winery, Napa
Newlan Vineyards and Winery, Napa
Newton Winery, St. Helena

Neyers Winery, St. Helena
Nichelini Vineyard, St. Helena
Niebaum-Coppola Estate, Rutherford
Charles Ortman Wines, St. Helena
Robert Pecota Winery, Calistoga
Peju Province, Rutherford
Robert Pepi Winery, Oakville
Perret Vineyards, Menlo Park
Joseph Phelps Vineyards, St. Helena
Piña Cellars, Rutherford
Pine Ridge Winery, Napa
Planet of the Grapes, St. Helena
Prager Winery and Port Works, St. Helena
Quail Ridge, Napa
Raymond Vineyard & Cellar, St. Helena
Ritchie Creek Vineyards, St. Helena
Roddis Cellar, Calistoga
Rombauer Vineyards, St. Helena
Don Charles Ross Winery, Napa
Round Hill Cellars, St. Helena
Rutherford Hill Winery, Rutherford
Rutherford Vintners, Rutherford
Saddleback Cellars, Oakville
Sage Canyon Winery, Rutherford
St. Andrews Winery, Napa
St. Clement Vineyards, St. Helena
Saintsbury Winery, Napa
V. Sattui Winery, St. Helena
Schramsberg Vineyards, Calistoga
Schug Cellars, Calistoga
Sequoia Grove Vineyards, Napa
Shafer Vineyards, Napa
Charles F. Shaw Vineyard, St. Helena
Shown and Sons Vineyards, Rutherford
Silver Oak Wine Cellars, Oakville
Silverado Vineyards, Napa
Smith-Madrone, St. Helena
Soleterra, St. Helena
Spottswoode Winery, St. Helena
Spring Mountain Vineyards, St. Helena
Stag's Leap Wine Cellars, Napa
Stags' Leap Winery, Napa
Steltzner Vineyards, Napa
Sterling Vineyards, Calistoga
Stonegate Winery, Calistoga
Stony Hill Vineyards, St. Helena
Storybook Mountain Vineyards, Calistoga
Stratford, St. Helena
Sullivan Vineyards Winery, Rutherford
Sutter Home Winery, St. Helena
Traulsen Vineyards, Calistoga
Trefethen Vineyards Winery, Napa
Tudal Winery, St. Helena
Tulocay Winery, Napa

Vichon Winery, Oakville
Villa Mount Eden Winery, Oakville
Vose Vineyards, Napa
Whitehall Lane Winery, St. Helena
Yverdon, St. Helena
ZD Wines, Napa

Nevada County
Nevada City Winery, Nevada City

Riverside County
Callaway Vineyards and Winery, Temecula
Cilurzo Vineyard and Winery, Temecula
Filsinger Vineyards and Winery, Temecula
Galleano Winery, Mira Loma
Hart Winery, Temecula
Mesa Verde Vineyards, Temecula
Mount Palomar Winery, Temecula
Noble Creek Vineyards, Cherry Valley
Opici Winery, Alta Loma
Piconi Winery, Temecula

Sacramento County
Frasinetti Winery, Sacramento

San Benito County
Calera Wine Company, Hollister
Enz Vineyards, Hollister

San Bernardino County
Brookside Vineyard Company, Guasti
J. Filippi Vintage Company, Fontana
Rancho de Philo, Alta Loma
Thomas Vineyards, Cucamonga

San Diego County
Bernardo Winery, San Diego
John Culbertson Winery, Fallbrook
Ferrara Winery, Escondido
Menghini Winery, Julian
Point Loma Winery, San Diego
San Pasqual Vineyards, Escondido
Santee Valley Winery, Santee

San Francisco County
Yerba Buena Winery, San Francisco

San Joaquin County
Bella Napoli Winery, Manteca
Borra's Cellar, Lodi
California Cellar Masters, Lodi
California Cooler, Stockton
Delicato Vineyards, Manteca

Franzia Winery, Ripon
Guild Wineries, Lodi
Lost Hills Vineyards, Acampo
The Lucas Winery, Lodi
Oak Ridge Vineyards, Lodi
Turner Winery, Woodbridge

San Luis Obispo County
Adelaida Cellars, Paso Robles
Belli and Sauret Vineyards, Paso Robles
Caparone Winery, Paso Robles
Chamisal Vineyard, San Luis Obispo
Claiborne & Churchill Vintners, San Luis Obispo
Corbett Canyon Vineyards, San Luis Obispo
Creston Manor Vineyards & Winery, Creston
Eberle Winery, Paso Robles
Edna Valley Vineyard, San Luis Obispo
El Paso de Robles Winery, Paso Robles
Estrella River Winery, Paso Robles
Farview Farm Vineyard, Templeton
HMR Estate Winery, Paso Robles
Martin Brothers Winery, Paso Robles
Mastantuono Winery, Paso Robles
Pesenti Winery, Templeton
Ranchita Oaks Winery, San Miguel
Ross-Keller Winery, Nipomo
Saucelito Canyon Vineyard, Arroyo Grande
Shadow Creek Champagne Cellars, San Luis Obispo
Tobias Vineyards, Paso Robles
Twin Hills Ranch Winery, Paso Robles
Watson Vineyards, Paso Robles
York Mountain Winery, Templeton

San Mateo County
Cronin Vineyards, Woodside
Thomas Fogarty Winery, Portola Valley
J. H. Gentili Wines, Redwood City
Obester Winery, Half Moon Bay

Santa Barbara County
Au Bon Climat, Los Olivos
Austin Cellars, Solvang
Babcock Vineyards, Lompoc
Ballard Canyon Winery, Solvang
The Brander Vineyard, Los Olivos
J. Carey Cellars, Solvang
Copenhagen Cellars, Solvang
The Firestone Vineyard, Los Olivos
Gainey Vineyards, Santa Ynez
Hale Cellars, Los Alamos
Houtz Vineyards, Los Olivos
Longoria Winery, Los Olivos
Los Vineros Winery, Santa Maria
Qupe, Los Olivos

Rancho Sisquoc Winery, Santa Maria
Sanford & Benedict, Lompoc
Sanford Winery, Buellton
Santa Barbara Winery, Santa Barbara
Santa Ynez Valley Winery, Santa Ynez
Tepusquet, Santa Maria
Vega Vineyards Winery, Buellton
Zaca Mesa Winery, Los Olivos

Santa Clara County

Almadén Vineyards, San Jose
Casa de Fruta, Hollister
Cloudstone Vineyards, Los Altos Hills
Congress Springs Vineyard, Saratoga
A. Conrotto Winery, Gilroy
Cygnet Cellars, Sunnyvale
Desantis Vineyards, Gilroy
Fortino Winery, Gilroy
Gemello Winery, Mountain View
Emilio Guglielmo Winery, Morgan Hill
Hecker Pass Winery, Gilroy
Kathryn Kennedy Winery, Saratoga
Kirigin Cellars, Gilroy
Thomas Kruse Winery, Gilroy
Ronald Lamb Winery, Morgan Hill
Live Oaks Winery, Gilroy
J. Lohr Winery, San Jose
M. Marion & Company, Saratoga
Paul Masson Vineyards, Saratoga
Mirassou Vineyards, San Jose
Mount Eden Vineyards, Saratoga
The Mountain View Winery, Mountain View
Novitiate Wines, Los Gatos
Page Mill Winery, Los Altos Hills
Pedrizzetti Winery, Morgan Hill
Pendleton Winery, Santa Clara
Rapazzini Winery, Gilroy
Martin Ray Vineyards, Saratoga
Ridge Vineyards, Cupertino
San Martin Winery, San Martin
Sarah's Vineyard, Gilroy
Sherrill Cellars, Woodside
Summerhill Vineyards, Gilroy
Sycamore Creek Vineyards, Morgan Hill
Villa Paradiso Vineyards, Morgan Hill
Woodside Vineyards, Woodside

Santa Cruz County

Ahlgren Vineyard, Boulder Creek
Bargetto Winery, Soquel
Bonny Doon Vineyard, Santa Cruz
David Bruce Winery, Los Gatos
Cook-Ellis Winery, Corraltos
Crescini Wines, Soquel
Devlin Wine Cellars, Soquel

Felton-Empire Vineyards, Felton
Frick Winery, Santa Cruz
Grover Gulch Winery, Soquel
McHenry Vineyards, Santa Cruz
Nicasio Vineyards, Soquel
River Run Vintners, Watsonville
Roudon-Smith Vineyards, Santa Cruz
Santa Cruz Mountain Vineyard, Santa Cruz
Silver Mountain Vineyards, Los Gatos
Smothers-Vine Hill Wines, Santa Cruz
P and M Staiger, Boulder Creek
Sunrise Winery, Cupertino
Walker Wines, Felton

Solano County

Cache Cellars, Davis
Cadenasso Winery, Fairfield
Château de Leu Winery, Suisun City
Susine Cellars, Suisun City
Wooden Valley Winery, Suisun City

Sonoma County

Adler Fels Winery, Santa Rosa
Alderbrook Winery, Healdsburg
Alexander Valley Vineyards, Healdsburg
Balverne Winery & Vineyards, Windsor
Bellerose Vineyard, Healdsburg
Belvedere Wine Company, Healdsburg
Brenner Cellars, Cotati
Buena Vista Winery, Sonoma
Davis Bynum Winery, Healdsburg
California Wine Company, Cloverdale
Cambiaso Vineyards, Healdsburg
Carano Cellars, Geyserville
Carmenet Vineyard, Sonoma
Caswell Vineyards, Sebastopol
Chanticleer Vineyards, Healdsburg
Château St. Jean, Kenwood
Clos du Bois Winery, Healdsburg
Colony, Asti
Cordtz Brothers Cellars, Cloverdale
H. Coturri and Sons, Glen Ellen
De Loach Vineyards, Santa Rosa
Dehlinger Winery, Sebastopol
Diamond Oaks Vineyard, Cloverdale
Domaine Laurier, Forestville
Donna Maria Vineyards, Healdsburg
Dry Creek Vineyard, Healdsburg
Georges Duboeuf & Son, Healdsburg
Duxoup Wine Works, Healdsburg
Field Stone Winery, Healdsburg
Fisher Vineyards, Santa Rosa
Louis Foppiano Wine Company, Healdsburg
Fritz Cellars, Cloverdale
Geyser Peak Winery, Geyserville

Glen Ellen Winery, Glen Ellen
Golden Creek Vineyard, Santa Rosa
Grand Cru Vineyards, Glen Ellen
Gundlach-Bundschu Winery, Vineburg
Hacienda del Rio Winery, Fulton
Hacienda Wine Cellars, Sonoma
Hafner Vineyard, Healdsburg
Hanzell Vineyards, Sonoma
Haywood Winery, Sonoma
Hop Kiln Winery, Healdsburg
Horizon Winery, Santa Rosa
Hultgren Samperton Winery, Healdsburg
Iron Horse Vineyards, Sebastopol
Johnson's Alexander Valley Winery, Healdsburg
Jordan Vineyard and Winery, Healdsburg
Kenwood Vineyards, Kenwood
Kistler Vineyards, Glen Ellen
F. Korbel and Brothers, Guerneville
La Crema Vinera, Petaluma
Lake Sonoma Winery, Healdsburg
Lambert Bridge, Healdsburg
Landmark Vineyards, Windsor
Las Montanas, Glen Ellen
Laurel Glen Vineyard, Glen Ellen
Lyeth Vineyard and Winery, Geyserville
Lytton Springs Winery, Healdsburg
Marietta Cellars, Healdsburg
Mark West Vineyards, Forestville
Martini and Prati, Santa Rosa
Matanzas Creek Winery, Santa Rosa
Matrose Wines, Geyserville
Merry Vintners, Santa Rosa
Michtom Vineyards, Healdsburg
Mill Creek Vineyards, Healdsburg
J. W. Morris Wineries, Healdsburg
Mountain House Winery, Cloverdale
Nervo Winery, Geyserville
Pastori Winery, Cloverdale
Pat Paulsen Vineyards, Cloverdale
J. Pedroncelli Winery, Geyserville
Pellegrini Brothers Winery, Santa Rosa
Piper-Sonoma, Healdsburg
Pommeraie Vineyards, Sebastopol
Preston Vineyards, Healdsburg
A. Rafanelli Winery, Healdsburg
Ravenswood, Sonoma
Richardson Vineyards, Sonoma
River Road Vineyards, Forestville
J. Rochioli Vineyards, Healdsburg
Rose Family Winery, Healdsburg
St. Francis Vineyards, Kenwood
Sausal Winery, Healdsburg
Sea Ridge Winery, Cazadero
Sebastiani Vineyards, Sonoma

Seghesio Winery, Cloverdale
Thomas Sellards Winery, Sebastopol
Simi Winery, Healdsburg
Soda Rock Winery, Healdsburg
Sonoma-Cutrer Vineyards, Windsor
Sonoma Hills Winery, Santa Rosa
Sonoma Vineyards, Windsor
Sotoyome Winery, Healdsburg
Souverain Cellars, Geyserville
Robert Stemmler Winery, Healdsburg
Joseph Swan Vineyards, Forestville
Taft Street Winery, Forestville
Topolos at Russian River, Forestville
Toyon Vineyards, Healdsburg
Trentadue Winery, Geyserville
Valfleur Winery, Healdsburg
Valley of the Moon, Glen Ellen
Van der Kamp Champagne Cellers, Kenwood
Vina Vista Vineyards, Cloverdale
Warnelius Winery, Cloverdale
William Wheeler Winery, Healdsburg
White Oak Vineyards, Healdsburg
Stephen Zellerbach Vineyard, Healdsburg

Stanislaus County

JFJ Bronco Winery, Ceres
Cosentino Wine Company, Modesto
E. & J. Gallo Winery, Modesto

Tulare County

Anderson Wine Cellars, Exeter
Arbor Knoll Winery, Springville
California Growers Winery, Cutler
Sierra Wine Corporation, Tulare

Tuolumne County

Yankee Hill Winery, Columbia

Ventura County

The Daume Winery, Camarillo
Leeward Winery, Ventura
The Old Creek Ranch Winery, Oakview
Rolling Hills Vineyard, Camarillo

Yolo County

Bogle Vineyards, Clarksburg
R. & J. Cook, Clarksburg
Harbor Winery, West Sacramento
Orleans Hill Vinicultural Corporation,
    Woodland
The R. H. Phillips Vineyards, Esparto
Satiety, Davis
Winters Winery, Winters

Oregon

Adelsheim Vineyard, Newberg

Alpine Vineyards, Alpine
Amity Vineyards, Amity
Arterberry Limited, McMinnville
Bjelland Vineyards, Roseburg
Château Benoit Winery, Carlton
Chehalen Mountain Winery, Newberg
Côte des Colombes Vineyard, Banks
Elk Cove Vineyards, Gaston
Ellendale Vineyards, Dallas
Henry Endress Winery, Oregon City
The Eyrie Vineyards, McMinnville
Forgeron Vineyard, Elmira
Glen Creek Winery, Salem
Henry Winery, Umpqua
Hidden Springs Winery, Amity
Hillcrest Vineyard, Roseburg
Hinman Vineyards, Eugene
Hood River Vineyards, Hood River
Jonicole Vineyards, Roseburg
Knudsen-Erath Winery, Dundee
Nehalem Bay Wine Company, Nehalem
Oak Knoll Winery, Hillsboro
Ponzi Vineyards, Beaverton
Serendipity Cellars Winery, Monmouth
Shafer Vineyard Cellars, Forest Grove
Siskiyou Vineyards, Cave Junction
Sokol Blosser Winery, Dundee
Tualatin Vineyards, Forest Grove
Valley View Vineyard, Jacksonville
Wasson Brothers Winery, Sandy

Washington

Arbor Crest, Spokane
Bainbridge Island Winery, Bainbridge Island
Blackwood Canyon Vintners, Benton City
Château Ste. Michelle, Woodinville
Champs de Brionne Winery, Quincy
Columbia Winery, Bellevue
Daquila Wines, Seattle
E. B. Foote Winery, Seattle
French Creek Cellars, Redmond
Gordon Brothers Cellars, Pasco
Haviland Vintners, Lynnwood
Hinzerling Vineyards, Prosser
The Hogue Cellars, Prosser
Hoodsport Winery, Hoodsport
Kiona Vineyards and Winery, Benton City
Franz Wilhelm Langguth Winery, Mattawa
Latah Creek Winery, Spokane
Leonetti Cellars, Walla Walla
Lost Mountain Winery, Sequim
Lowden Schoolhouse Winery, Lowden
Mont Elise Vineyards, Bingen
Mount Baker Vineyards, Everson
Neuharth Winery, Sequim

Preston Wine Cellars, Pasco
Quail Run Vintners, Zillah
Quilceda Creek Vintners, Snohomish
Salishan Vineyards, La Center
Snoqualmie Falls Winery, Issaquah
Stewart Vineyards, Sunnyside
Paul Thomas Wines, Bellevue
Tucker Cellars, Sunnyside
Vernier Wines, Seattle
Manfred Vierthaler Winery, Sumner
Waterbrook Winery, Lowden
Woodward Canyon Winery, Lowden
Worden's Washington Winery, Spokane
Yakima River Winery, Prosser

Rocky Mountain States

Colorado

Colorado Mountain Vineyards, Palisade

Idaho

Brundage Cellars, McCall
Camas Winery, Moscow
Louis Facelli Vineyards, Wilder
Pucci Winery, Sandpoint
Ste. Chapelle Winery, Caldwell
Weston Winery, Caldwell

Nevada

Woodhall Cellars, Sparks

Utah

Summum, Salt Lake City

Southern States

Alabama

Perdido Vineyards, Perdido

Arkansas

Cowie Wine Cellars, Paris
Mount Bethel Winery, Altus
Post Winery, Altus
Sax's Winery, Altus
Wiederkehr Wine Cellars, Franklin

Florida

Alaqua Vineyards Winery, Freeport
Florida Heritage Winery, Anthony
Fruit Wines of Florida, Tampa
Lafayette Vineyards, Tallahassee
The Wines of St. Augustine, Tampa

Georgia

Habersham Vintners, Baldwin
Happy B Farm Winery, Forsyth
Monarch Wine Company, Atlanta
B & B Rosser Winery, High Shoals

Maryland

Barrywine Plantations Winery, Mount Airy
Boordy Vineyards, Hydes
Byrd Vineyards, Myersville
Catoctin Vineyards, Brookeville
Montbray Wine Cellars, Westminster
Ziem Vineyards, Fairplay

Mississippi

Alamara Vineyards, Mathersville
Old South Winery, Natchez
Thousand Oaks Vineyard, Starkville
The Winery Rushing, Merigold

North Carolina

The Biltmore Estate Company, Asheville
Duplin Wine Cellars, Rose Hill
Germanton Vineyard and Winery, Germanton
LaRocca Wine Company, Fayetteville

South Carolina

Foxwood Wine Cellars, Woodruff
Truluck Vineyards & Winery, Lake City

Tennessee

Highland Manor Winery, Jamestown
Smokey Mountain Winery, Gatlinburg
Tennessee Valley Winery, Louden
Tiegs Vineyard, Lenoir City

Virginia

Bacchanal Vineyards, Afton
Barboursville Vineyards, Barboursville
Blenheim Vineyards, Charlottesville
Château Morrisette Winery, Meadows of Dan
Château Natural Vineyard, Rocky Mount
Chermont Winery, Esmont
Farfelu Vineyard, Flint Hill
Ingleside Plantation Winery, Oak Grove
La Abra Farm & Winery, Lovingston
Meredyth Vineyard, Middleburg
M J C Vineyards, Blacksburg
Montdomaine Cellars, Charlottesville

Naked Mountain Vineyard, Markham
Oakencroft Vineyards, Charlottesville
Oasis Vineyard, Hume
Prince Michel Vineyards, Culpeper
Rapidan River Vineyards, Culpeper
Rose Bower Vineyard & Winery, Hampden-
    Sydney
Shenandoah Vineyards, Edinburg
Tri Mountain Winery, Middletown
The Vineyard, Winchester

West Virginia

Fisher Ridge Wine Company, Liberty
West-Whitehill Winery, Keyser

Southwestern States

Arizona

Soñoito Vineyards, Tucson
R. W. Webb Winery, Tucson

New Mexico

Anderson Valley Vineyards, Albuquerque
La Chiripada Winery, Dixon
La Vina Winery, Chamberino
Sangre de Cristo Wines, Sapello
Viña Madre, Roswell

Oklahoma

Cimmaron Cellars, Caney
Pete Schwartz Winery, Okarche

Texas

Château Montgolfier Vineyards, Fort Worth
Cypress Valley Vineyards, Cypress Mill
Fall Creek Vineyards, Tow
Guadalupe Valley Winery, New Braunfels
La Buena Vida Vineyards, Springtown
Llano Estacado Winery, Lubbock
Messina Hof Wine Cellars, Bryan
Moyer Texas Champagne Company,
    New Braunfels
Oberhellmann Vineyards, Fredericksburg
Pheasant Ridge Winery, Lubbock
Sanchez-Gill-Richter-Cordier, Austin
Val Verde Winery, Del Rio
Wimberley Valley Wines, Conroe

Composition by Publisher's Typography, Agoura, California, using the
Penta System with the Mergenthaler Linotron 202.

Design by Robin Murawski and Randall Mize with the assistance of
Robert S. Tinnon.